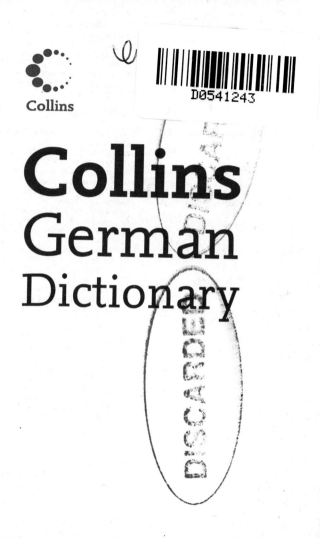

Collins
German
Dictionary

HarperCollins Publishers
Westerhill Road
Bishopbriggs
Glasgow
G64 2QT
Great Britain

Second Edition 2007

Reprint 10 9 8 7 6 5 4 3

© HarperCollins Publishers
2005, 2007

ISBN 978-0-00-725280-0

Collins® and Bank of English®
are registered trademarks of
HarperCollins Publishers Limited

www.collinslanguage.com

A catalogue record for this book is
available from the British Library

Dictionary text typeset by
RefineCatch Ltd, Bungay, Suffolk

Supplement text typeset by
Davidson Pre-Press, Glasgow

Printed in Italy by
Rotolito Lombarda S.p.A.

GENERAL EDITOR
Maree Airlie

CONTRIBUTORS
Daphne Day
Horst Kopleck
Joyce Littlejohn

EDITORIAL COORDINATION
Susie Beattie

SERIES EDITOR
Lorna Knight

Acknowledgements
We would like to thank those authors
and publishers who kindly gave
permission for copyright material to
be used in the Collins Word Web. We
would also like to thank Times
Newspapers Ltd for providing
valuable data.

This book is set in Collins Fedra, a
typeface specially created for Collins
Dictionaries by Peter Bil'ak

INHALT

CONTENTS

WARENZEICHEN

Warenzeichen, die unseres Wissens eingetragene Warenzeichen darstellen, sind als solche gekennzeichnet. Es ist jedoch zu beachten, dass weder das Vorhandensein noch das Fehlen derartiger Kennzeichnungen die Rechtslage hinsichtlich eingetragener Warenzeichen berührt.

NOTE ON TRADEMARKS

Words which we have reason to believe constitute trademarks have been designated as such. However, neither the presence nor the absence of such designation should be regarded as affecting the legal status of any trademark.

William Collins' dream of knowledge for all began with the publication of his first book in 1819. A self-educated mill worker, he not only enriched millions of lives, but also founded a flourishing publishing house. Today, staying true to this spirit, Collins books are packed with inspiration, innovation, and practical expertise. They place you at the centre of a world of possibility and give you exactly what you need to explore it.

Language is the key to this exploration, and at the heart of Collins Dictionaries is language as it is really used. New words, phrases, and meanings spring up every day, and all of them are captured and analysed by the Collins Word Web. Constantly updated, and with over 2.5 billion entries, this living language resource is unique to our dictionaries.

Words are tools for life. And a Collins Dictionary makes them work for you.

Collins. Do more.

EINFÜHRUNG

Wir freuen uns sehr, dass Sie sich zum Kauf eines Collins Wörterbuchs Deutsch entschlossen haben. Wir wünschen Ihnen viel Spaß beim Gebrauch in der Schule, zu Hause, im Urlaub und im Beruf.

Diese Einführung wird Ihnen einige nützliche Hinweise dazu geben, wie Sie am besten von Ihrem neuen Wörterbuch profitieren. Schließlich bietet Ihnen das Wörterbuch nicht nur Stichwörter und Übersetzungen, sondern auch zahlreiche Zusatzinformationen in jedem einzelnen Eintrag. Mit Hilfe all dieser Informationen können Sie zum einen modernes Deutsch lesen und verstehen, zum anderen auch aktiv auf Deutsch kommunizieren.

Das Collins Wörterbuch Deutsch gibt Ihnen vor dem eigentlichen Wörterbuchtextteil selbst eine Liste aller verwendeten Abkürzungen sowie eine Übersicht zu Aussprache und Gebrauch phonetischer Umschrift. Darüber hinaus finden Sie noch eine Auflistung zu den regelmäßigen deutschen Substantivendungen sowie zu unregelmäßigen englischen und deutschen Verben. Auf den letzten Seiten Ihres Wörterbuchs finden Sie in einem „kleinen Reise-ABC" zahlreiche nützliche Phrasen für verschiedenste Situationen am Urlaubsort.

WIE FINDE ICH WAS?

Die verschiedenen Schriftarten, Schriftgrößen, Symbole, Abkürzungen und Klammern helfen Ihnen dabei, sich innerhalb der Informationen, die das Wörterbuch bietet, zurechtzufinden. Die Konventionen, die diesem Wörterbuch zugrunde liegen, sowie auch der Gebrauch verschiedener Symbole werden im Folgenden näher erläutert.

STICHWÖRTER

Die Wörter, die Sie in Ihrem Wörterbuch nachschlagen, die Stichwörter, sind in alphabetischer Reihenfolge angeordnet. Sie sind **fett** gedruckt und in blauer Farbe, sodass Sie sie schnell finden. Die Stichwörter, die rechts und links oben auf jeder Seite erscheinen, sind das jeweils erste Stichwort einer Seite, wenn es sich dabei um eine linke Seite handelt, bzw. das letzte Stichwort einer Seite, wenn es sich um eine rechte Seite handelt. Informationen zu Form und Gebrauch des jeweiligen Stichworts werden im Anschluss an die Lautschrift in Klammern angegeben. Normalerweise sind diese Angaben in abgekürzter Form und *kursiver Schrift* (z.B. (*fam*) für umgangssprachlich oder (*Comm*) als Sachgebietsangabe für Wirtschaft).

Wo es sich anbietet, werden zusammengehörige Wörter und Wortgruppen in einem Eintrag zusammengefasst (z.B. **gather**, **gathering**; **höflich**, **Höflichkeit**). Hierbei sind die Stichwörter innerhalb des Nests von der Schriftgröße etwas kleiner als das erste Stichwort. Geläufige Ausdrücke, in denen das Stichwort vorkommt, erscheinen ebenfalls **fett**, aber in einer anderen Schriftgröße. Die Tilde (~) steht hierbei für das Hauptstichwort am Anfang eines Eintrags. So steht beispielsweise im Eintrag ‚Mitte' der Ausdruck ‚**~ Juni**' für ‚**Mitte Juni**'.

PHONETISCHE UMSCHRIFT

Die Aussprache jedes Stichworts findet sich in phonetischer Umschrift in eckigen Klammern jeweils direkt hinter dem Stichwort selbst (z.B. **mountain** [ˈmaʊntɪn]). Eine Liste der Lautschriftzeichen mit Erklärungen finden Sie auf S. xi.

BEDEUTUNGEN

Die Übersetzung der Stichwörter ist in Normalschrift angegeben. Gibt es mehrere Bedeutungen oder Gebrauchsmöglichkeiten, so sind diese durch einen Strichpunkt voneinander zu unterscheiden. Sie finden oft weitere Angaben in Klammern vor den jeweiligen Übersetzungen. Diese zeigen Ihnen typische Kontexte auf, in denen das Stichwort verwendet werden kann (z.B. **breakup** (*of meeting, organisation*)), oder sie liefern Synonyme (z.B. **fit** (*suitable*)).

GRAMMATISCHE HINWEISE

Die Wortartangabe finden Sie als Abkürzung und in *kursiver Schrift* direkt hinter der Ausspracheinformation zum jeweiligen Stichwort (z.B. *vt*, *adj*, *n*).

Die Genusangaben zu deutschen Substantiven werden wie folgt angegeben: *m* für Maskulinum, *f* für Femininum und *nt* für Neutrum. Darüber hinaus finden Sie neben dem Stichwort in Klammern Genitiv- und Pluralform (**Abenteuer** (*-s, -*)).

Die Genusangabe zur deutschen Übersetzung findet sich ebenfalls in *kursiver Schrift* direkt hinter dem Hauptbestandteil der Übersetzung.

INTRODUCTION

We are delighted you have decided to buy the Collins German Dictionary and hope you will enjoy and benefit from using it at school, at home, on holiday or at work.

This introduction gives you a few tips on how to get the most out of your dictionary - not simply from its comprehensive wordlist but also from the information provided in each entry. This will help you to read and understand modern German, as well as to communicate and express yourself in the language.

The Collins German Dictionary begins by listing the abbreviations used in the text and illustrating the sounds shown by the phonetic symbols. Next you will find regular German noun endings and English irregular verbs followed by a section on German irregular verbs. Finally, the new Phrasefinder supplement gives you hundreds of useful phrases which are intended to give you practical help in everyday situations when travelling.

USING YOUR COLLINS DICTIONARY

A wealth of information is presented in the dictionary, using various typefaces, sizes of type, symbols, abbreviations and brackets. The conventions and symbols used are explained in the following sections.

HEADWORDS

The words you look up in the dictionary – 'headwords' – are listed alphabetically. They are printed in **colour** for rapid identification. The headwords appearing at the top of each page indicate the first (if it appears on a left-hand page) and last word (if it appears on a right-hand page) dealt with on the page in question.

Information about the usage or form of certain headwords is given in brackets after the phonetic spelling. This usually appears in abbreviated form and in italics (e.g. (*fam*), (*Comm*)).

Where appropriate, words related to headwords are grouped in the same entry (**gather**, **gathering**; **höflich**, **Höflichkeit**) in a slightly smaller bold type than the headword. Common expressions in which the headword appears are shown in a different size of bold roman type. The swung dash, ~, represents the main headword at the start of each entry. For example, in the entry for '**Mitte**', the phrase '**~ Juni**' should be read '**Mitte Juni**'.

PHONETIC SPELLINGS

The phonetic spelling of each headword (indicating its pronunciation) is given in square brackets immediately after the headword (e.g. **mountain** ['maʊntɪn]). A list of these spellings is given on page xi.

MEANINGS

Headword translations are given in ordinary type and, where more than one meaning or usage exists, they are separated by a semicolon. You will often find other words in italics in brackets before the translations. These offer suggested contexts in which the headword might appear (e.g. **breakup** (*of meeting, organisation*)) or provide synonyms (e.g. **fit** (*suitable*)).

GRAMMATICAL INFORMATION

Parts of speech are given in abbreviated form in italics after the phonetic spellings of headwords (e.g. *vt*, *adj*, *n*).

Genders of German nouns are indicated as follows: *m* for a masculine, *f* for a feminine, and *nt* for a neuter noun. Genitive and plural forms of nouns are also shown next to the headword (**Abenteuer** (*-s*, *-*)).

The gender of the German translation appears in *italics* immediately following the key element of the translation.

ABKÜRZUNGEN

ABBREVIATIONS

auch	*a.*	also
Abkürzung	*abk, abbr*	abbreviation
Akronym	*acr*	acronym
Adjektiv	*adj*	adjective
Adverb	*adv*	adverb
Landwirtschaft	*Agr*	agriculture
Akkusativ	*akk*	accusative
Akronym	*akr*	acronym
Anatomie	*Anat*	anatomy
Artikel	*art*	article
Bildende Künste	*Art*	fine arts
Astronomie, Astrologie	*Astr*	astronomy, astrology
Auto, Verkehr	*Auto*	automobiles, traffic
Luftfahrt	*Aviat*	aviation
Biologie	*Bio*	biology
Botanik	*Bot*	botany
britisch	*BRIT*	British
schweizerisch	*CH*	Swiss
Chemie	*Chem*	chemistry
Film	*Cine*	cinema
Wirtschaft	*Comm*	commerce
Konjunktion	*conj*	conjunction
Dativ	*dat*	dative
Eisenbahn	*Eisenb*	railways
Elektrizität	*Elek, Elec*	electricity
besonders	*esp*	especially
und so weiter	*etc*	et cetera
etwas	*etw*	
Femininum	*f*	feminine
umgangssprachlich	*fam*	familiar, informal
übertragen	*fig*	figurative
Finanzen, Börse	*Fin*	finance
Fotografie	*Foto*	photography
Gastronomie	*Gastr*	cooking, gastronomy
Genitiv	*gen*	genitive
Geographie, Geologie	*Geo*	geography, geology
Geschichte	*Hist*	history
Imperativ	*imper*	imperative
Imperfekt	*imperf*	past tense
Informatik und Computer	*Inform*	computing
Interjektion, Ausruf	*interj*	interjection
unveränderlich	*inv*	invariable
unregelmäßig	*irr*	irregular
jemand, jemandem	*jd, jdm*	
jemanden, jemandes	*jdn, jds*	
Rechtsprechung	*Jur*	law

German	Abbreviation	English
Konjunktion	konj	conjunction
Bildende Künste	Kunst	fine arts
Sprachwissenschaft, Grammatik	Ling	linguistics, grammar
Maskulinum	m	masculine
Mathematik	Math	mathematics
Medizin	Med	medicine
Meteorologie	Meteo	meteorology
Maskulinum und Femininum	mf	masculine and feminine
Militär	Mil	military
Musik	Mus	music
Substantiv	n	noun
Seefahrt	Naut	nautical, naval
Neutrum	nt	neuter
Zahlwort	num	numeral
oder	o	or
pejorativ, abwertend	pej	pejorative
Physik	Phys	physics
Plural	pl	plural
Politik	Pol	politics
Partizip Perfekt	pp	past participle
Präfix	pref	prefix
Präposition	prep	preposition
Pronomen	pron	pronoun
1. Vergangenheit	pt	past tense
Eisenbahn	Rail	railways
Religion	Rel	religion
siehe	s.	see
	sb	someone, somebody
schottisch	Scot	Scottish
Singular	sing	singular
Skisport	Ski	skiing
	sth	something
Technik	Tech	technology
Nachrichtentechnik	Tel	telecommunications
Theater	Theat	theatre
Fernsehen	TV	television
Typographie, Buchdruck	Typo	printing
unpersönlich	unpers	impersonal
(nord)amerikanisch	US	(North) American
Verb	vb	verb
Hilfsverb	vb aux	auxiliary verb
intransitives Verb	vi	intransitive verb
reflexives Verb	vr	reflexive verb
transitives Verb	vt	transitive verb
vulgär	vulg	vulgar
Zoologie	Zool	zoology
ungefähre Entsprechung	≈	cultural equivalent
abtrennbares Präfix	|	separable prefix

LAUTSCHRIFT   PHONETIC SYMBOLS

[:] Längezeichen, length mark
['] Betonung, stress mark
[*] Bindungs-R, 'r' pronounced before a vowel

alle Vokallaute sind nur ungefähre Entsprechungen
all vowel sounds are approximate only

VOKALE UND DIPHTHONGE

plant, arm, father	[ɑ:]	Bahn
fiancé	[ɑ̃:]	Ensemble
life	[aɪ]	weit
house	[au]	Haut
man, sad	[æ]	
but, son	[ʌ]	Butler
get, bed	[e]	Metall
name, lame	[eɪ]	
ago, better	[ə]	bitte
bird, her	[ɜ:]	
there, care	[ɛə]	mehr
it, wish	[ɪ]	Bischof
bee, me, beat, belief	[i:]	viel
here	[ɪə]	Bier
no, low	[əʊ]	
not, long	[ɒ]	Post
law, all	[ɔ:]	Mond
boy, oil	[ɔɪ]	Heu
push, look	[ʊ]	Pult
you, do	[u:]	Hut
poor, sure	[ʊə]	

KONSONANTEN

been, blind	[b]	Ball
do, had	[d]	dann
jam, object	[dʒ]	
father, wolf	[f]	Fass
go, beg	[g]	Gast
house	[h]	Herr
youth, Indian	[j]	ja
keep, milk	[k]	kalt
lamp, oil, ill	[l]	Last
man, am	[m]	Mast
no, manner	[n]	Nuss
long, sing	[ŋ]	lang

El Niño	[ɲ]	El Niño
paper, happy	[p]	Pakt
red, dry	[r]	rot
stand, sand, yes	[s]	Rasse
ship, station	[ʃ]	Schal
tell, fat	[t]	Tal
thank, death	[θ]	
this, father	[ð]	
church, catch	[tʃ]	Rutsch
voice, live	[v]	was
water, we, which	[w]	
loch	[x]	Bach
zeal, these, gaze	[z]	Hase
pleasure	[ʒ]	Genie

REGULAR GERMAN NOUN ENDINGS

nominative		genitive	plural	nominative		genitive	plural
-ade	f	-ade	-aden	-ist	m	-isten	-isten
-ant	m	-anten	-anten	-ium	nt	-iums	-ien
-anz	f	-anz	-anzen	-ius	m	-ius	-iusse
-ar	m	-ars	-are	-ive	f	-ive	-iven
-är	m	-ärs	-äre	-keit	f	-keit	-keiten
-at	nt	-at(e)s	-ate	-lein	nt	-leins	-lein
-atte	f	-atte	-atten	-ling	m	-lings	-linge
-chen	nt	-chens	-chen	-ment	nt	-ments	-mente
-ei	f	-ei	-eien	-mus	m	-mus	-men
-elle	f	-elle	-ellen	-nis	f	-nis	-nisse
-ent	m	-enten	-enten	-nis	nt	-nisses	-nisse
-enz	f	-enz	-enzen	-nom	m	-nomen	-nomen
-ette	f	-ette	-etten	-rich	m	-richs	-riche
-eur	m	-eurs	-eure	-schaft	f	-schaft	-schaften
-euse	f	-euse	-eusen	-sel	nt	-sels	-sel
-heit	f	-heit	-heiten	-tät	f	-tät	-täten
-ie	f	-ie	-ien	-tiv	nt, m	-tivs	-tive
-ik	f	-ik	-iken	-tor	m	-tors	-toren
-in	f	-in	-innen	-tum	m, nt	-tums	-tümer
-ine	f	-ine	-inen	-ung	f	-ung	-ungen
-ion	f	-ion	-ionen	-ur	f	-ur	-uren

Substantive, die mit einem geklammerten 'r' oder 's' enden (z.B. **Angestellte(r)** mf, **Beamte(r)** m, **Gute(s)** nt) werden wie Adjektive dekliniert:

Nouns listed with an 'r' or an 's' in brackets (eg **Angestellte(r)** mf, **Beamte(r)** m, **Gute(s)** nt) take the same endings as adjectives:

der Angestellte m	**die Angestellte** f	**die Angestellten** pl
ein Angestellter m	**eine Angestellte** f	**Angestellte** pl
der Beamte m		**die Beamten** pl
ein Beamter m		**Beamte** pl
das Gute nt		
ein Gutes nt		

UNREGELMÄßIGE ENGLISCHE VERBEN

present	past tense	past participle	present	past tense	past participle
arise (arising)	arose	arisen	drink	drank	drunk
awake (awaking)	awoke	awaked	drive (driving)	drove	driven
be (am, is, are; being)	was, were	been	eat	ate	eaten
			fall	fell	fallen
			feed	fed	fed
bear	bore	born(e)	feel	felt	felt
beat	beat	beaten	fight	fought	fought
become (becoming)	became	become	find	found	found
			flee	fled	fled
begin (beginning)	began	begun	fling	flung	flung
			fly (flies)	flew	flown
bend	bent	bent	forbid (forbidding)	forbade	forbidden
bet (betting)	bet	bet			
bid (bidding)	bid	bid	foresee	foresaw	foreseen
bind	bound	bound	forget (forgetting)	forgot	forgotten
bite (biting)	bit	bitten			
bleed	bled	bled	forgive (forgiving)	forgave	forgiven
blow	blew	blown			
break	broke	broken	freeze (freezing)	froze	frozen
breed	bred	bred			
bring	brought	brought	get (getting)	got	got, (US) gotten
build	built	built			
burn	burnt (o burned)	burnt (o burned)	give (giving)	gave	given
burst	burst	burst	go (goes)	went	gone
buy	bought	bought	grind	ground	ground
can	could	(been able)	grow	grew	grown
cast	cast	cast	hang	hung (o hanged)	hung (o hanged)
catch	caught	caught			
choose (choosing)	chose	chosen	have (has; having)	had	had
cling	clung	clung	hear	heard	heard
come (coming)	came	come	hide (hiding)	hid	hidden
cost	cost	cost	hit (hitting)	hit	hit
creep	crept	crept	hold	held	held
cut (cutting)	cut	cut	hurt	hurt	hurt
deal	dealt	dealt	keep	kept	kept
dig (digging)	dug	dug	kneel	knelt (o kneeled)	knelt (o kneeled)
do (does)	did	done			
draw	drew	drawn	know	knew	known
dream	dreamed (o dreamt)	dreamed (o dreamt)	lay	laid	laid
			lead	led	led

present	past tense	past participle
lean	leant (o leaned)	leant (o leaned)
leap	leapt (o leaped)	leapt (o leaped)
learn	learnt (o learned)	learnt (o learned)
leave (leaving)	left	left
lend	lent	lent
let (letting)	let	let
lie (lying)	lay	lain
light	lit (o lighted)	lit (o lighted)
lose (losing)	lost	lost
make (making)	made	made
may	might	–
mean	meant	meant
meet	met	met
mow	mowed	mown (o mowed)
must	(had to)	(had to)
pay	paid	paid
put (putting)	put	put
quit (quitting)	quit (o quitted)	quit (o quitted)
read	read	read
rid (ridding)	rid	rid
ride (riding)	rode	ridden
ring	rang	rung
rise (rising)	rose	risen
run (running)	ran	run
saw	sawed	sawn
say	said	said
see	saw	seen
seek	sought	sought
sell	sold	sold
send	sent	sent
set (setting)	set	set
shake (shaking)	shook	shaken
shall	should	–
shine (shining)	shone	shone

present	past tense	past participle
shoot	shot	shot
show	showed	shown
shrink	shrank	shrunk
shut (shutting)	shut	shut
sing	sang	sung
sink	sank	sunk
sit (sitting)	sat	sat
sleep	slept	slept
slide (sliding)	slid	slid
sling	slung	slung
slit (slitting)	slit	slit
smell	smelt (o smelled)	smelt (o smelled)
sow	sowed	sown (o sowed)
speak	spoke	spoken
speed	sped (o speeded)	sped (o speeded)
spell	spelt (o spelled)	spelt (o spelled)
spend	spent	spent
spin (spinning)	spun	spun
spit (spitting)	spat	spat
split (splitting)	split	split
spoil	spoiled (o spoilt)	spoiled (o spoilt)
spread	spread	spread
spring	sprang	sprung
stand	stood	stood
steal	stole	stolen
stick	stuck	stuck
sting	stung	stung
stink	stank	stunk
strike (striking)	struck	struck
strive (striving)	strove	striven
swear	swore	sworn
sweep	swept	swept
swell	swelled	swollen (o swelled)

present	past tense	past participle	present	past tense	past participle
swim (swimming)	swam	swum	wake (waking)	woke (o waked)	woken (o waked)
swing	swung	swung	wear	wore	worn
take (taking)	took	taken	weave (weaving)	wove (o weaved)	woven (o weaved)
teach	taught	taught	weep	wept	wept
tear	tore	torn	win (winning)	won	won
tell	told	told			
think	thought	thought	wind	wound	wound
throw	threw	thrown	write (writing)	wrote	written
thrust	thrust	thrust			
tread	trod	trodden			

IRREGULAR GERMAN VERBS

Infinitiv	Präsens 2., 3. Singular	Imperfekt	Partizip Perfekt
backen	bäckst, bäckt	backte o buk	gebacken
befehlen	befiehlst, befiehlt	befahl	befohlen
beginnen	beginnst, beginnt	begann	begonnen
beißen	beißt, beißt	biss	gebissen
bergen	birgst, birgt	barg	geborgen
betrügen	betrügst, betrügt	betrog	betrogen
biegen	biegst, biegt	bog	gebogen
bieten	bietest, bietet	bot	geboten
binden	bindest, bindet	band	gebunden
bitten	bittest, bittet	bat	gebeten
blasen	bläst, bläst	blies	geblasen
bleiben	bleibst, bleibt	blieb	geblieben
braten	brätst, brät	briet	gebraten
brechen	brichst, bricht	brach	gebrochen
brennen	brennst, brennt	brannte	gebrannt
bringen	bringst, bringt	brachte	gebracht
denken	denkst, denkt	dachte	gedacht
dringen	dringst, dringt	drang	gedrungen
dürfen	darfst, darf	durfte	gedurft
erschrecken	erschrickst, erschrickt	erschrak	erschrocken
essen	isst, isst	aß	gegessen
fahren	fährst, fährt	fuhr	gefahren
fallen	fällst, fällt	fiel	gefallen
fangen	fängst, fängt	fing	gefangen
finden	findest, findet	fand	gefunden
fliegen	fliegst, fliegt	flog	geflogen
fließen	fließt, fließt	floss	geflossen
fressen	frisst, frisst	fraß	gefressen
frieren	frierst, friert	fror	gefroren
geben	gibst, gibt	gab	gegeben
gehen	gehst, geht	ging	gegangen
gelingen	–, gelingt	gelang	gelungen
gelten	giltst, gilt	galt	gegolten
genießen	genießt, genießt	genoss	genossen
geschehen	–, geschieht	geschah	geschehen
gewinnen	gewinnst, gewinnt	gewann	gewonnen
gießen	gießt, gießt	goss	gegossen
gleichen	gleichst, gleicht	glich	geglichen
gleiten	gleitest, gleitet	glitt	geglitten
graben	gräbst, gräbt	grub	gegraben
greifen	greifst, greift	griff	gegriffen
haben	hast, hat	hatte	gehabt
halten	hältst, hält	hielt	gehalten
hängen	hängst, hängt	hing	gehangen

Infinitiv	Präsens 2., 3. Singular	Imperfekt	Partizip Perfekt
heben	hebst, hebt	hob	gehoben
heißen	heißt, heißt	hieß	geheißen
helfen	hilfst, hilft	half	geholfen
kennen	kennst, kennt	kannte	gekannt
klingen	klingst, klingt	klang	geklungen
kommen	kommst, kommt	kam	gekommen
können	kannst, kann	konnte	gekonnt
kriechen	kriechst, kriecht	kroch	gekrochen
laden	lädst, lädt	lud	geladen
lassen	lässt, lässt	ließ	gelassen
laufen	läufst, läuft	lief	gelaufen
leiden	leidest, leidet	litt	gelitten
leihen	leihst, leiht	lieh	geliehen
lesen	liest, liest	las	gelesen
liegen	liegst, liegt	lag	gelegen
lügen	lügst, lügt	log	gelogen
mahlen	mahlst, mahlt	mahlte	gemahlen
meiden	meidest, meidet	mied	gemieden
messen	misst, misst	maß	gemessen
mögen	magst, mag	mochte	gemocht
müssen	musst, muss	musste	gemusst
nehmen	nimmst, nimmt	nahm	genommen
nennen	nennst, nennt	nannte	genannt
pfeifen	pfeifst, pfeift	pfiff	gepfiffen
raten	rätst, rät	riet	geraten
reiben	reibst, reibt	rieb	gerieben
reißen	reißt, reißt	riss	gerissen
reiten	reitest, reitet	ritt	geritten
rennen	rennst, rennt	rannte	gerannt
riechen	riechst, riecht	roch	gerochen
rufen	rufst, ruft	rief	gerufen
saufen	säufst, säuft	soff	gesoffen
saugen	saugst, saugt	sog o saugte	gesogen o gesaugt
schaffen	schaffst, schafft	schuf	geschaffen
scheiden	scheidest, scheidet	schied	geschieden
scheinen	scheinst, scheint	schien	geschienen
schieben	schiebst, schiebt	schob	geschoben
schießen	schießt, schießt	schoss	geschossen
schlafen	schläfst, schläft	schlief	geschlafen
schlagen	schlägst, schlägt	schlug	geschlagen
schleichen	schleichst, schleicht	schlich	geschlichen
schließen	schließt, schließt	schloss	geschlossen
schmeißen	schmeißt, schmeißt	schmiss	geschmissen
schmelzen	schmilzt, schmilzt	schmolz	geschmolzen
schneiden	schneidest, schneidet	schnitt	geschnitten

Infinitiv	Präsens 2., 3. Singular	Imperfekt	Partizip Perfekt
schreiben	schreibst, schreibt	schrieb	geschrieben
schreien	schreist, schreit	schrie	geschrie(e)n
schweigen	schweigst, schweigt	schwieg	geschwiegen
schwellen	schwillst, schwillt	schwoll	geschwollen
schwimmen	schwimmst, schwimmt	schwamm	geschwommen
schwören	schwörst, schwört	schwor	geschworen
sehen	siehst, sieht	sah	gesehen
sein	bist, ist	war	gewesen
senden	sendest, sendet	sandte	gesandt
singen	singst, singt	sang	gesungen
sinken	sinkst, sinkt	sank	gesunken
sitzen	sitzt, sitzt	saß	gesessen
sollen	sollst, soll	sollte	gesollt
sprechen	sprichst, spricht	sprach	gesprochen
springen	springst, springt	sprang	gesprungen
stechen	stichst, sticht	stach	gestochen
stehen	stehst, steht	stand	gestanden
stehlen	stiehlst, stiehlt	stahl	gestohlen
steigen	steigst, steigt	stieg	gestiegen
sterben	stirbst, stirbt	starb	gestorben
stinken	stinkst, stinkt	stank	gestunken
stoßen	stößt, stößt	stieß	gestoßen
streichen	streichst, streicht	strich	gestrichen
streiten	streitest, streitet	stritt	gestritten
tragen	trägst, trägt	trug	getragen
treffen	triffst, trifft	traf	getroffen
treiben	treibst, treibt	trieb	getrieben
treten	trittst, tritt	trat	getreten
trinken	trinkst, trinkt	trank	getrunken
tun	tust, tut	tat	getan
verderben	verdirbst, verdirbt	verdarb	verdorben
vergessen	vergisst, vergisst	vergaß	vergessen
verlieren	verlierst, verliert	verlor	verloren
verschwinden	verschwindest, verschwindet	verschwand	verschwunden
verzeihen	verzeihst, verzeiht	verzieh	verziehen
wachsen	wächst, wächst	wuchs	gewachsen
wenden	wendest, wendet	wandte	gewandt
werben	wirbst, wirbt	warb	geworben
werden	wirst, wird	wurde	geworden
werfen	wirfst, wirft	warf	geworfen
wiegen	wiegst, wiegt	wog	gewogen
wissen	weißt, weiß	wusste	gewusst
wollen	willst, will	wollte	gewollt
ziehen	ziehst, zieht	zog	gezogen
zwingen	zwingst, zwingt	zwang	gezwungen

a

à *prep* +*akk* at ... each; **4 Tickets ~ 8 Euro** 4 tickets at 8 euros each

A *abk* = **Autobahn** ≈ M (*Brit*), ≈ I (*US*)

Aal (-(e)s, -e) *m* eel

⬤ SCHLÜSSELWORT

ab *prep* +*dat* from; **Kinder ab 12 Jahren** children from the age of 12; **ab morgen** from tomorrow; **ab sofort** as of now
▷ *adv* **1** off; **links ab** to the left; **der Knopf ist ab** the button has come off; **ab nach Hause!** off you go home
2 (*zeitlich*) **von da ab** from then on; **von heute ab** from today, as of today
3 (*auf Fahrplänen*) **München ab 12.20** leaving Munich 12.20
4 ab und zu *o* **an** now and then *o* again

ab|bauen *vt* (*Zelt*) to take down; (*verringern*) to reduce
ab|beißen *irr vt* to bite off
ab|bestellen *vt* to cancel
ab|biegen *irr vi* to turn off; (*Straße*) to bend; **nach links/rechts ~** to turn left/right
Abbildung *f* illustration
ab|blasen *irr vt* (*fig*) to call off
ab|blenden *vt, vi* (*Auto*) (**die Scheinwerfer**) **~** to dip (*Brit*) (*o* to dim (*US*)) one's headlights; **Abblendlicht** *nt* dipped (*Brit*) (*o* dimmed (*US*)) headlights *pl*
ab|brechen *irr vt* to break off; (*Gebäude*) to pull down; (*aufhören*) to stop; (*Computerprogramm*) to abort
ab|bremsen *vi* to brake, to slow down
ab|bringen *irr vt*: **jdn von einer Idee ~** to talk sb out of an idea; **jdn vom Thema ~** to get sb away from the subject; **davon lasse ich mich nicht ~** nothing will make me change my mind about it
ab|buchen *vt* to debit (*von* to)
ab|danken *vi* to resign
ab|drehen *vt* (*Gas, Wasser*) to turn off; (*Licht*) to switch off ▷ *vi* (*Schiff, Flugzeug*) to change course
Abend (-s, -e) *m* evening; **am ~** in the evening; **zu ~ essen** to have dinner; **heute/morgen/gestern ~** this/tomorrow/yesterday evening; **guten ~!** good evening; **Abendbrot** *nt* supper; **Abendessen** *nt* dinner; **Abendgarderobe** *f* evening dress (*o* gown); **Abendkasse** *f* box office; **Abendkleid** *nt* evening dress (*o* gown); **Abendmahl** *nt*: **das ~** (Holy) Communion; **abends** *adv* in the evening; **montags ~** on Monday evenings
Abenteuer (-s, -) *nt* adventure; **Abenteuerurlaub** *m* adventure

holiday

aber conj but; (jedoch) however; **oder ~** alternatively; **~ ja!** (but) of course; **das ist ~ nett von Ihnen** that's really nice of you

abergläubisch adj superstitious

ab|fahren irr vi to leave (o to depart) (nach for); (Ski) to ski down; **Abfahrt** f departure; (von Autobahn) exit; (Ski) descent; (Piste) run; **Abfahrtslauf** m (Ski) downhill; **Abfahrtszeit** f departure time

Abfall m waste; (Müll) rubbish (Brit), garbage (US); **Abfalleimer** m rubbish bin (Brit), garbage can (US)

abfällig adj disparaging; **~ von jdm sprechen** to make disparaging remarks about sb

ab|färben vi (Wäsche) to run; (fig) to rub off

ab|fertigen vt (Pakete) to prepare for dispatch; (an der Grenze) to clear; **Abfertigungsschalter** m (am Flughafen) check-in desk

ab|finden irr vt to pay off ▷ vr: **sich mit etw ~** to come to terms with sth; **Abfindung** f (Entschädigung) compensation; (von Angestellten) redundancy payment

ab|fliegen irr vi (Flugzeug) to take off; (Passagier a.) to fly off; **Abflug** m departure; (Start) takeoff; **Abflughalle** f departure lounge; **Abflugzeit** f departure time

Abfluss m drain; (am Waschbecken) plughole (Brit); **Abflussrohr** nt waste pipe; (außen) drainpipe

ab|fragen vt to test; (Inform) to call up

ab|führen vi (Med) to have a laxative effect ▷ vt (Steuern, Gebühren) to pay; **jdn ~ lassen** to take sb into custody; **Abführmittel** nt laxative

Abgabe f handing in; (von Ball) pass; (Steuer) tax; (einer Erklärung) making; **abgabenfrei** adj tax-free; **abgabenpflichtig** adj liable to tax

Abgase pl (Auto) exhaust fumes pl; **Abgas(sonder)untersuchung** f exhaust emission test

ab|geben irr vt (Gepäck, Schlüssel) to leave (bei with); (Schularbeit etc) to hand in; (Wärme) to give off; (Erklärung, Urteil) to make ▷ vr: **sich mit jdm ~** to associate with sb; **sich mit etw ~** to bother with sth

abgebildet adj: **wie oben ~** as shown above

ab|gehen irr vi (Post) to go; (Knopf etc) to come off; (abgezogen werden) to be taken off; (Straße) to branch off; **von der Schule ~** to leave school; **sie geht mir ab** I really miss her; **was geht denn hier ab?** (fam) what's going on here?

abgehetzt adj exhausted, shattered

abgelaufen adj (Pass) expired; (Zeit, Frist) up; **die Milch ist ~** the milk is past its sell-by date

abgelegen adj remote

abgemacht interj OK, it's a deal, that's settled, then

abgeneigt adj **einer Sache** (dat) **~ sein** to be averse to sth; **ich wäre nicht ~, das zu tun** I wouldn't mind doing that

Abgeordnete(r) mf Member of Parliament

abgepackt adj prepacked

abgerissen adj: **der Knopf ist ~** the button has come off

abgesehen adj: **es auf jdn/etw ~ haben** to be after sb/sth; **~ von** apart from

abgespannt adj (Person) exhausted, worn out

abgestanden adj stale; (Bier) flat
abgestorben adj (Pflanze) dead; (Finger) numb
abgestumpft adj (Person) insensitive
abgetragen adj (Kleidung) worn
ab|gewöhnen vt: **jdm etw ~** to cure sb of sth; **sich etw ~** to give sth up
ab|haken vt to tick off; **das (Thema) ist schon abgehakt** that's been dealt with
ab|halten irr vt (Versammlung) to hold; **jdn von etw ~** (fernhalten) to keep sb away from sth; (hindern) to keep sb from sth
abhanden adj: **~ kommen** to get lost
Abhang m slope
ab|hängen vt (Bild) to take down; (Anhänger) to uncouple; (Verfolger) to shake off ▷ irr vi: **von jdm/etw ~** to depend on sb/sth; **das hängt davon ab, ob ...** it depends (on) whether ...; **abhängig** adj dependent (von on)
ab|hauen irr vt (abschlagen) to cut off ▷ vi (fam: verschwinden) to clear off; **hau ab!** get lost!, beat it!
ab|heben irr vt (Geld) to withdraw; (Telefonhörer, Spielkarte) to pick up ▷ vi (Flugzeug) to take off; (Rakete) to lift off; (Karten) to cut
ab|holen vt to collect; (am Bahnhof etc) to meet; (mit dem Auto) to pick up; **Abholmarkt** m cash and carry
ab|horchen vt (Med) to listen to
ab|hören vt (Vokabeln) to test; (Telefongespräch) to tap; (Tonband etc) to listen to
Abitur (-s, -e) nt German school-leaving examination, ≈ A-levels (Brit), ≈ High School Diploma (US)

● **ABITUR**
●
● The **Abitur** is the German
● school-leaving examination
● which is taken at the age of 18
● or 19 by pupils at a **Gymnasium**.
● It is taken in four subjects and is
● necessary for entry to
● university.

ab|kaufen vt: **jdm etw ~** to buy sth from sb; **das kauf ich dir nicht ab!** (fam: glauben) I don't believe you
ab|klingen irr vi (Schmerz) to ease; (Wirkung) to wear off
ab|kommen irr vi to get away; **von der Straße ~** to leave the road; **von einem Plan ~** to give up a plan; **vom Thema ~** to stray from the point
Abkommen (-s, -) nt agreement
ab|koppeln vt (Anhänger) to unhitch
ab|kratzen vt to scrape off ▷ vi (fam: sterben) to kick the bucket, to croak
ab|kühlen vi, vt to cool down ▷ vr: **sich ~** to cool down
ab|kürzen vt (Wort) to abbreviate; **den Weg ~** to take a short cut; **Abkürzung** f (Wort) abbreviation; (Weg) short cut
ab|laden irr vt to unload
Ablage f (für Akten) tray; (Aktenordnung) filing system
Ablauf m (Abfluss) drain; (von Ereignissen) course; (einer Frist, Zeit) expiry; **ab|laufen** irr vi (abfließen) to drain away; (Ereignisse) to happen; (Frist, Zeit, Pass) to expire
ab|legen vt to put down; (Kleider) to take off; (Gewohnheit) to get out of; (Prüfung) to take, to sit; (Akten) to file away ▷ vi (Schiff) to cast off
ab|lehnen vt to reject; (Einladung) to decline; (missbilligen)

to disapprove of; (*Bewerber*) to turn down ▷ *vi* to decline
ab|lenken *vt* to distract; **jdn von der Arbeit ~** to distract sb from their work; **vom Thema ~** to change the subject; **Ablenkung** *f* distraction
ab|lesen *vt* (*Text, Rede*) to read; **das Gas/den Strom ~** to read the gas/electricity meter
ab|liefern *vt* to deliver
ab|machen *vt* (*entfernen*) to take off; (*vereinbaren*) to agree; **Abmachung** *f* agreement
ab|melden *vt* (*Zeitung*) to cancel; (*Auto*) to take off the road ▷ *vr:* **sich ~** to give notice of one's departure; (*im Hotel*) to check out; (*vom Verein*) to cancel one's membership
ab|messen *irr vt* to measure
ab|nehmen *irr vt* to take off, to remove; (*Hörer*) to pick up; (*Führerschein*) to take away; (*Geld*) to get (*jdm* out of sb); (*kaufen, umg: glauben*) to buy (*jdm* from sb) ▷ *vi* to decrease; (*schlanker werden*) to lose weight; (*Tel*) to pick up the phone; **fünf Kilo ~** to lose five kilos
Abneigung *f* dislike (*gegen* of); (*stärker*) aversion (*gegen* to)
ab|nutzen *vt* to wear out ▷ *vr:* **sich ~** to wear out
Abonnement (*-s, -s*) *nt* subscription; **Abonnent(in)** *m(f)* subscriber; **abonnieren** *vt* to subscribe to
ab|raten *irr vi:* **jdm von etw ~** to advise sb against sth
ab|räumen *vt:* **den Tisch ~** to clear the table; **das Geschirr ~** to clear away the dishes; (*Preis etc*) to walk off with
Abrechnung *f* settlement; (*Rechnung*) bill
ab|regen *vr:* **sich ~** (*fam*) to calm

(*o* to cool) down; **reg dich ab!** take it easy
Abreise *f* departure; **ab|reisen** *vi* to leave (*nach* for); **Abreisetag** *m* day of departure
ab|reißen *irr vt* (*Haus*) to pull down; (*Blatt*) to tear off; **den Kontakt nicht ~ lassen** to stay in touch ▷ *vi* (*Knopf etc*) to come off
ab|runden *vt:* **eine Zahl nach oben/unten ~** to round a number up/down
abrupt *adj* abrupt
ABS *nt abk* = **Antiblockiersystem** (*Auto*) ABS
Abs. *abk* = **Absender** from
ab|sagen *vt* to cancel, to call off; (*Einladung*) to turn down ▷ *vi* (*ablehnen*) to decline; **ich muss leider ~** I'm afraid I can't come
Absatz *m* (*Comm*) sales *pl*; (*neuer Abschnitt*) paragraph; (*Schuh*) heel
ab|schaffen *vt* to abolish, to do away with
ab|schalten *vt, vi* (*a. fig*) to switch off
ab|schätzen *vt* to estimate; (*Lage*) to assess
abscheulich *adj* disgusting
ab|schicken *vt* to send off
ab|schieben *irr vt* (*ausweisen*) to deport
Abschied (*-(e)s, -e*) *m* parting; **~ nehmen** to say good-bye (*von jdm* to sb); **Abschiedsfeier** *f* farewell party
Abschlagszahlung *f* interim payment
Abschleppdienst *m* (*Auto*) breakdown service; **ab|schleppen** *vt* to tow; **Abschleppseil** *nt* towrope; **Abschleppwagen** *m* breakdown truck (*Brit*), tow truck (*US*)
ab|schließen *irr vt* (*Tür*) to lock; (*beenden*) to conclude, to finish; (*Vertrag, Handel*) to conclude;

Abschluss m (Beendigung) close, conclusion; (von Vertrag, Handel) conclusion

ab|schmecken vt (kosten) to taste; (würzen) to season

ab|schminken vr: **sich ~** to take one's make-up off ▷ vt (fam) **sich** (dat) **etw ~** to get sth out of one's mind

ab|schnallen vr: **sich ~** to undo one's seatbelt

ab|schneiden irr vt to cut off ▷ vi: **gut/schlecht ~** to do well/badly

Abschnitt m (von Buch, Text) section; (Kontrollabschnitt) stub

ab|schrauben vt to unscrew

ab|schrecken vt to deter, to put off

ab|schreiben irr vt to copy (bei, von from, off); (verloren geben) to write off; (Comm: absetzen) to deduct

abschüssig adj steep

ab|schwächen vt to lessen; (Behauptung, Kritik) to tone down

ab|schwellen irr vi (Entzündung) to go down; (Lärm) to die down

absehbar adj foreseeable: **in ~er Zeit** in the foreseeable future; **ab|sehen** irr vt (Ende, Folgen) to foresee ▷ vi: **von etw ~** to refrain from sth

abseits adv out of the way; (Sport) offside ▷ prep +gen away from; **Abseits** nt (Sport) offside; **Abseitsfalle** f (Sport) offside trap

ab|senden irr vt to send off; (Post) to post; **Absender(in)** (-s, -) m(f) sender

ab|setzen vt (Glas, Brille etc) to put down; (aussteigen lassen) to drop (off); (Comm) to sell; (Fin) to deduct; (streichen) to drop ▷ vr: **sich ~** (sich entfernen) to clear off; (sich ablagern) to be deposited

Absicht f intention; **mit ~** on purpose; **absichtlich** adj intentional, deliberate

absolut adj absolute

ab|specken vi (fam) to lose weight

ab|speichern vt (Inform) to save

ab|sperren vt to block (o to close) off; (Tür) to lock; **Absperrung** f (Vorgang) blocking (o closing) off; (Sperre) barricade

ab|spielen vt (CD etc) to play ▷ vr: **sich ~** to happen

ab|springen irr vi to jump down/off; (von etw Geplantem) to drop out (von of)

ab|spülen vt to rinse; (Geschirr) to wash (up)

Abstand m distance; (zeitlich) interval; **~ halten** to keep one's distance

ab|stauben vt, vi to dust; (fam: stehlen) to pinch

Abstecher (-s, -) m detour

ab|steigen irr vi (vom Rad etc) to get off, to dismount; (in Gasthof) to stay (in +dat at)

ab|stellen vt (niederstellen) to put down; (Auto) to park; (ausschalten) to turn (o to switch) off; (Missstand, Unsitte) to stop; **Abstellraum** m store room

Abstieg (-(e)s, -e) m (vom Berg) descent; (Sport) relegation

ab|stimmen vi to vote ▷ vt (Termine, Ziele) to fit in (auf +akk with); **Dinge aufeinander ~** to coordinate things ▷ vr: **sich ~** to come to an agreement (o arrangement)

abstoßend adj repulsive

abstrakt adj abstract

ab|streiten irr vt to deny

Abstrich m (Med) smear; **~e machen** to cut back (an +dat on); (weniger erwarten) to lower one's sights

Absturz m fall; (Aviat, Inform)

crash; **ab|stürzen** vi to fall; (Aviat, Inform) to crash

absurd adj absurd

Abszess (-es, -e) m abscess

ab|tauen vt, vi to thaw; (Kühlschrank) to defrost

Abtei (-, -en) f abbey

Abteil (-(e)s, -e) nt compartment

Abteilung f (in Firma, Kaufhaus) department; (in Krankenhaus) section

ab|treiben irr vt (Kind) to abort ▷ vi to be driven off course; (Med: Abtreibung vornehmen) to carry out an abortion; (Abtreibung vornehmen lassen) to have an abortion; **Abtreibung** f abortion

ab|trocknen vt to dry

ab|warten vt to wait for; **das bleibt abzuwarten** that remains to be seen ▷ vi to wait

abwärts adv down

Abwasch (-(e)s) m washing-up; **ab|waschen** irr vt (Schmutz) to wash off; (Geschirr) to wash (up)

Abwasser (-s, Abwässer) nt sewage

ab|wechseln vr: **sich ~** to alternate; **sich mit jdm ~** to take turns with sb; **abwechselnd** adv alternately; **Abwechslung** f change; **zur ~** for a change

ab|weisen irr vt to turn away; (Antrag) to turn down; **abweisend** adj unfriendly

abwesend adj absent; **Abwesenheit** f absence

ab|wiegen irr vt to weigh (out)

ab|wimmeln vt (fam) **jdn ~** to get rid of sb, to give sb the elbow

ab|wischen vt (Gesicht, Tisch etc) to wipe; (Schmutz) to wipe off

ab|zählen vt to count; (Geld) to count out

Abzeichen nt badge

ab|zeichnen vt to draw, to copy; (Dokument) to initial ▷ vr: **sich**

~ to stand out; (fig: bevorstehen) to loom

ab|ziehen irr vt to take off; (Bett) to strip; (Schlüssel) to take out; (subtrahieren) to take away, to subtract ▷ vi to go away

Abzug m (Foto) print; (Öffnung) vent; (Truppen) withdrawal; (Betrag) deduction; **nach ~ der Kosten** charges deducted; **abzüglich** prep +gen minus; **~ 20% Rabatt** less 20% discount

ab|zweigen vi to branch off ▷ vt to set aside; **Abzweigung** f junction

Accessoires pl accessories pl

ach interj oh; **~ so!** oh, I see; **~ was!** (Überraschung) really?; (Ärger) don't talk nonsense

Achse (-, -n) f axis; (Auto) axle

Achsel (-, -n) f shoulder; (Achselhöhle) armpit

Achsenbruch m (Auto) broken axle

acht num eight; **heute in ~ Tagen** in a week('s time), a week from today

Acht (-) f: **sich in ~ nehmen** to be careful (vor +dat of), to watch (vor +dat for); **etw außer ~ lassen** to disregard sth

achte(r, s) adj eighth; siehe auch **dritte**; **Achtel** (-s, -) nt (Bruchteil) eighth; (Wein etc) eighth of a litre; (Glas Wein) ≈ small glass

achten vt to respect ▷ vi to pay attention (auf +akk to)

Achterbahn f big dipper, roller coaster

acht|geben irr vi to take care (auf +akk of)

achthundert num eight hundred; **achtmal** adv eight times

Achtung f attention; (Ehrfurcht) respect ▷ interj look out

achtzehn num eighteen;

achtzehnte(r, s) *adj* eighteenth; *siehe auch* **dritte**; **achtzig** *num* eighty; **in den ~er Jahren** in the eighties; **achtzigste(r, s)** *adj* eightieth
Acker (*-s, Äcker*) *m* field
Action (*-, -s*) *f* (*fam*) action; **Actionfilm** *m* action film
Adapter (*-s, -*) *m* adapter
addieren *vt* to add (up)
Adel (*-s*) *m* nobility; **adelig** *adj* noble
Ader (*-, -n*) *f* vein
Adjektiv *nt* adjective
Adler (*-s, -*) *m* eagle
adoptieren *vt* to adopt; **Adoption** *f* adoption; **Adoptiveltern** *pl* adoptive parents *pl*; **Adoptivkind** *nt* adopted child
Adrenalin (*-s*) *nt* adrenalin
Adressbuch *nt* directory; (*persönliches*) address book; **Adresse** (*-, -n*) *f* address; **adressieren** *vt* to address (*an +akk* to)
Advent (*-s, -*) *m* Advent; **Adventskranz** *m* Advent wreath
Adverb *nt* adverb
Aerobic (*-s*) *nt* aerobics *sing*
Affäre (*-, -n*) *f* affair
Affe (*-n, -n*) *m* monkey
Afghanistan (*-s*) *nt* Afghanistan
Afrika (*-s*) *nt* Africa; **Afrikaner(in)** (*-s, -*) *m(f)* African; **afrikanisch** *adj* African
After (*-s, -*) *m* anus
Aftershave (*-(s), -s*) *nt* aftershave
AG (*-, -s*) *f abk =* **Aktiengesellschaft** plc (*Brit*), corp. (*US*)
Agent(in) *m(f)* agent; **Agentur** *f* agency
aggressiv *adj* aggressive
Ägypten (*-s*) *nt* Egypt

ah *interj* ah, ooh
äh *interj* (*Sprechpause*) er, um; (*angeekelt*) ugh
aha *interj* I see, aha
ähneln *vi +dat* to be like, to resemble ▷ *vr:* **sich ~** to be alike (*o* similar)
ahnen *vt* to suspect; **du ahnst es nicht!** would you believe it?
ähnlich *adj* similar (*dat* to); **jdm ~ sehen** to look like sb; **Ähnlichkeit** *f* similarity
Ahnung *f* idea; (*Vermutung*) suspicion; **keine ~!** no idea; **ahnungslos** *adj* unsuspecting
Ahorn (*-s, -e*) *m* maple
Aids (*-*) *nt* Aids; **aidskrank** *adj* suffering from Aids; **Aidstest** *m* Aids test
Airbag (*-s, -s*) *m* (*Auto*) airbag; **Airbus** *m* airbus
Akademie (*-, -n*) *f* academy; **Akademiker(in)** (*-s, -*) *m(f)* (university) graduate
akklimatisieren *vr:* **sich ~** to acclimatize oneself
Akkordeon (*-s, -s*) *nt* accordion
Akku (*-s, -s*) *m* (storage) battery
Akkusativ *m* accusative (case)
Akne (*-, -*) *f* acne
Akrobat(in) (*-s, -en*) *m(f)* acrobat
Akt (*-(e)s, -e*) *m* act; (*Kunst*) nude
Akte (*-, -n*) *f* file; **etw zu den ~n legen** (*a. fig*) to file sth away; **Aktenkoffer** *m* briefcase
Aktie (*-, -n*) *f* share; **Aktiengesellschaft** *f* public limited company (*Brit*), corporation (*US*)
Aktion *f* (*Kampagne*) campaign; (*Einsatz*) operation
Aktionär(in) (*-s, -e*) *m(f)* shareholder
aktiv *adj* active; **aktivieren** *vt* to activate
aktualisieren *vt* to update; **aktuell** *adj* (*Thema*) topical;

(*modern*) up-to-date; (*Problem*) current; **nicht mehr ~** no longer relevant

Akupunktur *f* acupuncture

akustisch *adj* acoustic; **Akustik** *f* acoustics *sing*

akut *adj* acute

AKW (*-s, -s*) *nt abk* = **Atomkraftwerk** nuclear power station

Akzent (*-(e)s, -e*) *m* accent; (*Betonung*) stress; **mit starkem schottischen ~** with a strong Scottish accent

akzeptieren *vt* to accept

Alarm (*-(e)s, -e*) *m* alarm; **Alarmanlage** *f* alarm system; **alarmieren** *vt* to alarm; **die Polizei ~** to call the police

Albanien (*-s*) *nt* Albania

Albatros (*-ses, -se*) *m* albatross

albern *adj* silly

Albtraum *m* nightmare

Album (*-s, Alben*) *nt* album

Algen (*-s*) *f* algae *pl*; (*Meeresalgen*) seaweed *sing*

Algerien (*-s*) *nt* Algeria

Alibi (*-s, -s*) *nt* alibi

Alimente *pl* maintenance *sing*

Alkohol (*-s, -e*) *m* alcohol; **alkoholfrei** *adj* non-alcoholic; **~es Getränk** soft drink; **Alkoholiker(in)** (*-s, -*) *m(f)* alcoholic; **alkoholisch** *adj* alcoholic; **Alkoholtest** *m* breathalyser® test (*Brit*), alcohol test

All (*-s*) *nt* universe

○ SCHLÜSSELWORT

alle(r, s) *adj* 1 (*sämtliche*) all; **wir alle** all of us; **alle Kinder waren da** all the children were there; **alle Kinder mögen ...** all children like ...; **alle beide** both of us/them; **sie kamen alle** they all came; **alles Gute** all the best; **alles**

in allem all in all

2 (*mit Zeit- oder Maßangaben*) every; **alle vier Jahre** every four years; **alle fünf Meter** every five metres

▷ *pron* everything; **alles, was er sagt** everything he says, all that he says

▷ *adv* (*zu Ende, aufgebraucht*) finished; **die Milch ist alle** the milk's all gone, there's no milk left; **etw alle machen** to finish sth up

Allee (*-, -n*) *f* avenue

allein *adj, adv* alone; (*ohne Hilfe*) on one's own, by oneself; **nicht ~** (*nicht nur*) not only; **alleinerziehend** *adj*: **~e Mutter** single mother; **Alleinerziehende(r)** *mf* single mother/father/parent; **alleinstehend** *adj* single, unmarried

allerbeste(r, s) *adj* very best

allerdings *adv* (*zwar*) admittedly; (*gewiss*) certainly, sure (*US*)

allererste(r, s) *adj* very first; **zu allererst** first of all

Allergie *f* allergy; **Allergiker(in)** (*-s, -*) *m(f)* allergy sufferer; **allergisch** *adj* allergic (*gegen* to)

allerhand *adj inv* (*fam*) all sorts of; **das ist doch ~!** (*Vorwurf*) that's the limit

Allerheiligen (*-*) *nt* All Saints' Day

allerhöchste(r, s) *adj* very highest; **allerhöchstens** *adv* at the very most; **allerlei** *adj inv* all sorts of; **allerletzte(r, s)** *adj* very last; **allerwenigste(r, s)** *adj* very least

alles *pron* everything; **~ in allem** all in all; *siehe auch* **alle**

Alleskleber (*-s, -*) *m* all-purpose glue

allgemein *adj* general; **im Allgemeinen** in general; **Allgemeinarzt** *m*,

Allgemeinärztin f GP (Brit), family practitioner (US)
Alligator (-s, -en) m alligator
alljährlich adj annual
allmählich adj gradual ▷ adv gradually
Allradantrieb m all-wheel drive
Alltag m everyday life; **alltäglich** adj everyday; (gewöhnlich) ordinary; (tagtäglich) daily
allzu adv all too
Allzweckreiniger (-s, -) m multi-purpose cleaner
Alpen pl: **die ~** the Alps pl
Alphabet (-(e)s, -e) nt alphabet; **alphabetisch** adj alphabetical
Alptraum m siehe **Albtraum**

SCHLÜSSELWORT

als konj 1 (zeitlich) when; (gleichzeitig) as; **damals, als ...** (in the days) when ...; **gerade, als ...** just as ...
2 (in der Eigenschaft) than; **als Antwort** as an answer; **als Kind** as a child
3 (bei Vergleichen) than; **ich kam später als er** I came later than he (did) o later than him; **lieber ... als ...** rather ... than ...; **nichts als Ärger** nothing but trouble
4 **als ob/wenn** as if

also conj (folglich) so, therefore ▷ adv, interj so; **~ gut** (o **schön**)! okay then
alt adj old; **wie ~ sind Sie?** how old are you?; **28 Jahre ~** 28 years old; **vier Jahre älter** four years older
Altar (-(e)s, Altäre) m altar
Alter (-s, -) nt age; (hohes) old age; **im ~ von** at the age of; **er ist in meinem ~** he's my age
alternativ adj alternative; (umweltbewusst) ecologically

minded; (Landwirtschaft) organic; **Alternative** f alternative
Altersheim nt old people's home
Altglas nt used glass; **Altglascontainer** m bottle bank; **altmodisch** adj old-fashioned; **Altpapier** nt waste paper; **Altstadt** f old town
Alt-Taste f Alt key
Alufolie f tin (o kitchen) foil
Aluminium (-s) nt aluminium (Brit), aluminum (US)
Alzheimerkrankheit f Alzheimer's (disease)
am kontr von **an dem**; **~ 2. Januar** on January 2(nd); **~ Morgen** in the morning; **~ Strand** on the beach; **~ Bahnhof** at the station; **was gefällt Ihnen ~ besten?** what do you like best?; **~ besten bleiben wir hier** it would be best if we stayed here
Amateur(in) m(f) amateur
ambulant adj outpatient; **kann ich ~ behandelt werden?** can I have it done as an outpatient?; **Ambulanz** f (Krankenwagen) ambulance; (in der Klinik) outpatients' department
Ameise (-, -n) f ant
amen interj amen
Amerika (-s) nt America; **Amerikaner(in)** (-s, -) m(f) American; **amerikanisch** adj American
Ampel (-, -n) f traffic lights pl
Amphitheater nt amphitheatre
Amsel (-, -n) f blackbird
Amt (-(e)s, Ämter) nt (Dienststelle) office, department; (Posten) post; **amtlich** adj official; **Amtszeichen** nt (Tel) dialling tone (Brit), dial tone (US)
amüsant adj amusing; **amüsieren** vt to amuse ▷ vr: **sich ~** to enjoy oneself, to have a good time

○ SCHLÜSSELWORT

an prep +dat **1** (räumlich) (wo?) at; (auf, bei) on; (nahe bei) near; **an diesem Ort** at this place; **an der Wand** on the wall; **zu nahe an etw** too near to sth; **unten am Fluss** down by the river; **Köln liegt am Rhein** Cologne is on the Rhine
2 (zeitlich: wann?) on; **an diesem Tag** on this day; **an Ostern** at Easter
3 arm an Fett low in fat; **an etw sterben** to die of sth; **an (und für) sich** actually
▷ prep +akk **1** (räumlich: wohin?) to; **er ging ans Fenster** he went (over) to the window; **etw an die Wand hängen/schreiben** to hang/write sth on the wall
2 (woran?) **an etw denken** to think of sth
3 (gerichtet an) to; **ein Gruß/eine Frage an dich** greetings/a question to you
▷ adv **1** (ungefähr) about: **an die hundert** about a hundred
2 (auf Fahrplänen) **Frankfurt an 18.30** arriving Frankfurt 18.30
3 (ab) **von dort/heute an** from there/today onwards
4 (angeschaltet, angezogen) on; **das Licht ist an** the light is on; **ohne etwas an** with nothing on; siehe auch **am**

anal adj anal
analog adj analogous; (Inform) analog
Analyse (-, -n) f analysis; **analysieren** vt to analyse
Ananas (-, - o -se) f pineapple
an|baggern vt (fam) to chat up (Brit), to come on to (US)
Anbau m (Agr) cultivation; (Gebäude) extension; **an|bauen** vt (Agr) to cultivate; (Gebäudeteil) to build on
an|behalten irr vt to keep on
anbei adv enclosed; **~ sende ich ...** please find enclosed ...
an|beten vt to worship
an|bieten irr vt to offer ▷ vr: **sich ~** to volunteer
an|binden irr vt to tie up
Anblick m sight
an|braten irr vt to brown
an|brechen irr vt to start; (Vorräte, Ersparnisse) to break into; (Flasche, Packung) to open ▷ vi to start; (Tag) to break; (Nacht) to fall
an|brennen irr vt, vi to burn; **das Fleisch schmeckt angebrannt** the meat tastes burnt
an|bringen irr vt (herbeibringen) to bring; (befestigen) to fix, to attach
Andacht (-, -en) f devotion; (Gottesdienst) prayers pl
an|dauern vi to continue, to go on; **andauernd** adj continual
Andenken (-s, -) nt memory; (Gegenstand) souvenir
andere(r, s) adj (weitere) other; (verschieden) different; (folgend) next; **am ~n Tag** the next day; **von etw/jmd ~m sprechen** to talk about sth/sb else; **unter ~m** among other things; **andererseits** adv on the other hand
ändern vt to alter, to change ▷ vr: **sich ~** to change
andernfalls adv otherwise
anders adv differently (als from); **jemand/irgendwo ~** someone/ somewhere else; **sie ist ~ als ihre Schwester** she's not like her sister; **es geht nicht ~** there's no other way; **anders(he)rum** adv the other way round; **anderswo** adv somewhere else
anderthalb num one and a half

Änderung f change, alteration

an|deuten vt to indicate; (Wink geben) to hint at

Andorra (-s) nt Andorra

Andrang m: **es herrschte großer ~** there was a huge crowd

an|drohen vt: **jdm etw ~** to threaten sb with sth

aneinander adv at/on/to one another (o each other); **~ denken** think of each other; **sich ~ gewöhnen** to get used to each other; **aneinander|geraten** irr vi to clash; **aneinander|legen** vt to put together

an|erkennen irr vt (Staat, Zeugnis etc) to recognize; (würdigen) to appreciate; **Anerkennung** f recognition; (Würdigung) appreciation

an|fahren irr vt (fahren gegen) to run into; (Ort, Hafen) to stop (o call) at; (liefern) to deliver; **jdn ~** (fig: schimpfen) to jump on sb ▷ vi to start; (losfahren) to drive off

Anfall m (Med) attack; **anfällig** adj delicate; (Maschine) temperamental; **~ für** prone to

Anfang (-(e)s, Anfänge) m beginning, start; **zu/am ~** to start with; **~ Mai** at the beginning of May; **sie ist ~ 20** she's in her early twenties; **an|fangen** irr vt, vi to begin, to start; **damit kann ich nichts ~** that's no use to me; **Anfänger(in)** (-s, -) m(f) beginner; **anfangs** adv at first; **Anfangsbuchstabe** m first (o initial) letter

an|fassen vt (berühren) to touch ▷ vi: **kannst du mal mit ~?** can you give me a hand?

Anflug m (Aviat) approach; (Hauch) trace

an|fordern vt to demand; **Anforderung** f request (von for); (Anspruch) demand

Anfrage f inquiry

an|freunden vr: **sich mit jdm ~** to make (o to become) friends with sb

an|fühlen vr: **sich ~** to feel; **es fühlt sich gut an** it feels good

Anführungszeichen pl quotation marks pl

Angabe f (Tech) specification; (fam: Prahlerei) showing off; (Tennis) serve; **~n** pl (Auskunft) particulars pl; **die ~n waren falsch** (Info) the information was wrong; **an|geben** irr vt (Name, Grund) to give; (zeigen) to indicate; (bestimmen) to set ▷ vi (fam: prahlen) to boast; (Sport) to serve; **Angeber(in)** (-s, -) m(f) (fam) show-off; **angeblich** adj alleged

angeboren adj inborn

Angebot nt offer; (Comm) supply (an +dat of); **~ und Nachfrage** supply and demand

angebracht adj appropriate

angebunden adj: **kurz ~** curt

angeheitert adj tipsy

an|gehen irr vt to concern; **das geht dich nichts an** that's none of your business; **ein Problem ~** to tackle a problem; **was ihn angeht** as far as he's concerned, as for him ▷ vi (Feuer) to catch; (fam: beginnen) to begin; **angehend** adj prospective

Angehörige(r) mf relative

Angeklagte(r) mf accused, defendant

Angel (-, -n) f fishing rod; (an der Tür) hinge

Angelegenheit f affair, matter

Angelhaken m fish hook; **angeln** vt to catch ▷ vi to fish; **Angeln** (-s) nt angling, fishing; **Angelrute** (-, -n) f fishing rod

angemessen adj appropriate, suitable

angenehm adj pleasant; **~!** (bei Vorstellung) pleased to meet you

angenommen adj assumed ▷ conj: **~, es regnet, was machen wir dann?** suppose it rains, what do we do then?

angesehen adj respected

angesichts prep +gen in view of, considering

Angestellte(r) mf employee

angetan adj: **von jdm/etw ~ sein** to be impressed by (o taken with) sb/sth

angewiesen adj: **auf jdn/etw ~ sein** to be dependent on sb/sth

an|gewöhnen vt: **sich etw ~** to get used to doing sth; **Angewohnheit** f habit

Angina (-, Anginen) f tonsillitis; **Angina Pectoris** (-) f angina

Angler(in) (-s, -) m(f) angler

Angora (-s) nt angora

an|greifen irr vt to attack; (anfassen) to touch; (beschädigen) to damage; **Angriff** m attack; **etw in ~ nehmen** to get started on sth

Angst (-, Ängste) f fear; **~ haben** to be afraid (o scared) (vor +dat of); **jdm ~ machen** to scare sb; **ängstigen** vt to frighten ▷ vr: **sich ~** to worry (um, wegen +dat about); **ängstlich** adj nervous; (besorgt) worried

an|haben irr vt (Kleidung) to have on, to wear; (Licht) to have on

an|halten irr vi to stop; (andauern) to continue; **anhaltend** adj continuous; **Anhalter(in)** (-s, -) m(f) hitch-hiker; **per ~ fahren** to hitch-hike

anhand prep +gen with; **~ von** by means of

an|hängen vt to hang up; (Eisenb: Wagen) to couple; (Zusatz) to add (on); **jdm etw ~** (fam: unterschieben) to pin sth on sb;

Anhänger (-s, -) m (Auto) trailer; (am Koffer) tag; (Schmuck) pendant; **Anhänger(in)** (-s, -) m(f) supporter; **Anhängerkupplung** f towbar; **anhänglich** adj affectionate; (pej) clinging

Anhieb m: **auf ~** straight away; **das kann ich nicht auf ~ sagen** I can't say offhand

an|himmeln vt to worship, to idolize

an|hören vt to listen to ▷ vr: **sich ~** to sound; **das hört sich gut an** that sounds good

Animateur(in) m(f) host/hostess

Anis (-es, -e) m aniseed

Anker (-s, -) m anchor; **ankern** vt, vi to anchor; **Ankerplatz** m anchorage

an|klicken vt (Inform) to click on

an|klopfen vi to knock (an +akk on)

an|kommen irr vi to arrive; **bei jdm gut ~** to go down well with sb; **es kommt darauf an** it depends (ob on whether); **darauf kommt es nicht an** that doesn't matter

an|kotzen vt (vulg) **es kotzt mich an** it makes me sick

an|kreuzen vt to mark with a cross

an|kündigen vt to announce

Ankunft (-, Ankünfte) f arrival; **Ankunftszeit** f arrival time

Anlage f (Veranlagung) disposition; (Begabung) talent; (Park) gardens pl, grounds pl; (zu Brief etc) enclosure; (Stereoanlage) stereo (system); (Tech) plant; (Fin) investment

Anlass (-es, Anlässe) m cause (zu for); (Ereignis) occasion; **aus diesem ~** for this reason; **an|lassen** irr vt (Motor) to start; (Licht, Kleidung) to leave on;

Anlasser (-s, -) m (Auto) starter; **anlässlich** prep +gen on the occasion of

Anlauf m run-up; **an|laufen** irr vi to begin; (Film) to open; (Fenster) to mist up; (Metall) to tarnish

an|legen vt to put (an +akk against/on); (Schmuck) to put on; (Garten) to lay out; (Geld) to invest; (Gewehr) to aim (auf +akk at); **es auf etw** (akk) **~** to be out for sth ▷ vi (Schiff) to berth, to dock ▷ vr: **sich mit jdm ~** (fam) to pick a quarrel with sb; **Anlegestelle** f moorings pl

an|lehnen vt to lean (an +akk against); (Tür) to leave ajar ▷ vr: **sich ~** to lean (an +akk against)

an|leiern vt: **etw ~** (fam) to get sth going

Anleitung f instructions pl

Anliegen (-s, -) nt matter; (Wunsch) request

Anlieger(in) (-s, -) m(f) resident; **~ frei** residents only

an|lügen irr vt to lie to

an|machen vt (befestigen) to attach; (einschalten) to switch on; (Salat) to dress; (fam: aufreizen) to turn on; (fam: ansprechen) to chat up (Brit), to come on to (US); (fam: beschimpfen) to have a go at

Anmeldeformular nt application form; (bei Amt) registration form; **an|melden** vt (Besuch etc) to announce ▷ vr: **sich ~** (beim Arzt etc) to make an appointment; (bei Amt, für Kurs etc) to register; **Anmeldeschluss** m deadline for applications, registration deadline; **Anmeldung** f registration; (Antrag) application

an|nähen vt: **einen Knopf (an den Mantel) ~** to sew a button on (one's coat)

annähernd adv roughly; **nicht ~** nowhere near

Annahme (-, -n) f acceptance; (Vermutung) assumption; **annehmbar** adj acceptable; **an|nehmen** irr vt to accept; (Namen) to take; (Kind) to adopt; (vermuten) to suppose, to assume

Annonce (-, -n) f advertisement

an|öden vt (fam) to bore stiff (o silly)

annullieren vt to cancel

anonym adj anonymous

Anorak (-s, -s) m anorak

an|packen vt (Problem, Aufgabe) to tackle; **mit ~** to lend a hand

an|passen vt (fig) to adapt (dat to) ▷ vr: **sich ~** to adapt (an +akk to)

an|pfeifen irr vt (Fußballspiel) **das Spiel ~** to start the game; **Anpfiff** m (Sport) (starting) whistle; (Beginn) kick-off; (fam: Tadel) roasting

an|probieren vt to try on

Anrede f form of address; **an|reden** vt to address

an|regen vt to stimulate; **Anregung** f stimulation; (Vorschlag) suggestion

Anreise f journey; **an|reisen** vi to arrive; **Anreisetag** m day of arrival

Anreiz m incentive

an|richten vt (Speisen) to prepare; (Schaden) to cause

Anruf m call; **Anrufbeantworter** (-s, -) m answering machine, answerphone; **an|rufen** irr vt (Tel) to call, to phone, to ring (Brit)

ans kontr von **an das**

Ansage f announcement; (auf Anrufbeantworter) recorded message; **an|sagen** vt to announce; **angesagt sein** to be recommended; (modisch sein) to be the in thing

an|schaffen vt to buy

an|schauen vt to look at

Anschein m appearance; **dem** (o **allem**) **~ nach ...** it looks as if ...; **den ~ erwecken, hart zu arbeiten** to give the impression of working hard; **anscheinend** adj apparent ▷ adv apparently

an|schieben irr vt: **könnten Sie mich mal ~?** (Auto) could you give me a push?

Anschlag m notice; (Attentat) attack; **an|schlagen** irr vt (Plakat) to put up; (beschädigen) to chip ▷ vi (wirken) to take effect; **mit etw an etw** (akk) **~** to bang sth against sth

an|schließen irr vt (Elek, Tech) to connect (an +akk to); (mit Stecker) to plug in ▷ vi, vr (sich) **an etw** (akk) **~** (Gebäude etc) to adjoin sth; (zeitlich) to follow sth ▷ vr: **sich ~** to join (jdm/einer Gruppe sb/a group); **anschließend** adj adjacent; (zeitlich) subsequent ▷ adv afterwards; **~ an** (+akk) following; **Anschluss** m (Elek, Eisenb) connection; (von Wasser, Gas etc) supply; **im ~ an** (+akk) following; **kein ~ unter dieser Nummer** (Tel) the number you have dialled has not been recognized; **Anschlussflug** m connecting flight

an|schnallen vt (Skier) to put on ▷ vr: **sich ~** to fasten one's seat belt

Anschrift f address

an|schwellen irr vi to swell (up)

an|sehen irr vt to look at; (bei etw zuschauen) to watch; **jdn/etw als etw ~** to look on sb/sth as sth; **das sieht man ihm an** he looks it

an sein irr vi siehe **an**

an|setzen vt (Termin) to fix; (zubereiten) to prepare ▷ vi (anfangen) to start, to begin; **zu etw ~** to prepare to do sth

Ansicht f (Meinung) view, opinion; (Anblick) sight; **meiner ~ nach** in my opinion; **zur ~** on approval; **Ansichtskarte** f postcard

ansonsten adv otherwise

an|spielen vi **auf etw** (akk) **~** to allude to sth; **Anspielung** f allusion (auf +akk to)

an|sprechen irr vt to speak to; (gefallen) to appeal to ▷ vi **auf etw** (akk) **~** (Patient) to respond to sth; **ansprechend** adj attractive; **Ansprechpartner(in)** m(f) contact

an|springen irr vi (Auto) to start

Anspruch m claim; (Recht) right (auf +akk to); **etw in ~ nehmen** to take advantage of sth; **~ auf etw haben** to be entitled to sth; **anspruchslos** adj undemanding; (bescheiden) modest; **anspruchsvoll** adj demanding

Anstalt (-, -en) f institution

Anstand m decency; **anständig** adj decent; (fig, fam) proper; (groß) considerable

an|starren vt to stare at

anstatt prep +gen instead of

an|stecken vt to pin on; (Med) to infect; **jdn mit einer Erkältung ~** to pass one's cold on to sb ▷ vr: **ich habe mich bei ihm angesteckt** I caught it from him ▷ vi (fig) to be infectious; **ansteckend** adj infectious; **Ansteckungsgefahr** f danger of infection

an|stehen irr vi (in Warteschlange) to queue (Brit), to stand in line (US); (erledigt werden müssen) to be on the agenda

anstelle prep +gen instead of

an|stellen vt (einschalten) to turn on; (Arbeit geben) to employ; (machen) to do; **was hast du**

wieder angestellt? what have you been up to now? ▷ vr: **sich ~** to queue (*Brit*), to stand in line (*US*); (*fam*) **stell dich nicht so an!** stop making such a fuss

Anstoß *m* impetus; (*Sport*) kick-off; **an|stoßen** *irr vt* to push; (*mit Fuß*) to kick ▷ vi to knock, to bump; (*mit Gläsern*) to drink (a toast) (*auf +akk* to); **anstößig** *adj* offensive; (*Kleidung etc*) indecent

an|strengen *vt* to strain ▷ vr: **sich ~** to make an effort; **anstrengend** *adj* tiring

Antarktis *f* Antarctic

Anteil *m* share (*an +dat* in); **~ nehmen an** (*+dat*) (*mitleidig*) to sympathize with; (*sich interessieren*) to take an interest in

Antenne (*-, -n*) *f* aerial

Antibabypille *f*: **die ~** the pill; **Antibiotikum** (*-s, Antibiotika*) *nt* (*Med*) antibiotic

antik *adj* antique

Antilope (*-, -n*) *f* antelope

Antiquariat *nt* (*für Bücher*) second-hand bookshop

Antiquitäten *pl* antiques *pl*; **Antiquitätenhändler(in)** *m(f)* antique dealer

an|törnen *vt* (*fam*) to turn on

Antrag (*-(e)s, Anträge*) *m* proposal; (*Pol*) motion; (*Formular*) application form; **einen ~ stellen auf** (*+akk*) to make an application for

an|treffen *irr vt* to find

an|treiben *irr vt* (*Tech*) to drive; (*anschwemmen*) to wash up; **jdn zur Arbeit ~** to make sb work

an|treten ~ *irr vt*: **eine Reise ~** to set off on a journey

Antrieb *m* (*Tech*) drive; (*Motivation*) impetus

an|tun *irr vt*: **jdm etwas ~** to do sth to sb; **sich** (*dat*) **etwas ~** (*Selbstmord begehen*) to kill

oneself

Antwort (*-, -en*) *f* answer, reply; **um ~ wird gebeten** RSVP (*répondez s'il vous plaît*); **antworten** *vi* to answer, to reply; **jdm ~** to answer sb; **auf etw** (*akk*) **~** to answer sth

an|vertrauen *vt*: **jdm etw ~** to entrust sb with sth

Anwalt (*-s, Anwälte*) *m*, **Anwältin** *f* lawyer

an|weisen *irr vt* (*anleiten*) to instruct; (*zuteilen*) to allocate (*jdm etw* sth to sb); **Anweisung** *f* instruction; (*von Geld*) money order

an|wenden *irr vt* to use; (*Gesetz, Regel*) to apply; **Anwender(in)** (*-s, -*) *m(f)* user; **Anwendung** *f* use; (*Inform*) application

anwesend *adj* present; **Anwesenheit** *f* presence

an|widern *vt* to disgust

Anwohner(in) (*-s, -*) *m(f)* resident

Anzahl *f* number (*an +dat* of); **an|zahlen** *vt* to pay a deposit on; **100 Euro ~** to pay 100 euros as a deposit; **Anzahlung** *f* deposit

Anzeichen *nt* sign; (*Med*) symptom

Anzeige (*-, -n*) *f* (*Werbung*) advertisement; (*elektronisch*) display; (*bei Polizei*) report; **an|zeigen** *vt* (*Temperatur, Zeit*) to indicate, to show; (*elektronisch*) to display; (*bekannt geben*) to announce; **jdn/einen Autodiebstahl bei der Polizei ~** to report sb/a stolen car to the police

an|ziehen *irr vt* to attract; (*Kleidung*) to put on; (*Schraube, Seil*) to tighten ▷ vr: **sich ~** to get dressed; **anziehend** *adj* attractive

Anzug *m* suit

anzüglich *adj* suggestive

an|zünden *vt* to light; (*Haus etc*)

to set fire to

an|zweifeln vt to doubt

Aperitif (-s, -s (o -e)) m aperitif

Apfel (-s, Äpfel) m apple;
Apfelbaum m apple tree;
Apfelkuchen m apple cake;
Apfelmus nt apple purée;
Apfelsaft m apple juice;
Apfelsine f orange; **Apfelwein** m cider

Apostroph (-s, -e) m apostrophe

Apotheke (-, -n) f chemist's (shop) (Brit), pharmacy (US);
apothekenpflichtig adj only available at the chemist's (o pharmacy); **Apotheker(in)** (-s, -) m(f) chemist (Brit), pharmacist (US)

Apparat (-(e)s, -e) m (piece of) apparatus; (Tel) telephone; (Radio, TV) set; **am ~!** (Tel) speaking; **am ~ bleiben** (Tel) to hold the line

Appartement (-s, -s) nt studio flat (Brit) (o apartment (US))

Appetit (-(e)s, -e) m appetite;
guten ~! bon appétit; **appetitlich** adj appetizing

Applaus (-es, -e) m applause

Aprikose (-, -n) f apricot

April (-(s), -e) m April; siehe auch **Juni; ~, ~!** April fool!; **Aprilscherz** (-es, -e) m April fool's joke

apropos adv by the way;
~ Urlaub ... while we're on the subject of holidays ...

Aquajogging nt aqua jogging;
Aquaplaning (-(s)) nt aquaplaning

Aquarell (-s, -e) nt watercolour

Aquarium (-s, Aquarien) nt aquarium

Äquator (-s, -) m equator

Araber(in) (-s, -) m(f) Arab;
arabisch adj Arab; (Ziffer, Sprache) Arabic; (Meer, Wüste) Arabian

Arbeit (-, -en) f work; (Stelle) job; (Erzeugnis) piece of work; **arbeiten**
vi to work; **Arbeiter(in)** (-s, -) m(f) worker; (ungelernt) labourer;
Arbeitgeber(in) (-s, -) m(f) employer;
Arbeitnehmer(in) (-s, -) m(f) employe
Arbeitsagentur f job agency (Brit), unemployment agency (US);
Arbeitsamt nt job centre (Brit), employment office (US);
Arbeitserlaubnis f work permit;
arbeitslos adj unemployed;
Arbeitslose(r) mf unemployed person; **die ~n** pl the unemployed pl; **Arbeitslosengeld** nt (income-related) unemployment benefit, job-seeker's allowance (Brit); **Arbeitslosenhilfe** f (non-income related) unemployment benefit;
Arbeitslosigkeit f unemployment; **Arbeitsplatz** m job; (Ort) workplace; **Arbeitsspeicher** m (Inform) main memory;
Arbeitszeit f working hours pl;
Arbeitszimmer nt study

Archäologe (-n, -n) m,
Archäologin f archaeologist

Architekt(in) (-en, -en) m(f) architect; **Architektur** f architecture

Archiv (-s, -e) nt archives pl

arg adj bad; (schrecklich) awful ▷ adv (sehr) terribly

Argentinien (-s) nt Argentina

Ärger (-s) m annoyance; (stärker) anger; (Unannehmlichkeiten) trouble; **ärgerlich** adj (zornig) angry; (lästig) annoying; **ärgern** vt to annoy ▷ vr: **sich ~** to get annoyed

Argument (-s, -e) nt argument

Arktis (-) f Arctic

arm adj poor

Arm (-(e)s, -e) m arm; (Fluss) branch

Armaturenbrett nt instrument panel; (Auto) dashboard

Armband nt bracelet;

Armbanduhr f (wrist)watch
Armee (-, -n) f army
Ärmel (-s, -) m sleeve;
Ärmelkanal m (English) Channel
Armut (-) f poverty
Aroma (-s, Aromen) nt aroma
arrogant adj arrogant
Arsch (-es, Ärsche) m (vulg) arse
(Brit), ass (US); **Arschloch** nt
(vulg: Person) arsehole (Brit),
asshole (US)
Art (-, -en) f (Weise) way; (Sorte)
kind, sort; (bei Tieren) species;
nach ~ des Hauses à la maison;
auf diese ~ (und Weise) in this
way; **das ist nicht seine ~** that's
not like him
Arterie (-, -n) f artery
artig adj good, well-behaved
Artikel (-s, -) m (Ware) article,
item; (Zeitung) article
Artischocke (-, -n) f artichoke
Artist(in) (-en, -en) m(f) (circus)
performer
Arznei f medicine; **Arzt** (-es,
Ärzte) m doctor; **Arzthelfer(in)**
m(f) doctor's assistant; **Ärztin** f
(female) doctor; **ärztlich** adj
medical; **sich ~ behandeln lassen**
to undergo medical treatment
Asche (-, -n) f ashes pl; (von
Zigarette) ash; **Aschenbecher** m
ashtray; **Aschermittwoch** m
Ash Wednesday
Asiat(in) (-en, -en) m(f) Asian;
asiatisch adj Asian; **Asien** (-s) nt
Asia
Aspekt (-(e)s, -e) m aspect
Asphalt (-(e)s, -e) m asphalt
Aspirin® (-s, -e) nt aspirin
aß imperf von **essen**
Ass (-es, -e) nt (Karten, Tennis) ace
Assistent(in) m(f) assistant
Ast (-(e)s, Äste) m branch
Asthma (-s) nt asthma
Astrologie f astrology;
Astronaut(in) (-en, -en) m(f)

astronaut; **Astronomie** f
astronomy
ASU (-, -s) f abk =
Abgassonderuntersuchung
exhaust emission test
Asyl (-s, -e) nt asylum; (Heim)
home; (für Obdachlose) shelter;
Asylant(in) m(f), **Asylbe-
werber(in)** m(f) asylum seeker
Atelier (-s, -s) nt studio
Atem (-s) m breath;
atemberaubend adj breathtaking; **Atembeschwerden** pl
breathing difficulties pl; **atemlos**
adj breathless; **Atempause** f
breather
Athen nt Athens
Äthiopien (-s) nt Ethiopia
Athlet(in) (-en, -en) m(f) athlete
Atlantik (-s) m Atlantic (Ocean)
Atlas (- o Atlasses, Atlanten) m
atlas
atmen vt, vi to breathe; **Atmung**
f breathing
Atom (-s, -e) nt atom;
Atombombe f atom bomb;
Atomkraftwerk nt nuclear
power station; **Atommüll** m
nuclear waste; **Atomwaffen** pl
nuclear weapons pl
Attentat (-(e)s, -e) nt
assassination (auf +akk of);
(Versuch) assassination attempt
Attest (-(e)s, -e) nt certificate
attraktiv adj attractive
Attrappe (-, -n) f dummy
ätzend adj (fam) revolting;
(schlecht) lousy
au interj ouch; **~ ja!** yeah
Aubergine (-, -n) f aubergine,
eggplant (US)

⊙ SCHLÜSSELWORT

auch adv **1** (ebenfalls) also, too, as
well; **das ist auch schön** that's
nice too o as well; **er kommt — ich**

auch he's coming — so am I, me too; **auch nicht** not ... either; **ich auch nicht** nor I, me neither; **oder auch** or; **auch das noch!** not that as well!

2 (*selbst, sogar*) even; **auch wenn das Wetter schlecht ist** even if the weather is bad; **ohne auch nur zu fragen** without even asking

3 (*wirklich*) really; **du siehst müde aus—bin ich auch** you look tired—(so) I am; **so sieht es auch aus** it looks like it too

4 (*auch immer*) **wer auch** whoever; **was auch** whatever; **wie dem auch sei** be that as it may; **wie sehr er sich auch bemühte** however much he tried

audiovisuell *adj* audiovisual

○ SCHLÜSSELWORT

auf *prep* +*dat* (*wo?*) on; **auf dem Tisch** on the table; **auf der Reise** on the way; **auf der Post/dem Fest** at the post office/party; **auf der Straße** on the road; **auf dem Land/der ganzen Welt** in the country/the whole world
▷ *prep* +*akk* 1 (*wohin?*) on(to); **auf den Tisch** on(to) the table; **auf die Post gehen** to go to the post office; **auf das Land** into the country; **etw auf einen Zettel schreiben** to write sth on a piece of paper

2 **auf Deutsch** in German; **auf Lebenszeit** for my/his lifetime; **bis auf ihn** except for him; **auf einmal** at once; **auf seinen Vorschlag (hin)** at his suggestion
▷ *adv* 1 (*offen*) open; **auf sein** (*fam*) (Tür, Geschäft) to be open; **das Fenster ist auf** the window is open

2 (*hinauf*) up; **auf und ab** up and down; **auf und davon** up and away; **auf!** (*los!*) come on!

3 (*aufgestanden*) up; **auf sein** to be up; **ist er schon auf?** is he up yet?
▷ *konj*: **auf dass** (so) that

auf|atmen *vi* to breathe a sigh of relief

auf|bauen *vt* (*errichten*) to put up; (*schaffen*) to build up; (*gestalten*) to construct; (*gründen*) to found, to base (*auf* +*akk* on); **sich eine Existenz ~** to make a life for oneself

auf|bewahren *vt* to keep, to store

auf|bleiben *irr vi* (Tür, Laden etc) to stay open; (Mensch) to stay up

auf|blenden *vi*, *vt*: (**die Scheinwerfer**) **~** to put one's headlights on full beam

auf|brechen *irr vt* to break open
▷ *vi* to burst open; (*gehen*) to leave; (*abreisen*) to set off

auf|drängen *vt*: **jdm etw ~** to force sth on sb ▷ *vr*: **sich ~** to intrude (*jdm* on sb); **aufdringlich** *adj* pushy

aufeinander *adv* (*übereinander*) on top of each other; **~ achten** to look after each other; **~ vertrauen** to trust each other; **aufeinan-der|folgen** *vi* to follow one another; **aufeinander|prallen** *vi* to crash into one another

Aufenthalt *m* stay; (Zug) stop; **Aufenthaltsgenehmigung** *f* residence permit; **Aufenthaltsraum** *m* lounge

auf|essen *irr vt* to eat up

auf|fahren *irr vi* (Auto) to run (*o* to crash) (*auf* +*akk* into); (*herankommen*) to drive up; **Auffahrt** *f* (am Haus) drive; (Autobahn) slip road (Brit), ramp (US); **Auffahrunfall** *m* rear-end collision; (*mehrere Fahrzeuge*) pile-up

auf|fallen *irr vi* to stand out; **jdm ~** to strike sb; **das fällt gar nicht auf** nobody will notice; **auffallend** *adj* striking; **auffällig** *adj* conspicuous; (*Kleidung, Farbe*) striking

auf|fangen *irr vt* (*Ball*) to catch; (*Stoß*) to cushion

auf|fassen *vt* to understand; **Auffassung** *f* view; (*Meinung*) opinion; (*Auslegung*) concept; (*Auffassungsgabe*) grasp

auf|fordern *vt* (*befehlen*) to call upon; (*bitten*) to ask

auf|frischen *vt* (*Kenntnisse*) to brush up

auf|führen *vt* (*Theat*) to perform; (*in einem Verzeichnis*) to list; (*Beispiel*) to give ▷ *vr*: **sich ~** (*sich benehmen*) to behave; **Aufführung** *f* (*Theat*) performance

Aufgabe *f* job, task; (*Schule*) exercise; (*Hausaufgabe*) homework

Aufgang *m* (*Treppe*) staircase

auf|geben *irr vt* (*verzichten auf*) to give up; (*Paket*) to post; (*Gepäck*) to check in; (*Bestellung*) to place; (*Inserat*) to insert; (*Rätsel, Problem*) to set ▷ *vi* to give up

auf|gehen *irr vi* (*Sonne, Teig*) to rise; (*sich öffnen*) to open; (*klar werden*) to dawn (*jdm on sb*)

aufgelegt *adj*: **gut/schlecht ~** in a good/bad mood

aufgeregt *adj* excited

aufgeschlossen *adj* open(minded)

aufgeschmissen *adj* (*fam*) in a fix

aufgrund, **auf Grund** *prep +gen* on the basis of; (*wegen*) because of

auf|haben *irr vt* (*Hut etc*) to have on; **viel ~** (*Schule*) to have a lot of homework to do ▷ *vi* (*Geschäft*) to be open

auf|halten *irr vt* (*jdn*) to detain; (*Entwicklung*) to stop; (*Tür, Hand*) to hold open; (*Augen*) to keep open ▷ *vr*: **sich ~** (*wohnen*) to live; (*vorübergehend*) to stay

auf|hängen *irr vt* to hang up

auf|heben *irr vt* (*vom Boden etc*) to pick up; (*aufbewahren*) to keep

auf|holen *vt* (*Zeit*) to make up ▷ *vi* to catch up

auf|hören *vi* to stop; **~, etw zu tun** to stop doing sth

auf|klären *vt* (*Geheimnis etc*) to clear up; **jdn ~** to enlighten sb; (*sexuell*) to tell sb the facts of life

Aufkleber (*-s, -*) *m* sticker

auf|kommen *irr vi* (*Wind*) to come up; (*Zweifel, Gefühl*) to arise; (*Mode etc*) to appear on the scene; **für den Schaden ~** to pay for the damage

auf|laden *irr vt* to load; (*Handy etc*) to charge; (*Handykarte etc*) to top up; **Aufladegerät** *nt* charger

Auflage *f* edition; (*von Zeitung*) circulation; (*Bedingung*) condition

auf|lassen *vt* (*Hut, Brille*) to keep on; (*Tür*) to leave open

Auflauf *m* (*Menschen*) crowd; (*Speise*) bake

auf|legen *vt* (*CD, Schminke etc*) to put on; (*Hörer*) to put down ▷ *vi* (*Tel*) to hang up

auf|leuchten *vi* to light up

auf|lösen *vt* (*in Flüssigkeit*) to dissolve ▷ *vr*: **sich ~** (*in Flüssigkeit*) to dissolve; **der Stau hat sich aufgelöst** traffic is back to normal; **Auflösung** *f* (*von Rätsel*) solution; (*von Bildschirm*) resolution

auf|machen *vt* to open; (*Kleidung*) to undo ▷ *vr*: **sich ~** to set out (*nach for*)

aufmerksam *adj* attentive; **jdn auf etw** (*akk*) **~ machen** to draw sb's attention to sth;

Aufmerksamkeit f attention; (Konzentration) attentiveness; (Geschenk) small token

auf|muntern vt (ermutigen) to encourage; (aufheitern) to cheer up

Aufnahme (-, -n) f (Foto) photo(graph); (einzelne) shot; (in Verein, Krankenhaus etc) admission; (Beginn) beginning; (auf Tonband etc) recording; **Aufnahmeprüfung** f entrance exam; **auf|nehmen** irr vt (in Krankenhaus, Verein etc) to admit; (Musik) to record; (beginnen) to take up; (in Liste) to include; (begreifen) to take in; **mit jdm Kontakt ~** to get in touch with sb

auf|passen vi (aufmerksam sein) to pay attention; (vorsichtig sein) to take care; **auf jdn/etw ~** to keep an eye on sb/sth

Aufprall (-s, -e) m impact; **auf|prallen** vi **auf etw** (akk) **~** to hit sth, to crash into sth

Aufpreis m extra charge

auf|pumpen vt to pump up

Aufputschmittel nt stimulant

auf|räumen vt, vi (Dinge) to clear away; (Zimmer) to tidy up

aufrecht adj upright

auf|regen vt to excite; (ärgern) to annoy ▷ vr: **sich ~** to get worked up; **aufregend** adj exciting; **Aufregung** f excitement

auf|reißen irr vt (Tüte) to tear open; (Tür) to fling open; (fam: Person) to pick up

Aufruf m (Aviat, Inform) call; (öffentlicher) appeal; **auf|rufen** irr vt (auffordern) to call upon (zu for); (Namen) to call out; (Aviat) to call; (Inform) to call up

auf|runden vt (Summe) to round up

aufs kontr von **auf das**

Aufsatz m essay

auf|schieben irr vt (verschieben) to postpone; (verzögern) to put off; (Tür) to slide open

Aufschlag m (auf Preis) extra charge; (Tennis) service; **auf|schlagen** irr vt (öffnen) to open; (verletzen) to cut open; (Zelt) to pitch, to put up; (Lager) to set up ▷ vi (Tennis) to serve; **auf etw** (+akk) **~** (aufprallen) to hit sth

auf|schließen irr vt to unlock, to open up ▷ vi (aufrücken) to close up

auf|schneiden irr vt to cut open; (in Scheiben) to slice ▷ vi (angeben) to boast, to show off

Aufschnitt m (slices pl of) cold meat; (bei Käse) (assorted) sliced cheeses pl

auf|schreiben irr vt to write down

Aufschrift f inscription; (Etikett) label

Aufschub m (Verzögerung) delay; (Vertagung) postponement

Aufsehen (-s) nt stir; **großes ~ erregen** to cause a sensation; **Aufseher(in)** (-s, -) m(f) guard; (im Betrieb) supervisor; (im Museum) attendant; (im Park) keeper

auf sein irr vi siehe **auf**

auf|setzen vt to put on; (Dokument) to draw up ▷ vi (Flugzeug) to touch down

Aufsicht f supervision; (bei Prüfung) invigilation; **die ~ haben** to be in charge

auf|spannen vt (Schirm) to put up

auf|sperren vt (Mund) to open wide; (aufschließen) to unlock

auf|springen irr vi to jump (auf +akk onto); (hochspringen) to jump up; (sich öffnen) to spring open

auf|stehen irr vi to get up; (Tür) to be open

auf|stellen vt (aufrecht stellen) to

put up; (*aufreihen*) to line up; (*nominieren*) to put up; (*Liste, Programm*) to draw up; (*Rekord*) to set up

Aufstieg (-(*e*)*s*, -*e*) *m* (*auf Berg*) ascent; (*Fortschritt*) rise; (*beruflich, im Sport*) promotion

Aufstrich *m* spread

auf|tanken *vt, vi* (*Auto*) to tank up; (*Flugzeug*) to refuel

auf|tauchen *vi* to turn up; (*aus Wasser etc*) to surface; (*Frage, Problem*) to come up

auf|tauen *vt* (*Speisen*) to defrost ▷ *vi* to thaw; (*fig: Person*) to unbend

Auftrag (-(*e*)*s*, *Aufträge*) *m* (*Comm*) order; (*Arbeit*) job; (*Anweisung*) instructions *pl*; (*Aufgabe*) task; **im ~ von** on behalf of; **auf|tragen** *irr vt* (*Salbe etc*) to apply; (*Essen*) to serve

auf|treten *irr vi* to appear; (*Problem*) to come up; (*sich verhalten*) to behave; **Auftritt** *m* (*des Schauspielers*) entrance; (*fig: Szene*) scene

auf|wachen *vi* to wake up

auf|wachsen *irr vi* to grow up

Aufwand (-(*e*)*s*) *m* expenditure; (*Kosten a.*) expense; (*Anstrengung*) effort; **aufwändig** *adj* costly; **das ist zu ~** that's too much trouble

auf|wärmen *vt* to warm up ▷ *vr*: **sich ~** to warm up

aufwärts *adv* upwards; **mit etw geht es ~** things are looking up for sth

auf|wecken *vt* to wake up

aufwendig *adj siehe* **aufwändig**

auf|wischen *vt* to wipe up; (*Fußboden*) to wipe

auf|zählen *vt* to list

auf|zeichnen *vt* to sketch; (*schriftlich*) to jot down; (*auf Band etc*) to record; **Aufzeichnung** *f*

(*schriftlich*) note; (*Tonband etc*) recording; (*Film*) record

auf|ziehen *irr vt* (*öffnen*) to pull open; (*Uhr*) to wind (up); (*fam: necken*) to tease; (*Kinder*) to bring up; (*Tiere*) to rear ▷ *vi* (*Gewitter*) to come up

Aufzug *m* (*Fahrstuhl*) lift (*Brit*), elevator (*US*); (*Kleidung*) get-up; (*Theat*) act

Auge (-*s*, -*n*) *nt* eye; **jdm etw aufs ~ drücken** (*fam*) to force sth on sb; **ins ~ gehen** (*fam*) to go wrong; **unter vier ~n** in private; **etw im ~ behalten** to keep sth in mind; **Augenarzt** *m*, **Augenärztin** *f* eye specialist, eye doctor (*US*); **Augenblick** *m* moment; **im ~** at the moment; **Augenbraue** (-, -*n*) *f* eyebrow; **Augenbrauenstift** *m* eyebrow pencil; **Augenfarbe** *f* eye colour; **seine ~** the colour of his eyes; **Augenlid** *nt* eyelid; **Augenoptiker(in)** (-*s*, -) *m(f)* optician; **Augentropfen** *pl* eyedrops *pl*; **Augenzeuge** *m*, **Augenzeugin** *f* eyewitness

August (-(*e*)*s o* -, -*e*) *m* August; *siehe auch* **Juni**

Auktion *f* auction

🅞 SCHLÜSSELWORT

aus *prep* +*dat* **1** (*räumlich*) out of; (*von ... her*) from; **er ist aus Berlin** he's from Berlin; **aus dem Fenster** out of the window

2 (*gemacht/hergestellt aus*) made of; **ein Herz aus Stein** a heart of stone

3 (*auf Ursache deutend*) out of; **aus Mitleid** out of sympathy; **aus Erfahrung** from experience; **aus Spaß** for fun

4 aus ihr wird nie etwas she'll never get anywhere

▷ *adv* **1** (*zu Ende*) finished, over; **aus sein** to be over; **aus und vorbei** over and done with
2 (*ausgeschaltet, ausgezogen*) out; (*Aufschrift an Geräten*) off; **aus sein** (*nicht brennen*) to be out; (*abgeschaltet sein: Radio, Herd*) to be off; **Licht aus!** lights out!
3 (*nicht zu Hause*) **aus sein** to be out
4 (*in Verbindung mit von*) **von Rom aus** from Rome; **vom Fenster aus** out of the window; **von sich aus** (*selbstständig*) of one's own accord; **von ihm aus** as far as he's concerned

Aus (-) *nt* (*Sport*) touch; (*fig*) end
aus|atmen *vi* to breathe out
aus|bauen *vt* (*Haus, Straße*) to extend; (*Motor etc*) to remove
aus|bessern *vt* to repair; (*Kleidung*) to mend
aus|bilden *vt* to educate; (*Lehrling etc*) to train; (*Fähigkeiten*) to develop; **Ausbildung** *f* education; (*von Lehrling etc*) training; (*von Fähigkeiten*) development
Ausblick *m* view; (*fig*) outlook
aus|brechen *irr vi* to break out; **in Tränen ~** to burst into tears; **in Gelächter ~** to burst out laughing
aus|breiten *vt* to spread (out); (*Arme*) to stretch out ▷ *vr:* **sich ~** to spread
Ausbruch *m* (*Krieg, Seuche etc*) outbreak; (*Vulkan*) eruption; (*Gefühle*) outburst; (*von Gefangenen*) escape
aus|buhen *vt* to boo
Ausdauer *f* perseverance; (*Sport*) stamina
aus|dehnen *vt* to stretch; (*fig: Macht*) to extend
aus|denken *irr vt* **sich** (*dat*) **etw ~** to come up with sth

Ausdruck *m* (*Ausdrücke*) expression *m* (*Ausdrucke, Computerausdruck*) print-out; **aus|drucken** *vt* (*Inform*) to print (out)
aus|drücken *vt* (*formulieren*) to express; (*Zigarette*) to put out; (*Zitrone etc*) to squeeze ▷ *vr:* **sich ~** to express oneself; **ausdrücklich** *adj* express ▷ *adv* expressly
auseinander *adv* (*getrennt*) apart; **~ schreiben** to write as separate words; **auseinander|gehen** *irr vi* (*Menschen*) to separate; (*Meinungen*) to differ; (*Gegenstand*) to fall apart; **auseinander|halten** *irr vt* to tell apart; **auseinander|setzen** *vt* (*erklären*) to explain; **auseinander|setzen** *vr:* **sich ~** (*sich beschäftigen*) to look (*mit* at); (*sich streiten*) to argue (*mit* with); **Auseinandersetzung** *f* (*Streit*) argument; (*Diskussion*) debate
Ausfahrt *f* (*des Zuges etc*) departure; (*Autobahn, Garage etc*) exit
aus|fallen *irr vi* (*Haare*) to fall out; (*nicht stattfinden*) to be cancelled; (*nicht funktionieren*) to break down; (*Strom*) to be cut off; (*Resultat haben*) to turn out; **groß/klein ~** (*Kleidung, Schuhe*) to be too big/too small
ausfindig machen *vt* to discover
aus|flippen *vi* (*fam*) to freak out
Ausflug *m* excursion, outing; **Ausflugsziel** *nt* destination
Ausfluss *m* (*Med*) discharge
aus|fragen *vt* to question
Ausfuhr (-, -en) *f* export
aus|führen *vt* (*verwirklichen*) to carry out; (*Person*) to take out; (*Comm*) to export; (*darlegen*) to explain

ausführlich adj detailed ▷ adv in detail

aus|füllen vt to fill up; (*Fragebogen etc*) to fill in (o out)

Ausgabe f (*Geld*) expenditure; (*Inform*) output; (*Buch*) edition; (*Nummer*) issue

Ausgang m way out, exit; (*Flugsteig*) gate; (*Ende*) end; (*Ergebnis*) result; **„kein ~"** "no exit"

aus|geben irr vt (*Geld*) to spend; (*austeilen*) to distribute; **jdm etw ~** (*spendieren*) to buy sb sth ▷ vr: **sich für etw/jdn ~** to pass oneself off as sth/sb

ausgebucht adj fully booked

ausgefallen adj (*ungewöhnlich*) unusual

aus|gehen irr vi (*abends etc*) to go out; (*Benzin, Kaffee etc*) to run out; (*Haare*) to fall out; (*Feuer, Licht etc*) to go out; (*Resultat haben*) to turn out; **davon ~, dass** to assume that; **ihm ging das Geld aus** he ran out of money

ausgelassen adj exuberant

ausgeleiert adj worn out

ausgenommen conj, prep +gen o dat except

ausgerechnet adv: **~ du** you of all people; **~ heute** today of all days

ausgeschildert adj signposted

ausgeschlafen adj: **bist du ~?** have you had enough sleep?

ausgeschlossen adj (*unmöglich*) impossible, out of the question

ausgesprochen adj (*absolut*) out-and-out; (*unverkennbar*) marked ▷ adv extremely; **~ gut** really good

ausgezeichnet adj excellent

ausgiebig adj (*Gebrauch*) thorough; (*Essen*) substantial

aus|gießen irr vt (*Getränk*) to pour out; (*Gefäß*) to empty

aus|gleichen irr vt to even out ▷ vi (*Sport*) to equalize

Ausguss m (*Spüle*) sink; (*Abfluss*) outlet

aus|halten irr vt to bear, to stand; **nicht auszuhalten sein** to be unbearable ▷ vi to hold out

aus|händigen vt: **jdm etw ~ to** hand sth over to sb

Aushang m notice

Aushilfe f temporary help; (*im Büro*) temp

aus|kennen irr vr: **sich ~ to** know a lot (*bei, mit* about); (*an einem Ort*) to know one's way around

aus|kommen irr vi: **gut/schlecht mit jdm ~** to get on well/badly with sb; **mit etw ~** to get by with sth

Auskunft (-, *Auskünfte*) f information; (*nähere*) details pl; (*Schalter*) information desk; (*Tel*) (directory) enquiries sing (*kein Artikel, Brit*), information (*US*)

aus|lachen vt to laugh at

aus|laden irr vt (*Gepäck etc*) to unload; **jdn ~** (*Gast*) to tell sb not to come

Auslage f window display; **~n** pl (*Kosten*) expenses

Ausland nt foreign countries pl; **im/ins ~** abroad; **Ausländer(in)** (*-s, -*) m(f) foreigner; **ausländerfeindlich** adj hostile to foreigners, xenophobic; **ausländisch** adj foreign; **Auslandsgespräch** nt international call; **Auslandskrankenschein** m health insurance certificate for foreign countries, ≈ E111 (*Brit*); **Auslandsschutzbrief** m international (motor) insurance cover (*documents pl*)

aus|lassen irr vt to leave out; (*Wort etc a.*) to omit; (*überspringen*) to skip; (*Wut, Ärger*) to vent (*an +dat* on) ▷ *vr* **sich über etw** (*akk*) ~ to speak one's mind about sth

aus|laufen *irr vi* (*Flüssigkeit*) to run out; (*Tank etc*) to leak; (*Schiff*) to leave port; (*Vertrag*) to expire

aus|legen *vt* (*Waren*) to display; (*Geld*) to lend; (*Text etc*) to interpret; (*technisch ausstatten*) to design (*für, auf +akk* for)

aus|leihen *irr vt* (*verleihen*) to lend; **sich** (*dat*) **etw** ~ to borrow sth

aus|loggen *vi* (*Inform*) to log out (*o off*)

aus|lösen *vt* (*Explosion, Alarm*) to set off; (*hervorrufen*) to cause; **Auslöser** (*-s, -*) *m* (*Foto*) shutter release

aus|machen *vt* (*Licht, Radio*) to turn off; (*Feuer*) to put out; (*Termin, Preis*) to fix; (*vereinbaren*) to agree; (*Anteil darstellen, betragen*) to represent; (*bedeuten*) to matter; **macht es Ihnen etwas aus, wenn ...?** would you mind if ...?; **das macht mir nichts aus** I don't mind

Ausmaß *nt* extent

Ausnahme (*-, -n*) *f* exception; **ausnahmsweise** *adv* as an exception, just this once

aus|nutzen *vt* (*Zeit, Gelegenheit, Einfluss*) to use; (*jdn, Gutmütigkeit*) to take advantage of

aus|packen *vt* to unpack

aus|probieren *vt* to try (out)

Auspuff (*-(e)s, -e*) *m* (*Tech*) exhaust; **Auspuffrohr** *nt* exhaust (pipe); **Auspufftopf** *m* (*Auto*) silencer (*Brit*), muffler (*US*)

aus|rauben *vt* to rob

aus|räumen *vt* (*Dinge*) to clear away; (*Schrank, Zimmer*) to empty; (*Bedenken*) to put aside

aus|rechnen *vt* to calculate, to work out

Ausrede *f* excuse

aus|reden *vi* to finish speaking ▷ *vt*: **jdm etw** ~ to talk sb out of sth

ausreichend *adj* sufficient, satisfactory; (*Schulnote*) ≈ D

Ausreise *f* departure; **bei der** ~ on leaving the country; **Ausreiseerlaubnis** *f* exit visa; **aus|reisen** *vi* to leave the country

aus|reißen *irr vt* to tear out ▷ *vi* to come off; (*fam: davonlaufen*) to run away

aus|renken *vt* **sich** (*dat*) **den Arm** ~ to dislocate one's arm

aus|richten *vt* (*Botschaft*) to deliver; (*Gruß*) to pass on; (*erreichen*) **ich konnte bei ihr nichts** ~ I couldn't get anywhere with her; **jdm etw** ~ to tell sb sth

aus|rufen *irr vt* (*über Lautsprecher*) to announce; **jdn** ~ **lassen** to page sb; **Ausrufezeichen** *nt* exclamation mark

aus|ruhen *vi* to rest ▷ *vr*: **sich** ~ to rest

Ausrüstung *f* equipment

aus|rutschen *vi* to slip

aus|schalten *vt* to switch off; (*fig*) to eliminate

Ausschau *f*: ~ **halten** to look out (*nach* for)

aus|scheiden *irr vt* (*Med*) to give off, to secrete ▷ *vi* to leave (*aus etw* sth); (*Sport*) to be eliminated

aus|schlafen *irr vi* to have a lie-in ▷ *vr*: **sich** ~ to have a lie-in ▷ *vt* to sleep off

Ausschlag *m* (*Med*) rash; **den** ~ **geben** (*fig*) to tip the balance; **aus|schlagen** *irr vt* (*Zahn*) to knock out; (*Einladung*) to turn down ▷ *vi* (*Pferd*) to kick out; **ausschlaggebend** *adj* decisive

aus|schließen *irr vt* to lock out; (*fig*) to exclude; **ausschließlich**

adv exclusively ▷ *prep +gen* excluding

Ausschnitt *m* (*Teil*) section; (*von Kleid*) neckline; (*aus Zeitung*) cutting

Ausschreitungen *pl* riots *pl*

aus|schütten *vt* (*Flüssigkeit*) to pour out; (*Gefäß*) to empty

aus|sehen *irr vi* to look; **krank ~** to look ill; **gut ~** (*Person*) to be good-looking; (*Sache*) to be looking good; **es sieht nach Regen aus** it looks like rain; **es sieht schlecht aus** things look bad

aus sein *irr vi siehe* **aus**

außen *adv* outside; **nach ~** outwards; **von ~** from (the) outside; **Außenbordmotor** *m* outboard motor; **Außenminister(in)** *m(f)* foreign minister, Foreign Secretary (*Brit*); **Außenseite** *f* outside; **Außenseiter(in)** *m(f)* outsider; **Außenspiegel** *m* wing mirror (*Brit*), side mirror (*US*)

außer *prep +dat* (*abgesehen von*) except (for); **nichts ~** nothing but; **~ Betrieb** out of order; **~ sich sein** to be beside oneself (*vor* with); **~ Atem** out of breath ▷ *conj* (*ausgenommen*) except; **~ wenn** unless; **~ dass** except; **außerdem** *conj* besides

äußere(r, s) *adj* outer, external

außergewöhnlich *adj* unusual ▷ *adv* exceptionally; **~ kalt** exceptionally cold; **außerhalb** *prep +gen* outside

äußerlich *adj* external

äußern *vt* to express; (*zeigen*) to show ▷ *vr*: **sich ~** to give one's opinion; (*sich zeigen*) to show itself

außerordentlich *adj* extraordinary; **außerplanmäßig** *adj* unscheduled

äußerst *adv* extremely;

äußerste(r, s) *adj* utmost; (*räumlich*) farthest; (*Termin*) last possible

Äußerung *f* remark

aus|setzen *vt* (*Kind, Tier*) to abandon; (*Belohnung*) to offer; **ich habe nichts daran auszusetzen** I have no objection to it ▷ *vi* (*aufhören*) to stop; (*Pause machen*) to drop out; (*beim Spiel*) to miss a turn

Aussicht *f* (*Blick*) view; (*Chance*) prospect; **aussichtslos** *adj* hopeless; **Aussichtsplattform** *f* observation platform; **Aussichtsturm** *m* observation tower

Aussiedler(in) (*-s, -*) *m(f)* émigré (*person of German descent from Eastern Europe*)

aus|spannen *vi* (*erholen*) to relax ▷ *vt*: **er hat ihm die Freundin ausgespannt** (*fam*) he's nicked his girlfriend

aus|sperren *vt* to lock out ▷ *vr*: **sich ~** to lock oneself out

Aussprache *f* (*von Wörtern*) pronunciation; (*Gespräch*) (frank) discussion; **aus|sprechen** *irr vt* to pronounce; (*äußern*) to express ▷ *vr*: **sich ~** to talk (*über +akk* about) ▷ *vi* (*zu Ende sprechen*) to finish speaking

aus|spülen *vt* to rinse (out)

Ausstattung *f* (*Ausrüstung*) equipment; (*Einrichtung*) furnishings *pl*; (*von Auto*) fittings *pl*

aus|stehen *irr vt* to endure; **ich kann ihn nicht ~** I can't stand him ▷ *vi* (*noch nicht da sein*) to be outstanding

aus|steigen *irr vi* to get out (*aus* of); **aus dem Bus/Zug ~** to get off the bus/train; **Aussteiger(in)** *m(f)* dropout

aus|stellen *vt* to display; (*auf Messe, in Museum etc*) to exhibit;

(*fam: ausschalten*) to switch off; (*Scheck etc*) to make out; (*Pass etc*) to issue; **Ausstellung** f exhibition

aus|sterben *irr vi* to die out

aus|strahlen *vt* to radiate; (*Programm*) to broadcast; **Ausstrahlung** f (*Radio, TV*) broadcast; (*fig: von Person*) charisma

aus|strecken *vr*: **sich ~** to stretch out ▷ *vt* (*Hand*) to reach out (*nach* for)

aus|suchen *vt* to choose

Austausch m exchange; **aus|tauschen** *vt* to exchange (*gegen* for)

aus|teilen *vt* to distribute; (*aushändigen*) to hand out

Auster (-, -n) f oyster; **Austernpilz** m oyster mushroom

aus|tragen *irr vt* (*Post*) to deliver; (*Wettkampf*) to hold

Australien (-s) *nt* Australia; **Australier(in)** (-s, -) *m(f)* Australian; **australisch** *adj* Australian

aus|trinken *irr vt* (*Glas*) to drain; (*Getränk*) to drink up ▷ *vi* to finish one's drink

aus|trocknen *vi* to dry out; (*Fluss*) to dry up

aus|üben *vt* (*Beruf, Sport*) to practise; (*Einfluss*) to exert

Ausverkauf m sale; **ausverkauft** *adj* (*Karten, Artikel*) sold out

Auswahl f selection, choice (*an* +*dat* of); **aus|wählen** *vt* to select, to choose

aus|wandern *vi* to emigrate

auswärtig *adj* (*nicht am/vom Ort*) not local; (*ausländisch*) foreign; **auswärts** *adv* (*außerhalb der Stadt*) out of town; (*Sport*) **~ spielen** to play away; **Auswärtsspiel** *nt* away match

aus|wechseln *vt* to replace; (*Sport*) to substitute

Ausweg m way out

aus|weichen *irr vi* to get out of the way; **jdm/einer Sache ~** to move aside for sb/sth; (*fig*) to avoid sb/sth

Ausweis (-es, -e) m (*Personalausweis*) identity card, ID; (*für Bibliothek etc*) card; **aus|weisen** *irr vt* to expel ▷ *vr*: **sich ~** to prove one's identity; **Ausweiskontrolle** f ID check; **Ausweispapiere** *pl* identification documents *pl*

auswendig *adv* by heart

aus|wuchten *vt* (*Auto: Räder*) to balance

aus|zahlen *vt* (*Summe*) to pay (out); (*Person*) to pay off ▷ *vr*: **sich ~** to be worth it

aus|zeichnen *vt* (*ehren*) to honour; (*Comm*) to price ▷ *vr*: **sich ~** to distinguish oneself

aus|ziehen *irr vt* (*Kleidung*) to take off ▷ *vr*: **sich ~** to undress ▷ *vi* (*aus Wohnung*) to move out

Auszubildende(r) *mf* trainee

authentisch *adj* authentic, genuine

Auto (-s, -s) *nt* car; **~ fahren** to drive; **Autoatlas** m road atlas; **Autobahn** f motorway (*Brit*), freeway (*US*); **Autobahnauffahrt** f motorway access road (*Brit*), on-ramp (*US*); **Autobahnausfahrt** f motorway exit (*Brit*), off-ramp (*US*); **Autobahngebühr** f toll; **Autobahnkreuz** *nt* motorway interchange; **Autobahnring** m motorway ring (*Brit*), beltway (*US*); **Autobombe** f car bomb; **Autofähre** f car ferry; **Autofahrer(in)** *m(f)* driver, motorist; **Autofahrt** f drive

Autogramm (-s, -e) *nt* autograph

Automarke f make of car
Automat (-en, -en) m vending machine
Automatik (-, -en) f (Auto) automatic transmission; **Automatikschaltung** f automatic gear change (Brit) (o shift (US)); **Automatikwagen** m automatic
automatisch adj automatic ▷ adv automatically
Automechaniker(in) m(f) car mechanic; **Autonummer** f registration (Brit) (o license (US)) number; **Autoradio** nt car radio; **Autoreifen** m car tyre; **Autoreisezug** m Motorail train® (Brit), auto train (US); **Autorennen** nt motor racing; (einzelnes Rennen) motor race; **Autoschlüssel** m car key; **Autotelefon** nt car phone; **Autounfall** m car accident; **Autoverleih** m, **Autovermietung** f car hire (Brit) (o rental (US)); (Firma) car hire (Brit) (o rental (US)) company; **Autowaschanlage** f car wash; **Autowerkstatt** f car repair shop, garage; **Autozubehör** nt car accessories pl
Avocado (-, -s) f avocado
Axt (-, Äxte) f axe
Azubi (-s, -s) m (-, -s) f akr = **Auszubildende** trainee

B abk = **Bundesstraße**
Baby (-s, -s) nt baby; **Babybett** nt cot (Brit), crib (US); **Babyfläschchen** nt baby's bottle; **Babynahrung** f baby food; **Babysitter(in)** m(f) babysitter; **Babysitz** m child seat; **Babywickelraum** m baby-changing room
Bach (-(e)s, Bäche) m stream
Backblech nt baking tray (Brit), cookie sheet (US)
Backbord nt port (side)
Backe (-, -n) f cheek
backen (backte, gebacken) vt, vi to bake
Backenzahn m molar
Bäcker(in) (-s, -) m(f) baker; **Bäckerei** f bakery; (Laden) baker's (shop)
Backofen m oven; **Backpulver** nt baking powder
Backspace-Taste f (Inform)

backspace key
Backstein *m* brick
Backwaren *pl* bread, cakes and pastries *pl*
Bad *(-(e)s, Bäder) nt* bath; *(Schwimmen)* swim; *(Ort)* spa; **ein ~ nehmen** to have (*o* take) a bath; **Badeanzug** *m* swimsuit, swimming costume (*Brit*); **Badehose** *f* swimming trunks *pl*; **Badekappe** *f* swimming cap; **Bademantel** *m* bathrobe; **Bademeister(in)** *m(f)* pool attendant; **Bademütze** *f* swimming cap
baden *vi* to have a bath; *(schwimmen)* to swim, to bathe (*Brit*) ▷ *vt* to bath (*Brit*), to bathe (*US*)
Baden-Württemberg *(-s) nt* Baden-Württemberg
Badeort *m* spa; **Badesachen** *pl* swimming things *pl*; **Badeschaum** *m* bubble bath, bath foam; **Badetuch** *nt* bath towel; **Badewanne** *f* bath (tub); **Badezeug** *nt* swimming gear; **Badezimmer** *nt* bathroom
Badminton *nt* badminton
baff *adj:* **~ sein** *(fam)* to be flabbergasted (*o* gobsmacked)
Bagger *(-s, -) m* excavator; **Baggersee** *m* artificial lake in quarry etc, used for bathing
Bahamas *pl:* **die ~** the Bahamas *pl*
Bahn *(-, -en) f (Eisenbahn)* railway (*Brit*), railroad (*US*); *(Rennbahn)* track; *(für Läufer)* lane; *(Astr)* orbit; **Deutsche ~** *Germany's main railway operator*; **bahnbrechend** *adj* groundbreaking; **BahnCard®** *(-, -s) f* rail card *(allowing 50% or 25% reduction on tickets)*; **Bahnfahrt** *f* railway (*Brit*) (*o* railroad (*US*)) journey; **Bahnhof** *m* station; **am** (*o* **auf dem**) **~** at the station;

Bahnlinie *f* railway (*Brit*) (*o* railroad (*US*)) line; **Bahnpolizei** *f* railway (*Brit*) (*o* railroad (*US*)) police; **Bahnsteig** *(-(e)s, -e) m* platform; **Bahnstrecke** *f* railway (*Brit*) (*o* railroad (*US*)) line; **Bahnübergang** *m* level crossing (*Brit*), grade crossing (*US*)
Bakterien *pl* bacteria *pl*, germs *pl*
bald *adv (zeitlich)* soon; *(beinahe)* almost; **bis ~!** see you soon (*o* later); **baldig** *adj* quick, speedy
Balkan *(-s) m:* **der ~** the Balkans *pl*
Balken *(-s, -) m* beam
Balkon *(-s, -s o -e) m* balcony
Ball *(-(e)s, Bälle) m* ball; *(Tanz)* dance, ball
Ballett *(-s) nt* ballet
Ballon *(-s, -s) m* balloon
Ballspiel *nt* ball game
Ballungsgebiet *nt* conurbation
Baltikum *(-s) nt:* **das ~** the Baltic States *pl*
Bambus *(-ses, -se) m* bamboo; **Bambussprossen** *pl* bamboo shoots *pl*
banal *adj* banal; *(Frage, Bemerkung)* trite
Banane *(-, -n) f* banana
band *imperf von* **binden**
Band *(-(e)s, Bände) m (Buch)* volume ▷ *(-(e)s, Bänder) nt (aus Stoff)* ribbon, tape; *(Fließband)* production line; *(Tonband)* tape; *(Anat)* ligament; **etw auf ~ aufnehmen** to tape sth ▷ *(-, -s) f (Musikgruppe)* band
Bandage *(-, -n) f* bandage; **bandagieren** *vt* to bandage
Bande *(-, -n) f (Gruppe)* gang
Bänderriss *m (Med)* torn ligament
Bandscheibe *f (Anat)* disc; **Bandwurm** *m* tapeworm
Bank *(-, Bänke) f (Sitzbank)* bench ▷ *(-, -en) f (Fin)* bank

Bankautomat *m* cash dispenser; **Bankkarte** *f* bank card; **Bankkonto** *nt* bank account; **Bankleitzahl** *f* bank sort code; **Banknote** *f* banknote; **Bankverbindung** *f* (*Kontonummer etc*) banking (*o* account) details *pl*

bar *adj*: **~es Geld** cash; **etw (in) ~ bezahlen** to pay sth (in) cash

Bar (-, -s) *f* bar

Bär (-en, -en) *m* bear

barfuß *adj* barefoot

barg *imperf von* **bergen**

Bargeld *nt* cash; **bargeldlos** *adj* non-cash

Barkeeper (-s, -) *m*, **Barmann** *m* barman, bartender (*US*)

barock *adj* baroque

Barometer (-s, -) *m* barometer

barsch *adj* brusque

Barsch (-(e)s, -e) *m* perch

Barscheck *m* open (*o* uncrossed) cheque

Bart (-(e)s, *Bärte*) *m* beard; **bärtig** *adj* bearded

Barzahlung *f* cash payment

Basar (-s, -e) *m* bazaar

Baseballmütze *f* baseball cap

Basel (-s) *nt* Basle

Basilikum (-s) *nt* basil

Basis (-, *Basen*) *f* basis

Baskenland *nt* Basque region

Basketball *m* basketball

Bass (-es, *Bässe*) *m* bass

basta *interj*: **und damit ~!** and that's that

basteln *vt* to make ▷ *vi* to make things, to do handicrafts

bat *imperf von* **bitten**

Batterie *f* battery; **batteriebetrieben** *adj* battery-powered

Bau (-(e)s) *m* (*Bauen*) building, construction; (*Aufbau*) structure; (*Baustelle*) building site ▷ *m* (*Baue*) (*Tier*) burrow ▷ *m* (*Bauten*) (*Gebäude*) building; **Bauarbeiten** *pl* construction work *sing*; (*Straßenbau*) roadworks *pl* (*Brit*), roadwork (*US*); **Bauarbeiter(in)** *m(f)* construction worker

Bauch (-(e)s, *Bäuche*) *m* stomach; **Bauchnabel** *m* navel; **Bauchredner(in)** *m(f)* ventriloquist; **Bauchschmerzen** *pl* stomach-ache *sing*; **Bauchspeicheldrüse** *f* pancreas; **Bauchtanz** *m* belly dance; (*das Tanzen*) belly dancing; **Bauchweh** (-s) *nt* stomach-ache

bauen *vt*, *vi* to build; (*Tech*) to construct

Bauer (-n *o* -s, -n) *m* farmer; (*Schach*) pawn; **Bäuerin** *f* farmer; (*Frau des Bauern*) farmer's wife; **Bauernhof** *m* farm

baufällig *adj* dilapidated; **Baujahr** *adj* year of construction; **der Wagen ist ~ 2002** the car is a 2002 model, the car was made in 2002

Baum (-(e)s, *Bäume*) *m* tree

Baumarkt *m* DIY centre

Baumwolle *f* cotton

Bauplatz *m* building site; **Baustein** *m* (*für Haus*) stone; (*Spielzeug*) brick; (*fig*) element; **elektronischer ~** chip; **Baustelle** *f* building site; (*bei Straßenbau*) roadworks *pl* (*Brit*), roadwork (*US*); **Bauteil** *nt* prefabricated part; **Bauunternehmer(in)** *m(f)* building contractor; **Bauwerk** *nt* building

Bayern (-s) *nt* Bavaria

beabsichtigen *vt* to intend

beachten *vt* (*Aufmerksamkeit schenken*) to pay attention to; (*Vorschrift etc*) to observe; **nicht ~** to ignore; **beachtlich** *adj* considerable

Beachvolleyball *nt* beach volleyball

Beamte(r) (-n, -n) m, **Beamtin** f
official; (Staatsbeamter) civil
servant

beanspruchen vt to claim; (Zeit,
Platz) to take up; **jdn ~** to keep sb
busy

beanstanden vt to complain
about; **Beanstandung** f
complaint

beantragen vt to apply for

beantworten vt to answer

bearbeiten vt to work; (Material,
Daten) to process; (Chem) to treat;
(Fall etc) to deal with; (Buch etc) to
revise; (fam: beeinflussen wollen) to
work on; **Bearbeitungsgebühr** f
handling (o service) charge

beatmen vt: **jdn ~** to give sb
artificial respiration

beaufsichtigen vt to supervise;
(bei Prüfung) to invigilate

beauftragen vt to instruct; **jdn
mit etw ~** to give sb the job of
doing sth

Becher (-s, -) m mug; (ohne
Henkel) tumbler; (für Jogurt) pot;
(aus Pappe) tub

Becken (-s, -) nt basin; (Spüle)
sink; (zum Schwimmen) pool; (Mus)
cymbal; (Anat) pelvis

bedanken vr: **sich ~** to say thank
you; **sich bei jdm für etw ~** to
thank sb for sth

Bedarf (-(e)s) m need (an +dat
for); (Comm) demand (an +dat for);
je nach ~ according to demand;
bei ~ if necessary;
Bedarfshaltestelle f request
stop, flag stop (US)

bedauerlich adj regrettable;
bedauern vt to regret;
(bemitleiden) to feel sorry for;
bedauernswert adj (Zustände)
regrettable; (Mensch) unfortunate

bedeckt adj covered; (Himmel)
overcast

bedenken irr vt to consider;

Bedenken (-s, -) nt (Überlegen)
consideration; (Zweifel) doubt;
(Skrupel) scruples pl; **bedenklich**
adj dubious; (Zustand) serious

bedeuten vt to mean; **jdm
nichts/viel ~** to mean nothing/a
lot to sb; **bedeutend** adj
important; (beträchtlich)
considerable; **Bedeutung** f
meaning; (Wichtigkeit) importance

bedienen vt to serve; (Maschine)
to operate ▷ vr: **sich ~** (beim Essen)
to help oneself; **Bedienung** f
service; (Kellner/Kellnerin)
waiter/waitress; (Verkäufer(in))
shop assistant; (Zuschlag) service
(charge); **Bedienungsanleitung**
f operating instructions pl;
Bedienungshandbuch nt
instruction manual; **Bedingung** f
condition; **unter der ~, dass** on
condition that; **unter diesen ~en**
under these circumstances

bedrohen vt to threaten

Bedürfnis nt need

beeilen vr: **sich ~** to hurry

beeindrucken vt to impress

beeinflussen vt to influence

beeinträchtigen vt to affect

beenden vt to end; (fertigstellen)
to finish

beerdigen vt to bury;
Beerdigung f burial; (Feier)
funeral

Beere (-, -n) f berry;
(Traubenbeere) grape

Beet (-(e)s, -e) nt bed

befahl imperf von **befehlen**

befahrbar adj passable; (Naut)
navigable; **befahren** irr vt
(Straße) to use; (Pass) to drive over;
(Fluss etc) to navigate ▷ adj:
stark/wenig ~ busy/quiet

Befehl (-(e)s, -e) m order; (Inform)
command; **befehlen** (befahl,
befohlen) vt to order; **jdm ~, etw
zu tun** to order sb to do sth ▷ vi

to give orders

befestigen vt to fix; (mit Schnur, Seil) to attach; (mit Klebestoff) to stick

befeuchten vt to moisten

befinden irr vr: **sich ~** to be

befohlen pp von **befehlen**

befolgen vt (Rat etc) to follow

befördern vt (transportieren) to transport; (beruflich) to promote; **Beförderung** f transport; (beruflich) promotion; **Beförderungsbedingungen** pl conditions pl of carriage

Befragung f questioning; (Umfrage) opinion poll

befreundet adj friendly; **~ sein** to be friends (mit jdm with sb)

befriedigen vt to satisfy; **befriedigend** adj satisfactory; (Schulnote) ≈ C; **Befriedigung** f satisfaction

befristet adj limited (auf +akk to)

befruchten vt to fertilize; (fig) to stimulate

Befund (-(e)s, -e) m findings pl; (Med) diagnosis

befürchten vt to fear

befürworten vt to support

begabt adj gifted, talented; **Begabung** f talent, gift

begann imperf von **beginnen**

begegnen vi to meet (jdm sb), to meet with (einer Sache dat sth)

begehen irr vt (Straftat) to commit; (Jubiläum etc) to celebrate

begehrt adj sought-after; (Junggeselle) eligible

begeistern vt to fill with enthusiasm; (inspirieren) to inspire ▷ vr: **sich für etw ~** to be/get enthusiastic about sth; **begeistert** adj enthusiastic

Beginn (-(e)s) m beginning; **zu ~** at the beginning; **beginnen** (begann, begonnen) vt, vi to start, to begin

beglaubigen vt to certify; **Beglaubigung** f certification

begleiten vt to accompany; **Begleiter(in)** m(f) companion; **Begleitung** f company; (Mus) accompaniment

beglückwünschen vt to congratulate (zu on)

begonnen pp von **beginnen**

begraben irr vt to bury; **Begräbnis** nt burial; (Feier) funeral

begreifen irr vt to understand

Begrenzung f boundary; (fig) restriction

Begriff (-(e)s, -e) m concept; (Vorstellung) idea; **im ~ sein, etw zu tun** to be on the point of doing sth; **schwer von ~ sein** to be slow on the uptake

begründen vt (rechtfertigen) to justify; **Begründung** f explanation; (Rechtfertigung) justification

begrüßen vt to greet; (willkommen heißen) to welcome; **Begrüßung** f greeting; (Empfang) welcome

behaart adj hairy

behalten irr vt to keep; (im Gedächtnis) to remember; **etw für sich ~** to keep sth to oneself

Behälter (-s, -) m container

behandeln vt to treat; **Behandlung** f treatment

behaupten vt to claim, to maintain ▷ vr: **sich ~** to assert oneself; **Behauptung** f claim

beheizen vt to heat

behelfen irr vr: **sich mit/ohne etw ~** to make do with/without sth

beherbergen vt to accommodate

beherrschen vt (Situation, Gefühle) to control; (Instrument) to master ▷ vr: **sich ~** to control oneself; **Beherrschung** f control (*über +akk* of); **die ~ verlieren** to lose one's self-control

behilflich adj helpful; **jdm ~ sein** to help sb (*bei* with)

behindern vt to hinder; (*Verkehr, Sicht*) to obstruct; **Behinderte(r)** mf disabled person; **behindertengerecht** adj suitable for disabled people

Behörde (-, -n) f authority; **die ~n** pl the authorities pl

SCHLÜSSELWORT

bei prep +dat **1** (*nahe bei*) near; (*zum Aufenthalt*) at, with; (*unter, zwischen*) among; **bei München** near Munich; **bei uns** at our place; **beim Friseur** at the hairdresser's; **bei seinen Eltern wohnen** to live with one's parents; **bei einer Firma arbeiten** to work for a firm; **etw bei sich haben** to have sth on one; **jdn bei sich haben** to have sb with one; **bei Goethe** in Goethe; **beim Militär** in the army **2** (*zeitlich*) at, on; (*während*) during; (*Zustand, Umstand*) in; **bei Nacht** at night; **bei Nebel** in fog; **bei Regen** if it rains; **bei solcher Hitze** in such heat; **bei meiner Ankunft** on my arrival; **bei der Arbeit** when I'm *etc* working; **beim Fahren** while driving

bei|behalten irr vt to keep

Beiboot nt dinghy

bei|bringen irr vt: **jdm etw ~** (*mitteilen*) to break sth to sb; (*lehren*) to teach sb sth

beide(s) pron both; **meine ~n Brüder** my two brothers, both my brothers; **wir ~** both (*o* the two) of us; **keiner von ~n** neither of them; **alle ~** both (of them); **~s ist sehr schön** both are very nice; **30**

~ (*beim Tennis*) 30 all

beieinander adv together

Beifahrer(in) m(f) passenger; **Beifahrerairbag** m passenger airbag; **Beifahrersitz** m passenger seat

Beifall (-(e)s) m applause

beige adj inv beige

Beigeschmack m aftertaste

Beil (-(e)s, -e) nt axe

Beilage f (*Gastr*) side dish; (*Gemüse*) vegetables pl; (*zu Buch etc*) supplement

beiläufig adj casual ▷ adv casually

Beileid nt condolences pl; (**mein**) **herzliches ~** please accept my sincere condolences

beiliegend adj enclosed

beim kontr von **bei dem**

Bein (-(e)s, -e) nt leg

beinah(e) adv almost, nearly

beinhalten vt to contain

Beipackzettel m instruction leaflet

beisammen adv together; **Beisammensein** (-s) nt get-together

beiseite adv aside; **beiseite|legen** vt: **etw ~** (*sparen*) to put sth by

Beispiel (-(e)s, -e) nt example; **sich** (*dat*) **an jdm/etw ein ~ nehmen** to take sb/sth as an example; **zum ~** for example

beißen (biss, gebissen) vt to bite ▷ vi to bite; (*stechen: Rauch, Säure*) to sting ▷ vr: **sich ~** (*Farben*) to clash

Beitrag (-(e)s, Beiträge) m contribution; (*für Mitgliedschaft*) subscription; (*Versicherung*) premium; **bei|tragen** irr vt, vi to contribute (*zu* to)

bekannt adj well-known; (*nicht fremd*) familiar; **mit jdm ~ sein** to know sb; **~ geben** to announce;

jdn mit jdm ~ machen to
introduce sb to sb; **Bekannte(r)**
mf friend; (*entfernter*)
acquaintance; **bekanntlich** *adv*
as everyone knows;
Bekanntschaft *f* acquaintance
bekiffen *vr*: **sich ~** (*fam*) to get
stoned
beklagen *vr*: **sich ~** to complain
Bekleidung *f* clothing
bekommen *irr vt* to get;
(*erhalten*) to receive; (*Kind*) to have;
(*Zug, Grippe*) to catch, to get; **wie
viel ~ Sie dafür?** how much is
that? ▷ *vi*: **jdm ~** (*Essen*) to agree
with sb; **wir ~ schon** (*bedient
werden*) we're being served
beladen *irr vt* to load
Belag (-(*e*)*s, Beläge*) *m* coating;
(*auf Zähnen*) plaque; (*auf Zunge*) fur
belasten *vt* to load; (*Körper*) to
strain; (*Umwelt*) to pollute; (*fig:
mit Sorgen etc*) to burden; (*Comm:
Konto*) to debit; (*Jur*) to incriminate
belästigen *vt* to bother; (*stärker*)
to pester; (*sexuell*) to harass;
Belästigung *f* annoyance;
sexuelle ~ sexual harassment
belebt *adj* (*Straße etc*) busy
Beleg (-(*e*)*s, -e*) *m* (*Comm*) receipt;
(*Beweis*) proof; **belegen** *vt* (*Brot*)
to spread; (*Platz*) to reserve; (*Kurs,
Vorlesung*) to register for; (*beweisen*)
to prove
belegt *adj* (*Tel*) engaged (*Brit*),
busy (*US*); (*Hotel*) full; (*Zunge*)
coated; **~es Brötchen** sandwich;
der Platz ist ~ this seat is taken;
Belegtzeichen *nt* (*Tel*) engaged
tone (*Brit*), busy tone (*US*)
beleidigen *vt* to insult; (*kränken*)
to offend; **Beleidigung** *f* insult;
(*Jur*) slander; (*schriftliche*) libel
beleuchten *vt* to light;
(*bestrahlen*) to illuminate; (*fig*) to
examine; **Beleuchtung** *f*
lighting; (*Bestrahlung*) illumination

Belgien (-*s*) *nt* Belgium;
Belgier(in) (-*s, -*) *m(f)* Belgian;
belgisch *adj* Belgian
belichten *vt* to expose;
Belichtung *f* exposure;
Belichtungsmesser (-*s, -*) *m* light
meter
Belieben *nt*: (**ganz**) **nach ~** (just)
as you wish
beliebig *adj*: **jedes ~e Muster**
any pattern; **jeder ~e** anyone
▷ *adv*: **~ lange** as long as you like;
~ viel as many (o much) as you like
beliebt *adj* popular; **sich bei jdm
~ machen** to make oneself
popular with sb
beliefern *vt* to supply
bellen *vi* to bark
Belohnung *f* reward
Belüftung *f* ventilation
belügen *irr vt* to lie to
bemerkbar *adj* noticeable; **sich
~ machen** (*Mensch*) to attract
attention; (*Zustand*) to become
noticeable; **bemerken** *vt*
(*wahrnehmen*) to notice; (*sagen*) to
remark; **bemerkenswert** *adj*
remarkable; **Bemerkung** *f*
remark
bemitleiden *vt* to pity
bemühen *vr*: **sich ~** to try (hard),
to make an effort; **Bemühung** *f*
effort
bemuttern *vt* to mother
benachbart *adj* neighbouring
benachrichtigen *vt* to inform;
Benachrichtigung *f* notification
benachteiligen *vt* to (put at a)
disadvantage; (*wegen Rasse etc*) to
discriminate against
benehmen *vr*: **sich ~** to
behave; **Benehmen** (-*s*) *nt*
behaviour
beneiden *vt* to envy; **jdn um etw
~** to envy sb sth
Beneluxländer *pl* Benelux
countries *pl*

benommen *adj* dazed
benötigen *vt* to need
benutzen *vt* to use;
  Benutzer(in) (*-s, -*) *m(f)* user;
  benutzerfreundlich *adj* user-friendly; **Benutzerhandbuch** *nt* user's guide; **Benutzerkennung** *f* user ID; **Benutzeroberfläche** *f* (*Inform*) user/system interface;
  Benutzung *f* use;
  Benutzungsgebühr *f* (hire) charge
Benzin (*-s, -e*) *nt* (*Auto*) petrol (*Brit*), gas (*US*); **Benzingutschein** *m* petrol (*Brit*) (*o* gas (*US*)) coupon; **Benzinkanister** *m* petrol (*Brit*) (*o* gas (*US*)) can; **Benzinpumpe** *f* petrol (*Brit*) (*o* gas (*US*)) pump; **Benzintank** *m* petrol (*Brit*) (*o* gas (*US*)) tank; **Benzinuhr** *f* fuel gauge
beobachten *vt* to observe;
  Beobachtung *f* observation
bequem *adj* comfortable;
  (*Ausrede*) convenient; (*faul*) lazy;
  machen Sie es sich ~ make yourself at home; **Bequemlichkeit** *f* comfort; (*Faulheit*) laziness
beraten *irr vt* to advise;
  (*besprechen*) to discuss ▷ *vr*: **sich ~** to consult; **Beratung** *f* advice;
  (*bei Arzt etc*) consultation
berauben *vt* to rob
berechnen *vt* to calculate;
  (*Comm*) to charge; **berechnend** *adj* (*Mensch*) calculating
berechtigen *vt* to entitle (*zu* to);
  (*fig*) to justify; **berechtigt** *adj* justified; **zu etw ~ sein** to be entitled to sth
bereden *vt* (*besprechen*) to discuss
Bereich (*-(e)s, -e*) *m* area;
  (*Ressort, Gebiet*) field
bereisen *vt* to travel through
bereit *adj* ready; **zu etw ~ sein** to be ready for sth; **sich ~ erklären, etw zu tun** to agree to do sth

bereiten *vt* to prepare; (*Kummer*) to cause; (*Freude*) to give
bereit|legen *vt* to lay out
bereit|machen *vr*: **sich ~** to get ready
bereits *adv* already
Bereitschaft *f* readiness;
  ~ haben (*Arzt*) to be on call
bereit|stehen *vi* to be ready
bereuen *vt* to regret
Berg (*-(e)s, -e*) *m* mountain;
  (*kleiner*) hill; **in die ~e fahren** to go to the mountains; **bergab** *adv* downhill; **bergauf** *adv* uphill;
  Bergbahn *f* mountain railway (*Brit*) (*o* railroad (*US*))
bergen (*barg, geborgen*) *vt* (*retten*) to rescue; (*enthalten*) to contain
Bergführer(in) *m(f)* mountain guide; **Berghütte** *f* mountain hut;
  bergig *adj* mountainous;
  Bergschuh *m* climbing boot;
  Bergsteigen (*-s*) *nt* mountaineering; **Bergsteiger(in)** (*-s, -*) *m(f)* mountaineer;
  Bergtour *f* mountain hike
Bergung *f* (*Rettung*) rescue; (*von Toten, Fahrzeugen*) recovery
Bergwacht (*-, -en*) *f* mountain rescue service; **Bergwerk** *nt* mine
Bericht (*-(e)s, -e*) *m* report;
  berichten *vt, vi* to report
berichtigen *vt* to correct
Bermudadreieck *nt* Bermuda triangle; **Bermudainseln** *pl* Bermuda *sing*; **Bermudashorts** *pl* Bermuda shorts *pl*
Bernstein *m* amber
berüchtigt *adj* notorious, infamous
berücksichtigen *vt* to take into account; (*Antrag, Bewerber*) to consider
Beruf (*-(e)s, -e*) *m* occupation;
  (*akademischer*) profession;
  (*Gewerbe*) trade; **was sind Sie von**

~? what do you do (for a living)?;
beruflich *adj* professional

Berufsausbildung *f* vocational
training; **Berufsschule** *f*
vocational college; **berufstätig**
adj employed; **Berufsverkehr** *m*
commuter traffic

beruhigen *vt* to calm ▷ *vr*: **sich
~** (*Mensch, Situation*) to calm down;
beruhigend *adj* reassuring;
Beruhigungsmittel *nt* sedative

berühmt *adj* famous

berühren *vt* to touch;
(*gefühlsmäßig bewegen*) to move;
(*betreffen*) to affect; (*flüchtig
erwähnen*) to mention, to touch on
▷ *vr*: **sich ~** to touch

besaufen *irr vr*: **sich ~** (*fam*) to
get plastered

beschädigen *vt* to damage

beschäftigen *vt* to occupy;
(*beruflich*) to employ ▷ *vr*: **sich mit
etw ~** to occupy oneself with sth;
(*sich befassen*) to deal with sth;
beschäftigt *adj* busy, occupied;
Beschäftigung *f* (*Beruf*)
employment; (*Tätigkeit*)
occupation; (*geistige*)
preoccupation (*mit* with)

Bescheid (*-(e)s, -e*) *m*
information; **~ wissen** to be
informed (*o* know) (*über +akk*
about); **ich weiß ~** I know; **jdm
~ geben** (*o* **sagen**) to let sb know

bescheiden *adj* modest

bescheinigen *vt* to certify;
(*bestätigen*) to acknowledge;
Bescheinigung *f* certificate;
(*Quittung*) receipt

bescheißen *irr vt* (*vulg*) to cheat
(*um* out of)

bescheuert *adj* (*fam, pej*) crazy

beschimpfen *vt* (*mit
Kraftausdrücken*) to swear at

Beschiss (*-es*) *m*: **das ist ~** (*vulg*)
that's a rip-off; **beschissen** *adj*
(*vulg*) shitty

beschlagnahmen *vt* to
confiscate

Beschleunigung *f* acceleration;
Beschleunigungsspur *f*
acceleration lane

beschließen *irr vt* to decide on;
(*beenden*) to end; **Beschluss** *m*
decision

beschränken *vt* to limit, to
restrict (*auf +akk* to) ▷ *vr*: **sich ~** to
restrict oneself (*auf +akk* to);
Beschränkung *f* limitation,
restriction

beschreiben *irr vt* to describe;
(*Papier*) to write on; **Beschreibung**
f description

beschuldigen *vt* to accuse (*gen*
of); **Beschuldigung** *f*
accusation

beschummeln *vt, vi* (*fam*) to
cheat (*um* out of)

beschützen *vt* to protect (*vor*
+*dat* from)

Beschwerde (*-, -n*) *f* complaint;
~n *pl* (*Leiden*) trouble *sing*;
beschweren *vt* to weight down;
(*fig*) to burden ▷ *vr*: **sich ~** to
complain

beschwipst *adj* tipsy

beseitigen *vt* to remove;
(*Problem*) to get rid of; (*Müll*) to
dispose of; **Beseitigung** *f*
removal; (*von Müll*) disposal

Besen (*-s, -*) *m* broom

besetzen *vt* (*Haus, Land*) to
occupy; (*Platz*) to take; (*Posten*) to
fill; (*Rolle*) to cast; **besetzt** *adj*
full; (*Tel*) engaged (*Brit*), busy (*US*);
(*Platz*) taken; (*WC*) engaged;
Besetztzeichen *nt* engaged tone
(*Brit*), busy tone (*US*)

besichtigen *vt* (*Museum*) to visit;
(*Sehenswürdigkeit*) to have a look at;
(*Stadt*) to tour

besiegen *vt* to defeat

Besitz (*-es*) *m* possession;
(*Eigentum*) property; **besitzen** *irr*

vt to own; (*Eigenschaft*) to have;
Besitzer(in) (*-s, -*) *m(f)* owner
besoffen *adj* (*fam*) plastered
besondere(r, s) *adj* special;
(*bestimmt*) particular;
(*eigentümlich*) peculiar; **nichts ~s**
nothing special; **Besonderheit** *f*
special feature; (*besondere
Eigenschaft*) peculiarity; **besonders**
adv especially, particularly;
(*getrennt*) separately
besorgen *vt* (*beschaffen*) to get
(*jdm* for sb); (*kaufen a.*) to purchase;
(*erledigen: Geschäfte*) to deal with
besprechen *irr vt* to discuss;
Besprechung *f* discussion;
(*Konferenz*) meeting; **Besprechungsraum** *m* consultation
room
besser *adj* better; **es geht ihm
~** he feels better; **~ gesagt** or
rather; **~ werden** to improve;
bessern *vt* to improve ▷ *vr*: **sich
~** to improve; (*Mensch*) to mend
one's ways; **Besserung** *f*
improvement; **gute ~!** get well
soon
beständig *adj* constant; (*Wetter*)
settled
Bestandteil *m* component
bestätigen *vt* to confirm;
(*Empfang, Brief*) to acknowledge;
Bestätigung *f* confirmation; (*von
Brief*) acknowledgement
beste(r, s) *adj* best; **das ~ wäre,
wir ...** it would be best if we ...
▷ *adv*: **sie singt am ~n** she sings
best; **so ist es am ~n** it's best that
way; **am ~n gehst du gleich** you'd
better go at once
bestechen *irr vt* to bribe;
Bestechung *f* bribery
Besteck (*-(e)s, -e*) *nt* cutlery
bestehen *irr vi* to be, to exist;
(*andauern*) to last; **~ auf** (*+dat*) to
insist on; **~ aus** to consist of ▷ *vt*
(*Probe, Prüfung*) to pass; (*Kampf*) to

win
bestehlen *irr vt* to rob
bestellen *vt* to order; (*reservieren*)
to book; (*Grüße, Auftrag*) to pass on
(*jdm* to sb); (*kommen lassen*) to send
for; **Bestellnummer** *f* order
number; **Bestellung** *f* (*Comm*)
order; (*das Bestellen*) ordering
bestens *adv* very well
bestimmen *vt* to determine;
(*Regeln*) to lay down; (*Tag, Ort*) to
fix; (*ernennen*) to appoint;
(*vorsehen*) to mean (*für* for);
bestimmt *adj* definite; (*gewiss*)
certain; (*entschlossen*) firm ▷ *adv*
definitely; (*wissen*) for sure;
Bestimmung *f* (*Verordnung*)
regulation; (*Zweck*) purpose
Best.-Nr. *abk* = **Bestellnummer**
order number
bestrafen *vt* to punish
bestrahlen *vt* to illuminate;
(*Med*) to treat with radiotherapy
bestreiten *irr vt* (*leugnen*) to
deny
Bestseller (*-s, -*) *m* bestseller
bestürzt *adj* dismayed
Besuch (*-(e)s, -e*) *m* visit; (*Mensch*)
visitor; **~ haben** to have visitors/a
visitor; **besuchen** *vt* to visit;
(*Schule, Kino etc*) to go to;
Besucher(in) (*-s, -*) *m(f)* visitor;
Besuchszeit *f* visiting hours *pl*
betäuben *vt* (*Med*) to
anaesthetize; **Betäubung** *f*
anaesthetic; **örtliche ~** local
anaesthetic; **Betäubungsmittel**
nt anaesthetic
Bete (*-, -n*) *f*: **Rote ~** beetroot
beteiligen *vr*: **sich an etw** (*dat*)
~ to take part in sth, to participate
in sth ▷ *vt*: **jdn an etw** (*dat*) **~** to
involve sb in sth; **Beteiligung** *f*
participation; (*Anteil*) share;
(*Besucherzahl*) attendance
beten *vi* to pray
Beton (*-s, -s*) *m* concrete

betonen *vt* to stress;
(*hervorheben*) to emphasize;
Betonung *f* stress; (*fig*)
emphasis

Betr. *abk* = **Betreff** re

Betracht *m*: **in ~ ziehen** to take
into consideration; **in ~ kommen**
to be a possibility; **nicht in
~ kommen** to be out of the
question; **betrachten** *vt* to look
at; **~ als** to regard as; **beträchtlich**
adj considerable

Betrag (-*(e)s*, *Beträge*) *m* amount,
sum; **betragen** *irr vt* to amount
(*o* come) to ▷ *vr*: **sich ~** to behave

betreffen *irr vt* to concern;
(*Regelung etc*) to affect; **was mich
betrifft** as for me; **betreffend** *adj*
relevant, in question

betreten *irr vt* to enter; (*Bühne
etc*) to step onto; „**Betreten
verboten**" "keep off/out"

betreuen *vt* to look after;
(*Reisegruppe, Abteilung*) to be in
charge of; **Betreuer(in)** (-*s*, -) *m(f)*
(*Pfleger*) carer; (*von Kind*) child
minder; (*von Reisegruppe*)
groupleader

Betrieb (-*(e)s*, -*e*) *m* (*Firma*) firm;
(*Anlage*) plant; (*Tätigkeit*)
operation; (*Treiben*) bustle; **außer
~ sein** to be out of order; **in ~ sein**
to be in operation; **betriebsbereit**
adj operational; **Betriebsrat** *m*
(*Gremium*) works council;
Betriebssystem *nt* (*Inform*)
operating system

betrinken *irr vr*: **sich ~** to get
drunk

betroffen *adj* (*bestürzt*) shaken;
von etw ~ werden/sein to be
affected by sth

betrog *imperf von* **betrügen**;
betrogen *pp von* **betrügen**

Betrug (-*(e)s*) *m* deception; (*Jur*)
fraud; **betrügen** (*betrog, betrogen*)
vt to deceive; (*Jur*) to defraud;

(*Partner*) to cheat on; **Betrüger(in)**
(-*s*, -) *m(f)* cheat

betrunken *adj* drunk

Bett (-*(e)s*, -*en*) *nt* bed; **ins** (*o* **zu**)
~ gehen to go to bed; **das
~ machen** to make the bed;
Bettbezug *m* duvet cover;
Bettdecke *f* blanket

betteln *vi* to beg

Bettlaken *nt* sheet

Bettler(in) (-*s*, -) *m(f)* beggar

Bettsofa *nt* sofa bed; **Betttuch**
nt sheet; **Bettwäsche** *f* bed
linen; **Bettzeug** *m* bedding

beugen *vt* to bend ▷ *vr*: **sich ~** to
bend; (*sich fügen*) to submit (*dat* to)

Beule (-, -*n*) *f* (*Schwellung*) bump;
(*Delle*) dent

beunruhigen *vt* to worry ▷ *vr*:
sich ~ to worry

beurteilen *vt* to judge

Beute (-) *f* (*von Dieb*) booty, loot;
(*von Tier*) prey

Beutel (-*s*, -) *m* bag

Bevölkerung *f* population

bevollmächtigt *adj* authorized
(*zu etw* to do sth)

bevor *conj* before; **bevor|stehen**
irr vi (*Schwierigkeiten*) to lie ahead;
(*Gefahr*) to be imminent; **jdm
~** (*Überraschung etc*) to be in store
for sb; **bevorstehend** *adj*
forthcoming; **bevorzugen** *vt* to
prefer

bewachen *vt* to guard; **bewacht**
adj: **~er Parkplatz** supervised car
park (*Brit*), guarded parking lot
(*US*)

bewegen *vt* to move; **jdn dazu ~,
etw zu tun** to get sb to do sth
▷ *vr*: **sich ~** to move; **es bewegt
sich etwas** (*fig*) things are
beginning to happen; **Bewegung**
f movement; (*Phys*) motion;
(*innere*) emotion; (*körperlich*)
exercise; **Bewegungsmelder**
(-*s*, -) *m* sensor (*which reacts to*

movement)

Beweis *(-es, -e)* m proof; *(Zeugnis)* evidence; **beweisen** *irr vt* to prove; *(zeigen)* to show

bewerben *irr vr:* **sich ~** to apply *(um* for); **Bewerbung** *f* application; **Bewerbungsun-terlagen** *pl* application documents *pl*

bewilligen *vt* to allow; *(Geld)* to grant

bewirken *vt* to cause, to bring about

bewohnen *vt* to live in; **Bewohner(in)** *(-s, -)* m(f) inhabitant; *(von Haus)* resident

bewölkt *adj* cloudy, overcast; **Bewölkung** *f* clouds *pl*

bewundern *vt* to admire; **bewundernswert** *adj* admirable

bewusst *adj* conscious; *(absichtlich)* deliberate; **sich** *(dat)* **einer Sache** *(gen)* **~ sein** to be aware of sth ▷ *adv* consciously; *(absichtlich)* deliberately; **bewusstlos** *adj* unconscious; **Bewusstlosigkeit** *f* unconscious-ness; **Bewusstsein** *(-s)* nt consciousness; **bei ~** conscious

bezahlen *vt* to pay; *(Ware, Leistung)* to pay for; **kann ich bar/mit Kreditkarte ~?** can I pay cash/by credit card?; **sich bezahlt machen** to be worth it; **Bezahlung** *f* payment

bezeichnen *vt (kennzeichnen)* to mark; *(nennen)* to call; *(beschreiben)* to describe; **Bezeichnung** *f (Name)* name; *(Begriff)* term

beziehen *irr vt (Bett)* to change; *(Haus, Position)* to move into; *(erhalten)* to receive; *(Zeitung)* to take; **einen Standpunkt ~** *(fig)* to take up a position ▷ *vr:* **sich ~** to refer *(auf* +*akk* to); **Beziehung** *f (Verbindung)* connection; *(Verhältnis)* relationship; **~en**

haben *(vorteilhaft)* to have connections *(o* contacts); **in dieser ~** in this respect; **beziehungsweise** *adv* or; *(genauer gesagt)* or rather

Bezirk *(-(e)s, -e)* m district

Bezug *(-(e)s, Bezüge)* m *(Überzug)* cover; *(von Kopfkissen)* pillowcase; **in ~ auf** *(+akk)* with regard to; **bezüglich** *prep* +*gen* concerning

bezweifeln *vt* to doubt

BH *(-s, -s)* m bra

Bhf. *abk* = **Bahnhof** station

Biathlon *(-s, -s)* m biathlon

Bibel *(-, -n)* f Bible

Biber *(-s, -)* m beaver

Bibliothek *(-, -en)* f library

biegen *(bog, gebogen)* *vt* to bend ▷ *vr:* **sich ~** to bend ▷ *vi* to turn *(in* +*akk* into); **Biegung** *f* bend

Biene *(-, -n)* f bee

Bier *(-(e)s, -e)* nt beer; **helles ~** ≈ lager *(Brit)*, beer *(US)*; **dunkles ~** ≈ brown ale *(Brit)*, dark beer *(US)*; **zwei ~, bitte!** two beers, please; **Biergarten** m beer garden; **Bierzelt** nt beer tent

bieten *(bot, geboten)* *vt* to offer; *(bei Versteigerung)* bid; **etw ~ lassen** to put up with sth ▷ *vr:* **sich ~** *(Gelegenheit)* to present itself *(dat* to)

Bikini *(-s, -s)* m bikini

Bild *(-(e)s, -er)* nt picture; *(gedankliches)* image; *(Foto)* photo

bilden *vt* to form; *(geistig)* to educate; *(ausmachen)* to constitute ▷ *vr:* **sich ~** *(entstehen)* to form; *(lernen)* to educate oneself

Bilderbuch nt picture book

Bildhauer(in) *(-s, -)* m(f) sculptor

Bildschirm m screen; **Bildschirmschoner** *(-s, -)* m screensaver; **Bildschirmtext** m viewdata, videotext

Bildung *f* formation; *(Wissen,*

Benehmen) education;
Bildungsurlaub m educational
holiday; (*von Firma*) study leave
Billard nt billiards *sing*
billig *adj* cheap; (*gerecht*) fair
Billigflieger m budget airline
Billigflug m cheap flight
Binde (-, -n) f bandage;
(*Armbinde*) band; (*Damenbinde*)
sanitary towel (*Brit*), sanitary
napkin (*US*)
Bindehautentzündung f
conjunctivitis
binden (*band, gebunden*) vt to tie;
(*Buch*) to bind; (*Soße*) to thicken
Bindestrich m hyphen
Bindfaden m string
Bindung f bond, tie; (*Skibindung*)
binding
Bio- *in zW* bio-; **Biokost** f health
food

- ● **BIOLADEN**
- ●
- ● A **Bioladen** is a shop which
- ● specializes in selling
- ● environmentally friendly
- ● products such as
- ● phosphate-free washing
- ● powders, recycled paper and
- ● organically grown vegetables.

Biologie f biology; **biologisch**
adj biological; (*Anbau*) organic
Birke (-, -n) f birch
Birne (-, -n) f (*Obst*) pear; (*Elek*)
(light) bulb

 SCHLÜSSELWORT

bis *prep +akk, adv* **1** (*zeitlich*) till,
until; (*bis spätestens*) by; **Sie haben
bis Dienstag Zeit** you have until *o*
till Tuesday; **bis Dienstag muss es
fertig sein** it must be ready by
Tuesday; **bis auf Weiteres** until
further notice; **bis in die Nacht**

into the night; **bis bald/gleich** see
you later/soon
2 (*räumlich*) (up) to; **ich fahre bis
Köln** I'm going to *o* I'm going as far
as Cologne; **bis an unser
Grundstück** (right *o* up) to our
plot; **bis hierher** this far
3 (*bei Zahlen*) up to; **bis zu** up to
4 bis auf etw *akk* (*außer*) except
sth; (*einschließlich*) including sth
▷ *konj* **1** (*mit Zahlen*) to; **10 bis 20** 10
to 20
2 (*zeitlich*) till, until; **bis es dunkel
wird** till *o* until it gets dark; **von ...
bis ...** from ... to ...

Bischof (-s, *Bischöfe*) m bishop
bisher *adv* up to now, so far
Biskuit (-(*e*)s, -s *o* -e) nt sponge
biss *imperf von* **beißen**
Biss (-es, -e) m bite
bisschen *adj*: **ein ~** a bit of; **ein
~ Salz/Liebe** a bit of salt/love; **ich
habe kein ~ Hunger** I'm not a bit
hungry ▷ *adv*: **ein ~** a bit; **kein
~** not at all
bissig *adj* (*Hund*) vicious;
(*Bemerkung*) cutting
Bit (-s, -s) nt (*Inform*) bit
bitte *interj* please; (*wie*) **~?** (I beg
your) pardon?; **~ (schön)!** (*als
Antwort auf Dank*) you're welcome,
that's alright; **hier, ~** here you are;
Bitte (-, -n) f request; **bitten**
(*bat, gebeten*) vt, vi to ask (*um* for)
bitter *adj* bitter
Blähungen *pl* (*Med*) wind *sing*
blamieren *vr*: **sich ~** to make a
fool of oneself ▷ *vt*: **jdn ~** to make
sb look a fool
Blankoscheck m blank cheque
Blase (-, -n) f bubble; (*Med*)
blister; (*Anat*) bladder
blasen (*blies, geblasen*) vi to blow;
jdm einen ~ (*vulg*) to give sb a
blow job
Blasenentzündung f cystitis

blass *adj* pale
Blatt *(-(e)s, Blätter) nt* leaf; *(von Papier)* sheet; **blättern** *vi (Inform)* to scroll; **in etw** *(dat)* ~ to leaf through sth; **Blätterteig** *m* puff pastry; **Blattsalat** *m* green salad; **Blattspinat** *m* spinach
blau *adj* blue; *(fam: betrunken)* plastered; *(Gastr)* boiled; **~es Auge** black eye; **~er Fleck** bruise; **Blaubeere** *f* bilberry, blueberry; **Blaulicht** *nt* flashing blue light; **blau|machen** *vi* to skip work; *(in Schule)* to skip school; **Blauschimmelkäse** *m* blue cheese
Blazer *(-s, -) m* blazer
Blech *(-(e)s, -e) nt* sheet metal; *(Backblech)* baking tray *(Brit)*, cookie sheet *(US)*; **Blechschaden** *m (Auto)* damage to the bodywork
Blei *(-(e)s, -e) nt* lead
bleiben *(blieb, geblieben) vi* to stay; **lass das ~!** stop it; **das bleibt unter uns** that's (just) between ourselves; **mir bleibt keine andere Wahl** I have no other choice
bleich *adj* pale; **bleichen** *vt* to bleach
bleifrei *adj (Benzin)* unleaded; **bleihaltig** *adj (Benzin)* leaded
Bleistift *m* pencil
Blende *(-, -n) f (Foto)* aperture
Blick *(-(e)s, -e) m* look; *(kurz)* glance; *(Aussicht)* view; **auf den ersten ~** at first sight; **einen ~ auf etw** *(akk)* **werfen** to have a look at sth; **blicken** *vi* to look; **sich ~ lassen** to show up
blieb *imperf von* **bleiben**
blies *imperf von* **blasen**
blind *adj* blind; *(Glas etc)* dull; **Blinddarm** *m* appendix; **Blinddarmentzündung** *f* appendicitis; **Blinde(r)** *mf* blind person/man/woman; **die ~n** *pl*

the blind *pl*; **Blindenhund** *m* guide dog; **Blindenschrift** *f* braille
blinken *vi (Stern, Lichter)* to twinkle; *(aufleuchten)* to flash; *(Auto)* to indicate; **Blinker** *(-s, -) m (Auto)* indicator *(Brit)*, turn signal *(US)*
blinzeln *vi (mit beiden Augen)* to blink; *(mit einem Auge)* to wink
Blitz *(-es, -e) m* (flash of) lightning; *(Foto)* flash; **blitzen** *vi (Foto)* to use a/the flash; **es blitzte und donnerte** there was thunder and lightning; **Blitzlicht** *nt* flash
Block *(-(e)s, Blöcke) m (a. fig)* block; *(von Papier)* pad; **Blockflöte** *f* recorder; **Blockhaus** *nt* log cabin; **blockieren** *vt* to block ▷ *vi* to jam; *(Räder)* to lock; **Blockschrift** *f* block letters *pl*
blöd *adj* stupid; **blödeln** *vi (fam)* to fool around
Blog *(-s, -s) nt (Inform)* blog
blond *adj* blond; *(Frau)* blonde

 SCHLÜSSELWORT

bloß *adj* 1 *(unbedeckt)* bare; *(nackt)* naked; **mit der bloßen Hand** with one's bare hand; **mit bloßem Auge** with the naked eye
2 *(alleinig, nur)* mere; **der bloße Gedanke** the very thought; **bloßer Neid** sheer envy
▷ *adv* only, merely; **lass das bloß!** just don't do that!; **wie ist das bloß passiert?** how on earth did that happen?

blühen *vi* to bloom; *(fig)* to flourish
Blume *(-, -n) f* flower; *(von Wein)* bouquet; **Blumengeschäft** *nt* florist's (shop); **Blumenkohl** *m* cauliflower; **Blumenladen** *m* flower shop; **Blumenstrauß** *m*

bunch of flowers; **Blumentopf** m
flowerpot; **Blumenvase** f vase
Bluse (-, -n) f blouse
Blut (-(e)s) nt blood; **Blutbild** nt
blood count; **Blutdruck** m blood
pressure; **Blutorange** f blood
orange
Blüte (-, -n) f (Pflanzenteil) flower,
bloom; (Baumblüte) blossom; (fig)
prime
bluten vi to bleed
Blütenstaub m pollen
Bluter (-s, -) m (Med)
haemophiliac; **Bluterguss** m
haematoma; (blauer Fleck) bruise;
Blutgruppe f blood group; **blutig**
adj bloody; **Blutkonserve** f unit
of stored blood; **Blutprobe** f
blood sample; **Blutspende** f
blood donation; **Bluttransfusion**
f blood transfusion; **Blutung** f
bleeding; **Blutvergiftung** f
blood poisoning; **Blutwurst** f
black pudding (Brit), blood
sausage (US)
BLZ abk = **Bankleitzahl**
Bob (-s, -s) m bob(sleigh)
Bock (-(e)s, Böcke) m (Reh) buck;
(Schaf) ram; (Gestell) trestle; (Sport)
vaulting horse; **ich hab keinen
~ (drauf)** (fam) I don't feel like it
Boden (-s, Böden) m ground;
(Fußboden) floor; (von Meer, Fass)
bottom; (Speicher) attic;
Bodennebel m ground mist;
Bodenpersonal nt ground staff;
Bodenschätze pl mineral
resources pl
Bodensee m: **der ~** Lake
Constance
Body (-s, -s) m body;
Bodybuilding (-s) nt
bodybuilding
bog imperf von **biegen**
Bogen (-s, -) m (Biegung) curve;
(in der Architektur) arch; (Waffe,
Instrument) bow; (Papier) sheet

Bohne (-, -n) f bean; **grüne ~n** pl
green (o French (Brit)) beans pl;
weiße ~n pl haricot beans pl;
Bohnenkaffee m real coffee;
Bohnensprosse f bean sprout
bohren vt to drill; **Bohrer** (-s, -)
m drill
Boiler (-s, -) m water heater
Boje (-, -n) f buoy
Bolivien (-s) nt Bolivia
Bombe (-, -n) f bomb
Bon (-s, -s) m (Kassenzettel)
receipt; (Gutschein) voucher,
coupon
Bonbon (-s, -s) nt sweet (Brit),
candy (US)
Bonus (- o -ses, -se o Boni) m
bonus; (Punktvorteil) bonus points
pl; (Schadenfreiheitsrabatt)
no-claims bonus
Boot (-(e)s, -e) nt boat;
Bootsverleih m boat hire (Brit) (o
rental (US))
Bord (-(e)s, -e) m: **an ~ (eines
Schiffes)** on board (a ship); **an
~ gehen** (Schiff) to go on board;
(Flugzeug) to board; **von ~ gehen**
to disembark; **Bordcomputer** m
dashboard computer
Bordell (-s, -e) nt brothel
Bordkarte f boarding card
Bordstein m kerb (Brit), curb (US)
borgen vt to borrow; **jdm etw
~** to lend sb sth; **sich** (dat) **etw ~** to
borrow sth
Börse (-, -n) f stock exchange;
(Geldbörse) purse
bös adj siehe **böse**; **bösartig** adj
malicious; (Med) malignant
Böschung f slope; (Uferböschung)
embankment
böse adj bad; (stärker) evil;
(Wunde) nasty; (zornig) angry; **bist
du mir ~?** are you angry with me?
boshaft adj malicious
Bosnien (-s) nt Bosnia;
Bosnien-Herzegowina (-s) nt

Bosnia-Herzegovina
böswillig *adj* malicious
bot *imperf von* **bieten**
botanisch *adj*: **~er Garten** botanical gardens *pl*
Botschaft *f* message; (*Pol*) embassy; **Botschafter(in)** *m(f)* ambassador
Botsuana (*-s*) *nt* Botswana
Bouillon (*-, -s*) *f* stock
Boutique (*-, -n*) *f* boutique
Bowle (*-, -n*) *f* punch
Box (*-, -en*) *f* (*Behälter, Pferdebox*) box; (*Lautsprecher*) speaker; (*bei Autorennen*) pit
boxen *vi* to box; **Boxer** (*-s, -*) *m* (*Hund, Sportler*) boxer; **Boxershorts** *pl* boxer shorts *pl*; **Boxkampf** *m* boxing match
Boykott (*-s, -e*) *m* boycott
brach *imperf von* **brechen**
brachte *imperf von* **bringen**
Brainstorming (*-s*) *nt* brainstorming
Branchenverzeichnis *nt* yellow pages® *pl*
Brand (*-(e)s, Brände*) *m* fire; **einen ~ haben** (*fam*) to be parched
Brandenburg (*-s*) *nt* Brandenburg
Brandsalbe *f* ointment for burns
Brandung *f* surf
Brandwunde *f* burn
brannte *imperf von* **brennen**
Brasilien (*-s*) *nt* Brazil
braten (*briet, gebraten*) *vt* to roast; (*auf dem Rost*) to grill; (*in der Pfanne*) to fry; **Braten** (*-s, -*) *m* roast; (*roher*) joint; **Bratensoße** *f* gravy; **Brathähnchen** *nt* roast chicken; **Bratkartoffeln** *pl* fried potatoes *pl*; **Bratpfanne** *f* frying pan; **Bratspieß** *m* spit; **Bratwurst** *f* fried sausage; (*gegrillte*) grilled sausage
Brauch (*-s, Bräuche*) *m* custom
brauchen *vt* (*nötig haben*) to need

(*für, zu* for); (*erfordern*) to require; (*Zeit*) to take; (*gebrauchen*) to use; **wie lange wird er ~?** how long will it take him?; **du brauchst es nur zu sagen** you only need to say; **das braucht (seine) Zeit** it takes time; **ihr braucht es nicht zu tun** you don't have (*o* need) to do it; **sie hätte nicht zu kommen ~** she needn't have come
brauen *vt* to brew; **Brauerei** *f* brewery
braun *adj* brown; (*von Sonne*) tanned; **Bräune** (*-, -n*) *f* brownness; (*von Sonne*) tan; **Bräunungsstudio** *nt* tanning studio
Brause (*-, -n*) *f* (*Dusche*) shower; (*Getränk*) fizzy drink (*Brit*), soda (*US*)
Braut (*-, Bräute*) *f* bride; **Bräutigam** (*-s, -e*) *m* bridegroom
brav *adj* (*artig*) good, well-behaved
bravo *interj* well done
BRD (*-*) *f abk* = **Bundesrepublik Deutschland** FRG

brechen (*brach, gebrochen*) *vt* to break; (*erbrechen*) to bring up; **sich** (*dat*) **den Arm ~** to break one's arm ▷ *vi* to break; (*erbrechen*) to vomit, to be sick; **Brechreiz** *m* nausea
Brei (*-(e)s, -e*) *m* (*Breimasse*) mush, pulp; (*Haferbrei*) porridge; (*für*

Kinder) pap
breit *adj* wide; *(Schultern)* broad;
zwei Meter ~ two metres wide;
Breite (-, -n) *f* breadth; *(bei
Maßangaben)* width; *(Geo)* latitude;
der ~ nach widthways;
Breitengrad *m* (degree of)
latitude
Bremen (-s) *nt* Bremen
Bremsbelag *m* brake lining;
Bremse (-, -n) *f* brake; *(Zool)*
horsefly; **bremsen** *vi* to brake
▷ *vt (Auto)* to brake; *(fig)* to slow
down; **Bremsflüssigkeit** *f* brake
fluid; **Bremslicht** *nt* brake light;
Bremspedal *nt* brake pedal;
Bremsspur *f* tyre marks *pl*;
Bremsweg *m* braking distance
brennen *(brannte, gebrannt) vi* to
burn; *(in Flammen stehen)* to be on
fire; **es brennt!** fire!; **mir ~ die
Augen** my eyes are smarting; **das
Licht ~ lassen** to leave the light
on; **Brennholz** *nt* firewood;
Brennnessel *f* stinging nettle;
Brennspiritus *m* methylated
spirits *pl*; **Brennstab** *m* fuel rod;
Brennstoff *m* fuel
Brett (-(e)s, -er) *nt* board; *(länger)*
plank; *(Regal)* shelf; *(Spielbrett)*
board; **Schwarzes ~** notice board,
bulletin board *(US)*; **~er** *pl (ski)* skis
pl; **Brettspiel** *nt* board game
Brezel (-, -n) *f* pretzel
Brief (-(e)s, -e) *m* letter;
Briefbombe *f* letter bomb;
Brieffreund(in) *m(f)* penfriend,
pen pal; **Briefkasten** *m* letterbox
(Brit), mailbox *(US)*;
elektronischer ~ electronic
mailbox; **Briefmarke** *f* stamp;
Briefpapier *nt* writing paper;
Brieftasche *f* wallet;
Briefträger(in) *m(f)* post-
man/-woman; **Briefumschlag** *m*
envelope; **Briefwaage** *f* letter
scales *pl*

briet *imperf von* **braten**
Brille (-, -n) *f* glasses *pl*;
(Schutzbrille) goggles *pl*; **Brillenetui**
nt glasses case
bringen *(brachte, gebracht) vt
(herbringen)* to bring; *(mitnehmen,
vom Sprecher weg)* to take; *(holen,
herbringen)* to get, to fetch; *(Theat,
Cine)* to show; *(Radio, TV)* to
broadcast; **~ Sie mir bitte noch
ein Bier** could you bring me
another beer, please?; **jdn nach
Hause ~** to take sb home; **jdn
dazu ~, etw zu tun** to make sb do
sth; **jdn auf eine Idee ~** to give sb
an idea
Brise (-, -n) *f* breeze
Brite (-n, -n) *m*, **Britin** *f* British
person, Briton; **er ist ~** he is
British; **die ~n** the British; **britisch**
adj British
Brocken (-s, -) *m* bit; *(größer)*
lump, chunk
Brokkoli *m* broccoli
Brombeere *f* blackberry
Bronchitis (-) *f* bronchitis
Bronze (-, -n) *f* bronze
Brosche (-, -n) *f* brooch
Brot (-(e)s, -e) *nt* bread; *(Laib)* loaf;
Brotaufstrich *m* spread;
Brötchen *nt* roll; **Brotzeit** *f
(Pause)* break; *(Essen)* snack;
~ machen to have a snack
Browser (-s, -) *m (Inform)*
browser
Bruch (-(e)s, Brüche) *m (Brechen)*
breaking; *(Bruchstelle; mit Partei,
Tradition etc)* break; *(Med:
Eingeweidebruch)* rupture, hernia;
(Knochenbruch) fracture; *(Math)*
fraction; **brüchig** *adj* brittle
Brücke (-, -n) *f* bridge
Bruder (-s, Brüder) *m* brother
Brühe (-, -n) *f (Suppe)* (clear)
soup; *(Grundlage)* stock; *(pej:
Getränk)* muck; **Brühwürfel** *m*
stock cube

brüllen *vi* to roar; (*Stier*) to bellow; (*vor Schmerzen*) to scream (with pain)

brummen *vi* (*Bär, Mensch*) to growl; (*brummeln*) to mutter; (*Insekt*) to buzz; (*Motor, Radio*) to drone ▷ *vt* to growl

brünett *adj* brunette

Brunnen (*-s, -*) *m* fountain; (*tief*) well; (*natürlich*) spring

Brust (*-, Brüste*) *f* breast; (*beim Mann*) chest; **Brustschwimmen** (*-s*) *nt* breaststroke; **Brustwarze** *f* nipple

brutal *adj* brutal

brutto *adv* gross

BSE (*-*) *nt* *abk* = **bovine spongiforme Enzephalopathie** BSE

Bube (*-n, -n*) *m* boy, lad; (*Karten*) jack

Buch (*-(e)s, Bücher*) *nt* book

Buche (*-, -n*) *f* beech (tree)

buchen *vt* to book; (*Betrag*) to enter

Bücherei *f* library

Buchfink *m* chaffinch

Buchhalter(in) *m(f)* accountant

Buchhandlung *f* bookshop

Büchse (*-, -n*) *f* tin (Brit), can

Buchstabe (*-ns, -n*) *m* letter; **buchstabieren** *vt* to spell

Bucht (*-, -en*) *f* bay

Buchung *f* booking; (*Comm*) entry

Buckel (*-s, -*) *m* hump

bücken *vr*: **sich ~** to bend down

Buddhismus (*-*) *m* Buddhism

Bude (*-, -en*) *f* (*auf Markt*) stall; (*fam: Wohnung*) pad, place

Büfett (*-s, -s*) *nt* sideboard; **kaltes ~** cold buffet

Büffel (*-s, -*) *m* buffalo

Bügel (*-s, -*) *m* (*Kleidung*) hanger; (*Steigbügel*) stirrup; (*Brille*) sidepiece; (*von Skilift*) T-bar; **Bügelbrett** *nt* ironing board;

Bügeleisen *nt* iron; **Bügelfalte** *f* crease; **bügelfrei** *adj* non-iron; **bügeln** *vt, vi* to iron

buh *interj* boo

Bühne (*-, -n*) *f* stage; **Bühnenbild** *nt* set

Bulgare (*-n, -n*) *m*, **Bulgarin** *f* Bulgarian; **Bulgarien** (*-s*) *nt* Bulgaria; **bulgarisch** *adj* Bulgarian; **Bulgarisch** *nt* Bulgarian

Bulimie *f* bulimia

Bulle (*-n, -n*) *m* bull; (*fam: Polizist*) cop

Bummel (*-s, -*) *m* stroll; **bummeln** *vi* to stroll; (*trödeln*) to dawdle; (*faulenzen*) to loaf around; **Bummelzug** *m* slow train

bums *interj* bang

bumsen *vi* (*vulg*) to screw

Bund (*-(e)s, Bünde*) *m* (*von Hose, Rock*) waistband; (*Freundschaftsbund*) bond; (*Organisation*) association; (*Pol*) confederation; **der ~** (*fam: Bundeswehr*) the army ▷ (*-(e)s, -e*) *nt* bunch; (*von Stroh etc*) bundle

Bundes- *in zW* Federal; (*auf Deutschland bezogen a.*) German; **Bundeskanzler(in)** *m(f)* Chancellor; **Bundesland** *nt* state, Land; **Bundesliga** *f*: **erste/zweite ~** First/Second Division; **Bundespräsident(in)** *m(f)* President; **Bundesrat** *m* (*in Deutschland*) Upper House (of the German Parliament); (*in der Schweiz*) Council of Ministers; **Bundesregierung** *f* Federal Government; **Bundesrepublik** *f* Federal Republic; **~ Deutschland** Federal Republic of Germany; **Bundesstraße** *f* ≈ A road (Brit), ≈ state highway (US); **Bundestag** *m* Lower House (of the German Parliament); **Bundeswehr** *f* (German) armed forces *pl*

● **BUNDESWEHR**
●
● The **Bundeswehr** is the name
● for the German armed forces. It
● was established in 1955, first of
● all for volunteers, but since 1956
● there has been compulsory
● military service for all
● able-bodied young men of 18. In
● peacetime the Defence Minister
● is the head of the 'Bundeswehr',
● but in wartime the
● **Bundeskanzler** takes over. The
● 'Bundeswehr' comes under the
● jurisdiction of NATO.

Bündnis _nt_ alliance
Bungalow (-s, -s) _m_ bungalow
Bungeejumping (-s) _nt_ bungee
jumping
bunt _adj_ colourful; (_von Programm
etc_) varied; **~e Farben** bright
colours ▷ _adv_ (_anstreichen_) in
bright colours; **Buntstift** _m_
crayon, coloured pencil
Burg (-, -en) _f_ castle
Bürger(in) (-s, -) _m(f)_ citizen;
bürgerlich _adj_ (_Rechte, Ehe etc_)
civil; (_vom Mittelstand_)
middle-class; (_pej_) bourgeois;
Bürgermeister(in) _m(f)_ mayor;
Bürgersteig (-(e)s, -e) _m_
pavement (_Brit_), sidewalk (_US_)
Büro (-s, -s) _nt_ office;
Büroklammer _f_ paper clip
Bürokratie _f_ bureaucracy
Bursche (-n, -n) _m_ lad; (_Typ_) guy
Bürste (-, -n) _f_ brush; **bürsten**
_vt_ to brush
Bus (-ses, -se) _m_ bus; (_Reisebus_)
coach (_Brit_), bus; **Busbahnhof** _m_
bus station
Busch (-(e)s, Büsche) _m_ bush;
(_Strauch_) shrub
Busen (-s, -) _m_ breasts _pl_, bosom
Busfahrer(in) _m(f)_ bus driver;
Bushaltestelle _f_ bus stop

Businessclass (-) _f_ business
class
Busreise _f_ coach tour (_Brit_), bus
tour
Bußgeld _nt_ fine
Büstenhalter (-s, -) _m_ bra
Busverbindung _f_ bus
connection
Butter (-) _f_ butter; **Butterbrot**
_nt_ slice of bread and butter;
Butterkäse _m_ type of mild, full-fat
cheese; **Buttermilch** _f_
buttermilk; **Butterschmalz** _nt_
clarified butter
Button (-s, -s) _m_ badge (_Brit_),
button (_US_)
b. w. _abk_ = **bitte wenden** pto
Byte (-s, -s) _nt_ byte
bzw. _adv abk_ = **beziehungsweise**

C

ca. *adv abk* = **circa** approx
Cabrio (-s, -s) *nt* convertible
Café (-s, -s) *nt* café
Cafeteria (-, -s) *f* cafeteria
Call-Center (-s, -) *nt* call centre
campen *vi* to camp; **Camping** (-s) *nt* camping; **Campingbus** *m* camper; **Campingplatz** *m* campsite, camping ground (*US*)
Cappuccino (-s, -) *m* cappuccino
Carving (-s) *nt* (*Ski*) carving; **Carvingski** *m* carving ski
CD (-, -s) *f abk* = **Compact Disc** CD; **CD-Brenner** (-s, -) *m* CD burner, CD writer; **CD-Player** (-s, -) *m* CD player; **CD-ROM** (-, -s) *f abk* = **Compact Disc Read Only Memory** CD-ROM; **CD-ROM-Laufwerk** *nt* CD-ROM drive, **CD-Spieler** *m* CD player
Cello (-s, -s *o* Celli) *nt* cello
Celsius *nt* celsius; **20 Grad ~** 20 degrees Celsius, 68 degrees Fahrenheit
Cent (-, -s) *m* (*von Dollar und Euro*) cent
Chamäleon (-s, -s) *nt* chameleon
Champagner (-s, -) *m* champagne
Champignon (-s, -s) *m* mushroom
Champions League (-, -s) *f* Champions League
Chance (-, -n) *f* chance; **die ~n stehen gut** the prospects are good
Chaos (-) *nt* chaos; **Chaot(in)** (-en, -en) *m(f)* (*fam*) disorganized person, scatterbrain; **chaotisch** *adj* chaotic
Charakter (-s, -e) *m* character; **charakteristisch** *adj* characteristic (*für* of)
Charisma (-s, Charismen *o* Charismata) *nt* charisma
charmant *adj* charming
Charterflug *m* charter flight; **chartern** *vt* to charter
Chat (-s, -s) *m* (*Inform*) chat; **chatten** *vi* (*Inform*) to chat
checken *vt* (*überprüfen*) to check; (*fam: verstehen*) to get
Check-in (-s, -s) *m* check-in; **Check-in-Schalter** *m* check-in desk
Chef(in) (-s, -s) *m(f)* boss; **Chefarzt** *m*, **Chefärztin** *f* senior consultant (*Brit*), medical director (*US*)
Chemie (-) *f* chemistry; **chemisch** *adj* chemical; **~e Reinigung** dry cleaning
Chemotherapie *f* chemotherapy
Chicoree (-s) *m* chicory
Chiffre (-, -n) *f* (*Geheimzeichen*) cipher; (*in Zeitung*) box number
Chile (-s) *nt* Chile
Chili (-s, -s) *m* chilli

China (-s) nt China; **Chinakohl** m Chinese leaves pl (Brit), bok choy (US); **Chinarestaurant** nt Chinese restaurant; **Chinese** (-n, -n) m Chinese; **Chinesin** (-, -nen) f Chinese (woman); **sie ist ~** she's Chinese; **chinesisch** adj Chinese; **Chinesisch** nt Chinese

Chip (-s, -s) m (Inform) chip; **Chipkarte** f smart card

Chips pl (Kartoffelchips) crisps pl (Brit), chips pl (US)

Chirurg(in) (-en, -en) m(f) surgeon

Chlor (-s) nt chlorine

Choke (-s, -s) m choke

Cholera (-) f cholera

Cholesterin (-s) nt cholesterol

Chor (-(e), Chöre) m choir; (Theat) chorus

Choreografie f choreography

Christ(in) (-en, -en) m(f) Christian; **Christbaum** m Christmas tree; **Christi Himmelfahrt** f the Ascension (of Christ); **Christkind** nt baby Jesus; (das Geschenke bringt) ≈ Father Christmas, Santa Claus; **christlich** adj Christian

Chrom (-s) nt chrome; (Chem) chromium

chronisch adj chronic

chronologisch adj chronological ▷ adv in chronological order

Chrysantheme (-, -n) f chrysanthemum

circa adv about, approximately

City (-) f city centre, downtown (US)

Clementine (-, -n) f clementine

clever adj clever, smart

Clique (-, -n) f group; (pej) clique; **David und seine ~** David and his lot o crowd

Clown (-s, -s) m clown

Club (-s, -s) m club; **Cluburlaub** m club holiday (Brit), club vacation (US)

Cocktail (-s, -s) m cocktail; **Cocktailtomate** f cherry tomato

Cognac (-s) m cognac

Cola (-, -s) f Coke®, cola

Comic (-s, -s) m comic strip; (Heft) comic

Compact Disc (-, -s) f compact disc

Computer (-s, -) m computer; **Computerfreak** m computer nerd; **computergesteuert** adj computer-controlled; **Computergrafik** f computer graphics pl; **computerlesbar** adj machine-readable; **Computerspiel** nt computer game; **Computertomografie** f computer tomography, scan; **Computervirus** m computer virus

Container (-s, -) m (zum Transport) container; (für Bauschutt etc) skip

Control-Taste f control key

Cookie (-s, -s) nt (Inform) cookie

cool adj (fam) cool

Cornflakes pl cornflakes pl

Couch (-, -en) f couch; **Couchtisch** m coffee table

Coupé (-s, -s) nt coupé

Coupon (-s, -s) m coupon

Cousin (-s, -s) m cousin; **Cousine** f cousin

Crack (-s) nt (Droge) crack

Creme (-, -s) f cream; (Gastr) mousse

Creutzfeld-Jakob-Krankheit f Creutzfeld-Jakob disease, CJD

Croissant (-s, -s) nt croissant

Curry (-s) m curry powder ▷ (-s) nt (indisches Gericht) curry; **Currywurst** f fried sausage with ketchup and curry powder

Cursor (-s, -) m (Inform) cursor

Cybercafé nt cybercafé; **Cyberspace** (-) m cyberspace

d

even though he has no idea; **ich finde nichts ~** I don't see anything wrong with it; **es bleibt ~** that's settled; **~ sein** (*anwesend*) to be present; (*beteiligt*) to be involved; **ich bin ~!** count me in; **er war gerade ~ zu gehen** he was just (*o* on the point of) leaving

dabei|bleiben *irr vi* to stick with it; **ich bleibe dabei** I'm not changing my mind

dabei|haben *irr vt:* **er hat seine Schwester dabei** he's brought his sister; **ich habe kein Geld dabei** I haven't got any money on me

Dach (*-(e)s, Dächer*) *nt* roof; **Dachboden** *m* attic, loft; **Dachgepäckträger** *m* roofrack; **Dachrinne** *f* gutter

Dachs (*-es, -e*) *m* badger

dachte *imperf von* **denken**

Dackel (*-s, -*) *m* dachshund

dadurch *adv* (*räumlich*) through it; (*durch diesen Umstand*) in that way; (*deshalb*) because of that, for that reason ▷ *conj:* **~, dass** because; **~, dass er hart arbeitete** (*indem*) by working hard

dafür *adv* for it; (*anstatt*) instead; **~ habe ich 50 Euro bezahlt** I paid 50 euros for it; **ich bin ~ zu bleiben** I'm for (*o* in favour of) staying; **~ ist er ja da** that's what he's there for; **er kann nichts ~** he can't help it

da *adv* **1** (*örtlich*) there; (*hier*) here; **da draußen** out there; **da sein** to be there; **da bin ich** here I am; **da, wo** where; **ist noch Milch da?** is there any milk left?

2 (*zeitlich*) then; (*folglich*) so

3 da haben wir Glück gehabt we were lucky there; **da kann man nichts machen** nothing can be done about it

▷ *konj* (*weil*) as, since

dabei *adv* (*räumlich*) close to it; (*zeitlich*) at the same time; (*obwohl, doch*) though; **sie hörte Radio und rauchte ~** she was listening to the radio and smoking (at the same time); **~ fällt mir ein ...** that reminds me ...; **~ kam es zu einem Unfall** this led to an accident; **... und ~ hat er gar keine Ahnung ...**

dagegen *adv* against it; (*im Vergleich damit*) in comparison; (*bei Tausch*) for it; **ich habe nichts ~** I don't mind

daheim *adv* at home

daher *adv* (*räumlich*) from there; (*Ursache*) that's why ▷ *conj* (*deshalb*) that's why

dahin *adv* (*räumlich*) there; (*zeitlich*) then; (*vergangen*) gone; **bis ~** (*zeitlich*) till then; (*örtlich*) up to there; **bis ~ muss die Arbeit fertig**

sein the work must be finished by then

dahinter adv behind it; **~ kommen** to find out

dahinterkommen vi to find out

Dahlie f dahlia

Dalmatiner (-s, -) m dalmatian

damals adv at that time, then

Dame (-, -n) f lady; (Karten) queen; (Spiel) draughts sing (Brit), checkers sing (US); **Damenbinde** f sanitary towel (Brit), sanitary napkin (US); **Damenkleidung** f ladies' wear; **Damentoilette** f ladies' toilet (o restroom (US))

damit adv with it; (begründend) by that; **was meint er ~?** what does he mean by that?; **genug ~!** that's enough ▷ conj so that

Damm (-(e)s, Dämme) m dyke; (Staudamm) dam; (am Hafen) mole; (Bahn-, Straßendamm) embankment

Dämmerung f twilight; (am Morgen) dawn; (am Abend) dusk

Dampf (-(e)s, Dämpfe) m steam; (Dunst) vapour; **Dampfbad** nt Turkish bath; **Dampfbügeleisen** nt steam iron; **dampfen** vi to steam

dämpfen vt (Gastr) to steam; (Geräusch) to deaden; (Begeisterung) to dampen

Dampfer (-s, -) m steamer

Dampfkochtopf m pressure cooker

danach adv after that; (zeitlich a.) afterwards; (demgemäß) accordingly; **mir ist nicht ~** I don't feel like it; **~ sieht es aus** that's what it looks like

Däne (-n, -n) m Dane

daneben adv beside it; (im Vergleich) in comparison

Dänemark (-s) nt Denmark; **Dänin** f Dane, Danish

woman/girl; **dänisch** adj Danish; **Dänisch** nt Danish

dank prep +dat o gen thanks to; **Dank** (-(e)s) m thanks pl; **vielen ~!** thank you very much; **jdm ~ sagen** to thank sb; **dankbar** adj grateful; (Aufgabe) rewarding; **danke** interj thank you, thanks; **nein ~!** no, thank you; **~, gerne!** yes, please; **~, gleichfalls!** thanks, and the same to you; **danken** vi: **jdm für etw ~** to thank sb for sth; **nichts zu ~!** you're welcome

dann adv then; **bis ~!** see you (later); **~ eben nicht** okay, forget it, suit yourself

daran adv (räumlich) on it; (befestigen) to it; (stoßen) against it; **es liegt ~, dass ...** it's because ...

darauf adv (räumlich) on it; (zielgerichtet) towards it; (danach) afterwards; **es kommt ganz ~ an, ob ...** it all depends whether ...; **ich freue mich ~** I'm looking forward to it; **am Tag ~** the next day; **~ folgend** (Tag, Jahr) next, following

darauffolgend adj (Tag, Jahr) next, following

daraus adv from it; **was ist ~ geworden?** what became of it?

darin adv in it; **das Problem liegt ~, dass ...** the basic problem is that ...

Darlehen (-s, -) nt loan

Darm (-(e)s, Därme) m intestine; (Wurstdarm) skin; **Darmgrippe** f gastroenteritis

darstellen vt to represent; (Theat) to play; (beschreiben) to describe; **Darsteller(in)** m(f) actor/actress; **Darstellung** f representation; (Beschreibung) description

darüber adv (räumlich) above it, over it; (fahren) over it; (mehr) more; (*währenddessen*) meanwhile; (*sprechen, streiten, sich freuen*) about it

darum *adv* (*deshalb*) that's why; **es geht ~, dass ...** the point (*o* thing) is that ...

darunter *adv* (*räumlich*) under it; (*dazwischen*) among them; (*weniger*) less; **was verstehen Sie ~?** what do you understand by that?; **~ fallen** to be included

darunterfallen *vi* to be included

das *art* the; **~ Auto da** that car; **er hat sich ~ Bein gebrochen** he's broken his leg; **vier Euro ~ Kilo** four euros a kilo ▷ *pron* that (one), this (one); (*relativ, Sache*) that, which; (*relativ, Person*) who, that; (*demonstrativ*) this/that one; **~ Auto da** that car; **ich nehme ~ da** I'll take that one; **~ Auto, ~ er kaufte** the car (that (*o* which)) he bought; **~ Mädchen, ~ nebenan wohnt** the girl who (*o* that) lives next door; **~ heißt** that is; **~ sind Amerikaner** they're American

da sein *irr vi siehe* **da**

dass *conj* that; **so ~** so that; **es sei denn, ~** unless; **ohne ~ er grüßte** without saying hello

dasselbe *pron* the same

Datei *f* (*Inform*) file; **Dateimanager** *m* file manager

Daten *pl* data *pl*; **Datenbank** *f* database; **Datenmissbrauch** *m* misuse of data; **Datenschutz** *m* data protection; **Datenträger** *m* data carrier; **Datenverarbeitung** *f* data processing

datieren *vt* to date

Dativ *m* dative (case)

Dattel (-, -n) *f* date

Datum (-s, *Daten*) *nt* date

Dauer (-, -n) *f* duration; (*Länge*) length; **auf die ~** in the long run; **für die ~ von zwei Jahren** for (a

period of) two years; **Dauerauftrag** *m* (*Fin*) standing order; **dauerhaft** *adj* lasting; (*Material*) durable; **Dauerkarte** *f* season ticket; **dauern** *vi* to last; (*Zeit benötigen*) to take; **es hat sehr lange gedauert, bis er ...** it took him a long time to ...; **wie lange dauert es denn noch?** how much longer will it be?; **das dauert mir zu lange** I can't wait that long; **dauernd** *adj* lasting; (*ständig*) constant ▷ *adv* always, constantly; **er lachte ~** he kept laughing; **unterbrich mich nicht ~** stop interrupting me; **Dauerwelle** *f* perm (*Brit*), permanent (*US*)

Daumen (-s, -) *m* thumb

Daunendecke *f* eiderdown

davon *adv* (*räumlich*) away; (*weg von*) from it; (*Grund*) because of it; **ich hätte gerne ein Kilo ~** I'd like one kilo of that; **~ habe ich gehört** I've heard of it; (*Geschehen*) I've heard about it; **das kommt ~, wenn ...** that's what happens when ...; **was habe ich ~?** what's the point?; **auf und ~** up and away; **davon|laufen** *irr vi* to run away

davor *adv* (*räumlich*) in front of it; (*zeitlich*) before; **ich habe Angst ~** I'm afraid of it

dazu *adv* (*zusätzlich*) on top of that, as well; (*zu diesem Zweck*) for it, for that purpose; **ich möchte Reis ~** I'd like rice with it; **und ~ noch** and in addition; **~ fähig sein, etw zu tun** to be capable of doing sth; **wie kam es ~?** how did it happen?; **dazu|gehören** *vi* to belong to it; **dazu|kommen** *irr vi* (*zu jdm ~*) to join sb; **kommt noch etwas dazu?** anything else?

dazwischen *adv* in between; (*Unterschied etc*) between them; (*in einer Gruppe*) among them

dazwischen|kommen *irr vi:*
wenn nichts dazwischenkommt
if all goes well; **mir ist etwas**
dazwischengekommen
something has cropped up
DDR (-) *f abk* = **Deutsche**
Demokratische Republik (*Hist*)
GDR
dealen *vi* (*fam: mit Drogen*) to deal
in drugs; **Dealer(in)** (-s, -) *m(f)*
(*fam*) dealer, pusher
Deck (-(e)s, -s o -e) *nt* deck
Decke (-, -n) *f* cover; (*für Bett*)
blanket; (*für Tisch*) tablecloth; (*von*
Zimmer) ceiling
Deckel (-s, -) *m* lid
decken *vt* to cover; (*Tisch*) to lay,
to set ▷ *vr:* **sich ~** (*Interessen*) to
coincide; (*Aussagen*) to correspond
▷ *vi* (*den Tisch decken*) to lay (o set)
the table
Decoder (-s, -) *m* decoder
defekt *adj* faulty; **Defekt** (-(e)s,
-e) *m* fault, defect
definieren *vt* to define;
Definition (-, -en) *f* definition
deftig *adj* (*Preise*) steep; **ein ~es**
Essen a good solid meal
dehnbar *adj* flexible, elastic;
dehnen *vt* to stretch ▷ *vr:* **sich**
~ to stretch
Deich (-(e)s, -e) *m* dyke
dein *pron* (*adjektivisch*) your;
deine(r, s) *pron* (*substantivisch*)
yours, of you; **deiner** *pron gen*
von **du**; of you; **deinetwegen** *adv*
(*wegen dir*) because of you; (*dir*
zuliebe) for your sake; (*um dich*)
about you
deinstallieren *vt* (*Programm*) to
uninstall
Dekolleté (-s, -s) *nt* low neckline
Dekoration *f* decoration; (*in*
Laden) window dressing;
dekorativ *adj* decorative;
dekorieren *vt* to decorate;
(*Schaufenster*) to dress

Delfin (-s, -e) *m* dolphin
delikat *adj* (*lecker*) delicious;
(*heikel*) delicate
Delikatesse (-, -n) *f* delicacy
Delle (-, -en) *f* (*fam*) dent
Delphin (-s, -e) *m* dolphin
dem *dat sing von* **der/das; wie**
~ auch sein mag be that as it may
demnächst *adv* shortly, soon
Demo (-, -s) *f* (*fam*) demo
Demokratie (-, -n) *f* democracy;
demokratisch *adj* democratic
demolieren *vt* to demolish
Demonstration *f* demonstration; **demonstrieren** *vt, vi* to
demonstrate
den *art akk sing, dat pl von* **der; sie**
hat sich ~ Arm gebrochen she's
broken her arm ▷ *pron* him;
(*Sache*) that one; (*relativ: Person*)
who, that, whom; (*relativ: Sache*)
which, that; **~ hab ich schon ewig**
nicht mehr gesehen I haven't
seen him in ages ▷ *pron* (*Person*)
who, that, whom; (*Sache*) which,
that; **der Typ, auf ~ sie steht** the
guy (who) she fancies; **der Berg,**
auf ~ wir geklettert sind the
mountain (that) we climbed
denkbar *adj:* **das ist ~** that's
possible ▷ *adv:* **~ einfach**
extremely simple; **denken** (*dachte,*
gedacht) *vt, vi* to think (*über +akk*
about); **an jdn/etw ~** to think of
sb/sth; (*sich erinnern,*
berücksichtigen) to remember
sb/sth; **woran denkst Du?** what
are you thinking about?; **denk an**
den Kaffee! don't forget the coffee
▷ *vr:* **sich ~** (*sich vorstellen*) to
imagine; **das kann ich mir ~** I can
(well) imagine
Denkmal (-s, Denkmäler) *nt*
monument; **Denkmalschutz** *m*
monument preservation; **unter**
~ stehen to be listed
denn *conj* for, because ▷ *adv*

then; (*nach Komparativ*) than; **was
ist ~?** what's wrong?; **ist das ~ so
schwierig?** is it really that
difficult?

dennoch *conj* still, nevertheless

Deo (*-s, -s*) *nt*, **Deodorant** (*-s, -s*)
nt deodorant; **Deoroller** *m*
roll-on deodorant; **Deospray** *m o*
nt deodorant spray

Deponie (*-, -n*) *f* waste disposal
site, tip

Depressionen *pl*: **an ~ leiden** to
suffer from depression *sing*;
deprimieren *vt* to depress

SCHLÜSSELWORT

der (*f* **die**, *nt* **das**, *gen* **des, der,
des**, *dat* **dem, der, dem**, *akk* **den,
die, das**, *pl* **die**) *def art* the; **der
Rhein** the Rhine; **der Klaus** (*fam*)
Klaus; **die Frau** (*im Allgemeinen*)
women; **der Tod/das Leben**
death/life; **der Fuß des Berges**
the foot of the hill; **gib es der Frau**
give it to the woman; **er hat sich
die Hand verletzt** he has hurt his
hand

▷ *relativ pron* (*bei Menschen*) who,
that; (*bei Tieren, Sachen*) which,
that; **der Mann, den ich gesehen
habe** the man who *o* whom *o* that
I saw

▷ *demonstrativ pron* he/she/it
(*jener, dieser*) that; (*pl*) those;
der/die war es it was him/her/;
der mit der Brille the one with
glasses; **ich will den (da)** I want
that one

derart *adv* so; (*solcher Art*) such;
derartig *adj*: **ein ~er Fehler** such
a mistake, a mistake like that

deren *gen von* **die** ▷ *pron* (*Person*)
her; (*Sache*) its; (*Plural*) their ▷ *pron*
(*Person*) whose; (*Sache*) of which;
meine Freundin und ~ Mutter my

friend and her mother; **das sind
~ Sachen** that's their stuff; **die
Frau, ~ Tochter ...** the woman
whose daughter ...; **ich bin mir
~ bewusst** I'm aware of that

dergleichen *pron*: **und ~ mehr**
and the like, and so on; **nichts
~** no such thing

derjenige *pron* the one; **~, der**
(*relativ*) the one who (*o* that)

dermaßen *adv* so much; (*mit Adj*)
so

derselbe *pron* the same
(person/thing)

deshalb *adv* therefore; **~ frage
ich ja** that's why I'm asking

Design (*-s, -s*) *nt* design;
Designer(in) (*-s, -*) *m(f)* designer

Desinfektionsmittel *nt*
disinfectant; **desinfizieren** *vt* to
disinfect

dessen *gen von* **der, das** ▷ *pron*
(*Person*) his; (*Sache*) its; **ich bin mir
~ bewusst** I'm aware of that
▷ *pron* (*Person*) whose; (*Sache*) of
which; **mein Freund und
~ Mutter** my friend and his
mother; **der Mann, ~ Tochter ...**
the man whose daughter ...; **ich
bin mir ~ bewusst** I'm aware of
that

Dessert (*-s, -s*) *nt* dessert; **zum**
(*o* **als**) **~** for dessert

destilliert *adj* distilled

desto *adv*: **je eher, ~ besser** the
sooner, the better

deswegen *conj* therefore

Detail (*-s, -s*) *nt* detail; **ins
~ gehen** to go into detail

Detektiv(in) (*-s, -e*) *m(f)*
detective

deutlich *adj* clear; (*Unterschied*)
distinct

deutsch *adj* German; **Deutsch** *nt*
German; **auf ~** in German; **ins ~e
übersetzen** to translate into
German; **Deutsche(r)** *mf*

German; **Deutschland** nt
Germany

Devise (-, -n) f motto; **~n** pl (Fin)
foreign currency sing;
Devisenkurs m exchange rate

Dezember (-(s), -) m December;
siehe auch **Juni**

dezent adj discreet

d.h. abk von **das heißt** i.e.
(gesprochen: i.e. oder that is)

Dia (-s, -s) nt slide

Diabetes (-, -) m (Med) diabetes;
Diabetiker(in) (-s, -) m(f)
diabetic

Diagnose (-, -n) f diagnosis

diagonal adj diagonal

Dialekt (-(e)s, -e) m dialect

Dialog (-(e)s, -e) m dialogue;
(Inform) dialog

Dialyse (-, -n) f (Med) dialysis

Diamant m diamond

Diaprojektor m slide projector

Diät (-, -en) f diet; **eine ~ machen**
to be on a diet; (anfangen) to go on
a diet

dich pron akk von **du** you;
~ (selbst) (reflexiv) yourself; **pass
auf ~ auf** look after yourself; **reg
~ nicht auf** don't get upset

dicht adj dense; (Nebel) thick;
(Gewebe) close; (wasserdicht)
watertight; (Verkehr) heavy ▷ adv:
~ an/bei close to; **~ bevölkert**
densely populated

Dichter(in) (-s, -) m(f) poet;
(Autor) writer

Dichtung f (Auto) gasket;
(Dichtungsring) washer; (Gedichte)
poetry

Dichtungsring m (Tech) washer

dick adj thick; (Person) fat; **jdn
~ haben** to be sick of sb;
Dickdarm m colon; **Dickkopf** m
stubborn (o pig-headed) person;
Dickmilch f sour milk

die art the; **~ arme Sarah** poor
Sarah ▷ pron (sing, Person, als

Subjekt) she; (Person, als Subjekt,
Plural) they; (Person, als Objekt) her;
(Person, als Objekt, Plural) them;
(Sache) that (one), this (one);
(Plural) those (ones); (Sache, Plural)
those (ones); (relativ, auf Person)
who, that; (relativ, auf Sache)
which, that; **~ mit den langen
Haaren** the one (o her) with the
long hair; **sie war ~ erste, ~ es
erfuhr** she was the first to know;
ich nehme ~ da I'll take that
one/those ▷ pl, von **der, die, das**

Dieb(in) (-(e)s, -e) m(f) thief;
Diebstahl (-(e)s, Diebstähle) m
theft; **Diebstahlsicherung** f
burglar alarm

diejenige pron the one; **~, die**
(relativ) the one who (o that); **~n** pl
those pl, the ones

Diele (-, -n) f hall

Dienst (-(e)s, -e) m service; **außer
~** retired; **~ haben** to be on duty

Dienstag m Tuesday; siehe auch
Mittwoch; **dienstags** adv on
Tuesdays; siehe auch **mittwochs**

Dienstbereitschaft f: **~ haben**
(Arzt) to be on call; **diensthabend**
adj: **der ~e Arzt** the doctor on
duty; **Dienstleistung** f service;
dienstlich adj official; **er ist
~ unterwegs** he's away on
business; **Dienstreise** f business
trip; **Dienststelle** f department;
Dienstwagen m company car;
Dienstzeit f office hours pl; (Mil)
period of service

diesbezüglich adj (formell) on
this matter

diese(r, s) pron this (one); pl
these; **~ Frau** this woman; **~r
Mann** this man; **~s Mädchen** this
girl; **~ Leute** these people; **ich
nehme ~/~n/~s** (hier) I'll take this
one; (dort) I'll take that one; **ich
nehme ~** pl (hier) I'll take these
ones; (dort) I'll take those (ones)

Diesel (-s, -) m (Auto) diesel

dieselbe pron the same; **es sind immer ~n** it's always the same people

Dieselmotor m diesel engine; **Dieselöl** nt diesel (oil)

diesig adj hazy, misty

diesmal adv this time

Dietrich (-s, -e) m skeleton key

Differenz (-, -en) f difference

digital adj digital; **Digital-** in zW (Anzeige etc) digital; **Digitalfernsehen** nt digital television, digital TV; **Digitalkamera** f digital camera

Diktat (-(e)s, -e) nt dictation

Diktatur f dictatorship

Dill (-s) m dill

DIN abk = **Deutsche Industrienorm** DIN; **~ A4** A4

Ding (-(e)s, -e) nt thing; **vor allen ~en** above all; **der Stand der ~e** the state of affairs; **das ist nicht mein ~** (fam) it's not my sort of thing (o cup of tea); **Dingsbums** (-) nt (fam) thingy, thingummybob

Dinkel (-s, -) m (Bot) spelt

Dinosaurier (-s, -) m dinosaur

Diphtherie (-, -n) f diphtheria

Diplom (-(e)s, -e) nt diploma

Diplomat(in) (-en, -en) m(f) diplomat

dir pron dat von **du** (to) you; **hat er ~ geholfen?** did he help you?; **ich werde es ~ erklären** I'll explain it to you; (reflexiv) **wasch ~ die Hände** go and wash your hands; **ein Freund von ~** a friend of yours

direkt adj direct; (Frage) straight; **~e Verbindung** through service ▷ adv directly; (sofort) immediately; **~ am Bahnhof** right next to the station; **Direktflug** m direct flight

Direktor(in) m(f) director; (Schule) headmaster/-mistress (Brit), principal (US)

Direktübertragung f live broadcast

Dirigent(in) m(f) conductor; **dirigieren** vt to direct; (Mus) to conduct

Discman® (-s, -s) m Discman®

Diskette f disk, diskette; **Diskettenlaufwerk** nt disk drive

Diskjockey (-s, -s) m disc jockey; **Disko** (-, -s) f (fam) disco, club; **Diskothek** (-, -en) f discotheque, club

diskret adj discreet

diskriminieren vt to discriminate against

Diskussion f discussion; **diskutieren** vt, vi to discuss

Display (-s, -s) nt display

disqualifizieren vt to disqualify

Distanz f distance

Distel (-, -n) f thistle

Disziplin (-, -en) f discipline

divers adj various

dividieren vt to divide (durch by); **8 dividiert durch 2 ist 4** 8 divided by 2 is 4

DJ (-s, -s) m abk = **Diskjockey** DJ

 SCHLÜSSELWORT

doch adv **1** (dennoch) after all; (sowieso) anyway; **er kam doch noch** he came after all; **du weißt es ja doch besser** you know better than I do anyway; **und doch ...** and yet ...

2 (als bejahende Antwort) yes I do/it does etc; **das ist nicht wahr — doch!** that's not true — yes it is!

3 (auffordernd) **komm doch** do come; **lass ihn doch** just leave him; **nicht doch!** oh no!

4 sie ist doch noch so jung but she's still so young; **Sie wissen doch, wie das ist** you know how

it is(, don't you?); **wenn doch** if only
▷ *konj* (*aber*) but; (*trotzdem*) all the same; **und doch hat er es getan** but still he did it

Doktor(in) *m(f)* doctor
Dokument *nt* document;
Dokumentarfilm *m* documentary (film); **dokumentieren** *vt* to document;
Dokumentvorlage *f* (*Inform*) document template
Dolch (*-(e)s, -e*) *m* dagger
Dollar (*-(s), -s*) *m* dollar
dolmetschen *vt, vi* to interpret;
Dolmetscher(in) (*-s, -*) *m(f)* interpreter
Dolomiten *pl* Dolomites *pl*
Dom (*-(e)s, -e*) *m* cathedral
Domäne (*-, -n*) *f* domain, province; (*Inform: Domain*) domain
Dominikanische Republik *f* Dominican Republic
Domino (*-s, -s*) *nt* dominoes *sing*
Donau (*-*) *f* Danube
Döner (*-s, -*) *m*, **Döner Kebab** (*-(s), -s*) *m* doner kebab
Donner (*-s, -*) *m* thunder;
donnern *vi*: **es donnert** it's thundering
Donnerstag *m* Thursday; *siehe auch* **Mittwoch**; **donnerstags** *adv* on Thursdays; *siehe auch* **mittwochs**
doof *adj* (*fam*) stupid
dopen *vt* to dope; **Doping** (*-s*) *nt* doping; **Dopingkontrolle** *f* drugs test
Doppel (*-s, -*) *nt* duplicate; (*Sport*) doubles *sing*; **Doppelbett** *nt* double bed; **Doppeldecker** *m* double-decker; **Doppelhaushälfte** *f* semi-detached house (*Brit*), duplex (*US*); **doppelklicken** *vi* to double-click; **Doppelname** *m* double-barrelled name;

Doppelpunkt *m* colon;
Doppelstecker *m* two-way adaptor; **doppelt** *adj* double; **in ~er Ausführung** in duplicate;
Doppelzimmer *nt* double room
Dorf (*-(e)s, Dörfer*) *nt* village
Dorn (*-(e)s, -en*) *m* (*Bot*) thorn
Dörrobst *nt* dried fruit
Dorsch (*-(e)s, -e*) *m* cod
dort *adv* there; **~ drüben** over there; **dorther** *adv* from there
Dose (*-, -n*) *f* box; (*Blechdose*) tin (*Brit*), can; (*Bierdose*) can
dösen *vi* to doze
Dosenbier *nt* canned beer;
Dosenmilch *f* canned milk, tinned milk (*Brit*); **Dosenöffner** *m* tin opener (*Brit*), can opener
Dotter (*-s, -*) *m* (egg) yolk
downloaden *vt* to download
Downsyndrom (*-s, -e*) *nt* (*Med*) Down's syndrome
Dozent(in) *m(f)* lecturer
Dr. *abk* = **Doktor**
Drache (*-n, -n*) *m* dragon;
Drachen (*-s, -*) *m* (*Spielzeug*) kite; (*Sport*) hang-glider;
Drachenfliegen (*-s*) *nt* hang-gliding; **Drachenflieger(in)** (*-s, -*) *m(f)* hang-glider
Draht (*-(e)s, Drähte*) *m* wire;
Drahtseilbahn *f* cable railway
Drama (*-s, Dramen*) *nt* drama;
dramatisch *adj* dramatic
dran *adv* (*fam*) *kontr von* **daran**;
gut ~ sein (*reich*) to be well-off; (*glücklich*) to be fortunate; (*gesundheitlich*) to be well;
schlecht ~ sein to be in a bad way; **wer ist ~?** whose turn is it?; **ich bin ~** it's my turn; **bleib ~!** (*Tel*) hang on
drang *imperf von* **dringen**
Drang (*-(e)s, Dränge*) *m* (*Trieb*) urge (*nach for*); (*Druck*) pressure
drängeln *vt, vi* to push
drängen *vt* (*schieben*) to push;

(*antreiben*) to urge ▷ *vi* (*eilig sein*) to be urgent; (*Zeit*) to press; **auf etw** (*akk*) **~** to press for sth
dran|kommen *irr vi*: **wer kommt dran?** who's turn is it?, who's next?
drauf (*fam*) *kontr von* **darauf**; **gut/schlecht ~ sein** to be in a good/bad mood
Draufgänger(in) (*-s, -*) *m(f)* daredevil
drauf|kommen *irr vi* to remember; **ich komme nicht drauf** I can't think of it
drauf|machen *vi* (*fam*) **einen ~** to go on a binge
draußen *adv* outside
Dreck (*-(e)s*) *m* dirt, filth; **dreckig** *adj* dirty, filthy
drehen *vt, vi* to turn; (*Zigaretten*) to roll; (*Film*) to shoot ▷ *vr*: **sich ~** to turn; (*um Achse*) to rotate; **sich ~ um** (*handeln von*) to be about
Drehstrom *m* three-phase current; **Drehtür** *f* revolving door; **Drehzahlmesser** *m* rev counter
drei *num* three; **~ viertel voll** three-quarters full; **es ist ~ viertel neun** it's a quarter to nine; **Drei** (*-, -en*) *f* three; (*Schulnote*) ≈ C; **Dreieck** *nt* triangle; **dreieckig** *adj* triangular; **dreifach** *adj* triple ▷ *adv* three times; **dreihundert** *num* three hundred; **Dreikönigstag** *m* Epiphany; **dreimal** *adv* three times; **Dreirad** *nt* tricycle; **dreispurig** *adj* three-lane
dreißig *num* thirty; **dreißigste(r, s)** *adj* thirtieth; *siehe auch* **dritte**
Dreiviertelstunde *f*: **eine ~** three quarters of an hour
dreizehn *num* thirteen; **dreizehnte(r, s)** *adj* thirteenth; *siehe auch* **dritte**
dressieren *vt* to train

Dressing (*-s, -s*) *nt* (salad) dressing
Dressman (*-s, Dressmen*) *m* (male) model
Dressur (*-, -en*) *f* training
drin (*fam*) *kontr von* **darin** in it; **mehr war nicht ~** that was the best I could do
dringen (*drang, gedrungen*) *vi* (*Wasser, Licht, Kälte*) to penetrate (*durch* through, *in +akk* into); **auf etw** (*akk*) **~** to insist on sth; **dringend, dringlich** *adj* urgent
drinnen *adv* inside
dritt *adv*: **wir sind zu ~** there are three of us; **dritte(r, s)** *adj* third; **die Dritte Welt** the Third World; **7. Juni** 7(th) June (*gesprochen: the seventh of June*); **am 7. Juni** on 7(th) June, on June 7(th) (*gesprochen: on the seventh of June*); **München, den 7. Juni** Munich, June 7(th); **Drittel** (*-s, -*) *nt* (*Bruchteil*) third; **drittens** *adv* thirdly
Droge (*-, -n*) *f* drug; **drogenabhängig, drogensüchtig** *adj* addicted to drugs
Drogerie *f* chemist's (*Brit*), drugstore (*US*); **Drogeriemarkt** *m* discount chemist's (*Brit*) (*o* drugstore (*US*))

- **DROGERIE**
-
- The **Drogerie** as opposed to the
- **Apotheke** sells medicines not
- requiring a prescription. It
- tends to be cheaper and also
- sells cosmetics, perfume and
- toiletries.

drohen *vi* to threaten (*jdm* sb); **mit etw ~** to threaten to do sth
dröhnen *vi* (*Motor*) to roar; (*Stimme, Musik*) to boom; (*Raum*) to resound
Drohung *f* threat

Drossel (-, -n) f thrush
drüben adv over there; (auf der anderen Seite) on the other side
drüber (fam) kontr von **darüber**
Druck (-(e)s, Drücke) m (Phys) pressure; (fig: Belastung) stress; **jdn unter ~ setzen** to put sb under pressure ▷ (-(e)s, -e) m (Typo: Vorgang) printing; (Produkt, Schriftart) print; **Druckbuchstabe** m block letter; **in ~n schreiben** to print; **drucken** vt, vi to print
drücken vt, vi (Knopf, Hand) to press; (zu eng sein) to pinch; (fig: Preise) to keep down; **jdm etw in die Hand ~** to press sth into sb's hand ▷ vr **sich vor etw** (dat) **~** to get out of sth; **drückend** adj oppressive
Drucker (-s, -) m (Inform) printer; **Druckertreiber** m printer driver
Druckknopf m press stud (Brit), snap fastener (US); **Drucksache** f printed matter; **Druckschrift** f block letters pl
drunten adv down there
drunter (fam) kontr von **darunter**
Drüse (-, -n) f gland
Dschungel (-s, -) m jungle
du pron you; **bist ~ es?** is it you?; **wir sind per ~** we're on first-name terms
Dübel (-s, -) m Rawlplug®
ducken vt to duck ▷ vr: **sich ~** to duck
Dudelsack m bagpipes pl
Duett (-s, -e) nt duet
Duft (-(e)s, Düfte) m scent; **duften** vi to smell nice; **es duftet nach ...** it smells of ...
dulden vt to tolerate
dumm adj stupid; **Dummheit** f stupidity; (Tat) stupid thing; **Dummkopf** m idiot
dumpf adj (Ton) muffled; (Erinnerung) vague; (Schmerz) dull
Düne (-, -n) f dune

Dünger (-s, -) m fertilizer
dunkel adj dark; (Stimme) deep; (Ahnung) vague; (rätselhaft) obscure; (verdächtig) dubious; **im Dunkeln tappen** (fig) to be in the dark; **dunkelblau** adj dark blue; **dunkelblond** adj light brown; **dunkelhaarig** adj dark-haired; **Dunkelheit** f darkness
dünn adj thin; (Kaffee) weak
Dunst (-es, Dünste) m haze; (leichter Nebel) mist; (Chem) vapour
dünsten vt (Gastr) to steam
Duo (-s, -s) nt duo
Dur (-) nt (Mus) major (key); **in G-~** in G major

SCHLÜSSELWORT

durch prep +akk **1** (hindurch) through; **durch den Urwald** through the jungle; **durch die ganze Welt reisen** to travel all over the world
2 (mittels) through, by (means of); (aufgrund) due to, owing to; **Tod durch Herzschlag/den Strang** death from a heart attack/by hanging; **durch die Post** by post; **durch seine Bemühungen** through his efforts
▷ adv **1** (hindurch) through; **die ganze Nacht durch** all through the night; **den Sommer durch** during the summer; **8 Uhr durch** past 8 o'clock; **durch und durch** completely
2 (durchgebraten etc) **(gut) durch** well-done

durchaus adv absolutely; **~ nicht** not at all
Durchblick m view; **den ~ haben** (fig) to know what's going on; **durch|blicken** vi to look through; (fam: verstehen) to understand (bei etw sth); **etw**

~ lassen (fig) to hint at sth

Durchblutung f circulation

durch|brennen irr vi (Sicherung) to blow; (Draht) to burn through; (fam: davonlaufen) to run away

durchdacht adv: **gut ~** well thought-out

durch|drehen vt (Fleisch) to mince ▷ vi (Räder) to spin; (fam: nervlich) to crack up

durcheinander adv in a mess; (fam: verwirrt) confused; **Durcheinander** (-s) nt (Verwirrung) confusion; (Unordnung) mess; **durcheinander|bringen** irr vt to mess up; (verwirren) to confuse; **durcheinander|reden** vi to talk all at the same time; **durcheinander|trinken** irr vi to mix one's drinks

Durchfahrt f way through; **„~ verboten!"** "no thoroughfare"

Durchfall m (Med) diarrhoea

durch|fallen irr vi to fall through; (in Prüfung) to fail

durch|fragen vr: **sich ~** to ask one's way

durch|führen vt to carry out

Durchgang m passage; (Sport) round; (bei Wahl) ballot; **Durchgangsverkehr** m through traffic

durchgebraten adj well done

durchgefroren adj frozen to the bone

durch|gehen irr vi to go through (durch etw sth); (ausreißen: Pferd) to break loose; (Mensch) to run away; **durchgehend** adj (Zug) through; **~ geöffnet** open all day

durch|halten irr vi to hold out ▷ vt (Tempo) to keep up; **etw ~** (bis zum Schluss) to see sth through

durch|kommen irr vi to get through; (Patient) to pull through

durch|lassen irr vt (jdn) to let through; (Wasser) to let in

durch|lesen irr vt to read through

durchleuchten vt to X-ray

durch|machen vt to go through; (Entwicklung) to undergo; **die Nacht ~** to make a night of it, to have an all-nighter

Durchmesser (-s, -) m diameter

Durchreise f journey through; **auf der ~** passing through; (Güter) in transit; **Durchreisevisum** nt transit visa

durch|reißen irr vt, vi to tear (in two)

durchs kontr von **durch das**

Durchsage (-, -n) f announcement

durchschauen vt (jdn, Lüge) to see through

durch|schlagen irr vr: **sich ~** to struggle through

durch|schneiden irr vt to cut (in two)

Durchschnitt m (Mittelwert) average; **im ~** on average; **durchschnittlich** adj average ▷ adv (im Durchschnitt) on average; **Durchschnittsgeschwindigkeit** f average speed

durch|setzen vt to get through ▷ vr: **sich ~** (Erfolg haben) to succeed; (sich behaupten) to get one's way

durchsichtig adj transparent, see-through

durch|stellen vt (Tel) to put through

durch|streichen irr vt to cross out

durchsuchen vt to search (nach for); **Durchsuchung** f search

durchwachsen adj (Speck) streaky; (fig: mittelmäßig) so-so

Durchwahl f direct dialling; (Nummer) extension

durch|ziehen *irr vt* (*Plan*) to carry through
Durchzug *m* draught

 SCHLÜSSELWORT

dürfen *unreg vi* **1** (*Erlaubnis haben*) to be allowed to; **ich darf das** I'm allowed to (do that); **darf ich?** may I?; **darf ich ins Kino?** can o may I go to the cinema?; **es darf geraucht werden** you may smoke **2** (*in Verneinungen*) **er darf das nicht** he's not allowed to (do that); **das darf nicht geschehen** that must not happen; **da darf sie sich nicht wundern** that shouldn't surprise her
3 (*in Höflichkeitsformeln*) **darf ich Sie bitten, das zu tun?** may o could I ask you to do that?; **was darf es sein?** what can I do for you?
4 (*können*) **das dürfen Sie mir glauben** you can believe me
5 (*Möglichkeit*) **das dürfte genug sein** that should be enough; **es dürfte Ihnen bekannt sein, dass ...** as you will probably know ...

dürftig *adj* (*ärmlich*) poor; (*unzulänglich*) inadequate
dürr *adj* dried-up; (*Land*) arid; (*mager*) skinny
Durst (*-(e)s*) *m* thirst; **~ haben** to be thirsty; **durstig** *adj* thirsty
Dusche (*-, -n*) *f* shower; **duschen** *vi* to have a shower ▷ *vr*: **sich ~** to have a shower; **Duschgel** *nt* shower gel; **Duschvorhang** *m* shower curtain
Düse (*-, -n*) *f* nozzle; (*Tech*) jet; **Düsenflugzeug** *nt* jet (aircraft)
Dussel (*-s, -*) *m* (*fam*) dope; **duss(e)lig** *adj* (*fam*) stupid

düster *adj* dark; (*Gedanken, Zukunft*) gloomy
Dutyfreeshop (*-s, -s*) *m* duty-free shop
Dutzend (*-s, -e*) *nt* dozen
duzen *vt* to address as "du" ▷ *vr*: **sich ~** (**mit jdm**) to address each other as "du", to be on first-name terms
DVD (*-, -s*) *f abk* = **Digital Versatile Disk** DVD; **DVD-Player** (*-s, -*) *m* DVD player; **DVD-Rekorder** (*-s, -*) *m* DVD recorder
dynamisch *adj* dynamic
Dynamo (*-s, -s*) *m* dynamo
D-Zug *m* fast train

e

Ebbe (-, -n) f low tide
eben adj level; (glatt) smooth
▷ adv just; (bestätigend) exactly
Ebene (-, -n) f plain; (fig) level
ebenfalls adv also, as well;
(Antwort: gleichfalls!) you too;
ebenso adv just as; **~ gut** just as
well; **~ viel** just as much
Eber (-s, -) m boar
EC (-, -s) m abk = **Eurocityzug**
Echo (-s, -s) nt echo
echt adj (Leder, Gold) real, genuine;
ein ~er Verlust a real loss
EC-Karte f ≈ debit card
Ecke (-, -n) f corner; (Math) angle;
an der ~ at the corner; **gleich um
die ~** just round the corner; **eckig**
adj rectangular; **Eckzahn** m
canine
Economyclass (-) f coach
(class), economy class
Ecstasy (-) f (Droge) ecstasy
edel adj noble; **Edelstein** m
precious stone
EDV (-) f abk = **elektronische
Datenverarbeitung** EDP
Efeu (-s) m ivy
Effekt (-s, -e) m effect
egal adj: **das ist ~** it doesn't
matter; **das ist mir ~** I don't care,
it's all the same to me; **~ wie teuer**
no matter how expensive
egoistisch adj selfish
ehe conj before
Ehe (-, -n) f marriage; **Ehefrau** f
wife; (verheiratete Frau) married
woman; **Eheleute** pl married
couple sing
ehemalig adj former; **ehemals**
adv formerly
Ehemann m husband;
(verheirateter Mann) married man;
Ehepaar nt married couple
eher adv (früher) sooner; (lieber)
rather, sooner; (mehr) more; **je ~,
desto besser** the sooner the
better
Ehering m wedding ring
eheste(r, s) adj (früheste) first
▷ adv: **am ~n** (am
wahrscheinlichsten) most likely
Ehre (-, -n) f honour; **ehren** vt
to honour; **ehrenamtlich** adj
voluntary; **Ehrengast** m guest
of honour; **Ehrenwort** nt word
of honour; **~!** I promise; **ich gebe
dir mein ~** I give you my word
ehrgeizig adj ambitious
ehrlich adj honest
Ei (-(e)s, -er) nt egg; **hart
gekochtes/weiches
~** hard-boiled/soft-boiled egg
Eiche (-, -n) f oak (tree); **Eichel**
(-, -n) f acorn
Eichhörnchen nt squirrel
Eid (-(e)s, -e) m oath
Eidechse (-, -n) f lizard
Eierbecher m eggcup; **Eierstock**
m ovary; **Eieruhr** f egg timer
Eifersucht f jealousy;

eifersüchtig adj jealous (auf +akk of)

Eigelb (-(e)s, -) nt egg yolk

eigen adj own; (typisch) characteristic (jdm of sb); (eigenartig) peculiar; **eigenartig** adj peculiar; **Eigenschaft** f quality; (Chem, Phys) property; (Merkmal) characteristic

eigentlich adj actual, real ▷ adv actually, really; **was denken Sie sich ~ dabei?** what on earth do you think you're doing?

Eigentum nt property; **Eigentümer(in)** m(f) owner; **Eigentumswohnung** f owner-occupied flat (Brit), condominium (US)

eignen vr: **sich ~ für** to be suited for; **er würde sich als Lehrer ~** he'd make a good teacher

Eilbrief m express letter, special-delivery letter; **Eile** (-) f hurry; **eilen** vi (dringend sein) to be urgent; **es eilt nicht** there's no hurry; **eilig** adj hurried; (dringlich) urgent; **es ~ haben** to be in a hurry

Eimer (-s, -) m bucket

ein adv: **nicht ~ noch aus wissen** not to know what to do; **~ - aus** (Schalter) on - off

ein(e) art a; (vor gesprochenem Vokal) an; **~ Mann** a man; **~ Apfel** an apple; **~e Stunde** an hour; **~ Haus** a house; **~ (gewisser) Herr Miller** a (certain) Mr Miller; **~es Tages** one day

einander pron one another, each other

ein|arbeiten vt to train ▷ vr: **sich ~** to get used to the work

ein|atmen vt, vi to breathe in

Einbahnstraße f one-way street

ein|bauen vt to build in; (Motor etc) to install, to fit; **Einbauküche** f fitted kitchen

ein|biegen irr vi to turn (in +akk into)

ein|bilden vt: **sich** (dat) **etw ~** to imagine sth

ein|brechen irr vi (in Haus) to break in; (Dach etc) to fall in, to collapse; **Einbrecher(in)** (-s, -) m(f) burglar

ein|bringen irr vt (Ernte) to bring in; (Gewinn) to yield; **jdm etw ~** to bring (o earn) sb sth ▷ vr: **sich in** (akk) **etw ~** to make a contribution to sth

Einbruch m (Haus) break-in, burglary; **bei ~ der Nacht** at nightfall

Einbürgerung f naturalization

ein|checken vt to check in

ein|cremen vt to put some cream on ▷ vr: **sich ~** to put some cream on

eindeutig adj clear, obvious ▷ adv clearly; **~ falsch** clearly wrong

ein|dringen irr vi (gewaltsam) to force one's way in (in +akk -to); (in Haus) to break in (in +akk -to); (Gas, Wasser) to get in (in +akk -to)

Eindruck m impression; **großen ~ auf jdn machen** to make a big impression on sb

eine(r, s) pron one; (jemand) someone; **~r meiner Freunde** one of my friends; **~r nach dem andern** one after the other

eineiig adj (Zwillinge) identical

eineinhalb num one and a half

einerseits adv on the one hand

einfach adj (nicht kompliziert) simple; (Mensch) ordinary; (Essen) plain; (nicht mehrfach) single; **~e Fahrkarte** single ticket (Brit), one-way ticket (US) ▷ adv simply; (nicht mehrfach) once

Einfahrt f (Vorgang) driving in; (eines Zuges) arrival; (Ort) entrance

Einfall m (Idee) idea; **ein|fallen** irr vi (Licht etc) to fall in; (einstürzen) to collapse; **ihm fiel ein, dass ...** it occurred to him that ...; **ich werde mir etwas ~ lassen** I'll think of something; **was fällt Ihnen ein!** what do you think you're doing?

Einfamilienhaus nt detached house

einfarbig adj all one colour; (Stoff etc) self-coloured

Einfluss m influence

ein|frieren irr vt, vi to freeze

ein|fügen vt to fit in; (zusätzlich) to add; (Inform) to insert; **Einfügetaste** f (Inform) insert key

Einfuhr (-, -en) f import; **Einfuhrbestimmungen** pl import regulations pl

ein|führen vt to introduce; (Ware) to import; **Einführung** f introduction

Eingabe f (Dateneingabe) input; **Eingabetaste** f (Inform) return (o enter) key

Eingang m entrance; **Eingangshalle** f entrance hall, lobby (US)

ein|geben irr vt (Daten etc) to enter, to key in

eingebildet adj imaginary; (eitel) arrogant

Eingeborene(r) mf native

ein|gehen irr vi (Sendung, Geld) to come in, to arrive; (Tier, Pflanze) to die; (Stoff) to shrink; **auf etw** (akk) **~ to** agree to sth; **auf jdn ~ to** respond to sb ▷ vt (Vertrag) to enter into; (Wette) to make; (Risiko) to take

eingelegt adj (in Essig) pickled

eingeschaltet adj (switched) on

eingeschlossen adj locked in; (inklusive) included

ein|gewöhnen vr: **sich ~ to** settle in

ein|gießen irr vt to pour

ein|greifen irr vi to intervene; **Eingriff** m intervention; (Operation) operation

ein|halten irr vt (Versprechen etc) to keep

einheimisch adj (Produkt, Mannschaft) local; **Einheimische(r)** mf local

Einheit f (Geschlossenheit) unity; (Maß) unit; **einheitlich** adj uniform

ein|holen vt (Vorsprung aufholen) to catch up with; (Verspätung) to make up for; (Rat, Erlaubnis) to ask for

Einhorn nt unicorn

einhundert num one (o a) hundred

einig adj (vereint) united; **sich** (dat) **~ sein** to agree

einige pron pl some; (mehrere) several ▷ adj some; **nach ~er Zeit** after some time; **~e hundert Euro** some hundred euros

einigen vr: **sich ~ to** agree (auf +akk on)

einigermaßen adv fairly, quite; (leidlich) reasonably

einiges pron something; (ziemlich viel) quite a bit; (mehreres) a few things; **es gibt noch ~ zu tun** there's still a fair bit to do

Einkauf m purchase; **Einkäufe** (**machen**) (to do one's) shopping; **ein|kaufen** vt to buy ▷ vi to go shopping; **Einkaufsbummel** m shopping trip; **Einkaufstasche** f, **Einkaufstüte** f shopping bag; **Einkaufswagen** m shopping trolley (Brit) (o cart (US)); **Einkaufszentrum** nt shopping centre (Brit) (o mall (US))

ein|klemmen vt to jam; **er hat sich** (dat) **den Finger eingeklemmt** he got his finger caught

Einkommen (-s, -) nt income

ein|laden *irr vt* (*jdn*) to invite; (*Gegenstände*) to load; **jdn zum Essen ~** to take sb out for a meal; **ich lade dich ein** (*bezahle*) it's my treat; **Einladung** *f* invitation

Einlass (*-es, Einlässe*) *m* admittance; **~ ab 18 Uhr** doors open at 6 pm; **ein|lassen** *irr vr* **sich mit jdm/auf etw** (*akk*) **~** to get involved with sb/sth

ein|leben *vr*: **sich ~** to settle down

ein|legen *vt* (*Film etc*) to put in; (*marinieren*) to marinate; **eine Pause ~** to take a break

ein|leiten *vt* to start; (*Maßnahmen*) to introduce; (*Geburt*) to induce; **Einleitung** *f* introduction; (*von Geburt*) induction

ein|leuchten *vi*: **jdm ~** to be (*o* become) clear to sb; **einleuchtend** *adj* clear

ein|loggen *vi* (*Inform*) to log on (*o* in)

ein|lösen *vt* (*Scheck*) to cash; (*Gutschein*) to redeem; (*Versprechen*) to keep

einmal *adv* once; (*früher*) before; (*in Zukunft*) some day; (*erstens*) first; **~ im Jahr** once a year; **noch ~** once more, again; **ich war schon ~ hier** I've been here before; **warst du schon ~ in London?** have you ever been to London?; **nicht ~** not even; **auf ~** suddenly; (*gleichzeitig*) at once; **einmalig** *adj* unique; (*einmal geschehend*) single; (*prima*) fantastic

ein|mischen *vr*: **sich ~** to interfere (*in +akk* with)

Einnahme (*-, -n*) *f* (*Geld*) takings *pl*; (*von Medizin*) taking; **ein|nehmen** *irr vt* (*Medizin*) to take; (*Geld*) to take in; (*Standpunkt, Raum*) to take up; **jdn für sich ~** to win sb over

ein|ordnen *vt* to put in order; (*klassifizieren*) to classify; (*Akten*) to file ▷ *vr*: **sich ~** (*Auto*) to get in lane; **sich rechts/links ~** to get into the right/left lane

ein|packen *vt* to pack (up)

ein|parken *vt, vi* to park

ein|planen *vt* to allow for

ein|prägen *vt* **sich** (*dat*) **etw ~** to remember (*o* memorize) sth

ein|räumen *vt* (*Bücher, Geschirr*) to put away; (*Schrank*) to put things in

ein|reden *vt*: **jdm/sich etw ~** to talk sb/oneself into (believing) sth

ein|reiben *irr vt*: **sich mit etw ~** to rub sth into one's skin

ein|reichen *vt* to hand in; (*Antrag*) to submit

Einreise *f* entry; **Einreisebestimmungen** *pl* entry regulations *pl*; **Einreiseerlaubnis** *f*, **Einreisegenehmigung** *f* entry permit; **ein|reisen** *vi* to enter (*in ein Land* a country); **Einreisevisum** *nt* entry visa

ein|renken *vt* (*Arm, Bein*) to set

ein|richten *vt* (*Wohnung*) to furnish; (*gründen*) to establish, to set up; (*arrangieren*) to arrange ▷ *vr*: **sich ~** (*in Haus*) to furnish one's home; (*sich vorbereiten*) to prepare oneself (*auf +akk* for); (*sich anpassen*) to adapt (*auf +akk* to); **Einrichtung** *f* (*Wohnung*) furnishings *pl*; (*öffentliche Anstalt*) institution; (*Schwimmbad etc*) facility

eins *num* one; **Eins** (*-, -en*) *f* one; (*Schulnote*) ≈ A

einsam *adj* lonely

ein|sammeln *vt* to collect

Einsatz *m* (*Teil*) insert; (*Verwendung*) use; (*Spieleinsatz*) stake; (*Risiko*) risk; (*Mus*) entry

ein|schalten *vt* (*Elek*) to switch on

ein|schätzen vt to estimate, to assess

ein|schenken vt to pour

ein|schiffen vr: **sich ~** to embark (nach for)

ein|schlafen irr vi to fall asleep, to drop off; **mir ist der Arm eingeschlafen** my arm's gone to sleep

ein|schlagen irr vt (Fenster) to smash; (Zähne, Schädel) to smash in; (Weg, Richtung) to take ▷ vi to hit (in etw akk sth, auf jdn sb); (Blitz) to strike; (Anklang finden) to be a success

ein|schließen irr vt (jdn) to lock in; (Gegenstand) to lock away; (umgeben) to surround; (fig: beinhalten) to include; **einschließlich** adv inclusive ▷ prep +gen including; **von Montag bis ~ Freitag** from Monday up to and including Friday, Monday through Friday (US)

ein|schränken vt to limit, to restrict; (verringern) to cut down on ▷ vr: **sich ~** to cut down (on expenditure)

ein|schreiben irr vr: **sich ~** to register; (Schule) to enrol; **Einschreiben** (-s, -) nt registered letter; **etw per ~ schicken** to send sth by special delivery

ein|schüchtern vt to intimidate

ein|sehen irr vt (verstehen) to see; (Fehler) to recognize; (Akten) to have a look at

einseitig adj one-sided

ein|senden irr vt to send in

ein|setzen vt to put in; (in Amt) to appoint; (Geld) to stake; (verwenden) to use ▷ vi (beginnen) to set in; (Mus) to enter, to come in ▷ vr: **sich ~** to work hard; **sich für jdn/etw ~** to support sb/sth

Einsicht f insight; **zu der ~ kommen, dass ...** to come to realize that ...

ein|sperren vt to lock up

ein|spielen vt (Geld) to bring in

ein|springen irr vi (aushelfen) to step in (für for)

Einspruch m objection (gegen to)

einspurig adj single-lane

Einstand m (Tennis) deuce

ein|stecken vt to pocket; (Elek: Stecker) to plug in; (Brief) to post, to mail (US); (mitnehmen) to take; (hinnehmen) to swallow

ein|steigen irr vi (in Auto) to get in; (in Bus, Zug, Flugzeug) to get on; (sich beteiligen) to get involved

ein|stellen vt (beenden) to stop; (Geräte) to adjust; (Kamera) to focus; (Sender, Radio) to tune in; (unterstellen) to put; (in Firma) to employ, to take on ▷ vr: **sich auf jdn/etw ~** to adapt to sb/prepare oneself for sth; **Einstellung** f (von Gerät) adjustment; (von Kamera) focusing; (von Arbeiter) taking on; (Meinung) attitude

ein|stürzen vi to collapse

eintägig adj one-day

ein|tauschen vt to exchange (gegen for)

eintausend num one (o a) thousand

ein|teilen vt (in Teile) to divide (up) (in +akk into); (Zeit) to organize

eintönig adj monotonous

Eintopf m stew

ein|tragen irr vt (in eine Liste) to put down, to enter ▷ vr: **sich ~** to put one's name down, to register

ein|treffen irr vi to happen; (ankommen) to arrive

ein|treten irr vi (hineingehen) to enter (in etw akk sth); (in Klub, Partei) to join (in etw akk sth); (sich ereignen) to occur; **~ für** to support; **Eintritt** m admission; **„~ frei"**

"admission free"; **Eintrittskarte** f (entrance) ticket; **Eintrittspreis** m admission charge

einverstanden interj okay, all right ▷ adj: **mit etwas ~ sein** to agree to sth, to accept sth

Einwanderer m, **Einwanderin** f immigrant; **ein|wandern** vi to immigrate

einwandfrei adj perfect, flawless

Einwegflasche f non-returnable bottle

ein|weichen vt to soak

ein|weihen vt (Gebäude) to inaugurate, to open; **jdn in etw** (akk) **~** to let sb in on sth; **Einweihungsparty** f house-warming party

ein|werfen irr vt (Ball, Bemerkung etc) to throw in; (Brief) to post, to mail (US); (Geld) to put in, to insert; (Fenster) to smash

ein|wickeln vt to wrap up; (fig) **jdn ~** to take sb in

Einwohner(in) (-s, -) m(f) inhabitant; **Einwohnermeldeamt** nt registration office for residents

Einwurf m (Öffnung) slot; (Sport) throw-in

Einzahl f singular

ein|zahlen vt to pay in (auf ein Konto -to an account)

Einzel (-s, -) nt (Tennis) singles sing; **Einzelbett** nt single bed; **Einzelfahrschein** m single ticket (Brit), one-way ticket (US); **Einzelgänger(in)** m(f) loner; **Einzelhandel** m retail trade; **Einzelkind** nt only child

einzeln adj individual; (getrennt) separate; (einzig) single; **~e ...** several ..., some ...; **der/die Einzelne** the individual; **im Einzelnen** in detail ▷ adv separately; (verpacken, aufführen) individually; **~ angeben** to specify; **~ eintreten** to enter one by one

Einzelzimmer nt single room; **Einzelzimmerzuschlag** m single-room supplement

ein|ziehen irr vt: **den Kopf ~** to duck ▷ vi (in ein Haus) to move in

einzig adj only; (einzeln) single; (einzigartig) unique; **kein ~er Fehler** not a single mistake; **das Einzige** the only thing; **der/die Einzige** the only person ▷ adv only; **die ~ richtige Lösung** the only correct solution; **einzigartig** adj unique

Eis (-es, -) nt ice; (Speiseeis) ice-cream; **Eisbahn** f ice(skating) rink; **Eisbär** m polar bear; **Eisbecher** m (ice-cream) sundae; **Eisberg** m iceberg; **Eisbergsalat** m iceberg lettuce; **Eiscafé** nt, **Eisdiele** f ice-cream parlour

Eisen (-s, -) nt iron; **Eisenbahn** f railway (Brit), railroad (US); **eisern** adj iron

eisgekühlt adj chilled; **Eishockey** nt ice hockey; **Eiskaffee** m iced coffee; **eiskalt** adj ice-cold; (Temperatur) freezing; **Eiskunstlauf** m figure skating; **eis|laufen** irr vi to skate; **Eisschokolade** f iced chocolate; **Eisschrank** m fridge, ice-box (US); **Eistee** m iced tea; **Eiswürfel** m ice cube; **Eiszapfen** m icicle

eitel adj vain

Eiter (-s) m pus

Eiweiß (-es, -e) nt egg white; (Chem, Bio) protein

ekelhaft, **ek(e)lig** adj disgusting, revolting; **ekeln** vr: **sich ~** to be disgusted (vor +dat at)

EKG (-s, -s) nt abk = **Elektrokardiogramm** ECG

Ekzem (-s, -e) nt (Med) eczema

elastisch adj elastic

Elch (-(e)s, -e) m elk; (nordamerikanischer) moose
Elefant m elephant
elegant adj elegant
Elektriker(in) (-s, -) m(f) electrician; **elektrisch** adj electric; **Elektrizität** f electricity; **Elektroauto** nt electric car; **Elektrogerät** nt electrical appliance; **Elektrogeschäft** nt electrical shop; **Elektroherd** m electric cooker; **Elektromotor** m electric motor; **Elektronik** f electronics sing; **elektronisch** adj electronic; **Elektrorasierer** (-s, -) m electric razor
Element (-(e)s, -e) nt element
elend adj miserable; **Elend** (-(e)s) nt misery
elf num eleven; **Elf** (-, -en) f (Sport) eleven
Elfenbein nt ivory
Elfmeter m (Sport) penalty (kick)
elfte(r, s) adj eleventh; siehe auch **dritte**
Ell(en)bogen m elbow
Elster (-, -n) f magpie
Eltern pl parents pl
EM f abk = **Europameisterschaft** European Championship(s)
E-Mail (-, -s) f (Inform) e-mail; **jdm eine ~ schicken** to e-mail sb, to send sb an e-mail; **jdm etwas per ~ schicken** to e-mail sth to sb; **E-Mail-Adresse** f e-mail address; **e-mailen** vt to e-mail
Emoticon (-s, -s) nt emoticon
emotional adj emotional
empfahl imperf von **empfehlen**
empfand imperf von **empfinden**
Empfang (-(e)s, Empfänge) m (Rezeption; Veranstaltung) reception; (Erhalten) receipt; **in ~ nehmen** to receive; **empfangen** (empfing, empfangen) vt to receive; **Empfänger(in)** (-s, -) m(f) recipient; (Adressat) addressee ▷ m

(Tech) receiver; **Empfängnisverhütung** f contraception; **Empfangshalle** f reception area
empfehlen (empfahl, empfohlen) vt to recommend; **Empfehlung** f recommendation
empfinden (empfand, empfunden) vt to feel; **empfindlich** adj (Mensch) sensitive; (Stelle) sore; (reizbar) touchy; (Material) delicate
empfing imperf von **empfangen**
empfohlen pp von **empfehlen**
empfunden pp von **empfinden**
empört adj indignant (über +akk at)
Ende (-s, -n) nt end; (Film, Roman) ending; **am ~** at the end; (schließlich) in the end; **~ Mai** at the end of May; **~ der Achtzigerjahre** in the late eighties; **sie ist ~ zwanzig** she's in her late twenties; **zu ~** over, finished; **enden** vi to end; **der Zug endet hier** this service (o train) terminates here; **endgültig** adj final; (Beweis) conclusive
Endivie f endive
endlich adv at last, finally; (am Ende) eventually; **Endspiel** nt final; (Endrunde) finals pl; **Endstation** f terminus; **Endung** f ending
Energie f energy; **~ sparend** energy-saving; **Energiebedarf** m energy requirement; **Energieverbrauch** m energy consumption
energisch adj (entschlossen) forceful
eng adj narrow; (Kleidung) tight; (fig: Freundschaft, Verhältnis) close; **das wird ~** (fam: zeitlich) we're running out of time, it's getting tight ▷ adv: **~ befreundet sein** to be close friends
engagieren vt to engage ▷ vr: **sich ~** to commit oneself, to be

committed (*für* to)

Engel (*-s, -*) *m* angel

England *nt* England;
Engländer(in) (*-s, -*) *m(f)*
Englishman/ -woman; **die ~** *pl* the
English *pl*; **englisch** *adj* English;
(*Gastr*) rare; **Englisch** *nt* English;
ins ~e übersetzen to translate
into English

Enkel (*-s, -*) *m* grandson; **Enkelin**
f granddaughter

enorm *adj* enormous; (*fig*)
tremendous

Entbindung *f* (*Med*) delivery

entdecken *vt* to discover;
Entdeckung *f* discovery

Ente (*-, -n*) *f* duck

Enter-Taste *f* (*Inform*) enter (*o*
return) key

entfernen *vt* to remove; (*Inform*)
to delete ▷ *vr*: **sich ~** to go away;
entfernt *adj* distant; **15 km von X
~** 15 km away from X; **20 km
voneinander ~** 20 km apart;
Entfernung *f* distance; **aus der
~** from a distance

entführen *vt* to kidnap;
Entführer(in) *m(f)* kidnapper;
Entführung *f* kidnapping

entgegen *prep* +*dat* contrary to
▷ *adv* towards; **dem Wind
~** against the wind;
entgegengesetzt *adj* (*Richtung*)
opposite; (*Meinung*) opposing;
entgegen|kommen *irr vi*: **jdm
~** to come to meet sb; (*fig*) to
accommodate sb;
entgegenkommend *adj* (*Verkehr*)
oncoming; (*fig*) obliging

entgegnen *vt* to reply (*auf* +*akk*
to)

entgehen *irr vi*: **jdm ~** to escape
sb's notice; **sich** (*dat*) **etw ~ lassen**
to miss sth

entgleisen *vi* (*Eisenb*) to be
derailed; (*fig: Mensch*) to
misbehave

Enthaarungscreme *f* hair
remover

enthalten *irr vt* (*Behälter*) to
contain; (*Preis*) to include ▷ *vr*:
sich ~ to abstain (*gen* from)

entkoffeiniert *adj*
decaffeinated

entkommen *irr vi* to escape

entkorken *vt* to uncork

entlang *prep* +*akk o dat* **~ dem
Fluss, den Fluss ~** along the river;
entlang|gehen *irr vi* to walk
along

entlassen *irr vt* (*Patient*) to
discharge; (*Arbeiter*) to dismiss

entlasten *vt*: **jdn ~** (*Arbeit
abnehmen*) to relieve sb of some of
his/her work

entmutigen *vt* to discourage

entnehmen *vt* to take (*dat* from)

entrahmt *adj* (*Milch*) skimmed

entschädigen *vt* to
compensate; **Entschädigung** *f*
compensation

entscheiden *irr vt, vi* to decide
▷ *vr*: **sich ~** to decide; **sich
für/gegen etw ~** to decide
on/against sth; **wir haben uns
entschieden, nicht zu gehen** we
decided not to go; **das
entscheidet sich morgen** that'll
be decided tomorrow;
entscheidend *adj* decisive;
(*Stimme*) casting; (*Frage, Problem*)
crucial; **Entscheidung** *f*
decision

entschließen *irr vr*: **sich ~** to
decide (*zu, für* on), to make up
one's mind; **Entschluss** *m*
decision

entschuldigen *vt* to excuse
▷ *vr*: **sich ~** to apologize; **sich bei
jdm für etw ~** to apologize to sb
for sth ▷ *vi*: **entschuldige!, ~ Sie!**
(*vor einer Frage*) excuse me;
(*Verzeihung!*) (I'm) sorry, excuse me
(*US*); **Entschuldigung** *f* apology;

(*Grund*) excuse; **jdn um ~ bitten** to apologize to sb; **~!** (*bei Zusammenstoß*) (I'm) sorry, excuse me (*US*); (*vor einer Frage*) excuse me; (*wenn man etw nicht verstanden hat*) (I beg your) pardon?

entsetzlich *adj* dreadful, appalling

entsorgen *vt* to dispose of

entspannen *vt* (*Körper*) to relax; (*Pol: Lage*) to ease ▷ *vr:* **sich ~** to relax; (*fam*) to chill out; **Entspannung** *f* relaxation

entsprechen *irr vi* +*dat* to correspond to; (*Anforderungen, Wünschen etc*) to comply with; **entsprechend** *adj* appropriate ▷ *adv* accordingly ▷ *prep* +*dat* according to, in accordance with

entstehen *vi* (*Schwierigkeiten*) to arise; (*gebaut werden*) to be built; (*hergestellt werden*) to be created

enttäuschen *vt* to disappoint; **Enttäuschung** *f* disappointment

entweder *conj:* **~ ... oder ...** either ... or ...; **~ oder!** take it or leave it

entwerfen *irr vt* (*Möbel, Kleider*) to design; (*Plan, Vertrag*) to draft

entwerten *vt* to devalue; (*Fahrschein*) to cancel; **Entwerter** (*-s, -*) *m* ticket-cancelling machine

entwickeln *vt* (*a. Foto*) to develop; (*Mut, Energie*) to show, to display ▷ *vr:* **sich ~** to develop; **Entwicklung** *f* development; (*Foto*) developing; **Entwicklungshelfer(in)** (*-s, -*) *m(f)* development worker; **Entwicklungsland** *nt* developing country

Entwurf *m* outline; (*Design*) design; (*Vertragsentwurf, Konzept*) draft

entzückend *adj* delightful, charming

Entzug *m* withdrawal;

(*Behandlung*) detox; **Entzugserscheinung** *f* withdrawal symptom

entzünden *vr:* **sich ~** to catch fire; (*Med*) to become inflamed; **Entzündung** *f* (*Med*) inflammation

Epidemie (*-, -n*) *f* epidemic

Epilepsie (*-, -n*) *f* epilepsy

epilieren *vt* to remove body hair, to depilate; **Epiliergerät** *nt* Ladyshave®

er *pron* (*Person*) he; (*Sache*) it; **er ist's** it's him; **wo ist mein Mantel? — ~ ist ...** where's my coat? — it's ...

Erbe (*-n, -n*) *m* heir ▷ (*-s*) *nt* inheritance; (*fig*) heritage; **erben** *vt* to inherit; **Erbin** *f* heiress; **erblich** *adj* hereditary

erbrechen *irr vt* to vomit ▷ *vr:* **sich ~** to vomit; **Erbrechen** *nt* vomiting

Erbschaft *f* inheritance

Erbse (*-, -n*) *f* pea

Erdapfel *m* potato; **Erdbeben** *nt* earthquake; **Erdbeere** *f* strawberry; **Erde** (*-, -n*) *f* (*Planet*) earth; (*Boden*) ground; **Erdgas** *nt* natural gas; **Erdgeschoss** *nt* ground floor (*Brit*), first floor (*US*); **Erdkunde** *f* geography; **Erdnuss** *f* peanut; **Erdöl** *nt* (*mineral*) oil; **Erdrutsch** *m* landslide; **Erdteil** *m* continent

ereignen *vr:* **sich ~** to happen, to take place; **Ereignis** *nt* event

erfahren *irr vt* to learn, to find out; (*erleben*) to experience ▷ *adj* experienced; **Erfahrung** *f* experience

erfinden *irr vt* to invent; **erfinderisch** *adj* inventive, creative; **Erfindung** *f* invention

Erfolg (*-(e)s, -e*) *m* success; (*Folge*) result; **~ versprechend** promising; **viel ~!** good luck;

erfolglos adj unsuccessful;
erfolgreich adj successful
erforderlich adj necessary
erforschen vt to explore;
(untersuchen) investigate
erfreulich adj pleasing, pleasant;
(Nachricht) good;
erfreulicherweise adv
fortunately
erfrieren irr vi to freeze to death;
(Pflanzen) to be killed by frost
Erfrischung f refreshment
erfüllen vt (Raum) to fill; (Bitte,
Wunsch etc) to fulfil ▷ vr: **sich ~** to
come true
ergänzen vt (hinzufügen) to add;
(vervollständigen) to complete ▷ vr:
sich ~ to complement one
another; **Ergänzung** f
completion; (Zusatz) supplement
ergeben irr vt (Betrag) to come
to; (zum Ergebnis haben) to result in
▷ irr vr: **sich ~** to surrender;
(folgen) to result (aus from) ▷ adj
devoted; (demütig) humble
Ergebnis nt result
ergreifen irr vt to seize; (Beruf) to
take up; (Maßnahme, Gelegenheit) to
take; (rühren) to move
erhalten irr vt (bekommen) to
receive; (bewahren) to preserve;
gut ~ sein to be in good
condition; **erhältlich** adj
available
erheblich adj considerable
erhitzen vt to heat (up)
erhöhen vt to raise; (verstärken)
to increase ▷ vr: **sich ~** to
increase
erholen vr: **sich ~** to recover; (sich
ausruhen) to have a rest; **erholsam**
adj restful; **Erholung** f recovery;
(Entspannung) relaxation, rest
erinnern vt to remind (an +akk
of) ▷ vr: **sich ~** to remember (an
etw akk sth); **Erinnerung** f
memory; (Andenken) souvenir;

(Mahnung) reminder
erkälten vr: **sich ~** to catch a
cold; **erkältet** adj: (**stark**) **~ sein**
to have a (bad) cold; **Erkältung** f
cold
erkennen irr vt to recognize;
(sehen, verstehen) to see; **~, dass ...**
to realize that ...; **erkenntlich**
adj: **sich ~ zeigen** to show one's
appreciation
Erker (-s, -) m bay
erklären vt to explain; (kundtun)
to declare; **Erklärung** f
explanation; (Aussage) declaration
erkundigen vr: **sich ~** to enquire
(nach about)
erlauben vt to allow, to permit;
jdm ~, etw zu tun to allow (o
permit) sb to do sth; **sich** (dat) **etw
~** to permit oneself sth; **~ Sie(,
dass ich rauche)?** do you mind (if I
smoke)?; **was ~ Sie sich?** what do
you think you're doing?; **Erlaubnis**
f permission
Erläuterung f explanation; (zu
Text) comment
erleben vt to experience; (schöne
Tage etc) to have; (Schlimmes) to go
through; (miterleben) to witness;
(noch miterleben) to live to see;
Erlebnis nt experience
erledigen vt (Angelegenheit,
Aufgabe) to deal with; (fam:
ruinieren) to finish; **erledigt** adj
(beendet) finished; (gelöst) dealt
with; (fam: erschöpft) whacked,
knackered (Brit)
erleichtert adj relieved
Erlös (-es, -e) m proceeds pl
ermahnen vt (warnend) to warn
ermäßigt adj reduced;
Ermäßigung f reduction
ermitteln vt to find out; (Täter)
to trace ▷ vi (Jur) to investigate
ermöglichen vt to make
possible (dat for)
ermorden vt to murder

ermüdend *adj* tiring
ermutigen *vt* to encourage
ernähren *vt* to feed; *(Familie)* to support ▷ *vr:* **sich ~** to support oneself; **sich ~ von** to live on; **Ernährung** *f (Essen)* food; **Ernährungsberater(in)** *m(f)* nutritional *(o* dietary) adviser
erneuern *vt* to renew; *(restaurieren)* to restore; *(renovieren)* to renovate; *(auswechseln)* to replace
ernst *adj* serious ▷ *adv:* **jdn/etw ~ nehmen** take sb/sth seriously; **Ernst** *(-es) m* seriousness; **das ist mein ~** I'm quite serious; **im ~?** seriously?; **ernsthaft** *adj* serious ▷ *adv* seriously
Ernte *(-, -n) f* harvest; **Erntedankfest** *nt* harvest festival *(Brit)*, Thanksgiving (Day) *(US: 4. Donnerstag im November)*; **ernten** *vt* to harvest; *(Lob etc)* to earn
erobern *vt* to conquer
eröffnen *vt* to open; **Eröffnung** *f* opening
erogen *adj* erogenous
erotisch *adj* erotic
erpressen *vt (jdn)* to blackmail; *(Geld etc)* to extort; **Erpressung** *f* blackmail; *(von Geld)* extortion
erraten *irr vt* to guess
erregen *vt* to excite; *(sexuell)* to arouse; *(ärgern)* to annoy; *(hervorrufen)* to arouse ▷ *vr:* **sich ~** to get worked up; **Erreger** *(-s, -) m (Med)* germ; *(Virus)* virus
erreichbar *adj:* **~ sein** to be within reach; *(Person)* to be available; **das Stadtzentrum ist zu Fuß/mit dem Wagen leicht ~** the city centre is within easy walking/driving distance; **erreichen** *vt* to reach; *(Zug etc)* to catch
Ersatz *(-es) m* replacement; *(auf*

Zeit) substitute; *(Ausgleich)* compensation; **Ersatzreifen** *m (Auto)* spare tyre; **Ersatzteil** *nt* spare (part)
erscheinen *irr vi* to appear; *(wirken)* to seem
erschöpft *adj* exhausted; **Erschöpfung** *f* exhaustion
erschrecken *vt* to frighten ▷ *(erschrak, erschrocken) vi* to get a fright; **erschreckend** *adj* alarming; **erschrocken** *adj* frightened
erschwinglich *adj* affordable
ersetzen *vt* to replace; *(Auslagen)* to reimburse

 SCHLÜSSELWORT

erst *adv* **1** first; **mach erst mal die Arbeit fertig** finish your work first; **wenn du das erst mal hinter dir hast** once you've got that behind you
2 *(nicht früher als, nur)* only; *(nicht bis)* not till; **erst gestern** only yesterday; **erst morgen** not until tomorrow; **erst als** only when, not until; **wir fahren erst später** we're not going until later; **er ist (gerade) erst angekommen** he's only just arrived
3 **wäre er doch erst zurück!** if only he were back!

erstatten *vt (Kosten)* to refund; **Bericht ~** to report *(über +akk* on); **Anzeige gegen jdn ~** to report sb to the police
erstaunlich *adj* astonishing; **erstaunt** *adj* surprised
erstbeste(r, s) *adj:* **das ~ Hotel** any old hotel; **der Erstbeste** just anyone
erste(r, s) *adj* first; *siehe auch* **dritte; zum ~n Mal** for the first time; **er wurde Erster** he came

first; **auf den ~n Blick** at first
sight
erstens *adv* first(ly), in the first
place
ersticken *vi* (*Mensch*) to
suffocate; **in Arbeit ~** to be
snowed under with work
erstklassig *adj* first-class;
erstmals *adv* for the first time
erstrecken *vr*: **sich ~** to extend,
to stretch (*auf +akk* to; *über +akk*
over)
ertappen *vt* to catch
erteilen *vt* (*Rat, Erlaubnis*) to give
Ertrag (*-(e)s, Erträge*) *m* yield;
(*Gewinn*) proceeds *pl*; **ertragen** *irr*
vt (*Schmerzen*) to bear, to stand;
(*dulden*) to put up with; **erträglich**
adj bearable; (*nicht zu schlecht*)
tolerable
ertrinken *irr vi* to drown
erwachsen *adj* grown-up;
~ werden to grow up;
Erwachsene(r) *mf* adult,
grown-up
erwähnen *vt* to mention
erwarten *vt* to expect; (*warten*
auf) to wait for; **ich kann den**
Sommer kaum ~ I can hardly wait
for the summer
erwerbstätig *adj* employed
erwidern *vt* to reply; (*Gruß,*
Besuch) to return
erwischen *vt* (*fam*) to catch (*bei*
etw doing sth)
erwünscht *adj* desired;
(*willkommen*) welcome
Erz (*-es, -e*) *nt* ore
erzählen *vt* to tell (*jdm etw* sb
sth); **Erzählung** *f* story, tale
erzeugen *vt* to produce; (*Strom*)
to generate; **Erzeugnis** *nt*
product
erziehen *irr vt* to bring up;
(*geistig*) to educate; (*Tier*) to train;
Erzieher(in) (*-s, -*) *m(f)* educator;
(*Kindergarten*) (nursery school)

teacher; **Erziehung** *f*
upbringing; (*Bildung*) education
es *pron* (*Sache, im Nom und Akk*) it;
(*Baby, Tier*) he/she; **ich bin ~** it's
me; **~ ist kalt** it's cold; **~ gibt ...**
there is .../there are ...; **ich hoffe**
~ I hope so; **ich kann ~** I can do it
Escape-Taste *f* (*Inform*) escape
key
Esel (*-s, -*) *m* donkey
Espresso (*-s, -*) *m* espresso
essbar *adj* edible; **essen** (*aß,*
gegessen) *vt, vi* to eat; **zu**
Mittag/Abend ~ to have
lunch/dinner; **was gibt's zu ~?**
what's for lunch/dinner?; **~ gehen**
to eat out; **gegessen sein** (*fig,*
fam) to be history; **Essen** (*-s, -*) *nt*
(*Mahlzeit*) meal; (*Nahrung*) food
Essig (*-s, -e*) *m* vinegar
Esslöffel *m* dessert spoon;
Esszimmer *nt* dining room
Estland *nt* Estonia
Etage (*-, -n*) *f* floor, storey; **in** (*o*
auf) **der ersten ~** on the first (*Brit*)
(*o* second (*US*)) floor; **Etagenbett**
nt bunk bed
Etappe (*-, -n*) *f* stage
ethnisch *adj* ethnic
Etikett (*-(e)s, -e*) *nt* label
etliche *pron pl* several, quite a
few; **etliches** *pron* quite a lot
etwa *adv* (*ungefähr*) about;
(*vielleicht*) perhaps; (*beispielsweise*)
for instance
etwas *pron* something;
(*verneinend, fragend*) anything; (*ein*
wenig) a little; **~ Neues**
something/anything new; **~ zu**
essen something to eat; **~ Salz**
some salt; **wenn ich noch ~ tun**
kann ... if I can do anything else ...
▷ *adv* a bit, a little; **~ mehr** a little
more
EU (*-*) *f abk* = **Europäische Union**
EU
euch *pron* *akk, dat von* **ihr**; you, (to)

you; **~ (selbst)** (*reflexiv*) yourselves; **wo kann ich ~ treffen?** where can I meet you?; **sie schickt es ~** she'll send it to you; **ein Freund von ~** a friend of yours; **setzt ~ bitte** please sit down; **habt ihr ~ amüsiert?** did you enjoy yourselves?

euer *pron* (*adjektivisch*) your; **~ David** (*am Briefende*) Yours, David ▷ *pron gen von* **ihr**; of you; **euere(r, s)** *pron siehe* **eure**

Eule (-, -*n*) *f* owl

eure(r, s) *pron* (*substantivisch*) yours; **das ist ~** that's yours; **euretwegen** *adv* (*wegen euch*) because of you; (*euch zuliebe*) for your sake; (*um euch*) about you

Euro (-, -) *m* (*Währung*) euro; **Eurocent** *m* eurocent; **Eurocity** (-(*s*), -*s*) *m*, **Eurocityzug** *m* European Intercity train; **Europa** (-*s*) *nt* Europe; **Europäer(in)** (-*s*, -) *m(f)* European; **europäisch** *adj* European; **Europäische Union** European Union; **Europameister(in)** *m(f)* European champion; (*Mannschaft*) European champions *pl*; **Europaparlament** *nt* European Parliament

Euter (-*s*, -) *nt* udder

evangelisch *adj* Protestant

eventuell *adj* possible ▷ *adv* possibly, perhaps

ewig *adj* eternal; **er hat ~ gebraucht** it took him ages; **Ewigkeit** *f* eternity

Ex *mf* ex

Ex- *in zW* ex-, former; **~frau** ex-wife; **~freund** *m* ex-boyfriend; **~minister** former minister

exakt *adj* precise

Examen (-*s*, -) *nt* exam

Exemplar (-*s*, -*e*) *nt* specimen; (*Buch*) copy

Exil (-*s*, -*e*) *nt* exile

Existenz *f* existence; (*Unterhalt*) livelihood, living; **existieren** *vi* to exist

exklusiv *adj* exclusive; **exklusive** *adv*, *prep* +*gen* excluding

exotisch *adj* exotic

Experte (-*n*, -*n*) *m*, **Expertin** *f* expert

explodieren *vi* to explode; **Explosion** *f* explosion

Export (-(*e*)*s*, -*e*) *m* export; **exportieren** *vt* to export

Express (-*es*) *m*, **Expresszug** *m* express (train)

extra *adj inv* (*fam: gesondert*) separate; (*zusätzlich*) extra ▷ *adv* (*gesondert*) separately; (*speziell*) specially; (*absichtlich*) on purpose; **Extra** (-*s*, -*s*) *nt* extra

extrem *adj* extreme ▷ *adv* extremely; **~ kalt** extremely cold

exzellent *adj* excellent

Eyeliner (-*s*, -) *m* eyeliner

f

fabelhaft *adj* fabulous, marvellous

Fabrik *f* factory

Fach *(-(e)s, Fächer) nt* compartment; (*Schulfach, Sachgebiet*) subject; **Facharzt** *m*, **Fachärztin** *f* specialist; **Fachausdruck** *(-s, Fachausdrücke) m* technical term

Fächer *(-s, -) m* fan

Fachfrau *f* specialist, expert; **Fachmann** *(-leute) m* specialist, expert; **Fachwerkhaus** *nt* half-timbered house

Fackel *(-, -n) f* torch

fad(e) *adj* (*Essen*) bland; (*langweilig*) dull

Faden *(-s, Fäden) m* thread

fähig *adj* capable (*zu, gen* of); **Fähigkeit** *f* ability

Fahndung *f* search

Fahne *(-, -n) f* flag

Fahrausweis *m* ticket

Fahrbahn *f* road; (*Spur*) lane

Fähre *(-, -n) f* ferry

fahren (*fuhr, gefahren*) *vt* to drive; (*Rad*) to ride; (*befördern*) to drive, to take; **50 km/h ~** to drive at (*o do*) 50 kph ▷ *vi* (*sich bewegen*) to go; (*Autofahrer*) to drive; (*Schiff*) to sail; (*abfahren*) to leave; **mit dem Auto/Zug ~** to go by car/train; **rechts ~!** keep to the right; **Fahrer(in)** *(-s, -) m(f)* driver; **Fahrerairbag** *m* driver airbag; **Fahrerflucht** *f:* **~ begehen** to fail to stop after an accident; **Fahrersitz** *m* driver's seat

Fahrgast *m* passenger; **Fahrgeld** *nt* fare; **Fahrgemeinschaft** *f* car pool; **Fahrkarte** *f* ticket; **Fahrkartenautomat** *m* ticket machine; **Fahrkartenschalter** *m* ticket office

fahrlässig *adj* negligent

Fahrlehrer(in) *m(f)* driving instructor; **Fahrplan** *m* timetable; **Fahrplanauszug** *m* individual timetable; **fahrplanmäßig** *adj* (*Eisenb*) scheduled; **Fahrpreis** *m* fare; **Fahrpreisermäßigung** *f* fare reduction; **Fahrrad** *nt* bicycle; **Fahrradschlauch** *m* bicycle tube; **Fahrradschloss** *nt* bicycle lock; **Fahrradverleih** *m* cycle hire (*Brit*) (*o rental* (*US*)); **Fahrradweg** *m* cycle path; **Fahrschein** *m* ticket; **Fahrscheinautomat** *m* ticket machine; **Fahrscheinentwerter** *m* ticket-cancelling machine; **Fahrschule** *f* driving school; **Fahrschüler(in)** *m(f)* learner (driver) (*Brit*), student driver (*US*); **Fahrspur** *f* lane; **Fahrstreifen** *m* lane; **Fahrstuhl** *m* lift (*Brit*), elevator (*US*)

Fahrt *(-, -en) f* journey; (*kurz*) trip; (*Auto*) drive; **auf der ~ nach London** on the way to London; **nach drei Stunden ~** after travelling for three hours; **gute ~!** have a good trip; **Fahrtkosten** *pl* travelling expenses *pl*; **Fahrtrichtung** *f* direction of travel

fahrtüchtig *f* (*Person*) fit to drive; (*Fahrzeug*) roadworthy

Fahrtunterbrechung *f* break in the journey, stop

Fahrverbot *nt*: **~ erhalten/ haben** to be banned from driving; **Fahrzeug** *nt* vehicle; **Fahrzeugbrief** *m* (vehicle) registration document; **Fahrzeughalter(in)** *m(f)* registered owner; **Fahrzeugpapiere** *pl* vehicle documents *pl*

fair *adj* fair

Fakultät *f* faculty

Falke (-n, -n) *m* falcon

Fall (-(e)s, Fälle) *m* (*Sturz*) fall; (*Sachverhalt, juristisch*) case; **auf jeden ~, auf alle Fälle** in any case; (*bestimmt*) definitely; **auf keinen ~** on no account; **für den ~, dass ...** in case ...

Falle (-, -n) *f* trap

fallen (fiel, gefallen) *vi* to fall; **etw ~ lassen** to drop sth

fällig *adj* due

falls *adv* if; (*für den Fall, dass*) in case

Fallschirm *m* parachute; **Fallschirmspringen** *nt* parachuting, parachute jumping; **Fallschirmspringer(in)** *m(f)* parachutist

falsch *adj* (*unrichtig*) wrong; (*unehrlich, unecht*) false; (*Schmuck*) fake; **~ verbunden** sorry, wrong number; **fälschen** *vt* to forge; **Falschfahrer(in)** *m(f)* *person driving the wrong way on the motorway*; **Falschgeld** *nt* counterfeit money; **Fälschung** *f* forgery, fake

Faltblatt *nt* leaflet

Falte (-, -n) *f* (*Knick*) fold; (*Haut*) wrinkle; (*Rock*) pleat; (*Bügel*) crease; **falten** *vt* to fold; **faltig** *adj* (*zerknittert*) creased; (*Haut, Gesicht*) wrinkled

Familie *f* family; **Familienangehörige(r)** *mf* family member; **Familienname** *m* surname; **Familienstand** *m* marital status

Fan (-s, -s) *m* fan

fand *imperf von* **finden**

fangen (fing, gefangen) *vt* to catch ▷ *vr*: **sich ~** (*nicht fallen*) to steady oneself; (*fig*) to compose oneself

Fantasie *f* imagination

fantastisch *adj* fantastic

Farbdrucker *m* colour printer; **Farbe** (-, -n) *f* colour; (*zum Malen etc*) paint; (*für Stoff*) dye; **färben** *vt* to colour; (*Stoff, Haar*) to dye; **Farbfernsehen** *nt* colour television; **Farbfilm** *m* colour film; **farbig** *adj* coloured; **Farbkopierer** *m* colour copier; **farblos** *adj* colourless; **Farbstoff** *m* dye; (*für Lebensmittel*) colouring

Farn (-(e)s, -e) *m* fern

Fasan (-(e)s, -e(n)) *m* pheasant

Fasching (-s, -e) *m* carnival, Mardi Gras (*US*); **Faschingsdienstag** (-s, -e) *m* Shrove Tuesday, Mardi Gras (*US*)

Faschismus *m* fascism

Faser (-, -n) *f* fibre

Fass (-es, Fässer) *nt* barrel; (*Öl*) drum

fassen *vt* (*ergreifen*) to grasp; (*enthalten*) to hold; (*Entschluss*) to take; (*verstehen*) to understand; **nicht zu ~!** unbelievable ▷ *vr*: **sich ~** to compose oneself; **Fassung** *f* (*Umrahmung*) mount; (*Brille*) frame; (*Lampe*) socket; (*Wortlaut*) version; (*Beherrschung*) composure; **jdn aus der ~ bringen**

to throw sb; **die ~ verlieren** to lose one's cool

fast *adv* almost, nearly

fasten *vi* to fast; **Fastenzeit** *f*: **die ~** (*christlich*) Lent; (*muslimisch*) Ramadan

Fast Food (*-s*) *nt* fast food

Fastnacht *f* (*Fasching*) carnival

fatal *adj* (*verhängnisvoll*) disastrous; (*peinlich*) embarrassing

faul *adj* (*Obst, Gemüse*) rotten; (*Mensch*) lazy; (*Ausreden*) lame; **faulen** *vi* to rot

faulenzen *vi* to do nothing, to hang around; **Faulheit** *f* laziness

faulig *adj* rotten; (*Geruch, Geschmack*) foul

Faust (*-, Fäuste*) *f* fist; **Fausthandschuh** *m* mitten

Fax (*-, -(e)*) *nt* fax; **faxen** *vi, vt* to fax; **Faxgerät** *nt* fax machine; **Faxnummer** *f* fax number

FCKW (*-, -s*) *nt abk* = **Fluorchlorkohlenwasserstoff** CFC

Februar (*-(s), -e*) *m* February; *siehe auch* **Juni**

Fechten *nt* fencing

Feder (*-, -n*) *f* feather; (*Schreibfeder*) (pen-)nib; (*Tech*) spring; **Federball** *m* (*Ball*) shuttlecock; (*Spiel*) badminton; **Federung** *f* suspension

Fee (*-, -n*) *f* fairy

fegen *vi, vt* to sweep

fehl *adj*: **~ am Platz** (*o Ort*) out of place

fehlen *vi* (*abwesend sein*) to be absent; **etw fehlt jdm** sb lacks sth; **was fehlt ihm?** what's wrong with him?; **du fehlst mir** I miss you; **es fehlt an ...** there's no...

Fehler (*-s, -*) *m* mistake, error; (*Mangel, Schwäche*) fault; **Fehlermeldung** *f* (*Inform*) error message

Fehlzündung *f* (*Auto*) misfire

Feier (*-, -n*) *f* celebration; (*Party*) party; **Feierabend** *m* end of the working day; **~ haben** to finish work; **nach ~** after work; **feierlich** *adj* solemn; **feiern** *vt, vi* to celebrate, to have a party; **Feiertag** *m* holiday; **gesetzlicher ~** public (*o bank* (*Brit*) *o legal* (*US*)) holiday

feig(e) *adj* cowardly

Feige (*-, -n*) *f* fig

Feigling *m* coward

Feile (*-, -n*) *f* file

fein *adj* fine; (*vornehm*) refined; **~!** great!; **das schmeckt ~** that tastes delicious

Feind(in) (*-(e)s, -e*) *m(f)* enemy; **feindlich** *adj* hostile

Feinkost (*-*) *f* delicacies *pl*; **Feinkostladen** *m* delicatessen; **Feinschmecker(in)** (*-s, -*) *m(f)* gourmet; **Feinstaub** *m* particulate matter; **Feinwaschmittel** *nt* washing powder for delicate fabrics

Feld (*-(e)s, -er*) *nt* field; (*Schach*) square; (*Sport*) pitch; **Feldsalat** *m* lamb's lettuce; **Feldweg** *m* path across the fields

Felge (*-, -n*) *f* (wheel) rim

Fell (*-(e)s, -e*) *nt* fur; (*von Schaf*) fleece

Fels (*-en, -en*) *m*, **Felsen** (*-s, -*) *m* rock; (*Klippe*) cliff; **felsig** *adj* rocky

feminin *adj* feminine; **Femininum** (*-s, Feminina*) *nt* (*Ling*) feminine noun

feministisch *adj* feminist

Fenchel (*-s, -*) *m* fennel

Fenster (*-s, -*) *nt* window; **Fensterbrett** *nt* windowsill; **Fensterladen** *m* shutter; **Fensterplatz** *m* windowseat; **Fensterscheibe** *f* windowpane

Ferien *pl* holidays *pl* (*Brit*), vacation *sing* (*US*); **~ haben/ machen** to be/go on holiday (*Brit*)

(o vacation (US)); **Ferienhaus** nt holiday (Brit) (o vacation (US)) home; **Ferienkurs** m holiday (Brit) (o vacation (US)) course; **Ferienlager** nt holiday camp (Brit), vacation camp (US); (für Kinder im Sommer) summer camp; **Ferienort** m holiday (Brit) (o vacation (US)) resort; **Ferienwohnung** f holiday flat (Brit), vacation apartment (US)

Ferkel (-s, -) nt piglet

fern adj distant, far-off; **von ~** from a distance; **Fernabfrage** f remote-control access; **Fernbedienung** f remote control; **Ferne** f distance; **aus der ~** from a distance

ferner adj, adv further; (außerdem) besides

Fernflug m long-distance flight; **Ferngespräch** nt long-distance call; **ferngesteuert** adj remote-controlled; **Fernglas** nt binoculars pl; **Fernlicht** nt full beam (Brit), high beam (US)

Fernsehapparat m TV (set); **fern|sehen** irr vi to watch television; **Fernsehen** nt television; **im ~** on television; **Fernseher** m TV (set); **Fernsehkanal** m TV channel; **Fernsehprogramm** nt (Sendung) TV programme; (Zeitschrift) TV guide; **Fernsehserie** f TV series sing; **Fernsehturm** m TV tower; **Fernsehzeitschrift** f TV guide

Fernstraße f major road; **Ferntourismus** m long-haul tourism; **Fernverkehr** m long-distance traffic

Ferse (-, -n) f heel

fertig adj (bereit) ready; (beendet) finished; (gebrauchsfertig) ready-made; **~ machen** (beenden) to finish; **sich ~ machen** to get ready; **mit etw ~ werden** to be

able to cope with sth; **auf die Plätze, ~, los!** on your marks, get set, go!; **Fertiggericht** nt ready meal; **fertig|machen** vt (jdn kritisieren) to give sb hell; (jdn zur Verzweiflung bringen) to drive sb mad; (jdn deprimieren) to get sb down

fest adj firm; (Nahrung) solid; (Gehalt) regular; (Schuhe) sturdy; (Schlaf) sound

Fest (-(e)s, -e) nt party; (Rel) festival

Festbetrag m fixed amount

fest|binden irr vt to tie (an +dat to); **fest|halten** irr vt to hold onto ▷ vr: **sich ~** to hold on (an +dat to)

Festiger (-s, -) m setting lotion

Festival (-s, -s) nt festival

Festland nt mainland; **das europäische ~** the (European) continent

fest|legen vt to fix ▷ vr: **sich ~** to commit oneself

festlich adj festive

fest|machen vt to fasten; (Termin etc) to fix; **fest|nehmen** irr vt to arrest; **Festnetz** nt (Tel) fixed-line network; **Festplatte** f (Inform) hard disk

fest|setzen vt to fix

Festspiele pl festival sing

fest|stehen irr vi to be fixed

fest|stellen vt to establish; (sagen) to remark

Feststelltaste f shift lock

Festung f fortress

Festzelt nt marquee

Fete (-, -n) f party

fett adj (dick) fat; (Essen etc) greasy; (Schrift) bold; **Fett** (-(e)s, -e) nt fat; (Tech) grease; **fettarm** adj low-fat; **fettig** adj fatty; (schmierig) greasy

feucht adj damp; (Luft) humid; **Feuchtigkeit** f dampness;

(*Luftfeuchtigkeit*) humidity; **Feuchtigkeitscreme** f moisturizing cream

Feuer (*-s, -*) nt fire; **haben Sie ~?** have you got a light?; **Feueralarm** m fire alarm; **feuerfest** adj fireproof; **Feuerlöscher** (*-s, -*) m fire extinguisher; **Feuermelder** (*-s, -*) m fire alarm; **Feuertreppe** f fire escape; **Feuerwehr** (*-, -en*) f fire brigade; **Feuerwehrfrau** f firewoman, fire fighter; **Feuerwehrmann** m fireman, fire fighter; **Feuerwerk** nt fireworks pl; **Feuerzeug** nt (cigarette) lighter

Fichte (*-, -n*) f spruce

ficken vt, vi (vulg) to fuck

Fieber (*-s, -*) nt temperature, fever; **~ haben** to have a high temperature; **Fieberthermometer** nt thermometer

fiel imperf von **fallen**

fies adj (fam) nasty

Figur (*-, -en*) f figure; (im Schach) piece

Filet (*-s, -s*) nt fillet; **filetieren** vt to fillet; **Filetsteak** nt fillet steak

Filiale (*-, -n*) f (Comm) branch

Film (*-(e)s, -e*) m film, movie; **filmen** vt, vi to film

Filter (*-s, -*) m filter; **Filterkaffee** m filter coffee; **filtern** vt to filter; **Filterpapier** nt filter paper

Filz (*-es, -e*) m felt; **Filzschreiber** m, **Filzstift** m felt(-tip) pen, felt-tip

Finale (*-s, -*) nt (Sport) final

Finanzamt nt tax office; **finanziell** adj financial; **finanzieren** vt to finance

finden (*fand, gefunden*) vt to find; (*meinen*) to think; **ich finde nichts dabei, wenn ...** I don't see what's wrong if ...; **ich finde es gut/schlecht** I like/don't like it ▷ vr: **es fanden sich nur wenige Helfer** there were only a few helpers

fing imperf von **fangen**

Finger (*-s, -*) m finger; **Fingerabdruck** m fingerprint; **Fingerhandschuh** m glove; **Fingernagel** m fingernail

Fink (*-en, -en*) m finch

Finne (*-n, -n*) m, **Finnin** f Finn, Finnish man/woman; **finnisch** adj Finnish; **Finnisch** nt Finnish; **Finnland** nt Finland

finster adj dark; (*verdächtig*) dubious; (*verdrossen*) grim; (*Gedanke*) dark; **Finsternis** f darkness

Firewall (*-, -s*) f (Inform) firewall

Firma (*-, Firmen*) f firm

Fisch (*-(e)s, -e*) m fish; **~e** pl (Astr) Pisces sing; **fischen** vt, vi to fish; **Fischer(in)** (*-s, -*) m(f) fisherman/-woman; **Fischerboot** nt fishing boat; **Fischgericht** nt fish dish; **Fischhändler(in)** m(f) fishmonger; **Fischstäbchen** nt fish finger (Brit) (o stick (US))

Fisole (*-, -n*) f French bean

fit adj fit; **Fitness** (*-*) f fitness; **Fitnesscenter** (*-s, -*) nt fitness centre; **Fitnesstrainer(in)** m(f) fitness trainer, personal trainer

fix adj (schnell) quick; **~ und fertig** exhausted

fixen vi (fam) to shoot up; **Fixer(in)** (*-s, -*) m(f) (fam) junkie

FKK f abk = **Freikörperkultur** nudism; **FKK-Strand** m nudist beach

flach adj flat; (*Gewässer; Teller*) shallow; **~er Absatz** low heel; **Flachbildschirm** m flat screen

Fläche (*-, -n*) f area; (*Oberfläche*) surface

Flagge (*-, -n*) f flag

flambiert *adj* flambé(ed)
Flamme (-, -n) *f* flame
Flanell (-s) *m* flannel
Flasche (-, -n) *f* bottle; **eine ~ sein** (*fam*) to be useless;
Flaschenbier *nt* bottled beer;
Flaschenöffner *m* bottle opener;
Flaschenpfand *nt* deposit;
Flaschentomate *f* plum tomato
flatterhaft *adj* fickle; **flattern** *vi* to flutter
flauschig *adj* fluffy
Flausen *pl* (*fam*) daft ideas *pl*
Flaute (-, -n) *f* calm; (*Comm*) recession
Flechte (-, -n) *f* plait; (*Med*) scab; (*Bot*) lichen; **flechten** (*flocht, geflochten*) *vt* to plait; (*Kranz*) to bind
Fleck (-(e)s, -e) *m*, **Flecken** (-s, -) *m* spot; (*Schmutz*) stain; (*Stoff~*) patch; (*Makel*) blemish;
Fleckentferner (-s, -) *m* stain remover; **fleckig** *adj* spotted; (*mit Schmutzflecken*) stained
Fledermaus *f* bat
Fleisch (-(e)s) *nt* flesh; (*Essen*) meat; **Fleischbrühe** *f* meat stock; **Fleischer(in)** (-s, -) *m(f)* butcher; **Fleischerei** *f* butcher's (shop); **Fleischtomate** *f* beef tomato
fleißig *adj* diligent, hard-working
flennen *vi* (*fam*) to cry, to howl
flexibel *adj* flexible
flicken *vt* to mend; **Flickzeug** *nt* repair kit
Flieder (-s, -) *m* lilac
Fliege (-, -n) *f* fly; (*Krawatte*) bow tie
fliegen (*flog, geflogen*) *vt, vi* to fly
Fliese (-, -n) *f* tile
Fließband *nt* conveyor belt; (*als Einrichtung*) production (*o* assembly) line; **fließen** (*floss, geflossen*) *vi* to flow; **fließend** *adj* (*Rede, Deutsch*) fluent; (*Übergänge*) smooth; **~(es) Wasser** running water
Flipper (-s, -) *m* pinball machine; **flippern** *vi* to play pinball
flippig *adj* (*fam*) eccentric
flirten *vi* to flirt
Flitterwochen *pl* honeymoon *sing*
flocht *imperf von* **flechten**
Flocke (-, -n) *f* flake
flog *imperf von* **fliegen**
Floh (-(e)s, Flöhe) *m* flea;
Flohmarkt *m* flea market
Flop (-s, -s) *m* flop
Floskel (-, -n) *f* empty phrase
floss *imperf von* **fließen**
Floß (-es, Flöße) *nt* raft
Flosse (-, -n) *f* fin; (*Schwimmflosse*) flipper
Flöte (-, -n) *f* flute; (*Blockflöte*) recorder
flott *adj* lively; (*elegant*) smart; (*Naut*) afloat
Fluch (-(e)s, Flüche) *m* curse; **fluchen** *vi* to swear, to curse
Flucht (-, -en) *f* flight; **flüchten** *vi* to flee (*vor +dat* from); **flüchtig** *adj*: **ich kenne ihn nur ~** I don't know him very well at all; **Flüchtling** *m* refugee
Flug (-(e)s, Flüge) *m* flight; **Flugbegleiter(in)** (-s, -) *m(f)* flight attendant; **Flugblatt** *nt* leaflet
Flügel (-s, -) *m* wing; (*Mus*) grand piano
Fluggast *m* passenger (*on a plane*); **Fluggesellschaft** *f* airline; **Flughafen** *m* airport; **Fluglotse** *m* air-traffic controller; **Flugnummer** *f* flight number; **Flugplan** *m* flight schedule; **Flugplatz** *m* airport; (*klein*) airfield; **Flugschein** *m* plane ticket; **Flugschreiber** *m* flight recorder, black box; **Flugsteig** (-s, -e) *m* gate; **Flugstrecke** *f* air route; **Flugticket** *nt* plane ticket; **Flugverbindung** *f* flight

connection; **Flugverkehr** m air
traffic; **Flugzeit** f flying time;
Flugzeug nt plane;
Flugzeugentführung f hijacking
Flunder (-, -n) f flounder
Fluor (-s) nt fluorine
Flur (-(e)s, -e) m hall
Fluss (-es, Flüsse) m river; (Fließen)
flow
flüssig adj liquid; **Flüssigkeit**
(-, -en) f liquid; **Flüssigseife** f
liquid soap
flüstern vt, vi to whisper
Flut (-, -(e)s, -e) m (a. fig) flood;
(Gezeiten) high tide; **Flutlicht** nt
floodlight
Fohlen (-s, -) nt foal
Föhn (-(e)s, -e) m hairdryer;
(Wind) foehn; **föhnen** vt to dry;
(beim Friseur) to blow-dry
Folge (-, -n) f (Reihe, Serie) series
sing; (Aufeinanderfolge) sequence;
(Fortsetzung eines Romans)
instalment; (Fortsetzung einer
Fernsehserie) episode; (Auswirkung)
result; **etw zur ~ haben** to result
in sth; **~n haben** to have
consequences; **folgen** vi to
follow (jdm sb); (gehorchen) to obey
(jdm sb); **jdm ~ können** (fig) to be
able to follow sb; **folgend** adj
following; **folgendermaßen** adv
as follows; **folglich** adv
consequently
Folie f foil; (für Projektor)
transparency
Fön® m siehe **Föhn**
Fondue (-s, -s) nt fondue
fönen vt siehe **föhnen**
fordern vt to demand
fördern vt to promote;
(unterstützen) to help
Forderung f demand
Forelle f trout
Form (-, -en) f form; (Gestalt)
shape; (Gussform) mould;
(Backform) baking tin (Brit) (o pan

(US)); **in ~ sein** to be in good form;
Formalität f formality; **Format**
nt format; **von internationalem
~** of international standing;
formatieren vt (Diskette) to
format; (Text) to edit
Formblatt nt form; **formen** vt
to form, to shape; **förmlich** adj
formal; (buchstäblich) real; **formlos**
adj informal; **Formular** (-s, -e) nt
form; **formulieren** vt to
formulate
forschen vi to search (nach for);
(wissenschaftlich) to (do) research;
Forscher(in) m(f) researcher;
Forschung f research
Förster(in) (-s, -) m(f) forester;
(für Wild) gamekeeper
fort adv away; (verschwunden)
gone; **fort|bewegen** vt to move
away ▷ vr: **sich ~** to move;
Fortbildung f further education;
(im Beruf) further training;
fort|fahren irr vi to go away;
(weitermachen) to continue;
fort|gehen irr vi to go away;
fortgeschritten adj advanced;
Fortpflanzung f reproduction
Fortschritt m progress; **~e
machen** to make progress;
fortschrittlich adj progressive
fort|setzen vt to continue;
Fortsetzung f continuation;
(folgender Teil) instalment; **~ folgt**
to be continued
Foto (-s, -s) nt photo ▷ (-s, -s) m
(Fotoapparat) camera; **Fotograf(in)**
(-en, -en) m(f) photographer;
Fotografie f photography; (Bild)
photograph; **fotografieren** vt
to photograph ▷ vi to take
photographs; **Fotohandy** nt
camera phone; **Fotokopie** f
photocopy; **fotokopieren** vt to
photocopy
Foul (-s, -s) nt foul
Foyer (-s, -s) nt foyer

Fr. f abk = **Frau** Mrs; (unverheiratet, neutral) Ms

Fracht (-, -en) f freight; (Naut) cargo; (Preis) carriage; **Frachter** (-s, -) m freighter

Frack (-(e)s, Fräcke) m tails pl

Frage (-, -n) f question; **das ist eine ~ der Zeit** that's a matter (o question) of time; **das kommt nicht in ~** that's out of the question; **Fragebogen** m questionnaire; **fragen** vt, vi to ask; **Fragezeichen** nt question mark; **fragwürdig** adj dubious

Franken (-s, -) m (Schweizer Währung) Swiss franc ▷ (-s) nt (Land) Franconia

frankieren vt to stamp; (maschinell) to frank

Frankreich (-s) nt France; **Franzose** (-n, -n) m, **Französin** f Frenchman/-woman; **die ~n** pl the French pl; **französisch** adj French; **Französisch** nt French

fraß imperf von **fressen**

Frau (-, -en) f woman; (Ehefrau) wife; (Anrede) Mrs; (unverheiratet, neutral) Ms; **Frauenarzt** m, **Frauenärztin** f gynaecologist; **Frauenbewegung** f women's movement; **frauenfeindlich** adj misogynous; **Frauenhaus** nt refuge (for battered women)

Fräulein nt (junge Dame) young lady; (veraltet als Anrede) Miss

Freak (-s, -s) m (fam) freak

frech adj cheeky; **Frechheit** f cheek; **so eine ~!** what a cheek

Freeclimbing (-s) nt free climbing

frei adj free; (Straße) clear; (Mitarbeiter) freelance; **ein ~er Tag** a day off; **~e Arbeitsstelle** vacancy; **Zimmer ~** room(s) to let (Brit), room(s) for rent (US); **im Freien** in the open air; **Freibad** nt open-air (swimming) pool;

freiberuflich adj freelance; **frei(g)ebig** adj generous; **Freiheit** f freedom; **Freikarte** f free ticket; **frei|lassen** irr vt to (set) free

freilich adv of course

Freilichtbühne f open-air theatre; **frei|machen** vr: **sich ~** to undress; **frei|nehmen** irr vt **sich (dat) einen Tag ~** to take a day off; **Freisprechanlage** f hands-free phone; **Freistoß** m free kick

Freitag m Friday; siehe auch **Mittwoch**; **freitags** adv on Fridays; siehe auch **mittwochs**

freiwillig adj voluntary

Freizeichen nt (Tel) ringing tone

Freizeit f spare (o free) time; **Freizeithemd** nt sports shirt; **Freizeitkleidung** f leisure wear; **Freizeitpark** m leisure park

fremd adj (nicht vertraut) strange; (ausländisch) foreign; (nicht eigen) someone else's; **Fremde(r)** mf (Unbekannter) stranger; (Ausländer) foreigner; **fremdenfeindlich** adj anti-foreigner, xenophobic; **Fremdenführer(in)** m(f) (tourist) guide; **Fremdenverkehr** m tourism; **Fremdenverkehrsamt** nt tourist information office; **Fremdenzimmer** nt (guest) room; **Fremdsprache** f foreign language; **Fremdsprachen-kenntnisse** pl knowledge sing of foreign languages; **Fremdwort** nt foreign word

Frequenz f (Radio) frequency

fressen (fraß, gefressen) vt, vi (Tier) to eat; (Mensch) to guzzle

Freude (-, -n) f joy, delight; **freuen** vt to please; **es freut mich, dass ...** I'm pleased that ... ▷ vr: **sich ~** to be delighted (über +akk about); **sich auf etw** (akk) **~** to look forward to sth

Freund (-(e)s, -e) m friend; (in Beziehung) boyfriend; **Freundin** f friend; (in Beziehung) girlfriend; **freundlich** adj friendly; (liebenswürdig) kind; **freundlicherweise** adv kindly; **Freundlichkeit** f friendliness; (Liebenswürdigkeit) kindness; **Freundschaft** f friendship

Frieden (-s, -) m peace; **Friedhof** m cemetery; **friedlich** adj peaceful

frieren (fror, gefroren) vt, vi to freeze; **ich friere, es friert mich** I'm freezing

Frikadelle f rissole

Frisbee® nt, **Frisbeescheibe®** f frisbee®

frisch adj fresh; (lebhaft) lively; „**~ gestrichen"** "wet paint"; **sich ~ machen** to freshen up; **Frischhaltefolie** f clingfilm® (Brit), plastic wrap (US); **Frischkäse** m cream cheese

Friseur(in) (-s, -e) m(f) hairdresser; **frisieren** vt: **jdn ~** to do sb's hair ▷ vr: **sich ~** to do one's hair

Frist (-, -en) f period; (Zeitpunkt) deadline; **innerhalb einer ~ von zehn Tagen** within a ten-day period; **eine ~ einhalten** to meet a deadline; **die ~ ist abgelaufen** the deadline has expired; **fristgerecht** adj, adv within the specified time; **fristlos** adj: **~e Entlassung** dismissal without notice

Frisur f hairdo, hairstyle

frittieren vt to deep-fry

Frl. f abk = **Fräulein** Miss

froh adj happy; **~e Weihnachten!** Merry Christmas

fröhlich adj happy, cheerful

Fronleichnam (-(e)s) m Corpus Christi

frontal adj frontal

fror imperf von **frieren**

Frosch (-(e)s, Frösche) m frog

Frost (-(e)s, Fröste) m frost; **bei ~** in frosty weather; **Frostschutzmittel** nt anti-freeze

Frottee nt terry(cloth); **Frottier(hand)tuch** nt towel

Frucht (-, Früchte) f (a. fig) fruit; (Getreide) corn; **Fruchteis** nt fruit-flavoured ice-cream; **Früchtetee** m fruit tea; **fruchtig** adj fruity; **Fruchtpresse** f juicer; **Fruchtsaft** m fruit juice; **Fruchtsalat** m fruit salad

früh adj, adv early; **heute ~** this morning; **um fünf Uhr ~** at five (o'clock) in the morning; **~ genug** soon enough; **früher** adj earlier; (ehemalig) former ▷ adv formerly, in the past; **frühestens** adv at the earliest

Frühjahr nt, **Frühling** m spring; **Frühlingsrolle** f spring roll; **Frühlingszwiebel** f spring onion (Brit), scallion (US)

frühmorgens adv early in the morning

Frühstück nt breakfast; **frühstücken** vi to have breakfast; **Frühstücksbüfett** nt breakfast buffet; **Frühstücksfernsehen** nt breakfast television; **Frühstücksspeck** m bacon

frühzeitig adj early

Frust (-s) m (fam) frustration; **frustrieren** vt to frustrate

Fuchs (-es, Füchse) m fox

fühlen vt, vi to feel ▷ vr: **sich ~** to feel

fuhr imperf von **fahren**

führen vt to lead; (Geschäft) to run; (Name) to bear; (Buch) to keep ▷ vi to lead, to be in the lead ▷ vr: **sich ~** to behave; **Führerschein** m driving licence (Brit), driver's license (US); **Führung** f leadership; (eines Unternehmens) management; (*Mil*) command; (*in Museum, Stadt*) guided tour; **in ~ liegen** to be in the lead

füllen *vt* to fill; (*Gastr*) to stuff ▷ *vr*: **sich ~** to fill

Füller (*-s, -*) *m*, **Füllfederhalter** (*-s, -*) *m* fountain pen

Füllung *f* filling

Fund (*-(e)s, -e*) *m* find; **Fundbüro** *nt* lost property office (*Brit*), lost and found (*US*); **Fundsachen** *pl* lost property *sing*

fünf *num* five; **Fünf** (*-, -en*) *f* five; (*Schulnote*) ≈ E; **fünfhundert** *num* five hundred; **fünfmal** *adv* five times; **fünfte(r, s)** *adj* fifth; *siehe auch* **dritte**; **Fünftel** (*-s, -*) *nt* (*Bruchteil*) fifth; **fünfzehn** *num* fifteen; **fünfzehnte(r, s)** *adj* fifteenth; *siehe auch* **dritte**; **fünfzig** *num* fifty; **fünfzigste(r, s)** *adj* fiftieth

Funk (*-s*) *m* radio; **über ~** by radio

Funke (*-ns, -n*) *m* spark; **funkeln** *vi* to sparkle

Funkgerät *nt* radio set; **Funktaxi** *nt* radio taxi, radio cab

Funktion *f* function; **funktionieren** *vi* to work, to function; **Funktionstaste** *f* (*Inform*) function key

für *prep* +*akk* for; **was ~ (ein) ...?** what kind (*o* sort) of ...?; **Tag ~ Tag** day after day

Furcht (*-*) *f* fear; **furchtbar** *adj* terrible; **fürchten** *vt* to be afraid of, to fear ▷ *vr*: **sich ~** to be afraid (*vor* +*dat* of); **fürchterlich** *adj* awful

füreinander *adv* for each other

fürs *kontr von* **für das**

Fürst(in) (*-en, -en*) *m(f)* prince/princess; **Fürstentum** *nt* principality; **fürstlich** *adj* (*fig*) splendid

Furunkel (*-s, -*) *nt* boil

Furz (*-es, -e*) *m* (*vulg*) fart; **furzen** *vi* (*vulg*) to fart

Fuß (*-es, Füße*) *m* foot; (*von Glas, Säule etc*) base; (*von Möbel*) leg; **zu ~** on foot; **zu ~ gehen** to walk; **Fußball** *m* football (*Brit*), soccer; **Fußballmannschaft** *f* football (*Brit*) (*o* soccer) team; **Fußballplatz** *m* football pitch (*Brit*), soccer field (*US*); **Fußballspiel** *nt* football (*Brit*) (*o* soccer) match; **Fußballspieler(in)** *m(f)* footballer (*Brit*), soccer player; **Fußboden** *m* floor; **Fußgänger(in)** (*-s, -*) *m(f)* pedestrian; **Fußgängerüberweg** *m* pedestrian crossing (*Brit*), crosswalk (*US*); **Fußgängerzone** *f* pedestrian precinct (*Brit*) (*o* zone (*US*)); **Fußgelenk** *nt* ankle; **Fußpilz** *m* athlete's foot; **Fußtritt** *m* kick; **jdm einen ~ geben** to give sb a kick, to kick sb; **Fußweg** *m* footpath

Futon (*-s, -s*) *m* futon

Futter (*-s, -*) *nt* feed; (*Heu etc*) fodder; (*Stoff*) lining; **füttern** *vt* to feed; (*Kleidung*) to line

Futur (*-s, -e*) *nt* (*Ling*) future (tense)

Fuzzi (*-s, -s*) *m* (*fam*) guy

g

gab imperf von **geben**
Gabe (-, -n) f gift
Gabel (-, -n) f fork; **Gabelung** f fork
gaffen vi to gape
Gage (-, -n) f fee
gähnen vi to yawn
Galerie f gallery
Galle (-, -n) f gall; (Organ) gall bladder; **Gallenstein** m gallstone
Galopp (-s) m gallop; **galoppieren** vi to gallop
galt imperf von **gelten**
Gameboy® (-s, -s) m Gameboy®
gammeln vi to loaf (o hang) around; **Gammler(in)** (-s, -) m(f) layabout
gang adj: ~ **und gäbe sein** to be quite normal
Gang (-(e)s, Gänge) m walk; (im Flugzeug) aisle; (Essen, Ablauf) course; (Flur etc) corridor; (Durchgang) passage; (Auto) gear; **den zweiten ~ einlegen** to change into second (gear); **etw in ~ bringen** to get sth going; **Gangschaltung** f gears pl; **Gangway** (-, -s) f (Aviat) steps pl; (Naut) gangway
Gans (-, Gänse) f goose; **Gänseblümchen** nt daisy; **Gänsehaut** f goose pimples pl (Brit), goose bumps pl (US)
ganz adj whole; (vollständig) complete; ~ **Europa** all of Europe; **sein ~es Geld** all his money; **den ~en Tag** all day; **die ~e Zeit** all the time ▷ adv quite; (völlig) completely; **es hat mir ~ gut gefallen** I quite liked it; ~ **schön viel** quite a lot; ~ **und gar nicht** not at all; **das ist etwas ~ anderes** that's a completely different matter; **ganztägig** adj all-day; (Arbeit, Stelle) full-time
gar adj done, cooked ▷ adv at all; ~ **nicht/nichts/keiner** not/nothing/nobody at all; ~ **nicht schlecht** not bad at all
Garage (-, -n) f garage
Garantie f guarantee; **garantieren** vt to guarantee
Garderobe (-, -n) f (Kleidung) wardrobe; (Abgabe) cloakroom
Gardine f curtain
Garn (-(e)s, -e) nt thread
Garnele (-, -n) f shrimp
garnieren vt to decorate; (Speisen) to garnish
Garten (-s, Gärten) m garden; **Gärtner(in)** (-s, -) m(f) gardener; **Gärtnerei** f nursery; (Gemüsegärtnerei) market garden (Brit), truck farm (US)
Garzeit f cooking time
Gas (-es, -e) nt gas; ~ **geben** (Auto) to accelerate; (fig) to get a move on; **Gasanzünder** m gas lighter; **Gasbrenner** m gas burner;

Gasflasche f gas bottle;
Gasheizung f gas heating;
Gasherd m gas stove, gas cooker
(Brit); **Gaskocher** (-s, -) m
camping stove; **Gaspedal** nt
accelerator, gas pedal (US)
Gasse (-, -n) f alley
Gast (-es, Gäste) m guest; **Gäste
haben** to have guests;
Gastarbeiter(in) m(f) foreign
worker; **Gästebett** nt spare bed;
Gästebuch nt visitors' book;
Gästehaus nt guest house;
Gästezimmer nt guest room;
gastfreundlich adj hospitable;
Gastgeber(in) (-s, -) m(f) host/
hostess; **Gasthaus** nt, **Gasthof** m
inn; **Gastland** nt host country
Gastritis (-) f gastritis
Gastronomie f (Gewerbe)
catering trade
Gastspiel nt (Sport) away game;
Gaststätte f restaurant;
(Trinklokal) pub (Brit), bar;
Gastwirt(in) m(f) landlord/-lady
GAU (-s, -s) m akr = **größter
anzunehmender Unfall** MCA
Gaumen (-s, -) m palate
Gaze (-, -n) f gauze
geb. adj abk = **geboren** b. ▷ adj
abk = **geborene** née; siehe **geboren**
Gebäck (-(e)s, -e) nt pastries pl;
(Kekse) biscuits pl (Brit), cookies pl
(US)
gebacken pp von **backen**
Gebärdensprache f sign
language
Gebärmutter f womb
Gebäude (-s, -) nt building
geben (gab, gegeben) vt, vi to give
(jdm etw sb sth, sth to sb); (Karten)
to deal; **lass dir eine Quittung
~** ask for a receipt ▷ vt impers: **es
gibt** there is/are; (in Zukunft) there
will be; **das gibt's nicht** I don't
believe it ▷ vr: **sich ~** (sich
verhalten) to behave, to act; **das**

gibt sich wieder it'll sort itself out
Gebet (-(e)s, -e) nt prayer
gebeten pp von **bitten**
Gebiet (-(e)s, -e) nt area;
(Hoheitsgebiet) territory; (fig) field
gebildet adj educated; (belesen)
well-read
Gebirge (-s, -) nt mountains pl;
gebirgig adj mountainous
Gebiss (-es, -e) nt teeth pl;
(künstlich) dentures pl; **gebissen**
pp von **beißen**; **Gebissreiniger** m
denture tablets pl
Gebläse (-s, -) nt fan, blower
geblasen pp von **blasen**
geblieben pp von **bleiben**
gebogen pp von **biegen**
geboren pp von **gebären** ▷ adj
born; **Andrea Jordan, geborene
Christian** Andrea Jordan, née
Christian
geborgen pp von **bergen** ▷ adj
secure, safe
geboten pp von **bieten**
gebracht pp von **bringen**
gebrannt pp von **brennen**
gebraten pp von **braten**
gebrauchen vt to use;
Gebrauchsanweisung f direc-
tions pl for use; **gebrauchsfertig**
adj ready to use; **gebraucht** adj
used; **etw ~ kaufen** to buy sth
secondhand; **Gebrauchtwagen**
m secondhand (o used) car
gebräunt adj tanned
gebrochen pp von **brechen**
Gebühr (-, -en) f charge; (Maut)
toll; (Honorar) fee; **Gebühren-
einheit** f (Tel) unit;
gebührenfrei adj free of charge;
(Telefonnummer) freefone® (Brit),
toll-free (US); **gebührenpflichtig**
adj subject to charges; **~e Straße**
toll road
gebunden pp von **binden**
Geburt (-, -en) f birth; **gebürtig**
adj: **er ist ~er Schweizer** he is

Swiss by birth; **Geburtsdatum**
nt date of birth; **Geburtsjahr** nt
year of birth; **Geburtsname** m
birth name; (einer Frau) maiden
name; **Geburtsort** m birthplace;
Geburtstag m birthday;
herzlichen Glückwunsch zum ~!
Happy Birthday; **Geburtsurkunde**
f birth certificate
Gebüsch (-(e)s, -e) nt bushes pl
gedacht pp von **denken**
Gedächtnis nt memory; **im
~ behalten** to remember
Gedanke (-ns, -n) m thought;
sich (dat) **über etw** (akk) **~n
machen** to think about sth;
(besorgt) to be worried about sth;
Gedankenstrich m dash
Gedeck (-(e)s, -e) nt place
setting; (Speisenfolge) set meal
Gedenkstätte f memorial;
Gedenktafel f commemorative
plaque
Gedicht (-(e)s, -e) nt poem
Gedränge (-s) nt crush, crowd
gedrungen pp von **dringen**
Geduld (-) f patience; **geduldig**
adj patient
gedurft pp von **dürfen**
geehrt adj: **Sehr ~er Herr Young**
Dear Mr Young
geeignet adj suitable
Gefahr (-, -en) f danger; **auf
eigene ~** at one's own risk; **außer
~** out of danger; **gefährden** vt to
endanger
gefahren pp von **fahren**
gefährlich adj dangerous
Gefälle (-s, -) nt gradient, slope
gefallen pp von **fallen** ▷ irr vi:
jdm ~ to please sb; **er/es gefällt
mir** I like him/it; **sich** (dat) **etw
~ lassen** to put up with sth
Gefallen (-s, -) m favour; **jdm
einen ~ tun** to do sb a favour
gefälligst adv ..., will you!; **sei
~ still!** be quiet, will you!

gefangen pp von **fangen**
Gefängnis nt prison
Gefäß (-es, -e) nt (Behälter)
container, receptacle; (Anat, Bot)
vessel
gefasst adj composed, calm; **auf
etw** (akk) **~ sein** to be prepared (o
ready) for sth
geflochten pp von **flechten**
geflogen pp von **fliegen**
geflossen pp von **fließen**
Geflügel (-s) nt poultry
gefragt adj in demand
gefressen pp von **fressen**
Gefrierbeutel m freezer bag;
gefrieren irr vi to freeze;
Gefrierfach nt freezer
compartment; **Gefrierschrank**
m (upright) freezer; **Gefriertruhe**
f (chest) freezer
gefroren pp von **frieren**
Gefühl (-(e)s, -e) nt feeling
gefunden pp von **finden**
gegangen pp von **gehen**
gegeben pp von **geben**;
gegebenenfalls adv if need
be

⊙ SCHLÜSSELWORT

gegen prep +akk **1** against; **nichts
gegen jdn haben** to have nothing
against sb; **X gegen Y** (Sport, Jur)
versus Y; **ein Mittel gegen
Schnupfen** something for colds
2 (in Richtung auf) towards; **gegen
Osten** to(wards) the east; **gegen
Abend** towards evening; **gegen
einen Baum fahren** to drive into a
tree
3 (ungefähr) round about; **gegen 3
Uhr** around 3 o'clock
4 (gegenüber) towards; (ungefähr)
around; **gerecht gegen alle** fair to
all
5 (im Austausch für) for; **gegen bar**
for cash; **gegen Quittung** against

a receipt
6 (*verglichen mit*) compared with

Gegend (-, -en) *f* area; **hier in der ~** around here
gegeneinander *adv* against one another
Gegenfahrbahn *f* opposite lane; **Gegenmittel** *nt* remedy (*gegen* for); **Gegenrichtung** *f* opposite direction; **Gegensatz** *m* contrast; **im ~ zu** in contrast to; **gegensätzlich** *adj* conflicting; **gegenseitig** *adj* mutual; **sich ~ helfen** to help each other
Gegenstand *m* object; (*Thema*) subject
Gegenteil *nt* opposite; **im ~** on the contrary; **gegenteilig** *adj* opposite, contrary
gegenüber *prep* +*dat* opposite; (*zu jdm*) to(wards); (*angesichts*) in the face of ▷ *adv* opposite; **gegenüber|stehen** *vt* to face; (*Problemen*) to be faced with; **gegenüber|stellen** *vt* to confront (*dat* with); (*fig*) compare (*dat* with)
Gegenverkehr *m* oncoming traffic; **Gegenwart** (-) *f* present (tense)
Gegenwind *m* headwind
gegessen *pp von* **essen**
geglichen *pp von* **gleichen**
geglitten *pp von* **gleiten**
Gegner(in) (-s, -) *m(f)* opponent
gegolten *pp von* **gelten**
gegossen *pp von* **gießen**
gegraben *pp von* **graben**
gegriffen *pp von* **greifen**
gehabt *pp von* **haben**
Gehackte(s) *nt* mince(d meat) (*Brit*), ground meat (*US*)
Gehalt (-(e)s, -e) *m* content ▷ (-(e)s, *Gehälter*) *nt* salary
gehalten *pp von* **halten**
gehangen *pp von* **hängen**
gehässig *adj* spiteful, nasty

gehauen *pp von* **hauen**
gehbehindert *adj*: **sie ist ~** she can't walk properly
geheim *adj* secret; **etw ~ halten** to keep sth secret; **Geheimnis** *nt* secret; (*rätselhaft*) mystery; **geheimnisvoll** *adj* mysterious; **Geheimnummer** *f*, **Geheimzahl** *f* (*von Kreditkarte*) PIN number
geheißen *pp von* **heißen**
gehen (*ging, gegangen*) *vt, vi* to go; (*zu Fuß*) to walk; (*funktionieren*) to work; **über die Straße ~** to cross the street; **~ nach** (*Fenster*) to face ▷ *vi impers*: **wie geht es** (**dir**)? how are you (o things)?; **mir/ihm geht es gut** I'm/he's (doing) fine; **geht das?** is that possible?; **geht's noch?** can you still manage?; **es geht** not too bad, OK; **das geht nicht** that's not on; **es geht um ...** it's about ...
Gehirn (-(e)s, -e) *nt* brain; **Gehirnerschütterung** *f* concussion
gehoben *pp von* **heben**
geholfen *pp von* **helfen**
Gehör (-(e)s) *nt* hearing
gehorchen *vi* to obey (*jdm* sb)
gehören *vi* to belong (*jdm* to sb); **wem gehört das Buch?** whose book is this?; **gehört es dir?** is it yours? ▷ *vr impers*: **das gehört sich nicht** it's not done
gehörlos *adj* deaf
gehorsam *adj* obedient
Gehsteig *m*
Gehweg (-(e)s, -e) *m* pavement (*Brit*), sidewalk (*US*)
Geier (-s, -) *m* vulture
Geige (-, -n) *f* violin
geil *adj* randy (*Brit*), horny (*US*); (*fam: toll*) fantastic
Geisel (-, -n) *f* hostage
Geist (-(e)s, -er) *m* spirit; (*Gespenst*) ghost; (*Verstand*) mind; **Geisterbahn** *f* ghost train, tunnel

of horror (US); **Geisterfahrer(in)**
m(f) *person driving the wrong way on
the motorway*
geizig *adj* stingy
gekannt *pp von* **kennen**
geklungen *pp von* **klingen**
geknickt *adj* (*fig*) dejected
gekniffen *pp von* **kneifen**
gekommen *pp von* **kommen**
gekonnt *pp von* **können** ▷ *adj*
skilful
gekrochen *pp von* **kriechen**
Gel (-s, -s) *nt* gel
Gelächter (-s, -) *nt* laughter
geladen *pp von* **laden** ▷ *adj*
loaded; (*Elek*) live; (*fig*) furious
gelähmt *adj* paralysed
Gelände (-s, -) *nt* land, terrain;
(*Fabrik, Sportgelände*) grounds *pl*;
(*Baugelände*) site
Geländer (-s, -) *nt* railing;
(*Treppengeländer*) banister
Geländewagen *m* off-road
vehicle
gelang *imperf von* **gelingen**
gelassen *pp von* **lassen** ▷ *adj*
calm, composed
Gelatine *f* gelatine
gelaufen *pp von* **laufen**
gelaunt *adj*: **gut/schlecht ~** in a
good/bad mood
gelb *adj* yellow; (*Ampel*) amber,
yellow (*US*); **gelblich** *adj*
yellowish; **Gelbsucht** *f* jaundice
Geld (-(e)s, -er) *nt* money;
Geldautomat *m* cash machine (*o*
dispenser (*Brit*), ATM (*US*);
Geldbeutel *m*, **Geldbörse** *f*
purse; **Geldbuße** *f* fine;
Geldschein *m* (bank)note (*Brit*),
bill (*US*); **Geldstrafe** *f* fine;
Geldstück *nt* coin; **Geldwechsel**
m exchange of money; (*Ort*)
bureau de change;
Geldwechselautomat *m*,
Geldwechsler (-s, -) *m* change
machine

Gelee (-s, -s) *nt* jelly
gelegen *pp von* **liegen** ▷ *adj*
situated; (*passend*) convenient;
etw kommt jdm ~ sth is
convenient for sb
Gelegenheit *f* opportunity;
(*Anlass*) occasion
gelegentlich *adj* occasional
▷ *adv* occasionally; (*bei
Gelegenheit*) some time (or other)
Gelenk (-(e)s, -e) *nt* joint
gelernt *adj* skilled
gelesen *pp von* **lesen**
geliehen *pp von* **leihen**
gelingen (*gelang, gelungen*) *vi* to
succeed; **es ist mir gelungen, ihn
zu erreichen** I managed to get
hold of him
gelitten *pp von* **leiden**
gelockt *adj* curly
gelogen *pp von* **lügen**
gelten (*galt, gegolten*) *vt* (*wert
sein*) to be worth; **jdm viel/wenig
~** to mean a lot/not to mean much
to sb ▷ *vi* (*gültig sein*) to be valid;
(*erlaubt sein*) to be allowed; **jdm
~** (*gemünzt sein auf*) to be meant for
(*o* aimed at) sb; **etw ~ lassen** to
accept sth; **als etw ~** to be
considered to be sth;
Geltungsdauer *f*: **eine ~ von
fünf Tagen haben** to be valid for
five days
gelungen *pp von* **gelingen**
gemahlen *pp von* **mahlen**
Gemälde (-s, -) *nt* painting,
picture
gemäß *prep* +*dat* in accordance
with ▷ *adj* appropriate (*dat* to)
gemein *adj* (*niederträchtig*) mean,
nasty; (*gewöhnlich*) common
Gemeinde (-, -n) *f* district,
community; (*Pfarrgemeinde*)
parish; (*Kirchengemeinde*)
congregation
gemeinsam *adj* joint, common
▷ *adv* together, jointly; **das Haus**

gehört uns beiden ~ the house belongs to both of us

Gemeinschaft f community; **~ Unabhängiger Staaten** Commonwealth of Independent States

gemeint pp von **meinen; das war nicht so ~** I didn't mean it like that

gemessen pp von **messen**

gemieden pp von **meiden**

gemischt adj mixed

gemocht pp von **mögen**

Gemüse (-s, -) nt vegetables pl; **Gemüsehändler(in)** m(f) greengrocer

gemusst pp von **müssen**

gemustert adj patterned

gemütlich adj comfortable, cosy; (Mensch) good-natured, easy-going; **mach es dir ~** make yourself at home

genannt pp von **nennen**

genau adj exact, precise ▷ adv exactly, precisely; **~ in der Mitte** right in the middle; **es mit etw ~ nehmen** to be particular about sth; **~ genommen** strictly speaking; **ich weiß es ~** I know for certain (o for sure); **genauso** adv exactly the same (way); **~ gut/viel/viele Leute** just as well/much/many people (wie as)

genehmigen vt to approve; **sich** (dat) **etw ~** to indulge in sth; **Genehmigung** f approval

Generalkonsulat nt consulate general

Generation f generation

Genf (-s) nt Geneva; **~er See** Lake Geneva

Genforschung f genetic research

genial adj brilliant

Genick (-(e)s, -e) nt (back of the) neck

Genie (-s, -s) nt genius

genieren vr: **sich ~** to feel awkward; **ich geniere mich vor ihm** he makes me feel embarrassed

genießen (genoss, genossen) vt to enjoy

Genitiv m genitive (case)

genmanipuliert adj genetically modified, GM

genommen pp von **nehmen**

genoss imperf von **genießen**

genossen pp von **genießen**

Gentechnik f genetic technology; **gentechnisch** adv: **~ verändert** genetically modified, GM

genug adv enough

genügen vi. to be enough (jdm for sb); **danke, das genügt** thanks, that's enough (o that will do)

Genuss (-es, Genüsse) m pleasure; (Zusichnehmen) consumption

geöffnet adj (Geschäft etc) open

Geografie f geography

Geologie f geology

Georgien (-s) nt Georgia

Gepäck (-(e)s) nt luggage (Brit), baggage; **Gepäckabfertigung** f luggage (Brit) (o baggage) check-in; **Gepäckablage** f luggage (Brit) (o baggage) rack; **Gepäckannahme** f (zur Beförderung) luggage (Brit) (o baggage) office; (zur Aufbewahrung) left-luggage office (Brit), baggage checkroom (US); **Gepäckaufbewahrung** f left-luggage office (Brit), baggage checkroom (US); **Gepäckausgabe** f luggage (Brit) (o baggage) office; (am Flughafen) baggage reclaim; **Gepäckband** nt luggage (Brit) (o baggage) conveyor; **Gepäckkontrolle** f luggage (Brit) (o baggage) check; **Gepäckstück** nt item of luggage (Brit) (o baggage (US)); **Gepäckträger** m porter; (an Fahrrad) carrier;

Gepäckversicherung f luggage (Brit) (o baggage) insurance;
Gepäckwagen m luggage van (Brit), baggage car (US)
gepfiffen pp von **pfeifen**
gepflegt adj well-groomed; (Park) well looked after
gequollen pp von **quellen**

○ SCHLÜSSELWORT

gerade adj straight; (aufrecht) upright; **eine gerade Zahl** an even number
▷ adv **1** (genau) just, exactly; (speziell) especially; **gerade deshalb** that's just o exactly why; **das ist es ja gerade!** that's just it!; **gerade du** you especially; **warum gerade ich?** why me (of all people)?; **jetzt gerade nicht!** not now!; **gerade neben** right next to **2** (eben, soeben) just; **er wollte gerade aufstehen** he was just about to get up; **gerade erst** only just; **gerade noch** (only) just

geradeaus adv straight ahead
gerannt pp von **rennen**
geraspelt adj grated
Gerät (-(e)s, -e) nt device, gadget; (Werkzeug) tool; (Radio, Fernseher) set; (Zubehör) equipment
geraten pp von **raten** ▷ irr vi to turn out; **gut/schlecht ~** to turn out well/badly; **an jdn ~** to come across sb; **in etw** (akk) **~** to get into sth
geräuchert adj smoked
geräumig adj roomy
Geräusch (-(e)s, -e) nt sound; (unangenehm) noise
gerecht adj fair; (Strafe, Belohnung) just; **jdm/einer Sache ~ werden** to do justice to sb/sth
gereizt adj irritable

Gericht (-(e)s, -e) nt (Jur) court; (Essen) dish
gerieben pp von **reiben**
gering adj small; (unbedeutend) slight; (niedrig) low; (Zeit) short; **geringfügig** adj slight, minor ▷ adv slightly
gerissen pp von **reißen**
geritten pp von **reiten**
gern(e) adv willingly, gladly; **etw ~ tun** to like doing sth; **~ geschehen** you're welcome; **gern|haben, gern mögen** irr vt to like
gerochen pp von **riechen**
Gerste (-, -n) f barley; **Gerstenkorn** nt (im Auge) stye
Geruch (-(e)s, Gerüche) m smell
Gerücht (-(e)s, -e) nt rumour
gerufen pp von **rufen**
Gerümpel (-s) nt junk
gerungen pp von **ringen**
Gerüst (-(e)s, -e) nt (auf Bau) scaffolding; (Gestell) trestle; (fig) framework (zu of)
gesalzen pp von **salzen**
gesamt adj whole, entire; (Kosten) total; (Werke) complete; **Gesamtschule** f ≈ comprehensive school
gesandt pp von **senden**
Gesäß (-es, -e) nt bottom
geschaffen pp von **schaffen**
Geschäft (-(e)s, -e) nt business; (Laden) shop; (Geschäftsabschluss) deal; **geschäftlich** adj commercial ▷ adv on business; **Geschäftsfrau** f businesswoman; **Geschäftsführer(in)** m(f) managing director; (von Laden) manager; **Geschäftsleitung** f executive board; **Geschäftsmann** m businessman; **Geschäftsreise** f business trip; **Geschäftsstraße** f shopping street; **Geschäftszeiten** pl business (o opening) hours pl

geschehen (*geschah, geschehen*) *vi* to happen

Geschenk (-(*e*)*s*, -*e*) *nt* present, gift; **Geschenkgutschein** *m* gift voucher; **Geschenkpapier** *nt* gift-wrapping paper, giftwrap

Geschichte (-, -*n*) *f* story; (*Sache*) affair; (*Hist*) history

geschickt *adj* skilful

geschieden *pp von* **scheiden** ▷ *adj* divorced

geschienen *pp von* **scheinen**

Geschirr (-(*e*)*s*, -*e*) *nt* crockery; (*zum Kochen*) pots and pans *pl*; (*von Pferd*) harness; **~ spülen** to do (*o* wash) the dishes, to do the washing-up (*Brit*);
Geschirrspülmaschine *f* dishwasher; **Geschirrspülmittel** *nt* washing-up liquid (*Brit*), dishwashing liquid (*US*);
Geschirrtuch *nt* tea towel (*Brit*), dish towel (*US*)

geschissen *pp von* **scheißen**

geschlafen *pp von* **schlafen**

geschlagen *pp von* **schlagen**

Geschlecht (-(*e*)*s*, -*er*) *nt* sex; (*Ling*) gender; **Geschlechtskrankheit** *f* sexually transmitted disease, STD; **Geschlechtsorgan** *nt* sexual organ;
Geschlechtsverkehr *m* sexual intercourse

geschlichen *pp von* **schleichen**

geschliffen *pp von* **schleifen**

geschlossen *adj* closed

Geschmack (-(*e*)*s*, *Geschmäcke*) *m* taste; **geschmacklos** *adj* tasteless; **Geschmack(s)sache** *f*: **das ist ~** that's a matter of taste; **geschmackvoll** *adj* tasteful

geschmissen *pp von* **schmeißen**

geschmolzen *pp von* **schmelzen**

geschnitten *pp von* **schneiden**

geschoben *pp von* **schieben**

Geschoss (-*es*, -*e*) *nt* (*Stockwerk*) floor

geschossen *pp von* **schießen**

Geschrei (-*s*) *nt* cries *pl*; (*fig*) fuss

geschrieben *pp von* **schreiben**

geschrie(e)n *pp von* **schreien**

geschützt *adj* protected

Geschwätz (-*es*) *nt* chatter; (*Klatsch*) gossip; **geschwätzig** *adj* talkative, gossipy

geschweige *adv*: **~ (denn)** let alone

geschwiegen *pp von* **schweigen**

Geschwindigkeit *f* speed; (*Phys*) velocity; **Geschwindigkeitsbegrenzung** *f* speed limit

Geschwister *pl* brothers and sisters *pl*

geschwollen *adj* (*angeschwollen*) swollen; (*Rede*) pompous

geschwommen *pp von* **schwimmen**

geschworen *pp von* **schwören**

Geschwulst (-, *Geschwülste*) *f* growth

Geschwür (-(*e*)*s*, -*e*) *nt* ulcer

gesehen *pp von* **sehen**

gesellig *adj* sociable;
Gesellschaft *f* society; (*Begleitung*) company; (*Abend~*) party; **~ mit beschränkter Haftung** limited company (*Brit*), limited corporation (*US*)

gesessen *pp von* **sitzen**

Gesetz (-*es*, -*e*) *nt* law; **gesetzlich** *adj* legal; **~er Feiertag** public (*o* bank (*Brit*) *o* legal (*US*)) holiday; **gesetzwidrig** *adj* illegal

Gesicht (-(*e*)*s*, -*er*) *nt* face; (*Miene*) expression; **mach doch nicht so ein ~!** stop pulling such a face; **Gesichtscreme** *f* face cream; **Gesichtswasser** *nt* toner

gesoffen *pp von* **saufen**

gesogen *pp von* **saugen**

gespannt *adj* tense; (*begierig*) eager; **ich bin ~, ob ...** I wonder if ...; **auf etw/jdn ~ sein** to look forward to sth/to seeing sb

Gespenst (-(e)s, -er) nt ghost

gesperrt adj closed

gesponnen pp von **spinnen**

Gespräch (-(e)s, -e) nt talk, conversation; (Diskussion) discussion; (Anruf) call

gesprochen pp von **sprechen**

gesprungen pp von **springen**

Gestalt (-, -en) f form, shape; (Mensch) figure

gestanden pp von **stehen, gestehen**

Gestank (-(e)s) m stench

gestatten vt to permit, to allow; ~ **Sie?** may I?

Geste (-, -n) f gesture

gestehen irr vt to confess

gestern adv yesterday; ~ **Abend/Morgen** yesterday evening/morning

gestiegen pp von **steigen**

gestochen pp von **stechen**

gestohlen pp von **stehlen**

gestorben pp von **sterben**

gestört adj disturbed; (Empfang) poor

gestoßen pp von **stoßen**

gestreift adj striped

gestrichen pp von **streichen**

gestritten pp von **streiten**

gestunken pp von **stinken**

gesund adj healthy; **wieder** ~ **werden** to get better; **Gesundheit** f health; ~! bless you!; **gesundheitsschädlich** adj unhealthy

gesungen pp von **singen**

gesunken pp von **sinken**

getan pp von **tun**

getragen pp von **tragen**

Getränk (-(e)s, -e) nt drink; **Getränkeautomat** m drinks machine; **Getränkekarte** f list of drinks

Getreide (-s, -) nt cereals pl, grain

getrennt adj separate; ~ **leben** to live apart; ~ **zahlen** to pay separately

getreten pp von **treten**

Getriebe (-s, -) nt (Auto) gearbox

getrieben pp von **treiben**

Getriebeschaden m gearbox damage

getroffen pp von **treffen**

getrunken pp von **trinken**

Getue nt fuss

geübt adj experienced

gewachsen pp von **wachsen** ▷ adj: **jdm/einer Sache** ~ **sein** to be a match for sb/up to sth

Gewähr (-) f guarantee; **keine** ~ **übernehmen für** to accept no responsibility for

Gewalt (-, -en) f (Macht) power; (Kontrolle) control; (große Kraft) force; (~taten) violence; **mit aller** ~ with all one's might; **gewaltig** adj tremendous; (Irrtum) huge

gewandt pp von **wenden** ▷ adj (flink) nimble; (geschickt) skilful

gewann imperf von **gewinnen**

gewaschen pp von **waschen**

Gewebe (-s, -) nt (Stoff) fabric; (Bio) tissue

Gewehr (-(e)s, -e) nt rifle, gun

Geweih (-(e)s, -e) nt antlers pl

gewellt adj (Haare) wavy

gewendet pp von **wenden**

Gewerbe (-s, -) nt trade; **Gewerbegebiet** nt industrial estate (Brit) (o park (US)); **gewerblich** adj commercial

Gewerkschaft f trade union

gewesen pp von **sein**

Gewicht (-(e)s, -e) nt weight; (fig) importance

gewiesen pp von **weisen**

Gewinn (-(e)s, -e) m profit; (bei Spiel) winnings pl; **gewinnen** (gewann, gewonnen) vt to win; (erwerben) to gain; (Kohle, Öl) to extract ▷ vi to win; (profitieren) to gain; **Gewinner(in)** (-s, -) m(f) winner

gewiss adj certain ▷ adv certainly

Gewissen (-s, -) nt conscience; **ein gutes/schlechtes ~ haben** to have a clear/bad conscience

Gewitter (-s, -) nt thunderstorm; **gewittern** vi impers: **es gewittert** it's thundering

gewogen pp von **wiegen**

gewöhnen vt **jdn an etw** (akk) **~** to accustom sb to sth ▷ vr: **sich an jdn/etw ~** to get used (o accustomed) to sb/sth; **Gewohnheit** f habit; (Brauch) custom; **gewöhnlich** adj usual; (durchschnittlich) ordinary; (pej) common; **wie ~** as usual; **gewohnt** adj usual; **etw ~ sein** to be used to sth

Gewölbe (-s, -) nt (Deckengewölbe) vault

gewonnen pp von **gewinnen**

geworben pp von **werben**

geworden pp von **werden**

geworfen pp von **werfen**

Gewürz (-es, -e) nt spice; **Gewürznelke** f clove; **gewürzt** adj seasoned

gewusst pp von **wissen**

Gezeiten pl tides pl

gezogen pp von **ziehen**

gezwungen pp von **zwingen**

Gibraltar (-s) nt Gibraltar

Gicht (-) f gout

Giebel (-s, -) m gable

gierig adj greedy

gießen (goss, gegossen) vt to pour; (Blumen) to water; (Metall) to cast; **Gießkanne** f watering can

Gift (-(e)s, -e) nt poison; **giftig** adj poisonous

Gigabyte nt gigabyte

Gin (-s, -s) m gin

ging imperf von **gehen**

Gin Tonic (-(s), -s) m gin and tonic

Gipfel (-s, -) m summit, peak; (Pol) summit; (fig: Höhepunkt) height

Gips (-es, -e) m (a. Med) plaster; **Gipsbein** nt: **sie hat ein ~** she's got her leg in plaster; **Gipsverband** m plaster cast

Giraffe (-, -n) f giraffe

Girokonto nt current account (Brit), checking account (US)

Gitarre (-, -n) f guitar

Gitter (-s, -) nt bars pl

glänzen vi (a. fig) to shine; **glänzend** adj shining; (fig) brilliant

Glas (-es, Gläser) nt glass; (Marmelade) jar; **zwei ~ Wein** two glasses of wine; **Glascontainer** m bottle bank; **Glaser(in)** m(f) glazier; **Glasscheibe** f pane (of glass); **Glassplitter** m splinter of glass

Glasur f glaze; (Gastr) icing

glatt adj smooth; (rutschig) slippery; (Lüge) downright; **Glatteis** nt (black) ice

Glatze (-, -n) f bald head; (fam: Skinhead) skinhead

glauben vt, vi to believe (an +akk in); (meinen) to think; **jdm ~** to believe sb

gleich adj equal; (identisch) same, identical; **alle Menschen sind ~** all people are the same; **es ist mir ~** it's all the same to me ▷ adv equally; (sofort) straight away; (bald) in a minute; **~ groß/alt** the same size/age; **~ nach/an** right after/at; **Gleichberechtigung** f equal rights pl; **gleichen** (glich, geglichen) vi: **jdm/einer Sache ~** to be like sb/sth ▷ vr: **sich ~** to be alike; **gleichfalls** adv likewise; **danke ~!** thanks, and the same to you; **gleichgültig** adj indifferent; **gleichmäßig** adj regular; (Verteilung) even, equal;

gleichzeitig adj simultaneous ▷ adv at the same time

Gleis (-es, -e) nt track, rails pl; (Bahnsteig) platform

gleiten (glitt, geglitten) vi to glide; (rutschen) to slide; **Gleitschirmfliegen** (-s) nt paragliding

Gletscher (-s, -) m glacier; **Gletscherskifahren** nt glacier skiing; **Gletscherspalte** f crevasse

glich imperf von **gleichen**

Glied (-(e)s, -er) nt (Arm, Bein) limb; (von Kette) link; (Penis) penis; **Gliedmaßen** pl limbs pl

glitschig adj slippery

glitt imperf von **gleiten**

glitzern vi to glitter; (Sterne) to twinkle

Glocke (-, -n) f bell; **Glockenspiel** nt chimes pl

Glotze (-, -n) f (fam: TV) box; **glotzen** vi (fam) to stare

Glück (-(e)s) nt luck; (Freude) happiness; **~ haben** to be lucky; **viel ~!** good luck; **zum ~** fortunately; **glücklich** adj lucky; (froh) happy; **glücklicherweise** adv fortunately; **Glückwunsch** m congratulations pl; **herzlichen ~ zur bestandenen Prüfung** congratulations on passing your exam; **herzlichen ~ zum Geburtstag!** Happy Birthday

Glühbirne f light bulb; **glühen** vi to glow; **Glühwein** m mulled wine

GmbH (-, -s) f abk = **Gesellschaft mit beschränkter Haftung** ≈ Ltd (Brit), ≈ Inc (US)

Gokart (-(s), -s) m go-kart

Gold (-(e)s) nt gold; **golden** adj gold; (fig) golden; **Goldfisch** m goldfish; **Goldmedaille** f gold medal; **Goldschmied(in)** m(f) goldsmith

Golf (-(e)s, -e) m gulf; **der ~ von Biskaya** the Bay of Biscay ▷ (-s) nt golf; **Golfplatz** m golf course; **Golfschläger** m golf club

Gondel (-, -n) f gondola; (Seilbahn) cable-car

gönnen vt: **ich gönne es ihm** I'm really pleased for him; **sich** (dat) **etw ~** to allow oneself sth

goss imperf von **gießen**

gotisch adj Gothic

Gott (-es, Götter) m God; (Gottheit) god; **Gottesdienst** m service; **Göttin** f goddess

Grab (-(e)s, Gräber) nt grave

graben (grub, gegraben) vt to dig; **Graben** (-s, Gräben) m ditch

Grabstein m gravestone

Grad (-(e)s, -e) m degree; **wir haben 30 ~ Celsius** it's 30 degrees Celsius, it's 86 degrees Fahrenheit; **bis zu einem gewissen ~** up to a certain extent

Graf (-en, -en) m count; (in Großbritannien) earl

Graffiti pl graffiti sing

Grafik (-, -en) f graph; (Kunstwerk) graphic; (Illustration) diagram; **Grafikkarte** f (Inform) graphics card; **Grafikprogramm** nt (Inform) graphics software

Gräfin (-, -nen) f countess

Gramm (-s) nt gram(me)

Grammatik f grammar

Grapefruit (-, -s) f grapefruit

Graphik f siehe **Grafik**

Gras (-es, Gräser) nt grass

grässlich adj horrible

Gräte (-, -n) f (fish)bone

gratis adj, adv free (of charge)

gratulieren vi: **jdm** (**zu etw**) **~** to congratulate sb (on sth); (**ich**) **gratuliere!** congratulations!

grau adj grey, gray (US); **grauhaarig** adj grey-haired

grausam adj cruel

gravierend adj (Fehler) serious
greifen (griff, gegriffen) vt to seize; **zu etw ~** (fig) to resort to sth ▷ vi (Regel etc) to have an effect (bei on)
grell adj harsh
Grenze (-, -n) f boundary; (Staat) border; (Schranke) limit; **grenzen** vi to border (an +akk on); **Grenzkontrolle** f border control; **Grenzübergang** m border crossing point; **Grenzverkehr** m border traffic
Grieche (-n, -n) m Greek; **Griechenland** nt Greece; **Griechin** f Greek; **griechisch** adj Greek; **Griechisch** nt Greek
griesgrämig adj grumpy
Grieß (-es, -e) m (Gastr) semolina
griff imperf von **greifen**
Griff (-(e)s, -e) m grip; (Tür etc) handle; **griffbereit** adj handy
Grill (-s, -s) m grill; (im Freien) barbecue
Grille (-, -n) f cricket
grillen vt to grill ▷ vi to have a barbecue; **Grillfest** nt, **Grillfete** f barbecue; **Grillkohle** f charcoal
grinsen vi to grin; (höhnisch) to sneer
Grippe (-, -n) f flu; **Grippeschutzimpfung** f flu vaccination
grob adj coarse; (Fehler, Verstoß) gross; (Einschätzung) rough
Grönland (-s) nt Greenland
groß adj big, large; (hoch) tall; (fig) great; (Buchstabe) capital; (erwachsen) grown-up; **im Großen und Ganzen** on the whole ▷ adv greatly; **großartig** adj wonderful
Großbritannien (-s) nt (Great) Britain
Großbuchstabe m capital letter
Größe (-, -n) f size; (Länge) height; (fig) greatness; **welche**

~ haben Sie? what size do you take?
Großeltern pl grandparents pl; **Großhandel** m wholesale trade; **Großmarkt** m hypermarket; **Großmutter** f grandmother; **Großraum** m: **der ~ Manchester** Greater Manchester; **groß|schreiben** irr vt to write with a capital letter; **Großstadt** f city; **Großvater** m grandfather; **großzügig** adj generous; (Planung) on a large scale
Grotte (-, -n) f grotto
grub imperf von **graben**
Grübchen nt dimple
Grube (-, -n) f pit
grüezi interj (schweizerisch) hello
Gruft (-, -en) f vault
grün adj green; **~e Bohnen** French beans; **der ~e Punkt** symbol for recyclable packaging; **im ~en Bereich** hunky-dory

● GRÜNER PUNKT
●
●   The **grüner Punkt** is the green
●   spot symbol which appears on
●   packaging, indicating that the
●   packaging should not be
●   thrown into the normal
●   household refuse but kept
●   separate to be recycled through
●   the **DSD** (Duales System
●   Deutschland) system. The
●   recycling is financed by licences
●   bought by the manufacturer
●   from the 'DSD' and the cost of
●   this is often passed on to the
●   consumer.

Grünanlage f park
Grund (-(e)s, Gründe) m (Ursache) reason; (Erdboden) ground; (See, Gefäß) bottom; (Grundbesitz) land, property; **aus gesundheitlichen**

Gründen for health reasons; **im ~e** basically; **aus diesem ~** for this reason

gründen vt to found; **Gründer(in)** m(f) founder

Grundgebühr f basic charge; **Grundgesetz** nt (German) Constitution

gründlich adj thorough

Gründonnerstag m Maundy Thursday

grundsätzlich adj fundamental, basic; **sie kommt ~ zu spät** she's always late; **Grundschule** f primary school; **Grundstück** nt plot; (Anwesen) estate; (Baugrundstück) site; **Grundwasser** nt ground water

Grüne(r) mf (Pol) Green; **die ~n** the Green Party

Gruppe (-, -n) f group; **Gruppenermäßigung** f group discount; **Gruppenreise** f group tour

Gruß (-es, Grüße) m greeting; **viele Grüße** best wishes; **Grüße an** (+akk) regards to; **mit freundlichen Grüßen** Yours sincerely (Brit), Sincerely yours (US); **sag ihm einen schönen ~ von mir** give him my regards; **grüßen** vt to greet; **grüß deine Mutter von mir** give your mother my regards; **Julia lässt (euch) ~** Julia sends (you) her regards

gucken vi to look

Gulasch (-(e)s, -e) nt goulash

gültig adj valid

Gummi (-s, -s) m o nt rubber; **Gummiband** nt rubber (o elastic (Brit)) band; **Gummibärchen** pl gums (in the shape of a bear) (Brit), gumdrops pl (in the shape of a bear) (US); **Gummihandschuhe** pl rubber gloves pl; **Gummistiefel** m wellington (boot) (Brit), rubber boot (US)

günstig adj favourable; (Preis) good

gurgeln vi to gurgle; (im Mund) to gargle

Gurke (-, -n) f cucumber; **saure ~** gherkin

Gurt (-(e)s, -e) m belt

Gürtel (-s, -) m belt; (Geo) zone; **Gürtelrose** f shingles sing

GUS (-) f akr = **Gemeinschaft Unabhängiger Staaten** CIS

O SCHLÜSSELWORT

gut adj good; **alles Gute** all the best; **also gut** all right then ▷ adv well; **gut gehen** to work, to come off; **es geht jdm gut** sb's doing fine; **gut gemeint** well meant; **gut schmecken** to taste good; **jdm guttun** to do sb good; **gut, aber ...** OK, but ...; **(na) gut, ich komme** all right, I'll come; **gut drei Stunden** a good three hours; **das kann gut sein** that may well be; **lass es gut sein** that'll do

Gutachten (-s, -) nt report; **Gutachter(in)** (-s, -) m(f) expert

gutartig adj (Med) benign

Güter pl goods pl; **Güterbahnhof** m goods station; **Güterzug** m goods train

gutgläubig adj trusting; **Guthaben** (-s) nt (credit) balance

gutmütig adj good-natured

Gutschein m voucher; **Gutschrift** f credit

Gymnasium nt ≈ grammar school (Brit), ≈ high school (US)

Gymnastik f exercises pl, keep-fit

Gynäkologe m, **Gynäkologin** f gynaecologist

Gyros (-, -) nt doner kebab

h

you mind if ...?; **was hast du denn?** what's the matter (with you)?

Haben nt (Comm) credit

Habicht (-(e)s, -e) m hawk

Hacke (-, -n) f (im Garten) hoe; (Ferse) heel; **hacken** vt to chop; (Loch) to hack; (Erde) to hoe; **Hacker(in)** (-s, -) m(f) (Inform) hacker; **Hackfleisch** nt mince(d meat) (Brit), ground meat (US)

Hafen (-s, Häfen) m harbour; (großer) port; **Hafenstadt** f port

Hafer (-s, -) m oats pl; **Haferflocken** pl rolled oats pl

Haft (-) f custody; **haftbar** adj liable, responsible; **haften** vi to stick; **~ für** to be liable (o responsible) for; **Haftnotiz** f Post-it®; **Haftpflichtversicherung** f third party insurance; **Haftung** f liability

Hagebutte (-, -n) f rose hip

Hagel (-s) m hail; **hageln** vi impers to hail

Hahn (-(e)s, Hähne) m cock; (Wasserhahn) tap (Brit), faucet (US); **Hähnchen** nt cockerel; (Gastr) chicken

Hai(fisch) (-(e)s, -e) m shark

häkeln vi, vt to crochet; **Häkelnadel** f crochet hook

Haken (-s, -) m hook; (Zeichen) tick

halb adj half; **~ eins** half past twelve; (fam) half twelve; **eine ~e Stunde** half an hour; **~ offen** half-open; **Halbfinale** nt semifinal; **halbieren** vt to halve; **Halbinsel** f peninsula; **Halbjahr** nt half-year; **halbjährlich** adj half-yearly; **Halbmond** m (Astr) half-moon; (Symbol) crescent; **Halbpension** f half board; **halbseitig** adj: **~ gelähmt** paralyzed on one side; **halbtags**

Haar (-(e)s, -e) nt hair; **um ein ~** nearly; **sich** (dat) **die ~e schneiden lassen** to have one's hair cut; **Haarbürste** f hairbrush; **Haarfestiger** m setting lotion; **Haargel** nt hair gel; **haarig** adj hairy; (fig) nasty; **Haarschnitt** m haircut; **Haarspange** f hair slide (Brit), barrette (US); **Haarspliss** m split ends pl; **Haarspray** nt hair spray; **Haartrockner** (-s, -) m hairdryer; **Haarwaschmittel** nt shampoo; **Haarwasser** nt hair tonic

haben (hatte, gehabt) vt, vaux to have; **Hunger/Angst ~** to be hungry/afraid; **Ferien ~** to be on holiday (Brit) (o vacation (US)); **welches Datum ~ wir heute?** what's the date today?; **ich hätte gerne ...** I'd like ...; **hätten Sie etwas dagegen, wenn ...?** would

adv (*arbeiten*) part-time; **halbwegs**
adv (*leidlich*) reasonably; **Halbzeit**
f half; (*Pause*) half-time
half *imperf von* **helfen**; **Hälfte**
(*-, -n*) *f* half
Halle (*-, -n*) *f* hall; **Hallenbad** *nt*
indoor (swimming) pool
hallo *interj* hello, hi
Halogenlampe *f* halogen lamp;
Halogenscheinwerfer *m* halogen headlight
Hals (*-es, Hälse*) *m* neck; (*Kehle*)
throat; **Halsband** *nt* (*für Tiere*)
collar; **Halsentzündung** *f* sore
throat; **Halskette** *f* necklace;
Hals-Nasen-Ohren-Arzt *m*,
Hals-Nasen-Ohren-Ärztin *f* ear,
nose and throat specialist;
Halsschmerzen *pl* sore throat
sing; **Halstuch** *nt* scarf
halt *interj* stop ▷ *adv*: **das ist ~ so**
that's just the way it is; **Halt** (*-(e)s,
-e*) *m* stop; (*fester*) hold; (*innerer*)
stability
haltbar *adj* durable; (*Lebensmittel*)
non-perishable; **Haltbarkeitsdatum** *nt* best-before
date
halten (*hielt, gehalten*) *vt* to keep;
(*festhalten*) to hold; **~ für** to regard
as; **~ von** to think of; **den
Elfmeter ~** to save the penalty;
eine Rede ~ to give (*o* make) a
speech ▷ *vi* to hold; (*frisch bleiben*)
to keep; (*stoppen*) to stop; **zu jdm
~** to stand by sb ▷ *vr*: **sich ~** (*frisch
bleiben*) to keep; (*sich behaupten*) to
hold out
Haltestelle *f* stop; **Halteverbot**
nt: **hier ist ~** you can't stop here
Haltung *f* (*Körper*) posture; (*fig*)
attitude; (*Selbstbeherrschung*)
composure; **~ bewahren** to keep
one's composure
Hamburg (*-s*) *nt* Hamburg;
Hamburger (*-s, -*) *m* (*Gastr*)
hamburger

Hammelfleisch *nt* mutton
Hammer (*-s, Hämmer*) *m* hammer; (*fig, fam: Fehler*) howler; **das
ist der ~** (*unerhört*) that's a bit
much
Hämorr(ho)iden *pl* haemorrhoids *pl*, piles *pl*
Hamster (*-s, -*) *m* hamster
Hand (*-, Hände*) *f* hand; **jdm die
~ geben** to shake hands with sb;
jdn bei der ~ nehmen to take sb
by the hand; **eine ~ voll
Reis/Leute** a handful of
rice/people; **zu Händen von**
attention; **Handarbeit** *f*
(*Schulfach*) handicraft; **~ sein** to be
handmade; **Handball** *m*
handball; **Handbremse** *f*
handbrake; **Handbuch** *nt*
handbook, manual; **Handcreme**
f hand cream; **Händedruck** *m*
handshake
Handel (*-s*) *m* trade; (*Geschäft*)
transaction; **handeln** *vi* to act;
(*Comm*) to trade; **~ von** to be
about ▷ *vr impers*: **sich ~ um** to
be about; **es handelt sich um ...**
it's about ...; **Handelskammer** *f*
chamber of commerce;
Handelsschule *f* business school
Handfeger (*-s, -*) *m* brush;
Handfläche *f* palm; **Handgelenk**
nt wrist; **handgemacht** *adj*
handmade; **Handgepäck** *nt*
hand luggage (*Brit*) (*o* baggage)
Händler(in) (*-s, -*) *m(f)* dealer
handlich *adj* handy
Handlung *f* act, action; (*von
Roman, Film*) plot
Handschellen *pl* handcuffs *pl*;
Handschrift *f* handwriting;
Handschuh *m* glove;
Handschuhfach *nt* glove
compartment; **Handtasche** *f*
handbag, purse (*US*); **Handtuch**
nt towel; **Handwerk** *nt* trade;
(*Kunst~*) craft; **Handwerker** (*-s, -*)

m workman

Handy (*-s, -s*) *nt* mobile (phone) (*Brit*), cell phone (*US*); **Handynummer** *f* mobile number (*Brit*), cell phone number (*US*)

Hanf (*-(e)s*) *m* hemp

Hang (*-(e)s, Hänge*) *m* (*Abhang*) slope; (*fig*) tendency

Hängebrücke *f* suspension bridge; **Hängematte** *f* hammock

hängen (*hing, gehangen*) *vi* to hang; **an der Wand/an der Decke ~** to hang on the wall/from the ceiling; **an jdm ~** (*fig*) to be attached to sb; **~ bleiben** to get caught (*an +dat* on); (*fig*) to get stuck ▷ *vt* to hang (*an +akk* on)

Hantel (*-, -n*) *f* dumbbell

Hardware (*-, -s*) *f* (*Inform*) hardware

Harfe (*-, -n*) *f* harp

harmlos *adj* harmless

harmonisch *adj* harmonious

Harn (*-(e)s, -e*) *m* urine; **Harnblase** *f* bladder

Harpune (*-, -n*) *f* harpoon

hart *adj* hard; (*fig*) harsh; **zu jdm ~ sein** to be hard on sb; **~ gekocht** (*Ei*) hard-boiled; **hartnäckig** *adj* stubborn

Haschee (*-s, -s*) *nt* hash

Haschisch (*-*) *nt* hashish

Hase (*-n, -n*) *m* hare

Haselnuss *f* hazelnut

Hasenscharte *f* (*Med*) harelip

Hass (*-es*) *m* hatred (*auf, gegen +akk* of), hate; **einen ~ kriegen** (*fam*) to see red; **hassen** *vt* to hate

hässlich *adj* ugly; (*gemein*) nasty

Hast (*-*) *f* haste, hurry; **hastig** *adj* hasty

hatte *imperf von* **haben**

Haube (*-, -n*) *f* hood; (*Mütze*) cap; (*Auto*) bonnet (*Brit*), hood (*US*)

Hauch (*-(e)s, -e*) *m* breath; (*Luft~*) breeze; (*fig*) trace; **hauchdünn** *adj* (*Schicht, Scheibe*) wafer-thin

hauen (*haute, gehauen*) *vt* to hit

Haufen (*-s, -*) *m* pile; **ein ~ Geld** (*viel Geld*) a lot of money

häufig *adj* frequent ▷ *adv* frequently, often

Haupt- *in zW* main: **Hauptbahnhof** *m* central (*o* main) station; **Hauptdarsteller(in)** *m(f)* leading actor/lady; **Haupteingang** *m* main entrance; **Hauptgericht** *nt* main course; **Hauptgeschäftszeiten** *pl* peak shopping hours *pl*; **Hauptgewinn** *m* first prize

Häuptling *m* chief

Hauptquartier *nt* headquarters *pl*; **Hauptreisezeit** *f* peak tourist season; **Hauptrolle** *f* leading role; **Hauptsache** *f* main thing; **hauptsächlich** *adv* mainly, chiefly; **Hauptsaison** *f* high (*o* peak) season; **Hauptsatz** *m* main clause; **Hauptschule** *f* ≈ secondary school (*Brit*), ≈ junior high school (*US*); **Hauptspeicher** *m* (*Inform*) main storage (*o* memory); **Hauptstadt** *f* capital; **Hauptstraße** *f* main road; (*im Stadtzentrum*) main street; **Hauptverkehrszeit** *f* rush hour

Haus (*-es, Häuser*) *nt* house; **nach ~e** home; **zu ~e** at home; **jdn nach ~e bringen** to take sb home; **bei uns zu ~e** (*Heimat*) where we come from; (*Familie*) in my family; (*Haus*) at our place; **Hausarbeit** *f* housework; **Hausaufgabe** *f* (*Schule*) homework; **~n** *pl* homework *sing*; **Hausbesitzer(in)** (*-s, -*) *m(f)* house owner; (*Vermieter*) landlord/-lady; **Hausbesuch** *m* home visit; **Hausbewohner(in)** (*-s, -*) *m(f)* occupan **Hausflur** *m* hall; **Hausfrau** *f* housewife; **hausgemacht** adj homemade; **Haushalt** m household; (Pol) budget; **Hausherr(in)** m(f) host/hostess; (Vermieter) landlord/-lady

häuslich adj domestic

Hausmann m house-husband; **Hausmannskost** f good plain cooking; **Hausmeister(in)** m(f) caretaker (Brit), janitor (US); **Hausnummer** f house number; **Hausordnung** f (house) rules pl; **Hausschlüssel** m front-door key; **Hausschuh** m slipper; **Haustier** nt pet; **Haustür** f front door

Haut (-, Häute) f skin; (Tier) hide; **Hautarzt** m, **Hautärztin** f dermatologist; **Hautausschlag** m skin rash; **Hautcreme** f skin cream; **Hautfarbe** f skin colour; **Hautkrankheit** f skin disease

Hawaii (-s) nt Hawaii

Hbf. abk = **Hauptbahnhof** central station

Hebamme (-, -n) f midwife

Hebel (-s, -) m lever

heben (hob, gehoben) vt to raise, to lift

Hebräisch (-) nt Hebrew

Hecht (-(e)s, -e) m pike

Heck (-(e)s, -e) nt (von Boot) stern; (von Auto) rear; **Heckantrieb** m rear-wheel drive

Hecke (-, -n) f hedge

Heckklappe f tailgate; **Hecklicht** nt tail-light; **Heckscheibe** f rear window

Hefe (-, -n) f yeast

Heft (-(e)s, -e) nt notebook, exercise book; (Ausgabe) issue

heftig adj violent; (Kritik, Streit) fierce

Heftklammer f paper clip; **Heftpflaster** nt plaster (Brit), Band-Aid® (US)

Heide (-, -n) f heath, moor; **Heidekraut** nt heather

Heidelbeere f bilberry, blueberry

heidnisch adj (Brauch) pagan

heikel adj (Angelegenheit) awkward; (wählerisch) fussy

heil adj (Sache) in one piece, intact; (Person) unhurt; **heilbar** adj curable

Heilbutt (-(e)s, -e) m halibut

heilen vt to cure ▷ vi to heal

heilig adj holy; **Heiligabend** m Christmas Eve; **Heilige(r)** mf saint

Heilmittel n remedy, cure (gegen for); **Heilpraktiker(in)** (-s, -) m(f) non-medical practitioner

heim adv home; **Heim** (-(e), -e) nt home

Heimat (-, -en) f home (town/country); **Heimatland** nt home country

heim|fahren irr vi to drive home; **Heimfahrt** f journey home; **heimisch** adj (Bevölkerung, Brauchtum) local; (Tiere, Pflanzen) native; **heim|kommen** irr vi to come (o return) home

heimlich adj secret

Heimreise f journey home; **Heimspiel** nt (Sport) home game; **Heimvorteil** m (Sport) home advantage; **Heimweg** m way home; **Heimweh** (-s) nt homesickness; **~ haben** to be homesick; **Heimwerker(in)** m(f) DIY enthusiast

Heirat (-, -en) f marriage; **heiraten** vi to get married ▷ vt to marry; **Heiratsantrag** m proposal; **er hat ihr einen ~ gemacht** he proposed to her

heiser adj hoarse

heiß adj hot; (Diskussion) heated; **mir ist ~** I'm hot

heißen (hieß, geheißen) vi to be called; (bedeuten) to mean; **ich heiße Tom** my name is Tom; **wie**

~ Sie? what's your name?; **wie heißt sie mit Nachnamen?** what's her surname?; **wie heißt das auf Englisch?** what's that in English? ▷ *vi impers:* **es heißt** (*man sagt*) it is said; **es heißt in dem Brief ...** it says in the letter ...; **das heißt** that is

Heißluftherd *m* fan-assisted oven

heiter *adj* cheerful; (*Wetter*) bright

heizen *vt* to heat; **Heizkissen** *m* (*Med*) heated pad; **Heizkörper** *m* radiator; **Heizöl** *nt* fuel oil; **Heizung** *f* heating

Hektar (*-s, -*) *nt* hectare

Hektik (*-, -en*) *f:* **nur keine ~!** take it easy; **hektisch** *adj* hectic

Held (*-en, -en*) *m* hero; **Heldin** *f* heroine

helfen (*half, geholfen*) *vi* to help (*jdm bei etw* sb with sth); (*nützen*) to be of use; **sie weiß sich** (*dat*) **zu ~** she can manage ▷ *vi impers:* **es hilft nichts, du musst ...** it's no use, you have to ...; **Helfer(in)** *m(f)* helper; (*Mitarbeiter*) assistant

Helikopter-Skiing (*-s*) *nt* heliskiing, helicopter skiing

hell *adj* bright; (*Farbe*) light; (*Hautfarbe*) fair; **hellblau** *adj* light blue; **hellblond** *adj* ash-blond; **hellgelb** *adj* pale yellow; **hellgrün** *adj* light green; **Hellseher(in)** *m(f)* clairvoyant

Helm (*-(e)s, -e*) *m* helmet; **Helmpflicht** *f* compulsory wearing of helmets

Hemd (*-(e)s, -en*) *nt* shirt; (*Unter~*) vest

hemmen *vt* to check; (*behindern*) to hamper; **gehemmt sein** to be inhibited; **Hemmung** *f* (*psychisch*) inhibition; **sie hatte keine ~, ihn zu betrügen** she had no scruples about deceiving him; (*moralisch*) scruple

Henkel (*-s, -*) *m* handle

Henna (*-s*) *nt* henna

Henne (*-, -n*) *f* hen

Hepatitis (*-, Hepatitiden*) *f* hepatitis

○ **SCHLÜSSELWORT**

her *adv* **1** (*Richtung*) **komm her zu mir** come here (to me); **von England her** from England; **von weit her** from a long way away; **her damit!** hand it over!; **wo hat er das her?** where did he get that from?; **wo bist du her?** where do you come from?

2 (*Blickpunkt*) **von der Form her** as far as the form is concerned

3 (*zeitlich*) **das ist 5 Jahre her** that was 5 years ago; **ich kenne ihn von früher her** I know him from before

herab *adv* down; **herablassend** *adj* (*Bemerkung*) condescending; **herab|sehen** *irr vt:* **auf jdn ~** to look down on sb; **herab|setzen** *vt* to reduce; (*fig*) to disparage

heran *adv:* **näher ~!** come closer; **heran|kommen** *irr vi* to approach; **~ an** (*+akk*) to be able to get at; (*fig*) to be able to get hold of; **heran|wachsen** *irr vi* to grow up

herauf *adv* up; **herauf|beschwören** *irr vt* to evoke; (*verursachen*) to cause; **herauf|ziehen** *irr vt* to pull up ▷ *vi* to approach; (*Sturm*) to gather

heraus *adv* out; **heraus|bekommen** *irr vt* (*Geheimnis*) to find out; (*Rätsel*) to solve; **ich bekomme noch zwei Euro heraus** I've got two euros change to come; **heraus|bringen** *irr vt* to bring out; **heraus|finden**

irr vt to find out; **heraus|fordern** *vt* to challenge; **Herausforderung** *f* challenge; **heraus|geben** *irr vt* (*Buch*) to edit; (*veröffentlichen*) to publish; **jdm zwei Euro ~** to give sb two euros change; **geben Sie mir bitte auf 20 Euro heraus** could you give me change for 20 euros, please?; **heraus|holen** *vt* to get out (*aus* of); **heraus|- kommen** *irr vi* to come out; **dabei kommt nichts heraus** nothing will come of it; **heraus|stellen** *vr:* **sich ~** to turn out (*als* to be); **heraus|ziehen** *irr vt* to pull out

Herbst (*-(e)s, -e*) *m* autumn, fall (*US*)

Herd (*-(e)s, -e*) *m* cooker, stove

Herde (*-, -n*) *f* herd; (*Schafe*) flock

herein *adv* in; **~!** come in; **herein|fallen** *irr vi:* **wir sind auf einen Betrüger hereingefallen** we were taken in by a swindler; **herein|legen** *vt:* **jdn ~** (*fig*) to take sb for a ride

Herfahrt *f* journey here; **auf der ~** on the way here

Hergang *m* course (of events); **schildern Sie mir den ~** tell me what happened

Hering (*-s, -e*) *m* herring

her|kommen *irr vi* to come; **wo kommt sie her?** where does she come from?

Heroin (*-s*) *nt* heroin

Herpes (*-*) *m* (*Med*) herpes

Herr (*-(e)n, -en*) *m* (*vor Namen*) Mr; (*Mann*) gentleman; (*Adliger, Gott*) Lord; **mein ~!** sir; **meine ~en!** gentlemen; **Sehr geehrte Damen und ~en** Dear Sir or Madam; **herrenlos** *adj* (*Gepäckstück*) abandoned; (*Tier*) stray; **Herrentoilette** *f* men's toilet, gents

her|richten *vt* to prepare

herrlich *adj* marvellous, splendid

Herrschaft *f* rule; (*Macht*) power; **meine ~en!** ladies and gentlemen!

herrschen *vi* to rule; (*bestehen*) to be

her|stellen *vt* to make; (*industriell*) to manufacture; **Hersteller(in)** *m(f)* manufacturer; **Herstellung** *f* production

herüber *adv* over

herum *adv* around; (*im Kreis*) round; **um etw ~** around sth; **du hast den Pulli falsch ~ an** you're wearing your sweater inside out; **anders ~** the other way round; **herum|fahren** *irr vi* to drive around; **herum|führen** *vt:* **jdn in der Stadt ~** to show sb around the town ▷ *vi:* **die Straße führt um das Zentrum herum** the road goes around the city centre; **herum|kommen** *irr vi:* **sie ist viel in der Welt herumgekommen** she's been around the world; **um etw ~** (*vermeiden*) to get out of sth; **herum|kriegen** *vt* to talk round; **herum|treiben** *irr vr:* **sich ~** to hang around

herunter *adv* down; **heruntergekommen** *adj* (*Gebäude, Gegend*) run-down; (*Person*) down-at-heel; **herunter|handeln** *vt* to get down; **herunter|holen** *vt* to bring down; **herunter|kommen** *irr vi* to come down; **herunter|laden** *irr vt* (*Inform*) to download

hervor *adv* out; **hervor|bringen** *irr vt* to produce; (*Wort*) to utter; **hervor|heben** *irr vt* to emphasize, to stress; **hervorragend** *adj* excellent; **hervor|rufen** *irr vt* to cause, to give rise to

Herz (*-ens, -en*) *nt* heart; (*Karten*)

hearts pl; **von ganzem ~en** wholeheartedly; **sich** (dat) **etw zu ~en nehmen** to take sth to heart; **Herzanfall** m heart attack; **Herzbeschwerden** pl heart trouble sing; **Herzfehler** m heart defect; **herzhaft** adj (Essen) substantial; **~ lachen** to have a good laugh; **Herzinfarkt** m heart attack; **Herzklopfen** (-s) nt (Med) palpitations pl; **ich hatte ~** (vor Aufregung) my heart was pounding (with excitement); **herzkrank** adj: **sie ist ~** she's got a heart condition; **herzlich** adj (Empfang, Mensch) warm; **~en Glückwunsch** congratulations

Herzog(in) (-s, Herzöge) m(f) duke/duchess

Herzschlag m heartbeat; (Herzversagen) heart failure; **Herzschrittmacher** m pacemaker; **Herzstillstand** m cardiac arrest

Hessen (-s) nt Hessen

heterosexuell adj heterosexual; **Heterosexuelle(r)** mf heterosexual

Hetze (-, -n) f (Eile) rush; **hetzen** vt to rush ▷ vr: **sich ~** to rush

Heu (-(e)s) nt hay

heuer adv this year

heulen vi to howl; (weinen) to cry

Heuschnupfen m hay fever; **Heuschrecke** (-, -n) f grasshopper; (größer) locust

heute adv today; **~ Abend/früh** this evening/morning; **~ Nacht** tonight; (letzte Nacht) last night; **~ in acht Tagen** a week (from) today; **sie hat bis ~ nicht bezahlt** she hasn't paid to this day; **heutig** adj: **die ~e Zeitung/Generation** today's paper/generation; **heutzutage** adv nowadays

Hexe (-, -n) f witch; **Hexenschuss** m lumbago

hielt imperf von **halten**

hier adv here; **~ entlang** this way; **ich bin auch nicht von ~** I'm a stranger here myself; **hier|bleiben** irr vi to stay here; **hier|lassen** irr vt to leave here; **hierher** adv here; **das gehört nicht ~** that doesn't belong here; **hiermit** adv with this; **hierzulande** adv in this country

hiesig adj local

hieß imperf von **heißen**

Hi-Fi-Anlage f hi-fi (system)

high adj (fam) high; **Highlife** (-s) nt high life; **~ machen** to live it up; **Hightech** (-s) nt high tech

Hilfe (-, -n) f help; (für Notleidende, finanziell) aid; **~!** help!; **Erste ~ leisten** to give first aid; **um ~ bitten** to ask for help; **hilflos** adj helpless; **hilfsbereit** adj helpful; **Hilfsmittel** nt aid

Himbeere f raspberry

Himmel (-s, -) m sky; (Rel) heaven; **Himmelfahrt** f Ascension; **Himmelsrichtung** f direction; **himmlisch** adj heavenly

○ SCHLÜSSELWORT

hin adv 1 (Richtung) **hin und zurück** there and back; **hin und her** to and fro; **bis zur Mauer hin** up to the wall; **wo ist er hin?** where has he gone?; **Geld hin, Geld her** money or no money

2 (auf ... hin) **auf meine Bitte hin** at my request; **auf seinen Rat hin** on the basis of his advice

3 **mein Glück ist hin** my happiness has gone

hinab adv down; **hinab|gehen** irr vi to go down

hinauf adv up; **hinauf|gehen** irr

vi, vt to go up; **hinauf|steigen** *irr*
vi to climb (up)
hinaus *adv* out; **hinaus|gehen** *irr*
vi to go out; **das Zimmer geht auf**
den See hinaus the room looks
out onto the lake; **~ über** (+*akk*) to
exceed; **hinaus|laufen** *irr vi* to
run out; **~ auf** (+*akk*) to come to, to
amount to; **hinaus|schieben** *irr*
vi to put off, to postpone;
hinaus|werfen *irr vt* to throw
out; (*aus Firma*) to fire, to sack
(*Brit*); **hinaus|zögern** *vr*: **sich**
~ to take longer than expected
Hinblick *m* **in** (*o* **im**) **~ auf** (+*akk*)
with regard to; (*wegen*) in view of
hin|bringen *irr vt*: **ich bringe Sie**
hin I'll take you there
hindern *vt* to prevent; **jdn daran**
~, etw zu tun to stop (*o* prevent)
sb from doing sth; **Hindernis** *nt*
obstacle
Hinduismus *m* Hinduism
hindurch *adv* through; **das**
ganze Jahr ~ throughout the year,
all year round; **die ganze Nacht**
~ all night (long)
hinein *adv* in; **hinein|gehen** *irr vi*
to go in; **~ in** (+*akk*) to go into, to
enter; **hinein|passen** *vi* to fit in;
~ in (+*akk*) to fit into
hin|fahren *irr vi* to go there ▷ *vt*
to take there; **Hinfahrt** *f*
outward journey
hin|fallen *irr vi* to fall (down)
Hinflug *m* outward flight
hing *imperf von* **hängen**
hin|gehen *irr vi* to go there;
(*Zeit*) to pass; **hin|halten** *irr vt* to
hold out; (*warten lassen*) to put off
hinken *vi* to limp; **der Vergleich**
hinkt the comparison doesn't
work
hin|knien *vr*: **sich ~** to kneel
down; **hin|legen** *vt* to put down
▷ *vr*: **sich ~** to lie down;
hin|nehmen *irr vt* (*fig*) to put up

with, to take; **Hinreise** *f*
outward journey; **hin|setzen** *vr*:
sich ~ to sit down; **hinsichtlich**
prep +*gen* with regard to;
hin|stellen *vt* to put (down) ▷ *vr*:
sich ~ to stand
hinten *adv* at the back; (*im Auto*)
in the back; (*dahinter*) behind
hinter *prep* +*dat o akk* behind;
(*nach*) after; **~ jdm her sein** to be
after sb; **etw ~ sich** (*akk*) **bringen**
to get sth over (and done) with;
Hinterachse *f* rear axle;
Hinterausgang *m* rear exit;
Hinterbein *nt* hind leg;
Hinterbliebene(r) *mf* dependant;
hintere(r, s) *adj* rear, back;
hintereinander *adv* (*in einer*
Reihe) one behind the other;
(*hintereinander her*) one after the
other; **drei Tage ~** three days
running (*o* in a row);
Hintereingang *m* rear entrance;
Hintergedanke *m* ulterior
motive; **hintergehen** *irr vt* to
deceive; **Hintergrund** *m*
background; **hinterher** *adv*
(*zeitlich*) afterwards; **los, ~!** come
on, after him/her/them;
Hinterkopf *m* back of the head;
hinterlassen *vt* to leave; **jdm**
eine Nachricht ~ to leave a
message for sb; **hinterlegen** *vt*
to leave (*bei* with)
Hintern (-, -) *m* (*fam*) backside,
bum
Hinterradantrieb *m* (*Auto*)
rear-wheel drive; **Hinterteil** *nt*
back (part); (*Hintern*) behind;
Hintertür *f* back door
hinüber *adv* over; **~ sein** (*fam*:
kaputt) to be ruined; (*verdorben*) to
have gone bad; **hinüber|gehen** *irr*
vi to go over
hinunter *adv* down;
hinunter|gehen *irr vi, vt* to go
down; **hinunter|schlucken** *vt*

(*a. fig*) to swallow

Hinweg *m* outward journey

hinweg|setzen *vr* **sich über etw** (*akk*) **~** to ignore sth

Hinweis (*-es, -e*) *m* (*Andeutung*) hint; (*Anweisung*) instruction; (*Verweis*) reference; **hin|weisen** *irr vi* **jdn auf etw** (*acc*) **~** to point sth out to sb; **jdn nochmal auf etw ~** to remind sb of sth

hinzu *adv* in addition; **hinzu|fügen** *vt* to add; **hinzu|kommen** *irr vi:* **zu jdm ~** to join sb; **es war kalt, hinzu kam, dass es auch noch regnete** it was cold, and on top of that it was raining

Hirn (*-(e)s, -e*) *nt* brain; (*Verstand*) brains *pl;* **Hirnhautentzündung** *f* meningitis; **hirnverbrannt** *adj* crazy

Hirsch (*-(e)s, -e*) *m* deer; (*als Speise*) venison

Hirse (*-, -n*) *f* millet

Hirte (*-n, -n*) *m* shepherd

historisch *adj* historical

Hit (*-s, -s*) *m* (*fig, Mus, Inform*) hit; **Hitliste** *f*, **Hitparade** *f* charts *pl*

Hitze (*-*) *f* heat; **hitzebeständig** *adj* heat-resistant; **Hitzewelle** *f* heatwave; **hitzig** *adj* hot-tempered; (*Debatte*) heated; **Hitzschlag** *m* heatstroke

HIV (*-(s), -(s)*) *nt abk* = **Human Immunodeficiency Virus** HIV; **HIV-negativ** *adj* HIV-negative; **HIV-positiv** *adj* HIV-positive

H-Milch *f* long-life milk

hob *imperf von* **heben**

Hobby (*-s, -s*) *nt* hobby

Hobel (*-s, -*) *m* plane

hoch *adj* high; (*Baum, Haus*) tall; (*Schnee*) deep; **der Zaun ist drei Meter ~** the fence is three metres high; **~ auflösend** high-resolution; **~ begabt** extremely gifted; **das ist mir zu ~** that's above my head;

~ soll sie leben!, sie lebe ~! three cheers for her; **4 ~ 2 ist 16** 4 squared is 16; **4 ~ 5** 4 to the power of 5

Hoch (*-s, -s*) *nt* (*Ruf*) cheer; (*Meteo*) high; **hochachtungsvoll** *adv* (*in Briefen*) Yours faithfully; **Hochbetrieb** *m:* **es herrscht ~** they/we are extremely busy; **Hochdeutsch** *nt* High German; **Hochgebirge** *nt* high mountains *pl;* **Hochgeschwindigkeitszug** *m* high-speed train; **Hochhaus** *nt* high rise; **hoch|heben** *irr vt* to lift (up); **hochprozentig** *adj* (*Alkohol*) high-proof; **Hochsaison** *f* high season; **Hochschule** *f* college; (*Universität*) university; **hochschwanger** *adj* heavily pregnant; **Hochsommer** *m* midsummer; **Hochspannung** *f* great tension; (*Elek*) high voltage; **Hochsprung** *m* high jump

höchst *adv* highly, extremely; **höchste(r, s)** *adj* highest; (*äußerste*) extreme; **höchstens** *adv* at the most; **Höchstgeschwindigkeit** *f* maximum speed; **Höchstparkdauer** *f* maximum stay

Hochstuhl *m* high chair

höchstwahrscheinlich *adv* very probably

Hochwasser *nt* high water; (*Überschwemmung*) floods *pl;* **hochwertig** *adj* high-quality

Hochzeit (*-, -en*) *f* wedding; **Hochzeitsnacht** *f* wedding night; **Hochzeitsreise** *f* honeymoon; **Hochzeitstag** *m* wedding day; (*Jahrestag*) wedding anniversary

hocken *vi* to squat, to crouch

Hocker (*-s, -*) *m* stool

Hockey (*-s*) *nt* hockey

Hoden (*-s, -*) *m* testicle

Hof (*-(e)s, Höfe*) *m* (*Hinterhof*) yard;

(*Innenhof*) courtyard; (*Bauernhof*) farm; (*Königshof*) court

hoffen *vi* to hope (*auf +akk* for); **ich hoffe es** I hope so; **hoffentlich** *adv* hopefully; **~ nicht** I hope not; **Hoffnung** *f* hope; **hoffnungslos** *adj* hopeless

höflich *adj* polite; **Höflichkeit** *f* politeness

hohe(r, s) *adj siehe* **hoch**

Höhe (-, -n) *f* height; (*Anhöhe*) hill; (*einer Summe*) amount; **in einer ~ von 5000 Metern** at an altitude of 5,000 metres; (*Flughöhe*) altitude; **Höhenangst** *f* vertigo

Höhepunkt *m* (*einer Reise*) high point; (*einer Veranstaltung*) highlight; (*eines Films; sexuell*) climax

höher *adj, adv* higher

hohl *adj* hollow

Höhle (-, -n) *f* cave

holen *vt* to get, to fetch; (*abholen*) to pick up; (*Atem*) to catch; **die Polizei ~** to call the police; **jdn/etw ~ lassen** to send for sb/sth

Holland *nt* Holland; **Holländer(in)** (-s, -) *m(f)* Dutchman/ -woman; **holländisch** *adj* Dutch

Hölle (-, -n) *f* hell

Hologramm *nt* hologram

holperig *adj* bumpy

Holunder (-s, -) *m* elder

Holz (-es, *Hölzer*) *nt* wood; **Holzboden** *m* wooden floor; **hölzern** *adj* wooden; **holzig** *adj* (*Stängel*) woody; **Holzkohle** *f* charcoal

Homebanking (-s) *nt* home banking, online banking; **Homepage** (-, -s) *f* home page; **Hometrainer** *m* exercise machine

Homoehe *f* (*fam*) gay marriage

homöopathisch *adj* homeopathic

homosexuell *adj* homosexual; **Homosexuelle(r)** *mf* homosexual

Honig (-s, -e) *m* honey; **Honigmelone** *f* honeydew melon

Honorar (-s, -e) *nt* fee

Hopfen (-s, -) *m* (*Bot*) hop; (*beim Brauen*) hops *pl*

hoppla *interj* whoops, oops

horchen *vi* to listen (*auf +akk* to); (*an der Tür*) to eavesdrop

hören *vt, vi* (*passiv, mitbekommen*) to hear; (*zufällig*) to overhear; (*aufmerksam zuhören; Radio, Musik*) to listen to; **ich habe schon viel von Ihnen gehört** I've heard a lot about you; **Hörer** *m* (*Tel*) receiver; **Hörer(in)** *m(f)* listener; **Hörgerät** *nt* hearing aid

Horizont (-(e)s, -e) *m* horizon; **das geht über meinen ~** that's beyond me

Hormon (-s, -e) *nt* hormone

Hornhaut *f* hard skin; (*des Auges*) cornea

Hornisse (-, -n) *f* hornet

Horoskop (-s, -e) *nt* horoscope

Hörsaal *m* lecture hall; **Hörsturz** *m* acute hearing loss; **Hörweite** *f*: **in/außer ~** within/out of earshot

Höschenwindel (-, -n) *f* nappy (*Brit*), diaper (*US*)

Hose (-, -n) *f* trousers *pl* (*Brit*), pants *pl* (*US*); (*Unterhose*) (under)pants *pl*; **eine ~** a pair of trousers/pants; **kurze ~** (pair of) shorts *pl*; **Hosenanzug** *m* trouser suit (*Brit*), pantsuit (*US*); **Hosenschlitz** *m* fly, flies (*Brit*); **Hosentasche** *f* trouser pocket (*Brit*), pant pocket (*US*); **Hosenträger** *m* braces *pl* (*Brit*), suspenders *pl* (*US*)

Hospital (-s, *Hospitäler*) *nt* hospital

Hotdog (-s, -s) *nt o m* hot dog

Hotel (-s, -s) nt hotel; **in welchem ~ seid ihr?** which hotel are you staying at?; **Hoteldirektor(in)** m(f) hotel manager; **Hotelkette** f hotel chain; **Hotelzimmer** nt hotel room

Hotline (-, -s) f hot line

Hubraum m cubic capacity

hübsch adj (Mädchen, Kind, Kleid) pretty; (gutaussehend; Mann, Frau) good-looking, cute

Hubschrauber (-s, -) m helicopter

Huf (-(e)s, -e) m hoof; **Hufeisen** nt horseshoe

Hüfte (-, -n) f hip

Hügel (-s, -) m hill; **hügelig** adj hilly

Huhn (-(e)s, Hühner) nt hen; (Gastr) chicken; **Hühnchen** nt chicken; **Hühnerauge** nt corn; **Hühnerbrühe** f chicken broth

Hülle (-, -n) f cover; (für Ausweis) case; (Zellophan) wrapping

Hummel (-, -n) f bumblebee

Hummer (-s, -) m lobster; **Hummerkrabbe** f king prawn

Humor (-s) m humour; **~ haben** to have a sense of humour; **humorvoll** adj humorous

humpeln vi hobble

Hund (-(e)s, -e) m dog; **Hundeleine** f dog lead (Brit), dog leash (US)

hundert num hundred; **Hundertjahrfeier** f centenary; **hundertprozentig** adj, adv one hundred per cent; **hundertste(r, s)** adj hundredth

Hündin f bitch

Hunger (-s) m hunger; **~ haben/bekommen** to be/get hungry; **hungern** vi to go hungry; (ernsthaft, dauernd) to starve

Hupe (-, -n) f horn; **hupen** vi to sound one's horn

Hüpfburg f bouncy castle®; **hüpfen** vi to hop; (springen) to jump

Hürde (-, -n) f hurdle

Hure (-, -n) f whore

hurra interj hooray

husten vi to cough; **Husten** (-s) m cough; **Hustenbonbon** nt cough sweet; **Hustensaft** m cough mixture

Hut (-(e)s, Hüte) m hat

hüten vt to look after ▷ vr: **sich ~** to watch out; **sich ~, etw zu tun** to take care not to do sth; **sich ~ vor** (+dat) to beware of

Hütte (-, -n) f hut, cottage; **Hüttenkäse** m cottage cheese

Hyäne (-, -n) f hyena

Hydrant m hydrant

hygienisch adj hygienic

Hyperlink (-s, -s) m hyperlink

Hypnose (-, -n) f hypnosis; **Hypnotiseur(in)** m(f) hypnotist; **hypnotisieren** vt to hypnotize

Hypothek (-, -en) f mortgage

hysterisch adj hysterical

I

i. A. abk = **im Auftrag** pp
IC (-, -s) m abk = **Intercityzug** Intercity (train)
ICE (-, -s) m abk = **Intercityexpresszug** German high-speed train
ich pron I; **~ bin's** it's me; **~ nicht** not me; **du und ~** you and me; **hier bin ~!** here I am; **~ Idiot!** stupid me
Icon (-s, -s) nt (Inform) icon
IC-Zuschlag m Intercity supplement
ideal adj ideal; **Ideal** (-s, -e) nt ideal
Idee (-, -n) f idea
identifizieren vt to identify
▷ vr: **sich mit jdm/etw ~** to identify with sb/sth
identisch adj identical
Idiot(in) (-en, -en) m(f) idiot; **idiotisch** adj idiotic
Idol (-s, -e) nt idol
Idylle f idyll; **idyllisch** adj idyllic

Igel (-s, -) m hedgehog
ignorieren vt to ignore
ihm pron dat sing von **er/es**; (to) him, (to) it; **wie geht es ~?** how is he?; **ein Freund von ~** a friend of his ▷ pron dat von **es**; (to) it
ihn pron akk sing von **er**; (Person) him; (Sache) it
ihnen pron dat pl von **sie**; (to) them; **wie geht es ~?** how are they?; **ein Freund von ~** a friend of theirs
Ihnen pron dat sing u pl von **Sie**; (to) you; **wie geht es ~?** how are you?; **ein Freund von ~** a friend of yours

SCHLÜSSELWORT

ihr pron **1** (nom pl) you; **ihr seid es** it's you
2 (dat von sie) to her; **gib es ihr** give it to her; **er steht neben ihr** he is standing beside her
▷ possessiv pron **1** (sg) her; (bei Tieren, Dingen) its; **ihr Mann** her husband
2 (pl) their; **die Bäume und ihre Blätter** the trees and their leaves

Ihr pron von **Sie**; (adjektivisch) your; **~(e) XY** (am Briefende) Yours, XY
ihre(r, s) pron (substantivisch, sing) hers; (pl) theirs; **das ist ~/~r/ihr(e)s** that's hers; (pl) that's theirs
Ihre(r, s) pron (substantivisch) yours; **das ist ~/~r/Ihr(e)s** that's yours
ihretwegen adv (wegen ihr) because of her; (ihr zuliebe) for her sake; (um sie) about her; (von ihr aus) as far as she is concerned
▷ adv (wegen ihnen) because of them; (ihnen zuliebe) for their sake; (um sie) about them; (von ihnen aus)

as far as they are concerned;
Ihretwegen adv (wegen Ihnen)
because of you; (Ihnen zuliebe) for
your sake; (um Sie) about you; (von
Ihnen aus) as far as you are
concerned
Ikone (-, -n) f icon
illegal adj illegal
Illusion f illusion; **sich** (dat) **~en
machen** to delude oneself;
illusorisch adj illusory
Illustration f illustration
Illustrierte (-n, -n) f (glossy)
magazine
im kontr von **in dem**; **~ Bett** in bed;
~ Fernsehen on TV; **~ Radio** on
the radio; **~ Bus/Zug** on the
bus/train; **~ Januar** in January;
~ Stehen (while) standing up
Imbiss (-es, -e) m snack;
Imbissbude f, **Imbissstube** f
snack bar
Imbusschlüssel m hex key
immer adv always; **~ mehr** more
and more; **~ wieder** again and
again; **~ noch** still; **~ noch nicht**
still not; **für ~** forever; **~ wenn
ich …** every time I …; **~ schöner/
trauriger** more and
more beautiful/sadder and
sadder; **was/wer/wo/wann**
(**auch**) **~** whatever/whoever/
wherever/whenever; **immerhin**
adv after all; **immerzu** adv all the
time
Immigrant(in) m(f) immigrant
Immobilien pl property sing, real
estate sing; **Immobilien-
makler(in)** m(f) estate
agent (Brit), realtor (US)
immun adj immune (gegen to);
Immunschwäche f immunodeficiency; **Immun-
schwächekrankheit** f immune
deficiency syndrome;
Immunsystem nt immune
system

impfen vt to vaccinate; **ich muss
mich gegen Pocken ~ lassen** I've
got to get myself vaccinated
against smallpox; **Impfpass** m
vaccination card; **Impfstoff** m
vaccine; **Impfung** f vaccination
imponieren vi to impress (jdm
sb)
Import (-(e)s, -e) m import;
importieren vt to import
impotent adj impotent
imstande adj: **~ sein** to be
in a position; (fähig) to be
able

○ SCHLÜSSELWORT

in prep +akk **1** (räumlich: wohin?) in,
into; **in die Stadt** into town; **in die
Schule gehen** to go to school
2 (zeitlich) **bis ins 20. Jahrhundert**
into o up to the 20th century
▷ prep +dat **1** (räumlich: wo?) in; **in
der Stadt** in town; **in der Schule
sein** to be at school
2 (zeitlich: wann?) **in diesem Jahr**
this year; (in jenem Jahr) in that
year; **heute in zwei Wochen** two
weeks today

inbegriffen adj included
indem conj: **sie gewann, ~ sie
mogelte** she won by cheating
Inder(in) (-s, -) m(f) Indian
Indianer(in) (-s, -) m(f)
American Indian, Native
American; **indianisch** adj
American Indian, Native American
Indien (-s) nt India
indirekt adj indirect
indisch adj Indian
indiskret adj indiscreet
individuell adj individual
Indonesien (-s) nt Indonesia
Industrie f industry; **Industrie-
in** zW industrial; **Industriegebiet**
nt industrial area; **industriell** adj

industrial
ineinander adv in(to) one
another (o each other)
Infarkt (-(e)s, -e) m (Herzinfarkt)
heart attack
Infektion f infection;
Infektionskrankheit f infectious
disease; **infizieren** vt to infect
▷ vr: **sich ~** to be infected
Info (-, -s) f (fam) info
infolge prep +gen as a result of,
owing to; **infolgedessen** adv
consequently
Infomaterial nt (fam) bumf, info
Informatik f computer science;
Informatiker(in) (-s, -) m(f)
computer scientist
Information f information;
Informationsschalter m information desk; **informieren** vt to
inform; **falsch ~** to misinform
▷ vr: **sich ~** to find out (über +akk
about)
infrage adv: **das kommt nicht
~** that's out of the question; **etw
~ stellen** to question sth
Infrastruktur f infrastructure
Infusion f infusion
Ingenieur(in) m(f) engineer
Ingwer (-s) m ginger
Inhaber(in) (-s, -) m(f) owner;
(Haus~) occupier; (von Lizenz)
holder; (Fin) bearer
Inhalt (-(e)s, -e) m contents pl;
(eines Buchs etc) content; (Math)
volume; (Flächeninhalt) area;
Inhaltsangabe f summary;
Inhaltsverzeichnis nt table of
contents
Initiative f initiative; **die
~ ergreifen** to take the initiative
Injektion f injection
inklusive adv, prep inclusive (gen
of)
inkonsequent adj inconsistent
Inland nt (Pol, Comm) home; **im
~** at home; (Geo) inland;

inländisch adj domestic;
Inlandsflug m domestic flight;
Inlandsgespräch nt national call
Inliner pl, **Inlineskates** pl
(Sport) Rollerblades® pl, in-line
skates pl
innen adv inside;
Innenarchitekt(in) m(f) interior
designer; **Innenhof** m (inner)
courtyard; **Innenminister(in)**
m(f) minister of the interior,
Home Secretary (Brit); **Innenseite**
f inside; **Innenspiegel** m
rearview mirror; **Innenstadt** f
town centre; (von Großstadt) city
centre
innere(r, s) adj inner; (im Körper,
inländisch) internal; **Innere(s)** nt
inside; (Mitte) centre; (fig) heart
Innereien pl innards pl
innerhalb adv, prep +gen within;
(räumlich) inside
innerlich adj internal; (geistig)
inner
innerste(r, s) adj innermost
Innovation f innovation;
innovativ adj innovative
inoffiziell adj unofficial;
(zwanglos) informal
ins kontr von **in das**
Insasse (-n, -n) m, **Insassin** f
(Auto) passenger; (Anstalt) inmate
insbesondere adv particularly,
in particular
Inschrift f inscription
Insekt (-(e)s, -en) nt insect, bug
(US); **Insektenschutzmittel** nt
insect repellent; **Insektenstich**
m insect bite
Insel (-, -n) f island
Inserat nt advertisement
insgesamt adv altogether, all in
all
Insider(in) (-s, -) m(f) insider
insofern adv in that respect;
(deshalb) (and) so ▷ conj if; **~ als** in
so far as

Installateur(in) m(f) (Klempner)
plumber; (Elektroinstallateur)
electrician; **installieren** vt
(Inform) to install
Instinkt (-(e)s, -e) m instinct
Institut (-(e)s, -e) nt institute
Institution f institution
Instrument nt instrument
Insulin (-s) nt insulin
Inszenierung f production
intakt adj intact
intellektuell adj intellectual
intelligent adj intelligent;
Intelligenz f intelligence
intensiv adj (gründlich) intensive;
(Gefühl, Schmerz) intense;
Intensivkurs m crash course;
Intensivstation f intensive care
unit
interaktiv adj interactive
Intercityexpress(zug) m German
high-speed train; **Intercityzug** m
Intercity (train);
Intercityzuschlag m Intercity
supplement
interessant adj interesting;
Interesse (-s, -n) nt interest;
~ haben an (+dat) to be interested
in; **interessieren** vt to interest
▷ vr: **sich ~** to be interested (für in)
Interface (-, -s) nt (Inform)
interface
Internat nt boarding school
international adj international
Internet (-s) nt internet, net; **im
~** on the internet; **im ~ surfen** to
surf the net; **Internetanschluss**
m internet connection;
Internetauktion f internet
auction; **Internetcafé** nt
internet café, cybercafé;
Internetfirma f dotcom
company; **Internethandel** m
e-commerce; **Internetseite** f
web page; **Internetzugang** m
internet access
interpretieren vt to interpret

(als as)
Interpunktion f punctuation
Interview (-s, -s) nt interview;
interviewen vt to interview
intim adj intimate
intolerant adj intolerant
investieren vt to invest
inwiefern adv in what way; (in
welchem Ausmaß) to what extent;
inwieweit adv to what extent
inzwischen adv meanwhile
Irak (-(s)) m: (**der**) **~** Iraq
Iran (-(s)) m: (**der**) **~** Iran
Ire (-n, -n) m Irishman
irgend adv: **~ so ein Idiot** some
idiot; **wenn ~ möglich** if at all
possible; **irgendein** pron,
irgendeine(r, s) adj some;
(fragend, im Bedingungssatz; beliebig)
any; **irgendetwas** pron
something; (fragend, im
Bedingungssatz) anything;
irgendjemand pron somebody;
(fragend, im Bedingungssatz)
anybody; **irgendwann** adv
sometime; (zu beliebiger Zeit) any
time; **irgendwie** adv somehow;
irgendwo adv somewhere;
(fragend, im Bedingungssatz)
anywhere
Irin f Irishwoman; **irisch** adj
Irish; **Irland** nt Ireland
ironisch adj ironic
irre adj crazy, mad; (toll) terrific;
Irre(r) mf lunatic; **irreführen** irr
vt to mislead; **irremachen** vt to
confuse; **irren** vi to be mistaken;
(umherirren) to wander ▷ vr: **sich
~** to be mistaken; **wenn ich mich
nicht irre** if I'm not mistaken; **sich
in der Nummer ~** (Telefon) to get
the wrong number; **irrsinnig** adj
mad, crazy; **Irrtum** (-s, -tümer) m
mistake, error; **irrtümlich** adj
mistaken ▷ adv by mistake
ISBN (-) nt abk = **industrial
standard business network** ISBN

▷ (-) *f abk* = **Internationale Standard Buchnummer** ISBN
Ischias (-) *m* sciatica
ISDN (-) *nt abk* = **integrated services digital network** ISDN
Islam (-s) *m* Islam; **islamisch** *adj* Islamic
Island *nt* Iceland; **Isländer(in)** (-s, -) *m(f)* Icelander; **isländisch** *adj* Icelandic; **Isländisch** *nt* Icelandic
Isolierband *nt* insulating tape; **isolieren** *vt* to isolate; (*Elek*) to insulate
Isomatte *f* thermomat, karrymat®
Israel (-s) *nt* Israel; **Israeli** (-(s), -(s)) *m* (-, -(s)) *f* Israeli; **israelisch** *adj* Israeli
IT (-) *f abk* = **Informationstechnologie** IT
Italien (-s) *nt* Italy; **Italiener(in)** (-s, -) *m(f)* Italian; **italienisch** *adj* Italian; **Italienisch** *nt* Italian

J

○ SCHLÜSSELWORT

ja *adv* **1** yes; **haben Sie das gesehen? — ja** did you see it? — yes(, I did); **ich glaube ja** (yes,) I think so
2 (*fragend*) really?; **ich habe gekündigt — ja?** I've quit — have you?; **du kommst, ja?** you're coming, aren't you?
3 sei ja vorsichtig do be careful; **Sie wissen ja, dass ...** as you know, ...; **tu das ja nicht!** don't do that!; **ich habe es ja gewusst** I just knew it; **ja, also ...** well you see ...
Jacht (-, -en) *f* yacht; **Jachthafen** *m* marina
Jacke (-, -n) *f* jacket; (*Wolljacke*) cardigan
Jackett (-s, -s *o* -e) *nt* jacket
Jagd (-, -en) *f* hunt; (*Jagen*) hunting; **jagen** *vi* to hunt ▷ *vt* to

hunt; (*verfolgen*) to chase; **Jäger(in)** *m(f)* hunter
Jaguar (*-s, -e*) *m* jaguar
Jahr (*-(e)s, -e*) *nt* year; **ein halbes ~** six months *pl*; **Anfang der neunziger ~** in the early nineties; **mit sechzehn ~en** at (the age of) sixteen; **Jahrestag** *m* anniversary; **Jahreszahl** *f* date, year; **Jahreszeit** *f* season; **Jahrgang** *m* (*Wein*) year, vintage; **der ~ 1989** (*Personen*) those born in 1989; **Jahrhundert** (*-s, -e*) *nt* century; **jährlich** *adj* yearly, annual; **Jahrmarkt** *m* fair; **Jahrtausend** *nt* millennium; **Jahrzehnt** *nt* decade
jähzornig *adj* hot-tempered
Jakobsmuschel *f* scallop
Jalousie *f* (venetian) blind
Jamaika (*-s*) *nt* Jamaica
jämmerlich *adj* pathetic
jammern *vi* to moan
Januar (*-(s), -e*) *m* January; *siehe auch* **Juni**
Japan (*-s*) *nt* Japan; **Japaner(in)** (*-s, -*) *m(f)* Japanese; **japanisch** *adj* Japanese; **Japanisch** *nt* Japanese
jaulen *vi* to howl
jawohl *adv* yes (of course)
Jazz (*-*) *m* jazz

○ SCHLÜSSELWORT

je *adv* 1 (*jemals*) ever; **hast du so was je gesehen?** did you ever see anything like it?
2 (*jeweils*) every, each; **sie zahlten je 3 Euro** they paid 3 euros each
▷ *konj* 1 **je nach** depending on; **je nachdem** it depends; **je nachdem, ob ...** depending on whether ...
2 **je eher, desto** *o* **umso besser** the sooner the better

Jeans (*-, -*) *f* jeans *pl*

jede(r, s) *unbest Zahlwort* (*insgesamt gesehen*) every; (*einzeln gesehen*) each; (*jede(r, s) beliebige*) any; **~s Mal** every time, each time; **~n zweiten Tag** every other day; **sie hat an ~m Finger einen Ring** she's got a ring on each finger; **~r Computer reicht aus** any computer will do; **bei ~m Wetter** in any weather ▷ *pron* everybody; (*jeder Einzelne*) each; **~r von euch/uns** each of you/us; **jedenfalls** *adv* in any case; **jederzeit** *adv* at any time; **jedesmal** *adv* every time
jedoch *adv* however
jemals *adv* ever
jemand *pron* somebody; (*in Frage und Verneinung*) anybody
Jemen (*-(s)*) *m* Yemen
jene(r, s) *adj* that, those *pl* ▷ *pron* that (one), those *pl*
jenseits *adv* on the other side ▷ *prep* +*gen* on the other side of; (*fig*) beyond
Jetlag (*-s*) *m* jet lag
jetzig *adj* present
jetzt *adv* now; **erst ~** only now; **~ gleich** right now; **bis ~** so far, up to now; **von ~ an** from now on
jeweils *adv*: **~ zwei zusammen** two at a time; **zu ~ 5 Euro** at 5 euros each
Job (*-s, -s*) *m* job; **jobben** *vi* (*fam*) to work, to have a job
Jod (*-(e)s*) *nt* iodine
joggen *vi* to jog; **Jogging** (*-s*) *nt* jogging; **Jogginganzug** *m* jogging suit, tracksuit; **Jogginghose** *f* jogging pants *pl*
Jog(h)urt (*-s, -s*) *m o nt* yoghurt
Johannisbeere *f*: **Schwarze ~** blackcurrant; **Rote ~** redcurrant
Joint (*-s, -s*) *m* (*fam*) joint
jonglieren *vi* to juggle
Jordanien (*-s*) *nt* Jordan
Journalist(in) *m(f)* journalist

Joystick (-s, -s) m (Inform) joystick

jubeln vi to cheer

Jubiläum (-s, Jubiläen) nt jubilee; (Jahrestag) anniversary

jucken vi to itch ▷ vt: **es juckt mich am Arm** my arm is itching; **das juckt mich nicht** (fam) I couldn't care less; **Juckreiz** m itch

Jude (-n, -n) m, **Jüdin** f Jew; **sie ist Jüdin** she's Jewish; **jüdisch** adj Jewish

Judo (-(s)) nt judo

Jugend (-) f youth; **jugendfrei** adj: **ein ~er Film** a U-rated film (Brit), a G-rated film (US); **ein nicht ~er Film** an X-rated film; **Jugendgruppe** f youth group; **Jugendherberge** (-, -n) f youth hostel; **Jugendherbergsausweis** m youth hostel card; **jugendlich** adj youthful; **Jugendliche(r)** mf young person; **Jugendstil** m art nouveau; **Jugendzentrum** nt youth centre

Jugoslawien (-s) nt (Hist) Yugoslavia; **das ehemalige ~** the former Yugoslavia

Juli (-(s), -s) m July; siehe auch **Juni**

jung adj young

Junge (-n, -n) m boy

Junge(s) (-n, -n) nt young animal; **die ~n** pl the young pl

Jungfrau f virgin; (Astr) Virgo

Junggeselle (-n, -n) m bachelor; **Junggesellin** f single woman

Juni (-(s), -s) m June; **im ~** in June; **am 4. ~** on 4(th) June, on June 4(th) (gesprochen: on the fourth of June); **Anfang/Mitte/Ende ~** at the beginning/in the middle/at the end of June; **letzten/nächsten ~** last/next June

Jupiter (-s) m Jupiter

Jura ohne Artikel (Studienfach) law; **~ studieren** to study law; **Jurist(in)** m(f) lawyer; **juristisch** adj legal

Justiz (-) f justice; **Justizminister(in)** m(f) minister of justice

Juwel (-s, -en) nt jewel; **Juwelier(in)** (-s, -e) m(f) jeweller

K

Kabel (-s, -) nt (Elek) wire; (stark) cable; **Kabelfernsehen** nt cable television

Kabeljau (-s, -e o -s) m cod

Kabine f cabin; (im Schwimmbad) cubicle

Kabrio (-s, -s) nt convertible

Kachel (-, -n) f tile; **Kachelofen** m tiled stove

Käfer (-s, -) m beetle, bug (US)

Kaff (-s, -s) nt dump, hole

Kaffee (-s, -s) m coffee; **~ kochen** to make some coffee; **Kaffeefilter** m coffee filter; **Kaffeekanne** f coffeepot; **Kaffeeklatsch** (-(e)s, -e) m chat over coffee and cakes, coffee klatch (US); **Kaffeelöffel** m coffee spoon; **Kaffeemaschine** f coffee maker (o machine); **Kaffeetasse** f coffee cup

Käfig (-s, -e) m cage

kahl adj (Mensch, Kopf) bald; (Baum, Wand) bare

Kahn (-(e)s, Kähne) m boat; (Lastkahn) barge

Kai (-s, -e o -s) m quay

Kaiser (-s, -) m emperor; **Kaiserin** f empress; **Kaiserschnitt** m (Med) caesarean (section)

Kajak (-s, -s) nt kayak; **Kajakfahren** nt kayaking

Kajal (-s) m kohl

Kajüte (-, -n) f cabin

Kakao (-s, -s) m cocoa; (Getränk) (hot) chocolate

Kakerlake (-, -n) f cockroach

Kaki (-, -s) f kaki

Kaktee (-, -n) f, **Kaktus** (-, -se) m cactus

Kalb (-(e)s, Kälber) nt calf; **Kalbfleisch** nt veal; **Kalbsbraten** m roast veal; **Kalbsschnitzel** nt veal cutlet; (paniert) escalope of veal

Kalender (-s, -) m calendar; (Taschenkalender) diary

Kalk (-(e)s, -e) m lime; (in Knochen) calcium

Kalorie f calorie; **kalorienarm** adj low-calorie

kalt adj cold; **mir ist (es) ~** I'm cold; **kaltblütig** adj cold-blooded; **Kälte** (-) f cold; (fig) coldness

kam imperf von **kommen**

Kambodscha (-s) nt Cambodia

Kamel (-(e)s, -e) nt camel

Kamera (-, -s) f camera

Kamerad(in) (-en, -en) m(f) friend; (als Begleiter) companion

Kamerafrau f, **Kameramann** m camerawoman/-man

Kamille (-, -n) f camomile; **Kamillentee** m camomile tea

Kamin (-s, -e) m (außen) chimney; (innen) fireplace

Kamm (-(e)s, Kämme) m comb; (Berg) ridge; (Hahn) crest; **kämmen** vr **sich ~, sich** (dat) **die Haare ~** to

comb one's hair; **Kammermusik**
f chamber music
Kampf (-(e)s, Kämpfe) m fight;
(Schlacht) battle; (Wettbewerb)
contest; (fig: Anstrengung)
struggle; (fig: **kämpfen** vi to fight
(für, um for); **Kampfsport** m
martial art
Kanada (-s) nt Canada;
Kanadier(in) (-s, -) m(f) Cana-
dian; **kanadisch** adj Canadian
Kanal (-s, Kanäle) m (Fluss) canal;
(Rinne, TV) channel; (für Abfluss)
drain; **der ~** (Ärmelkanal) the
(English) Channel; **Kanalinseln**
pl Channel Islands pl;
Kanalisation f sewerage system;
Kanaltunnel m Channel Tunnel
Kanarienvogel m canary
Kandidat(in) (-en, -en) m(f)
candidate
Kandis(zucker) (-) m rock
candy
Känguru (-s, -s) nt kangaroo
Kaninchen nt rabbit
Kanister (-s, -) m can
Kännchen nt pot; **ein
~ Kaffee/Tee** a pot of coffee/tea;
Kanne (-, -n) f (Krug) jug;
(Kaffeekanne) pot; (Milchkanne)
churn; (Gießkanne) can
kannte imperf von **kennen**
Kante (-, -n) f edge
Kantine f canteen
Kanton (-s, -e) m canton
Kanu (-s, -s) nt canoe
Kanzler(in) (-s, -) m(f)
chancellor
Kap (-s, -s) nt cape
Kapazität f capacity; (Fachmann)
authority
Kapelle f (Gebäude) chapel; (Mus)
band
Kaper (-, -n) f caper
kapieren vt, vi (fam) to
understand; **kapiert?** got it?
Kapital (-s, -e o -ien) nt capital

Kapitän (-s, -e) m captain
Kapitel (-s, -) nt chapter
Kappe (-, -n) f cap
Kapsel (-, -n) f capsule
kaputt adj (fam) broken; (Mensch)
exhausted; **kaputt|gehen** irr vi
to break; (Schuhe) to fall apart;
(Firma) to go bust; (Stoff) to wear
out; **kaputt|machen** vt to
break; (jdn) to wear out
Kapuze (-, -n) f hood
Kap Verde (-s) nt Cape Verde
Karaffe (-, -n) f carafe; (mit
Stöpsel) decanter
Karamell (-s) m caramel, toffee
Karaoke (-(s)) nt karaoke
Karat (-s, -e) nt carat
Karate (-s) nt karate
Kardinal (-s, Kardinäle) m
cardinal
Karfreitag m Good Friday
kariert adj checked; (Papier)
squared
Karies (-) f (tooth) decay
Karikatur f caricature
Karneval (-s, -e o -s) m carnival

● **KARNEVAL**

Karneval is the name given to
the days immediately before
Lent when people gather to
sing, dance, eat, drink and
generally make merry before the
fasting begins. **Rosenmontag**,
the day before Shrove Tuesday,
is the most important day of
'Karneval' on the Rhine. Most
firms take a day's holiday on
that day to enjoy the parades
and revelry. In South Germany
'Karneval' is called **Fasching**.

Kärnten (-s) nt Carinthia
Karo (-s, -s) nt square; (Karten)
diamonds pl
Karosserie f (Auto) body(work)

Karotte (-, -n) f carrot
Karpfen (-s, -) m carp
Karriere (-, -n) f career
Karte (-, -n) f card; (Landkarte) map; (Speisekarte) menu; (Eintrittskarte, Fahrkarte) ticket; **mit ~ bezahlen** to pay by credit card; **~n spielen** to play cards; **die ~n mischen/geben** to shuffle/deal the cards
Kartei f card index; **Karteikarte** f index card
Kartenspiel nt card game; **Kartentelefon** nt cardphone; **Kartenvorverkauf** m advance booking
Kartoffel (-, -n) f potato; **Kartoffelbrei** m mashed potatoes pl; **Kartoffelchips** pl crisps pl (Brit), chips pl (US); **Kartoffelpuffer** m potato cake (made from grated potatoes); **Kartoffelpüree** nt mashed potatoes pl; **Kartoffelsalat** m potato salad
Karton (-s, -s) m cardboard; (Schachtel) (cardboard) box
Kartusche (-, -n) f cartridge
Karussell (-s, -s) nt roundabout (Brit), merry-go-round
Kaschmir (-s, e) m (Stoff) cashmere
Käse (-s, -) m cheese; **Käsekuchen** m cheesecake; **Käseplatte** f cheeseboard
Kasino (-s, -s) nt (Spielkasino) casino
Kaskoversicherung f comprehensive insurance
Kasper(l) (-s, -) m Punch; (fig) clown; **Kasperl(e)theater** nt (Vorstellung) Punch and Judy show; (Gebäude) Punch and Judy theatre
Kasse (-, -n) f (in Geschäft) till, cash register; (im Supermarkt) checkout; (Geldkasten) cashbox;

(Theater) box office; (Kino) ticket office; (Krankenkasse) health insurance; (Spar~) savings bank; **Kassenbon** (-s, -s) m, **Kassenzettel** m receipt
Kassette f (small) box; (Tonband) cassette; **Kassettenrekorder** m cassette recorder
kassieren vt to take ▷ vi: **darf ich ~?** would you like to pay now?; **Kassierer(in)** m(f) cashier
Kastanie f chestnut
Kasten (-s, Kästen) m (Behälter) box; (Getränkekasten) crate
Kat m abk = **Katalysator**
Katalog (-(e)s, -e) m catalogue
Katalysator m (Auto) catalytic converter; (Phys) catalyst
Katar (-s) nt Qatar
Katarr(h) (-s, -e) m catarrh
Katastrophe (-, -n) f catastrophe, disaster
Kategorie (-, -n) f category
Kater (-s, -) m tomcat; (fam: nach zu viel Alkohol) hangover
Kathedrale (-, -n) f cathedral
Katholik(in) m(f) Catholic; **katholisch** adj Catholic
Katze (-, -n) f cat
Kauderwelsch (-(s)) nt (unverständlich) gibberish; (Fachjargon) jargon
kauen vt, vi to chew
Kauf (-(e)s, Käufe) m purchase; (Kaufen) buying; **ein guter ~** a bargain; **etw in ~ nehmen** to put up with sth; **kaufen** vt to buy; **Käufer(in)** m(f) buyer; **Kauffrau** f businesswoman; **Kaufhaus** nt department store; **Kaufmann** m businessman; (im Einzelhandel) shopkeeper (Brit), storekeeper (US); **Kaufpreis** m purchase price; **Kaufvertrag** m purchase agreement
Kaugummi m chewing gum
Kaulquappe (-, -n) f tadpole

kaum *adv* hardly, scarcely
Kaution *f* deposit; (*Jur*) bail
Kaviar *m* caviar
KB (-, -) *nt*, **Kbyte** (-, -) *nt abk* = **Kilobyte** KB
Kebab (-(s), -s) *m* kebab
Kegel (-s, -) *m* skittle; (*beim Bowling*) pin; (*Math*) cone; **Kegelbahn** *f* bowling alley; **kegeln** *vi* to play skittles; (*bowlen*) to bowl
Kehle (-, -n) *f* throat; **Kehlkopf** *m* larynx
Kehre (-, -n) *f* sharp bend
kehren *vt* (*fegen*) to sweep
Keilriemen *m* (*Auto*) fan belt
kein *pron* no, not ... any; **ich habe ~ Geld** I have no money, I don't have money; **~ Mensch** no one; **du bist ~ Kind mehr** you're not a child any more; **keine(r, s)** *pron* (*Person*) no one, nobody; (*Sache*) not ... any, none; **~r von ihnen** none of them; (*bei zwei Personen/Sachen*) neither of them; **ich will keins von beiden** I don't want either (of them); **keinesfalls** *adv* on no account, under no circumstances
Keks (-es, -e) *m* biscuit (*Brit*), cookie (*US*); **jdm auf den ~ gehen** (*fam*) to get on sb's nerves
Keller (-s, -) *m* cellar; (*Geschoss*) basement
Kellner (-s, -) *m* waiter; **Kellnerin** *f* waitress
Kenia (-s) *nt* Kenya
kennen (*kannte, gekannt*) *vt* to know; **wir ~ uns seit 1990** we've known each other since 1990; **wir ~ uns schon** we've already met; **kennst du mich noch?** do you remember me?; **kennen|lernen** *vt* to get to know; **sich ~** to get to know each other; (*zum ersten Mal*) to meet
Kenntnis *f* knowledge; **seine ~se**

his knowledge
Kennwort *nt* (*a. Inform*) password; **Kennzeichen** *nt* mark, sign; (*Auto*) number plate (*Brit*), license plate (*US*); **besondere ~** distinguishing marks
Kerl (-s, -e) *m* guy, bloke (*Brit*)
Kern (-(e)s, -e) *m* (*Obst*) pip; (*Pfirsich, Kirsche etc*) stone; (*Nuss*) kernel; (*Atomkern*) nucleus; (*fig*) heart, core
Kernenergie *f* nuclear energy; **Kernkraft** *f* nuclear power; **Kernkraftwerk** *nt* nuclear power station
Kerze (-, -n) *f* candle; (*Zündkerze*) plug
Ket(s)chup (-(s), -s) *m o nt* ketchup
Kette (-, -n) *f* chain; (*Halskette*) necklace
keuchen *vi* to pant; **Keuchhusten** *m* whooping cough
Keule (-, -n) *f* club; (*Gastr*) leg; (*von Hähnchen a.*) drumstick
Keyboard (-s, -s) *nt* (*Mus*) keyboard
Kfz *nt abk* = **Kraftfahrzeug**
Kfz-Brief *m* ≈ logbook
Kfz-Steuer *f* ≈ road tax (*Brit*), vehicle tax (*US*)
KG (-, -s) *f abk* = **Kommanditgesellschaft** limited partnership
Kichererbse *f* chick pea
kichern *vi* to giggle
Kickboard® (-s, -s) *nt* micro scooter
Kicker (-s, -) *m* (*Spiel*) table football (*Brit*), foosball (*US*)
kidnappen *vt* to kidnap
Kidney-Bohne *f* kidney bean
Kiefer (-s, -) *m* jaw ▷ (-, -n) *f* pine; **Kieferchirurg(in)** *m(f)* oral surgeon

Kieme (-, -n) f gill
Kies (-es, -e) m gravel; **Kiesel** (-s, -) m, **Kieselstein** m pebble
kiffen vi (fam) to smoke pot
Kilo (-s, -(s)) nt kilo; **Kilobyte** nt kilobyte; **Kilogramm** nt kilogram; **Kilometer** m kilometre; **Kilometerstand** m ≈ mileage; **Kilometerzähler** m ≈ mileometer; **Kilowatt** nt kilowatt
Kind (-(e)s, -er) nt child; **sie bekommt ein ~** she's having a baby; **Kinderarzt** m, **Kinderärztin** f paediatrician; **Kinderbetreuung** f childcare; **Kinderbett** nt cot (Brit), crib (US); **Kinderfahrkarte** f child's ticket; **Kindergarten** m nursery school, kindergarten; **Kindergärtner(in)** m(f) nursery-school teacher; **Kindergeld** nt child benefit; **Kinderkrankheit** f children's illness; **Kinderkrippe** f crèche (Brit), daycare center (US); **Kinderlähmung** f polio; **Kindermädchen** nt nanny (Brit), nurse(maid); **kindersicher** adj childproof; **Kindersicherung** f childproof safety catch; (an Flasche) childproof cap; **Kindersitz** m child seat; **Kindertagesstätte** nt day nursery; **Kinderteller** m (im Restaurant) children's portion; **Kinderwagen** m pram (Brit), baby carriage (US); **Kinderzimmer** nt children's (bed)room; **Kindheit** f childhood; **kindisch** adj childish; **kindlich** adj childlike
Kinn (-(e)s, -e) nt chin
Kino (-s, -s) nt cinema (Brit), movie theater (US); **ins ~ gehen** to go to the cinema (Brit) (o to the movies (US))
Kiosk (-(e)s, -e) m kiosk
Kippe f (fam: Zigarettenstummel) cigarette end, fag end (Brit)

kippen vi to tip over ▷ vt to tilt; (Regierung, Minister) to topple
Kirche (-, -n) f church; **Kirchturm** m church tower; (mit Spitze) steeple
Kirmes (-, -sen) f fair
Kirsche (-, -n) f cherry; **Kirschtomate** f cherry tomato
Kissen (-s, -) nt cushion; (Kopfkissen) pillow; **Kissenbezug** m cushion cover; (für Kopfkissen) pillowcase
Kiste (-, -n) f box; (Truhe) chest
KITA (-, -s) f abk = **Kindertagesstätte** day-care centre (Brit), day-care center (US)
kitschig adj kitschy, cheesy
kitzelig adj (a. fig) ticklish; **kitzeln** vt, vi to tickle
Kiwi (-, -s) f (Frucht) kiwi (fruit)
Klage (-, -n) f complaint; (Jur) lawsuit; **klagen** vi to complain (über +akk about, bei to); **kläglich** adj wretched
Klammer (-, -n) f (in Text) bracket; (Büroklammer) clip; (Wäscheklammer) peg (Brit), clothespin (US); (Zahnklammer) brace; **Klammeraffe** m (fam) at-sign, @; **klammern** vr: **sich ~** to cling (an +akk to)
klang imperf von **klingen**
Klang (-(e)s, Klänge) m sound
Klappbett nt folding bed
klappen vi impers (gelingen) to work; **es hat gut geklappt** it went well
klappern vi to rattle; (Geschirr) to clatter; **Klapperschlange** f rattlesnake
Klappfahrrad nt folding bicycle; **Klappstuhl** m folding chair
klar adj clear; **sich** (dat) **im Klaren sein** to be clear (über +akk about); **alles ~?** everything okay?
klären vt (Flüssigkeit) to purify; (Probleme, Frage) to clarify ▷ vr:

sich ~ to clear itself up
Klarinette (-, -n) f clarinet
klar|kommen irr vi: **mit etw ~** to cope with something; **kommst du klar?** are you managing all right?; **mit jdm ~** to get along with sb; **klar|machen** vt: **jdm etw ~** to make sth clear to sb; **klar|stellen** vt to clarify
Klärung f (von Frage, Problem) clarification
klasse adj inv (fam) great, brilliant
Klasse (-, -n) f class; (Schuljahr) form (Brit), grade (US); **erster ~ reisen** to travel first class; **in welche ~ gehst du?** which form (Brit) (o grade (US)) are you in?; **Klassenarbeit** f test; **Klassenlehrer(in)** m(f) class teacher; **Klassenzimmer** nt classroom
Klassik f (Zeit) classical period; (Musik) classical music
Klatsch (-(e)s, -e) m (Gerede) gossip; **klatschen** vi (schlagen) to smack; (Beifall) to applaud, to clap; (reden) to gossip; **Klatschmohn** m (corn) poppy; **klatschnass** adj soaking (wet)
Klaue (-, -n) f claw; (fam: Schrift) scrawl; **klauen** vt (fam) to pinch
Klavier (-s, -e) nt piano
Klebeband nt adhesive tape; **kleben** vt to stick (an +akk to) ▷ vi (klebrig sein) to be sticky; **klebrig** adj sticky; **Klebstoff** m glue; **Klebstreifen** m adhesive tape
Klecks (-es, -e) m blob; (Tinte) blot
Klee (-s) m clover
Kleid (-(e)s, -er) nt (Frauen~) dress; **~er** pl (Kleidung) clothes pl; **Kleiderbügel** m coat hanger; **Kleiderschrank** m wardrobe (Brit), closet (US); **Kleidung** f clothing
klein adj small, little; (Finger) little; **mein ~er Bruder** my little (o younger) brother; **als ich noch ~ war** when I was a little boy/girl; **etw ~ schneiden** to chop sth up; **Kleinanzeige** f classified ad; **Kleinbuchstabe** m small letter; **Kleinbus** m minibus; **Kleingeld** nt change; **Kleinigkeit** f trifle; (Zwischenmahlzeit) snack; **Kleinkind** nt toddler; **klein|schreiben** vt (mit kleinem Anfangsbuchstaben) to write with a small letter; **Kleinstadt** f small town
Kleister (-s, -) m paste
Klempner(in) m(f) plumber
klettern vi to climb
Klettverschluss m Velcro® fastening
klicken vi (a. Inform) to click
Klient(in) (-en, -en) m(f) client
Klima (-s, -s) nt climate; **Klimaanlage** f air conditioning; **klimatisiert** adj air-conditioned
Klinge (-, -n) f blade
Klingel (-, -n) f bell; **klingeln** vi to ring
klingen (klang, geklungen) vi to sound
Klinik f clinic; (Krankenhaus) hospital
Klinke (-, -n) f handle
Klippe (-, -n) f cliff; (im Meer) reef; (fig) hurdle
Klischee (-s, -s) nt (fig) cliché
Klo (-s, -s) nt (fam) loo (Brit), john (US); **Klobrille** f toilet seat; **Klopapier** nt toilet paper
klopfen vt, vi to knock; (Herz) to thump
Kloß (-es, Klöße) m (im Hals) lump; (Gastr) dumpling
Kloster (-s, Klöster) nt (für Männer) monastery; (für Frauen) convent
Klub (-s, -s) m club
klug adj clever
knabbern vt, vi to nibble

Knäckebrot nt crispbread
knacken vt, vi to crack
Knall (-(e)s, -e) m bang; **knallen**
vi to bang
knapp adj (kaum ausreichend)
scarce; (Sieg) narrow; **~ bei Kasse
sein** to be short of money; **~ zwei
Stunden** just under two hours
Knauf (-s, Knäufe) m knob
kneifen (kniff, gekniffen) vt, vi to
pinch; (sich drücken) to back out
(vor +dat of); **Kneifzange** f
pincers pl
Kneipe (-, -n) f (fam) pub (Brit),
bar
Knete (-) f (fam: Geld) dough;
kneten vt to knead; (formen) to
mould
knicken vt, vi (brechen) to break;
(Papier) to fold; **geknickt sein** (fig)
to be downcast
Knie (-s, -) nt knee; **in die
~ gehen** to bend one's knees;
Kniebeuge f knee bend;
Kniegelenk nt knee joint;
Kniekehle f back of the knee;
knien vi to kneel; **Kniescheibe** f
kneecap; **Knieschoner** (-s, -) m,
Knieschützer (-s, -) m knee pad;
Kniestrumpf m knee-length sock
kniff imperf von **kneifen**
knipsen vt to punch; (Foto) to
snap ▷ vi (Foto) to take snaps
knirschen vi to crunch; **mit den
Zähnen ~** to grind one's teeth
knitterfrei adj non-crease;
knittern vi to crease
Knoblauch m garlic;
Knoblauchbrot nt garlic bread;
Knoblauchzehe f clove of garlic
Knöchel (-s, -) m (Finger)
knuckle; (Fuß) ankle
Knochen (-s, -) m bone;
Knochenbruch m fracture;
Knochenmark nt marrow
Knödel (-s, -) m dumpling
Knollensellerie m celeriac

Knopf (-(e)s, Knöpfe) m button;
Knopfdruck m: **auf ~** at the
touch of a botton; **Knopfloch** nt
buttonhole
Knospe (-, -n) f bud
knoten vt to knot; **Knoten** (-s, -)
m knot; (Med) lump
Know-how (-(s)) nt know-how,
expertise
knurren vi (Hund) to growl;
(Magen) to rumble; (Mensch) to
grumble
knusprig adj crisp; (Keks) crunchy
knutschen vi (fam) to smooch
k. o. adj inv (Sport) knocked out;
(fig) knackered
Koalition f coalition
Koch (-(e)s, Köche) m cook;
Kochbuch nt cookery book,
cookbook; **kochen** vt, vi to cook;
(Wasser) to boil; (Kaffee, Tee) to
make; **Köchin** f cook;
Kochlöffel m wooden spoon;
Kochnische f kitchenette;
Kochplatte f hotplate;
Kochrezept nt recipe; **Kochtopf**
m saucepan
Kode (-s, -s) m code
Köder (-s, -) m bait
Koffein (-s) nt caffeine;
koffeinfrei adj decaffeinated
Koffer (-s, -) m (suit)case;
Kofferraum m (Auto) boot (Brit),
trunk (US)
Kognak (-s, -s) m brandy
Kohl (-(e)s, -e) m cabbage
Kohle (-, -n) f coal; (Holzkohle)
charcoal; (Chem) carbon; (fam:
Geld) cash, dough; **Kohlehydrat**
nt carbohydrate; **Kohlendioxid**
nt carbon dioxide; **Kohlensäure**
f (in Getränken) fizz; **ohne ~** still,
non-carbonated (US); **mit
~** sparkling, carbonated (US);
Kohletablette f charcoal tablet
Kohlrabi (-(s), -(s)) m kohlrabi
Koje (-, -n) f cabin; (Bett) bunk

Kokain (-s) nt cocaine
Kokosnuss f coconut
Kolben (-s, -) m (Tech) piston; (Mais~) cob
Kolik (-, -en) f colic
Kollaps (-es, -e) m collapse
Kollege (-n, -n) m, **Kollegin** f colleague
Köln (-s) nt Cologne
Kolonne (-, -n) f convoy; **in ~ fahren** to drive in convoy
Kölsch (-, -) nt (Bier) (strong) lager (from the Cologne region)
Kolumbien (-s) nt Columbia
Koma (-s, -s) nt coma
Kombi (-(s), -s) m estate (car) (Brit), station wagon (US); **Kombination** f combination; (Folgerung) deduction; (Hemdhose) combinations pl; (Aviat) flying suit; **kombinieren** vt to combine ▷ vi to reason; (vermuten) to guess; **Kombizange** f (pair of) pliers pl
Komfort (-s) m conveniences pl; (Bequemlichkeit) comfort
Komiker(in) m(f) comedian, comic; **komisch** adj funny
Komma (-s, -s) nt comma
Kommanditgesellschaft f limited partnership
kommen (kam, gekommen) vi to come; (näher kommen) to approach; (passieren) to happen; (gelangen, geraten) to get; (erscheinen) to appear; (in die Schule, das Gefängnis etc) to go; **~ lassen** to send for; **zu sich ~** to come round (o to); **zu etw ~** (bekommen) to acquire sth; (Zeit dazu finden) to get round to sth; **wer kommt zuerst?** who's first?; **kommend** adj coming; **~e Woche** next week; **in den ~en Jahren** in the years to come
Kommentar m commentary; **kein ~** no comment
Kommilitone (-n, -n) m, **Kommilitonin** f fellow student

Kommissar(in) m(f) inspector
Kommode (-, -n) f chest of drawers
Kommunikation f communication
Kommunion f (Rel) communion
Kommunismus m communism
Komödie f comedy
kompakt adj compact
Kompass (-es, -e) m compass
kompatibel adj compatible
kompetent adj competent
komplett adj complete
Kompliment nt compliment; **jdm ein ~ machen** to pay sb a compliment; **~!** congratulations
Komplize (-n, -n) m accomplice
kompliziert adj complicated
Komponist(in) m(f) composer
Kompost (-(e)s, -e) m compost; **Komposthaufen** m compost heap; **kompostierbar** adj biodegradable
Kompott (-(e)s, -e) nt stewed fruit
Kompresse (-, -n) f compress
Kompromiss (-es, -e) m compromise
Kondensmilch f condensed milk, evaporated milk
Kondition f (Leistungsfähigkeit) condition; **sie hat eine gute ~** she's in good shape
Konditorei f cake shop; (mit Café) café
Kondom (-s, -e) nt condom
Konfektionsgröße f size
Konferenz f conference
Konfession f religion; (christlich) denomination
Konfetti (-(s)) nt confetti
Konfirmation f (Rel) confirmation
Konfitüre (-, -n) f jam
Konflikt (-(e)s, -e) m conflict
konfrontieren vt to confront
Kongo (-s) m Congo

Kongress (-es, -e) m conference; **der ~** (Parlament der USA) Congress

König (-(e)s, -e) m king; **Königin** f queen; **königlich** adj royal; **Königreich** nt kingdom

Konkurrenz f competition

 SCHLÜSSELWORT

können (pt **konnte**, pp **gekonnt** o (als Hilfsverb) **können**) vt, vi **1** to be able to; **ich kann es machen** I can do it, I am able to do it; **ich kann es nicht machen** I can't do it, I'm not able to do it; **ich kann nicht ...** I can't ..., I cannot ...; **ich kann nicht mehr** I can't go on **2** (wissen, beherrschen) to know; **können Sie Deutsch?** can you speak German?; **er kann gut Englisch** he speaks English well; **sie kann keine Mathematik** she can't do mathematics **3** (dürfen) to be allowed to; **kann ich gehen?** can I go?; **könnte ich ...?** could I ...?; **kann ich mit?** (fam) can I come with you? **4** (möglich sein) **Sie könnten recht haben** you may be right; **das kann sein** that's possible; **kann sein** maybe

konsequent adj consistent; **Konsequenz** f consequence

konservativ adj conservative

Konserven pl tinned food sing (Brit), canned food sing; **Konservendose** f tin (Brit), can

konservieren vt to preserve; **Konservierungsmittel** nt preservative

Konsonant m consonant

Konsul(in) (-s, -n) m(f) consul; **Konsulat** nt consulate

Kontakt (-(e)s, -e) m contact; **kontaktarm** adj: **er ist ~** he lacks

contact with other people; **kontaktfreudig** adj sociable; **Kontaktlinsen** pl contact lenses pl

Kontinent m continent

Konto (-s, Konten) nt account; **Kontoauszug** m (bank) statement; **Kontoauszugsdrucker** m bank-statement machine; **Kontoinhaber(in)** m(f) account holder; **Kontonummer** f account number; **Kontostand** m balance

Kontrabass m double bass

Kontrast (-(e)s, -e) m contrast

Kontrolle (-, -n) f control; (Aufsicht) supervision; (Passkontrolle) passport control; **kontrollieren** vt to control; (nachprüfen) to check

Konzentration f concentration; **Konzentrationslager** nt (Hist) concentration camp; **konzentrieren** vt to concentrate ▷ vr: **sich ~** to concentrate

Konzept (-(e)s, -e) nt rough draft; **jdn aus dem ~ bringen** to put sb off

Konzern (-(e)s, -e) m firm

Konzert (-(e)s, -e) nt concert; (Stück) concerto; **Konzertsaal** m concert hall

koordinieren vt to coordinate

Kopf (-(e)s, Köpfe) m head; **pro ~** per person; **sich den ~ zerbrechen** to rack one's brains; **Kopfhörer** m headphones pl; **Kopfkissen** nt pillow; **Kopfsalat** m lettuce; **Kopfschmerzen** pl headache sing; **Kopfstütze** f headrest; **Kopftuch** nt headscarf; **kopfüber** adv headfirst

Kopie f copy; **kopieren** vt (a. Inform) to copy; **Kopierer** (-s, -) m, **Kopiergerät** nt copier

Kopilot(in) m(f) co-pilot
Koralle (-, -n) f coral
Koran (-s) m (Rel) Koran
Korb (-(e)s, Körbe) m basket; **jdm einen ~ geben** (fig) to turn sb down
Kord (-(e)s, -e) m corduroy
Kordel (-, -n) f cord
Kork (-(e)s, -e) m cork; **Korken** (-s, -) m cork; **Korkenzieher** (-s, -) m corkscrew
Korn (-(e)s, Körner) nt grain; **Kornblume** f cornflower
Körper (-s, -) m body; **Körperbau** m build; **Körpergeruch** m body odour; **Körpergröße** f height; **körperlich** adj physical; **Körperteil** m part of the body; **Körperverletzung** f physical injury
korrekt adj correct
Korrespondent(in) m(f) correspondent; **Korrespondenz** f correspondence
korrigieren vt to correct
Kosmetik f cosmetics pl; **Kosmetikkoffer** m vanity case; **Kosmetiksalon** m beauty parlour; **Kosmetiktuch** nt paper tissue
Kost (-) f (Nahrung) food; (Verpflegung) board
kostbar adj precious; (teuer) costly, expensive
kosten vt to cost ▷ vt, vi (versuchen) to taste; **Kosten** pl costs pl, cost; (Ausgaben) expenses pl; **auf ~ von** at the expense of; **kostenlos** adj free (of charge); **Kostenvoranschlag** m estimate
köstlich adj (Essen) delicious; (Einfall) delightful; **sich ~ amüsieren** to have a marvellous time
Kostprobe f taster; (fig) sample; **kostspielig** adj expensive
Kostüm (-s, -e) nt costume;

(Damenkostüm) suit
Kot (-(e)s) m excrement
Kotelett (-(e)s, -e o -s) nt chop, cutlet
Koteletten pl sideboards pl (Brit), sideburns pl (US)
Kotflügel m (Auto) wing
kotzen vi (vulg) to puke, to throw up
Krabbe (-, -n) f shrimp; (größer) prawn; (Krebs) crab
krabbeln vi to crawl
Krach (-(e)s, -s o -e) m crash; (andauernd) noise; (fam: Streit) row
Kraft (-, Kräfte) f strength; (Pol, Phys) force; (Fähigkeit) power; (Arbeits~) worker; **in ~ treten** to come into effect; **Kraftausdruck** m swearword; **Kraftfahrzeug** nt motor vehicle; **Kraftfahrzeugbrief** m ≈ logbook; **Kraftfahrzeugschein** m vehicle registration document; **Kraftfahrzeugsteuer** f ≈ road tax (Brit), vehicle tax (US); **Kraftfahrzeugversicherung** f car insurance; **kräftig** adj strong; (gesund) healthy; (Farben) intense, strong; **Kraftstoff** m fuel; **Kraftwerk** nt power station
Kragen (-s, -) m collar
Krähe (-, -n) f crow
Kralle (-, -n) f claw; (Parkkralle) wheel clamp
Kram (-(e)s) m stuff
Krampf (-(e)s, Krämpfe) m cramp; (zuckend) spasm; **Krampfader** f varicose vein
Kran (-(e)s, Kräne) m crane
Kranich (-s, -e) m (Zool) crane
krank adj ill, sick
kränken vt to hurt
Krankengymnastik f physiotherapy; **Krankenhaus** nt hospital; **Krankenkasse** f health insurance; **Krankenpfleger** (-s, -) m (male) nurse;

Krankenschein m *health insurance certificate*; **Krankenschwester** f nurse; **Krankenversicherung** f health insurance; **Krankenwagen** m ambulance; **Krankheit** f illness; *(durch Infektion hervorgerufen)* disease

Kränkung f insult

Kranz *(-es, Kränze)* m wreath

krass *adj* crass; *(fam: toll)* wicked

kratzen *vt, vi* to scratch; **Kratzer** *(-s, -)* m scratch

kraulen *vi (schwimmen)* to do the crawl ▷ *vt (streicheln)* to pet

Kraut *(-(e)s, Kräuter)* nt plant; *(Gewürz)* herb; *(Gemüse)* cabbage; **Kräuter** pl herbs pl; **Kräuterbutter** f herb butter; **Kräutertee** m herbal tea; **Krautsalat** m coleslaw

Krawatte f tie

kreativ *adj* creative

Krebs *(-es, -e)* m *(Zool)* crab; *(Med)* cancer; *(Astr)* Cancer

Kredit *(-(e)s, -e)* m credit; **auf ~ on** credit; **einen ~ aufnehmen** to take out a loan; **Kreditkarte** f credit card

Kreide *(-, -n)* f chalk

Kreis *(-es, -e)* m circle; *(Bezirk)* district

kreischen *vi* to shriek; *(Bremsen, Säge)* to screech

Kreisel *(-s, -)* m *(Spielzeug)* top; *(Verkehrskreisel)* roundabout *(Brit)*, traffic circle *(US)*

Kreislauf m *(Med)* circulation; *(fig: der Natur etc)* cycle; **Kreislaufstörungen** pl *(Med)* **ich habe ~** I've got problems with my circulation; **Kreisverkehr** m roundabout *(Brit)*, traffic circle *(US)*

Kren *(-s)* m horseradish

Kresse *(-, -n)* f cress

Kreuz *(-es, -e)* nt cross; *(Anat)* small of the back; *(Karten)* clubs pl;

mir tut das ~ weh I've got backache; **Kreuzband** m cruciate ligament; **kreuzen** *vt* to cross ▷ *vr:* **sich ~** to cross ▷ *vi (Naut)* to cruise; **Kreuzfahrt** f cruise; **Kreuzgang** *m* cloisters pl; **Kreuzotter** *(-, -n)* f adder; **Kreuzschlitzschraubenzieher** m Phillips® screwdriver; **Kreuzschlüssel** m *(Auto)* wheel brace; **Kreuzschmerzen** pl backache sing; **Kreuzung** f *(Verkehrskreuzung)* crossroads sing, intersection; *(Züchtung)* cross; **Kreuzworträtsel** nt crossword (puzzle)

kriechen *(kroch, gekrochen)* vi to crawl; *(unauffällig)* to creep; *(fig, pej)* **(vor jdm)** ~ to crawl (to sb); **Kriechspur** f crawler lane

Krieg *(-(e)s, -e)* m war

kriegen *vt (fam)* to get; *(erwischen)* to catch; **sie kriegt ein Kind** she's having a baby; **ich kriege noch Geld von dir** you still owe me some money

Krimi *(-s, -s)* m *(fam)* thriller; **Kriminalität** f criminality; **Kriminalpolizei** f detective force, ≈ CID *(Brit)*, ≈ FBI *(US)*; **Kriminalroman** m detective novel; **kriminell** *adj* criminal

Krippe *(-, -n)* f *(Futterkrippe)* manger; *(Weihnachtskrippe)* crib *(Brit)*, crèche *(US)*; *(Kinderkrippe)* crèche *(Brit)*, daycare center *(US)*

Krise *(-, -n)* f crisis

Kristall *(-s, -e)* m crystal ▷ *(-s)* nt *(Glas)* crystal

Kritik f criticism; *(Rezension)* review; **Kritiker(in)** *m(f)* critic; **kritisch** *adj* critical

kritzeln *vt, vi* to scribble, to scrawl

Kroate *(-n, -n)* m Croat; **Kroatien** *(-s)* nt Croatia; **Kroatin** f Croat; **kroatisch** *adj* Croatian;

Kroatisch nt Croatian
kroch imperf von **kriechen**
Krokodil (-s, -e) nt crocodile
Krokus (-, - o -se) m crocus
Krone (-, -n) f crown;
Kronleuchter m chandelier
Kropf (-(e)s, Kröpfe) m (Med)
goitre; (von Vogel) crop
Kröte (-, -n) f toad
Krücke (-, -n) f crutch
Krug (-(e)s, Krüge) m jug;
(Bierkrug) mug
Krümel (-s, -) m crumb
krumm adj crooked
Krüppel (-s, -) m cripple
Kruste (-, -n) f crust
Kruzifix (-es, -e) nt crucifix
Kuba (-s) nt Cuba
Kübel (-s, -) m tub; (Eimer) bucket
Kubikmeter m cubic metre
Küche (-, -n) f kitchen; (Kochen)
cooking
Kuchen (-s, -) m cake; (mit
Teigdeckel) pie; **Kuchengabel** f
cake fork
Küchenmaschine f food
processor; **Küchenpapier** nt
kitchen roll; **Küchenschrank** m
(kitchen) cupboard
Kuckuck (-s, -e) m cuckoo
Kugel (-, -n) f ball; (Math) sphere;
(Mil) bullet; (Weihnachtskugel)
bauble; **Kugellager** nt ball
bearing; **Kugelschreiber** m
(ball-point) pen, biro® (Brit);
Kugelstoßen (-s) nt shot put
Kuh (-, Kühe) f cow
kühl adj cool; **Kühlakku** (-s, -s) m
ice pack; **Kühlbox** f cool box;
kühlen vt to cool; **Kühler** (-s, -)
m (Auto) radiator; **Kühlerhaube**
f (Auto) bonnet (Brit), hood (US);
Kühlschrank m fridge,
refrigerator; **Kühltasche** f cool
bag; **Kühltruhe** f freezer;
Kühlwasser nt (Auto) radiator
water

Kuhstall m cowshed
Küken (-s, -) nt chick
Kuli (-s, -s) m (fam: Kugelschreiber)
pen, biro® (Brit)
Kulisse (-, -n) f scenery
Kult (-s, -e) m cult; **Kultfigur** f
cult figure
Kultur f culture; (Lebensform)
civilization; **Kulturbeutel** m
toilet bag (Brit), washbag;
kulturell adj cultural
Kümmel (-s, -) m caraway
seeds pl
Kummer (-s) m grief, sorrow
kümmern vr: **sich um jdn ~** to
look after sb; **sich um etw ~** to see
to sth ▷ vt to concern; **das
kümmert mich nicht** that doesn't
worry me
Kumpel (-s, -) m (fam) mate, pal
Kunde (-n, -n) m customer;
Kundendienst m after-sales (o
customer) service;
Kunden(kredit)karte f storecard, chargecard; **Kunden-
nummer** f customer number
kündigen vi to hand in one's
notice; (Mieter) to give notice that
one is moving out; **jdm ~** to give
sb his/her notice; (Vermieter) to
give sb notice to quit ▷ vt to
cancel; (Vertrag) to terminate; **jdm
die Stellung ~** to give sb his/her
notice; **jdm die Wohnung ~** to
give sb notice to quit; **Kündigung**
f (Arbeitsverhältnis) dismissal;
(Vertrag) termination;
(Abonnement) cancellation; (Frist)
notice; **Kündigungsfrist** f
period of notice
Kundin f customer; **Kundschaft**
f customers pl
künftig adj future
Kunst (-, Künste) f art; (Können)
skill; **Kunstausstellung** f art
exhibition; **Kunstgewerbe** nt arts
and crafts pl; **Künstler(in)** (-s, -)

m(f) artist; **künstlerisch** *adj* artistic
künstlich *adj* artificial
Kunststoff *m* synthetic material; **Kunststück** *nt* trick; **Kunstwerk** *nt* work of art
Kupfer (*-s, -*) *nt* copper
Kuppel (*-, -n*) *f* dome
kuppeln *vi* (*Auto*) to operate the clutch; **Kupplung** *f* coupling; (*Auto*) clutch
Kur (*-, -en*) *f* course of treatment; (*am Kurort*) cure
Kür (*-, -en*) *f* (*Sport*) free programme
Kurbel (*-, -n*) *f* crank; (*von Rollo, Fenster*) winder
Kürbis (*-ses, -se*) *m* pumpkin
Kurierdienst *m* courier service
kurieren *vt* to cure
Kurort *m* health resort
Kurs (*-es, -e*) *m* course; (*Fin*) rate; (*Wechselkurs*) exchange rate
kursiv *adj* italic ▷ *adv* in italics
Kursleiter(in) *m(f)* course tutor; **Kursteilnehmer(in)** *m(f)* (*course*) participant; **Kurswagen** *m* (*Eisenb*) through carriage
Kurve (*-, -n*) *f* curve; (*Straßenkurve*) bend; **kurvenreich** *adj* (*Straße*) winding
kurz *adj* short; (*zeitlich a.*) brief; **~ vorher/darauf** shortly before/after; **kannst du ~ kommen?** could you come here for a minute?; **~ gesagt** in short; **kurzärmelig** *adj* short-sleeved; **kürzen** *vt* to cut short; (*in der Länge*) to shorten; (*Gehalt*) to reduce; **kurzerhand** *adv* on the spot; **kurzfristig** *adj* short-term; **das Konzert wurde ~ abgesagt** the concert was called off at short notice; **Kurzgeschichte** *f* short story; **kurzhaarig** *adj* short-haired; **kürzlich** *adv* recently; **Kurzparkzone** *f*

short-stay (*Brit*) (*o* short-term (*US*)) parking zone; **Kurzschluss** *m* (*Elek*) short circuit; **kurzsichtig** *adj* short-sighted; **Kurztrip** *m* trip, break; **Kurzurlaub** *m* short holiday (*Brit*), short vacation (*US*); **Kurzwelle** *f* short wave
Kusine *f* cousin
Kuss (*-es, Küsse*) *m* kiss; **küssen** *vt* to kiss ▷ *vr:* **sich ~** to kiss
Küste (*-, -n*) *f* coast; (*Ufer*) shore; **Küstenwache** *f* coastguard
Kutsche (*-, -n*) *f* carriage; (*geschlossene*) coach
Kuvert (*-s, -s*) *nt* envelope
Kuvertüre (*-, -n*) *f* coating
Kuwait (*-s*) *nt* Kuwait
KZ (*-s, -s*) *nt* *abk =* **Konzentrationslager** (*Hist*) concentration camp

Labor (-s, -e o -s) nt lab
Labyrinth (-s, -e) nt maze
Lache (-, -n) f (Pfütze) puddle; (Blut~, Öl~) pool
lächeln vi to smile; **Lächeln** (-s) nt smile; **lachen** vi to laugh; **lächerlich** adj ridiculous
Lachs (-es, -e) m salmon
Lack (-(e)s, -e) m varnish; (Farblack) lacquer; (an Auto) paint; **lackieren** vt to varnish; (Auto) to spray; **Lackschaden** m scratch (on the paintwork)
Ladegerät nt (battery) charger; **laden** (lud, geladen) vt (a. Inform) to load; (einladen) to invite; (Handy etc) to charge
Laden (-s, Läden) m shop; (Fensterladen) shutter; **Ladendieb(in)** m(f) shoplifter; **Ladendiebstahl** m shoplifting; **Ladenschluss** m closing time
Ladung f load; (Naut, Aviat)

cargo; (Jur) summons sing
lag imperf von **liegen**
Lage (-, -n) f position, situation; (Schicht) layer; **in der ~ sein zu** to be in a position to
Lager (-s, -) nt camp; (Comm) warehouse; (Tech) bearing; **Lagerfeuer** nt campfire; **lagern** vi (Dinge) to be stored; (Menschen) to camp ▷ vt to store
Lagune f lagoon
lahm adj lame; (langweilig) dull; **lähmen** vt to paralyse; **Lähmung** f paralysis
Laib (-s, -e) m loaf
Laie (-n, -n) m layman
Laken (-s, -) nt sheet
Lakritze (-, -n) f liquorice
Lamm (-(e)s, Lämmer) nt lamb
Lampe (-, -n) f lamp; (Glühbirne) bulb; **Lampenfieber** nt stage fright; **Lampenschirm** m lampshade
Lampion (-s, -s) m Chinese lantern
Land (-(e)s, Länder) nt (Gelände) land; (Nation) country; (Bundesland) state, Land; **auf dem ~(e)** in the country

- LAND
-
- A **Land** (plural **Länder**) is a
- member state of the **BRD**. There
- are 16 **Länder**, namely
- Baden-Württemberg, Bayern,
- Berlin, Brandenburg, Bremen,
- Hamburg, Hessen,
- Mecklenburg-Vorpommern,
- Niedersachsen,
- Nordrhein-Westfalen,
- Rheinland-Pfalz, Saarland,
- Sachsen, Sachsen-Anhalt,
- Schleswig-Holstein and
- Thüringen. Each "Land" has its
- own parliament and
- constitution.

Landebahn f runway; **landen** vt, vi to land; (Schiff) to dock

Länderspiel nt international (match)

Landesgrenze f national border, frontier; **Landesinnere** nt interior; **landesüblich** adj customary; **Landeswährung** f national currency; **landesweit** adj nationwide

Landhaus nt country house; **Landkarte** f map; **Landkreis** m administrative region, ≈ district

ländlich adj rural

Landschaft f countryside; (schöne) scenery; (Kunst) landscape; **Landstraße** f country road, B road (Brit)

Landung f landing; **Landungsbrücke** f, **Landungssteg** m gangway

Landwirt(in) m(f) farmer; **Landwirtschaft** f agriculture, farming; **landwirtschaftlich** adj agricultural

lang adj long; (Mensch) tall; **ein zwei Meter ~er Tisch** a table two metres long; **den ganzen Tag ~** all day long; **die Straße ~** along the street; **langärmelig** adj long-sleeved; **lange** adv (for) a long time; **ich musste ~ warten** I had to wait (for) a long time; **ich bleibe nicht ~** I won't stay long; **es ist ~ her, dass wir uns gesehen haben** it's a long time since we saw each other; **Länge** (-, -n) f length; (Geo) longitude

langen vi (fam: ausreichen) to be enough; (fam: fassen) to reach (nach for); **mir langt's** I've had enough

Langeweile f boredom

langfristig adj long-term ▷ adv in the long term

Langlauf m cross-country skiing

längs prep +gen **die Bäume ~ der Straße** the trees along(side) the road ▷ adv: **die Streifen laufen ~ über das Hemd** the stripes run lengthways down the shirt

langsam adj slow ▷ adv slowly

Langschläfer(in) (-s, -) m(f) late riser

längst adv: **das ist ~ fertig** that was finished a long time ago; **sie sollte ~ da sein** she should have been here long ago; **als sie kam, waren wir ~ weg** when she arrived we had long since left

Langstreckenflug m long-haul flight

Languste (-, -n) f crayfish, crawfish (US)

langweilen vt to bore; **ich langweile mich** I'm bored; **langweilig** adj boring; **Langwelle** f long wave

Laos (-) nt Laos

Lappen (-s, -) m cloth, rag; (Staublappen) duster

läppisch adj silly; (Summe) ridiculous

Laptop (-s, -s) m laptop

Lärche (-, -n) f larch

Lärm (-(e)s) m noise

las imperf von **lesen**

Lasche (-, -n) f flap

Laser (-s, -) m laser; **Laserdrucker** m laser printer

⭕ SCHLÜSSELWORT

lassen (pt **ließ**, pp **gelassen** o (als Hilfsverb) **lassen**) vt 1 (unterlassen) to stop; (momentan) to leave; **lass das (sein)!** don't (do it)!; (hör auf!) stop it!; **lass mich!** leave me alone; **lassen wir das!** let's leave it; **er kann das Trinken nicht lassen** he can't stop drinking

2 (zurücklassen) to leave; **etw lassen, wie es ist** to leave sth (just) as it is

3 (*überlassen*) **jdn ins Haus lassen** to let sb into the house
▷ *vi* ; **lass mal, ich mache das schon** leave it, I'll do it
▷ *Hilfsverb* **1** (*veranlassen*) **etw machen lassen** to have *o* get sth done; **sich** *dat* **etw schicken lassen** to have sth sent (to one) **2** (*zulassen*) **jdn etw wissen lassen** to let sb know sth; **das Licht brennen lassen** to leave the light on; **jdn warten lassen** to keep sb waiting; **das lässt sich machen** that can be done
3 lass uns gehen let's go

lässig *adj* casual
Last (-, *-en*) *f* load; (*Bürde*) burden; (*Naut, Aviat*) cargo
Laster (-s, -) *nt* vice; (*fam*) truck, lorry (*Brit*)
lästern *vi*: **über jdn/etw ~** to make nasty remarks about sb/sth
lästig *adj* annoying; (*Person*) tiresome
Last-Minute-Angebot *nt* last-minute offer; **Last-Minute-Flug** *m* last-minute flight; **Last-Minute-Ticket** *nt* last-minute ticket
Lastwagen *m* truck, lorry (*Brit*)
Latein (-s) *nt* Latin
Laterne (-, *-n*) *f* lantern; (*Straßenlaterne*) streetlight
Latte (-, *-n*) *f* slat; (*Sport*) bar
Latz (*-es, Lätze*) *m* bib; **Lätzchen** *nt* bib; **Latzhose** *f* dungarees *pl*
lau *adj* (*Wind, Luft*) mild
Laub (*-(e)s*) *nt* foliage; **Laubfrosch** *m* tree frog; **Laubsäge** *f* fretsaw
Lauch (*-(e)s, -e*) *m* leeks *pl*; **eine Stange ~** a leek; **Lauchzwiebel** *f* spring onions *pl* (*Brit*), scallions *pl* (*US*)
Lauf (*-(e)s, Läufe*) *m* run; (*Wettlauf*) race; (*Entwicklung*) course; (*von*

Gewehr) barrel; **Laufbahn** *f* career; **laufen** (*lief, gelaufen*) *vi, vt* to run; (*gehen*) to walk; (*funktionieren*) to work; **mir läuft die Nase** my nose is running; **was läuft im Kino?** what's on at the cinema?; **wie läuft's so?** how are things?; **laufend** *adj* running; (*Monat, Ausgaben*) current; **auf dem Laufenden sein/halten** to be/to keep up-to-date; **Läufer** (-s, -) *m* (*Teppich*) rug; (*Schach*) bishop; **Läufer(in)** *m(f)* (*Sport*) runner; **Laufmasche** *f* ladder (*Brit*), run (*US*); **Laufwerk** *nt* (*Inform*) drive
Laune (-, *-n*) *f* mood; **gute/schlechte ~ haben** to be in a good/bad mood; **launisch** *adj* moody
Laus (-, *Läuse*) *f* louse
lauschen *vi* to listen; (*heimlich*) to eavesdrop
laut *adj* loud ▷ *adv* loudly; (*lesen*) aloud ▷ *prep* +*gen o dat* according to
läuten *vt, vi* to ring
lauter *adv* (*fam: nichts als*) nothing but
Lautsprecher *m* loudspeaker; **Lautstärke** *f* loudness; (*Radio, TV*) volume
lauwarm *adj* lukewarm
Lava (-, *Laven*) *f* lava
Lavendel (-s, -) *m* lavender
Lawine *f* avalanche
LCD-Anzeige *f* LCD-display
leasen *vt* to lease; **Leasing** (-s) *nt* leasing
leben *vt, vi* to live; (*am Leben sein*) to be alive; **wie lange ~ Sie schon hier?** how long have you been living here?; **von ... ~** (*Nahrungsmittel etc*) to live on ...; (*Beruf, Beschäftigung*) to make one's living from ...; **Leben** (-s, -) *nt* life; **lebend** *adj* living; **lebendig** *adj* alive; (*lebhaft*) lively;

lebensgefährlich adj very dangerous; (Verletzung) critical;
Lebensgefährte m,
Lebensgefährtin f partner;
Lebenshaltungskosten pl cost sing of living; **lebenslänglich** adj for life; **~ bekommen** to get life;
Lebenslauf m curriculum vitae (Brit), CV (Brit), resumé (US);
Lebensmittel pl food sing;
Lebensmittelgeschäft nt grocer's (shop); **Lebensmittelvergiftung** f food poisoning;
lebensnotwendig adj vital;
Lebensretter(in) m(f) rescuer;
Lebensstandard m standard of living; **Lebensunterhalt** m livelihood; **Lebensversicherung** f life insurance (o assurance (Brit));
Lebenszeichen nt sign of life
Leber (-, -n) f liver; **Leberfleck** m mole; **Leberpastete** f liver pâté
Lebewesen nt living being
lebhaft adj lively; (Erinnerung, Eindruck) vivid; **Lebkuchen** m gingerbread; **ein ~** a piece of gingerbread; **leblos** adj lifeless
Leck nt leak
lecken vi (Loch haben) to leak ▷ vt, vi (schlecken) to lick
lecker adj delicious, tasty
Leder (-s, -) nt leather
ledig adj single
leer adj empty; (Seite) blank; (Batterie) dead; **leeren** vt to empty ▷ vr: **sich ~** to empty;
Leerlauf m (Gang) neutral;
Leertaste f space bar; **Leerung** f emptying; (Briefkasten) collection; **Leerzeichen** nt blank, space
legal adj legal, lawful
legen vt to put, to place; (Eier) to lay ▷ vr: **sich ~** to lie down; (Sturm, Begeisterung) to die down; (Schmerz, Gefühl) to wear off

Legende (-, -n) f legend
leger adj casual
Lehm (-(e)s, -e) m loam; (Ton) clay
Lehne (-, -n) f arm(rest); (Rückenlehne) back(rest); **lehnen** vt to lean ▷ vr: **sich ~** to lean (an/gegen +akk against); **Lehnstuhl** m armchair
Lehrbuch nt textbook; **Lehre** (-, -n) f teaching; (beruflich) apprenticeship; (moralisch) lesson; **lehren** vt to teach; **Lehrer(in)** (-s, -) m(f) teacher; **Lehrgang** m course; **Lehrling** m apprentice; **lehrreich** adj instructive
Leib (-(e)s, -er) m body; **Leibgericht** nt, **Leibspeise** f favourite dish; **Leibwächter(in)** m(f) bodyguard
Leiche (-, -n) f corpse; **Leichenhalle** f mortuary; **Leichenwagen** m hearse
leicht adj light; (einfach) easy, simple; (Erkrankung) slight; **es sich** (dat) **~ machen** to take the easy way out ▷ adv (mühelos, schnell) easily; (geringfügig) slightly; **Leichtathletik** f athletics sing; **leicht|fallen** irr vi: **jdm ~** to be easy for sb; **leichtsinnig** adj careless; (stärker) reckless
leid adj: **jdn/etw ~ sein** to be tired of sb/sth; **Leid** (-(e)s) nt grief, sorrow; **leiden** (litt, gelitten) vi, vt to suffer (an, unter +dat from); **ich kann ihn/es nicht ~** I can't stand him/it; **Leiden** (-s, -) nt suffering; (Krankheit) illness
Leidenschaft f passion; **leidenschaftlich** adj passionate
leider adv unfortunately; **wir müssen jetzt ~ gehen** I'm afraid we have to go now; **~ ja/nein** I'm afraid so/not
leid|tun irr vi: **es tut mir/ihm leid** I'm/he's sorry; **er tut mir leid** I'm sorry for him

Leihbücherei f lending library
leihen (lieh, geliehen) vt: **jdm etw ~** to lend sb sth; **sich** (dat) **etw von jdm ~** to borrow sth from sb; **Leihfrist** f lending period; **Leihgebühr** f hire charge; (für Buch) lending charge; **Leihwagen** m hire car (Brit), rental car (US)
Leim (-(e)s, -e) m glue
Leine (-, -n) f cord; (für Wäsche) line; (Hundeleine) lead (Brit), leash (US)
Leinen (-s, -) nt linen; **Leintuch** nt (für Bett) sheet; **Leinwand** f (Kunst) canvas; (Cine) screen
leise adj quiet; (sanft) soft ▷ adv quietly
Leiste (-, -n) f ledge; (Zierleiste) strip; (Anat) groin
leisten vt (Arbeit) to do; (vollbringen) to achieve; **jdm Gesellschaft ~** to keep sb company; **sich** (dat) **etw ~** (gönnen) to treat oneself to sth; **ich kann es mir nicht ~** I can't afford it
Leistenbruch m hernia
Leistung f performance; (gute) achievement
Leitartikel m leading article (Brit), editorial (US)
leiten vt to lead; (Firma) to run; (in eine Richtung) to direct; (Elek) to conduct
Leiter (-, -n) f ladder
Leiter(in) (-s, -) m(f) (von Geschäft) manager
Leitplanke (-, -n) f crash barrier
Leitung f (Führung) direction; (Tel) line; (von Firma) management; (Wasserleitung) pipe; (Kabel) cable; **eine lange ~ haben** to be slow on the uptake; **Leitungswasser** nt tap water
Lektion f lesson
Lektüre (-, -n) f (Lesen) reading; (Lesestoff) reading matter

Lende (-, -n) f (Speise) loin; (vom Rind) sirloin; **die ~n** pl (Med) the lumbar region sing
lenken vt to steer; (Blick) to direct (auf +akk towards); **jds Aufmerksamkeit auf etw** (akk) **~** to draw sb's attention to sth; **Lenker** m (von Fahrrad, Motorrad) handlebars pl; **Lenkrad** nt steering wheel; **Lenkradschloss** nt steering lock; **Lenkstange** f handlebars pl
Leopard (-en, -en) m leopard
Lepra (-) f leprosy
Lerche (-, -n) f lark
lernen vt, vi to learn; (für eine Prüfung) to study, to revise
lesbisch adj lesbian
Lesebuch nt reader; **lesen** (las, gelesen) vi, vt to read; (ernten) to pick; **Leser(in)** m(f) reader; **Leserbrief** m letter to the editor; **leserlich** adj legible; **Lesezeichen** nt bookmark
Lettland nt Latvia
letzte(r, s) adj last; (neueste) latest; (endgültig) final; **zum ~n Mal** for the last time; **am ~n Montag** last Monday; **in ~r Zeit** lately, recently; **letztens** adv (vor kurzem) recently; **letztere(r, s)** adj the latter
Leuchtanzeige f illuminated display; **Leuchte** (-, -n) f lamp, light; **leuchten** vi to shine; (Feuer, Zifferblatt) to glow; **Leuchter** (-s, -) m candlestick; **Leuchtfarbe** f fluorescent colour; (Anstrichfarbe) luminous paint; **Leuchtreklame** f neon sign; **Leuchtstoffröhre** f strip light; **Leuchtturm** m lighthouse
leugnen vt to deny ▷ vi to deny everything
Leukämie f leukaemia (Brit), leukemia (US)

Leukoplast® (-(e)s, -e) nt
Elastoplast® (Brit), Band-Aid®
(US)

Leute pl people pl

Lexikon (-s, Lexika) nt encyclopaedia (Brit), encyclopedia (US);
(Wörterbuch) dictionary

Libanon (-s) m: **der ~** Lebanon

Libelle f dragonfly

liberal adj liberal

Libyen (-s) nt Libya

Licht (-(e)s, -er) nt light;
Lichtblick m ray of hope;
lichtempfindlich adj sensitive to
light; **Lichtempfindlichkeit** f
(Foto) speed; **Lichthupe** f: **die
~ betätigen** to flash one's lights;
Lichtjahr nt light year;
Lichtmaschine f dynamo;
Lichtschalter m light switch;
Lichtschranke f light barrier;
Lichtschutzfaktor m sun
protection factor, SPF

Lichtung f clearing

Lid (-(e)s, -er) nt eyelid;
Lidschatten m eyeshadow

lieb adj (nett) nice; (teuer, geliebt)
dear; (liebenswert) sweet; **das ist
~ von dir** that's nice of you; **Lieber
Herr X** Dear Mr X; **Liebe** (-, -n) f
love; **lieben** vt to love; (sexuell) to
make love to; **liebenswürdig** adj
kind; **lieber** adv rather; **ich
möchte ~ nicht** I'd rather not;
welches ist dir ~? which one do
you prefer?; siehe auch **gern, lieb**;
Liebesbrief m love letter;
Liebeskummer m: **~ haben** to be
lovesick; **Liebespaar** nt lovers pl;
liebevoll adj loving;
Liebhaber(in) (-s, -) m(f) lover;
lieblich adj lovely; (Wein) sweet;
Liebling m darling; (Günstling)
favourite; **Lieblings-** in zW
favourite; **liebste(r, s)** adj
favourite; **liebsten** adv: **am
~ esse ich ...** my favourite food

is ...; **am ~ würde ich bleiben** I'd
really like to stay

Liechtenstein (-s) nt
Liechtenstein

Lied (-(e)s, -er) nt song; (Rel) hymn

lief imperf von **laufen**

Lieferant(in) m(f) supplier

lieferbar adj available

liefern vt to deliver; (beschaffen)
to supply

Lieferschein m delivery note;
Lieferung f delivery;
Lieferwagen m delivery van

Liege (-, -n) f (beim Arzt) couch;
(Notbett) campbed; (Gartenliege)
lounger; **liegen** (lag, gelegen) vi to
lie; (sich befinden) to be; **mir liegt
nichts/viel daran** it doesn't
matter to me/it matters a lot to
me; **woran liegt es nur, dass ...?**
why is it that ...?; **~ bleiben**
(Mensch) to stay lying down; (im
Bett) to stay in bed; (Ding) to be left
(behind); **~ lassen** (vergessen) to
leave behind; **Liegestuhl** m deck
chair; **Liegestütz** m press-up
(Brit), push-up (US); **Liegewagen**
m (Eisenb) couchette car

lieh imperf von **leihen**

ließ imperf von **lassen**

Lift (-(e)s, -e o -s) m lift, elevator
(US)

Liga (-, Ligen) f league, division

light adj (Cola) diet; (fettarm)
low-fat; (kalorienarm) low-calorie;
(Zigaretten) mild

Likör (-s, -e) m liqueur

lila adj inv purple

Lilie f lily

Limette (-, -n) f lime

Limo (-, -s) f (fam) fizzy drink
(Brit), soda (US); **Limonade** f
fizzy drink (Brit), soda (US); (mit
Zitronengeschmack) lemonade

Limone (-, -n) f lime

Limousine (-, -n) f saloon (car)
(Brit), sedan (US); (fam) limo

Linde (-, -n) f lime tree
lindern vt to relieve, to soothe
Lineal (-s, -e) nt ruler
Linie f line; **Linienflug** m
scheduled flight; **liniert** adj
ruled, lined
Link (-s, -s) m (Inform) link
Linke (-n, -n) f left-hand side;
(Hand) left hand; (Pol) left (wing);
linke(r, s) adj left; **auf der ~n
Seite** on the left, on the left-hand
side; **links** adv on the left;
~ abbiegen to turn left; **~ von** to
the left of; **~ oben** at the top left;
Linkshänder(in) (-s, -) m(f) left-
hander; **linksherum** adv to the
left, anticlockwise; **Linksverkehr**
m driving on the left
Linse (-, -n) f lentil; (optisch) lens
Lippe (-, -n) f lip; **Lipgloss** nt lip
gloss; **Lippenstift** m lipstick
lispeln vi to lisp
List (-, -en) f cunning; (Trick)
trick
Liste (-, -n) f list
Litauen (-s) nt Lithuania
Liter (-s, -) m o nt litre
literarisch adj literary; **Literatur**
f literature
Litschi (-, -s) f lychee, litchi
litt imperf von **leiden**
live adv (Radio, TV) live
Lizenz f licence
Lkw (-(s), -(s)) m abk =
Lastkraftwagen truck, lorry (Brit);
Lkw-Maut f heavy goods vehicle
toll
Lob (-(e)s) nt praise; **loben** vt to
praise
Loch (-(e)s, Löcher) nt hole;
lochen vt to punch; **Locher** (-s, -)
m (hole) punch
Locke (-, -n) f curl; **locken** vt
(anlocken) to lure; (Haare) to curl;
Lockenstab m curling tongs pl
(Brit), curling irons pl (US);
Lockenwickler (-s, -) m curler

locker adj (Schraube, Zahn) loose;
(Haltung) relaxed; (Person)
easy-going; **das schaffe ich
~** (fam) I'll manage it, no problem;
lockern vt to loosen ▷ vr: **sich
~** to loosen
lockig adj curly
Löffel (-s, -) m spoon; **einen
~ Mehl zugeben** add a spoonful of
flour; **Löffelbiskuit** (-s, -s) m
sponge finger
log imperf von **lügen**
Loge (-, -n) f (Theat) box
logisch adj logical
Logo (-s, -s) nt logo
Lohn (-(e)s, Löhne) m reward;
(Arbeitslohn) pay, wages pl
lohnen vr: **sich ~** to be worth it;
es lohnt sich nicht zu warten it's
no use waiting
Lohnerhöhung f pay rise (Brit),
pay raise (US); **Lohnsteuer** f
income tax
Lokal (-(e)s, -e) nt (Gaststätte)
restaurant; (Kneipe) pub (Brit), bar
Lokomotive f locomotive
London (-s) nt London
Lorbeer (-s, -en) m laurel;
Lorbeerblatt nt (Gastr) bay leaf
los adj loose; **~!** go on!; **jdn/etw
~ sein** to be rid of sb/sth; **was ist
~?** what's the matter?, what's up?;
dort ist nichts/viel ~ there's
nothing/a lot going on there
Los (-es, -e) nt (Schicksal) lot, fate;
(Lotterie etc) ticket
los|binden irr vt to untie
löschen vt (Feuer, Licht) to put
out, to extinguish; (Durst) to
quench; (Tonband) to erase; (Daten,
Zeile) to delete; **Löschtaste** f
delete key
lose adj loose
Lösegeld nt ransom
losen vi to draw lots
lösen vt (lockern) to loosen;
(Rätsel) to solve; (Chem) to

dissolve; (*Fahrkarte*) to buy ▷ *vr:*
sich ~ (*abgehen*) to come off;
(*Zucker etc*) to dissolve; (*Problem,
Schwierigkeit*) to (re)solve itself
los|fahren *irr vi* to leave;
los|gehen *irr vi* to set out;
(*anfangen*) to start; **los|lassen** *irr
vt* to let go
löslich *adj* soluble
Lösung *f* (*eines Rätsels, Problems,
Flüssigkeit*) solution
los|werden *irr vt* to get rid of
Lotterie *f* lottery; **Lotto** (*-s*) *nt*
National Lottery; **~ spielen** to play
the lottery
Löwe (*-n, -n*) *m* (*Zool*) lion; (*Astr*)
Leo; **Löwenzahn** *m* dandelion
Luchs (*-es, -e*) *m* lynx
Lücke (*-, -n*) *f* gap;
Lückenbüßer(in) (*-s, -*) *m(f)*
stopgap
lud *imperf von* **laden**
Luft (*-, Lüfte*) *f* air; (*Atem*) breath;
Luftballon *m* balloon; **Luftblase**
f (air) bubble; **luftdicht** *adj*
airtight; **Luftdruck** *m* (*Meteo*)
atmospheric pressure; (*in Reifen*)
air pressure
lüften *vt* to air; (*Geheimnis*) to
reveal
Luftfahrt *f* aviation;
Luftfeuchtigkeit *f* humidity;
Luftfilter *m* air filter; **Luftfracht**
f air freight; **Luftkissenfahrzeug**
nt hovercraft; **Luftlinie** *f:* **10 km
~** 10 km as the crow flies;
Luftmatratze *f* airbed;
Luftpirat(in) *m(f)* hijacker;
Luftpost *f* airmail; **Luftpumpe**
f (bicycle) pump; **Luftröhre** *f*
windpipe
Lüftung *f* ventilation
Luftveränderung *f* change of
air; **Luftverschmutzung** *f* air
pollution; **Luftwaffe** *f* air force;
Luftzug *m* draught (*Brit*), draft
(*US*)

Lüge (*-, -n*) *f* lie; **lügen** (*log,
gelogen*) *vi* to lie; **Lügner(in)** (*-s, -*)
m(f) liar
Luke (*-, -n*) *f* hatch
Lumpen (*-s, -*) *m* rag
Lunchpaket *nt* packed lunch
Lunge (*-, -n*) *f* lungs *pl;*
Lungenentzündung *f*
pneumonia
Lupe (*-, -n*) *f* magnifying glass;
etw unter die ~ nehmen (*fig*) to
have a close look at sth
Lust (*-, Lüste*) *f* joy, delight;
(*Neigung*) desire; **~ auf etw** (*akk*)
haben to feel like sth; **~ haben,
etw zu tun** to feel like doing sth
lustig *adj* (*komisch*) amusing,
funny; (*fröhlich*) cheerful
lutschen *vt* to suck ▷ *vi* **~ an**
(*+dat*) to suck; **Lutscher** (*-s, -*) *m*
lollipop
Luxemburg (*-s*) *nt* Luxembourg
luxuriös *adj* luxurious
Luxus (*-*) *m* luxury
Lymphdrüse *f* lymph gland;
Lymphknoten *m* lymph node
Lyrik (*-*) *f* poetry

m

machbar *adj* feasible

 SCHLÜSSELWORT

machen *vt* **1** to do; (*herstellen, zubereiten*) to make; **was machst du da?** what are you doing (there)?; **das ist nicht zu machen** that can't be done; **das Radio leiser machen** to turn the radio down; **aus Holz gemacht** made of wood

2 (*verursachen, bewirken*) to make; **jdm Angst machen** to make sb afraid; **das macht die Kälte** it's the cold that does that

3 (*ausmachen*) to matter; **das macht nichts** that doesn't matter; **die Kälte macht mir nichts** I don't mind the cold

4 (*kosten, ergeben*) to be; **3 und 5 macht 8** 3 and 5 is o are 8; **was** o **wie viel macht das?** how much does that make?

5 was macht die Arbeit? how's the work going?; **was macht dein Bruder?** how is your brother doing?; **das Auto machen lassen** to have the car done; **mach's gut!** take care!; (*viel Glück*) good luck! ▷ *vi*: **mach schnell!** hurry up!; **Schluss machen** to finish (off); **mach schon!** come on!; **das macht müde** it makes you tired; **in etw** *dat* **machen** to be o deal in sth ▷ *vr* to come along (nicely); **sich an etw** *akk* **machen** to set about sth; **sich verständlich machen** to make o.s. understood; **sich** *dat* **viel aus jdm/etw machen** to like sb/sth

Macho (*-s, -s*) *m* (*fam*) macho (type)

Macht (*-s, Mächte*) *f* power; **mächtig** *adj* powerful; (*fam: ungeheuer*) enormous; **machtlos** *adj* powerless; **da ist man ~** there's nothing you can do (about it)

Mädchen *nt* girl; **Mädchenname** *m* maiden name

Made (*-, -n*) *f* maggot

Magazin (*-s, -e*) *nt* magazine

Magen (*-s, - o Mägen*) *m* stomach; **Magenbeschwerden** *pl* stomach trouble *sing*; **Magen-Darm-Infektion** *f* gastroenteritis; **Magengeschwür** *nt* stomach ulcer; **Magenschmerzen** *pl* stomach-ache *sing*

mager *adj* (*Fleisch, Wurst*) lean; (*Person*) thin; (*Käse, Joghurt*) low-fat; **Magermilch** *f* skimmed milk; **Magersucht** *f* anorexia; **magersüchtig** *adj* anorexic

magisch *adj* magical

Magnet (*-s o -en, -en*) *m* magnet

mähen *vt, vi* to mow

mahlen (*mahlte, gemahlen*) *vt* to grind

Mahlzeit *f* meal; (*für Baby*) feed ▷ *interj* (*guten Appetit*) enjoy your meal

Mähne (-, -*n*) *f* mane

mahnen *vt* to urge; **jdn schriftlich ~** to send sb a reminder; **Mahngebühr** *f* fine; **Mahnung** *f* warning; (*schriftlich*) reminder

Mai (-(*s*), -*e*) *m* May; *siehe auch* **Juni**; **Maifeiertag** *m* May Day; **Maiglöckchen** *nt* lily of the valley; **Maikäfer** *m* cockchafer

Mail (-, -*s*) *f* e-mail; **jdm eine~ schicken** to mail sb, to e-mail sb; **Mailbox** *f* (*Inform*) mailbox; **mailen** *vi*, *vt* to e-mail

Mais (-*es*, -*e*) *m* maize, corn (*US*); **Maiskolben** *m* corn cob; (*Gastr*) corn on the cob

Majestät (-, -*en*) *f* Majesty

Majonäse (-, -*n*) *f* mayonnaise

Majoran (-*s*, -*e*) *m* marjoram

makaber *adj* macabre

Make-up (-*s*, -*s*) *nt* make-up

Makler(in) (-*s*, -) *m(f)* broker; (*Immobilienmakler*) estate agent (*Brit*), Realtor® (*US*)

Makrele (-, -*n*) *f* mackerel

Makro (-*s*, -*s*) *nt* (*Inform*) macro

Makrone (-, -*n*) *f* macaroon

mal *adv* (*beim Rechnen*) times, multiplied by; (*beim Messen*) by; (*fam: einmal = früher*) once; (*einmal = zukünftig*) some day; **4 ~ 3 ist 12** 4 times 3 is (*o equals*) twelve; **da habe ich ~ gewohnt** I used to live there; **irgendwann ~ werde ich dort hinfahren** I'll go there one day; **das ist nun ~ so** well, that's just the way it is (*o goes*); **Mal** (-(*e*)*s*, -*e*) *nt* (*Zeitpunkt*) time; (*Markierung*) mark; **jedes ~** every time; **ein paar ~** a few times; **ein einziges ~** just once

Malaria (-) *f* malaria

Malaysia (-*s*) *nt* Malaysia

Malbuch *nt* colouring book

Malediven *pl* Maldives *pl*

malen *vt*, *vi* to paint; **Maler(in)** (-*s*, -) *m(f)* painter; **Malerei** *f* painting; **malerisch** *adj* picturesque

Mallorca (-*s*) *nt* Majorca, Mallorca

mal|nehmen *irr vt* to multiply (*mit* by)

Malta (-*s*) *nt* Malta

Malventee *m* mallow tea

Malz (-*es*) *nt* malt; **Malzbier** *nt* malt beer

Mama (-, -*s*) *f* mum(my) (*Brit*), mom(my) (*US*)

man *pron* you; (*förmlich*) one; (*jemand*) someone, somebody; (*die Leute*) they, people *pl*; **wie schreibt ~ das?** how do you spell that?; **~ hat ihr das Fahrrad gestohlen** someone stole her bike; **~ sagt, dass ...** they (*o people*) say that ...

managen *vt* (*fam*) to manage; **Manager(in)** (-*s*, -) *m(f)* manager

manche(r, s) *adj* many a; (*mit pl*) a number of, some ▷ *pron* (*einige*) some; (*viele*) many; **~ Politiker** many politicians *pl*, many a politician; **manchmal** *adv* sometimes

Mandant(in) *m(f)* client

Mandarine *f* mandarin, tangerine

Mandel (-, -*n*) *f* almond; **~n** (*Anat*) tonsils *pl*; **Mandelentzündung** *f* tonsillitis

Manege (-, -*n*) *f* ring

Mangel (-*s*, *Mängel*) *m* (*Fehlen*) lack; (*Knappheit*) shortage (*an +dat* of); (*Fehler*) defect, fault; **mangelhaft** *adj* (*Ware*) faulty; (*Schulnote*) ≈ E

Mango (-, -*s*) *f* mango

Mangold (-*s*) *m* mangel(wurzel)

Manieren *pl* manners *pl*

Maniküre (-, -n) *f* manicure

manipulieren *vt* to manipulate

Manko (-s, -s) *nt* deficiency

Mann (-(e)s, *Männer*) *m* man; (*Ehemann*) husband; **Männchen** *nt*: **es ist ein ~** (*Tier*) it's a he; **männlich** *adj* masculine; (*Bio*) male

Mannschaft *f* (*Sport, fig*) team; (*Naut, Aviat*) crew

Mansarde (-, -n) *f* attic

Manschettenknopf *m* cufflink

Mantel (-s, *Mäntel*) *m* coat; (*Tech*) casing, jacket

Mappe (-, -n) *f* briefcase; (*Aktenmappe*) folder

Maracuja (-, -s) *f* passion fruit

Marathon (-s, -s) *m* marathon

Märchen *nt* fairy tale

Marder (-s, -) *m* marten

Margarine *f* margarine

Marienkäfer *m* ladybird (*Brit*), ladybug (*US*)

Marihuana (-s) *nt* marijuana

Marille (-, -n) *f* apricot

Marinade *f* marinade

Marine *f* navy

marinieren *vt* to marinate

Marionette *f* puppet

Mark (-(e)s) *nt* (*Knochenmark*) marrow; (*Fruchtmark*) pulp

Marke (-, -n) *f* (*Warensorte*) brand; (*Fabrikat*) make; (*Briefmarke*) stamp; (*Essenmarke*) voucher, ticket; (*aus Metall etc*) disc; (*Messpunkt*) mark; **Markenartikel** *m* branded item, brand name product; **Markenzeichen** *nt* trademark

markieren *vt* to mark; **Markierung** *f* marking; (*Zeichen*) mark

Markise (-, -n) *f* awning

Markt (-(e)s, *Märkte*) *m* market; **auf den ~ bringen** to launch; **Markthalle** *f* covered market;

Marktlücke *f* gap in the market; **Marktplatz** *m* market place; **Marktwirtschaft** *f* market economy

Marmelade *f* jam; (*Orangenmarmelade*) marmalade

Marmor (-s, -e) *m* marble; **Marmorkuchen** *m* marble cake

Marokko (-s) *nt* Morocco

Marone (-, -n) *f* chestnut

Mars (-) *m* Mars

Marsch (-(e)s, *Märsche*) *m* march

Märtyrer(in) (-s, -) *m(f)* martyr

März (-(es), -e) *m* March; *siehe auch* **Juni**

Marzipan (-s, -e) *nt* marzipan

Maschine *f* machine; (*Motor*) engine; **maschinell** *adj* mechanical, machine-; **Maschinenbau** *m* mechanical engineering

Masern *pl* (*Med*) measles *sing*

Maske (-, -n) *f* mask; **Maskenball** *m* fancy-dress ball; **maskieren** *vr*: **sich ~** (*Maske aufsetzen*) to put on a mask; (*verkleiden*) to dress up

Maskottchen *nt* mascot

maß *imperf von* **messen**

Maß (-es, -e) *nt* measure; (*Mäßigung*) moderation; (*Grad*) degree, extent; **~e** (*Person*) measurements; (*Raum*) dimensions; **in gewissem/hohem ~e** to a certain/high degree; **in zunehmendem ~e** increasingly

Mass (-, -(en)) *f* (*Bier*) litre of beer

Massage (-, -n) *f* massage

Masse (-, -n) *f* mass; (*von Menschen*) crowd; (*Großteil*) majority; **massenhaft** *adv* masses (*o* loads) of; **am See sind ~ Mücken** there are masses of mosquitoes at the lake; **Massenkarambolage** *f* pile-up; **Massenmedien** *pl* mass media *pl*; **Massenproduktion** *f* mass

production; **Massentourismus**
m mass tourism
Masseur(in) *m(f)*
masseur/masseuse
maßgeschneidert *adj (Kleidung)* made-to-measure
massieren *vt* to massage
mäßig *adj* moderate
massiv *adj* solid; *(fig)* massive
maßlos *adj* extreme
Maßnahme (-, -n) *f* measure,
step
Maßstab *m* rule, measure; *(fig)*
standard; **im ~ von 1:5** on a scale
of 1:5
Mast (-(e)s, -e(n)) *m* mast; *(Elek)*
pylon
Material (-s, -ien) *nt* material;
(Arbeitsmaterial) materials *pl*;
materialistisch *adj* materialistic
Materie *f* matter; **materiell** *adj*
material
Mathematik *f* mathematics
sing; **Mathematiker(in)** *m(f)*
mathematician
Matinee (-, -n) *f* ≈ matinee
Matratze (-, -n) *f* mattress
Matrose (-n, -n) *m* sailor
Matsch (-(e)s) *m* mud; *(Schnee)*
slush; **matschig** *adj (Boden)*
muddy; *(Schnee)* slushy; *(Obst)*
mushy
matt *adj* weak; *(glanzlos)* dull;
(Foto) matt; *(Schach)* mate
Matte (-, -n) *f* mat
Matura (-) *f* Austrian
school-leaving examination; ≈
A-levels *(Brit)*, ≈ High School
Diploma *(US)*
Mauer (-, -n) *f* wall
Maul (-(e)s, *Mäuler)* *nt* mouth;
(fam) gob; **halt's ~!** shut your face
(*o* gob); **Maulbeere** *f* mulberry;
Maulesel *m* mule; **Maulkorb** *m*
muzzle; **Maul- und Klauenseuche**
f foot-and-mouth disease;
Maulwurf *m* mole

Maurer(in) (-s, -) *m(f)* bricklayer
Mauritius (-) *nt* Mauritius
Maus (-, *Mäuse)* *f* mouse;
Mausefalle *f* mousetrap;
Mausklick (-s, -s) *m* mouse click;
Mauspad (-s, -s) *nt* mouse mat (*o*
pad); **Maustaste** *f* mouse key (*o*
button)
Maut (-, -en) *f* toll; **Mautgebühr**
f toll; **mautpflichtig** *adj*: **~e
Straße** toll road, turnpike *(US)*;
Mautstelle *f* tollbooth, tollgate;
Mautstraße *f* toll road, turnpike
(US)
maximal *adv*: **ihr habt ~ zwei
Stunden Zeit** you've got two
hours at (the) most; **~ vier Leute** a
maximum of four people
Mayonnaise *f siehe* **Majonäse**
Mazedonien (-s) *nt* Macedonia
MB (-, -) *nt*, **Mbyte** (-, -) *nt abk* =
Megabyte MB
Mechanik *f* mechanics *sing*;
(Getriebe) mechanics *pl*;
Mechaniker(in) (-s, -) *m(f)* mechanic;
mechanisch *adj* mechanical;
Mechanismus *m* mechanism
meckern *vi (Ziege)* to bleat; *(fam:
schimpfen)* to moan
Mecklenburg-Vorpommern
(-s) *nt* Mecklenburg-Western
Pomerania
Medaille (-, -n) *f* medal
Medien *pl* media *pl*
Medikament *nt* medicine
Meditation *f* meditation;
meditieren *vi* to meditate
medium *adj (Steak)* medium
Medizin (-, -en) *f* medicine *(gegen*
for); **medizinisch** *adj* medical
Meer (-(e)s, -e) *nt* sea; **am ~** by
the sea; **Meerenge** *f* straits *pl*;
Meeresfrüchte *pl* seafood *sing*;
Meeresspiegel *m* sea level;
Meerrettich *m* horseradish;
Meerschweinchen *nt* guinea
pig; **Meerwasser** *nt* seawater

Megabyte *nt* megabyte;
Megahertz *nt* megahertz
Mehl *(-(e)s, -e)* *nt* flour;
Mehlspeise *f* sweet dish made from flour, eggs and milk
mehr *pron, adv* more; **~ will ich nicht ausgeben** I don't want to spend any more, that's as much as I want to spend; **was willst du ~?** what more do you want? ▷ *adv*: **immer ~ (Leute)** more and more (people); **~ als fünf Minuten** more than five minutes; **je ~ …, desto besser** the more …, the better; **ich kann nicht ~ stehen** I can't stand any more (o longer); **es ist kein Brot ~ da** there's no bread left; **nie ~** never again; **mehrdeutig** *adj* ambiguous; **mehrere** *pron* several; **mehreres** *pron* several things; **mehrfach** *adj* multiple; *(wiederholt)* repeated;
Mehrfachstecker *m* multiple plug; **Mehrheit** *f* majority; **mehrmals** *adv* repeatedly; **mehrsprachig** *adj* multilingual; **Mehrwegflasche** *f* returnable bottle, deposit bottle; **Mehrwertsteuer** *f* value added tax, VAT; **Mehrzahl** *f* majority; *(Plural)* plural
meiden *(mied, gemieden)* *vt* to avoid
Meile *(-, -n)* *f* mile
mein *pron (adjektivisch)* my; **meine(r, s)** *pron (substantivisch)* mine
meinen *vt, vi (glauben, der Ansicht sein)* to think; *(sagen)* to say; *(sagen wollen, beabsichtigen)* to mean; **das war nicht so gemeint** I didn't mean it like that
meinetwegen *adv (wegen mir)* because of me; *(mir zuliebe)* for my sake; *(von mir aus)* as far as I'm concerned
Meinung *f* opinion; **meiner**

~ nach in my opinion;
Meinungsumfrage *f* opinion poll; **Meinungsverschiedenheit** *f* disagreement *(über +akk* about)
Meise *(-, -n)* *f* tit; **eine ~ haben** *(fam)* to be crazy
Meißel *(-s, -)* *m* chisel
meist *adv* mostly; **meiste(r, s)** *pron (adjektivisch)* most; **die ~n (Leute)** most people; **die ~ Zeit** most of the time; **das ~ (davon)** most of it; **die ~n von ihnen** most of them; *(substantivisch)* most of them; **am ~n** (the) most; **meistens** *adv* mostly; *(zum größten Teil)* for the most part
Meister(in) *(-s, -)* *m(f)* master; *(Sport)* champion; **Meisterschaft** *f* championship; **Meisterwerk** *nt* masterpiece
melden *vt* to report ▷ *vr*: **sich ~** to report *(bei* to); *(Schule)* to put one's hand up; *(freiwillig)* to volunteer; *(auf etw, am Telefon)* to answer; **Meldung** *f* announcement; *(Bericht)* report; *(Inform)* message
Melodie *f* tune, melody
Melone *(-, -n)* *f* melon
Memoiren *pl* memoirs *pl*
Menge *(-, -n)* *f* quantity; *(Menschen)* crowd; **eine ~ (große Anzahl)** a lot *(gen* of); **Mengenrabatt** *m* bulk discount
Meniskus *(-, Menisken)* *m* meniscus
Mensa *(-, Mensen)* *f* canteen, cafeteria (US)
Mensch *(-en, -en)* *m* human being, man; *(Person)* person; **kein ~** nobody; **~!** *(bewundernd)* wow!; *(verärgert)* bloody hell!; **Menschenmenge** *f* crowd; **Menschenrechte** *pl* human rights *pl*; **Menschenverstand** *m*: **gesunder ~** common sense; **Menschheit** *f* humanity,

mankind; **menschlich** adj
human; (human) humane
Menstruation f menstruation
Mentalität f mentality, mindset
Menthol (-s) nt menthol
Menü (-s, -s) nt set meal; (Inform)
menu; **Menüleiste** f (Inform)
menu bar
Merkblatt nt leaflet; **merken** vt
(bemerken) to notice; **sich** (dat) **etw
~ to** remember sth; **Merkmal** nt
feature
Merkur (-s) m Mercury
merkwürdig adj odd
Messbecher m measuring jug
Messe (-, -n) f fair; (Rel) mass;
Messebesucher(in) m(f) visitor
to a/the fair; **Messegelände** nt
exhibition site
messen (maß, gemessen) vt to
measure; (Temperatur, Puls) to take
▷ vr: **sich ~** to compete; **sie kann
sich mit ihm nicht ~** she's no
match for him
Messer (-s, -) nt knife
Messgerät nt measuring device,
gauge
Messing (-s) nt brass
Metall (-s, -e) nt metal
Meteorologe m, **Meteorologin**
f meteorologist
Meter (-s, -) m o nt metre;
Metermaß nt tape measure
Methode (-, -n) f method
Metzger(in) (-s, -) m(f) butcher;
Metzgerei f butcher's (shop)
Mexiko (-s) nt Mexico
MEZ f abk = **mitteleuropäische
Zeit** CET
miau interj miaow
mich pron akk von **ich** me;
~ (selbst) (reflexiv) myself; **stell
dich hinter ~** stand behind me;
ich fühle ~ wohl I feel fine
mied imperf von **meiden**
Miene (-, -n) f look, expression
mies adj (fam) lousy

Miesmuschel f mussel
Mietauto nt siehe **Mietwagen**;
Miete (-, -n) f rent; **mieten** vt to
rent; (Auto) to hire (Brit), to rent
(US); **Mieter(in)** (-s, -) m(f)
tenant; **Mietshaus** nt block of
flats (Brit), apartment house (US);
Mietvertrag m rental
agreement; **Mietwagen** m hire
car (Brit), rental car (US); **sich** (dat)
einen ~ nehmen to hire (Brit) (o
rent (US)) a car
Migräne (-, -n) f migraine
Migrant(in) (-en, -en) m(f)
migrant (worker)
Mikrofon (-s, -e) nt microphone
Mikrowelle (-, -n) f,
Mikrowellenherd m microwave
(oven)
Milch (-) f milk; **Milcheis** nt
ice-cream (made with milk);
Milchglas nt (dickes, trübes Glas)
frosted glass; **Milchkaffee** m
milky coffee; **Milchprodukte** pl
dairy products pl; **Milchpulver** nt
powdered milk; **Milchreis** m rice
pudding; **Milchshake** m milk
shake; **Milchstraße** f Milky Way
mild adj mild; (Richter) lenient;
(freundlich) kind
Militär (-s) nt military, army
Milliarde (-, -n) f billion;
Milligramm nt milligram;
Milliliter m millilitre; **Millimeter**
m millimetre; **Million** f million;
Millionär(in) m(f) millionaire
Milz (-, -en) f spleen
Mimik f facial expression(s)
Minderheit f minority
minderjährig adj underage
minderwertig adj inferior;
Minderwertigkeitskomplex m
inferiority complex
Mindest- in zW minimum;
mindeste(r, s) adj least;
mindestens adv at least;
Mindesthaltbarkeitsdatum nt

best-before date, sell-by date (*Brit*)

Mine (-, -n) f mine; (*Bleistift*) lead; (*Kugelschreiber*) refill

Mineralwasser nt mineral water

Minibar f minibar; **Minigolf** nt miniature golf, crazy golf (*Brit*)

minimal adj minimal

Minimum (-s, *Minima*) nt minimum

Minirock m miniskirt

Minister(in) (-s, -) m(f) minister; **Ministerium** nt ministry; **Ministerpräsident(in)** m(f) (*von Bundesland*) Minister President (*Prime Minister of a Bundesland*)

minus adv minus; **Minus** (-, -) nt deficit; **im ~ sein** to be in the red; (*Konto*) to be overdrawn

Minute (-, -n) f minute

Minze (-, -n) f mint

Mio. nt abk von **Million(en)** m

mir pron dat von **ich** (to) me; **kannst du ~ helfen?** can you help me?; **kannst du es ~ erklären?** can you explain it to me?; **ich habe ~ einen neuen Rechner gekauft** I bought (myself) a new computer; **ein Freund von ~** a friend of mine

Mirabelle (-, -n) f mirabelle (*small yellow plum*)

mischen vt to mix; (*Karten*) to shuffle; **Mischmasch** m (*fam*) hotchpotch; **Mischung** f mixture (*aus* of)

missachten vt to ignore; **Missbrauch** m abuse; (*falscher Gebrauch*) misuse; **missbrauchen** vt to misuse (*zu* for); (*sexuell*) to abuse; **Misserfolg** m failure; **Missgeschick** nt (*Panne*) mishap; **misshandeln** vt to ill-treat

Mission f mission

misslingen (*misslang, misslungen*) vi to fail; **der Versuch ist mir misslungen** my attempt failed;

misstrauen vt +*dat* to distrust; **Misstrauen** (-s) nt mistrust, suspicion (*gegenüber* of); **misstrauisch** adj distrustful; (*argwöhnisch*) suspicious; **Missverständnis** nt misunderstanding; **missverstehen** irr vt to misunderstand

Mist (-(e)s) m (*fam*) rubbish; (*von Kühen*) dung; (*als Dünger*) manure

Mistel (-, -n) f mistletoe

mit prep +*dat* with; (*mittels*) by; **~ der Bahn** by train; **~ der Kreditkarte bezahlen** to pay by credit card; **~ 10 Jahren** at the age of 10; **wie wärs ~ ...?** how about ...? ▷ adv along, too; **wollen Sie ~?** do you want to come along?

Mitarbeiter(in) m(f) (*Angestellter*) employee; (*an Projekt*) collaborator; (*freier*) freelancer

mit|bekommen irr vt (*fam: aufschnappen*) to catch; (*hören*) to hear; (*verstehen*) to get

mit|benutzen vt to share

Mitbewohner(in) m(f) (*in Wohnung*) flatmate (*Brit*), roommate (*US*)

mit|bringen irr vt to bring along; **Mitbringsel** (-s, -) nt small present

miteinander adv with one another; (*gemeinsam*) together

mit|erleben vt to see (with one's own eyes)

Mitesser (-s, -) m blackhead

Mitfahrgelegenheit f ≈ lift, ride (*US*); **Mitfahrzentrale** f *agency for arranging lifts*

mit|geben irr vt: **jdm etw ~** to give sb sth (to take along)

Mitgefühl nt sympathy

mit|gehen irr vi to go/come along

mitgenommen adj worn out, exhausted

Mitglied nt member

mithilfe *prep +gen* ~ **von** with the help of

mit|kommen *irr vi* to come along; (*verstehen*) to follow

Mitleid *nt* pity; ~ **haben mit** to feel sorry for

mit|machen *vt* to take part in ▷ *vi* to take part

mit|nehmen *irr vt* to take along; (*anstrengen*) to wear out, to exhaust

mit|schreiben *irr vi* to take notes ▷ *vt* to take down

Mitschüler(in) *m(f)* schoolmate

mit|spielen *vi* (*in Mannschaft*) to play; (*bei Spiel*) to join in; **in einem Film/Stück** ~ to act in a film/play

Mittag *m* midday; **gestern** ~ at midday yesterday, yesterday lunchtime; **über** ~ **geschlossen** closed at lunchtime; **zu** ~ **essen** to have lunch; **Mittagessen** *nt* lunch; **mittags** *adv* at lunchtime, at midday; **Mittagspause** *f* lunch break

Mitte (-, -n) *f* middle; ~ **Juni** in the middle of June; **sie ist** ~ **zwanzig** she's in her mid-twenties

mit|teilen *vt*: **jdm etw** ~ to inform sb of sth; **Mitteilung** *f* notification

Mittel (-s -) *nt* means *sing*; (*Maßnahme, Methode*) method; (*Med*) remedy (*gegen* for); **das ist ein gutes ~, (um) junge Leute zu erreichen** that's a good way of engaging with young people

Mittelalter *nt* Middle Ages *pl*; **mittelalterlich** *adj* medieval; **Mittelamerika** *nt* Central America; **Mitteleuropa** *nt* Central Europe; **Mittelfeld** *nt* midfield; **Mittelfinger** *m* middle finger; **mittelmäßig** *adj* mediocre; **Mittelmeer** *nt* Mediterranean (Sea);

Mittelohrentzündung *f* inflammation of the middle ear; **Mittelpunkt** *m* centre; **im** ~ **stehen** to be the centre of attention

mittels *prep +gen* by means of

Mittelstreifen *m* central reservation (*Brit*), median (*US*); **Mittelstürmer(in)** *m(f)* striker, centre-forward; **Mittelwelle** *f* medium wave

mitten *adv* in the middle; ~ **auf der Straße/in der Nacht** in the middle of the street/night

Mitternacht *f* midnight

mittlere(r, s) *adj* middle; (*durchschnittlich*) average

mittlerweile *adv* meanwhile

Mittwoch (-s, -e) *m* Wednesday; (**am**) ~ on Wednesday; (**am**) ~ **Morgen/Nachmittag/Abend** (on) Wednesday morning/afternoon/evening; **diesen/letzten/nächsten** ~ this/last/next Wednesday; **jeden** ~ every Wednesday; ~ **in einer Woche** a week on Wednesday, Wednesday week; **mittwochs** *adv* on Wednesdays; ~ **abends** (*jeden Mittwochabend*) on Wednesday evenings

mixen *vt* to mix; **Mixer** (-s, -) *m* (*Küchengerät*) blender

MKS *f abk* = **Maul- und Klauenseuche** FMD

mobben *vt* to harass (*o* to bully) (at work)

Mobbing (-s) *nt* workplace bullying (*o* harassment)

Möbel (-s, -) *nt* piece of furniture; **die** ~ *pl* the furniture *sing*; **Möbelwagen** *m* removal van

mobil *adj* mobile

Mobilfunknetz *nt* cellular network; **Mobiltelefon** *nt* mobile phone

möblieren *vt* to furnish

mochte *imperf von* **mögen**
Mode (-, -n) *f* fashion
Model (-s, -s) *nt* model
Modell (-s, -e) *nt* model
Modem (-s, -s) *nt* (*Inform*) modem
Mode(n)schau *f* fashion show
Moderator(in) *m(f)* presenter
modern *adj* modern; (*modisch*) fashionable
Modeschmuck *m* costume jewellery; **modisch** *adj* fashionable
Modus (-, *Modi*) *m* (*Inform*) mode; (*fig*) way
Mofa (-s, -s) *nt* moped
mogeln *vi* to cheat

 SCHLÜSSELWORT

mögen (*pt* **mochte**, *pp* **gemocht** *o* (*als Hilfsverb*) **mögen**) *vt, vi* to like; **magst du/mögen Sie ihn?** do you like him?; **ich möchte ...** I would like ..., I'd like ...; **er möchte in die Stadt** he'd like to go into town; **ich möchte nicht, dass du ...** I wouldn't like you to ...; **ich mag nicht mehr** I've had enough ▷ *Hilfsverb* to like to; (*wollen*) to want; **möchtest du etwas essen?** would you like something to eat?; **sie mag nicht bleiben** she doesn't want to stay; **das mag wohl sein** that may well be; **was mag das heißen?** what might that mean?; **Sie möchten zu Hause anrufen** could you please call home?

möglich *adj* possible; **so bald wie ~** as soon as possible; **möglicherweise** *adv* possibly; **Möglichkeit** *f* possibility; **möglichst** *adv* as ... as possible
Mohn (-(e)s, -e) *m* (*Blume*) poppy; (*Samen*) poppy seed

Möhre (-, -n) *f*, **Mohrrübe** *f* carrot
Mokka (-s, -s) *m* mocha
Moldawien (-s) *nt* Moldova
Molkerei (-, -en) *f* dairy
Moll (-) *nt* minor (key); **a-~** A minor
mollig *adj* cosy; (*dicklich*) plump
Moment (-(e)s, -e) *m* moment; **im ~** at the moment; **einen ~ bitte!** just a minute; **momentan** *adj* momentary ▷ *adv* at the moment
Monaco (-s) *nt* Monaco
Monarchie *f* monarchy
Monat (-(e)s, -e) *m* month; **sie ist im dritten ~** (*schwanger*) she's three months pregnant; **monatlich** *adj, adv* monthly; **~ 100 Euro zahlen** to pay 100 euros a month (*o* every month); **Monatskarte** *f* monthly season ticket
Mönch (-s, -e) *m* monk
Mond (-(e)s, -e) *m* moon; **Mondfinsternis** *f* lunar eclipse
Mongolei (-) *f*: **die ~** Mongolia
Monitor *m* (*Inform*) monitor
monoton *adj* monotonous
Monsun (-s, -e) *m* monsoon
Montag *m* Monday; *siehe auch* **Mittwoch**; **montags** *adv* on Mondays; *siehe auch* **mittwochs**
Montenegro (-s) *nt* Montenegro
Monteur(in) (-s, -e) *m(f)* fitter; **montieren** *vt* to assemble, to set up
Monument *nt* monument
Moor (-(e)s, -e) *nt* moor
Moos (-es, -e) *nt* moss
Moped (-s, -s) *nt* moped
Moral (-) *f* (*Werte*) morals *pl*; (*einer Geschichte*) moral; **moralisch** *adj* moral
Mord (-(e)s, -e) *m* murder;

Mörder(in) (-s, -) m(f) murderer/murderess

morgen adv tomorrow; **~ früh** tomorrow morning

Morgen (-s, -) m morning; **am ~** in the morning; **Morgenmantel** m, **Morgenrock** m dressing gown; **Morgenmuffel** m: **er ist ein ~** he's not a morning person; **morgens** adv in the morning; **um 3 Uhr ~** at 3 (o'clock) in the morning, at 3 am

Morphium (-s) nt morphine

morsch adj rotten

Mosaik (-s, -e(n)) nt mosaic

Mosambik (-s) nt Mozambique

Moschee (-, -n) f mosque

Moskau (-s) nt Moscow

Moskito (-s, -s) m mosquito; **Moskitonetz** nt mosquito net

Moslem (-s, -s) m, **Moslime** (-, -n) f Muslim

Most (-(e)s, -e) m (unfermented) fruit juice; (Apfelwein) cider

Motel (-s, -s) nt motel

motivieren vt to motivate

Motor m engine; (Elek) motor; **Motorboot** nt motorboat; **Motorenöl** nt engine oil; **Motorhaube** f bonnet (Brit), hood (US); **Motorrad** nt motorbike, motorcycle; **Motorradfahrer(in)** m(f) motorcyclist; **Motorroller** m (motor) scooter; **Motorschaden** m engine trouble

Motte (-, -n) f moth

Motto (-s, -s) nt motto

Mountainbike (-s, -s) nt mountain bike

Möwe (-, -n) f (sea)gull

MP3-Player (-s, -) m MP3 player

Mrd. f abk = **Milliarde(n)**

MS (-) f abk = **multiple Sklerose** MS

Mücke (-, -n) f midge; (tropische) mosquito; **Mückenstich** m mosquito bite

müde adj tired

muffig adj (Geruch) musty; (Gesicht, Mensch) grumpy

Mühe (-, -n) f trouble, pains pl; **sich** (dat) **große ~ geben** to go to a lot of trouble

muhen vi to moo

Mühle (-, -n) f mill; (Kaffeemühle) grinder

Müll (-(e)s) m rubbish (Brit), garbage (US); **Müllabfuhr** f rubbish (Brit) (o garbage (US)) disposal

Mullbinde f gauze bandage

Müllcontainer m waste container; **Mülldeponie** f rubbish (Brit) (o garbage (US)) dump; **Mülleimer** m rubbish bin (Brit), garbage can (US); **Mülltonne** f dustbin (Brit), garbage can (US); **Mülltrennung** f sorting and collecting household waste according to type of material; **Müllverbrennungsanlage** f incineration plant; **Müllwagen** m dustcart (Brit), garbage truck (US)

multikulturell adj multicultural

Multimedia- in zW multimedia

Multiple-Choice-Verfahren nt multiple choice

multiple Sklerose (-n, -n) f multiple sclerosis

Multiplexkino nt multiplex (cinema)

multiplizieren vt to multiply (mit by)

Mumie f mummy

Mumps (-) m mumps sing

München (-s) nt Munich

Mund (-(e)s, Münder) m mouth; **halt den ~!** shut up; **Mundart** f dialect; **Munddusche** f dental water jet

münden vi to flow (in +akk into)

Mundgeruch m bad breath; **Mundharmonika** (-, -s) f mouth organ

mündlich adj oral
Mundschutz m mask;
Mundwasser nt mouthwash
Munition f ammunition
Münster (-s, -) nt minster,
cathedral
munter adj lively
Münzautomat m vending
machine; **Münze** (-, -n) f coin;
Münzeinwurf m slot;
Münzrückgabe f coin return;
Münztelefon nt pay phone;
Münzwechsler m change
machine
murmeln vt, vi to murmur, to
mutter
Murmeltier nt marmot
mürrisch adj sullen, grumpy
Mus (-es, -e) nt puree
Muschel (-, -n) f mussel; (~schale)
shell
Museum (-s, Museen) nt
museum
Musical (-s, -s) nt musical
Musik f music; **musikalisch** adj
musical; **Musiker(in)** (-s, -) m(f)
musician; **Musikinstrument** nt
musical instrument; **musizieren**
vi to play music
Muskat (-(e)s) m nutmeg
Muskel (-s, -n) m muscle;
Muskelkater m: **~ haben** to be
stiff; **Muskelriss** m torn muscle;
Muskelzerrung f pulled muscle;
muskulös adj muscular
Müsli (-s, -) nt muesli
Muslim(in) (-s, -s) m(f) Muslim
Muss (-) nt must

SCHLÜSSELWORT

müssen (pt **musste**, pp **gemusst**
o (als Hilfsverb) **müssen**) vi
1 (Zwang) must; (nur im Präsens) to
have to; **ich muss es tun** I must do
it, I have to do it; **ich musste es
tun** I had to do it; **er muss es**

nicht tun he doesn't have to do it;
muss ich? must I?, do I have to?;
wann müsst ihr zur Schule?
when do you have to go to
school?; **er hat gehen müssen** he
(has) had to go; **muss das sein?** is
that really necessary?; **ich muss
mal** (fam) I need the toilet
2 (sollen) **das musst du nicht tun!**
you oughtn't to o shouldn't do
that; **Sie hätten ihn fragen
müssen** you should have asked
him
3 es muss geregnet haben it
must have rained; **es muss nicht
wahr sein** it needn't be true

Muster (-s, -) nt (Dessin) pattern,
design; (Probe) sample; (Vorbild)
model; **mustern** vt to have a
close look at; **jdn ~** to look sb up
and down
Mut (-(e)s) m courage; **jdm
~ machen** to encourage sb; **mutig**
adj brave, courageous
Mutter (-, Mütter) f mother
▷ (-, -n) f (Schraubenmutter) nut;
Muttersprache f mother
tongue; **Muttertag** m Mother's
Day; **Mutti** f mum(my) (Brit),
mom(my) (US)
mutwillig adj deliberate
Mütze (-, -n) f cap
MwSt. abk = **Mehrwertsteuer**
VAT
Myanmar (-s) nt Myanmar

n

N *abk* = **Nord** N
na *interj*: **~ also!**, **~ bitte!** see?, what did I tell you?; **~ ja** well; **~ und?** so what?
Nabel (-s, -) *m* navel

O **SCHLÜSSELWORT**

nach *prep +dat* **1** (*örtlich*) to; **nach Berlin** to Berlin; **nach links/rechts** (to the) left/right; **nach oben/hinten** up/back
2 (*zeitlich*) after; **einer nach dem anderen** one after the other; **nach Ihnen!** after you!; **zehn (Minuten) nach drei** ten (minutes) past three
3 (*gemäß*) according to; **nach dem Gesetz** according to the law; **dem Namen nach** judging by his/her name; **nach allem, was ich weiß** as far as I know
▷ *adv*: **ihm nach!** after him!; **nach**

und nach gradually, little by little; **nach wie vor** still

nach|ahmen *vt* to imitate
Nachbar(in) (-n, -n) *m(f)* neighbour; **Nachbarschaft** *f* neighbourhood
nach|bestellen *vt* to order some more
nachdem *conj* after; (*weil*) since; **je ~ (ob/wie)** depending on (whether/how)
nach|denken *irr vi* to think (*über +akk* about); **nachdenklich** *adj* thoughtful
nacheinander *adv* one after another (*o* the other)
Nachfolger(in) (-s, -) *m(f)* successor
nach|forschen *vt* to investigate
Nachfrage *f* inquiry; (*Comm*) demand; **nach|fragen** *vi* to inquire
nach|geben *irr vi* to give in (*jdm* to sb)
Nachgebühr *f* surcharge; (*für Briefe etc*) excess postage
nach|gehen *irr vi* to follow (*jdm* sb); (*erforschen*) to inquire (*einer Sache dat* into sth); **die Uhr geht (zehn Minuten) nach** this watch is (ten minutes) slow
nachher *adv* afterwards; **bis ~!** see you later
Nachhilfe *f* extra tuition
nach|holen *vt* to catch up with; (*Versäumtes*) to make up for
nach|kommen *irr vi* to follow; **einer Verpflichtung** (*dat*) **~ to** fulfil an obligation
nach|lassen *irr vt* (*Summe*) to take off ▷ *vi* to decrease, to ease off; (*schlechter werden*) to deteriorate; **nachlässig** *adj* negligent, careless
nach|laufen *irr vi* to run after, to chase (*jdm* sb)

nach|lösen vt: **eine Fahrkarte
~** to buy a ticket on the bus/train
nach|machen vt to imitate, to
copy (jdm etw sth from sb);
(fälschen) to counterfeit
Nachmittag m afternoon;
heute ~ this afternoon; **am ~** in
the afternoon; **nachmittags** adv
in the afternoon; **um 3 Uhr ~** at 3
(o'clock) in the afternoon, at 3 pm
Nachnahme (-, -n) f cash on
delivery; **per ~** COD
Nachname m surname
nach|prüfen vt to check
nach|rechnen vt to check
Nachricht (-, -en) f (piece of)
news sing; (Mitteilung) message;
Nachrichten pl news sing
Nachsaison f off-season
nach|schauen vi: **jdm ~** to
gaze after sb ▷ vt (prüfen)
to check
nach|schicken vt to forward
nach|schlagen irr vt to look
up
nach|sehen irr vt (prüfen) to
check
Nachspeise f dessert
nächstbeste(r, s) adj: **der
~ Zug/Job** the first train/job that
comes along; **nächste(r, s)** adj
next; (nächstgelegen) nearest
Nacht (-, Nächte) f night; **in der
~** during the night; (bei Nacht) at
night; **Nachtclub** m nightclub;
Nachtdienst m night duty;
~ haben (Apotheke) to be open all
night
Nachteil m disadvantage
Nachtflug m night flight;
Nachtfrost m overnight frost;
Nachthemd nt (für Damen)
nightdress; (für Herren) nightshirt
Nachtigall (-, -en) f nightingale
Nachtisch m dessert, sweet
(Brit), pudding (Brit); **Nachtleben**
nt nightlife

nach|tragen irr vt: **jdm etw
~** (übel nehmen) to hold sth
against sb
nachträglich adv: **~ alles Gute
zum Geburtstag!** Happy belated
birthday
nachts adv at night; **um 11 Uhr
~** at 11 (o'clock) at night, at 11 pm;
um 2 Uhr ~ at 2 (o'clock) in the
morning, at 2 am; **Nachtschicht**
f night shift; **Nachttarif** m
off-peak rate; **Nachttisch** m
bedside table; **Nachtzug** m
night train
Nachweis (-es, -e) m proof
Nachwirkung f after-effect
nach|zahlen vi to pay extra ▷ vt:
20 Euro ~ to pay 20 euros extra
nach|zählen vt to check
Nacken (-s, -) m (nape of the)
neck
nackt adj naked; (Tatsachen)
plain, bare; **Nacktbadestrand** m
nudist beach
Nadel (-, -n) f needle; (Stecknadel)
pin; **Nadelstreifen** pl pinstripes
pl
Nagel (-s, Nägel) m nail;
Nagelbürste f nail brush;
Nagelfeile f nail-file; **Nagellack**
m nail varnish (o polish);
Nagellackentferner (-s, -) m nail-
varnish (o nail-polish) remover;
Nagelschere f nail scissors pl
nah(e) adj, adv (räumlich) near(by);
(zeitlich) near; (Verwandte, Freunde)
close; **Nähe** (-) f (Umgebung)
vicinity; **in der ~** nearby; **in der
~ von** near to; **nahe|gehen** irr vi:
jdm ~ to upset sb; **nahe|legen**
vt: **jdm etw ~** to suggest sth to sb;
nahe|liegen irr vi to be obvious
▷ prep +dat near (to), close to
nähen vt, vi to sew
nähere(r, s) adj (Erklärung,
Erkundigung) more detailed; **die
~ Umgebung** the immediate area;

Nähere(s) nt details pl; **nähern** vr: **sich ~** to approach

nahezu adv virtually, almost

nahm imperf von **nehmen**

Nähmaschine f sewing machine

nahrhaft adj nourishing, nutritious; **Nahrung** f food; **Nahrungsmittel** nt food

Naht (-, Nähte) f seam; (Med) stitches pl, suture; (Tech) join

Nahverkehr m local traffic; **Nahverkehrszug** m local train

Nähzeug nt sewing kit

naiv adj naive

Name (-ns, -n) m name

nämlich adv that is to say, namely; (denn) since

nannte imperf von **nennen**

Napf (-(e)s, Näpfe) m bowl, dish

Narbe (-, -n) f scar

Narkose (-, -n) f anaesthetic

Narzisse (-, -n) f narcissus

naschen vt, vi to nibble; **Naschkatze** f (fam) nibbler; **eine ~ sein** to have a sweet tooth

Nase (-, -n) f nose; **Nasenbluten** (-s) nt nosebleed; **~ haben** to have a nosebleed; **Nasenloch** nt nostril; **Nasentropfen** pl nose drops pl

Nashorn nt rhinoceros

nass adj wet; **Nässe** (-) f wetness; **nässen** vi (Wunde) to weep

Nation (-, -en) f nation; **national** adj national; **Nationalfeiertag** m national holiday; **Nationalhymne** (-, -n) f national anthem; **Nationalität** f nationality; **Nationalmannschaft** f national team; **Nationalpark** m National Park; **Nationalspieler(in)** m(f) international (player)

NATO (-) f abk = **North Atlantic Treaty Organization** NATO, Nato

Natur f nature; **Naturkost** f health food; **natürlich** adj natural ▷ adv naturally; (selbstverständlich) of course; **Naturpark** m nature reserve; **naturrein** adj natural, pure; **Naturschutz** m conservation; **Naturschutzgebiet** nt nature reserve; **Naturwissenschaft** f (natural) science; **Naturwissenschaftler(in)** m(f) scientist

Navigationssystem nt (Auto) navigation system

n. Chr. abk = **nach Christus** AD

Nebel (-s, -) m fog, mist; **nebelig** adj foggy, misty; **Nebelscheinwerfer** m foglamp; **Nebelschlussleuchte** f (Auto) rear foglight

neben prep +akk o dat next to; (außer) apart from, besides; **nebenan** adv next door; **Nebenausgang** m side exit; **nebenbei** adv at the same time; (außerdem) additionally; (beiläufig) incidentally; **nebeneinander** adv side by side; **Nebeneingang** m side entrance; **Nebenfach** nt subsidiary subject

nebenher adv (zusätzlich) besides; (gleichzeitig) at the same time; (daneben) alongside

Nebenkosten pl extra charges pl, extras pl; **Nebensache** f minor matter; **nebensächlich** adj minor; **Nebensaison** f low season; **Nebenstraße** f side street; **Nebenwirkung** f side effect

neblig adj foggy, misty

necken vt to tease

Neffe (-n, -n) m nephew

negativ adj negative; **Negativ** nt (Foto) negative

nehmen (nahm, genommen) vt to take; **wie man's nimmt** it depends on how you look at it; **den Bus/Zug ~** to take the bus/train; **jdn/etw ernst ~** to take sb/sth seriously; **etw zu sich ~** to eat sth; **jdn zu sich ~** to have sb come and live with one; **jdn an die Hand ~** to take sb by the hand

neidisch *adj* envious

neigen *vi*: **zu etw ~** to tend towards sth; **Neigung** *f* (*des Geländes*) slope; (*Tendenz*) inclination; (*Vorliebe*) liking

nein *adv* no

Nektarine *f* nectarine

Nelke (-, -n) *f* carnation; (*Gewürz*) clove

nennen (*nannte, genannt*) *vt* to name; (*mit Namen*) to call

Neonazi (-s, -s) *m* neo-Nazi

Nepal (-s) *nt* Nepal

Neptun (-s) *m* Neptune

Nerv (-s, -en) *m* nerve; **jdm auf die ~en gehen** to get on sb's nerves; **nerven** *vt*: **jdn ~** (*fam*) to get on sb's nerves; **Nerven-zusammenbruch** *m* nervous breakdown; **nervös** *adj* nervous

Nest (-(e)s, -er) *nt* nest; (*pej: Ort*) dump

nett *adj* nice; (*freundlich*) kind; **sei so ~ und ...** do me a favour and ...

netto *adv* net

Netz (-es, -e) *nt* net; (*für Einkauf*) string bag; (*System*) network; (*Stromnetz*) mains, power (*US*); **Netzanschluss** *m* mains connection; **Netzbetreiber(in)** *m(f)* network operator; (*Inform*) Internet (*o* Net) operator; **Netzgerät** *nt* power pack; **Netzkarte** *f* season ticket; **Netzwerk** *nt* (*Inform*) network; **Netzwerkkarte** *f* network card

neu *adj* new; (*Sprache, Geschichte*) modern; **die ~esten Nachrichten** the latest news; **Neubau** *m* new building; **neuerdings** *adv* recently; **Neueröffnung** *f* (*Geschäft*) new business;

Neuerung *f* innovation; (*Reform*) reform

Neugier *f* curiosity; **neugierig** *adj* curious (*auf +akk* about); **ich bin ~, ob ...** I wonder whether (*o* if) ...; **ich bin ~ , was du dazu sagst** I'll be interested to hear what you have to say about it

Neuheit *f* novelty; **Neuigkeit** *f* news *sing*; **eine ~** a piece of news; **Neujahr** *nt* New Year; **prosit ~!** Happy New Year; **neulich** *adv* recently, the other day; **Neumond** *m* new moon

neun *num* nine; **neunhundert** *num* nine hundred; **neunmal** *adv* nine times; **neunte(r, s)** *adj* ninth; *siehe auch* **dritte**; **Neuntel** (-s, -) *nt* ninth; **neunzehn** *num* nineteen; **neunzehnte(r, s)** *adj* nineteenth; *siehe auch* **dritte**; **neunzig** *num* ninety; **in den ~er Jahren** in the nineties; **Neunzigerjahre** *pl* nineties *pl*; **neunzigste(r, s)** *adj* ninetieth

neureich *adj* nouveau riche

Neurologe *m*, **Neurologin** *f* neurologist; **Neurose** (-, -n) *f* neurosis; **neurotisch** *adj* neurotic

Neuseeland *nt* New Zealand

Neustart *m* (*Inform*) restart, reboot

neutral *adj* neutral

neuwertig *adj* nearly new

Nicaragua (-s) *nt* Nicaragua

⭕ SCHLÜSSELWORT

nicht *adv* **1** (*Verneinung*) not; **er ist es nicht** it's not him, it isn't him; **er raucht nicht** (*gerade*) he isn't smoking; (*gewöhnlich*) he doesn't smoke; **ich kann das nicht — ich auch nicht** I can't do it — neither *o* nor can I; **es regnet nicht mehr** it's not raining any more; **nicht rostend** stainless

2 (*Bitte, Verbot*) **nicht!** don't!, no!; **nicht berühren!** do not touch!; **nicht doch!** don't!

3 (*rhetorisch*) **du bist müde, nicht (wahr)?** you're tired, aren't you?; **das ist schön, nicht (wahr)?** it's nice, isn't it?

4 was du nicht sagst! the things you say!

Nichte (-, -n) *f* niece
Nichtraucher(in) *m(f)* non-smoker; **Nichtraucherabteil** *nt* non-smoking compartment; **Nichtraucherzone** *f* non-smoking area
nichts *pron* nothing; **für ~ und wieder ~** for nothing at all; **ich habe ~ gesagt** I didn't say anything; **macht ~** never mind
Nichtschwimmer(in) *m(f)* non-swimmer
nichtssagend *adj* meaningless
nicken *vi* to nod
Nickerchen *nt* nap
nie *adv* never; **~ wieder** (*o* **mehr**) never again; **fast ~** hardly ever
nieder *adj* (*niedrig*) low; (*gering*) inferior ▷ *adv* down; **niedergeschlagen** *adj* depressed; **Niederlage** *f* defeat
Niederlande *pl* Netherlands *pl*; **Niederländer(in)** *m(f)* Dutchman/Dutchwoman; **niederländisch** *adj* Dutch; **Niederländisch** *nt* Dutch
Niederlassung *f* branch
Niederösterreich *nt* Lower Austria; **Niedersachsen** *nt* Lower Saxony
Niederschlag *m* (*Meteo*) precipitation; (*Regen*) rainfall
niedlich *adj* sweet, cute
niedrig *adj* low; (*Qualität*) inferior
niemals *adv* never
niemand *pron* nobody, no one;

ich habe ~en gesehen I haven't seen anyone; **~ von ihnen** none of them
Niere (-, -n) *f* kidney; **Nierenentzündung** *f* kidney infection; **Nierensteine** *pl* kidney stones *pl*
nieseln *vi impers* to drizzle; **Nieselregen** *m* drizzle
niesen *vi* to sneeze
Niete (-, -n) *f* (*Los*) blank; (*Reinfall*) flop; (*pej: Mensch*) failure; (*Tech*) rivet
Nigeria (-s) *nt* Nigeria
Nikotin (-s) *nt* nicotine
Nilpferd *nt* hippopotamus
nippen *vi* to sip; **an etw** (*dat*) **~** to sip sth
nirgends *adv* nowhere
Nische (-, -n) *f* niche
Niveau (-s, -s) *nt* level; **sie hat ~** she's got class
nobel *adj* (*großzügig*) generous; (*fam: luxuriös*) classy, posh; **Nobelpreis** *m* Nobel Prize

○ SCHLÜSSELWORT

noch *adv* **1** (*weiterhin*) still; **noch nicht** not yet; **noch nie** never (yet); **noch immer** *o* **immer noch** still; **bleiben Sie doch noch** stay a bit longer

2 (*in Zukunft*) still, yet; **das kann noch passieren** that might still happen; **er wird noch kommen** he'll come (yet)

3 (*nicht später als*) **noch vor einer Woche** only a week ago; **noch am selben Tag** the very same day; **noch im 19. Jahrhundert** as late as the 19th century; **noch heute** today

4 (*zusätzlich*) **wer war noch da?** who else was there?; **noch einmal** once more, again; **noch dreimal** three more times; **noch einer** another one

5 (*bei Vergleichen*) **noch größer** even bigger; **das ist noch besser** that's better still; **und wenn es noch so schwer ist** however hard it is

6 Geld noch und noch heaps (and heaps) of money; **sie hat noch und noch versucht, ...** she tried again and again to ...

▷ *konj:* **weder A noch B** neither A nor B

nochmal(s) *adv* again, once more

Nominativ *m* nominative (case)

Nonne (-, -n) *f* nun

Nonstop-Flug *m* nonstop flight

Nord north; **Nordamerika** *nt* North America; **Norddeutschland** *nt* Northern Germany; **Norden** (-s) *m* north; **im ~ Deutschlands** in the north of Germany; **Nordeuropa** *nt* Northern Europe

Nordic Walking *nt* (*Sport*) Nordic Walking

Nordirland *nt* Northern Ireland; **nordisch** *adj* (*Völker, Sprache*) Nordic; **Nordkorea** (-s) *nt* North Korea; **nördlich** *adj* northern; (*Kurs, Richtung*) northerly; **Nordost(en)** *m* northeast; **Nordpol** *m* North Pole; **Nordrhein-Westfalen** (-s) *nt* North Rhine-Westphalia; **Nordsee** *f* North Sea; **nordwärts** *adv* north, northwards; **Nordwest(en)** *m* northwest; **Nordwind** *m* north wind

nörgeln *vi* to grumble

Norm (-, -en) *f* norm; (*Größenvorschrift*) standard

normal *adj* normal; **Normalbenzin** *nt* regular (petrol (*Brit*) o gas (*US*)); **normalerweise** *adv* normally

normen *vt* to standardize

Norwegen (-s) *nt* Norway;

Norweger(in) *m(f)* Norwegian; **norwegisch** *adj* Norwegian; **Norwegisch** *nt* Norwegian

Not (-, *Nöte*) *f* need; (*Armut*) poverty; (*Elend*) hardship; (*Bedrängnis*) trouble; (*Mangel*) want; (*Mühe*) trouble; (*Zwang*) necessity; **zur ~** if necessary; (*gerade noch*) just about

Notar(in) *m(f)* public notary; **notariell** *adj:* **~ beglaubigt** attested by a notary

Notarzt *m*, **Notärztin** *f* emergency doctor; **Notarztwagen** *m* emergency ambulance; **Notaufnahme** *f* A&E, casualty (*Brit*), emergency room (*US*); **Notausgang** *m* emergency exit; **Notbremse** *f* emergency brake; **Notdienst** *m* emergency service, after-hours service; **notdürftig** *adj* scanty; (*behelfsmäßig*) makeshift

Note (-, -n) *f* note; (*in Schule*) mark, grade (*US*); (*Mus*) note

Notebook (-(s), -s) *nt* (*Inform*) notebook

Notfall *m* emergency; **notfalls** *adv* if necessary

notieren *vt* to note down

nötig *adj* necessary; **etw ~ haben** to need sth

Notiz (-, -en) *f* note; (*Zeitungs~*) item; **Notizblock** *m* notepad; **Notizbuch** *nt* notebook

Notlage *f* crisis; (*Elend*) plight; **notlanden** *vi* to make a forced (*o* emergency) landing; **Notlandung** *f* emergency landing; **Notruf** *m* emergency call; **Notrufnummer** *f* emergency number; **Notrufsäule** *f* emergency telephone

notwendig *adj* necessary

Nougat (-s, -s) *m od nt* nougat

November (-(s), -) *m* November; *siehe auch* **Juni**

Nr. *abk* = **Nummer** No., no.
Nu *m*: **im ~** in no time
nüchtern *adj* sober; (*Magen*) empty
Nudel (-, -n) *f* noodle; **~n** *pl* (*italienische*) pasta *sing*
null *num* zero; (*Tel*) O (*Brit*), zero (*US*); **~ Fehler** no mistakes; **~ Uhr** midnight; **Null** (-, -en) *f* nought, zero; (*pej: Mensch*) dead loss; **Nulltarif** *m*: **zum ~** free of charge
Numerus clausus (-) *m* restriction on the number of students allowed to study a particular subject
Nummer (-, -n) *f* number; **nummerieren** *vt* to number; **Nummernschild** *nt* (*Auto*) number plate (*Brit*), license plate (*US*)
nun *adv* now; **von ~ an** from now on ▷ *interj* well; **~ gut!** all right, then; **es ist ~ mal so** that's the way it is
nur *adv* only; **nicht ~ ..., sondern auch ...** not only ..., but also ...; **~ Anna nicht** except Anna
Nürnberg (-s) *nt* Nuremberg
Nuss (-, *Nüsse*) *f* nut; **Nussknacker** (-s, -) *m* nut-cracker; **Nuss-Nougat-Creme** *f* chocolate nut cream
Nutte (-, -n) *f* (*fam*) tart
nutz, nütze *adj*: **zu nichts ~ sein** to be useless; **nutzen, nützen** *vt* to use (*zu etw* for sth); **was nützt es?** what use is it? ▷ *vi* to be of use; **das nützt nicht viel** that doesn't help much; **es nützt nichts(, es zu tun)** it's no use (doing it); **Nutzen** (-s, -) *m* usefulness; (*Gewinn*) profit; **nützlich** *adj* useful
Nylon (-s) *nt* nylon

o *interj* oh
O *abk* = **Ost** E
Oase (-, -n) *f* oasis
ob *conj* if, whether; **so als ~** as if; **er tut so, als ~ er krank wäre** he's pretending to be sick; **und ~!** you bet
obdachlos *adj* homeless
oben *adv* (*am oberen Ende*) at the top; (*obenauf*) on (the) top; (*im Haus*) upstairs; (*in einem Text*) above; **~ erwähnt** (*o genannt*) above-mentioned; **mit dem Gesicht nach ~** face up; **da ~** up there; **von ~ bis unten** from top to bottom; **siehe ~** see above
Ober (-s, -) *m* waiter
obere(r, s) *adj* upper, top
Oberfläche *f* surface; **oberflächlich** *adj* superficial; **Obergeschoss** *nt* upper floor
oberhalb *adv*, *prep* +*gen* above
Oberhemd *nt* shirt; **Oberkörper**

m upper body; **Oberlippe** *f* upper lip; **Oberösterreich** *nt* Upper Austria; **Oberschenkel** *m* thigh

oberste(r, s) *adj* very top, topmost

Oberteil *nt* top; **Oberweite** *f* bust/chest measurement

obig *adj* above(-mentioned)

Objekt (-(e)s, -e) *nt* object

objektiv *adj* objective; **Objektiv** *nt* lens

obligatorisch *adj* compulsory, obligatory

Oboe (-, -n) *f* oboe

Observatorium *nt* observatory

Obst (-(e)s) *nt* fruit; **Obstkuchen** *m* fruit tart; **Obstsalat** *m* fruit salad

obszön *adj* obscene

obwohl *conj* although

Ochse (-n, -n) *m* ox; **Ochsenschwanzsuppe** *f* oxtail soup

ocker *adj* ochre

öd(e) *adj* waste; (*unbebaut*) barren; (*fig*) dull

oder *conj* or; **~ aber** or else; **er kommt doch, ~?** he's coming, isn't he?

Ofen (-s, Öfen) *m* oven; (*Heizofen*) heater; (*Kohleofen*) stove; (*Herd*) cooker, stove; **Ofenkartoffel** *f* baked (*o* jacket) potato

offen *adj* open; (*aufrichtig*) frank; (*Stelle*) vacant ▷ *adv* frankly; **~ gesagt** to be honest

offenbar *adj* obvious; **offensichtlich** *adj* evident, obvious

öffentlich *adj* public; **Öffentlichkeit** *f* (*Leute*) public; (*einer Versammlung etc*) public nature

offiziell *adj* official

offline *adv* (*Inform*) offline

öffnen *vt* to open ▷ *vr:* **sich ~** to open; **Öffner** (-s, -) *m* opener;

Öffnung *f* opening; **Öffnungszeiten** *pl* opening times *pl*

oft *adv* often; **schon ~** many times; **öfter** *adv* more often (*o* frequently); **öfters** *adv* often, frequently

ohne *conj, prep* +*akk* without; **~ weiteres** without a second thought; (*sofort*) immediately; **~ ein Wort zu sagen** without saying a word; **~ mich** count me out

Ohnmacht (-machten) *f* unconsciousness; (*Hilflosigkeit*) helplessness; **in ~ fallen** to faint; **ohnmächtig** *adj* unconscious; **sie ist ~** she has fainted

Ohr (-(e)s, -en) *nt* ear; (*Gehör*) hearing

Öhr (-(e)s, -e) *nt* eye

Ohrenarzt *m*, **Ohrenärztin** *f* ear specialist; **Ohrenschmerzen** *pl* earache; **Ohrentropfen** *pl* ear drops *pl*; **Ohrfeige** *f* slap (in the face); **Ohrläppchen** *nt* earlobe; **Ohrringe** *pl* earrings *pl*

oje *interj* oh dear

okay *interj* OK, okay

Ökoladen *m* health food store; **ökologisch** *adj* ecological; **~e Landwirtschaft** organic farming

ökonomisch *adj* economic; (*sparsam*) economical

Ökosystem *nt* ecosystem

Oktanzahl *f* (*bei Benzin*) octane rating

Oktober (-(s), -) *m* October; *siehe auch* **Juni**

- **OKTOBERFEST**
-
- The annual October beer
- festival, the **Oktoberfest**,
- takes place in Munich on a
- huge field where beer tents,
- roller coasters and many other

amusements are set up. People
sit at long wooden tables, drink
beer from enormous litre beer
mugs, eat pretzels and listen
to brass bands. It is a great
attraction for tourists and locals
alike.

Öl (-(e)s, -e) nt oil; **Ölbaum** m
olive tree; **ölen** vt to oil; (Tech) to
lubricate; **Ölfarbe** f oil paint;
Ölfilter m oil filter; **Ölgemälde**
nt oil painting; **Ölheizung** f
oil-fired central heating; **ölig** adj
oily

oliv adj inv olive-green; **Olive**
(-, -n) f olive; **Olivenöl** nt olive
oil

Ölmessstab m dipstick; **Ölofen**
m oil stove; **Ölpest** f oil
pollution; **Ölsardine** f sardine in
oil; **Ölstandanzeiger** m (Auto)
oil gauge; **Ölteppich** m oil slick;
Ölwechsel m oil change

Olympiade f Olympic Games pl;
olympisch adj Olympic

Oma f, **Omi** (-s, -s) f grandma,
gran(ny)

Omelett (-(e)s, -s) nt, **Omelette**
f omelette

Omnibus m bus

onanieren vi to masturbate

Onkel (-s, -) m uncle

online adv (Inform) online;
Onlinedienst m (Inform) online
service

OP (-s, -s) m abk =
Operationssaal operating
theatre (Brit) (o room (US))

Opa m, **Opi** (-s, -s) m grandpa,
grandad

Open-Air-Konzert nt open-air
concert

Oper (-, -n) f opera; (Gebäude)
opera house

Operation f operation

Operette f operetta

operieren vi to operate ▷ vt to
operate on

Opernhaus nt opera house,
opera; **Opernsänger(in)** m(f)
opera singer

Opfer (-s, -) nt sacrifice; (Mensch)
victim; **ein ~ bringen** to make a
sacrifice

Opium (-s) nt opium

Opposition f opposition

Optiker(in) (-s, -) m(f) optician

optimal adj optimal, optimum

optimistisch adj optimistic

oral adj oral; **Oralverkehr** m
oral sex

orange adj inv orange; **Orange**
(-, -n) f orange; **Orangenmarmelade** f marmalade;
Orangensaft m orange juice

Orchester (-s, -) nt orchestra

Orchidee (-, -n) f orchid

Orden (-s, -) m (Rel) order; (Mil)
decoration

ordentlich adj (anständig)
respectable; (geordnet) tidy, neat;
(fam: annehmbar) not bad; (fam:
tüchtig) proper ▷ adv properly

ordinär adj common, vulgar;
(Witz) dirty

ordnen vt to sort out; **Ordner**
(-s, -) m (bei Veranstaltung)
steward; (Aktenordner) file;
Ordnung f order; (Geordnetsein)
tidiness; (**geht**) **in ~!** (that's) all
right; **mit dem Drucker ist etwas
nicht in ~** there's something
wrong with the printer

Oregano (-s) m oregano

Organ (-s, -e) nt organ; (Stimme)
voice

Organisation f organization;
organisieren vt to organize;
(fam: beschaffen) to get hold of
▷ vr: **sich ~** to organize

Organismus m organism

Orgasmus m orgasm

Orgel (-, -n) f organ

Orgie f orgy
orientalisch adj oriental
orientieren vr: **sich ~** to get one's bearings; **Orientierung** f orientation; **Orientierungssinn** m sense of direction
original adj original; (echt) genuine; **Original** (-s, -e) nt original
originell adj original; (komisch) witty
Orkan (-(e)s, -e) m hurricane
Ort (-(e)s, -e) m place; (Dorf) village; **an ~ und Stelle, vor ~** on the spot
Orthopäde (-n, -n) m, **Orthopädin** f orthopaedist
örtlich adj local; **Ortschaft** f village, small town; **Ortsgespräch** nt local call; **Ortstarif** m local rate; **Ortszeit** f local time

---

* OSSI
*
* **Ossi** is a colloquial and rather
* derogatory word used to
* describe a German from the
* former **DDR**.

Ost east; **Ostdeutschland** nt (als Landesteil) Eastern Germany; (Hist) East Germany; **Osten** (-s) m east
Osterei nt Easter egg; **Osterglocke** f daffodil; **Osterhase** m Easter bunny; **Ostermontag** m Easter Monday; **Ostern** (-, -) nt Easter; **an** (o **zu**) **~** at Easter; **frohe ~** Happy Easter
Österreich (-s) nt Austria; **Österreicher(in)** (-s, -) m(f) Austrian; **österreichisch** adj Austrian
Ostersonntag m Easter Sunday
Osteuropa nt Eastern Europe; **Ostküste** f east coast; **östlich** adj eastern; (Kurs, Richtung) easterly; **Ostsee** f: **die ~** the

Baltic (Sea); **Ostwind** m east(erly) wind
OSZE (-) f abk = **Organisation für Sicherheit und Zusammenarbeit in Europa** OSCE
Otter (-s, -) m otter
out adj (fam) out; **outen** vt to out
oval adj oval
Overheadprojektor m overhead projector
Ozean (-s, -e) m ocean; **der Stille ~** the Pacific (Ocean)
Ozon (-s) nt ozone; **Ozonbelastung** f ozone level; **Ozonloch** nt hole in the ozone layer; **Ozonschicht** f ozone layer; **Ozonwerte** pl ozone levels pl

paar *adj inv* **ein ~** a few; **ein ~ Mal** a few times; **ein ~ Äpfel** some apples

Paar *(-(e)s, -e) nt* pair; *(Ehepaar)* couple; **ein ~ Socken** a pair of socks .

pachten *vt* to lease

Päckchen *nt* package; *(Zigaretten)* packet; *(zum Verschicken)* small parcel; **packen** *vt* to pack; *(fassen)* to grasp, to seize; *(fam: schaffen)* to manage; *(fig: fesseln)* to grip; **Packpapier** *nt* brown paper; **Packung** *f* packet, pack *(US)*;
Packungsbeilage *f* package insert, patient information leaflet

Pädagoge *(-n, -n) m*, **Pädagogin** *f* teacher; **pädagogisch** *adj* educational; **~e Hochschule** college of education

Paddel *(-s, -) nt* paddle; **Paddelboot** *nt* canoe; **paddeln**
vi to paddle

Paket *(-(e)s, -e) nt* packet; *(Postpaket)* parcel; *(Inform)* package; **Paketbombe** *f* parcel bomb; **Paketkarte** *f* dispatch form *(to be filled in with details of the sender and the addressee when handing in a parcel at the post office)*

Pakistan *(-s) nt* Pakistan

Palast *(-es, Paläste) m* palace

Palästina *(-s) nt* Palestine; **Palästinenser(in)** *(-s, -) m(f)* Palestinian

Palatschinken *pl* filled pancakes *pl*

Palette *f (von Maler)* palette; *(Ladepalette)* pallet; *(Vielfalt)* range

Palme *(-, -n) f* palm (tree); **Palmsonntag** *m* Palm Sunday

Pampelmuse *(-, -n) f* grapefruit

pampig *adj (fam: frech)* cheeky; *(breiig)* gooey

Panda(bär) *(-s, -s) m* panda

Pandemie *(-, -n) f* pandemic

panieren *vt (Gastr)* to coat with breadcrumbs; **paniert** *adj* breaded

Panik *f* panic

Panne *(-, -n) f (Auto)* breakdown; *(Missgeschick)* slip; **Pannendienst** *m*, **Pannenhilfe** *f* breakdown *(o rescue)* service

Pant(h)er *(-s, -) m* panther

Pantomime *(-, -n) f* mime

Panzer *(-s, -) m (Panzerung)* armour (plating); *(Mil)* tank

Papa *(-s, -s) m* dad(dy), pa *(US)*

Papagei *(-s, -en) m* parrot

Papaya *(-, -s) f* papaya

Papier *(-s, -e) nt* paper; **~e** *pl (Ausweispapiere)* papers *pl*; *(Dokumente, Urkunden)* papers *pl*, documents *pl*; **Papiercontainer** *m* paper bank; **Papierformat** *nt* paper size; **Papiergeld** *nt* paper money; **Papierkorb** *m* wastepaper basket; *(Inform)*

recycle bin; **Papiertaschentuch** nt (paper) tissue; **Papiertonne** f paper bank

Pappbecher m paper cup; **Pappe** (-, -n) f cardboard; **Pappkarton** m cardboard box; **Pappteller** m paper plate

Paprika (-s, -s) m (Gewürz) paprika; (Schote) pepper

Papst (-(e)s, Päpste) m pope

Paradeiser (-s, -) m tomato

Paradies (-es, -e) nt paradise

Paragliding (-s) nt paragliding

Paragraph (-en, -en) m paragraph; (Jur) section

parallel adj parallel

Paranuss f Brazil nut

Parasit (-en, -en) m parasite

parat adj ready; **etw ~ haben** to have sth ready

Pärchen nt couple

Parfüm (-s, -s o -e) nt perfume; **Parfümerie** f perfumery; **parfümieren** vt to scent, to perfume

Pariser (-s, -) m (fam: Kondom) rubber

Park (-s, -s) m park

Park-and-ride-System nt park-and-ride system; **Parkbank** f park bench; **Parkdeck** nt parking level; **parken** vt, vi to park

Parkett (-s, -e) nt parquet flooring; (Theat) stalls pl (Brit), parquet (US)

Parkhaus nt multi-storey car park (Brit), parking garage (US)

parkinsonsche Krankheit f Parkinson's disease

Parkkralle f (Auto) wheel clamp; **Parklicht** nt parking light; **Parklücke** f parking space; **Parkplatz** m (für ein Auto) parking space; (für mehrere Autos) car park (Brit), parking lot (US); **Parkscheibe** f parking disc; **Parkscheinautomat** m pay

point; (Parkscheinausgabegerät) ticket machine; **Parkuhr** f parking meter; **Parkverbot** nt (Stelle) no-parking zone; **hier ist ~** you can't park here

Parlament nt parliament

Parmesan (-s) m Parmesan (cheese)

Partei f party

Parterre (-s, -s) nt ground floor (Brit), first floor (US)

Partie f part; (Spiel) game; (Mann, Frau) catch; **mit von der ~ sein** to be in on it

Partitur f (Mus) score

Partizip (-s, -ien) nt participle

Partner(in) (-s, -) m(f) partner; **Partnerschaft** f partnership; **eingetragene ~** civil partnership; **Partnerstadt** f twin town

Party (-, -s) f party; **Partymuffel** (-s, -) m party pooper; **Partyservice** m catering service

Pass (-es, Pässe) m pass; (Ausweis) passport

passabel adj reasonable

Passagier (-s, -e) m passenger

Passamt nt passport office

Passant(in) m(f) passer-by; **Passbild** nt passport photo

passen vi (Größe) to fit; (Farbe, Stil) to go (zu with); (auf Frage) to pass; **passt (es) dir morgen?** does tomorrow suit you?; **das passt mir gut** that suits me fine; **passend** adj suitable; (zusammenpassend) matching; (angebracht) fitting; (Zeit) convenient; **haben Sie es nicht ~?** (Kleingeld) have you got the right change?

passieren vi to happen

passiv adj passive

Passkontrolle f passport control

Passwort nt password

Paste (-, -n) f paste

Pastellfarbe f pastel colour
Pastete (-, -n) f (warmes Gericht)
pie; (Pastetchen) vol-au-vent; (ohne
Teig) pâté
Pastor, in (-s, -en) m(f) minister,
vicar
Pate (-n, -n) m godfather;
Patenkind nt godchild
Patient(in) m(f) patient
Patin f godmother
Patrone (-, -n) f cartridge
patsch interj splat; **patschnass**
adj soaking wet
pauschal adj (Kosten) inclusive;
(Urteil) sweeping; **Pauschale**
(-, -n) f, **Pauschalgebühr** f flat
rate (charge); **Pauschalpreis** m
flat rate; (für Hotel, Reise)
all-inclusive price; **Pauschalreise**
f package tour
Pause (-, -n) f break; (Theat)
interval; (Kino etc) intermission;
(Innehalten) pause
Pavian (-s, -e) m baboon
Pavillon (-s, -s) m pavilion
Pay-TV (-s) nt pay-per-view
television, pay TV
Pazifik (-s) m Pacific (Ocean)
PC (-s, -s) m abk = **Personal
Computer** PC
Pech (-s, -e) nt (fig) bad luck;
~ haben to be unlucky; **~ gehabt!**
tough (luck)
Pedal (-s, -e) nt pedal
Pediküre (-, -en) f pedicure
Peeling (-s, -s) nt (facial/body)
scrub
peinlich adj (unangenehm)
embarrassing, awkward; (genau)
painstaking; **es war mir sehr ~** I
was totally embarrassed
Peitsche (-, -n) f whip
Pelikan (-s, -e) m pelican
Pellkartoffeln pl potatoes pl
boiled in their skins
Pelz (-es, -e) m fur; **pelzig** adj
(Zunge) furred

pendeln vi (Zug, Bus) to shuttle;
(Mensch) to commute;
Pendelverkehr m shuttle traffic;
(für Pendler) commuter traffic;
Pendler(in) (-s, -) m(f)
commuter
penetrant adj sharp; (Mensch)
pushy
Penis (-, -se) m penis
Pension f (Geld) pension;
(Ruhestand) retirement; (für Gäste)
guesthouse, B&B; **pensioniert**
adj retired; **Pensionsgast** m
guest (in a guesthouse)
Peperoni (-, -) f chilli
per prep +akk by, per; (pro) per; (bis)
by
perfekt adj perfect
Pergamentpapier nt grease-
proof paper
Periode (-, -n) f period
Perle (-, -n) f (a. fig) pearl
perplex adj dumbfounded
Person (-, -en) f person; **ein Tisch
für drei ~en** a table for three;
Personal (-s) nt staff, personnel;
(Bedienung) servants pl;
Personalausweis m identity
card; **Personalien** pl particulars
pl; **Personenschaden** m injury
to persons; **Personenwaage** f
(bathroom) scales pl;
Personenzug m passenger train;
persönlich adj personal; (auf
Briefen) private ▷ adv personally;
(selbst) in person; **Persönlichkeit**
f personality
Peru (-s) nt Peru
Perücke (-, -n) f wig
pervers adj perverted
pessimistisch adj pessimistic
Pest (-) f plague
Petersilie f parsley
Petroleum (-s) nt paraffin (Brit),
kerosene (US)
Pfad (-(e)s, -e) m path;
Pfadfinder (-s, -) m boy scout;

Pfadfinderin f girl guide
Pfahl (-(e)s, Pfähle) m post, stake
Pfand (-(e)s, Pfänder) nt security; (Flaschenpfand) deposit; (im Spiel) forfeit; **Pfandflasche** f returnable bottle
Pfanne (-, -n) f (frying) pan
Pfannkuchen m pancake
Pfarrei f parish; **Pfarrer(in)** (-s, -) m(f) priest
Pfau (-(e)s, -en) m peacock
Pfeffer (-s, -) m pepper; **Pfefferkuchen** m gingerbread; **Pfefferminze** (-e) f peppermint; **Pfefferminztee** m peppermint tea; **Pfeffermühle** f pepper mill; **pfeffern** vt to put pepper on/in; **Pfefferstreuer** (-s, -) m pepper pot
Pfeife (-, -n) f whistle; (für Tabak, von Orgel) pipe; **pfeifen** (pfiff, gepfiffen) vt, vi to whistle
Pfeil (-(e)s, -e) m arrow
Pfeiltaste f (Inform) arrow key
Pferd (-(e)s, -e) nt horse; **Pferdeschwanz** m (Frisur) ponytail; **Pferdestall** m stable; **Pferdestärke** f horsepower
pfiff imperf von **pfeifen**
Pfifferling m chanterelle
Pfingsten (-, -) nt Whitsun, Pentecost (US); **Pfingstmontag** m Whit Monday; **Pfingstsonntag** m Whit Sunday, Pentecost (US)
Pfirsich (-s, -e) m peach
Pflanze (-, -n) f plant; **pflanzen** vt to plant; **Pflanzenfett** nt vegetable fat
Pflaster (-s, -) nt (für Wunde) plaster, Band Aid® (US); (Straßenpflaster) road surface, pavement (US)
Pflaume (-, -n) f plum
Pflege (-, -n) f care; (Krankenpflege) nursing; (von Autos, Maschinen) maintenance; **pflegebedürftig** adj in need of

care; **pflegeleicht** adj easy-care; (fig) easy to handle; **pflegen** vt to look after; (Kranke) to nurse; (Beziehungen) to foster; (Fingernägel, Gesicht) to take care of; (Daten) to maintain; **Pflegepersonal** nt nursing staff; **Pflegeversicherung** f long-term care insurance
Pflicht (-, -en) f duty; (Sport) compulsory section; **pflicht-bewusst** adj conscientious; **Pflichtfach** nt (Schule) compulsory subject; **Pflicht-versicherung** f compulsory insurance
pflücken vt to pick
Pforte (-, -n) f gate; **Pförtner(in)** (-s, -) m(f) porter
Pfosten (-s, -) m post
Pfote (-, -n) f paw
pfui interj ugh
Pfund (-(e)s, -e) nt pound
pfuschen vi (fam) to be sloppy
Pfütze (-, -n) f puddle
Phantasie f siehe **Fantasie**; **phantastisch** adj siehe **fantastisch**
Phase (-, -n) f phase
Philippinen pl Philippines pl
Philosophie f philosophy
Photo nt siehe **Foto**
pH-neutral adj pH-balanced; **pH-Wert** m pH-value
Physalis (-, Physalen) f physalis
Physik f physics sing
physisch adj physical
Pianist(in) (-en, -en) m(f) pianist
Pickel (-s, -) m pimple; (Werkzeug) pickaxe; (Berg~) ice-axe
Picknick (-s, -e o -s) nt picnic; **ein ~ machen** to have a picnic
piepsen vi to chirp
piercen vt: **sich die Nase ~ lassen** to have one's nose pierced; **Piercing** (-s) nt (body) piercing
pieseln vi (fam) to pee

Pik (-, -) nt (Karten) spades pl
pikant adj spicy
Pilates nt (Sport) Pilates
Pilger(in) m(f) pilgrim;
Pilgerfahrt f pilgrimage
Pille (-, -n) f pill; **sie nimmt die
~** she's on the pill
Pilot(in) (-en, -en) m(f) pilot
Pilz (-es, -e) m (essbar) mushroom;
(giftig) toadstool; (Med) fungus
PIN (-, -s) f PIN (number)
pingelig adj (fam) fussy
Pinguin (-s, -e) m penguin
Pinie f pine; **Pinienkern** m pine
nut
pink adj shocking pink
pinkeln vi (fam) to pee
Pinsel (-s, -) m (paint)brush
Pinzette f tweezers pl
Pistazie f pistachio
Piste (-, -n) f (Ski) piste; (Aviat)
runway
Pistole (-, -n) f pistol
Pixel (-s) nt (Inform) pixel
Pizza (-, -s) f pizza; **Pizzaservice**
m pizza delivery service; **Pizzeria**
(-, Pizzerien) f pizzeria
Pkw (-(s), -(s)) m abk =
Personenkraftwagen car
Plakat nt poster
Plakette f (Schildchen) badge;
(Aufkleber) sticker
Plan (-(e)s, Pläne) m plan; (Karte)
map; **planen** vt to plan
Planet (-en, -en) m planet;
Planetarium nt planetarium
planmäßig adj scheduled
Plan(t)schbecken nt paddling
pool; **plan(t)schen** vi to splash
around
Planung f planning
Plastik f sculpture ▷ (-s) nt
(Kunststoff) plastic; **Plastikfolie** f
plastic film; **Plastiktüte** f
plastic bag
Platin (-s) nt platinum
platsch interj splash

platt adj flat; (fam: überrascht)
flabbergasted; (fig: geistlos) flat,
boring
Platte (-, -n) f (Foto, Tech, Gastr)
plate; (Steinplatte) flag;
(Schallplatte) record;
Plattenspieler m record player
Plattform f platform; **Plattfuß**
m flat foot; (Reifen) flat (tyre)
Platz (-es, Plätze) m place;
(Sitzplatz) seat; (freier Raum) space,
room; (in Stadt) square; (Sportplatz)
playing field; **nehmen Sie ~** please
sit down, take a seat; **ist dieser
~ frei?** is this seat taken?;
Platzanweiser(in) m(f)
usher/usherette
Plätzchen nt spot; (Gebäck)
biscuit
platzen vi to burst; (Bombe) to
explode
Platzkarte f seat reservation;
Platzreservierung f seat
reservation; **Platzverweis** m: **er
erhielt einen ~** he was sent off;
Platzwunde f laceration, cut
plaudern vi to chat, to talk
pleite adj (fam) broke; **Pleite**
(-, -n) f (Bankrott) bankruptcy;
(fam: Reinfall) flop
Plombe (-, -n) f lead seal;
(Zahnplombe) filling; **plombieren**
vt (Zahn) to fill
plötzlich adj sudden ▷ adv suddenly,
all at once
plump adj clumsy; (Hände)
ungainly; (Körper) shapeless
plumps interj thud; (in Flüssigkeit)
plop
Plural (-s, -e) m plural
plus adv plus; **fünf ~ sieben ist
zwölf** five plus seven is (o are)
twelve; **zehn Grad ~** ten degrees
above zero; **Plus** (-, -) nt plus;
(Fin) profit; (Vorteil) advantage
Plüsch (-(e)s, -e) m plush
Pluto (-) m Pluto

PLZ *abk* = **Postleitzahl** postcode (*Brit*), zip code (*US*)

Po (*-s, -s*) *m* (*fam*) bottom, bum

Pocken *pl* smallpox *sing*

poetisch *adj* poetic

Pointe (*-, -n*) *f* punch line

Pokal (*-s, -e*) *m* goblet; (*Sport*) cup

pökeln *vt* to pickle

Pol (*-s, -e*) *m* pole

Pole (*-n, -n*) *m* Pole; **Polen** (*-s*) *nt* Poland

Police (*-, -n*) *f* (insurance) policy

polieren *vt* to polish

Polin *f* Pole, Polish woman

Politik *f* politics *sing*; (*eine bestimmte*) policy; **Politiker(in)** *m(f)* politician; **politisch** *adj* political

Politur *f* polish

Polizei *f* police *pl*; **Polizeibeamte(r)** *m*, **Polizeibeamtin** *f* police officer; **polizeilich** *adj* police; **sie wird ~ gesucht** the police are looking for her; **Polizeirevier** *nt*, **Polizeiwache** *f* police station; **Polizeistunde** *f* closing time; **Polizeiwache** *f* police station; **Polizist(in)** *m(f)* policeman/ -woman

Pollen (*-s, -*) *m* pollen; **Pollenflug** (*-s*) *m* pollen count

polnisch *adj* Polish; **Polnisch** *nt* Polish

Polo (*-s*) *nt* polo; **Polohemd** *nt* polo shirt

Polster (*-s, -*) *nt* cushion; (*Polsterung*) upholstery; (*in Kleidung*) padding; (*fig: Geld*) reserves *pl*; **Polstergarnitur** *f* living-room suite; **Polstermöbel** *pl* upholstered furniture *sing*; **polstern** *vt* to upholster; (*Kleidung*) to pad

Polterabend *m* party prior to a wedding, at which old crockery is smashed to bring good luck

poltern *vi* (*Krach machen*) to crash; (*schimpfen*) to rant

Polyester (*-s, -*) *m* polyester

Polypen *pl* (*Med*) adenoids *pl*

Pommes frites *pl* chips *pl* (*Brit*), French fries *pl* (*US*)

Pony (*-s, -s*) *m* (*Frisur*) fringe (*Brit*), bangs *pl* (*US*) ▷ (*-s, -s*) *nt* (*Pferd*) pony

Popcorn (*-s*) *nt* popcorn

Popmusik *f* pop (music)

populär *adj* popular

Pore (*-, -n*) *f* pore

Pornografie *f* pornography

Porree (*-s, -s*) *m* leeks *pl*; **eine Stange ~** a leek

Portemonnaie, **Portmonee** (*-s, -s*) *nt* purse

Portier (*-s, -s*) *m* porter; *siehe auch* **Pförtner**

Portion *f* portion, helping

Porto (*-s, -s*) *nt* postage

Portrait, **Porträt** (*-s, -s*) *nt* portrait

Portugal (*-s*) *nt* Portugal; **Portugiese** (*-n, -n*) *m* Portuguese; **Portugiesin** (*-, -nen*) *f* Portuguese; **portugiesisch** *adj* Portuguese; **Portugiesisch** *nt* Portuguese

Portwein (*-s, -e*) *m* port

Porzellan (*-s, -e*) *nt* china

Posaune (*-, -n*) *f* trombone

Position *f* position

positiv *adj* positive

Post® (*-, -en*) *f* post office; (*Briefe*) post (*Brit*), mail; **Postamt** *nt* post office; **Postanweisung** *f* postal order (*Brit*), money order (*US*); **Postbank** *f* German post office bank; **Postbote** *m*, **-botin** *f* postman/-woman

Posten (*-s, -*) *m* post, position; (*Comm*) item; (*auf Liste*) entry

Poster (*-s, -*) *nt* poster

Postfach *nt* post-office box, PO box; **Postkarte** *f* postcard;

postlagernd adv poste restante;
Postleitzahl f postcode (Brit), zip
code (US)
postmodern adj postmodern
Postsparkasse f post office
savings bank; **Poststempel** m
postmark; **Postweg** m: **auf dem
~ by mail**
Potenz f (Math) power; (eines
Mannes) potency
PR (-, -s) f abk = **Public Relations**
PR
prächtig adj splendid
prahlen vi to boast, to brag
Praktikant(in) m(f) trainee;
Praktikum (-s, Praktika) nt prac-
tical training; **praktisch** adj
practical; **~er Arzt** general
practitioner
Praline f chocolate
Prämie f (bei Versicherung)
premium; (Belohnung) reward; (von
Arbeitgeber) bonus
Präparat nt (Med) medicine; (Bio)
preparation
Präservativ nt condom
Präsident(in) m(f) president
Praxis (-, Praxen) f practice;
(Behandlungsraum) surgery; (von
Anwalt) office; **Praxisgebühr** f
surgery surcharge
präzise adj precise, exact
predigen vt, vi to preach; **Predigt**
(-, -en) f sermon
Preis (-es, -e) m (zu zahlen) price;
(bei Sieg) prize; **den ersten
~ gewinnen** to win first prize;
Preisausschreiben nt
competition
Preiselbeere f cranberry
preisgünstig adj inexpensive;
Preislage f price range; **Preisliste**
f price list; **Preisschild** nt price
tag; **Preisträger(in)** m(f)
prizewinner; **preiswert** adj
inexpensive
Prellung f bruise

Premiere (-, -n) f premiere, first
night
Premierminister(in) m(f) prime
minister, premier
Prepaidhandy nt prepaid
mobile (Brit), prepaid cell phone
(US); **Prepaidkarte** f prepaid
card
Presse (-, -n) f press
pressen vt to press
prickeln vi to tingle
Priester(in) (-s, -) m(f) priest/(woman)
priest
Primel (-, -n) f primrose
primitiv adj primitive
Prinz (-en, -en) m prince;
Prinzessin f princess
Prinzip (-s, -ien) nt principle; **im
~ basically**; **aus ~** on principle
Priorität f priority
privat adj private;
Privatfernsehen nt commercial
television; **Privatgrundstück** nt
private property; **privatisieren**
vt to privatize
pro prep +akk per; **5 Euro
~ Stück/Person** 5 euros each/per
person; **Pro** (-s) nt pro
Probe (-, -n) f test; (Teststück)
sample; (Theat) rehearsal;
Probefahrt f test drive; **eine
~ machen** to go for a test drive;
Probezeit f trial period;
probieren vt, vi to try; (Wein,
Speise) to taste, to sample
Problem (-s, -e) nt problem
Produkt (-(e)s, -e) nt product;
Produktion f production;
(produzierte Menge) output;
produzieren vt to produce
Professor(in) (-s, -en) m(f)
professor
Profi (-s, -s) m pro
Profil (-s, -e) nt profile; (von
Reifen, Schuhsohle) tread
Profit (-(e)s, -e) m profit;
profitieren vi to profit (von from)

Prognose (-, -n) f prediction; (*Wetter*) forecast

Programm (-s, -e) nt programme; (*Inform*) program; (*TV*) channel; **Programmheft** nt programme; **programmieren** vt to program; **Programmierer(in)** (-s, -) m(f) programmer; **Programmkino** nt arts (o repertory (*US*)) cinema

Projekt (-(e)s, -e) nt project

Projektor m projector

Promenade (-, -n) f promenade

Promille (-(s)) nt (blood) alcohol level; **o,8 ~** 0,08 per cent; **Promillegrenze** f legal alcohol limit

prominent adj prominent; **Prominenz** f VIPs pl, prominent figures pl; (*fam*: *Stars*) the glitterati pl

Propeller (-s, -) m propeller

prosit interj cheers

Prospekt (-(e)s, -e) m leaflet, brochure

prost interj cheers

Prostituierte(r) mf prostitute

Protest (-(e)s, -e) m protest

Protestant(in) m(f) Protestant; **protestantisch** adj Protestant

protestieren vi to protest (*gegen* against)

Prothese (-, -n) f artificial arm/leg; (*Gebiss*) dentures pl

Protokoll (-s, -e) nt (*bei Sitzung*) minutes pl; (*diplomatisch, Inform*) protocol; (*bei Polizei*) statement

protzen vi to show off; **protzig** adj flashy

Proviant (-s, -e) m provisions pl

Provider (-s, -) m (*Inform*) (service) provider

Provinz (-, -en) f province

Provision f (*Comm*) commission

provisorisch adj provisional; **Provisorium** (-s, Provisorien) nt stopgap; (*Zahn*) temporary filling

provozieren vt to provoke

Prozent (-(e)s, -e) nt per cent

Prozess (-es, -e) m (*Vorgang*) process; (*Jur*) trial; (*Rechtsfall*) (court) case; **prozessieren** vi to go to law (*mit* against)

Prozession f procession

Prozessor (-s, -en) m (*Inform*) processor

prüde adj prudish

prüfen vt to test; (*nachprüfen*) to check; **Prüfung** f (*Schule*) exam; (*Überprüfung*) check; **eine ~ machen** (*Schule*) to take an exam

Prügelei f fight; **prügeln** vt to beat ▷ vr: **sich ~** to fight

PS abk = **Pferdestärke** hp; = **Postskript(um)** PS

pseudo- präf pseudo; **Pseudokrupp** (-s) m (*Med*) pseudocroup; **Pseudonym** (-s, -e) nt pseudonym

pst interj ssh

Psychiater(in) (-s, -) m(f) psychiatrist; **psychisch** adj psychological; (*Krankheit*) mental; **Psychoanalyse** f psychoanalysis; **Psychologe** (-n, -n) m, **Psychologin** f psychologist; **Psychologie** f psychology

Psychopharmaka pl mind-affecting drugs pl, psychotropic drugs pl; **psychosomatisch** adj psychosomatic; **Psychoterror** m psychological intimidation; **Psychotherapie** f psychotherapy

Pubertät f puberty

Publikum (-s) nt audience; (*Sport*) crowd

Pudding (-s, -e o -s) m blancmange

Pudel (-s, -) m poodle

Puder (-s, -) m powder; **Puderzucker** m icing sugar

Puerto Rico (-s) nt Puerto Rico

Pulli (-s, -s) m, **Pullover** (-s, -) m sweater, pullover, jumper (*Brit*)

Puls *(-es, -e)* *m* pulse
Pulver *(-s, -)* *nt* powder;
 Pulverkaffee *m* instant coffee;
 Pulverschnee *m* powder snow
pummelig *adj* chubby
Pumpe *(-, -n)* *f* pump; **pumpen**
 vt to pump; *(fam: verleihen)* to lend;
 (fam: sich ausleihen) to borrow
Pumps *pl* court shoes *pl* (Brit),
 pumps *pl* (US)
Punk *(-s, -s)* *m* *(Musik, Mensch)*
 punk
Punkt *(-(e)s, -e)* *m* point; *(bei
 Muster)* dot; *(Satzzeichen)* full stop
 (Brit), period (US); **~ zwei Uhr** at
 two o'clock sharp
pünktlich *adj* punctual, on time;
 Pünktlichkeit *f* punctuality
Punsch *(-(e)s, -e)* *m* punch
Pupille *(-, -n)* *f* pupil
Puppe *(-, -n)* *f* doll
pur *adj* pure; *(völlig)* sheer;
 (Whisky) neat
Püree *(-s, -s)* *nt* puree;
 (Kartoffelpüree) mashed potatoes *pl*
Puste *(-)* *f* *(fam)* puff; **außer
 ~ sein** to be puffed
Pustel *(-, -n)* *f* pustule; *(Pickel)*
 pimple; **pusten** *vi* to blow;
 (keuchen) to puff
Pute *(-, -n)* *f* turkey;
 Putenschnitzel *nt* turkey
 escalope
Putsch *(-es, -e)* *m* putsch
Putz *(-es)* *m* *(Mörtel)* plaster
putzen *vt* to clean; **sich** *(dat)* **die
 Nase ~** to blow one's nose; **sich**
 (dat) **die Zähne ~** to brush one's
 teeth; **Putzfrau** *f* cleaner;
 Putzlappen *m* cloth, **Putzmann**
 m cleaner; **Putzmittel** *nt*
 cleaning agent, cleaner
Puzzle *(-s, -s)* *nt* jigsaw (puzzle)
Pyjama *(-s, -s)* *m* pyjamas *pl*
Pyramide *(-, -n)* *f* pyramid
Python *(-s, -s)* *m* python

Quadrat *nt* square; **quadratisch**
 adj square; **Quadratmeter** *m*
 square metre
quaken *vi* *(Frosch)* to croak; *(Ente)*
 to quack
Qual *(-, -en)* *f* pain, agony;
 (seelisch) anguish; **quälen** *vt* to
 torment ▷ *vr*: **sich ~** to struggle;
 (geistig) to torment oneself;
 Quälerei *f* torture, torment
qualifizieren *vt* to qualify;
 (einstufen) to label ▷ *vr*: **sich ~** to
 qualify
Qualität *f* quality
Qualle *(-, -n)* *f* jellyfish
Qualm *(-(e)s)* *m* thick smoke;
 qualmen *vt, vi* to smoke
Quantität *f* quantity
Quarantäne *(-, -n)* *f* quarantine
Quark *(-s)* *m* quark; *(fam: Unsinn)*
 rubbish
Quartett *(-s, -e)* *nt* quartet;
 (Kartenspiel) happy families *sing*

Quartier (*-s, -e*) *nt* accommodation

quasi *adv* more or less

Quatsch (*-es*) *m* (*fam*) rubbish; **quatschen** *vi* (*fam*) to chat

Quecksilber *nt* mercury

Quelle (*-, -n*) *f* spring; (*eines Flusses*) source

quellen *vi* to pour

quer *adv* crossways, diagonally; (*rechtwinklig*) at right angles; **~ über die Straße** straight across the street; **querfeldein** *adv* across country; **Querflöte** *f* flute; **Querschnitt** *m* cross section; **querschnittsgelähmt** *adj* paraplegic; **Querstraße** *f* side street

quetschen *vt* to squash, to crush; (*Med*) to bruise; **Quetschung** *f* bruise

Queue (*-s, -s*) *m* (billiard) cue

quietschen *vi* to squeal; (*Tür, Bett*) to squeak; (*Bremsen*) to screech

quitt *adj* quits, even

Quitte (*-, -n*) *f* quince

Quittung *f* receipt

Quiz (*-, -*) *nt* quiz

Quote (*-, -n*) *f* rate; (*Comm*) quota

r

Rabatt (*-(e)s, -e*) *m* discount

Rabbi (*-(s), -s*) *m* rabbi; **Rabbiner** (*-s, -*) *m* rabbi

Rabe (*-n, -n*) *m* raven

Rache (*-*) *f* revenge, vengeance

Rachen (*-s, -*) *m* throat

rächen *vt* to avenge ▷ *vr*: **sich ~** to take (one's) revenge (*an +dat* on)

Rad (*-(e)s, Räder*) *nt* wheel; (*Fahrrad*) bike; **~ fahren** to cycle; **mit dem ~ fahren** to go by bike

Radar (*-s*) *m o nt* radar; **Radarfalle** *f* speed trap; **Radarkontrolle** *f* radar speed check

radeln *vi* (*fam*) to cycle; **Radfahrer(in)** *m(f)* cyclist; **Radfahrweg** *m* cycle track (*o* path)

Radicchio (*-s*) *m* (*Salatsorte*) radicchio

radieren *vt* to rub out, to erase; **Radiergummi** *m* rubber (*Brit*), eraser; **Radierung** *f* (*Kunst*) etching

Radieschen *nt* radish

radikal *adj* radical

Radio (*-s, -s*) *nt* radio; **im ~** on the radio

radioaktiv *adj* radioactive

Radiologe (*-n, -n*) *m*, **Radiologin** *f* radiologist

Radiorekorder *m* radio cassette recorder; **Radiosender** *m* radio station; **Radiowecker** *m* radio alarm (clock)

Radkappe *f* (*Auto*) hub cap

Radler(in) (*-s, -*) *m(f)* cyclist

Radler (*-s, -*) *nt* ≈ shandy

Radlerhose *f* cycling shorts *pl*; **Radrennen** *nt* cycle racing; (*einzelnes Rennen*) cycle race; **Radtour** *f* cycling tour; **Radweg** *m* cycle track (*o* path)

raffiniert *adj* crafty, cunning; (*Zucker*) refined

Rafting (*-s*) *nt* white water rafting

Ragout (*-s, -s*) *nt* ragout

Rahm (*-s*) *m* cream

rahmen *vt* to frame; **Rahmen** (*-s, -*) *m* frame

Rakete (*-, -n*) *f* rocket

rammen *vt* to ram

Rampe (*-, -n*) *f* ramp

ramponieren *vt* (*fam*) to damage, to batter

Ramsch (*-(e)s, -e*) *m* junk

ran (*fam*) *kontr von* **heran**

Rand (*-(e)s, Ränder*) *m* edge; (*von Brille, Tasse etc*) rim; (*auf Papier*) margin; (*Schmutzrand, unter Augen*) ring; (*fig*) verge, brink

randalieren *vi* to (go on the) rampage; **Randalierer(in)** (*-s, -*) *m(f)* hooligan

Randstein *m* kerb (*Brit*), curb (*US*); **Randstreifen** *m* shoulder

rang *imperf von* **ringen**

Rang (*-(e)s, Ränge*) *m* rank; (*in Wettbewerb*) place; (*Theat*) circle

rannte *imperf von* **rennen**

ranzig *adj* rancid

Rap (*-(s), -s*) *m* (*Mus*) rap; **rappen** *vi* (*Mus*) to rap; **Rapper(in)** (*-s, -*) *m(f)* (*Mus*) rapper

rar *adj* rare, scarce

rasant *adj* quick, rapid

rasch *adj* quick

rascheln *vi* to rustle

rasen *vi* (*sich schnell bewegen*) to race; (*toben*) to rave; **gegen einen Baum ~** to crash into a tree

Rasen (*-s, -*) *m* lawn

rasend *adj* (*vor Wut*) furious

Rasenmäher (*-s, -*) *m* lawnmower

Rasierapparat *m* razor; (*elektrischer*) shaver; **Rasiercreme** *f* shaving cream; **rasieren** *vt* to shave ▷ *vr*: **sich ~** to shave; **Rasierer** *m* shaver; **Rasiergel** *nt* shaving gel; **Rasierklinge** *f* razor blade; **Rasiermesser** *nt* (cutthroat) razor; **Rasierpinsel** *m* shaving brush; **Rasierschaum** *m* shaving foam; **Rasierzeug** *nt* shaving tackle, shaving equipment

Rasse (*-, -n*) *f* race; (*Tiere*) breed

Rassismus *m* racism; **Rassist(in)** *m(f)* racist; **rassistisch** *adj* racist

Rast (*-, -en*) *f* rest, break; **~ machen** to have a rest (*o* break); **rasten** *vi* to rest; **Rastplatz** *m* (*Auto*) rest area; **Raststätte** *f* (*Auto*) service area; (*Gaststätte*) motorway (*Brit*) (*o* highway (*US*)) restaurant

Rasur *f* shave

Rat (*-(e)s, Ratschläge*) *m* (piece of) advice; **sie hat mir einen ~ gegeben** she gave me some advice; **um ~ fragen** to ask for advice

Rate (-, -n) f instalment; **etw auf ~n kaufen** to buy sth in instalments (Brit), to buy sth on the instalment plan (US)

raten (riet, geraten) vt, vi to guess; (empfehlen) to advise (jdm sb)

Rathaus nt town hall

Ration f ration

ratlos adj at a loss, helpless; **ratsam** adj advisable

Rätsel (-s, -) nt puzzle; (Worträtsel) riddle; **das ist mir ein ~** it's a mystery to me; **rätselhaft** adj mysterious

Ratte (-, -n) f rat

rau adj rough, coarse; (Wetter) harsh

Raub (-(e)s) m robbery; (Beute) loot, booty; **rauben** vt to steal; **jdm etw ~** to rob sb of sth; **Räuber(in)** (-s, -) m(f) robber; **Raubfisch** m predatory fish; **Raubkopie** f piracy; **Raubmord** m robbery with murder; **Raubtier** nt predator; **Raubüberfall** m mugging; **Raubvogel** m bird of prey

Rauch (-(e)s) m smoke; (Abgase) fumes pl; **rauchen** vt, vi to smoke; **Raucher(in)** (-s, -) m(f) smoker; **Raucherabteil** nt smoking compartment

Räucherlachs m smoked salmon; **räuchern** vt to smoke

rauchig adj smoky; **Rauchmelder** m smoke detector; **Rauchverbot** nt smoking ban; **hier ist ~** there's no smoking here

rauf (fam) kontr von **herauf**

rauh adj siehe **rau**; **Rauhreif** m siehe **Raureif**

Raum (-(e)s, Räume) m space; (Zimmer, Platz) room; (Gebiet) area

räumen vt to clear; (Wohnung, Platz) to vacate; (wegbringen) to

shift, to move; (in Schrank etc) to put away

Raumfähre f space shuttle; **Raumfahrt** f space travel; **Raumschiff** nt spacecraft, spaceship; **Raumsonde** f space probe; **Raumstation** f space station

Raumtemperatur f room temperature

Räumungsverkauf m clearance sale, closing-down sale

Raupe (-, -n) f caterpillar

Raureif m hoarfrost

raus (fam) kontr von **heraus, hinaus**; **~!** (get) out!

Rausch (-(e)s, Räusche) m intoxication; **einen ~ haben/kriegen** to be/get drunk

rauschen vi (Wasser) to rush; (Baum) to rustle; (Radio etc) to hiss; **Rauschgift** nt drug; **Rauschgiftsüchtige(r)** mf drug addict

raus|fliegen irr vi (fam) to be kicked out

raus|halten irr vr (fam) **halt du dich da raus!** you (just) keep out of it

räuspern vr: **sich ~** to clear one's throat

raus|schmeißen irr vt (fam) to throw out

Razzia (-, Razzien) f raid

reagieren vi to react (auf +akk to); **Reaktion** f reaction

real adj real; **realisieren** vt (merken) to realize; (verwirklichen) to implement; **realistisch** adj realistic; **Realität** (-, -en) f reality; **Reality-TV** (-s) nt reality TV

Realschule f ≈ secondary school, junior high (school) (US)

Rebe (-, -n) f vine

rebellieren vi to rebel

Rebhuhn nt partridge

rechnen *vt, vi* to calculate; **~ mit** to expect; (*bauen auf*) to count on ▷ *vr*: **sich ~** to pay off, to turn out to be profitable; **Rechner** (*-s, -*) *m* calculator; (*Computer*) computer; **Rechnung** *f* calculation(s); (*Comm*) bill (*Brit*), check (*US*); **die ~, bitte!** can I have the bill, please?; **das geht auf meine ~** this is on me

recht *adj* (*richtig, passend*) right; **~ haben** to be right; **jdm ~ geben** to agree with sb; **mir soll's ~ sein** it's alright by me; **mir ist es ~** I don't mind ▷ *adv* really, quite; (*richtig*) right(ly); **ich weiß nicht ~** I don't really know; **es geschieht ihm ~** it serves him right

Recht (*-(e)s, -e*) *nt* right; (*Jur*) law

Rechte (*-n, -n*) *f* right-hand side; (*Hand*) right hand; (*Pol*) right (wing); **rechte(r, s)** *adj* right; **auf der ~n Seite** on the right, on the right-hand side; **Rechte(s)** *nt* right thing; **etwas/nichts ~s** something/nothing proper

Rechteck (*-s, -e*) *nt* rectangle; **rechteckig** *adj* rectangular

rechtfertigen *vt* to justify ▷ *vr*: **sich ~** to justify oneself

rechtlich *adj* legal; **rechtmäßig** *adj* legal, lawful

rechts *adv* on the right; **~ abbiegen** to turn right; **~ von** to the right of; **~ oben** at the top right

Rechtsanwalt *m*, **-anwältin** *f* lawyer

Rechtschreibung *f* spelling

Rechtshänder(in) (*-s, -*) *m(f)* right-hander; **rechtsherum** *adv* to the right, clockwise; **rechtsradikal** *adj* (*Pol*) extreme right-wing

Rechtsschutzversicherung *f* legal costs insurance

Rechtsverkehr *m* driving on the right

rechtswidrig *adj* illegal

rechtwinklig *adj* right-angled; **rechtzeitig** *adj* timely ▷ *adv* in time

recycelbar *adj* recyclable; **recyceln** *vt* to recycle; **Recycling** (*-s*) *nt* recycling; **Recyclingpapier** *nt* recycled paper

Redakteur(in) *m(f)* editor; **Redaktion** *f* editing; (*Leute*) editorial staff; (*Büro*) editorial office(s)

Rede (*-, -n*) *f* speech; (*Gespräch*) talk; **eine ~ halten** to make a speech; **reden** *vi* to talk, to speak ▷ *vt* to say; (*Unsinn etc*) to talk; **Redewendung** *f* idiom; **Redner(in)** *m(f)* speaker

reduzieren *vt* to reduce

Referat (*-s, -e*) *nt* paper; **ein ~ halten** to give a paper (*über +akk* on)

reflektieren *vt* to reflect

Reform (*-, -en*) *f* reform; **Reformhaus** *nt* health food shop; **reformieren** *vt* to reform

Regal (*-s, -e*) *nt* shelf; (*Möbelstück*) shelves *pl*

Regel (*-, -n*) *f* rule; (*Med*) period; **regelmäßig** *adj* regular; **regeln** *vt* to regulate, to control; (*Angelegenheit*) to settle ▷ *vr*: **sich von selbst ~** to sort itself out; **Regelung** *f* regulation

Regen (*-s, -*) *m* rain; **Regenbogen** *m* rainbow; **Regenmantel** *m* raincoat; **Regenrinne** *f* gutter; **Regenschauer** *m* shower; **Regenschirm** *m* umbrella; **Regenwald** *m* rainforest; **Regenwurm** *m* earthworm

Regie *f* direction

regieren *vt, vi* to govern, to rule;

Regierung f government; (von Monarch) reign

Region f region; **regional** adj regional

Regisseur(in) m(f) director

registrieren vt to register; (bemerken) to notice

regnen vi impers to rain; **regnerisch** adj rainy

regulär adj regular; **regulieren** vt to regulate, to adjust

Reh (-(e)s, -e) nt deer; (Fleisch) venison

Rehabilitationszentrum nt (Med) rehabilitation centre

Reibe (-, -n) f, **Reibeisen** nt grater; **reiben** (rieb, gerieben) vt to rub; (Gastr) to grate; **reibungslos** adj smooth

reich adj rich

Reich (-(e)s, -e) nt empire; (eines Königs) kingdom

reichen vi to reach; (genügen) to be enough, to be sufficient (jdm for sb) ▷ vt to hold out; (geben) to pass, to hand; (anbieten) to offer

reichhaltig adj ample, rich; **reichlich** adj (Trinkgeld) generous; (Essen) ample; **~ Zeit** plenty of time; **Reichtum** (-s, -tümer) m wealth

reif adj ripe; (Mensch, Urteil) mature

Reif (-(e)s) m (Raureif) hoarfrost ▷ (-(e)s, -e) m (Ring) ring, hoop

reifen vi to mature; (Obst) to ripen

Reifen (-s, -) m ring, hoop; (von Auto) tyre; **Reifendruck** m tyre pressure; **Reifenpanne** f puncture; **Reifenwechsel** m tyre change

Reihe (-, -n) f row; (von Tagen etc, fam: Anzahl) series sing; **der ~ nach** one after the other; **er ist an der ~** it's his turn; **Reihenfolge** f

order, sequence; **Reihenhaus** nt terraced house (Brit), row house (US)

Reiher (-s, -) m heron

rein (fam) kontr von **herein, hinein** ▷ adj pure; (sauber) clean

Reinfall m (fam) letdown; **rein|fallen** irr vi (fam) **auf etw** (akk) **~** to fall for sth

reinigen vt to clean; **Reinigung** f cleaning; (Geschäft) (dry) cleaner's; **Reinigungsmittel** nt cleaning agent, cleaner

rein|legen vt: **jdn ~** to take sb for a ride

Reis (-es, -e) m rice

Reise (-, -n) f journey; (auf Schiff) voyage; **Reiseapotheke** f first-aid kit; **Reisebüro** nt travel agent's; **Reisebus** m coach; **Reiseführer(in)** m(f) (Mensch) courier; (Buch) guide(book); **Reisegepäck** nt luggage (Brit), baggage; **Reisegesellschaft** f (Veranstalter) tour operator; **Reisegruppe** f tourist party; (mit Reisebus) coach party; **Reiseleiter(in)** m(f) courier; **reisen** vi to travel; **~ nach** to go to; **Reisende(r)** mf traveller; **Reisepass** m passport; **Reiseroute** f route, itinerary; **Reiserücktrittversicherung** f holiday cancellation insurance; **Reisescheck** m traveller's cheque; **Reisetasche** f holdall (Brit), carryall (US); **Reiseveranstalter** m tour operator; **Reiseverkehr** m holiday traffic; **Reiseversicherung** f travel insurance; **Reiseziel** nt destination

Reiskocher (-s, -) m rice steamer

reißen (riss, gerissen) vt, vi to tear; (ziehen) to pull, to drag; (Witz) to crack

Reißnagel *m* drawing pin (*Brit*), thumbtack (*US*); **Reißverschluss** *m* zip (*Brit*), zipper (*US*); **Reißzwecke** *f* drawing pin (*Brit*), thumbtack (*US*)

reiten (*ritt, geritten*) *vt, vi* to ride; **Reiter(in)** *m(f)* rider; **Reithose** *f* riding breeches *pl*; **Reitsport** *m* riding; **Reitstiefel** *m* riding boot

Reiz (*-es, -e*) *m* stimulus; (*angenehm*) charm; (*Verlockung*) attraction; **reizen** *vt* to stimulate; (*unangenehm*) to annoy; (*verlocken*) to appeal to, to attract; **reizend** *adj* charming; **Reizgas** *nt* irritant gas; **Reizung** *f* irritation

Reklamation *f* complaint

Reklame (*-, -n*) *f* advertising; (*Einzelwerbung*) advertisement; (*im Fernsehen*) commercial

reklamieren *vi* to complain (*wegen* about)

Rekord (*-(e)s, -e*) *m* record

relativ *adj* relative ▷ *adv* relatively

relaxen *vi* to relax, to chill out

Religion *f* religion; **religiös** *adj* religious

Remoulade (*-, -n*) *f* tartar sauce

Renaissance *f* renaissance, revival; (*Hist*) Renaissance

Rennbahn *f* racecourse; (*Auto*) racetrack; **rennen** (*rannte, gerannt*) *vt, vi* to run; **Rennen** (*-s, -*) *nt* running; (*Wettbewerb*) race; **Rennfahrer(in)** *m(f)* racing driver; **Rennrad** *nt* racing bike; **Rennwagen** *m* racing car

renommiert *adj* famous, noted (*wegen, für* for)

renovieren *vt* to renovate; **Renovierung** *f* renovation

rentabel *adj* profitable

Rente (*-, -n*) *f* pension; **Rentenversicherung** *f* pension scheme

Rentier *nt* reindeer

rentieren *vr:* **sich ~** to pay, to be profitable

Rentner(in) (*-s, -*) *m(f)* pensioner, senior citizen

Reparatur *f* repair; **Reparaturwerkstatt** *f* repair shop; (*Auto*) garage; **reparieren** *vt* to repair

Reportage *f* report; **Reporter(in)** (*-s, -*) *m(f)* reporter

Reptil (*-s, -ien*) *nt* reptile

Republik *f* republic

Reservat (*-s, -e*) *nt* nature reserve; (*für Ureinwohner*) reservation; **Reserve** (*-, -n*) *f* reserve; **Reservekanister** *m* spare can; **Reserverad** *nt* (*Auto*) spare wheel; **reservieren** *vt* to reserve; **Reservierung** *f* reservation

resignieren *vi* to give up; **resigniert** *adj* resigned

Respekt (*-(e)s*) *m* respect; **respektieren** *vt* to respect

Rest (*-(e)s, -e*) *m* rest, remainder; (*Überreste*) remains *pl*; **der ~ ist für Sie** (*zur Bedienung*) keep the change

Restaurant (*-s, -s*) *nt* restaurant

restaurieren *vt* to restore

Restbetrag *m* balance; **restlich** *adj* remaining; **restlos** *adj* complete

Resultat *nt* result

retten *vt* to save, to rescue

Rettich (*-s, -e*) *m* radish (*large white or red variety*)

Rettung *f* rescue; (*Hilfe*) help; (*Rettungsdienst*) ambulance service; **Rettungsboot** *nt* lifeboat; **Rettungshubschrauber** *m* rescue helicopter; **Rettungsring** *m* lifebelt, life preserver (*US*); **Rettungswagen** *m* ambulance

Reue (*-*) *f* remorse; (*Bedauern*)

regret; **reuen** vt: **es reut ihn** he regrets it

revanchieren vr: **sich ~** (sich rächen) to get one's own back, to get one's revenge; (für Hilfe etc) to return the favour

Revolution f revolution

Rezept (-(e)s, -e) nt (Gastr) recipe; (Med) prescription; **rezeptfrei** adj over-the-counter, non-prescription

Rezeption f (im Hotel) reception

rezeptpflichtig adj available only on prescription

R-Gespräch nt reverse-charge (Brit) (o collect (US)) call

Rhabarber (-s) m rhubarb

Rhein (-s) m Rhine; **Rheinland-Pfalz** (-) nt Rhineland-Palatinate

Rheuma (-s) nt rheumatism

Rhythmus m rhythm

richten vt (lenken) to direct (auf +akk to); (Waffe, Kamera) to point (auf +akk at); (Brief, Anfrage) to address (an +akk to); (einstellen) to adjust; (instand setzen) to repair; (zurechtmachen) to prepare ▷ vr: **sich ~ nach** (Regel etc) to keep to; (Mode, Beispiel) to follow; (abhängen von) to depend on

Richter(in) (-s, -) m(f) judge

Richtgeschwindigkeit f recommended speed

richtig adj right, correct; (echt) proper ▷ adv (fam: sehr) really; **richtig|stellen** vt: **etw ~** (berichtigen) to correct sth

Richtlinie f guideline

Richtung f direction; (Tendenz) tendency

rieb imperf von **reiben**

riechen (roch, gerochen) vt, vi to smell; **nach etw ~** to smell of sth; **an etw** (dat) **~** to smell sth

rief imperf von **rufen**

Riegel (-s, -) m bolt; (Gastr) bar

Riemen (-s, -) m strap; (Gürtel) belt

Riese (-n, -n) m giant; **Riesengarnele** f king prawn; **riesengroß** adj gigantic, huge; **Riesenrad** nt big wheel; **riesig** adj enormous, huge

riet imperf von **raten**

Riff (-(e)s, -e) nt reef

Rind (-(e)s, -er) nt cow; (Bulle) bull; (Gastr) beef; **~er** pl cattle pl

Rinde (-, -n) f (Baum) bark; (Käse) rind; (Brot) crust

Rinderbraten m roast beef; **Rinderwahn(sinn)** m mad cow disease; **Rindfleisch** nt beef

Ring (-(e)s, -e) m ring; (Straße) ring road; **Ringbuch** nt ring binder

ringen (rang, gerungen) vi to wrestle; **Ringer(in)** m(f) wrestler; **Ringfinger** m ring finger; **Ringkampf** m wrestling match; **ringsherum** adv round about

Rippe (-, -n) f rib; **Rippenfellentzündung** f pleurisy

Risiko (-s, -s o Risiken) nt risk; **auf eigenes ~** at one's own risk; **riskant** adj risky; **riskieren** vt to risk

riss imperf von **reißen**

Riss (-es, -e) m tear; (in Mauer, Tasse etc) crack; **rissig** adj cracked; (Haut) chapped

ritt imperf von **reiten**

Ritter (-s, -) m knight

Rivale (-n, -n) m, **Rivalin** f rival

Rizinusöl nt castor oil

Robbe (-, -n) f seal

Roboter (-s, -) m robot

robust adj robust

roch imperf von **riechen**

Rock (-(e)s, Röcke) m skirt

Rockband f (Musikgruppe) rock band; **Rockmusik** f rock (music)

Rodelbahn f toboggan run; **rodeln** vi to toboggan

Roggen (-s, -) m rye; **Roggenbrot** nt rye bread

roh adj raw; (Mensch) coarse, crude; **Rohkost** f raw vegetables and fruit pl

Rohr (-(e)s, -e) nt pipe; (Bot) cane; (Schilf) reed; **Röhre** (-, -n) f tube; (Leitung) pipe; (Elek) valve; (Backröhre) oven; **Rohrzucker** m cane sugar

Rohstoff m raw material

Rokoko (-s) nt rococo

Rolle (-, -n) f (etw Zusammengerolltes) roll; (Theat) role

rollen vt, vi to roll

Roller (-s, -) m scooter

Rollerblades® pl Rollerblades® pl; **Rollerskates** pl roller skates pl

Rollkragenpullover m poloneck (Brit) (o turtleneck (US)) sweater; **Rollladen** m, **Rollo** (-s, -s) m (roller) shutters pl; **Rollschuh** m roller skate; **Rollstuhl** m wheelchair; **rollstuhlgerecht** adj suitable for wheelchairs; **Rolltreppe** f escalator

Roman (-s, -e) m novel

Romantik f romance; **romantisch** adj romantic

römisch-katholisch adj Roman Catholic

röntgen vt to X-ray; **Röntgenaufnahme** f, **Röntgenbild** nt X-ray; **Röntgenstrahlen** pl X-rays pl

rosa adj inv pink

Rose (-, -n) f rose

Rosenkohl m (Brussels) sprouts pl

Rosé(wein) m rosé (wine)

rosig adj rosy

Rosine f raisin

Rosmarin (-s) m rosemary

Rosskastanie f horse chestnut

Rost (-(e)s, -e) m rust; (zum Braten) grill, gridiron; **Rostbratwurst** f grilled sausage; **rosten** vi to rust; **rösten** vt to roast, to grill; (Brot) to toast; **rostfrei** adj rustproof; (Stahl) stainless; **rostig** adj rusty; **Rostschutz** m rustproofing

rot adj red; **~ werden** to blush; **Rote Karte** red card; **Rote Bete** beetroot; **bei Rot über die Ampel fahren** to jump the lights; **das Rote Kreuz** the Red Cross

Röteln pl German measles sing

röten vt to redden ▷ vr: **sich ~ to** redden

rothaarig adj red-haired

rotieren vi to rotate; **am Rotieren sein** (fam) to be rushing around like a mad thing

Rotkehlchen nt robin; **Rotkohl** m, **Rotkraut** nt red cabbage; **Rotlichtviertel** nt red-light district; **Rotwein** m red wine

Rouge (-s, -s) nt rouge

Route (-, -n) f route

Routine f experience; (Trott) routine

Rubbellos nt scratchcard; **rubbeln** vt to rub

Rübe (-, -n) f turnip; **Gelbe ~** carrot; **Rote ~** beetroot

rüber (fam) kontr von **herüber, hinüber**

rückbestätigen vt (Flug etc) to reconfirm

rücken vt, vi to move; **könntest du ein bisschen ~?** could you move over a bit?

Rücken (-s, -) m back; **Rückenlehne** f back(rest); **Rückenmark** nt spinal cord; **Rückenschmerzen** pl backache sing; **Rückenschwimmen** (-s) nt backstroke; **Rückenwind** m tailwind

Rückerstattung f refund;
Rückfahrkarte f return ticket
(*Brit*), round-trip ticket (*US*);
Rückfahrt f return journey;
Rückfall m relapse; **Rückflug** m
return flight; **Rückgabe** f return;
rückgängig adj: **etw ~ machen**
to cancel sth; **Rückgrat** (-(e)s, -e)
nt spine, backbone; **Rückkehr**
(-, -en) f return; **Rücklicht** nt
rear light; **Rückreise** f return
journey; **auf der ~** on the way
back
Rucksack m rucksack, backpack;
Rucksacktourist(in) m(f)
backpacker
Rückschritt m step back;
Rückseite f back; (*hinterer Teil*)
rear; **siehe ~** see overleaf;
Rücksicht f consideration;
~ nehmen auf (+*akk*) to show
consideration for; **rücksichtslos**
adj inconsiderate; (*Fahren*)
reckless; (*unbarmherzig*) ruthless;
rücksichtsvoll adj considerate;
Rücksitz m back seat;
Rückspiegel m (*Auto*) rear-view
mirror; **Rückstand** m: **sie sind
zwei Tore im ~** they're two goals
down; **im ~ sein mit** (*Arbeit, Miete*)
to be behind with; **Rücktaste** f
backspace key; **Rückvergütung**
f refund; **rückwärts** adv
backwards, back; **Rückwärtsgang** m (*Auto*) reverse (gear);
Rückweg m return journey, way
back; **Rückzahlung** f repayment
Ruder (-s, -) nt oar; (*Steuer*)
rudder; **Ruderboot** nt rowing
boat (*Brit*), rowboat (*US*); **rudern**
vt, vi to row
Ruf (-(e)s, -e) m call, cry; (*Ansehen*)
reputation; **rufen** (*rief, gerufen*) vt,
vi to call; (*schreien*) to cry;
Rufnummer f telephone number
Ruhe (-) f rest; (*Ungestörtheit*)
peace, quiet; (*Gelassenheit, Stille*)

calm; (*Schweigen*) silence; **lass
mich in ~!** leave me alone; **ruhen**
vi to rest; **Ruhestand** m
retirement; **im ~ sein** to be retired;
Ruhestörung f disturbance of
the peace; **Ruhetag** m closing
day; **montags ~ haben** to be
closed on Mondays
ruhig adj quiet; (*bewegungslos*)
still; (*Hand*) steady; (*gelassen*) calm
Ruhm (-(e)s) m fame, glory
Rührei nt scrambled egg(s);
rühren vt to move; (*umrühren*) to
stir ▷ vr: **sich ~** to move; (*sich
bemerkbar machen*) to say
something; **rührend** adj
touching, moving; **Rührung** f
emotion
Ruine (-, -n) f ruin; **ruinieren** vt
to ruin
rülpsen vi to burp, to belch
rum (*fam*) *kontr von* **herum**
Rum (-s, -s) m rum
Rumänien (-s) nt Romania
Rummel (-s) m (*Trubel*) hustle
and bustle; (*Jahrmarkt*) fair;
(*Medienrummel*) hype;
Rummelplatz m fairground
rumoren vi: **es rumort in
meinem Bauch/Kopf** my
stomach is rumbling/my head is
spinning
Rumpf (-(e)s, *Rümpfe*) m (*Anat*)
trunk; (*Aviat*) fuselage; (*Naut*)
hull
rümpfen vt: **die Nase ~** to turn
one's nose up (*über* at)
Rumpsteak nt rump steak
rund adj round ▷ adv (*etwa*)
around; **~ um etw** (a)round sth;
Runde (-, -n) f round; (*in Rennen*)
lap; **Rundfahrt** f tour (*durch* of);
Rundfunk m broadcasting;
(*Rundfunkanstalt*) broadcasting
service; **im ~** on the radio;
Rundgang m tour (*durch* of); (*von
Wächter*) round

rundlich *adj* plump; **Rundreise** *f* tour (*durch* of)

runter (*fam*) *kontr von* **herunter, hinunter**; **runterscrollen** *vt* (*Inform*) to scroll down

runzeln *vt*: **die Stirn ~** to frown; **runzelig** *adj* wrinkled

ruppig *adj* gruff

Rüsche (-, -n) *f* frill

Ruß (-es) *m* soot

Russe (-n, -n) *m* Russian

Rüssel (-s, -) *m* (*Elefant*) trunk; (*Schwein*) snout

Russin *f* Russian; **russisch** *adj* Russian; **Russisch** *nt* Russian; **Russland** *nt* Russia

Rüstung *f* (*mit Waffen*) arming; (*Ritterrüstung*) armour; (*Waffen*) armaments *pl*

Rutsch (-(e)s, -e) *m*: **guten ~ (ins neue Jahr)!** Happy New Year; **Rutschbahn** *f*, **Rutsche** *f* slide; **rutschen** *vi* to slide; (*ausrutschen*) to slip; **rutschig** *adj* slippery

rütteln *vt, vi* to shake

S

S *abk* = **Süd** S

s. *abk* = **siehe** see; = **Seite** p.

Saal (-(e)s, *Säle*) *m* hall; (*für Sitzungen*) room

Saarland *nt* Saarland

sabotieren *vt* to sabotage

Sache (-, -n) *f* thing; (*Angelegenheit*) affair, business; (*Frage*) matter; **bei der ~ bleiben** to keep to the point; **sachkundig** *adj* competent; **Sachlage** *f* situation; **sachlich** *adj* (*objektiv*) objective; (*nüchtern*) matter-of-fact; (*inhaltlich*) factual; **sächlich** *adj* (*Ling*) neuter; **Sachschaden** *m* material damage

Sachsen (-s) *nt* Saxony; **Sachsen-Anhalt** (-s) *nt* Saxony-Anhalt

sacht(e) *adv* softly, gently

Sachverständige(r) *mf* expert

Sack (-(e)s, *Säcke*) *m* sack; (*pej:*

Mensch) bastard, bugger;
Sackgasse f dead end, cul-de-sac
Safe (-s, -s) m safe
Safer Sex m safe sex
Safran (-s, -e) m saffron
Saft (-(e)s, Säfte) m juice; **saftig**
adj juicy
Sage (-, -n) f legend
Säge (-, -n) f saw; **Sägemehl** nt
sawdust
sagen vt, vi to say (jdm to sb),
to tell (jdm sb); **wie sagt man ...
auf Englisch?** what's ... in
English?
sägen vt, vi to saw
sagenhaft adj legendary; (fam:
großartig) fantastic
sah imperf von **sehen**
Sahne (-) f cream
Saison (-, -s) f season;
außerhalb der ~ out of season
Saite (-, -n) f string
Sakko (-s, -s) nt jacket
Salami (-, -s) f salami
Salat (-(e)s, -e) m salad;
(Kopfsalat) lettuce; **Salatbar** f
salad bar; **Salatschüssel** f salad
bowl; **Salatsoße** f salad
dressing
Salbe (-, -n) f ointment
Salbei (-s) m sage
Salmonellenvergiftung f
salmonella (poisoning)
salopp adj (Kleidung) casual;
(Sprache) slangy
Salsamusik f salsa (music)
Salto (-s, -s) m somersault
Salz (-es, -e) nt salt; **salzarm** adj
low-salt; **salzen** (salzte, gesalzen)
vt to salt; **Salzgurke** f pickled
gherkin; **Salzhering** m pickled
herring; **salzig** adj salty;
Salzkartoffeln pl boiled potatoes
pl; **Salzstange** f pretzel stick;
Salzstreuer m salt cellar (Brit) (o
shaker (US)); **Salzwasser** nt salt
water

Samba (-, -s) f samba
Samen (-s, -) m seed; (Sperma)
sperm
sammeln vt to collect;
Sammler(in) m(f) collector;
Sammlung f collection;
(Ansammlung, Konzentration)
concentration
Samstag m Saturday; siehe auch
Mittwoch; **samstags** adv on
Saturdays; siehe auch **mittwochs**
samt prep +dat (along) with,
together with
Samt (-(e)s, -e) m velvet
sämtliche(r, s) adj all (the)
Sanatorium (-s, Sanatorien) nt
sanatorium (Brit), sanitarium (US)
Sand (-(e)s, -e) m sand
Sandale (-, -n) f sandal
sandig adj sandy; **Sandkasten**
m sandpit (Brit), sandbox (US);
Sandpapier nt sandpaper;
Sandstrand m sandy beach
sandte imperf von **senden**
sanft adj soft, gentle
sang imperf von **singen**;
Sänger(in) (-s, -) m(f) singer
Sangria (-, -s) f sangria
sanieren vt to redevelop;
(Gebäude) to renovate; (Betrieb) to
restore to profitability
sanitär adj sanitary; **~e Anlagen**
pl sanitation
Sanitäter(in) (-s, -) m(f) ambu-
lance man/woman, paramedic
sank imperf von **sinken**
Sankt Gallen (-s) nt St Gallen
Saphir (-s, -e) m sapphire
Sardelle f anchovy
Sardine f sardine
Sarg (-(e)s, Särge) m coffin
saß imperf von **sitzen**
Satellit (-en, -en) m satellite;
Satellitenfernsehen nt satellite
TV; **Satellitenschüssel** f (fam)
satellite dish
Satire (-, -n) f satire (auf +akk on)

satt *adj* full; (*Farbe*) rich, deep;
~ **sein** (*gesättigt*) to be full;
~ **machen** to be filling; **jdn/etw**
~ **sein** to be fed up with sb/sth
Sattel (*-s, Sättel*) *m* saddle
satt|haben *irr vt:* **jdn/etw**
~ (*nicht mehr mögen*) to be fed up
with sb/sth
Saturn (*-s*) *m* Saturn
Satz (*-es, Sätze*) *m* (*Ling*) sentence;
(*Mus*) movement; (*Tennis*) set;
(*Kaffee*) grounds *pl*; (*Comm*) rate;
(*Sprung*) jump; (*Comm*) rate
Satzzeichen *nt* punctuation
mark
Sau (*-, Säue*) *f* sow; (*pej: Mensch*)
dirty bugger
sauber *adj* clean; (*ironisch*) fine;
~ **machen** to clean; **Sauberkeit** *f*
cleanness; (*von Person*) cleanliness;
säubern *vt* to clean
saublöd *adj* (*fam*) really stupid,
dumb
Sauce (*-, -n*) *f* sauce; (*zu Braten*)
gravy
Saudi-Arabien (*-s*) *nt* Saudi
Arabia
sauer *adj* sour; (*Chem*) acid; (*fam:
verärgert*) cross; **saurer Regen** acid
rain; **Sauerkirsche** *f* sour
cherry; **Sauerkraut** *nt*
sauerkraut; **säuerlich** *adj*
slighthly sour; **Sauermilch** *f*
sour milk; **Sauerrahm** *m* sour
cream; **Sauerstoff** *m* oxygen
saufen (*soff, gesoffen*) *vt* to drink;
(*fam: Mensch*) to knock back ▷ *vi*
to drink; (*fam: Mensch*) to booze
saugen (*sog o saugte, gesogen o
gesaugt*) *vt, vi* to suck; (*mit
Staubsauger*) to vacuum, to hoover
(*Brit*); **Sauger** (*-s, -*) *m* (*auf Flasche*)
teat; **Säugetier** *nt* mammal;
Säugling *m* infant, baby
Säule (*-, -n*) *f* column, pillar
Saum (*-s, Säume*) *m* hem; (*Naht*)
seam

Sauna (*-, -s*) *f* sauna
Säure (*-, -n*) *f* acid
sausen *vi* (*Ohren*) to buzz; (*Wind*)
to howl; (*Mensch*) to rush
Saustall *m* pigsty; **Sauwetter**
nt: **was für ein** ~ (*fam*) what lousy
weather
Saxophon (*-s, -e*) *nt* saxophone
S-Bahn *f* suburban railway;
S-Bahn-Haltestelle *f*, **S-Bahnhof**
m suburban (train) station
scannen *vt* to scan; **Scanner**
(*-s, -*) *m* scanner
schäbig *adj* shabby
Schach (*-s, -s*) *nt* chess; (*Stellung*)
check; **Schachbrett** *nt*
chessboard; **Schachfigur** *f*
chess piece; **schachmatt** *adj*
checkmate
Schacht (*-(e)s, Schächte*) *m* shaft
Schachtel (*-, -n*) *f* box
schade *interj* what a pity
Schädel (*-s, -*) *m* skull;
Schädelbruch *m* fractured skull
schaden *vi* to damage, to harm
(*jdm sb*); **das schadet nichts** it
won't do any harm; **Schaden**
(*-s, Schäden*) *m* damage;
(*Verletzung*) injury; (*Nachteil*)
disadvantage; **einen**
~ **verursachen** to cause damage;
Schadenersatz *m* compensation, damages *pl*; **schadhaft** *adj*
faulty; (*beschädigt*) damaged;
schädigen *vt* to damage; (*jdn*) to
do harm to, to harm; **schädlich**
adj harmful (*für to*); **Schadstoff**
m harmful substance;
schadstoffarm *adj* low-emission
Schaf (*-(e)s, -e*) *nt* sheep;
Schafbock *m* ram; **Schäfer** (*-s, -*)
m shepherd; **Schäferhund** *m*
Alsatian (*Brit*), German shepherd;
Schäferin *f* shepherdess
schaffen (*schuf, geschaffen*) *vt* to
create; (*Platz*) to make ▷ *vt*
(*erreichen*) to manage, to do;

(*erledigen*) to finish; (*Prüfung*) to
pass; (*transportieren*) to take;
jdm zu ~ machen to cause sb
trouble
Schaffner(in) (*-s, -*) *m(f)* (*in Bus*)
conductor/conductress; (*Eisenb*)
guard
Schafskäse *m* sheep's (milk)
cheese
schal *adj* (*Getränk*) flat
Schal (*-s, -e o -s*) *m* scarf
Schälchen *nt* (small) bowl
Schale (*-, -n*) *f* skin; (*abgeschält*)
peel; (*Nuss, Muschel, Ei*) shell;
(*Geschirr*) bowl, dish
schälen *vt* to peel; (*Tomate,
Mandel*) to skin; (*Erbsen, Eier, Nüsse*)
to shell; (*Getreide*) to husk ▷ *vr:*
sich ~ to peel
Schall (*-(e)s, -e*) *m* sound;
Schalldämpfer (*-s, -*) *m* (*Auto*)
silencer (*Brit*), muffler (*US*);
Schallplatte *f* record
Schalotte (*-, -n*) *f* shallot
schalten *vt* to switch ▷ *vi* (*Auto*)
to change gear; (*fam: begreifen*) to
catch on; **Schalter** (*-s, -*) *m* (*auf
Post, Bank*) counter; (*an Gerät*)
switch; **Schalterhalle** *f* main
hall; **Schalteröffnungszeiten** *pl*
business hours *pl*
Schaltfläche *f* (*Inform*) button;
Schalthebel *m* gear lever (*Brit*) (o
shift (*US*)); **Schaltjahr** *nt* leap
year; **Schaltknüppel** *m* gear
lever (*Brit*) (o shift (*US*)); **Schaltung**
f gear change (*Brit*), gearshift (*US*)
Scham (*-*) *f* shame; (*Schamgefühl*)
modesty; **schämen** *vr:* **sich ~** to
be ashamed
Schande (*-*) *f* disgrace
Schanze (*-, -n*) *f* ski jump
Schar (*-, -en*) *f* (*von Vögeln*) flock;
(*Menge*) crowd; **in ~en** in droves
scharf *adj* (*Messer, Kritik*) sharp;
(*Essen*) hot; **auf etw** (*akk*) **~ sein**
(*fam*) to be keen on sth

Schärfe (*-, -n*) *f* sharpness;
(*Strenge*) rigour; (*Foto*) focus
Scharlach (*-s*) *m* (*Med*) scarlet
fever
Scharnier (*-s, -e*) *nt* hinge
Schaschlik (*-s, -s*) *m* o *nt* (shish)
kebab
Schatten (*-s, -*) *m* shadow; **30
Grad im ~** 30 degrees in the shade;
schattig *adj* shady
Schatz (*-es, Schätze*) *m* treasure;
(*Mensch*) love
schätzen *vt* (*abschätzen*) to
estimate; (*Gegenstand*) to value;
(*würdigen*) to value, to esteem;
(*vermuten*) to reckon; **Schätzung**
f estimate; (*das Schätzen*)
estimation; (*von Wertgegenstand*)
valuation; **schätzungsweise** *adv*
roughly, approximately
Schau (*-, -en*) *f* show;
(*Ausstellung*) exhibition
schauen *vi* to look; **ich schau
mal, ob ...** I'll go and have a look
whether ...; **schau, dass ...** see
(to it) that ...
Schauer (*-s, -*) *m* (*Regen*) shower;
(*Schreck*) shudder
Schaufel (*-, -n*) *f* shovel;
~ und Besen dustpan and
brush; **schaufeln** *vt* to shovel;
Schnee ~ to clear the snow
away
Schaufenster *nt* shop window;
Schaufensterbummel *m*
window-shopping expedition
Schaukel (*-, -n*) *f* swing;
schaukeln *vi* to rock; (*mit
Schaukel*) to swing
Schaulustige(r) *mf* gawper
(*Brit*), rubbernecker (*US*)
Schaum (*-(e)s, Schäume*) *m* foam;
(*Seifenschaum*) lather; (*Bierschaum*)
froth; **Schaumbad** *nt* bubble
bath; **schäumen** *vi* to foam;
Schaumfestiger (*-s, -*) *m* styling
mousse; **Schaumgummi** *m*

foam (rubber); **Schaumwein** m sparkling wine

Schauplatz m scene; **Schauspiel** nt spectacle; (Theat) play; **Schauspieler(in)** m(f) actor/actress

Scheck (-s, -s) m cheque; **Scheckheft** nt chequebook; **Scheckkarte** f cheque card

Scheibe (-, -n) f disc; (von Brot, Käse etc) slice; (Glasscheibe) pane; **Scheibenbremse** f (Auto) disc brake; **Scheibenwaschanlage** f (Auto) windscreen (Brit) (o windshield (US)) washer unit; **Scheibenwischer** (-s, -) m (Auto) windscreen (Brit) (o windshield (US)) wiper

Scheich (-s, -s) m sheik(h)

Scheide (-, -n) f (Anat) vagina

scheiden (schied, geschieden) vt (trennen) to separate; (Ehe) to dissolve; **sich ~ lassen** to get a divorce; **sie hat sich von ihm ~ lassen** she divorced him; **Scheidung** f divorce

Schein (-(e)s, -e) m light; (Anschein) appearance; (Geld) (bank)note; **scheinbar** adj apparent; **scheinen** (schien, geschienen) vi (Sonne) to shine; (den Anschein haben) to seem; **Scheinwerfer** (-s, -) m flood-light; (Theat) spotlight; (Auto) headlight

Scheiß- in zW (vulg) damned, bloody (Brit); **Scheiße** (-) f (vulg) shit, crap; **scheißegal** adj (vulg) **das ist mir ~** I don't give a damn (o toss); **scheißen** (schiss, geschissen) vi (vulg) to shit

Scheitel (-s, -) m parting (Brit), part (US)

scheitern vi to fail (an +dat because of)

Schellfisch m haddock

Schema (-s, -s o Schemata) nt

scheme, plan; (Darstellung) diagram

Schenkel (-s, -) m thigh

schenken vt to give; **er hat es mir geschenkt** he gave it to me (as a present); **sich** (dat) **etw ~** (fam: weglassen) to skip sth

Scherbe (-, -n) f broken piece, fragment

Schere (-, -n) f scissors pl; (groß) shears pl; **eine ~** a pair of scissors/shears

Scherz (-es, -e) m joke

scheu adj shy

scheuen vr **sich ~ vor** (+dat) to be afraid of, to shrink from ▷ vt to shun ▷ vi (Pferd) to shy

scheuern vt to scrub; **jdm eine ~** (fam) to slap sb in the face

Scheune (-, -n) f barn

scheußlich adj dreadful

Schi (-s, -er) m siehe **Ski**

Schicht (-, -en) f layer; (in Gesellschaft) class; (in Fabrik etc) shift

schick adj stylish, chic

schicken vt to send ▷ vr: **sich ~** (sich beeilen) to hurry up

Schickimicki (-(s), -s) m (fam) trendy

Schicksal (-s, -e) nt fate

Schiebedach nt (Auto) sunroof; **schieben** (schob, geschoben) vt, vi to push; **die Schuld auf jdn ~** to put the blame on sb; **Schiebetür** f sliding door

schied imperf von **scheiden**

Schiedsrichter(in) m(f) referee; (Tennis) umpire; (Schlichter) arbitrator

schief adj crooked; (Blick) funny ▷ adv crooked(ly); **schief|gehen** irr vi (fam: misslingen) to go wrong

schielen vi to squint

schien imperf von **scheinen**

Schienbein nt shin

Schiene (-, -n) f rail; (Med) splint

schier *adj* pure; (*fig*) sheer ▷ *adv* nearly, almost

schießen (*schoss, geschossen*) *vt* to shoot; (*Ball*) to kick; (*Tor*) to score; (*Foto*) to take ▷ *vi* to shoot (*auf +akk* at)

Schiff (*-(e)s, -e*) *nt* ship; (*in Kirche*) nave; **Schifffahrt** *f* shipping; **Schiffsreise** *f* voyage

schikanieren *vt* to harass; (*Schule*) to bully

Schild (*-(e)s, -e*) *m* (*Schutz*) shield ▷ (*-(e)s, -er*) *nt* sign; **was steht auf dem ~?** what does the sign say?

Schilddrüse *f* thyroid gland

schildern *vt* to describe

Schildkröte *f* tortoise; (*Wasserschildkröte*) turtle

Schimmel (*-s, -*) *m* mould; (*Pferd*) white horse; **schimmeln** *vi* to go mouldy

schimpfen *vt* to tell off ▷ *vi* (*sich beklagen*) to complain; **mit jdm ~** to tell sb off; **Schimpfwort** *nt* swearword

Schinken (*-s, -*) *m* ham

Schirm (*-(e)s, -e*) *m* (*Regenschirm*) umbrella; (*Sonnenschirm*) parasol, sunshade

schiss *imperf von* **scheißen**

Schlacht (*-, -en*) *f* battle; **schlachten** *vt* to slaughter; **Schlachter(in)** (*-s, -*) *m(f)* butcher

Schlaf (*-(e)s*) *m* sleep; **Schlafanzug** *m* pyjamas *pl*; **Schlafcouch** *f* bed settee

Schläfe (*-, -n*) *f* temple

schlafen (*schlief, geschlafen*) *vi* to sleep; **schlaf gut!** sleep well; **hast du gut geschlafen?** did you sleep all right?; **er schläft noch** he's still asleep; **~ gehen** to go to bed

schlaff *adj* slack; (*kraftlos*) limp; (*erschöpft*) exhausted

Schlafgelegenheit *f* place to sleep; **Schlaflosigkeit** *f*

sleeplessness; **Schlafmittel** *nt* sleeping pill; **schläfrig** *adj* sleepy

Schlafsaal *m* dormitory; **Schlafsack** *m* sleeping bag; **Schlaftablette** *f* sleeping pill; **er ist eine richtige ~** (*fam: langweilig*) he's such a bore; **Schlafwagen** *m* sleeping car, sleeper; **Schlafzimmer** *nt* bedroom

Schlag (*-(e)s, Schläge*) *m* blow; (*Puls*) beat; (*Elek*) shock; (*fam: Portion*) helping; (*Art*) kind, type; **Schlagader** *f* artery; **Schlaganfall** *m* (*Med*) stroke; **schlagartig** *adj* sudden

schlagen (*schlug, geschlagen*) *vt* to hit; (*besiegen*) to beat; (*Sahne*) to whip; **jdn zu Boden ~** to knock sb down ▷ *vi* (*Herz*) to beat; (*Uhr*) to strike; **mit dem Kopf gegen etw ~** to bang one's head against sth ▷ *vr*: **sich ~** to fight

Schläger (*-s, -*) *m* (*Sport*) bat; (*Tennis*) racket; (*Golf*) (golf) club; (*Hockey*) hockey stick; (*Mensch*) brawler; **Schlägerei** *f* fight, brawl

schlagfertig *adj* quick-witted; **Schlagloch** *nt* pothole; **Schlagsahne** *f* whipping cream; (*geschlagen*) whipped cream; **Schlagzeile** *f* headline; **Schlagzeug** *nt* drums *pl*; (*in Orchester*) percussion

Schlamm (*-(e)s, -e*) *m* mud

schlampig *adj* (*fam*) sloppy

schlang *imperf von* **schlingen**

Schlange (*-, -n*) *f* snake; (*von Menschen*) queue (*Brit*), line (*US*); **~ stehen** to queue (*Brit*), to stand in line (*US*); **Schlangenlinie** *f* wavy line; **in ~n fahren** to swerve about

schlank *adj* slim

schlapp *adj* limp; (*locker*) slack

Schlappe (*-, -n*) *f* (*fam*) setback

schlau adj clever, smart; (*raffiniert*) crafty, cunning

Schlauch (-(*e*)*s*, *Schläuche*) m hose; (*in Reifen*) inner tube; **Schlauchboot** nt rubber dinghy

schlecht adj bad; **mir ist ~** I feel sick; **die Milch ist ~** the milk has gone off ▷ adv badly; **es geht ihm ~** he's having a hard time; (*gesundheitlich*) he's not feeling well; (*finanziell*) he's pretty hard up; **schlecht|machen** vt: **jdn ~** (*herabsetzen*) to run sb down

schleichen (*schlich, geschlichen*) vi to creep

Schleier (-*s*, -) m veil

Schleife (-, -*n*) f (*Inform, Aviat, Elek*) loop; (*Band*) bow

schleifen vt (*ziehen, schleppen*) to drag ▷ (*schliff, geschliffen*) vt (*schärfen*) to grind; (*Edelstein*) to cut

Schleim (-(*e*)*s*, -*e*) m slime; (*Med*) mucus; **Schleimer** (-*s*, -) m (*fam*) creep; **Schleimhaut** f mucous membrane

schlendern vi to stroll

schleppen vt to drag; (*Auto, Schiff*) to tow; (*tragen*) to lug; **Schlepplift** m ski tow

Schleswig-Holstein (-*s*) nt Schleswig-Holstein

Schleuder (-, -*n*) f catapult; (*für Wäsche*) spin-dryer; **schleudern** vt to hurl; (*Wäsche*) to spin-dry ▷ vi (*Auto*) to skid; **Schleudersitz** m ejector seat

schlich imperf von **schleichen**

schlicht adj simple, plain

schlichten vt (*Streit*) to settle

schlief imperf von **schlafen**

schließen (*schloss, geschlossen*) vt, vi to close, to shut; (*beenden*) to close; (*Freundschaft, Ehe*) to enter into; (*folgern*) to infer (*aus* from) ▷ vr: **sich ~** to close, to shut; **Schließfach** nt locker

schließlich adv finally; (*schließlich doch*) after all

schliff imperf von **schleifen**

schlimm adj bad; **schlimmer** adj worse; **schlimmste(r, s)** adj worst; **schlimmstenfalls** adv at (the) worst

Schlinge (-, -*n*) f loop; (*Med*) sling

Schlips (-*es*, -*e*) m tie

Schlitten (-*s*, -) m sledge, toboggan; (*mit Pferden*) sleigh; **Schlittenfahren** (-*s*) nt tobogganing

Schlittschuh m ice skate; **~ laufen** to ice-skate

Schlitz (-*es*, -*e*) m slit; (*für Münze*) slot; (*an Hose*) flies pl

schloss imperf von **schließen**

Schloss (-*es*, *Schlösser*) nt lock; (*Burg*) castle

Schlosser(in) m(f) mechanic

Schlucht (-, -*en*) f gorge, ravine

schluchzen vi to sob

Schluck (-(*e*)*s*, -*e*) m swallow; **Schluckauf** (-*s*) m hiccups pl; **schlucken** vt, vi to swallow

schludern vi (*fam*) to do sloppy work

schlug imperf von **schlagen**

Schlüpfer (-*s*, -) m panties pl

schlürfen vt, vi to slurp

Schluss (-*es*, *Schlüsse*) m end; (*Schlussfolgerung*) conclusion; **am ~** at the end; **mit jdm ~ machen** to finish (*o* split up) with sb

Schlüssel (-*s*, -) m (*a. fig*) key; **Schlüsselbein** nt collarbone; **Schlüsselbund** m bunch of keys; **Schlüsseldienst** m key-cutting service; **Schlüsselloch** nt keyhole

Schlussfolgerung f conclusion; **Schlusslicht** nt tail-light; (*fig*) tail-ender; **Schlussverkauf** m clearance sale

schmächtig adj frail

schmal adj narrow; (*Mensch, Buch etc*) slim; (*karg*) meagre

Schmalz (-es, -e) nt dripping, lard; (fig: Sentimentalitäten) schmaltz

schmatzen vi to eat noisily

schmecken vt, vi to taste (nach of); **es schmeckt ihm** he likes it; **lass es dir ~!** bon appétit

Schmeichelei f flattery; **schmeichelhaft** adj flattering; **schmeicheln** vi: **jdm ~** to flatter sb

schmeißen (schmiss, geschmissen) vt (fam) to chuck, to throw

schmelzen (schmolz, geschmolzen) vt, vi to melt; (Metall, Erz) to smelt; **Schmelzkäse** m cheese spread

Schmerz (-es, -en) m pain; (Trauer) grief; **~en haben** to be in pain; **~en im Rücken haben** to have a pain in one's back; **schmerzen** vt, vi to hurt; **Schmerzensgeld** nt compensation; **schmerzhaft, schmerzlich** adj painful; **schmerzlos** adj painless; **Schmerzmittel** nt painkiller; **schmerzstillend** adj painkilling; **Schmerztablette** f painkiller

Schmetterling m butterfly

Schmied(in) (-(e)s, -e) m(f) blacksmith; **schmieden** vt to forge; (Pläne) to make

schmieren vt to smear; (ölen) to lubricate, to grease; (bestechen) to bribe ▷ vt, vi (unsauber schreiben) to scrawl; **Schmiergeld** nt (fam) bribe; **schmierig** adj greasy; **Schmierseife** f soft soap

Schminke (-, -n) f make-up; **schminken** vr: **sich ~** to put one's make-up on

schmiss imperf von **schmeißen**

schmollen vi to sulk; **schmollend** adj sulky

schmolz imperf von **schmelzen**

Schmuck (-(e)s, -e) m jewellery (Brit), jewelry (US); (Verzierung) decoration; **schmücken** vt to decorate

schmuggeln vt, vi to smuggle

schmunzeln vi to smile

schmusen vi to (kiss and) cuddle

Schmutz (-es) m dirt, filth; **schmutzig** adj dirty

Schnabel (-s, Schnäbel) m beak, bill; (Ausguss) spout

Schnake (-, -n) f mosquito

Schnalle (-, -n) f buckle

Schnäppchen nt (fam) bargain; **schnappen** vt (fangen) to catch ▷ vi: **nach Luft ~** to gasp for breath; **Schnappschuss** m (Foto) snap(shot)

Schnaps (-es, Schnäpse) m schnapps

schnarchen vi to snore

schnaufen vi to puff, to pant

Schnauzbart m moustache; **Schnauze** (-, -n) f snout, muzzle; (Ausguss) spout; (fam: Mund) trap; **die ~ voll haben** to have had enough

schnäuzen vr: **sich ~** to blow one's nose

Schnecke (-, -n) f snail; **Schneckenhaus** nt snail's shell

Schnee (-s) m snow; **Schneeball** m snowball; **Schneebob** m snowmobile; **Schneebrille** f snow goggles pl; **Schneeflocke** f snowflake; **Schneegestöber** (-s, -) nt snow flurry; **Schneeglöckchen** nt snowdrop; **Schneegrenze** f snowline; **Schneekanone** f snow thrower; **Schneekette** f (Auto) snow chain; **Schneemann** m snowman; **Schneepflug** m snowplough; **Schneeregen** m sleet; **Schneeschmelze** f thaw; **Schneesturm** m snowstorm, blizzard; **Schneetreiben** nt light blizzards pl; **Schneewehe** f snowdrift

Schneide (-, -n) f edge; (*Klinge*) blade; **schneiden** (*schnitt, geschnitten*) vt to cut; **sich** (*dat*) **die Haare ~ lassen** to have one's hair cut ▷ vr: **sich ~** to cut oneself; **Schneider(in)** (-s, -) m(f) tailor; (*für Damenmode*) dressmaker; **Schneiderin** f dressmaker; **Schneidezahn** m incisor

schneien vi impers to snow

schnell adj quick, fast ▷ adv quickly, fast; **mach ~!** hurry up; **Schnelldienst** m express service; **Schnellhefter** m loose-leaf binder; **Schnellimbiss** m snack bar; **Schnellkochtopf** m pressure cooker; **Schnellreinigung** f express dry cleaning; (*Geschäft*) express (dry) cleaner's; **Schnellstraße** f expressway; **Schnellzug** m fast train

schneuzen vr siehe **schnäuzen**

schnitt imperf von **schneiden**

Schnitt (-(e)s, -e) m cut; (*Schnittpunkt*) intersection; (*Querschnitt*) (cross) section; (*Durchschnitt*) average; (*eines Kleides*) style; **Schnitte** (-, -n) f slice; (*belegt*) sandwich; **Schnittkäse** m cheese slices pl; **Schnittlauch** m chives pl; **Schnittmuster** nt pattern; **Schnittstelle** f (*Inform, fig*) interface; **Schnittwunde** f cut, gash

Schnitzel (-s, -) nt (*Papier*) scrap; (*Gastr*) escalope

schnitzen vt to carve

Schnorchel (-s, -) m snorkel; **schnorcheln** vi to go snorkelling, to snorkel

schnüffeln vi to sniff

Schnuller (-s, -) m dummy (*Brit*), pacifier (*US*)

Schnulze (-, -n) f (*Film, Roman*) weepie

Schnupfen (-s, -) m cold

schnuppern vi to sniff

Schnur (-, Schnüre) f string, cord; (*Elek*) lead; **schnurlos** adj (*Telefon*) cordless

Schnurrbart m moustache

schnurren vi to purr

Schnürsenkel (-s, -) m shoelace

schob imperf von **schieben**

Schock (-(e)s, -e) m shock; **unter ~ stehen** to be in a state of shock; **schockieren** vt to shock

Schokolade f chocolate; **Schokoriegel** m chocolate bar

Scholle (-, -n) f (*Fisch*) plaice; (*Eis*) ice floe

 SCHLÜSSELWORT

schon adv **1** (*bereits*) already; **er ist schon da** he's there already, he's already there; **ist er schon da?** is he there yet?; **warst du schon einmal da?** have you ever been there?; **ich war schon einmal da** I've been there before; **das war schon immer so** that has always been the case; **schon oft** often; **hast du schon gehört?** have you heard?

2 (*bestimmt*) all right; **du wirst schon sehen** you'll see (all right); **das wird schon noch gut** that'll be OK

3 (*bloß*) just; **allein schon das Gefühl ...** just the very feeling ...; **schon der Gedanke** the very thought; **wenn ich das schon höre** I only have to hear that

4 (*einschränkend*) **ja schon, aber ...** yes (well), but ...

5 schon möglich possible; **schon gut!** OK!; **du weißt schon** you know; **komm schon!** come on!

schön adj beautiful; (*nett*) nice; (*Frau*) beautiful, pretty; (*Mann*) beautiful, handsome; (*Wetter*) fine; **~e Grüße** best wishes; **-es Wochenende** have a nice weekend

schonen *vt (pfleglich behandeln)* to look after ▷ *vr:* **sich ~** to take it easy

Schönheit *f* beauty

Schonkost *f* light diet

schöpfen *vt* to scoop; (*mit Kelle*) to ladle; **Schöpfkelle** *f*, **Schöpflöffel** *m* ladle

Schöpfung *f* creation

Schoppen (*-s, -*) *m* glass (of wine)

Schorf (*-(e)s, -e*) *m* scab

Schorle (*-, -n*) *f* spritzer

Schornstein *m* chimney; **Schornsteinfeger(in)** (*-s, -*) *m(f)* chimney sweep

schoss *imperf von* **schießen**

Schoß (*-es, Schöße*) *m* lap

Schotte (*-n, -n*) *m* Scot, Scotsman; **Schottin** *f* Scot, Scotswoman; **schottisch** *adj* Scottish, Scots; **Schottland** *nt* Scotland

schräg *adj* slanting; (*Dach*) sloping; (*Linie*) diagonal; (*fam: unkonventionell*) wacky

Schrank (*-(e)s, Schränke*) *m* cupboard; (*Kleiderschrank*) wardrobe (*Brit*), closet (*US*)

Schranke (*-, -n*) *f* barrier

Schrankwand *f* wall unit

Schraube (*-, -n*) *f* screw; **schrauben** *vt* to screw; **Schraubendreher** (*-s, -*) *m* screwdriver; **Schraubenschlüssel** *m* spanner; **Schraubenzieher** (*-s, -*) *m* screwdriver; **Schraubverschluss** *m* screw top, screw cap

Schreck (*-(e)s, -e*) *m*, **Schrecken** (*-s, -*) *m* terror; (*Angst*) fright; **jdm einen ~ einjagen** to give sb a fright; **schreckhaft** *adj* jumpy; **schrecklich** *adj* terrible, dreadful

Schrei (*-(e)s, -e*) *m* scream; (*Ruf*) shout

Schreibblock *m* writing pad; **schreiben** (*schrieb, geschrieben*) *vt, vi* to write; (*buchstabieren*) to spell; **wie schreibt man ...?** how do you spell ...?; **Schreiben** (*-s, -*) *nt* writing; (*Brief*) letter; **Schreibfehler** *m* spelling mistake; **schreibgeschützt** *adj* (*Diskette*) write-protected; **Schreibtisch** *m* desk; **Schreibwaren** *pl* stationery *sing*; **Schreibwarenladen** *m* stationer's

schreien (*schrie, geschrie(e)n*) *vt, vi* to scream; (*rufen*) to shout

Schreiner(in) *m(f)* joiner; **Schreinerei** *f* joiner's workshop

schrie *imperf von* **schreien**

schrieb *imperf von* **schreiben**

Schrift (*-, -en*) *f* writing; (*Handschrift*) handwriting; (*Schriftart*) typeface; (*Schrifttyp*) font; **schriftlich** *adj* written ▷ *adv* in writing; **würden Sie uns das bitte ~ geben?** could we have that in writing, please?; **Schriftsteller(in)** (*-s, -*) *m(f)* writer

Schritt (*-(e)s, -e*) *m* step; **~ für ~** step by step; **-e gegen etw unternehmen** to take steps against sth; **Schrittgeschwindigkeit** *f* walking speed; **Schrittmacher** *m* (*Med*) pacemaker

Schrott (*-(e)s, -e*) *m* scrap metal; (*fig*) rubbish

schrubben *vi, vt* to scrub; **Schrubber** (*-s, -*) *m* scrubbing brush

schrumpfen *vi* to shrink

Schubkarren (*-s, -*) *m* wheelbarrow; **Schublade** *f* drawer

schubsen *vt* to shove, to push

schüchtern *adj* shy

schuf *imperf von* **schaffen**

Schuh (-(e)s, -e) m shoe;
Schuhcreme f shoe polish;
Schuhgeschäft nt shoe shop;
Schuhgröße f shoe size;
Schuhlöffel m shoehorn
Schulabschluss m school-
leaving qualification
schuld adj: **wer ist ~ daran?**
whose fault is it?; **er ist ~** it's his
fault, he's to blame; **Schuld** (-) f
guilt; (Verschulden) fault; **~ haben**
to be to blame (an +dat for); **er hat
~** it's his fault; **sie gibt mir die
~ an dem Unfall** she blames me
for the accident; **schulden** vt to
owe (jdm etw sb sth); **Schulden** pl
debts pl; **~ haben** to be in debt;
~ machen to run up debts; **seine
~ bezahlen** to pay off one's debts;
schuldig adj guilty (an +dat of);
(gebührend) due; **jdm etw ~ sein** to
owe sb sth
Schule (-, -n) f school; **in der ~** at
school; **in die ~ gehen** to go to
school; **Schüler(in)** (-s, -) m(f)
(jüngerer) pupil; (älterer) student;
Schüleraustausch m school
exchange; **Schulfach** nt subject;
Schulferien pl school holidays pl
(Brit) (o vacation (US)); **schulfrei**
adj: **morgen ist ~** there's no school
tomorrow; **Schulfreund(in)** m(f)
schoolmate; **Schuljahr** nt school
year; **Schulkenntnisse** pl: **~ in
Französisch** school(-level) French;
Schulklasse f class; **Schul-
leiter(in)** m(f) headmaster/
headmistress (Brit), principal (US)
Schulter (-, -n) f shoulder;
Schulterblatt nt shoulder blade
Schulung f training;
(Veranstaltung) training course
schummeln vi (fam) to cheat
Schuppe (-, -n) f (von Fisch) scale;
schuppen vt to scale ▷ vr: **sich
~** to peel; **Schuppen** pl (im Haar)
dandruff sing

Schürfwunde f graze
Schürze (-, -n) f apron
Schuss (-es, Schüsse) m shot; **mit
einem ~ Wodka** with a dash of
vodka
Schüssel (-, -n) f bowl
Schuster(in) (-s, -) m(f)
shoemaker
Schutt (-(e)s) m rubble
Schüttelfrost m shivering fit;
schütteln vt to shake ▷ vr: **sich
~** to shake
schütten vt to pour; (Zucker, Kies
etc) to tip ▷ vi impers to pour
(down)
Schutz (-es) m protection (gegen,
vor against, from); (Unterschlupf)
shelter; **jdn in ~ nehmen** to stand
up for sb; **Schutzblech** nt
mudguard; **Schutzbrief** m travel
insurance document for drivers;
Schutzbrille f (safety) goggles pl
Schütze (-n, -n) m (beim Fußball)
scorer; (Astr) Sagittarius
schützen vt: **jdn gegen/vor etw
~** to protect sb against/from sth;
Schutzimpfung f inoculation,
vaccination
schwach adj weak; **~e Augen**
poor eyesight sing; **Schwäche**
(-, -n) f weakness; **Schwachstelle**
f weak point; **Schwachstrom** m
low-voltage current
Schwager (-s, Schwäger) m
brother-in-law; **Schwägerin** f
sister-in-law
Schwalbe (-, -n) f swallow; (beim
Fußball) dive
schwamm imperf von
schwimmen
Schwamm (-(e)s, Schwämme) m
sponge; **~ drüber!** (fam) let's forget
it!
Schwan (-(e)s,
Schwäne) m swan
schwanger adj pregnant; **im
vierten Monat ~ sein** to be four

months pregnant; **Schwanger-schaft** f pregnancy; **Schwanger-schaftsabbruch** m abortion; **Schwangerschaftstest** m pregnancy test

schwanken vi to sway; (*Preise, Zahlen*) to fluctuate; (*zögern*) to hesitate; (*taumeln*) to stagger; **ich schwanke zwischen A und B** I can't decide between A and B

Schwanz (-es, Schwänze) m tail; (*vulg: Penis*) cock

Schwarm (-(e)s, Schwärme) m swarm; (*fam: angehimmelte Person*) heartthrob; **schwärmen** vi to swarm; **~ für** to be mad about

schwarz adj black; **mir wurde ~ vor Augen** everything went black; **Schwarzarbeit** f illicit work; **Schwarzbrot** nt black bread; **schwarz|fahren** irr vi to travel without a ticket; (*ohne Führerschein*) to drive without a licence; **Schwarzfahrer(in)** m(f) fare-dodger; **Schwarzmarkt** m black market; **schwarz|sehen** irr vi (*fam: pessimistisch sein*) to be pessimistic (*für about*); **Schwarzwald** m Black Forest; **schwarzweiß** adj black and white; **Schwarzwurzel** f black salsify

schwatzen vi to chatter; **Schwätzer(in)** (-s, -) m(f) chatterbox; (*Schwafler*) gasbag; (*Klatschmaul*) gossip

Schwebebahn f suspension railway; **schweben** vi to float; (*hoch*) to soar

Schwede (-n, -n) m Swede; **Schweden** (-s) nt Sweden; **Schwedin** f Swede; **schwedisch** adj Swedish; **Schwedisch** nt Swedish

Schwefel (-s) m sulphur

schweigen (schwieg, geschwiegen) vi to be silent; (*nicht mehr reden*) to stop talking; **Schweigen** (-s) nt silence; **Schweigepflicht** f duty of confidentiality; **die ärztliche ~** medical confidentiality

Schwein (-(e)s, -e) nt pig; (*fam: Glück*) luck; (*fam: gemeiner Mensch*) swine; **Schweinebraten** m roast pork; **Schweinefleisch** nt pork; **Schweinerei** f mess; (*Gemeinheit*) dirty trick

Schweiß (-es) m sweat

schweißen vt, vi to weld

Schweiz (-) f: **die ~** Switzerland; **Schweizer(in)** (-s, -) m(f) Swiss; **Schweizerdeutsch** nt Swiss German; **schweizerisch** adj Swiss

Schwelle (-, -n) f doorstep; (*a. fig*) threshold

schwellen vi to swell (up); **Schwellung** f swelling

schwer adj heavy; (*schwierig*) difficult, hard; (*schlimm*) serious, bad; **er ist ~ zu verstehen** it's difficult to understand what he's saying ▷ adv (*sehr*) really; (*verletzt etc*) seriously, badly; **etw ~ nehmen** to take sth hard; **Schwerbehinderte(r)** mf severely disabled person; **schwer|fallen** irr vi (*Schwierigkeiten bereiten*) **jdm ~** to be difficult for sb; **schwerhörig** adj hard of hearing

Schwert (-(e)s, -er) nt sword; **Schwertlilie** f iris

Schwester (-, -n) f sister; (*Med*) nurse

schwieg imperf von **schweigen**

Schwiegereltern pl parents-in-law pl; **Schwiegermutter** f mother-in-law; **Schwiegersohn** m son-in-law; **Schwiegertochter** f daughter-in-law; **Schwiegervater** m father-in-law

schwierig adj difficult, hard; **Schwierigkeit** f difficulty; **in ~en kommen** to get into trouble; **jdm**

~en machen to make things difficult for sb

Schwimmbad *nt* swimming pool; **Schwimmbecken** *nt* swimming pool; **schwimmen** (*schwamm, geschwommen*) *vi* to swim; (*treiben*) to float; (*fig: unsicher sein*) to be all at sea; **Schwimmer(in)** *m(f)* swimmer; **Schwimmflosse** *f* flipper; **Schwimmflügel** *m* water wing; **Schwimmreifen** *m* rubber ring; **Schwimmweste** *f* life jacket

Schwindel (-s) *m* dizziness; (*Anfall*) dizzy spell; (*Betrug*) swindle; **schwindelfrei** *adj*: **nicht ~ sein** to suffer from vertigo; **~ sein** to have a head for heights; **schwindlig** *adj* dizzy; **mir ist ~** I feel dizzy

Schwips *m*: **einen ~ haben** to be tipsy

schwitzen *vi* to sweat

schwoll *imperf von* **schwellen**

schwor *imperf von* **schwören**

schwören (*schwor, geschworen*) *vt, vi* to swear; **einen Eid ~** to take an oath

schwul *adj* gay

schwül *adj* close

Schwung (-(e)s, *Schwünge*) *m* swing; (*Triebkraft*) momentum; (*fig: Energie*) energy; (*fam: Menge*) batch; **in ~ kommen** to get going

Schwur (-s, *Schwüre*) *m* oath

scrollen *vi* (*Inform*) to scroll

sechs *num* six; **Sechs** (-, *-en*) *f* six; (*Schulnote*) ≈ F; **Sechserpack** *m* sixpack; **sechshundert** *num* six hundred; **sechsmal** *adv* six times; **sechste(r, s)** *adj* sixth; *siehe auch* **dritte**; **Sechstel** (-s, -) *nt* sixth; **sechzehn** *num* sixteen; **sechzehnte(r, s)** *adj* sixteenth; *siehe auch* **dritte**; **sechzig** *num* sixty; **in den ~er Jahren** in the sixties; **sechzigste(r, s)** *adj* sixtieth

Secondhandladen *m* second-hand shop

See (-, *-n*) *f* sea; **an der ~** by the sea ▷ (-s, *-n*) *m* lake; **am ~** by the lake; **Seegang** *m* waves; **hoher/schwerer/leichter ~** rough/heavy/calm seas *pl*; **Seehund** *m* seal; **Seeigel** *m* sea urchin; **seekrank** *adj* seasick

Seele (-, *-n*) *f* soul

Seeleute *pl* seamen *pl*, sailors *pl*

seelisch *adj* mental, psychological

Seelöwe *m* sea lion; **Seemann** *m* sailor, seaman; **Seemeile** *f* nautical mile; **Seemöwe** *f* seagull; **Seenot** *f* distress (at sea); **Seepferdchen** *nt* sea horse; **Seerose** *f* water lily; **Seestern** *m* starfish; **Seezunge** *f* sole

Segel (-s, -) *nt* sail; **Segelboot** *nt* yacht; **Segelfliegen** (-s) *nt* gliding; **Segelflugzeug** *nt* glider; **segeln** *vt, vi* to sail; **Segelschiff** *nt* sailing ship

sehbehindert *adj* partially sighted

sehen (*sah, gesehen*) *vt, vi* to see; (*in bestimmte Richtung*) to look; **gut/schlecht ~** to have good/bad eyesight; **auf die Uhr ~** to look at one's watch; **kann ich das mal ~?** can I have a look at it?; **wir ~ uns morgen!** see you tomorrow; **ich kenne sie nur vom Sehen** I only know her by sight; **Sehenswürdigkeiten** *pl* sights *pl*

Sehne (-, *-n*) *f* tendon; (*an Bogen*) string

sehnen *vr*: **sich ~** to long (*nach* for)

Sehnenscheidenentzündung *f* (*Med*) tendovaginitis;

Sehnenzerrung f (Med) pulled tendon
Sehnsucht f longing; **sehnsüchtig** adj longing
sehr adv (vor Adjektiv, Adverb) very; (mit Verben) a lot, very much; **zu ~** too much
seicht adj shallow
Seide (-, -n) f silk
Seife (-, -n) f soap; **Seifenoper** f soap (opera); **Seifenschale** f soap dish
Seil (-(e)s, -e) nt rope; (Kabel) cable; **Seilbahn** f cable railway

 SCHLÜSSELWORT

sein¹ (pt **war**, pp **gewesen**) vi **1** to be; **ich bin** I am; **du bist** you are; **er/sie/es ist** he/she/it is; **wir sind/ihr seid/sie sind** we/you/they are; **wir waren** we were; **wir sind gewesen** we have been

2 seien Sie nicht böse don't be angry; **sei so gut und ...** be so kind as to ...; **das wäre gut** that would o that'd be a good thing; **wenn ich Sie wäre** if I were o was you; **das wär's** that's all, that's it; **morgen bin ich in Rom** tomorrow I'll o I will o I shall be in Rome; **waren Sie mal in Rom?** have you ever been to Rome?

3 wie ist das zu verstehen? how is that to be understood?; **er ist nicht zu ersetzen** he cannot be replaced; **mit ihr ist nicht zu reden** you can't talk to her

4 mir ist kalt I'm cold; **was ist?** what's the matter?, what is it?; **ist was?** is something the matter?; **es sei denn, dass ...** unless ...; **wie dem auch sei** be that as it may; **wie wäre es mit ...?** how o what about ...?; **lass das sein!** stop that!

sein² pron possessiv von **er**; (adjektivisch) his ▷ pron possessiv von **es**; (adjektivisch) its; (adjektivisch, männlich) his; (weiblich) her; (sächlich) its; **das ist ~e Tasche** that's his bag; **jeder hat ~e Sorgen** everyone has their problems; **seine(r, s)** pron possessiv von **er**; (substantivisch) his ▷ pron possessiv von **es**; (substantivisch) its; (substantivisch, männlich) his; **das ist ~r/~/~s** that's his/hers; **seiner** pron gen von **er**; of him ▷ pron gen von **es**; of it; **seinetwegen** adv (wegen ihm) because of him; (ihm zuliebe) for his sake; (um ihn) about him; (von ihm aus) as far as he is concerned
seit conj (bei Zeitpunkt) since; (bei Zeitraum) for; **er ist ~ Montag hier** he's been here since Monday; **er ist ~ einer Woche hier** he's been here for a week; **~ langem** for a long time; **seitdem** adv, conj since
Seite (-, -n) f side; (in Buch) page; **zur ~ gehen** to step aside; **Seitenairbag** m side-impact airbag; **Seitenaufprallschutz** m (Auto) side-impact protection; **Seitensprung** m affair; **Seitenstechen** (-s) nt: **~ haben/ bekommen** to have/get a stitch; **Seitenstraße** f side street; **Seitenstreifen** m hard shoulder (Brit), shoulder (US); **Seitenwind** m crosswind
seither adv since (then)
seitlich adj side
Sekretär(in) m(f) secretary; **Sekretariat** (-s, -e) nt secretary's office
Sekt (-(e)s, -e) m sparkling wine (similar to champagne)
Sekte (-, -n) f sect

Sekunde (-, -n) f second;
Sekundenkleber (-s, -) m superglue; **Sekundenschnelle** f: **es
geschah alles in ~** it was all over
in a matter of seconds

⬤ SCHLÜSSELWORT

selbst pron **1** **ich/er/wir selbst** I
myself/he himself/we ourselves;
sie ist die Tugend selbst she's
virtue itself; **er braut sein Bier
selbst** he brews his own beer; **wie
geht's? — gut, und selbst?** how
are things? — fine, and yourself?
2 (ohne Hilfe) alone, on
my/his/one's etc own; **von selbst**
by itself; **er kam von selbst** he
came of his own accord; **selbst
gemacht** home-made
▷ adv even; **selbst wenn** even if;
selbst Gott even God (himself)

selbständig adj siehe
selbstständig
Selbstauslöser (-s, -) m (Foto)
self-timer; **Selbstbedienung** f
self-service; **Selbstbefriedigung** f
masturbation;
Selbstbeherrschung f
self-control; **Selbstbeteiligung** f
(einer Versicherung) excess;
selbstbewusst adj
(self-)confident; **Selbstbräuner**
(-s, -) m self-tanning lotion;
selbstgemacht adj self-made;
selbstklebend adj self-adhesive;
Selbstlaut m vowel; **Selbstmord**
m suicide; **Selbstmordattentat**
nt suicide bombing; **Selbstmord-
attentäter(in)** m(f) suicide
bomber; **selbstsicher** adj
self-assured; **selbstständig** adj
independent; (arbeitend)
self-employed; **Selbstverpflegung**
f self-catering;
selbstverständlich adj obvious;

ich halte das für ~ I take that for
granted ▷ adv naturally;
Selbstvertrauen nt
self-confidence
Sellerie (-s, -(s)) m (-, -n) f (Knollensellerie) celeriac; (Stangensellerie)
celery
selten adj rare ▷ adv seldom,
rarely
seltsam adj strange;
~ schmecken/riechen to
taste/smell strange
Semester (-s, -) nt semester;
Semesterferien pl vacation sing
Semikolon (-s, Semikola) nt
semicolon
Seminar (-s, -e) nt seminar
Semmel (-, -n) f roll;
Semmelbrösel pl breadcrumbs
Senat (-(e)s, -e) m senate
senden (sandte, gesandt) vt to
send ▷ vt, vi (Radio, TV) to
broadcast; **Sender** (-s, -) m (TV)
channel; (Radio) station; (Anlage)
transmitter; **Sendung** f (Radio,
TV) broadcasting; (Programm)
programme
Senf (-(e)s, -e) m mustard
Senior(in) m(f) senior citizen;
Seniorenpass m senior citizen's
travel pass
senken vt to lower ▷ vr: **sich
~** to sink
senkrecht adj vertical
Sensation (-, -en) f sensation
sensibel adj sensitive
sentimental adj sentimental
separat adj separate
September (-(s), -) m
September; siehe auch **Juni**
Serbien (-s) nt Serbia
Serie f series sing
seriös adj (ernsthaft) serious;
(anständig) respectable
Serpentine f hairpin (bend)
Serum (-s, Seren) nt serum
Server (-s, -) m (Inform) server

Service (-(s), -) nt (Geschirr)
service ▷ (-, -s) m service
servieren vt, vi to serve
Serviette f napkin, serviette
Servolenkung f (Auto) power
steering
Sesam (-s, -s) m sesame seeds pl
Sessel (-s, -) m armchair;
Sessellift m chairlift
Set (-s, -s) m o nt set; (Tischset)
tablemat
setzen vt to put; (Baum etc) to
plant; (Segel) to set ▷ vr: **sich ~** to
settle; (hinsetzen) to sit down; **~ Sie
sich doch** please sit down
Seuche (-, -n) f epidemic
seufzen vt, vi to sigh
Sex (-(es)) m sex; **Sexismus** m
sexism; **sexistisch** adj sexist;
Sextourismus m sex tourism;
Sexualität f sexuality; **sexuell**
adj sexual
Seychellen pl Seychelles pl
sfr abk = **Schweizer Franken** Swiss
franc(s)
Shampoo (-s, -s) nt shampoo
Shareware (-, -s) f (Inform)
shareware
Shorts pl shorts pl
Shuttlebus m shuttle bus

 SCHLÜSSELWORT

sich pron 1 (akk) **er/sie/es ... sich**
he/she/it ... himself/herself/itself;
sie pl/**man ... sich** they/one ...
themselves/oneself; **Sie ... sich**
you ... yourself/yourselves pl; **sich
wiederholen** to repeat
oneself/itself
2 (dat) **er/sie/es ... sich** he/she/it
... to himself/herself/itself; **sie**
pl/**man ... sich** they/one ... to
themselves/oneself; **Sie ... sich**
you ... to yourself/yourselves pl;
**sie hat sich einen Pullover
gekauft** she bought herself a

jumper; **sich die Haare waschen**
to wash one's hair
3 (mit Präposition) **haben Sie Ihren
Ausweis bei sich?** do you have
your pass on you?; **er hat nichts
bei sich** he's got nothing on him;
sie bleiben gern unter sich they
keep themselves to themselves
4 (einander) each other, one
another; **sie bekämpfen sich** they
fight each other o one another
5 **dieses Auto fährt sich gut** this
car drives well; **hier sitzt es sich
gut** it's good to sit here

sicher adj safe (vor +dat from);
(gewiss) certain (gen of);
(zuverlässig) reliable; (selbstsicher)
confident; **aber ~!** of course, sure;
Sicherheit f safety; (Aufgabe von
Sicherheitsbeamten) (Fin) security;
(Gewissheit) certainty;
(Selbstsicherheit) confidence; **mit
~** definitely; **Sicherheitsabstand**
m safe distance; **Sicherheitsgurt**
m seat belt; **sicherheitshalber**
adv just to be on the safe side;
Sicherheitsnadel f safety pin;
Sicherheitsvorkehrung f safety
precaution; **sicherlich** adv
certainly; (wahrscheinlich) probably
sichern vt to secure (gegen
against); (schützen) to protect;
(Daten) to back up; **Sicherung** f
(Sichern) securing; (Vorrichtung)
safety device; (an Waffen) safety
catch; (Elek) fuse; (Inform) backup;
die ~ ist durchgebrannt the fuse
has blown
Sicht (-) f sight; (Aussicht) view;
sichtbar adj visible; **sichtlich**
adj evident, obvious;
Sichtverhältnisse pl visibility
sing; **Sichtweite** f: **in/außer
~** within/out of sight
sie pron (3. Person sing) she; (3.
Person pl) they; (akk von sing) her;

(*akk von pl*) them; (*für eine Sache*) it;
da ist ~ ja there she is; **da sind ~ ja**
there they are; **ich kenne ~** (*Frau*) I
know her; (*mehrere Personen*) I
know them; **~ lag gerade noch
hier** (*meine Jacke, Uhr*) it was here
just a minute ago; **ich hab
~ gefunden** (*meine Jacke, Uhr*) I've
found it; **hast du meine
Brille/Hose gesehen? — ich kann
~ nirgends finden** have you seen
my glasses/trousers? — I can't
find them anywhere
Sie *pron* (*Höflichkeitsform, Nom und
Akk*) you
Sieb (*-(e)s, -e*) *nt* sieve; (*Teesieb*)
strainer
sieben *num* seven;
siebenhundert *num* seven
hundred; **siebenmal** *adv* seven
times; **siebte(r, s)** *adj* seventh;
siehe auch **dritte**; **Siebtel** (*-s, -*) *nt*
seventh; **siebzehn** *num*
seventeen; **siebzehnte(r, s)** *adj*
seventeenth; *siehe auch* **dritte**;
siebzig *num* seventy; **in den ~er
Jahren** in the seventies;
siebzigste(r, s) *adj*
seventieth
Siedlung (*-, -en*) *f* (*Wohngebiet*)
housing estate (*Brit*) (*o*
development (*US*))
Sieg (*-(e)s, -e*) *m* victory; **siegen**
vi to win; **Sieger(in)** (*-s, -*) *m(f)*
winner; **Siegerehrung** *f*
presentation ceremony
siehe *imper* see
siezen *vt* to address as "Sie"
Signal (*-s, -e*) *nt* signal
Silbe (*-, -n*) *f* syllable
Silber (*-s*) *nt* silver;
Silberhochzeit *f* silver wedding;
Silbermedaille *f* silver medal
Silikon (*-s, -e*) *nt* silicone
Silvester (*-s, -*) *nt*,
Silvesterabend *m* New Year's
Eve, Hogmanay (*Scot*)

⚬ **SILVESTER**
⚬
⚬ **Silvester** is the German name
⚬ for New Year's Eve. Although
⚬ not an official holiday, most
⚬ businesses close early and
⚬ shops shut at midday. Most
⚬ Germans celebrate in the
⚬ evening and at midnight they
⚬ let off fireworks and rockets;
⚬ the revelry usually lasts until the
⚬ early hours of the morning.

Simbabwe (*-s*) *nt* Zimbabwe
simpel *adj* simple
simultan *adj* simultaneous
simsen *vt, vi* (*fam*) to text
Sinfonie (*-, -n*) *f* symphony;
Sinfonieorchester *nt* symphony
orchestra
Singapur (*-s*) *nt* Singapore
singen (*sang, gesungen*) *vt, vi* to
sing; **richtig/falsch ~** to sing in
tune/out of tune
Single (*-, -s*) *f* (*CD*) single ▷ (*-s, -s*)
m (*Mensch*) single
Singular *m* singular
sinken (*sank, gesunken*) *vi* to sink;
(*Preise etc*) to fall, to go down
Sinn (*-(e)s, -e*) *m* (*Denken*) mind;
(*Wahrnehmung*) sense; (*Bedeutung*)
sense, meaning; **~ machen** to
make sense; **das hat keinen ~** it's
no use; **sinnlich** *adj* sensuous;
(*erotisch*) sensual; (*Wahrnehmung*)
sensory; **sinnlos** *adj* (*unsinnig*)
stupid; (*Verhalten*) senseless;
(*zwecklos*) pointless; (*bedeutungslos*)
meaningless; **sinnvoll** *adj*
meaningful; (*vernünftig*) sensible
Sirup (*-s, -e*) *m* syrup
Sitte (*-, -n*) *f* custom
Situation *f* situation
Sitz (*-es, -e*) *m* seat; **sitzen** (*saß,
gesessen*) *vi* to sit; (*Bemerkung,
Schlag*) to strike home; (*Gelerntes*)
to have sunk in; **der Rock sitzt**

gut the skirt is a good fit;
Sitzgelegenheit f place to sit
down; **Sitzplatz** m seat; **Sitzung**
f meeting
Sizilien (-s) nt Sicily
Skandal (-s, -e) m scandal
Skandinavien (-s) nt
Scandinavia
Skateboard (-s, -s) nt
skateboard
Skelett (-s, -e) nt skeleton
skeptisch adj sceptical
Ski (-s, -er) m ski; **~ laufen** (o
fahren) to ski; **Skianzug** m ski
suit; **Skibrille** f ski goggles pl;
Skifahren (-s) nt skiing; **Skigebiet**
(-s, -e) nt skiing area; **Skihose** f
skiing trousers pl; **Skikurs** m
skiing course; **Skilanglauf** m
cross-country skiing; **Skiläufer(in)**
m(f) skier; **Skilehrer(in)** m(f) ski
instructor; **Skilift** m ski-lift
Skinhead (-s, -s) m skinhead
Skipiste f ski run; **Skischanze**
(-, -n) f ski jump; **Skischuh** m
ski boot; **Skischule** f ski school;
Skispringen (-s, -n) nt ski
jumping; **Skistiefel** (-s, -) m ski
boot; **Skistock** m ski pole;
Skiträger m ski rack; **Skiurlaub**
m skiing holiday (Brit) (o vacation
(US))
Skizze (-, -n) f sketch
Skonto (-s, -s) m o nt discount
Skorpion (-s, -e) m (Zool)
scorpion; (Astr) Scorpio
Skulptur (-, -en) f sculpture
S-Kurve f double bend
Slalom (-s, -s) m slalom
Slip (-s, -s) m (pair of) briefs pl;
Slipeinlage f panty liner
Slowakei (-) f Slovakia;
slowakisch adj Slovakian;
Slowakische Republik Slovak
Republic; **Slowakisch** nt
Slovakian
Slowenien (-s) nt Slovenia;

slowenisch adj Slovenian;
Slowenisch nt Slovenian
Smiley (-s, -s) m smiley
Smog (-s) m smog; **Smogalarm**
m smog alert
Smoking (-s, -s) m dinner jacket
(Brit), tuxedo (US)
SMS nt abk = **Short Message**
Service ▷ f (Nachricht) text
message; **ich schicke dir eine ~** I'll
text you, I'll send you a text
(message)
Snowboard (-s, -s) nt snow-
board; **Snowboardfahren** (-s) nt
snowboarding;
Snowboardfahrer(in) m(f)
snowboarder

SCHLÜSSELWORT

SO adv **1** (so sehr) so; **so groß/schön**
etc so big/nice etc; **so groß/schön**
wie ... as big/nice as ...; **so viel**
(wie) as much as; **rede nicht so**
viel don't talk so much; **so weit**
sein to be ready; **so weit wie** o **als**
möglich as far as possible; **ich bin**
so weit zufrieden by and large I'm
quite satisfied; **so wenig (wie)** as
little (as); **das hat ihn so**
geärgert, dass ... that annoyed
him so much that ...; **so einer wie**
ich somebody like me; **na so was!**
well, well!
2 (auf diese Weise) like this; **mach**
es nicht so don't do it like that; **so**
oder so in one way or the other;
und so weiter and so on; **... oder**
so was ... or something like that;
das ist gut so that's fine
3 (fam) (umsonst) **ich habe es so**
bekommen I got it for nothing
▷ konj: **sodass** so that; **so wie es**
jetzt ist as things are at the
moment
▷ excl: **so?** really?; **so, das wär's**
so, that's it then

s. o. *abk = siehe oben* see above
sobald *conj* as soon as
Socke (-, -n) *f* sock
Sodbrennen (-s) *nt* heartburn
Sofa (-s, -s) *nt* sofa
sofern *conj* if, provided (that)
soff *imperf von* **saufen**
sofort *adv* immediately, at once;
  Sofortbildkamera *f* instant
  camera
Softeis *nt* soft ice-cream
Software (-, -s) *f* software
sog *imperf von* **saugen**
sogar *adv* even; **kalt, ~ sehr kalt**
  cold, in fact very cold
sogenannt *adj* so-called
Sohle (-, -n) *f* sole
Sohn (-(e)s, Söhne) *m* son
Soja (-, Sojen) *f* soya;
  Sojasprossen *pl* bean sprouts *pl*
solang(e) *conj* as long as
Solarium *nt* solarium
Solarzelle *f* solar cell
solche(r, s) *pron* such; **eine**
  ~ Frau, solch eine Frau such a
  woman, a woman like that;
  ~ Sachen things like that, such
  things; **ich habe ~ Kopfschmerz-**
  en I've got such a headache; **ich**
  habe ~n Hunger I'm so hungry
Soldat(in) (-en, -en) *m(f)* soldier
solidarisch *adj* showing
  solidarity; **sich ~ erklären mit** to
  declare one's solidarity with
solid(e) *adj* solid; (*Leben, Mensch*)
  respectable
Soll (-(s), -(s)) *nt* (*Fin*) debit;
  (*Arbeitsmenge*) quota, target

○ SCHLÜSSELWORT

sollen (*pt* **sollte**, *pp* **gesollt** *o* (*als*
  Hilfsverb) **sollen**) *Hilfsverb* 1 (*Pflicht,*
  Befehl) to be supposed to; **du**
  hättest nicht gehen sollen you
  shouldn't have gone, you oughtn't
  to have gone; **soll ich?** shall I?; **soll**
  ich dir helfen? shall I help you?;
  sag ihm, er soll warten tell him
  he's to wait; **was soll ich**
  machen? what should I do?
  2 (*Vermutung*) **sie soll verheiratet**
  sein she's said to be married; **was**
  soll das heißen? what's that
  supposed to mean?; **man sollte**
  glauben, dass ... you would think
  that ...; **sollte das passieren, ...** if
  that should happen ...
  ▷ *vt, vi:* **was soll das?** what's all
  this?; **das sollst du nicht** you
  shouldn't do that; **was soll's?**
  what the hell!

Solo (-s, -) *nt* solo
Sommer (-s, -) *m* summer;
  Sommerfahrplan *m* summer
  timetable; **Sommerferien** *pl*
  summer holidays *pl* (*Brit*) (*o*
  vacation *sing* (*US*)); **sommerlich**
  adj summery; (*Sommer-*) summer;
  Sommerreifen *m* normal tyre;
  Sommersprossen *pl* freckles *pl*;
  Sommerzeit *f* summertime;
  (*Uhrzeit*) daylight saving
  time
Sonderangebot *nt* special
  offer; **sonderbar** *adj* strange,
  odd; **Sondermarke** *f* special
  stamp; **Sondermaschine** *f*
  special plane; **Sondermüll** *m*
  hazardous waste
sondern *conj* but; **nicht nur ...,**
  ~ auch not only ..., but also
Sonderpreis *m* special price;
  Sonderschule *f* special school;
  Sonderzeichen *nt* (*Inform*)
  special character; **Sonderzug** *m*
  special train
Song (-s, -s) *m* song
Sonnabend *m* Saturday; *siehe*
  auch **Mittwoch**; **sonnabends** *adv*
  on Saturdays; **~ morgens** on
  Saturday mornings; *siehe auch*
  mittwochs

Sonne (-, -n) f sun; **sonnen** vr:
sich ~ to sunbathe;
Sonnenallergie f sun allergy;
Sonnenaufgang m sunrise;
Sonnenblume f sunflower;
Sonnenblumenkern m sunflower seed; **Sonnenbrand** m
sunburn; **Sonnenbrille** f
sunglasses pl, shades pl;
Sonnencreme f sun cream;
Sonnendach nt (an Haus)
awning; (Auto) sunroof; **Sonnen-
deck** nt sun deck; **Sonnenmilch** f
suntan lotion; **Sonnenöl** nt
suntan oil; **Sonnenschein** m
sunshine; **Sonnenschirm** m
parasol, sunshade; **Sonnenschutz-
creme** f sunscreen; **Sonnenstich**
m sunstroke; **Sonnenstudio** nt
solarium; **Sonnenuhr** f sundial;
Sonnenuntergang m sunset;
sonnig adj sunny
Sonntag m Sunday; siehe auch
Mittwoch; **sonntags** adv on
Sundays; siehe auch **mittwochs**
sonst adv, conj (außerdem) else;
(andernfalls) otherwise, (or) else;
(mit Pron, in Fragen) else;
(normalerweise) normally, usually;
~ noch etwas? anything else?;
~ nichts nothing else
sooft conj whenever
Sopran (-s, -e) m soprano
Sorge (-, -n) f worry; (Fürsorge)
care; **sich** (dat) **um jdn ~n machen**
to be worried about sb; **sorgen**
vi: **für jdn ~** to look after sb; **für
etw ~** to take care of sth, to see to
sth ▷ vr: **sich ~** to worry (um
about); **sorgfältig** adj careful
sortieren vt to sort (out)
Sortiment nt assortment
sosehr conj however much
Soße (-, -n) f sauce; (zu Braten)
gravy
Soundkarte f (Inform) sound
card

Souvenir (-s, -s) nt souvenir
soviel conj as far as
soweit conj as far as
sowie conj (wie auch) as well as;
(sobald) as soon as
sowohl conj: **~ ... als** (o **wie**) **auch**
both ... and
sozial adj social; **Sozialhilfe** f
income support (Brit), welfare
(aid) (US); **Sozialismus** m
socialism; **Sozialversicherung** f
social security; **Sozialwohnung**
f council flat (Brit),
state-subsidized apartment (US)
Soziologie f sociology
sozusagen adv so to speak
Spachtel (-s, -) m spatula
Spag(h)etti pl spaghetti sing
Spalte (-, -n) f crack; (Gletscher)
crevasse; (in Text) column
spalten vt to split ▷ vr: **sich ~** to
split
Spange (-, -n) f clasp;
(Haarspange) hair slide (Brit),
barrette (US)
Spanien (-s) nt Spain;
Spanier(in) (-s, -) m(f) Spaniard;
spanisch adj Spanish; **Spanisch**
nt Spanish
spann imperf von **spinnen**
spannen vt (straffen) to tighten;
(befestigen) to brace ▷ vi to be
tight
spannend adj exciting, gripping;
Spannung f tension; (Elek)
voltage; (fig) suspense
Sparbuch nt savings book;
(Konto) savings account; **sparen**
vt, vi to save
Spargel (-s, -) m asparagus;
Spargelsuppe f asparagus soup
Sparkasse f savings bank;
Sparkonto nt savings account
spärlich adj meagre; (Bekleidung)
scanty
sparsam adj economical;
Sparschwein nt piggy bank

Spaß (*-es, Späße*) *m* joke; (*Freude*) fun; **es macht mir ~** I enjoy it, it's (great) fun; **viel ~!** have fun

spät *adj, adv* late; **zu ~ kommen** to be late

Spaten (*-s, -*) *m* spade

später *adj, adv* later; **spätestens** *adv* at the latest; **Spätlese** *f* late vintage (wine); **Spätvorstellung** *f* late-night performance

Spatz (*-en, -en*) *m* sparrow

spazieren *vi* to stroll, to walk; **~ gehen** to go for a walk; **Spaziergang** *m* walk

Specht (*-(e)s, -e*) *m* woodpecker

Speck (*-(e)s, -e*) *m* bacon fat; (*durchwachsen*) bacon

Spedition *f* (*für Umzug*) removal firm

Speiche (*-, -n*) *f* spoke

Speichel (*-s*) *m* saliva

Speicher (*-s, -*) *m* storehouse; (*Dachboden*) attic; (*Inform*) memory; **speichern** *vt* (*Inform*) to store; (*sichern*) to save

Speise (*-, -n*) *f* food; (*Gericht*) dish; **Speisekarte** *f* menu; **Speiseröhre** *f* gullet, oesophagus; **Speisesaal** *m* dining hall; **Speisewagen** *m* dining car

Spende (*-, -n*) *f* donation; **spenden** *vt* to donate, to give

spendieren *vt*: **jdm etw ~** to treat sb to sth

Sperre (*-, -n*) *f* barrier; (*Verbot*) ban; **sperren** *vt* to block; (*Sport*) to suspend; (*verbieten*) to ban

Sperrgepäck *m* bulky luggage; **Sperrmüll** *m* bulky refuse; **Sperrstunde** *f* closing time; **Sperrung** *f* closing

Spesen *pl* expenses *pl*

spezialisieren *vr*: **sich ~** to specialize (*auf +akk* in); **Spezialist(in)** *m(f)* specialist; **Spezialität** *f* speciality (*Brit*), specialty (*US*); **speziell** *adj* special ▷ *adv* especially

Spiegel (*-s, -*) *m* mirror; **Spiegelei** *nt* fried egg (sunny-side up (*US*)); **spiegelglatt** *adj* very slippery; **Spiegelreflexkamera** *f* reflex camera

Spiel (*-(e)s, -e*) *nt* game; (*Tätigkeit*) play(ing); (*Karten*) pack, deck; (*Tech*) (free) play; **Spielautomat** *m* (*ohne Geldgewinn*) gaming machine; (*mit Geldgewinn*) slot machine; **spielen** *vt, vi* to play; (*um Geld*) to gamble; (*Theat*) to perform, to act; **Klavier ~** to play the piano; **spielend** *adv* easily; **Spieler(in)** (*-s, -*) *m(f)* player; (*um Geld*) gambler; **Spielfeld** *nt* (*für Fußball, Hockey*) field; (*für Basketball*) court; **Spielfilm** *m* feature film; **Spielkasino** *nt* casino; **Spielplatz** *m* playground; **Spielraum** *m* room to manoeuvre; **Spielregel** *f* rule; **sich an die ~n halten** to stick to the rules; **Spielsachen** *pl* toys *pl*; **Spielzeug** *nt* toys *pl*; (*einzelnes*) toy

Spieß (*-es, -e*) *m* spear; (*Bratspieß*) spit; **Spießer(in)** (*-s, -*) *m(f)* square, stuffy type; **spießig** *adj* square, uncool

Spikes *pl* (*Sport*) spikes *pl*; (*Auto*) studs *pl*

Spinat (*-(e)s, -e*) *m* spinach

Spinne (*-, -n*) *f* spider; **spinnen** (*spann, gesponnen*) *vt, vi* to spin; (*fam: Unsinn reden*) to talk rubbish; (*verrückt sein*) to be crazy; **du spinnst!** you must be mad; **Spinnwebe** (*-, -n*) *f* cobweb

Spion(in) (*-s, -e*) *m(f)* spy; **spionieren** *vi* to spy; (*fig*) to snoop around

Spirale (*-, -n*) *f* spiral; (*Med*) coil

Spirituosen *pl* spirits *pl*, liquor *sing* (*US*)

Spiritus (-, -se) m spirit
spitz adj (Nase, Kinn) pointed; (Bleistift, Messer) sharp; (Winkel) acute; **Spitze** (-, -n) f point; (von Finger, Nase) tip; (Bemerkung) taunt, dig; (erster Platz) lead; (Gewebe) lace; **Spitzer** (-s, -) m pencil sharpener; **Spitzname** m nickname
Spliss (-) m split ends pl
sponsern vt to sponsor; **Sponsor(in)** (-s, -en) m(f) sponsor
spontan adj spontaneous
Sport (-(e)s, -e) m sport; **~ treiben** to do sport; **Sportanlage** f sports grounds pl; **Sportart** f sport; **Sportbekleidung** f sportswear; **Sportgeschäft** nt sports shop; **Sporthalle** f gymnasium, gym; **Sportlehrer(in)** (-s, -) m(f) sports instructor; (Schule) PE teacher; **Sportler(in)** (-s, -) m(f) sportsman/-woman; **sportlich** adj sporting; (Mensch) sporty; **Sportplatz** m playing field; **Sporttauchen** nt (skin-)diving; (mit Gerät) scuba-diving; **Sportverein** m sports club; **Sportwagen** m sports car
sprach imperf von **sprechen**
Sprache (-, -n) f language; (Sprechen) speech; **Sprachenschule** f language school; **Sprachführer** m phrasebook; **Sprachkenntnisse** pl knowledge sing of languages; **gute englische ~ haben** to have a good knowledge of English; **Sprachkurs** m language course; **Sprachunterricht** m language teaching
sprang imperf von **springen**
Spray (-s, -s) m o nt spray
Sprechanlage f intercom; **sprechen** (sprach, gesprochen) vt, vi

to speak (jdn, mit jdm to sb); (sich unterhalten) to talk (mit to, über, von about); **~ Sie Deutsch?** do you speak German?; **kann ich bitte mit David ~?** (am Telefon) can I speak to David, please?; **Sprecher(in)** m(f) speaker; (Ansager) announcer; **Sprechstunde** f consultation; (Arzt) surgery hours pl; (Anwalt etc) office hours pl; **Sprechzimmer** nt consulting room
Sprengstoff m explosive
Sprichwort nt proverb
Springbrunnen m fountain
springen (sprang, gesprungen) vi to jump; (Glas) to crack; (mit Kopfsprung) to dive
Sprit (-(e)s, -e) m (fam: Benzin) petrol (Brit), gas (US)
Spritze (-, -n) f (Gegenstand) syringe; (Injektion) injection; (an Schlauch) nozzle; **spritzen** vt to spray; (Med) to inject ▷ vi to splash; (Med) to give injections
Spruch (-(e)s, Sprüche) m saying
Sprudel (-s, -) m sparkling mineral water; (süßer) fizzy drink (Brit), soda (US); **sprudeln** vi to bubble
Sprühdose f aerosol (can); **sprühen** vt, vi to spray; (fig) to sparkle; **Sprühregen** m drizzle
Sprung (-(e)s, Sprünge) m jump; (Riss) crack; **Sprungbrett** nt springboard; **Sprungschanze** f ski jump; **Sprungturm** m diving platforms pl
Spucke (-) f spit; **spucken** vt, vi to spit; (fam: sich erbrechen) to vomit; **Spucktüte** f sick bag
spuken vi (Geist) to walk; **hier spukt es** this place is haunted
Spülbecken nt sink
Spule (-, -n) f spool; (Elek) coil
Spüle (-, -n) f sink; **spülen** vt, vi to rinse; (Geschirr) to wash up;

(Toilette) to flush; **Spülmaschine** *f* dishwasher; **Spülmittel** *nt* washing-up liquid *(Brit)*, dishwashing liquid *(US)*; **Spültuch** *nt* dishcloth; **Spülung** *f* *(von WC)* flush

Spur (-, -en) *f* trace; *(Fußspur, Radspur)* track; *(Fährte)* trail; *(Fahrspur)* lane; **die ~ wechseln** to change lanes *pl*

spüren *vt* to feel; *(merken)* to notice; **Spürhund** *m* sniffer dog

Squash (-) *nt* squash; **Squashschläger** *m* squash racket

Sri Lanka (-s) *nt* Sri Lanka

Staat (-(e)s, -en) *m* state; **staatlich** *adj* state(-); *(vom Staat betrieben)* state-run; **Staatsangehörigkeit** *f* nationality; **Staatsanwalt** *m*, **-anwältin** *f* prosecuting counsel *(Brit)*, district attorney *(US)*; **Staatsbürger(in)** *m(f)* citizen; **Staatsbürgerschaft** *f* national-ity; **doppelte ~** dual nationality; **Staatsexamen** *nt* final exam taken by trainee teachers, medical and law students

Stab (-(e)s, Stäbe) *m* rod; *(Gitter)* bar; **Stäbchen** *nt* *(Essstäbchen)* chopstick; **Stabhochsprung** *m* pole vault

stabil *adj* stable; *(Möbel)* sturdy

stach *imperf von* **stechen**

Stachel (-s, -n) *m* spike; *(von Tier)* spine; *(von Insekten)* sting; **Stachelbeere** *f* gooseberry; **Stacheldraht** *m* barbed wire; **stachelig** *adj* prickly

Stadion (-s, Stadien) *nt* stadium

Stadt (-, Städte) *f* town; *(groß)* city; **in der ~** in town; **Stadtautobahn** *f* urban motorway *(Brit)* (o expressway *(US)*); **Stadtbummel** (-s, -) *m*: **einen ~ machen** to go round town; **Stadtführer** *m* *(Heft)* city

guide; **Stadtführung** *f* city sightseeing tour; **Stadthalle** *f* municipal hall; **städtisch** *adj* municipal; **Stadtmauer** *f* city wall(s); **Stadtmitte** *f* town/city centre, downtown *(US)*; **Stadtplan** *m* (street) map; **Stadtrand** *m* outskirts *pl*; **Stadtrundfahrt** *f* city tour; **Stadtteil** *m*, **Stadtviertel** *nt* district, part of town; **Stadtzentrum** *nt* town/city centre, downtown *(US)*

stahl *imperf von* **stehlen**

Stahl (-(e)s, Stähle) *m* steel

Stall (-(e)s, Ställe) *m* stable; *(Kaninchen)* hutch; *(Schweine)* pigsty; *(Hühner)* henhouse

Stamm (-(e)s, Stämme) *m* *(Baum)* trunk; *(von Menschen)* tribe; **stammen** *vi*: **~ aus** to come from; **Stammgast** *m* regular (guest); **Stammkunde** *m*, **Stammkundin** *f* regular (customer); **Stammtisch** *m* table reserved for regulars

stampfen *vt, vi* to stamp; *(mit Werkzeug)* to pound; *(stapfen)* to tramp

stand *imperf von* **stehen**

Stand (-(e)s, Stände) *m* *(Wasser, Benzin)* level; *(Stehen)* standing position; *(Zustand)* state; *(Spielstand)* score; *(auf Messe etc)* stand; *(Klasse)* class; **im ~e sein** to be in a position; *(fähig)* to be able

Stand-by-Betrieb *m* stand-by; **Stand-by-Ticket** *nt* stand-by ticket

Ständer (-s, -) *m* *(Gestell)* stand; *(fam: Erektion)* hard-on

Standesamt *nt* registry office

ständig *adj* permanent; *(ununterbrochen)* constant, continual

Standlicht *nt* sidelights *pl* *(Brit)*, parking lights *pl* *(US)*; **Standort** *m* position; **Standpunkt** *m*

standpoint; **Standspur** f (Auto)
hard shoulder (Brit), shoulder
(US)

Stange (-, -n) f stick; (Stab) pole;
(Metall) bar; (Zigaretten) carton;
Stangenbohne f runner (Brit) (o
string (US)) bean; **Stangenbrot**
nt French stick; **Stangensellerie**
m celery

stank imperf von **stinken**

Stapel (-s, -) m pile

Star (-(e)s, -e) m (Vogel) starling;
(Med) cataract ▷ (-s, -s) m (in Film
etc) star

starb imperf von **sterben**

stark adj strong; (heftig, groß)
heavy; (Maßangabe) thick; **Stärke**
(-, -n) f strength; (Dicke)
thickness; (Wäschestärke,
Speisestärke) starch; **stärken** vt
to strengthen; (Wäsche) to starch;
Starkstrom m high-voltage
current; **Stärkung** f
strengthening; (Essen)
refreshment

starr adj stiff; (unnachgiebig) rigid;
(Blick) staring

starren vi to stare

Start (-(e)s, -e) m start; (Aviat)
takeoff; **Startautomatik** f
automatic choke; **Startbahn** f
runway; **starten** vt, vi to start;
(Aviat) to take off; **Starthilfekabel**
nt jump leads pl (Brit), jumper
cables pl (US); **Startmenü** nt
(Inform) start menu

Station f (Haltestelle) stop;
(Bahnhof) station; (im Krankenhaus)
ward; **stationär** adj stationary;
~e Behandlung in-patient
treatment; **jdn ~ behandeln** to
treat sb as an in-patient

Statistik f statistics pl

Stativ nt tripod

statt conj, prep +gen o dat instead
of; **~ zu arbeiten** instead of
working

statt|finden irr vi to take place

Statue (-, -n) f statue

Statusleiste f, **Statuszeile** f
(Inform) status bar

Stau (-(e)s, -e) m (im Verkehr)
(traffic) jam; **im ~ stehen** to be
stuck in a traffic jam

Staub (-(e)s) m dust; **~ wischen**
to dust; **staubig** adj dusty;
staubsaugen vt, vi to vacuum, to
hoover (Brit); **Staubsauger** m
vacuum cleaner, Hoover® (Brit);
Staubtuch nt duster

Staudamm m dam

staunen vi to be astonished (über
+akk at)

Stausee m reservoir; **Stauung** f
(von Wasser) damming-up; (von
Blut, Verkehr) congestion;
Stauwarnung f traffic report

Std. abk = **Stunde** h

Steak (-s, -s) nt steak

stechen (stach, gestochen) vt, vi
(mit Nadel etc) to prick; (mit Messer)
to stab; (mit Finger) to poke; (Biene)
to sting; (Mücke) to bite; (Sonne) to
burn; (Kartenspiel) to trump;
Stechen (-s, -) nt sharp pain,
stabbing pain; **Stechmücke** f
mosquito

Steckdose f socket; **stecken** vt
to put; (Nadel) to stick; (beim
Nähen) to pin ▷ vi (festsitzen) to be
stuck; (Nadeln) to be (sticking); **der
Schlüssel steckt** the key is in the
door; **Stecker** (-s, -) m plug;
Steckrübe f swede (Brit),
rutabaga (US)

Steg (-s, -e) m bridge

stehen (stand, gestanden) vi to
stand (zu by); (sich befinden) to be;
(stillstehen) to have stopped; **was
steht im Brief?** what does it say in
the letter?; **jdm** (gut) **~** to suit sb;
~ bleiben (Uhr) to stop; **~ lassen**
to leave ▷ vi impers: **wie steht's?**
(Sport) what's the score?

stehlen (*stahl, gestohlen*) *vt* to steal

Stehplatz *m* (*im Konzert etc*) standing ticket

Steiermark (-) *f* Styria

steif *adj* stiff

steigen (*stieg, gestiegen*) *vi* (*Preise, Temperatur*) to rise; (*klettern*) to climb; **~ in/auf** (+*akk*) to get in/on

steigern *vt* to increase ▷ *vr*: **sich ~** to increase

Steigung *f* incline, gradient

steil *adj* steep; **Steilhang** *m* steep slope; **Steilküste** *f* steep coast

Stein (-(*e*)*s*, -*e*) *m* stone; **Steinbock** *m* (*Zool*) ibex; (*Astr*) Capricorn; **steinig** *adj* stony; **Steinschlag** *m* falling rocks *pl*

Stelle (-, -*n*) *f* place, spot; (*Arbeit*) post, job; (*Amt*) office; **ich an deiner ~** if I were you; **auf der ~** straightaway; **stellen** *vt* to put; (*Uhr etc*) to set (*auf* +*akk* to); (*zur Verfügung stellen*) to provide ▷ *vr*: **sich ~** (*bei Polizei*) to give oneself up; **sich schlafend ~** to pretend to be asleep; **Stellenangebot** *nt* job offer, vacancy; **stellenweise** *adv* in places; **Stellenwert** *m* (*fig*) status; **einen hohen ~ haben** to play an important role; **Stellplatz** *m* parking space; **Stellung** *f* position; **zu etw ~ nehmen** to comment on sth; **Stellvertreter(in)** *m(f)* representative; (*amtlich*) deputy; (*von Arzt*) locum (*Brit*), locum tenens (*US*)

Stempel (-*s*, -) *m* stamp; **stempeln** *vt* to stamp; (*Briefmarke*) to cancel

sterben (*starb, gestorben*) *vi* to die

Stereoanlage *f* stereo (system)

steril *adj* sterile; **sterilisieren** *vt* to sterilize

Stern (-(*e*)*s*, -*e*) *m* star; **ein Hotel mit vier ~en** a four-star hotel; **Sternbild** *nt* constellation; (*Sternzeichen*) star sign, sign of the zodiac; **Sternfrucht** *f* star fruit; **Sternschnuppe** (-, -*n*) *f* shooting star; **Sternwarte** (-*e*, -*n*) *f* observatory; **Sternzeichen** *nt* star sign, sign of the zodiac; **welches ~ bist du?** what's your star sign?

stets *adv* always

Steuer (-*s*, -) *nt* (*Auto*) steering wheel ▷ (-, -*n*) *f* tax; **Steuerberater(in)** *m(f)* tax adviser; **Steuerbord** *nt* starboard; **Steuererklärung** *f* tax declaration; **steuerfrei** *adj* tax-free; (*Waren*) duty-free; **Steuerknüppel** *m* control column; (*Aviat, Inform*) joystick; **steuern** *vt, vi* to steer; (*Flugzeug*) to pilot; (*Entwicklung, Tonstärke*) (*Inform*) to control; **steuerpflichtig** *adj* taxable; **Steuerung** *f* (*Auto*) steering; (*Vorrichtung*) controls *pl*; (*Aviat*) piloting; (*fig*) control; **Steuerungstaste** *f* (*Inform*) control key

Stich (-(*e*)*s*, -*e*) *m* (*von Insekt*) sting; (*von Mücke*) bite; (*durch Messer*) stab; (*beim Nähen*) stitch; (*Färbung*) tinge; (*Kartenspiel*) trick; (*Kunst*) engraving

sticken *vt, vi* to embroider

Sticker (-*s*, -) *m* sticker

Stickerei *f* embroidery

stickig *adj* stuffy, close

Stiefbruder *m* stepbrother

Stiefel (-*s*, -) *m* boot

Stiefmutter *f* stepmother

Stiefmütterchen *nt* pansy

Stiefschwester *f* stepsister; **Stiefsohn** *m* stepson; **Stieftochter** *f* stepdaughter; **Stiefvater** *m* stepfather

stieg *imperf von* **steigen**

Stiege (-, -n) f steps pl
Stiel (-(e)s, -e) m handle; (Bot) stalk; **ein Eis am ~** an ice lolly (Brit), a Popsicle® (US)
Stier (-(e)s, -e) m (Zool) bull; (Astr) Taurus; **Stierkampf** m bullfight
stieß imperf von **stoßen**
Stift (-(e)s, -e) m (aus Holz) peg; (Nagel) tack; (zum Schreiben) pen; (Farbstift) crayon; (Bleistift) pencil
Stil (-s, -e) m style
still adj quiet; (unbewegt) still
stillen vt (Säugling) to breast-feed
still|halten irr vi to keep still;
still|stehen irr vi to stand still
Stimme (-, -n) f voice; (bei Wahl) vote
stimmen vi to be right; **stimmt!** that's right; **hier stimmt was nicht** there's something wrong here; **stimmt so!** (beim Bezahlen) keep the change
Stimmung f mood; (Atmosphäre) atmosphere
Stinkefinger m (fam) **jdm den ~ zeigen** to give sb the finger (o bird (US))
stinken (stank, gestunken) vi to stink (nach of)
Stipendium nt scholarship; (als Unterstützung) grant
Stirn (-, -en) f forehead; **Stirnhöhle** f sinus
Stock (-(e)s, Stöcke) m stick; (Bot) stock ▷ m (Stockwerke) floor, storey; **Stockbett** nt bunk bed; **Stöckelschuhe** pl high-heels; **Stockwerk** nt floor; **im ersten ~** on the first floor (Brit), on the second floor (US)
Stoff (-(e)s, -e) m (Gewebe) material; (Materie) matter; (von Buch etc) subject (matter); (fam: Rauschgift) stuff
stöhnen vi to groan (vor with)
stolpern vi to stumble, to trip
stolz adj proud

stopp interj hold it; (Moment mal!) hang on a minute; **stoppen** vt, vi to stop; (mit Uhr) to time; **Stoppschild** nt stop sign; **Stoppuhr** f stopwatch
Stöpsel (-s, -) m plug; (für Flaschen) stopper
Storch (-(e)s, Störche) m stork
stören vt to disturb; (behindern) to interfere with; **darf ich dich kurz ~?** can I trouble you for a minute?; **stört es dich, wenn ...?** do you mind if ...?
stornieren vt to cancel; **Stornogebühr** f cancellation fee
Störung f disturbance; (in der Leitung) fault
Stoß (-es, Stöße) m (Schub) push; (Schlag) blow; (mit Fuß) kick; (Haufen) pile; **Stoßdämpfer** (-s, -) m shock absorber
stoßen (stieß, gestoßen) vt (mit Druck) to shove, to push; (mit Schlag) to knock; (mit Fuß) to kick; (anstoßen) to bump; (zerkleinern) to pulverize ▷ vr: **sich ~** to bang oneself; **sich ~ an** (+dat) (fig) to take exception to
Stoßstange f (Auto) bumper
stottern vt, vi to stutter
Str. abk von **Straße** St, Rd
Strafe (-, -n) f punishment; (Sport) penalty; (Gefängnisstrafe) sentence; (Geldstrafe) fine; **strafen** vt to punish; **Straftat** f (criminal) offence; **Strafzettel** m ticket
Strahl (-s, -en) m ray, beam; (Wasser) jet; **strahlen** vi to radiate; (fig) to beam
Strähne (-, -n) f strand; (weiß, gefärbt) streak
Strand (-(e)s, Strände) m beach; **am ~** on the beach; **Strandcafé** nt beach café; **Strandkorb** m wicker beach chair with a hood; **Strandpromenade** f promenade

strapazieren vt (*Material*) to be hard on; (*Mensch, Kräfte*) to be a strain on

Straße (-, -n) f road; (*in der Stadt*) street; **Straßenarbeiten** pl roadworks pl (*Brit*), road repairs pl (*US*); **Straßenbahn** f tram (*Brit*), streetcar (*US*); **Straßencafé** nt pavement café (*Brit*), sidewalk café (*US*); **Straßenfest** nt street party; **Straßenglätte** f slippery roads pl; **Straßenkarte** f road map; **Straßenrand** m: **am ~** at the roadside; **Straßenschild** nt street sign; **Straßensperre** f roadblock; **Straßenverhältnisse** pl road conditions pl

Strategie (-, -n) f strategy

Strauch (-(e)s, Sträucher) m bush, shrub; **Strauchtomate** f vine-ripened tomato

Strauß (-es, Sträuße) m bunch; (*als Geschenk*) bouquet ▷ m (*Strauße*) (*Vogel*) ostrich

Strecke (-, -n) f route; (*Entfernung*) distance; (*Eisenb*) line

strecken vt to stretch ▷ vr: **sich ~** to stretch

streckenweise adv (*teilweise*) in parts; (*zeitweise*) at times

Streich (-(e)s, -e) m trick, prank

streicheln vt to stroke

streichen (strich, gestrichen) vt (*anmalen*) to paint; (*berühren*) to stroke; (*auftragen*) to spread; (*durchstreichen*) to delete; (*nicht genehmigen*) to cancel

Streichholz nt match; **Streichholzschachtel** f matchbox; **Streichkäse** m cheese spread

Streifen (-s, -) m (*Linie*) stripe; (*Stück*) strip; (*Film*) film

Streifenwagen m patrol car

Streik (-(e)s, -s) m strike; **streiken** vi to be on strike

Streit (-(e)s, -e) m argument (*um, wegen* about, over); **streiten** (stritt, gestritten) vi to argue (*um, wegen* about, over) ▷ vr: **sich ~** to argue (*um, wegen* about, over)

streng adj (*Blick*) severe; (*Lehrer*) strict; (*Geruch*) sharp

Stress (-es) m stress; **stressen** vt to stress (out); **stressig** adj (*fam*) stressful

Stretching (-s) nt (*Sport*) stretching exercises pl

streuen vt to scatter; **die Straßen ~** to grit the roads; (*mit Salz*) to put salt down on the roads; **Streufahrzeug** nt gritter lorry (*Brit*), salt truck (*US*)

strich imperf von **streichen**

Strich (-(e)s, -e) m (*Linie*) line; **Stricher** m (*fam: Strichjunge*) rent boy (*Brit*), boy prostitute; **Strichkode** (-s, -s) m bar code; **Stricherin** f (*fam: Strichmädchen*) hooker; **Strichpunkt** m semicolon

Strick (-(e)s, -e) m rope

stricken vt, vi to knit; **Strickjacke** f cardigan; **Stricknadel** f knitting needle

String (-s, -s) m, **Stringtanga** m G-string

Stripper(in) m(f) stripper; **Striptease** (-) m striptease

stritt imperf von **streiten**

Stroh (-(e)s) nt straw; **Strohdach** nt thatched roof; **Strohhalm** m (*drinking*) straw

Strom (-(e)s, Ströme) m river; (*fig*) stream; (*Elek*) current; **Stromanschluss** m connection; **Stromausfall** m power failure

strömen vi to stream, to pour; **Strömung** f current

Stromverbrauch m power consumption; **Stromzähler** m electricity meter

Strophe (-, -n) f verse

Strudel (-s, -) m (in Fluss) whirlpool; (Gebäck) strudel

Struktur f structure; (von Material) texture

Strumpf (-(e)s, Strümpfe) m (Damenstrumpf) stocking; (Socke) sock; **Strumpfhose** f (pair of) tights pl (Brit), pantyhose (US)

Stück (-(e)s, -e) nt piece; (von Zucker) lump; (etwas) bit; (Zucker) lump; (Theat) play; **ein ~ Käse** a piece of cheese

Student(in) m(f) student; **Studentenausweis** m student card; **Studentenwohnheim** nt hall of residence (Brit), dormitory (US); **Studienabschluss** m qualification (at the end of a course of higher education); **Studienfahrt** f study trip; **Studienplatz** m university/college place; **studieren** vt, vi to study; **Studium** nt studies pl; **während seines ~s** while he is/was studying

Stufe (-, -n) f step; (Entwicklungsstufe) stage

Stuhl (-(e)s, Stühle) m chair

stumm adj silent; (Med) dumb

stumpf adj blunt; (teilnahmslos, glanzlos) dull; **stumpfsinnig** adj dull

Stunde (-, -n) f hour; (Unterricht) lesson; **eine halbe ~** half an hour; **Stundenkilometer** m: **80 ~** 80 kilometres an hour; **stundenlang** adv for hours; **Stundenlohn** m hourly wage; **Stundenplan** m timetable; **stündlich** adj hourly

Stuntman (-s, Stuntmen) m stuntman; **Stuntwoman** (-, Stuntwomen) f stuntwoman

stur adj stubborn; (stärker) pigheaded

Sturm (-(e)s, Stürme) m storm; **stürmen** vi (Wind) to blow hard; (rennen) to storm; **Stürmer(in)** m(f) striker, forward; **Sturmflut** f storm tide; **stürmisch** adj stormy; (fig) tempestuous; (Zeit) turbulent; (Liebhaber) passionate; (Beifall, Begrüßung) tumultuous; **Sturmwarnung** f gale warning

Sturz (-es, Stürze) m fall; (Pol) overthrow; **stürzen** vt (werfen) to hurl; (Pol) to overthrow; (umkehren) to overturn ▷ vi to fall; (rennen) to dash; **Sturzhelm** m crash helmet

Stute (-, -n) f mare

Stütze (-, -n) f support; (Hilfe) help; (fam: Arbeitslosenunterstützung) dole (Brit), welfare (US)

stützen vt to support; (Ellbogen) to prop

stutzig adj perplexed, puzzled; (misstrauisch) suspicious

Styropor® (-s) nt polystyrene (Brit), styrofoam (US)

subjektiv adj subjective

Substanz (-, -en) f substance

subtrahieren vt to subtract

Subvention f subsidy; **subventionieren** vt to subsidize

Suche f search (nach for); **auf der ~ nach etw sein** to be looking for sth; **suchen** vt to look for; (Inform) to search ▷ vi to look, to search (nach for); **Suchmaschine** f (Inform) search engine

Sucht (-, Süchte) f mania; (Med) addiction; **süchtig** adj addicted; **Süchtige(r)** mf addict

Süd south; **Südafrika** nt South Africa; **Südamerika** nt South America; **Süddeutschland** nt Southern Germany; **Süden** (-s) m south; **im ~ Deutschlands** in the south of Germany; **Südeuropa** nt Southern Europe; **Südkorea** (-s) nt South Korea; **südlich** adj southern; (Kurs, Richtung) southerly; **Verkehr in ~er**

Richtung southbound traffic; **Südost(en)** m southeast; **Südpol** m South Pole; **Südstaaten** pl (der USA) the Southern States pl, the South sing; **südwärts** adv south, southwards; **Südwest(en)** m southwest; **Südwind** m south wind

Sülze (-, -n) f jellied meat

Summe (-, -n) f sum; (Gesamtsumme) total

summen vi, vt to hum; (Insekt) to buzz

Sumpf (-(e)s, Sümpfe) m marsh; (subtropischer) swamp; **sumpfig** adj marshy

Sünde (-, -n) f sin

super adj (fam) super, great; **Super** (-s) nt (Benzin) four star (petrol) (Brit), premium (US); **Supermarkt** m supermarket

Suppe (-, -n) f soup; **Suppengrün** nt bunch of herbs and vegetables for flavouring soup; **Suppenlöffel** m soup spoon; **Suppenschüssel** f soup tureen; **Suppentasse** f soup cup; **Suppenteller** m soup plate; **Suppenwürfel** m stock cube

Surfbrett nt surfboard; **surfen** vi to surf; **im Internet ~** to surf the Internet; **Surfer(in)** (-s, -) m(f) surfer

Surrealismus m surrealism

Sushi (-s, -s) nt sushi

süß adj sweet; **süßen** vt to sweeten; **Süßigkeit** f (Bonbon etc) sweet (Brit), candy (US); **Süßkartoffel** f sweet potato (Brit), yam (US); **süßsauer** adj sweet-and-sour; **Süßspeise** f dessert; **Süßstoff** m sweetener; **Süßwasser** nt fresh water

Sweatshirt (-s, -s) nt sweatshirt

Swimmingpool (-s, -s) m (swimming) pool

Sylvester nt siehe **Silvester**

Symbol (-s, -e) nt symbol; **Symbolleiste** f (Inform) toolbar

Symmetrie (-, -n) f symmetry; **symmetrisch** adj symmetrical

sympathisch adj nice; **jdn ~ finden** to like sb

Symphonie (-, -n) f symphony

Symptom (-s, -e) nt symptom (für of)

Synagoge (-, -n) f synagogue

synchronisiert adj (Film) dubbed; **Synchronstimme** f dubbing voice

Synthetik (-, -en) f synthetic (fibre); **synthetisch** adj synthetic

Syrien (-s) nt Syria

System (-s, -e) nt system; **systematisch** adj systematic; **Systemsteuerung** f (Inform) control panel

Szene (-, -n) f scene

t

Tabak (*-s, -e*) *m* tobacco;
  Tabakladen *m* tobacconist's
Tabelle *f* table
Tablett (*-s, -s*) *nt* tray
Tablette *f* tablet, pill
Tabulator *m* tabulator, tab
Tacho(meter) (*-s, -*) *m* (*Auto*)
  speedometer
Tafel (*-, -n*) *f* (*a. Math*) table;
  (*Anschlagtafel*) board; (*Wandtafel*)
  blackboard; (*Schiefer~*) slate;
  (*Gedenktafel*) plaque; **eine
  ~ Schokolade** a bar of chocolate;
  Tafelwasser *nt* table water;
  Tafelwein *m* table wine
Tag (*-(e)s, -e*) *m* day; (*Tageslicht*)
  daylight; **guten ~!** good
  morning/afternoon; **am ~** during
  the day; **sie hat ihre ~e** she's got
  her period; **eines ~es** one day;
  ~ der Arbeit Labour Day;
  Tagebuch *nt* diary; **tagelang**
  adj for days (on end);

Tagesanbruch *m* daybreak;
Tagesausflug *m* day trip;
Tagescreme *f* day cream;
Tagesdecke *f* bedspread;
Tagesgericht *nt* dish of the day;
Tageskarte *f* (*Fahrkarte*) day
ticket; **die ~** (*Speisekarte*) today's
menu; **Tageslicht** *nt* daylight;
Tagesmutter *f* child minder;
Tagesordnung *f* agenda;
Tagestour *f* day trip;
Tageszeitung *f* daily newspaper;
täglich *adj, adv* daily; **tags(über)**
adv during the day; **Tagung** *f*
conference
Tai Chi (*-*) *nt* tai chi
Taille (*-, -n*) *f* waist
Taiwan (*-s*) *nt* Taiwan
Takt (*-(e)s, -e*) *m* (*Taktgefühl*) tact;
  (*Mus*) time
Taktik (*-, -en*) *f* tactics *pl*
taktlos *adj* tactless; **taktvoll** *adj*
  tactful
Tal (*-(e)s, Täler*) *nt* valley
Talent (*-(e)s, -e*) *nt* talent;
  talentiert *adj* talented
Talkmaster(in) (*-s, -*) *m(f)* talk-show
  host; **Talkshow** (*-, -s*) *f* talkshow
Tampon (*-s, -s*) *m* tampon
Tandem (*-s, -s*) *nt* tandem
Tang (*-s, -e*) *m* seaweed
Tanga (*-s, -s*) *m* thong
Tank (*-s, -s*) *m* tank;
  Tankanzeige *f* fuel gauge;
  Tankdeckel *m* fuel cap; **tanken** *vi*
  to get some petrol (*Brit*) (*o* gas
  (*US*)); (*Aviat*) to refuel; **Tanker**
  (*-s, -*) *m* (oil) tanker; **Tankstelle** *f*
  petrol station (*Brit*), gas station
  (*US*); **Tankwart(in)** (*-s, -e*) *m(f)*
  petrol pump attendant (*Brit*), gas
  station attendant (*US*)
Tanne (*-, -n*) *f* fir; **Tannenzapfen**
  m fir cone
Tansania (*-s*) *nt* Tanzania
Tante (*-, -n*) *f* aunt;
  Tante-Emma-Laden *m* corner

shop (Brit), grocery store (US)

Tanz (-es, Tänze) m dance; **tanzen** vt, vi to dance; **Tänzer(in)** m(f) dancer; **Tanzfläche** f dance floor; **Tanzkurs** m dancing course; **Tanzlehrer(in)** m(f) dancing instructor; **Tanzstunde** f dancing lesson

Tapete (-, -n) f wallpaper; **tapezieren** vt, vi to wallpaper

Tarantel (-, -n) f tarantula

Tarif (-s, -e) m tariff, (scale of) fares/charges pl

Tasche (-, -n) f bag; (Hosentasche) pocket; (Handtasche) bag (Brit), purse (US)

Taschen- in zW pocket; **Taschenbuch** nt paperback; **Taschendieb(in)** m(f) pickpocket; **Taschengeld** nt pocket money; **Taschenlampe** f torch (Brit), flashlight (US); **Taschenmesser** nt penknife; **Taschenrechner** m pocket calculator; **Taschentuch** nt handkerchief

Tasse (-, -n) f cup; **eine ~ Kaffee** a cup of coffee

Tastatur f keyboard; **Taste** (-, -n) f button; (von Klavier, Computer) key; **Tastenkombination** f (Inform) shortcut

tat imperf von **tun**

Tat (-, -en) f action

Tatar (-s, -s) nt raw minced beef

Täter(in) (-s, -) m(f) culprit

tätig adj active; **in einer Firma ~ sein** to work for a firm; **Tätigkeit** f activity; (Beruf) occupation

tätowieren vt to tattoo; **Tätowierung** f tattoo (an +dat on)

Tatsache f fact; **tatsächlich** adj actual ▷ adv really

Tau (-(e)s, -e) nt (Seil) rope ▷ (-(e)s) m dew

taub adj deaf; (Füße etc) numb (vor Kälte with cold)

Taube (-, -n) f pigeon; (Turtel~, fig: Friedenssymbol) dove

taubstumm adj deaf-and-dumb; **Taubstumme(r)** mf deaf-mute

tauchen vt to dip ▷ vi to dive; (Naut) to submerge; **Tauchen** (-s) nt diving; **Taucher(in)** (-s, -) m(f) diver; **Taucheranzug** m diving (o wet) suit; **Taucherbrille** f diving goggles pl; **Tauchermaske** f diving mask; **Tauchkurs** m diving course; **Tauchsieder** (-s, -) m portable immersion coil for heating water

tauen vi impers to thaw

Taufe (-, -n) f baptism; **taufen** vt to baptize; (nennen) to christen

taugen vi to be suitable (für for); **nichts ~** to be no good

Tausch (-(e)s, -e) m exchange; **tauschen** vt to exchange, to swap

täuschen vt to deceive ▷ vi to be deceptive ▷ vr: **sich ~** to be wrong; **täuschend** adj deceptive; **Täuschung** f deception; (optisch) illusion

tausend num a thousand; **vier~** four thousand; **~ Dank!** thanks a lot; **tausendmal** adv a thousand times; **tausendste(r, s)** adj thousandth; **Tausendstel** (-s, -) nt (Bruchteil) thousandth

Taxi nt taxi; **Taxifahrer(in)** m(f) taxi driver; **Taxistand** m taxi rank (Brit), taxi stand (US)

Team (-s, -s) nt team; **Teamarbeit** f team work; **teamfähig** adj able to work in a team

Technik f technology; (angewandte) engineering; (Methode) technique; **Techniker(in)** (-s, -) m(f) engineer; (Sport, Mus) technician;

technisch adj technical
Techno (-s) m (Mus) techno
Teddybär m teddy bear
Tee (-s, -s) m tea; **Teebeutel** m
teabag; **Teekanne** f teapot;
Teelöffel m teaspoon
Teer (-(e)s, -e) m tar
Teesieb nt tea strainer; **Teetasse**
f teacup
Teich (-(e)s, -e) m pond
Teig (-(e)s, -e) m dough;
Teigwaren pl pasta sing
Teil (-(e)s, -e) m part; (Anteil)
share; **zum ~** partly ▷ (-(e)s, -e) nt
part; (Bestandteil) component;
teilen vt to divide; (mit jdm) to
share (mit with); **20 durch 4 ~** to
divide 20 by 4 ▷ vr: **sich ~** to
divide
Teilkaskoversicherung f third
party, fire and theft insurance
teilmöbliert adj partly furnished
Teilnahme (-, -n) f participation
(an +dat in); **teil|nehmen** irr vi to
take part (an +dat in); **Teilneh-
mer(in)** (-s, -) m(f) participant
teils adv partly; **teilweise** adv
partially, in part; **Teilzeit** f:
~ arbeiten to work part-time
Teint (-s, -s) m complexion
Tel. abk von **Telefon** tel.
Telefon (-s, -e) nt telephone;
Telefonanruf m, **Telefonat** nt
(tele)phone call;
Telefonanschluss m telephone
connection; **Telefonauskunft** f
directory enquiries pl (Brit),
directory assistance (US);
Telefonbuch nt telephone
directory; **Telefongebühren** pl
telephone charges pl;
Telefongespräch nt telephone
conversation; **telefonieren** vi:
ich telefoniere gerade (mit ...)
I'm on the phone (to ...);
telefonisch adj telephone;
(Benachrichtigung) by telephone;

Telefonkarte f phonecard;
Telefonnummer f (tele)phone
number; **Telefonrechnung** f
phone bill; **Telefonverbindung** f
telephone connection;
Telefonzelle f phone box (Brit),
phone booth; **Telefonzentrale** f
switchboard; **über die ~** through
the switchboard
Telegramm nt telegram;
Teleobjektiv nt telephoto lens;
Teleshopping (-s) nt teleshopping; **Teleskop** (-s, -e) nt
telescope
Teller (-s, -) m plate
Tempel (-s, -) m temple
Temperament nt temperament; (Schwung) liveliness;
temperamentvoll adj lively
Temperatur f temperature; **bei
~en von 30 Grad** at temperatures
of 30 degrees; **~ haben** to have a
temperature; **~ bei jdm messen** to
take sb's temperature
Tempo (-s, -s) nt (Geschwindigkeit)
speed; **Tempolimit** (-s, -s) nt
speed limit
Tempotaschentuch® nt
(Papiertaschentuch) (paper) tissue,
≈ Kleenex®
Tendenz f tendency; (Absicht)
intention
Tennis (-) nt tennis; **Tennisball**
m tennis ball; **Tennisplatz** m
tennis court; **Tennisschläger** m
tennis racket; **Tennisspieler(in)**
m(f) tennis player
Tenor (-s, Tenöre) m tenor
Teppich (-s, -e) m carpet;
Teppichboden m (wall-to-wall)
carpet
Termin (-s, -e) m (Zeitpunkt) date;
(Frist) deadline; (Arzttermin etc)
appointment
Terminal (-s, -s) nt (Inform, Aviat)
terminal
Terminkalender m diary;

Terminplaner m (in Buchform) personal organizer, Filofax®; (Taschencomputer) personal digital assistant, PDA

Terpentin (-s, -e) nt turpentine, turps sing

Terrasse (-, -n) f terrace; (hinter einem Haus) patio

Terror (-s) m terror; **Terroranschlag** m terrorist attack; **terrorisieren** vt to terrorize; **Terrorismus** m terrorism; **Terrorist(in)** m(f) terrorist

Tesafilm® m ≈ sellotape® (Brit), ≈ Scotch tape® (US)

Test (-s, -s) m test

Testament nt will; **das Alte/Neue ~** the Old/New Testament

testen vt to test; **Testergebnis** nt test results pl

Tetanus (-) m tetanus; **Tetanusimpfung** f (anti-)tetanus injection

teuer adj expensive, dear (Brit)

Teufel (-s, -) m devil; **was/wo zum ~** what/where the devil; **Teufelskreis** m vicious circle

Text (-(e)s, -e) m text; (Liedertext) words pl, lyrics pl; **Textmarker** (-s, -) m highlighter; **Textverarbeitung** f word processing; **Textverarbeitungsprogramm** nt word processing program

Thailand nt Thailand

Theater (-s, -) nt theatre; (fam) fuss; **ins ~ gehen** to go to the theatre; **Theaterkasse** f box office; **Theaterstück** nt (stage) play; **Theatervorstellung** f (stage) performance

Theke (-, -n) f (Schanktisch) bar; (Ladentisch) counter

Thema (-s, Themen) nt subject, topic; **kein ~!** no problem

Themse (-) f Thames

Theologie f theology

theoretisch adj theoretical; **~ stimmt das** that's right in theory; **Theorie** f theory

Therapeut(in) m(f) therapist; **Therapie** f therapy; **eine ~ machen** to undergo therapy

Thermalbad nt thermal bath; (Ort) thermal spa; **Thermometer** (-s, -) nt thermometer

Thermosflasche® f, **Thermoskanne®** f Thermos® (flask); **Thermostat** (-(e)s, -e) m thermostat

These (-, -n) f theory

Thron (-(e)s, -e) m throne

Thunfisch m tuna

Thüringen (-s) nt Thuringia

Thymian (-s, -e) m thyme

Tick (-(e)s, -s) m tic; (Eigenart) quirk; (Fimmel) craze; **ticken** vi to tick; **er tickt nicht ganz richtig** he's off his rocker

Ticket (-s, -s) nt (plane) ticket

tief adj deep; (Ausschnitt, Ton, Sonne) low; **2 Meter ~** 2 metres deep; **Tief** (-s, -s) nt (Meteo) low; (seelisch) depression; **Tiefdruck** m (Meteo) low pressure; **Tiefe** (-, -n) f depth; **Tiefgarage** f underground car park (Brit) (o garage (US)); **tiefgekühlt** adj frozen; **Tiefkühlfach** nt freezer compartment; **Tiefkühlkost** f frozen food; **Tiefkühltruhe** f freezer; **Tiefpunkt** m low

Tier (-(e)s, -e) nt animal; **Tierarzt** m, **Tierärztin** f vet; **Tiergarten** m zoo; **Tierhandlung** f pet shop; **Tierheim** nt animal shelter; **tierisch** adj animal ▷ adv (fam) really; **~ ernst** deadly serious; **ich hatte ~ Angst** I was dead scared; **Tierkreiszeichen** nt sign of the zodiac; **Tierpark** m zoo; **Tierquälerei** f cruelty to animals;

Tierschützer(in) (-s, -) m(f) animal rights campaigner; **Tierversuch** m animal experiment

Tiger (-s, -) m tiger

timen vt to time; **Timing** (-s) nt timing

Tinte (-, -n) f ink; **Tintenfisch** m cuttlefish; (klein) squid; (achtfüßig) octopus; **Tintenfischringe** pl calamari pl; **Tintenstrahldrucker** m ink-jet printer

Tipp (-s, -s) m tip; **tippen** vt, vi to tap; (fam: schreiben) to type; (fam: raten) to guess

Tirol (-s) nt Tyrol

Tisch (-(e)s, -e) m table; **Tischdecke** f tablecloth; **Tischlerei** f joiner's workshop; (Arbeit) joinery; **Tischtennis** nt table tennis; **Tischtennisschläger** m table-tennis bat

Titel (-s, -) m title; **Titelbild** nt cover picture

Toast (-(e)s, -s) m toast; **toasten** vt to toast; **Toaster** (-s, -) m toaster

Tochter (-, Töchter) f daughter

Tod (-(e)s, -e) m death; **Todesopfer** nt casualty; **Todesstrafe** f death penalty; **todkrank** adj terminally ill; (sehr krank) seriously ill; **tödlich** adj deadly, fatal; **er ist ~ verunglückt** he was killed in an accident; **todmüde** adj (fam) dead tired; **todsicher** adj (fam) dead certain

Tofu (-(s)) m tofu, bean curd

Toilette f toilet, restroom (US); **Toilettenpapier** nt toilet paper

toi, toi, toi interj good luck

tolerant adj tolerant (gegen of)

toll adj mad; (Treiben) wild; (fam: großartig) great; **Tollkirsche** f deadly nightshade; **Tollwut** f rabies sing

Tomate (-, -n) f tomato; **Tomatenmark** nt tomato purée (Brit) (o paste (US)); **Tomatensaft** m tomato juice

Tombola (-, -s) f raffle, tombola (Brit)

Ton (-(e)s, -e) m (Erde) clay ▷ m (Töne, Laut) sound; (Mus) note; (Redeweise) tone; (Farbton, Nuance) shade; **Tonband** nt tape; **Tonbandgerät** nt tape recorder

tönen vi to sound ▷ vt to shade; (Haare) to tint

Toner (-s, -) m toner; **Tonerkassette** f toner cartridge

Tonne (-, -n) f (Fass) barrel; (Gewicht) tonne, metric ton

Tontechniker(in) m(f) sound engineer

Tönung f hue; (für Haar) rinse

Top (-s, -s) nt top

Topf (-(e)s, Töpfe) m pot

Töpfer(in) (-s, -) m(f) potter; **Töpferei** f pottery; (Gegenstand) piece of pottery

Tor (-(e)s, -e) nt gate; (Sport) goal; **ein ~ schießen** to score a goal; **Torhüter(in)** m(f) goalkeeper

torkeln vi to stagger

Tornado (-s, -s) m tornado

Torschütze m, **Torschützin** f (goal)scorer

Torte (-, -n) f cake; (Obsttorte) flan; (Sahnetorte) gateau

Torwart(in) (-s, -e) m(f) goalkeeper

tot adj dead; **~er Winkel** blind spot

total adj total, complete; **Totalschaden** m complete write-off

Tote(r) mf dead man/woman; (Leiche) corpse; **töten** vt, vi to kill; **Totenkopf** m skull

tot|lachen vr: **sich ~** to kill oneself laughing

Toto (-s, -s) m o nt pools pl

tot|schlagen *irr vt* to beat to death; **die Zeit ~** to kill time

Touchscreen (-s, -s) *m* touch screen

Tour (-, -en) *f* trip; (*Rundfahrt*) tour; **eine ~ nach York machen** to go on a trip to York; **Tourenski** *m* touring ski

Tourismus *m* tourism; **Tourist(in)** *m(f)* tourist; **Touristenklasse** *f* tourist class; **touristisch** *adj* tourist; (*pej*) touristy

traben *vi* to trot

Tournee (-, -n) *f* tour

Tracht (-, -en) *f* (*Kleidung*) traditional costume

Trackball (-s, -s) *m* (*Inform*) trackball

Tradition *f* tradition; **traditionell** *adj* traditional

traf *imperf von* **treffen**

Trafik (-, -en) *f* tobacconist's

Tragbahre (-, -n) *f* stretcher

tragbar *adj* portable

träge *adj* sluggish, slow

tragen (*trug, getragen*) *vt* to carry; (*Kleidung, Brille, Haare*) to wear; (*Namen, Früchte*) to bear; **Träger** (-s, -) *m* (*an Kleidung*) strap; (*Hosen~*) braces *pl* (*Brit*), suspenders *pl* (*US*); (*in der Architektur*) beam; (*Stahl~, Eisen~*) girder

Tragfläche *f* wing; **Tragflügelboot** *nt* hydrofoil

tragisch *adj* tragic; **Tragödie** *f* tragedy

Trainer(in) (-s, -) *m(f)* trainer, coach; **trainieren** *vt, vi* to train; (*jdn a.*) to coach; (*Übung*) to practise; **Training** (-s, -s) *nt* training; **Trainingsanzug** *m* tracksuit

Traktor *m* tractor

Trambahn *f* tram (*Brit*), streetcar (*US*)

trampen *vi* to hitchhike; **Tramper(in)** *m(f)* hitchhiker

Träne (-, -n) *f* tear; **tränen** *vi* to water; **Tränengas** *nt* teargas

trank *imperf von* **trinken**

Transfusion *f* transfusion

Transitverkehr *m* transit traffic; **Transitvisum** *nt* transit visa

Transplantation *f* transplant; (*Hauttransplantation*) graft

Transport (-(e)s, -e) *m* transport; **transportieren** *vt* to transport; **Transportmittel** *nt* means *sing* of transport; **Transportunternehmen** *nt* haulage firm

Transvestit (-en, -en) *m* transvestite

trat *imperf von* **treten**

Traube (-, -n) *f* (*einzelne Beere*) grape; (*ganze Frucht*) bunch of grapes; **Traubensaft** *m* grape juice; **Traubenzucker** *m* glucose

trauen *vi*: **jdm/einer Sache ~** to trust sb/sth; **ich traute meinen Ohren nicht** I couldn't believe my ears ▷ *vr*: **sich ~** to dare ▷ *vt* to marry; **sich ~ lassen** to get married

Trauer (-) *f* sorrow; (*für Verstorbenen*) mourning

Traum (-(e)s, Träume) *m* dream; **träumen** *vt, vi* to dream (*von* of, about); **traumhaft** *adj* dreamlike; (*fig*) wonderful

traurig *adj* sad (*über* +*akk* about)

Trauschein *m* marriage certificate; **Trauung** *f* wedding ceremony; **Trauzeuge** *m*, **Trauzeugin** *f* witness (*at wedding ceremony*), ≈ best man/maid of honour

Travellerscheck *m* traveller's cheque

treffen (*traf, getroffen*) *vr*: **sich ~** to meet ▷ *vt, vi* to hit; (*Bemerkung*) to hurt; (*begegnen*) to meet; (*Entscheidung*) to make; (*Maßnahmen*) to take; **Treffen** (*-s, -*) *nt* meeting; **Treffer** (*-s, -*) *m* (*Tor*) goal; **Treffpunkt** *m* meeting place

treiben (*trieb, getrieben*) *vt* to drive; (*Sport*) to do ▷ *vi* (*im Wasser*) to drift; (*Pflanzen*) to sprout; (*Tee, Kaffee*) to be diuretic; **Treiber** (*-s, -*) *m* (*Inform*) driver

Treibgas *nt* propellant; **Treibhaus** *nt* greenhouse; **Treibstoff** *m* fuel

trennen *vt* to separate; (*teilen*) to divide ▷ *vr*: **sich ~** to separate; **sich von jdm ~** to leave sb; **sich von etw ~** to part with sth; **Trennung** *f* separation

Treppe (*-, -n*) *f* stairs *pl*; (*im Freien*) steps *pl*; **Treppengeländer** *nt* banister; **Treppenhaus** *nt* staircase

Tresen (*-s, -*) *m* (*in Kneipe*) bar; (*in Laden*) counter

Tresor (*-s, -e*) *m* safe

Tretboot *nt* pedal boat; **treten** (*trat, getreten*) *vi* to step; **mit jdm in Verbindung ~** to get in contact with sb ▷ *vt* to kick; (*nieder~*) to tread

treu *adj* (*gegenüber Partner*) faithful; (*Kunde, Fan*) loyal; **Treue** (*-*) *f* (*eheliche*) faithfulness; (*von Kunde, Fan*) loyalty

Triathlon (*-s, -s*) *m* triathlon

Tribüne (*-, -n*) *f* stand; (*Rednertribüne*) platform

Trick (*-s, -e o -s*) *m* trick; **Trickfilm** *m* cartoon

trieb *imperf von* **treiben**

Trieb (*-(e)s, -e*) *m* urge; (*Instinkt*) drive; (*Neigung*) inclination; (*an Baum etc*) shoot; **Triebwerk** *nt* engine

Trikot (*-s, -s*) *nt* shirt, jersey

Trimm-Dich-Pfad *m* fitness trail

trinkbar *adj* drinkable; **trinken** (*trank, getrunken*) *vt, vi* to drink; **einen ~ gehen** to go out for a drink; **Trinkgeld** *nt* tip; **Trinkhalm** *m* (drinking) straw; **Trinkwasser** *nt* drinking water

Trio (*-s, -s*) *nt* trio

Tripper (*-s, -*) *m* gonorrhoea

Tritt (*-(e)s, -e*) *m* (*Schritt*) step; (*Fußtritt*) kick; **Trittbrett** *nt* running board

Triumph (*-(e)s, -e*) *m* triumph; **triumphieren** *vi* to triumph (*über +akk* over)

trivial *adj* trivial

trocken *adj* dry; **Trockenhaube** *f* hair-dryer; **Trockenheit** *f* dryness; **trocken|legen** *vt* (*Baby*) to change; **trocknen** *vt, vi* to dry; **Trockner** (*-s, -*) *m* dryer

Trödel (*-s*) *m* (*fam*) junk; **Trödelmarkt** *m* flea market

trödeln *vi* (*fam*) to dawdle

Trommel (*-, -n*) *f* drum; **Trommelfell** *nt* eardrum; **trommeln** *vt, vi* to drum

Trompete (*-, -n*) *f* trumpet

Tropen *pl* tropics *pl*

Tropf (*-(e)s, -e*) *m* (*Med*) drip; **am ~ hängen** to be on a drip; **tröpfeln** *vi* to drip; **es tröpfelt** it's drizzling; **tropfen** *vt, vi* to drip; **Tropfen** (*-s, -*) *m* drop; **tropfenweise** *adv* drop by drop; **tropfnass** *adj* dripping wet; **Tropfsteinhöhle** *f* stalactite cave

tropisch *adj* tropical

Trost (*-es*) *m* consolation, comfort; **trösten** *vt* to console, to comfort; **trostlos** *adj* bleak; (*Verhältnisse*) wretched; **Trostpreis** *m* consolation prize

Trottoir (*-s, -s*) *nt* pavement (*Brit*), sidewalk (*US*)

trotz *prep +gen o dat* in spite of; **Trotz** (*-es*) *m* defiance; **trotzdem** *adv* nevertheless ▷ *conj* although;

trotzig *adj* defiant
trüb *adj* dull; (*Flüssigkeit, Glas*)
cloudy; (*fig*) gloomy
Trüffel (-, -n) *f* truffle
trug *imperf von* **tragen**
trügerisch *adj* deceptive
Truhe (-, -n) *f* chest
Trümmer *pl* wreckage *sing*;
(*Bau~*) ruins *pl*
Trumpf (-(e)s, Trümpfe) *m* trump
Trunkenheit *f* intoxication;
~ am Steuer drink driving (*Brit*),
drunk driving (*US*)
Truthahn *m* turkey
Tscheche (-n, -n) *m*, **Tschechin**
f Czech; **Tschechien** (-s) *nt*
Czech Republic; **tschechisch** *adj*
Czech; **Tschechische Republik**
Czech Republic; **Tschechisch** *nt*
Czech
Tschetschenien (-s) *nt*
Chechnya
tschüs(s) *interj* bye
T-Shirt (-s, -s) *nt* T-shirt
Tube (-, -n) *f* tube
Tuberkulose (-, -n) *f* tubercu-
losis, TB
Tuch (-(e)s, Tücher) *nt* cloth;
(*Halstuch*) scarf; (*Kopftuch*)
headscarf
tüchtig *adj* competent; (*fleißig*)
efficient; (*fam: kräftig*) good
Tugend (-, -en) *f* virtue;
tugendhaft *adj* virtuous
Tulpe (-, -n) *f* tulip
Tumor (-s, -en) *m* tumour
tun (tat, getan) *vt* (*machen*) to do;
(*legen*) to put; **was tust du da?**
what are you doing?; **das tut man
nicht** you shouldn't do that; **jdm
etw ~** (*antun*) to do sth to sb; **das
tut es auch** that'll do ▷ *vi* to act;
so ~, als ob to act as if ▷ *vr impers*:
es tut sich etwas/viel
something/a lot is happening
Tuner (-s, -) *m* tuner
Tunesien (-s) *nt* Tunisia

Tunfisch *m siehe* **Thunfisch**
tuna
Tunnel (-s, -s o -) *m* tunnel
Tunte (-, -n) *f* (*pej, fam*) fairy
tupfen *vt, vi* to dab; (*mit Farbe*) to
dot; **Tupfen** (-s, -) *m* dot
Tür (-, -en) *f* door; **vor/an der ~** at
the door; **an die ~ gehen** to
answer the door
Türke (-n, -n) *m* Turk; **Türkei** (-) *f*:
die ~ Turkey; **Türkin** *f* Turk
Türkis (-es, -e) *m* turquoise
türkisch *adj* Turkish; **Türkisch**
nt Turkish
Turm (-(e)s, Türme) *m* tower;
(*spitzer Kirchturm*) steeple; (*Sprung~*)
diving platform; (*Schach*) rook,
castle
turnen *vi* to do gymnastics;
Turnen (-s) *nt* gymnastics *sing*;
(*Schule*) physical education, PE;
Turner(in) *m(f)* gymnast;
Turnhalle *f* gym(nasium);
Turnhose *f* gym shorts *pl*
Turnier (-s, -e) *nt* tournament
Turnschuh *m* gym shoe, sneaker
(*US*)
Türschild *nt* doorplate;
Türschloss *nt* lock
tuscheln *vt, vi* to whisper
Tussi (-, -s) *f* (*pej, fam*) chick
Tüte (-, -n) *f* bag
TÜV (-s, -s) *m akr* = **Technischer
Überwachungsverein** ≈ MOT
(*Brit*), vehicle inspection (*US*)

○ TÜV
○
○ The **TÜV** is the organization
○ responsible for checking the
○ safety of machinery, particularly
○ vehicles. Cars over three years
○ old have to be examined every
○ two years for their safety and
○ for their exhaust emissions.
○ **TÜV** is also the name given to
○ the test itself.

TÜV-Plakette *f* badge attached to a vehicle's numberplate, indicating that it has passed the "TÜV"

Tweed *(-s, -s) m* tweed

Typ *(-s, -en) m* type; *(Auto)* model; *(Mann)* guy, bloke

Typhus *(-) m* typhoid

typisch *adj* typical *(für* of); **ein ~er Fehler** a common mistake; **~ Marcus!** that's just like Marcus; **~ amerikanisch!** that's so American

u. *abk* = **und**

u. a. *abk* = **und andere(s)** and others; = **unter anderem, unter anderen** among other things

u. A. w. g. *abk* = **um Antwort wird gebeten** RSVP

U-Bahn *f* underground *(Brit)*, subway *(US)*

übel *adj* bad; *(moralisch)* wicked; **mir ist ~** I feel sick; **diese Bemerkung hat er mir ~ genommen** he took offence at my remark; **Übelkeit** *f* nausea

üben *vt, vi* to practise

⬤ SCHLÜSSELWORT

über *prep +dat* **1** *(räumlich)* over, above; **zwei Grad über null** two degrees above zero
2 *(zeitlich)* over; **über der Arbeit einschlafen** to fall asleep over one's work

▷ prep +akk **1** (räumlich) over; (hoch über auch) above; (quer über auch) across

2 (zeitlich) over; **über Weihnachten** over Christmas; **über kurz oder lang** sooner or later

3 (mit Zahlen) **Kinder über 12 Jahren** children over o above 12 years of age; **ein Scheck über 200 Euro** a cheque for 200 euros

4 (auf dem Wege) via; **nach Köln über Aachen** to Cologne via Aachen; **ich habe es über die Auskunft erfahren** I found out from information

5 (betreffend) about; **ein Buch über ...** a book about o on ...; **über jdn/etw lachen** to laugh about o at sb/sth

6 Macht über jdn haben to have power over sb; **sie liebt ihn über alles** she loves him more than everything

▷ adv over; **über und über** over and over; **den ganzen Tag über** all day long; **jdm in etw** dat **über sein** to be superior to sb in sth

überall adv everywhere
überanstrengen vr: **sich ~ to** overexert oneself
überbacken adj: (mit Käse) **~** au gratin; **überbelichten** vt (Foto) to overexpose; **überbieten** irr vt to outbid; (übertreffen) to surpass; (Rekord) to break
Überbleibsel (-s, -) nt remnant
Überblick m overview; (fig: in Darstellung) survey; (Fähigkeit zu verstehen) grasp (über +akk of)
überbuchen vt to overbook; **Überbuchung** f overbooking
überdurchschnittlich adj above average
übereinander adv on top of each other; (sprechen etc) about

each other
überein|stimmen vi to agree (mit with)
überempfindlich adj hypersensitive
überfahren irr vt (Auto) to run over; **Überfahrt** f crossing
Überfall m (Banküberfall) robbery; (Mil) raid; (auf jdn) assault; **überfallen** irr vt to attack; (Bank) to raid
überfällig adj overdue
überfliegen irr vt to fly over; (Buch) to skim through
Überfluss m overabundance, excess (an +dat of); **überflüssig** adj superfluous
überfordern vt to demand too much of; (Kräfte) to overtax; **da bin ich überfordert** (bei Antwort) you've got me there
Überführung f (Brücke) flyover (Brit), overpass (US)
überfüllt adj overcrowded
Übergabe f handover
Übergang m crossing; (Wandel, Überleitung) transition; **Übergangslösung** f temporary solution, stopgap
übergeben irr vt to hand over
▷ vr: **sich ~** to be sick, to vomit
Übergepäck nt excess baggage
Übergewicht nt excess weight; (**10 Kilo**) **~ haben** to be (10 kilos) overweight
überglücklich adj overjoyed; (fam) over the moon
Übergröße f outsize
überhaupt adv at all; (im Allgemeinen) in general; (besonders) especially; **was willst du ~?** what is it you want?
überheblich adj arrogant
überholen vt to overtake; (Tech) to overhaul; **Überholspur** f overtaking (Brit) (o passing (US)) lane; **überholt** adj outdated

Überholverbot *nt*: **hier herrscht ~** you can't overtake here

überhören *vt* to miss, not to catch; (*absichtlich*) to ignore; **überladen** *irr vt* to overload ▷ *adj* (*fig*) cluttered; **überlassen** *irr vt*: **jdm etw ~** to leave sth to sb; **über|laufen** *irr vi* (*Flüssigkeit*) to overflow

überleben *vt, vi* to survive; **Überlebende(r)** *mf* survivor

überlegen *vt* to consider; **sich** (*dat*) **etw ~** to think about sth; **er hat es sich** (*dat*) **anders überlegt** he's changed his mind ▷ *adj* superior (*dat* to); **Überlegung** *f* consideration

überm *kontr von* **über dem**

übermäßig *adj* excessive

übermorgen *adv* the day after tomorrow

übernächste(r, s) *adj*: **~ Woche** the week after next

übernachten *vi* to spend the night (*bei jdm* at sb's place); **übernächtigt** *adj* bleary-eyed, very tired; **Übernachtung** *f* overnight stay; **~ mit Frühstück** bed and breakfast

übernehmen *irr vt* to take on; (*Amt, Geschäft*) to take over ▷ *vr*: **sich ~** to take on too much

überprüfen *vt* to check; **Überprüfung** *f* check; (*Überprüfen*) checking

überqueren *vt* to cross

überraschen *vt* to surprise; **Überraschung** *f* surprise

überreden *vt* to persuade; **er hat mich überredet** he talked me into it

überreichen *vt* to hand over

übers *kontr von* **über das**

überschätzen *vt* to overestimate; **überschlagen** *irr vt* (*berechnen*) to estimate; (*auslassen: Seite*) to skip ▷ *vr*: **sich**

~ to somersault; (*Auto*) to overturn; (*Stimme*) to crack; **überschneiden** *irr vr*: **sich ~** (*Linien etc*) to intersect; (*Termine*) to clash

Überschrift *f* heading

Überschwemmung *f* flood

Übersee *f*: **nach/in ~** overseas

übersehen *irr vt* (*Gelände*) to look (out) over; (*nicht beachten*) to overlook

übersetzen *vt* to translate (*aus* from, *in* +akk into); **Übersetzer(in)** (*-s, -*) *m(f)* translator; **Übersetzung** *f* translation

Übersicht *f* overall view; (*Darstellung*) survey; **übersichtlich** *adj* clear

überstehen *irr vt* (*durchstehen*) to get over; (*Winter etc*) to get through

Überstunden *pl* overtime *sing*

überstürzt *adj* hasty

überteuert *adj* overpriced

übertragbar *adj* transferable; (*Med*) infectious; **übertragen** *irr vt* to transfer (*auf* +akk to); (*Radio*) to broadcast; (*Krankheit*) to transmit ▷ *vr* to spread (*auf* +akk to) ▷ *adj* figurative; **Übertragung** *f* (*Radio*) broadcast; (*von Daten*) transmission

übertreffen *irr vt* to surpass

übertreiben *irr vt, vi* to exaggerate, to overdo; **Übertreibung** *f* exaggeration; **übertrieben** *adj* exaggerated, overdone

überwachen *vt* to supervise; (*Verdächtigen*) to keep under surveillance

überwand *imperf von* **überwinden**

überweisen *irr vt* to transfer; (*Patienten*) to refer (*an* +akk to); **Überweisung** *f* transfer; (*von Patienten*) referral

überwiegend *adv* mainly
überwinden (*überwand*, *überwunden*) *vt* to overcome ▷ *vr*: **sich ~** to make an effort, to force oneself; **überwunden** *pp von* **überwinden**
Überzelt *nt* flysheet
überzeugen *vt* to convince; **Überzeugung** *f* conviction
überziehen *irr vt* (*bedecken*) to cover; (*Jacke etc*) to put on; (*Konto*) to overdraw; **die Betten frisch ~** to change the sheets
üblich *adj* usual
übrig *adj* remaining; **ist noch Saft ~?** is there any juice left?; **die Übrigen** *pl* the rest *pl*; **im Übrigen** besides; **~ bleiben** to be left (over); **mir blieb nichts anderes ~(, als zu gehen)** I had no other choice (but to go); **übrigens** *adv* besides; (*nebenbei bemerkt*) by the way; **übrig|haben** *irr vt*: **für jdn etwas ~** (*fam*: *jdn mögen*) to have a soft spot for sb
Übung *f* practice; (*im Sport, Aufgabe etc*) exercise
Ufer (*-s, -*) *nt* (*Fluss*) bank; (*Meer, See*) shore; **am ~** on the bank/shore
Ufo (*-(s), -s*) *nt akr* = **unbekanntes Flugobjekt** UFO
Uhr (*-, -en*) *f* clock; (*am Arm*) watch; **wie viel ~ ist es?** what time is it?; **1 ~** 1 o'clock; **20 ~** 8 o'clock, 8 pm; **Uhrzeigersinn** *m*: **im ~** clockwise; **gegen den ~** anticlockwise (*Brit*), counterclockwise (*US*); **Uhrzeit** *f* time (of day)
Ukraine (*-*) *f*: **die ~** the Ukraine
UKW *abk* = **Ultrakurzwelle** VHF
Ulme (*-, -n*) *f* elm
Ultrakurzwelle *f* very high frequency; **Ultraschallaufnahme** *f* (*Med*) scan

○ SCHLÜSSELWORT

um *prep* +*akk* **1** (*um herum*) (a)round; **um Weihnachten** around Christmas; **er schlug um sich** he hit about him
2 (*mit Zeitangabe*) at; **um acht (Uhr)** at eight (o'clock)
3 (*mit Größenangabe*) by; **etw um 4 cm kürzen** to shorten sth by 4 cm; **um 10% teurer** 10% more expensive; **um vieles besser** better by far; **um so besser** so much the better
4 **der Kampf um den Titel** the battle for the title; **um Geld spielen** to play for money; **Stunde um Stunde** hour after hour; **Auge um Auge** an eye for an eye
▷ *prep* +*gen*: **um ... willen** for the sake of ...; **um Gottes willen** for goodness' *o* (*stärker*) God's sake
▷ *konj*: **um ... zu** (in order) to ...; **zu klug, um zu ...** too clever to ...; *siehe* **umso**
▷ *adv* **1** (*ungefähr*) about; **um (die) 30 Leute** about *o* around 30 people
2 (*vorbei*) **die 2 Stunden sind um** the two hours are up

umarmen *vt* to embrace
Umbau *m* rebuilding; (*zu etwas*) conversion (*zu into*); **um|bauen** *vt* to rebuild; (*zu etwas*) to convert (*zu into*)
um|blättern *vt, vi* to turn over
um|bringen *irr vt* to kill
um|buchen *vi* to change one's reservation/flight
um|drehen *vt* to turn (round); (*obere Seite nach unten*) to turn over ▷ *vr*: **sich ~** to turn (round); **Umdrehung** *f* turn; (*Phys, Auto*) revolution
um|fahren *irr vt* to knock down

um|fallen *irr vi* to fall over
Umfang *m* (*Ausmaß*) extent; (*von Buch*) size; (*Reichweite*) range; (*Math*) circumference;
umfangreich *adj* extensive
Umfeld *nt* environment
Umfrage *f* survey
Umgang *m* company; (*mit jdm*) dealings *pl*; **umgänglich** *adj* sociable; **Umgangssprache** *f* colloquial language, slang
Umgebung *f* surroundings *pl*; (*Milieu*) environment; (*Personen*) people around one
umgehen *irr vi* (*Gerücht*) to go round; **~** (**können**) **mit** (know how to) handle **▷** *irr vt* to avoid; (*Schwierigkeit, Verbot*) to get round
um|gehen *irr vi*: **mit etw ~** to handle sth; **Umgehungsstraße** *f* bypass
umgekehrt *adj* reverse; (*gegenteilig*) opposite **▷** *adv* the other way round; **und ~** and vice versa
um|hören *vr*: **sich ~** to ask around; **um|kehren** *vi* to turn back **▷** *vt* to reverse; (*Kleidungsstück*) to turn inside out; **um|kippen** *vt* to tip over **▷** *vi* to overturn; (*fig*) to change one's mind; (*fam: ohnmächtig werden*) to pass out
Umkleidekabine *f* changing cubicle (*Brit*), dressing room (*US*); **Umkleideraum** *m* changing room
Umkreis *m* neighbourhood; **im ~ von** within a radius of
um|leiten *vt* to divert; **Umleitung** *f* diversion
um|rechnen *vt* to convert (*in +akk* into); **Umrechnung** *f* conversion; **Umrechnungskurs** *m* rate of exchange
Umriss *m* outline
um|rühren *vi, vt* to stir

ums *kontr von* **um das**
Umsatz *m* turnover
um|schalten *vi* to turn over
Umschlag *m* cover; (*Buch*) jacket; (*Med*) compress; (*Brief*) envelope
Umschulung *f* retraining
um|sehen *irr vr*: **sich ~** to look around; (*suchen*) to look out (*nach* for)
umso *adv* all the; **~ mehr** all the more; **~ besser** so much the better
umsonst *adv* (*vergeblich*) in vain; (*gratis*) for nothing
Umstand *m* circumstance; **Umstände** (*pl*) (*fig*) fuss; **in anderen Umständen sein** to be pregnant; **jdm Umstände machen** to cause sb a lot of trouble; **machen Sie bitte keine Umstände** please, don't put yourself out; **unter diesen/ keinen Umständen** under these/no circumstances; **unter Umständen** possibly; **umständlich** *adj* (*Methode*) complicated; (*Ausdrucksweise*) long-winded; (*Mensch*) ponderous; **Umstandsmode** *f* maternity wear
um|steigen *irr vi* to change (trains/buses)
um|stellen *vt* (*an anderen Ort*) to change round; (*Tech*) to convert **▷** *vr*: **sich ~** to adapt (*auf +akk* to); **Umstellung** *f* change; (*Umgewöhnung*) adjustment; (*Tech*) conversion
Umtausch *m* exchange; **um|tauschen** *vt* to exchange; (*Währung*) to change
Umweg *m* detour
Umwelt *f* environment; **Umweltbelastung** *f* ecological damage; **umweltbewusst** *adj* environmentally aware;

umweltfreundlich *adj*
environment-friendly;
Umweltpapier *nt* recycled paper;
umweltschädlich *adj* harmful to
the environment; **Umweltschutz**
m environmental protection;
Umweltschützer(in) (*-s, -*) *m(f)*
environmentalist;
Umweltverschmutzung *f*
pollution; **umweltverträglich** *adj*
environment-friendly

um|werfen *irr vt* to knock over;
(*fig: ändern*) to upset; (*fig, fam: jdn*)
to flabbergast

um|ziehen *irr vt* to change ▷ *vr:*
sich ~ to change ▷ *vi* to move
(house); **Umzug** *m*
(*Straßenumzug*) procession;
(*Wohnungsumzug*) move

unabhängig *adj* independent;
Unabhängigkeitstag *m*
Independence Day, Fourth of July
(*US*)

unabsichtlich *adv*
unintentionally

unangenehm *adj* unpleasant;
Unannehmlichkeit *f* inconvenience;
~en *pl* trouble *sing*

unanständig *adj* indecent;
unappetitlich *adj* (*Essen*)
unappetizing; (*abstoßend*)
off-putting; **unbeabsichtigt** *adj*
unintentional; **unbedeutend** *adj*
insignificant, unimportant;
(*Fehler*) slight

unbedingt *adj* unconditional
▷ *adv* absolutely

unbefriedigend *adj* unsatisfactory; **unbegrenzt** *adj*
unlimited; **unbekannt** *adj*
unknown; **unbeliebt** *adj*
unpopular; **unbemerkt** *adj*
unnoticed; **unbequem** *adj*
(*Stuhl, Mensch*) uncomfortable;
(*Regelung*) inconvenient;
unbeständig *adj* (*Wetter*)
unsettled; (*Lage*) unstable;

(*Mensch*) unreliable; **unbestimmt**
adj indefinite; **unbeteiligt** *adj*
(*nicht dazugehörig*) uninvolved;
(*innerlich nicht berührt*) indifferent,
unconcerned; **unbewacht** *adj*
unguarded; **unbewusst** *adj*
unconscious; **unbezahlt** *adj*
unpaid; **unbrauchbar** *adj*
useless

und *conj* and; **~ so weiter** and so
on; **na ~?** so what?

undankbar *adj* (*Person*)
ungrateful; (*Aufgabe*) thankless;
undenkbar *adj* inconceivable;
undeutlich *adj* indistinct;
undicht *adj* leaky; **uneben** *adj*
uneven; **unecht** *adj* (*Schmuck etc*)
fake; **unehelich** *adj* (*Kind*)
illegitimate; **unendlich** *adj*
endless; (*Math*) infinite;
unentbehrlich *adj* indispensable;
unentgeltlich *adj* free (of charge)

unentschieden *adj* undecided;
~ enden (*Sport*) to end in a draw

unerfreulich *adj* unpleasant

unerhört *adj* unheard-of; (*Bitte*)
outrageous; **unerlässlich** *adj*
indispensable; **unerträglich** *adj*
unbearable; **unerwartet** *adj*
unexpected

unerwünscht *adj* unwelcome;
(*Eigenschaften*) undesirable;
unfähig *adj* incompetent; **~ sein,
etw zu tun** to be incapable of
doing sth; **unfair** *adj* unfair

Unfall *m* accident; **Unfallbericht**
m accident report; **Unfallflucht** *f*
failure to stop after an accident;
Unfallhergang *m:* **den
~ schildern** to give details of the
accident; **Unfallstation** *f*
casualty ward; **Unfallstelle** *f*
scene of the accident;
Unfallversicherung *f* accident
insurance

unfreundlich *adj* unfriendly

Ungarn (*-s*) *nt* Hungary

Ungeduld *f* impatience;
ungeduldig *adj* impatient
ungeeignet *adj* unsuitable
ungefähr *adj* approximate ▷ *adv*
approximately; **~ 10 Kilometer**
about 10 kilometres; **wann ~?**
about what time?; **wo ~?**
whereabouts?
ungefährlich *adj* harmless;
(*sicher*) safe
ungeheuer *adj* huge ▷ *adv* (*fam*)
enormously; **Ungeheuer** (*-s, -*) *nt*
monster
ungehorsam *adj* disobedient
(*gegenüber* to)
ungelegen *adj* inconvenient;
ungemütlich *adj* unpleasant;
(*Mensch*) disagreeable;
ungenießbar *adj* inedible;
(*Getränk*) undrinkable;
ungenügend *adj* unsatisfactory;
(*Schulnote*) ≈ F; **ungepflegt** *adj*
(*Garten*) untended; (*Aussehen*)
unkempt; (*Hände*) neglected;
ungerade *adj* odd
ungerecht *adj* unjust;
ungerechtfertigt *adj* unjusti-
fied; **Ungerechtigkeit** *f*
injustice, unfairness
ungern *adv* reluctantly;
ungeschickt *adj* clumsy;
ungeschminkt *adj* without
make-up; **ungesund** *adj*
unhealthy; **ungewiss** *adj*
uncertain; **ungewöhnlich** *adj*
unusual
Ungeziefer (*-s*) *nt* vermin *pl*
ungezogen *adj* ill-mannered
ungezwungen *adj* relaxed
ungiftig *adj* non-toxic
unglaublich *adj* incredible
Unglück (*-(e)s, -e*) *nt* (*Unheil*)
misfortune; (*Pech*) bad luck;
(*Unglücksfall*) disaster; (*Verkehrs~*)
accident; **das bringt ~** that's
unlucky; **unglücklich** *adj*
unhappy; (*erfolglos*) unlucky;

(*unerfreulich*) unfortunate;
unglücklicherweise *adv*
unfortunately
ungültig *adj* invalid
ungünstig *adj* inconvenient
unheilbar *adj* incurable; **~ krank
sein** to be terminally ill
unheimlich *adj* eerie ▷ *adv* (*fam*)
incredibly
unhöflich *adj* impolite
uni *adj* plain
Uni (*-, -s*) *f* uni
Uniform (*-, -en*) *f* uniform
Universität *f* university
Unkenntnis *f* ignorance
unklar *adj* unclear
Unkosten *pl* expenses *pl*;
Unkostenbeitrag *m* contribution (towards expenses)
Unkraut *nt* weeds *pl*, ~art, weed
unlogisch *adj* illogical
unmissverständlich *adj*
unambiguous
unmittelbar *adj* immediate;
~ darauf immediately afterwards
unmöbliert *adj* unfurnished
unmöglich *adj* impossible
unnahbar *adj* unapproachable
unnötig *adj* unnecessary
UNO (*-*) *f* *akr* = **United Nations
Organization** UN
unordentlich *adj* untidy;
Unordnung *f* disorder
unpassend *adj* inappropriate;
(*Zeit*) inconvenient; **unpersönlich**
adj impersonal; **unpraktisch** *adj*
impractical
Unrecht *nt* wrong; **zu ~** wrongly;
im ~ sein to be wrong; **unrecht**
adj wrong; **~ haben** to be
wrong
unregelmäßig *adj* irregular;
unreif *adj* unripe; **unruhig** *adj*
restless; **~ schlafen** to have a bad
night
uns *pron* *akk, dat von* **wir**; us, (to)
us; **~ (selbst)** (*reflexiv*) ourselves;

sehen Sie ~? can you see us?; **er schickte es ~** he sent it to us; **lasst ~ in Ruhe** leave us alone; **ein Freund von ~** a friend of ours; **wir haben ~ hingesetzt** we sat down; **wir haben ~ amüsiert** we enjoyed ourselves; **wir mögen ~** we like each other

unscharf *adj* (*Foto*) blurred, out of focus

unscheinbar *adj* insignificant; (*Aussehen*) unprepossessing

unschlüssig *adj* undecided

unschuldig *adj* innocent

unser *pron* (*adjektivisch*) our ▷ *pron gen von* **wir**; of us; **unsere(r, s)** *pron* (*substantivisch*) ours; **unseretwegen** *adv* (*wegen uns*) because of us; (*uns zuliebe*) for our sake; (*um uns*) about us; (*von uns aus*) as far as we are concerned

unseriös *adj* dubious; **unsicher** *adj* (*ungewiss*) uncertain; (*Person, Job*) insecure

Unsinn *m* nonsense

unsterblich *adj* immortal; **~ verliebt** madly in love

unsympathisch *adj* unpleasant; **er ist mir ~** I don't like him

unten *adv* below; (*im Haus*) downstairs; (*an der Treppe etc*) at the bottom; **nach ~** down

 SCHLÜSSELWORT

unter *prep* +*dat* **1** (*räumlich, mit Zahlen*) under; (*drunter*) underneath, below; **unter 18 Jahren** under 18 years **2** (*zwischen*) among(st); **sie waren unter sich** they were by themselves; **einer unter ihnen** one of them; **unter anderem** among other things
▷ *prep* +*akk* under, below

Unterarm *m* forearm

unterbelichtet *adj* (*Foto*) underexposed

Unterbewusstsein *nt* subconscious

unterbrechen *irr vt* to interrupt; **Unterbrechung** *f* interruption; **ohne ~** nonstop

unterdrücken *vt* to suppress; (*Leute*) to oppress

unterdurchschnittlich *adj* below average

untere(r, s) *adj* lower

untereinander *adv* (*räumlich*) one below the other; (*gegenseitig*) each other; (*miteinander*) among themselves/yourselves/ourselves

Unterführung *f* underpass

unter|gehen *irr vi* to go down; (*Sonne*) to set; (*Volk*) to perish; (*Welt*) to come to an end; (*im Lärm*) to be drowned out

Untergeschoss *nt* basement; **Untergewicht** *nt*: (**3 Kilo**) **~ haben** to be (3 kilos) underweight; **Untergrund** *m* foundation; (*Pol*) underground; **Untergrundbahn** *f* underground (*Brit*), subway (*US*)

unterhalb *adv, prep* +*gen* below; **~ von** below

Unterhalt *m* maintenance; **unterhalten** *irr vt* to maintain; (*belustigen*) to entertain ▷ *vr*: **sich ~** to talk; (*sich belustigen*) to enjoy oneself; **Unterhaltung** *f* (*Belustigung*) entertainment; (*Gespräch*) talk, conversation

Unterhemd *nt* vest (*Brit*), undershirt (*US*); **Unterhose** *f* underpants *pl*; (*für Damen*) briefs *pl*

unterirdisch *adj* underground

Unterkiefer *m* lower jaw

Unterkunft (-, -künfte) *f* accommodation

Unterlage *f* (*Beleg*) document; (*Schreibunterlage*) pad

unterlassen *irr vt*: **es ~, etw zu tun** (*versäumen*) to fail to do sth; (*bleiben lassen*) to refrain from doing sth

unterlegen *adj* inferior (*dat* to); (*besiegt*) defeated

Unterleib *m* abdomen

Unterlippe *f* lower lip

Untermiete *f*: **zur ~ wohnen** to be a subtenant; **Untermieter(in)** *m(f)* subtenant

unternehmen *irr vt* (*Reise*) to go on; (*Versuch*) to make; **etwas ~ to** do something (*gegen* about); **Unternehmen** (*-s, -*) *nt* undertaking; (*Comm*) company; **Unternehmensberater(in)** (*-s, -*) *m(f)* management consultant; **Unternehmer(in)** (*-s, -*) *m(f)* entrepreneur

Unterricht (*-(e)s, -e*) *m* lessons *pl*; **unterrichten** *vt* to teach

unterschätzen *vt* to underestimate

unterscheiden *irr vt* to distinguish (*von* from, *zwischen* +*dat* between) ▷ *vr*: **sich ~ to** differ (*von* from)

Unterschenkel *m* lower leg

Unterschied (*-(e)s, -e*) *m* difference; **im ~ zu dir** unlike you; **unterschiedlich** *adj* different

unterschreiben *irr vt* to sign; **Unterschrift** *f* signature

Untersetzer (*-s, -*) *m* tablemat; (*für Gläser*) coaster

unterste(r, s) *adj* lowest, bottom

unter|stellen *vr*: **sich ~ to** take shelter

unterstellen *vt* (*rangmäßig*) to subordinate (*dat* to); (*fig*) to impute (*jdm etw* sth to sb)

unterstreichen *irr vt* (*a. fig*) to underline

Unterstrich *m* (*Inform*) underscore

unterstützen *vt* to support; **Unterstützung** *f* support

untersuchen *vt* (*Med*) to examine; (*Polizei*) to investigate; **Untersuchung** *f* examination; (*polizeiliche*) investigation

untertags *adv* during the day

Untertasse *f* saucer

Unterteil *nt* lower part, bottom

Untertitel *m* subtitle

untervermieten *vt* to sublet

Unterwäsche *f* underwear

unterwegs *adv* on the way

unterzeichnen *vt* to sign

untreu *adj* unfaithful

untröstlich *adj* inconsolable; **unüberlegt** *adj* ill-considered ▷ *adv* without thinking; **unüblich** *adj* unusual; **unverantwortlich** *adj* irresponsible; (*unentschuldbar*) inexcusable

unverbindlich *adj* not binding; (*Antwort*) noncommittal ▷ *adv* (*Comm*) without obligation

unverbleit *adj* unleaded; **unverheiratet** *adj* unmarried, single; **unvermeidlich** *adj* unavoidable; **unvernünftig** *adj* silly; **unverschämt** *adj* impudent; **unverständlich** *adj* incomprehensible; **unverträglich** *adj* (*Person*) quarrelsome; (*Essen*) indigestible

unverwüstlich *adj* indestructible; (*Mensch*) irrepressible

unverzeihlich *adj* unpardonable; **unverzüglich** *adj* immediate; **unvollständig** *adj* incomplete; **unvorsichtig** *adj* careless

unwahrscheinlich *adj* improbable, unlikely ▷ *adv* (*fam*) incredibly

Unwetter *nt* thunderstorm

unwichtig *adj* unimportant

unwiderstehlich *adj* irresistible

unwillkürlich adj involuntary
▷ adv instinctively; **ich musste ~ lachen** I couldn't help laughing
unwohl adj unwell, ill
unzählig adj innumerable, countless
unzerbrechlich adj unbreakable; **unzertrennlich** adj inseparable; **unzufrieden** adj dissatisfied; **unzugänglich** adj inaccessible; **unzumutbar** adj unacceptable
unzusammenhängend adj disconnected; (Äußerung) incoherent; **unzutreffend** adj inapplicable; (unwahr) incorrect; **unzuverlässig** adj unreliable
Update (-s, -s) nt (Inform) update
üppig adj (Essen) lavish; (Vegetation) lush
uralt adj ancient, very old
Uran (-s) nt uranium
Uranus (-) m Uranus
Uraufführung f premiere
Urenkel m great-grandson; **Urenkelin** f great-granddaughter; **Urgroßeltern** pl great-grandparents pl; **Urgroßmutter** f great-grandmother; **Urgroßvater** m great-grandfather
Urheber(in) (-s, -) m(f) originator; (Autor) author
Urin (-s, -e) m urine; **Urinprobe** f urine specimen
Urkunde (-, -n) f document
Urlaub (-(e)s, -e) m holiday (Brit), vacation (US); **im ~** on holiday (Brit), on vacation (US); **in ~ fahren** to go on holiday (Brit) (o vacation (US)); **Urlauber(in)** (-s, -) m(f) holiday-maker (Brit), vacationer (US); **Urlaubsort** m holiday resort; **urlaubsreif** adj ready for a holiday (Brit) (o vacation (US)); **Urlaubszeit** f holiday season (Brit), vacation period (US)

Urne (-, -n) f urn
Urologe m, **Urologin** f urologist
Ursache f cause (für of); **keine ~!** not at all; (bei Entschuldigung) that's all right
Ursprung m origin; (von Fluss) source; **ursprünglich** adj original ▷ adv originally; **Ursprungsland** adj country of origin
Urteil (-s, -e) nt (Meinung) opinion; (Jur) verdict; (Strafmaß) sentence; **urteilen** vi to judge
Uruguay (-s) nt Uruguay
Urwald m jungle
USA pl USA sing
User(in) (-s, -) m(f) (Inform) user
usw. abk = **und so weiter** etc
Utensilien pl utensils pl

V

vage *adj* vague
Vagina (-, *Vaginen*) *f* vagina
Valentinstag *m* St Valentine's Day
Vandalismus *m* vandalism
Vanille (-) *f* vanilla
variieren *vt, vi* to vary
Vase (-, -n) *f* vase
Vaseline (-) *f* Vaseline®
Vater (-s, *Väter*) *m* father; **väterlich** *adj* paternal; **Vaterschaft** *f* fatherhood; (*Jur*) paternity; **Vatertag** *m* Father's Day; **Vaterunser** *nt*: **das ~** (**beten**) (to say) the Lord's Prayer
V-Ausschnitt *m* V-neck
v. Chr. *abk* = **vor Christus** BC
Veganer(in) (-s, -) *m(f)* vegan; **Vegetarier(in)** (-s, -) *m(f)* vegetarian; **vegetarisch** *adj* vegetarian
Veilchen *nt* violet
Velo (-s, -s) *nt* (*schweizerisch*) bicycle
Vene (-, -n) *f* vein
Venedig (-s) *nt* Venice
Venezuela (-s) *nt* Venezuela
Ventil (-s, -e) *nt* valve
Ventilator *m* ventilator
Venus (-) *f* Venus
Venusmuschel *f* clam
verabreden *vt* to arrange ▷ *vr:* **sich ~** to arrange to meet (*mit jdm* sb); **ich bin schon verabredet** I'm already meeting someone; **Verabredung** *f* arrangement; (*Termin*) appointment; (*zum Ausgehen*) date
verabschieden *vt* (*Gäste*) to say goodbye to; (*Gesetz*) to pass ▷ *vr:* **sich ~** to say goodbye
verachten *vt* to despise; **verächtlich** *adj* contemptuous; (*verachtenswert*) contemptible; **Verachtung** *f* contempt
verallgemeinern *vt* to generalize
Veranda (-, *Veranden*) *f* veranda, porch (*US*)
veränderlich *adj* changeable; **verändern** *vt* to change ▷ *vr:* **sich ~** to change; **Veränderung** *f* change
veranlassen *vt* to cause
veranstalten *vt* to organize; **Veranstalter(in)** (-s, -) *m(f)* organizer; **Veranstaltung** *f* event; **Veranstaltungsort** *m* venue
verantworten *vt* to take responsibility for ▷ *vr:* **sich für etw ~** to answer for sth; **verantwortlich** *adj* responsible (*für* for); **Verantwortung** *f* responsibility (*für* for)
verärgern *vt* to annoy
verarschen *vt* (*fam*) to take the piss out of (*Brit*), to make a sucker out of (*US*)
Verb (-s, -en) *nt* verb

Verband m (Med) bandage; (Bund) association; **Verband(s)kasten** m first-aid box; **Verband(s)zeug** nt dressing material

verbergen irr vt to hide (vor +dat from) ▷ vr: **sich ~** to hide (vor +dat from)

verbessern vt to improve; (berichtigen) to correct ▷ vr: **sich ~** to improve; (berichtigen) to correct oneself; **Verbesserung** f improvement; (Berichtigung) correction

verbiegen irr vi to bend ▷ vr: **sich ~** to bend

verbieten irr vt to forbid; **jdm ~, etw zu tun** to forbid sb to do sth

verbinden irr vt to connect; (kombinieren) to combine; (Med) to bandage; **können Sie mich mit ... ~?** (Tel) can you put me through to ...?; **ich verbinde** (Tel) I'm putting you through ▷ vr (Chem) **sich ~** to combine

verbindlich adj binding; (freundlich) friendly; **Verbindung** f connection

verbleit adj leaded

verblüffen vt to amaze

verblühen vi to fade

verborgen adj hidden

Verbot (-(e)s, -e) nt ban (für, von on); **verboten** adj forbidden; **es ist ~** it's not allowed; **es ist ~, hier zu parken** you're not allowed to park here; **Rauchen ~** no smoking

verbrannt adj burnt

Verbrauch (-(e)s) m consumption; **verbrauchen** vt to use up; **Verbraucher(in)** (-s, -) m(f) consumer

Verbrechen (-s, -) nt crime; **Verbrecher(in)** (-s, -) m(f) criminal

verbreiten vt to spread ▷ vr: **sich ~** to spread

verbrennen irr vt to burn; **Verbrennung** f burning; (in Motor) combustion

verbringen irr vt to spend

verbunden adj: **falsch ~** sorry, wrong number

Verdacht (-(e)s) m suspicion; **verdächtig** adj suspicious; **verdächtigen** vt to suspect

verdammt interj (fam) damn

verdanken vt: **jdm etw ~** to owe sth to sb

verdarb imperf von **verderben**

verdauen vt (a. fig) to digest; **verdaulich** adj digestible; **das ist schwer ~** that is hard to digest; **Verdauung** f digestion

Verdeck (-(e)s, -e) nt top

verderben (verdarb, verdorben) vt to spoil; (schädigen) to ruin; (moralisch) to corrupt; **es sich** (dat) **mit jdm ~** to get into sb's bad books; **ich habe mir den Magen verdorben** I've got an upset stomach ▷ vi (Lebensmittel) to go off

verdienen vt to earn; (moralisch) to deserve; **Verdienst** (-(e)s, -e) m earnings pl ▷ (-(e)s, -e) nt merit; (Leistung) service (um to)

verdoppeln vt to double

verdorben pp von **verderben** ▷ adj spoilt; (geschädigt) ruined; (moralisch) corrupt

verdrehen vt to twist; (Augen) to roll; **jdm den Kopf ~** (fig) to turn sb's head

verdünnen vt to dilute

verdunsten vi to evaporate

verdursten vi to die of thirst

verehren vt to admire; (Rel) to worship; **Verehrer(in)** (-s, -) m(f) admirer

Verein (-(e)s, -e) m association; (Klub) club

vereinbar adj compatible

vereinbaren vt to arrange; **Vereinbarung** f agreement, arrangement

vereinigen vt to unite ▷ vr: **sich ~** to unite; **Vereinigtes Königreich** nt United Kingdom; **Vereinigte Staaten (von Amerika)** pl United States sing (of America); **Vereinigung** f union; (*Verein*) association; **Vereinte Nationen** pl United Nations pl

vereisen vi (*Straße*) to freeze over; (*Fenster*) to ice up ▷ vt (*Med*) to freeze

vererben vt: **jdm etw ~** to leave sth to sb; (*Bio*) to pass sth on to sb ▷ vr: **sich ~** to be hereditary; **vererblich** adj hereditary

verfahren irr vi to proceed ▷ vr: **sich ~** to get lost; **Verfahren** (*-s, -*) nt procedure; (*Tech*) method; (*Jur*) proceedings pl

verfallen irr vi to decline; (*Haus*) to be falling apart; (*Fin*) to lapse; (*Fahrkarte etc*) to expire; **~ in** (*+akk*) to lapse into; **Verfallsdatum** nt expiry (*Brit*) (*o* expiration (*US*)) date; (*von Lebensmitteln*) best-before date

verfärben vr: **sich ~** to change colour; (*Wäsche*) to discolour

Verfasser(in) (*-s, -*) m(f) author, writer; **Verfassung** f (*gesundheitlich*) condition; (*Pol*) constitution

verfaulen vi to rot

verfehlen vt to miss

verfeinern vt to refine

Verfilmung f film (*o* screen) version

verfluchen vt to curse

verfolgen vt to pursue; (*Pol*) to persecute

verfügbar adj available; **verfügen** vi **über etw** (*akk*) **~** to have sth at one's disposal;

Verfügung f order; **jdm zur ~ stehen** to be at sb's disposal; **jdm etw zur ~ stellen** to put sth at sb's disposal

verführen vt to tempt; (*sexuell*) to seduce; **verführerisch** adj seductive

vergangen adj past; **~e Woche** last week; **Vergangenheit** f past

Vergaser (*-s, -*) m (*Auto*) carburettor

vergaß imperf von **vergessen**

vergeben irr vt to forgive (*jdm etw* sb for sth); (*weggeben*) to award, to allocate; **vergebens** adv in vain; **vergeblich** adv in vain ▷ adj vain, futile

vergehen irr vi to pass ▷ vr: **sich an jdm ~** to indecently assault sb; **Vergehen** (*-s, -*) nt offence

Vergeltung f retaliation

vergessen (*vergaß, vergessen*) vt to forget; **vergesslich** adj forgetful

vergeuden vt to squander, to waste

vergewaltigen vt to rape; **Vergewaltigung** f rape

vergewissern vr: **sich ~** to make sure

vergiften vt to poison; **Vergiftung** f poisoning

Vergissmeinnicht (*-(e)s, -e*) nt forget-me-not

Vergleich (*-(e)s, -e*) m comparison; (*Jur*) settlement; **im ~ zu** compared to (*o* with); **vergleichen** irr vt to compare (*mit* to, with)

Vergnügen (*-s, -*) nt pleasure; **viel ~!** enjoy yourself; **vergnügt** adj cheerful; **Vergnügungspark** m amusement park

vergoldet adj gold-plated

vergriffen adj (*Buch*) out of print; (*Ware*) out of stock

vergrößern vt to enlarge; (*Menge*) to increase; (*mit Lupe*) to magnify; **Vergrößerung** f enlargement; (*Menge*) increase; (*mit Lupe*) magnification; **Vergrößerungsglas** nt magnifying glass

verh. adj abk = **verheiratet** married

verhaften vt to arrest

verhalten irr vr: **sich ~** (*sich benehmen*) to behave; (*Sache*) to be; **Verhalten** (-s) nt behaviour

Verhältnis nt relationship (*zu* with); (*Math*) ratio; **~se** pl circumstances pl, conditions pl; **im ~ von 1 zu 2** in a ratio of 1 to 2; **verhältnismäßig** adj relative ▷ adv relatively

verhandeln vi to negotiate (*über etw akk* sth); **Verhandlung** f negotiation

verheimlichen vt to keep secret (*jdm* from sb)

verheiratet adj married

verhindern vt to prevent; **sie ist verhindert** she can't make it

Verhör (-(e)s, -e) nt interrogation; (*gerichtlich*) examination; **verhören** vt to interrogate; (*bei Gericht*) to examine ▷ vr: **sich ~** to mishear

verhungern vi to starve to death

verhüten vt to prevent; **Verhütung** f prevention; (*mit Pille, Kondom etc*) contraception; **Verhütungsmittel** nt contraceptive

verirren vr: **sich ~** to get lost

Verkauf m sale; **verkaufen** vt to sell; **zu ~** for sale; **Verkäufer(in)** m(f) seller; (*beruflich*) salesperson; (*in Laden*) shop assistant (*Brit*), salesperson (*US*); **verkäuflich** adj for sale

Verkehr (-s, -e) m traffic; (*Sex*) intercourse; (*Umlauf*) circulation; **verkehren** vi (*Bus etc*) to run; **~ in** to frequent; **~ mit** to associate (*o* mix) with; **Verkehrsampel** f traffic lights pl; **Verkehrsamt** nt tourist information office; **verkehrsfrei** adj traffic-free; **Verkehrsfunk** m travel news sing; **Verkehrsinsel** f traffic island; **Verkehrsmeldung** f traffic report; **Verkehrsmittel** nt means sing of transport; **öffentliche ~** pl public transport sing; **Verkehrsschild** nt traffic sign; **Verkehrstote(r)** mf road casualty; **die Zahl der ~n** the number of deaths on the road; **Verkehrsunfall** m road accident; **Verkehrszeichen** nt traffic sign

verkehrt adj wrong; (*verkehrt herum*) the wrong way round; (*Pullover etc*) inside out; **du machst es ~** you're doing it wrong

verklagen vt to take to court

verkleiden vt to dress up (*als* as) ▷ vr: **sich ~** to dress up (*als* as); (*um unerkannt zu bleiben*) to disguise oneself; **Verkleidung** f (*Karneval*) fancy dress; (*um nicht erkannt zu werden*) disguise

verkleinern vt to reduce; (*Zimmer, Gebiet etc*) to make smaller

verkneifen irr vt **sich** (*dat*) **etw ~** (*Lachen*) to stifle sth; (*Schmerz*) to hide sth; (*sich versagen*) to do without sth; **verkommen** irr vi to deteriorate; (*Mensch*) to go downhill ▷ adj (*Haus*) dilapidated; (*moralisch*) depraved; **verkraften** vt to cope with

verkratzt adj scratched

verkühlen vr: **sich ~** to get a chill

verkürzen vt to shorten

Verlag (-(e)s, -e) m publishing company

verlangen vt (*fordern*) to

demand; (*wollen*) to want; (*Preis*) to ask; (*Qualifikation*) to require; (*erwarten*) to ask (*von* of); (*fragen nach*) to ask for; (*Pass etc*) to ask to see; **~ Sie Herrn X** ask for Mr X ▷ *vi:* **~ nach** to ask for

verlängern *vt* to extend; (*Pass, Erlaubnis*) renew; **Verlängerung** *f* extension; (*Sport*) extra time; (*von Pass, Erlaubnis*) renewal; **Verlängerungsschnur** *f* extension cable; **Verlängerungswoche** *f* extra week

verlassen *irr vt* to leave ▷ *irr vr:* **sich ~** to rely (*auf +akk* on) ▷ *adj* desolate; (*Mensch*) abandoned; **verlässlich** *adj* reliable

Verlauf *m* course; **verlaufen** *irr vi* (*Weg, Grenze*) to run (*entlang* along); (*zeitlich*) to pass; (*Farben*) to run ▷ *vr:* **sich ~** to get lost; (*Menschenmenge*) to disperse

verlegen *vt* to move; (*verlieren*) to mislay; (*Buch*) to publish ▷ *adj* embarrassed; **Verlegenheit** *f* embarrassment; (*Situation*) difficulty

Verleih (*-(e)s, -e*) *m* (*Firma*) hire company (*Brit*), rental company (*US*); **verleihen** *irr vt* to lend; (*vermieten*) to hire (out) (*Brit*), to rent (out) (*US*); (*Preis, Medaille*) to award

verleiten *vt:* **jdn dazu ~, etw zu tun** to induce sb to do sth

verlernen *vt* to forget

verletzen *vt* to injure; (*fig*) to hurt; **Verletzte(r)** *mf* injured person; **Verletzung** *f* injury; (*Verstoß*) violation

verlieben *vr:* **sich ~** to fall in love (*in jdn* with sb); **verliebt** *adj* in love

verlieren (*verlor, verloren*) *vt, vi* to lose

verloben *vr:* **sich ~** to get engaged (*mit* to); **Verlobte(r)** *mf*

fiancé/fiancée; **Verlobung** *f* engagement

verlor *imperf von* **verlieren**

verloren *pp von* **verlieren** ▷ *adj* lost; (*Eier*) poached; **~ gehen** to go missing

verlosen *vt* to raffle; **Verlosung** *f* raffle

Verlust (*-(e)s, -e*) *m* loss

vermehren *vt* to multiply; (*Menge*) to increase ▷ *vr:* **sich ~** to multiply; (*Menge*) to increase

vermeiden *irr vt* to avoid

vermeintlich *adj* supposed

vermieten *vt* to rent (out), to let (out) (*Brit*); (*Auto*) to hire (out) (*Brit*), to rent (out) (*US*); **Vermieter(in)** *m(f)* landlord/-lady

vermischen *vt* to mix ▷ *vr:* **sich ~** to mix

vermissen *vt* to miss; **vermisst** *adj* missing; **jdn als ~ melden** to report sb missing

Vermittlung *f* (*bei Streit*) mediation; (*Herbeiführung*) arranging; (*Stelle*) agency

Vermögen (*-s, -*) *nt* fortune

vermuten *vt* to suppose; (*argwöhnen*) to suspect; **vermutlich** *adj* probable ▷ *adv* probably; **Vermutung** *f* supposition; (*Verdacht*) suspicion

vernachlässigen *vt* to neglect

vernichten *vt* to destroy; **vernichtend** *adj* (*fig*) crushing; (*Blick*) withering; (*Kritik*) scathing

Vernunft (*-*) *f* reason; **ich kann ihn nicht zur ~ bringen** I can't make him see reason; **vernünftig** *adj* sensible; (*Preis*) reasonable

veröffentlichen *vt* to publish

verordnen *vt* (*Med*) to prescribe; **Verordnung** *f* order; (*Med*) prescription

verpachten *vt* to lease (out) (*an +akk* to)

verpacken vt to pack; (einwickeln) to wrap up

Verpackung f packaging; **Verpackungskosten** pl packing charges pl

verpassen vt to miss

verpflegen vt to feed; **Verpflegung** f feeding; (Kost) food; (in Hotel) board

verpflichten vt to oblige; (anstellen) to engage ▷ vr: **sich ~** to commit oneself (etw zu tun to doing sth)

verprügeln vt to beat up

verraten irr vt to betray; (Geheimnis) to divulge; **aber nicht ~!** but don't tell anyone ▷ vr: **sich ~** to give oneself away

verrechnen vt: **~ mit** to set off against ▷ vr: **sich ~** to miscalculate; **Verrechnungsscheck** m crossed cheque (Brit), check for deposit only (US)

verregnet adj rainy

verreisen vi to go away (nach to); **sie ist (geschäftlich) verreist** she's away (on business);

verrenken vt to contort; (Med) to dislocate; **sich** (dat) **den Knöchel ~** to sprain (o twist) one's ankle; **verringern** vt to reduce

verrostet adj rusty

verrückt adj mad, crazy; **es macht mich ~** it's driving me mad

versagen vi to fail; **Versagen** (-s) nt failure; **Versager(in)** (-s, -) m(f) failure

versalzen irr vt to put too much salt in/on

versammeln vt to assemble, to gather ▷ vr: **sich ~** to assemble, to gather; **Versammlung** f meeting

Versand (-(e)s) m dispatch; (Abteilung) dispatch department; **Versandhaus** nt mail-order company

versäumen vt to miss; (unterlassen) to neglect; **~, etw zu tun** to fail to do sth

verschätzen vr: **sich ~** to miscalculate

verschenken vt to give away; (Chance) to waste

verschicken vt to send off

verschieben vt irr (auf später) to postpone, to put off; (an anderen Ort) to move

verschieden adj (unterschiedlich) different; (mehrere) various; **sie sind ~ groß** they are of different sizes; **Verschiedene** pl various people/things pl; **Verschiedenes** various things pl

verschimmelt adj mouldy

verschlafen irr vt to sleep through; (fig) to miss ▷ vi to oversleep

verschlechtern vr: **sich ~** to deteriorate, to get worse; **Verschlechterung** f deterioration

Verschleiß (-es) m wear and tear

verschließbar adj lockable; **verschließen** irr vt to close; (mit Schlüssel) to lock

verschlimmern vt to make worse ▷ vr: **sich ~** to get worse

verschlossen adj locked; (fig) reserved

verschlucken vt to swallow ▷ vr: **sich ~** to choke (an +dat on)

Verschluss m lock; (von Kleid) fastener; (Foto) shutter; (Stöpsel) stopper

verschmutzen vt to get dirty; (Umwelt) to pollute

verschnaufen vi: **ich muss mal ~** I need to get my breath back

verschneit adj snow-covered

verschnupft adj: **~ sein** to have a cold; (fam: beleidigt) to be peeved

verschonen vt to spare (jdn mit etw sb sth)

verschreiben *irr vt (Med)* to prescribe;
verschreibungspflichtig *adj* available only on prescription
verschwand *imperf von* **verschwinden**
verschweigen *irr vt* to keep secret; **jdm etw ~** to keep sth from sb
verschwenden *vt* to waste; **Verschwendung** *f* waste
verschwiegen *adj* discreet; *(Ort)* secluded
verschwinden *(verschwand, verschwunden) vi* to disappear, to vanish; **verschwinde!** get lost!; **verschwunden** *pp von* **verschwinden**
Versehen *(-s, -) nt*: **aus ~** by mistake; **versehentlich** *adv* by mistake
versenden *irr vt* to send off
versessen *adj* **~ auf** *(+akk)* mad about
versetzen *vt* to transfer; *(verpfänden)* to pawn; *(fam: bei Verabredung)* to stand up ▷ *vr*: **sich in jdn** *(o* **jds Lage) ~** to put oneself in sb's place
verseuchen *vt* to contaminate
versichern *vt* to insure; *(bestätigen)* to assure; **versichert sein** to be insured; **Versichertenkarte** *f* health-insurance card; **Versicherung** *f* insurance; **Versicherungskarte** *f*: **grüne ~** green card *(Brit)*, *insurance document for driving abroad*; **Versicherungspolice** *f* insurance policy
versilbert *adj* silver-plated
versinken *irr vi* to sink
Version *f* version
versöhnen *vt* to reconcile ▷ *vr*: **sich ~** to become reconciled
versorgen *vt* to provide, to supply *(mit with)*; *(Familie)* to look after ▷ *vr*: **sich ~** to look after oneself; **Versorgung** *f* provision; *(Unterhalt)* maintenance; *(für Alter etc)* benefit
verspäten *vr*: **sich ~** to be late; **verspätet** *adj* late; **Verspätung** *f* delay; **(eine Stunde) ~ haben** to be (an hour) late
versprechen *irr vt* to promise ▷ *vr*: **ich habe mich versprochen** I didn't mean to say that
Verstand *m* mind; *(Vernunft)* (common) sense; **den ~ verlieren** to lose one's mind; **verständigen** *vt* to inform ▷ *vr*: **sich ~** to communicate; *(sich einigen)* to come to an understanding; **Verständigung** *f* communication; **verständlich** *adj* understandable; **Verständnis** *nt* understanding *(für of)*; *(Mitgefühl)* sympathy; **verständnisvoll** *adj* understanding
verstauchen *vt* to sprain; **verstaucht** *pp von* **verstauchen** sprained
Versteck *(-(e)s, -e) nt* hiding place; **~ spielen** to play hide-and-seek; **verstecken** *vt* to hide *(vor +dat from)* ▷ *vr*: **sich ~** to hide *(vor +dat from)*
verstehen *irr vt* to understand; **falsch ~** to misunderstand ▷ *vr*: **sich ~** to get on *(mit with)*
Versteigerung *f* auction
verstellbar *adj* adjustable; **verstellen** *vt* to move; *(Uhr)* to adjust; *(versperren)* to block; *(Stimme, Handschrift)* to disguise ▷ *vr*: **sich ~** to pretend, to put on an act
verstopfen *vt* to block up; *(Med)* to constipate; **Verstopfung** *f* obstruction; *(Med)* constipation
Verstoß *m* infringement, violation *(gegen of)*

Versuch (-(e)s, -e) m attempt; (wissenschaftlich) experiment; **versuchen** vt to try

vertauschen vt to exchange; (versehentlich) to mix up

verteidigen vt to defend; **Verteidiger(in)** (-s, -) m(f) (Sport) defender; (Jur) defence counsel; **Verteidigung** f defence

verteilen vt to distribute

Vertrag (-(e)s, Verträge) m contract; (Pol) treaty

vertragen irr vt to stand, to bear ▷ vr: **sich ~** to get along (with each other); (sich aussöhnen) to make it up

verträglich adj (Mensch) good-natured; (Speisen) digestible

vertrauen vi: **jdm/einer Sache ~** to trust sb/sth; **Vertrauen** (-s) nt trust (in +akk in, zu in); **ich habe kein ~ zu ihm** I don't trust him; **ich hab's ihm im ~ gesagt** I told him in confidence; **vertraulich** adj (geheim) confidential; **vertraut** adj: **sich mit etw ~ machen** to familiarize oneself with sth

vertreten irr vt to represent; (Ansicht) to hold; **Vertreter(in)** (-s, -) m(f) representative

Vertrieb (-(e)s, -e) m (Abteilung) sales department

vertrocknen vi to dry up

vertun irr vr: **sich ~** to make a mistake

vertuschen vt to cover up

verunglücken vi to have an accident; **tödlich ~** to be killed in an accident

verunsichern vt to make uneasy

verursachen vt to cause

verurteilen vt to condemn

vervielfältigen vt to make copies of

verwählen vr: **sich ~** to dial the wrong number

verwalten vt to manage; (behördlich) to administer; **Verwalter(in)** (-s, -) m(f) manager; (Vermögens~) trustee; **Verwaltung** f management; (amtlich) administration

verwandt adj related (mit to); **Verwandte(r)** mf relative, relation; **Verwandtschaft** f relationship; (Menschen) relations pl

verwarnen vt to warn; (Sport) to caution

verwechseln vt to confuse (mit with); (halten für) to mistake (mit for)

verweigern vt to refuse

verwenden vt to use; (Zeit) to spend; **Mühe auf etw** (akk) **~** to take trouble over sth; **Verwendung** f use

verwirklichen vt to realize; **sich selbst ~** to fulfil oneself

verwirren vt to confuse; **Verwirrung** f confusion

verwitwet adj widowed

verwöhnen vt to spoil

verwunderlich adj surprising; **Verwunderung** f astonishment

verwüsten vt to devastate

verzählen vr: **sich ~** to miscount

verzehren vt to consume

Verzeichnis nt (Liste) list; (Katalog) catalogue; (in Buch) index; (Inform) directory

verzeihen (verzieh, verziehen) vt, vi to forgive (jdm etw sb for sth); **~ Sie bitte, ...** (vor Frage etc) excuse me, ...; **~ Sie die Störung** sorry to disturb you; **Verzeihung** f: **~!** sorry; **~, ...** (vor Frage etc) excuse me, ...; (jdn) **um ~ bitten** to apologize (to sb)

verzichten vi **auf etw** (akk) **~** to do without sth; (aufgeben) to give sth up

verzieh *imperf von* **verzeihen**

verziehen *pp von* **verzeihen**

verziehen *irr vt* (*Kind*) to spoil; **das Gesicht ~** to pull a face ▷ *vr:* **sich ~** to go out of shape; (*Gesicht*) to contort; (*verschwinden*) to disappear

verzieren *vt* to decorate

verzögern *vt* to delay ▷ *vr:* **sich ~** to be delayed; **Verzögerung** *f* delay

verzweifeln *vi* to despair (*an* +*dat* of); **verzweifelt** *adj* desperate; **Verzweiflung** *f* despair

Veterinär(in) (*-s, -e*) *m(f)* veterinary surgeon (*Brit*), veterinarian (*US*)

Vetter (*-s, -n*) *m* cousin

vgl. *abk* = **vergleiche** cf

Viagra® (*-s*) *nt* Viagra®

Vibrator (*-s, -en*) *m* vibrator; **vibrieren** *vi* to vibrate

Video (*-s, -s*) *nt* video; **auf ~ aufnehmen** to video; **Videoclip** (*-s, -s*) *m* video clip; **Videofilm** *m* video; **Videogerät** *nt* video (recorder); **Videokamera** *f* video camera; **Videokassette** *f* video (cassette); **Videorekorder** *m* video recorder; **Videospiel** *nt* video game; **Videothek** (*-, -en*) *f* video library

Vieh (*-(e)s*) *nt* cattle

viel *pron* a lot (of), lots of; **~ Arbeit** a lot of work, lots of work; **~e Leute** a lot of people, lots of people, many people; **zu ~** too much; **zu ~e** too many; **sehr ~** a great deal of; **sehr ~e** a great many; **ziemlich ~/~e** quite a lot of; **nicht ~** not much, not a lot of; **nicht ~e** not many, not a lot of ▷ *pron:* **sie sagt nicht ~** she doesn't say a lot; **nicht ~** not much, not a lot of; **nicht ~e** not many, not a lot of; **gibt es ~?** is

there much?, is there a lot?; **gibt es ~e?** are there many?, are there a lot? ▷ *adv* a lot; **er geht ~ ins Kino** he goes a lot to the cinema; **sehr ~** a great deal; **ziemlich ~** quite a lot; **~ besser** much better; **~ teurer** much more expensive; **~ zu ~** far too much

vielleicht *adv* perhaps; **~ ist sie krank** perhaps she's ill, she might be ill; **weißt du ~, wo er ist?** do you know where he is (by any chance)?

vielmal(s) *adv* many times; **danke ~s** many thanks; **vielmehr** *adv* rather; **vielseitig** *adj* very varied; (*Mensch, Gerät*) versatile

vier *num* four; **auf allen ~en** on all fours; **unter ~ Augen** in private, privately; **Vier** (*-, -en*) *f* four; (*Schulnote*) ≈ D; **Vierbettzimmer** *nt* four-bed room; **Viereck** (*-(e)s, -e*) *nt* four-sided figure; (*Quadrat*) square; **viereckig** *adj* four-sided; (*quadratisch*) square; **vierfach** *adj:* **die ~e Menge** four times the amount; **vierhundert** *num* four hundred; **viermal** *adv* four times; **vierspurig** *adj* four-lane

viert *adv:* **wir sind zu ~** there are four of us; **vierte(r, s)** *adj* fourth; *siehe auch* **dritte**

Viertel (*-s, -*) *nt* (*Stadtviertel*) quarter, district; (*Bruchteil*) quarter; (*Viertelliter*) quarter-litre; (*Uhrzeit*) quarter; **vor/nach drei** a quarter to/past three; **viertel drei** a quarter past two; **drei viertel drei** a quarter to three; **Viertelfinale** *nt* quarter-final; **vierteljährlich** *adj* quarterly; **Viertelstunde** *f* quarter of an hour

vierzehn *num* fourteen; **in ~ Tagen** in two weeks, in a fortnight (*Brit*); **vierzehntägig** *adj* two-week, fortnightly (*Brit*);

vierzehnte(r, s) adj fourteenth; siehe auch **dritte**; **vierzig** num forty; **vierzigste(r, s)** adj fortieth
Vietnam (-s) nt Vietnam
Vignette f (Autobahn~) motorway (Brit) (o freeway (US)) permit
Villa (-, Villen) f villa
violett adj purple
Violine f violin
Virus (-, Viren) m o nt virus
Visitenkarte f card
Visum (-s, Visa o Visen) nt visa
Vitamin (-s, -e) nt vitamin
Vitrine (-, -n) f (glass) cabinet; (Schaukasten) display case
Vogel (-s, Vögel) m bird; **Vogelgrippe** f bird flu, avian flu; **vögeln** vi, vt (vulg) to screw
Voicemail (-, -s) f voice mail
Vokal (-s, -e) m vowel
Volk (-(e)s, Völker) nt people pl; (Nation) nation; **Volksfest** nt festival; (Jahrmarkt) funfair; **Volkshochschule** f adult education centre; **Volkslied** nt folksong; **Volksmusik** f folk music; **volkstümlich** adj (einfach und beliebt) popular; (herkömmlich) traditional; (Kunst) folk
voll adj full (von of); **voll|machen** vt to fill (up); **voll|tanken** vi to fill up
Vollbart m beard; **Vollbremsung** f: **eine ~ machen** to slam on the brakes; **vollends** adv completely
Volleyball m volleyball
Vollgas nt: **mit ~** at full throttle; **~ geben** to step on it
völlig adj complete ▷ adv completely
volljährig adj of age; **Vollkaskoversicherung** f fully comprehensive insurance; **vollklimatisiert** adj fully

air-conditioned; **vollkommen** adj perfect; **~er Unsinn** complete rubbish ▷ adv completely
Vollkornbrot nt wholemeal (Brit) (o whole wheat (US)) bread
Vollmacht (-, -en) f authority; (Urkunde) power of attorney
Vollmilch f full-fat milk (Brit), whole milk (US); **Vollmilchschokolade** f milk chocolate; **Vollmond** m full moon; **Vollnarkose** f general anaesthetic; **Vollpension** f full board
vollständig adj complete
Volltreffer m direct hit; **Vollwertkost** f wholefood; **vollzählig** adj complete
Volt (-, -) nt volt
Volumen (-s, -) nt volume
vom kontr von **von dem** (räumlich, zeitlich, Ursache) from; **ich kenne sie nur ~ Sehen** I only know her by sight

○ SCHLÜSSELWORT

von prep +dat 1 (Ausgangspunkt) from; **von ... bis ...** from ... to; **von morgens bis abends** from morning till night; **von ... nach ...** from ... to ...; **von ... an** from ...; **von ... aus** from ...; **von dort aus** from there; **etw von sich aus tun** to do sth of one's own accord; **von mir aus** (fam) if you like, I don't mind; **von wo/wann ...?** where/when ... from?
2 (Ursache, im Passiv) by; **ein Gedicht von Schiller** a poem by Schiller; **von etw müde** tired from sth
3 (als Genitiv) of; **ein Freund von mir** a friend of mine; **nett von dir** nice of you; **jeweils zwei von zehn** two out of every ten
4 (über) about; **er erzählte vom**

Urlaub he talked about his holiday
5 von wegen! (*fam*) no way!

voneinander *adv* from each
other

 SCHLÜSSELWORT

vor *prep* +dat **1** (*räumlich*) in front
of; **vor der Kirche links abbiegen**
turn left before the church
2 (*zeitlich*) before; **ich war vor ihm
da** I was there before him; **vor 2
Tagen** 2 days ago; **5 (Minuten) vor
4** 5 (minutes) to 4; **vor Kurzem** a
little while ago
3 (*Ursache*) with; **vor Wut/Liebe**
with rage/love; **vor Hunger
sterben** to die of hunger; **vor
lauter Arbeit** because of work
4 vor allem, vor allen Dingen
most of all
▷ *prep* +akk (*räumlich*) in front of
▷ *adv*: **vor und zurück** backwards
and forwards

voran|gehen *irr vi* to go ahead;
einer Sache (*dat*) **~** to precede sth;
voran|kommen *irr vi* to make
progress
Vorarlberg (-s) *nt* Vorarlberg
voraus *adv* ahead ; **im Voraus** in
advance; **voraus|fahren** *irr vi* to
drive on ahead; **vorausgesetzt**
conj provided (that); **Voraussage**
f prediction; (*Wetter*) forecast;
voraus|sagen *vt* to predict;
voraus|sehen *irr vt* to foresee;
voraus|sein *irr vi*: **jdm ~** to be
ahead of sb; **voraus|setzen** *vt* to
assume; **Voraussetzung** *f*
requirement, prerequisite;
voraussichtlich *adj* expected
▷ *adv* probably; **voraus|zahlen**
vt to pay in advance
Vorbehalt (-(e)s, -e) *m*
reservation; **vor|behalten** *irr vt*:

sich/jdm etw ~ to reserve sth (for
oneself)/for sb
vorbei *adv* past, over, finished;
vorbei|bringen *irr vt* to drop by
(*o in*); **vorbei|fahren** *irr vi* to
drive past; **vorbei|gehen** *irr vi* to
pass by, to go past; (*verstreichen,
aufhören*) to pass; **vorbei|kommen**
irr vi to drop by; **vorbei|lassen** *irr
vt*: **kannst du die Leute ~?** would
you let these people pass?; **lässt
du mich bitte mal vorbei?** can I
get past, please?; **vorbei|reden**
vi: **aneinander ~** to talk at
cross-purposes
vor|bereiten *vt* to prepare ▷ *vr*:
sich ~ to get ready (*auf* +akk, **für**
for); **Vorbereitung** *f* preparation
vor|bestellen *vt* to book in
advance; (*Essen*) to order in
advance; **Vorbestellung** *f*
booking, reservation
vor|beugen *vi* to prevent (*dat*
sth); **vorbeugend** *adj* preven-
tive; **Vorbeugung** *f* prevention
Vorbild *nt* (role) model;
vorbildlich *adj* model, ideal
Vorderachse *f* front axle;
vordere(r, s) *adj* front;
Vordergrund *m* foreground;
Vorderradantrieb *m* (*Auto*)
front-wheel drive; **Vorderseite** *f*
front; **Vordersitz** *m* front seat;
Vorderteil *m o nt* front (part)
Vordruck *m* form
voreilig *adj* hasty, rash; **~e
Schlüsse ziehen** to jump to
conclusions; **voreingenommen**
adj biased
vor|enthalten *irr vt*: **jdm etw
~** to withhold sth from sb
vorerst *adv* for the moment
vor|fahren *irr vi* (*vorausfahren*) to
drive on ahead; **vor das Haus ~** to
drive up to the house; **fahren Sie
bis zur Ampel vor** drive as far as
the traffic lights

Vorfahrt f (*Auto*) right of way; **~ achten** give way (*Brit*), yield (*US*); **Vorfahrtsschild** nt give way (*Brit*) (*o* yield (*US*)) sign; **Vorfahrtsstraße** f major road

Vorfall m incident

vor|führen vt to demonstrate; (*Film*) to show; (*Theaterstück, Trick*) to perform

Vorgänger(in) m(f) predecessor

vor|gehen irr vi (*vorausgehen*) to go on ahead; (*nach vorn*) to go forward; (*handeln*) to act, to proceed; (*Uhr*) to be fast; (*Vorrang haben*) to take precedence; (*passieren*) to go on; **Vorgehen** (-s) nt procedure

Vorgesetzte(r) mf superior

vorgestern adv the day before yesterday

vor|haben irr vt to plan; **hast du schon was vor?** have you got anything on?; **ich habe vor, nach Rom zu fahren** I'm planning to go to Rome

vor|halten irr vt: **jdm etw ~** to accuse sb of sth

Vorhand f forehand

vorhanden adj existing; (*erhältlich*) available

Vorhang m curtain

Vorhaut f foreskin

vorher adv before; **zwei Tage ~** two days before; **~ essen wir** we'll eat first; **Vorhersage** f forecast; **vorher|sehen** irr vt to foresee

vorhin adv just now, a moment ago

Vorkenntnisse pl previous knowledge *sing*

vor|kommen irr vi (*nach vorne kommen*) to come forward; (*geschehen*) to happen; (*sich finden*) to occur; (*scheinen*) to seem (to be); **sich** (*dat*) **dumm ~** to feel stupid

Vorlage f model

vor|lassen irr vt: **jdn ~** to let sb go first

vorläufig adj temporary

vor|lesen irr vt to read out

Vorlesung f lecture

vorletzte(r, s) adj last but one; **am ~n Samstag** (on) the Saturday before last

Vorliebe f preference

vor|machen vt: **kannst du es mir ~?** can you show me how to do it?; **jdm etwas ~** (*fig: täuschen*) to fool sb

vor|merken vt to note down; (*Plätze*) to book

Vormittag m morning; **am ~** in the morning; **heute ~** this morning; **vormittags** adv in the morning; **um 9 Uhr ~** at 9 (o'clock) in the morning, at 9 am

vorn(e) adv in front; **von ~ anfangen** to start at the beginning; **nach ~** to the front; **weiter ~** further up; **von ~ bis hinten** from beginning to end

Vorname m first name; **wie heißt du mit ~** what's your first name?

vornehm adj (*von Rang*) distinguished; (*Benehmen*) refined; (*fein, elegant*) elegant

vor|nehmen irr vt **sich** (*dat*) **etw ~** to start on sth; **sich** (*dat*) **~, etw zu tun** (*beschließen*) to decide to do sth

vornherein adv: **von ~** from the start

Vorort m suburb

vorrangig adj priority

Vorrat m stock, supply; **vorrätig** adj in stock

Vorrecht nt privilege

Vorruhestand m early retirement

Vorsaison f early season

Vorsatz m intention; (*Jur*) intent;

vorsätzlich adj intentional; (Jur) premeditated

Vorschau f preview; (Film) trailer

Vorschlag m suggestion, proposal; **vorschlagen** irr vt to suggest, to propose; **ich schlage vor, dass wir gehen** I suggest we go

vor|schreiben irr vt (befehlen) to stipulate; **jdm etw ~** to dictate sth to sb

Vorschrift f regulation, rule; (Anweisung) instruction; **vorschriftsmäßig** adj correct

Vorschule f nursery school, pre-school (US)

Vorsicht f care; **~!** look out; (Schild) caution; **~ Stufe!** mind the step; **vorsichtig** adj careful; **vorsichtshalber** adv just in case

Vorsorge f precaution; (Vorbeugung) prevention; **Vorsorgeuntersuchung** f checkup; **vorsorglich** adv as a precaution

Vorspann (-(e)s, -e) m credits pl

Vorspeise f starter

Vorsprung m projection; (Abstand) lead

vor|stellen vt (bekannt machen) to introduce; (Uhr) to put forward; (vor etw) to put in front; **sich** (dat) **etw ~** to imagine sth; **Vorstellung** f (Bekanntmachen) introduction; (Theat) performance; (Gedanke) idea; **Vorstellungsgespräch** nt interview

vor|täuschen vt to feign

Vorteil m advantage (gegenüber over); **die Vor- und Nachteile** the pros and cons; **vorteilhaft** adj advantageous

Vortrag (-(e)s, Vorträge) m talk (über +akk on); (akademisch) lecture; **einen ~ halten** to give a talk

vorüber adv over; **vorüber|gehen** irr vi to pass; **vorübergehend** adj temporary

▷ adv temporarily, for the time being

Vorurteil nt prejudice

Vorverkauf m advance booking

vor|verlegen vt to bring forward

Vorwahl f (Tel) dialling code (Brit), area code (US)

Vorwand (-(e)s, Vorwände) m pretext, excuse; **unter dem ~, dass** with the excuse that

vorwärts adv forward; **vorwärts|gehen** irr vi (fig) to progress

vorweg adv in advance; **vorweg|nehmen** irr vt to anticipate

Vorweihnachtszeit f pre-Christmas period, run-up to Christmas (Brit)

vor|werfen irr vt: **jdm etw ~** to accuse sb of sth

vorwiegend adv mainly

Vorwort nt preface

Vorwurf m reproach; **sich** (dat) **Vorwürfe machen** to reproach oneself; **jdm Vorwürfe machen** to accuse sb; **vorwurfsvoll** adj reproachful

vor|zeigen vt to show

vorzeitig adj premature, early

vor|ziehen irr vt (lieber haben) to prefer

Vorzug m preference; (gute Eigenschaft) merit; (Vorteil) advantage

vorzüglich adj excellent

vulgär adj vulgar

Vulkan (-s, -e) m volcano; **Vulkanausbruch** m volcanic eruption

W

W *abk* = **West** W

Waage (-, -n) *f* scales *pl*; (*Astr*) Libra; **waagerecht** *adj* horizontal

wach *adj* awake; **~ werden** to wake up; **Wache** (-, -n) *f* guard

Wachs (-es, -e) *nt* wax

wachsen (*wuchs, gewachsen*) *vi* to grow

wachsen *vt* (*Skier*) to wax

Wachstum *nt* growth

Wachtel (-, -n) *f* quail

Wächter(in) (-s, -) *m(f)* guard; (*auf Parkplatz*) attendant

wackelig *adj* wobbly; (*fig*) shaky; **Wackelkontakt** *m* loose connection; **wackeln** *vi* (*Stuhl*) to be wobbly; (*Zahn, Schraube*) to be loose; **mit dem Kopf ~** to waggle one's head

Wade (-, -n) *f* (*Anat*) calf

Waffe (-, -n) *f* weapon

Waffel (-, -n) *f* waffle; (*Keks, Eiswaffel*) wafer

wagen *vt* to risk; **es ~, etw zu tun** to dare to do sth

Wagen (-s, -) *m* (*Auto*) car; (*Eisenb*) carriage; **Wagenheber** (-s, -) *m* jack; **Wagentyp** *m* model, make

Wahl (-, -en) *f* choice; (*Pol*) election

wählen *vt* to choose; (*Tel*) to dial; (*Pol*) to vote for; (*durch Wahl ermitteln*) to elect ▷ *vi* to choose; (*Tel*) to dial; (*Pol*) to vote; **Wähler(in)** (-s, -) *m(f)* voter; **wählerisch** *adj* choosy

Wahlkampf *m* election campaign; **wahllos** *adv* at random; **Wahlwiederholung** *f* redial

Wahnsinn *m* madness; **~!** amazing!; **wahnsinnig** *adj* insane, mad ▷ *adv* (*fam*) incredibly

wahr *adj* true; **das darf doch nicht ~ sein!** I don't believe it; **nicht ~?** that's right, isn't it?

während *prep* +gen during ▷ *conj* while; **währenddessen** *adv* meanwhile, in the meantime

Wahrheit *f* truth

wahrnehmbar *adj* noticeable, perceptible; **wahr|nehmen** *irr vt* to perceive

Wahrsager(in) (-s, -) *m(f)* fortune-teller

wahrscheinlich *adj* probable, likely ▷ *adv* probably; **ich komme ~ zu spät** I'll probably be late; **Wahrscheinlichkeit** *f* probability

Währung *f* currency

Wahrzeichen *nt* symbol

Waise (-, -n) *f* orphan

Wal (-(e)s, -e) *m* whale

Wald (-(e)s, *Wälder*) *m* wood; (*groß*) forest; **Waldbrand** *m* forest fire; **Waldsterben** (-s) *nt* forest dieback

Wales (-) nt Wales; **Waliser(in)** m(f) Welshman/Welshwoman; **walisisch** adj Welsh; **Walisisch** nt Welsh

Walkie-Talkie (-(s), -s) nt walkie-talkie

Walkman® (-s, -s) m walkman®, personal stereo

Wall (-(e)s, Wälle) m embankment

Wallfahrt f pilgrimage; **Wallfahrtsort** m place of pilgrimage

Walnuss f walnut

Walross (-es, -e) nt walrus

wälzen vt to roll; (Bücher) to pore over; (Probleme) to deliberate on ▷ vr: **sich ~** to wallow; (vor Schmerzen) to roll about; (im Bett) to toss and turn

Walzer (-s, -) m waltz

Wand (-, Wände) f wall; (Trenn~) partition; (Berg~) (rock) face

Wandel (-s) m change; **wandeln** vt to change ▷ vr: **sich ~** to change

Wanderer (-s, -) m, **Wanderin** f hiker; **Wanderkarte** f hiking map; **wandern** vi to hike; (Blick) to wander; (Gedanken) to stray; **Wanderschuh** m walking shoe; **Wanderstiefel** m hiking boot; **Wanderung** f hike; **eine ~ machen** to go on a hike; **Wanderweg** m walking (o hiking) trail

Wandleuchte f wall lamp; **Wandmalerei** f mural; **Wandschrank** m built-in cupboard (Brit), closet (US)

wandte imperf von **wenden**

Wange (-, -n) f cheek

wann adv when; **seit ~ ist sie da?** how long has she been here?; **bis ~ bleibt ihr?** how long are you staying?

Wanne (-, -n) f (bath) tub

Wappen (-s, -) nt coat of arms

war imperf von **sein**

warb imperf von **werben**

Ware (-, -n) f product; **~n** goods pl; **Warenhaus** nt department store; **Warenprobe** f sample; **Warenzeichen** nt trademark

warf imperf von **werfen**

warm adj warm; (Essen) hot; **~ laufen** to warm up; **mir ist es zu ~** I'm too warm; **Wärme** (-, -n) f warmth; **wärmen** vt to warm; (Essen) to warm (o to heat) up ▷ vi (Kleidung, Sonne) to be warm ▷ vr: **sich ~** to warm up; (gegenseitig) to keep each other warm; **Wärmflasche** f hot-water bottle; **Warmstart** m (Inform) warm start

Warnblinkanlage f (Auto) warning flasher; **Warndreieck** nt (Auto) warning triangle; **warnen** vt to warn (vor +dat about, of); **Warnung** f warning

Warteliste f waiting list; **warten** vi to wait (auf +akk for); **warte mal!** wait (o hang on) a minute ▷ vt (Tech) to service

Wärter(in) m(f) attendant

Wartesaal m, **Wartezimmer** nt waiting room

Wartung f service; (das Warten) servicing

warum adv why

Warze (-, -n) f wart

was pron what; (fam: etwas) something; **~ kostet das?** what does it cost? how much is it?; **~ für ein Auto ist das?** what kind of car is that?; **~ für eine Farbe/Größe?** what colour/size?; **~?** (fam: wie bitte?) what?; **~ ist/gibt's?** what is it? what's up? **du weißt, ~ ich meine** you know what I mean; **~ (auch) immer** whatever; **soll ich dir ~ mitbringen?** do you want me to bring you anything?; **alles, ~ er hat** everything he's got

Waschanlage f (*Auto*) car wash; **waschbar** adj washable; **Waschbär** m raccoon; **Waschbecken** nt washbasin

Wäsche (-, -n) f washing; (*schmutzig*) laundry; (*Bettwäsche*) linen; (*Unterwäsche*) underwear; **in der ~** in the wash; **Wäscheklammer** f clothes peg (*Brit*) (o pin (*US*)); **Wäscheleine** f clothesline

waschen (*wusch, gewaschen*) vt, vi to wash; **Waschen und Legen** shampoo and set ▷ vr: **sich ~** to (have a) wash; **sich** (*dat*) **die Haare ~** to wash one's hair

Wäscherei f laundry; **Wäscheständer** m clothes horse; **Wäschetrockner** m tumble-drier

Waschgelegenheit f washing facilities pl; **Waschlappen** m flannel (*Brit*), washcloth (*US*); (*fam: Mensch*) wet blanket; **Waschmaschine** f washing machine; **Waschmittel** nt, **Waschpulver** nt washing powder; **Waschraum** m washroom; **Waschsalon** (-s, -s) m launderette (*Brit*), laundromat (*US*); **Waschstraße** f car wash

Wasser (-s, -) nt water; **fließendes ~** running water; **Wasserball** m (*Sport*) water polo; **Wasserbob** m jet ski; **wasserdicht** adj watertight; (*Uhr etc*) waterproof; **Wasserfall** m waterfall; **Wasserfarbe** f watercolour; **wasserfest** adj watertight, waterproof; **Wasserhahn** m tap (*Brit*), faucet (*US*); **wässerig** adj watery; **Wasserkessel** (-s, -) m kettle; **Wasserkocher** (-s, -) m electric kettle; **Wasserleitung** f water pipe; **wasserlöslich** adj water-soluble; **Wassermann** m (*Astr*) Aquarius; **Wassermelone** f

water melon; **Wasserrutschbahn** f water chute; **Wasserschaden** m water damage; **wasserscheu** adj scared of water; **Wasserski** nt water-skiing; **Wasserspiegel** m surface of the water; (*Wasserstand*) water level; **Wassersport** m water sports pl; **wasserundurchlässig** adj watertight, waterproof; **Wasserverbrauch** m water consumption; **Wasserversorgung** f water supply; **Wasserwaage** f spirit level; **Wasserwerk** nt waterworks pl

waten vi to wade

Watt (-(e)s, -en) nt (*Geo*) mud flats pl ▷ (-s, -) nt (*Elek*) watt

Watte (-, -n) f cotton wool; **Wattepad** (-s, -s) m cotton pad; **Wattestäbchen** nt cotton bud, Q-tip® (*US*)

WC (-s, -s) nt toilet, restroom (*US*); **WC-Reiniger** m toilet cleaner

Web (-s) nt (*Inform*) Web; **Webseite** f (*Inform*) web page

Wechsel (-s, -) m change; (*Spieler~: Sport*) substitution; **Wechselgeld** nt change; **wechselhaft** adj (*Wetter*) changeable; **Wechseljahre** pl menopause sing; **Wechselkurs** m exchange rate; **wechseln** vt to change; (*Blicke*) to exchange; **Geld ~** to change some money; (*in Kleingeld*) to get some change; **Euro in Pfund ~** to change euros into pounds ▷ vi to change; **kannst du ~?** can you change this?; **Wechselstrom** m alternating current, AC; **Wechselstube** f bureau de change

Weckdienst m wake-up call service; **wecken** vt to wake (up);

Wecker (-s, -) m alarm clock;
Weckruf m wake-up call
wedeln vi (Ski) to wedel; **mit etw
~ to** wave sth; **mit dem Schwanz
~** to wag its tail; **der Hund
wedelte mit dem Schwanz** the
dog wagged its tail
weder conj: **~ ... noch ...** neither
... nor ...
weg adv (entfernt, verreist) away;
(los, ab) off; **er war schon ~** he had
already left (o gone); **Hände ~!**
hands off; **weit ~** a long way away
(o off)
Weg (-(e)s, -e) m way; (Pfad) path;
(Route) route; **jdn nach dem
~ fragen** to ask sb the way; **auf
dem ~ sein** to be on the way
weg|bleiben irr vi to stay away;
weg|bringen irr vt to take away
wegen prep +gen o dat because of
weg|fahren irr vi to drive away;
(abfahren) to leave; (in Urlaub) to go
away; **Wegfahrsperre** f (Auto)
(engine) immobilizer; **weg|gehen**
irr vi to go away; **weg|kommen**
irr vi to get away; (fig)
gut/schlecht ~ to come off
well/badly; **weg|lassen** irr vt to
leave out; **weg|laufen** irr vi to
run away; **weg|legen** vt to put
aside; **weg|machen** vt (fam) to
get rid of; **weg|müssen** irr vi: **ich
muss weg** I've got to go;
weg|nehmen irr vt to take away;
weg|räumen vt to clear away;
weg|rennen irr vi to run away;
weg|schicken vt to send away;
weg|schmeißen irr vt to throw
away; **weg|sehen** irr vi to look
away; **weg|tun** irr vt to put away
Wegweiser (-s, -) m signpost
weg|werfen irr vt to throw
away; **weg|wischen** vt to wipe
off; **weg|ziehen** irr vi to move
(away)
weh adj sore; siehe auch **wehtun**

wehen vt, vi to blow; (Fahne) to
flutter
Wehen pl labour pains pl
Wehrdienst m military service
wehren vr: **sich ~** to defend
oneself
weh|tun irr vi to hurt; **jdm/sich
~** to hurt sb/oneself
Weibchen nt: **es ist ein ~** (Tier)
it's a she; **weiblich** adj feminine;
(Bio) female
weich adj soft; **~ gekocht** (Ei)
soft-boiled
Weichkäse m soft cheese;
(Streichkäse) cheese spread;
weichlich adj soft; (körperlich)
weak; **Weichspüler** (-s, -) m (für
Wäsche) (fabric) softener
Weide (-, -n) f (Baum) willow;
(Grasfläche) meadow
weigern vr: **sich ~** to refuse;
Weigerung f refusal
Weiher (-s, -) m pond
Weihnachten (-, -) nt Christ-
mas; **Weihnachtsabend** m
Christmas Eve; **Weihnachtsbaum**
m Christmas tree;
Weihnachtsfeier f Christmas
party; **Weihnachtsferien** pl
Christmas holidays pl (Brit),
Christmas vacation sing (US);
Weihnachtsgeld nt Christmas
bonus; **Weihnachtsgeschenk** nt
Christmas present;
Weihnachtskarte f Christmas
card; **Weihnachtslied** nt
Christmas carol;
Weihnachtsmann m Father
Christmas, Santa (Claus)

● **WEIHNACHTSMARKT**

● The **Weihnachtsmarkt** is a
● market held in most large
● towns in Germany in the weeks
● prior to Christmas. People visit
● it to buy presents, toys and

- Christmas decorations, and to
- enjoy the festive atmosphere.
- Food and drink associated with
- the Christmas festivities can
- also be eaten and drunk there,
- for example, gingerbread and
- mulled wine.

Weihnachtsstern m (Bot)
poinsettia; **Weihnachtstag** m:
erster ~ Christmas Day; **zweiter
~** Boxing Day; **Weihnachtszeit** f
Christmas season
weil conj because
Weile (-) f while, short time; **es
kann noch eine ~ dauern** it could
take some time
Wein (-(e)s, -e) m wine; (Pflanze)
vine; **Weinbeere** f grape;
Weinberg m vineyard;
Weinbergschnecke f snail;
Weinbrand m brandy
weinen vt, vi to cry
Weinglas nt wine glass;
Weinkarte f wine list;
Weinkeller m wine cellar;
Weinlese (-, -n) f vintage;
Weinprobe f wine tasting;
Weintraube f grape
weise adj wise
Weise (-, -n) f manner, way; **auf
diese** (**Art und**) **~** this way
weisen (wies, gewiesen) vt to
show
Weisheit f wisdom;
Weisheitszahn m wisdom
tooth
weiß adj white; **Weißbier** nt ≈
wheat beer; **Weißbrot** nt white
bread; **weißhaarig** adj
white-haired; **Weißkohl** m,
Weißkraut nt (white) cabbage;
Weißwein m white wine
weit adj wide; (Begriff) broad;
(Reise, Wurf) long; (Kleid) loose; **wie
~ ist es ...?** how far is it ...?; **so
~ sein** to be ready ▷ adv far;

~ verbreitet widespread;
~ gereist widely travelled; **~ offen**
wide open; **das geht zu ~** that's
going too far, that's pushing it
weiter adj wider; (~ weg) farther
(away); (zusätzlich) further; **~e
Informationen** further
information sing ▷ adv further; **~!**
go on; (weitergehen!) keep moving;
~ nichts/niemand
nothing/nobody else; **und so
~** and so on; **weiter|arbeiten** vi
to carry on working;
Weiterbildung f further training
(o education); **weiter|empfehlen**
irr vt to recommend;
weiter|erzählen vt: **nicht ~!**
don't tell anyone; **weiter|fahren**
irr vi to go on (nach to, bis as far
as); **weiter|geben** irr vt to pass
on; **weiter|gehen** irr vi to go on;
weiter|helfen irr vi: **jdm ~** to
help sb; **weiterhin** adv: **etw
~ tun** to go on doing sth;
weiter|machen vt, vi to
continue; **weiter|reisen** vi to
continue one's journey
weitgehend adj considerable
▷ adv largely; **weitsichtig** adj
long-sighted; (fig) far-sighted;
Weitsprung m long jump;
Weitwinkelobjektiv nt (Foto)
wide-angle lens
Weizen (-s, -) m wheat;
Weizenbier nt ≈ wheat beer

○ SCHLÜSSELWORT

welche(r, s) interrogativ pron
which; **welcher von beiden?**
which (one) of the two?; **welchen
hast du genommen?** which (one)
did you take?; **welche eine ...!**
what a ...!; **welche Freude!** what
joy! ▷ indef pron some; (in Fragen)
any; **ich habe welche** I have some;
haben Sie welche? do you have

any? ▷ *relativ pron* (*bei Menschen*)
who; (*bei Sachen*) which, that;
welche(r, s) auch immer
whoever/whichever/whatever

welk *adj* withered; **welken** *vi* to
wither
Welle (-, -n) *f* wave; **Wellengang**
m waves *pl*; **starker ~** heavy seas
pl; **Wellenlänge** *f* (*a. fig*)
wavelength; **Wellenreiten** *nt*
surfing; **Wellensittich** (-*s*, -*e*) *m*
budgerigar, budgie; **wellig** *adj*
wavy
Wellness *f* health and beauty
(*Brit*), wellness (*US*)
Welpe (-*n*, -*n*) *m* puppy
Welt (-, -*en*) *f* world; **auf der ~** in
the world; **auf die ~ kommen** to
be born; **Weltall** *nt* universe;
weltbekannt, **weltberühmt** *adj*
world-famous; **Weltkrieg** *m*
world war; **Weltmacht** *f* world
power; **Weltmeister(in)** *m(f)*
world champion;
Weltmeisterschaft *f* world
championship; (*im Fußball*) World
Cup; **Weltraum** *m* space;
Weltreise *f* trip round the world;
Weltrekord *m* world record;
Weltstadt *f* metropolis;
weltweit *adj* worldwide, global
wem *pron dat von* **wer** who ... to,
(to) whom; **~ hast du's gegeben?**
who did you give it to?; **~ gehört
es?** who does it belong to?, whose
is it?; **~ auch immer es gehört**
whoever it belongs to
wen *pron akk von* **wer** who, whom;
~ hast du besucht? who did you
visit?; **~ möchten Sie sprechen?**
who would you like to speak to?
Wende (-, -*n*) *f* turning point;
(*Veränderung*) change; **die ~** (*Hist*)
the fall of the Berlin Wall; **Wende-
kreis** *m* (*Auto*) turning circle
Wendeltreppe *f* spiral staircase

wenden (*wendete o wandte,
gewendet o gewandt*) *vt*, *vi* to turn
(round); (*um 180°*) to make a
U-turn; **sich an jdn ~** to turn to sb;
bitte ~! please turn over, PTO ▷ *vr*:
sich ~ to turn; **sich an jdn ~** to
turn to sb
wenig *pron*, *adv* little; **~(e)** *pl* few;
(*nur*) **ein (klein) ~** (just) a little
(bit); **ein ~ Zucker** a little bit of
sugar, a little sugar; **wir haben
~ Zeit** we haven't got much time;
zu ~ too little; *pl* too few; **nur
~ wissen** only a few know ▷ *adv*:
er spricht ~ he doesn't talk much;
~ bekannt little known; **wenige**
pron pl few *pl*; **wenigste(r, s)** *adj*
least; **wenigstens** *adv* at least

SCHLÜSSELWORT

wenn *konj* **1** (*falls, bei Wünschen*) if;
wenn auch ..., selbst wenn ...
even if ...; **wenn ich doch ...** if
only I ...
2 (*zeitlich*) when; **immer wenn**
whenever

wennschon *adv*: **na ~** so what?
wer *pron* who; **~ war das?** who
was that?; **~ von euch?** which
(one) of you? ▷ *pron* anybody
who, anyone who; **~ das glaubt,
ist dumm** anyone who believes
that is stupid; **~ auch immer**
whoever ▷ *pron* somebody,
someone; (*in Fragen*) anybody,
anyone; **ist da ~?** is (there)
anybody there?
Werbefernsehen *nt* TV
commercials *pl*; **Werbegeschenk**
nt promotional gift; **werben**
(*warb, geworben*) *vt* to win;
(*Mitglied*) to recruit ▷ *vi* to
advertise; **Werbespot** (-*s*, -*s*) *m*
commercial; **Werbung** *f*
advertising

○ SCHLÜSSELWORT

werden (*pt* **wurde**, *pp* **geworden** *o* (*bei Passiv*) **worden**) *vi* to become; **was ist aus ihm/aus der Sache geworden?** what became of him/it?; **es ist nichts/gut geworden** it came to nothing/turned out well; **es wird Nacht/Tag** it's getting dark/light; **mir wird kalt** I'm getting cold; **mir wird schlecht** I feel ill; **Erster werden** to come *o* be first; **das muss anders werden** that'll have to change; **rot/zu Eis werden** to turn red/to ice; **was willst du (mal) werden?** what do you want to be?; **die Fotos sind gut geworden** the photos have come out nicely

▷ *als Hilfsverb* 1 (*bei Futur*) **er wird es tun** he will *o* he'll do it; **er wird das nicht tun** he will not *o* he won't do it; **es wird gleich regnen** it's going to rain

2 (*bei Konjunktiv*) **ich würde ...** I would ...; **er würde gern ...** he would *o* he'd like to ...; **ich würde lieber ...** I would *o* I'd rather ...

3 (*bei Vermutung*) **sie wird in der Küche sein** she will be in the kitchen

4 (*bei Passiv*) **gebraucht werden** to be used; **er ist erschossen worden** he has *o* he's been shot; **mir wurde gesagt, dass ...** I was told that ...

werfen (*warf, geworfen*) *vt* to throw

Werft (*-, -en*) *f* shipyard, dockyard

Werk (*-(e)s, -e*) *nt* (*Kunstwerk, Buch etc*) work; (*Fabrik*) factory; (*Mechanismus*) works *pl*; **Werkstatt** (*-, -stätten*) *f* workshop; (*Auto*) garage; **Werktag** *m* working day; **werktags** *adv* on weekdays, during the week; **Werkzeug** *nt* tool; **Werkzeugkasten** *m* toolbox

wert *adj* worth; **es ist etwa 50 Euro ~** it's worth about 50 euros; **das ist nichts ~** it's worthless; **Wert** (*-(e)s, -e*) *m* worth; (*Zahlen~*) (*Fin*) value; **~ legen auf** (+*akk*) to attach importance to; **es hat doch keinen ~** (*Sinn*) it's pointless; **Wertangabe** *f* declaration of value; **Wertbrief** *m* insured letter; **Wertgegenstand** *m* valuable object; **wertlos** *adj* worthless; **Wertmarke** *f* token; **Wertpapiere** *pl* securities *pl*; **Wertsachen** *pl* valuables *pl*; **Wertstoff** *m* recyclable waste; **wertvoll** *adj* valuable

Wesen (*-s, -*) *nt* being; (*Natur, Charakter*) nature

wesentlich *adj* significant; (*beträchtlich*) considerable ▷ *adv* considerably

weshalb *adv* why

Wespe (*-, -n*) *f* wasp; **Wespenstich** *m* wasp sting

wessen *pron gen von* **wer**; whose

● WESSI
●
● A **Wessi** is a colloquial and often
● derogatory word used to
● describe a German from the
● former West Germany. The
● expression 'Besserwessi' is used
● by East Germans to describe a
● West German who is considered
● to be a know-all.

West west; **Westdeutschland** *nt* (*als Landesteil*) Western Germany; (*Hist*) West Germany

Weste (*-, -n*) *f* waistcoat (*Brit*), vest (*US*); (*Wollweste*) cardigan

Westen (-s) *m* west; **im ~ Englands** in the west of England; **der Wilde ~** the Wild West; **Westeuropa** *nt* Western Europe; **Westküste** *f* west coast; **westlich** *adj* western; (*Kurs, Richtung*) westerly; **Westwind** *m* west(erly) wind

weswegen *adv* why

Wettbewerb *m* competition; **Wettbüro** *nt* betting office; **Wette** (-, -n) *f* bet; **eine ~ abschließen** to make a bet; **die ~ gilt!** you're on; **wetten** *vt, vi* to bet (*auf +akk* on); **ich habe mit ihm gewettet, dass ...** I bet him that ...; **ich wette mit dir um 50 Euro** I'll bet you 50 euros; **~, dass?** wanna bet?

Wetter (-s, -) *nt* weather; **Wetterbericht** *m*, **Wettervorhersage** *f* weather forecast; **Wetterkarte** *f* weather map; **Wetterlage** *f* weather situation; **Wettervorhersage** *f* weather forecast

Wettkampf *m* contest; **Wettlauf** *m* race; **Wettrennen** *nt* race

WG (-, -s) *f abk =* **Wohngemeinschaft**

Whirlpool® (-s, -s) *m* jacuzzi®

Whisky (-s, -s) *m* (*schottisch*) whisky; (*irisch, amerikanisch*) whiskey

wichtig *adj* important

wickeln *vt* (*Schnur*) to wind (*um* round); (*Schal, Decke*) to wrap (*um* round); **ein Baby ~** to change a baby's nappy (*Brit*) (*o* diaper (*US*)); **Wickelraum** *m* baby-changing room; **Wickeltisch** *m* baby-changing table

Widder (-s, -) *m* (*Zool*) ram; (*Astr*) Aries *sing*

wider *prep +akk* against

widerlich *adj* disgusting

widerrufen *irr vt* to withdraw; (*Auftrag, Befehl etc*) to cancel

widersprechen *irr vi* to contradict (*jdm* sb); **Widerspruch** *m* contradiction

Widerstand *m* resistance; **widerstandsfähig** *adj* resistant (*gegen* to)

widerwärtig *adj* disgusting

widerwillig *adj* unwilling, reluctant

widmen *vt* to dedicate ▷ *vr*: **sich jdm/etw ~** to devote oneself to sb/sth; **Widmung** *f* dedication

⭕ SCHLÜSSELWORT

wie *adv* how; **wie groß/schnell?** how big/fast?; **wie wär's?** how about it?; **wie ist er?** what's he like?; **wie gut du das kannst!** you're very good at it; **wie bitte?** pardon?; (*entrüstet*) I beg your pardon!; **und wie!** and how!; **wie viel** how much; **wie viele Menschen** how many people; **wie weit** to what extent
▷ *konj* 1 (*bei Vergleichen*) **so schön wie ...** as beautiful as ...; **wie ich schon sagte** as I said; **wie du** like you; **singen wie ein ...** to sing like a ...; **wie (zum Beispiel)** such as (for example)
2 (*zeitlich*) **wie er das hörte, ging er** when he heard that he left; **er hörte, wie der Regen fiel** he heard the rain falling

wieder *adv* again; **~ ein(e) ...** another ...; **~ erkennen** to recognize; **etw ~ gutmachen** to make up for sth; **~ verwerten** to recycle

wieder|bekommen *irr vt* to get back

wiederholen vt to repeat;
Wiederholung f repetition
Wiederhören nt (Tel) **auf
~** goodbye
wieder|kommen irr vi to come
back
wieder|sehen irr vt to see
again; (wieder treffen) to meet
again; **Wiedersehen** (-s) nt
reunion; **auf ~!** goodbye
Wiedervereinigung f
reunification
Wiege (-, -n) f cradle; **wiegen**
(wog, gewogen) vt, vi (Gewicht) to
weigh
Wien (-s) nt Vienna
wies imperf von **weisen**
Wiese (-, -n) f meadow
Wiesel (-s, -) nt weasel
wieso adv why
wievielmal adv how often;
wievielte(r, s) adj: **zum ~n Mal?**
how many times?; **den
Wievielten haben wir heute?**
what's the date today?; **am
Wievielten hast du Geburtstag?**
which day is your birthday?
wieweit conj to what extent
wild adj wild
Wild (-(e)s) nt game
wildfremd adj (fam) **ein ~er
Mensch** a complete (o total)
stranger; **Wildleder** nt suede;
Wildpark m game park;
Wildschwein nt (wild) boar;
Wildwasserfahren (-s) nt
whitewater canoeing (o
rafting)
Wille (-ns, -n) m will
willen prep +gen **um ... ~** for the
sake of ...; **um Himmels ~!**
(vorwurfsvoll) for heaven's sake;
(betroffen) goodness me
willkommen adj welcome
Wimper (-, -n) f eyelash;
Wimperntusche f mascara
Wind (-(e)s, -e) m wind

Windel (-, -n) f nappy (Brit),
diaper (US)
windgeschützt adj sheltered
from the wind; **windig** adj windy;
(fig) dubious; **Windjacke** f
windcheater; **Windmühle** f
windmill; **Windpocken** pl
chickenpox sing;
Windschutzscheibe f (Auto)
windscreen (Brit), windshield (US);
Windstärke f wind force;
Windsurfen (-s) nt windsurfing;
Windsurfer(in) m(f) windsurfer
Winkel (-s, -) m (Math) angle;
(Gerät) set square; (in Raum)
corner; **im rechten ~ zu** at right
angles to
winken vt, vi to wave
Winter (-s, -) m winter;
Winterausrüstung f (Auto)
winter equipment;
Winterfahrplan m winter
timetable; **winterlich** adj
wintry; **Wintermantel** m winter
coat; **Winterreifen** m winter
tyre; **Winterschlussverkauf** m
winter sales pl; **Wintersport** m
winter sports pl
Winterzeit f (Uhrzeit) winter
time (Brit), standard time (US)
winzig adj tiny
wir pron we; **~ selbst** we
ourselves; **~ alle** all of us; **~ drei**
the three of us; **~ sind's** it's us;
~ nicht not us
Wirbel (-s, -) m whirl; (Trubel)
hurly-burly; (Aufsehen) fuss; (Anat)
vertebra; **Wirbelsäule** f spine
wirken vi to be effective;
(erfolgreich sein) to work; (scheinen)
to seem
wirklich adj real; **Wirklichkeit** f
reality
wirksam adj effective; **Wirkung**
f effect
wirr adj confused; **Wirrwarr** (-s)
m confusion

Wirsing (-s) m savoy cabbage
Wirt (-(e)s, -e) m landlord; **Wirtin** f landlady
Wirtschaft f (Comm) economy; (Gaststätte) pub; **wirtschaftlich** adj (Pol, Comm) economic; (sparsam) economical
Wirtshaus nt pub
wischen vt, vi to wipe; **Wischer** (-s, -) m wiper
wissen (wusste, gewusst) vt to know; **weißt du schon, ...?** did you know ...?; **woher weißt du das?** how do you know?; **das musst du selbst ~** that's up to you; **Wissen** (-s) nt knowledge
Wissenschaft f science; **Wissenschaftler(in)** (-s, -) m(f) scientist; (Geisteswissenschaftler) academic; **wissenschaftlich** adj scientific; (geisteswissenschaftlich) academic
Witwe (-, -n) f widow; **Witwer** (-s, -) m widower
Witz (-(e)s, -e) m joke; **mach keine ~e!** you're kidding!; **das soll wohl ein ~ sein** you've got to be joking; **witzig** adj funny
wo adv where; **zu einer Zeit, ~ ...** at a time when ...; **überall, ~ ich hingehe** wherever I go ▷ conj: **jetzt, ~ du da bist** now that you're here; **~ ich dich gerade spreche** while I'm talking to you; **woanders** adv somewhere else
wobei adv: **~ mir einfällt ...** which reminds me ...
Woche (-, -n) f week; **während** (o **unter**) **der ~** during the week; **einmal die ~** once a week; **Wochenende** nt weekend; **am ~** at (Brit) (o on (US)) the weekend; **wir fahren übers ~ weg** we're going away for the weekend; **Wochenendhaus** nt weekend cottage; **Wochenendtrip** m weekend trip; **Wochenendurlaub**

m weekend break; **Wochenkarte** f weekly (season) ticket; **wochenlang** adv for weeks (on end); **Wochenmarkt** m weekly market; **Wochentag** m weekday; **wöchentlich** adj, adv weekly
Wodka (-s, -s) m vodka
wodurch adv: **~ unterscheiden sie sich?** what's the difference between them?; **~ hast du es gemerkt?** how did you notice?; **wofür** adv (relativ) for what; (Frage) what ... for; **~ brauchst du das?** what do you need that for?
wog imperf von **wiegen**
woher adv where ... from; **wohin** adv where ... to

◯ SCHLÜSSELWORT

wohl adv 1 **wohl oder übel** whether one likes it or not
2 (wahrscheinlich) probably; (gewiss) certainly; (vielleicht) perhaps; **sie ist wohl zu Hause** she's probably at home; **das ist doch wohl nicht dein Ernst!** surely you're not serious; **das mag wohl sein** that may well be; **ob das wohl stimmt?** I wonder if that's true; **er weiß das sehr wohl** he knows that perfectly well

Wohl (-(e)s) nt: **zum ~!** cheers; **wohlbehalten** adv safe and sound; **wohl|fühlen** vr: **sich ~** (zufrieden) to feel happy; (gesundheitlich) to feel well; **Wohlstand** m prosperity, affluence; **wohl|tun** irr vi: **jdm ~** to do sb good; **Wohlwollen** nt goodwill
Wohnblock m block of flats (Brit), apartment house (US); **wohnen** vi to live; **Wohngemeinschaft** f shared flat

(Brit) (o apartment (US)); **ich wohne in einer ~** I share a flat (o apartment); **wohnhaft** adj resident; **Wohnküche** f kitchen-cum-living-room; **Wohnmobil** (-s, -e) nt camper, RV (US); **Wohnort** m place of residence; **Wohnsitz** m place of residence; **Wohnung** f flat (Brit), apartment (US); **Wohnungstür** f front door; **Wohnwagen** m caravan; **Wohnzimmer** nt living room

Wolf (-(e)s, Wölfe) m wolf

Wolke (-, -n) f cloud; **Wolkenkratzer** m skyscraper; **wolkenlos** adj cloudless; **wolkig** adj cloudy

Wolldecke f (woollen) blanket; **Wolle** (-, -n) f wool

⭕ SCHLÜSSELWORT

wollen (pt **wollte**, pp **gewollt** o (als Hilfsverb) **wollen**) vt, vi to want; **ich will nach Hause** I want to go home; **er will nicht** he doesn't want to; **er wollte das nicht** he didn't want it; **wenn du willst** if you like; **ich will, dass du mir zuhörst** I want you to listen to me ▷ Hilfsverb: **er will ein Haus kaufen** he wants to buy a house; **ich wollte, ich wäre ...** I wish I were ...; **etw gerade tun wollen** to be going to do sth

Wolljacke f cardigan

womit adv what ... with; **~ habe ich das verdient?** what have I done to deserve that?

womöglich adv possibly

woran adv: **~ denkst du?** what are you thinking of?; **~ ist er gestorben?** what did he die of?; **~ sieht man das?** how can you tell?

worauf adv: **~ wartest du?** what are you waiting for?

woraus adv: **~ ist das gemacht?** what is it made of?

Workshop (-s, -s) m workshop

World Wide Web nt World Wide Web

Wort (-(e)s, Wörter) nt (Vokabel) word ▷ (-(e)s, -e) nt (Äußerung) word; **mit anderen ~en** in other words; **jdn beim ~ nehmen** to take sb at his/her word; **Wörterbuch** nt dictionary; **wörtlich** adj literal

worüber adv: **~ redet sie?** what is she talking about?

worum adv: **~ gehts?** what is it about?

worunter adv: **~ leidet er?** what is he suffering from?

wovon adv (relativ) from which; **~ redest du?** what are you talking about?; **wozu** adv (relativ) to/for which; (interrogativ) what ... for/to; (warum) why; **~?** what for?; **~ brauchst du das?** what do you need it for?; **~ soll das gut sein?** what's it for?; **~ hast du Lust?** what do you feel like doing?

Wrack (-(e)s, -s) nt wreck

Wucher (-s) m profiteering; **das ist ~!** that's daylight robbery!

wuchs imperf von **wachsen**

wühlen vi to rummage; (Tier) to root; (Maulwurf) to burrow

Wühltisch m bargain counter

wund adj sore; **Wunde** (-, -n) f wound

Wunder (-s, -) nt miracle; **es ist kein ~** it's no wonder; **wunderbar** adj wonderful, marvellous; **Wunderkerze** f sparkler; **Wundermittel** nt wonder cure; **wundern** vr: **sich ~** to be surprised (über +akk at) ▷ vt to surprise; **wunderschön** adj

beautiful; **wundervoll** *adj*
wonderful

Wundsalbe *f* antiseptic
ointment; **Wundstarrkrampf** *m*
tetanus

Wunsch (-(e)s, *Wünsche*) *m* wish
(*nach* for); **wünschen** *vt* to wish;
sich (*dat*) **etw ~** to want sth; **ich
wünsche dir alles Gute** I wish you
all the best; **wünschenswert** *adj*
desirable

wurde *imperf von* **werden**

Wurf (-s, *Würfe*) *m* throw; (*Zool*)
litter

Würfel (-s, -) *m* dice; (*Math*)
cube; **würfeln** *vi* to throw (the
dice); (*Würfel spielen*) to play dice
▷ *vt* (*Zahl*) to throw; (*Gastr*) to
dice; **Würfelzucker** *m* lump
sugar

Wurm (-(e)s, *Würmer*) *m* worm

Wurst (-, *Würste*) *f* sausage; **das
ist mir ~** (*fam*) I couldn't care less

Würstchen *nt* frankfurter

Würze (-, -n) *f* seasoning, spice

Wurzel (-, -n) *f* root;
Wurzelbehandlung *f* root canal
treatment

würzen *vt* to season, to spice;
würzig *adj* spicy

wusch *imperf von* **waschen**

wusste *imperf von* **wissen**

wüst *adj* (*unordentlich*) chaotic;
(*ausschweifend*) wild; (*öde*)
desolate; (*fam: heftig*) terrible

Wüste (-, -n) *f* desert

Wut (-) *f* rage, fury; **ich habe eine
~ auf ihn** I'm really mad at him;
wütend *adj* furious

WWW (-) *nt abk* = **World Wide
Web** WWW

X-Beine *pl* knock-knees *pl*;
x-beinig *adj* knock-kneed

x-beliebig *adj*: **ein ~es Buch** any
book (you like)

x-mal *adv* umpteen times

Xylophon (-s, -e) *nt* xylophone

Yoga *(-(s))* *m o nt* yoga
Yuppie *(-s, -s)* *m (-, -s)* *f* yuppie

zackig *adj (Linie etc)* jagged; *(fam: Tempo)* brisk
zaghaft *adj* timid
zäh *adj* tough; *(Flüssigkeit)* thick
Zahl *(-, -en)* *f* number; **zahlbar** *adj* payable; **zahlen** *vt, vi* to pay; **~ bitte!** could I have the bill *(Brit)* *(o* check *(US))* please?; **bar ~** to pay cash; **zählen** *vt, vi* to count *(auf +akk* on); **~ zu** to be one of; **Zahlenschloss** *nt* combination lock; **Zähler** *(-s, -)* *m (Gerät)* counter; *(für Strom, Wasser)* meter; **zahlreich** *adj* numerous; **Zahlung** *f* payment; **Zahlungsanweisung** *f* money order; **Zahlungsbedingungen** *pl* terms *pl* of payment
zahm *adj* tame; **zähmen** *vt* to tame
Zahn *(-(e)s, Zähne)* *m* tooth; **Zahnarzt** *m*, **Zahnärztin** *f* dentist; **Zahnbürste** *f*

toothbrush; **Zahncreme** f toothpaste; **Zahnersatz** m dentures pl; **Zahnfleisch** nt gums pl; **Zahnfleischbluten** nt bleeding gums pl; **Zahnfüllung** f filling; **Zahnklammer** f brace; **Zahnpasta** f, **Zahnpaste** f toothpaste; **Zahnradbahn** f rack railway (Brit) (o railroad (US)); **Zahnschmerzen** pl toothache sing; **Zahnseide** f dental floss; **Zahnspange** f brace; **Zahnstocher** (-s, -) m toothpick

Zange (-, -n) f pliers pl; (Zuckerzange) tongs pl; (Beißzange, Zool) pincers pl; (Med) forceps pl

zanken vi to quarrel ▷ vr: **sich ~** to quarrel

Zäpfchen nt (Anat) uvula; (Med) suppository

zapfen vt (Bier) to pull; **Zapfsäule** f petrol (Brit) (o gas (US)) pump

zappeln vi to wriggle; (unruhig sein) to fidget

zappen vi to zap, to channel-hop

zart adj (weich, leise) soft; (Braten etc) tender; (fein, schwächlich) delicate; **zartbitter** adj (Schokolade) plain, dark

zärtlich adj tender, affectionate; **Zärtlichkeit** f tenderness; **~en** pl hugs and kisses pl

Zauber (-s, -) m magic; (Bann) spell; **Zauberei** f magic; **Zauberer** (-s, -) m magician; (Künstler) conjuror; **Zauberformel** f (magic) spell; **zauberhaft** adj enchanting; **Zauberin** f sorceress; **Zauberkünstler(in)** m(f) magician, conjuror; **Zaubermittel** nt magic cure; **zaubern** vi to do magic; (Künstler) to do conjuring tricks; **Zauberspruch** m (magic) spell

Zaun (-(e)s, Zäune) m fence

z. B. abk = **zum Beispiel** e.g., eg

Zebra (-s, -s) nt zebra;

Zebrastreifen m zebra crossing (Brit), crosswalk (US)

Zecke (-, -n) f tick

Zehe (-, -n) f toe; (Knoblauch) clove; **Zehennagel** m toenail; **Zehenspitze** f tip of the toes

zehn num ten; **Zehnerkarte** f ticket valid for ten trips; **Zehnkampf** m decathlon; **Zehnkämpfer(in)** m(f) decathlete; **zehnmal** adv ten times; **zehntausend** num ten thousand; **zehnte(r, s)** adj tenth; siehe auch **dritte**; **Zehntel** (-s, -) nt (Bruchteil) tenth; **Zehntelsekunde** f tenth of a second

Zeichen (-s, -) nt sign; (Schriftzeichen) character; **Zeichenblock** m sketch pad; **Zeichenerklärung** f key; **Zeichensetzung** f punctuation; **Zeichensprache** f sign language; **Zeichentrickfilm** m cartoon

zeichnen vt, vi to draw; **Zeichnung** f drawing

Zeigefinger m index finger; **zeigen** vt to show; **sie zeigte uns die Stadt** she showed us around the town; **zeig mal!** let me see ▷ vi to point (auf +akk to, at) ▷ vr: **sich ~** to show oneself; **es wird sich ~** time will tell; **Zeiger** (-s, -) m pointer; (Uhr) hand

Zeile (-, -n) f line

Zeit (-, -en) f time; **ich habe keine ~** I haven't got time; **lass dir ~** take your time; **das hat ~** there's no rush; **von ~ zu ~** from time to time; **Zeitansage** f (Tel) speaking clock (Brit), correct time (US); **Zeitarbeit** f temporary work; **zeitgenössisch** adj contemporary, modern; **zeitgleich** adj simultaneous ▷ adv at exactly the same time; **zeitig** adj early; **Zeitkarte** f season ticket; **zeitlich** adj (Reihenfolge) chronological; **es passt ~ nicht** it isn't a convenient time; **ich schaff es ~ nicht** I'm not going to make it; **Zeitlupe** f slow motion; **Zeitplan** m schedule; **Zeitpunkt** m point in time; **Zeitraum** m period (of time); **Zeitschrift** f magazine; (wissenschaftliche) periodical

Zeitung f newspaper; **es steht in der ~** it's in the paper(s); **Zeitungsanzeige** f newspaper advertisement; **Zeitungsartikel** m newspaper article; **Zeitungskiosk** m, **Zeitungsstand** m newsstand

Zeitunterschied m time difference; **Zeitverschiebung** f time lag; **Zeitvertreib** (-(e)s, -e) m: **zum ~** to pass the time; **zeitweise** adv occasionally; **Zeitzone** f time zone

Zelle (-, -n) f cell

Zellophan® (-s) nt cellophane®

Zelt (-(e)s, -e) nt tent; **zelten** vi to camp, to go camping; **Zeltplatz** m campsite, camping site

Zement (-(e)s, -e) m cement

Zentimeter m o nt centimetre

Zentner (-s, -) m (metric) hundredweight; (in Deutschland) fifty kilos; (in Österreich und der Schweiz) one hundred kilos

zentral adj central; **Zentrale** (-, -n) f central office; (Tel) exchange; **Zentralheizung** f central heating; **Zentralverriegelung** f (Auto) central locking; **Zentrum** (-s, Zentren) nt centre

zerbrechen irr vt, vi to break; **zerbrechlich** adj fragile

Zeremonie (-, -n) f ceremony

zergehen irr vi to dissolve; (schmelzen) to melt

zerkleinern vt to cut up; (zerhacken) to chop (up);

zerkratzen vt to scratch; **zerlegen** vt to take to pieces; (Fleisch) to carve; (Gerät, Maschine) to dismantle; **zerquetschen** vt to squash; **zerreißen** irr vt to tear to pieces ▷ vi to tear

zerren vt to drag; **sich** (dat) **einen Muskel ~** to pull a muscle ▷ vi to tug (an +dat at); **Zerrung** f (Med) pulled muscle

zerschlagen irr vt to smash ▷ vr: **sich ~** to come to nothing

zerschneiden irr vt to cut up

zerstören vt to destroy; **Zerstörung** f destruction

zerstreuen vt to scatter; (Menge) to disperse; (Zweifel etc) to dispel ▷ vr: **sich ~** (Menge) to disperse; **zerstreut** adj scattered; (Mensch) absent-minded; (kurzfristig) distracted

zerteilen vt to split up

Zertifikat (-(e)s, -e) nt certificate

Zettel (-s, -) m piece of paper; (Notizzettel) note

Zeug (-(e)s, -e) nt (fam) stuff; (Ausrüstung) gear; **dummes ~** nonsense

Zeuge (-n, -n) m, **Zeugin** f witness

Zeugnis nt certificate; (Schule) report; (Referenz) reference

z. H(d). abk = **zu Händen von** attn

zickig adj (fam) touchy, bitchy

Zickzack (-(e)s, -e) m: **im ~ fahren** to zigzag (across the road)

Ziege (-, -n) f goat

Ziegel (-s, -) m brick; (Dach) tile

Ziegenkäse m goat's cheese; **Ziegenpeter** m mumps

ziehen (zog, gezogen) vt to draw; (zerren) to pull; (Spielfigur) to move; (züchten) to rear ▷ vi (zerren) to pull; (sich bewegen) to move; (Rauch, Wolke etc) to drift; **den Tee**

~ lassen to let the tea stand ▷ *vi impers*: **es zieht** there's a draught ▷ *vr*: **sich ~** (*Treffen, Rede*) to drag on

Ziel (*-(e)s, -e*) *nt* (*Reise*) destination; (*Sport*) finish; (*Absicht*) goal, aim; **zielen** *vi* to aim (*auf +akk* at); **Zielgruppe** *f* target group; **ziellos** *adj* aimless; **Zielscheibe** *f* target

ziemlich *adj* considerable; **ein ~es Durcheinander** quite a mess; **mit ~er Sicherheit** with some certainty ▷ *adv* rather, quite; **~ viel** quite a lot

zierlich *adj* dainty; (*Frau*) petite

Ziffer (*-, -n*) *f* figure; **arabische/römische ~n** *pl* Arabic/Roman numerals *pl*; **Zifferblatt** *nt* dial, face

zig *adj* (*fam*) umpteen

Zigarette *f* cigarette; **Zigarettenautomat** *m* cigarette machine; **Zigarettenpapier** *nt* cigarette paper; **Zigarettenschachtel** *f* cigarette packet; **Zigarettenstummel** *m* cigarette end; **Zigarillo** (*-s, -s*) *m* cigarillo; **Zigarre** (*-, -n*) *f* cigar

Zigeuner(in) (*-s, -*) *m(f)* gipsy

Zimmer (*-s, -*) *nt* room; **haben Sie ein ~ für zwei Personen?** do you have a room for two?; **Zimmerlautstärke** *f* reasonable volume; **Zimmermädchen** *nt* chambermaid; **Zimmermann** *m* carpenter; **Zimmerpflanze** *f* house plant; **Zimmerschlüssel** *m* room key; **Zimmerservice** *m* room service; **Zimmervermittlung** *f* accommodation agency

Zimt (*-(e)s, -e*) *m* cinnamon; **Zimtstange** *f* cinnamon stick

Zink (*-(e)s*) *nt* zinc

Zinn (*-(e)s*) *nt* (*Element*) tin; (*legiertes*) pewter

Zinsen *pl* interest *sing*

Zipfel (*-s, -*) *m* corner; (*spitz*) tip; (*Hemd*) tail; (*Wurst*) end; **Zipfelmütze** *f* pointed hat

zirka *adv* about, approximately

Zirkel (*-s, -*) *m* (*Math*) (pair of) compasses *pl*

Zirkus (*-, -se*) *m* circus

zischen *vi* to hiss

Zitat (*-(e)s, -e*) *nt* quotation (*aus* from); **zitieren** *vt* to quote

Zitronat *nt* candied lemon peel; **Zitrone** (*-, -n*) *f* lemon; **Zitronenlimonade** *f* lemonade; **Zitronensaft** *m* lemon juice

zittern *vi* to tremble (*vor +dat* with)

zivil *adj* civilian; (*Preis*) reasonable; **Zivil** (*-s*) *nt* plain clothes *pl*; (*Mil*) civilian clothes *pl*; **Zivildienst** *m* community service (*for conscientious objectors*)

zocken *vi* (*fam*) to gamble

Zoff (*-s*) *m* (*fam*) trouble

zog *imperf von* **ziehen**

zögerlich *adj* hesitant; **zögern** *vi* to hesitate

Zoll (*-(e)s, Zölle*) *m* customs *pl*; (*Abgabe*) duty; **Zollabfertigung** *f* customs clearance; **Zollamt** *nt* customs office; **Zollbeamte(r)** *m*, **-beamtin** *f* customs official; **Zollerklärung** *f* customs declaration; **zollfrei** *adj* duty-free; **Zollgebühren** *pl* customs duties *pl*; **Zollkontrolle** *f* customs check; **Zöllner(in)** *m(f)* customs officer; **zollpflichtig** *adj* liable to duty

Zone (*-, -n*) *f* zone

Zoo (*-s, -s*) *m* zoo

Zoom (*-s, -s*) *nt* zoom (shot); (*Objektiv*) zoom (lens)

Zopf (*-(e)s, Zöpfe*) *m* plait (*Brit*), braid (*US*)

Zorn (*-(e)s*) *m* anger; **zornig** *adj* angry (*über etw akk* about sth, *auf jdn* with sb)

zu *prep* +*dat* **1** (*örtlich*) to; **zum Bahnhof/Arzt gehen** to go to the station/doctor; **zur Schule/Kirche gehen** to go to school/church; **sollen wir zu euch gehen?** shall we go to your place?; **sie sah zu ihm hin** she looked towards him; **zum Fenster herein** through the window; **zu meiner Linken** to *o* on my left

2 (*zeitlich*) at; **zu Ostern** at Easter; **bis zum 1. Mai** until May 1st; (*nicht später als*) by May 1st; **zu meiner Zeit** in my time

3 (*Zusatz*) with; **Wein zum Essen trinken** to drink wine with one's meal; **sich zu jdm setzen** to sit down beside sb; **setz dich doch zu uns** (come and) sit with us; **Anmerkungen zu etw** notes on sth

4 (*Zweck*) for; **Wasser zum Waschen** water for washing; **Papier zum Schreiben** paper to write on; **etw zum Geburtstag bekommen** to get sth for one's birthday

5 (*Veränderung*) into; **zu etw werden** to turn into sth; **jdn zu etw machen** to make sb (into) sth; **zu Asche verbrennen** to burn to ashes

6 (*mit Zahlen*) **3 zu 2** (*Sport*) 3-2; **das Stück zu 5 Euro** at 5 euros each; **zum ersten Mal** for the first time

7 zu meiner Freude *etc* to my joy *etc*; **zum Glück** luckily; **zu Fuß** on foot; **es ist zum Weinen** it's enough to make you cry

▷ *konj* to; **etw zu essen** sth to eat; **um besser sehen zu können** in order to see better; **ohne es zu wissen** without knowing it; **noch zu bezahlende Rechnungen** bills

that are still to be paid

▷ *adv* **1** (*allzu*) too; **zu sehr** too much; **zu viel** too much; **zu wenig** too little

2 (*örtlich*) toward(s); **er kam auf mich zu** he came up to me

3 (*geschlossen*) shut, closed; **die Geschäfte haben zu** the shops are closed; **„auf/zu"** (*Wasserhahn etc*) "on/off"

4 (*fam*) (*los*) **nur zu!** just keep on!; **mach zu!** hurry up!

zuallererst *adv* first of all; **zuallerletzt** *adv* last of all

Zubehör (*-(e)s, -e*) *nt* accessories *pl*

zu|bereiten *vt* to prepare; **Zubereitung** *f* preparation

zu|binden *irr vt* to do (*o* tie) up

Zucchini *pl* courgettes *pl* (*Brit*), zucchini *pl* (*US*)

züchten *vt* (*Tiere*) to breed; (*Pflanzen*) to grow

zucken *vi* to jerk; (*krampfhaft*) to twitch; (*Strahl etc*) to flicker; **mit den Schultern ~** to shrug (one's shoulders)

Zucker (*-s, -*) *m* sugar; (*Med*) diabetes *sing*; **Zuckerdose** *f* sugar bowl; **zuckerkrank** *adj* diabetic; **Zuckerrohr** *nt* sugar cane; **Zuckerrübe** *f* sugar beet; **Zuckerwatte** *f* candy-floss (*Brit*), cotton candy (*US*)

zu|decken *vt* to cover up

zu|drehen *vt* to turn off

zueinander *adv* to one other; (*mit Verb*) together; **zueinander|halten** *irr vi* to stick together

zuerst *adv* first; (*zu Anfang*) at first; **~ einmal** first of all

Zufahrt *f* access; (*Einfahrt*) drive(way); **Zufahrtsstraße** *f* access road; (*Autobahn*) slip road (*Brit*), ramp (*US*)

Zufall *m* chance; (*Ereignis*) coincidence; **durch ~** by accident; **so ein ~!** what a coincidence; **zufällig** *adj* chance ▷ *adv* by chance; **weißt du ~, ob ...?** do you happen to know whether ...?

zufrieden *adj* content(ed); (*befriedigt*) satisfied; **lass sie ~** leave her alone (*o* in peace); **zufrieden|geben** *irr vr:* **sich mit etw ~** to settle for sth; **Zufriedenheit** *f* contentment; (*Befriedigtsein*) satisfaction; **zufrieden|stellen** *vt:* **sie ist schwer zufriedenzustellen** she is hard to please

zu|fügen *vt* to add (*dat* to); **jdm Schaden/Schmerzen ~** to cause sb harm/pain

Zug (-(e)s, Züge) *m* (*Eisenb*) train; (*Luft*) draught; (*Ziehen*) pull; (*Gesichtszug*) feature; (*Schach*) move; (*Charakterzug*) trait; (*an Zigarette*) puff, drag; (*Schluck*) gulp

Zugabe *f* extra; (*in Konzert etc*) encore

Zugabteil *nt* train compartment

Zugang *m* access; **„kein ~!"** "no entry!"

Zugauskunft *f* (*Stelle*) train information office/desk; **Zugbegleiter(in)** *m(f)* guard (*Brit*), conductor (*US*)

zu|geben *irr vt* (*zugestehen*) admit; **zugegeben** *adv* admittedly

zu|gehen *irr vi* (*schließen*) to shut; **auf jdn/etw ~** to walk towards sb/sth; **dem Ende ~** to be coming to a close ▷ *vi impers* (*sich ereignen*) to happen; **es ging lustig zu** we/they had a lot of fun; **dort geht es streng zu** it's strict there

Zügel (-s, -) *m* rein

Zugführer(in) *m(f)* guard (*Brit*), conductor (*US*)

zugig *adj* draughty

zügig *adj* speedy

Zugluft *f* draught

Zugpersonal *nt* train staff

zu|greifen *irr vi* (*fig*) to seize the opportunity; (*beim Essen*) to help oneself; **~ auf** (+*akk*) (*Inform*) to access

Zugrestauraunt *nt* dining car, diner (*US*)

Zugriffsberechtigung *f* (*Inform*) access right

zugrunde *adv:* **~ gehen** to perish; **~ gehen an** (+*dat*) (*sterben*) to die of

Zugschaffner(in) *m(f)* ticket inspector; **Zugunglück** *nt* train crash

zugunsten *prep* +*gen o dat* in favour of

Zugverbindung *f* train connection

zu|haben *irr vi* to be closed

zu|halten *irr vt:* **sich** (*dat*) **die Nase ~** to hold one's nose; **sich** (*dat*) **die Ohren ~** to hold one's hands over one's ears; **die Tür ~** to hold the door shut

Zuhause (-s) *nt* home

zu|hören *vi* to listen (*dat* to); **Zuhörer(in)** *m(f)* listener

zu|kleben *vt* to seal

zu|kommen *irr vi* to come up (*auf* +*akk* to); **jdm etw ~ lassen** to give/send sb sth; **etw auf sich** (*akk*) **~ lassen** to take sth as it comes

zu|kriegen *vt:* **ich krieg den Koffer nicht zu** I can't shut the case

Zukunft (-, Zukünfte) *f* future; **zukünftig** *adj* future ▷ *adv* in future

zu|lassen *irr vt* (*hereinlassen*) to admit; (*erlauben*) to permit; (*Auto*) to license; (*fam: nicht öffnen*) to keep shut; **zulässig** *adj* permissible, permitted

zuletzt *adv* finally, at last

zuliebe *adv*: **jdm ~** for sb's sake

zum *kontr von* **zu dem**; **~ dritten Mal** for the third time; **~ Scherz** as a joke; **~ Trinken** for drinking

zu|machen *vt* to shut; (*Kleidung*) to do up ▷ *vi* to shut

zumindest *adv* at least

zu|muten *vt*: **jdm etw ~** to expect sth of sb ▷ *vr*: **sich** (*dat*) **zu viel ~** to overdo things

zunächst *adv* first of all; **~ einmal** to start with

Zunahme (-, -n) *f* increase

Zuname *m* surname, last name

zünden *vt, vi* (*Auto*) to ignite, to fire; **Zündkabel** *f* (*Auto*) ignition cable; **Zündkerze** *f* (*Auto*) spark plug; **Zündschloss** *nt* ignition lock; **Zündschlüssel** *m* ignition key; **Zündung** *f* ignition

zu|nehmen *irr vi* to increase; (*Mensch*) to put on weight ▷ *vt*: **5 Kilo ~** to put on 5 kilos

Zunge (-, -n) *f* tongue

Zungenkuss *m* French kiss

zunichte|machen *vt* (*zerstören*) to ruin

zunutze *adv* **sich** (*dat*) **etw ~ machen** to make use of sth

zu|parken *vt* to block

zur *kontr von* **zu der**

zurecht|finden *irr vr*: **sich ~** to find one's way around;
zurecht|kommen *irr vi* to cope (*mit etw* with sth);
zurecht|machen *vt* to prepare ▷ *vr*: **sich ~** to get ready

Zürich (-s) *nt* Zurich

zurück *adv* back

zurück|bekommen *irr vt* to get back; **zurück|blicken** *vi* to look back (*auf +akk* at); **zurück|bringen** *irr vt* (*hierhin*) to bring back; (*woandershin*) to take back;
zurück|erstatten *vt* to refund;
zurück|fahren *irr vi* to go back;

zurück|geben *irr vt* to give back; (*antworten*) to answer;
zurück|gehen *irr vi* to go back; (*zeitlich*) to date back (*auf +akk* to)

zurück|halten *irr vt* to hold back; (*hindern*) to prevent ▷ *vr*: **sich ~** to hold back;
zurückhaltend *adj* reserved

zurück|holen *vt* to fetch back;
zurück|kommen *irr vi* to come back; **auf etw** (*akk*) **~** to return (*o* get back) to sth; **zurück|lassen** *irr vt* to leave behind; **zurück|legen** *vt* to put back; (*Geld*) to put by; (*reservieren*) to keep back; (*Strecke*) to cover; **zurück|nehmen** *irr vt* to take back; **zurück|rufen** *irr vt* to call back; **zurück|schicken** *vt* to send back; **zurück|stellen** *vt* to put back; **zurück|treten** *irr vi* to step back; (*von Amt*) to retire;
zurück|verlangen *vt*: **etw ~** to ask for sth back; **zurück|zahlen** *vt* to pay back

zurzeit *adv* at present

Zusage *f* promise; (*Annahme*) acceptance; **zu|sagen** *vt* to promise ▷ *vi* to accept; **jdm ~** (*gefallen*) to appeal to sb

zusammen *adv* together

Zusammenarbeit *f* collaboration; **zusammen|arbeiten** *vi* to work together

zusammen|brechen *irr vi* to collapse; (*psychisch*) to break down; **Zusammenbruch** *m* collapse; (*psychischer*) breakdown

zusammen|fassen *vt* to summarize; (*vereinigen*) to unite; **zusammenfassend** *adj* summarizing ▷ *adv* to summarize; **Zusammenfassung** *f* summary

zusammen|gehören *vi* to belong together;
zusammen|halten *irr vi* to stick together

Zusammenhang m connection; **im/aus dem ~** in/out of context; **zusammen|hängen** irr vi to be connected; **zusammenhängend** adj coherent; **zusammenhang(s)los** adj incoherent
zusammen|klappen vi, vt to fold up
zusammen|knüllen vt to screw up
zusammen|kommen irr vi to meet; (sich ereignen) to happen together; **zusammen|legen** vt to fold up ▷ vi (Geld sammeln) to club together; **zusammen|nehmen** irr vt to summon up; **alles zusammengenommen** all in all ▷ vr: **sich ~** to pull oneself together; (fam) to get a grip, to get one's act together; **zusammen|passen** vi to go together; (Personen) to be suited; **zusammen|rechnen** vt to add up
Zusammensein (-s) nt get-together
zusammen|setzen vt to put together ▷ vr: **sich ~ aus** to be composed of; **Zusammensetzung** f composition
Zusammenstoß m crash, collision; **zusammen|stoßen** irr vi to crash (mit into)
zusammen|zählen vt to add up
zusammen|ziehen irr vi (in Wohnung etc) to move in together
Zusatz m addition; **zusätzlich** adj additional ▷ adv in addition
zu|schauen vi to watch; **Zuschauer(in)** (-s, -) m(f) spectator; **die ~** (pl) (Theat) the audience sing; **Zuschauertribüne** f stand
zu|schicken vt to send
Zuschlag m extra charge; (Fahrkarte) supplement

zuschlagpflichtig adj subject to an extra charge; (Eisenb) subject to a supplement
zu|schließen irr vt to lock up
zu|sehen irr vi to watch (jdm sb); **~, dass** (dafür sorgen) to make sure that
zu|sichern vt: **jdm etw ~** to assure sb of sth
Zustand m state, condition; **sie bekommt Zustände, wenn sie das sieht** (fam) she'll have a fit if she sees that
zustande adv: **~ bringen** to bring about; **~ kommen** to come about
zuständig adj (Behörde) relevant; **~ für** responsible for
Zustellung f delivery
zu|stimmen vi to agree (einer Sache dat to sth, jdm with sb); **Zustimmung** f approval
zu|stoßen irr vi (fig) to happen (jdm to sb)
Zutaten pl ingredients pl
zu|trauen vt: **jdm etw ~** to think sb is capable of sth; **das hätte ich ihm nie zugetraut** I'd never have thought he was capable of it; **ich würde es ihr ~** (etw Negatives) I wouldn't put it past her; **Zutrauen** (-s) nt confidence (zu in); **zutraulich** adj trusting; (Tier) friendly
zu|treffen irr vi to be correct; **~ auf** (+akk) to apply to; **Zutreffendes bitte streichen** please delete as applicable
Zutritt m entry; (Zugang) access; **~ verboten!** no entry
zuverlässig adj reliable; **Zuverlässigkeit** f reliability
Zuversicht f confidence; **zuversichtlich** adj confident
zuvor adv before; (zunächst) first; **zuvor|kommen** irr vi: **jdm ~** to

beat sb to it; **zuvorkommend**
adj obliging
Zuwachs *(-es, Zuwächse) m*
increase, growth; *(fam: Baby)*
addition to the family
zuwider *adv:* **es ist mir ~** I hate (*o*
detest) it
zuzüglich *prep +gen* plus
zwang *imperf von* **zwingen**
Zwang *(-(e)s, Zwänge) m (innerer)*
compulsion; *(Gewalt)* force
zwängen *vt* to squeeze (*in +akk*
into) ▷ *vr:* **sich ~** to squeeze (*in*
+akk into)
zwanglos *adj* informal
zwanzig *num* twenty;
zwanzigste(r, s) *adj* twentieth;
siehe auch **dritte**
zwar *adv:* **und ~ ...** *(genauer)* ...,
to be precise; **das ist ~ schön,**
aber ... it is nice, but ...; **ich kenne**
ihn ~, aber ... I know him all right,
but ...
Zweck *(-(e)s, -e) m* purpose;
zwecklos *adj* pointless
zwei *num* two; **Zwei** *(-, -en) f*
two; *(Schulnote)* ≈ B;
Zweibettzimmer *nt* twin room;
zweideutig *adj* ambiguous;
(unanständig) suggestive;
zweifach *adj, adv* double
Zweifel *(-s, -) m* doubt;
zweifellos *adv* undoubtedly;
zweifeln *vi* to doubt (*an etw dat*
sth); **Zweifelsfall** *m:* **im ~** in case
of doubt
Zweig *(-(e)s, -e) m* branch
Zweigstelle *f* branch
zweihundert *num* two hundred;
zweimal *adv* twice; **zweisprachig**
adj bilingual; **zweispurig** *adj*
(Auto) two-lane; **zweit** *adv:* **wir**
sind zu ~ there are two of us;
zweite(r, s) *adj* second; *siehe*
auch **dritte eine ~ Portion** a
second helping; **zweitens** *adv*
secondly; *(bei Aufzählungen)*

second; **zweitgrößte(r, s)** *adj*
second largest; **Zweitschlüssel**
m spare key
Zwerchfell *nt* diaphragm
Zwerg(in) *(-(e)s, -e) m(f)* dwarf
Zwetschge *(-, -n) f* plum
zwicken *vt* to pinch
Zwieback *(-(e)s, -e) m* rusk
Zwiebel *(-, -n) f* onion; *(von*
Blume) bulb; **Zwiebelsuppe** *f*
onion soup
Zwilling *(-s, -e) m* twin; **~e** *(pl)*
(Astr) Gemini *sing*
zwingen *(zwang, gezwungen) vt*
to force
zwinkern *vi* to blink; *(absichtlich)*
to wink
zwischen *prep +akk o dat*
between
Zwischenablage *f (Inform)*
clipboard
zwischendurch *adv* in between
Zwischenfall *m* incident
Zwischenlandung *f* stopover
zwischenmenschlich *adj*
interpersonal
Zwischenraum *m* space
Zwischenstopp *(-s, -s) m*
stopover
Zwischensumme *f* subtotal
Zwischenzeit *f:* **in der ~** in the
meantime
zwitschern *vt, vi* to twitter, to
chirp
zwölf *num* twelve; **zwölfte(r, s)**
adj twelfth; *siehe auch* **dritte**
Zylinder *(-s, -) m* cylinder; *(Hut)*
top hat
zynisch *adj* cynical
Zypern *(-s) nt* Cyprus
Zyste *(-, -n) f* cyst

VERB TABLES

Introduction

The **Verb Tables** in the following section contain 31 tables of German verbs in alphabetical order. Each table shows you the following forms: **Present, Perfect, Future, Subjunctive, Imperfect, Conditional, Imperative** and the **Present** and **Past Participles**.

In order to help you use the verbs shown in the Verb Tables correctly, there are also a number of example phrases at the bottom of each page to show the verb as it is used in context.

In German there are **regular** verbs or **weak** verbs (their forms follow the normal rules) and **irregular** or **strong** verbs (their forms do not follow the normal rules) and **mixed** verbs (their forms have features of both **weak** and **strong** verbs).

The **Verb Tables** given show one **weak** verb – machen, Verb Table 19 and three **mixed** verbs – bringen, Verb Table 2; denken, Verb Table 3 and kennen Verb Table 13. The rest of the verbs shown are **strong** verbs.

▶ bleiben (to remain)

PRESENT

ich	bleibe
du	bleibst
er	bleibt
wir	bleiben
ihr	bleibt
sie	bleiben

PRESENT SUBJUNCTIVE

ich	bleibe
du	bleibest
er	bleibe
wir	bleiben
ihr	bleibet
sie	bleiben

PERFECT

ich	bin geblieben
du	bist geblieben
er	ist geblieben
wir	sind geblieben
ihr	seid geblieben
sie	sind geblieben

IMPERFECT

ich	blieb
du	bliebst
er	blieb
wir	blieben
ihr	bliebt
sie	blieben

FUTURE

ich	werde bleiben
du	wirst bleiben
er	wird bleiben
wir	werden bleiben
ihr	werdet bleiben
sie	werden bleiben

CONDITIONAL

ich	würde bleiben
du	würdest bleiben
er	würde bleiben
wir	würden bleiben
ihr	würdet bleiben
sie	würden bleiben

IMPERATIVE

bleib(e)!/bleiben wir!/bleibt!
bleiben Sie!

PAST PARTICIPLE

geblieben

PRESENT PARTICIPLE

bleibend

EXAMPLE PHRASES

*Hoffentlich **bleibt** das Wetter schön.* I hope the weather will stay fine.
*Vom Kuchen **ist** nur noch ein Stück **geblieben**.* There's only one piece of cake left.
*Dieses Erlebnis **blieb** in meiner Erinnerung.* This experience stayed with me.

ich = I **du** = you **er** = he **wir** = we/one **ihr** = you **sie** = they

▶ **bringen** (to bring)

PRESENT		PRESENT SUBJUNCTIVE	
ich	bringe	ich	bringe
du	bringst	du	bringest
er	bringt	er	bringe
wir	bringen	wir	bringen
ihr	bringt	ihr	bringet
sie	bringen	sie	bringen

PERFECT		IMPERFECT	
ich	habe gebracht	ich	brachte
du	hast gebracht	du	brachtest
er	hat gebracht	er	brachte
wir	haben gebracht	wir	brachten
ihr	habt gebracht	ihr	brachtet
sie	haben gebracht	sie	brachten

FUTURE		CONDITIONAL	
ich	werde bringen	ich	würde bringen
du	wirst bringen	du	würdest bringen
er	wird bringen	er	würde bringen
wir	werden bringen	wir	würden bringen
ihr	werdet bringen	ihr	würdet bringen
sie	werden bringen	sie	würden bringen

IMPERATIVE

bring(e)!/bringen wir!/bringt!
bringen Sie!

PAST PARTICIPLE

gebracht

PRESENT PARTICIPLE

bringend

EXAMPLE PHRASES

*Kannst du mich zum Flughafen **bringen**?* Can you take me to the airport?
*Max **hat** mir Blumen **gebracht**.* Max brought me flowers.
*Das **brachte** mich auf eine Idee.* It gave me an idea.

ich = I **du** = you **er** = he **wir** = we/one **ihr** = you **sie** = they

▶ **denken** (to think)

PRESENT		PRESENT SUBJUNCTIVE	
ich	denke	ich	denke
du	denkst	du	denkest
er	denkt	er	denke
wir	denken	wir	denken
ihr	denkt	ihr	denket
sie	denken	sie	denken

PERFECT		IMPERFECT	
ich	habe gedacht	ich	dachte
du	hast gedacht	du	dachtest
er	hat gedacht	er	dachte
wir	haben gedacht	wir	dachten
ihr	habt gedacht	ihr	dachtet
sie	haben gedacht	sie	dachten

FUTURE		CONDITIONAL	
ich	werde denken	ich	würde denken
du	wirst denken	du	würdest denken
er	wird denken	er	würde denken
wir	werden denken	wir	würden denken
ihr	werdet denken	ihr	würdet denken
sie	werden denken	sie	würden denken

IMPERATIVE

denk(e)!/denken wir!/denkt!
denken Sie!

PAST PARTICIPLE

gedacht

PRESENT PARTICIPLE

denkend

EXAMPLE PHRASES

*Wie **denken** Sie darüber?* What do you think about it?
*Das war für ihn **gedacht**.* It was meant for him.
*Es war das Erste, woran ich **dachte**.* It was the first thing I thought of.

ich = I **du** = you **er** = he **wir** = we/one **ihr** = you **sie** = they

▶ dürfen (to be allowed to)

PRESENT		PRESENT SUBJUNCTIVE	
ich	darf	ich	dürfe
du	darfst	du	dürfest
er	darf	er	dürfe
wir	dürfen	wir	dürfen
ihr	dürft	ihr	dürfet
sie	dürfen	sie	dürfen

PERFECT		IMPERFECT	
ich	habe gedurft/dürfen	ich	durfte
du	hast gedurft/dürfen	du	durftest
er	hat gedurft/dürfen	er	durfte
wir	haben gedurft/dürfen	wir	durften
ihr	habt gedurft/dürfen	ihr	durftet
sie	haben gedurft/dürfen	sie	durften

FUTURE		CONDITIONAL	
ich	werde dürfen	ich	würde dürfen
du	wirst dürfen	du	würdest dürfen
er	wird dürfen	er	würde dürfen
wir	werden dürfen	wir	würden dürfen
ihr	werdet dürfen	ihr	würdet dürfen
sie	werden dürfen	sie	würden dürfen

IMPERATIVE

PAST PARTICIPLE

gedurft/dürfen*

PRESENT PARTICIPLE

dürfend

The second form is used when combined with an infinitive construction.

EXAMPLE PHRASES

Darf ich ins Kino? Can I go to the cinema?
Das **würde** ich zu Hause nicht dürfen. I wouldn't be allowed to do that at home.
Das **dürfen** Sie mir glauben. You can take my word for it.

ich = I **du** = you **er** = he **wir** = we/one **ihr** = you **sie** = they

▶ fahren (to drive/to go)

PRESENT

ich	fahre
du	fährst
er	fährt
wir	fahren
ihr	fahrt
sie	fahren

PRESENT SUBJUNCTIVE

ich	fahre
du	fahrest
er	fahre
wir	fahren
ihr	fahret
sie	fahren

PERFECT

ich	bin gefahren*
du	bist gefahren
er	ist gefahren
wir	sind gefahren
ihr	seid gefahren
sie	sind gefahren

IMPERFECT

ich	fuhr
du	fuhrst
er	fuhr
wir	fuhren
ihr	fuhrt
sie	fuhren

FUTURE

ich	werde fahren
du	wirst fahren
er	wird fahren
wir	werden fahren
ihr	werdet fahren
sie	werden fahren

CONDITIONAL

ich	würde fahren
du	würdest fahren
er	würde fahren
wir	würden fahren
ihr	würdet fahren
sie	würden fahren

IIMPERATIVE

fahr(e)!/fahren wir!/fahrt!
fahren Sie!
OR: ich habe/hätte gefahren
etc (*when transitive*).

PAST PARTICIPLE

gefahren

PRESENT PARTICIPLE

fahrend

EXAMPLE PHRASES

*Sie **fahren** mit dem Bus in die Schule.* They go to school by bus.
*Rechts **fahren**!* Drive on the right!
*Ich **bin** mit der Familie nach Spanien **gefahren**.* I went to Spain with my family.

ich = I   **du** = you   **er** = he   **wir** = we/one   **ihr** = you   **sie** = they

▶ **fallen** (to fall)

PRESENT

ich	falle
du	fällst
er	fällt
wir	fallen
ihr	fallt
sie	fallen

PRESENT SUBJUNCTIVE

ich	falle
du	fallest
er	falle
wir	fallen
ihr	fallet
sie	fallen

PERFECT

ich	bin gefallen
du	bist gefallen
er	ist gefallen
wir	sind gefallen
ihr	seid gefallen
sie	sind gefallen

IMPERFECT

ich	fiel
du	fielst
er	fiel
wir	fielen
ihr	fielt
sie	fielen

FUTURE

ich	werde fallen
du	wirst fallen
er	wird fallen
wir	werden fallen
ihr	werdet fallen
sie	werden fallen

CONDITIONAL

ich	würde fallen
du	würdest fallen
er	würde fallen
wir	würden fallen
ihr	würdet fallen
sie	würden fallen

IMPERATIVE

fall(e)!/fallen wir!/fallt!
fallen Sie!

PAST PARTICIPLE

gefallen

PRESENT PARTICIPLE

fallend

EXAMPLE PHRASES

*Er **fiel** vom Fahrrad.* He fell off his bike.
*Ich **bin** durch die Prüfung **gefallen**.* I failed my exam.
*Die Aktien **fielen** im Kurs.* Share prices went down.

ich = I **du** = you **er** = he **wir** = we/one **ihr** = you **sie** = they

▶ **finden** (to find)

PRESENT

ich	finde
du	findest
er	findet
wir	finden
ihr	findet
sie	finden

PRESENT SUBJUNCTIVE

ich	finde
du	findest
er	finde
wir	finden
ihr	findet
sie	finden

PERFECT

ich	habe gefunden
du	hast gefunden
er	hat gefunden
wir	haben gefunden
ihr	habt gefunden
sie	haben gefunden

IMPERFECT

ich	fand
du	fand(e)st
er	fand
wir	fanden
ihr	fandet
sie	fanden

FUTURE

ich	werde finden
du	wirst finden
er	wird finden
wir	werden finden
ihr	werdet finden
sie	werden finden

CONDITIONAL

ich	würde finden
du	würdest finden
er	würde finden
wir	würden finden
ihr	würdet finden
sie	würden finden

IMPERATIVE

find(e)!/finden wir!/findet!
finden Sie!

PAST PARTICIPLE

gefunden

PRESENT PARTICIPLE

findend

EXAMPLE PHRASES

*Hast du deine Brieftasche **gefunden**?* Have you found your wallet?
*Er **fand** den Mut, sie zu fragen.* He found the courage to ask her.
*Ich **finde**, sie ist eine gute Lehrerin.* I think she's a good teacher.

---

ich = I   **du** = you   **er** = he   **wir** = we/one   **ihr** = you   **sie** = they

▶ **geben** (to give)

PRESENT

ich	gebe
du	gibst
er	gibt
wir	geben
ihr	gebt
sie	geben

PRESENT SUBJUNCTIVE

ich	gebe
du	gebest
er	gebe
wir	geben
ihr	gebet
sie	geben

PERFECT

ich	habe gegeben
du	hast gegeben
er	hat gegeben
wir	haben gegeben
ihr	habt gegeben
sie	haben gegeben

IMPERFECT

ich	gab
du	gabst
er	gab
wir	gaben
ihr	gabt
sie	gaben

FUTURE

ich	werde geben
du	wirst geben
er	wird geben
wir	werden geben
ihr	werdet geben
sie	werden geben

CONDITIONAL

ich	würde geben
du	würdest geben
er	würde geben
wir	würden geben
ihr	würdet geben
sie	würden geben

IMPERATIVE

gib!/geben wir!/gebt!
geben Sie!

PAST PARTICIPLE

gegeben

PRESENT PARTICIPLE

gebend

EXAMPLE PHRASES

*Er **gab** mir das Geld für die Bücher.* He gave me the money for the books.
*Was **gibt** es im Kino?* What's on at the cinema?
*Wir **würden** alles darum **geben**, ins Finale zu kommen.* We would give anything
to reach the finals.

ich =

ich = I **du** = you **er** = he **wir** = we/one **ihr** = you **sie** = they

▶ gehen (to go)

PRESENT		PRESENT SUBJUNCTIVE	
ich	gehe	ich	gehe
du	gehst	du	gehest
er	geht	er	gehe
wir	gehen	wir	gehen
ihr	geht	ihr	gehet
sie	gehen	sie	gehen

PERFECT		IMPERFECT	
ich	bin gegangen	ich	ging
du	bist gegangen	du	gingst
er	ist gegangen	er	ging
wir	sind gegangen	wir	gingen
ihr	seid gegangen	ihr	gingt
sie	sind gegangen	sie	gingen

FUTURE		CONDITIONAL	
ich	werde gehen	ich	würde gehen
du	wirst gehen	du	würdest gehen
er	wird gehen	er	würde gehen
wir	werden gehen	wir	würden gehen
ihr	werdet gehen	ihr	würdet gehen
sie	werden gehen	sie	würden gehen

IMPERATIVE

geh(e)!/gehen wir!/geht!
gehen Sie!

PAST PARTICIPLE

gegangen

PRESENT PARTICIPLE

gehend

EXAMPLE PHRASES

*Die Kinder **gingen** ins Haus.* The children went into the house.
*Wie **geht** es dir?* How are you?
*Wir **sind** gestern schwimmen **gegangen**.* We went swimming yesterday.

du = you **er** = he **wir** = we/one **ihr** = you **sie** = they

▶ haben (to have)

PRESENT

ich	habe
du	hast
er	hat
wir	haben
ihr	habt
sie	haben

PRESENT SUBJUNCTIVE

ich	habe
du	habest
er	habe
wir	haben
ihr	habet
sie	haben

PERFECT

ich	habe gehabt
du	hast gehabt
er	hat gehabt
wir	haben gehabt
ihr	habt gehabt
sie	haben gehabt

IMPERFECT

ich	hatte
du	hattest
er	hatte
wir	hatten
ihr	hattet
sie	hatten

FUTURE

ich	werde haben
du	wirst haben
er	wird haben
wir	werden haben
ihr	werdet haben
sie	werden haben

CONDITIONAL

ich	würde haben
du	würdest haben
er	würde haben
wir	würden haben
ihr	würdet haben
sie	würden haben

IMPERATIVE

hab(e)!/haben wir!/habt!
haben Sie!

PAST PARTICIPLE

gehabt

PRESENT PARTICIPLE

habend

EXAMPLE PHRASES

Hast du eine Schwester? Have you got a sister?
Er hatte Hunger. He was hungry.
Ich hätte gern ein Eis. I'd like an ice cream.
Sie hat heute Geburtstag. It's her birthday today.

ich = I **du** = you **er** = he **wir** = we/one **ihr** = you **sie** = they

▶ **halten** (to hold)

PRESENT

ich	halte
du	hältst
er	hält
wir	halten
ihr	haltet
sie	halten

PRESENT SUBJUNCTIVE

ich	halte
du	haltest
er	halte
wir	halten
ihr	haltet
sie	halten

PERFECT

ich	habe gehalten
du	hast gehalten
er	hat gehalten
wir	haben gehalten
ihr	habt gehalten
sie	haben gehalten

IMPERFECT

ich	hielt
du	hielt(e)st
er	hielt
wir	hielten
ihr	hieltet
sie	hielten

FUTURE

ich	werde halten
du	wirst halten
er	wird halten
wir	werden halten
ihr	werdet halten
sie	werden halten

CONDITIONAL

ich	würde halten
du	würdest halten
er	würde halten
wir	würden halten
ihr	würdet halten
sie	würden halten

IMPERATIVE

halt(e)!/halten wir!/haltet!
halten Sie!

PAST PARTICIPLE

gehalten

PRESENT PARTICIPLE

haltend

EXAMPLE PHRASES

*Kannst du das mal **halten**?* Can you hold that for a moment?
*Der Bus **hielt** vor dem Rathaus.* The bus stopped in front of the town hall.
*Ich **habe** sie für deine Mutter **gehalten**.* I took her for your mother.

I **du** = you **er** = he **wir** = we/one **ihr** = you **sie** = they

▶ **helfen** (to help)

PRESENT

ich	helfe
du	hilfst
er	hilft
wir	helfen
ihr	helft
sie	helfen

PRESENT SUBJUNCTIVE

ich	helfe
du	helfest
er	helfe
wir	helfen
ihr	helfet
sie	helfen

PERFECT

ich	habe geholfen
du	hast geholfen
er	hat geholfen
wir	haben geholfen
ihr	habt geholfen
sie	haben geholfen

IMPERFECT

ich	half
du	halfst
er	half
wir	halfen
ihr	halft
sie	halfen

FUTURE

ich	werde helfen
du	wirst helfen
er	wird helfen
wir	werden helfen
ihr	werdet helfen
sie	werden helfen

CONDITIONAL

ich	würde helfen
du	würdest helfen
er	würde helfen
wir	würden helfen
ihr	würdet helfen
sie	würden helfen

IMPERATIVE

hilf!/helfen wir!/helft!
helfen Sie!

PAST PARTICIPLE

geholfen

PRESENT PARTICIPLE

helfend

EXAMPLE PHRASES

*Er **hat** mir dabei **geholfen**.* He helped me with it.
*Diese Arznei **hilft** gegen Kopfschmerzen.* This medicine is good for headaches.
*Sein Vorschlag **half** mir wenig.* His suggestion was not much help to me.

ich = I **du** = you **er** = he **wir** = we/one **ihr** = you **sie** = they

▶ **kennen** (to know) *(be acquainted with)*

PRESENT

ich	kenne
du	kennst
er	kennt
wir	kennen
ihr	kennt
sie	kennen

PRESENT SUBJUNCTIVE

ich	kenne
du	kennest
er	kenne
wir	kennen
ihr	kennet
sie	kennen

PERFECT

ich	habe gekannt
du	hast gekannt
er	hat gekannt
wir	haben gekannt
ihr	habt gekannt
sie	haben gekannt

IMPERFECT

ich	kannte
du	kanntest
er	kannte
wir	kannten
ihr	kanntet
sie	kannten

FUTURE

ich	werde kennen
du	wirst kennen
er	wird kennen
wir	werden kennen
ihr	werdet kennen
sie	werden kennen

CONDITIONAL

ich	würde kennen
du	würdest kennen
er	würde kennen
wir	würden kennen
ihr	würdet kennen
sie	würden kennen

IMPERATIVE

kenn(e)!/kennen wir!/kennt!
kennen Sie!

PAST PARTICIPLE

gekannt

PRESENT PARTICIPLE

kennend

EXAMPLE PHRASES

*Ich **kenne** ihn nicht.* I don't know him.
*Er **kannte** kein Erbarmen.* He knew no mercy.
***Kennst** du mich noch?* Do you remember me?

ich = I **du** = you **er** = he **wir** = we/one **ihr** = you **sie** = they

▶ **kommen** (to come)

PRESENT

ich	komme
du	kommst
er	kommt
wir	kommen
ihr	kommt
sie	kommen

PRESENT SUBJUNCTIVE

ich	komme
du	kommest
er	komme
wir	kommen
ihr	kommet
sie	kommen

PERFECT

ich	bin gekommen
du	bist gekommen
er	ist gekommen
wir	sind gekommen
ihr	seid gekommen
sie	sind gekommen

IMPERFECT

ich	kam
du	kamst
er	kam
wir	kamen
ihr	kamt
sie	kamen

FUTURE

ich	werde kommen
du	wirst kommen
er	wird kommen
wir	werden kommen
ihr	werdet kommen
sie	werden kommen

CONDITIONAL

ich	würde kommen
du	würdest kommen
er	würde kommen
wir	würden kommen
ihr	würdet kommen
sie	würden kommen

IMPERATIVE

komm(e)!/kommen wir!
kommt!/kommen Sie!

PAST PARTICIPLE

gekommen

PRESENT PARTICIPLE

kommend

EXAMPLE PHRASES

*Er **kam** die Straße entlang.* He was coming along the street.
*Ich **komme** zu deiner Party.* I'm coming to your party.
*Woher **kommst** du?* Where do you come from?

ich = I **du** = you **er** = he **wir** = we/one **ihr** = you **sie** = they

▶ **können** (to be able to)

PRESENT

ich	kann
du	kannst
er	kann
wir	können
ihr	könnt
sie	können

PRESENT SUBJUNCTIVE

ich	könne
du	könnest
er	könne
wir	können
ihr	könnet
sie	können

PERFECT

ich	habe gekonnt/können
du	hast gekonnt/können
er	hat gekonnt/können
wir	haben gekonnt/können
ihr	habt gekonnt/können
sie	haben gekonnt/können

IMPERFECT

ich	konnte
du	konntest
er	konnte
wir	konnten
ihr	konntet
sie	konnten

FUTURE

ich	werde können
du	wirst können
er	wird können
wir	werden können
ihr	werdet können
sie	werden können

CONDITIONAL

ich	würde können
du	würdest können
er	würde können
wir	würden können
ihr	würdet können
sie	würden können

IMPERATIVE

PAST PARTICIPLE

gekonnt/können*

PRESENT PARTICIPLE

könnend

*The second form is used when combined with an infinitive construction.

EXAMPLE PHRASES

Er **kann** gut schwimmen. He can swim well.
Sie **konnte** kein Wort Deutsch. She couldn't speak a word of German.
Kann ich gehen? Can I go?

ich = I **du** = you **er** = he **wir** = we/one **ihr** = you **sie** = they

▶ **lassen** (to leave; to allow)

PRESENT		**PRESENT SUBJUNCTIVE**	
ich	lasse	ich	lasse
du	lässt	du	lassest
er	lässt	er	lasse
wir	lassen	wir	lassen
ihr	lasst	ihr	lasset
sie	lassen	sie	lassen

PERFECT		**IMPERFECT**	
ich	habe gelassen	ich	ließ
du	hast gelassen	du	ließest
er	hat gelassen	er	ließ
wir	haben gelassen	wir	ließen
ihr	habt gelassen	ihr	ließt
sie	haben gelassen	sie	ließen

FUTURE		**CONDITIONAL**	
ich	werde lassen	ich	würde lassen
du	wirst lassen	du	würdest lassen
er	wird lassen	er	würde lassen
wir	werden lassen	wir	würden lassen
ihr	werdet lassen	ihr	würdet lassen
sie	werden lassen	sie	würden lassen

IMPERATIVE

lass!/lassen wir!/lasst!
lassen Sie!

PAST PARTICIPLE

gelassen/lassen*

PRESENT PARTICIPLE

lassend

The second form is used when combined with an infinitive construction.

EXAMPLE PHRASES

*Sie **ließ** uns warten.* She kept us waiting.
*Ich **lasse** den Hund nicht auf das Sofa.* I won't let the dog get up on the sofa.
*Sie **haben** ihn allein im Auto **gelassen**.* They left him alone in the car.

ich = I **du** = you **er** = he **wir** = we/one **ihr** = you **sie** = they

▶ **laufen** (to run)

PRESENT		PRESENT SUBJUNCTIVE	
ich	laufe	ich	laufe
du	läufst	du	laufest
er	läuft	er	laufe
wir	laufen	wir	laufen
ihr	lauft	ihr	laufet
sie	laufen	sie	laufen

PERFECT		IMPERFECT	
ich	bin gelaufen	ich	lief
du	bist gelaufen	du	liefst
er	ist gelaufen	er	lief
wir	sind gelaufen	wir	liefen
ihr	seid gelaufen	ihr	lieft
sie	sind gelaufen	sie	liefen

FUTURE		CONDITIONAL	
ich	werde laufen	ich	würde laufen
du	wirst laufen	du	würdest laufen
er	wird laufen	er	würde laufen
wir	werden laufen	wir	würden laufen
ihr	werdet laufen	ihr	würdet laufen
sie	werden laufen	sie	würden laufen

IIMPERATIVE

lauf(e)!/laufen wir!/lauft!
laufen Sie!

PAST PARTICIPLE

gelaufen

PRESENT PARTICIPLE

laufend

EXAMPLE PHRASES

Er **lief** so schnell er konnte. He ran as fast as he could.
Sie **läuft** ständig zur Polizei. She's always going to the police.
Das Schiff **ist** auf Grund **gelaufen**. The ship ran aground.

ich = I **du** = you **er** = he **wir** = we/one **ihr** = you **sie** = they

▶ liegen (to lie)

PRESENT

ich	liege
du	liegst
er	liegt
wir	liegen
ihr	liegt
sie	liegen

PRESENT SUBJUNCTIVE

ich	liege
du	liegest
er	liege
wir	liegen
ihr	lieget
sie	liegen

PERFECT

ich	habe gelegen
du	hast gelegen
er	hat gelegen
wir	haben gelegen
ihr	habt gelegen
sie	haben gelegen

IMPERFECT

ich	lag
du	lagst
er	lag
wir	lagen
ihr	lagt
sie	lagen

FUTURE

ich	werde liegen
du	wirst liegen
er	wird liegen
wir	werden liegen
ihr	werdet liegen
sie	werden liegen

CONDITIONAL

ich	würde liegen
du	würdest liegen
er	würde liegen
wir	würden liegen
ihr	würdet liegen
sie	würden liegen

IMPERATIVE

lieg(e)!/liegen wir!/liegt!
liegen Sie!

PAST PARTICIPLE

gelegen

PRESENT PARTICIPLE

liegend

EXAMPLE PHRASES

*Wir **lagen** den ganzen Tag am Strand.* We lay on the beach all day.
*Köln **liegt** am Rhein.* Cologne is on the Rhine.
*Es **hat** daran **gelegen**, dass ich krank war.* It was because I was ill.

---

ich = I **du** = you **er** = he **wir** = we/one **ihr** = you **sie** = they

▶ **machen** (to do *or* to make)

PRESENT

ich	mache
du	machst
er	macht
wir	machen
ihr	macht
sie	machen

PRESENT SUBJUNCTIVE

ich	mache
du	machest
er	mache
wir	machen
ihr	machet
sie	machen

PERFECT

ich	habe gemacht
du	hast gemacht
er	hat gemacht
wir	haben gemacht
ihr	habt gemacht
sie	haben gemacht

IMPERFECT

ich	machte
du	machtest
er	machte
wir	machten
ihr	machtet
sie	machten

FUTURE

ich	werde machen
du	wirst machen
er	wird machen
wir	werden machen
ihr	werdet machen
sie	werden machen

CONDITIONAL

ich	würde machen
du	würdest machen
er	würde machen
wir	würden machen
ihr	würdet machen
sie	würden machen

IMPERATIVE

mach!/macht!/machen Sie!

PAST PARTICIPLE

gemacht

PRESENT PARTICIPLE

machend

EXAMPLE PHRASES

*Was **machst** du?* What are you doing?
*Ich **habe** die Betten **gemacht**.* I made the beds.
*Ich **werde** es morgen **machen**.* I'll do it tomorrow.

---

ich = I   **du** = you   **er** = he   **wir** = we/one   **ihr** = you   **sie** = they

► mögen (to like)

PRESENT

ich	mag
du	magst
er	mag
wir	mögen
ihr	mögt
sie	mögen

PRESENT SUBJUNCTIVE

ich	möge
du	mögest
er	möge
wir	mögen
ihr	möget
sie	mögen

PERFECT

ich	habe gemocht/mögen
du	hast gemocht/mögen
er	hat gemocht/mögen
wir	haben gemocht/mögen
ihr	habt gemocht/mögen
sie	haben gemocht/mögen

IMPERFECT

ich	mochte
du	mochtest
er	mochte
wir	mochten
ihr	mochtet
sie	mochten

FUTURE

ich	werde mögen
du	wirst mögen
er	wird mögen
wir	werden mögen
ihr	werdet mögen
sie	werden mögen

CONDITIONAL

ich	würde mögen
du	würdest mögen
er	würde mögen
wir	würden mögen
ihr	würdet mögen
sie	würden mögen

IMPERATIVE

PAST PARTICIPLE

gemocht/mögen*

PRESENT PARTICIPLE

mögend

The second form is used when combined with an infinitive construction.

EXAMPLE PHRASES

*Ich **mag** gern Vanilleeis.* I like vanilla ice cream.
*Er **mochte** sie nicht danach fragen.* He didn't want to ask her about it.
*Ich **habe** ihn noch nie **gemocht**.* I never liked him.

ich = I **du** = you **er** = he **wir** = we/one **ihr** = you **sie** = they

▶ müssen (to have to)

PRESENT

ich	muss
du	musst
er	muss
wir	müssen
ihr	müsst
sie	müssen

PRESENT SUBJUNCTIVE

ich	müsse
du	müssest
er	müsse
wir	müssen
ihr	müsset
sie	müssen

PERFECT

ich	habe gemusst/müssen
du	hast gemusst/müssen
er	hat gemusst/müssen
wir	haben gemusst/müssen
ihr	habt gemusst/müssen
sie	haben gemusst/müssen

IMPERFECT

ich	musste
du	musstest
er	musste
wir	mussten
ihr	musstet
sie	mussten

FUTURE

ich	werde müssen
du	wirst müssen
er	wird müssen
wir	werden müssen
ihr	werdet müssen
sie	werden müssen

CONDITIONAL

ich	würde müssen
du	würdest müssen
er	würde müssen
wir	würden müssen
ihr	würdet müssen
sie	würden müssen

IMPERATIVE

PAST PARTICIPLE

gemusst/müssen*

PRESENT PARTICIPLE

müssend

The second form is used when combined with an infinitive construction.

EXAMPLE PHRASES

Ich **muss** *aufs Klo.* I must go to the loo.
Wir **müssen** *jeden Abend unsere Hausaufgaben machen.* We have to do our homework every night.
Sie **hat** *abwaschen* **müssen.** She had to wash up.

ich = I **du** = you **er** = he **wir** = we/one **ihr** = you **sie** = they

▶ **nehmen** (to take)

PRESENT

ich	nehme
du	nimmst
er	nimmt
wir	nehmen
ihr	nehmt
sie	nehmen

PRESENT SUBJUNCTIVE

ich	nehme
du	nehmest
er	nehme
wir	nehmen
ihr	nehmet
sie	nehmen

PERFECT

ich	habe genommen
du	hast genommen
er	hat genommen
wir	haben genommen
ihr	habt genommen
sie	haben genommen

IMPERFECT

ich	nahm
du	nahmst
er	nahm
wir	nahmen
ihr	nahmt
sie	nahmen

FUTURE

ich	werde nehmen
du	wirst nehmen
er	wird nehmen
wir	werden nehmen
ihr	werdet nehmen
sie	werden nehmen

CONDITIONAL

ich	würde nehmen
du	würdest nehmen
er	würde nehmen
wir	würden nehmen
ihr	würdet nehmen
sie	würden nehmen

IMPERATIVE

nimm!/nehmen wir!/nehmt!
nehmen Sie!

PAST PARTICIPLE

genommen

PRESENT PARTICIPLE

nehmend

EXAMPLE PHRASES

Hast du den Bus in die Stadt genommen? Did you take the bus into town?
Wie viel nimmst du dafür? How much will you take for it?
Er nahm sich vom Brot. He helped himself to bread.

---

ich = I **du** = you **er** = he **wir** = we/one **ihr** = you **sie** = they

▶ sein (to be)

PRESENT		PRESENT SUBJUNCTIVE	
ich	bin	ich	sei
du	bist	du	sei(e)st
er	ist	er	sei
wir	sind	wir	seien
ihr	seid	ihr	seiet
sie	sind	sie	seien

PERFECT		IMPERFECT	
ich	bin gewesen	ich	war
du	bist gewesen	du	warst
er	ist gewesen	er	war
wir	sind gewesen	wir	waren
ihr	seid gewesen	ihr	wart
sie	sind gewesen	sie	waren

FUTURE		CONDITIONAL	
ich	werde sein	ich	würde sein
du	wirst sein	du	würdest sein
er	wird sein	er	würde sein
wir	werden sein	wir	würden sein
ihr	werdet sein	ihr	würdet sein
sie	werden sein	sie	würden sein

IMPERATIVE

sei!/seien wir!/seid!/seien Sie!

PAST PARTICIPLE

gewesen

PRESENT PARTICIPLE

seiend

EXAMPLE PHRASES

Er ist zehn Jahre alt. He is ten years old.
Mir ist kalt. I'm cold.
Wir waren gestern im Theater. We were at the theatre yesterday.
Seid ruhig! Be quiet!

---

ich = I **du** = you **er** = he **wir** = we/one **ihr** = you **sie** = they

▶ **sitzen** (to sit)

PRESENT		PRESENT SUBJUNCTIVE	
ich	sitze	ich	sitze
du	sitzt	du	sitzest
er	sitzt	er	sitze
wir	sitzen	wir	sitzen
ihr	sitzt	ihr	sitzet
sie	sitzen	sie	sitzen

PERFECT		IMPERFECT	
ich	habe gesessen	ich	saß
du	hast gesessen	du	saßest
er	hat gesessen	er	saß
wir	haben gesessen	wir	saßen
ihr	habt gesessen	ihr	saßt
sie	haben gesessen	sie	saßen

FUTURE		CONDITIONAL	
ich	werde sitzen	ich	würde sitzen
du	wirst sitzen	du	würdest sitzen
er	wird sitzen	er	würde sitzen
wir	werden sitzen	wir	würden sitzen
ihr	werdet sitzen	ihr	würdet sitzen
sie	werden sitzen	sie	würden sitzen

IMPERATIVE

sitz(e)!/sitzen wir!/sitzt!
sitzen Sie!

PAST PARTICIPLE

gesessen

PRESENT PARTICIPLE

sitzend

EXAMPLE PHRASES

*Er **saß** auf meinem Stuhl.* He was sitting on my chair.
*Deine Krawatte **sitzt** nicht richtig.* Your tie isn't straight.
*Ich **habe** zwei Jahre über dieser Arbeit **gesessen**.* I've spent two years on this piece of work.

ich = I **du** = you **er** = he **wir** = we/one **ihr** = you **sie** = they

▶ **sprechen** (to speak)

PRESENT

ich	spreche
du	sprichst
er	spricht
wir	sprechen
ihr	sprecht
sie	sprechen

PRESENT SUBJUNCTIVE

ich	spreche
du	sprechest
er	spreche
wir	sprechen
ihr	sprechet
sie	sprechen

PERFECT

ich	habe gesprochen
du	hast gesprochen
er	hat gesprochen
wir	haben gesprochen
ihr	habt gesprochen
sie	haben gesprochen

IMPERFECT

ich	sprach
du	sprachst
er	sprach
wir	sprachen
ihr	spracht
sie	sprachen

FUTURE

ich	werde sprechen
du	wirst sprechen
er	wird sprechen
wir	werden sprechen
ihr	werdet sprechen
sie	werden sprechen

CONDITIONAL

ich	würde sprechen
du	würdest sprechen
er	würde sprechen
wir	würden sprechen
ihr	würdet sprechen
sie	würden sprechen

IMPERATIVE

sprich!/sprechen wir!/sprecht!
sprechen Sie!

PAST PARTICIPLE

gesprochen

PRESENT PARTICIPLE

sprechend

EXAMPLE PHRASES

*Er **spricht** kein Italienisch.* He doesn't speak Italian.
*Ich **würde** dich gern privat **sprechen**.* I would like to speak to you privately.
*Hast du mit ihr **gesprochen**?* Have you spoken to her?

ich = I **du** = you **er** = he **wir** = we/one **ihr** = you **sie** = they

▶ stehen (to stand)

PRESENT

ich	stehe
du	stehst
er	steht
wir	stehen
ihr	steht
sie	stehen

PRESENT SUBJUNCTIVE

ich	stehe
du	stehest
er	stehe
wir	stehen
ihr	stehet
sie	stehen

PERFECT

ich	habe gestanden
du	hast gestanden
er	hat gestanden
wir	haben gestanden
ihr	habt gestanden
sie	haben gestanden

IMPERFECT

ich	stand
du	stand(e)st
er	stand
wir	standen
ihr	standet
sie	standen

FUTURE

ich	werde stehen
du	wirst stehen
er	wird stehen
wir	werden stehen
ihr	werdet stehen
sie	werden stehen

CONDITIONAL

ich	würde stehen
du	würdest stehen
er	würde stehen
wir	würden stehen
ihr	würdet stehen
sie	würden stehen

IMPERATIVE

steh(e)!/stehen wir!/steht!
stehen Sie!

PAST PARTICIPLE

gestanden

PRESENT PARTICIPLE

stehend

EXAMPLE PHRASES

*Wir **standen** an der Bushaltestelle.* We stood at the bus stop.
*Es **hat** in der Zeitung **gestanden**.* It was in the newspaper.
*Dieses Kleid **würde** dir gut **stehen**.* This dress would suit you.

---

ich = I **du** = you **er** = he **wir** = we/one **ihr** = you **sie** = they

▶ **tragen** (to wear, to carry)

PRESENT

ich	trage
du	trägst
er	trägt
wir	tragen
ihr	tragt
sie	tragen

PRESENT SUBJUNCTIVE

ich	trage
du	tragest
er	trage
wir	tragen
ihr	traget
sie	tragen

PERFECT

ich	habe getragen
du	hast getragen
er	hat getragen
wir	haben getragen
ihr	habt getragen
sie	haben getragen

IMPERFECT

ich	trug
du	trugst
er	trug
wir	trugen
ihr	trugt
sie	trugen

FUTURE

ich	werde tragen
du	wirst tragen
er	wird tragen
wir	werden tragen
ihr	werdet tragen
sie	werden tragen

CONDITIONAL

ich	würde tragen
du	würdest tragen
er	würde tragen
wir	würden tragen
ihr	würdet tragen
sie	würden tragen

IMPERATIVE

trag(e)!/tragen wir!/tragt!
tragen Sie!

PAST PARTICIPLE

getragen

PRESENT PARTICIPLE

tragend

EXAMPLE PHRASES

*Ich **trug** ihren Koffer zum Bahnhof.* I carried her case to the station.
*Du **trägst** die ganze Verantwortung dafür.* You bear the full responsibility for it.
*Ich **würde** meine Haare gern länger **tragen**.* I'd like to wear my hair longer.

---

ich = I **du** = you **er** = he **wir** = we/one **ihr** = you **sie** = they

▶ **tun** (to do)

PRESENT

ich	tue
du	tust
er	tut
wir	tun
ihr	tut
sie	tun

PRESENT SUBJUNCTIVE

ich	tue
du	tuest
er	tue
wir	tuen
ihr	tuet
sie	tuen

PERFECT

ich	habe getan
du	hast getan
er	hat getan
wir	haben getan
ihr	habt getan
sie	haben getan

IMPERFECT

ich	tat
du	tat(e)st
er	tat
wir	taten
ihr	tatet
sie	taten

FUTURE

ich	werde tun
du	wirst tun
er	wird tun
wir	werden tun
ihr	werdet tun
sie	werden tun

CONDITIONAL

ich	würde tun
du	würdest tun
er	würde tun
wir	würden tun
ihr	würdet tun
sie	würden tun

IMPERATIVE

tu(e)!/tun wir!/tut!/tun Sie!

PAST PARTICIPLE

getan

PRESENT PARTICIPLE

tuend

EXAMPLE PHRASES

*Ich **werde** das auf keinen Fall **tun**.* There is no way I'll do that.
*So etwas **tut** man nicht!* That is just not done!
*Sie **tat**, als ob sie schliefe.* She pretended to be sleeping.

ich = I **du** = you **er** = he **wir** = we/one **ihr** = you **sie** = they

▶ **werden** (to become)

PRESENT

ich	werde
du	wirst
er	wird
wir	werden
ihr	werdet
sie	werden

PRESENT SUBJUNCTIVE

ich	werde
du	werdest
er	werde
wir	werden
ihr	werdet
sie	werden

PERFECT

ich	bin geworden/worden
du	bist geworden/worden
er	ist geworden/worden
wir	sind geworden/worden
ihr	seid geworden/worden
sie	sind geworden/worden

IMPERFECT

ich	wurde
du	wurdest
er	wurde
wir	wurden
ihr	wurdet
sie	wurden

FUTURE

ich	werde werden
du	wirst werden
er	wird werden
wir	werden werden
ihr	werdet werden
sie	werden werden

CONDITIONAL

ich	würde werden
du	würdest werden
er	würde werden
wir	würden werden
ihr	würdet werden
sie	würden werden

IMPERATIVE

werde!/werden wir!/werdet!
werden Sie!

PAST PARTICIPLE

geworden/worden*

PRESENT PARTICIPLE

werdend

*The second form is used when combined with an infinitive construction.

EXAMPLE PHRASES

*Mir **wird** schlecht.* I feel ill.
*Ich will Lehrerin **werden**.* I want to be a teacher.
*Der Kuchen **ist** gut **geworden**.* The cake turned out well.

ich = I **du** = you **er** = he **wir** = we/one **ihr** = you **sie** = they

▶ wissen (to know)

PRESENT

ich	weiß
du	weißt
er	weiß
wir	wissen
ihr	wisst
sie	wissen

PRESENT SUBJUNCTIVE

ich	wisse
du	wissest
er	wisse
wir	wissen
ihr	wisset
sie	wissen

PERFECT

ich	habe gewusst
du	hast gewusst
er	hat gewusst
wir	haben gewusst
ihr	habt gewusst
sie	haben gewusst

IMPERFECT

ich	wusste
du	wusstest
er	wusste
wir	wussten
ihr	wusstet
sie	wussten

FUTURE

ich	werde wissen
du	wirst wissen
er	wird wissen
wir	werden wissen
ihr	werdet wissen
sie	werden wissen

CONDITIONAL

ich	würde wissen
du	würdest wissen
er	würde wissen
wir	würden wissen
ihr	würdet wissen
sie	würden wissen

IMPERATIVE

wisse!/wissen wir!/wisset!
wissen Sie!

PAST PARTICIPLE

gewusst

PRESENT PARTICIPLE

wissend

EXAMPLE PHRASES

*Ich **weiß** nicht.* I don't know.
*Er **hat** nichts davon **gewusst**.* He didn't know anything about it.
*Sie **wussten**, wo das Kino war.* They knew where the cinema was.

ich = I **du** = you **er** = he **wir** = we/one **ihr** = you **sie** = they

▶ wollen (to want)

PRESENT

ich	will
du	willst
er	will
wir	wollen
ihr	wollt
sie	wollen

PRESENT SUBJUNCTIVE

ich	wolle
du	wollest
er	wolle
wir	wollen
ihr	wollet
sie	wollen

PERFECT

ich	habe gewollt/wollen
du	hast gewollt/wollen
er	hat gewollt/wollen
wir	haben gewollt/wollen
ihr	habt gewollt/wollen
sie	haben gewollt/wollen

IMPERFECT

ich	wollte
du	wolltest
er	wollte
wir	wollten
ihr	wolltet
sie	wollten

FUTURE

ich	werde wollen
du	wirst wollen
er	wird wollen
wir	werden wollen
ihr	werdet wollen
sie	werden wollen

CONDITIONAL

ich	würde wollen
du	würdest wollen
er	würde wollen
wir	würden wollen
ihr	würdet wollen
sie	würden wollen

IMPERATIVE

wolle!/wollen wir!/wollt!
wollen Sie!

PAST PARTICIPLE

gewollt/wollen*

PRESENT PARTICIPLE

wollend

---

*The second form is used when combined with an infinitive construction.

EXAMPLE PHRASES

Er **will** nach London gehen. He wants to go to London.
Das **habe** ich nicht **gewollt**. I didn't want this to happen.
Sie **wollten** nur mehr Geld. All they wanted was more money.

---

ich = I **du** = you **er** = he **wir** = we/one **ihr** = you **sie** = they

a

a [eɪ, ə; æn, ən] (*before vowel or silent h:* **an**) *indef art* **1** ein, eine; **a woman** eine Frau; **a book** ein Buch; **an eagle** ein Adler; **she's a doctor** sie ist Ärztin
2 (*instead of the number "one"*) ein, eine; **a year ago** vor einem Jahr; **a hundred/thousand** *etc* **pounds** (ein) hundert/(ein) tausend *etc* Pfund
3 (*in expressing ratios, prices etc*) pro; **3 a day/week** 3 pro Tag/Woche, 3 am Tag/in der Woche; **10 km an hour** 10 km pro Stunde/in der Stunde

AA *abbr* = **Automobile Association** *britischer Automobilklub,* ≈ ADAC *m*
aback *adv*: **taken ~** erstaunt

abandon [ə'bændən] *vt* (*desert*) verlassen; (*give up*) aufgeben
abbey ['æbɪ] *n* Abtei *f*
abbreviate [əbriːvɪ'eɪt] *vt* abkürzen; **abbreviation** [əbriːvɪ'eɪʃən] *n* Abkürzung *f*
ABC ['eɪbiː'siː] *n* (*a. fig*) Abc *nt*
abdicate ['æbdɪkeɪt] *vi* (*king*) abdanken; **abdication** [æbdɪ'keɪʃən] *n* Abdankung *f*
abdomen ['æbdəmən] *n* Unterleib *m*
ability [ə'bɪlɪtɪ] *n* Fähigkeit *f*; **able** ['eɪbl] *adj* fähig; **to be ~ to do sth** etw tun können
abnormal [æb'nɔːml] *adj* anormal
aboard [ə'bɔːd] *adv, prep* an Bord +*gen*
abolish [ə'bɒlɪʃ] *vt* abschaffen
aborigine [æbə'rɪdʒɪniː] *n* Ureinwohner(in) *m(f)* (Australiens)
abort [ə'bɔːt] *vt* (*Med: foetus*) abtreiben; (*Space: mission*) abbrechen; **abortion** [ə'bɔːʃən] *n* Abtreibung *f*

about [ə'baʊt] *adv* **1** (*approximately*) etwa, ungefähr; **about a hundred/thousand** *etc* etwa hundert/tausend *etc*; **at about 2 o'clock** etwa um 2 Uhr; **I've just about finished** ich bin gerade fertig
2 (*referring to place*) herum, umher; **to leave things lying about** Sachen herumliegen lassen; **to run/walk** *etc* **about** herumrennen/gehen *etc*
3 to be about to do sth im Begriff sein, etw zu tun; **he was about to go to bed** er wollte gerade ins Bett gehen

▷ prep **1** (relating to) über +akk; **a book about London** ein Buch über London; **what is it about?** worum geht es?; (book etc) wovon handelt es?; **we talked about it** wir haben darüber geredet; **what o how about doing this?** wollen wir das machen?
2 (referring to place) um (… herum); **to walk about the town** in der Stadt herumgehen; **her clothes were scattered about the room** ihre Kleider waren über das ganze Zimmer verstreut

above [əˈbʌv] adv oben; **children aged 8 and ~** Kinder ab 8 Jahren; **on the floor ~** ein Stockwerk höher ▷ prep über; **~ 40 degrees** über 40 Grad; **~ all** vor allem ▷ adj obig

abroad [əˈbrɔːd] adv im Ausland; **to go ~** ins Ausland gehen

abrupt [əˈbrʌpt] adj (sudden) plötzlich, abrupt

abscess [ˈæbsɪs] n Geschwür nt

absence [ˈæbsəns] n Abwesenheit f; **absent** [ˈæbsənt] adj abwesend; **to be ~** fehlen; **absent-minded** adj zerstreut

absolute [ˈæbsəluːt] adj absolut; (power) unumschränkt; (rubbish) vollkommen, total; **absolutely** adv absolut; (true, stupid) vollkommen; **~!** genau!; **you're ~ right** du hast/Sie haben völlig recht

absorb [əbˈzɔːb] vt absorbieren; (fig: information) in sich aufnehmen; **absorbed** adj: **~ in sth** in etw vertieft; **absorbent** adj absorbierend; **~ cotton** (US) Watte f; **absorbing** adj (fig) faszinierend, fesselnd

abstain [əbˈsteɪn] vi: **to ~ (from voting)** sich (der Stimme) enthalten

abstract [ˈæbstrækt] adj abstrakt

absurd [əbˈsɜːd] adj absurd

abundance [əˈbʌndəns] n Reichtum m (of an +dat)

abuse [əˈbjuːs] n (rude language) Beschimpfungen pl; (mistreatment) Missbrauch m ▷ [əˈbjuːz] vt (misuse) missbrauchen; **abusive** [əˈbjuːsɪv] adj beleidigend

AC abbr = **alternating current** Wechselstrom m ▷ abbr = **air conditioning** Klimaanlage

a/c abbr = **account** Kto.

academic [ækəˈdemɪk] n Wissenschaftler(in) m(f) ▷ adj akademisch, wissenschaftlich

accelerate [ækˈseləreɪt] vi (car etc) beschleunigen; (driver) Gas geben; **acceleration** [əksɛləˈreɪʃən] n Beschleunigung f; **accelerator** [əkˈseləreɪtə*] n Gas(pedal) nt

accent [ˈæksent] n Akzent m

accept [əkˈsept] vt annehmen; (agree to) akzeptieren; (responsibility) übernehmen; **acceptable** [əkˈseptəbl] adj annehmbar

access [ˈækses] n Zugang m; (Inform) Zugriff m; **accessible** [ækˈsesəbl] adj (leicht) zugänglich/erreichbar; (place) (leicht) erreichbar

accessory [ækˈsesərɪ] n Zubehörteil nt

access road n Zufahrtsstraße f

accident [ˈæksɪdənt] n Unfall m; **by ~** zufällig; **accidental** [æksɪˈdentl] adj unbeabsichtigt; (meeting) zufällig; (death) durch Unfall; **~ damage** Unfallschaden m; **accident-prone** adj vom Pech verfolgt

acclimatize [əˈklaɪmətaɪz] vt: **to ~ oneself** sich gewöhnen (to an +akk)

accommodate [ə'kɒmədeɪt] *vt*
unterbringen;
accommodation(s)
[əkɒmə'deɪʃən(z)] *n* Unterkunft *f*
accompany [ə'kʌmpənɪ] *vt*
begleiten
accomplish [ə'kʌmplɪʃ] *vt*
erreichen
accord [ə'kɔːd] *n*: **of one's own**
~ freiwillig; **according to** *prep*
nach, laut +*dat*
account [ə'kaʊnt] *n* (*in bank etc*)
Konto *nt*; (*narrative*) Bericht *m*; **on**
~ **of** wegen; **on no** ~ auf keinen
Fall; **to take into** ~
berücksichtigen, in Betracht
ziehen; **accountant** [ə'kaʊntənt]
n Buchhalter(in) *m(f)*; **account for**
vt (*explain*) erklären; (*expenditure*)
Rechenschaft ablegen für;
account number *n*
Kontonummer *f*
accumulate [ə'kjuːmjʊleɪt] *vt*
ansammeln ▷ *vi* sich ansammeln
accuracy ['ækjʊrəsɪ] *n*
Genauigkeit *f*; **accurate** ['ækjʊrɪt]
adj genau
accusation [ækjʊ'zeɪʃən] *n*
Anklage *f*, Beschuldigung *f*
accusative [ə'kjuːzətɪv] *n*
Akkusativ *m*
accuse [ə'kjuːz] *vt* beschuldigen;
(*Jur*) anklagen (*of* wegen +*gen*); ~ **sb**
of doing sth jdn beschuldigen,
etw getan zu haben; **accused** *n*
(*Jur*) Angeklagte(r) *mf*
accustom [ə'kʌstəm] *vt*
gewöhnen (*to an* +*akk*);
accustomed *adj* gewohnt; **to get**
~ **to sth** sich an etw *akk* gewöhnen
ace [eɪs] *n* Ass *nt* ▷ *adj* Star-
ache [eɪk] *n* Schmerz *m* ▷ *vi*
wehtun
achieve [ə'tʃiːv] *vt* erreichen;
achievement *n* Leistung *f*
acid ['æsɪd] *n* Säure *f* ▷ *adj* sauer;
~ **rain** saurer Regen

acknowledge [ək'nɒlɪdʒ] *vt*
(*recognize*) anerkennen; (*admit*)
zugeben; (*receipt of letter etc*)
bestätigen; **acknowledgement** *n*
Anerkennung *f*; (*of letter*)
Empfangsbestätigung *f*
acne ['æknɪ] *n* Akne *f*
acorn ['eɪkɔːn] *n* Eichel *f*
acoustic [ə'kuːstɪk] *adj* akustisch; **acoustics** [ə'kuːstɪks] *npl*
Akustik *f*
acquaintance [ə'kweɪntəns] *n*
(*person*) Bekannte(r) *mf*
acquire [ə'kwaɪə*] *vt* erwerben,
sich aneignen; **acquisition**
[ækwɪ'zɪʃn] *n* (*of skills etc*) Erwerb
m; (*object*) Anschaffung *f*
acrobat ['ækrəbæt] *n* Akrobat(in)
m(f)
across [ə'krɒs] *prep* über +*akk*; **he**
lives ~ **the street** er wohnt auf der
anderen Seite der Straße ▷ *adv*
hinüber, herüber; **100m** ~ 100m
breit
act [ækt] *n* (*deed*) Tat *f*; (*Jur: law*)
Gesetz *nt*; (*Theat*) Akt *m*; (*fig:
pretence*) Schau *f*; **it's all an** ~ es ist
alles nur Theater; **to be in the** ~ **of**
doing sth gerade dabei sein, etw
zu tun ▷ *vi* (*take action*) handeln;
(*behave*) sich verhalten; (*Theat*) spielen;
to ~ **as** (*person*) fungieren als; (*thing*)
dienen als ▷ *vt* (*a part*) spielen
action ['ækʃən] *n* (*of play, novel*
etc) Handlung *f*; (*in film etc*) Action
f; (*Mil*) Kampf *m*; **to take** ~ etwas
unternehmen; **out of** ~ (*machine*)
außer Betrieb; **to put a plan into**
~ einen Plan in die Tat umsetzen;
action replay *n* (*Sport, TV*)
Wiederholung *f*
activate ['æktɪveɪt] *vt* aktivieren;
active ['æktɪv] *adj* aktiv; (*child*)
lebhaft; **activity** [æk'tɪvɪtɪ] *n*
Aktivität *f*; (*occupation*)
Beschäftigung *f*; (*organized event*)
Veranstaltung *f*

actor ['æktə*] n Schauspieler(in) m(f); **actress** ['æktrɪs] n Schauspielerin f

actual ['æktjʊəl] adj wirklich; **actually** adv eigentlich; (said in surprise) tatsächlich

acupuncture ['ækjʊpʌŋktʃə*] n Akupunktur f

acute [ə'kjuːt] adj (pain) akut; (sense of smell) fein; (Math: angle) spitz

ad [æd] abbr = **advertisement**

AD abbr = **Anno Domini** nach Christi, n. Chr.

adapt [ə'dæpt] vi sich anpassen (to +dat) ▷ vt anpassen (to +dat); (rewrite) bearbeiten (for für); **adaptable** adj anpassungsfähig; **adaptation** n (of book etc) Bearbeitung f; **adapter** n (Elec) Zwischenstecker m, Adapter m

add [æd] vt (ingredient) hinzufügen; (numbers) addieren; **add up** vi (make sense) stimmen ▷ vt (numbers) addieren

addict ['ædɪkt] n Süchtige(r) mf; **addicted** [ə'dɪktɪd] adj: ~ **to alcohol/drugs** alkohol-/ drogensüchtig

addition [ə'dɪʃən] n Zusatz m; (to bill) Aufschlag m; (Math) Addition f; **in** ~ außerdem, zusätzlich (to zu); **additional** adj zusätzlich, weiter; **additive** ['ædɪtɪv] n Zusatz m; **add-on** ['ædɒn] n Zusatzgerät nt

address [ə'dres] n Adresse f ▷ vt (letter) adressieren; (person) anreden

adequate ['ædɪkwɪt] adj (appropriate) angemessen; (sufficient) ausreichend; (time) genügend

adhesive [əd'hiːsɪv] n Klebstoff m; **adhesive tape** n Klebstreifen m

adjacent [ə'dʒeɪsənt] adj benachbart

adjective ['ædʒəktɪv] n Adjektiv nt

adjoining [ə'dʒɔɪnɪŋ] adj benachbart, Neben-

adjust [ə'dʒʌst] vt einstellen; (put right also) richtig stellen; (speed, flow) regulieren; (in position) verstellen ▷ vi sich anpassen (to +dat); **adjustable** adj verstellbar

admin [əd'mɪn] n (fam) Verwaltung f; **administration** [ədmɪnɪs'treɪʃən] n Verwaltung f; (Pol) Regierung f

admirable ['ædmərəbl] adj bewundernswert; **admiration** [ædmɪ'reɪʃən] n Bewunderung f; **admire** [əd'maɪə*] vt bewundern

admission [əd'mɪʃən] n (entrance) Zutritt m; (to university etc) Zulassung f; (fee) Eintritt m; (confession) Eingeständnis nt; **admission charge, admission fee** n Eintrittspreis m; **admit** [əd'mɪt] vt (let in) hereinlassen (to in +akk); (to university etc) zulassen; (confess) zugeben, gestehen; **to be ~ted to hospital** ins Krankenhaus eingeliefert werden

adolescent [ædə'lesnt] n Jugendliche(r) mf

adopt [ə'dɒpt] vt (child) adoptieren; (idea) übernehmen; **adoption** [ə'dɒptʃn] n (of child) Adoption f; (of idea) Übernahme f

adorable [ə'dɔːrəbl] adj entzückend; **adore** [ə'dɔː*] vt anbeten; (person) über alles lieben, vergöttern

adult ['ædʌlt] adj (person) erwachsen; (film etc) für Erwachsene ▷ n Erwachsene(r) mf

adultery [ə'dʌltərɪ] n Ehebruch m

advance [əd'vɑːns] n (money) Vorschuss m; (progress) Fortschritt

m; **in ~** im Voraus; **to book in ~**
vorbestellen ▷ vi (*move forward*)
vorrücken ▷ vt (*money*)
vorschießen; **advance booking** n
Reservierung f; (*Theat*) Vorverkauf
m; **advanced** adj (*modern*)
fortschrittlich; (*course, study*) für
Fortgeschrittene; **advance
payment** n Vorauszahlung f

advantage [əd'vɑːntɪdʒ] n
Vorteil m; **to take ~ of** (*exploit*)
ausnutzen; (*profit from*) Nutzen
ziehen aus; **it's to your ~** es ist in
deinem/Ihrem Interesse

adventure [əd'ventʃə*] n
Abenteuer nt; **adventure holiday**
n Abenteuerurlaub m; **adventure
playground** n Abenteuerspiel-
platz m; **adventurous**
[əd'ventʃərəs] adj (*person*)
abenteuerlustig

adverb ['ædvɜːb] n Adverb nt

adverse ['ædvɜːs] adj (*conditions
etc*) ungünstig; (*effect, comment etc*)
negativ

advert ['ædvɜːt] n Anzeige f;
advertise ['ædvətaɪz] vt werben
für; (*in newspaper*) inserieren; (*job*)
ausschreiben ▷ vi Reklame
machen; (*in newspaper*)
annoncieren (*for* für);
advertisement [əd'vɜːtɪsmənt]
n Werbung f; (*announcement*)
Anzeige f; **advertising** n
Werbung f

advice [əd'vaɪs] n Rat(schlag) m;
word o **piece of ~** Ratschlag m;
take my ~ hör auf mich;
advisable [əd'vaɪzəbl] adj ratsam; **advise** [əd'vaɪz] vt raten
(*sb* jdm); **to ~ sb to do sth/not to
do sth** jdm zuraten/abraten, etw
zu tun

Aegean [iː'dʒiːən] n: **the ~ (Sea)**
die Ägäis

aerial ['ɛərɪəl] n Antenne f ▷ adj
Luft-

aerobatics [ɛərəʊ'bætɪks] npl
Kunstfliegen nt

aerobics [ɛə'rəʊbɪks] nsing
Aerobic nt

aeroplane ['ɛərəpleɪn] n
Flugzeug nt

afaik abbr = **as far as I know**;
(*SMS*) ≈ soweit ich weiß

affair [ə'fɛə*] n (*matter, business*)
Sache f, Angelegenheit f; (*scandal*)
Affäre f; (*love affair*) Verhältnis nt

affect [ə'fekt] vt (*influence*)
(ein)wirken auf +akk; (*health,
organ*) angreifen; (*move deeply*)
berühren; (*concern*) betreffen;
affection [ə'fekʃən] n Zuneigung
f; **affectionate** [ə'fekʃənɪt] adj
liebevoll

affluent ['æflʊənt] adj
wohlhabend

afford [ə'fɔːd] vt sich leisten; **I
can't ~ it** ich kann es mir nicht
leisten; **affordable** [ə'fɔːdəbl]
adj erschwinglich

Afghanistan [æf'gænɪstæn] n
Afghanistan nt

aforementioned
[əfɔː'menʃənd] adj oben genannt

afraid [ə'freɪd] adj: **to be ~** Angst
haben (*of* vor +dat); **to be ~ that ...**
fürchten, dass ...; **I'm ~ I don't
know** das weiß ich leider nicht

Africa ['æfrɪkə] n Afrika nt;
African adj afrikanisch ▷ n
Afrikaner(in) m(f); **African
American**, **Afro-American** n
Afroamerikaner(in) m(f)

after ['ɑːftə*] prep nach; **ten
~ five** (*US*) zehn nach fünf; **to be
~ sb/sth** (*following, seeking*) hinter
jdm/etw her sein; **~ all**
schließlich; (*in spite of everything*)
(schließlich) doch ▷ conj
nachdem ▷ adv: **soon ~** bald
danach; **aftercare** n
Nachbehandlung f; **after-effect** n
Nachwirkung f

afternoon n Nachmittag m; **~, good ~** guten Tag!; **in the ~** nachmittags

afters npl Nachtisch m; **after-sales service** n Kundendienst m; **after-shave (lotion)** n Rasierwasser nt; **afterwards** adv nachher; (after that) danach

again [ə'gen] adv wieder; (one more time) noch einmal; **not ~!** (nicht) schon wieder!; **~ and ~** immer wieder; **the same ~ please** das Gleiche noch mal bitte

against [ə'genst] prep gegen; **~ my will** wider Willen; **~ the law** unrechtmäßig, illegal

age [eɪdʒ] n Alter nt; (period of history) Zeitalter nt; **at the ~ of four** im Alter von vier (Jahren); **what ~ is she?, what is her ~?** wie alt ist sie?; **to come of ~** volljährig werden; **under ~** minderjährig ▷ vi altern, alt werden; **aged** adj: **~ thirty** dreißig Jahre alt; **a son ~ twenty** ein zwanzigjähriger Sohn ▷ adj ['eɪdʒɪd] (elderly) betagt; **age group** n Altersgruppe f; **ageism** n Diskriminierung f aufgrund des Alters; **age limit** n Altersgrenze f

agency ['eɪdʒənsɪ] n Agentur f

agenda [ə'dʒendə] n Tagesordnung f

agent ['eɪdʒənt] n (Comm) Vertreter(in) m(f); (for writer, actor etc) Agent(in) m(f)

aggression [ə'greʃn] n Aggression f; **aggressive** [ə'gresɪv] adj aggressiv

agitated adj aufgeregt; **to get ~** sich aufregen

AGM abbr = **Annual General Meeting** JHV f

ago [ə'gəʊ] adv: **two days ~** heute vor zwei Tagen; **not long ~** (erst) vor Kurzem

agonize ['ægənaɪz] vi sich den Kopf zerbrechen (over über dat); **agonizing** adj qualvoll; **agony** ['ægənɪ] n Qual f

agree [ə'griː] vt (date, price etc) vereinbaren; **to ~ to do sth** sich bereit erklären, etw zu tun; **to ~ that ...** sich dat einig sein, dass ...; (decide) beschließen, dass ...; (admit) zugeben, dass ... ▷ vi (have same opinion, correspond) übereinstimmen, (with mit); (consent) zustimmen; (come to an agreement) sich einigen (about, on auf +akk); (food) **not to ~ with sb** jdm nicht bekommen; **agreement** n (agreeing) Übereinstimmung f; (contract) Abkommen nt, Vereinbarung f

agricultural [ægrɪ'kʌltʃərəl] adj landwirtschaftlich, Landwirtschafts-; **agriculture** ['ægrɪkʌltʃə*] n Landwirtschaft f

ahead [ə'hed] adv: **to be ~** führen, vorne liegen; **~ of** vor +dat; **to be ~ of sb** (person) jdm voraus sein; (thing) vor jdm liegen; **to be 3 metres ~** 3 Meter Vorsprung haben

aid [eɪd] n Hilfe f; **in ~ of** zugunsten +gen; **with the ~ of** mithilfe +gen ▷ vt helfen +dat; (support) unterstützen

Aids [eɪdz] n acr = **acquired immune deficiency syndrome** Aids nt

aim [eɪm] vt (gun, camera) richten (at auf +akk) ▷ vi: **to ~ at** (with gun etc) zielen auf +akk; (fig) abzielen auf +akk; **to ~ to do sth** beabsichtigen, etw zu tun ▷ n Ziel nt

air [ɛə*] n Luft f; **in the open ~** im Freien; (Radio, TV) **to be on the ~** (programme) auf Sendung sein;

(*station*) senden ▷ *vt* lüften;
airbag *n* (*Auto*) Airbag *m*;
air-conditioned *adj* mit
Klimaanlage; **air-conditioning** *n*
Klimaanlage *f*; **aircraft** *n*
Flugzeug *nt*; **airfield** *n* Flugplatz
m; **air force** *n* Luftwaffe *f*;
airgun *n* Luftgewehr *nt*;
airline *n* Fluggesellschaft *f*;
airmail *n* Luftpost *f*; **by ~** mit
Luftpost; **airplane** *n* (*US*)
Flugzeug *nt*; **air pollution** *n*
Luftverschmutzung *f*; **airport** *n*
Flughafen *m*; **airsick** *adj*
luftkrank; **airtight** *adj* luftdicht;
air-traffic controller *n* Fluglotse
m, Fluglotsin *f*; **airy** *adj* luftig;
(*manner*) lässig
aisle [aɪl] *n* Gang *m*; (*in church*)
Seitenschiff *nt*; **~ seat** Sitz *m* am
Gang
ajar [ə'dʒɑː*] *adj* (*door*) angelehnt
alarm [ə'lɑːm] *n* (*warning*) Alarm
m; (*bell etc*) Alarmanlage *f* ▷ *vt*
beunruhigen; **alarm clock** *n*
Wecker *m*; **alarmed** *adj* (*protected*)
alarmgesichert; **alarming** *adj*
beunruhigend
Albania [æl'beɪnɪə] *n* Albanien
nt; **Albanian** *adj* albanisch ▷ *n*
(*person*) Albaner(in) *m(f)*; (*language*)
Albanisch *nt*
album ['ælbəm] *n* Album *nt*
alcohol ['ælkəhɒl] *n* Alkohol *m*;
alcohol-free *adj* alkoholfrei;
alcoholic [ælkə'hɒlɪk] *adj* (*drink*)
alkoholisch ▷ *n* Alkoholiker(in)
m(f); **alcoholism** *n* Alkoholismus
m
ale [eɪl] *n* Ale *nt* (*helles englisches
Bier*)
alert [ə'lɜːt] *adj* wachsam ▷ *n*
Alarm *m* ▷ *vt* warnen (*to* vor +*dat*)
algebra ['ældʒɪbrə] *n* Algebra *f*
Algeria [æl'dʒɪərɪə] *n* Algerien *nt*
alibi ['ælɪbaɪ] *n* Alibi *nt*
alien ['eɪlɪən] *n* (*foreigner*)

Ausländer(in) *m(f)*; (*from space*)
Außerirdische(r) *mf*
align [ə'laɪn] *vt* ausrichten (*with*
auf +*akk*)
alike [ə'laɪk] *adj, adv* gleich;
(*similar*) ähnlich
alive [ə'laɪv] *adj* lebendig; **to
keep sth ~** etw am Leben
erhalten; **he's still ~** er lebt noch

KEYWORD

all [ɔːl] *adj* alle(r, s); **all day/night**
den ganzen Tag/die ganze Nacht;
all men are equal alle Menschen
sind gleich; **all five came** alle fünf
kamen; **all the books/food** die
ganzen Bücher/das ganze Essen;
all the time die ganze Zeit (über);
all his life sein ganzes Leben
(lang)
▷ *pron* 1 alles; **I ate it all, I ate all of
it** ich habe alles gegessen; **all of
us/the boys went** wir gingen
alle/alle Jungen gingen; **we all sat
down** wir setzten uns alle
2 (*in phrases*): **above all** vor allem;
after all schließlich; **at all**: **not at
all** (*in answer to question*)
überhaupt nicht; (*in answer to
thanks*) gern geschehen; **I'm not at
all tired** ich bin überhaupt nicht
müde; **anything at all will do** es
ist egal, welche(r, s); **all in all** alles
in allem
▷ *adv* ganz; **all alone** ganz allein;
it's not as hard as all that so
schwer ist es nun auch wieder
nicht; **all the more/the better**
umso mehr/besser; **all but** fast;
the score is 2 all es steht 2 zu 2

allegation [ælɪ'geɪʃən] *n*
Behauptung *f*; **alleged** *adj*
angeblich
allergic [ə'lɜːdʒɪk] *adj* allergisch

(to gegen); **allergy** ['ælədʒɪ] n
Allergie f
alleviate [ə'liːvɪeɪt] vt (pain)
lindern
alley ['ælɪ] n (enge) Gasse;
(passage) Durchgang m; (bowling)
Bahn f
alliance [ə'laɪəns] n Bündnis nt
alligator ['ælɪgeɪtə°] n Alligator
m
all-night adj (café, cinema) die
ganze Nacht geöffnet
allocate ['æləkeɪt] vt zuweisen,
zuteilen (to dat)
allotment n (plot)
Schrebergarten m
allow [ə'laʊ] vt (permit) erlauben
(sb jdm); (grant) bewilligen; (time)
einplanen; **allow for** vt
berücksichtigen; (cost etc)
einkalkulieren; **allowance** n (from
state) Beihilfe f; (from parent)
Unterhaltsgeld nt
all right ['ɔːl'raɪt] adj okay, in
Ordnung; **I'm ~** mir geht's gut
▷ adv (satisfactorily) ganz gut
▷ interj okay
all-time adj (record, high) aller
Zeiten
allusion [ə'luːʒn] n Anspielung f
(to auf +akk)
ally ['ælaɪ] n Verbündete(r) mf;
(Hist) Alliierte(r) mf
almond ['ɑːmənd] n Mandel f
almost ['ɔːlməʊst] adv fast
alone [ə'ləʊn] adj, adv allein
along [ə'lɒŋ] prep entlang
+akk; **~ the river** den Fluss
entlang; (position) am Fluss
entlang ▷ adv (onward) weiter;
~ with zusammen mit; **all ~** die
ganze Zeit, von Anfang an;
alongside prep neben +dat ▷ adv
(walk) nebenher
aloud [ə'laʊd] adv laut
alphabet ['ælfəbet] n Alphabet
nt

alpine ['ælpaɪn] adj alpin; **Alps**
[ælps] npl: **the ~** die Alpen
already [ɔːl'redɪ] adv schon,
bereits
Alsace ['ælsæs] n Elsass nt;
Alsatian [æl'seɪʃən] adj
elsässisch ▷ n Elsässer(in) m(f);
(Brit: dog) Schäferhund m
also ['ɔːlsəʊ] adv auch
altar ['ɔːltə°] n Altar m
alter ['ɔːltə°] vt ändern;
alteration [ɔːltə'reɪʃən] n
Änderung f; **~s** (to building) Umbau
m
alternate [ɔːl'tɜːnət] adj
abwechselnd ▷ ['ɔːltəneɪt] vi
abwechseln (with mit);
alternating current n
Wechselstrom m
alternative [ɔːl'tɜːnətɪv] adj
Alternativ- ▷ n Alternative f
although [ɔːl'ðəʊ] conj obwohl
altitude ['æltɪtjuːd] n Höhe f
altogether [ɔːltə'geðə°] adv (in
total) insgesamt; (entirely) ganz
und gar
aluminium, aluminum (US)
[æljʊ'mɪnɪəm, ə'luːmɪnəm] n
Aluminium nt
always ['ɔːlweɪz] adv immer
am [æm] present of **be**; bin
am, a.m. abbr = **ante meridiem**
vormittags, morgens
amateur ['æmətə°] n Ama-
teur(in) m(f) ▷ adj Amateur-;
(theatre, choir) Laien-
amaze [ə'meɪz] vt erstaunen;
amazed adj erstaunt (at über
+akk); **amazing** adj erstaunlich
Amazon ['æməzən] n: **~ (river)**
Amazonas m
ambassador [æm'bæsədə°] n
Botschafter m
amber ['æmbə°] n Bernstein m
ambiguity [æmbɪ'gjʊɪti] n
Zweideutigkeit f; **ambiguous**
[æm'bɪgjʊəs] adj zweideutig

ambition [æm'bɪʃən] n Ambition f; (ambitious nature) Ehrgeiz m; **ambitious** [æm'bɪʃəs] adj ehrgeizig

ambulance ['æmbjʊləns] n Krankenwagen m

amend [ə'mend] vt (law etc) ändern

America [ə'merɪkə] n Amerika nt; **American** adj amerikanisch ▷ n Amerikaner(in) m(f); **native ~** Indianer(in) m(f)

amiable ['eɪmɪəbl] adj liebenswürdig

amicable ['æmɪkəbl] adj freundlich; (relations) freundschaftlich; (Jur: settlement) gütlich

amnesia [æm'niːzɪə] n Gedächtnisverlust m

among(st) [ə'mʌŋ(st)] prep unter +dat

amount [ə'maʊnt] n (quantity) Menge f; (of money) Betrag m; **a large/small ~ of ...** ziemlich viel/wenig ... ▷ vi: **to ~ to** (total) sich belaufen auf +akk

amp, ampere [æmp, 'æmpɛə*] n Ampere nt

amplifier ['æmplɪfaɪə*] n Verstärker m

amputate ['æmpjʊteɪt] vt amputieren

Amtrak® ['æmtræk] n amerikanische Eisenbahngesellschaft

amuse [ə'mjuːz] vt amüsieren; (entertain) unterhalten; **amused** adj: **I'm not ~** das finde ich gar nicht lustig; **amusement** n (enjoyment) Vergnügen nt; (recreation) Unterhaltung f; **amusement arcade** n Spielhalle f; **amusement park** n Vergnügungspark m; **amusing** adj amüsant

an [æn, ən] art ein(e)

anaemic [ə'niːmɪk] adj blutarm

anaesthetic [ænɪs'θetɪk] n

Narkose f; (substance) Narkosemittel nt

analyse, analyze ['ænəlaɪz] vt analysieren; **analysis** [ə'næləsɪs] n Analyse f

anatomy [ə'nætəmɪ] n Anatomie f; (structure) Körperbau m

ancestor ['ænsestə*] n Vorfahr m

anchor ['æŋkə*] n Anker m ▷ vt verankern; **anchorage** n Ankerplatz m

anchovy ['æntʃəvɪ] n Sardelle f

ancient ['eɪnʃənt] adj alt; (fam: person, clothes etc) uralt

and [ænd, ənd] conj und

Andorra [æn'dɔːrə] n Andorra nt

anemic adj (US) see **anaemic**

anesthetic n (US) see **anaesthetic**

angel ['eɪndʒəl] n Engel m

anger ['æŋgə*] n Zorn m ▷ vt ärgern

angina, angina pectoris [æn'dʒaɪnə('pektərɪs)] n Angina Pectoris f

angle ['æŋgl] n Winkel m; (fig) Standpunkt m

angler ['æŋglə*] n Angler(in) m(f); **angling** ['æŋglɪŋ] n Angeln nt

angry ['æŋgrɪ] adj verärgert; (stronger) zornig; **to be ~ with sb** auf jdn böse sein

angular ['æŋgjʊlə*] adj eckig; (face) kantig

animal ['ænɪməl] n Tier nt; **animal rights** npl Tierrechte pl

animated ['ænɪmeɪtɪd] adj lebhaft; **~ film** Zeichentrickfilm m

aniseed ['ænɪsiːd] n Anis m

ankle ['æŋkl] n (Fuß)knöchel m

annex ['æneks] n Anbau m

anniversary [ænɪ'vɜːsərɪ] n Jahrestag m

announce [ə'naʊns] vt bekannt geben; (officially) bekannt machen; (on radio, TV etc) (Radio,

TV) ansagen; **announcement** *n*
Bekanntgabe *f*; (*official*)
Bekanntmachung *f*; (*Radio, TV*)
Ansage *f*; **announcer** *n* (*Radio, TV*)
Ansager(in) *m(f)*

annoy [ə'nɔɪ] *vt* ärgern;
annoyance *n* Ärger *m*; **annoyed**
adj ärgerlich; **to be ~ with sb**
(**about sth**) sich über jdn (über
etw) ärgern; **annoying** *adj*
ärgerlich; (*person*) lästig, nervig

annual ['ænjʊəl] *adj* jährlich
▷ *n* Jahrbuch *nt*

anonymous [ə'nɒnɪməs] *adj*
anonym

anorak ['ænəræk] *n* Anorak *m*;
(*Brit fam: pej*) Freak *m*

anorexia [ænə'reksɪə] *n* Magersucht *f*; **anorexic** *adj*
magersüchtig

another [ə'nʌðə°] *adj, pron*
(*different*) ein(e) andere(r, s);
(*additional*) noch eine(r, s); **let me
put it ~ way** lass es mich anders
sagen

answer ['ɑ:nsə°] *n* Antwort *f* (*to*
auf +*akk*); (*solution*) Lösung *f* +*gen*
▷ *vi* antworten; (*on phone*) sich
melden ▷ *vt* (*person*) antworten
+*dat*; (*letter, question*) beantworten;
(*telephone*) gehen an +*akk*,
abnehmen; (*door*) öffnen; **answer
back** *vi* widersprechen;
answering machine,
answerphone *n* Anrufbeant-
worter *m*

ant [ænt] *n* Ameise *f*

Antarctic [ænt'ɑ:ktɪk] *n*
Antarktis *f*; **Antarctic Circle** *n*
südlicher Polarkreis

antelope ['æntɪləʊp] *n* Antilope *f*

antenna [æn'tenə] (*pl* **antennae**)
n (*Zool*) Fühler *m*; (*Radio*) Antenne *f*

anti- ['æntɪ] *pref* Anti-, anti-;
antibiotic ['æntɪbaɪ'ɒtɪk] *n*
Antibiotikum *n*

anticipate [æn'tɪsɪpeɪt] *vt* (*expect:*

trouble, question) erwarten,
rechnen mit; **anticipation**
[æntɪsɪ'peɪʃən] *n* Erwartung *f*

anticlimax [æntɪ'klaɪmæks] *n*
Enttäuschung *f*; **anticlockwise**
[æntɪ'klɒkwaɪz] *adv* entgegen
dem Uhrzeigersinn

antidote ['æntɪdəʊt] *n* Gegenmittel *nt*; **antifreeze** *n*
Frostschutzmittel *nt*

Antipodes [æn'tɪpədiːz] *npl*
Australien und Neuseeland

antiquarian [æntɪ'kwɛərɪən]
adj: **~ bookshop** Antiquariat *nt*

antique [æn'tiːk] *n* Antiquität *f*
▷ *adj* antik; **antique shop** *n*
Antiquitätengeschäft *nt*

anti-Semitism [æntɪ'semɪtɪzm]
n Antisemitismus *m*; **antiseptic**
[æntɪ'septɪk] *n* Antiseptikum *nt*
▷ *adj* antiseptisch; **antisocial** *adj*
(*person*) ungesellig; (*behaviour*)
unsozial, asozial

antlers ['æntləz] *npl* Geweih *nt*

anxiety [æŋ'zaɪətɪ] *n* Sorge *f*
(*about* um); **anxious** ['æŋkʃəs] *adj*
besorgt (*about* um); (*apprehensive*)
ängstlich

KEYWORD

any ['enɪ] *adj* **1** (*in questions etc*)
have you any butter? haben Sie
(etwas) Butter?; **have you any
children?** haben Sie Kinder?; **if
there are any tickets left** falls
noch Karten da sind
2 (*with negative*) **I haven't any
money/books** ich habe kein
Geld/keine Bücher
3 (*no matter which*) jede(r, s)
(beliebige); **any colour (at all)**
jede beliebige Farbe; **choose any
book you like** nehmen Sie ein
beliebiges Buch
4 (*in phrases*) **in any case** in jedem

Fall; **any day now** jeden Tag; **at any moment** jeden Moment; **at any rate** auf jeden Fall
▷ *pron* **1** (*in questions etc*) **have you got any?** haben Sie welche?; **can any of you sing?** kann (irgend)einer von euch singen?
2 (*with negative*) **I haven't any (of them)** ich habe keinen/keines (davon)
3 (*no matter which one(s)*): **take any of those books (you like)** nehmen Sie irgendeines dieser Bücher
▷ *adv* **1** (*in questions etc*) **do you want any more soup/sandwiches?** möchten Sie noch Suppe/Brote?; **are you feeling any better?** fühlen Sie sich etwas besser?
2 (*with negative*) **I can't hear him any more** ich kann ihn nicht mehr hören

anybody *pron* (*whoever one likes*) irgendjemand; (*everyone*) jeder; (*in question*) jemand;
  anyhow *adv*: **I don't want to talk about it, not now ~** ich möchte nicht darüber sprechen, jedenfalls nicht jetzt; **they asked me not to go, but I went ~** sie baten mich, nicht hinzugehen, aber ich bin trotzdem hingegangen; **anyone** *pron* (*whoever one likes*) irgendjemand; (*everyone*) jeder; (*in question*) jemand; **isn't there ~ you can ask?** gibt es denn niemanden, den du fragen kannst/den Sie fragen können?; **anyplace** *adv* (*US*) irgendwo; (*direction*) irgendwohin; (*everywhere*) überall

KEYWORD

anything ['ɛnɪθɪŋ] *pron* **1** (*in questions etc*) (irgend)etwas; **can**
you see anything? können Sie etwas sehen?
2 (*with negative*) **I can't see anything** ich kann nichts sehen
3 (*no matter what*) **you can say anything you like** Sie können sagen, was Sie wollen; **anything will do** irgendetwas (wird genügen), irgendeine(r, s) (wird genügen); **he'll eat anything** er isst alles

anytime *adv* jederzeit; **anyway** *adv*: **I didn't want to go there ~** ich wollte da sowieso nicht hingehen; **thanks ~** trotzdem danke; **~, as I was saying, ...** jedenfalls, wie ich schon sagte, ...;
  anywhere *adv* irgendwo; (*direction*) irgendwohin; (*everywhere*) überall
apart [ə'pɑːt] *adv* auseinander; **~ from** außer; **live ~** getrennt leben
apartment [ə'pɑːtmənt] *n* (*esp US*) Wohnung *f*; **apartment block** *n* (*esp US*) Wohnblock *m*
ape [eɪp] *n* (Menschen)affe *m*
aperitif [ə'pɛrɪtɪf] *n* Aperitif *m*
aperture ['æpətjʊə*] *n* Öffnung *f*; (*Foto*) Blende *f*
apologize [ə'pɒlədʒaɪz] *vi* sich entschuldigen; **apology** *n* Entschuldigung *f*
apostrophe [ə'pɒstrəfɪ] *n* Apostroph *m*
appalled [ə'pɔːld] *adj* entsetzt (*at* über +*akk*); **appalling** *adj* entsetzlich
apparatus [æpə'reɪtəs] *n* Apparat *m*; (*piece of apparatus*) Gerät *nt*
apparent [ə'pærənt] *adj* (*obvious*) offensichtlich (*to* für); (*seeming*) scheinbar; **apparently** *adv* anscheinend
appeal [ə'piːl] *vi* (dringend)

bitten (for um, to +akk); (Jur) Berufung einlegen; **to ~ to sb** (be attractive) jdm zusagen ▷ n Aufruf m (to an +akk); (Jur) Berufung f; (attraction) Reiz m; **appealing** adj ansprechend, attraktiv

appear [ə'pɪə°] vi erscheinen; (Theat) auftreten; (seem) scheinen; **appearance** n Erscheinen nt; (Theat) Auftritt m; (look) Aussehen nt

appendicitis [əpendɪ'saɪtɪs] n Blinddarmentzündung f; **appendix** [ə'pendɪks] n Blinddarm m; (to book) Anhang m

appetite ['æpɪtaɪt] n Appetit m; (fig: desire) Verlangen nt; (sexual) Lust f; **appetizing** ['æpɪtaɪzɪŋ] adj appetitlich, appetitanregend

applause [ə'plɔːz] n Beifall m, Applaus m

apple ['æpl] n Apfel m; **apple crumble** n mit Streuseln bestreutes Apfeldessert; **apple juice** n Apfelsaft m; **apple pie** n gedeckter Apfelkuchen m; **apple puree, apple sauce** n Apfelmus nt; **apple tart** n Apfelkuchen m; **apple tree** n Apfelbaum m

appliance [ə'plaɪəns] n Gerät nt; **applicable** [ə'plɪkəbl] adj anwendbar; (on forms) zutreffend; **applicant** ['æplɪkənt] n Bewerber(in) m(f); **application** [æplɪ'keɪʃən] n (request) Antrag m (for auf +akk); (for job) Bewerbung f (for um); **application form** n Anmeldeformular nt; **apply** [ə'plaɪ] vi (be relevant) zutreffen (to auf +akk); (for job etc) sich bewerben (for um) ▷ vt (cream, paint etc) auftragen; (put into practice) anwenden; (brakes) betätigen

appoint [ə'pɔɪnt] vt (to post) ernennen; **appointment** n Verabredung f; (at doctor, hairdresser

etc, in business) Termin m; **by ~** nach Vereinbarung

appreciate [ə'priːʃɪeɪt] vt (value) zu schätzen wissen; (understand) einsehen; **to be much ~d** richtig gewürdigt werden ▷ vi (increase in value) im Wert steigen; **appreciation** [əpriːʃɪ'eɪʃən] n (esteem) Anerkennung f, Würdigung f; (of person also) Wertschätzung f

apprehensive [æprɪ'hensɪv] adj ängstlich

apprentice [ə'prentɪs] n Lehrling m

approach [ə'prəʊtʃ] vi sich nähern ▷ vt (place) sich nähern +dat; (person) herantreten an +akk; (problem) angehen

appropriate [ə'prəʊprɪət] adj passend; (to occasion) angemessen; (remark) treffend; **appropriately** adv passend; (expressed) treffend

approval [ə'pruːvəl] n (show of satisfaction) Anerkennung f; (permission) Zustimmung f (of zu); **approve** [ə'pruːv] vt billigen ▷ vi: **to ~ of sth/sb** etw billigen/von jdm etwas halten; **I don't ~** ich missbillige das

approx [ə'prɒks] abbr = **approximately** ca.; **approximate** [ə'prɒksɪmɪt] adj ungefähr; **approximately** adv ungefähr, circa

apricot ['eɪprɪkɒt] n Aprikose f

April ['eɪprəl] n April m; see also **September**

apron ['eɪprən] n Schürze f

aptitude [æptɪtjuːd] n Begabung f

aquaplaning ['ækwəpleɪnɪŋ] n (Auto) Aquaplaning nt

aquarium [ə'kwɛərɪəm] n Aquarium nt

Aquarius [ə'kwɛərɪəs] n (Astr) Wassermann m

Arab ['ærəb] n Araber(in) m(f); (horse) Araber m; **Arabian** [ə'reɪbɪən] adj arabisch; **Arabic** ['ærəbɪk] n (language) Arabisch nt ▷ adj arabisch

arbitrary ['ɑːbɪtrərɪ] adj willkürlich

arcade [ɑːˈkeɪd] n Arkade f; (shopping arcade) Einkaufspassage f

arch [ɑːtʃ] n Bogen m

archaeologist, archeologist (US) [ɑːkɪˈɒlədʒɪst] n Archäologe m, Archäologin f; **archaeology, archeology** (US) [ɑːkɪˈɒlədʒɪ] n Archäologie f

archaic [ɑːˈkeɪɪk] adj veraltet

archbishop [ɑːtʃˈbɪʃəp] n Erzbischof m

archery ['ɑːtʃərɪ] n Bogenschießen nt

architect ['ɑːkɪtekt] n Architekt(in) m(f); **architecture** [ɑːkɪˈtektʃə] n Architektur f

archive(s) ['ɑːkaɪv(z)] n(pl) Archiv nt

archway ['ɑːtʃweɪ] n Torbogen m

Arctic ['ɑːktɪk] n Arktis f; **Arctic Circle** n nördlicher Polarkreis

are [ə, unstressed ɑː*] present of **be**

area ['ɛərɪə] n (region, district) Gebiet nt, Gegend f; (amount of space) Fläche f; (part of building etc) Bereich m, Zone f; (fig: field) Bereich m; **the London ~** der Londoner Raum; **area code** n (US) Vorwahl f

aren't [ɑːnt] contr of **are not**

Argentina [ɑːdʒən'tiːnə] n Argentinien nt

argue ['ɑːgjuː] vi streiten (about, over über +akk); **to ~ that ...** behaupten, dass ...; **to ~ for/against ...** sprechen für/gegen ...; **argument** n (reasons) Argument nt; (quarrel)

Streit m; **to have an ~** sich streiten

Aries ['ɛəriːz] nsing (Astr) Widder m

arise [əˈraɪz] (**arose, arisen**) vi sich ergeben, entstehen; (problem, question, wind) aufkommen

aristocracy [ærɪsˈtɒkrəsɪ] n (class) Adel m; **aristocrat** ['ærɪstəkræt] n Adlige(r) mf; **aristocratic** [ærɪstəˈkrætɪk] adj aristokratisch, adlig

arm [ɑːm] n Arm m; (sleeve) Ärmel m; (of armchair) Armlehne f ▷ vt bewaffnen; **armchair** ['ɑːmtʃɛə*] n Lehnstuhl m

armed [ɑːmd] adj bewaffnet

armpit ['ɑːmpɪt] n Achselhöhle f

arms [ɑːmz] npl Waffen pl

army ['ɑːmɪ] n Armee f, Heer nt

A road ['eɪrəʊd] n (Brit) ≈ Bundesstraße f

aroma [əˈrəʊmə] n Duft m, Aroma nt; **aromatherapy** [ərəʊməˈθerəpɪ] n Aromatherapie f

arose [əˈrəʊz] pt of **arise**

around [əˈraʊnd] adv herum, umher; (present) hier (irgendwo); (approximately) ungefähr; (with time) gegen; **he's ~ somewhere** er ist hier irgendwo in der Nähe ▷ prep (surrounding) um ... (herum); (about in) in ... herum

arr. abbr = **arrival, arrives** Ank.

arrange [əˈreɪndʒ] vt (put in order) (an)ordnen; (alphabetically) ordnen; (artistically) arrangieren; (agree to: meeting etc) vereinbaren, festsetzen; (holidays) festlegen; (organize) planen; **to ~ that ...** es so einrichten, dass ...; **we ~d to meet at eight o'clock** wir haben uns für acht Uhr verabredet; **it's all ~d** es ist alles arrangiert; **arrangement** n (layout) Anordnung f; (agreement)

Vereinbarung f, Plan m; **make ~s** Vorbereitungen treffen

arrest [ə'rest] vt (person) verhaften ▷ n Verhaftung f; **under ~** verhaftet

arrival [ə'raɪvəl] n Ankunft f; **new ~** (person) Neuankömmling m; **arrivals** n (airport) Ankunftshalle f; **arrive** [ə'raɪv] vi ankommen (at bei, in +dat); **to ~ at a solution** eine Lösung finden

arrogant ['ærəgənt] adj arrogant

arrow ['ærəʊ] n Pfeil m

arse [ɑːs] n (vulg) Arsch m

art [ɑːt] n Kunst f, **the ~s** (pl) Geisteswissenschaften pl

artery ['ɑːtərɪ] n Schlagader f, Arterie f

art gallery n Kunstgalerie f, Kunstmuseum nt

arthritis [ɑː'θraɪtɪs] n Arthritis f

artichoke ['ɑːtɪtʃəʊk] n Artischocke f

article ['ɑːtɪkl] n Artikel m; (object) Gegenstand m

artificial [ɑːtɪ'fɪʃəl] adj künstlich, Kunst-; (smile etc) gekünstelt

artist ['ɑːtɪst] n Künstler(in) m(f); **artistic** [ɑː'tɪstɪk] adj künstlerisch

KEYWORD

as [æz, əz] conj 1 (referring to time) als; **as the years went by** mit den Jahren; **he came in as I was leaving** als er hereinkam, ging ich gerade; **as from tomorrow** ab morgen

2 (in comparisons) **as big as** so groß wie; **twice as big as** zweimal so groß wie; **as much/many as** so viel/so viele wie; **as soon as** sobald

3 (since, because) da; **he left early as he had to be home by 10** er

ging früher, da er um 10 zu Hause sein musste

4 (referring to manner, way) wie; **do as you wish** mach was du willst; **as she said** wie sie sagte

5 (concerning) **as for o as to that** was das betrifft o angeht

6 **as if o though** als ob

▷ prep als; see also **long**; **he works as a driver** er arbeitet als Fahrer; see also **such**; **he gave it to me as a present** er hat es mir als Geschenk gegeben; see also **well**

asap [eɪeseɪ'piː, 'eɪsæp] acr = **as soon as possible** möglichst bald

ascertain [æsə'teɪn] vt feststellen

ash [æʃ] n (dust) Asche f; (tree) Esche f

ashamed [ə'ʃeɪmd] adj beschämt; **to be ~** (of sb/sth) sich (für jdn/etw) schämen

ashore [ə'ʃɔː*] adv an Land

ashtray ['æʃtreɪ] n Aschenbecher m

Asia ['eɪʃə] n Asien nt; **Asian** adj asiatisch ▷ n Asiat(in) m(f)

aside [ə'saɪd] adv beiseite, zur Seite; **~ from** (esp US) außer

ask [ɑːsk] vt, vi fragen; (question) stellen; (request) bitten um; (invite) einladen; **to ~ sb the way** jdn nach dem Weg fragen; **to ~ sb to do sth** jdn darum bitten, etw zu tun; **ask for** vt bitten um

asleep [ə'sliːp] adj, adv: **to be ~** schlafen; **to fall ~** einschlafen

asparagus [əs'pærəgəs] n Spargel m

aspect ['æspekt] n Aspekt m

aspirin ['æsprɪn] n Aspirin® nt

ass [æs] n (a. fig) Esel m; (US vulg) Arsch m

assassinate [ə'sæsɪneɪt] vt ermorden; **assassination**

[ə'sæsɪneɪʃn] n Ermordung f; **~ attempt** Attentat nt

assault [ə'sɔːlt] n Angriff m; (Jur) Körperverletzung f ▷ vt überfallen, herfallen über +akk

assemble [ə'sembl] vt (parts) zusammensetzen; (people) zusammenrufen ▷ vi sich versammeln; **assembly** [ə'semblɪ] n (of people) Versammlung f; (putting together) Zusammensetzen nt; **assembly hall** n Aula f

assert [ə'sɜːt] vt behaupten; **assertion** [ə'sɜːʃən] n Behauptung f

assess [ə'ses] vt einschätzen; **assessment** n Einschätzung f

asset ['æset] n Vermögenswert m; (fig) Vorteil m; **~s** pl Vermögen nt

assign [ə'saɪn] vt zuweisen; **assignment** n Aufgabe f; (mission) Auftrag m

assist [ə'sɪst] vt helfen +dat; **assistance** n Hilfe f; **assistant** n Assistent(in) m(f), Mitarbeiter(in) m(f); (in shop) Verkäufer(in) m(f); **assistant referee** n (Sport) Schiedsrichterassistent(in) m(f)

associate [ə'səʊʃɪeɪt] vt verbinden (with mit); **association** [əsəʊsɪ'eɪʃən] n (organization) Verband m, Vereinigung f; **in ~ with ...** in Zusammenarbeit mit ...

assorted [ə'sɔːtɪd] adj gemischt; **assortment** n Auswahl f (of an +dat); (of sweets) Mischung f

assume [ə'sjuːm] vt annehmen (that ... dass ...); (role, responsibility) übernehmen; **assumption** [ə'sʌmpʃən] n Annahme f

assurance [ə'ʃʊərəns] n Versicherung f; (confidence) Zuversicht f; **assure** [ə'ʃʊə°] vt (say confidently) versichern +dat; **to**

~ sb of sth jdm etw zusichern; **to be ~d of sth** einer Sache sicher sein

asterisk ['æstərɪsk] n Sternchen nt

asthma ['æsmə] n Asthma nt

astonish [əs'tɒnɪʃ] vt erstaunen; **astonished** adj erstaunt (at über); **astonishing** adj erstaunlich; **astonishment** n Erstaunen nt

astound [ə'staʊnd] vt sehr erstaunen; **astounding** adj erstaunlich

astray [ə'streɪ] adv: **to go ~** (letter etc) verloren gehen; (person) vom Weg abkommen; **to lead ~** irreführen, verführen

astrology [əs'trɒlədʒɪ] n Astrologie f

astronaut ['æstrənɔːt] n Astronaut(in) m(f)

astronomy [əs'trɒnəmɪ] n Astronomie f

asylum [ə'saɪləm] n (home) Anstalt f; (political asylum) Asyl nt; **asylum seeker** n Asylbewerber(in) m(f)

KEYWORD

at [æt] prep 1 (referring to position, direction) an +dat; bei +dat; (with place) in +dat; **at the top** an der Spitze; **at home/school** zu Hause, zuhause (österreichisch, schweizerisch)/in der Schule; **at the baker's** beim Bäcker; **to look at sth** auf etw akk blicken; **to throw sth at sb** etw nach jdm werfen
2 (referring to time) **at 4 o'clock** um 4 Uhr; **at night** bei Nacht; **at Christmas** zu Weihnachten; **at times** manchmal
3 (referring to rates, speed etc) **at £1 a kilo** zu £1 pro Kilo; **two at a time**

zwei auf einmal; **at 50 km/h** mit 50 km/h
4 (*referring to manner*) **at a stroke** mit einem Schlag; **at peace** in Frieden
5 (*referring to activity*) **to be at work** bei der Arbeit sein; **to play at cowboys** Cowboy spielen; **to be good at sth** gut in etw *dat* sein
6 (*referring to cause*) **shocked/surprised/annoyed at sth** schockiert/überrascht/ verärgert über etw *akk*; **I went at his suggestion** ich ging auf seinen Vorschlag hin

ate [et, eɪt] *pt of* **eat**
athlete ['æθliːt] *n* Athlet(in) *m(f)*; (*track and field*) Leichtathlet(in) *m(f)*; (*sportsman*) Sportler(in) *m(f)*; **~'s foot** Fußpilz *m*; **athletic** [æθ'letɪk] *adj* sportlich; (*build*) athletisch; **athletics** *npl* Leichtathletik *f*
Atlantic [ət'læntɪk] *n*: **the ~ (Ocean)** der Atlantik
atlas ['ætləs] *n* Atlas *m*
ATM *abbr* = **automated teller machine** Geldautomat *m*
atmosphere ['ætməsfɪə*] *n* Atmosphäre *f*; (*fig*) Stimmung *f*
atom ['ætəm] *n* Atom *nt*; **atom(ic) bomb** *n* Atombombe *f*; **atomic** [ə'tɒmɪk] *adj* Atom-; **~ energy** Atomenergie *f*; **~ power** Atomkraft *f*
A to Z® ['eɪtə'zed] *n* Stadtplan *m* (*in Buchform*)
atrocious [ə'trəʊʃəs] *adj* grauenhaft; **atrocity** [ə'trɒsɪtɪ] *n* Grausamkeit *f*; (*deed*) Gräueltat *f*
attach [ə'tætʃ] *vt* befestigen, anheften (*to* an +*dat*); **to ~ importance to sth** Wert auf etw *akk* legen; **to be ~ed to sb/sth** an jdm/etw hängen; **attachment** [ə'tætʃmənt] *n* (*affection*)

Zuneigung *f*; (*Inform*) Attachment *nt*, Anhang *m*, Anlage *f*
attack [ə'tæk] *vt, vi* angreifen ▷ *n* Angriff +*akk* (*on* auf *m*); (*Med*) Anfall *m*
attempt [ə'tempt] *n* Versuch *m*; **to make an ~ to do sth** versuchen, etw zu tun ▷ *vt* versuchen
attend [ə'tend] *vt* (*go to*) teilnehmen an +*dat*; (*lectures, school*) besuchen ▷ *vi* (*be present*) anwesend sein; **attend to** *vt* sich kümmern um; (*customer*) bedienen; **attendance** *n* (*presence*) Anwesenheit *f*; (*people present*) Teilnehmerzahl *f*; **attendant** *n* (*in car park etc*) Wächter(in) *m(f)*; (*in museum*) Aufseher(in) *m(f)*
attention [ə'tenʃən] *n* Aufmerksamkeit *f*; (**your**) **~ please** Achtung!; **to pay ~ to sth** etw beachten; **to pay ~ to sb** jdm aufmerksam zuhören; (*listen*) jdm/etw aufmerksam zuhören; **for the ~ of ...** zu Händen von ...; **attentive** [ə'tentɪv] *adj* aufmerksam
attic ['ætɪk] *n* Dachboden *m*; (*lived in*) Mansarde *f*
attitude ['ætɪtjuːd] *n* (*mental*) Einstellung *f* (*to, towards* zu); (*more general, physical*) Haltung *f*
attorney [ə'tɜːnɪ] *n* (*US: lawyer*) Rechtsanwalt *m*, Rechtsanwältin *f*
attract [ə'trækt] *vt* anziehen; (*attention*) erregen; **to be ~ed to o by sb** sich zu jdm hingezogen fühlen; **attraction** [ə'trækʃən] *n* Anziehungskraft *f*; (*thing*) Attraktion *f*; **attractive** *adj* attraktiv; (*thing, idea*) reizvoll
aubergine ['əʊbəʒiːn] *n* Aubergine *f*
auction ['ɔːkʃən] *n* Versteigerung *f*, Auktion *f* ▷ *vt* versteigern

audible ['ɔ:dɪbl] *adj* hörbar
audience ['ɔ:dɪəns] *n* Publikum
nt; (*Radio*) Zuhörer *pl*; (*TV*)
Zuschauer *pl*
audio ['ɔ:dɪəʊ] *adj* Ton-
audition [ɔ:'dɪʃən] *n* Probe *f* ▷ *vi*
(*Theat*) vorspielen, vorsingen
auditorium [ɔ:dɪ'tɔ:rɪəm] *n*
Zuschauerraum *m*
Aug *abbr* = **August**
August ['ɔ:gəst] *n* August *m*; *see*
also **September**
aunt [ɑ:nt] *n* Tante *f*
au pair [əʊ'peə*] *n*
Aupairmädchen *nt*, Aupairjunge *m*
Australia [ɒ'streɪlɪə] *n* Australien *nt*; **Australian** *adj* australisch
▷ *n* Australier(in) *m(f)*
Austria ['ɒstrɪə] *n* Österreich *nt*;
Austrian *adj* österreichisch ▷ *n*
Österreicher(in) *m(f)*
authentic [ɔ:'θentɪk] *adj* echt;
(*signature*) authentisch;
authenticity [ɔ:θen'tɪsɪtɪ] *n*
Echtheit *f*
author ['ɔ:θə*] *n* Autor(in) *m(f)*;
(*of report etc*) Verfasser(in) *m(f)*
authority [ɔ:'θɒrɪtɪ] *n* (*power,*
expert) Autorität *f*; **an ~ on sth**
eine Autorität auf dem Gebiet
einer Sache; **the authorities** (*pl*)
die Behörden *pl*; **authorize**
['ɔ:θəraɪz] *vt* (*permit*)
genehmigen; **to be ~d to do sth**
offiziell berechtigt sein, etw zu
tun
auto ['ɔ:təʊ] (*pl* **-s**) *n* (*US*) Auto *nt*
autobiography [ɔ:təʊbaɪ'ɒgrəfɪ]
n Autobiographie *f*; **autograph**
['ɔ:təgrɑ:f] *n* Autogramm *nt*
automatic [ɔ:tə'mætɪk] *adj*
automatisch; **~ gear change**
(*Brit*), **~ gear shift** (*US*)
Automatikschaltung *f* ▷ *n* (*car*)
Automatikwagen *m*
automobile ['ɔ:təməbi:l] *n* (*US*)
Auto(mobil) *nt*; **autotrain**

['ɔ:təʊtreɪn] *n* (*US*) Autoreisezug
m
autumn ['ɔ:təm] *n* (*Brit*) Herbst
m
auxiliary [ɔ:g'zɪlɪərɪ] *adj* Hilfs-;
~ verb Hilfsverb *nt* ▷ *n* Hilfskraft *f*
availability [əveɪlə'bɪlɪtɪ] *n* (*of*
product) Lieferbarkeit *f*; (*of*
resources) Verfügbarkeit *f*;
available *adj* erhältlich; (*existing*)
vorhanden; (*product*) lieferbar;
(*person*) erreichbar; **to be/make**
~ to sb jdm zur Verfügung
stehen/stellen; **they're only ~ in**
black es gibt sie nur in Schwarz,
sie sind nur in Schwarz erhältlich
avalanche ['ævəlɑ:nʃ] *n* Lawine *f*
Ave *abbr* = **avenue**
avenue ['ævənju:] *n* Allee *f*
average ['ævrɪdʒ] *n* Durchschnitt *m*; **on ~** im Durchschnitt
▷ *adj* durchschnittlich; **~ speed**
Durchschnittsgeschwindigkeit *f*;
of ~ height von mittlerer Größe
avian flu ['eɪvɪən'flu:] *n*
Vogelgrippe *f*
aviation [eɪvɪ'eɪʃən] *n* Luftfahrt *f*
avocado [ævə'kɑ:dəʊ] (*pl* **-s**) *n*
Avocado *f*
avoid [ə'vɔɪd] *vt* vermeiden; **to**
~ sb jdm aus dem Weg gehen;
avoidable *adj* vermeidbar
awake [ə'weɪk] (**awoke,**
awoken) *vi* aufwachen ▷ *adj*
wach
award [ə'wɔ:d] *n* (*prize*) Preis *m*;
(*for bravery etc*) Auszeichnung *f*
▷ *vt* zuerkennen (*to sb* jdm);
(*present*) verleihen (*to sb* jdm)
aware [ə'weə*] *adj* bewusst; **to**
be ~ of sth sich *dat* einer Sache *gen*
bewusst sein; **I was not ~ that ...**
es war mir nicht klar, dass ...
away [ə'weɪ] *adv* weg; **to look**
~ wegsehen; **he's ~** er ist nicht da;
(*on a trip*) er ist verreist; (*from*
school, work) er fehlt; (*Sport*) **they**

are (**playing**) ~ sie spielen
auswärts; (*with distance*) **three
miles** ~ drei Meilen (von hier)
entfernt; **to work** ~ drauflos
arbeiten
awful ['ɔːful] *adj* schrecklich,
furchtbar; **awfully** *adv* furchtbar
awkward ['ɔːkwəd] *adj* (*clumsy*)
ungeschickt; (*embarrassing*)
peinlich; (*difficult*) schwierig
awning ['ɔːnɪŋ] *n* Markise *f*
awoke [ə'wəʊk] *pt of* **awake**;
awoken [ə'wəʊkən] *pp of* **awake**
ax (*US*), **axe** [æks] *n* Axt *f*
axle ['æksl] *n* (*Tech*) Achse *f*

BA *abbr* = **Bachelor of Arts**
BSc *abbr* = **Bachelor of Science**
babe [beɪb] *n* (*fam*) Baby *nt*;
(*fam: affectionate*) Schatz *m*,
Kleine(r) *mf*
baby ['beɪbɪ] *n* Baby *nt*; (*of animal*)
Junge(s) *nt*; (*fam: affectionate*)
Schatz *m*, Kleine(r) *mf*; **to have a
~** ein Kind bekommen; **it's your
~** (*fam: responsibility*) das ist dein
Bier; **baby carriage** *n* (*US*)
Kinderwagen *m*; **baby food** *n*
Babynahrung *f*; **babyish** *adj*
kindisch; **baby shower** *n* (*US*)
Party für die werdende Mutter;
baby-sit *irr vi* babysitten;
baby-sitter *n* Babysitter(in) *m(f)*
bachelor ['bætʃələ*] *n* Junggeselle *m*; **Bachelor of
Arts/Science** *erster akademischer
Grad*, ≈ Magister/Diplom;
bachelorette *n* Junggesellin *f*;
bachelorette party *n* (*US*)

Junggesellinnenabschied; **bachelor party** *n* (US) *Junggesellenabschied*
back [bæk] *n* (*of person, animal*) Rücken *m*; (*of house, coin etc*) Rückseite *f*; (*of chair*) Rückenlehne *f*; (*of car*) Rücksitz *m*; (*of train*) Ende *nt*; (*Sport: defender*) Verteidiger(in) *m(f)*; **at the ~ of ...**, (US) **in ~ of** (*inside*) hinten in ...; (*outside*) hinter ...; **~ to front** verkehrt herum ▷ *vt* (*support*) unterstützen; (*car*) rückwärtsfahren ▷ *vi* (*go backwards*) rückwärtsgehen *o* rückwärtsfahren ▷ *adj* Hinter-; **~ wheel** Hinterrad *nt* ▷ *adv* zurück; **they're ~** sie sind wieder da; **back away** *vi* sich zurückziehen; **back down** *vi* nachgeben; **back up** *vi* (*car etc*) zurücksetzen ▷ *vt* (*support*) unterstützen; (*Inform*) sichern; (*car*) zurückfahren
backache *n* Rückenschmerzen *pl*; **backbone** *n* Rückgrat *nt*; **backdate** *vt* zurückdatieren; **backdoor** *n* Hintertür *f*; **backfire** *vi* (*plan*) fehlschlagen; (*Auto*) fehlzünden; **background** *n* Hintergrund *m*; **backhand** *n* (*Sport*) Rückhand *f*; **backlog** *n* (*of work*) Rückstand *m*; **backpack** *n* (US) Rucksack *m*; **backpacker** *n* Rucksacktourist(in) *m(f)*; **backpacking** *n* Rucksacktourismus *m*; **back seat** *n* Rücksitz *m*; **backside** *n* (*fam*) Po *m*; **back street** *n* Seitensträßchen *nt*; **backstroke** *n* Rückenschwimmen *nt*; **back-up** *n* (*support*) Unterstützung *f*; **~** (**copy**) (*Inform*) Sicherungskopie *f*; **backward** *adj* (*child*) zurückgeblieben; (*region*) rückständig; **~ movement** Rückwärtsbewegung *f*; **backwards** *adv* rückwärts; **backyard** *n* Hinterhof *m*

bacon ['beɪkən] *n* Frühstücksspeck *m*
bacteria [bæk'tɪərɪə] *npl* Bakterien *pl*
bad [bæd] (**worse, worst**) *adj* schlecht, schlimm; (*smell*) übel; **I have a ~ back** mir tut der Rücken weh; **I'm ~ at maths/sport** ich bin schlecht in Mathe/Sport; **to go ~** schlecht werden, verderben
badge [bædʒ] *n* Abzeichen *nt*
badger ['bædʒə°] *n* Dachs *m*
badly ['bædlɪ] *adv* schlecht; **~ wounded** schwer verwundet; **to need sth ~** etw dringend brauchen; **bad-tempered** ['bæd'tempəd] *adj* schlecht gelaunt
bag [bæg] *n* (*small*) Tüte *f*; (*larger*) Beutel *m*; (*handbag*) Tasche *f*; **my ~s** (*luggage*) mein Gepäck
baggage ['bægɪdʒ] *n* Gepäck *nt*; **baggage allowance** *n* Freigepäck *nt*; **baggage (re)claim** *n* Gepäckrückgabe *f*
baggy ['bægɪ] *adj* (zu) weit; (*trousers, suit*) ausgebeult
bag lady ['bægleɪdɪ] *n* Stadtstreicherin *f*
bagpipes ['bægpaɪps] *npl* Dudelsack *m*
Bahamas [bə'hɑːməz] *npl*: **the ~** die Bahamas *pl*
bail [beɪl] *n* (*money*) Kaution *f*
bait [beɪt] *n* Köder *m*
bake [beɪk] *vt, vi* backen; **baked beans** *npl weiße Bohnen in Tomatensoße*; **baked potato** (*pl* **-es**) *n* in der Schale gebackene Kartoffel, Ofenkartoffel *f*; **baker** *n* Bäcker(in) *m(f)*; **bakery** ['beɪkərɪ] *n* Bäckerei *f*; **baking powder** *n* Backpulver *nt*
balance ['bæləns] *n* (*equilibrium*) Gleichgewicht *nt* ▷ *vt* (*make up for*) ausgleichen; **balanced** *adj*

ausgeglichen; **balance sheet** n
Bilanz f
balcony ['bælkənı] n Balkon m
bald [bɔːld] adj kahl; **to be ~** eine
Glatze haben
Balkans ['bɔːlkənz] npl: **the ~**
der Balkan, die Balkanländer pl
ball [bɔːl] n Ball m; **to have a ~**
(fam) sich prima amüsieren
ballet ['bæleɪ] n Ballett nt; **ballet
dancer** n Balletttänzer(in) m(f)
balloon [bə'luːn] n (Luft)ballon
m
ballot ['bælət] n (geheime)
Abstimmung; **ballot box** n
Wahlurne f; **ballot paper** n
Stimmzettel m
ballpoint (pen) ['bɔːlpɔɪnt] n
Kugelschreiber m
ballroom ['bɔːlruːm] n Tanzsaal
m
Baltic ['bɔːltɪk] adj: **~ Sea** Ostsee
f; **the ~ States** die baltischen
Staaten
Baltics ['bɔːltɪks] n: **the ~** das
Baltikum nt
bamboo [bæm'buː] n Bambus m;
bamboo shoots npl
Bambussprossen pl
ban [bæn] n Verbot nt ⊳ vt
verbieten
banana [bə'nɑːnə] n Banane f;
he's ~s er ist völlig durchgeknallt;
banana split n Bananensplit nt
band [bænd] n (group) Gruppe f;
(of criminals) Bande f; (Mus) Kapelle
f; (pop, rock etc) Band f; (strip) Band
nt
bandage ['bændɪdʒ] n Verband
m; (elastic) Bandage f ⊳ vt
verbinden
B & B abbr = **bed and breakfast**
bang [bæŋ] n (noise) Knall m;
(blow) Schlag m ⊳ vt, vi knallen;
(door) zuschlagen, zuknallen;
banger ['bæŋə*] n (Brit fam:
firework) Knallkörper m; (sausage)

Würstchen nt; (fam: old car)
Klapperkiste f
bangs [bæŋz] npl (US: of hair)
Pony m
banish ['bænɪʃ] vt verbannen
banister(s) ['bænɪstə*] n (Treppen)geländer nt
bank [bæŋk] n (Fin) Bank f; (of
river etc) Ufer nt; **bank account** n
Bankkonto nt; **bank balance** n
Kontostand m; **bank card** n
Bankkarte f; **bank code** n
Bankleitzahl f; **bank holiday** n
gesetzlicher Feiertag

> ● **BANK HOLIDAY**
>
> ● Als **bank holiday** wird in
> ● Großbritannien ein gesetzlicher
> ● Feiertag bezeichnet, an dem die
> ● Banken geschlossen sind. Die
> ● meisten dieser Feiertage,
> ● abgesehen von Weihnachten
> ● und Ostern, fallen auf Montage
> ● im Mai und August. An diesen
> ● langen Wochenenden (bank
> ● holiday weekends) fahren viele
> ● Briten in Urlaub, sodass dann
> ● auf den Straßen, Flughäfen und
> ● bei der Bahn sehr viel Betrieb
> ● ist.

bank manager n Filialleiter(in)
m(f); **banknote** n Banknote f
bankrupt vt ruinieren; **to go
~** Pleite gehen
bank statement n
Kontoauszug m
baptism ['bæptɪzəm] n Taufe f;
baptize ['bæptaɪz] vt taufen
bar [bɑː*] n (for drinks) Bar f; (less
smart) Lokal nt; (rod) Stange f; (of
chocolate etc) Riegel m, Tafel f; (of
soap) Stück nt; (counter) Theke f
⊳ prep außer; **~ none** ohne
Ausnahme
barbecue ['bɑːbɪkjuː] n (device)

Grill *m*; (*party*) Barbecue *nt*,
Grillfete *f*; **to have a ~** grillen
barbed wire ['bɑːbd'waɪə*] *n*
Stacheldraht *m*
barber ['bɑːbə*] *n* (Herren)friseur
m
bar code ['bɑːkəʊd] *n*
Strichkode *m*
bare [bɛə*] *adj* nackt; **~ patch**
kahle Stelle; **barefoot** *adj, adv*
barfuß; **bareheaded** *adj, adv*
ohne Kopfbedeckung; **barely** *adv*
kaum; (*with age*) knapp
bargain ['bɑːgɪn] *n* (*cheap offer*)
günstiges Angebot, Schnäppchen
nt; (*transaction*) Geschäft *nt*; **what
a ~** das ist aber günstig! ▷ *vi*
(ver)handeln
barge [bɑːdʒ] *n* (*for freight*)
Lastkahn *m*; (*unpowered*)
Schleppkahn *m*
bark [bɑːk] *n* (*of tree*) Rinde *f*;
(*of dog*) Bellen *nt* ▷ *vi* (*dog*)
bellen
barley ['bɑːlɪ] *n* Gerste *f*
barmaid ['bɑːmeɪd] *n* Bar-
keeperin *f*; **barman** ['bɑːmən] (*pl*
-men) *n* Barkeeper *m*
barn [bɑːn] *n* Scheune *f*
barometer [bə'rɒmɪtə*] *n* Barometer *nt*
baroque [bə'rɒk] *adj* barock,
Barock-
barracks ['bærəks] *npl* Kaserne *f*
barrel ['bærəl] *n* Fass *nt*; **barrel
organ** *n* Drehorgel *f*
barricade [bærɪ'keɪd] *n* Bar-
rikade *f*
barrier ['bærɪə*] *n* (*obstruction*)
Absperrung *f*, Barriere *f*; (*across
road etc*) Schranke *f*
barrow ['bærəʊ] *n* (*cart*)
Schubkarren *m*
bartender ['bɑːtendə*] *n* (*US*)
Barkeeper(in) *m(f)*
base [beɪs] *n* Basis *f*; (*of lamp,
pillar etc*) Fuß *m*; (*Mil*) Stützpunkt *m*

▷ *vt* gründen (*on* auf +*akk*); **to be
~d on sth** auf etw *dat* basieren;
baseball *n* Baseball *m*; **baseball
cap** *n* Baseballmütze *f*;
basement *n* Kellergeschoss *nt*
bash [bæʃ] *n* Schlag *m*; (*fam*)
Party *f* ▷ *vt* hauen
basic ['beɪsɪk] *adj* einfach;
(*fundamental*) Grund-; (*importance,
difference*) grundlegend; (*in
principle*) grundsätzlich; **the
accomodation is very ~** die
Unterkunft ist sehr bescheiden;
basically *adv* im Grunde; **basics**
npl: **the ~** das Wesentliche
basil ['bæzl] *n* Basilikum *nt*
basin ['beɪsn] *n* (*for washing,
valley*) (Wasch)becken *nt*
basis ['beɪsɪs] *n* Basis *f*; **on the
~ of** aufgrund +*gen*; **on a monthly
~** monatlich
basket ['bɑːskɪt] *n* Korb *m*;
basketball *n* Basketball *m*
Basque [bæsk] *n* (*person*) Baske
m, Baskin *f*; (*language*) Baskisch *nt*
▷ *adj* baskisch
bass [beɪs] *n* (*Mus*) Bass *m*; (*Zool*)
Barsch *m* ▷ *adj* (*Mus*) Bass-
bastard ['bɑːstəd] *n* (*vulg: awful
person*) Arschloch *nt*
bat [bæt] *n* (*Zool*) Fledermaus *f*;
(*Sport: cricket, baseball*) Schlagholz
nt; (*table tennis*) Schläger *m*
batch [bætʃ] *n* Schwung *m*; (*fam:
of letters, books etc*) Stoß *m*
bath [bɑːθ] *n* Bad *nt*; (*tub*)
Badewanne *f*; **to have a ~** baden
▷ *vt* (*child etc*) baden
bathe [beɪð] *vt, vi* (*wound etc*)
baden; **bath foam** ['bɑːθfəʊm] *n*
Badeschaum *m*; **bathing cap** *n*
Badekappe *f*; **bathing costume**,
bathing suit (*US*) *n* Badeanzug *m*
bathmat ['bɑːθmæt] *n* Badevor-
leger *m*; **bathrobe** *n* Bademantel
m; **bathroom** *n* Bad(ezimmer) *nt*;
baths [bɑːðz] *npl* (Schwimm)bad

nt; **bath towel** *n* Badetuch *nt;*
bathtub *n* Badewanne *f*

baton ['bætən] *n* (*Mus*) Taktstock
m; (*police*) Schlagstock *m*

batter ['bætə*] *n* Teig *m* ▷ *vt*
heftig schlagen; **battered** *adj*
übel zugerichtet; (*hat, car*)
verbeult; (*wife, baby*) misshandelt

battery ['bætərɪ] *n* (*Elec*) Batterie
f; **battery charger** *n* Ladegerät *nt*

battle ['bætl] *n* Schlacht *f;* (*fig*)
Kampf *m* (*for* um +*akk*); **battlefield**
n Schlachtfeld *nt;* **battlements**
npl Zinnen *pl*

Bavaria [bə'veərɪə] *n* Bayern *nt;*
Bavarian *adj* bay(e)risch ▷ *n*
Bayer(in) *m(f)*

bay [beɪ] *n* (*of sea*) Bucht *f;* (*on
house*) Erker *m;* (*tree*) Lorbeerbaum
m; **bay leaf** *n* Lorbeerblatt *nt;* **bay
window** *n* Erkerfenster *nt*

BBC *abbr* = **British Broadcasting
Corporation** BBC *f*

BC *abbr* = **before Christ** vor Christi
Geburt, v. Chr.

⭕ **KEYWORD**

be [biː] (*pt* **was**, **were**, *pp* **been**) *vb
aux* **1** (*with present participle: forming
continuous tenses*): **what are you
doing?** was machst du (gerade)?;
it is raining es regnet; **I've been
waiting for you for hours** ich
warte schon seit Stunden auf dich
2 (*with pp: forming passives*): **to be
killed** getötet werden; **the thief
was nowhere to be seen** der Dieb
war nirgendwo zu sehen
3 (*in tag questions*) **it was fun,
wasn't it?** es hat Spaß gemacht,
nicht wahr?
4 (+*to* +*infin*) **the house is to be
sold** das Haus soll verkauft
werden; **he's not to open it** er darf
es nicht öffnen
▷ *vb* +complement **1** (*usu*) sein; **I'm**

tired ich bin müde; **I'm hot/cold**
mir ist heiß/kalt; **he's a doctor** er
ist Arzt; **2 and 2 are 4** 2 und 2 ist 0
sind 4; **she's tall/pretty** sie ist
groß/hübsch; **be careful/quiet**
sei vorsichtig/ruhig
2 (*of health*) **how are you?** wie geht
es dir?; **he's very ill** er ist sehr
krank; **I'm fine now** jetzt geht es
mir gut
3 (*of age*) **how old are you?** wie alt
bist du?; **I'm sixteen (years old)**
ich bin sechzehn (Jahre alt)
4 (*cost*) **how much was the meal?**
was 0 wie viel hat das Essen
gekostet?; **that'll be £5.75, please**
das macht £5.75, bitte
▷ *vi* **1** (*exist, occur etc*) sein; **is there
a God?** gibt es einen Gott?; **be
that as it may** wie dem auch sei;
so be it also gut
2 (*referring to place*) sein; **I won't be
here tomorrow** ich werde morgen
nicht hier sein
3 (*referring to movement*) **where
have you been?** wo bist du
gewesen?; **I've been in the
garden** ich war im Garten
▷ *impers vb* **1** (*referring to time,
distance, weather*) sein; **it's 5
o'clock** es ist 5 Uhr; **it's 10 km to
the village** es sind 10 km bis zum
Dorf; **it's too hot/cold** es ist zu
heiß/kalt
2 (*emphatic*) **it's me** ich bin's; **it's
the postman** es ist der Briefträger

beach [biːtʃ] *n* Strand *m;*
beachwear *n* Strandkleidung *f*

bead [biːd] *n* (*of glass, wood etc*)
Perle *f;* (*drop*) Tropfen *m*

beak [biːk] *n* Schnabel *m*

beam [biːm] (*of wood etc*) Balken
m; (*of light*) Strahl *m* ▷ *vi* (*smile etc*)
strahlen

bean [biːn] *n* Bohne *f;* **bean curd**
n Tofu *m*

bear [bɛə*] (**bore, borne**) vt
(carry) tragen; (tolerate) ertragen
▷ n Bär m; **bearable** adj
erträglich
beard [bɪəd] n Bart m
beast [biːst] n Tier nt; (brutal
person) Bestie f; (disliked person)
Biest nt
beat [biːt] (**beat, beaten**) vt
schlagen; (as punishment) prügeln;
to ~ sb at tennis jdn im Tennis
schlagen ▷ n (of heart, drum etc)
Schlag m; (Mus) Takt m; (type of
music) Beat m; **beat up** vt
zusammenschlagen
beaten ['biːtn] pp of **beat**; **off the
~ track** abgelegen
beautiful ['bjuːtɪfʊl] adj schön;
(splendid) herrlich; **beauty** ['bjuːtɪ]
n Schönheit f; **beauty spot** n
(place) lohnendes Ausflugsziel
beaver ['biːvə*] n Biber m
became [bɪ'keɪm] pt of **become**
because [bɪ'kɒz] adv, conj weil
▷ prep: **~ of** wegen +gen o dat
become [bɪ'kʌm] (**became,
become**) vt werden; **what's ~ of
him?** was ist aus ihm geworden?
bed [bed] n Bett nt; (in garden)
Beet nt; **bed and breakfast** n
Übernachtung f mit Frühstück;
bedclothes npl Bettwäsche f;
bedding n Bettzeug nt; **bed linen**
n Bettwäsche f; **bedroom** n
Schlafzimmer nt; **bed-sit(ter)** n
(fam) möblierte
Einzimmerwohnung; **bedspread**
n Tagesdecke f; **bedtime** n
Schlafenszeit f
bee [biː] n Biene f
beech [biːtʃ] n Buche f
beef [biːf] n Rindfleisch nt;
beefburger n Hamburger m; **beef
tomato** (pl **-es**) n Fleischtomate
f
beehive ['biːhaɪv] n Bienenstock
m

been [biːn] pp of **be**
beer [bɪə*] n Bier nt; **beer garden**
n Biergarten m
beetle ['biːtl] n Käfer m
beetroot ['biːtruːt] n Rote Bete f
before [bɪ'fɔː*] prep vor; **the year
~ last** vorletztes Jahr; **the day
~ yesterday** vorgestern ▷ conj
bevor ▷ adv (of time) vorher; **have
you been there ~?** waren
Sie/warst du schon einmal dort?;
beforehand adv vorher
beg [beg] vt: **to ~ sb to do sth** jdn
inständig bitten, etw zu tun ▷ vi
(beggar) betteln (for um +akk)
began [bɪ'gæn] pt of **begin**
beggar ['begə*] n Bettler(in) m(f)
begin [bɪ'gɪn] (**began, begun**) vt,
vi anfangen, beginnen; **to ~ to do
sth** anfangen, etw zu tun;
beginner n Anfänger(in) m(f);
beginning n Anfang m
begun [bɪ'gʌn] pp of **begin**
behalf [bɪ'hɑːf] n: **on ~ of, in ~ of**
(US) im Namen/Auftrag von; **on
my ~** für mich
behave [bɪ'heɪv] vi sich
benehmen; **~ yourself!** benimm
dich!; **behavior** (US), **behaviour**
[bɪ'heɪvjə*] n Benehmen nt
behind [bɪ'haɪnd] prep hinter;
to be ~ time Verspätung haben
▷ adv hinten; **to be ~ with one's
work** mit seiner Arbeit im
Rückstand sein ▷ n (fam)
Hinterteil nt
beige [beɪʒ] adj beige
being ['biːɪŋ] n (existence) Dasein
nt; (person) Wesen nt
Belarus [belə'rʊs] n Weißruss-
land nt
belch [beltʃ] n Rülpser m ▷ vi
rülpsen
belfry ['belfrɪ] n Glockenturm m
Belgian ['beldʒən] adj belgisch
▷ n Belgier(in) m(f); **Belgium**
['beldʒəm] n Belgien nt

belief [bɪ'liːf] *n* Glaube *m* (*in an* +*akk*); (*conviction*) Überzeugung *f*; **it's my ~ that ...** ich bin der Überzeugung, dass ...; **believe** [bɪ'liːv] *vt* glauben; **believe in** *vi* glauben an +*akk*; **believer** *n* (*Rel*) Gläubige(r) *mf*

bell [bel] *n* (*church*) Glocke *f*; (*bicycle, door*) Klingel *f*; **bellboy** ['belbɔɪ] *n* (*esp US*) Page *m*

bellows ['beləʊz] *npl* (*for fire*) Blasebalg *m*

belly ['belɪ] *n* Bauch *m*; **bellyache** *n* Bauchweh *nt* ▷ *vi* (*fam*) meckern; **belly button** *n* (*fam*) Bauchnabel *m*; **bellyflop** *n* (*fam*) Bauchklatscher *m*

belong [bɪ'lɒŋ] *vi* gehören (*to sb* jdm); (*to club*) angehören +*dat*; **belongings** *npl* Habe *f*

below [bɪ'ləʊ] *prep* unter ▷ *adv* unten

belt [belt] *n* (*round waist*) Gürtel *m*; (*safety belt*) Gurt *m*; **below the ~** unter der Gürtellinie ▷ *vi* (*fam: go fast*) rasen, düsen; **beltway** *n* (*US*) Umgehungsstraße *f*

bench [bentʃ] *n* Bank *f*

bend [bend] *n* Biegung *f*; (*in road*) Kurve *f* ▷ *vt* (**bent, bent**) (*curve*) biegen; (*head, arm*) beugen ▷ *vi* sich biegen; (*person*) sich beugen; **bend down** *vi* sich bücken

beneath [bɪ'niːθ] *prep* unter ▷ *adv* darunter

beneficial [benɪ'fɪʃl] *adj* gut, nützlich (*to* für); **benefit** ['benɪfɪt] *n* (*advantage*) Vorteil *m*; (*profit*) Nutzen *m*; **for your/his ~** deinetwegen/seinetwegen; **unemployment ~** Arbeitslosengeld *nt* ▷ *vt* guttun +*dat* ▷ *vi* Nutzen ziehen (*from* aus)

benign [bɪ'naɪn] *adj* (*person*) gütig; (*climate*) mild; (*Med*) gutartig

bent [bent] *pt, pp of* **bend** ▷ *adj* krumm; (*fam*) korrupt

beret ['bereɪ] *n* Baskenmütze *f*

Bermuda [bə'mjuːdə] *n* **the ~s** *pl* die Bermudas *pl* ▷ *adj* **~ shorts** *pl* Bermudashorts *pl*; **the ~ triangle** das Bermudadreieck

berry ['berɪ] *n* Beere *f*

berth [bɜːθ] *n* (*for ship*) Ankerplatz *m*; (*in ship*) Koje *f*; (*in train*) Bett *nt* ▷ *vt* am Kai festmachen ▷ *vi* anlegen

beside [bɪ'saɪd] *prep* neben; **~ the sea/lake** am Meer/See; **besides** [bɪ'saɪdz] *prep* außer ▷ *adv* außerdem

besiege [bɪ'siːdʒ] *vt* belagern

best [best] *adj* beste(r, s); **my ~ friend** mein bester *o* engster Freund; **the ~ thing (to do) would be to ...** das Beste wäre zu ...; (*on food packaging*) **~ before ...** mindestens haltbar bis ... ▷ *n* der/die/das Beste; **all the ~** alles Gute; **to make the ~ of it** das Beste daraus machen ▷ *adv* am besten; **I like this ~** das mag ich am liebsten; **best-before date** *n* Mindesthaltbarkeitsdatum *nt*; **best man** ['best'mæn] (*pl* **men**) *n* Trauzeuge *m*; **bestseller** ['bestselə*] *n* Bestseller *m*

bet [bet] *n* (**bet, bet**) *vt, vi* wetten (*on* auf +*akk*); **I ~ him £5 that ...** ich habe mit ihm um 5 Pfund gewettet, dass ...; **you ~** (*fam*) und ob!; **I ~ he'll be late** er kommt mit Sicherheit zu spät ▷ *n* Wette *f*

betray [bɪ'treɪ] *vt* verraten; **betrayal** *n* Verrat *m*

better ['betə*] *adj, adv* besser; **to get ~** (*healthwise*) sich erholen, wieder gesund werden; (*improve*) sich verbessern; **I'm much ~ today** es geht mir heute viel besser; **you'd ~ go** du solltest/Sie sollten lieber gehen; **a change for the ~** eine Wendung zum Guten

betting ['bɛtɪŋ] n Wetten nt; **betting shop** n Wettbüro nt

between [bɪ'twiːn] prep zwischen; (among) unter; **~ you and me, ...** unter uns gesagt, ... ▷ adv: (**in**) **~** dazwischen

beverage ['bɛvərɪdʒ] n (formal) Getränk nt

beware [bɪ'wɛə°] vt: **to ~ of sth** sich vor etw +dat hüten; **"~ of the dog"** „Vorsicht, bissiger Hund!"

bewildered [bɪ'wɪldəd] adj verwirrt

beyond [bɪ'jɒnd] prep (place) jenseits +gen; (time) über ... hinaus; (out of reach) außerhalb +gen; **it's ~ me** da habe ich keine Ahnung, da bin ich überfragt ▷ adv darüber hinaus

bias ['baɪəs] n (prejudice) Vorurteil nt, Voreingenommenheit f

bias(s)ed adj voreingenommen

bib [bɪb] n Latz m

Bible ['baɪbl] n Bibel f

bicycle ['baɪsɪkl] n Fahrrad nt

bid [bɪd] n (bid, bid) vt (offer) bieten ▷ n (attempt) Versuch m; (offer) Gebot nt

big [bɪg] adj groß; **it's no ~ deal** (fam) es ist nichts Besonderes; **big dipper** n (Brit) Achterbahn f; **big-headed** [bɪg'hɛdɪd] adj eingebildet

bike [baɪk] n (fam) Rad nt

bikini [bɪ'kiːnɪ] n Bikini m

bilberry ['bɪlbərɪ] n Heidelbeere f

bilingual [baɪ'lɪŋgwəl] adj zweisprachig

bill [bɪl] n (account) Rechnung f; (US: banknote) Banknote f; (Pol) Gesetzentwurf m; (Zool) Schnabel m; **billfold** ['bɪlfəʊld] n (US) Brieftasche f

billiards ['bɪlɪədz] nsing Billard nt; **billiard table** Billardtisch m

billion ['bɪlɪən] n Milliarde f

bin [bɪn] n Behälter m; (rubbish bin) (Müll)eimer m; (for paper) Papierkorb m

bind [baɪnd] (bound, bound) vt binden; (bind together) zusammenbinden; (wound) verbinden; **binding** n (ski) Bindung f; (book) Einband m

binge [bɪndʒ] n (fam: drinking) Sauferei f; **to go on a ~** auf Sauftour gehen

bingo ['bɪŋgəʊ] n Bingo nt

binoculars [bɪ'nɒkjʊləz] npl Fernglas nt

biodegradable ['baɪəʊdɪ'greɪdəbl] adj biologisch abbaubar

biography [baɪ'ɒgrəfɪ] n Biografie f

biological [baɪə'lɒdʒɪkəl] adj biologisch; **biology** [baɪ'ɒlədʒɪ] n Biologie f

birch [bɜːtʃ] n Birke f

bird [bɜːd] n Vogel m; (Brit fam: girl, girlfriend) Tussi f; **bird flu** n Vogelgrippe f; **bird watcher** n Vogelbeobachter(in) m(f)

birth [bɜːθ] n Geburt f; **birth certificate** n Geburtsurkunde f; **birth control** n Geburtenkontrolle f; **birthday** n Geburtstag m; **happy ~** herzlichen Glückwunsch zum Geburtstag; **birthday card** n Geburtstagskarte f; **birthday party** n Geburtstagsfeier f; **birthplace** n Geburtsort m

biscuit ['bɪskɪt] n (Brit) Keks m

bisexual [baɪ'sɛksjʊəl] adj bisexuell

bishop ['bɪʃəp] n Bischof m; (in chess) Läufer m

bit [bɪt] pt of **bite** ▷ n (piece) Stück(chen) nt; (Inform) Bit nt; **a ~ (of ...)** (small amount) ein bisschen ...; **a ~ tired** etwas müde;

~ by ~ allmählich; (*time*) **for a ~** ein Weilchen; **quite a ~** (*a lot*) ganz schön viel

bitch [bɪtʃ] *n* (*dog*) Hündin *f*; (*pej: woman*) Miststück *nt*, Schlampe *f*; **son of a ~** (*US: vulg*) Hurensohn *m*, Scheißkerl *m*; **bitchy** *adj* gemein, zickig

bite [baɪt] (**bit, bitten**) *vt, vi* beißen ▷ *n* Biss *m*; (*mouthful*) Bissen *m*; (*insect*) Stich *m*; **to have a ~** eine Kleinigkeit essen; **bitten** *pp of* **bite**

bitter ['bɪtə*] *adj* bitter; (*memory etc*) schmerzlich ▷ *n* (*Brit: beer*) halbdunkles Bier; **bitter lemon** *n* Bitter Lemon *nt*

bizarre [bɪ'zɑː*] *adj* bizarr

black [blæk] *adj* schwarz; **blackberry** *n* Brombeere *f*; **blackbird** *n* Amsel *f*; **blackboard** *n* (Wand)tafel *f*; **black box** *n* (*Aviat*) Flugschreiber *m*; **blackcurrant** *n* Schwarze Johannisbeere; **black eye** *n* blaues Auge; **Black Forest** *n* Schwarzwald *m*; **Black Forest gateau** *n* Schwarzwälder Kirschtorte *f*; **blackmail** *n* Erpressung *f* ▷ *vt* erpressen; **black market** *n* Schwarzmarkt *m*; **blackout** *n* (*Med*) Ohnmacht *f*; **to have a ~** ohnmächtig werden; **black pudding** *n* ≈ Blutwurst *f*; **Black Sea** *n*: **the ~** das Schwarze Meer; **blacksmith** *n* Schmied(in) *m(f)*; **black tie** *n* Abendanzug *m*, Smoking *m*; **is it ~?** ist/besteht da Smokingzwang?

bladder ['blædə*] *n* Blase *f*

blade [bleɪd] *n* (*of knife*) Klinge *f*; (*of propeller*) Blatt *nt*; (*of grass*) Halm *m*

blame [bleɪm] *n* Schuld *f* ▷ *vt*: **to ~ sth on sb** jdm die Schuld an etw *dat* geben; **he is to ~** er ist daran schuld

bland [blænd] *adj* (*taste*) fade; (*comment*) nichtssagend

blank [blæŋk] *adj* (*page, space*) leer, unbeschrieben; (*look*) ausdruckslos; **~ cheque** Blankoscheck *m*

blanket ['blæŋkɪt] *n* (Woll)decke *f*

blast [blɑːst] *n* (*of wind*) Windstoß *m*; (*of explosion*) Druckwelle *f* ▷ *vt* (*blow up*) sprengen; **~!** (*fam*) Mist!, verdammt!

blatant ['bleɪtənt] *adj* (*undisguised*) offen; (*obvious*) offensichtlich

blaze [bleɪz] *vi* lodern; (*sun*) brennen ▷ *n* (*building*) Brand *m*; (*other fire*) Feuer *nt*; **a ~ of colour** eine Farbenpracht

blazer ['bleɪzə*] *n* Blazer *m*

bleach [bliːtʃ] *n* Bleichmittel *nt* ▷ *vt* bleichen

bleak [bliːk] *adj* öde, düster; (*future*) trostlos

bleary ['blɪərɪ] *adj* (*eyes*) trübe, verschlafen

bleed [bliːd] (**bled, bled**) *vi* bluten

blend [blend] *n* Mischung *f* ▷ *vt* mischen ▷ *vi* sich mischen; **blender** *n* Mixer *m*

bless [bles] *vt* segnen; **~ you!** Gesundheit!; **blessing** *n* Segen *m*

blew [bluː] *pt of* **blow**

blind [blaɪnd] *adj* blind; (*corner*) unübersichtlich; **to turn a ~ eye to sth** bei etw ein Auge zudrücken ▷ *n* (*for window*) Rollo *nt* ▷ *vt* blenden; **blind alley** *n* Sackgasse *f*; **blind spot** *n* (*Auto*) toter Winkel; (*fig*) schwacher Punkt

blink [blɪŋk] *vi* blinzeln; (*light*) blinken

bliss [blɪs] *n* (Glück)seligkeit *f*

blister ['blɪstə*] *n* Blase *f*

blizzard ['blɪzəd] n Schneesturm m

bloated ['bləʊtɪd] adj aufgedunsen

block [blɒk] n (of wood, stone, ice) Block m, Klotz m; (of buildings) Häuserblock m; **~ of flats** (Brit) Wohnblock m ▷ vt (road etc) blockieren; (pipe, nose) verstopfen; **blockage** ['blɒkɪdʒ] n Verstopfung f; **blockbuster** ['blɒkbʌstə°] n Knüller m; **block letters** npl Blockschrift f

blog [blɒg] n (Inform) Blog nt

bloke [bləʊk] n (Brit fam) Kerl m, Typ m

blond(e) [blɒnd] adj blond ▷ n (person) Blondine f, blonder Typ

blood [blʌd] n Blut nt; **blood count** n Blutbild nt; **blood donor** n Blutspender(in) m(f); **blood group** n Blutgruppe f; **blood orange** n Blutorange f; **blood poisoning** n Blutvergiftung f; **blood pressure** n Blutdruck m; **blood sample** n Blutprobe f; **bloodsports** npl Sportarten, bei denen Tiere getötet werden; **bloodthirsty** adj blutrünstig; **bloody** adj (Brit fam) verdammt, Scheiß-; (literal sense) blutig

bloom [blu:m] n Blüte f ▷ vi blühen

blossom ['blɒsəm] n Blüte f ▷ vi blühen

blot [blɒt] n (of ink) Klecks m; (fig) Fleck m

blouse [blaʊz] n Bluse f; **big girl's ~** (fam) Schwächling m, femininer Typ

blow [bləʊ] n Schlag m ▷ vi, vt (**blew, blown**) (wind) wehen, blasen; (person: trumpet etc) blasen; **to ~ one's nose** sich dat die Nase putzen; **blow out** vt (candle etc) ausblasen; **blow up** vi explodieren ▷ vt sprengen;

(balloon, tyre) aufblasen; (Foto: enlarge) vergrößern; **blow-dry** vt föhnen; **blowjob** n (fam) **to give sb a ~** jdm einen blasen; **blown** [bləʊn] pp of **blow**; **blow-out** n (Auto) geplatzter Reifen

BLT n abbr = **bacon, lettuce and tomato sandwich** mit Frühstücksspeck, Kopfsalat und Tomaten belegtes Sandwich

blue [blu:] adj blau; (fam: unhappy) trübsinnig, niedergeschlagen; (film) pornografisch; (joke) anzüglich; (language) derb; **bluebell** n Glockenblume f; **blueberry** n Blaubeere f; **blue cheese** n Blauschimmelkäse m; **blues** npl: **the ~** (Mus) der Blues; **to have the ~** (fam) niedergeschlagen sein

blunder ['blʌndə°] n Schnitzer m

blunt [blʌnt] adj (knife) stumpf; (fig) unverblümt; **bluntly** adv geradeheraus

blurred [blɜ:d] adj verschwommen, unklar

blush [blʌʃ] vi erröten

board [bɔ:d] n (of wood) Brett nt; (committee) Ausschuss m; (of firm) Vorstand m; **~ and lodging** Unterkunft und Verpflegung; **on ~** an Bord ▷ vt (train, bus) einsteigen in +akk; (ship) an Bord +gen gehen; **boarder** n Pensionsgast m; (school) Internatsschüler(in) m(f); **board game** n Brettspiel nt; **boarding card**, **boarding pass** n Bordkarte f, Einsteigekarte f; **boarding school** n Internat nt; **board meeting** n Vorstandssitzung f; **boardroom** n Sitzungssaal m (des Vorstands)

boast [bəʊst] vi prahlen (about mit) ▷ n Prahlerei f

boat [bəʊt] n Boot nt; (ship) Schiff nt; **boatman** n (hirer)

Bootsverleiher m; **boat race** n
Regatta f; **boat train** n Zug m mit
Schiffsanschluss
bob(sleigh) ['bɒbsleɪ] n Bob m
bodily ['bɒdɪlɪ] adj körperlich
▷ adv (forcibly) gewaltsam; **body**
['bɒdɪ] n Körper m; (dead) Leiche f;
(of car) Karosserie f; **bodybuilding**
n Bodybuilding nt; **bodyguard** n
Leibwächter m; (group) Leibwache
f; **body jewellery** n
Intimschmuck m; **body odour** n
Körpergeruch m; **body piercing** n
Piercing nt; **bodywork** n
Karosserie f
boil [bɔɪl] vt, vi kochen ▷ n (Med)
Geschwür nt; **boiler** n Boiler m;
boiling adj (water etc) kochend
(heiß); **I was ~** (hot) mir war
fürchterlich heiß; (with rage) ich
kochte vor Wut; **boiling point** n
Siedepunkt m
bold [bəʊld] adj kühn, mutig;
(colours) kräftig; (type) fett
Bolivia [bə'lɪvɪə] n Bolivien nt
bolt [bəʊlt] n (lock) Riegel m;
(screw) Bolzen m ▷ vt verriegeln
bomb [bɒm] n Bombe f ▷ vt
bombardieren
bond [bɒnd] n (link) Bindung f;
(Fin) Obligation f
bone [bəʊn] n Knochen m; (of
fish) Gräte f; **boner** n (US fam)
Schnitzer m; (vulg: erection) Ständer
m
bonfire ['bɒnfaɪə*] n Feuer nt
(im Freien)
bonnet ['bɒnɪt] n (Brit Auto)
Haube f; (for baby) Häubchen nt
bonny ['bɒnɪ] adj (esp Scottish)
hübsch
bonus ['bəʊnəs] n Bonus m,
Prämie f
boo [bu:] vt auspfeifen,
ausbuhen ▷ vi buhen ▷ n Buhruf
m
book [bʊk] n Buch nt; (of tickets,

stamps) Heft nt ▷ vt (ticket etc)
bestellen; (hotel, flight etc) buchen;
(Sport) verwarnen; **fully ~ed (up)**
ausgebucht; (performance)
ausverkauft; **book in** vt
eintragen; **to be ~ed in at a hotel**
ein Zimmer in einem Hotel
bestellt haben; **bookcase** n
Bücherregal nt; **booking** n
Buchung f; **booking office** n
(Rail) Fahrkartenschalter m; (Theat)
Vorverkaufsstelle f; **book-keeping**
n Buchhaltung f; **booklet** n
Broschüre f; **bookmark** n (a.
Inform) Lesezeichen nt; **bookshelf**
n Bücherbord nt; **bookshelves**
Bücherregal nt; **bookshop,**
bookstore n (esp US)
Buchhandlung f
boom [bu:m] n (of business)
Boom m; (noise) Dröhnen nt ▷ vi
(business) boomen; (fam) florieren;
(voice etc) dröhnen
boomerang ['bu:məræŋ] n
Bumerang m
boost [bu:st] n Auftrieb m ▷ vt
(production, sales) ankurbeln;
(power, profits etc) steigern;
booster (injection) n
Wiederholungsimpfung f
boot [bu:t] n Stiefel m; (Brit Auto)
Kofferraum m ▷ vt (Inform) laden,
booten
booth [bu:ð] n (at fair etc) Bude f;
(at trade fair etc) Stand m
booze [bu:z] n (fam) Alkohol m
▷ vi (fam) saufen
border ['bɔ:də*] n Grenze f; (edge)
Rand m; **north/south of the**
Border in Schottland/England;
borderline n Grenze f
bore [bɔ:*] pt of **bear** ▷ vt (hole
etc) bohren; (person) langweilen
▷ n (person) Langweiler(in) m(f),
langweiliger Mensch; (thing)
langweilige Sache; **bored** adj: **to**
be ~ sich langweilen; **boredom** n

Langeweile f; **boring** adj
langweilig
born [bɔːn] adj: **he was ~ in
London** er ist in London geboren
borne [bɔːn] pp of **bear**
borough ['bʌrə] n Stadtbezirk m
borrow ['bɒrəʊ] vt borgen
Bosnia-Herzegovina
['bɒznɪəhɜːtsəgəʊ'viːnə] n
Bosnien-Herzegowina nt; **Bosnian**
['bɒznɪən] adj bosnisch ▷ n
Bosnier(in) m(f)
boss [bɒs] n Chef(in) m(f), Boss
m; **boss around** vt
herumkommandieren; **bossy** adj
herrisch
botanical [bə'tænɪkəl] adj botanisch; **~ garden(s)** botanischer
Garten
both [bəʊθ] adj beide; **~ the
books** beide Bücher ▷ pron
(people) beide; (things) beides;
~ (of) the boys die beiden Jungs; **I
like ~ of them** ich mag sie (alle)
beide ▷ adv: **~ X and Y** sowohl X
als auch Y
bother ['bɒðə*] vt ärgern,
belästigen; **it doesn't ~ me** das
stört mich nicht; **he can't be ~ed
with details** mit Details gibt er
sich nicht ab; **I'm not ~ed** das ist
mir egal ▷ vi sich kümmern
(about um); **don't ~** (das ist) nicht
nötig, lass es! ▷ n (trouble) Mühe f;
(annoyance) Ärger m
bottle ['bɒtl] n Flasche f ▷ vt (in
Flaschen) abfüllen; **bottle out** vi
(fam) den Mut verlieren, aufgeben;
bottle bank n Altglascontainer
m; **bottled** adj in Flaschen; **~ beer**
Flaschenbier nt; **bottleneck** n
(fig) Engpass m; **bottle opener** n
Flaschenöffner m
bottom ['bɒtəm] n (of container)
Boden m; (underside) Unterseite f;
(fam: of person) Po m; **at the ~ of
the sea/table/page** auf dem

Meeresgrund/am Tabellen-
ende/unten auf der Seite ▷ adj
unterste(r, s); **to be ~ of the
class/league** Klassen-
letzte(r)/Tabellenletzte(r) sein;
~ gear (Auto) erster Gang
bought [bɔːt] pt, pp of **buy**
bounce [baʊns] vi (ball)
springen, aufprallen; (cheque)
platzen; **~ up and down** (person)
herumhüpfen; **bouncy** adj (ball)
gut springend; (person) munter;
bouncy castle® n Hüpfburg f
bound [baʊnd] pt, pp of **bind**
▷ adj (tied up) gebunden; (obliged)
verpflichtet; **to be ~ to do sth** (sure
to) etw bestimmt tun (werden);
(have to) etw tun müssen; **it's ~ to
happen** es muss so kommen; **to
be ~ for ...** auf dem Weg nach ...
sein; **boundary** ['baʊndərɪ] n
Grenze f
bouquet [bʊ'keɪ] n (flowers)
Strauß m; (of wine) Blume f
boutique [buː'tiːk] n Boutique f
bow [bəʊ] n (ribbon) Schleife f;
(instrument, weapon) Bogen m
▷ [baʊ] vi sich verbeugen ▷ [baʊ]
n (with head) Verbeugung f; (of
ship) Bug m
bowels ['baʊəlz] npl Darm m
bowl [bəʊl] n (basin) Schüssel f;
(shallow) Schale f; (for animal) Napf
m ▷ vt, vi (in cricket) werfen
bowler ['bəʊlə*] n (in cricket)
Werfer(in) m(f); (hat) Melone f
bowling ['bəʊlɪŋ] n Kegeln nt;
bowling alley n Kegelbahn f;
bowling green n Rasen m zum
Bowling-Spiel; **bowls** [bəʊlz]
nsing (game) Bowling-Spiel nt
bow tie [bəʊ'taɪ] n Fliege f
box [bɒks] n Schachtel f;
(cardboard) Karton m; (bigger)
Kasten m; (space on form) Kästchen
nt; (Theat) Loge f; **boxer** n
Boxer(in) m(f); **boxers, boxer**

shorts npl Boxershorts pl; **boxing** n (Sport) Boxen nt; **Boxing Day** n zweiter Weihnachtsfeiertag

● **BOXING DAY**
●
● **Boxing Day** ist ein Feiertag in
● Großbritannien. Fällt
● Weihnachten auf ein
● Wochenende, wird der Feiertag
● am nächsten Wochentag
● nachgeholt. Der Name geht auf
● einen alten Brauch zurück:
● früher erhielten Händler und
● Lieferanten an diesem Tag ein
● Geschenk, die sogenannte
● Christmas Box.

boxing gloves npl Boxhandschuhe pl; **boxing ring** n Boxring m
box number n Chiffre f
box office n (cinema, theatre) Kasse f
boy [bɔɪ] n Junge m
boycott ['bɔɪkɒt] n Boykott m ▷ vt boykottieren
boyfriend ['bɔɪfrend] n (fester) Freund m; **boy scout** n Pfadfinder m
bra [brɑː] n BH m
brace [breɪs] n (on teeth) Spange f
bracelet ['breɪslɪt] n Armband nt
braces ['breɪsɪz] npl (Brit) Hosenträger pl
bracket ['brækɪt] n (in text) Klammer f; (Tech) Träger m ▷ vt einklammern
brag [bræg] vi angeben
Braille [breɪl] n Blindenschrift f
brain [breɪn] n (Anat) Gehirn nt; (mind) Verstand m; **~s** (pl) (intelligence) Grips m; **brainwave** n Geistesblitz m; **brainy** adj schlau, clever
braise [breɪz] vt schmoren
brake [breɪk] n Bremse f ▷ vi

bremsen; **brake fluid** n Bremsflüssigkeit f; **brake light** n Bremslicht nt; **brake pedal** n Bremspedal nt
branch [brɑːntʃ] n (of tree) Ast m; (of family, subject) Zweig m; (of firm) Filiale f, Zweigstelle f; **branch off** vi (road) abzweigen
brand [brænd] n (Comm) Marke f
brand-new ['brænd'njuː] adj (funkel)nagelneu
brandy ['brændɪ] n Weinbrand m
brass [brɑːs] n Messing nt; (Brit fam: money) Knete f; **brass band** n Blaskapelle f
brat [bræt] n (pej, fam) Gör nt
brave [breɪv] adj tapfer, mutig; **bravery** ['breɪvərɪ] n Mut m
brawl [brɔːl] n Schlägerei f
brawn [brɔːn] n (strength) Muskelkraft f; (Gastr) Sülze f; **brawny** adj muskulös
Brazil [brə'zɪl] n Brasilien nt; **Brazilian** adj brasilianisch ▷ n Brasilianer(in) m(f); **brazil nut** n Paranuss f
bread [bred] n Brot nt; **breadbin** (Brit), **breadbox** (US) n Brotkasten m; **breadcrumbs** npl Brotkrumen pl; (Gastr) Paniermehl nt; **breaded** adj paniert; **breadknife** n Brotmesser nt
breadth [bredθ] n Breite f
break [breɪk] n (fracture) Bruch m; (rest) Pause f; (short holiday) Kurzurlaub m; **give me a ~** gib mir eine Chance, hör auf damit! ▷ vt (**broke, broken**) (fracture) brechen; (in pieces) zerbrechen; (toy, device) kaputt machen; (promise) nicht halten; (silence) brechen; (law) verletzen; (journey) unterbrechen; (news) mitteilen (to sb jdm); **I broke my leg** ich habe mir das Bein gebrochen; **he broke it to her gently** er hat es ihr schonend beigebracht ▷ vi (come apart)

(auseinander)brechen; (*in pieces*) zerbrechen; (*toy, device*) kaputtgehen; (*person*) zusammenbrechen; (*day, dawn*) anbrechen; (*news*) bekannt werden; **break down** *vi* (*car*) eine Panne haben; (*machine*) versagen; (*person*) zusammenbrechen; **break in** *vi* (*burglar*) einbrechen; **break into** *vt* einbrechen in +*akk*; **break off** *vi, vt* abbrechen; **break out** *vi* ausbrechen; **to ~ in a rash** einen Ausschlag bekommen; **break up** *vi* aufbrechen; (*meeting, organisation*) sich auflösen; (*marriage*) in die Brüche gehen; (*couple*) sich trennen; **school breaks up on Friday** am Freitag beginnen die Ferien ⊳ *vt* aufbrechen; (*marriage*) zerstören; (*meeting*) auflösen; **breakable** *adj* zerbrechlich; **breakage** *n* Bruch *m*; **breakdown** *n* (*of car*) Panne *f*; (*of machine*) Störung *f*; (*of person, relations, system*) Zusammenbruch *m*; **breakdown service** *n* Pannendienst *m*; **breakdown truck** *n* Abschleppwagen *m*

breakfast ['brɛkfəst] *n* Frühstück *nt*; **to have ~** frühstücken; **breakfast cereal** *n* Cornflakes, Muesli etc; **breakfast television** *n* Frühstücksfernsehen *nt*

break-in ['breɪkɪn] *n* Einbruch *m*; **breakup** ['breɪkʌp] *n* (*of meeting, organization*) Auflösung *f*; (*of marriage*) Zerrüttung *f*

breast [brɛst] *n* Brust *f*; **breastfeed** *vt* stillen; **breaststroke** *n* Brustschwimmen *nt*

breath [brɛθ] *n* Atem *m*; **out of ~** außer Atem; **breathalyse**, **breathalyze** ['brɛθəlaɪz] *vt* (ins Röhrchen) blasen lassen; **breathalyser**, **breathalyzer** *n* Promillemesser *m*; **breathe** [briːð]

vt, vi atmen; **breathe in** *vt, vi* einatmen; **breathe out** *vt, vi* ausatmen; **breathless** ['brɛθlɪs] *adj* atemlos; **breathtaking** ['brɛθteɪkɪŋ] *adj* atemberaubend

bred [brɛd] *pt, pp of* **breed**

breed [briːd] *n* (*race*) Rasse *f* ⊳ *vi* (**bred, bred**) sich vermehren ⊳ *vt* züchten; **breeder** *n* Züchter(in) *m(f)*; (*fam*) Hetero *m*; **breeding** *n* (*of animals*) Züchtung *f*; (*of person*) (gute) Erziehung

breeze [briːz] *n* Brise *f*

brevity ['brɛvɪtɪ] *n* Kürze *f*

brew [bruː] *vt* (*beer*) brauen; (*tea*) kochen; **brewery** *n* Brauerei *f*

bribe ['braɪb] *n* Bestechungsgeld *nt* ⊳ *vt* bestechen; **bribery** ['braɪbərɪ] *n* Bestechung *f*

brick [brɪk] *n* Backstein *m*; **bricklayer** *n* Maurer(in) *m(f)*

bride [braɪd] *n* Braut *f*; **bridegroom** *n* Bräutigam *m*; **bridesmaid** *n* Brautjungfer *f*

bridge [brɪdʒ] *n* Brücke *f*; (*cards*) Bridge *nt*

brief [briːf] *adj* kurz ⊳ *vt* instruieren (*on* über +*akk*); **briefcase** *n* Aktentasche *f*; **briefs** *npl* Slip *m*

bright [braɪt] *adj* hell; (*colour*) leuchtend; (*cheerful*) heiter; (*intelligent*) intelligent; (*idea*) glänzend; **brighten up** *vt* aufhellen; (*person*) aufheitern ⊳ *vi* sich aufheitern; (*person*) fröhlicher werden

brilliant ['brɪljənt] *adj* (*sunshine, colour*) strahlend; (*person*) brillant; (*idea*) glänzend; (*Brit fam*) **it was ~** es war fantastisch

brim [brɪm] *n* Rand *m*

bring [brɪŋ] (**brought, brought**) *vt* bringen; (*with one*) mitbringen; **bring about** *vt* herbeiführen, bewirken; **bring back** *vt* zurückbringen; (*memories*) wecken; **bring down** *vt* (*reduce*)

senken; (*government etc*) zu Fall
bringen; **bring in** *vt*
hereinbringen; (*introduce*)
einführen; **bring out** *vt*
herausbringen; **bring round**,
bring to *vt* wieder zu sich
bringen; **bring up** *vt* (*child*)
aufziehen; (*question*) zur Sprache
bringen
brisk [brɪsk] *adj* (*trade*) lebhaft;
(*wind*) frisch
bristle [ˈbrɪsl] *n* Borste f
Brit [brɪt] *n* (*fam*) Brite m, Britin f;
Britain [ˈbrɪtn] *n* Großbritannien
nt; **British** [ˈbrɪtɪʃ] *adj* britisch;
the ~ Isles (*pl*) die Britischen
Inseln *pl* ▷ *n* **the ~** (*pl*) die Briten *pl*
brittle [ˈbrɪtl] *adj* spröde
broad [brɔːd] *adj* breit; (*accent*)
stark; **in ~ daylight** am helllichten
Tag ▷ *n* (*US fam*) Frau f
B road [ˈbiːrəʊd] *n* (*Brit*) ≈
Landstraße f
broadcast [ˈbrɔːdkɑːst] *n*
Sendung f ▷ *irr* *vt*, *vi* senden;
(*event*) übertragen
broaden [ˈbrɔːdn] *vt*: **to ~ the
mind** den Horizont erweitern;
broad-minded *adj* tolerant
broccoli [ˈbrɒkəlɪ] *n* Brokkoli *pl*
brochure [ˈbrəʊʃjʊəʳ] *n* Prospekt
m, Broschüre f
broke [brəʊk] *pt of* **break** ▷ *adj*
(*Brit fam*) pleite; **broken**
[ˈbrəʊkən] *pp of* **break**;
broken-hearted *adj* untröstlich
broker [ˈbrəʊkəʳ] *n* Makler(in)
m(f)
brolly [ˈbrɒlɪ] *n* (*Brit*) Schirm m
bronchitis [brɒŋˈkaɪtɪs] *n*
Bronchitis f
bronze [brɒnz] *n* Bronze f
brooch [brəʊtʃ] *n* Brosche f
broom [bruːm] *n* Besen m
Bros [brɒs] *abbr* = **brothers** Gebr.
broth [brɒθ] *n* Fleischbrühe f
brothel [ˈbrɒθl] *n* Bordell *nt*

brother [ˈbrʌðəʳ] *n* Bruder m; **~s**
(*pl*) (*Comm*) Gebrüder *pl*; **brother-
in-law** (*pl* **brothers-in-law**) *n*
Schwager m
brought [brɔːt] *pt*, *pp of* **bring**
brow [braʊ] *n* (*eyebrow*)
(Augen)braue f; (*forehead*) Stirn f
brown [braʊn] *adj* braun; **brown
bread** *n* Mischbrot *nt*; (*wholemeal*)
Vollkornbrot *nt*; **brownie**
[ˈbraʊnɪ] *n* (*Gastr*) Brownie m;
(*Brit*) junge Pfadfinderin; **brown
paper** *n* Packpapier *nt*; **brown
rice** *n* Naturreis m; **brown sugar**
n brauner Zucker
browse [braʊz] *vi* (*in book*)
blättern; (*in shop*) schmökern,
herumschauen; **browser** *n*
(*Inform*) Browser m
bruise [bruːz] *n* blauer Fleck
▷ *vt*: **to ~ one's arm** sich *dat* einen
blauen Fleck (am Arm) holen
brunette [bruˈnet] *n* Brünette
f
brush [brʌʃ] *n* Bürste f; (*for
sweeping*) Handbesen m; (*for
painting*) Pinsel m ▷ *vt* bürsten;
(*sweep*) fegen; **to ~ one's teeth**
sich *dat* die Zähne putzen; **brush
up** *vt* (*French etc*) auffrischen
Brussels sprouts
[ˈbrʌslˈspraʊts] *npl* Rosenkohl m,
Kohlsprossen *pl*
brutal [ˈbruːtl] *adj* brutal;
brutality [bruːˈtælɪtɪ] *n* Bru-
talität f
BSE *abbr* = **bovine spongiform
encephalopathy** BSE f
bubble [ˈbʌbl] *n* Blase f; **bubble
bath** *n* Schaumbad *nt*,
Badeschaum m; **bubbly** [ˈbʌblɪ]
adj sprudelnd; (*person*)
temperamentvoll ▷ *n* (*fam*)
Champus m
buck [bʌk] *n* (*animal*) Bock m; (*US
fam*) Dollar m
bucket [ˈbʌkɪt] *n* Eimer m

buckle ['bʌkl] n Schnalle f ▷ vi
(Tech) sich verbiegen ▷ vt
zuschnallen
bud [bʌd] n Knospe f
Buddhism ['bʊdɪzəm] n Buddhismus m; **Buddhist** adj
buddhistisch ▷ n Buddhist(in)
m(f)
buddy ['bʌdɪ] n (fam) Kumpel m
budget ['bʌdʒɪt] n Budget nt
▷ adj preisgünstig; **budget airline**
n Billigflieger m
budgie ['bʌdʒɪ] n Wellensittich m
buff [bʌf] adj (US) muskulös; **in
the ~** nackt ▷ n (enthusiast) Fan m
buffalo ['bʌfələʊ] (pl **-es**) n
Büffel m
buffer ['bʌfə°] n (a. Inform) Puffer m
buffet ['bʊfeɪ] n (food) (kaltes)
Büfett nt
bug [bʌg] n (Inform) Bug m,
Programmfehler m; (listening
device) Wanze f; (US: insect) Insekt
nt; (fam: illness) Infektion f ▷ vt
(fam) nerven
bugger ['bʌgə°] n (vulg)
Scheißkerl m ▷ interj (vulg)
Scheiße f; **bugger off** vi (vulg)
abhauen, Leine ziehen
buggy® ['bʌgɪ] n (for baby)
Buggy® m

build [bɪld] (**built, built**) vt
bauen; **build up** vt aufbauen;
builder n Bauunternehmer(in)
m(f); **building** n Gebäude nt;
building site n Baustelle f;
building society n Bausparkasse f
built pt, pp of **build**; **built-in** adj
(cupboard) Einbau-, eingebaut
bulb [bʌlb] n (Bot)
(Blumen)zwiebel f; (Elec)
Glühbirne f
Bulgaria [bʌl'gɛərɪə] n Bulgarien nt; **Bulgarian** adj
bulgarisch ▷ n (person) Bulgare m,
Bulgarin f; (language) Bulgarisch nt
bulimia [bə'lɪmɪə] n Bulimie f
bulk [bʌlk] n (size) Größe f;
(greater part) Großteil m (of +gen); **in
~** en gros; **bulky** adj (goods)
sperrig; (person) stämmig
bull [bʊl] n Stier m; **bulldog** n
Bulldogge f; **bulldoze** ['bʊldəʊz]
vt planieren; **bulldozer** n
Planierraupe f
bullet ['bʊlɪt] n Kugel f
bulletin ['bʊlɪtɪn] n Bulletin nt;
(announcement) Bekanntmachung
f; (Med) Krankenbericht m; **bulletin
board** n (US: Inform) schwarzes
Brett
bullfight ['bʊlfaɪt] n Stierkampf
m; **bullshit** n (fam) Scheiß m
bully ['bʊlɪ] n Tyrann m
bum [bʌm] n (Brit fam: backside)
Po m; (US: vagrant) Penner m;
(worthless person) Rumtreiber m;
bum around vi herumgammeln
bumblebee ['bʌmblbiː] n
Hummel f
bumf [bʌmf] (fam) n
Infomaterial nt, Papierkram m
bump [bʌmp] n (fam: swelling)
Beule f; (road) Unebenheit f; (blow)
Stoß m ▷ vt stoßen; **to ~ one's
head** sich am Kopf
anschlagen (on an +dat); **bump
into** vt stoßen gegen; (fam: meet)

(zufällig) begegnen +dat; **bumper** n (Auto) Stoßstange f ▷ adj (edition etc) Riesen-; (crop etc) Rekord-; **bumpy** ['bʌmpɪ] adj holp(e)rig

bun [bʌn] n süßes Brötchen

bunch [bʌntʃ] n (of flowers) Strauß m; (fam: of people) Haufen m; **~ of keys** Schlüsselbund m; **~ of grapes** Weintraube f

bundle ['bʌndl] n Bündel nt

bungalow ['bʌŋgələʊ] n Bungalow m

bungee jumping ['bʌndʒɪ-dʒʌmpɪŋ] n Bungeejumping nt

bunk [bʌŋk] n Koje f; **bunk bed(s)** n(pl) Etagenbett nt

bunker ['bʌŋkə*] n (Mil) Bunker m

bunny ['bʌnɪ] n Häschen nt

buoy [bɔɪ] n Boje f; **buoyant** ['bɔɪənt] adj (floating) schwimmend

BUPA ['buːpə] abbr (Brit) private Krankenkasse

burden ['bɜːdn] n Last f

bureau ['bjʊərəʊ] n Büro nt; (government department) Amt nt; **bureaucracy** [bjʊ'rɒkrəsɪ] n Bürokratie f; **bureaucratic** [bjʊərə'krætɪk] adj bürokratisch; **bureau de change** ['bjʊərəʊ də 'ʃɑ̃ʒ] n Wechselstube f

burger ['bɜːgə*] n Hamburger m

burglar ['bɜːglə*] n Einbrecher(in) m(f); **burglar alarm** n Alarmanlage f; **burglarize** vt (US) einbrechen in +akk; **burglary** n Einbruch m; **burgle** ['bɜːgl] vt einbrechen in +akk

burial ['berɪəl] n Beerdigung f

burn [bɜːn] (**burnt** o **burned**, **burnt** o **burned**) vt verbrennen; (food, slightly) anbrennen; **to ~ one's hand** sich dat die Hand verbrennen ▷ vi brennen ▷ n (injury) Brandwunde f; (on material)

verbrannte Stelle; **burn down** vt, vi abbrennen

burp [bɜːp] vi rülpsen ▷ vt (baby) aufstoßen lassen

bursary ['bɜːsərɪ] n Stipendium nt

burst [bɜːst] (**burst, burst**) vt platzen lassen ▷ vi platzen; **to ~ into tears** in Tränen ausbrechen

bury ['berɪ] vt begraben; (in grave) beerdigen; (hide) vergraben

bus [bʌs] n Bus m; **bus driver** n Busfahrer(in) m(f)

bush [bʊʃ] n Busch m

business ['bɪznɪs] n Geschäft nt; (enterprise) Unternehmen nt; (concern, affair) Sache f; **I'm here on ~** ich bin geschäftlich hier; **it's none of your ~** das geht dich nichts an; **business card** n Visitenkarte f; **business class** n (Aviat) Businessclass f; **businessman** (pl **-men**) n Geschäftsmann m; **business studies** npl Betriebswirtschaftslehre f; **businesswoman** (pl **-women**) n Geschäftsfrau f

bus service n Busverbindung f; **bus shelter** n Wartehäuschen nt; **bus station** n Busbahnhof m; **bus stop** n Bushaltestelle f

bust [bʌst] n Büste f ▷ adj (broken) kaputt; **to go ~** Pleite gehen; **bust-up** n (fam) Krach m

busy ['bɪzɪ] adj beschäftigt; (street, place) belebt; (esp US: telephone) besetzt; **~ signal** (US) Besetztzeichen nt

⭕ **KEYWORD**

but [bʌt, bət] conj 1 (yet) aber; **not X but Y** nicht X sondern Y

2 (however) **I'd love to come, but I'm busy** ich würde gern kommen, bin aber beschäftigt

3 (showing disagreement, surprise etc)

but that's fantastic! (aber) das ist ja fantastisch!
▷ *prep* (*apart from, except*): **nothing but trouble** nichts als Ärger; **no-one but him can do it** niemand außer ihm kann es machen; **but for you/your help** ohne dich/deine Hilfe; **anything but that** alles, nur das nicht
▷ *adv* (*just, only*) **she's but a child** sie ist noch ein Kind; **had I but known** wenn ich es nur gewusst hätte; **I can but try** ich kann es immerhin versuchen; **all but finished** so gut wie fertig

butcher ['bʊtʃə*] *n* Fleischer(in) *m(f)*, Metzger(in) *m(f)*
butler ['bʌtlə*] *n* Butler *m*
butt [bʌt] (*US fam*) *n* Hintern *m*
butter ['bʌtə*] *n* Butter *f* ▷ *vt* buttern; **buttercup** *n* Butterblume *f*; **butterfly** *n* Schmetterling *m*
buttocks ['bʌtəks] *npl* Gesäß *nt*
button ['bʌtn] *n* Knopf *m*; (*badge*) Button *m* ▷ *vt* zuknöpfen; **buttonhole** *n* Knopfloch *nt*
buy [baɪ] *n* Kauf *m* ▷ *vt* (**bought, bought**) kaufen (*from* von); **he bought me a ring** er hat mir einen Ring gekauft; **buyer** *n* Käufer(in) *m(f)*
buzz [bʌz] *n* Summen *nt*; **to give sb a ~** (*fam*) jdn anrufen ▷ *vi* summen; **buzzer** ['bʌzə*] *n* Summer *m*; **buzz word** *n* (*fam*) Modewort *nt*

◯ **KEYWORD**

by [baɪ] *prep* **1** (*referring to cause, agent*) von, durch; **killed by lightning** vom Blitz getötet; **a painting by Picasso** ein Gemälde von Picasso
2 (*referring to method, manner*) **by**

bus/car/train mit dem Bus/Auto/Zug; **to pay by cheque** per Scheck bezahlen; **by moonlight** bei Mondschein; **by saving hard, he ...** indem er eisern sparte, ... er ...
3 (*via, through*) über +*akk*; **he came in by the back door** er kam durch die Hintertür herein
4 (*close to, past*) bei, an +*dat*; **a holiday by the sea** ein Urlaub am Meer; **she rushed by me** sie eilte an mir vorbei
5 (*not later than*) **by 4 o'clock** bis 4 Uhr; **by this time tomorrow** morgen um diese Zeit; **by the time I got here it was too late** als ich hier ankam, war es zu spät
6 (*during*) **by day** bei Tag
7 (*amount*) **by the kilo/metre** kiloweise/meterweise; **paid by the hour** stundenweise bezahlt
8 (*math, measure*) **to divide by 3** durch 3 teilen; **to multiply by 3** mit 3 malnehmen; **a room 3 metres by 4** ein Zimmer 3 mal 4 Meter; **it's broader by a metre** es ist (um) einem Meter breiter
9 (*according to*) nach; **it's all right by me** von mir aus gern
10 (**all**) **by oneself** *etc* ganz allein
11 **by the way** übrigens
▷ *adv* **1** *see* **go**; **pass** *etc*
2 **by and by** irgendwann; (*with past tenses*) nach einiger Zeit; **by and large** (*on the whole*) im Großen und Ganzen

bye-bye ['baɪ'baɪ] *interj* (*fam*) Wiedersehen, tschüss
by-election *n* Nachwahl *f*; **bypass** *n* Umgehungsstraße *f*; (*Med*) Bypass *m*; **byproduct** *n* Nebenprodukt *nt*; **byroad** *n* Nebenstraße *f*; **bystander** *n* Zuschauer(in) *m(f)*
byte [baɪt] *n* Byte *nt*

C

C [siː] *abbr* = **Celsius** C

c *abbr* = **circa** ca

cab [kæb] *n* Taxi *nt*

cabbage ['kæbɪdʒ] *n* Kohl *m*

cabin ['kæbɪn] *n* (*Naut*) Kajüte *f*; (*Aviat*) Passagierraum *m*; (*wooden house*) Hütte *f*; **cabin crew** *n* Flugbegleitpersonal *nt*; **cabin cruiser** *n* Kajütboot *nt*

cabinet ['kæbɪnɪt] *n* Schrank *m*; (*for display*) Vitrine *f*; (*Pol*) Kabinett *nt*

cable ['keɪbl] *n* (*Elec*) Kabel *nt*; **cable-car** *n* Seilbahn *f*; **cable railway** *n* Drahtseilbahn *f*; **cable television**, **cablevision** (*US*) *n* Kabelfernsehen *nt*

cactus ['kæktəs] *n* Kaktus *m*

CAD *abbr* = **computer-aided design** CAD *nt*

Caesarean [siːˈzɛərɪən] *adj*: **~ (section)** Kaiserschnitt *m*

café ['kæfeɪ] *n* Café *nt*; **cafeteria** [kæfɪˈtɪərɪə] *n* Cafeteria *f*; **cafetiere** [kæfəˈtjɛəʳ] *n* Kaffeebereiter *m*

cage [keɪdʒ] *n* Käfig *m*

Cairo ['kaɪərəʊ] *n* Kairo *nt*

cake [keɪk] *n* Kuchen *m*; **cake shop** *n* Konditorei *f*

calamity [kəˈlæmɪtɪ] *n* Katastrophe *f*

calculate ['kælkjʊleɪt] *vt* berechnen; (*estimate*) kalkulieren; **calculating** *adj* berechnend; **calculation** [kælkjʊˈleɪʃən] *n* Berechnung *f*; (*estimate*) Kalkulation *f*; **calculator** ['kælkjʊleɪtəʳ] *n* Taschenrechner *m*

calendar ['kælɪndəʳ] *n* Kalender *m*

calf [kɑːf] (*pl* **calves**) *n* Kalb *nt*; (*Anat*) Wade *f*

California [kælɪˈfɔːnɪə] *n* Kalifornien *nt*

call [kɔːl] *vt* rufen; (*name, describe as*) nennen; (*Tel*) anrufen; (*Inform, Aviat*) aufrufen; **what's this ~ed?** wie heißt das?; **that's what I ~ service** das nenne ich guten Service ▷ *vi* (*shout*) rufen (*for help* um Hilfe); (*visit*) vorbeikommen; **to ~ at the doctor's** beim Arzt vorbeigehen; (*of train*) **to ~ at ...** in ... halten ▷ *n* (*shout*) Ruf *m*; (*Tel*) Anruf *m*; (*Inform, Aviat*) Aufruf *m*; **to make a ~** telefonieren; **to give sb a ~** jdn anrufen; **to be on ~** Bereitschaftsdienst haben; **call back** *vt*, *vi* zurückrufen; **call for** *vt* (*come to pick up*) abholen; (*demand, require*) verlangen; **call off** *vt* absagen

call centre *n* Callcenter *nt*; **caller** *n* Besucher(in) *m(f)*; (*Tel*) Anrufer(in) *m(f)*

calm [kɑːm] *n* Stille *f*; (*also of person*) Ruhe *f*; (*of sea*) Flaute *f* ▷ *vt* beruhigen ▷ *adj* ruhig; **calm down** *vi* sich beruhigen

calorie ['kælərɪ] *n* Kalorie *f*

calves [kɑːvz] *pl of* **calf**

Cambodia [kæm'bəʊdɪə] *n* Kambodscha *nt*

camcorder ['kæmkɔːdə*] *n* Camcorder *m*

came [keɪm] *pt of* **come**

camel ['kæməl] *n* Kamel *nt*

camera ['kæmərə] *n* Fotoapparat *m*, Kamera *f*; **camera phone** ['kæmərəfəʊn] *n* Fotohandy *nt*

camomile ['kæməmaɪl] *n* Kamille *f*

camouflage ['kæməflɑːʒ] *n* Tarnung *f*

camp [kæmp] *n* Lager *nt*; (*camping place*) Zeltplatz *m* ▷ *vi* zelten, campen ▷ *adj* (*fam*) theatralisch, tuntig

campaign [kæm'peɪn] *n* Kampagne *f*; (*Pol*) Wahlkampf *m* ▷ *vi* sich einsetzen (*for/against* für/gegen)

campbed ['kæmpbed] *n* Campingliege *f*; **camper** ['kæmpə*] *n* (*person*) Camper(in) *m(f)*; (*van*) Wohnmobil *nt*; **camping** ['kæmpɪŋ] *n* Zelten *nt*, Camping *nt*; **campsite** ['kæmpsaɪt] *n* Zeltplatz *m*, Campingplatz *m*

campus ['kæmpəs] *n* (*of university*) Universitätsgelände *nt*, Campus *m*

○ **KEYWORD**

can [kæn] (*negative* **cannot, can't**, *conditional* **could**) *vb aux* **1** (*be able to, know how to*) können; **I can see you tomorrow, if you like** ich könnte Sie morgen sehen, wenn Sie wollen; **I can swim** ich kann schwimmen; **can you speak German?** sprechen Sie Deutsch?

2 (*may*) können, dürfen; **could I have a word with you?** könnte ich Sie kurz sprechen?

Canada ['kænədə] *n* Kanada *nt*; **Canadian** [kə'neɪdjən] *adj* kanadisch ▷ *n* Kanadier(in) *m(f)*

canal [kə'næl] *n* Kanal *m*

canary [kə'nɛərɪ] *n* Kanarienvogel *m*

cancel ['kænsəl] *vt* (*plans*) aufgeben; (*meeting, event*) absagen; (*Comm: order etc*) stornieren; (*contract*) kündigen; (*Inform*) löschen; (*Aviat: flight*) streichen; **to be ~led** (*event, train, bus*) ausfallen; **cancellation** [kænsə'leɪʃən] *n* Absage *f*; (*Comm*) Stornierung *f*; (*Aviat*) gestrichener Flug

cancer ['kænsə*] *n* (*Med*) Krebs *m*; **Cancer** *n* (*Astr*) Krebs *m*

candid ['kændɪd] *adj* (*person, conversation*) offen

candidate ['kændɪdət] *n* (*for post*) Bewerber(in) *m(f)*; (*Pol*) Kandidat(in) *m(f)*

candle ['kændl] *n* Kerze *f*; **candlelight** *n* Kerzenlicht *nt*; **candlestick** *n* Kerzenhalter *m*

candy ['kændɪ] *n* (*US*) Bonbon *nt*; (*quantity*) Süßigkeiten *pl*; **candy-floss** *n* (*Brit*) Zuckerwatte *f*

cane [keɪn] *n* Rohr *nt*; (*stick*) Stock *m*

cannabis ['kænəbɪs] *n* Cannabis *m*

canned [kænd] *adj* Dosen-

cannot ['kænɒt] *contr of* **can not**

canny ['kænɪ] *adj* (*shrewd*) schlau

canoe [kə'nuː] *n* Kanu *nt*; **canoeing** *n* Kanufahren *nt*

can opener ['kænəʊpnə*] *n* Dosenöffner *m*

canopy ['kænəpɪ] *n* Baldachin *m*; (*awning*) Markise *f*; (*over entrance*) Vordach *nt*

can't [kɑːnt] *contr of* **can not**

canteen [kæn'tiːn] *n* (*in factory*) Kantine *f*; (*in university*) Mensa *f*

canvas ['kænvəs] *n* (*for sails, shoes*) Segeltuch *nt*; (*for tent*) Zeltstoff *m*; (*for painting*) Leinwand *f*

canvass ['kænvəs] *vi* um Stimmen werben (*for* für)

canyon ['kænjən] *n* Felsenschlucht *f*; **canyoning** ['kænjənɪŋ] *n* Canyoning *nt*

cap [kæp] *n* Mütze *f*; (*lid*) Verschluss *m*, Deckel *m*

capability [keɪpə'bɪlɪtɪ] *n* Fähigkeit *f*; **capable** ['keɪpəbl] *adj* fähig; **to be ~ of sth** zu etw fähig (*o* imstande) sein; **to be ~ of doing sth** etw tun können

capacity [kə'pæsɪtɪ] *n* (*of building, container*) Fassungsvermögen *nt*; (*ability*) Fähigkeit *f*; (*function*) **in his ~ as ...** in seiner Eigenschaft als ...

cape [keɪp] *n* (*garment*) Cape *nt*, Umhang *m*; (*Geo*) Kap *nt*

caper ['keɪpə*] *n* (*for cooking*) Kaper *f*

capital ['kæpɪtl] *n* (*Fin*) Kapital *nt*; (*letter*) Großbuchstabe *m*; **~ (city)** Hauptstadt *f*; **capitalism** *n* Kapitalismus *m*; **capital punishment** *n* die Todesstrafe

Capricorn ['kæprɪkɔːn] *n* (*Astr*) Steinbock *m*

capsize [kæp'saɪz] *vi* kentern

capsule ['kæpsjuːl] *n* Kapsel *f*

captain ['kæptɪn] *n* Kapitän *m*; (*army*) Hauptmann *m*

caption ['kæpʃən] *n* Bildunterschrift *f*

captive ['kæptɪv] *n* Gefangene(r) *mf*; **capture** ['kæptʃə*] *vt* (*person*) fassen, gefangen nehmen; (*town etc*) einnehmen; (*Inform: data*) erfassen ▷ *n* Gefangennahme *f*; (*Inform*) Erfassung *f*

car [kɑː*] *n* Auto *nt*; (*US Rail*) Wagen *m*

carafe [kə'ræf] *n* Karaffe *f*

caramel ['kærəmel] *n* Karamelle *f*

caravan ['kærəvæn] *n* Wohnwagen *m*; **caravan site** *n* Campingplatz *m* für Wohnwagen

caraway (seed) ['kærəweɪ] *n* Kümmel *m*

carbohydrate [kɑːbəʊ'haɪdreɪt] *n* Kohle(n)hydrat *nt*

car bomb *n* Autobombe *f*

carbon ['kɑːbən] *n* Kohlenstoff *m*

car boot sale *n auf einem Parkplatz stattfindender Flohmarkt*

carburettor, carburetor (*US*) ['kɑːbjʊretə*] *n* Vergaser *m*

card [kɑːd] *n* Karte *f*; (*material*) Pappe *f*; **cardboard** *n* Pappe *f*; **~ (box)** Karton *m*; (*smaller*) Pappschachtel *f*; **card game** *n* Kartenspiel *nt*

cardigan ['kɑːdɪgən] *n* Strickjacke *f*

card index *n* Kartei *f*; **cardphone** ['kɑːdfəʊn] *n* Kartentelefon *nt*

care [keə*] *n* (*worry*) Sorge *f*; (*carefulness*) Sorgfalt *f*; (*looking after things, people*) Pflege *f*; **with ~** sorgfältig; (*cautiously*) vorsichtig; **to take ~** (*watch out*) vorsichtig sein; (*in address*) **to take ~ of** sorgen für, sich kümmern um ▷ *vi*: **I don't ~** es ist mir egal; **to ~ about sth** Wert auf etw *akk* legen; **he ~s about her** sie liegt ihm am Herzen; **care for** *vt* (*look after*) sorgen für, sich kümmern um; (*like*) mögen

career [kə'rɪə*] *n* Karriere *f*, Laufbahn *f*; **career woman** (*pl* **women**) *n* Karrierefrau *f*; **careers adviser** *n* Berufsberater(in) *m(f)*

carefree ['keəfriː] *adj* sorgenfrei; **careful, carefully** *adj, adv* sorgfältig; (*cautious, cautiously*) vorsichtig; **careless, carelessly** *adj, adv* nachlässig; (*driving etc*) leichtsinnig; (*remark*) unvorsichtig; **carer** ['kɛərə*] *n* Betreuer(in) *m(f)*, Pfleger(in) *m(f)*; **caretaker** ['kɛəteɪkə*] *n* Hausmeister(in) *m(f)*; **careworker** *n* Pfleger(in) *m(f)*

car-ferry ['kɑːferɪ] *n* Autofähre *f*

cargo ['kɑːgəʊ] (*pl* -(**e**)**s**) *n* Ladung *f*

car hire, car hire company *n* Autovermietung *f*

Caribbean [kærɪˈbiːən] *n* Karibik *f* ▷ *adj* karibisch

caring ['kɛərɪŋ] *adj* mitfühlend; (*parent, partner*) liebevoll; (*looking after sb*) fürsorglich

car insurance *n* Kraftfahrzeugversicherung *f*

carnation [kɑːˈneɪʃən] *n* Nelke *f*

carnival ['kɑːnɪvəl] *n* Volksfest *nt*; (*before Lent*) Karneval *m*

carol ['kærəl] *n* Weihnachtslied *nt*

carp [kɑːp] *n* (*fish*) Karpfen *m*

car park *n* (*Brit*) Parkplatz *m*; (*multi-storey car park*) Parkhaus *nt*

carpenter ['kɑːpəntə*] *n* Zimmermann *m*

carpet ['kɑːpɪt] *n* Teppich *m*

car phone *n* Autotelefon *nt*; **carpool** *n* Fahrgemeinschaft *f*; (*vehicles*) Fuhrpark *m* ▷ *vi* eine Fahrgemeinschaft bilden; **car rental** *n* Autovermietung *f*

carriage ['kærɪdʒ] *n* (*Brit Rail: coach*) Wagen *m*; (*compartment*) Abteil *nt*; (*horse-drawn*) Kutsche *f*; (*transport*) Beförderung *f*; **carriageway** *n* (*Brit: on road*) Fahrbahn *f*

carrier ['kærɪə*] *n* (*Comm*) Spediteur(in) *m(f)*; **carrier bag** *n* Tragetasche *f*

carrot ['kærət] *n* Karotte *f*

carry ['kærɪ] *vt* tragen; (*in vehicle*) befördern; (*have on one*) bei sich

haben; **carry on** *vi* (*continue*) weitermachen; (*fam: make a scene*) ein Theater machen ▷ *vt* (*continue*) fortführen; **to ~ on working** weiter arbeiten; **carry out** *vt* (*orders, plan*) ausführen, durchführen

carrycot *n* Babytragetasche *f*

carsick ['kɑːsɪk] *adj*: **he gets ~** ihm wird beim Autofahren übel

cart [kɑːt] *n* Wagen *m*, Karren *m*; (*US: shopping trolley*) Einkaufswagen *m*

carton ['kɑːtən] *n* (*Papp*)karton *m*; (*of cigarettes*) Stange *f*

cartoon [kɑːˈtuːn] *n* Cartoon *m* o *nt*; (*one drawing*) Karikatur *f*; (*film*) (Zeichen)trickfilm *m*

cartridge ['kɑːtrɪdʒ] *n* (*for film*) Kassette *f*; (*for gun, pen, printer*) Patrone *f*; (*for copier*) Kartusche *f*

carve [kɑːv] *vt, vi* (*wood*) schnitzen; (*stone*) meißeln; (*meat*) schneiden, tranchieren; **carving** *n* (*in wood*) Schnitzerei *f*; (*in stone*) Skulptur *f*; (*Ski*) Carving *nt*

car wash *n* Autowaschanlage *f*

case [keɪs] *n* (*crate*) Kiste *f*; (*box*) Schachtel *f*; (*for jewels*) Schatulle *f*; (*for spectacles*) Etui *nt*; (*Jur, matter*) Fall *m*; **in ~** falls; **in that ~** in dem Fall; **in ~ of fire** bei Brand; **it's a ~ of ...** es handelt sich hier um ...

cash [kæʃ] *n* Bargeld *nt*; **in ~** bar; **~ on delivery** per Nachnahme ▷ *vt* (*cheque*) einlösen; **cash desk** *n* Kasse *f*; **cash dispenser** *n* Geldautomat *m*; **cashier** [kæˈʃɪə*] *n* Kassierer(in) *m(f)*; **cash machine** *n* (*Brit*) Geldautomat *m*

cashmere ['kæʃmɪə*] *n* Kaschmirwolle *f*

cash payment *n* Barzahlung *f*; **cashpoint** *n* (*Brit*) Geldautomat *m*

casing ['keɪsɪŋ] *n* Gehäuse *nt*

casino [kəˈsiːnəʊ] (*pl* -**s**) *n* Kasino *nt*

cask [kɑːsk] *n* Fass *nt*

casserole [ˈkæsərəʊl] *n* Kasserole *f*; (*food*) Schmortopf *m*

cassette [kæˈset] *n* Kassette *f*; **cassette recorder** *n* Kassettenrekorder *m*

cast [kɑːst] (**cast, cast**) *vt* (*throw*) werfen; (*Theat, Cine*) besetzen; (*roles*) verteilen ▷ *n* (*Theat, Cine*) Besetzung *f*; (*Med*) Gipsverband *m*; **cast off** *vi* (*Naut*) losmachen

caster [ˈkɑːstə*] *n*: **~ sugar** Streuzucker *m*

castle [ˈkɑːsl] *n* Burg *f*

castrate [kæsˈtreɪt] *vt* kastrieren

casual [ˈkæʒjʊəl] *adj* (*arrangement, remark*) beiläufig; (*attitude, manner*) (nach)lässig, zwanglos; (*dress*) leger; (*work, earnings*) Gelegenheits-; (*look, glance*) flüchtig; **~ wear** Freizeitkleidung *f*; **~ sex** Gelegenheitssex *m*; **casually** *adv* (*remark, say*) beiläufig; (*meet*) zwanglos; (*dressed*) leger

casualty [ˈkæʒjʊəltɪ] *n* Verletzte(r) *mf*; (*dead*) Tote(r) *mf*; (*department in hospital*) Notaufnahme *f*

cat [kæt] *n* Katze *f*; (*male*) Kater *m*

catalog (*US*), **catalogue** [ˈkætəlɒg] *n* Katalog *m* ▷ *vt* katalogisieren

cataract [ˈkætərækt] *n* Wasserfall *m*; (*Med*) grauer Star

catarrh [kəˈtɑː*] *n* Katarr(h) *m*

catastrophe [kəˈtæstrəfɪ] *n* Katastrophe *f*

catch [kætʃ] *n* (*fish etc*) Fang *m* ▷ *vt* (**caught, caught**) fangen; (*thief*) fassen; (*train, bus etc*) nehmen; (*not miss*) erreichen; **to ~ a cold** sich erkälten; **to ~ fire** Feuer fangen; **I didn't ~ that** das habe ich nicht verstanden; **catch on** *vi* (*become popular*) Anklang finden; **catch up** *vt, vi*: **to ~ with**

sb jdn einholen; **to ~ on sth** etw nachholen; **catching** *adj* ansteckend

category [ˈkætɪgərɪ] *n* Kategorie *f*

cater [ˈkeɪtə*] *vi* die Speisen und Getränke liefern (*for* für); **cater for** *vt* (*have facilities for*) eingestellt sein auf +*akk*; **catering** *n* Versorgung *f* mit Speisen und Getränken, Gastronomie *f*; **catering service** *n* Partyservice *m*

caterpillar [ˈkætəpɪlə*] *n* Raupe *f*

cathedral [kəˈθiːdrəl] *n* Kathedrale *f*, Dom *m*

Catholic [ˈkæθəlɪk] *adj* katholisch ▷ Katholik(in) *m(f)*

cat nap *n* (*Brit*) kurzer Schlaf; **cat's eyes** [ˈkætsaɪz] *npl* (*in road*) Katzenaugen *pl*, Reflektoren *pl*

catsup [ˈkætsəp] *n* (*US*) Ketschup *nt o m*

cattle [ˈkætl] *npl* Vieh *nt*

caught [kɔːt] *pt, pp of* **catch**

cauliflower [ˈkɒlɪflaʊə*] *n* Blumenkohl *m*; **cauliflower cheese** *n* Blumenkohl *m* in Käsesoße

cause [kɔːz] *n* (*origin*) Ursache *f* (*of* für); (*reason*) Grund *m* (*for* zu); (*purpose*) Sache *f*; **for a good ~** für wohltätige Zwecke; **no ~ for alarm/complaint** kein Grund zur Aufregung/Klage ▷ *vt* verursachen

causeway [ˈkɔːzweɪ] *n* Damm *m*

caution [ˈkɔːʃən] *n* Vorsicht *f*; (*Jur, Sport*) Verwarnung *f* ▷ *vt* (ver)warnen; **cautious** [ˈkɔːʃəs] *adj* vorsichtig

cave [keɪv] *n* Höhle *f*; **cave in** *vi* einstürzen

cavity [ˈkævɪtɪ] *n* Hohlraum *m*; (*in tooth*) Loch *nt*

cayenne (pepper) [keɪˈen] *n* Cayennepfeffer *m*

CCTV *abbr* = **closed circuit television** Videoüberwachungsanlage *f*

CD *abbr* = **Compact Disc** CD *f*; **CD player** *n* CD-Spieler *m*; **CD-ROM** *abbr* = **Compact Disc Read Only Memory** CD-ROM *f*; **CD-RW** *abbr* = **Compact Disc Rewritable** CD-RW *f*

cease [siːs] *vi* aufhören ▷ *vt* beenden; **to ~ doing sth** aufhören, etw zu tun; **cease fire** *n* Waffenstillstand *m*

ceiling ['siːlɪŋ] *n* Decke *f*

celebrate ['selɪbreɪt] *vt, vi* feiern; **celebrated** *adj* gefeiert; **celebration** [selɪ'breɪʃən] *n* Feier *f*; **celebrity** [sɪ'lebrɪtɪ] *n* Berühmtheit *f*, Star *m*

celeriac [sə'lerɪæk] *n* (Knollen)sellerie *m* o *f*; **celery** ['selərɪ] *n* (Stangen)sellerie *m* o *f*

cell [sel] *n* Zelle *f*; (US) see **cellphone**

cellar ['selə*] *n* Keller *m*

cello ['tʃeləʊ] (*pl* **-s**) *n* Cello *nt*

cellphone ['selfəʊn], **cellular phone** ['seljʊlə* 'fəʊn] *n* Mobiltelefon *nt*, Handy *nt*

Celt [kelt] *n* Kelte *m*, Keltin *f*; **Celtic** ['keltɪk] *adj* keltisch ▷ *n* (*language*) Keltisch *nt*

cement [sɪ'ment] *n* Zement *m*

cemetery ['semɪtrɪ] *n* Friedhof *m*

censorship ['sensəʃɪp] *n* Zensur *f*

cent [sent] *n* (of dollar, euro etc) Cent *m*

center *n* (US) see **centre**

centiliter (US), **centilitre** ['sentɪliːtə*] *n* Zentiliter *m*; **centimeter** (US), **centimetre** ['sentɪmiːtə*] *n* Zentimeter *m*

central ['sentrəl] *adj* zentral; **Central America** *n* Mittelamerika *nt*; **Central Europe** *n* Mitteleuropa *nt*; **central heating** *n* Zentralheizung *f*; **centralize** *vt* zentralisieren; **central locking** *n* (Auto) Zentralverriegelung *f*; **central reservation** *n* (Brit) Mittelstreifen *m*; **central station** *n* Hauptbahnhof *m*

centre ['sentə*] *n* Mitte *f*; (building, of city) Zentrum *nt* ▷ *vt* zentrieren; **centre forward** *n* (Sport) Mittelstürmer *m*

century ['sentjʊrɪ] *n* Jahrhundert *nt*

ceramic [sɪ'ræmɪk] *adj* keramisch

cereal ['sɪərɪəl] *n* (any grain) Getreide *nt*; (breakfast cereal) Frühstücksflocken *pl*

ceremony ['serɪmənɪ] *n* Feier *f*, Zeremonie *f*

certain ['sɜːtən] *adj* sicher (of +gen); (particular) bestimmt; **for ~** mit Sicherheit; **certainly** *adv* sicher; (without doubt) bestimmt; **~!** aber sicher!; **~ not** ganz bestimmt nicht!

certificate [sə'tɪfɪkɪt] *n* Bescheinigung *f*; (in school, qualification) Zeugnis *nt*; **certify** ['sɜːtɪfaɪ] *vt, vi* bescheinigen

cervical smear ['sɜːvɪkəl smɪə*] *n* Abstrich *m*

CFC *abbr* = **chlorofluorocarbon** FCKW *nt*

chain [tʃeɪn] *n* Kette *f* ▷ *vt*: **to ~ (up)** anketten; **chain reaction** *n* Kettenreaktion *f*; **chain store** *n* Kettenladen *m*

chair [tʃeə*] *n* Stuhl *m*; (university) Lehrstuhl *m*; (armchair) Sessel *m*; (chairperson) Vorsitzende(r) *mf*; **chairlift** *n* Sessellift *m*; **chairman** (*pl* **-men**) *n* Vorsitzende(r) *m*; (of firm) Präsident *m*; **chairperson** *n* Vorsitzende(r) *mf*; (of firm) Präsident(in) *m(f)*; **chairwoman**

(pl **-women**) n Vorsitzende f; (of firm) Präsidentin f

chalet ['ʃæleɪ] n (in mountains) Berghütte f; (holiday dwelling) Ferienhäuschen nt

chalk ['tʃɔːk] n Kreide f

challenge ['tʃælɪndʒ] n Herausforderung f ▷ vt (person) herausfordern; (statement) bestreiten

chambermaid ['tʃeɪmbə*meɪd] n Zimmermädchen nt

chamois leather ['ʃæmwɑː'leðə*] n (for windows) Fensterleder nt

champagne [ʃæm'peɪn] n Champagner m

champion ['tʃæmpiən] n (Sport) Meister(in) m(f); **championship** n Meisterschaft f

chance [tʃɑːns] n (fate) Zufall m; (possibility) Möglichkeit f; (opportunity) Gelegenheit f; (risk) Risiko nt; **by ~** zufällig; **he doesn't stand a ~ (of winning)** er hat keinerlei Chance(, zu gewinnen)

chancellor ['tʃɑːnsələ*] n Kanzler(in) m(f)

chandelier [ʃændɪ'lɪə*] n Kronleuchter m

change [tʃeɪndʒ] vt verändern; (alter) ändern; (money, wheel, nappy) wechseln; (exchange) (um)tauschen; **to ~ one's clothes** sich umziehen; **to ~ trains** umsteigen; **to ~ gear** (Auto) schalten ▷ vi sich ändern; (esp outwardly) sich verändern; (get changed) sich umziehen ▷ n Veränderung f; (alteration) Änderung f; (money) Wechselgeld nt; (coins) Kleingeld nt; **for a ~** zur Abwechslung; **can you give me ~ for £10?** können Sie mir auf 10 Pfund herausgeben?; **change down** vi (Brit Auto) herunterschalten; **change over** vi

sich umstellen (to auf +akk); **change up** vi (Brit Auto) hochschalten

changeable adj (weather) veränderlich, wechselhaft; **change machine** n Geldwechsler m; **changing room** n Umkleideraum m

channel ['tʃænl] n Kanal m; (Radio, TV) Kanal m, Sender m; **the (English) Channel** der Ärmelkanal; **the Channel Islands** die Kanalinseln; **the Channel Tunnel** der Kanaltunnel; **channel-hopping** n Zappen nt

chaos ['keɪɒs] n Chaos nt; **chaotic** [keɪ'ɒtɪk] adj chaotisch

chap [tʃæp] n (Brit fam) Bursche m, Kerl m

chapel ['tʃæpəl] n Kapelle f

chapped ['tʃæpt] adj (lips) aufgesprungen

chapter ['tʃæptə*] n Kapitel nt

character ['kærəktə*] n Charakter m, Wesen nt; (in a play, novel etc) Figur f; (Typo) Zeichen nt; **he's a real ~** er ist ein echtes Original; **characteristic** [kærəktə'rɪstɪk] n typisches Merkmal

charcoal ['tʃɑːkəʊl] n Holzkohle f

charge [tʃɑːdʒ] n (cost) Gebühr f; (Jur) Anklage f; **free of ~** gratis, kostenlos; **to be in ~ of** verantwortlich sein für ▷ vt (money) verlangen; (Jur) anklagen; (battery) laden; **charge card** n Kundenkreditkarte f

charity ['tʃærɪtɪ] n (institution) wohltätige Organisation f; **a collection for ~** eine Sammlung für wohltätige Zwecke; **charity shop** n Geschäft einer 'charity', in dem freiwillige Helfer gebrauchte Kleidung, Bücher etc verkaufen

charm [tʃɑːm] n Charme m ▷ vt bezaubern; **charming** adj reizend, charmant

chart [tʃɑːt] n Diagramm nt; (map) Karte f; **the ~s** pl die Charts, die Hitliste

charter ['tʃɑːtə°] n Urkunde f ▷ vt (Naut, Aviat) chartern; **charter flight** n Charterflug m

chase [tʃeɪs] vt jagen, verfolgen ▷ n Verfolgungsjagd f; (hunt) Jagd f

chassis ['ʃæsɪ] n (Auto) Fahrgestell nt

chat [tʃæt] vi plaudern; (Inform) chatten ▷ n Plauderei f; **chat up** vt anmachen, anbaggern; **chatroom** n (Inform) Chatroom m; **chat show** n Talkshow f; **chatty** adj geschwätzig

chauffeur ['ʃəʊfə°] n Chauffeur(in) m(f), Fahrer(in) m(f)

cheap [tʃiːp] adj billig; (of poor quality) minderwertig

cheat [tʃiːt] vt, vi betrügen; (in school, game) mogeln

Chechen ['tʃetʃen] adj tschetschenisch ▷ n Tschetschene m, Tschetschenin f; **Chechnya** ['tʃetʃnɪə] n Tschetschenien nt

check [tʃek] vt (examine) überprüfen (for auf +akk); (Tech: adjustment etc) kontrollieren; (US: tick) abhaken; (Aviat: luggage) einchecken; (US: coat) abgeben ▷ n (examination, restraint) Kontrolle f; (US: restaurant bill) Rechnung f; (pattern) Karo(muster) nt; (US) see **cheque**; **check in** vt, vi (Aviat) einchecken; (into hotel) sich anmelden; **check out** vi sich abmelden, auschecken; **check up** vi nachprüfen; **to ~ on sb** Nachforschungen über jdn anstellen

checkers ['tʃekəz] nsing (US) Damespiel n

check-in ['tʃekɪn] n (airport) Check-in m; (hotel) Anmeldung f; **check-in desk** n

Abfertigungsschalter m; **checking account** n (US) Scheckkonto nt; **check list** n Kontrollliste f; **checkout** n (supermarket) Kasse f; **checkout time** n (hotel) Abreise(zeit) f; **checkpoint** n Kontrollpunkt m; **checkroom** n (US) Gepäckaufbewahrung f; **checkup** n (Med) (ärztliche) Untersuchung

cheddar ['tʃedə°] n Cheddarkäse m

cheek [tʃiːk] n Backe f, Wange f; (insolence) Frechheit f; **what a ~** so eine Frechheit!; **cheekbone** n Backenknochen m; **cheeky** adj frech

cheer [tʃɪə°] n Beifallsruf m; **~s** (when drinking) prost!; (Brit fam: thanks) danke; (Brit: goodbye) tschüs ▷ vt zujubeln +dat ▷ vi jubeln; **cheer up** vt aufmuntern ▷ vi fröhlicher werden; **~!** Kopf hoch!; **cheerful** ['tʃɪəfʊl] adj fröhlich

cheese [tʃiːz] n Käse m; **cheeseboard** n Käsebrett nt; (as course) (gemischte) Käseplatte; **cheesecake** n Käsekuchen m

chef [ʃef] n Koch m; (in charge of kitchen) Küchenchef(in) m(f)

chemical ['kemɪkəl] adj chemisch ▷ Chemikalie f; **chemist** ['kemɪst] n (pharmacist) Apotheker(in) m(f); (industrial chemist) Chemiker(in) m(f); **~'s** (shop) Apotheke f; **chemistry** n Chemie f

cheque [tʃek] n (Brit) Scheck m; **cheque account** n (Brit) Girokonto nt; **cheque book** n (Brit) Scheckheft nt; **cheque card** n (Brit) Scheckkarte f

chequered ['tʃekəd] adj kariert

cherish ['tʃerɪʃ] vt (look after) liebevoll sorgen für; (hope) hegen; (memory) bewahren

cherry ['tʃerɪ] n Kirsche f; **cherry tomato** (pl **-es**) n Kirschtomate f

chess [tʃes] n Schach nt; **chessboard** n Schachbrett nt

chest [tʃest] n Brust f; (box) Kiste f; **~ of drawers** Kommode f

chestnut ['tʃesnʌt] n Kastanie f

chew [tʃuː] vt, vi kauen; **chewing gum** n Kaugummi m

chick [tʃɪk] n Küken nt; **chicken** n Huhn nt; (food: roast) Hähnchen nt; (coward) Feigling m; **chicken breast** n Hühnerbrust f; **chicken Kiev** n paniertes Hähnchen, mit Knoblauchbutter gefüllt; **chickenpox** n Windpocken pl; **chickpea** n Kichererbse f

chicory ['tʃɪkərɪ] n Chicorée f

chief [tʃiːf] n (of department etc) Leiter(in) m(f); (boss) Chef(in) m(f); (of tribe) Häuptling m ⊳ adj Haupt-; **chiefly** adv hauptsächlich

child [tʃaɪld] (pl **children**) n Kind nt; **child abuse** n Kindesmisshandlung f; **child allowance, child benefit** (Brit) n Kindergeld nt; **childbirth** n Geburt f, Entbindung f; **childhood** n Kindheit f; **childish** adj kindisch; **child lock** n Kindersicherung f; **childproof** adj kindersicher; **children** ['tʃɪldrən] pl of **child**; **child seat** n Kindersitz m

Chile ['tʃɪlɪ] n Chile nt

chill [tʃɪl] n Kühle f; (Med) Erkältung f ⊳ vt (wine) kühlen; **chill out** vi (fam) chillen, relaxen; **chilled** adj gekühlt

chilli ['tʃɪlɪ] n Pepperoni pl; (spice) Chili m; **chilli con carne** ['tʃɪlɪkɒn'kɑːnɪ] n Chili con carne nt

chilly ['tʃɪlɪ] adj kühl, frostig

chimney ['tʃɪmnɪ] n Schornstein m; **chimneysweep** n Schornsteinfeger(in) m(f)

chimpanzee [tʃɪmpæn'ziː] n Schimpanse m

chin [tʃɪn] n Kinn nt

china ['tʃaɪnə] n Porzellan nt

China ['tʃaɪnə] n China nt; **Chinese** [tʃaɪ'niːz] adj chinesisch ⊳ n (person) Chinese m, Chinesin f; (language) Chinesisch nt; **Chinese leaves** npl Chinakohl m

chip [tʃɪp] n (of wood etc) Splitter m; (damage) angeschlagene Stelle; (Inform) Chip m; **~s** (Brit: potatoes) Pommes (frites) pl; (US: crisps) Kartoffelchips pl ⊳ vt anschlagen, beschädigen; **chippie** (fam), **chip shop** n Frittenbude f

chiropodist [kɪ'rɒpədɪst] n Fußpfleger(in) m(f)

chirp [tʃɜːp] vi zwitschern

chisel ['tʃɪzl] n Meißel m

chitchat ['tʃɪttʃæt] n Gerede nt

chives [tʃaɪvz] npl Schnittlauch m

chlorine ['klɔːriːn] n Chlor nt

chocaholic, chocoholic [tʃɒkə'hɒlɪk] n Schokoladenfreak m; **choc-ice** ['tʃɒkaɪs] n Eis nt mit Schokoladenüberzug; **chocolate** ['tʃɒklɪt] n Schokolade f; (chocolate-coated sweet) Praline f; **a bar of ~** eine Tafel Schokolade; **a box of ~s** eine Schachtel Pralinen; **chocolate cake** n Schokoladenkuchen m; **chocolate sauce** n Schokoladensoße f

choice [tʃɔɪs] n Wahl f; (selection) Auswahl f ⊳ adj auserlesen; (product) Qualitäts-

choir ['kwaɪə°] n Chor m

choke [tʃəʊk] vi sich verschlucken; (Sport) die Nerven verlieren ⊳ vt erdrosseln ⊳ n (Auto) Choke m

cholera ['kɒlərə] n Cholera f
cholesterol [kə'lestərəl] n
Cholesterin nt
choose [tʃuːz] (**chose, chosen**)
vt wählen; (pick out) sich
aussuchen; **there are three to
~ from** es stehen drei zur
Auswahl
chop [tʃɒp] vt (zer)hacken; (meat
etc) klein schneiden ▷ n (meat)
Kotelett nt; **to get the ~** gefeuert
werden; **chopper** n Hackbeil nt;
(fam: helicopter) Hubschrauber m;
chopsticks npl Essstäbchen pl
chorus ['kɔːrəs] n Chor m; (in
song) Refrain m
chose, chosen [tʃəuz, 'tʃəuzn] pt,
pp of **choose**
chowder ['tʃaudə*] n (US) dicke
Suppe mit Meeresfrüchten
christen ['krɪsn] vt taufen;
christening n Taufe f; **Christian**
['krɪstɪən] adj christlich ▷ n
Christ(in) m(f); **Christian name** n
(Brit) Vorname m
Christmas ['krɪsməs] n
Weihnachten pl; **Christmas bonus**
n Weihnachtsgeld nt; **Christmas
card** n Weihnachtskarte f;
Christmas carol n
Weihnachtslied nt; **Christmas
Day** n der erste Weihnachtstag;
Christmas Eve n Heiligabend m;
Christmas pudding n
Plumpudding m; **Christmas tree**
n Weihnachtsbaum m
chronic ['krɒnɪk] adj (Med, fig)
chronisch; (fam: very bad)
miserabel
chrysanthemum
[krɪ'sænθɪməm] n Chrysantheme
f
chubby ['tʃʌbɪ] adj (child)
pummelig; (adult) rundlich
chuck [tʃʌk] vt (fam) schmeißen;
chuck in vt (fam: job)
hinschmeißen; **chuck out** vt

(fam) rausschmeißen; **chuck up** vi
(fam) kotzen
chunk [tʃʌŋk] n Klumpen m;
(of bread) Brocken m; (of meat)
Batzen m; **chunky** adj (person)
stämmig
Chunnel ['tʃʌnəl] n (fam)
Kanaltunnel m
church [tʃɜːtʃ] n Kirche f;
churchyard n Kirchhof m
chute [ʃuːt] n Rutsche f
chutney ['tʃʌtnɪ] n Chutney m
CIA abbr = **Central Intelligence
Agency** (US) CIA f
CID abbr = **Criminal Investigation
Department** (Brit) ≈ Kripo f
cider ['saɪdə*] n ≈ Apfelmost m
cigar [sɪ'gɑː*] n Zigarre f;
cigarette [sɪgə'ret] n Zigarette f
cinema ['sɪnəmə] n Kino nt
cinnamon ['sɪnəmən] n Zimt m
circle ['sɜːkl] n Kreis m ▷ vi
kreisen; **circuit** ['sɜːkɪt] n
Rundfahrt f; (on foot) Rundgang m;
(for racing) Rennstrecke f; (Elec)
Stromkreis m; **circular** ['sɜːkjulə*]
adj (kreis)rund, kreisförmig ▷ n
Rundschreiben nt; **circulation**
[sɜːkju'leɪʃən] n (of blood)
Kreislauf m; (of newspaper) Auflage f
circumstances
['sɜːkəmstənsəz] npl (facts)
Umstände pl; (financial condition)
Verhältnisse pl; **in/under the
~** unter den Umständen; **under no
~** auf keinen Fall
circus ['sɜːkəs] n Zirkus m
cissy ['sɪsɪ] n (fam) Weichling m
cistern ['sɪstən] n Zisterne f; (of
WC) Spülkasten m
citizen ['sɪtɪzn] n Bürger(in) m(f);
(of nation) Staatsangehörige(r) mf;
citizenship n Staatsangehörigkeit f
city ['sɪtɪ] n Stadt f; (large)
Großstadt f; **the ~** (London's
financial centre) die (Londoner)

City; **city centre** n Innenstadt f,
Zentrum nt

civil ['sɪvɪl] adj (of town) Bürger-;
(of state) staatsbürgerlich; (not
military) zivil; **civil ceremony** n
standesamtliche Hochzeit; **civil
engineering** n Hoch- und Tiefbau
m, Bauingenieurwesen nt; **civilian**
[sɪ'vɪljən] n Zivilist(in) m(f);
civilization [sɪvɪlaɪ'zeɪʃən] n
Zivilisation f, Kultur f; **civilized**
['sɪvɪlaɪzd] adj zivilisiert,
kultiviert; **civil partnership** n
eingetragene Partnerschaft; **civil
rights** npl Bürgerrechte pl; **civil
servant** n (Staats)beamte(r) m,
(Staats)beamtin f; **civil service** n
Staatsdienst m; **civil war** n
Bürgerkrieg m

CJD abbr = **Creutzfeld-Jakob
disease** Creutzfeld-
Jakob-Krankheit f

cl abbr = **centilitre(s)** cl

claim [kleɪm] vt beanspruchen;
(apply for) beantragen; (demand)
fordern; (assert) behaupten (that
dass) ▷ n (demand) Forderung f
(for für); (right) Anspruch m (to auf
+akk); **~ for damages**
Schadenersatzforderung f; **to
make** o **put in a ~** (insurance)
Ansprüche geltend machen;
claimant n Antragsteller(in) m(f)

clam [klæm] n Venusmuschel f;
clam chowder n (US) dicke
Muschelsuppe (mit Sellerie, Zwiebeln
etc)

clap [klæp] vi (Beifall) klatschen

claret ['klærɪt] n roter
Bordeaux(wein)

clarify ['klærɪfaɪ] vt klären

clarinet [klærɪ'net] n Klarinette f

clarity ['klærɪtɪ] n Klarheit f

clash [klæʃ] vi (physically)
zusammenstoßen (with mit);
(argue) sich auseinandersetzen
(with mit); (fig: colours) sich beißen

▷ n Zusammenstoß m; (argument)
Auseinandersetzung f

clasp [klɑːsp] n (on belt) Schnalle f

class [klɑːs] n Klasse f ▷ vt
einordnen, einstufen

classic ['klæsɪk] adj (mistake,
example etc) klassisch ▷ n
Klassiker m; **classical** ['klæsɪkəl]
adj (music, ballet etc) klassisch

classification [klæsɪfɪ'keɪʃn] n
Klassifizierung f; **classify**
['klæsɪfaɪ] vt klassifizieren;
classified advertisement
Kleinanzeige f

classroom ['klɑːsrʊm] n Klassenzimmer nt

classy ['klɑːsɪ] adj (fam) nobel,
exklusiv

clatter ['klætə*] vi klappern

clause [klɔːz] n (Ling) Satz m; (Jur)
Klausel f

claw [klɔː] n Kralle f

clay [kleɪ] n Lehm m; (for pottery)
Ton m

clean [kliːn] adj sauber;
~ driving licence Führerschein
ohne Strafpunkte ▷ vt sauber
machen; (carpet etc) reinigen;
(window, shoes, vegetables) putzen;
(wound) säubern; **clean up** vt
sauber machen ▷ vi aufräumen;
cleaner n (person) Putzmann m,
Putzfrau f; (substance) Putzmittel
nt; **~'s** (firm) Reinigung f

cleanse [klenz] vt reinigen;
(wound) säubern; **cleanser** n
Reinigungsmittel nt

clear ['klɪə*] adj klar; (distinct)
deutlich; (conscience) rein; (free,
road etc) frei; **to be ~ about sth**
sich über etw im Klaren sein
▷ adv: **to stand ~** zurücktreten
▷ vt (road, room etc) räumen; (table)
abräumen; (Jur: find innocent)
freisprechen (of von) ▷ vi (fog,
mist) sich verziehen; (weather)
aufklaren; **clear away** vt

wegräumen; (*dishes*) abräumen;
clear off *vi* (*fam*) abhauen; **clear
up** *vi* (*tidy up*) aufräumen;
(*weather*) sich aufklären ▷ *vt*
(*room*) aufräumen; (*litter*)
wegräumen; (*matter*) klären
clearance sale *n*
Räumungsverkauf *m*; **clearing** *n*
Lichtung *f*; **clearly** *adv* klar;
(*speak, remember*) deutlich;
(*obviously*) eindeutig; **clearout**
n Entrümpelungsaktion *f*;
clearway *n* (*Brit*) Straße *f* mit
Halteverbot *nt*
clench [klentʃ] *vt* (*fist*) ballen;
(*teeth*) zusammenbeißen
clergyman [ˈklɜːdʒɪmæn] (*pl*
-men) *n* Geistliche(r) *m*;
clergywoman [ˈklɜːdʒɪwʊmən] (*pl*
-women) *n* Geistliche *f*
clerk [klɑːk], (*US*) [klɜːk] *n* (*in
office*) Büroangestellte(r) *mf*; (*US:
salesperson*) Verkäufer(in) *m(f)*
clever [ˈklevə*] *adj* schlau, klug;
(*idea*) clever
cliché [ˈkliːʃeɪ] *n* Klischee *nt*
click [klɪk] *n* Klicken *nt*; (*Inform*)
Mausklick *m* ▷ *vi* klicken; **to ~ on
sth** (*Inform*) etw anklicken; **it ~ed**
(*fam*) ich hab's/er hat's etc
geschnallt, es hat gefunkt, es hat
Klick gemacht; **they ~ed** sie haben
sich gleich verstanden; **click on** *vt*
(*Inform*) anklicken
client [ˈklaɪənt] *n* Kunde *m*,
Kundin *f*; (*Jur*) Mandant(in) *m(f)*
cliff [klɪf] *n* Klippe *f*
climate [ˈklaɪmɪt] *n* Klima *nt*
climax [ˈklaɪmæks] *n* Höhepunkt
m
climb [klaɪm] *vi* (*person*) klettern;
(*aircraft, sun*) steigen; (*road*)
ansteigen ▷ *vt* (*mountain*)
besteigen; (*tree etc*) klettern auf
+*akk* ▷ *n* Aufstieg *m*; **climber** *n*
(*mountaineer*) Bergsteiger(in) *m(f)*;
climbing *n* Klettern *nt*,

Bergsteigen *nt*; **climbing frame** *n*
Klettergerüst *nt*
cling [klɪŋ] (**clung, clung**) *vi*
sich klammern (*to* an +*akk*); **cling
film®** *n* Frischhaltefolie *f*
clinic [ˈklɪnɪk] *n* Klinik *f*; **clinical**
adj klinisch
clip [klɪp] *n* Klammer *f* ▷ *vt* (*fix*)
anklemmen (*to* an +*akk*);
(*fingernails*) schneiden; **clipboard**
n Klemmbrett *nt*; **clippers** *npl*
Schere *f*; (*for nails*) Zwicker *m*
cloak [kləʊk] *n* Umhang *m*;
cloakroom *n* (*for coats*)
Garderobe *f*
clock [klɒk] *n* Uhr *f*; (*Auto: fam*)
Tacho *m*; **round the ~** rund um die
Uhr; **clockwise** *adv* im
Uhrzeigersinn
clog [klɒg] *n* Holzschuh *m* ▷ *vt*
verstopfen
cloister [ˈklɔɪstə*] *n* Kreuzgang
m
clone [kləʊn] *n* Klon *m* ▷ *vt*
klonen
close [kləʊs] *adj* nahe (*to* +*dat*);
(*friend, contact*) eng; (*resemblance*)
groß; **~ to the beach** in der Nähe
des Strandes; **~ win** knapper Sieg;
on ~r examination *o*
genauerer Untersuchung ▷ *adv*
[kləʊs] dicht; **he lives ~ by** er
wohnt ganz in der Nähe ▷ *vt*
[kləʊz] schließen; (*road*) sperren;
(*discussion, matter*) abschließen-
▷ *vi* [kləʊz] schließen
rtrir; *n* [kləʊz] Ende *nt*; **close
down** *vi* schließen; (*factory*)
stillgelegt werden ▷ *vt* (*shop*)
schließen; (*factory*) stilllegen;
closed *adj* (*road*) gesperrt;
(*shop etc*) geschlossen; **closed
circuit television** *n*
Videoüberwachungsanlage *f*;
closely *adv* (*related*) eng, nah;
(*packed, follow*) dicht; (*attentively*)
genau

closet ['klɒzɪt] *n* (*esp US*) Schrank *m*

close-up ['kləʊsʌp] *n* Nahaufnahme *f*

closing ['kləʊzɪŋ] *adj*: **~ date** letzter Termin; (*for competition*) Einsendeschluss *m*; **~ time** (*of shop*) Ladenschluss *m*; (*Brit: of pub*) Polizeistunde *f*

closure ['kləʊʒə*] *n* Schließung *f*; Abschluss *m*; **to look for ~** mit etw abschließen wollen

clot [klɒt] (**blood**) **~** Blutgerinnsel *nt*; (*fam: idiot*) Trottel *m* ▷ *vi* (*blood*) gerinnen

cloth [klɒθ] *n* (*material*) Tuch *nt*; (*for cleaning*) Lappen *m*

clothe [kləʊð] *vt* kleiden; **clothes** [kləʊðz] *npl* Kleider *pl*, Kleidung *f*; **clothes line** *n* Wäscheleine *f*; **clothes peg**, **clothespin** (*US*) *n* Wäscheklammer *f*; **clothing** ['kləʊðɪŋ] *n* Kleidung *f*

clotted ['klɒtɪd] *adj*: **~ cream** dicke Sahne (*aus erhitzter Milch*)

cloud [klaʊd] *n* Wolke *f*; **cloudy** *adj* (*sky*) bewölkt; (*liquid*) trüb

clove [kləʊv] *n* Gewürznelke *f*; **~ of garlic** Knoblauchzehe *f*

clover ['kləʊvə*] *n* Klee *m*; **cloverleaf** (*pl* **-leaves**) *n* Kleeblatt *nt*

clown [klaʊn] *n* Clown *m*

club [klʌb] *n* (*weapon*) Knüppel *m*; (*society*) Klub *m*, Verein *m*; (*nightclub*) Disko *f*; (*golf club*) Golfschläger *m*; **~s** (*Cards*) Kreuz *nt*; **clubbing** *n*: **to go ~** in die Disko gehen; **club class** *n* (*Aviat*) Businessclass *f*

clue [kluː] *n* Anhaltspunkt *m*, Hinweis *m*; **he hasn't a ~** er hat keine Ahnung

clumsy ['klʌmzɪ] *adj* unbeholfen, ungeschickt

clung [klʌŋ] *pt*, *pp of* **cling**

clutch [klʌtʃ] *n* (*Auto*) Kupplung *f* ▷ *vt* umklammern; (*book etc*) an sich *akk* klammern

cm *abbr* = **centimetre(s)** cm

c/o *abbr* = **care of** bei

Co *abbr* = **company** Co

coach [kəʊtʃ] *n* (*Brit: bus*) Reisebus *m*; (*Rail*) (Personen)wagen *m*; (*Sport: trainer*) Trainer(in) *m(f)* ▷ *vt* Nachhilfeunterricht geben +*dat*; (*Sport*) trainieren; **coach (class)** *n* (*Aviat*) Economyclass *f*; **coach driver** *n* Busfahrer(in) *m(f)*; **coach party** *n* Reisegruppe *f* (*Bus*) ; **coach station** *n* Busbahnhof *m*; **coach trip** *n* Busfahrt *f*; (*tour*) Busreise *f*

coal [kəʊl] *n* Kohle *f*

coalition [kəʊə'lɪʃən] *n* (*Pol*) Koalition *f*

coalmine ['kəʊlmaɪn] *n* Kohlenbergwerk *nt*; **coalminer** *n* Bergarbeiter *m*

coast [kəʊst] *n* Küste *f*; **coastguard** *n* Küstenwache *f*; **coastline** *n* Küste *f*

coat [kəʊt] *n* Mantel *m*; (*jacket*) Jacke *f*; (*on animals*) Fell *nt*, Pelz *m*; (*of paint*) Schicht *f*; **~ of arms** Wappen *nt*; **coathanger** *n* Kleiderbügel *m*; **coating** *n* Überzug *m*; (*layer*) Schicht *f*

cobble(stone)s ['kɒbl(stəʊn)z] *npl* Kopfsteine *pl*; (*surface*) Kopfsteinpflaster *nt*

cobweb ['kɒbweb] *n* Spinnennetz *nt*

cocaine [kə'keɪn] *n* Kokain *nt*

cock [kɒk] *n* Hahn *m*; (*vulg: penis*) Schwanz *m*; **cock up** *vt* (*Brit fam*) vermasseln, versauen; **cockerel** ['kɒkərəl] *n* junger Hahn

cockle ['kɒkl] *n* Herzmuschel *f*

cockpit ['kɒkpɪt] *n* (*in plane, racing car*) Cockpit *nt*; **cockroach** ['kɒkrəʊtʃ] *n* Kakerlake *f*; **cocktail**

['kɒkteɪl] n Cocktail m; **cock-up** n (Brit fam) **to make a ~ of sth** bei etw Mist bauen; **cocky** ['kɒkɪ] adj großspurig, von sich selbst überzeugt
cocoa ['kəʊkəʊ] n Kakao m
coconut ['kəʊkənʌt] n Kokos- nuss f
cod [kɒd] n Kabeljau m
COD abbr = **cash on delivery** per Nachnahme
code [kəʊd] n Kode m
coeducational [kəʊedjʊ'keɪʃənl] adj (school) gemischt
coffee ['kɒfɪ] n Kaffee m; **coffee bar** nt; **coffee break** n Kaffeepause f; **coffee maker** n Kaffeemaschine f; **coffee pot** n Kaffeekanne f; **coffee shop** n Café nt; **coffee table** n Couchtisch m
coffin ['kɒfɪn] n Sarg m
coil [kɔɪl] n Rolle f; (Elec) Spule f; (Med) Spirale f
coin [kɔɪn] n Münze f
coincide [kəʊɪn'saɪd] vi (happen together) zusammenfallen (with mit); **coincidence** [kəʊ'ɪnsɪdəns] n Zufall m
coke [kəʊk] n Koks m; **Coke®** Cola f
cola ['kəʊlə] n Cola f
cold [kəʊld] adj kalt; **I'm ~** mir ist kalt, ich friere ▷ n Kälte f; (illness) Erkältung f, Schnupfen m; **to catch a ~** sich erkälten; **cold box** n Kühlbox f; **cold sore** n Herpes m; **cold turkey** n (fam) Totalentzug m; (symptoms) Entzugserscheinungen pl
coleslaw ['kəʊlslɔː] n Krautsalat m
collaborate [kə'læbəreɪt] vi zusammenarbeiten (with mit); **collaboration** [kəlæbə'reɪʃən] n Zusammenarbeit f; (of one party) Mitarbeit f

collapse [kə'læps] vi zusam- menbrechen; (building etc) einstürzen ▷ n Zusammenbruch m; (of building) Einsturz m; **collapsible** [kə'læpsəbl] adj zusammenklappbar
collar ['kɒlə°] n Kragen m; (for dog, cat) Halsband nt; **collarbone** n Schlüsselbein nt
colleague ['kɒliːg] n Kollege m, Kollegin f
collect [kə'lekt] vt sammeln; (fetch) abholen ▷ vi sich sammeln; **collect call** n (US) R-Gespräch nt; **collected** adj (works) gesammelt; (person) gefasst; **collector** n Sammler(in) m(f); **collection** [kə'lekʃən] n Sammlung f; (Rel) Kollekte f; (from postbox) Leerung f
college ['kɒlɪdʒ] n (residential) College nt; (specialist) Fachhochschule f; (vocational) Berufsschule f; (US: university) Universität f; **to go to ~** (US) studieren
collide [kə'laɪd] vi zusam- menstoßen; **collision** [kə'lɪʒən] n Zusammenstoß m
colloquial [kə'ləʊkwɪəl] adj umgangssprachlich
Cologne [kə'ləʊn] n Köln nt
colon ['kəʊlən] n (punctuation mark) Doppelpunkt m
colonial [kə'ləʊnɪəl] adj Kolo- nial-; **colonize** ['kɒlənaɪz] vt kolonisieren; **colony** ['kɒlənɪ] n Kolonie f
color n (US), **colour** ['kʌlə°] n Farbe f; (of skin) Hautfarbe f ▷ vt anmalen; (bias) färben; **colour-blind** adj farbenblind; **coloured** adj farbig; (biased) gefärbt; **colour film** n Farbfilm m; **colourful** adj (lit, fig) bunt; (life, past) bewegt; **colouring** n (in food etc) Farbstoff m; (complexion) Gesichtsfarbe f; **colourless** adj

(lit, fig) farblos; **colour photo(graph)** n Farbfoto nt; **colour television** n Farbfernsehen nt

column ['kɒləm] n Säule f; (of print) Spalte f

comb [kəʊm] n Kamm m ▷ vt kämmen; **to ~ one's hair** sich kämmen

combination [kɒmbɪ'neɪʃən] n Kombination f; (mixture) Mischung f (of aus); **combine** [kəm'baɪn] vt verbinden (with mit); (two things) kombinieren

come [kʌm] (**came**, **come**) vi kommen; (arrive) ankommen; (on list, in order) stehen; (with adjective: become) werden; **~ and see us** besuchen Sie uns mal; **coming** ich komm ja schon!; **to ~ first/second** erster/zweiter werden; **to ~ true** wahr werden; **to ~ loose** sich lockern; **the years to ~** die kommenden Jahre; **there's one more to ~** es kommt noch eins/noch einer; **how ~ ...?** (fam) wie kommt es, dass ...?; **~ to think of it** (fam) wo es mir gerade einfällt; **come across** vt (find) stoßen auf +akk; **come back** vi zurückkommen; **I'll ~ to that** ich komme darauf zurück; **come down** vi herunterkommen; (rain, snow, price) fallen; **come from** vt (result) kommen von; **where do you ~?** wo kommen Sie her?; **I ~ London** ich komme aus London; **come in** vi hereinkommen; (arrive) ankommen; (in race) **to ~ fourth** Vierter werden; **come off** vi (button, handle etc) abgehen; (succeed) gelingen; **to ~ well/badly** gut/schlecht wegkommen; **come on** vi (progress) vorankommen; **~!** komm!; (hurry) beeil dich!; (encouraging) los!; **come out** vi

herauskommen; (photo) was werden; (homosexual) sich outen; **come round** vi (visit) vorbeikommen; (regain consciousness) wieder zu sich kommen; **come to** vi (regain consciousness) wieder zu sich kommen ▷ vt (sum) sich belaufen auf +akk; **when it comes to ...** wenn es um ... geht; **come up** vi hochkommen; (sun, moon) aufgehen; **to ~ (for discussion)** zur Sprache kommen; **come up to** vt (approach) zukommen auf +akk; (water) reichen bis zu; (expectations) entsprechen +dat; **come up with** vt (idea) haben; (solution, answer) kommen auf +akk; **to ~ a suggestion** einen Vorschlag machen

comedian [kə'miːdɪən] n Komiker(in) m(f)

comedown ['kʌmdaʊn] n Abstieg m

comedy ['kɒmədɪ] n Komödie f, Comedy f

comfort ['kʌmfət] n Komfort m; (consolation) Trost m ▷ vt trösten; **comfortable** adj bequem; (income) ausreichend; (temperature, life) angenehm; **comforting** adj tröstlich

comic ['kɒmɪk] n (magazine) Comic(heft) nt; (comedian) Komiker(in) m(f) ▷ adj komisch

coming ['kʌmɪŋ] adj kommend; (event) bevorstehend

comma ['kɒmə] n Komma nt

command [kə'maːnd] n Befehl m; (control) Führung f; (Mil) Kommando nt ▷ vt befehlen +dat

commemorate [kə'meməreɪt] vt gedenken +gen; **commemoration** [kəmemə'reɪʃən] n: **in ~ of** in Gedenken an +akk

comment ['kɒment] n (remark)

Bemerkung *f*; (*note*) Anmerkung *f*; (*official*) Kommentar *m* (on zu); **no ~** kein Kommentar ▷ *vi* sich äußern (on zu); **commentary** ['kɒməntrɪ] *n* Kommentar *m* (on zu); (*TV*, *Sport*) Livereportage *f*; **commentator** ['kɒmənteɪtə°] *n* Kommentator(in) *m(f)*; (*TV*, *Sport*) Reporter(in) *m(f)*

commerce ['kɒmɜːs] *n* Handel *m*; **commercial** [kə'mɜːʃəl] *adj* kommerziell; (*training*) kaufmännisch; **~ break** Werbepause *f*; **~ vehicle** Lieferwagen *m* ▷ *n* (*TV*) Werbespot *m*

commission [kə'mɪʃən] *n* Auftrag *m*; (*fee*) Provision *f*; (*reporting body*) Kommission *f* ▷ *vt* beauftragen

commit [kə'mɪt] *vt* (*crime*) begehen ▷ *vr*: **to ~ oneself** (*undertake*) sich verpflichten (to zu); **commitment** *n* Verpflichtung *f*; (*Pol*) Engagement *nt*

committee [kə'mɪtɪ] *n* Ausschuss *m*, Komitee *nt*

commodity [kə'mɒdɪtɪ] *n* Ware *f*

common ['kɒmən] *adj* (*experience*) allgemein, alltäglich; (*shared*) gemeinsam; (*widespread, frequent*) häufig; (*pej*) gewöhnlich, ordinär; **to have sth in ~** etw gemein haben ▷ *n* (*Brit: land*) Gemeindewiese *f*; **commonly** *adv* häufig, allgemein; **commonplace** *adj* alltäglich; (*pej*) banal; **commonroom** *n* Gemeinschaftsraum *m*; **Commons** *n* (*Brit Pol*) **the** (**House of**) **~** das Unterhaus; **common sense** *n* gesunder Menschenverstand; **Commonwealth** *n* Commonwealth *nt*; **~ of Independent**

States Gemeinschaft *f* Unabhängiger Staaten

communal ['kɒmjʊnl] *adj* gemeinsam; (*of a community*) Gemeinschafts-, Gemeinde-

communicate [kə'mjuːnɪkeɪt] *vi* kommunizieren (with mit); **communication** [kəmjuːnɪ'keɪʃən] *n* Kommunikation *f*, Verständigung *f*; **communications satellite** *n* Nachrichtensatellit *m*; **communications technology** *n* Nachrichtentechnik *f*; **communicative** *adj* gesprächig

communion [kə'mjuːnɪən] *n*: (**Holy**) **Communion** Heiliges Abendmahl; (*Catholic*) Kommunion *f*

communism ['kɒmjʊnɪzəm] *n* Kommunismus *m*; **communist** ['kɒmjʊnɪst] *adj* kommunistisch ▷ *n* Kommunist(in) *m(f)*

community [kə'mjuːnɪtɪ] *n* Gemeinschaft *f*; **community centre** *n* Gemeindezentrum *nt*; **community service** *n* (*Jur*) Sozialdienst *m*

commutation ticket [kɒmjʊ'teɪʃəntɪkɪt] *n* (*US*) Zeitkarte *f*; **commute** [kə'mjuːt] *vi* pendeln; **commuter** *n* Pendler(in) *m(f)*

compact [kəm'pækt] *adj* kompakt ▷ ['kɒmpækt] *n* (*for make-up*) Puderdose *f*; (*US: car*) ≈ Mittelklassewagen *m*; **compact camera** *n* Kompaktkamera *f*; **compact disc** *n* Compact Disc *f*, CD *f*

companion [kəm'pænɪən] *n* Begleiter(in) *m(f)*

company ['kʌmpənɪ] *n* Gesellschaft *f*; (*Comm*) Firma *f*; **to keep sb ~** jdm Gesellschaft leisten; **company car** *n* Firmenauto *nt*

comparable ['kɒmpərəbl] *adj*
vergleichbar (*with*, *to* mit)

comparative [kəm'pærətɪv] *adj*
relativ ▷ *n* (*Ling*) Komparativ *m*;
comparatively *adv*
verhältnismäßig

compare [kəm'pεə°] *vt* vergleichen (*with*, *to* mit); **~d with**
o **to** im Vergleich zu; **beyond**
~ unvergleichlich; **comparison**
[kəm'pærɪsn] *n* Vergleich *m*; **in**
~ with im Vergleich mit (*o* zu)

compartment [kəm'pɑːtmənt]
n (*Rail*) Abteil *nt*; (*in desk etc*) Fach
nt

compass ['kʌmpəs] *n* Kompass
m; **~es** *pl* Zirkel *m*

compassion [kəm'pæʃən] *n*
Mitgefühl *nt*

compatible [kəm'pætɪbl] *adj*
vereinbar (*with* mit); (*Inform*)
kompatibel; **we're not ~** wir
passen nicht zueinander

compensate ['kɒmpenseɪt] *vt*
(*person*) entschädigen (*for* für) ▷ *vi*:
to ~ for sth Ersatz für etw leisten;
(*make up for*) etw ausgleichen;
compensation [kɒmpen'seɪʃən]
n Entschädigung *f*; (*money*)
Schadenersatz *m*; (*Jur*) Abfindung *f*

compete [kəm'piːt] *vi* konkur-
rieren (*for* um); (*Sport*) kämpfen (*for*
um); (*take part*) teilnehmen (*in* an
+*dat*)

competence ['kɒmpɪtəns] *n*
Fähigkeit *f*; (*Jur*) Zuständigkeit *f*;
competent *adj* fähig; (*Jur*)
zuständig

competition [kɒmpɪ'tɪʃən] *n*
(*contest*) Wettbewerb *m*; (*Comm*)
Konkurrenz *f* (*for* um);
competitive [kəm'petɪtɪv] *adj*
(*firm*, *price*, *product*)
konkurrenzfähig; **competitor**
[kəm'petɪtə°] *n* (*Comm*)
Konkurrent(in) *m(f)*; (*Sport*)
Teilnehmer(in) *m(f)*

complain [kəm'pleɪn] *vi* klagen;
(*formally*) sich beschweren (*about*
über +*akk*); **complaint** *n* Klage *f*;
Beanstandung *f*; (*formal*)
Beschwerde *f*; (*Med*) Leiden *nt*

complement *vt* ergänzen

complete [kəm'pliːt] *adj* vollständig; (*finished*) fertig; (*failure*,
disaster) total; (*happiness*)
vollkommen; **are we ~?** sind wir
vollzählig? ▷ *vt* vervollständigen;
(*finish*) beenden; (*form*) ausfüllen;
completely *adv* völlig; **not ~ ...**
nicht ganz ...

complex ['kɒmpleks] *adj* komplex; (*task*, *theory etc*) kompliziert
▷ *n* Komplex *m*

complexion [kəm'plekʃən] *n*
Gesichtsfarbe *f*, Teint *m*

complicated ['kɒmplɪkeɪtɪd] *adj*
kompliziert; **complication**
['kɒmplɪkeɪʃən] *n* Komplikation
f

compliment ['kɒmplɪmənt] *n*
Kompliment *nt*; **complimentary**
[kɒmplɪ'mentərɪ] *adj* lobend;
(*free of charge*) Gratis-; **~ ticket**
Freikarte *f*

comply [kəm'plaɪ] *vi*: **to ~ with**
the regulations den Vorschriften
entsprechen

component [kəm'pəʊnənt] *n*
Bestandteil *m*

compose [kəm'pəʊz] *vt* (*music*)
komponieren; **to ~ oneself** sich
zusammennehmen; **composed**
adj gefasst; **to be ~ of** bestehen
aus; **composer** *n* Komponist(in)
m(f); **composition** [kɒmpə'zɪʃən]
n (*of a group*) Zusammensetzung *f*;
(*Mus*) Komposition *f*

comprehend [kɒmprɪ'hend] *vt*
verstehen; **comprehension**
[kɒmprɪ'henʃən] *n* Verständnis *nt*

comprehensive
[kɒmprɪ'hensɪv] *adj* umfassend;
~ school Gesamtschule *f*

compress [kəm'pres] *vt* komprimieren

comprise [kəm'praɪz] *vt* umfassen, bestehen aus

compromise ['kɒmprəmaɪz] *n* Kompromiss *m* ▷ *vi* einen Kompromiss schließen

compulsory [kəm'pʌlsərɪ] *adj* obligatorisch; **~ subject** Pflichtfach *nt*

computer [kəm'pju:tə⁎] *n* Computer *m*; **computer-aided** *adj* computergestützt; **computer-controlled** *adj* rechnergesteuert; **computer game** *n* Computerspiel *nt*; **computer-literate** *adj*: **to be ~** mit dem Computer umgehen können; **computer scientist** *n* Informatiker(in) *m(f)*; **computing** *n* (*subject*) Informatik *f*

con [kɒn] (*fam*) *n* Schwindel *m* ▷ *vt* betrügen (*out of* um)

conceal [kən'si:l] *vt* verbergen (*from* vor +*dat*)

conceivable [kən'si:vəbl] *adj* denkbar, vorstellbar; **conceive** [kən'si:v] *vt* (*imagine*) sich vorstellen; (*child*) empfangen

concentrate ['kɒnsəntreɪt] *vi* sich konzentrieren (*on* auf +*akk*); **concentration** [kɒnsən'treɪʃən] *n* Konzentration *f*

concept ['kɒnsept] *n* Begriff *m*

concern [kən'sɜ:n] *n* (*affair*) Angelegenheit *f*; (*worry*) Sorge *f*; (*Comm: firm*) Unternehmen *nt*; **it's not my ~** das geht mich nichts an; **there's no cause for ~** kein Grund zur Beunruhigung ▷ *vt* (*affect*) angehen; (*have connection with*) betreffen; (*be about*) handeln von; **those ~ed** die Betroffenen; **as far as I'm ~ed** was mich betrifft; **concerned** *adj* (*anxious*) besorgt; **concerning** *prep* bezüglich, hinsichtlich +*gen*

concert ['kɒnsət] *n* Konzert *nt*; **~ hall** Konzertsaal *m*

concession [kən'seʃən] *n* Zugeständnis *nt*; (*reduction*) Ermäßigung *f*

concise [kən'saɪs] *adj* knapp gefasst, prägnant

conclude [kən'klu:d] *vt* (*end*) beenden, (ab)schließen; (*infer*) folgern (*from* aus); **to ~ that ...** zu dem Schluss kommen, dass ...; **conclusion** [kən'klu:ʒən] *n* Schluss *m*, Schlussfolgerung *f*

concrete ['kɒŋkri:t] *n* Beton *m* ▷ *adj* konkret

concussion [kɒn'kʌʃən] *n* Gehirnerschütterung *f*

condemn [kən'dem] *vt* verdammen; (*esp Jur*) verurteilen

condensed milk *n* Kondensmilch *f*, Dosenmilch *f*

condition [kən'dɪʃən] *n* (*state*) Zustand *m*; (*requirement*) Bedingung *f*; **on ~ that ...** unter der Bedingung, dass ...; **~s** *pl* (*circumstances, weather*) Verhältnisse *pl*; **conditional** *adj* bedingt; (*Ling*) Konditional-; **conditioner** *n* Weichspüler *m*; (*for hair*) Pflegespülung *f*

condo ['kɒndəʊ] (*pl* -s) *n see* condominium

condolences [kən'dəʊlənsɪz] *npl* Beileid *nt*

condom ['kɒndəm] *n* Kondom *nt*

condominium [kɒndə'mɪnɪəm] *n* (*US: apartment*) Eigentumswohnung *f*

conduct ['kɒndʌkt] *n* (*of behaviour*) Verhalten *nt* ▷ [kən'dʌkt] *vt* führen, leiten; (*orchestra*) dirigieren; **conductor** [kən'dʌktə⁎] *n* (*of orchestra*) Dirigent(in) *m(f)*; (*Brit: in bus*) Schaffner(in) *m(f)*; (*US: on train*) Zugführer(in) *m(f)*

cone [kəʊn] n Kegel m; (for ice cream) Waffeltüte f; (fir cone) (Tannen)zapfen m

conference ['kɒnfərəns] n Konferenz f

confess [kən'fes] vt, vi: **to ~ that ...** gestehen, dass ...; **confession** [kən'feʃən] n Geständnis nt; (Rel) Beichte f

confetti [kən'fetɪ] n Konfetti nt

confidence ['kɒnfɪdəns] n Vertrauen nt (in zu); (assurance) Selbstvertrauen nt; **confident** adj (sure) zuversichtlich (that ... dass ...), überzeugt (of von); (self-assured) selbstsicher; **confidential** [kɒnfɪ'denʃəl] adj vertraulich

confine [kən'faɪn] vt beschränken (to auf +akk)

confirm [kən'fɜːm] vt bestätigen; **confirmation** [kɒnfə'meɪʃən] n Bestätigung f; (Rel) Konfirmation f; **confirmed** adj überzeugt; (bachelor) eingefleischt

confiscate ['kɒnfɪskeɪt] vt beschlagnahmen, konfiszieren

conflict ['kɒnflɪkt] n Konflikt m

confuse [kən'fjuːz] vt verwirren; (sth with sth) verwechseln (with mit); (several things) durcheinanderbringen; **confused** adj (person) konfus, verwirrt; (account) verworren; **confusing** adj verwirrend; **confusion** [kən'fjuːʒən] n Verwirrung f; (of two things) Verwechslung f; (muddle) Chaos nt

congested [kən'dʒestɪd] adj verstopft; (overcrowded) überfüllt; **congestion** [kən'dʒestʃən] n Stau m

congratulate [kən'grætjʊleɪt] vt gratulieren (on zu); **congratulations** [kəngrætjʊ'leɪʃənz] npl Glück-

wünsche pl; **~!** gratuliere!, herzlichen Glückwunsch!

congregation [kɒngrɪ'geɪʃən] n (Rel) Gemeinde f

congress ['kɒngres] n Kongress m; (US) **Congress** der Kongress; **congressman** (pl **-men**), **congresswoman** (pl **-women**) n (US) Mitglied nt des Repräsentantenhauses

conifer ['kɒnɪfə°] n Nadelbaum m

conjunction [kən'dʒʌŋkʃən] n (Ling) Konjunktion f; **in ~ with** in Verbindung mit

conk out [kɒŋk 'aʊt] vi (fam: appliance, car) den Geist aufgeben, streiken; (person: die) ins Gras beißen

connect [kə'nekt] vt verbinden (with, to mit); (Elec, Tech: appliance etc) anschließen (to an +akk) ▷ vi (train, plane) Anschluss haben (with an +akk); **~ing flight** Anschlussflug m; **~ing train** Anschlusszug m; **connection** [kə'nekʃən] n Verbindung f; (link) Zusammenhang m; (for train, plane, electrical appliance) Anschluss m (with, to an +akk); (business etc) Beziehung f; **in ~ with** in Zusammenhang mit; **bad ~** (Tel) schlechte Verbindung; (Elec) Wackelkontakt m; **connector** n (Inform: computer) Stecker m

conscience ['kɒnʃəns] n Gewissen nt; **conscientious** [kɒnʃɪ'enʃəs] adj gewissenhaft

conscious ['kɒnʃəs] adj (act) bewusst; (Med) bei Bewusstsein; **to be ~** bei Bewusstsein sein; **consciousness** n Bewusstsein nt

consecutive [kən'sekjʊtɪv] adj aufeinanderfolgend

consent [kən'sent] n Zustimmung f ▷ vi zustimmen (to dat)

consequence ['kɒnsɪkwəns] n
Folge f, Konsequenz f;
consequently ['kɒnsɪkwəntlɪ]
adv folglich, deshalb

conservation [kɒnsə'veɪʃən] n
Erhaltung f; (nature conservation)
Naturschutz m; **conservation
area** n Naturschutzgebiet nt

conservative, (Pol) **Conservative**
[kən'sɜːvətɪv] adj konservativ

conservatory [kən'sɜːvətrɪ] n
(greenhouse) Gewächshaus nt;
(room) Wintergarten m

consider [kən'sɪdə*] vt (reflect
on) nachdenken über, sich
überlegen; (take into account) in
Betracht ziehen; (regard) halten
für; **he is ~ed (to be) ...** er gilt als
...; **considerable** [kən'sɪdərəbl]
adj beträchtlich; **considerate**
[kən'sɪdərɪt] adj aufmerksam,
rücksichtsvoll; **consideration**
[kənsɪdə'reɪʃən] n (thoughtfulness)
Rücksicht f; (thought) Überlegung
f; **to take sth into** ~ etw in
Betracht ziehen; **considering**
[kən'sɪdərɪŋ] prep in Anbetracht
+gen ▷ conj da

consist [kən'sɪst] vi: **to ~ of ...**
bestehen aus ...

consistent [kən'sɪstənt] adj
(behaviour, process etc)
konsequent; (statements)
übereinstimmend; (argument)
folgerichtig; (performance, results)
beständig

consolation [kɒnsə'leɪʃən] n
Trost m; **console** [kən'səʊl] vt
trösten

consolidate [kən'sɒlɪdeɪt] vt
festigen

consonant ['kɒnsənənt] n
Konsonant m

conspicuous [kən'spɪkjʊəs] adj
auffällig, auffallend

conspiracy [kən'spɪrəsɪ] n
Komplott nt; **conspire**

[kən'spaɪə*] vi sich verschwören
(against gegen)

constable ['kʌnstəbl] n (Brit)
Polizist(in) m(f)

Constance ['kɒnstəns] n Kon-
stanz nt; **Lake ~** der Bodensee

constant ['kɒnstənt] adj (continual) ständig, dauernd;
(unchanging) gleichbleibend; **constantly** adv
dauernd

consternation [kɒnstə'neɪʃən]
n (dismay) Bestürzung f

constituency [kən'stɪtjʊənsɪ]
n Wahlkreis m

constitution [kɒnstɪ'tjuːʃən] n
Verfassung f; (of person)
Konstitution f

construct [kən'strʌkt] vt bauen;
construction [kən'strʌkʃən] n
(process, result) Bau m; (method)
Bauweise f; **under ~** im Bau
befindlich; **construction site** n
Baustelle f; **construction worker**
n Bauarbeiter(in) m(f)

consulate ['kɒnsjʊlət] n Konsulat nt

consult [kən'sʌlt] vt um Rat
fragen; (doctor) konsultieren;
(book) nachschlagen in +dat;
consultant n (Med) Facharzt m,
Fachärztin f; **consultation**
[kɒnsəl'teɪʃən] n Beratung f;
(Med) Konsultation f; ~ **room**
Besprechungsraum;
Sprechzimmer

consume [kən'sjuːm] vt verbrauchen; (food) konsumieren;
consumer n Verbraucher(in)
m(f); **consumer-friendly** adj
verbraucherfreundlich

contact ['kɒntækt] n (touch)
Berührung f; (communication)
Kontakt m; (person) Kontaktperson
f; **to be/keep in ~ (with sb)** (mit
jdm) in Kontakt sein/bleiben ▷ vt
sich in Verbindung setzen mit;

contact lenses *npl* Kontaktlinsen *pl*

contagious [kən'teɪdʒəs] *adj* ansteckend

contain [kən'teɪn] *vt* enthalten; **container** *n* Behälter *m*; (*for transport*) Container *m*

contaminate [kən'tæmɪneɪt] *vt* verunreinigen; (*chemically*) verseuchen; **~d by radiation** strahlenverseucht, verstrahlt; **contamination** [kəntæmɪ'neɪʃən] *n* Verunreinigung *f*; (*by radiation*) Verseuchung *f*

contemporary [kən'tempərərɪ] *adj* zeitgenössisch

contempt [kən'tempt] *n* Verachtung *f*; **contemptuous** *adj* verächtlich; **to be ~** voller Verachtung sein (*of* für)

content [kən'tent] *adj* zufrieden

content(s) ['kɒntent(s)] *n pl* Inhalt *m*

contest ['kɒntest] *n* (Wett)kampf *m* (*for* um); (*competition*) Wettbewerb *m* ▷ [kən'test] *vt* kämpfen um +*akk*; (*dispute*) bestreiten; **contestant** [kən'testənt] *n* Teilnehmer(in) *m(f)*

context ['kɒntekst] *n* Zusammenhang *m*; **out of ~** aus dem Zusammenhang gerissen

continent ['kɒntɪnənt] *n* Kontinent *m*, Festland *nt*; **the Continent** (*Brit*) das europäische Festland, der Kontinent; **continental** [kɒntɪ'nentl] *adj* kontinental; **~ breakfast** kleines Frühstück mit Brötchen und Marmelade, Kaffee oder Tee

continual [kən'tɪnjʊəl] *adj* (*endless*) ununterbrochen; (*constant*) dauernd, ständig; **continually** *adv* dauernd; (*again and again*) immer wieder; **continuation** [kəntɪnjʊ'eɪʃən] *n*

Fortsetzung *f*; **continue** [kən'tɪnjuː] *vi* weitermachen (*with* mit); (*esp talking*) fortfahren (*with* mit); (*travelling*) weiterfahren; (*state, conditions*) fortdauern, anhalten ▷ *vt* fortsetzen; **to be ~d** Fortsetzung folgt; **continuous** [kən'tɪnjʊəs] *adj* (*endless*) ununterbrochen; (*constant*) ständig

contraceptive [kɒntrə'septɪv] *n* Verhütungsmittel *nt*

contract ['kɒntrækt] *n* Vertrag *m*

contradict [kɒntrə'dɪkt] *vt* widersprechen +*dat*; **contradiction** [kɒntrə'dɪkʃən] *n* Widerspruch *m*

contrary ['kɒntrərɪ] *n* Gegenteil *nt*; **on the ~** im Gegenteil ▷ *adj*: **~ to** entgegen +*dat*

contrast ['kɒntrɑːst] *n* Kontrast *m*, Gegensatz *m*; **in ~ to** im Gegensatz zu ▷ [kən'trɑːst] *vt* entgegensetzen

contribute [kən'trɪbjuːt] *vt, vi* beitragen (*to* zu); (*money*) spenden (*to* für); **contribution** [kɒntrɪ'bjuːt] *n* Beitrag *m*

control [kən'trəʊl] *vt* (*master*) beherrschen; (*temper etc*) im Griff haben; (*esp Tech*) steuern; **to ~ oneself** sich beherrschen ▷ *n* Kontrolle *f*; (*mastery*) Beherrschung *f*; (*esp Tech*) Steuerung *f*; **~s** *pl* (*knobs, switches etc*) Bedienungselemente *pl*; (*collectively*) Steuerung *f*; **to be out of ~** außer Kontrolle sein; **control knob** *n* Bedienungsknopf *m*; **control panel** *n* Schalttafel *f*

controversial [kɒntrə'vɜːʃəl] *adj* umstritten

convalesce [kɒnvə'les] *vi* gesund werden; **convalescence** *n* Genesung *f*

convenience [kən'viːnɪəns] *n* (*quality, thing*) Annehmlichkeit *f*; **at**

your ~ wann es Ihnen passt; **with all modern ~s** mit allem Komfort; **convenience food** n Fertiggericht nt; **convenient** adj günstig, passend

convent ['kɒnvənt] n Kloster nt

convention [kən'venʃən] n (custom) Konvention f; (meeting) Konferenz f; **the Geneva Convention** die Genfer Konvention; **conventional** adj herkömmlich, konventionell

conversation [kɒnvə'seɪʃən] n Gespräch nt, Unterhaltung f

conversion [kən'vɜːʃən] n Umwandlung f (into in +akk); (of building) Umbau m (into zu); (calculation) Umrechnung f; **conversion table** n Umrechnungstabelle f; **convert** [kən'vɜːt] vt umwandeln; (person) bekehren; (Inform) konvertieren; **to ~ into euros** in Euro umrechnen; **convertible** n (Auto) Kabrio nt ▷ adj umwandelbar

convey [kən'veɪ] vt (carry) befördern; (feelings) vermitteln; **conveyor belt** n Förderband nt, Fließband nt

convict [kən'vɪkt] vt verurteilen (of wegen) ▷ ['kɒnvɪkt] n Strafgefangene(r) mf; **conviction** n (Jur) Verurteilung f; (strong belief) Überzeugung f

convince [kən'vɪns] vt überzeugen (of von); **convincing** adj überzeugend

cook [kʊk] vt, vi kochen ▷ n Koch m, Köchin f; **cookbook** n Kochbuch nt; **cooker** n Herd m; **cookery** n Kochkunst f; **~ book** Kochbuch nt; **cookie** n (US) Keks m; **cooking** n Kochen nt; (style of cooking) Küche f

cool [kuːl] adj kühl, gelassen; (fam: brilliant) cool, stark ▷ vt, vi (ab)kühlen; **~ it** reg dich ab! ▷ n:

to keep/lose one's ~ (fam) ruhig bleiben/durchdrehen; **cool down** vi abkühlen; (calm down) sich beruhigen

cooperate [kəʊ'ɒpəreɪt] vi zusammenarbeiten, kooperieren; **cooperation** [kəʊɒpə'reɪʃən] n Zusammenarbeit f, Kooperation f; **cooperative** [kəʊ'ɒpərətɪv] adj hilfsbereit ▷ n Genossenschaft f

coordinate [kəʊ'ɔːdɪneɪt] vt koordinieren

cop [kɒp] n (fam: policeman) Bulle m

cope [kəʊp] vi zurechtkommen, fertig werden (with mit)

Copenhagen [kəʊpən'heɪgən] n Kopenhagen nt

copier ['kɒpɪə*] n Kopierer m

copper ['kɒpə*] n Kupfer nt; (Brit fam: policeman) Bulle m; (fam: coin) Kupfermünze f; **~s** Kleingeld nt

copy ['kɒpɪ] n Kopie f; (of book) Exemplar nt ▷ vt kopieren; (imitate) nachahmen; **copyright** n Urheberrecht nt

coral ['kɒrəl] n Koralle f

cord [kɔːd] n Schnur f; (material) Kordsamt m; **cordless** ['kɔːdlɪs] adj (phone) schnurlos

core [kɔː*] n (a. fig) Kern m; (of apple, pear) Kerngehäuse nt; **core business** n Kerngeschäft nt

cork [kɔːk] n (material) Kork m; (stopper) Korken m; **corkscrew** ['kɔːkskruː] n Korkenzieher m

corn [kɔːn] n Getreide nt, Korn nt; (US: maize) Mais m; (on foot) Hühnerauge nt; **~ on the cob** (gekochter) Maiskolben; **corned beef** n Cornedbeef nt

corner ['kɔːnə*] n Ecke f; (on road) Kurve f; (Sport) Eckstoß m ▷ vt in die Enge treiben; **corner shop** n Laden m an der Ecke

cornflakes ['kɔːfleɪks] npl Cornflakes pl

Cornish ['kɔːnɪʃ] adj kornisch;
~ **pasty** mit Fleisch und Kartoffeln
gefüllte Pastete; **Cornwall**
['kɔːnwəl] n Cornwall nt
coronation [kɒrə'neɪʃən] n
Krönung f
corporation [kɔːpə'reɪʃən] n
(US Comm) Aktiengesellschaft f
corpse [kɔːps] n Leiche f
correct [kə'rekt] adj (accurate)
richtig; (proper) korrekt ▷ vt
korrigieren, verbessern;
correction n (esp written)
Korrektur f
correspond [kɒrɪ'spɒnd] vi
entsprechen (to dat); (two things)
übereinstimmen; (exchange letters)
korrespondieren; **corresponding**
adj entsprechend
corridor ['kɒrɪdɔː°] n (in building)
Flur m; (in train) Gang m
corrupt [kə'rʌpt] adj korrupt
cosmetic [kɒz'metɪk] adj kos-
metisch; **cosmetics** npl
Kosmetika pl; **cosmetic surgeon**
n Schönheitschirurg(in) m(f);
cosmetic surgery n
Schönheitschirurgie f
cosmopolitan [kɒzmə'pɒlɪtən]
adj international; (attitude)
weltoffen
cost [kɒst] (**cost, cost**) vt kosten
▷ n Kosten pl; **at all ~s, at any**
~ um jeden Preis; ~ **of living**
Lebenshaltungskosten pl; **costly**
adj kostspielig
costume ['kɒstjuːm] n (Theat)
Kostüm nt
cosy ['kəʊzɪ] adj gemütlich
cot [kɒt] n (Brit) Kinderbett nt;
(US) Campingliege f
cottage ['kɒtɪdʒ] n kleines Haus;
(country cottage) Landhäuschen nt;
cottage cheese n Hüttenkäse m;
cottage pie n Hackfleisch mit
Kartoffelbrei überbacken
cotton ['kɒtn] n Baumwolle f;

cotton candy n (US) Zuckerwatte
f; **cotton wool** n (Brit) Watte f
couch [kaʊtʃ] n Couch f; (sofa)
Sofa nt; **couchette** [kuː'ʃet] n
Liegewagen(platz) m
cough [kɒf] vi husten ▷ n Husten m; **cough mixture** n
Hustensaft m; **cough sweet** n
Hustenbonbon m
could [kʊd] pt of **can** konnte;
conditional könnte; ~ **you come**
earlier? könntest du/könnten Sie
früher kommen?
couldn't contr of **could not**
council ['kaʊnsl] n (Pol) Rat m;
(local ~) Gemeinderat m; (town ~)
Stadtrat m; **council estate** n
Siedlung f des sozialen
Wohnungsbaus; **council house** n
Sozialwohnung f; **councillor**
['kaʊnsɪlə°] n Gemeinderat m,
Gemeinderätin f; **council tax** n
Gemeindesteuer f
count [kaʊnt] vt, vi zählen;
(include) mitrechnen ▷ n Zählung
f; (noble) Graf m; **count on** vt (rely
on) sich verlassen auf +akk; (expect)
rechnen mit
counter ['kaʊntə°] n (in shop)
Ladentisch m; (in café) Theke f; (in
bank, post office) Schalter m;
counter attack n Gegenangriff m
▷ vi zurückschlagen;
counter-clockwise adv (US)
entgegen dem Uhrzeigersinn
counterpart ['kaʊntəpɒːt] n
Gegenstück nt (of zu)
countess n Gräfin f
countless ['kaʊntlɪs] adj zahl-
los, unzählig
country ['kʌntrɪ] n Land nt; **in**
the ~ auf dem Land(e); **in this**
~ hierzulande; **country cousin** n
(fam) Landei nt; **country dancing**
n Volkstanz m; **country house** n
Landhaus nt; **countryman** n
(compatriot) Landsmann m;

country music n Countrymusic f;
country road n Landstraße f;
countryside n Landschaft f; (*rural area*) Land nt

county ['kaʊntɪ] n (*Brit*) Grafschaft f; (*US*) Verwaltungsbezirk m; **county town** n (*Brit*) ≈ Kreisstadt f

couple ['kʌpl] n Paar nt; **a ~ of** ein paar

coupon ['kuːpɒn] n (*voucher*) Gutschein m

courage ['kʌrɪdʒ] n Mut m; **courageous** [kə'reɪdʒəs] adj mutig

courgette [kʊə'ʒet] n (*Brit*) Zucchini f

courier ['kʊrɪə*] n (*for tourists*) Reiseleiter(in) m(f); (*messenger*) Kurier m

course [kɔːs] n (*of study*) Kurs m; (*for race*) Strecke f; (*Naut, Aviat*) Kurs m; (*at university*) Studiengang m; (*in meal*) Gang m; **of ~** natürlich; **in the ~ of** während

court [kɔːt] n (*Sport*) Platz m; (*Jur*) Gericht nt

courteous ['kɜːtɪəs] adj höflich; **courtesy** ['kɜːtəsɪ] n Höflichkeit f; **~ bus/coach** (gebührenfreier) Zubringerbus

courthouse ['kɔːthaʊs] n (*US*) Gerichtsgebäude nt; **court order** n Gerichtsbeschluss m; **courtroom** n Gerichtssaal m

courtyard ['kɔːtjɑːd] n Hof m

cousin ['kʌzn] n (*male*) Cousin m; (*female*) Cousine f

cover ['kʌvə*] vt bedecken (*in, with* mit); (*distance*) zurücklegen; (*loan, costs*) decken ▷ n (*bed etc*) Decke f; (*of cushion*) Bezug m; (*lid*) Deckel m; (*of book*) Umschlag m; (**insurance**) **~** Versicherungsschutz m; **cover up** vt zudecken; (*error etc*) vertuschen; **coverage** n Berichterstattung f (*of* über +*akk*);

cover charge n Kosten pl für ein Gedeck; **covering** n Decke f; **covering letter** n Begleitbrief m; **cover story** n (*newspaper*) Titelgeschichte f

cow [kaʊ] n Kuh f

coward ['kaʊəd] n Feigling m; **cowardly** adj feig(e)

cowboy ['kaʊbɔɪ] n Cowboy m

coy [kɔɪ] adj gespielt schüchtern, kokett

cozy ['kəʊzɪ] adj (*US*) gemütlich

CPU abbr = **central processing unit** Zentraleinheit f

crab [kræb] n Krabbe f

crabby ['kræbɪ] adj mürrisch, reizbar

crack [kræk] n Riss m; (*in pottery, glass*) Sprung m; (*drug*) Crack nt; **to have a ~ at sth** etw ausprobieren ▷ vi (*pottery, glass*) einen Sprung bekommen; (*wood, ice etc*) einen Riss bekommen; **to get ~ing** (*fam*) loslegen ▷ vt (*bone*) anbrechen; (*nut, code*) knacken

cracker ['krækə*] n (*biscuit*) Kräcker m; (*Christmas ~*) Knallbonbon nt; **crackers** adj (*fam*) verrückt, bekloppt; **he's ~** er hat nicht alle Tassen im Schrank

crackle ['krækl] vi knistern; (*telephone, radio*) knacken; **crackling** n (*Gastr*) Kruste f (*des Schweinebratens*)

cradle ['kreɪdl] n Wiege f

craft [krɑːft] n Handwerk nt; (*art*) Kunsthandwerk nt; (*Naut*) Boot nt; **craftsman** (*pl* **-men**) n Handwerker m; **craftsmanship** n Handwerkskunst f; (*ability*) handwerkliches Können

crafty ['krɑːftɪ] adj schlau

cram [kræm] vt stopfen (*into* in +*akk*); **to be ~med with ...** mit ... vollgestopft sein ▷ vi (*revise for exam*) pauken (*for* für)

cramp [kræmp] n Krampf m

cranberry ['krænbərɪ] *n* Preiselbeere *f*

crane [kreɪn] *n* (*machine*) Kran *m*; (*bird*) Kranich *m*

crap [kræp] *n* (*vulg*) Scheiße *f*; (*rubbish*) Mist *m* ▷ *adj* beschissen, Scheiß-

crash [kræʃ] *vi* einen Unfall haben; (*two vehicles*) zusammenstoßen; (*plane, computer*) abstürzen; (*economy*) zusammenbrechen; **to ~ into sth** gegen etw knallen ▷ *vt* einen Unfall haben mit ▷ *n* (*car*) Unfall *m*; (*train*) Unglück *nt*; (*collision*) Zusammenstoß *m*; (*Aviat, Inform*) Absturz *m*; (*noise*) Krachen *nt*; **crash barrier** *n* Leitplanke *f*; **crash course** *n* Intensivkurs *m*; **crash helmet** *n* Sturzhelm *m*; **crash landing** *n* Bruchlandung *f*

crate [kreɪt] *n* Kiste *f*; (*of beer*) Kasten *m*

crater ['kreɪtə°] *n* Krater *m*

craving [kreɪvɪŋ] *n* starkes Verlangen, Bedürfnis *nt*

crawl [krɔ:l] *vi* kriechen; (*baby*) krabbeln ▷ *n* (*swimming*) Kraul *nt*; **crawler lane** *n* Kriechspur *f*

crayfish ['kreɪfɪʃ] *n* Languste *f*

crayon ['kreɪən] *n* Buntstift *m*

crazy ['kreɪzɪ] *adj* verrückt (*about* nach)

cream [kri:m] *n* (*from milk*) Sahne *f*, Rahm *m*; (*polish, cosmetic*) Creme *f* ▷ *adj* cremefarben; **cream cake** *n* (*small*) Sahnetörtchen *nt*; (*big*) Sahnetorte *f*; **cream cheese** *n* Frischkäse *m*; **creamer** *n* Kaffeeweißer *m*; **cream tea** *n* (*Brit*) Nachmittagstee mit Törtchen, Marmelade und Schlagsahne; **creamy** *adj* sahnig

crease [kri:s] *n* Falte *f* ▷ *vt* falten; (*untidy*) zerknittern

create [kri:'eɪt] *vt* schaffen; (*cause*) verursachen; **creative**

[kri:'eɪtɪv] *adj* schöpferisch; (*person*) kreativ; **creature** ['kri:tʃə°] *n* Geschöpf *nt*

crèche [kreʃ] *n* Kinderkrippe *f*

credible ['kredɪbl] *adj* (*person*) glaubwürdig; **credibility** *n* Glaubwürdigkeit *f*

credit ['kredɪt] *n* (*Fin: amount allowed*) Kredit *m*; (*amount possessed*) Guthaben *nt*; (*recognition*) Anerkennung *f*; **~s** (*of film*) Abspann *m*; **credit card** *n* Kreditkarte *f*

creep [kri:p] (**crept, crept**) *vi* kriechen; **creeps** *n*: **he gives me the ~** er ist mir nicht ganz geheuer; **creepy** ['kri:pɪ] *adj* (*frightening*) gruselig, unheimlich

crept [krept] *pt, pp of* **creep**

cress [kres] *n* Kresse *f*

crest [krest] *n* Kamm *m*; (*coat of arms*) Wappen *nt*

crew [kru:] *n* Besatzung *f*, Mannschaft *f*

crib [krɪb] *n* (*US*) Kinderbett *nt*

cricket ['krɪkɪt] *n* (*insect*) Grille *f*; (*game*) Kricket *nt*

crime [kraɪm] *n* Verbrechen *nt*; **criminal** ['krɪmɪnl] *n* Verbrecher(in) *m(f)* ▷ *adj* kriminell, strafbar

cripple ['krɪpl] *n* Krüppel *m* ▷ *vt* verkrüppeln, lähmen

crisis ['kraɪsɪs] *n* (*pl* **crises**) *n* Krise *f*

crisp [krɪsp] *adj* knusprig; **crisps** *npl* (*Brit*) Chips *pl*; **crispbread** *n* Knäckebrot *nt*

criterion [kraɪ'tɪərɪən] *n* Kriterium *nt*; **critic** ['krɪtɪk] *n* Kritiker(in) *m(f)*; **critical** *adj* kritisch; **critically** *adv* kritisch; **~ ill/injured** schwer krank/verletzt; **criticism** ['krɪtɪsɪzəm] *n* Kritik *f*; **criticize** ['krɪtɪsaɪz] *vt* kritisieren

Croat ['krəʊæt] *n* Kroate *m*,

Kroatin f; **Croatia** [krəʊ'eɪʃə] n
Kroatien nt; **Croatian** [krəʊ'eɪʃən]
adj kroatisch
crockery ['krɒkərɪ] n Geschirr nt
crocodile ['krɒkədaɪl] n Krokodil
nt
crocus ['krəʊkəs] n Krokus m
crop [krɒp] n (harvest) Ernte f;
crops npl Getreide nt; **crop up** vi
auftauchen
croquette [krə'ket] n Krokette f
cross [krɒs] n Kreuz nt; **to mark
sth with a ~** etw ankreuzen ▷ vt
(road, river etc) überqueren; (legs)
übereinanderschlagen; **it ~ed my
mind** es fiel mir ein; **to ~ one's
fingers** die Daumen drücken
▷ adj ärgerlich, böse; **cross out** vt
durchstreichen
crossbar n (of bicycle) Stange f;
(Sport) Querlatte f; **cross-country**
adj: **~ running** Geländelauf m;
~ skiing Langlauf m;
cross-examination n Kreuz-
verhör nt; **cross-eyed** adj: **to be
~** schielen; **crossing** n (crossroads)
(Straßen)kreuzung f; (for
pedestrians) Fußgängerüberweg m;
(on ship) Überfahrt f; **crossroads**
nsing o pl Straßenkreuzung f; **cross
section** n Querschnitt m;
crosswalk n (US)
Fußgängerüberweg m; **crossword
(puzzle)** n Kreuzworträtsel nt
crouch [kraʊtʃ] vi hocken
crouton ['kru:tɒn] n Croûton m
crow [krəʊ] n Krähe f
crowbar [krəʊbɑ:°] n Brecheisen
nt
crowd [kraʊd] n Menge f ▷ vi
sich drängen (into in +akk; round
um); **crowded** adj überfüllt
crown [kraʊn] n Krone f ▷ vt
krönen; (fam) **and to ~ it all ...** und
als Krönung ...
crucial ['kru:ʃəl] adj
entscheidend

crude [kru:d] adj primitiv;
(humour, behaviour) derb, ordinär
▷ n: **~ (oil)** Rohöl nt
cruel ['krʊəl] adj grausam (to zu,
gegen); (unfeeling) gefühllos;
cruelty n Grausamkeit f; **~ to
animals** Tierquälerei f
cruise [kru:z] n Kreuzfahrt f ▷ vi
(ship) kreuzen; (car) mit
Reisegeschwindigkeit fahren;
cruise liner n Kreuzfahrtschiff nt;
cruise missile n
Marschflugkörper m; **cruising
speed** n Reisegeschwindigkeit f
crumb [krʌm] n Krume f
crumble ['krʌmbl] vt, vi
zerbröckeln ▷ n mit Streuseln
überbackenes Kompott
crumpet ['krʌmpɪt] n weiches
Hefegebäck zum Toasten; (fam:
attractive woman) Schnecke f
crumple ['krʌmpl] vt
zerknittern
crunchy ['krʌntʃɪ] adj (Brit)
knusprig
crusade [kru:'seɪd] n Kreuzzug
m
crush [krʌʃ] vt zerdrücken;
(finger etc) quetschen; (spices,
stone) zerstoßen ▷ n: **to have a
~ on sb** in jdn verknallt sein;
crushing adj (defeat, remark)
vernichtend
crust [krʌst] n Kruste f; **crusty**
adj knusprig
crutch [krʌtʃ] n Krücke f
cry [kraɪ] vi (call) rufen; (scream)
schreien; (weep) weinen ▷ n (call)
Ruf m; (louder) Schrei m
crypt [krɪpt] n Krypta f
crystal ['krɪstl] n Kristall m
cu abbr = **see you** (SMS, e-mail) bis
bald
Cuba ['kju:bə] n Kuba nt
cube [kju:b] n Würfel m
cubic ['kju:bɪk] adj Kubik-
cubicle ['kju:bɪkl] n Kabine f

cuckoo ['kuku:] n Kuckuck m
cucumber ['kju:kʌmbə*] n Salatgurke f
cuddle ['kʌdl] vt in den Arm nehmen; (amorously) schmusen mit ▷ n Liebkosung f, Umarmung f; **to have a ~** schmusen; **cuddly** adj verschmust; **cuddly toy** n Plüschtier nt
cuff [kʌf] n Manschette f; (US: trouser ~) Aufschlag m; **off the ~** aus dem Stegreif; **cufflink** n Manschettenknopf m
cuisine [kwɪ'zi:n] n Kochkunst f, Küche f
cul-de-sac ['kʌldəsæk] n (Brit) Sackgasse f
culprit ['kʌlprɪt] n Schuldige(r) mf; (fig) Übeltäter(in) m(f)
cult [kʌlt] n Kult m
cultivate ['kʌltɪveɪt] vt (Agr: land) bebauen; (crop) anbauen; **cultivated** adj (person) kultiviert, gebildet
cultural ['kʌltʃərəl] adj kulturell, Kultur-; **culture** ['kʌltʃə*] n Kultur f; **cultured** adj gebildet, kultiviert; **culture vulture** (Brit fam) n Kulturfanatiker(in) m(f)
cumbersome ['kʌmbəsəm] adj (object) unhandlich
cumin ['kʌmɪn] n Kreuzkümmel m
cunning ['kʌnɪŋ] adj schlau; (person a.) gerissen
cup [kʌp] n Tasse f; (prize) Pokal m; **it's not his ~ of tea** das ist nicht sein Fall; **cupboard** ['kʌbəd] n Schrank m; **cup final** n Pokalendspiel nt; **cup tie** n Pokalspiel m
cupola ['kju:pələ] n Kuppel f
curable ['kjʊrəbəl] adj heilbar
curb [kɜ:b] n (US) see **kerb**
curd [kɜ:d] n: **~ cheese**, **~s** ≈ Quark m
cure [kjʊə*] n Heilmittel nt (for

gegen); (process) Heilung f ▷ vt heilen; (Gastr) pökeln; (smoke) räuchern
curious ['kjʊərɪəs] adj neugierig; (strange) seltsam
curl [kɜ:l] n Locke f ▷ vi sich kräuseln; **curly** adj lockig
currant ['kʌrənt] n (dried) Korinthe f; (red, black) Johannisbeere f
currency ['kʌrənsɪ] n Währung f; **foreign ~** Devisen pl
current ['kʌrənt] n (in water) Strömung f; (electric ~) Strom m ▷ adj (issue, affairs) aktuell, gegenwärtig; (expression) gängig; **current account** n Girokonto nt; **currently** adv zur Zeit
curriculum [kə'rɪkjʊləm] n Lehrplan m; **curriculum vitae** [kə'rɪkjʊləm'vi:taɪ] n (Brit) Lebenslauf m
curry ['kʌrɪ] n Currygericht nt; **curry powder** n Curry(pulver) nt
curse [kɜ:s] vi (swear) fluchen (at auf +akk) ▷ n Fluch m
cursor ['kɜ:sə*] n (Inform) Cursor m
curt [kɜ:t] adj schroff, kurz angebunden
curtain ['kɜ:tn] n Vorhang m; **it was ~s for Benny** für Benny war alles vorbei
curve [kɜ:v] n Kurve f ▷ vi einen Bogen machen; **curved** adj gebogen
cushion ['kʊʃən] n Kissen nt
custard ['kʌstəd] n dicke Vanillesoße, die warm oder kalt zu vielen englischen Nachspeisen gegessen wird
custom ['kʌstəm] n Brauch m; (habit) Gewohnheit f; **customary** ['kʌstəmrɪ] adj üblich; **custom-built** adj nach Kundenangaben gefertigt; **customer** ['kʌstəmə*] n Kunde

m, Kundin *f*; **customer loyalty card** *n* Kundenkarte *f*; **customer service** *n* Kundendienst *m*

customs ['kʌstəmz] *npl* (*organization, location*) Zoll *m*; **to pass through** ~ durch den Zoll gehen; **customs officer** *n* Zollbeamte(r) *m*, Zollbeamtin *f*

cut [kʌt] (**cut, cut**) *vt* schneiden; (*cake*) anschneiden; (*wages, benefits*) kürzen; (*prices*) heruntersetzen; **I ~ my finger** ich habe mir in den Finger geschnitten ▷ *n* Schnitt *m*; (*wound*) Schnittwunde *f*; (*reduction*) Kürzung *f* (*in gen*); **price/tax ~** Preissenkung/Steuersenkung *f*; **to be a ~ above the rest** eine Klasse besser als die anderen sein; **cut back** *vt* (*workforce etc*) reduzieren; **cut down** *vt* (*tree*) fällen; **to ~ on sth** etwas einschränken; **cut in** *vi* (*Auto*) scharf einscheren; **to ~ on sb** jdn schneiden; **cut off** *vt* abschneiden; (*gas, electricity*) abdrehen, abstellen; (*Tel*) **I was ~** ich wurde unterbrochen

cutback *n* Kürzung *f*

cute [kjuːt] *adj* putzig, niedlich; (*US: shrewd*) clever

cutlery ['kʌtlərɪ] *n* Besteck *nt*

cutlet ['kʌtlɪt] *n* (*pork*) Kotelett *nt*; (*veal*) Schnitzel *nt*

cut-price *adj* verbilligt

cutting ['kʌtɪŋ] *n* (*from paper*) Ausschnitt *m*; (*of plant*) Ableger *m* ▷ *adj* (*comment*) verletzend

CV *abbr* = **curriculum vitae**

cwt *abbr* = **hundredweight** ≈ Zentner, Ztr.

cybercafé [saɪbə'kæfeɪ] *n* Internetcafé *nt*; **cyberspace** *n* Cyberspace *m*

cycle ['saɪkl] *n* Fahrrad *nt* ▷ *vi* Rad fahren; **cycle lane**, **cycle path** *n* Radweg *m*; **cycling** *n*

Radfahren *nt*; **cyclist** ['saɪklɪst] *n* Radfahrer(in) *m(f)*

cylinder ['sɪlɪndə°] *n* Zylinder *m*

cynical ['sɪnɪkəl] *adj* zynisch

cypress ['saɪprɪs] *n* Zypresse *f*

Cypriot ['sɪprɪət] *adj* zypriotisch ▷ *n* Zypriote *m*, Zypriotin *f*; **Cyprus** ['saɪprəs] *n* Zypern *nt*

czar [zɑː°] *n* Zar *m*; **czarina** [zɑ'riːnə] *n* Zarin *f*

Czech [tʃek] *adj* tschechisch ▷ *n* (*person*) Tscheche *m*, Tschechin *f*; (*language*) Tschechisch *nt*; **Czech Republic** *n* Tschechische Republik, Tschechien *nt*

d

dab [dæb] *vt* (*wound, nose etc*) betupfen (*with* mit)

dachshund ['dækshʊnd] *n* Dackel *m*

dad(dy) ['dæd(ɪ)] *n* Papa *m*, Vati *m*; **daddy-longlegs** *nsing* (*Brit*) Schnake; (*US*) Weberknecht *m*

daffodil ['dæfədɪl] *n* Osterglocke *f*

daft [dɑːft] *adj* (*fam*) blöd, doof

dahlia ['deɪlɪə] *n* Dahlie *f*

daily ['deɪlɪ] *adj, adv* täglich ▷ *n* (*paper*) Tageszeitung *f*

dairy ['dɛərɪ] *n* (*on farm*) Molkerei *f*; **dairy products** *npl* Milchprodukte *pl*

daisy ['deɪzɪ] *n* Gänseblümchen *nt*

dam [dæm] *n* Staudamm *m* ▷ *vt* stauen

damage ['dæmɪdʒ] *n* Schaden *m*; **~s** *pl* (*Jur*) Schadenersatz *m* ▷ *vt* beschädigen; (*reputation, health*) schädigen, schaden +*dat*

damn [dæm] *adj* (*fam*) verdammt ▷ *vt* (*condemn*) verurteilen; **~ (it)!** verflucht! ▷ *n*: **he doesn't give a ~** es ist ihm völlig egal

damp [dæmp] *adj* feucht ▷ *n* Feuchtigkeit *f*; **dampen** ['dæmpən] *vt* befeuchten

dance [dɑːns] *n* Tanz *m*; (*event*) Tanzveranstaltung *f* ▷ *vi* tanzen; **dance floor** *n* Tanzfläche *f*; **dancer** *n* Tänzer(in) *m(f)*; **dancing** *n* Tanzen *nt*

dandelion ['dændɪlaɪən] *n* Löwenzahn *m*

dandruff ['dændrəf] *n* Schuppen *pl*

Dane [deɪn] *n* Däne *m*, Dänin *f*

danger ['deɪndʒə*] *n* Gefahr *f*; **~** (*sign*) Achtung!; **to be in ~** in Gefahr sein; **dangerous** *adj* gefährlich

Danish ['deɪnɪʃ] *adj* dänisch ▷ *n* (*language*) Dänisch *nt*; **the ~** *pl* die Dänen; **Danish pastry** *n* Plundergebäck *nt*

Danube ['dænjuːb] *n* Donau *f*

dare [dɛə*] *vi*: **to ~ (to) do sth** es wagen, etw zu tun; **I didn't ~ ask** ich traute mich nicht, zu fragen; **how ~ you** was fällt dir ein!; **daring** *adj* (*person*) mutig; (*film, clothes etc*) gewagt

dark [dɑːk] *adj* dunkel; (*gloomy*) düster, trübe; (*sinister*) finster; **~ chocolate** Bitterschokolade *f*; **~ green/blue** dunkelgrün/dunkelblau ▷ *n* Dunkelheit *f*; **in the ~** im Dunkeln; **dark glasses** *npl* Sonnenbrille *f*; **darkness** *n* Dunkelheit *f*

darling ['dɑːlɪŋ] *n* Schatz *m*; (*also favourite*) Liebling *m*

darts [dɑːts] *nsing* (*game*) Darts *nt*

dash [dæʃ] *vi* stürzen, rennen

▷ vt: **to ~ hopes** Hoffnungen zerstören ▷ n (in text) Gedankenstrich m; (of liquid) Schuss m; **dashboard** n Armaturenbrett nt

data ['deɪtə] npl Daten pl; **data bank, data base** n Datenbank f; **data capture** n Datenerfassung f; **data processing** n Datenverarbeitung f; **data protection** n Datenschutz m

date [deɪt] n Datum nt; (for meeting, delivery etc) Termin m; (with person) Verabredung f; (with girlfriend/boyfriend etc) Date nt; (fruit) Dattel f; **what's the ~ (today)?** der Wievielte ist heute?; **out of ~** adj veraltet; **up to ~** adj (news) aktuell; (fashion) zeitgemäß ▷ vt (letter etc) datieren; (person) gehen mit; **dated** adj altmodisch; **date of birth** n Geburtsdatum nt; **dating agency** n Partnervermittlung f

dative ['deɪtɪv] n Dativ m

daughter ['dɔːtə°] n Tochter f; **daughter-in-law** (pl **daughters-in-law**) n Schwiegertochter f

dawn [dɔːn] n Morgendämmerung f ▷ vi dämmern; **it ~ed on me** mir ging ein Licht auf

day [deɪ] n Tag m; **one ~** eines Tages; **by ~** bei Tage; **~ after ~, ~ by ~** Tag für Tag; **the ~ after/before** am Tag danach/zuvor; **the ~ before yesterday** vorgestern; **the ~ after tomorrow** übermorgen; **these ~s** heutzutage; **in those ~s** damals; **let's call it a ~** Schluss für heute!; **daybreak** n Tagesanbruch m; **day-care center** (US), **day-care centre** n (Brit) Kita f (Kindertagesstätte); **daydream** n Tagtraum m ▷ vi (mit offenen Augen) träumen; **daylight** n

Tageslicht nt; **in ~** bei Tage; **day nursery** n Kita f (Kindertagesstätte); **day return** n (Brit Rail) Tagesrückfahrkarte f; **daytime** n: **in the ~** bei Tage, tagsüber; **daytrip** n Tagesausflug m

dazed [deɪzd] adj benommen

dazzle ['dæzl] vt blenden; **dazzling** adj blendend, glänzend

dead [ded] adj tot; (limb) abgestorben ▷ adv genau; (fam) total, völlig; **~ tired** adj todmüde; **~ slow** (sign) Schritt fahren; **dead end** n Sackgasse f; **deadline** n Termin m; (period) Frist f; **~ for applications** Anmeldeschluss m; **deadly** adj tödlich ▷ adv: **~ dull** todlangweilig

deaf [def] adj taub; **deafen** vt taub machen; **deafening** adj ohrenbetäubend

deal [diːl] (**dealt, dealt**) vt, vi (cards) geben, austeilen ▷ n (business ~) Geschäft nt; (agreement) Abmachung f; **it's a ~** abgemacht!; **a good/great ~ of** ziemlich/sehr viel; **deal in** vt handeln mit; **deal with** vt (matter) sich beschäftigen mit; (book, film) behandeln; (successfully: person, problem) fertig werden mit; (matter) erledigen; **dealer** n (Comm) Händler(in) m(f); (drugs) Dealer(in) m(f); **dealings** npl (Comm) Geschäfte pl

dealt [delt] pt, pp of **deal**

dear [dɪə°] adj lieb, teuer; **Dear Sir or Madam** Sehr geehrte Damen und Herren; **Dear David** Lieber David ▷ n Schatz m; (as address) mein Schatz, Liebling; **dearly** adv (love) (heiß und) innig; (pay) teuer

death [deθ] n Tod m; (of project, hopes) Ende nt; (in accident etc) Todesfall m, Todesopfer nt; **death certificate** n Totenschein m;

death penalty n Todesstrafe f;
death toll n Zahl f der
Todesopfer; **death trap** n
Todesfalle f

debatable [dɪ'beɪtəbl] adj
fraglich; (question) strittig; **debate**
[dɪ'beɪt] n Debatte f ▷ vt
debattieren

debauched [dɪ'bɔ:tʃt] adj
ausschweifend

debit ['debɪt] n Soll nt ▷ vt
(account) belasten; **debit card** n
Geldkarte f

debris ['debri:] n Trümmer pl

debt [det] n Schuld f; **to be in
~** verschuldet sein

decade ['dekeɪd] n Jahrzehnt nt

decadent ['dekədənt] adj
dekadent

decaff ['di:kæf] n (fam)
koffeinfreier Kaffee;
decaffeinated [di:'kæfɪneɪtɪd]
adj koffeinfrei

decanter [dɪ'kæntə*] n Dekanter
m, Karaffe f

decay [dɪ'keɪ] n Verfall m;
(rotting) Verwesung f; (of tooth)
Karies f ▷ vi verfallen; (rot)
verwesen; (wood) vermodern;
(teeth) faulen; (leaves) verrotten

deceased [dɪ'si:st] n: **the ~**
der/die Verstorbene

deceit [dɪ'si:t] n Betrug m;
deceive [dɪ'si:v] vt täuschen

December [dɪ'sembə*] n
Dezember m; see also **September**

decent ['di:sənt] adj anständig

deception [dɪ'sepʃən] n Betrug
m; **deceptive** [dɪ'septɪv] adj
täuschend, irreführend

decide [dɪ'saɪd] vt (question)
entscheiden; (body of people)
beschließen; **I can't ~ what to do**
ich kann mich nicht entscheiden,
was ich tun soll ▷ vi sich
entscheiden; **to ~ on sth** (in favour
of sth) sich für etw entscheiden,

sich zu etw entschließen; **decided**
adj entschieden; (clear) deutlich;
decidedly adv entschieden

decimal ['desɪməl] adj Dezimal-;
decimal system n
Dezimalsystem nt

decipher [dɪ'saɪfə*] vt entziffern

decision [dɪ'sɪʒən] n Entscheidung f (on über +akk); (of committee,
jury etc) Beschluss m; **to make a
~** eine Entscheidung treffen;
decisive [dɪ'saɪsɪv] adj entscheidend; (person)
entscheidungsfreudig

deck [dek] n (Naut) Deck nt; (of
cards) Blatt nt; **deckchair** n
Liegestuhl m

declaration [deklə'reɪʃən] n
Erklärung f; **declare** [dɪ'klɛə*] vt
erklären; (state) behaupten (that
dass); (at customs) **have you
anything to ~?** haben Sie etwas
zu verzollen?

decline [dɪ'klaɪn] n Rückgang m
▷ vt (invitation, offer) ablehnen ▷ vi
(become less) sinken, abnehmen;
(health) sich verschlechtern

decode [di:'kəʊd] vt
entschlüsseln

decompose [di:kəm'pəʊz] vi sich
zersetzen

decontaminate
[di:kən'tæmɪneɪt] vt entgiften;
(from radioactivity) entseuchen

decorate ['dekəreɪt] vt
(aus)schmücken; (wallpaper)
tapezieren; (paint) anstreichen;
decoration [dekə'reɪʃən] n
Schmuck m; (process) Schmücken
nt; (wallpapering) Tapezieren nt;
(painting) Anstreichen nt;
Christmas ~s Weihnachts-
schmuck m; **decorator** n
Maler(in) m(f)

decrease ['di:kri:s] n Abnahme f
▷ [di:'kri:s] vi abnehmen

dedicate ['dedɪkeɪt] vt widmen

(to sb jdm); **dedicated** adj (person) engagiert; **dedication** [dedɪ'keɪʃən] n Widmung f; (commitment) Hingabe f, Engagement nt

deduce [dɪ'djuːs] vt folgern, schließen (from aus, that dass)

deduct [dɪ'dʌkt] vt abziehen (from von); **deduction** [dɪ'dʌkʃən] n (of money) Abzug m; (conclusion) (Schluss)folgerung f

deed [diːd] n Tat f

deep [diːp] adj tief; **deepen** vt vertiefen; **deep-freeze** n Tiefkühltruhe f; (upright) Gefrierschrank m; **deep-fry** vt frittieren

deer [dɪə*] n Reh nt; (with stag) Hirsch m

defeat [dɪ'fiːt] n Niederlage f; **to admit ~** sich geschlagen geben ▷ vt besiegen

defect [di:fekt] n Defekt m, Fehler m; **defective** [dɪ'fektɪv] adj fehlerhaft

defence [dɪ'fens] n Verteidigung f; **defend** [dɪ'fend] vt verteidigen; **defendant** [dɪ'fendənt] n (Jur) Angeklagte(r) mf; **defender** n (Sport) Verteidiger(in) m(f); **defensive** [dɪ'fensɪv] adj defensiv

deficiency [dɪ'fɪʃənsɪ] n Mangel m; **deficient** adj mangelhaft; **deficit** ['defɪsɪt] n Defizit nt

define [dɪ'faɪn] vt (word) definieren; (duties, powers) bestimmen; **definite** ['defɪnɪt] adj (clear) klar, eindeutig; (certain) sicher; **it's ~** es steht fest; **definitely** adv bestimmt; **definition** [defɪ'nɪʃən] n Definition f; (Foto) Schärfe f

defrost [di:'frɒst] vt (fridge) abtauen; (food) auftauen

degrading [dɪ'greɪdɪŋ] adj erniedrigend

degree [dɪ'griː] n Grad m; (at university) akademischer Grad; **a certain/high ~ of** ein gewisses/hohes Maß an +dat; **to a certain ~** einigermaßen; **I have a ~ in chemistry** ≈ ich habe einen Abschluss in Chemie

dehydrated [di:haɪ'dreɪtɪd] adj (food) getrocknet, Trocken-; (person) ausgetrocknet

de-ice [di:'aɪs] vt enteisen

delay [dɪ'leɪ] vt (postpone) verschieben, aufschieben; **to be ~ed** (event) sich verzögern; **the train/flight was ~ed** der Zug/die Maschine hatte Verspätung ▷ vi warten; (hesitate) zögern ▷ n Verzögerung f; (of train etc) Verspätung f; **without ~** unverzüglich; **delayed** adj (train etc) verspätet

delegate n ['delɪgət] Delegierte(r) mf ▷ ['delɪgeɪt] vt delegieren; **delegation** [delɪ'geɪʃən] n Abordnung f; (foreign) Delegation f

delete [dɪ'liːt] vt (aus)streichen; (Inform) löschen; **deletion** n Streichung f; (Inform) Löschung f

deli ['delɪ] n (fam) Feinkostgeschäft nt

deliberate [dɪ'lɪbərət] adj (intentional) absichtlich; **deliberately** adv mit Absicht, extra

delicate ['delɪkɪt] adj (fine) fein; (fragile) zart; (a. Med) empfindlich; (situation) heikel

delicatessen [delɪkə'tesn] nsing Feinkostgeschäft nt

delicious [dɪ'lɪʃəs] adj köstlich, lecker

delight [dɪ'laɪt] n Freude f ▷ vt entzücken; **delighted** adj sehr erfreut (with über +akk); **delightful** adj entzückend; (weather, meal etc) herrlich

deliver [dɪ'lɪvə*] vt (goods) liefern
(to sb jdm); (letter, parcel) zustellen;
(speech) halten; (baby) entbinden;
delivery n Lieferung f; (of letter,
parcel) Zustellung f; (of baby)
Entbindung f; **delivery van** n
Lieferwagen m

delude [dɪ'luːd] vt täuschen;
don't ~ yourself mach dir nichts
vor; **delusion** n Irrglaube m

de luxe [dɪ'lʌks] adj Luxus-

demand [dɪ'mɑːnd] vt verlangen
(from von); (time, patience etc)
erfordern ▷ n (request) Forderung
f, Verlangen nt (for nach); (Comm:
for goods) Nachfrage f; **on ~** auf
Wunsch; **very much in ~** sehr
gefragt; **demanding** adj
anspruchsvoll

demented [dɪ'mentɪd] adj
wahnsinnig

demerara [demə'rɛərə] n:
~ (sugar) brauner Zucker

demister n Defroster m

demo ['deməʊ] (pl **-s**) n (fam)
Demo f

democracy [dɪ'mɒkrəsɪ] n
Demokratie f; **democrat,
Democrat** (US Pol) ['deməkræt]
Demokrat(in) m(f); **democratic**
adj demokratisch; **the
Democratic Party** (US Pol) die
Demokratische Partei

demolish [dɪ'mɒlɪʃ] vt abreißen;
(fig) zerstören; **demolition**
[demə'lɪʃən] n Abbruch m

demonstrate ['demənstreɪt] vt,
vi demonstrieren, beweisen;
demonstration n Demonstration f

demoralize [dɪ'mɒrəlaɪz] vt
demoralisieren

denial [dɪ'naɪəl] n Leugnung f;
(official ~) Dementi nt

denim ['denɪm] n Jeansstoff m;
denim jacket n Jeansjacke f;
denims npl Bluejeans pl

Denmark ['denmɑːk] n Dänemark nt

denomination [dɪnɒmɪ'neɪʃən]
n (Rel) Konfession f; (Comm)
Nennwert m

dense [dens] adj dicht; (fam:
stupid) schwer von Begriff; **density**
['densɪtɪ] n Dichte f

dent [dent] n Beule f, Delle f ▷ vt
einbeulen

dental ['dentl] adj Zahn-; **~ care**
Zahnpflege f; **~ floss** Zahnseide f;
dentist ['dentɪst] n Zahnarzt m,
Zahnärztin; **dentures** ['dentʃəz]
npl Zahnprothese f; (full) Gebiss nt

deny [dɪ'naɪ] vt leugnen,
bestreiten; (refuse) ablehnen

deodorant [diː'əʊdərənt] n
Deo(dorant) nt

depart [dɪ'pɑːt] vi abreisen; (bus,
train) abfahren (for nach, from von);
(plane) abfliegen (for nach, from
von)

department [dɪ'pɑːtmənt] n
Abteilung f; (at university) Institut
nt; (Pol: ministry) Ministerium nt;
department store n Kaufhaus nt

departure [dɪ'pɑːtʃə*] n (of
person) Weggang m; (on journey)
Abreise f (for nach); (of train etc)
Abfahrt f (for nach); (of plane)
Abflug m (for nach); **departure
lounge** n (Aviat) Abflughalle f;
departure time n Abfahrtzeit f;
(Aviat) Abflugzeit f

depend [dɪ'pend] vi: **it ~s** es
kommt darauf an (whether, if ob);
depend on vt (thing) abhängen
von; (person: rely on) sich verlassen
auf +akk; (person, area etc)
angewiesen sein auf +akk; **it ~s on
the weather** es kommt auf das
Wetter an; **dependable** adj
zuverlässig; **dependence** n
Abhängigkeit f (on von);
dependent adj abhängig (on von)

deport [dɪ'pɔːt] vt ausweisen,

abschieben; **deportation**
[di:pɔːˈteɪʃən] *n* Abschiebung *f*
deposit [dɪˈpɒzɪt] *n* (*down payment*) Anzahlung *f*; (*security*) Kaution *f*; (*for bottle*) Pfand *nt*; (*to bank account*) Einzahlung *f*; (*in river etc*) Ablagerung *f* ▷ *vt* (*put down*) abstellen, absetzen; (*to bank account*) einzahlen; (*sth valuable*) deponieren; **deposit account** *n* Sparkonto *nt*
depot [ˈdepəʊ] *n* Depot *nt*
depreciate [dɪˈpriːʃɪeɪt] *vi* an Wert verlieren
depress [dɪˈpres] *vt* (*in mood*) deprimieren; **depressed** *adj* (*person*) niedergeschlagen, deprimiert; **~ area** Notstandsgebiet *nt*; **depressing** *adj* deprimierend; **depression** [dɪˈpreʃən] *n* (*mood*) Depression *f*; (*Meteo*) Tief *nt*
deprive [dɪˈpraɪv] *vt*: **to ~ sb of sth** jdn einer Sache berauben; **deprived** *adj* (*child*) (sozial) benachteiligt
dept *abbr* = **department** Abt.
depth [depθ] *n* Tiefe *f*
deputy [ˈdepjʊtɪ] *adj* stellvertretend, Vize- ▷ *n* Stellvertreter(in) *m(f)*; (*US Pol*) Abgeordnete(r) *mf*
derail [dɪˈreɪl] *vt* entgleisen lassen; **to be ~ed** entgleisen
deranged [dɪˈreɪndʒd] *adj* geistesgestört
derivation [derɪˈveɪʃən] *n* Ableitung *f*; **derive** [dɪˈraɪv] *vt* ableiten (*from* von) ▷ abstammen (*from* von)
dermatitis [dɜːməˈtaɪtɪs] *n* Hautentzündung *f*
derogatory [dɪˈrɒgətərɪ] *adj* abfällig
descend [dɪˈsend] *vt, vi* hinabsteigen, hinuntergehen; (*person*) **to ~** *o* **be ~ed from**

abstammen von; **descendant** *n* Nachkomme*m*; **descent** [dɪˈsent] *n* (*coming down*) Abstieg *m*; (*origin*) Abstammung *f*
describe [dɪsˈkraɪb] *vt* beschreiben; **description** [dɪsˈkrɪpʃən] *n* Beschreibung *f*
desert [ˈdezət] *n* Wüste *f* ▷ [dɪˈzɜːt] *vt* verlassen; (*abandon*) im Stich lassen; **deserted** *adj* verlassen; (*empty*) menschenleer
deserve [dɪˈzɜːv] *vt* verdienen
design [dɪˈzaɪn] *n* (*plan*) Entwurf *m*; (*of vehicle, machine*) Konstruktion *f*; (*of object*) Design *nt*; (*planning*) Gestaltung *f* ▷ *vt* entwerfen; (*machine etc*) konstruieren; **~ed for sb/sth** (*intended*) für jdn/etw konzipiert
designate [ˈdezɪgneɪt] *vt* bestimmen
designer [dɪˈzaɪnə*] *n* Designer(in) *m(f)*; (*Tech*) Konstrukteur(in) *m(f)*; **designer drug** *n* Designerdroge *f*
desirable [dɪˈzaɪərəbl] *n* wünschenswert; (*person*) begehrenswert; **desire** [dɪˈzaɪə*] *n* Wunsch *m* (*for* nach); (*esp sexual*) Begierde *f* (*for* nach) ▷ *vt* wünschen; (*ask for*) verlangen; **if ~d** auf Wunsch
desk [desk] *n* Schreibtisch *m*; (*reception ~*) Empfang *m*; (*at airport etc*) Schalter *m*; **desktop publishing** *n* Desktoppublishing *nt*
desolate [ˈdesəlɪt] *adj* trostlos
despair [dɪsˈpeə*] *n* Verzweiflung *f* (*at* über +*akk*) ▷ *vi* verzweifeln (*of* an +*dat*)
despatch [dɪsˈpætʃ] *see* **dispatch**
desperate [ˈdespərɪt] *adj* verzweifelt; (*situation*) hoffnungslos; **to be ~ for sth** etw dringend brauchen, unbedingt wollen; **desperation**

[despə'reɪʃən] n Verzweiflung f

despicable [dɪ'spɪkəbl] adj verachtenswert; **despise** [dɪ'spaɪz] vt verachten

despite [dɪ'spaɪt] prep trotz +gen

dessert [dɪ'zɜ:t] n Nachtisch m; **dessert spoon** n Dessertlöffel m

destination [destɪ'neɪʃən] n (of person) (Reise)ziel nt; (of goods) Bestimmungsort m

destiny ['destɪnɪ] n Schicksal nt

destroy [dɪ'strɔɪ] vt zerstören; (completely) vernichten; **destruction** [dɪ'strʌkʃən] n Zerstörung f; (complete) Vernichtung f; **destructive** [dɪ'strʌktɪv] adj zerstörerisch; (esp fig) destruktiv

detach [dɪ'tætʃ] vt abnehmen; (from form etc) abtrennen; (free) lösen (from von); **detachable** adj abnehmbar; (from form etc) abtrennbar; **detached** adj (attitude) distanziert, objektiv; **~ house** Einzelhaus nt

detail ['di:teɪl, (US) di:'teɪl] n Einzelheit f, Detail nt; (further) **~s from ...** Näheres erfahren Sie bei ...; **to go into ~** ins Detail gehen; **in ~** ausführlich; **detailed** adj detailliert, ausführlich

detain [dɪ'teɪn] vt aufhalten; (police) in Haft nehmen

detect [dɪ'tekt] vt entdecken; (notice) wahrnehmen; **detective** [dɪ'tektɪv] n Detektiv(in) m(f); **detective story** n Krimi m

detention [dɪ'tenʃən] n Haft f; (Sch) Nachsitzen nt

deter [dɪ'tɜ:*] vt abschrecken (from von)

detergent [dɪ'tɜ:dʒənt] n Reinigungsmittel nt; (soap powder) Waschmittel nt

deteriorate [dɪ'tɪərɪəreɪt] vi sich verschlechtern

determination [dɪtɜ:mɪ'neɪʃən] n Entschlossenheit f; **determine** [dɪ'tɜ:mɪn] vt bestimmen; **determined** adj (fest) entschlossen

deterrent [dɪ'terənt] n Abschreckungsmittel nt

detest [dɪ'test] vt verabscheuen; **detestable** adj abscheulich

detour ['di:tuə*] n Umweg m; (of traffic) Umleitung f

deuce [dju:s] n (Tennis) Einstand m

devalue [di:'vælju:] vt abwerten

devastate ['devəsteɪt] vt verwüsten; **devastating** ['devəsteɪtɪŋ] adj verheerend

develop [dɪ'veləp] vt entwickeln; (illness) bekommen ▷ vi sich entwickeln; **developing country** n Entwicklungsland nt; **development** n Entwicklung f; (of land) Erschließung f

device [dɪ'vaɪs] n Vorrichtung f, Gerät nt

devil ['devl] n Teufel m; **devilish** adj teuflisch

devote [dɪ'vəut] vt widmen (to dat); **devoted** adj liebend; (servant etc) treu ergeben; **devotion** n Hingabe f

devour [dɪ'vauə*] vt verschlingen

dew [dju:] n Tau m

diabetes [daɪə'bi:ti:z] n Diabetes m, Zuckerkrankheit f; **diabetic** [daɪə'betɪk] adj zuckerkrank, für Diabetiker ▷ n Diabetiker(in) m(f)

diagnosis (diagnoses) [daɪəg'nəusɪs] (pl **diagnoses**) n Diagnose f

diagonal [daɪ'ægənl] adj diagonal

diagram ['daɪəgræm] n Diagramm nt

dial ['daɪəl] n Skala f; (of clock)

Zifferblatt nt ▷ vt (Tel) wählen; **dial code** n (US) Vorwahl f

dialect ['daɪəlekt] n Dialekt m

dialling code n (Brit) Vorwahl f; **dialling tone** n (Brit) Amtszeichen nt

dialogue, **dialog** (US) ['daɪəlɒg] n Dialog m

dial tone n (US) Amtszeichen nt

dialysis [daɪˈæləsɪs] n (Med) Dialyse f

diameter [daɪˈæmɪtə*] n Durchmesser m

diamond ['daɪəmənd] n Diamant m; (Cards) Karo nt

diaper ['daɪpə*] n (US) Windel f

diarrhoea [daɪəˈriːə] n Durchfall m

diary ['daɪərɪ] n (Taschen)kalender m; (account) Tagebuch nt

dice [daɪs] npl Würfel pl; **diced** adj in Würfel geschnitten

dictate [dɪkˈteɪt] vt diktieren; **dictation** [dɪkˈteɪʃən] n Diktat nt

dictator [dɪkˈteɪtə*] n Diktator(in) m(f); **dictatorship** [dɪkˈteɪtəʃɪp] n Diktatur f

dictionary ['dɪkʃənrɪ] n Wörterbuch nt

did [dɪd] pt of **do**

didn't ['dɪdnt] contr of **did not**

die [daɪ] vi sterben (of an +dat); (plant, animal) eingehen; (engine) absterben; **to be dying to do sth** darauf brennen, etw zu tun; **I'm dying for a drink** ich brauche unbedingt was zu trinken; **die away** vi schwächer werden; (wind) sich legen; **die down** vi nachlassen; **die out** vi aussterben

diesel ['diːzəl] n (fuel, car) Diesel m; **~ engine** Dieselmotor m

diet ['daɪət] n Kost f; (special food) Diät f; **to go on a ~** eine Diät machen

differ ['dɪfə*] vi (be different) sich unterscheiden; (disagree) anderer Meinung sein; **difference** ['dɪfrəns] n Unterschied m; **it makes no ~ (to me)** es ist (mir) egal; **it makes a big ~** es macht viel aus; **different** adj andere(r, s); (with pl) verschieden; **to be quite ~** ganz anders sein (from als); (two people, things) völlig verschieden sein; **a ~ person** ein anderer Mensch; **differentiate** [dɪfəˈrenʃɪeɪt] vt, vi unterscheiden; **differently** ['dɪfrəntlɪ] adv anders (from als); (from one another) unterschiedlich

difficult ['dɪfɪkəlt] adj schwierig; **I find it ~** es fällt mir schwer; **difficulty** n Schwierigkeit f; **with ~** nur schwer; **to have ~ in doing sth** etw nur mit Mühe machen können

dig [dɪg] (**dug, dug**) vt, vi (hole) graben; **dig in** vi (fam: to food) reinhauen; **~!** greif(t) zu!; **dig up** vt ausgraben

digest [daɪˈdʒest] vt (a. fig) verdauen; **digestible** [dɪˈdʒestəbl] adj verdaulich; **digestion** [dɪˈdʒestʃən] n Verdauung f; **digestive** [dɪˈdʒestɪv] adj: **~ biscuit** (Brit) Vollkornkeks m

digit ['dɪdʒɪt] n Ziffer f; **digital** ['dɪdʒɪtəl] adj digital; **~ computer** Digitalrechner m; **~ watch/clock** Digitaluhr f; **digital camera** n Digitalkamera f; **digital television**, **digital TV** n Digitalfernsehen nt

dignified ['dɪgnɪfaɪd] adj würdevoll; **dignity** ['dɪgnɪtɪ] n Würde f

dilapidated [dɪˈlæpɪdeɪtɪd] adj baufällig

dilemma [daɪˈlemə] n Dilemma nt

dill [dɪl] n Dill m

dilute [daɪˈluːt] vt verdünnen

dim [dɪm] adj (light) schwach; (outline) undeutlich; (stupid)

schwer von Begriff ▷ vt
verdunkeln; (US Auto) abblenden;
~med headlights (US)
Abblendlicht nt
dime [daɪm] n (US)
Zehncentstück nt
dimension [daɪˈmenʃən] n
Dimension f; **~s** pl Maße pl
diminish [dɪˈmɪnɪʃ] vt
verringern ▷ vi sich verringern
dimple [ˈdɪmpl] n Grübchen nt
dine [daɪn] vi speisen; **dine out**
vi außer Haus essen; **diner** n Gast
m; (Rail) Speisewagen m; (US)
Speiselokal nt
dinghy [ˈdɪŋɡɪ] n Ding(h)i nt;
(inflatable) Schlauchboot nt
dingy [ˈdɪndʒɪ] adj düster; (dirty)
schmuddelig
dining car [ˈdaɪnɪŋkaː*] n
Speisewagen m; **dining room** n
Esszimmer nt; (in hotel)
Speiseraum m; **dining table** n
Esstisch m
dinner [ˈdɪnə*] n Abendessen nt;
(lunch) Mittagessen nt; (public)
Diner nt; **to be at ~** beim Essen
sein; **to have ~** zu Abend/Mittag
essen; **dinner jacket** n Smoking
m; **dinner party** n
Abendgesellschaft f (mit Essen);
dinnertime n Essenszeit f
dinosaur [ˈdaɪnəsɔː*] n Dinosaurier m
dip [dɪp] vt tauchen (in in +akk);
to ~ (one's headlights) (Brit Auto)
abblenden; **~ped headlights**
Abblendlicht nt ▷ n (in ground)
Bodensenke f; (sauce) Dip m
diploma [dɪˈpləʊmə] n Diplom
nt
diplomat [ˈdɪpləmæt] n Diplo-
mat(in) m(f); **diplomatic**
[dɪpləˈmætɪk] adj diplomatisch
dipstick [ˈdɪpstɪk] n Ölmessstab
m
direct [daɪˈrekt] adj direkt;

(cause, consequence) unmittelbar;
~ debit (mandate)
Einzugsermächtigung f;
(transaction) Abbuchung f im
Lastschriftverfahren; **~ train**
durchgehender Zug ▷ vt (aim,
send) richten (at, to an +akk); (film)
die Regie führen bei; (traffic)
regeln; **direct current** (Elec)
Gleichstrom m
direction [dɪˈrekʃən] n (course)
Richtung f; (Cine) Regie f; **in
the ~ of ...** in Richtung ...; **~s**
pl (to a place) Wegbeschreibung f
directly [dɪˈrektlɪ] adv direkt; (at
once) sofort
director [dɪˈrektə*] n Direk-
tor(in) m(f), Leiter(in) m(f); (of film)
Regisseur(in) m(f)
directory [dɪˈrektərɪ] n Adressbuch nt; (Tel) Telefonbuch nt;
~ enquiries o (US) **assistance** (Tel)
Auskunft f
dirt [dɜːt] n Schmutz m, Dreck m;
dirt cheap adj spottbillig; **dirt
road** n unbefestigte Straße; **dirty**
adj schmutzig
disability [dɪsəˈbɪlɪtɪ] n
Behinderung f; **disabled**
[dɪsˈeɪbld] adj behindert,
Behinderten- ▷ npl: **the ~** die
Behinderten
disadvantage [dɪsədˈvaːntɪdʒ]
n Nachteil m; **at a ~** benachteiligt;
disadvantageous [dɪsædvaːn-
ˈteɪdʒəs] adj unvorteilhaft,
ungünstig
disagree [dɪsəˈgriː] vi anderer
Meinung sein; (two people) sich
nicht einig sein; (two reports etc)
nicht übereinstimmen; **to ~ with
sb** mit jdm nicht übereinstimmen;
(food) jdm nicht bekommen;
disagreeable [dɪsəˈgriːəbl] adj unangenehm;
(person) unsympathisch;
disagreement n Meinungsverschiedenheit f

disappear [dɪsə'pɪə*] *vi* verschwinden; **disappearance** *n* Verschwinden *nt*

disappoint [dɪsə'pɔɪnt] *vt* enttäuschen; **disappointing** *adj* enttäuschend; **disappointment** *n* Enttäuschung *f*

disapproval [dɪsə'pruːvl] *n* Missbilligung *f*; **disapprove** [dɪsə'pruːv] *vi* missbilligen (*of akk*)

disarm [dɪs'ɑːm] *vt* entwaffnen ▷ *vi* (*Pol*) abrüsten; **disarmament** *n* Abrüstung *f*; **disarming** *adj* (*smile, look*) gewinnend

disaster [dɪ'zɑːstə*] *n* Katastrophe *f*; **disastrous** [dɪ'zɑːstrəs] *adj* katastrophal

disbelief [dɪsbə'liːf] *n* Ungläubigkeit *f*

disc [dɪsk] *n* Scheibe *f*, CD *f*; *see also* **disk**; (*Anat*) Bandscheibe *f*; **disc brake** *n* Scheibenbremse *f*

discharge ['dɪstʃɑːdʒ] *n* (*Med*) Ausfluss *m* ▷ [dɪs'tʃɑːdʒ] *vt* (*person*) entlassen; (*emit*) ausstoßen; (*Med*) ausscheiden

discipline ['dɪsɪplɪn] *n* Disziplin *f*

disc jockey ['dɪskdʒɒkɪ] *n* Diskjockey *m*

disclose [dɪs'kləʊz] *vt* bekannt geben; (*secret*) enthüllen

disco ['dɪskəʊ] (*pl* **-s**) *n* Disko *f*, Diskomusik *f*

discomfort [dɪs'kʌmfət] *n* (*slight pain*) leichte Schmerzen *pl*; (*unease*) Unbehagen *nt*

disconnect [dɪskə'nekt] *vt* (*electricity, gas, phone*) abstellen; (*unplug*) **to ~ the TV (from the mains)** den Stecker des Fernsehers herausziehen; (*Tel*) **I've been ~ed** das Gespräch ist unterbrochen worden

discontent [dɪskən'tent] *n* Unzufriedenheit *f*; **discontented** *adj* unzufrieden

discontinue [dɪskən'tɪnjuː] *vt* einstellen; (*product*) auslaufen lassen

discount ['dɪskaʊnt] *n* Rabatt *m*

discover [dɪs'kʌvə*] *vt* entdecken; **discovery** *n* Entdeckung *f*

discredit [dɪs'kredɪt] *vt* in Verruf bringen ▷ *n* Misskredit *m*

discreet [dɪs'kriːt] *adj* diskret

discrepancy [dɪs'krepənsɪ] *n* Unstimmigkeit *f*, Diskrepanz *f*

discriminate [dɪs'krɪmɪneɪt] *vi* unterscheiden; **to ~ against sb** jdn diskriminieren; **discrimination** [dɪskrɪmɪ'neɪʃən] *n* (*different treatment*) Diskriminierung *f*

discus ['dɪskəs] *n* Diskus *m*

discuss [dɪs'kʌs] *vt* diskutieren, besprechen; **discussion** [dɪs'kʌʃən] *n* Diskussion *f*

disease [dɪ'ziːz] *n* Krankheit *f*

disembark [dɪsɪm'bɑːk] *vi* von Bord gehen

disentangle ['dɪsɪn'tæŋgl] *vt* entwirren

disgrace [dɪs'greɪs] *n* Schande *f* ▷ *vt* Schande machen +*dat*; (*family etc*) Schande bringen über +*akk*; (*less strong*) blamieren; **disgraceful** *adj* skandalös

disguise [dɪs'gaɪz] *vt* verkleiden; (*voice*) verstellen ▷ *n* Verkleidung *f*; **in ~** verkleidet

disgust [dɪs'gʌst] *n* Abscheu *m*; (*physical*) Ekel *m* ▷ *vt* anekeln, anwidern; **disgusting** *adj* widerlich; (*physically*) ekelhaft

dish [dɪʃ] *n* Schüssel *f*; (*food*) Gericht *nt*; **~es** *pl* (*crockery*) Geschirr *nt*; **to do/wash the ~es** abwaschen; **dishcloth** *n* (*for washing*) Spültuch *nt*; (*for drying*) Geschirrtuch *nt*

dishearten [dɪs'hɑːtən] vt entmutigen; **don't be ~ed** lass den Kopf nicht hängen!

dishonest [dɪs'ɒnɪst] adj unehrlich

dishonour [dɪs'ɒnə°] n Schande f

dish towel n (US) Geschirrtuch nt; **dish washer** n Geschirrspülmaschine f

dishy ['dɪʃɪ] adj (Brit fam) gut aussehend

disillusioned [dɪsɪ'luːʒənd] adj desillusioniert

disinfect [dɪsɪn'fekt] vt desinfizieren; **disinfectant** n Desinfektionsmittel nt

disintegrate [dɪs'ɪntɪgreɪt] vi zerfallen; (group) sich auflösen

disjointed [dɪs'dʒɔɪntɪd] adj unzusammenhängend

disk [dɪsk] n (Inform: floppy) Diskette f; **disk drive** n Diskettenlaufwerk nt; **diskette** [dɪ'sket] n Diskette f

dislike [dɪs'laɪk] n Abneigung f ▷ vt nicht mögen; **to ~ doing sth** etw ungern tun

dislocate ['dɪsləʊkeɪt] vt (Med) verrenken, ausrenken

dismal ['dɪzməl] adj trostlos

dismantle [dɪs'mæntl] vt auseinandernehmen; (machine) demontieren

dismay [dɪs'meɪ] n Bestürzung f; **dismayed** adj bestürzt

dismiss [dɪs'mɪs] vt (employee) entlassen; **dismissal** n Entlassung f

disobedience [dɪsə'biːdɪəns] n Ungehorsam m; **disobedient** adj ungehorsam; **disobey** [dɪsə'beɪ] vt nicht gehorchen +dat

disorder [dɪs'ɔːdə°] n (mess) Unordnung f; (riot) Aufruhr m; (Med) Störung f, Leiden nt

disorganized [dɪs'ɔːgənaɪzd] adj chaotisch

disparaging adj geringschätzig

dispatch [dɪ'spætʃ] vt abschicken, abfertigen

dispensable [dɪ'spensəbl] adj entbehrlich; **dispense** vt verteilen; **dispense with** vt verzichten auf +akk; **dispenser** n Automat m

disperse [dɪ'spɜːs] vi sich zerstreuen

display [dɪ'spleɪ] n (exhibition) Ausstellung f, Show f; (of goods) Auslage f; (Tech) Anzeige f, Display nt ▷ vt zeigen; (goods) ausstellen

disposable [dɪ'spəʊzəbl] adj (container, razor etc) Wegwerf-; **~ nappy** Wegwerfwindel f; **disposal** [dɪ'spəʊzəl] n Loswerden nt; (of waste) Beseitigung f; **to be at sb's ~** jdm zur Verfügung stehen; **to have at one's ~** verfügen über; **dispose of** vt loswerden; (waste etc) beseitigen

dispute [dɪ'spjuːt] n Streit m; (industrial) Auseinandersetzung f ▷ vt bestreiten

disqualification [dɪskwɒlɪfɪ'keɪʃən] n Disqualifikation f; **disqualify** [dɪs'kwɒlɪfaɪ] vt disqualifizieren

disregard [dɪsrɪ'gɑːd] vt nicht beachten

disreputable [dɪs'repjʊtəbl] adj verrufen

disrespect [dɪsrɪ'spekt] n Respektlosigkeit f

disrupt [dɪs'rʌpt] vt stören; (interrupt) unterbrechen; **disruption** [dɪs'rʌpʃən] n Störung f; (interruption) Unterbrechung f

dissatisfied [dɪs'sætɪsfaɪd] adj unzufrieden

dissent [dɪ'sent] n Widerspruch m

dissolve [dɪ'zɒlv] vt auflösen
▷ vi sich auflösen

dissuade [dɪ'sweɪd] vt (davon abbringen) **to ~ sb from doing sth** jdn davon abbringen, etw zu tun

distance ['dɪstəns] n Entfernung f; **in the/from a ~** in/aus der Ferne; **distant** adj (a. in time) fern; (relative etc) entfernt; (person) distanziert

distaste [dɪs'teɪst] n Abneigung f (for gegen)

distil [dɪs'tɪl] vt destillieren; **distillery** n Brennerei f

distinct [dɪs'tɪŋkt] adj verschieden; (clear) klar, deutlich; **distinction** [dɪs'tɪŋkʃən] n (difference) Unterschied m; (in exam etc) Auszeichnung f; **distinctive** adj unverkennbar; **distinctly** adv deutlich

distinguish [dɪs'tɪŋgwɪʃ] vt unterscheiden (sth from sth etw von etw)

distort [dɪs'tɔːt] vt verzerren; (truth) verdrehen

distract [dɪs'trækt] vt ablenken; **distraction** [dɪs'trækʃən] n Ablenkung f; (diversion) Zerstreuung f

distress [dɪs'tres] n (need, danger) Not f; (suffering) Leiden nt; (mental) Qual f; (worry) Kummer m ▷ vt mitnehmen, erschüttern; **distressed area** n Notstandsgebiet nt; **distress signal** n Notsignal nt

distribute [dɪ'strɪbjuːt] vt verteilen; (Comm: goods) vertreiben; **distribution** [dɪstrɪ'bjuːʃən] n Verteilung f; (Comm: of goods) Vertrieb m; **distributor** [dɪ'strɪbjʊtə*] n (Auto) Verteiler m; (Comm) Händler(in) m(f)

district ['dɪstrɪkt] n Gegend f; (administrative) Bezirk m; **district attorney** n (US) Staatsanwalt m, Staatsanwältin f

distrust [dɪs'trʌst] vt misstrauen +dat ▷ n Misstrauen nt

disturb [dɪs'tɜːb] vt stören; (worry) beunruhigen; **disturbance** n Störung f; **disturbing** adj beunruhigend

ditch [dɪtʃ] n Graben m ▷ vt (fam: person) den Laufpass geben +dat; (plan etc) verwerfen

ditto ['dɪtəʊ] adv dito, ebenfalls

dive [daɪv] n (into water) Kopfsprung m; (Aviat) Sturzflug m; (fam) zwielichtiges Lokal ▷ vi (under water) tauchen; **diver** n Taucher(in) m(f)

diverse [daɪ'vɜːs] adj verschieden; **diversion** [daɪ'vɜːʃən] n (of traffic) Umleitung f; (distraction) Ablenkung f; **divert** [daɪ'vɜːt] vt ablenken; (traffic) umleiten

divide [dɪ'vaɪd] vt teilen; (in several parts, between people) aufteilen ▷ vi sich teilen; **dividend** ['dɪvɪdend] n Dividende f

divine [dɪ'vaɪn] adj göttlich

diving ['daɪvɪŋ] n (Sport)tauchen nt; (jumping in) Springen nt; (Sport: from board) Kunstspringen nt; **diving board** n Sprungbrett nt; **diving goggles** npl Taucherbrille f; **diving mask** n Tauchermaske f

division [dɪ'vɪʒən] n Teilung f; (Math) Division f; (department) Abteilung f; (Sport) Liga f

divorce [dɪ'vɔːs] n Scheidung f ▷ vt sich scheiden lassen von; **divorced** adj geschieden; **to get ~** sich scheiden lassen; **divorcee** [dɪvɔː'siː] n Geschiedene(r) mf

DIY [diːaɪ'waɪ] abbr =

do-it-yourself; **DIY centre** *n* Baumarkt *m*

dizzy ['dɪzɪ] *adj* schwindlig

DJ [diː'dʒeɪ] *abbr* = **dinner jacket** Smoking *m* ▷ *abbr* = **disc jockey** Diskjockey *m*, DJ *m*

DNA *abbr* = **desoxyribonucleic acid** DNS *f*

KEYWORD

do [duː] (*pt* **did**, *pp* **done**) *n* (*inf*) (*party etc*) Fete *f*
▷ *vb aux* **1** (*in negative constructions and questions*) **I don't understand** ich verstehe nicht; **didn't you know?** wusstest du das nicht?; **what do you think?** was meinen Sie?
2 (*for emphasis, in polite phrases*) **she does seem rather tired** sie scheint wirklich sehr müde zu sein; **do sit down/help yourself** setzen Sie sich doch hin/greifen Sie doch zu
3 (*used to avoid repeating vb*) **she swims better than I do** sie schwimmt besser als ich; **she lives in Glasgow — so do I** sie wohnt in Glasgow — ich auch
4 (*in tag questions*) **you like him, don't you?** du magst/Sie mögen ihn doch, oder?
▷ *vt* **1** (*carry out, perform etc*) tun, machen; **what are you doing tonight?** was machst du/machen Sie heute Abend?; **I've got nothing to do** ich habe nichts zu tun; **to do one's hair/nails** sich die Haare/Nägel machen
2 (*car etc*) fahren
▷ *vi* **1** (*act, behave*) **do as I do** mach es wie ich
2 (*get on, fare*) **he's doing well/badly at school** er ist gut/schlecht in der Schule; **how do you do?** guten Tag

3 (*be suitable*) gehen; (*be sufficient*) reichen; **to make do (with)** auskommen mit

do away with *vt* (*kill*) umbringen; (*abolish: law etc*) abschaffen

do up *vt* (*laces, dress, buttons*) zumachen; (*renovate: room, house*) renovieren

do with *vt* (*need*) brauchen; (*be connected*) zu tun haben mit

do without *vt*, *vi* auskommen ohne

do up *vt* (*fasten*) zumachen; (*parcel*) verschnüren; (*renovate*) wiederherrichten

do with *vt* (*need*) brauchen; **I could ~ a drink** ich könnte einen Drink gebrauchen

do without *vt* auskommen ohne; **I can ~ your comments** auf deine Kommentare kann ich verzichten

dock [dɒk] *n* Dock *nt*; (*Jur*) Anklagebank *f*; **docker** *n* Hafenarbeiter *m*; **dockyard** *n* Werft *f*

doctor ['dɒktə*] *n* Arzt *m*, Ärztin; (*in title, also academic*) Doktor *m*

document ['dɒkjumənt] *n* Dokument *nt*; **documentary** [dɒkjʊ'mentərɪ] *n* Dokumentarfilm *m*; **documentation** [dɒkjumen'teɪʃən] *n* Dokumentation *f*

docusoap ['dɒkjʊsəʊp] *n* Reality-Serie *f*, Dokusoap *f*

doddery ['dɒdərɪ] *adj* tatterig

dodgem ['dɒdʒəm] *n* Autoskooter *m*

dodgy [dɒdʒɪ] *adj* nicht ganz in Ordnung; (*dishonest, unreliable*) zwielichtig; **he has a ~ stomach** er hat sich den Magen verdorben

dog [dɒg] *n* Hund *m*; **dog food** *n* Hundefutter *nt*; **doggie bag**

['dʊgɪˈbæg] *n* Tüte oder Box, in der Essensreste aus dem Restaurant mit nach Hause genommen werden können

do-it-yourself ['duːɪtjəˈself] *n* Heimwerken *nt*, Do-it-yourself *nt* ▷ *adj* Heimwerker-; **do-it-yourselfer** *n* Bastler(in) *m(f)*, Heimwerker(in) *m(f)*

doll [dɒl] *n* Puppe *f*

dollar ['dɒlə*] *n* Dollar *m*

dolphin ['dɒlfɪn] *n* Delphin *m*

domain *n* Domäne *f*; (*Inform*) Domain *f*

dome [dəʊm] *n* Kuppel *f*

domestic [dəˈmestɪk] *adj* häuslich; (*within country*) Innen-, Binnen-; **domestic animal** *n* Haustier *nt*; **domesticated** [dəˈmestɪkeɪtɪd] *adj* (*person*) häuslich; (*animal*) zahm; **domestic flight** *n* Inlandsflug *m*

domicile ['dɒmɪsaɪl] *n* (ständiger) Wohnsitz

dominant ['dɒmɪnənt] *adj* dominierend, vorherrschend; **dominate** ['dɒmɪneɪt] *vt* beherrschen

dominoes ['dɒmɪnəʊz] *npl* Domino(spiel) *nt*

donate [dəʊˈneɪt] *vt* spenden; **donation** *n* Spende *f*

done [dʌn] *pp of* **do** ▷ *adj* (*cooked*) gar; **well ~** durchgebraten

döner (kebab) ['dɒnəkəˈbæb] *n* Döner (Kebab) *m*

donkey ['dɒŋkɪ] *n* Esel *m*

donor ['dəʊnə] *n* Spender(in) *m(f)*

don't [dəʊnt] *contr of* **do not**

doom [duːm] *n* Schicksal *nt*; (*downfall*) Verderben *nt*

door [dɔː*] *n* Tür *f*; **doorbell** *n* Türklingel *f*; **door handle** *n* Türklinke *f*; **doorknob** *n* Türknauf *m*; **doormat** *n* Fußabtreter *m*; **doorstep** *n* Türstufe *f*; **right**

on our ~ direkt vor unserer Haustür

dope [dəʊp] (*Sport*) *n* (*for athlete*) Aufputschmittel *nt* ▷ *vt* dopen

dormitory ['dɔːmɪtrɪ] *n* Schlafsaal *m*; (*US*) Studentenwohnheim *nt*

dosage ['dəʊsɪdʒ] *n* Dosierung *f*; **dose** [dəʊs] *n* Dosis *f* ▷ *vt* dosieren

dot [dɒt] *n* Punkt *m*; **on the ~** auf die Minute genau, pünktlich

dotcom ['dɒtkɒm] *n*: **~ (company)** Internetfirma *f*, Dotcom-Unternehmen *nt*

dote on [dəʊt ɒn] *vt* abgöttisch lieben

dotted line *n* punktierte Linie

double ['dʌbl] *adj*, *adv* doppelt; **~ the quantity** die zweifache Menge, doppelt so viel ▷ *vt* verdoppeln ▷ *n* (*person*) Doppelgänger(in) *m(f)*; (*Cine*) Double *nt*; **double bass** *n* Kontrabass *m*; **double bed** *n* Doppelbett *nt*; **double-click** *vt* (*Inform*) doppelklicken; **double cream** *n* Sahne mit hohem Fettgehalt; **doubledecker** *n* Doppeldecker *m*; **double glazing** *n* Doppelverglasung *f*; **double-park** *vi* in zweiter Reihe parken; **double room** *n* Doppelzimmer *nt*; **doubles** *npl* (*Sport: also match*) Doppel *nt*

doubt [daʊt] *n* Zweifel *m*; **no ~** ohne Zweifel, zweifellos, wahrscheinlich; **to have one's ~s** Bedenken haben ▷ *vt* bezweifeln; (*statement, word*) anzweifeln; **I ~ it** das bezweifle ich; **doubtful** *adj* zweifelhaft, zweifelnd; **it is ~ whether ...** es ist fraglich, ob ...; **doubtless** *adv* ohne Zweifel, sicherlich

dough [dəʊ] *n* Teig *m*; **doughnut** *n* Donut *m* (*rundes Hefegebäck*)

dove [dʌv] n Taube f
down [daʊn] n Daunen pl; (fluff)
Flaum m ▷ adv unten; (motion)
nach unten; (towards speaker)
herunter; (away from speaker)
hinunter; **~ here/there** hier/dort
unten; (downstairs) **they came
~ for breakfast** sie kamen zum
Frühstück herunter; (southwards)
he came ~ from Scotland er kam
von Schottland herunter ▷ prep
(towards speaker) herunter; (away
from speaker) hinunter; **to drive
~ the hill/road** den Berg/die
Straße hinunter fahren; (along) **to
walk ~ the street** die Straße
entlang gehen; **he's ~ the pub**
(fam) er ist in der Kneipe ▷ vt
(fam: drink) runterkippen ▷ adj
niedergeschlagen, deprimiert
down-and-out adj
heruntergekommen ▷ n
Obdachlose(r) mf, Penner(in) m(f);
downcast adj niedergeschlagen;
downfall n Sturz m;
down-hearted adj entmutigt;
downhill adv bergab; **he's going
~** (fig) mit ihm geht es bergab

- **DOWNING STREET**
-
- **Downing Street** ist die Straße
- in London, die von Whitehall
- zum St James's Park führt, und
- in der sich der offizielle
- Wohnsitz des Premierministers
- (Nr. 10) und des Finanzministers
- (Nr. 11) befindet. Im weiteren
- Sinne bezieht sich der Begriff
- „Downing Street" auf die
- britische Regierung.

download ['daʊnləʊd] vt
downloaden, herunterladen;
downmarket adj für den
Massenmarkt; **down payment** n
Anzahlung f; **downpour** n

Platzregen m; **downs** npl
Hügelland nt; **downsize** vt
(business) verkleinern ▷ vi sich
verkleinern
Down's syndrome
['daʊnz'sɪndrəʊm] n (Med)
Downsyndrom nt
downstairs [daʊn'stɛəz] adv
unten; (motion) nach unten;
downstream adv flussabwärts;
downtime n Ausfallzeit f;
downtown adv (be, work etc) in
der Innenstadt; (go) in die
Innenstadt ▷ adj (US) in der
Innenstadt; **~ Chicago** die
Innenstadt von Chicago; **down
under** adv (fam: in/to Australia)
in/nach Australien; (in/to New
Zealand) in/nach Neuseeland;
downwards adv, adj nach unten;
(movement, trend) Abwärts-
doze [dəʊz] vi dösen ▷ n Nickerchen nt
dozen ['dʌzn] n Dutzend nt; **two
~ eggs** zwei Dutzend Eier; **~s of
times** x-mal
DP abbr = **data processing** DV f
drab [dræb] adj trist; (colour)
düster
draft [drɑ:ft] n (outline) Entwurf
m; (US Mil) Einberufung f
drag [dræg] vt schleppen ▷ n (fam)
to be a ~ (boring) stinklangweilig
sein; (laborious) ein ziemlicher
Schlauch sein; **drag on** vi sich in
die Länge ziehen
dragon ['drægən] n Drache m;
dragonfly n Libelle f
drain [dreɪn] n Abfluss m ▷ vt
(water, oil) ablassen; (vegetables etc)
abgießen; (land) entwässern,
trockenlegen ▷ vi (of water)
abfließen; **drainpipe** n
Abflussrohr nt
drama ['drɑ:mə] n (a. fig) Drama
nt; **dramatic** [drə'mætɪk] adj
dramatisch

drank [dræŋk] *pt of* **drink**
drapes [dreɪps] *npl* (*US*)
Vorhänge *pl*
drastic ['dræstɪk] *adj* drastisch
draught [drɑːft] *n* (Luft)zug *m*;
there's a ~ es zieht; **on ~** (*beer*)
vom Fass; **draughts** *nsing*
Damespiel *nt*; **draughty** *adj*
zugig
draw [drɔː] (**drew, drawn**) *vt*
(*pull*) ziehen; (*crowd*) anlocken,
anziehen; (*picture*) zeichnen ▷ *vi*
(*Sport*) unentschieden spielen ▷ *n*
(*Sport*) Unentschieden *nt*;
(*attraction*) Attraktion *f*; (*for lottery*)
Ziehung *f*; **draw out** *vt*
herausziehen; (*money*) abheben;
draw up *vt* (*formulate*) entwerfen;
(*list*) erstellen ▷ *vi* (*car*) anhalten;
drawback *n* Nachteil *m*;
drawbridge *n* Zugbrücke *f*
drawer ['drɔː*] *n* Schublade *f*
drawing ['drɔːɪŋ] *n* Zeichnung *f*;
drawing pin *n* Reißzwecke *f*
drawn [drɔːn] *pp of* **draw**
dread [dred] *n* Furcht *f* (*of* vor
+*dat*) ▷ *vt* sich fürchten vor +*dat*;
dreadful *adj* furchtbar;
dreadlocks *npl* Rastalocken *pl*
dream [driːm] (**dreamed** *o*
dreamt, dreamed *o* **dreamt**) *vt, vi*
träumen (*about* von) ▷ *n* Traum *m*;
dreamt [dremt] *pt, pp of* **dream**
dreary ['drɪərɪ] *adj* (*weather*,
place) trostlos; (*book etc*) langweilig
drench [drentʃ] *vt* durchnässen
dress [dres] *n* Kleidung *f*;
(*garment*) Kleid *nt* ▷ *vt* anziehen;
(*Med: wound*) verbinden; **to get
~ed** sich anziehen; **dress up** *vi*
sich fein machen; (*in costume*) sich
verkleiden (*as* als); **dress circle** *n*
(*Theat*) erster Rang; **dresser** *n*
Anrichte *f*; (*US: dressing table*)
(Frisier)kommode *f*; **dressing** *n*
(*Gastr*) Dressing *nt*, Soße *f*; (*Med*)
Verband *m*; **dressing gown** *n*

Bademantel *m*; **dressing room** *n*
(*Theat*) Künstlergarderobe *f*;
dressing table *n*
Frisierkommode *f*; **dress
rehearsal** *n* (*Theat*) Generalprobe
f
drew [druː] *pt of* **draw**
dried [draɪd] *adj* getrocknet;
(*milk, flowers*) Trocken-; **~ fruit**
Dörrobst *nt*; **drier** ['draɪə*] *n see*
dryer
drift [drɪft] *vi* treiben ▷ *n* (*of*
snow) Verwehung *f*; (*fig*) Tendenz *f*;
if you get my ~ wenn du mich
richtig verstehst/wenn Sie mich
richtig verstehen
drill [drɪl] *n* Bohrer *m* ▷ *vt, vi*
bohren
drink [drɪŋk] (**drank, drunk**) *vt,*
vi trinken ▷ *n* Getränk *nt*;
(*alcoholic*) Drink *m*; **drink-driving**
n (*Brit*) Trunkenheit *f* am Steuer;
drinking water *n* Trinkwasser
nt
drip [drɪp] *n* Tropfen *m* ▷ *vi*
tropfen; **drip-dry** *adj* bügelfrei;
dripping *n* Bratenfett *nt* ▷ *adj*:
~ (wet) tropfnass
drive [draɪv] (**drove, driven**) *vt*
(*car, person in car*) fahren; (*force:*
person, animal) treiben; (*Tech*)
antreiben; **to ~ sb mad** jdn
verrückt machen ▷ *vi* fahren ▷ *n*
Fahrt *f*; (*entrance*) Einfahrt *f*,
Auffahrt *f*; (*Inform*) Laufwerk *nt*; **to
go for a ~** spazieren fahren; **drive
away, drive off** *vi* wegfahren
▷ *vt* vertreiben
drive-in *adj* Drive-in-; **~ cinema**
(*US*) Autokino *nt*
driven ['drɪvn] *pp of* **drive**
driver ['draɪvə*] *n* Fahrer(in)
m(f); (*Inform*) Treiber *m*; **~'s license**
(*US*) Führerschein *m*; **~'s seat**
Fahrersitz *m*; **driving** ['draɪvɪŋ]
n (Auto)fahren *nt*; **he likes ~** er
fährt gern Auto; **driving lesson** *n*

Fahrstunde f; **driving licence** n (Brit) Führerschein m; **driving school** n Fahrschule f; **driving seat** n (Brit) Fahrersitz m; **to be in the ~** alles im Griff haben; **driving test** n Fahrprüfung f

drizzle ['drɪzl] n Nieselregen m ▷ vi nieseln

drop [drɒp] n (of liquid) Tropfen m; (fall in price etc) Rückgang m ▷ vt (a. fig: give up) fallen lassen ▷ vi (fall) herunterfallen; (figures, temperature) sinken, zurückgehen; **drop by, drop in** vi vorbeikommen; **drop off** vi (to sleep) einnicken; **drop out** vi (withdraw) aussteigen; (university) das Studium abbrechen; **dropout** n Aussteiger(in) m(f)

drought [draut] n Dürre f

drove [drəuv] pt of **drive**

drown [draun] vi ertrinken ▷ vt ertränken

drowsy ['drauzɪ] adj schläfrig

drug [drʌg] n (Med) Medikament nt, Arznei f; (addictive) Droge f; (narcotic) Rauschgift nt; **to be on ~s** drogensüchtig sein ▷ vt (mit Medikamenten) betäuben; **drug addict** n Rauschgiftsüchtige(r) mf; **drug dealer** n Drogenhändler(in) m(f); **druggist** n (US) Drogist(in) m(f); **drugstore** n (US) Drogerie f

drum [drʌm] n Trommel f; **~s** pl Schlagzeug nt; **drummer** n Schlagzeuger(in) m(f)

drunk [drʌŋk] pp of **drink** ▷ adj betrunken; **to get ~** sich betrinken ▷ n Betrunkene(r) mf; (alcoholic) Trinker(in) m(f); **drunk-driving** n (US) Trunkenheit f am Steuer; **drunken** adj betrunken, besoffen

dry [draɪ] adj trocken ▷ vt trocknen; (dishes, oneself, one's hands etc) abtrocknen ▷ vi trocknen, trocken werden; **dry out** vi trocknen; **dry up** vi austrocknen; **dry-clean** vt chemisch reinigen; **dry-cleaning** n chemische Reinigung; **dryer** n Trockner m; (for hair) Föhn m; (over head) Trockenhaube f

DTP abbr = **desktop publishing** DTP nt

dual ['djʊəl] adj doppelt; **~ carriageway** (Brit) zweispurige Schnellstraße f; **~ nationality** doppelte Staatsangehörigkeit

dubbed [dʌbd] adj (film) synchronisiert

dubious ['dju:bɪəs] adj zweifelhaft

duchess ['dʌtʃəs] n Herzogin f

duck [dʌk] n Ente f

dude [du:d] n (US fam) Typ m; **a cool ~** ein cooler Typ

due [dju:] adj (time) fällig; (fitting) angemessen; **in ~ course** zu gegebener Zeit; **~ to** infolge +gen, wegen +gen ▷ adv: **~ south/north** etc direkt nach Norden/Süden etc

dug [dʌg] pt, pp of **dig**

duke [dju:k] n Herzog m

dull [dʌl] adj (colour, light, weather) trübe; (boring) langweilig

duly ['dju:lɪ] adv ordnungsgemäß; (as expected) wie erwartet

dumb [dʌm] adj stumm; (fam: stupid) doof, blöde

dumb-bell ['dʌmbel] n Hantel f

dummy ['dʌmɪ] n (sham) Attrappe f; (in shop) Schaufensterpuppe f; (Brit: teat) Schnuller m; (fam: person) Dummkopf m ▷ adj unecht, Schein-; **~ run** Testlauf m

dump [dʌmp] n Abfallhaufen m; (fam: place) Kaff nt ▷ vt (lit, fig) abladen; (fam) **he ~ed her** er hat mir ihr Schluss gemacht

dumpling ['dʌmplɪŋ] n Kloß m, Knödel m

dune [dju:n] n Düne f

dung [dʌŋ] n (manure) Mist m
dungarees [dʌŋgə'riːz] npl
Latzhose f
dungeon ['dʌndʒən] n Kerker m
duplex ['djuːpleks] n
zweistöckige Wohnung; (US)
Doppelhaushälfte f
duplicate ['djuːplɪkɪt] n Dup-
likat nt ▷ ['djuːplɪkeɪt] vt (make
copies of) kopieren; (repeat)
wiederholen
durable ['djʊərəbl] adj haltbar;
duration [djʊə'reɪʃən] n Dauer f
during ['djʊərɪŋ] prep (time)
während +gen
dusk [dʌsk] n Abenddämmerung f
dust [dʌst] n Staub m ▷ vt
abstauben; **dustbin** n (Brit)
Mülleimer m; **dustcart** n (Brit)
Müllwagen m; **duster** n
Staubtuch nt; **dust jacket** n
Schutzumschlag m; **dustman** n
(Brit) Müllmann m; **dustpan** n
Kehrschaufel f; **dusty** adj staubig
Dutch [dʌtʃ] adj holländisch ▷ n
(language) Holländisch nt; **to
speak/talk double ~** (fam)
Quatsch reden; **the ~** pl die
Holländer; **Dutchman** (pl **-men**)
n Holländer m; **Dutchwoman** (pl
-women) n Holländerin f
duty ['djuːtɪ] n Pflicht f; (task)
Aufgabe f; (tax) Zoll m; **on/off ~** im
Dienst/nicht im Dienst; **to be on
~** Dienst haben; **duty-free** adj
zollfrei; **~ shop** Dutyfreeshop m
duvet ['duːveɪ] n Federbett nt
DVD n abbr = **digital versatile
disk** DVD f; **DVD player** n
DVD-Player m; **DVD recorder** n
DVD-Rekorder m
dwelling ['dwelɪŋ] n Wohnung f
dwindle ['dwɪndl] vi schwinden
dye [daɪ] n Farbstoff m ▷ vt
färben
dynamic [daɪ'næmɪk] adj
dynamisch

dynamo ['daɪnəməʊ] n Dynamo m
dyslexia [dɪs'leksɪə] n Legasthenie
f; **dyslexic** adj legasthenisch; **to
be ~** Legastheniker(in) sein

e

E [iː] *abbr* = **east** (*geo*) O; *abbr* =
ecstasy (*drug*) Ecstasy *nt*

E111 form *n* ≈
Auslandskrankenschein *m*

each [iːtʃ] *adj* jeder/jede/jedes
▷ *pron* jeder/jede/jedes; **I'll have
one of ~** ich nehme von jedem
eins; **they ~ have a car** jeder von
ihnen hat ein Auto; **~ other**
einander, sich; **for/against
~ other** füreinander/
gegeneinander ▷ *adv* je; **they
cost 10 euros ~** sie kosten je 10
Euro, sie kosten 10 Euro das Stück

eager ['iːgə*] *adj* eifrig; **to be ~ to
do sth** darauf brennen, etw zu tun

eagle ['iːgl] *n* Adler *m*

ear [ɪə*] *n* Ohr *nt*; **earache** *n*
Ohrenschmerzen *pl*; **eardrum** *n*
Trommelfell *nt*

earl [ɜːl] *n* Graf *m*

early ['ɜːlɪ] *adj, adv* früh; **to be 10
minutes ~** 10 Minuten zu früh

kommen; **at the earliest**
frühestens; **in ~ June/2008**
Anfang Juni/2008; **~ retirement**
vorzeitiger Ruhestand; **~ warning
system** Frühwarnsystem *nt*

earn [ɜːn] *vt* verdienen

earnest ['ɜːnɪst] *adj* ernst; **in
~** im Ernst

earnings ['ɜːnɪŋz] *npl* Verdienst
m, Einkommen *nt*

earplug *n* Ohrenstöpsel *m*,
Ohropax® *nt*; **earring** *n* Ohrring
m

earth [ɜːθ] *n* Erde *f*; **what on
~ ...?** was in aller Welt ...? ▷ *vt*
erden; **earthenware** *n* Tonwaren
pl; **earthquake** *n* Erdbeben *nt*

earwig ['ɪəwɪg] *n* Ohrwurm *m*

ease [iːz] *vt* (*pain*) lindern;
(*burden*) erleichtern ▷ *n* (*easiness*)
Leichtigkeit *f*; **to feel at ~** sich
wohlfühlen; **to feel ill at ~** sich
nicht wohlfühlen; **easily** ['iːzɪlɪ]
adv leicht; **he is ~ the best** er ist
mit Abstand der Beste

east [iːst] *n* Osten *m*; **to the ~ of**
östlich von ▷ *adv* (*go, face*) nach
Osten ▷ *adj* Ost-; **~ wind** Ostwind
m; **eastbound** *adj* (in) Richtung
Osten

Easter ['iːstə*] *n* Ostern *nt*; **at
~** zu Ostern; **Easter egg** *n* Osterei
nt; **Easter Sunday** *n*
Ostersonntag *m*

eastern ['iːstən] *adj* Ost-,
östlich; **Eastern Europe**
Osteuropa *nt*; **East Germany** *n*
Ostdeutschland *nt*; **former ~** die
ehemalige DDR, die neuen
Bundesländer; **eastwards**
['iːstwədz] *adv* nach Osten

easy ['iːzɪ] *adj* leicht; (*task,
solution*) einfach; (*life*) bequem;
(*manner*) ungezwungen;
easy-going *adj* gelassen

eat [iːt] (**ate, eaten**) *vt* essen;
(*animal*) fressen; **eat out** *vi* zum

Essen ausgehen; **eat up** vt
aufessen; (*animal*) auffressen
eaten ['i:tn] pp of **eat**
eavesdrop ['i:vzdrɒp] vi (heimlich) lauschen; **to ~ on sb** jdn
belauschen
eccentric [ɪk'sentrɪk] adj
exzentrisch
echo ['ekəʊ] (pl **-es**) n Echo nt
▷ vi widerhallen
ecological [i:kə'lɒdʒɪkl] adj
ökologisch; **~ disaster**
Umweltkatastrophe f; **ecology**
[ɪ'kɒlədʒɪ] n Ökologie f
economic [i:kə'nɒmɪk] adj
wirtschaftlich, Wirtschafts-; **~ aid**
Wirtschaftshilfe f; **economical** adj
wirtschaftlich; (*person*) sparsam;
economics nsing o pl
Wirtschaftswissenschaft f;
economist [ɪ'kɒnəmɪst] n
Wirtschaftswissenschaftler(in)
m(f); **economize** [ɪ'kɒnəmaɪz] vi
sparen (on an +dat); **economy**
[ɪ'kɒnəmɪ] n (of state) Wirtschaft
f; (*thrift*) Sparsamkeit f; **economy
class** n (Aviat) Economyclass f
ecstasy ['ekstəsɪ] n Ekstase f;
(*drug*) Ecstasy f
eczema ['eksɪmə] n Ekzem nt
edge [edʒ] n Rand m; (of knife)
Schneide f; **on ~** nervös; **edgy**
['edʒɪ] adj nervös
edible ['edɪbl] adj essbar
Edinburgh ['edɪnbərə] n Edin-
burg nt
edit ['edɪt] vt (*series, newspaper
etc*) herausgeben; (*text*) redigieren;
(*film*) schneiden; (*Inform*)
editieren; **edition** [ɪ'dɪʃən] n
Ausgabe f; **editor** n Redakteur(in)
m(f); (of series etc) Herausgeber(in)
m(f); **editorial** [edɪ'tɔ:rɪəl] adj
Redaktions- ▷ n Leitartikel m
educate ['edjʊkeɪt] vt (*child*)
erziehen; (*at school, university*)
ausbilden; (*public*) aufklären;

educated adj gebildet;
education [edjʊ'keɪʃən] n
Erziehung f; (*studies, training*)
Ausbildung f; (*subject of study*)
Pädagogik f; (*system*) Schulwesen
nt; (*knowledge*) Bildung f;
educational adj pädagogisch;
(*instructive*) lehrreich; **~ television**
Schulfernsehen nt
eel [i:l] n Aal m
eerie ['ɪərɪ] adj unheimlich
effect [ɪ'fekt] n Wirkung f (on auf
+akk); **to come into ~** in Kraft
treten; **effective** adj wirksam,
effektiv
effeminate [ɪ'femɪnət] adj (of
man) tuntig
efficiency [ɪ'fɪʃənsɪ] n Leistungsfähigkeit f; (of method)
Wirksamkeit f; **efficient** adj
(Tech) leistungsfähig; (method)
wirksam, effizient
effort ['efət] n Anstrengung f;
(*attempt*) Versuch m; **to make an
~** sich anstrengen; **effortless** adj
mühelos
e.g. abbr = **exempli gratia (for
example)** z. B.
egg [eg] n Ei nt; **eggcup** n
Eierbecher m; **eggplant** n (US)
Aubergine f; **eggshell** n
Eierschale f
ego ['i:gəʊ] (pl **-s**) n Ich nt;
(*self-esteem*) Selbstbewusstsein nt;
ego(t)ist ['egəʊ(t)ɪst] n Ego-
zentriker(in) m(f)
Egypt ['i:dʒɪpt] n Ägypten nt;
Egyptian [ɪ'dʒɪpʃən] adj
ägyptisch ▷ n Ägypter(in) m(f)
eiderdown ['aɪdədaʊn] n
Daunendecke f
eight [eɪt] num acht; **at the age
of ~** im Alter von acht Jahren; **it's
~ (o'clock)** es ist acht Uhr ▷ n (a.
bus etc) Acht f; (boat) Achter m;
eighteen [eɪ'ti:n] num achtzehn
▷ n Achtzehn f; see also **eight**;

eighteenth adj achtzehnte(r, s);
see also **eighth**; **eighth** [eɪtθ] adj
achte(r, s); **the ~ of June** der achte
Juni ▷ n (fraction) Achtel nt; **an
~ of a litre** ein Achtelliter;
eightieth ['eɪtɪəθ] adj achtzig-
ste(r, s); see also **eighth**; **eighty**
['eɪtɪ] num achtzig ▷ n Achtzig f;
see also **eight**

Eire ['ɛərə] n die Republik Irland

either ['aɪðə°] conj: **~ ... or**
entweder ... oder ▷ pron: **~ of the
two** eine(r, s) von beiden ▷ adj:
on ~ side auf beiden Seiten ▷ adv:
I won't go ~ ich gehe auch nicht

eject [ɪ'dʒekt] vt ausstoßen;
(person) vertreiben

elaborate [ɪ'læbərət] adj (complex) kompliziert; (plan)
ausgeklügelt; (decoration)
kunstvoll ▷ vi [ɪ'læbəreɪt] **could
you ~ on that?** könntest
du/könnten Sie mehr darüber
sagen?

elastic [ɪ'læstɪk] adj elastisch;
~ band Gummiband nt

elbow ['elbəʊ] n Ellbogen m; **to
give sb the ~** (fam) jdm den
Laufpass geben

elder ['eldə°] adj (of two) älter ▷ n
Ältere(r) mf; (Bot) Holunder m;
elderly adj ältere(r, s) ▷ n: **the
~** die älteren Leute; **eldest**
['eldɪst] adj älteste(r, s)

elect [ɪ'lekt] vt wählen; **he was
~ed chairman** er wurde zum
Vorsitzenden gewählt; **election**
[ɪ'lekʃən] n Wahl f; **election
campaign** n Wahlkampf m;
electioneering [ɪlekʃə'nɪərɪŋ] n
Wahlpropaganda f; **electorate**
[ɪ'lektərɪt] n Wähler pl

electric [ɪ'lektrɪk] adj elektrisch;
(car, motor, razor etc) Elektro-;
~ blanket Heizdecke f; **~ cooker**
Elektroherd m; **~ current**
elektrischer Strom; **~ shock**
Stromschlag m; **electrical** adj
elektrisch; **~ goods/appliances**
Elektrogeräte; **electrician**
[ɪlek'trɪʃən] n Elektriker(in) m(f);
electricity [ɪlek'trɪsɪtɪ] n Elektrizität f; **electrocute**
[ɪ'lektrəkjuːt] vt durch einen
Stromschlag töten; **electronic**
[ɪlek'trɒnɪk] adj elektronisch

elegance ['elɪɡəns] n Eleganz f;
elegant adj elegant

element ['elɪmənt] n Element
nt; **an ~ of truth** ein Körnchen
Wahrheit; **elementary**
[elɪ'mentərɪ] adj einfach; (basic)
grundlegend; **~ stage**
Anfangsstadium nt; **~ school** (US)
Grundschule f; **~ maths/French**
Grundkenntnisse in
Mathematik/Französisch

elephant ['elɪfənt] n Elefant m

elevator ['elɪveɪtə°] n (US)
Fahrstuhl m

eleven [ɪ'levn] num elf
▷ n (team, bus etc) Elf f see
eight; **eleventh** [ɪ'levnθ] adj
elfte(r, s) ▷ n (fraction) Elftel nt
see **eighth**

eligible ['elɪdʒəbl] adj infrage
kommend; (for grant etc)
berechtigt; **~ for a
pension/competition**
pensions-/teilnahmeberechtigt;
~ bachelor begehrter Junggeselle

eliminate [ɪ'lɪmɪneɪt] vt
ausschließen (from aus),
ausschalten; (problem etc)
beseitigen; **elimination** n
Ausschluss m (from aus); (of problem
etc) Beseitigung f

elm [elm] n Ulme f

elope [ɪ'ləʊp] vi durchbrennen
(with sb mit jdm)

eloquent ['eləkwənt] adj
redegewandt

else [els] adv: **anybody/any-
thing ~** (in addition) sonst (noch)

jemand/etwas; (*other*) ein anderer/etwas anderes;
somebody ~ jemand anders;
everyone ~ alle anderen; **or ~**; **elsewhere** *adv* anderswo, woanders; (*direction*) woandershin

ELT *abbr* = **English Language Teaching**

e-mail, E-mail ['i:meɪl] *vi, vt* mailen (*sth to sb* jdm etw) ▷ *n* E-Mail *f*; **e-mail address** *n* E-Mail-Adresse *f*

emancipated [ɪ'mænsɪpeɪtɪd] *adj* emanzipiert

embankment [ɪm'bæŋkmənt] *n* Böschung *f*; (*for railway*) Bahndamm *m*

embargo [ɪm'bɑːgəʊ] (*pl* **-es**) *n* Embargo *nt*

embark [ɪm'bɑːk] *vi* an Bord gehen

embarrass [ɪm'bærəs] *vt* in Verlegenheit bringen;
embarrassed *adj* verlegen;
embarrassing *adj* peinlich

embassy ['embəsɪ] *n* Botschaft *f*

embrace [ɪm'breɪs] *vt* umarmen ▷ *n* Umarmung *f*

embroider [ɪm'brɔɪdə*] *vt* besticken; **embroidery** *n* Stickerei *f*

embryo ['embrɪəʊ] (*pl* **-s**) *n* Embryo *m*

emerald ['emərəld] *n* Smaragd *m*

emerge [ɪ'mɜːdʒ] *vi* auftauchen;
it ~d that ... es stellte sich heraus, dass ...

emergency [ɪ'mɜːdʒənsɪ] *n* Notfall *m* ▷ *adj* Not-; **~ exit** Notausgang *m*; **~ landing** Notlandung *f*; **~ room** (*US*) Unfallstation *f*; **~ service** Notdienst *m*; **~ stop** Vollbremsung *f*

emigrate ['emɪɡreɪt] *vi* auswandern

emit [ɪ'mɪt] *vt* ausstoßen; (*heat*) abgeben

emotion [ɪ'məʊʃən] *n* Emotion *f*, Gefühl *nt*; **emotional** *adj* (*person*) emotional; (*experience, moment, scene*) ergreifend

emperor ['empərə*] *n* Kaiser *m*

emphasis ['emfəsɪs] *n* Betonung *f*; **emphasize** ['emfəsaɪz] *vt* betonen; **emphatic, emphatically** [ɪm'fætɪk, -lɪ] *adj, adv* nachdrücklich

empire ['empaɪə*] *n* Reich *nt*

employ [ɪm'plɔɪ] *vt* beschäftigen; (*hire*) anstellen; (*use*) anwenden; **employee** [emplɔɪ'i:] *n* Angestellte(r) *mf*; **employer** *n* Arbeitgeber(in) *m(f)*;
employment *n* Beschäftigung *f*; (*position*) Stellung *f*; **employment agency** *n* Stellenvermittlung *f*

empress ['emprɪs] *n* Kaiserin *f*

empty ['emptɪ] *adj* leer ▷ *vt* (*contents*) leeren; (*container*) ausleeren

enable [ɪ'neɪbl] *vt*: **to ~ sb to do sth** es jdm ermöglichen, etw zu tun

enamel [ɪ'næməl] *n* Email *nt*; (*of teeth*) Zahnschmelz *m*

enchanting [ɪn'tʃɑːntɪŋ] *adj* bezaubernd

enclose [ɪn'kləʊz] *vt* einschließen; (*in letter*) beilegen (*in, with dat*); **enclosure** [ɪn'kləʊʒə*] *n* (*for animals*) Gehege *nt*; (*in letter*) Anlage *f*

encore ['ɒŋkɔː*] *n* Zugabe *f*

encounter [ɪn'kaʊntə*] *n* Begegnung *f* ▷ *vt* (*person*) begegnen +*dat*; (*difficulties*) stoßen auf +*akk*

encourage [ɪn'kʌrɪdʒ] *vt* ermutigen; **encouragement** *n* Ermutigung *f*

encyclopaedia
[ensaɪklə(ʊ)'piːdɪə] n Lexikon nt,
Enzyklopädie f
end [end] n Ende nt; (of film, play
etc) Schluss m; (purpose) Zweck m;
at the ~ of May Ende Mai; **in the
~** schließlich; **to come to an ~** zu
Ende gehen ▷ vt beenden ▷ vi
enden; **end up** vi enden
endanger [ɪn'deɪndʒə°] vt
gefährden; **~ed species** vom
Aussterben bedrohte Art
endeavour [ɪn'devə°] n Bemühung f ▷ vt sich bemühen
(to do sth etw zu tun)
ending ['endɪŋ] n (of book)
Ausgang m; (last part) Schluss m;
(of word) Endung f; **endless**
['endlɪs] adj endlos; (possibilities)
unendlich
endurance [ɪn'djʊərəns] n
Ausdauer f; **endure** [ɪn'djʊə°] vt
ertragen
enemy ['enɪmɪ] n Feind(in) m(f)
▷ adj feindlich
energetic [enə'dʒetɪk] adj
energiegeladen; (active) aktiv;
energy ['enədʒɪ] n Energie f
enforce [ɪn'fɔːs] vt durchsetzen;
(obedience) erzwingen
engage [ɪn'geɪdʒ] vt (employ)
einstellen; (singer, performer)
engagieren; **engaged** adj verlobt;
(toilet, telephone line) besetzt; **to
get ~** sich verloben (to mit);
engaged tone n (Brit Tel)
Belegtzeichen nt; **engagement** n
(to marry) Verlobung f; **~ ring**
Verlobungsring m; **engaging** adj
gewinnend
engine ['endʒɪn] n (Auto) Motor
m; (Rail) Lokomotive f; **~ failure**
(Auto) Motorschaden m; **~ trouble**
(Auto) Defekt m am Motor;
engineer [endʒɪ'nɪə°] n In-
genieur(in) m(f); (US Rail)
Lokomotivführer(in) m(f);

engineering [endʒɪ'nɪərɪŋ] n
Technik f; (mechanical ~)
Maschinenbau m; (subject)
Ingenieurwesen nt; **engine
immobilizer** n (Auto)
Wegfahrsperre f
England ['ɪŋglənd] n England
nt; **English** adj englisch; **he's ~** er
ist Engländer; **the ~ Channel** der
Ärmelkanal ▷ n (language)
Englisch nt; **in ~** auf Englisch; **to
translate into ~** ins Englische
übersetzen; **the ~** pl die
Engländer; **Englishman** (pl -men)
n Engländer m; **Englishwoman**
(pl -women) n Engländerin f
engrave [ɪn'greɪv] vt ein-
gravieren; **engraving** n Stich
m
engrossed [ɪn'grəʊst] adj
vertieft (in sth in etw akk)
enigma [ɪ'nɪgmə] n Rätsel nt
enjoy [ɪn'dʒɔɪ] vt genießen; **I
~ reading** ich lese gern; **he ~s
teasing her** es macht ihm Spaß,
sie aufzuziehen; **did you ~ the
film?** hat dir der Film gefallen?;
enjoyable adj angenehm;
(entertaining) unterhaltsam;
enjoyment n Vergnügen nt;
(stronger) Freude f (of an +dat)
enlarge [ɪn'lɑːdʒ] vt vergrößern;
(expand) erweitern; **enlargement**
n Vergrößerung f
enormous, enormously
[ɪ'nɔːməs, -lɪ] adj, adv riesig,
ungeheuer
enough [ɪ'nʌf] adj genug; **that's
~** das reicht!; (stop it) Schluss
damit!; **I've had ~** das hat mir
gereicht; (to eat) ich bin satt ▷ adv
genug, genügend
enquire [ɪn'kwaɪə°] vi sich
erkundigen (about nach); **enquiry**
[ɪn'kwaɪərɪ] n (question) Anfrage
f; (for information) Erkundigung f
(about über +akk); (investigation)

Untersuchung f; **"Enquiries"** „Auskunft"

enrol [ɪnˈrəʊl] vi sich einschreiben; (for course, school) sich anmelden; **enrolment** n Einschreibung f, Anmeldung f

en suite [ɒnˈswiːt] adj, n: **room with ~** (**bathroom**) Zimmer nt mit eigenem Bad

ensure [ɪnˈʃʊə°] vt sicherstellen

enter [ˈentə°] vt eintreten in +akk, betreten; (drive into) einfahren in +akk; (country) einreisen in +akk; (in list) eintragen; (Inform) eingeben; (race, contest) teilnehmen an +dat ▷ vi (towards speaker) hereinkommen; (away from speaker) hineingehen

enterprise [ˈentəpraɪz] n (Comm) Unternehmen nt

entertain [entəˈteɪn] vt (guest) bewirten; (amuse) unterhalten; **entertaining** adj unterhaltsam; **entertainment** n (amusement) Unterhaltung f

enthusiasm [ɪnˈθjuːzɪæzəm] n Begeisterung f; **enthusiastic** [ɪnθjuːzɪˈæstɪk] adj begeistert (about von)

entice [ɪnˈtaɪs] vt locken; (lead astray) verleiten

entire, **entirely** [ɪnˈtaɪə°, -lɪ] adj, adv ganz

entitle [ɪnˈtaɪtl] vt (qualify) berechtigen (to zu); (name) betiteln

entrance [ˈentrəns] n Eingang m; (for vehicles) Einfahrt f; (entering) Eintritt m; (Theat) Auftritt m; **entrance exam** n Aufnahmeprüfung f; **entrance fee** n Eintrittsgeld nt

entrust [ɪnˈtrʌst] vt: **to ~ sb with sth** jdm etw anvertrauen

entry [ˈentrɪ] n (way in) Eingang m; (entering) Eintritt m; (in vehicle) Einfahrt f; (into country) Einreise f; (admission) Zutritt m; (in diary, accounts) Eintrag m; **"no ~"** „Eintritt verboten"; (for vehicles) „Einfahrt verboten"; **entry phone** n Türsprechanlage f

E-number n (food additive) E-Nummer f

envelope [ˈenvələʊp] n (Brief)umschlag m

enviable [ˈenvɪəbl] adj beneidenswert; **envious** [ˈenvɪəs] adj neidisch

environment [ɪnˈvaɪərənmənt] n Umgebung f; (ecology) Umwelt f; **environmental** [ɪnvaɪərənˈmentəl] adj Umwelt-; **~ pollution** Umweltverschmutzung f; **environmentalist** n Umweltschützer(in) m(f)

envy [ˈenvɪ] n Neid m (of auf +akk) ▷ vt beneiden (sb sth jdn um etw)

epic [ˈepɪk] n Epos nt; (film) Monumentalfilm m

epidemic [epɪˈdemɪk] n Epidemie f

epilepsy [ˈepɪlepsɪ] n Epilepsie f; **epileptic** [epɪˈleptɪk] adj epileptisch

episode [ˈepɪsəʊd] n Episode f; (TV) Folge f

epoch [ˈiːpɒk] n Zeitalter nt, Epoche f

equal [ˈiːkwl] adj gleich (to +dat) ▷ n Gleichgestellte(r) mf ▷ vt gleichen; (match) gleichkommen +dat; **two times two ~s four** zwei mal zwei ist gleich vier; **equality** [ɪˈkwɒlɪtɪ] n Gleichheit f; (equal rights) Gleichberechtigung f; **equalize** vi (Sport) ausgleichen; **equalizer** n (Sport) Ausgleichstreffer m; **equally** adv gleich; (on the other hand) andererseits; **equation** [ɪˈkweɪʒən] n (Math) Gleichung f

equator [ɪˈkweɪtə°] n Äquator m

equilibrium [iːkwɪˈlɪbrɪəm] *n*
Gleichgewicht *nt*

equip [ɪˈkwɪp] *vt* ausrüsten;
(*kitchen*) ausstatten; **equipment** *n*
Ausrüstung *f*; (*for kitchen*)
Ausstattung *f*; **electrical**
~ Elektrogeräte *pl*

equivalent [ɪˈkwɪvələnt] *adj*
gleichwertig (*to dat*);
(*corresponding*) entsprechend (*to dat*) ▷ *n* Äquivalent *nt*; (*amount*)
gleiche Menge; (*in money*)
Gegenwert *m*

era [ˈɪərə] *n* Ära *f*, Zeitalter *nt*

erase [ɪˈreɪz] *vt* ausradieren;
(*tape, disk*) löschen; **eraser** *n*
Radiergummi *m*

erect [ɪˈrekt] *adj* aufrecht ▷ *vt*
(*building, monument*) errichten;
(*tent*) aufstellen; **erection** *n*
Errichtung *f*; (*Anat*) Erektion *f*

erode [ɪˈrəʊd] *vt* zerfressen;
(*land*) auswaschen; (*rights, power*)
aushöhlen; **erosion** [ɪˈrəʊʒən] *n*
Erosion *f*

erotic [ɪˈrɒtɪk] *adj* erotisch

err [ɜː*] *vi* sich irren

errand [ˈerənd] *n* Besorgung *f*

erratic [ɪˈrætɪk] *adj* (*behaviour*)
unberechenbar; (*bus link etc*)
unregelmäßig; (*performance*)
unbeständig

error [ˈerə*] *n* Fehler *m*; **in**
~ irrtümlicherweise; **error**
message *n* (*Inform*)
Fehlermeldung *f*

erupt [ɪˈrʌpt] *vi* ausbrechen

escalator [ˈeskəleɪtə*] *n* Rolltreppe *f*

escalope [ˈeskəlɒp] *n* Schnitzel
nt

escape [ɪˈskeɪp] *n* Flucht *f*; (*from
prison etc*) Ausbruch *m*; **to have a**
narrow ~ gerade noch
davonkommen; **there's no ~** (*fig*)
es gibt keinen Ausweg ▷ *vt*
(*pursuers*) entkommen +*dat*;

(*punishment etc*) entgehen +*dat* ▷ *vi*
(*from pursuers*) entkommen (*from
dat*); (*from prison etc*) ausbrechen
(*from dat*); (*leak: gas*) ausströmen;
(*water*) auslaufen

escort [ˈeskɔːt] *n* (*companion*)
Begleiter(in) *m(f)*; (*guard*) Eskorte *f*
▷ *vt* [ɪˈskɔːt] (*lady*) begleiten

especially [ɪˈspeʃəlɪ] *adv*
besonders

espionage [ˈespɪənɑːʒ] *n* Spio-
nage *f*

Esquire [ɪˈskwaɪə*] *n* (*Brit: in
address*): **J. Brown, Esq** Herrn J.
Brown

essay [ˈeseɪ] *n* Aufsatz *m*;
(*literary*) Essay *m*

essential [ɪˈsenʃəl] *adj* (*necessary*) unentbehrlich,
unverzichtbar; (*basic*) wesentlich
▷ *n* **the ~s** *pl* das Wesentliche;
essentially *adv* im Wesentlichen

establish [ɪˈstæblɪʃ] *vt* (*set up*)
gründen; (*introduce*) einführen;
(*relations*) aufnehmen; (*prove*)
nachweisen; **to ~ that ...**
feststellen, dass ...;
establishment *n* Institution *f*;
(*business*) Unternehmen *nt*

estate [ɪˈsteɪt] *n* Gut *nt*; (*of
deceased*) Nachlass *m*; (*housing ~*)
Siedlung *f*; (*country house*) Landsitz
m; **estate agent** *n* (*Brit*)
Grundstücksmakler(in) *m(f)*,
Immobilienmakler(in) *m(f)*; **estate**
car *n* (*Brit*) Kombiwagen *m*

estimate [ˈestɪmət] *n* Schätzung
f; (*Comm: of price*)
Kostenvoranschlag *m* ▷ [ˈestɪmeɪt]
vt schätzen

Estonia [eˈstəʊnɪə] *n* Estland *nt*;
Estonian [eˈstəʊnɪən] ▷ *adj*
estnisch; ▷ *n* (*person*) Este *m*;
Estin *f*; (*language*) Estnisch *nt*

estuary [ˈestjʊərɪ] *n* Mündung *f*

etching [ˈetʃɪŋ] *n* Radierung *f*

eternal, **eternally** [ɪˈtɜːnl, -nəlɪ]

adj, adv ewig; **eternity** *n* Ewigkeit *f*

ethical ['eθɪkəl] *adj* ethisch; **ethics** ['eθɪks] *npl* Ethik *f*

Ethiopia [iːθɪ'əʊpɪə] *n* Äthiopien *nt*

ethnic ['eθnɪk] *adj* ethnisch; (*clothes etc*) landesüblich; **~ minority** ethnische Minderheit

EU *abbr* = **European Union** EU *f*

euphemism ['juːfɪmɪzəm] *n* Euphemismus *m*

euro ['jʊərəʊ] (*pl* **-s**) *n* (*Fin*) Euro *m*; **~ symbol** Eurozeichen *nt*; **Eurocheque** ['jʊərəʊtʃek] *n* Euroscheck *m*; **Europe** ['jʊərəp] *n* Europa *nt*; **European** [jʊərə'piːən] *adj* europäisch; **~ Parliament** Europäisches Parlament; **~ Union** Europäische Union ▷ *n* Europäer(in) *m(f)*; **Eurosceptic** ['jʊərəʊskeptɪk] *n* Euroskeptiker(in) *m(f)*; **Eurotunnel** *n* Eurotunnel *m*

evacuate [ɪ'vækjʊeɪt] *vt* (*place*) räumen; (*people*) evakuieren

evade [ɪ'veɪd] *vt* ausweichen +*dat*; (*pursuers*) sich entziehen +*dat*

evaluate [ɪ'væljʊeɪt] *vt* auswerten

evaporate [ɪ'væpəreɪt] *vi* verdampfen; (*fig*) verschwinden; **~d milk** Kondensmilch *f*

even ['iːvən] *adj* (*flat*) eben; (*regular*) gleichmäßig; (*equal*) gleich; (*number*) gerade; **the score is ~** es steht unentschieden ▷ *adv* sogar; **~ you** selbst (o sogar) du/Sie; **~ if** selbst wenn, wenn auch; **~ though** obwohl; **not ~** nicht einmal; **~ better** noch besser; **even out** *vi* (*prices*) sich einpendeln

evening ['iːvnɪŋ] *n* Abend *m*; **in the ~** abends, am Abend; **this ~** heute Abend; **evening class** *n* Abendkurs *m*; **evening dress** *n*

(*generally*) Abendkleidung *f*; (*woman's*) Abendkleid *nt*

evenly ['iːvənlɪ] *adv* gleichmäßig

event [ɪ'vent] *n* Ereignis *nt*; (*organized*) Veranstaltung *f*; (*Sport: discipline*) Disziplin *f*; **in the ~ of** im Falle +*gen*; **eventful** *adj* ereignisreich

eventual [ɪ'ventʃʊəl] *adj* (*final*) letztendlich; **eventually** [ɪ'ventʃʊəlɪ] *adv* (*at last*) am Ende; (*given time*) schließlich

ever ['evə*] *adv* (*at any time*) je(mals); **don't ~ do that again** tu das ja nie wieder; **he's the best ~** er ist der Beste, den es je gegeben hat; **have you ~ been to the States?** bist du schon einmal in den Staaten gewesen?; **for ~** (für) immer; **for ~ and ~** auf immer und ewig; **~ so ...** (*fam*) äußerst ...; **~ so drunk** ganz schön betrunken

every ['evrɪ] *adj* jeder/jede/ jedes; **~ day** jeden Tag; **~ other day** jeden zweiten Tag; **~ five days** alle fünf Tage; **I have ~ reason to believe that ...** ich habe allen Grund anzunehmen, dass ...; **everybody** *pron* jeder, alle *pl*; **everyday** *adj* (*commonplace*) alltäglich; (*clothes, language etc*) Alltags-; **everyone** *pron* jeder, alle *pl*; **everything** *pron* alles; **everywhere** *adv* überall; (*with direction*) überallhin

evidence ['evɪdəns] *n* Beweise *pl*; (*single piece*) Beweis *m*; (*testimony*) Aussage *f*; (*signs*) Spuren *pl*; **evident, evidently** *adj, adv* offensichtlich

evil ['iːvl] *adj* böse ▷ *n* Böse(s) *nt*; **an ~** ein Übel

evolution [iːvə'luːʃən] *n* Entwicklung *f*; (*of life*) Evolution *f*; **evolve** [ɪ'vɒlv] *vi* sich entwickeln

ex- [eks] *pref* Ex-, ehemalig;

~boyfriend Exfreund *m*; **~wife** frühere Frau, Exfrau *f*; **ex** *n* (*fam*) Verflossene(r) *mf*, Ex *mf*

exact [ɪg'zækt] *adj* genau; **exactly** *adv* genau; **not ~ fast** nicht gerade schnell

exaggerate [ɪg'zædʒəreɪt] *vt, vi* übertreiben; **exaggerated** *adj* übertrieben; **exaggeration** *n* Übertreibung *f*

exam [ɪg'zæm] *n* Prüfung *f*; **examination** [ɪgzæmɪ'neɪʃən] *n* (*Med etc*) Untersuchung *f*, Prüfung *f*; (*at university*) Examen *nt*; (*at customs etc*) Kontrolle *f*; **examine** [ɪg'zæmɪn] *vt* untersuchen (*for* auf +*akk*); (*check*) kontrollieren, prüfen; **examiner** *n* Prüfer(in) *m(f)*

example [ɪg'zɑːmpl] *n* Beispiel *nt* (*of* für +*akk*); **for ~** zum Beispiel

excavation [ekskə'veɪʃən] *n* Ausgrabung *f*

exceed [ɪk'siːd] *vt* überschreiten, übertreffen; **exceedingly** *adv* äußerst

excel [ɪk'sel] *vt* übertreffen; **he ~led himself** er hat sich selbst übertroffen ▷ *vi* sich auszeichnen (*in* in +*dat*, *at* bei); **excellent, excellently** ['eksələnt, -lɪ] *adj, adv* ausgezeichnet

except [ɪk'sept] *prep*: **~** außer +*dat*; **~ for** abgesehen von ▷ *vt* ausnehmen; **exception** [ɪk'sepʃən] *n* Ausnahme *f*; **exceptional, exceptionally** [ɪk'sepʃənl, -nəlɪ] *adj, adv* außergewöhnlich

excess [ek'ses] *n* Übermaß *nt* (*of* an +*dat*); **excess baggage** *n* Übergepäck *nt*; **excesses** *npl* Exzesse *pl*; (*drink, sex*) Ausschweifungen *pl*; **excessive, excessively** *adj, adv* übermäßig; **excess weight** *n* Übergewicht *nt*

exchange [ɪks'tʃeɪndʒ] *n* Austausch *m* (*for* gegen); (*of bought items*) Umtausch *m* (*for* gegen); (*Fin*) Wechsel *m*; (*Tel*) Vermittlung *f*, Zentrale *f* ▷ *vt* austauschen; (*goods*) tauschen; (*bought items*) umtauschen (*for* gegen); (*money, blows*) wechseln; **exchange rate** *n* Wechselkurs *m*

excite [ɪk'saɪt] *vt* erregen; **excited** *adj* aufgeregt; **to get ~** sich aufregen; **exciting** *adj* aufregend; (*book, film*) spannend

exclamation [eksklə'meɪʃən] *n* Ausruf *m*; **exclamation mark**, **exclamation point** (*US*) *n* Ausrufezeichen *nt*

exclude [ɪks'kluːd] *vt* ausschließen; **exclusion** [ɪks'kluːʒən] *n* Ausschluss *m*; **exclusive** [ɪks'kluːsɪv] *adj* (*select*) exklusiv; (*sole*) ausschließlich; **exclusively** *adv* ausschließlich

excrement ['ekskrɪmənt] *n* Kot *m*, Exkremente *pl*

excruciating [ɪks'kruːʃieɪtɪŋ] *adj* fürchterlich, entsetzlich

excursion [ɪks'kɜːʃən] *n* Ausflug *m*

excusable [ɪks'kjuːzəbl] *adj* entschuldbar; **excuse** [ɪks'kjuːz] *vt* entschuldigen; **~ me** Entschuldigung!; **to ~ sb for sth** jdm etw verzeihen; **to ~ sb from sth** jdn von etw befreien ▷ [ɪks'kjuːs] *n* Entschuldigung *f*, Ausrede *f*

ex-directory [eksdaɪ'rektərɪ] *adj*: **to be ~** (*Brit Tel*) nicht im Telefonbuch stehen

execute ['eksɪkjuːt] *vt* (*carry out*) ausführen; (*kill*) hinrichten; **execution** *n* (*killing*) Hinrichtung *f*; (*carrying out*) Ausführung *f*; **executive** [ɪg'zekjʊtɪv] *n* (*Comm*) leitender Angestellter, leitende Angestellte

exemplary [ɪgˈzemplərɪ] *adj* beispielhaft

exempt [ɪgˈzempt] *adj* befreit (*from* von) ▷ *vt* befreien

exercise [ˈeksəsaɪz] *n* (*in school, sports*) Übung *f*; (*movement*) Bewegung *f*; **to get more ~** mehr Sport treiben; **exercise bike** *n* Heimtrainer *m*; **exercise book** *n* Heft *nt*

exert [ɪgˈzɜːt] *vt* (*influence*) ausüben

exhaust [ɪgˈzɔːst] *n* (*fumes*) Abgase *pl*; (*Auto*) **~ (pipe)** Auspuff *m*; **exhausted** *adj* erschöpft; **exhausting** *adj* anstrengend

exhibit [ɪgˈzɪbɪt] *n* (*in exhibition*) Ausstellungsstück *nt*; **exhibition** [eksɪˈbɪʃən] *n* Ausstellung *f*; **exhibitionist** [eksɪˈbɪʃənɪst] *n* Selbstdarsteller(in) *m(f)*; **exhibitor** *n* Aussteller(in) *m(f)*

exhilarating [ɪgˈzɪləreɪtɪŋ] *adj* belebend, erregend

exile [ˈeksaɪl] *n* Exil *nt*; (*person*) Verbannte(r) *mf* ▷ *vt* verbannen

exist [ɪgˈzɪst] *vi* existieren; (*live*) leben (*on* von); **existence** *n* Existenz *f*; **to come into ~** entstehen; **existing** *adj* bestehend

exit [ˈeksɪt] *n* Ausgang *m*; (*for vehicles*) Ausfahrt *f*; **exit poll** *n* Umfrage direkt nach dem Wahlgang

exorbitant [ɪgˈzɔːbɪtənt] *adj* astronomisch

exotic [ɪgˈzɒtɪk] *adj* exotisch

expand [ɪksˈpænd] *vt* ausdehnen, erweitern ▷ *vi* sich ausdehnen; **expansion** [ɪksˈpænʃən] *n* Expansion *f*, Erweiterung *f*

expect [ɪkˈspekt] *vt* erwarten; (*suppose*) annehmen; **he ~s me to do it** er erwartet, dass ich es mache; **I ~ it'll rain** es wird wohl regnen; **I ~ so** ich denke schon

▷ *vi*: **she's ~ing** sie bekommt ein Kind

expedition [ekspɪˈdɪʃən] *n* Expedition *f*

expenditure [ɪkˈspendɪtʃə°] *n* Ausgaben *pl*

expense [ɪkˈspens] *n* Kosten *pl*; (*single cost*) Ausgabe *f*; (**business**) **~s** *pl* Spesen *pl*; **at sb's ~** auf jds Kosten; **expensive** [ɪkˈspensɪv] *adj* teuer

experience [ɪkˈspɪərɪəns] *n* Erfahrung *f*; (*particular incident*) Erlebnis *nt*; **by/from ~** aus Erfahrung ▷ *vt* erfahren, erleben; (*hardship*) durchmachen; **experienced** *adj* erfahren

experiment [ɪkˈsperɪmənt] *n* Versuch *m*, Experiment *nt* ▷ *vi* experimentieren

expert [ˈekspɜːt] *n* Experte *m*, Expertin *f*; (*professional*) Fachmann *m*, Fachfrau *f*; (*Jur*) Sachverständige(r) *mf* ▷ *adj* fachmännisch, Fach-; **expertise** [ekspəˈtiːz] *n* Sachkenntnis *f*

expire [ɪkˈspaɪə°] *vi* (*end*) ablaufen; **expiry date** [ɪkˈspaɪərɪdeɪt] *n* Verfallsdatum *nt*

explain [ɪkˈspleɪn] *vt* erklären (*sth to sb* jdm etw); **explanation** [ekspləˈneɪʃən] *n* Erklärung *f*

explicit [ɪkˈsplɪsɪt] *adj* ausdrücklich, eindeutig

explode [ɪkˈspləʊd] *vi* explodieren

exploit [ɪkˈsplɔɪt] *vt* ausbeuten

explore [ɪkˈsplɔː°] *vt* erforschen

explosion [ɪkˈspləʊʒən] *n* Explosion *f*; **explosive** [ɪkˈspləʊsɪv] *adj* explosiv ▷ *n* Sprengstoff *m*

export [ekˈspɔːt] *vt*, *vi* exportieren ▷ [ˈekspɔːt] *n* Export *m* ▷ *adj* (*trade*) Export-

expose [ɪkˈspəʊz] *vt* (*to danger*

etc) aussetzen (to dat); (uncover) freilegen; (imposter) entlarven; **exposed** adj (position) ungeschützt; **exposure** [ɪkˈspəʊʒəʳ] n (Med) Unterkühlung f; (Foto: time) Belichtung(szeit) f; **24 ~s** 24 Aufnahmen

express [ɪkˈspres] adj (speedy) Express-, Schnell-; **~ delivery** Eilzustellung f ▷ n (Rail) Schnellzug m ▷ vt ausdrücken ▷ vr: **to ~ oneself** sich ausdrücken; **expression** [ɪkˈspreʃən] n (phrase) Ausdruck m; (look) Gesichtsausdruck m; **expressive** adj ausdrucksvoll; **expressway** n (US) Schnellstraße f

extend [ɪkˈstend] vt (arms) ausstrecken; (lengthen) verlängern; (building) vergrößern, ausbauen; (business, limits) erweitern; **extension** [ɪkˈstenʃən] n (lengthening) Verlängerung f; (of building) Anbau m; (Tel) Anschluss m; (of business, limits) Erweiterung f; **extensive** [ɪkˈstensɪv] adj (knowledge) umfangreich; (use) häufig; **extent** [ɪkˈstent] n (length) Länge f; (size) Ausdehnung f; (scope) Umfang m, Ausmaß nt; **to a certain/large ~** in gewissem/hohem Maße

exterior [ekˈstɪərɪəʳ] n Äußere(s) nt

external [ekˈstɜːnl] adj äußere(r, s), Außen-; **externally** adv äußerlich

extinct [ɪkˈstɪŋkt] adj (species) ausgestorben

extinguish [ɪkˈstɪŋgwɪʃ] vt löschen; **extinguisher** n Löschgerät nt

extra [ˈekstrə] adj zusätzlich; **~ charge** Zuschlag m; **~ time** (Sport) Verlängerung f ▷ adv

besonders; **~ large** (clothing) übergroß ▷ npl: **~s** zusätzliche Kosten pl; (food) Beilagen pl; (accessories) Zubehör nt; (for car etc) Extras pl

extract [ɪkˈstrækt] vt herausziehen (from aus); (tooth) ziehen ▷ [ˈekstrækt] n (from book etc) Auszug m

extraordinary [ɪkˈstrɔːdnrɪ] adj außerordentlich; (unusual) ungewöhnlich; (amazing) erstaunlich

extreme [ɪkˈstriːm] adj äußerste(r, s); (drastic) extrem ▷ n Extrem nt; **extremely** adv äußerst, höchst; **extreme sports** npl Extremsportarten pl; **extremist** [ɪkˈstriːmɪst] adj extremistisch ▷ n Extremist m

extricate [ˈekstrɪkeɪt] vt befreien (from aus)

extrovert [ˈekstrəʊvɜːt] adj extrovertiert

exuberance [ɪgˈzuːbərəns] n Überschwang m; **exuberant** adj überschwänglich

exultation [egzʌlˈteɪʃən] n Jubel m

eye [aɪ] n Auge nt; **to keep an ~ on sb/sth** auf jdn/etw aufpassen ▷ vt mustern; **eyebrow** n Augenbraue f; **eyelash** n Wimper f; **eyelid** n Augenlid nt; **eyeliner** n Eyeliner m; **eyeopener** n: **that was an ~** das hat mir die Augen geöffnet; **eyeshadow** n Lidschatten m; **eyesight** n Sehkraft f; **eyesore** n Schandfleck m; **eye witness** n Augenzeuge m, Augenzeugin f

f

fabric ['fæbrɪk] *n* Stoff *m*
fabulous ['fæbjʊləs] *adj* sagenhaft
façade [fə'sɑːd] *n* (*a. fig*) Fassade *f*
face [feɪs] *n* Gesicht *nt*; (*of clock*) Zifferblatt *nt*; (*of mountain*) Wand *f*; **in the ~ of** trotz +*gen*; **to be ~ to ~** (*people*) einander gegenüberstehen ▷ *vt, vi* (*person*) gegenüberstehen +*dat*; (*at table*) gegenübersitzen +*dat*; **to ~ north** (*room*) nach Norden gehen; **to ~ (up to) the facts** den Tatsachen ins Auge sehen; **to be ~d with sth** mit etw konfrontiert sein; **face lift** *n* Gesichtsstraffung *f*; (*fig*) Verschönerung *f*; **face powder** *n* Gesichtspuder *m*
facet ['fæsɪt] *n* (*fig*) Aspekt *m*
face value *n* Nennwert *m*
facial ['feɪʃəl] *adj* Gesichts- ▷ *n* (*fam*) (kosmetische) Gesichtsbehandlung

facilitate [fə'sɪlɪteɪt] *vt* erleichtern
facility [fə'sɪlɪtɪ] *n* (*building etc to be used*) Einrichtung *f*, Möglichkeit *f*; (*installation*) Anlage *f*; (*skill*) Gewandtheit *f*
fact [fækt] *n* Tatsache *f*; **as a matter of ~, in ~** eigentlich, tatsächlich
factor ['fæktə*] *n* Faktor *m*
factory ['fæktərɪ] *n* Fabrik *f*; **factory outlet** *n* Fabrikverkauf *m*
factual ['fæktjʊəl] *adj* sachlich
faculty ['fækəltɪ] *n* Fähigkeit *f*; (*at university*) Fakultät *f*; (*US: teaching staff*) Lehrkörper *m*
fade [feɪd] *vi* (*a. fig*) verblassen; **faded** *adj* verblasst, verblichen
faff about ['fæfəbaʊt] *vi* (*Brit fam*) herumwursteln
fag [fæg] *n* (*Brit fam: cigarette*) Kippe *f*; (*US fam pej*) Schwule(r) *m*
Fahrenheit ['færənhaɪt] *n* Fahrenheit
fail [feɪl] *vt* (*exam*) nicht bestehen ▷ *vi* versagen; (*plan, marriage*) scheitern; (*student*) durchfallen; (*eyesight*) nachlassen; **words ~ me** ich bin sprachlos; **failing** *n* Schwäche *f*; **failure** ['feɪljə*] *n* (*person*) Versager(in) *m(f)*; (*act, a. Tech*) Versagen *nt*; (*of engine etc*) Ausfall *m*; (*of plan, marriage*) Scheitern *nt*
faint [feɪnt] *adj* schwach; (*sound*) leise; (*fam*) **I haven't the ~est** (**idea**) ich habe keinen blassen Schimmer ▷ *vi* ohnmächtig werden (*with* vor +*dat*); **faintness** *n* (*Med*) Schwächegefühl *nt*
fair [fɛə*] *adj* (*hair*) (dunkel)blond; (*skin*) hell; (*just*) gerecht, fair; (*reasonable*) ganz ordentlich; (*in school*) befriedigend; (*weather*) schön; (*wind*) günstig; **a ~ number/amount of** ziemlich viele/viel ▷ *adv*: **to play ~** fair

spielen; (fig) fair sein; **~ enough** in Ordnung! ▷ n (fun~) Jahrmarkt m; (Comm) Messe f; **fair-haired** adj (dunkel)blond; **fairly** adv (honestly) fair; (rather) ziemlich

fairy ['fɛərɪ] n Fee f; **fairy tale** n Märchen nt

faith [feɪθ] n (trust) Vertrauen nt (in sb zu jdm); (Rel) Glaube m; **faithful, faithfully** adj, adv treu; **Yours ~ly** Hochachtungsvoll

fake [feɪk] n (thing) Fälschung f ▷ adj vorgetäuscht ▷ vt fälschen

falcon ['fɔːlkən] n Falke m

fall [fɔːl] (**fell, fallen**) vi fallen; (from a height, badly) stürzen; **to ~ ill** krank werden; **to ~ asleep** einschlafen; **to ~ in love** sich verlieben ▷ n Fall m; (accident, fig: of regime) Sturz m; (decrease) Sinken nt (in +gen); (US: autumn) Herbst m; **fall apart** vi auseinanderfallen; **fall behind** vi zurückbleiben; (with work, rent) in Rückstand geraten; **fall down** vi (person) hinfallen; **fall off** vi herunterfallen; (decrease) zurückgehen; **fall out** vi herausfallen; (quarrel) sich streiten; **fall over** vi hinfallen; **fall through** vi (plan etc) ins Wasser fallen

fallen ['fɔːlən] pp of **fall**

fallout ['fɔːlaʊt] n radioaktiver Niederschlag, Fall-out m

false [fɔːls] adj falsch; (artificial) künstlich; **false alarm** n blinder Alarm; **false start** n (Sport) Fehlstart m; **false teeth** npl (künstliches) Gebiss

fame [feɪm] n Ruhm m

familiar [fə'mɪlɪə*] adj vertraut, bekannt; **to be ~ with** vertraut sein mit, gut kennen; **familiarity** [fəmɪlɪ'ærɪtɪ] n Vertrautheit f

family ['fæmɪlɪ] n Familie f; (including relations) Verwandtschaft f; **family man** n Familienvater m; **family name** n Familienname m, Nachname m; **family practitioner** n (US) Allgemeinarzt m, Allgemeinärztin f

famine ['fæmɪn] n Hungersnot f; **famished** ['fæmɪʃt] adj ausgehungert

famous ['feɪməs] adj berühmt

fan [fæn] n (hand-held) Fächer m; (Elec) Ventilator m; (admirer) Fan m

fanatic [fə'nætɪk] n Fanatiker(in) m(f)

fancy ['fænsɪ] adj (elaborate) kunstvoll; (unusual) ausgefallen ▷ vt (like) gernhaben; **he fancies her** er steht auf sie; **~ that** stell dir vor!, so was!; **fancy dress** n Kostüm nt, Verkleidung f

fan heater ['fænhiːtə*] n Heizlüfter m; **fanlight** n Oberlicht m

fan mail n Fanpost f

fantasise ['fæntəsaɪz] vi träumen (about von); **fantastic** [fæn'tæstɪk] adj (a. fam) fantastisch; **that's ~** (fam) das ist ja toll!; **fantasy** ['fæntəzɪ] n Fantasie f

far [fɑː*] (**further** o **farther, furthest** o **farthest**) adj weit; **the ~ end of the room** das andere Ende des Zimmers; **the Far East** der Ferne Osten ▷ adv weit; **~ better** viel besser; **by ~ the best** bei weitem der/die/das Beste; **as ~ as …** bis zum o zur …; (with place name) bis nach …; **as ~ as I'm concerned** was mich betrifft, von mir aus; **so ~** soweit, bisher; **faraway** adj weit entfernt; (look) verträumt

fare [fɛə*] n Fahrpreis m; (money) Fahrgeld nt

farm [fɑːm] n Bauernhof m, Farm f; **farmer** n Bauer m, Bäuerin f, Landwirt(in) m(f); **farmhouse** n

Bauernhaus nt; **farming** n
Landwirtschaft f; **farmland** n
Ackerland nt; **farmyard** n Hof m

far-reaching ['fɑːriːtʃɪŋ] adj
weit reichend; **far-sighted** adj
weitsichtig; (fig) weitblickend

fart [fɑːt] n (fam) Furz m; **old
~** (fam: person) alter Sack ▷ vi (fam)
furzen

farther ['fɑːðə*] adj, adv
comparative of **far**; see **further**

farthest ['fɑːðɪst] adj, adv
superlative of **far**; see **furthest**

fascinating ['fæsɪneɪtɪŋ] adj
faszinierend; **fascination** n
Faszination f

fascism ['fæʃɪzəm] n Faschismus
m; **fascist** ['fæʃɪst] adj
faschistisch ▷ Faschist(in) m(f)

fashion ['fæʃən] n (clothes) Mode
f; (manner) Art (und Weise) f; **to be
in ~** (in) Mode sein; **out of
~** unmodisch; **fashionable,
fashionably** adj, adv (clothes,
person) modisch; (author, pub etc) in
Mode

fast [fɑːst] adj schnell; **to be
~** (clock) vorgehen ▷ adv schnell;
(firmly) fest; **to be ~ asleep** fest
schlafen ▷ n Fasten nt ▷ vi
fasten; **fastback** n (Auto)
Fließheck nt

fasten ['fɑːsn] vt (attach)
befestigen (to an +dat); (do up)
zumachen; **~ your seatbelts** bitte
anschnallen; **fastener, fastening**
n Verschluss m

fast food n Fast Food nt; **fast
forward** n (for tape)
Schnellvorlauf m; **fast lane** n
Überholspur f

fat [fæt] adj dick; (meat) fett ▷ n
Fett nt

fatal ['feɪtl] adj tödlich

fate [feɪt] n Schicksal nt

fat-free adj (food) fettfrei

father ['fɑːðə*] n Vater m; (priest)

Pfarrer m ▷ vt (child) zeugen;
Father Christmas n der
Weihnachtsmann; **father-in-law**
(pl **fathers-in-law**) n
Schwiegervater m

fatigue [fə'tiːg] n Ermüdung
f

fattening ['fætnɪŋ] adj: **to be
~** dick machen; **fatty** ['fætɪ] adj
(food) fettig

faucet ['fɔːsɪt] n (US)
Wasserhahn m

fault [fɔːlt] n Fehler m; (Tech)
Defekt m; (Elec) Störung f; (blame)
Schuld f; **it's your ~** du bist daran
schuld; **faulty** adj fehlerhaft;
(Tech) defekt

favor (US), **favour** ['feɪvə*] n
(approval) Gunst f; (kindness)
Gefallen m; **in ~ of** für; **I'm in ~ (of
going)** ich bin dafür(, dass wir
gehen); **to do sb a ~** jdm einen
Gefallen tun ▷ vt (prefer)
vorziehen; **favourable** adj
günstig (to, for für); **favourite**
['feɪvərɪt] n Liebling m,
Favorit(in) m(f) ▷ adj Lieblings-

fax [fæks] vt faxen ▷ n Fax nt;
fax number n Faxnummer f

faze [feɪz] vt (fam) aus der
Fassung bringen

FBI abbr = **Federal Bureau of
Investigation** FBI nt

fear [fɪə*] n Angst f (of vor +dat)
▷ vt befürchten; **fearful** adj
(timid) ängstlich, furchtsam;
(terrible) fürchterlich; **fearless** adj
furchtlos

feasible ['fiːzəbl] adj machbar

feast [fiːst] n Festessen nt

feather ['feðə*] n Feder f

feature ['fiːtʃə*] n (facial)
(Gesichts)zug m; (characteristic)
Merkmal nt; (of car etc)
Ausstattungsmerkmal nt; (in the
press) (Cine) Feature nt ▷ vt
bringen, (als Besonderheit)

zeigen; **feature film** n Spielfilm
m

February ['februərɪ] n Februar
m; see also **September**

fed [fed] pt, pp of **feed**

federal ['fedərəl] adj Bundes-;
**the Federal Republic of
Germany** die Bundesrepublik
Deutschland

fed-up [fed'ʌp] adj: **to be ~ with
sth** etw satthaben; **I'm ~** ich habe
die Nase voll

fee [fiː] n Gebühr f; (of doctor,
lawyer) Honorar m

feeble ['fiːbl] adj schwach

feed [fiːd] (**fed, fed**) vt (baby,
animal) füttern; (support) ernähren
▷ n (for baby) Mahlzeit f; (for
animals) Futter nt; (Inform: paper ~)
Zufuhr f; **feed in** vt (information)
eingeben; **feedback** n
(information) Feed-back nt

feel [fiːl] (**felt, felt**) vt (sense)
fühlen; (pain) empfinden; (touch)
anfassen; (think) meinen ▷ vi
(person) sich fühlen; **I ~ cold** mir ist
kalt; **do you ~ like a walk?** hast du
Lust, spazieren zu gehen?; **feeling**
n Gefühl nt

feet [fiːt] pl of **foot**

fell [fel] pt of **fall** ▷ vt (tree) fällen

fellow ['feləu] n Kerl m, Typ m;
~ citizen Mitbürger(in) m(f);
~ countryman Landsmann m;
~ worker Mitarbeiter(in) m(f)

felt [felt] pt, pp of **feel** ▷ n Filz m;
felt tip, felt-tip pen n Filzstift m

female ['fiːmeɪl] n (of animals)
Weibchen nt ▷ adj weiblich;
~ doctor Ärztin f; **feminine**
['femɪnɪn] adj weiblich; **feminist**
['femɪnɪst] n Feminist(in) m(f)
▷ adj feministisch

fence [fens] n Zaun m

fencing n (Sport) Fechten nt

fender ['fendə*] n (US Auto)
Kotflügel m

fennel ['fenl] n Fenchel m

fern [fɜːn] n Farn m

ferocious [fə'rəuʃəs] adj wild

ferry ['ferɪ] n Fähre f ▷ vt
übersetzen

fertile ['fɜːtaɪl] adj fruchtbar;
fertility [fə'tɪlɪtɪ] n Fruchtbarkeit
f; **fertilize** ['fɜːtɪlaɪz] vt (Bio)
befruchten; (Agr: land) düngen;
fertilizer n Dünger m

festival ['festɪvəl] n (Rel) Fest nt;
(Art, Mus) Festspiele pl; (pop music)
Festival nt; **festive** ['festɪv] adj
festlich; **festivities** [fe'stɪvɪtɪz] n
Feierlichkeiten pl

fetch [fetʃ] vt holen; (collect)
abholen; (in sale, money)
einbringen; **fetching** adj reizend

fetish ['fetɪʃ] n Fetisch m

fetus ['fiːtəs] n (US) Fötus m

fever ['fiːvə*] n Fieber nt;
feverish adj (Med) fiebrig; (fig)
fieberhaft

few [fjuː] adj, pron pl wenige pl; **a
~ pl** ein paar; **fewer** adj weniger;
fewest adj wenigste(r, s)

fiancé [fɪ'ɑ̃seɪ] n Verlobte(r) m;
fiancée n Verlobte f

fiasco [fɪ'æskəu] (pl -s o US -es) n
Fiasko nt

fiber (US), **fibre** ['faɪbə*] n
Faser f; (material) Faserstoff m

fickle ['fɪkl] adj unbeständig

fiction ['fɪkʃən] n (novels)
Prosaliteratur f; **fictional**,
fictitious [fɪk'tɪʃəs] adj erfunden

fiddle ['fɪdl] n Geige f; (trick)
Betrug m ▷ vt (accounts, results)
frisieren; **fiddle with** vt
herumfummeln an +dat; **fiddly**
adj knifflig

fidelity [fɪ'delɪtɪ] n Treue f

fidget ['fɪdʒɪt] vi zappeln;
fidgety adj zappelig

field [fiːld] n Feld nt;
(grass-covered) Wiese f; (fig: of work)
(Arbeits)gebiet nt

fierce [fɪəs] *adj* heftig; (*animal, appearance*) wild; (*criticism, competition*) scharf

fifteen [fɪf'tiːn] *num* fünfzehn ▷ *n* Fünfzehn *f*; *see also* **eight**; **fifteenth** *adj* fünfzehnte(r, s); *see also* **eighth**; **fifth** [fɪfθ] *adj* fünfte(r, s) ▷ *n* (*fraction*) Fünftel *nt*; *see also* **eighth**; **fifty** ['fɪftɪ] *num* fünfzig ▷ *n* Fünfzig *f*; *see also* **eight**; **fiftieth** *adj* fünfzigste(r, s); *see also* **eighth**

fig [fɪg] *n* Feige *f*

fight [faɪt] (**fought, fought**) *vi* kämpfen (*with, against* gegen, *for, over* um) ▷ *vt* (*person*) kämpfen mit; (*fig: disease, fire etc*) bekämpfen ▷ *n* Kampf *m*; (*brawl*) Schlägerei *f*; (*argument*) Streit *m*; **fight back** *vi* zurückschlagen; **fight off** *vt* abwehren; **fighter** *n* Kämpfer(in) *m(f)*

figurative ['fɪgərətɪv] *adj* übertragen

figure ['fɪgə°] *n* (*person*) Gestalt *f*; (*of person*) Figur *f*; (*number*) Zahl *f*, Ziffer *f*; (*amount*) Betrag *m*; **a four-figure sum** eine vierstellige Summe ▷ *vt* (*US: think*) glauben ▷ *vi* (*appear*) erscheinen; **figure out** *vt* (*work out*) herausbekommen; **I can't figure him out** ich werde aus ihm nicht schlau; **figure skating** *n* Eiskunstlauf *m*

file [faɪl] *n* (*tool*) Feile *f*; (*dossier*) Akte *f*; (*Inform*) Datei *f*; (*folder*) Aktenordner *m*; **on ~** in den Akten ▷ *vt* (*metal, nails*) feilen; (*papers*) ablegen (*under* unter) ▷ *vi*: **to ~ in/out** hintereinander hereinkommen/hinausgehen; **filing cabinet** *n* Aktenschrank *m*

fill [fɪl] *vt* füllen; (*tooth*) plombieren; (*post*) besetzen; **fill in** *vt* (*hole*) auffüllen; (*form*) ausfüllen; (*tell*) informieren (*on* über); **fill out**

vt (*form*) ausfüllen; **fill up** *vi* (*Auto*) volltanken

fillet ['fɪlɪt] *n* Filet *nt*

filling ['fɪlɪŋ] *n* (*Gastr*) Füllung *f*; (*for tooth*) Plombe *f*; **filling station** *n* Tankstelle *f*

film [fɪlm] *n* Film *m* ▷ *vt* (*scene*) filmen; **film star** *n* Filmstar *m*; **film studio** *n* Filmstudio *nt*

filter ['fɪltə°] *n* Filter *m*; (*traffic lane*) Abbiegespur *f* ▷ *vt* filtern

filth [fɪlθ] *n* Dreck *m*; **filthy** *adj* dreckig

fin [fɪn] *n* Flosse *f*

final ['faɪnl] *adj* letzte(r, s); (*stage, round*) End-; (*decision, version*) endgültig; **~ score** Schlussstand *m* ▷ *n* (*Sport*) Endspiel *nt*; (*competition*) Finale *nt*; **~s** *pl* Abschlussexamen *nt*; **finalize** *vt* die endgültige Form geben +*dat*; **finally** *adv* (*lastly*) zuletzt; (*eventually*) schließlich, endlich

finance [faɪ'næns] *n* Finanzwesen *nt*; **~s** *pl* Finanzen *pl* ▷ *vt* finanzieren; **financial** [faɪ'nænʃəl] *adj* finanziell; (*adviser, crisis, policy etc*) Finanz-

find [faɪnd] (**found, found**) *vt* finden; **he was found dead** er wurde tot aufgefunden; **I ~ myself in difficulties** ich befinde mich in Schwierigkeiten; **she ~s it difficult/easy** es fällt ihr schwer/leicht; **find out** *vt* herausfinden; **findings** *npl* (*Jur*) Ermittlungsergebnis *nt*; (*of report, Med*) Befund *m*

fine [faɪn] *adj* (*thin*) dünn, fein; (*good*) gut; (*splendid*) herrlich; (*clothes*) elegant; (*weather*) schön; **I'm ~** es geht mir gut; **that's ~** das ist OK ▷ *adv* (*well*) gut ▷ *n* (*Jur*) Geldstrafe *f* ▷ *vt* (*Jur*) mit einer Geldstrafe belegen; **fine arts** *npl*: **the ~** die schönen Künste *pl*;

finely *adv* (*cut*) dünn; (*ground*) fein

finger ['fɪŋgə*] *n* Finger *m* ▷ *vt* herumfingern an +*dat*; **fingernail** *n* Fingernagel *m*; **fingerprint** *n* Fingerabdruck *m*; **fingertip** *n* Fingerspitze *f*

finicky ['fɪnɪkɪ] *adj* (*person*) pingelig; (*work*) knifflig

finish ['fɪnɪʃ] *n* Ende *nt*; (*Sport*) Finish *nt*; (*line*) Ziel *nt*; (*of product*) Verarbeitung *f* ▷ *vt* beenden; (*book etc*) zu Ende lesen; (*food*) aufessen; (*drink*) austrinken ▷ *vi* zu Ende gehen; (*song, story*) enden; (*person*) fertig sein; (*stop*) aufhören; **have you ~ed?** bist du fertig?; **to ~ first/second** (*Sport*) als erster/zweiter durchs Ziel gehen; **finishing line** *n* Ziellinie *f*

Finland ['fɪnlənd] *n* Finnland *nt*; **Finn** *n* Finne *m*, Finnin *f*; **Finnish** *adj* finnisch ▷ *n* (*language*) Finnisch *nt*

fir [fɜ:*] *n* Tanne *f*

fire [faɪə*] *n* Feuer *nt*; (*house etc*) Brand *m*; **to set ~ to sth** etw in Brand stecken; **to be on ~** brennen ▷ *vt* (*bullets, rockets*) abfeuern; (*fam: dismiss*) feuern ▷ *vi* (*Auto: engine*) zünden; **to ~ at sb** auf jdn schießen; **fire alarm** *n* Feuermelder *m*; **fire brigade** *n* Feuerwehr *f*; **fire engine** *n* Feuerwehrauto *nt*; **fire escape** *n* Feuerleiter *f*; **fire extinguisher** *n* Feuerlöscher *m*; **firefighter** *n* Feuerwehrmann *m*, Feuerwehrfrau *f*; **fireman** *n* Feuerwehrmann *m*; **fireplace** *n* (offener) Kamin; **fireproof** *adj* feuerfest; **fire station** *n* Feuerwache *f*; **firewood** *n* Brennholz *nt*; **fireworks** *npl* Feuerwerk *nt*

firm [fɜ:m] *adj* fest; (*person*) **to be ~** entschlossen auftreten ▷ *n* Firma *f*

first [fɜ:st] *adj* erste(r, s) ▷ *adv* (*at first*) zuerst; (*firstly*) erstens; (*arrive, finish*) zum ersten Mal; **~ of all** zuallererst ▷ *n* (*person*) Erste(r) *mf*; (*Auto: gear*) erster Gang; **at ~** zuerst, anfangs; **first aid** *n* erste Hilfe; **first-class** *adj* erstklassig; (*compartment, ticket*) erster Klasse; **~ mail** (*Brit*) *bevorzugt beförderte Post* ▷ *adv* (*travel*) erster Klasse; **first floor** *n* (*Brit*) erster Stock; (*US*) Erdgeschoss *nt*; **first lady** *n* (*US*) Frau *f* des Präsidenten; **firstly** *adv* erstens; **first name** *n* Vorname *m*; **first night** *n* (*Theat*) Premiere *f*; **first-rate** *adj* erstklassig

fir tree *n* Tannenbaum *m*

fish [fɪʃ] *n* Fisch *m*; **~ and chips** (*Brit*) frittierter Fisch mit Pommes frites ▷ *vi* fischen; (*with rod*) angeln; **to go ~ing** fischen/angeln gehen; **fishbone** *n* Gräte *f*; **fishcake** *n* Fischfrikadelle *f*; **fish farm** *n* Fischzucht *f*; **fish finger** *n* (*Brit*) Fischstäbchen *nt*; **fishing** ['fɪʃɪŋ] *n* Fischen *nt*; (*with rod*) Angeln *nt*; (*as industry*) Fischerei *f*; **fishing boat** *n* Fischerboot *nt*; **fishing line** *n* Angelschnur *f*; **fishing rod** *n* Angelrute *f*; **fishing village** *n* Fischerdorf *nt*; **fishmonger** ['fɪʃmʌŋgə*] *n* Fischhändler(in) *m(f)*; **fish stick** *n* (*US*) Fischstäbchen *nt*; **fish tank** *n* Aquarium *nt*

fishy ['fɪʃɪ] *adj* (*fam: suspicious*) faul

fist [fɪst] *n* Faust *f*

fit [fɪt] *adj* (*Med*) gesund; (*Sport*) in Form, fit; (*suitable*) geeignet; **to keep ~** sich in Form halten ▷ *vt* passen +*dat*; (*attach*) anbringen (*to* an +*dat*); (*install*) einbauen (*in* in +*akk*) ▷ *vi* passen; (*in space, gap*) hineinpassen ▷ *n* (*of clothes*) Sitz *m*; (*Med*) Anfall *m*; **it's a good ~** es passt gut; **fit in** vt (accommodate) unterbringen; (find time for) einschieben ▷ vi (in space) hineinpassen; (plans, ideas) passen; **he doesn't ~** (here) er passt nicht hierher; **to ~ with sb's plans** sich mit jds Plänen vereinbaren lassen; **fitness** n (Med) Gesundheit f; (Sport) Fitness f; **fitness trainer** n (Sport) Fitnesstrainer(in) m(f); **fitted carpet** n Teppichboden m; **fitted kitchen** n Einbauküche f; **fitting** adj passend ▷ n (of dress) Anprobe f; **~s** pl Ausstattung f

five [faɪv] num fünf ▷ n Fünf f; see also **eight**; **fiver** n (Brit fam) Fünfpfundschein m

fix [fɪks] vt befestigen (to an +dat); (settle) festsetzen; (place, time) ausmachen; (repair) reparieren; **fixer** n (drug addict) Fixer(in) m(f); **fixture** ['fɪkstʃə*] n (Sport) Veranstaltung f; (match) Spiel nt; (in building) Installationsteil nt; **~s (and fittings)** pl Ausstattung f

fizzy ['fɪzɪ] adj sprudelnd; **~ drink** Limo f

flabbergasted ['flæbəgɑːstɪd] adj (fam) platt

flabby ['flæbɪ] adj (fat) wabbelig

flag [flæg] n Fahne f; **flagstone** n Steinplatte f

flake [fleɪk] n Flocke f ▷ vi: **to ~ (off)** abblättern

flamboyant [flæm'bɔɪənt] adj extravagant

flame [fleɪm] n Flamme f; (person) **an old ~** eine alte Liebe

flan [flæn] n (fruit ~) Obstkuchen m

flannel ['flænl] n Flanell m; (Brit: face~) Waschlappen m; (fam: waffle) Geschwafel nt ▷ vi herumlabern

flap [flæp] n Klappe f; (fam) **to be in a ~** rotieren ▷ vt (wings) schlagen mit ▷ vi flattern

flared [flɛəd] adj (trousers) mit Schlag; **flares** npl Schlaghose f

flash [flæʃ] n Blitz m; (news ~) Kurzmeldung f; (Foto) Blitzlicht nt; **in a ~** im Nu ▷ vt: **to ~ one's (head)lights** die Lichthupe betätigen ▷ vi aufblinken; (brightly) aufblitzen; **flashback** n Rückblende f, Flashback m; **flashlight** ['flæʃlaɪt] n (Photo) Blitzlicht nt; (US: torch) Taschenlampe f; **flashy** adj grell, schrill; (pej) protzig

flat [flæt] adj flach; (surface) eben; (drink) abgestanden; (tyre) platt; (battery) leer; (refusal) glatt ▷ n (Brit: rooms) Wohnung f; (Auto) Reifenpanne f; **flat screen** n (Inform) Flachbildschirm m; **flatten** vt platt machen, einebnen

flatter ['flætə*] vt schmeicheln +dat; **flattering** adj schmeichelhaft

flatware ['flætwɛə] n (US) Besteck nt

flavor (US), **flavour** ['fleɪvə*] n Geschmack m ▷ vt Geschmack geben +dat; (with spices) würzen; **flavouring** n Aroma nt

flaw [flɔː] n Fehler m; **flawless** adj fehlerlos; (complexion) makellos

flea [fliː] n Floh m

fled [fled] pt, pp of **flee**

flee [fliː] (**fled, fled**) vi fliehen

fleece [fliːs] n (of sheep) Vlies nt; (soft material) Fleece m; (jacket) Fleecejacke f

fleet [fliːt] n Flotte f

Flemish ['flemɪʃ] adj flämisch ▷ n (language) Flämisch nt

flesh [fleʃ] n Fleisch nt

flew [fluː] pt of **fly**

flex [fleks] n (Brit Elec) Schnur f

flexibility [fleksɪ'bɪlɪtɪ] n Biegsamkeit f; (fig) Flexibilität f; **flexible** ['fleksɪbl] adj biegsam;

(*plans, person*) flexibel; **flexitime** *n* gleitende Arbeitszeit, Gleitzeit *f*

flicker ['flɪkə*] *vi* flackern; (*TV*) flimmern

flies [flaɪz] *pl of* **fly** ▷ *n*

flight [flaɪt] *n* Flug *m*; (*escape*) Flucht *f*; **~ of stairs** Treppe *f*; **flight attendant** *n* Flugbegleiter(in) *m(f)*; **flight recorder** *n* Flugschreiber *m*

flimsy ['flɪmzɪ] *adj* leicht gebaut, nicht stabil; (*thin*) hauchdünn; (*excuse*) fadenscheinig

fling [flɪŋ] (**flung, flung**) *vt* schleudern ▷ *n*: **to have a ~** eine (kurze) Affäre haben

flip [flɪp] *vt* schnippen; **to ~ a coin** eine Münze werfen; **flip through** *vt* (*book*) durchblättern; **flipchart** *n* Flipchart *nt*

flipper ['flɪpə*] *n* Flosse *f*

flirt [flɜːt] *vi* flirten

float [fləʊt] *n* (*for fishing*) Schwimmer *m*; (*in procession*) Festwagen *m*; (*money*) Wechselgeld *nt* ▷ *vi* schwimmen; (*in air*) schweben

flock [flɒk] *n* (*of sheep*) (*Rel*) Herde *f*; (*of birds*) Schwarm *m*; (*of people*) Schar *f*

flog [flɒg] *vt* auspeitschen; (*Brit fam*) verscheuern

flood [flʌd] *n* Hochwasser *nt*, Überschwemmung *f*; (*fig*) Flut *f* ▷ *vt* überschwemmen; **floodlight** *n* Flutlicht *nt*; **floodlit** *adj* (*building*) angestrahlt

floor [flɔː*] *n* Fußboden *m*; (*storey*) Stock *m*; **ground ~** (*Brit*), **first ~** (*US*) Erdgeschoss *nt*; **first ~** (*Brit*), **second ~** (*US*) erster Stock; **floorboard** *n* Diele *f*

flop [flɒp] *n* (*fam: failure*) Reinfall *m*, Flop *m* ▷ *vi* misslingen, floppen

floppy disk ['flɒpɪ'dɪsk] *n* Diskette *f*

Florence ['flɒrəns] *n* Florenz *nt*

florist ['flɒrɪst] *n* Blumenhändler(in) *m(f)*; **florist's (shop)** ['flɒrɪsts] *n* Blumengeschäft *m(f)*

flounder ['flaʊndə*] *n* (*fish*) Flunder *f*

flour ['flaʊə*] *n* Mehl *nt*

flourish ['flʌrɪʃ] *vi* gedeihen; (*business*) gut laufen; (*boom*) florieren ▷ *vt* (*wave about*) schwenken; **flourishing** *adj* blühend

flow [fləʊ] *n* Fluss *m*; **to go with the ~** mit dem Strom schwimmen ▷ *vi* fließen

flower ['flaʊə*] *n* Blume *f* ▷ *vi* blühen; **flower bed** *n* Blumenbeet *nt*; **flowerpot** *n* Blumentopf *m*

flown [fləʊn] *pp of* **fly**

flu [fluː] *n* (*fam*) Grippe *f*

fluent *adj* (*Italian etc*) fließend; **to be ~ in German** fließend Deutsch sprechen

fluid ['fluːɪd] *n* Flüssigkeit *f* ▷ *adj* flüssig

flung [flʌŋ] *pt, pp of* **fling**

fluorescent [fluə'resnt] *adj* fluoreszierend, Leucht-

flush [flʌʃ] *n* (*lavatory*) Wasserspülung *f*; (*blush*) Röte *f* ▷ *vi* (*lavatory*) spülen

flute [fluːt] *n* Flöte *f*

fly [flaɪ] (**flew, flown**) *vt, vi* fliegen; **how time flies** wie die Zeit vergeht! ▷ *n* (*insect*) Fliege *f*; **~/flies** (*pl*) (*on trousers*) Hosenschlitz *m*; **fly-drive** *n* Urlaub *m* mit Flug und Mietwagen; **flyover** *n* (*Brit*) Straßenüberführung *f*, Eisenbahnüberführung *f*; **flysheet** *n* Überzelt *nt*

FM *abbr* = **frequency modulation** ≈ UKW

FO *abbr* = **Foreign Office** ≈ AA *nt*

foal [fəʊl] *n* Fohlen *nt*

foam [fəʊm] n Schaum m ▷ vi schäumen

fob off [fɒb ɒf] vt: **to fob sb off with sth** jdm etw andrehen

focus ['fəʊkəs] n Brennpunkt m; **in/out of ~** (photo) scharf/unscharf; (camera) scharf/unscharf eingestellt ▷ vt (camera) scharf stellen ▷ vi sich konzentrieren (on auf +akk)

foetus ['fiːtəs] n Fötus m

fog [fɒg] n Nebel m; **foggy** adj neblig; **fog light** n (Auto: at rear) Nebelschlussleuchte f

foil [fɔɪl] vt vereiteln ▷ n Folie f

fold [fəʊld] vt falten ▷ vi (fam: business) eingehen ▷ n Falte f; **fold up** vt (map etc) zusammenfalten; (chair etc) zusammenklappen ▷ vi (fam: business) eingehen ▷ n (portfolio) Aktenmappe f; (pamphlet) Broschüre f; (Inform) Ordner m; **folding** adj zusammenklappbar; (bicycle, chair) Klapp-

folk [fəʊk] n Leute pl; (Mus) Folk m; **my ~s** pl (fam) meine Leute ▷ adj Volks-

follow ['fɒləʊ] vt folgen +dat; (pursue) verfolgen; (understand) folgen können +dat; (career, news etc) verfolgen; **as ~s** wie folgt ▷ vi folgen; (result) sich ergeben (from aus); **follow up** vt (request, rumour) nachgehen +dat, weiter verfolgen; **follower** n Anhänger(in) m(f); **following** adj folgend; **the ~ day** am (darauf)folgenden Tag ▷ prep nach; **follow up** n (event, book etc) Fortsetzung f

fond [fɒnd] adj: **to be ~ of** gernhaben; **fondly** adv (with love) liebevoll; **fondness** n Vorliebe f; (for people) Zuneigung f

fondue ['fɒnduː] n Fondue nt

font [fɒnt] n Taufbecken nt; (Typo) Schriftart f

food [fuːd] n Essen nt, Lebensmittel pl; (for animals) Futter nt; (groceries) Lebensmittel pl; **food poisoning** n Lebensmittelvergiftung f; **food processor** n Küchenmaschine f; **foodstuff** n Lebensmittel nt

fool [fuːl] n Idiot m, Narr m; **to make a ~ of oneself** sich blamieren ▷ vt (deceive) hereinlegen ▷ vi: **to ~ around** herumalbern; (waste time) herumtrödeln; **foolish** adj dumm; **foolproof** adj idiotensicher

foot [fʊt] (pl **feet** [fiːt]) n Fuß m; (measure) Fuß m (30,48 cm); **on ~** zu Fuß ▷ vt (bill) bezahlen; **foot-and-mouth disease** n Maul- und Klauenseuche f; **football** n Fußball m; (US: American ~) Football m; **footballer** n Fußballspieler(in) m(f); **footbridge** n Fußgängerbrücke f; **footing** n (hold) Halt m; **footlights** npl Rampenlicht nt; **footnote** n Fußnote f; **footpath** n Fußweg m; **footprint** n Fußabdruck m; **footwear** n Schuhwerk nt

○ KEYWORD

for [fɔː*] prep **1** für; **is this for me?** ist das für mich?; **the train for London** der Zug nach London; **he went for the paper** er ging die Zeitung holen; **give it to me — what for?** gib es mir — warum? **2** (because of) wegen; **for this reason** aus diesem Grunde **3** (referring to distance) **there are roadworks for 5 km** die Baustelle ist 5 km lang; **we walked for miles** wir sind meilenweit gegangen

4 (*referring to time*) seit; (*with future sense*) für; **he was away for 2 years** er war zwei Jahre lang weg **5** (+*infin clauses*) **it is not for me to decide** das kann ich nicht entscheiden; **for this to be possible ...** damit dies möglich wird/wurde ... **6** (*in spite of*) trotz +*gen o* (*inf*) *dat*; **for all his complaints** obwohl er sich ständig beschwert
▷ *conj* denn

forbade [fə'bæd] *pt of* **forbid**
forbid [fə'bɪd] (**forbade, forbidden**) *vt* verbieten
force [fɔːs] *n* Kraft *f*; (*compulsion*) Zwang *m*, Gewalt; **to come into ~ in** Kraft treten; **the Forces** *pl* die Streitkräfte ▷ *vt* zwingen; **forced** *adj* (*smile*) gezwungen; **~ landing** Notlandung *f*; **forceful** *adj* kraftvoll
forceps ['fɔːseps] *npl* Zange *f*
forearm ['fɔːrɑːm] *n* Unterarm *m*
forecast ['fɔːkɑːst] *vt* voraussagen; (*weather*) vorhersagen ▷ *n* Vorhersage *f*
forefinger ['fɔːfɪŋɡə'] *n* Zeigefinger *m*
foreground ['fɔːɡraʊnd] *n* Vordergrund *m*
forehand ['fɔːhænd] *n* (*Sport*) Vorhand *f*
forehead ['fɔːhed, 'fɒrɪd] *n* Stirn *f*
foreign ['fɒrən] *adj* ausländisch; **foreigner** *n* Ausländer(in) *m(f)*; **foreign exchange** *n* Devisen *pl*; **foreign language** *n* Fremdsprache *f*; **foreign minister** *n* Außenminister(in) *m(f)*; **Foreign Office** *n* (*Brit*) Außenministerium *nt*; **Foreign Secretary** *n* (*Brit*) Außenminister(in) *m(f)*; **foreign policy** *n* Außenpolitik *f*

foremost ['fɔːməʊst] *adj* erste(r, s); (*leading*) führend
forerunner ['fɔːrʌnə'] *n* Vorläufer(in) *m(f)*
foresee [fɔː'siː] *irr vt* vorhersehen; **foreseeable** *adj* absehbar
forest ['fɒrɪst] *n* Wald *m*; **forestry** ['fɒrɪstrɪ] *n* Forstwirtschaft *f*
forever [fə'revə'] *adv* für immer
forgave [fə'ɡeɪv] *pt of* **forgive**
forge [fɔːdʒ] *n* Schmiede *f* ▷ *vt* schmieden; (*fake*) fälschen; **forger** *n* Fälscher(in) *m(f)*; **forgery** *n* Fälschung *f*
forget [fə'ɡet] (**forgot, forgotten**) *vt, vi* vergessen; **to ~ about sth** etw vergessen; **forgetful** *adj* vergesslich; **forgetfulness** *n* Vergesslichkeit *f*; **forget-me-not** *n* Vergissmeinnicht *nt*
forgive [fə'ɡɪv] (**forgave, forgiven**) *irr vt* verzeihen; **to ~ sb for sth** jdm etw verzeihen
forgot [fə'ɡɒt] *pt of* **forget**
forgotten [fə'ɡɒtn] *pp of* **forget**
fork [fɔːk] *n* Gabel *f*; (*in road*) Gabelung *f* ▷ *vi* (*road*) sich gabeln
form [fɔːm] *n* (*shape*) Form *f*, Klasse *f*; (*document*) Formular *nt*; (*person*) **to be in** (**good**) **~** in Form sein ▷ *vt* bilden
formal ['fɔːməl] *adj* förmlich, formell; **formality** [fɔː'mælɪtɪ] *n* Formalität *f*
format ['fɔːmæt] *n* Format *nt* ▷ *vt* (*Inform*) formatieren
former ['fɔːmə'] *adj* frühere(r, s); (*opposite of latter*) erstere(r, s); **formerly** *adv* früher
formidable ['fɔːmɪdəbl] *adj* gewaltig; (*opponent*) stark
formula ['fɔːmjʊlə] *n* Formel *f*
formulate ['fɔːmjʊleɪt] *vt* formulieren

forth [fɔ:θ] adv: **and so ~** und so weiter; **forthcoming** [fɔ:θˈkʌmɪŋ] adj kommend, bevorstehend

fortify [ˈfɔ:tɪfaɪ] vt verstärken; (for protection) befestigen

fortieth [ˈfɔ:tɪəθ] adj vierzigste(r, s); see also **eighth**

fortnight [ˈfɔ:tnaɪt] n vierzehn Tage pl

fortress [ˈfɔ:trɪs] n Festung f

fortunate [ˈfɔ:tʃənɪt] adj glücklich; **I was ~** ich hatte Glück; **fortunately** adv zum Glück; **fortune** [ˈfɔ:tʃən] n (money) Vermögen nt; **good ~** Glück nt; **fortune-teller** n Wahrsager(in) m(f)

forty [ˈfɔ:tɪ] num vierzig ▷ n Vierzig f; see also **eight**

forward [ˈfɔ:wəd] adv vorwärts ▷ n (Sport) Stürmer(in) m(f) ▷ vt (send on) nachsenden; (Inform) weiterleiten; **forwards** adv vorwärts

foster child [ˈfɒstətʃaɪld] n Pflegekind nt; **foster parents** npl Pflegeeltern pl

fought [fɔ:t] pt, pp of **fight**

foul [faʊl] adj (weather) schlecht; (smell) übel ▷ n (Sport) Foul nt

found [faʊnd] pt, pp of **find** ▷ vt (establish) gründen; **foundations** [faʊnˈdeɪʃənz] npl Fundament nt

fountain [ˈfaʊntɪn] n Springbrunnen m; **fountain pen** n Füller m

four [fɔ:*] num vier ▷ n Vier f; see also **eight**; **fourteen** [ˈfɔ:ti:n] num vierzehn ▷ n Vierzehn f; see also **eight**; **fourteenth** adj vierzehnte(r, s); see also **eighth**; **fourth** [fɔ:θ] adj vierte(r, s); see also **eighth**

four-wheel drive n Allradantrieb m; (car) Geländewagen m

fowl [faʊl] n Geflügel nt

fox [fɒks] n (a. fig) Fuchs m

fraction [ˈfrækʃən] n (Math) Bruch m; (part) Bruchteil m; **fracture** [ˈfræktʃə*] n (Med) Bruch m ▷ vt brechen

fragile [ˈfrædʒaɪl] adj zerbrechlich

fragment [ˈfrægmənt] n Bruchstück nt

fragrance [ˈfreɪgrəns] n Duft m; **fragrant** adj duftend

frail [freɪl] adj gebrechlich

frame [freɪm] n Rahmen m; (of spectacles) Gestell nt; **~ of mind** Verfassung f ▷ vt einrahmen; **to ~ sb** (fam: incriminate) jdm etwas anhängen; **framework** n Rahmen m, Struktur f

France [frɑ:ns] n Frankreich nt

frank [fræŋk] adj offen

frankfurter [ˈfræŋkfɜ:tə*] n (Frankfurter) Würstchen nt

frankly [ˈfræŋklɪ] adv offen gesagt; **quite ~** ganz ehrlich; **frankness** n Offenheit f

frantic [ˈfræntɪk] adj (activity) hektisch; (effort) verzweifelt; **~ with worry** außer sich vor Sorge

fraud [frɔ:d] n (trickery) Betrug m; (person) Schwindler(in) m(f)

freak [fri:k] n Anomalie f; (animal, person) Missgeburt f; (fam: fan) Fan m, Freak m ▷ adj (conditions) außergewöhnlich, seltsam; **freak out** vi (fam) ausflippen

freckle [ˈfrekl] n Sommersprosse f

free [fri:] adj, adv frei; (without payment) gratis, kostenlos; **for ~** umsonst ▷ vt befreien; **freebie** [ˈfri:bɪ] n (fam) Werbegeschenk nt; **it was a ~** es war gratis; **freedom** [ˈfri:dəm] n Freiheit f; **freefone** [ˈfri:fəʊn] adj: **a ~ number** eine gebührenfreie

Nummer; **free kick** n (Sport)
Freistoß m
freelance ['fri:lɑ:ns] adj
freiberuflich tätig; (artist)
freischaffend ▷ n Freiberufler(in)
m(f)
free-range ['fri:reɪndʒ] adj (hen)
frei laufend; **~ eggs** pl Freilandeier
pl
freeway ['fri:weɪ] n (US)
(gebührenfreie) Autobahn
freeze [fri:z] n (froze, frozen) vi
(feel cold) frieren; (of lake etc)
zufrieren; (water etc) gefrieren ▷ vt
einfrieren; **freezer** n
Tiefkühltruhe f; (in fridge)
Gefrierfach nt; **freezing** adj
eiskalt; **I'm ~** mir ist eiskalt;
freezing point n Gefrierpunkt m
freight [freɪt] n (goods) Fracht f;
(money charged) Frachtgebühr f;
freight car n (US) Güterwagen m;
freight train n (US) Güterzug m
French [frentʃ] adj französisch
▷ n (language) Französisch nt; **the
~** pl die Franzosen; **French bean** n
grüne Bohne; **French bread** n
Baguette f; **French dressing** n
Vinaigrette f; **French fries** (US)
npl Pommes frites pl; **French kiss**
n Zungenkuss m; **Frenchman** (pl
-men) n Franzose m; **French
toast** n (US) in Ei und Milch
getunktes gebratenes Brot; **French
window(s)** n(pl) Balkontür f,
Terrassentür f; **Frenchwoman** (pl
-women) n Französin f
frequency ['fri:kwənsɪ] n
Häufigkeit f; (Phys) Frequenz f;
frequent ['fri:kwənt] adj häufig;
frequently adv häufig
fresco ['freskəʊ] n (pl **-es**) n Fresko
nt
fresh [freʃ] adj frisch; (new) neu;
freshen vi: **to ~ (up)** (person) sich
frisch machen; **fresher, freshman**
(pl **-men**) n Erstsemester nt;

freshwater fish n
Süßwasserfisch m
Fri abbr = **Friday** Fr
friction ['frɪkʃən] n (a. fig)
Reibung f
Friday ['fraɪdeɪ] n Freitag m; see
also **Tuesday**
fridge [frɪdʒ] n Kühlschrank m
fried [fraɪd] adj gebraten;
~ potatoes Bratkartoffeln pl;
~ egg Spiegelei nt; **~ rice**
gebratener Reis
friend [frend] n Freund(in) m(f);
(less close) Bekannte(r) mf; **to make
~s with sb** sich mit jdm
anfreunden; **we're good ~s** wir
sind gut befreundet; **friendly** adj
freundlich; **to be ~ with sb** mit
jdm befreundet sein ▷ n (Sport)
Freundschaftsspiel nt; **friendship**
['frendʃɪp] n Freundschaft f
fright [fraɪt] n Schrecken m;
frighten vt erschrecken; **to be
~ed** Angst haben; **frightening** adj
beängstigend
frill [frɪl] n Rüsche f; **~s** (fam)
Schnickschnack m
fringe [frɪndʒ] n (edge) Rand m;
(on shawl etc) Fransen pl; (hair)
Pony m
frivolous ['frɪvələs] adj leichtsinnig; (remark) frivol
frizzy ['frɪzɪ] adj kraus
frog [frɒg] n Frosch m

◯ KEYWORD

from [frɒm] prep **1** (indicating
starting place) von; (indicating origin
etc) aus +dat; **a letter/telephone
call from my sister** ein
Brief/Anruf von meiner
Schwester; **where do you come
from?** woher kommen Sie?; **to
drink from the bottle** aus der
Flasche trinken

2 (*indicating time*) von ... an; (*past*) seit; **from one o'clock to** *o* **until** *o* **till two** von ein Uhr bis zwei; **from January (on)** ab Januar

3 (*indicating distance*) von ... (entfernt)

4 (*indicating price, number etc*) ab +*dat*; **from £10** ab £10; **there were from 20 to 30 people there** es waren zwischen 20 und 30 Leute da

5 (*indicating difference*) **he can't tell red from green** er kann nicht zwischen Rot und Grün unterscheiden; **to be different from sb/sth** anders sein als jd/etw

6 (*because of, based on*) **from what he says** aus dem, was er sagt; **weak from hunger** schwach vor Hunger

front [frʌnt] *n* Vorderseite *f*; (*of house*) Fassade *f*; (*in war, of weather*) Front *f*; (*at seaside*) Promenade *f*; **in ~, at the ~** vorne; **in ~ of** vor; **up ~** (*in advance*) vorher, im Voraus ▷ *adj* vordere(r, s), Vorder-; (*first*) vordere(r, s); **~ door** Haustür *f*; **~ page** Titelseite *f*; **~ seat** Vordersitz *m*; **~ wheel** Vorderrad *nt*

frontier ['frʌntɪə*] *n* Grenze *f*

front-wheel drive *n* (*Auto*) Frontantrieb *m*

frost [frɒst] *n* Frost *m*; (*white ~*) Reif *m*; **frosting** *n* (*US*) Zuckerguss *m*; **frosty** *adj* frostig

froth [frɒθ] *n* Schaum *m*; **frothy** *adj* schaumig

frown [fraʊn] *vi* die Stirn runzeln

froze [frəʊz] *pt of* **freeze**

frozen ['frəʊzn] *pp of* **freeze** ▷ *adj* (*food*) tiefgekühlt, Tiefkühl-

fruit [fruːt] *n* (*as collective, a. type*) Obst *nt*; (*single ~, a. fig*) Frucht *f*;

fruit machine *n* Spielautomat *m*; **fruit salad** *n* Obstsalat *m*

frustrated [frʌ'streɪtɪd] *adj* frustriert; **frustratration** *n* Frustration *f*, Frust *m*

fry [fraɪ] *vt* braten; **frying pan** *n* Bratpfanne *f*

fuchsia ['fjuːʃə] *n* Fuchsie *f*

fuck [fʌk] *vt* (*vulg*) ficken; **~ off** verpiss dich!; **fucking** *adj* (*vulg*) Scheiß-

fudge [fʌdʒ] *n* weiche Karamellsüßigkeit

fuel [fjʊəl] *n* Kraftstoff *m*; (*for heating*) Brennstoff *m*; **fuel consumption** *n* Kraftstoffverbrauch *m*; **fuel gauge** *n* Benzinuhr *f*; **fuel oil** *n* Gasöl *nt*; **fuel rod** *n* Brennstab *m*; **fuel tank** *n* Tank *m*; (*for oil*) Öltank *m*

fugitive ['fjuːdʒɪtɪv] *n* Flüchtling *m*

fulfil [fʊl'fɪl] *vt* erfüllen

full [fʊl] *adj* voll; (*person: satisfied*) satt; (*member, employment*) Voll(zeit)-; (*complete*) vollständig; **~ of ...** voller ... *gen*; **full beam** *n* (*Auto*) Fernlicht *nt*; **full moon** *n* Vollmond *m*; **full stop** *n* Punkt *m*; **full-time** *adj*: **~ job** Ganztagsarbeit *f*; **fully** *adv* völlig; (*recover*) voll und ganz; (*discuss*) ausführlich

fumble ['fʌmbl] *vi* herumfummeln (*with, at* an +*dat*)

fumes [fjuːmz] *npl* Dämpfe *pl*; (*of car*) Abgase *pl*

fun [fʌn] *n* Spaß *m*; **for ~** zum Spaß; **it's ~** es macht Spaß; **to make ~ of** sich lustig machen über +*akk*

function ['fʌŋkʃən] *n* Funktion *f*; (*event*) Feier *f*; (*reception*) Empfang *m* ▷ *vi* funktionieren; **function key** *n* (*Inform*) Funktionstaste *f*

fund [fʌnd] *n* Fonds *m*; **~s** *pl* Geldmittel *pl*

fundamental [fʌndə'mentl] *adj* grundlegend; **fundamentally** *adv* im Grunde

funding ['fʌndɪŋ] *n* finanzielle Unterstützung

funeral ['fjuːnərəl] *n* Beerdigung *f*

funfair ['fʌnfeə°] *n* Jahrmarkt *m*

fungus ['fʌŋɡəs] (*pl* **fungi** *o* **funguses**) *n* Pilz *m*

funicular [fjuː'nɪkjʊlə°] *n* Seilbahn *f*

funnel ['fʌnl] *n* Trichter *m*; (*of steamer*) Schornstein *m*

funny ['fʌnɪ] *adj* (*amusing*) komisch, lustig; (*strange*) seltsam

fur [fɜː°] *n* Pelz *m*; (*of animal*) Fell *nt*

furious ['fjʊərɪəs] *adj* wütend (*with sb* auf jdn)

furnished ['fɜːnɪʃd] *adj* möbliert; **furniture** ['fɜːnɪtʃə°] *n* Möbel *pl*; **piece of ~** Möbelstück *nt*

further ['fɜːðə°] *comparative of* **far** ▷ *adj* weitere(r, s); **~ education** Weiterbildung *f*; **until ~ notice** bis auf weiteres ▷ *adv* weiter; **furthest** ['fɜːðɪst] *superlative of* **far** ▷ *adj* am weitesten entfernt ▷ *adv* am weitesten

fury ['fjʊərɪ] *n* Wut *f*

fuse [fjuːz] *n* (*Elec*) Sicherung *f* ▷ *vi* (*Elec*) durchbrennen; **fuse box** *n* Sicherungskasten *m*

fuss [fʌs] *n* Theater *nt*; **to make a ~** (ein) Theater machen; **fussy** *adj* (*difficult*) schwierig, kompliziert; (*attentive to detail*) pingelig

future ['fjuːtʃə°] *adj* künftig ▷ *n* Zukunft *f*

fuze (*US*) *see* **fuse**

fuzzy ['fʌzɪ] *adj* (*indistinct*) verschwommen; (*hair*) kraus

gable ['ɡeɪbl] *n* Giebel *m*

gadget ['ɡædʒɪt] *n* Vorrichtung *f*, Gerät *nt*

Gaelic ['ɡeɪlɪk] *adj* gälisch ▷ *n* (*language*) Gälisch *nt*

gain [ɡeɪn] *vt* (*obtain, win*) gewinnen; (*advantage, respect*) sich verschaffen; (*wealth*) erwerben; (*weight*) zunehmen ▷ *vi* (*improve*) gewinnen (*in an* +*dat*); (*clock*) vorgehen ▷ *n* Gewinn *m* (*in an* +*dat*)

gale [ɡeɪl] *n* Sturm *m*

gall bladder ['ɡɔːlblædə°] *n* Gallenblase *f*

gallery ['ɡælərɪ] *n* Galerie *f*, Museum *nt*

gallon ['ɡælən] *n* Gallone *f*; ((*Brit*) 4,546 l, (*US*) 3,79 l)

gallop ['ɡæləp] *n* Galopp *m* ▷ *vi* galoppieren

gallstone ['ɡɔːlstəʊn] *n* Gallenstein *m*

Gambia ['gæmbɪə] n Gambia nt
gamble ['gæmbl] vi um Geld spielen, wetten ▷ n: **it's a ~** es ist riskant; **gambling** n Glücksspiel nt
game [geɪm] n Spiel nt; (animals) Wild nt; **a ~ of chess** eine Partie Schach; **~s** (in school) Sport m; **game show** n (TV) Gameshow f
gammon ['gæmən] n geräucherter Schinken
gang [gæŋ] n (of criminals, youths) Bande f, Gang f, Clique f ▷ vt: **to ~ up on** sich verschwören gegen
gangster ['gæŋstə°] n Gangster m
gangway ['gæŋweɪ] n (for ship) Gangway f; (Brit: aisle) Gang m, Gangway f
gap [gæp] n (hole) Lücke f; (in time) Pause f; (in age) Unterschied m
gape [geɪp] vi (mit offenem Mund) starren
gap year n Jahr zwischen Schulabschluss und Studium, das oft zu Auslandsaufenthalten genutzt wird
garage ['gærɑːʒ] n Garage f; (for repair) (Auto)werkstatt f; (for fuel) Tankstelle f
garbage ['gɑːbɪdʒ] n (US) Müll m; (fam: nonsense) Quatsch m; **garbage can** n (US) Mülleimer m; (outside) Mülltonne f; **garbage truck** n (US) Müllwagen m
garden ['gɑːdn] n Garten m; (**public**) **~s** Park m; **garden centre** n Gartencenter nt; **gardener** n Gärtner(in) m(f); **gardening** n Gartenarbeit f
gargle ['gɑːgl] vi gurgeln
gargoyle ['gɑːgɔɪl] n Wasserspeier m
garlic ['gɑːlɪk] n Knoblauch m; **garlic bread** n Knoblauchbrot nt; **garlic butter** n Knoblauchbutter f
gas [gæs] n Gas nt; (US: petrol)

Benzin nt; **to step on the ~** Gas geben; **gas cooker** n Gasherd m; **gas cylinder** n Gasflasche f; **gas fire** n Gasofen m
gasket ['gæskɪt] n Dichtung f
gas lighter n (for cigarettes) Gasfeuerzeug nt; **gas mask** n Gasmaske f; **gas meter** n Gaszähler m
gasoline ['gæsəliːn] n (US) Benzin nt
gasp [gɑːsp] vi keuchen; (in surprise) nach Luft schnappen
gas pedal n (US) Gaspedal nt; **gas pump** n (US) Zapfsäule f; **gas station** n (US) Tankstelle f; **gas tank** n (US) Benzintank m
gastric ['gæstrɪk] adj Magen-; **~ flu** Magen-Darm-Grippe f; **~ ulcer** Magengeschwür nt
gasworks ['gæswɜːks] n Gaswerk nt
gate [geɪt] n Tor nt; (barrier) Schranke f; (Aviat) Gate nt, Flugsteig m
gateau ['gætəʊ] (pl **gateaux**) n Torte f
gateway n Tor nt
gather ['gæðə°] vt (collect) sammeln; **to ~ speed** beschleunigen ▷ vi (assemble) sich versammeln; (understand) schließen (from aus); **gathering** n Versammlung f
gauge [geɪdʒ] n Meßgerät nt
gauze [gɔːz] n Gaze f; (for bandages) Mull m
gave [geɪv] pt of **give**
gay [geɪ] adj (homosexual) schwul; **~ marriage** (fam) Homoehe f
gaze [geɪz] n Blick m ▷ vi starren
GCSE abbr = **general certificate of secondary education** (school) Abschlussprüfung f der Sekundarstufe, ≈ mittlere Reife
gear [gɪə°] n (Auto) Gang m; (equipment) Ausrüstung f; (clothes)

Klamotten *pl*; **to change ~** schalten; **gearbox** *n* Getriebe *nt*; **gear change**, **gear shift** (US) *n* Gangschaltung *f*; **gear lever**, **gear stick** (US) *n* Schalthebel *m*

geese [giːs] *pl of* **goose**

gel [dʒel] *n* Gel *nt* ▷ *vi* gelieren; **they really ~led** sie verstanden sich auf Anhieb

gem [dʒem] *n* Edelstein *m*; (*fig*) Juwel *nt*

Gemini ['dʒemɪniː] *nsing* (*Astr*) Zwillinge *pl*

gender ['dʒendə*] *n* Geschlecht *nt*

gene [dʒiːn] *n* Gen *nt*

general ['dʒenərəl] *adj* allgemein; **~ knowledge** Allgemeinbildung *f*; **~ election** Parlamentswahlen *pl*; **generalize** ['dʒenrəlaɪz] *vi* verallgemeinern; **generally** ['dʒenrəlɪ] *adv* im Allgemeinen

generation [dʒenə'reɪʃən] *n* Generation *f*; **generation gap** *n* Generationsunterschied *m*

generator ['dʒenəreɪtə*] *n* Generator *m*

generosity [dʒenə'rɔsɪtɪ] *n* Großzügigkeit *f*; **generous** ['dʒenərəs] *adj* großzügig; (*portion*) reichlich

genetic [dʒɪ'netɪk] *adj* genetisch; **~ research** Genforschung *f*; **~ technology** Gentechnik *f*; **genetically modified** *adj* gentechnisch verändert, genmanipuliert; *see also* **GM**

Geneva [dʒɪ'niːvə] *n* Genf *nt*; **Lake ~** der Genfer See

genitals ['dʒenɪtlz] *npl* Geschlechtsteile *pl*

genitive ['dʒenɪtɪv] *n* Genitiv *m*

genius ['dʒiːnɪəs] *n* Genie *nt*

gentle ['dʒentl] *adj* sanft; (*touch*) zart; **gentleman** (*pl* **-men**) *n*

Herr *m*; (*polite man*) Gentleman *m*

gents [dʒents] *n*: **"~"** (*lavatory*) „Herren"; **the ~** *pl* die Herrentoilette

genuine ['dʒenjʊɪn] *adj* echt

geographical [dʒɪə'græfɪkəl] *adj* geografisch; **geography** [dʒɪ'ɒgrəfɪ] *n* Geografie *f*; (*at school*) Erdkunde *f*

geological [dʒɪəʊ'lɒdʒɪkəl] *adj* geologisch; **geology** [dʒɪ'ɒlədʒɪ] *n* Geologie *f*

geometry [dʒɪ'ɒmɪtrɪ] *n* Geometrie *f*

geranium [dʒɪ'reɪnɪəm] *n* Geranie *f*

gerbil ['dʒɜːbəl] *n* (*Zool*) Wüstenrennmaus *f*

germ [dʒɜːm] *n* Keim *m*; (*Med*) Bazillus *m*

German ['dʒɜːmən] *adj* deutsch; **she's ~** sie ist Deutsche; **~ shepherd** Deutscher Schäferhund ▷ *n* (*person*) Deutsche(r) *mf*; (*language*) Deutsch *nt*; **in ~** auf Deutsch; **German measles** *n sing* Röteln *pl*; **Germany** ['dʒɜːmənɪ] *n* Deutschland *nt*

gesture ['dʒestʃə*] *n* Geste *f*

◯ **KEYWORD**

get [get] (*pt, pp* **got**, *pp* **gotten** (US)) *vi* **1** (*become, be*) werden; **to get old/tired** alt/müde werden; **to get married** heiraten
2 (*go*) (an)kommen, gehen
3 (*begin*) **to get to know sb** jdn kennenlernen; **let's get going** *o* **started!** fangen wir an!
4 (*modal vb aux*) **you've got to do it** du musst/Sie müssen es tun
▷ *vt* **1 to get sth done** (*do*) etw machen; (*have done*) etw machen lassen; **to get sth going** *o* **to go** etw in Gang bringen *o* bekommen;

to get sb to do sth jdn dazu bringen, etw zu tun
2 (*obtain: money, permission, results*) erhalten; (*find: job, flat*) finden; (*fetch: person, object*) holen; **to get sth for sb** jdm etw besorgen; **get me Mr Jones, please** (*Tel*) verbinde/verbinden Sie mich bitte mit Mr Jones; **get a life!** (*annoyed*) mach dich mal locker!, reg dich bloß ab!
3 (*receive: present, letter*) bekommen, kriegen; (*acquire: reputation etc*) erwerben
4 (*catch*) bekommen, kriegen; (*hit*) (*target etc*) treffen, erwischen; **get him!** (*to dog*) fass!
5 (*take, move*) bringen; **to get sth to sb** jdm etw bringen
6 (*understand*) verstehen; (*hear*) mitbekommen; **I've got it!** ich hab's!
7 (*have, possess*) **to have got sth** etw haben
get about vi herumkommen, (*news*) sich verbreiten
get across vi: **to sth** über etw *akk* kommen; vt: **to get sth across** (*communicate*) etw klarmachen
get along vi (*people*) (*gut*) zurecht-/auskommen (*with*) mit; (*depart*) sich *akk* auf den Weg machen
get at vt (*reach*) herankommen an +*akk*; (*facts*) herausbekommen; **what are you getting at?** worauf wollen Sie hinaus?, was meinst du damit?; **to get at sb** (*nag*) an jdm herumnörgeln
get away vi (*leave*) sich *akk* davonmachen, wegkommen (*escape*); **to get away from sth** von etw *dat* entkommen; **to get away with sth** mit etw davonkommen
get back vi (*return*) zurückkommen; (*Tel*) **to get back**

to s.o. jdn zurückrufen
▷ vt zurückbekommen
get by vi (*pass*) vorbeikommen; (*manage*) zurecht-/auskommen (*on*) mit
get down vi (*her)untergehen*; **to get down to** in Angriff nehmen, (*find time to do*) kommen zu;
▷ vt (*depress*) fertigmachen; **it gets me down** (*fam*) es macht mich fertig; **to get sth down** (*write*) etw aufschreiben
get in vi (*train*) ankommen; (*arrive home*) heimkommen
get into vt (*enter*) hinein-/ hereinkommen in +*akk*; (*car, train etc*) einsteigen in +*akk*; (*clothes*) anziehen; (*rage, panic etc*) geraten in +*akk*; **to get into trouble** in Schwierigkeiten kommen
get off vi (*from train etc*) aussteigen; (*from horse etc*) absteigen; (*fam: be enthusiastic*) **to get off on sth** auf etw abfahren;
▷ vt (*nail, sticker*) los-/abbekommen; (*clothes*) ausziehen
get on vi (*progress*) vorankommen; (*be friends*) auskommen; (*age*) alt werden; (*onto train etc*) einsteigen; (*onto horse etc*) aufsteigen
▷ vt etw +*akk* vorantreiben, mit etw *akk* loslegen
get out vi (*of house*) herauskommen; (*of vehicle*) aussteigen; **get out!** raus!
▷ vt (*take out*) herausholen; (*stain, nail*) herausbekommen
get out of vi (*duty etc*) herumkommen um
get over vi (*illness*) sich *akk* erholen von; (*surprise*) verkraften; (*news*) fassen; (*loss*) sich abfinden mit
get round vi herumkommen um; vt (*fig*) (*person*) herumkriegen

get through vi (Tel) durchkommen (to) zu
get together vi zusammenkommen
get up vi aufstehen ▷ vt hinaufbringen; (go up) hinaufgehen; (organize) auf die Beine stellen
get up to vi (reach) erreichen; (prank etc) anstellen

getaway n Flucht f;
get-together n Treffen nt
Ghana ['gɑːnə] n Ghana nt
gherkin ['gɜːkɪn] n Gewürzgurke f
ghetto ['getəʊ] (pl -es) n Ghetto nt
ghost [gəʊst] n Gespenst nt; (of sb) Geist m
giant ['dʒaɪənt] n Riese m ▷ adj riesig
giblets ['dʒɪblɪts] npl Geflügelinnereien pl
Gibraltar [dʒɪ'brɔːltə*] n Gibraltar nt
giddy ['gɪdɪ] adj schwindlig
gift [gɪft] n Geschenk nt; (talent) Begabung f; **gifted** adj begabt; **giftwrap** vt als Geschenk verpacken
gigantic [dʒaɪ'gæntɪk] adj riesig
giggle ['gɪgl] vi kichern ▷ n Gekicher nt
gill [gɪl] n (of fish) Kieme f
gimmick ['gɪmɪk] n (for sales, publicity) Gag m
gin [dʒɪn] n Gin m
ginger ['dʒɪndʒə*] n Ingwer m ▷ adj (colour) kupferrot; (cat) rötlichgelb; **ginger ale** n Gingerale nt; **ginger beer** n Ingwerlimonade f; **gingerbread** n Lebkuchen m (mit Ingwergeschmack); **ginger(-haired)** adj rotblond; **gingerly** adv (move) vorsichtig

gipsy ['dʒɪpsɪ] n Zigeuner(in) m(f)
giraffe [dʒɪ'rɑːf] n Giraffe f
girl [gɜːl] n Mädchen nt; **girlfriend** n (feste) Freundin f; **girl guide** n (Brit), **girl scout** (US) Pfadfinderin f
gist [dʒɪst] n: **to get the ~ (of it)** das Wesentliche verstehen
give [gɪv] (**gave, given**) vt geben; (as present) schenken (to sb jdm); (state: name etc) angeben; (speech) halten; (blood) spenden; **to ~ sb sth** jdm etw geben/schenken ▷ vi (yield) nachgeben; **give away** vt (give free) verschenken; (secret) verraten; **give back** vt zurückgeben; **give in** vi aufgeben; **give up** vt, vi aufgeben; **give way** vi (collapse, yield) nachgeben; (traffic) die Vorfahrt beachten
given ['gɪvn] pp of **give** ▷ adj (fixed) festgesetzt; (certain) bestimmt; **~ name** (US) Vorname m ▷ conj: **~ that ...** angesichts der Tatsache, dass ...
glacier ['glæsɪə*] n Gletscher m
glad [glæd] adj froh (about über); **I was ~ (to hear) that ...** es hat mich gefreut, dass ...; **gladly** ['glædlɪ] adv gerne
glance [glɑːns] n Blick m ▷ vi einen Blick werfen (at auf +akk)
gland [glænd] n Drüse f; **glandular fever** n Drüsenfieber nt
glare [gleə*] n grelles Licht; (stare) stechender Blick ▷ vi (angrily) **to ~ at sb** jdn böse anstarren; **glaring** adj (mistake) krass
glass [glɑːs] n Glas nt; **~es** pl Brille f
glen [glen] n (Scot) (enges) Bergtal nt

glide [glaɪd] *vi* gleiten; (*hover*) schweben; **glider** *n* Segelflugzeug *nt*; **gliding** *n* Segelfliegen *nt*

glimmer ['glɪmə*] *n* (*of hope*) Schimmer *m*

glimpse [glɪmps] *n* flüchtiger Blick

glitter ['glɪtə*] *vi* glitzern; (*eyes*) funkeln

glitzy [glɪtsɪ] *adj* (*fam*) glanzvoll, Schickimicki-

global ['gləʊbəl] *adj* global, Welt-; **~ warming** die Erwärmung der Erdatmosphäre; **globe** [gləʊb] spz; *n* (*sphere*) Kugel *f*; (*world*) Erdball *m*; (*map*) Globus *m*

gloomily ['gluːmɪlɪ] , **gloomy** *adv, adj* düster

glorious ['glɔːrɪəs] *adj* (*victory, past*) ruhmreich; (*weather, day*) herrlich; **glory** ['glɔːrɪ] *n* Herrlichkeit *f*

gloss [glɒs] *n* (*shine*) Glanz *m*

glossary ['glɒsərɪ] *n* Glossar *nt*

glossy ['glɒsɪ] *adj* (*surface*) glänzend ▷ *n* (*magazine*) Hochglanzmagazin *nt*

glove [glʌv] *n* Handschuh *m*; **glove compartment** *n* Handschuhfach *nt*

glow [gləʊ] *vi* glühen

glucose ['gluːkəʊs] *n* Trauben-zucker *m*

glue [gluː] *n* Klebstoff *m* ▷ *vt* kleben

glutton ['glʌtn] *n* Vielfraß *m*; **a ~ for punishment** (*fam*) Masochist *m*

GM *abbr* = **genetically modified** Gen-; **~ foods** gentechnisch veränderte Lebensmittel

GMT *abbr* = **Greenwich Mean Time** WEZ *f*

go [gəʊ] (**went**, **gone**) *vi* gehen; (*in vehicle, travel*) fahren; (*plane*) fliegen; (*road*) führen (*to* nach); (*depart: train, bus*) (ab)fahren; (*person*) (fort)gehen; (*disappear*) verschwinden; (*time*) vergehen; (*function*) gehen, funktionieren; (*machine, engine*) laufen; (*fit, suit*) passen (*with* zu); (*fail*) nachlassen; **I have to ~ to the doctor/to London** ich muss zum Arzt/nach London; **to ~ shopping** einkaufen gehen; **to ~ for a walk/swim** spazieren/schwimmen gehen; **has he gone yet?** ist er schon weg?; **the wine ~es in the cupboard** der Wein kommt in den Schrank; **to get sth ~ing** etw in Gang setzen; **to keep ~ing** weitermachen; (*machine etc*) weiterlaufen; **how's the job ~ing?** was macht der Job?; **his memory/eyesight is going** sein Gedächtnis lässt nach/seine Augen werden schwach; **to ~ deaf/mad/grey** taub/verrückt/grau werden ▷ *vb aux*: **to be ~ing to do sth** etw tun werden; **I was ~ing to do it** ich wollte es tun ▷ *n* (*pl* **-es**) (*attempt*) Versuch *m*; **can I have another ~?** darf ich noch mal (probieren)?; **it's my ~** ich bin dran; **in one ~** auf einen Schlag; (*drink*) in einem Zug; **go after** *vt* nachlaufen +*dat*; (*in vehicle*) nachfahren +*dat*; **go ahead** *vi* (*in front*) vorausgehen; (*start*) anfangen; **go away** *vi* weggehen; (*on holiday, business*) verreisen; **go back** *vi* (*return*) zurückgehen; **we ~ a long way** (*fam*) wir kennen uns schon ewig; **go by** *vi* vorbeigehen; (*vehicle*) vorbeifahren; (*years, time*) vergehen ▷ *vt* (*judge by*) gehen nach; **go down** *vi* (*sun, ship*) untergehen; (*flood, temperature*) zurückgehen; (*price*) sinken; **to ~ well/badly** gut/schlecht ankommen; **go in** *vi* hineingehen; **go into** *vt* (*enter*) hineingehen in +akk; (crash) fahren gegen, hineinfahren in +akk; **to ~ teaching/politics/the army** Lehrer werden/in die Politik gehen/zum Militär gehen; **go off** vi (depart) weggehen; (in vehicle) wegfahren; (lights) ausgehen; (milk etc) sauer werden; (gun, bomb, alarm) losgehen ▷ vt (dislike) nicht mehr mögen; **go on** vi (continue) weitergehen; (lights) angehen; **to ~ with** o **doing sth** etw weitermachen; **go out** vi (leave house) hinausgehen; (fire, light, person socially) ausgehen; **to ~ for a meal** essen gehen; **go up** vi (temperature, price) steigen; (lift) hochfahren; **go without** vt verzichten auf +akk; (food, sleep) auskommen ohne

go-ahead ['gəʊəhed] adj (progressive) fortschrittlich ▷ n grünes Licht

goal [gəʊl] n (aim) Ziel nt; (Sport) Tor nt; **goalie, goalkeeper** n Torwart m, Torfrau f; **goalpost** n Torpfosten m

goat [gəʊt] n Ziege f

gob [gɒb] n (Brit fam) Maul nt; **shut your ~** halt's Maul! ▷ vi spucken; **gobsmacked** (fam: surprised) platt

god [gɒd] n Gott m; **thank God** Gott sei Dank; **godchild** (pl **-children**) n Patenkind nt; **goddaughter** n Patentochter f; **goddess** ['gɒdes] n Göttin f; **godfather** n Pate m; **godmother** n Patin f; **godson** n Patensohn m

goggles npl Schutzbrille f; (for skiing) Skibrille f; (for diving) Taucherbrille f

going ['gəʊɪŋ] adj (rate) üblich; **goings-on** npl Vorgänge pl

go-kart ['gəʊkɑːt] n Gokart m

gold [gəʊld] n Gold nt; **golden** adj golden; **goldfish** n Goldfisch m; **gold-plated** adj vergoldet

golf [gɒlf] n Golf nt; **golf ball** n Golfball m; **golf club** n Golfschläger m; (association) Golfklub m; **golf course** n Golfplatz m; **golfer** n Golfspieler(in) m(f)

gone [gɒn] pp of **go; he's ~** er ist weg ▷ prep: **just ~ three** kurz nach drei

good [gʊd] n (benefit) Wohl nt; (morally good things) Gute(s) nt; **for the ~ of** zum Wohle +gen; **it's for your own ~** es ist zu deinem/Ihrem Besten o Vorteil; **it's no ~** (doing sth) es hat keinen Sinn o Zweck; (thing) es taugt nichts; **for ~** für immer ▷ adj (better, best) gut; (suitable) passend; (thorough) gründlich; (well-behaved) brav; (kind) nett, lieb; **to be ~ at sport/maths** gut in Sport/Mathe sein; **to be no ~ at sport/maths** schlecht in Sport/Mathe sein; **it's ~ for you** es tut dir gut; **this is ~ for colds** das ist gut gegen Erkältungen; **too ~ to be true** zu schön, um wahr zu sein; **this is just not ~ enough** so geht das nicht; **a ~ three hours** gute drei Stunden; **~ morning/evening** guten Morgen/Abend; **~ night** gute Nacht; **to have a ~ time** sich gut amüsieren

goodbye [gʊd'baɪ] interj auf Wiedersehen

Good Friday n Karfreitag m

good-looking adj gut aussehend

goods [gʊdz] npl Waren pl, Güter pl; **goods train** n (Brit) Güterzug m

goodwill [gʊd'wɪl] n Wohlwollen nt

goose [guːs] (pl **geese**) n Gans f

▷ vt (fam) **to ~ s.o.** jdn in den Arsch kneifen; **gooseberry** ['gʊzbərɪ] n Stachelbeere f; **goose bumps** n, **goose pimples** npl Gänsehaut f

gorge [gɔːdʒ] n Schlucht f

gorgeous ['gɔːdʒəs] adj wunderschön; **he's ~** er sieht toll aus

gorilla [gəˈrɪlə] n Gorilla m

gossip ['gɒsɪp] n (talk) Klatsch m; (person) Klatschtante f ▷ vi klatschen, tratschen

got [gɒt] pt, pp of **get**

gotten ['gɒtn] (US) pp of **get**

govern ['gʌvən] vt regieren; (province etc) verwalten; **government** n Regierung f; **governor** n Gouverneur(in) m(f); **govt** abbr = **government** Regierung f

gown [gaʊn] n Abendkleid nt; (academic) Robe f

GP abbr = **General Practitioner** Allgemeinarzt, Allgemeinärztin

GPS n abbr = **global positioning system** GPS nt

grab [græb] vt packen; (person) schnappen

grace [greɪs] n Anmut f; (prayer) Tischgebet nt; **5 days' ~** 5 Tage Aufschub; **graceful** adj anmutig

grade [greɪd] n Niveau nt; (of goods) Güteklasse f; (mark) Note f; (US: year) Klasse f; **to make the ~** es schaffen; **grade crossing** n (US) Bahnübergang m; **grade school** n (US) Grundschule f

gradient ['greɪdɪənt] n (upward) Steigung f; (downward) Gefälle nt

gradual, gradually ['grædjʊəl, -lɪ] adj, adv allmählich

graduate ['grædjuɪt] n Uniabsolvent(in) m(f), Hochschulabsolvent(in) m(f) ▷ ['grædjʊeɪt] vi einen akademischen Grad erwerben

grain [greɪn] n (cereals) Getreide nt; (of corn, sand) Korn nt; (in wood) Maserung f

gram [græm] n Gramm nt

grammar ['græmə*] n Grammatik f; **grammar school** n (Brit) ≈ Gymnasium nt

gran [græn] n (fam) Oma f

grand [grænd] adj (a) (pej) hochnäsig; (posh) vornehm ▷ n (fam) 1000 Pfund bzw. 1000 Dollar

grand(d)ad n (fam) Opa m; **granddaughter** n Enkelin f; **grandfather** n Großvater m; **grandma** n (fam) Oma f; **grandmother** n Großmutter f; **grandpa** n (fam) Opa m; **grandparents** npl Großeltern pl; **grandson** n Enkel m

grandstand n (Sport) Tribüne f

granny ['grænɪ] n (fam) Oma f

grant [grɑːnt] vt gewähren (sb sth jdm etw); **to take sb/sth for ~ed** jdn/etw als selbstverständlich hinnehmen ▷ n Subvention f, finanzielle Unterstützung f; (for university) Stipendium nt

grape [greɪp] n Weintraube f; **grapefruit** n Grapefruit f; **grape juice** n Traubensaft m

graph [grɑːf] n Diagramm nt; **graphic** ['græfɪk] adj grafisch; (description) anschaulich

grasp [grɑːsp] vt ergreifen; (understand) begreifen

grass [grɑːs] n (lawn) Gras nt; (lawn) Rasen m; **grasshopper** n Heuschrecke f

grate [greɪt] n Feuerrost m ▷ vi kratzen ▷ vt (cheese) reiben

grateful, gratefully ['greɪtfʊl, -fəlɪ] adj, adv dankbar

grater ['greɪtə*] n Reibe f

gratifying ['grætɪfaɪɪŋ] adj erfreulich

gratitude ['grætɪtjuːd] n Dankbarkeit f

grave [greɪv] n Grab nt ▷ adj
ernst; (mistake) schwer
gravel ['grævəl] n Kies m
graveyard ['greɪvjɑːd] n Friedhof m
gravity ['grævɪtɪ] n Schwerkraft
f; (seriousness) Ernst m
gravy ['greɪvɪ] n Bratensoße
f
gray [greɪ] adj (US) grau
graze [greɪz] vi (of animals)
grasen ▷ vt (touch) streifen; (Med)
abschürfen ▷ n (Med)
Abschürfung f
grease [griːs] n (fat) Fett nt;
(lubricant) Schmiere f ▷ vt
einfetten; (Tech) schmieren;
greasy ['griːsɪ] adj fettig; (hands,
tools) schmierig; (fam: person)
schleimig
great [greɪt] adj groß; (fam: good)
großartig, super; **a ~ deal of** viel;
Great Britain ['greɪt'brɪtn] n
Großbritannien nt;
great-grandfather n Urgroßvater m; **great-grandmother** n
Urgroßmutter f; **greatly** adv sehr;
~ disappointed zutiefst
enttäuscht
Greece [griːs] n Griechenland nt
greed [griːd] n Gier f (for nach);
(for food) Gefräßigkeit f; **greedy**
adj gierig; (for food) gefräßig
Greek [griːk] adj griechisch ▷ n
(person) Grieche m, Griechin f;
(language) Griechisch nt; **it's all
~ to me** ich verstehe nur
Bahnhof
green [griːn] adj grün; **~ with
envy** grün/gelb vor Neid ▷ n
(colour; for golf) Grün nt; (village ~)
Dorfwiese f; **~s** (vegetables) grünes
Gemüse; **the Greens, the Green
Party** (Pol) die Grünen; **green card**
n (US: work permit)
Arbeitserlaubnis f; (Brit: for car)
grüne Versicherungskarte;

greengage n Reneklode f;
greengrocer n Obst- und
Gemüsehändler(in) m(f);
greenhouse n Gewächshaus nt;
~ effect Treibhauseffekt m;
Greenland n Grönland nt; **green
pepper** n grüner Paprika; **green
salad** n grüner Salat
Greenwich Mean Time
['grenɪdʒ'miːntaɪm] n west-
europäische Zeit
greet [griːt] vt grüßen; **greeting**
n Gruß m
grew [gruː] pt of **grow**
grey [greɪ] adj grau; **grey-haired**
adj grauhaarig; **greyhound** n
Windhund m
grid [grɪd] n Gitter nt; **gridlock** n
Verkehrsinfarkt m; **gridlocked** adj
(roads) völlig verstopft; (talks)
festgefahren
grief [griːf] n Kummer m; (over
loss) Trauer f
grievance ['griːvəns] n
Beschwerde f
grieve [griːv] vi trauern (for um)
grill [grɪl] n (on cooker) Grill m ▷ vt
grillen
grim [grɪm] adj (face, humour)
grimmig; (situation, prospects)
trostlos
grin [grɪn] n Grinsen nt ▷ vi
grinsen
grind [graɪnd] (**ground, ground**)
vt mahlen; (sharpen) schleifen; (US:
meat) durchdrehen, hacken
grip [grɪp] n Griff m; **get a
~** nimm dich zusammen!; **to get
to ~s with sth** etw in den Griff
bekommen ▷ vt packen; **gripping**
adj (exciting) spannend
groan [grəʊn] vi stöhnen (with
vor +dat)
grocer ['grəʊsə*] n Lebensmit-
telhändler(in) m(f); **groceries** npl
Lebensmittel pl
groin [grɔɪn] n (Anat) Leiste f;

groin strain n (Med) Leistenbruch m

groom [gruːm] n Bräutigam m ▷ vt: **well -ed** gepflegt

grope [grəʊp] vi tasten ▷ vt (sexually harrass) befummeln

gross [grəʊs] adj (coarse) derb; (extreme: negligence, error) grob; (disgusting) ekelhaft; (Comm) brutto; **~ national product** Bruttosozialprodukt nt; **~ salary** Bruttogehalt nt

grotty ['grɒtɪ] adj (fam) mies, vergammelt

ground [graʊnd] pt, pp of **grind** ▷ n Boden m, Erde f; (Sport) Platz m; **~s** pl (around house) (Garten)anlagen pl; (reasons) Gründe pl; (of coffee) Satz m; **on (the) ~s of** aufgrund von; **ground floor** n (Brit) Erdgeschoss nt; **ground meat** n (US) Hackfleisch nt

group [gruːp] n Gruppe f ▷ vt gruppieren

grouse [graʊs] (pl -) n (bird) Schottisches Moorhuhn; (complaint) Nörgelei f

grow [grəʊ] (**grew, grown**) vi wachsen; (increase) zunehmen (in an); (become) werden; **to ~ old** alt werden; **to ~ into ...** sich entwickeln zu ... ▷ vt (crop, plant) ziehen; (commercially) anbauen; **I'm ~ing a beard** ich lasse mir einen Bart wachsen; **grow up** vi aufwachsen; (mature) erwachsen werden; **growing** adj wachsend; **a ~ number of people** immer mehr Leute

growl [graʊl] vi knurren

grown [grəʊn] pp of **grow**

grown-up [grəʊnˈʌp] adj erwachsen ▷ n Erwachsene(r) mf; **growth** [grəʊθ] n Wachstum nt; (increase) Zunahme f; (Med) Wucherung f

grubby ['grʌbɪ] adj schmuddelig

grudge [grʌdʒ] n Abneigung f (against gegen) ▷ vt: **to ~ sb sth** jdm etw nicht gönnen

gruelling ['grʊəlɪŋ] adj aufreibend; (pace) mörderisch

gruesome ['gruːsəm] adj grausig

grumble ['grʌmbl] vi murren (about über +akk)

grumpy ['grʌmpɪ] adj (fam) mürrisch, grantig

grunt [grʌnt] vi grunzen

G-string ['dʒiːstrɪŋ] n String m, Stringtanga m

guarantee [gærənˈtiː] n Garantie f (of für); **it's still under ~** es ist noch Garantie darauf ▷ vt garantieren

guard [gɑːd] n (sentry) Wache f; (in prison) Wärter(in) m(f); (Brit Rail) Schaffner(in) m(f) ▷ vt bewachen; **a closely ~ed secret** ein streng gehütetes Geheimnis

guardian ['gɑːdɪən] n Vormund m; **~ angel** Schutzengel m

guess [ges] n Vermutung f; (estimate) Schätzung f; **have a ~ rate mal!** ▷ vt, vi raten; (estimate) schätzen; **I ~ you're right** du hast wohl recht; **I ~ so** ich glaube schon

guest [gest] n Gast m; **be my ~** nur zu!; **guest-house** n Pension f; **guest room** n Gästezimmer nt

guidance ['gaɪdəns] n (direction) Leitung f; (advice) Rat m; (counselling) Beratung f; **for your ~** zu Ihrer Orientierung; **guide** [gaɪd] n (person) Führer(in) m(f); (tour) Reiseleiter(in) m(f); (book) Führer m; (girl ~) Pfadfinderin f ▷ vt führen; **guidebook** n Reiseführer m; **guide dog** n Blindenhund m; **guided tour** n

guilt |

Führung f (of durch); **guidelines** npl Richtlinien pl

guilt [gɪlt] n Schuld f; **guilty** adj schuldig (of gen); (look) schuldbewusst; **to have a ~ conscience** ein schlechtes Gewissen haben

guinea pig ['gɪnɪ pɪg] n Meerschweinchen nt; (person) Versuchskaninchen nt

guitar [gɪ'tɑː°] n Gitarre f

gulf [gʌlf] n Golf m; (gap) Kluft f; **Gulf States** npl Golfstaaten pl

gull [gʌl] n Möwe f

gullible ['gʌlɪbl] adj leichtgläubig

gulp [gʌlp] n (kräftiger) Schluck ▷ vi schlucken

gum [gʌm] n (around teeth, usu pl) Zahnfleisch nt; (chewing ~) Kaugummi m

gun [gʌn] n Schusswaffe f; (rifle) Gewehr nt; (pistol) Pistole f; **gunfire** n Schüsse pl, Geschützfeuer nt; **gunpowder** n Schießpulver nt; **gunshot** n Schuss m

gush [gʌʃ] vi (heraus)strömen (from aus)

gut [gʌt] n Darm m; **~s** pl (intestines) Eingeweide; (courage) Mumm m

gutter ['gʌtə°] n (for roof) Dachrinne f; (in street) Rinnstein m, Gosse f; **gutter press** n Skandalpresse f

guy [gaɪ] n (man) Typ m, Kerl m; **~s** pl (US) Leute pl

gym [dʒɪm] n Turnhalle f; (for working out) Fitnesscenter nt; **gymnasium** [dʒɪm'neɪzɪəm] n Turnhalle f; **gymnastics** [dʒɪm'næstɪks] nsing Turnen nt; **gym-toned** adj durchtrainiert

gynaecologist [gaɪnɪ'kɒlədʒɪst] n Frauenarzt m, Frauenärztin f, Gynäkologe m, Gynäkologin f;

gynaecology n Gynäkologie f, Frauenheilkunde f

gypsy ['dʒɪpsɪ] n Zigeuner(in) m(f)

h

habit ['hæbɪt] n Gewohnheit f; **habitual** [hə'bɪtjʊəl] adj gewohnt; (drinker, liar) gewohnheitsmäßig

hack [hæk] vt hacken; **hacker** n (Inform) Hacker(in) m(f)

had [hæd] pt, pp of **have**

haddock ['hædək] n Schellfisch m

hadn't ['hædnt] contr of **had not**

haemophiliac, hemophiliac (US) [hi:məʊ'fɪlɪæk] n Bluter(in) m(f); **haemorrhage, hemorrhage** (US) ['hemərɪdʒ] n Blutung f ▷ vi bluten; **haemorrhoids, hemorrhoids** (US) ['hemərɔɪdz] npl Hämorrhoiden pl

haggis ['hægɪs] n (Scot) mit gehackten Schafsinnereien und Haferschrot gefüllter Schafsmagen

Hague [heɪg] n: **the ~** Den Haag

hail [heɪl] n Hagel m ▷ vi hageln ▷ vt: **to ~ sb as sth** jdn als etw

feiern; **hailstone** n Hagelkorn nt; **hailstorm** n Hagelschauer m

hair [hɛə°] n Haar nt, Haare pl; **to do one's ~** sich frisieren; **to get one's ~ cut** sich dat die Haare schneiden lassen; **hairbrush** n Haarbürste f; **hair conditioner** n Haarspülung f; **haircut** n Haarschnitt m; **to have a ~** sich dat die Haare schneiden lassen; **hairdo** (pl -s) n Frisur f; **hairdresser** n Friseur m, Friseuse f; **hairdryer** n Haartrockner m; (hand-held) Fön® m; (over head) Trockenhaube f; **hair gel** n Haargel nt; **hairpin** n Haarnadel f; **hair remover** n Enthaarungsmittel nt; **hair spray** n Haarspray nt; **hair style** n Frisur f; **hairy** adj haarig, behaart; (fam: dangerous) brenzlig

hake [heɪk] n Seehecht m

half [hɑ:f] (pl **halves**) n Hälfte f; (Sport: of game) Halbzeit f; **to cut in ~** halbieren ▷ adj halb; **three and a ~ pounds** dreieinhalb Pfund; **~ an hour, a ~ hour** eine halbe Stunde; **one and a ~** eineinhalb, anderthalb ▷ adv halb, zur Hälfte; **~ past three, ~ three** halb vier; **at ~ past** um halb; **~ asleep** fast eingeschlafen; **she's ~ German** sie ist zur Hälfte Deutsche; **~ as big (as)** halb so groß (wie); **half board** n Halbpension f; **half fare** n halber Fahrpreis; **half-hearted** adj halbherzig; **half-hour** n halbe Stunde; **half moon** n Halbmond m; **half pint** n ≈ Viertelliter m o nt; **half price** n: **(at) ~** zum halben Preis; **half-term** n (at school) Ferien pl in der Mitte des Trimesters; **half-time** n Halbzeit f; **halfway** adv auf halbem Wege; **halfwit** n (fam) Trottel m

halibut ['hælɪbət] n Heilbutt m

hall [hɔ:l] n (building) Halle f; (for

audience) Saal *m*; (*entrance* ~) Flur *m*; (*large*) Diele *f*; **~ of residence** (*Brit*) Studentenwohnheim *nt*

hallmark ['hɔːlmɑːk] *n* Stempel *m*; (*fig*) Kennzeichen *nt*

hallo [hʌ'ləʊ] *interj* hallo

Hallowe'en [hæləʊ'iːn] *n* Halloween *nt* (*Tag vor Allerheiligen, an dem sich Kinder verkleiden und von Tür zu Tür gehen*)

halo ['heɪləʊ] (*pl* **-es**) *n* (*of saint*) Heiligenschein *m*

halt [hɔːlt] *n* Pause *f*, Halt *m*; **to come to a ~** zum Stillstand kommen ▷ *vt, vi* anhalten

halve [hɑːv] *vt* halbieren

ham [hæm] *n* Schinken *m*; **~ and eggs** Schinken mit Spiegelei

hamburger ['hæmbɜːgə°] *n* (*Gastr*) Hamburger *m*

hammer ['hæmə°] *n* Hammer *m* ▷ *vt, vi* hämmern

hammock ['hæmək] *n* Hängematte *f*

hamper ['hæmpə°] *vt* behindern ▷ *n* (*as gift*) Geschenkkorb *m*; (*for picnic*) Picknickkorb *m*

hamster ['hæmstə°] *n* Hamster *m*

hand [hænd] *n* Hand *f*; (*of clock, instrument*) Zeiger *m*; (*in card game*) Blatt *nt*; **to be made by**

~ Handarbeit sein; **~s up!** Hände hoch!; (*at school*) meldet euch!; **~s off!** Finger weg!; **on the one ~ ..., on the other ~...** einerseits ..., andererseits ...; **to give sb a ~** jdm helfen (*with bei*); **it's in his ~s** er hat es in der Hand; **to be in good ~s** gut aufgehoben sein; **to get out of ~** außer Kontrolle geraten ▷ *vt* (*pass*) reichen (*to sb jdm*); **hand down** *vt* (*tradition*) überliefern; (*heirloom*) vererben; **hand in** *vt* einreichen; (*at school, university etc*) abgeben; **hand out** *vt* verteilen; **hand over** *vt* übergeben

handbag *n* Handtasche *f*; **handbook** *n* Handbuch *nt*; **handbrake** *n* (*Brit*) Handbremse *f*; **handcuffs** *npl* Handschellen *pl*; **handful** *n* Handvoll *f*; **handheld PC** *n* Handheld *m*

handicap ['hændɪkæp] *n* Behinderung *f*, Handikap *nt* ▷ *vt* benachteiligen; **handicapped** *adj* behindert; **the ~** die Behinderten

handicraft ['hændɪkrɑːft] *n* Kunsthandwerk *nt*

handkerchief ['hæŋkətʃɪf] *n* Taschentuch *nt*

handle ['hændl] *n* Griff *m*; (*of door*) Klinke *f*; (*of cup etc*) Henkel *m*; (*for winding*) Kurbel *f* ▷ *vt* (*touch*) anfassen; (*deal with: matter*) sich befassen mit; (*people, machine etc*) umgehen mit; (*situation, problem*) fertig werden mit; **handlebars** *npl* Lenkstange *f*

hand luggage ['hændlʌgɪdʒ] *n* Handgepäck *nt*; **handmade** *adj* handgefertigt; **to be ~** Handarbeit sein; **handout** *n* (*sheet*) Handout *nt*, Thesenpapier *nt*; **handset** *n* Hörer *m*; **please replace the ~** bitte legen Sie auf; **hands-free phone** *n* Freisprechanlage *f*; **handshake** *n* Händedruck *m*

handsome ['hænsəm] *adj* (*man*) gut aussehend

hands-on [hændz'ɒn] *adj* praxisorientiert; **~ experience** praktische Erfahrung

handwriting ['hændraɪtɪŋ] *n* Handschrift *f*

handy ['hændɪ] *adj* (*useful*) praktisch

hang [hæŋ] (**hung, hung**) *vt* (auf)hängen; (*execute: hanged, hanged*) hängen; **to ~ sth on sth** etw an etw *akk* hängen ▷ *vi* hängen ▷ *n*: **he's got the ~ of it** er hat den Dreh raus; **hang about** *vi* sich herumtreiben, rumhängen; **hang on** *vi* sich festhalten (*to* an *+dat*); (*fam: wait*) warten; **to ~ to sth** etw behalten; **hang up** *vi* (*Tel*) auflegen ▷ *vt* aufhängen

hangar ['hæŋə*] *n* Flugzeughalle *f*

hanger ['hæŋə*] *n* Kleiderbügel *m*

hang glider ['hæŋglaɪdə*] *n* (*Flug*)drachen *m*; (*person*) Drachenflieger(in) *m(f)*; **hang-gliding** *n* Drachenfliegen *nt*

hangover ['hæŋəʊvə*] *n* (*bad head*) Kater *m*; (*relic*) Überbleibsel *nt*

hankie ['hæŋki] *n* (*fam*) Taschentuch *nt*

happen ['hæpən] *vi* geschehen; (*sth strange, unpleasant*) passieren; **if anything should ~ to me** wenn mir etwas passieren sollte; **it won't ~ again** es wird nicht wieder vorkommen; **I ~ed to be passing** ich kam zufällig vorbei; **happening** *n* Ereignis *nt*, Happening *nt*

happily ['hæpɪlɪ] *adv* fröhlich, glücklich; (*luckily*) glücklicherweise; **happiness** ['hæpɪnəs] *n* Glück *nt*; **happy** ['hæpɪ] *adj* glücklich; (*satisfied*)

~ with sth mit etw zufrieden; (*willing*) **to be ~ to do sth** etw gerne tun; **Happy Christmas** fröhliche Weihnachten!; **Happy New Year** ein glückliches Neues Jahr!; **Happy Birthday** herzlichen Glückwunsch zum Geburtstag!; **happy hour** *n* Happy Hour *f* (*Zeit, in der man in Bars Getränke zu günstigeren Preisen bekommt*)

harass ['hærəs] *vt* (ständig) belästigen; **harassment** *n* Belästigung *f*; (*at work*) Mobbing *nt*; **sexual ~** sexuelle Belästigung

harbor (*US*), **harbour** ['hɑːbə*] *n* Hafen *m*

hard [hɑːd] *adj* hart; (*difficult*) schwer, schwierig; (*harsh*) hart(herzig); **don't be ~ on him** sei nicht zu streng zu ihm; **it's ~ to believe** es ist kaum zu glauben ▷ *adv* (*work*) schwer; (*run*) schnell; (*rain, snow*) stark; **to try ~/~er** sich *dat* große/mehr Mühe geben; **hardback** *n* gebundene Ausgabe; **hard-boiled** *adj* (*egg*) hart gekocht; **hard copy** *n* (*Inform*) Ausdruck *m*; **hard disk** *n* (*Inform*) Festplatte *f*; **harden** *vt* härten ▷ *vi* hart werden; **hardened** *adj* (*person*) abgehärtet (*to* gegen); **hard-hearted** *adj* hartherzig; **hardliner** *n* Hardliner(in) *m(f)*; **hardly** ['hɑːdlɪ] *adv* kaum; **~ ever** fast nie; **hardship** ['hɑːdʃɪp] *n* Not *f*; **hard shoulder** *n* (*Brit*) Standspur *f*; **hardware** *n* (*Inform*) Hardware *f*, Haushalts- und Eisenwaren *pl*; **hard-working** *adj* fleißig, tüchtig

hare [hɛə*] *n* Hase *m*

harm [hɑːm] *n* Schaden *m*; (*bodily*) Verletzung *f*; **it wouldn't do any ~** es würde nicht schaden ▷ *vt* schaden *+dat*; (*person*) verletzen; **harmful** *adj* schädlich; **harmless** *adj* harmlos

harp [hɑːp] n Harfe f
harsh [hɑːʃ] adj (climate, voice) rau; (light, sound) grell; (severe) hart, streng
harvest ['hɑːvɪst] n Ernte f; (time) Erntezeit f ▷ vt ernten
has [hæz] pres of **have**
hash [hæʃ] n (Gastr) Haschee nt; (fam: hashish) Haschisch nt; **to make a ~ of sth** etw vermasseln; **hash browns** npl (US) ≈ Kartoffelpuffer/Rösti mit Zwiebeln pl
hassle ['hæsl] n Ärger m; (fuss) Theater nt; **no ~** kein Problem ▷ vt bedrängen
hasn't ['hæznt] contr of **has not**
haste [heɪst] n Eile f; **hastily**, **hasty** adv, adj hastig; (rash) vorschnell
hat [hæt] n Hut m
hatch [hætʃ] n (Naut) Luke f; (in house) Durchreiche f; **hatchback** ['hætʃbæk] n (car) Wagen m mit Hecktür
hate [heɪt] vt hassen; **I ~ doing this** ich mache das sehr ungern ▷ n Hass m (of auf +akk)
haul [hɔːl] vt ziehen, schleppen ▷ n (booty) Beute f; **haulage** ['hɔːlɪdʒ] n Transport m; (trade) Spedition f; **haunted** adj: **a ~ house** ein Haus, in dem es spukt

◯ **KEYWORD**

have [hæv] (pt, pp **had**) vb aux **1** haben; (esp with vbs of motion) sein; **to have arrived/slept** angekommen sein/geschlafen haben; **to have been** gewesen sein; **having eaten** o **when he had eaten, he left** nachdem er gegessen hatte, ging er
2 (in tag questions) **you've done it, haven't you?** du hast/Sie haben es doch gemacht, oder nicht?

3 (in short answers and questions) **you've made a mistake — so I have/no I haven't** du hast/Sie haben einen Fehler gemacht — ja, stimmt/nein; **we haven't paid — yes we have!** wir haben nicht bezahlt — doch!; **I've been there before, have you?** ich war schon einmal da, du/Sie auch?
▷ modal vb aux (be obliged): **to have (got) to do sth** etw tun müssen; **you haven't to tell her** du darfst es ihr nicht erzählen
▷ vt **1** (possess) haben; **he has (got) blue eyes** er hat blaue Augen; **I have (got) an idea** ich habe eine Idee
2 (referring to meals etc) **to have breakfast/a cigarette** frühstücken/eine Zigarette rauchen
3 (receive, obtain etc) haben; **may I have your address?** kann ich deine/Ihre Adresse haben?; **to have a baby** ein Kind bekommen
4 (maintain, allow) **he will have it that he is right** er besteht darauf, dass er recht hat; **I won't have it** das lasse ich mir nicht bieten
5 to have sth done etw machen lassen; **to have sb do sth** jdn etw machen lassen; **he soon had them all laughing** er brachte sie alle zum Lachen
6 (experience, suffer) **she had her bag stolen** man hat ihr die Tasche gestohlen; **he had his arm broken** er hat sich den Arm gebrochen
7 (+noun: take, hold etc) **to have a walk/rest** spazieren gehen/sich ausruhen; **to have a meeting/party** eine Besprechung/Party haben;
have on vt (be wearing) anhaben; (have arranged) vorhaben; (Brit) **you're having me on** du verarschst mich doch;

have out vt: **to have it out with sb** (settle problem) etw mit jdm bereden

Hawaii [hə'waɪiː] n Hawaii nt
hawk [hɔːk] n Habicht m
hay [heɪ] n Heu nt; **hay fever** n Heuschnupfen m
hazard ['hæzəd] n Gefahr f; (risk) Risiko nt; **hazardous** adj gefährlich; ~ **waste** Sondermüll m; **hazard warning lights** npl Warnblinkanlage f
haze [heɪz] n Dunst m
hazelnut ['heɪzlnʌt] n Haselnuss f
hazy ['heɪzɪ] adj (misty) dunstig; (vague) verschwommen
he [hiː] pron er
head [hed] n Kopf m; (leader) Leiter(in) m(f); (at school) Schulleiter(in) m(f); ~ **of state** Staatsoberhaupt nt; **at the ~ of** an der Spitze von; (tossing coin) ~**s or tails?** Kopf oder Zahl? ▷ adj (leading) Ober-; ~ **boy** Schulsprecher m; ~ **girl** Schulsprecherin f ▷ vt anführen; (organization) leiten; **head for** vt zusteuern auf +akk; **he's heading for trouble** er wird Ärger bekommen
headache ['hedeɪk] n Kopfschmerzen pl, Kopfweh nt; **header** n (football) Kopfball m; (dive) Kopfsprung m; **headfirst** adj kopfüber; **headhunt** vt (Comm) abwerben; **heading** n Überschrift f; **headlamp, headlight** n Scheinwerfer m; **headline** n Schlagzeile f; **headmaster** n Schulleiter m; **headmistress** n Schulleiterin f; **head-on collision** adj Frontalzusammenstoß m; **headphones** npl Kopfhörer m; **headquarters** npl (of firm) Zentrale f; **headrest**, **head**

restraint n Kopfstütze f; **headscarf** (pl **-scarves**) n Kopftuch nt; **head teacher** n Schulleiter(in) m(f)
heal [hiːl] vt, vi heilen
health [helθ] n Gesundheit f; **good/bad for one's** ~ gesund/ungesund; **your ~!** zum Wohl!; ~ **and beauty** Wellness; **health centre** n Ärztezentrum nt; **health club** n Fitnesscenter nt; **health food** n Reformkost f; ~ **shop**, ~ **store** Bioladen m; **health insurance** n Krankenversicherung f; **health service** n Gesundheitswesen nt; **healthy** adj gesund
heap [hiːp] n Haufen m; ~**s of** (fam) jede Menge ▷ vt, vi häufen
hear [hɪə*] (**heard, heard**) vt, vi hören; **to ~ about sth** von etw erfahren; **I've ~d of it/him** ich habe schon davon/von ihm gehört; **hearing** n Gehör nt; (Jur) Verhandlung f; **hearing aid** n Hörgerät nt; **hearsay** n: **from** ~ vom Hörensagen
heart [hɑːt] n Herz nt; **to lose/take** ~ den Mut verlieren/Mut fassen; **to learn by** ~ auswendig lernen; (cards) ~**s** Herz nt; **queen of** ~**s** Herzdame f; **heart attack** n Herzanfall m; **heartbeat** n Herzschlag m; **heartbreaking** adj herzzerreißend; **heartbroken** adj todunglücklich, untröstlich; **heartburn** n Sodbrennen nt; **heart failure** n Herzversagen nt; **heartfelt** adj tief empfunden; **heartless** adj herzlos; **heart-throb** n (fam) Schwarm m; **heart-to-heart** n offene Aussprache; **hearty** [hɑːtɪ] adj (meal, appetite) herzhaft; (welcome) herzlich
heat [hiːt] n Hitze f; (pleasant) Wärme f; (temperature) Temperatur

f; (Sport) Vorlauf m ▷ vt (house,
room) heizen; **heat up** vi warm
werden ▷ vt aufwärmen; **heated**
adj beheizt; (fig) hitzig; **heater** n
Heizofen m; (Auto) Heizung f

heath [hi:θ] n (Brit) Heide f;
heather ['heðə*] n Heidekraut
nt

heating ['hi:tɪŋ] n Heizung f;
heat resistant adj
hitzebeständig; **heatwave** n
Hitzewelle f

heaven ['hevn] n Himmel m;
heavenly adj himmlisch

heavily ['hevɪlɪ] adv (rain, drink
etc) stark; **heavy** ['hevɪ] adj
schwer; (rain, traffic, smoker etc)
stark; **heavy goods vehicle** n
Lastkraftwagen m

Hebrew ['hi:bru:] adj hebräisch
▷ n (language) Hebräisch nt

hectic ['hektɪk] adj hektisch

he'd [hi:d] contr of **he had**; **he
would**

hedge [hedʒ] n Hecke f

hedgehog ['hedʒhɒg] n Igel
m

heel [hi:l] n (Anat) Ferse f; (of
shoe) Absatz m

hefty ['heftɪ] adj schwer; (person)
stämmig; (fine, amount) saftig

height [haɪt] n Höhe f; (of person)
Größe f

heir [eə*] n Erbe m; **heiress**
['eərɪs] n Erbin f

held [held] pt, pp of **hold**

helicopter ['helɪkɒptə*] n
Hubschrauber m; **heliport**
['helɪpɔːt] n Hubschrauber-
landeplatz m

hell [hel] n Hölle f; **go to ~** scher
dich zum Teufel ▷ interj
verdammt; **that's a ~ of a lot of
money** das ist verdammt viel Geld

he'll [hi:l] contr of **he will**; **he
shall**

hello [hʌ'ləʊ] interj hallo

helmet ['helmɪt] n Helm m

help [help] n Hilfe f ▷ vt, vi
helfen +dat (with bei); **to ~ sb (to)
do sth** jdm helfen, etw zu tun; **can
I ~?** kann ich (Ihnen) behilflich
sein?; **I couldn't ~ laughing** ich
musste einfach lachen; **I can't ~ it**
ich kann nichts dafür; **~ yourself**
bedienen Sie sich; **helpful** adj
(person) hilfsbereit; (useful)
nützlich; **helping** n Portion f;
helpless adj hilflos

hem [hem] n Saum m

hemophiliac [hi:məʊ'fɪlɪæk] n
(US) Bluter m; **hemorrhage**
['hemərɪdʒ] n (US) Blutung f;
hemorrhoids ['hemərɔɪdz] npl
(US) Hämorrhoiden pl

hen [hen] n Henne f

hen night n (Brit)
Junggesellinnenabschied m

hence [hens] adv (reason) daher

henpecked ['henpekt] adj: **to
be ~** unter dem Pantoffel stehen

hepatitis [hepə'taɪtɪs] n Hepatitis f

her [hɜː*] adj ihr; **she's hurt ~ leg**
sie hat sich dat das Bein verletzt
▷ pron (direct object) sie; (indirect
object) ihr; **do you know ~?** kennst
du sie?; **can you help ~?** kannst du
ihr helfen?; **it's ~** sie ist's

herb [hɜːb] n Kraut nt

herbal medicine ['hɜːbəl-] n
Pflanzenheilkunde f; **herbal tea** n
Kräutertee m

herd [hɜːd] n Herde f; **herd
instinct** n Herdentrieb m

here [hɪə*] adv hier; (to this place)
hierher; **come ~** komm her; **I
won't be ~ for lunch** ich bin zum
Mittagessen nicht da; **~ and there**
hier und da, da und dort

hereditary [hɪ'redɪtərɪ] adj
erblich; **hereditary disease** n
Erbkrankheit f; **heritage**
['herɪtɪdʒ] n Erbe nt

hernia ['hɜːnɪə] n Leistenbruch
m, Eingeweidebruch m
hero ['hɪərəʊ] (pl **-es**) n Held m
heroin ['herəʊɪn] n Heroin nt
heroine ['herəʊɪn] n Heldin f;
heroism ['herəʊɪzəm] n
Heldentum nt
herring ['herɪŋ] n Hering m
hers [hɜːz] pron ihre(r, s); **this is**
~ das gehört ihr; **a friend of** ~ ein
Freund von ihr
herself [hɜː'self] pron (reflexive)
sich; **she's bought** ~ **a flat** sie hat
sich eine Wohnung gekauft; **she**
needs it for ~ sie braucht es für
sich (selbst); (emphatic) **she did it**
~ sie hat es selbst gemacht; (**all**)
by ~ allein
he's [hiːz] contr of **he is**; **he has**
hesitant ['hezɪtənt] adj zögernd;
hesitate ['hezɪteɪt] vi zögern;
don't ~ **to ask** fragen Sie ruhig;
hesitation n Zögern nt; **without**
~ ohne zu zögern
heterosexual [hetərəʊ'seksʊəl]
adj heterosexuell ▷ n Hetero-
sexuelle(r) mf
HGV abbr = **heavy goods vehicle**
LKW m
hi [haɪ] interj hi, hallo
hiccup ['hɪkʌp] n Schluckauf m;
(minor problem) Problemchen nt; **to**
have (the) ~**s** Schluckauf haben
hid [hɪd] pt of **hide**
hidden ['hɪdn] pp of **hide**
hide [haɪd] (**hid, hidden**) vt
verstecken (from vor +dat); (feelings,
truth) verbergen; (cover) verdecken
▷ vi sich verstecken (from vor +dat)
hideous ['hɪdɪəs] adj scheußlich
hiding ['haɪdɪŋ] n (beating)
Tracht f Prügel; (concealment) **to be**
in ~ sich versteckt halten; **hiding**
place n Versteck nt
hi-fi ['haɪfaɪ] n Hi-Fi nt; (system)
Hi-Fi-Anlage f
high [haɪ] adj hoch; (wind) stark;

(living) im großen Stil; (on drugs)
high ▷ adv hoch ▷ n (Meteo)
Hoch nt; **highchair** n Hochstuhl
m; **higher** adj höher; **higher**
education n Hochschulbildung f;
high flier n Hochbegabte(r) (m)f;
high heels npl Stöckelschuhe pl;
high jump n Hochsprung m;
Highlands npl (schottisches)
Hochland nt; **highlight** n (in hair)
Strähnchen nt; (fig) Höhepunkt m
▷ vt (with pen) hervorheben;
highlighter n Textmarker m;
highly adj hoch, sehr; ~ **paid**
hoch bezahlt; **I think** ~ **of him** ich
habe eine hohe Meinung von ihm;
high-performance adj Hoch-
leistungs-; **high school** n (US)
Highschool f, ≈ Gymnasium nt;
high-speed adj Schnell-; ~ **train**
Hochgeschwindigkeitszug m;
high street n Hauptstraße f; **high**
tech adj Hightech- ▷ n Hightech
nt; **high tide** n Flut f; **highway** n
(US) ≈ Autobahn f; (Brit)
Landstraße f
hijack ['haɪdʒæk] vt entführen,
hijacken; **hijacker** n
Entführer(in) m(f), Hijacker m
hike [haɪk] vi wandern ▷ n
Wanderung f; **hiker** n Wanderer
m, Wanderin f; **hiking** n Wandern
nt
hilarious [hɪ'leərɪəs] adj zum
Schreien komisch
hill [hɪl] n Hügel m; (higher) Berg
m; **hilly** adj hügelig
him [hɪm] pron (direct object) ihn;
(indirect object) ihm; **do you know**
~? kennst du ihn?; **can you help** ~?
kannst du ihm helfen?; **it's** ~ er
ist's; ~ **too** er auch
himself [hɪm'self] pron (reflexive)
sich; **he's bought** ~ **a flat** er hat
sich eine Wohnung gekauft; **he**
needs it for ~ er braucht es für
sich (selbst); (emphatic) **he did it**

~ er hat es selbst gemacht; (**all**) **by** ~ allein

hinder ['hɪndə°] vt behindern; **hindrance** ['hɪndrəns] n Behinderung f

Hindu ['hɪnduː] adj hinduistisch ▷ n Hindu m; **Hinduism** ['hɪnduːɪzəm] n Hinduismus m

hinge [hɪndʒ] n Scharnier nt; (on door) Angel f

hint [hɪnt] n Wink m, Andeutung f; (trace) Spur f ▷ vi andeuten (at akk)

hip [hɪp] n Hüfte f

hippopotamus [hɪpə'pɒtəməs] n Nilpferd nt

hire ['haɪə°] vt (worker) anstellen; (car, bike etc) mieten ▷ n Miete f; **for** ~ (taxi) frei; **hire car** n Mietwagen m; **hire charge** n Benutzungsgebühr f; **hire purchase** n Ratenkauf m

his [hɪz] adj sein; **he's hurt** ~ **leg** er hat sich dat das Bein verletzt ▷ pron seine(r, s); **it's** ~ es gehört ihm; **a friend of** ~ ein Freund von ihm

historic [hɪ'stɒrɪk] adj (significant) historisch; **historical** adj (monument etc) historisch; (studies etc) geschichtlich; **history** ['hɪstərɪ] n Geschichte f

hit [hɪt] n (blow) Schlag m; (on target) Treffer m; (successful film, CD etc) Hit m ▷ vt (**hit, hit**) schlagen; (bullet, stone etc) treffen; **the car** ~ **the tree** das Auto fuhr gegen einen Baum; **to** ~ **one's head on sth** sich dat den Kopf an etw dat stoßen; **hit (up)on** vt stoßen auf +akk; **hit-and-run** adj: ~ **accident** Unfall m mit Fahrerflucht

hitch [hɪtʃ] vt (pull up) hochziehen ▷ n Schwierigkeit f; **without a** ~ reibungslos

hitch-hike ['hɪtʃhaɪk] vi trampen; **hitch-hiker** n Tramper(in)

m(f); **hitchhiking** n Trampen nt

HIV abbr = **human immunodeficiency virus** HIV nt; ~ **positive/negative** HIV-positiv/negativ

hive [haɪv] n Bienenstock m

HM abbr = **His/Her Majesty**

HMS abbr = **His/Her Majesty's Ship**

hoarse [hɔːs] adj heiser

hoax [həʊks] n Streich m, Jux m; (false alarm) blinder Alarm

hob [hɒb] n (of cooker) Kochfeld nt

hobble ['hɒbl] vi humpeln

hobby ['hɒbɪ] n Hobby nt

hobo ['həʊbəʊ] (pl -**es**) n (US) Penner(in) m(f)

hockey ['hɒkɪ] n Hockey nt

hold [həʊld] (**held, held**) vt halten; (contain) enthalten; (be able to contain) fassen; (post, office) innehaben; (value) behalten; (meeting) abhalten; (person as prisoner) gefangen halten; **to** ~ **one's breath** den Atem anhalten; **to** ~ **hands** Händchen halten; ~ **the line** (Tel) bleiben Sie am Apparat ▷ vi halten; (weather) sich halten ▷ n (grasp) Halt m; (of ship, aircraft) Laderaum m; **hold back** vt zurückhalten; (keep secret) verheimlichen; **hold on** vi sich festhalten; (wait) warten; (Tel) dranbleiben; **to** ~ **to sth** etw festhalten; **hold out** vt ausstrecken; (offer) hinhalten; (offer) bieten ▷ vi durchhalten; **hold up** vt hochhalten; (support) stützen; (delay) aufhalten; **holdall** n Reisetasche f; **holder** n (person) Inhaber(in) m(f); **holdup** n (in traffic) Stau m; (robbery) Überfall m

hole [həʊl] n Loch nt; (of fox, rabbit) Bau m; ~ **in the wall** (cash dispenser) Geldautomat m

holiday ['hɒlɪdəɪ] *n* (*day off*) freier Tag; (*public* ~) Feiertag *m*; (*vacation*) Urlaub *m*; (*at school*) Ferien *pl*; **on** ~ im Urlaub; **to go on** ~ Urlaub machen; **holiday camp** *n* Ferienlager *nt*; **holiday home** *n* Ferienhaus *nt*; (*flat*) Ferienwohnung *f*; **holidaymaker** *n* Urlauber(in) *m(f)*; **holiday resort** *n* Ferienort *m*

Holland ['hɒlənd] *n* Holland *nt*

hollow ['hɒləʊ] *adj* hohl; (*words*) leer ▷ *n* Vertiefung *f*

holly ['hɒlɪ] *n* Stechpalme *f*

holy ['həʊlɪ] *adj* heilig; **Holy Week** *n* Karwoche *f*

home [həʊm] *n* Zuhause *nt*; (*area, country*) Heimat *f*; (*institution*) Heim *nt*; **at** ~ zu Hause; **to make oneself at** ~ es sich *dat* bequem machen; **away from** ~ verreist ▷ *adv* **to go** ~ nach Hause gehen/fahren; **home address** *n* Heimatadresse *f*; **home country** *n* Heimatland *nt*; **home game** *n* (*Sport*) Heimspiel *nt*; **homeless** *adj* obdachlos; **homely** *adj* häuslich; (*US: ugly*) unscheinbar; **home-made** *adj* selbst gemacht; **home movie** *n* Amateurfilm *m*; **Home Office** *n* (*Brit*) Innenministerium *nt*

homeopathic *adj* (*US*) *see* **homoeopathic**

home page ['həʊmpeɪdʒ] *n* (*Inform*) Homepage *f*; **Home Secretary** *n* (*Brit*) Innenminister(in) *m(f)*; **homesick** *adj*: **to be** ~ Heimweh haben; **home town** *n* Heimatstadt *f*; **homework** *n* Hausaufgaben *pl*

homicide ['hɒmɪsaɪd] *n* (*US*) Totschlag *m*

homoeopathic [həʊmɪəʊ'pæθɪk] *adj* homöopathisch

homosexual [hɒməʊ'sekʃʊəl] *adj* homosexuell ▷ *n* Homosexuelle(r) *mf*

Honduras [hɒn'djʊərəs] *n* Honduras *nt*

honest ['ɒnɪst] *adj* ehrlich; **honesty** *n* Ehrlichkeit *f*

honey ['hʌnɪ] *n* Honig *m*; **honeycomb** *n* Honigwabe *f*; **honeydew melon** *n* Honigmelone *f*; **honeymoon** *n* Flitterwochen *pl*

Hong Kong [hɒŋ 'kɒŋ] *n* Hongkong *nt*

honor (*US*) *see* **honour**; **honorary** ['ɒnərərɪ] *adj* (*member, title etc*) Ehren-, ehrenamtlich; **honour** ['ɒnə*] *vt* ehren; (*cheque*) einlösen; (*contract*) einhalten ▷ *n* Ehre *f*; **in** ~ **of** zu Ehren von; **honourable** *adj* ehrenhaft; **honours degree** *n* *akademischer Grad mit Prüfung im Spezialfach*

hood [hʊd] *n* Kapuze *f*; (*Auto*) Verdeck *nt*; (*US Auto*) Kühlerhaube *f*

hoof [hu:f] *n* (*pl* **hooves**) *n* Huf *m*

hook [hʊk] *n* Haken *m*; **hooked** *adj* (*keen*) besessen (*on* von); (*drugs*) abhängig sein (*on* von)

hooligan ['hu:lɪɡən] *n* Hooligan *m*

hoot [hu:t] *vi* (*Auto*) hupen

Hoover® ['hu:və] *n* Staubsauger *m*; **hoover** *vi, vt* staubsaugen

hop [hɒp] *vi* hüpfen ▷ *n* (*Bot*) Hopfen *m*

hope [həʊp] *vi, vt* hoffen (*for* auf +*akk*); **I** ~ **so/**~ **not** hoffentlich/hoffentlich nicht; **I** ~ (**that**) **we'll meet** ich hoffe, dass wir uns sehen werden ▷ *n* Hoffnung *f*; **there's no** ~ es ist aussichtslos; **hopeful** *adj* hoffnungsvoll; **hopefully** *adv* (*full of hope*) hoffnungsvoll; (*I hope so*) hoffentlich; **hopeless** *adj* hoffnungslos; (*incompetent*) miserabel

horizon [hə'raɪzn] *n* Horizont *m*; **horizontal** [hɒrɪ'zɒntl] *adj* horizontal

hormone ['hɔːməʊn] *n* Hormon *nt*

horn [hɔːn] *n* Horn *nt*; (*Auto*) Hupe *f*

hornet ['hɔːnɪt] *n* Hornisse *f*

horny ['hɔːnɪ] *adj* (*fam*) geil

horoscope ['hɒrəskəʊp] *n* Horoskop *nt*

horrible, horribly ['hɒrɪbl, -blɪ] *adj, adv* schrecklich; **horrid, horridly** ['hɒrɪd, -lɪ] *adj, adv* abscheulich; **horrify** ['hɒrɪfaɪ] *vt* entsetzen; **horror** ['hɒrə*] *n* Entsetzen *nt*; **~s** (*things*) Schrecken *pl*

hors d'oeuvre [ɔː'dɜːvr] *n* Vorspeise *f*

horse [hɔːs] *n* Pferd *nt*; **horse chestnut** *n* Rosskastanie *f*; **horsepower** *n* Pferdestärke *f*, PS *nt*; **horse racing** *n* Pferderennen *nt*; **horseradish** *n* Meerrettich *m*; **horse riding** *n* Reiten *nt*; **horseshoe** *n* Hufeisen *nt*

horticulture ['hɔːtɪkʌltʃə*] *n* Gartenbau *m*

hose, hosepipe ['həʊz, 'həʊzpaɪp] *n* Schlauch *m*

hospitable [hɒ'spɪtəbl] *adj* gastfreundlich

hospital ['hɒspɪtl] *n* Krankenhaus *nt*

hospitality [hɒspɪ'tælɪtɪ] *n* Gastfreundschaft *f*

host [həʊst] *n* Gastgeber *m*; (*TV: of show*) Moderator(in) *m(f)*, Talkmaster(in) *m(f)* ▷ *vt* (*party*) geben; (*TV: TV show*) moderieren

hostage ['hɒstɪdʒ] *n* Geisel *f*

hostel ['hɒstəl] *n* Wohnheim *nt*; (*youth ~*) Jugendherberge *f*

hostess ['həʊstɪs] *n* (*of a party*) Gastgeberin *f*

hostile ['hɒstaɪl] *adj* feindlich; **hostility** [hɒs'tɪlɪtɪ] *n* Feindseligkeit *f*

hot [hɒt] *adj* heiß; (*drink, food, water*) warm; (*spiced*) scharf; **I'm (feeling) ~** mir ist heiß; **hot cross bun** *n* Rosinenbrötchen mit einem Kreuz darauf, hauptsächlich zu Ostern gegessen; **hot dog** *n* Hotdog *nt*

hotel [həʊ'tel] *n* Hotel *nt*; **hotel room** *n* Hotelzimmer *nt*

hothouse *n* Treibhaus *nt*; **hotline** *n* Hotline *f*; **hotplate** *n* Kochplatte *f*; **hotpot** *n* Fleischeintopf mit Kartoffeleinlage; **hot-water bottle** *n* Wärmflasche *f*

hour ['aʊə*] *n* Stunde *f*; **to wait for ~s** stundenlang warten; **~s** *pl* (*of shops etc*) Geschäftszeiten *pl*; **hourly** *adj* stündlich

house [haʊs] (*pl* **houses**) *n* Haus *nt*; **at my ~** bei mir (zu Hause); **to my ~** zu mir (nach Hause); **on the ~** auf Kosten des Hauses; **the House of Commons/Lords** das britische Unterhaus/Oberhaus; **the Houses of Parliament** das britische Parlamentsgebäude ▷ [haʊz] *vt* unterbringen; **houseboat** *n* Hausboot *nt*; **household** *n* Haushalt *m*; **~ appliance** Haushaltsgerät *nt*; **house-husband** *n* Hausmann *m*; **housekeeping** *n* Haushaltung *f*; (*money*) Haushaltsgeld *nt*; **house-trained** *adj* stubenrein; **house-warming (party)** *n* Einzugsparty *f*; **housewife** (*pl* **-wives**) *n* Hausfrau *f*; **house wine** *n* Hauswein *m*; **housework** *n* Hausarbeit *f*

housing ['haʊzɪŋ] *n* (*houses*) Wohnungen *pl*; (*house building*) Wohnungsbau *m*; **housing**

benefit n Wohngeld nt; **housing development, housing estate** (Brit) n Wohnsiedlung f

hover ['hɒvə*] vi schweben; **hovercraft** n Luftkissenboot nt

how [haʊ] adv wie; **~ many** wie viele; **~ much** wie viel; **~ are you?** wie geht es Ihnen?; **~ are things?** wie geht's?; **~'s work?** was macht die Arbeit?; **~ about ...?** wie wäre es mit ...?; **however** [haʊ'evə*] conj (but) jedoch, aber ▷ adv (no matter how) wie ... auch; **~ much it costs** wie viel es auch kostet; **~ you do it** wie man es auch macht

howl [haʊl] vi heulen; **howler** ['haʊlə*] n (fam) grober Schnitzer

HP, hp n (Brit) abbr = **hire purchase** Ratenkauf m ▷ abbr = **horsepower** PS

HQ abbr = **headquarters**

hubcap ['hʌbkæp] n Radkappe f

hug [hʌg] vt umarmen ▷ n Umarmung f

huge [hjuːdʒ] adj riesig

hum [hʌm] vi, vt summen

human ['hjuːmən] adj menschlich; **~ rights** Menschenrechte pl ▷ n: **~ (being)** Mensch m; **humanitarian** [hjuːmænɪ'tɛərɪən] adj humanitär; **humanity** [hjuː'mænɪtɪ] n Menschheit f; (kindliness) Menschlichkeit f; **humanities** Geisteswissenschaften pl

humble ['hʌmbl] adj demütig; (modest) bescheiden

humid ['hjuːmɪd] adj feucht; **humidity** [hjuː'mɪdɪtɪ] n (Luft)feuchtigkeit f

humiliate [hjuː'mɪlɪeɪt] vt demütigen; **humiliation** [hjuːmɪlɪ'eɪʃn] n Erniedrigung f, Demütigung f

humor (US) see **humour**;

humorous ['hjuːmərəs] adj humorvoll; (story) lustig, witzig; **humour** ['hjuːmə*] n Humor m; **sense of ~** Sinn m für Humor

hump [hʌmp] n Buckel m

hunch [hʌntʃ] n Gefühl nt, Ahnung f ▷ vt (back) krümmen; **hunchback** n Bucklige(r) mf

hundred ['hʌndrəd] num: **one ~, a ~** (ein)hundert; **~ and one** hundert(und)eins; **two ~** zweihundert; **hundredth** adj hundertste(r, s) ▷ n (fraction) Hundertstel nt; **hundredweight** n Zentner m (50,8 kg)

hung [hʌŋ] pt, pp of **hang**

Hungarian [hʌŋ'gɛərɪən] adj ungarisch ▷ n (person) Ungar(in) m(f); (language) Ungarisch nt; **Hungary** ['hʌŋgərɪ] n Ungarn nt

hunger ['hʌŋgə*] n Hunger m; **hungry** ['hʌŋgrɪ] adj hungrig; **to be ~** Hunger haben

hunk [hʌŋk] n (fam) gut gebauter Mann; **hunky** ['hʌŋkɪ] adj (fam) gut gebaut

hunt [hʌnt] n Jagd f; (search) Suche f (for nach) ▷ vt, vi jagen; (search) suchen (for nach); **hunting** n Jagen nt, Jagd f

hurdle ['hɜːdl] n (a. fig) Hürde f; **the 400m ~s** der 400m-Hürdenlauf

hurl [hɜːl] vt schleudern

hurricane ['hʌrɪkən] n Orkan m

hurried ['hʌrɪd] adj eilig; **hurry** ['hʌrɪ] n Eile f; **to be in a ~** es eilig haben; **there's no ~** es eilt nicht ▷ vi sich beeilen; **~ (up)** mach schnell! ▷ vt antreiben

hurt [hɜːt] (**hurt, hurt**) vt wehtun +dat; (wound: person, feelings) verletzen; **I've ~ my arm** ich habe mir am Arm wehgetan ▷ vi wehtun; **my arm ~s** mir tut der Arm weh

husband ['hʌzbənd] n Ehemann m

husky ['hʌskɪ] adj rau ▷ n Schlittenhund m

hut [hʌt] n Hütte f

hyacinth ['haɪəsɪnθ] n Hyazinthe f

hybrid ['haɪbrɪd] n Kreuzung f

hydroelectric ['haɪdrəʊ'lektrɪk] adj: **~ power station** Wasserkraftwerk nt

hydrofoil ['haɪdrəʊfɔɪl] n Tragflächenboot nt

hydrogen ['haɪdrədʒən] n Wasserstoff m

hygiene ['haɪdʒiːn] n Hygiene f; **hygienic** [haɪ'dʒiːnɪk] adj hygienisch

hymn [hɪm] n Kirchenlied nt

hypermarket ['haɪpəmɑːkɪt] n Großmarkt m; **hypersensitive** adj überempfindlich

hyphen ['haɪfən] n Bindestrich m

hypnosis [hɪp'nəʊsɪs] n Hypnose f; **hypnotize** ['hɪpnətaɪz] vt hypnotisieren

hypochondriac [haɪpəʊ'kɒndrɪæk] n eingebildete(r) Kranke(r), eingebildete Kranke

hypocrisy [hɪ'pɒkrəsɪ] n Heuchelei f; **hypocrite** ['hɪpəkrɪt] n Heuchler(in) m(f)

hypodermic [haɪpə'dɜːmɪk] adj, n: **~ (needle)** Spritze f

hypothetical [haɪpəʊ'θetɪkəl] adj hypothetisch

hysteria [hɪ'stɪərɪə] n Hysterie f; **hysterical** [hɪ'sterɪkəl] adj hysterisch; (amusing) zum Totlachen

I [aɪ] pron ich

ice [aɪs] n Eis nt ▷ vt (cake) glasieren; **iceberg** n Eisberg m; **iceberg lettuce** n Eisbergsalat m; **icebox** n (US) Kühlschrank m; **icecold** adj eiskalt; **ice cream** n Eis nt; **ice cube** n Eiswürfel m; **iced** adj eisgekühlt; (coffee, tea) Eis-; (cake) glasiert; **ice hockey** n Eishockey nt

Iceland ['aɪslənd] n Island nt; **Icelander** n Isländer(in) m(f); **Icelandic** [aɪs'lændɪk] adj isländisch ▷ n (language) Isländisch nt

ice lolly ['aɪslɒlɪ] n (Brit) Eis nt am Stiel; **ice rink** n Kunsteisbahn f; **ice skating** n Schlittschuhlaufen nt

icing ['aɪsɪŋ] n (on cake) Zuckerguss m

icon ['aɪkɒn] n Ikone f; (Inform) Icon nt, Programmsymbol nt

icy ['aɪsɪ] *adj* (*slippery*) vereist;
(*cold*) eisig

I'd [aɪd] *contr of* **I would; I had**

ID *abbr* = **identification** Ausweis *m*

idea [aɪ'dɪə] *n* Idee *f*; (**I've**) **no
~** (ich habe) keine Ahnung; **that's
my ~ of ...** so stelle ich mir ... vor

ideal [aɪ'dɪəl] *n* Ideal *nt* ▷ *adj*
ideal; **ideally** *adv* ideal; (*before
statement*) idealerweise

identical [aɪ'dentɪkəl] *adj*
identisch; **~ twins** eineiige
Zwillinge

identify [aɪ'dentɪfaɪ] *vt* identi-
fizieren; **identity** [aɪ'dentɪtɪ] *n*
Identität *f*; **identity card** *n*
Personalausweis *m*

idiom ['ɪdɪəm] *n* Redewendung
f; **idiomatic** *adj* idiomatisch

idiot ['ɪdɪət] *n* Idiot(in) *m(f)*

idle ['aɪdl] *adj* (*doing nothing*)
untätig; (*worker*) unbeschäftigt;
(*machines*) außer Betrieb; (*lazy*)
faul; (*promise, threat*) leer

idol ['aɪdl] *n* Idol *nt*; **idolize**
['aɪdəlaɪz] *vt* vergöttern

idyllic [ɪ'dɪlɪk] *adj* idyllisch

i.e. *abbr* = **id est** d.h.

⬤   **KEYWORD**

if [ɪf] *conj* **1** wenn; (*in case also*)
falls; **if I were you** wenn ich Sie
wäre
2 (*although*) (**even**) **if** (selbst *o*
auch) wenn
3 (*whether*) ob
4 if so/not wenn ja/nicht; **if
only ...** wenn ... doch nur ...; **if
only I could** wenn ich doch nur
könnte; *see also* **as**

ignition [ɪg'nɪʃən] *n* Zündung *f*;
ignition key *n* (*Auto*)
Zündschlüssel *m*

ignorance ['ɪgnərəns] *n*
Unwissenheit *f*; **ignorant** *adj*

unwissend; **ignore** [ɪg'nɔː*] *vt*
ignorieren, nicht beachten

I'll [aɪl] *contr of* **I will; I shall**

ill [ɪl] *adj* krank; **~ at ease**
unbehaglich

illegal [ɪ'liːgəl] *adj* illegal

illegitimate [ɪlɪ'dʒɪtɪmət] *adj*
unzulässig; (*child*) unehelich

illiterate [ɪ'lɪtərət] *adj*: **to be
~** Analphabet(in) sein

illness ['ɪlnəs] *n* Krankheit *f*

illuminate [ɪ'luːmɪneɪt] *vt*
beleuchten; **illuminating** *adj*
(*remark*) aufschlussreich

illusion [ɪ'luːʒən] *n* Illusion *f*; **to
be under the ~ that ...** sich
einbilden, dass ...

illustrate ['ɪləstreɪt] *vt*
illustrieren; **illustration** *n*
Abbildung *f*, Bild *nt*

I'm [aɪm] *contr of* **I am**

image ['ɪmɪdʒ] *n* Bild *nt*; (*public ~*)
Image *nt*; **imaginable**
[ɪ'mædʒɪnəbl] *adj* denkbar;
imaginary [ɪ'mædʒɪnərɪ] *adj*
eingebildet; **~ world** Fantasiewelt
f; **imagination** [ɪmædʒɪ'neɪʃən]
n Fantasie *f*; (*mistaken*) Einbildung
f; **imaginative** [ɪ'mædʒɪnətɪv]
adj fantasievoll; **imagine**
[ɪ'mædʒɪn] *vt* sich vorstellen;
(*wrongly*) sich einbilden; **~!** stell dir
vor!

imbecile ['ɪmbəsiːl] *n* Trottel *m*

imitate ['ɪmɪteɪt] *vt* nachah-
men, nachmachen; **imitation** *n*
Nachahmung *f* ▷ *adj* imitiert,
Kunst-

immaculate [ɪ'mækjʊlɪt] *adj*
tadellos; (*spotless*) makellos

immature [ɪmə'tjʊə*] *adj* unreif

immediate [ɪ'miːdɪət] *adj*
unmittelbar; (*instant*) sofortig;
(*reply*) umgehend; **immediately**
adv sofort

immense, immensely [ɪ'mens,
-lɪ] *adj, adv* riesig, enorm

immersion heater [ɪˈmɜːʃn
hiːtə] n Boiler m
immigrant [ˈɪmɪɡrənt] n Ein-
wanderer m, Einwanderin f;
immigration [ɪmɪˈɡreɪʃən] n
Einwanderung f; (facility)
Einwanderungskontrolle f
immobilize [ɪˈməʊbɪlaɪz] vt
lähmen; **immobilizer** n (Auto)
Wegfahrsperre f
immoral [ɪˈmɒrəl] adj
unmoralisch
immortal [ɪˈmɔːtl] adj
unsterblich
immune [ɪˈmjuːn] adj (Med)
immun (from, to gegen); **immune
system** n Immunsystem nt
impact [ˈɪmpækt] n Aufprall m;
(effect) Auswirkung f (on auf +akk)
impatience [ɪmˈpeɪʃəns] n
Ungeduld f; **impatient,
impatiently** adj, adv ungeduldig
impeccable [ɪmˈpekəbl] adj
tadellos
impede [ɪmˈpiːd] vt behindern
imperative [ɪmˈperətɪv] adj
unbedingt erforderlich ▷ n (Ling)
Imperativ m
imperfect [ɪmˈpɜːfɪkt] adj
unvollkommen; (goods) fehlerhaft
▷ n (Ling) Imperfekt nt;
imperfection [ɪmpəˈfekʃən] n
Unvollkommenheit f; (fault) Fehler
m
imperial [ɪmˈpɪərɪəl] adj kaiser-
lich, Reichs-; **imperialism** n
Imperialismus m
impertinence [ɪmˈpɜːtɪnəns] n
Unverschämtheit f, Zumutung f;
impertinent adj unverschämt
implant [ˈɪmplɑːnt] n (Med)
Implantat nt
implausible [ɪmˈplɔːzəbl] adj
unglaubwürdig
implement [ˈɪmplɪmənt] n
Werkzeug nt, Gerät nt
▷ [ˈɪmplɪˈment] vt durchführen

implication [ɪmplɪˈkeɪʃən] n
Folge f, Auswirkung f; (logical)
Schlussfolgerung f; **implicit**
[ɪmˈplɪsɪt] adj implizit,
unausgesprochen; **imply**
[ɪmˈplaɪ] vt (indicate) andeuten;
(mean) bedeuten; **are you ~ing
that ...** wollen Sie damit sagen,
dass ...
impolite [ɪmpəˈlaɪt] adj
unhöflich
import [ɪmˈpɔːt] vt einführen,
importieren ▷ n [ˈɪmpɔːt] Einfuhr f, Import m
importance [ɪmˈpɔːtəns] n
Bedeutung f; **of no ~** unwichtig;
important adj wichtig (to sb für
jdn); (significant) bedeutend;
(influential) einflussreich
import duty [ˈɪmpɔːt djuːtɪ] n
Einfuhrzoll m; **import licence** n
Einfuhrgenehmigung f
impose [ɪmˈpəʊz] vt (conditions)
auferlegen (on dat); (penalty,
sanctions) verhängen (on gegen);
imposing [ɪmˈpəʊzɪŋ] adj eindrucksvoll, imposant
impossible [ɪmˈpɒsəbl] adj
unmöglich
impotence [ˈɪmpətəns] n
Machtlosigkeit f; (sexual)
Impotenz f; **impotent** adj
machtlos; (sexually) impotent
impractical [ɪmˈpræktɪkəl] adj
unpraktisch; (plan)
undurchführbar
impress [ɪmˈpres] vt beeindrucken; **impression** [ɪmˈpreʃən]
n Eindruck m; **impressive** adj
eindrucksvoll
imprison [ɪmˈprɪzn] vt inhaf-
tieren; **imprisonment** n
Inhaftierung f
improbability [ɪmprɒbəˈbɪlɪtɪ]
n Unwahrscheinlichkeit f;
improbable [ɪmˈprɒbəbl] adj
unwahrscheinlich

improper [ɪm'prɒpə°] *adj*
(*indecent*) unanständig; (*use*)
unsachgemäß

improve [ɪm'pruːv] *vt*
verbessern ▷ *vi* sich verbessern,
besser werden; (*patient*)
Fortschritte machen;
improvement *n* Verbesserung *f*
(*in* +*gen*; *on* gegenüber); (*in
appearance*) Verschönerung *f*

improvise ['ɪmprəvaɪz] *vt, vi*
improvisieren

impulse ['ɪmpʌls] *n* Impuls *m*;
impulsive [ɪm'pʌlsɪv] *adj*
impulsiv

O KEYWORD

in [ɪn] *prep* **1** (*indicating place,
position*) in +*dat*; (*with motion*) in
+*akk*; **in here/there** hier/dort; **in
London** in London; **in the United
States** in den Vereinigten Staaten
2 (*indicating time: during*) in +*dat*; **in
summer** im Sommer; **in 1988** (im
Jahre) 1988; **in the afternoon**
nachmittags, am Nachmittag
3 (*indicating time: in the space of*)
innerhalb von; **I'll see you in 2
weeks** *o* **in 2 weeks' time** ich sehe
dich/Sie in zwei Wochen
4 (*indicating manner, circumstances,
state etc*) in +*dat*; **in the sun/rain**
in der Sonne/im Regen; **in
English/French** auf
Englisch/Französisch; **in a
loud/soft voice** mit lauter/leiser
Stimme
5 (*with ratios, numbers*) **1 in 10** jeder
Zehnte; **20 pence in the pound** 20
Pence pro Pfund; **they lined up in
twos** sie stellten sich in
Zweierreihe auf
6 (*referring to people, works*) **the
disease is common in children**
die Krankheit ist bei Kindern
häufig; **in Dickens** bei Dickens;

we have a loyal friend in him er
ist uns ein treuer Freund
7 (*indicating profession etc*) **to be in
teaching/the army** Lehrer,
Lehrerin/beim Militär sein; **to be
in publishing** im Verlagswesen
arbeiten
8 (*with present participle*) **in saying
this, I ...** wenn ich das sage, ... ich;
in accepting this view, he ... weil
er diese Meinung akzeptierte, ...
er
▷ *adv*: **to be in** (*person: at home,
work*) da sein; (*train, ship, plane*)
angekommen sein; (*in fashion*) in
sein; **to ask sb in** jdn hereinbitten;
to run/limp *etc* **in**
hereingerannt/gehumpelt *etc*
kommen
▷ *n*: **the ins and outs** (*of proposal,
situation etc*) die Feinheiten

inability [ɪnə'bɪlɪtɪ] *n* Unfähig-
keit *f*

inaccessible [ɪnæk'sesəbl] *adj*
(*a. fig*) unzugänglich

inaccurate [ɪn'ækjʊrɪt] *adj*
ungenau

inadequate [ɪn'ædɪkwət] *adj*
unzulänglich

inapplicable [ɪnə'plɪkəbl] *adj*
unzutreffend

inappropriate [ɪnə'prəupriət]
adj unpassend; (*clothing*)
ungeeignet; (*remark*)
unangebracht

inborn ['ɪn'bɔːn] *adj* angeboren

incapable [ɪn'keɪpəbl] *adj*
unfähig (*of* zu); **to be ~ of doing
sth** nicht imstande sein, etw zu
tun

incense ['ɪnsens] *n* Weihrauch
m

incentive [ɪn'sentɪv] *n* Anreiz *m*

incessant, **incessantly** [ɪn'sesnt,
-lɪ] *adj, adv* unaufhörlich

incest ['ɪnsest] *n* Inzest *m*

inch [ɪntʃ] *n* Zoll *m* (2,54 cm)
incident ['ɪnsɪdənt] *n* Vorfall *m*; (*disturbance*) Zwischenfall *m*; **incidentally** [ɪnsɪ'dentlɪ] *adv* nebenbei bemerkt, übrigens
inclination [ɪnklɪ'neɪʃən] *n* Neigung *f*; **inclined** ['ɪnklaɪnd] *adj*: **to be ~ to do sth** dazu neigen, etw zu tun
include [ɪn'kluːd] *vt* einschließen; (*on list, in group*) aufnehmen; **including** *prep* einschließlich (+*gen*); **not ~ service** Bedienung nicht inbegriffen; **inclusive** [ɪn'kluːsɪv] *adj* einschließlich (*of* +*gen*); (*price*) Pauschal-
incoherent [ɪnkəʊ'hɪərənt] *adj* zusammenhanglos
income ['ɪnkʌm] *n* Einkommen *nt*; (*from business*) Einkünfte *pl*; **income tax** *n* Einkommensteuer *f*; (*on wages, salary*) Lohnsteuer *f*; **incoming** ['ɪnkʌmɪŋ] *adj* ankommend; (*mail*) eingehend
incompatible [ɪnkəm'pætəbl] *adj* unvereinbar; (*people*) unverträglich; (*Inform*) nicht kompatibel
incompetent [ɪn'kɒmpɪtənt] *adj* unfähig
incomplete [ɪnkəm'pliːt] *adj* unvollständig
incomprehensible [ɪnkɒmprɪ'hensəbl] *adj* unverständlich
inconceivable [ɪnkən'siːvəbl] *adj* unvorstellbar
inconsiderate [ɪnkən'sɪdərət] *adj* rücksichtslos
inconsistency [ɪnkən'sɪstənsɪ] *n* Inkonsequenz *f*; (*contradictory*) Widersprüchlichkeit *f*; **inconsistent** *adj* inkonsequent; (*contradictory*) widersprüchlich; (*work*) unbeständig

inconvenience [ɪnkən'viːnɪəns] *n* Unannehmlichkeit *f*; (*trouble*) Umstände *pl*; **inconvenient** *adj* ungünstig, unbequem; (*time*) **it's ~ for me** es kommt mir ungelegen; **if it's not too ~ for you** wenn es dir/Ihnen passt
incorporate [ɪn'kɔːpəreɪt] *vt* aufnehmen (*into* in +*akk*); (*include*) enthalten
incorrect ['ɪnkərekt] *adj* falsch; (*improper*) inkorrekt
increase ['ɪnkriːs] *n* Zunahme *f* (*in* an +*dat*); (*in amount, speed*) Erhöhung *f* (*in* +*gen*) ▷ [ɪn'kriːs] *vt* (*price, taxes, salary, speed etc*) erhöhen; (*wealth*) vermehren; (*number*) vergrößern; (*business*) erweitern ▷ *vi* zunehmen (*in* an +*dat*); (*prices*) steigen; (*in size*) größer werden; (*in number*) sich vermehren; **increasingly** [ɪn'kriːsɪŋlɪ] *adv* zunehmend
incredible, incredibly [ɪn'kredəbl, -blɪ] *adj, adv* unglaublich; (*very good*) fantastisch
incredulous [ɪn'kredjʊləs] *adj* ungläubig, skeptisch
incriminate [ɪn'krɪmɪneɪt] *vt* belasten
incubator ['ɪnkjʊbeɪtə°] *n* Brutkasten *m*
incurable [ɪn'kjʊərəbl] *adj* unheilbar
indecent [ɪn'diːsnt] *adj* unanständig
indecisive [ɪndɪ'saɪsɪv] *adj* (*person*) unentschlossen; (*result*) nicht entscheidend
indeed [ɪn'diːd] *adv* tatsächlich; (*as answer*) allerdings; **very hot ~** wirklich sehr heiß
indefinite [ɪn'defɪnɪt] *adj* unbestimmt; **indefinitely** *adv* endlos; (*postpone*) auf unbestimmte Zeit

independence [ɪndɪˈpendəns]
n Unabhängigkeit *f*

independent [ɪndɪˈpendənt]
adj unabhängig (*of* von); (*person*)
selbstständig
indescribable [ɪndɪˈskraɪbəbl]
adj unbeschreiblich
index [ˈɪndeks] *n* Index *m*,
Verzeichnis *nt*; **index finger** *n*
Zeigefinger *m*
India [ˈɪndɪə] *n* Indien *nt*; **Indian**
[ˈɪndɪən] *adj* indisch; (*Native
American*) indianisch ▷ *n* Inder(in)
m(f); (*Native American*) Indianer(in)
m(f); **Indian Ocean** *n* Indischer
Ozean; **Indian summer** *n* Spät-
sommer *m*, Altweibersommer *m*
indicate [ˈɪndɪkeɪt] *vt* (*show*)
zeigen; (*instrument*) anzeigen;
(*suggest*) hinweisen auf +*akk* ▷ *vi*
(*Auto*) blinken; **indication**
[ɪndɪˈkeɪʃn] *n* (*sign*) Anzeichen *nt*
(*of* für); **indicator** [ˈɪndɪkeɪtə*] *n*
(*Auto*) Blinker *m*
indifferent [ɪnˈdɪfrənt] *adj* (*not
caring*) gleichgültig (*to, towards*
gegenüber); (*mediocre*)
mittelmäßig
indigestible [ɪndɪˈdʒestəbl] *adj*
unverdaulich; **indigestion**
[ɪndɪˈdʒestʃən] *n* Verdau-
ungsstörung *f*
indignity [ɪnˈdɪgnɪtɪ] *n* Demütigung *f*

indirect, indirectly [ɪndɪˈrekt, -lɪ]
adj, adv indirekt
indiscreet [ɪndɪˈskriːt] *adj*
indiskret
indispensable [ɪndɪˈspensəbl]
adj unentbehrlich
indisposed [ɪndɪˈspəʊzd] *adj*
unwohl
indisputable [ɪndɪˈspjuːtəbl]
adj unbestreitbar; (*evidence*)
unanfechtbar
individual [ɪndɪˈvɪdjʊəl] *n*
Einzelne(r) *mf* ▷ *adj* einzeln;
(*distinctive*) eigen, individuell;
~ case Einzelfall *m*; **individually**
adv (*separately*) einzeln
Indonesia [ɪndəʊˈniːzjə] *n*
Indonesien *nt*
indoor [ˈɪndɔː*] *adj* (*shoes*)
Haus-; (*plant, games*) Zimmer-;
(*Sport: football, championship, record
etc*) Hallen-; **indoors** *adv* drinnen,
im Haus
indulge [ɪnˈdʌldʒ] *vi*: **to ~ in sth**
sich *dat* etw gönnen; **indulgence**
n Nachsicht *f*; (*enjoyment*)
(übermäßiger) Genuss; (*luxury*)
Luxus *m*; **indulgent** *adj*
nachsichtig (*with* gegenüber)
industrial [ɪnˈdʌstrɪəl] *adj*
Industrie-, industriell; **~ estate**
Industriegebiet *nt*; **industry**
[ˈɪndəstrɪ] *n* Industrie *f*
inedible [ɪnˈedɪbl] *adj* nicht
essbar, ungenießbar
ineffective [ɪnɪˈfektɪv] *adj*
unwirksam, wirkungslos;
inefficient *adj* unwirksam; (*use,
machine*) unwirtschaftlich; (*method
etc*) unrationell
ineligible [ɪnˈelɪdʒəbl] *adj* nicht
berechtigt (*for* zu)
inequality [ɪnɪˈkwɒlɪtɪ] *n*
Ungleichheit *f*
inevitable [ɪnˈevɪtəbl] *adj*
unvermeidlich; **inevitably** *adv*
zwangsläufig

inexcusable [ɪnɪksˈkjuːzəbl]
adj unverzeihlich; **that's ~** das
kann man nicht verzeihen
inexpensive [ɪnɪksˈpensɪv] *adj*
preisgünstig
inexperience [ɪnɪksˈpɪərɪəns]
n Unerfahrenheit *f*;
inexperienced *adj* unerfahren
inexplicable [ɪnɪksˈplɪkəbl] *adj*
unerklärlich
infallible [ɪnˈfæləbl] *adj*
unfehlbar
infamous [ˈɪnfəməs] *adj* (*person*)
berüchtigt (*for* wegen); (*deed*)
niederträchtig
infancy [ˈɪnfənsɪ] *n* frühe
Kindheit; **infant** [ˈɪnfənt] *n*
Säugling *m*; (*small child*)
Kleinkind *nt*; **infant school** *n*
Vorschule *f*
infatuated [ɪnˈfætjʊeɪtɪd] *adj*
vernarrt (*with* in +*akk*), verknallt
(*with* in +*akk*)
infect [ɪnˈfekt] *vt* (*person*)
anstecken; (*wound*) infizieren;
infection [ɪnˈfekʃən] *n* Infektion
f; **infectious** [ɪnˈfekʃəs] *adj*
ansteckend
inferior [ɪnˈfɪərɪə°] *adj* (*in quality*)
minderwertig; (*in rank*)
untergeordnet; **inferiority**
[ɪnfɪərɪˈɒrɪtɪ] *n* Minderwertigkeit
f; **~ complex** Minderwertigkeitskomplex *m*
infertile [ɪnˈfɜːtaɪl] *adj*
unfruchtbar
infidelity [ɪnfɪˈdelɪtɪ] *n* Untreue
f
infinite [ˈɪnfɪnɪt] *adj* unendlich
infinitive [ɪnˈfɪnɪtɪv] *n* (*Ling*)
Infinitiv *m*
infinity [ɪnˈfɪnɪtɪ] *n* Unend-
lichkeit *f*
infirmary [ɪnˈfɜːmərɪ] *n*
Krankenhaus *nt*
inflame [ɪnˈfleɪm] *vt* (*Med*)
entzünden; **inflammation**

[ɪnfləˈmeɪʃən] *n* (*Med*)
Entzündung *f*
inflatable [ɪnˈfleɪtəbl] *adj* auf-
blasbar; **~ dinghy** Schlauchboot
nt; **inflate** [ɪnˈfleɪt] *vt*
aufpumpen; (*by blowing*)
aufblasen; (*prices*) hochtreiben
inflation [ɪnˈfleɪʃən] *n* Inflation
f
inflexible [ɪnˈfleksəbl] *adj*
unflexibel
inflict [ɪnˈflɪkt] *vt*: **to ~ sth on sb**
jdm etw zufügen; (*punishment*)
jdm etw auferlegen; (*wound*) jdm
etw beibringen
in-flight [ɪnˈflaɪt] *adj* (*catering*,
magazine) Bord-; **~ entertainment**
Bordprogramm *nt*
influence [ˈɪnflʊəns] *n* Einfluss
m (*on* auf +*akk*) ▷ *vt* beeinflussen;
influential [ɪnflʊˈenʃəl] *adj*
einflussreich
influenza [ɪnflʊˈenzə] *n* Grippe
f
inform [ɪnˈfɔːm] *vt* informieren
(*of*, *about* über +*akk*); **to keep sb**
~ed jdn auf dem Laufenden halten
informal [ɪnˈfɔːməl] *adj* zwanglos, ungezwungen
information [ɪnfəˈmeɪʃən] *n*
Auskunft *f*, Informationen *pl*; **for**
your ~ zu deiner/Ihrer
Information; **further ~** weitere
Informationen, Weiteres;
information desk *n*
Auskunftsschalter *m*; **information**
technology *n* Informations-
technik *f*; **informative**
[ɪnˈfɔːmətɪv] *adj* aufschlussreich
infra-red [ˈɪnfrəˈred] *adj* infrarot
infrastructure *n* Infrastruktur
f
infuriate [ɪnˈfjʊərɪeɪt] *vt* wütend
machen; **infuriating** *adj* äußerst
ärgerlich
infusion [ɪnˈfjuːʒən] *n* (*herbal*
tea) Aufguss *m*; (*Med*) Infusion *f*

ingenious [ɪn'dʒiːnɪəs] *adj* (*person*) erfinderisch; (*device*) raffiniert; (*idea*) genial
ingredient [ɪn'griːdɪənt] *n* (*Gastr*) Zutat *f*
inhabit [ɪn'hæbɪt] *vt* bewohnen; **inhabitant** *n* Einwohner(in) *m(f)*
inhale [ɪn'heɪl] *vt* einatmen; (*cigarettes, Med*) inhalieren; **inhaler** *n* Inhalationsgerät *nt*
inherit [ɪn'herɪt] *vt* erben; **inheritance** *n* Erbe *nt*
inhibited [ɪn'hɪbɪtɪd] *adj* gehemmt; **inhibition** [ɪnhɪ'bɪʃən] *n* Hemmung *f*
in-house [ˈɪnhaʊs] *adj* intern
inhuman [ɪn'hjuːmən] *adj* unmenschlich
initial [ɪ'nɪʃəl] *adj* anfänglich; **~ stage** Anfangsstadium *nt* ▷ *vt* mit Initialen unterschreiben; **initially** *adv* anfangs; **initials** *npl* Initialen *pl*
initiative [ɪ'nɪʃətɪv] *n* Initiative *f*
inject [ɪn'dʒekt] *vt* (*drug etc*) einspritzen; **to ~ sb with sth** jdm etw (ein)spritzen; **injection** *n* Spritze *f*, Injektion *f*
in-joke [ˈɪndʒəʊk] *n* Insiderwitz *m*
injure [ˈɪndʒə*] *vt* verletzen; **to ~ one's leg** sich *dat* das Bein verletzen; **injury** [ˈɪndʒərɪ] *n* Verletzung *f*
injustice [ɪn'dʒʌstɪs] *n* Ungerechtigkeit *f*
ink [ɪŋk] *n* Tinte *f*; **ink-jet printer** *n* Tintenstrahldrucker *m*
inland [ˈɪnlənd] *adj* Binnen- ▷ *adv* landeinwärts; **inland revenue** [*Brit*] Finanzamt *nt*
in-laws [ˈɪnlɔːz] *npl* (*fam*) Schwiegereltern *pl*
inline skates [ˈɪnlaɪnskeɪts] *npl* Inlineskates *pl*, Inliner *pl*
inmate [ˈɪnmeɪt] *n* Insasse *m*
inn [ɪn] *n* Gasthaus *nt*

innate [ɪ'neɪt] *adj* angeboren
inner [ˈɪnə*] *adj* innere(r, s); **~ city** Innenstadt *f*
innocence [ˈɪnəsns] *n* Unschuld *f*; **innocent** *adj* unschuldig
innovation [ɪnəʊ'veɪʃən] *n* Neuerung *f*
innumerable [ɪ'njuːmərəbl] *adj* unzählig
inoculate [ɪ'nɒkjʊleɪt] *vt* impfen (*against* gegen); **inoculation** [ɪnɒkjʊ'leɪʃən] *n* Impfung *f*
in-patient [ˈɪnpeɪʃənt] *n* stationärer Patient, stationäre Patientin
input [ˈɪnpʊt] *n* (*contribution*) Beitrag *m*; (*Inform*) Eingabe *f*
inquest [ˈɪnkwest] *n* gerichtliche Untersuchung (einer Todesursache)
inquire [ɪn'kwaɪə*] *see* **enquire**; **inquiry** [ɪn'kwaɪrɪ] *see* **enquiry**
insane [ɪn'seɪn] *adj* wahnsinnig; (*Med*) geisteskrank; **insanity** [ɪn'sænɪtɪ] *n* Wahnsinn *m*
insatiable [ɪn'seɪʃəbl] *adj* unersättlich
inscription [ɪn'skrɪpʃən] *n* (*on stone etc*) Inschrift *f*
insect [ˈɪnsekt] *n* Insekt *nt*; **insecticide** [ɪn'sektɪsaɪd] *n* Insektenbekämpfungsmittel *nt*; **insect repellent** *n* Insektenschutzmittel *nt*
insecure [ɪnsɪ'kjʊə*] *adj* (*person*) unsicher; (*shelves*) instabil
insensitive [ɪn'sensɪtɪv] *adj* unempfindlich (*to* gegen); (*unfeeling*) gefühllos; **insensitivity** [ɪnsensɪ'tɪvɪtɪ] *n* Unempfindlichkeit *f* (*to* gegen); (*unfeeling nature*) Gefühllosigkeit *f*
inseparable [ɪn'sepərəbl] *adj* unzertrennlich
insert [ɪn'sɜːt] *vt* einfügen; (*coin*) einwerfen; (*key etc*) hineinstecken

▷ n (in magazine) Beilage f;
insertion n (in text) Einfügen nt
inside ['ɪn'saɪd] n: **the ~** das
Innere; (surface) die Innenseite;
from the ~ von innen ▷ adj
innere(r, s), Innen-; **~ lane** (Auto)
Innenspur f; (Sport) Innenbahn f
▷ adv (place) innen; (direction)
hinein; **to go ~** hineingehen
▷ prep (place) in +dat; (into) in +akk
... hinein; (time, within) innerhalb
+gen; **inside out** adv verkehrt
herum; (know) in- und auswendig;
insider n Eingeweihte(r) mf,
Insider(in) m(f)
insight ['ɪnsaɪt] n Einblick m
(into in +akk)
insignificant [ɪnsɪg'nɪfɪkənt]
adj unbedeutend
insincere [ɪnsɪn'sɪə*] adj un-
aufrichtig, falsch
insinuate [ɪn'sɪnjʊeɪt] vt
andeuten; **insinuation**
[ɪnsɪnjʊ'eɪʃən] n Andeutung f
insist [ɪn'sɪst] vi darauf bestehen;
to ~ on sth auf etw dat bestehen;
insistent adj hartnäckig
insoluble [ɪn'sɒljʊbl] adj
unlösbar
insomnia [ɪn'sɒmnɪə] n Schlaflosigkeit f
inspect [ɪn'spekt] vt prüfen,
kontrollieren; **inspection** n
Prüfung f; (check) Kontrolle f;
inspector n (police ~)
Inspektor(in) m(f); (senior)
Kommissar(in) m(f); (on bus etc)
Kontrolleur(in) m(f)
inspiration [ɪnspɪ'reɪʃən] n
Inspiration f; **inspire** [ɪn'spaɪə*]
vt (respect) einflößen (in dat);
(person) inspirieren
install [ɪn'stɔːl] vt (software)
installieren; (furnishings) einbauen
installment, **instalment**
[ɪn'stɔːlmənt] n Rate f; (of story)
Folge f; **to pay in ~s** auf Raten

zahlen; **installment plan** n (US)
Ratenkauf m
instance ['ɪnstəns] n (of
discrimination) Fall m; (example)
Beispiel nt (of für +akk); **for ~** zum
Beispiel
instant ['ɪnstənt] n Augenblick
m ▷ adj sofortig; **instant coffee**
n löslicher Kaffee m; **instantly** adv
sofort
instead [ɪn'sted] adv stattdes-
sen; **instead of** prep (an)statt
+gen; **~ of me** an meiner Stelle;
~ of going (an)statt zu gehen
instinct ['ɪnstɪŋkt] n Instinkt m;
instinctive, **instinctively**
[ɪn'stɪŋktɪv, -lɪ] adj, adv
instinktiv
institute ['ɪnstɪtjuːt] n Institut
nt; **institution** [ɪnstɪ'tjuːʃən] n
(organisation) Institution f,
Einrichtung f; (home) Anstalt f
instruct [ɪn'strʌkt] vt anweisen;
instruction [ɪn'strʌkʃən] n
(teaching) Unterricht m; (command)
Anweisung f; **~s for use**
Gebrauchsanweisung f;
instructor n Lehrer(in) m(f); (US)
Dozent(in) m(f)
instrument ['ɪnstrʊmənt] n
Instrument nt; **instrument panel**
n Armaturenbrett nt
insufficient [ɪnsə'fɪʃənt] adj
ungenügend
insulate ['ɪnsjʊleɪt] vt (Elec)
isolieren; **insulating tape** n
Isolierband nt; **insulation**
[ɪnsjʊ'leɪʃən] n Isolierung f
insulin ['ɪnsjʊlɪn] n Insulin nt
insult ['ɪnsʌlt] n Beleidigung f
▷ [ɪn'sʌlt] vt beleidigen;
insulting [ɪn'sʌltɪŋ] adj
beleidigend
insurance [ɪn'ʃʊərəns] n Versicherung f; **~ company**
Versicherungsgesellschaft f;
~ policy Versicherungspolice f;

insure [ɪn'ʃʊə°] *vt* versichern (*against* gegen)

intact [ɪn'tækt] *adj* intakt

intake ['ɪnteɪk] *n* Aufnahme *f*

integrate [ɪntɪ'greɪt] *vt* integrieren (*into* in +*akk*); **integration** *n* Integration *f*

integrity [ɪn'tegrətɪ] *n* Integrität *f*, Ehrlichkeit *f*

intellect ['ɪntɪlekt] *n* Intellekt *m*; **intellectual** [ɪntɪ'lektjʊəl] *adj* intellektuell; (*interests etc*) geistig

intelligence [ɪn'telɪdʒəns] *n* (*understanding*) Intelligenz *f*; **intelligent** *adj* intelligent

intend [ɪn'tend] *vt* beabsichtigen; **to ~ to do sth** vorhaben, etw zu tun

intense [ɪn'tens] *adj* intensiv; (*pressure*) enorm; (*competition*) heftig; **intensity** *n* Intensität *f*; **intensive** *adj* intensiv; **intensive care unit** *n* Intensivstation *f*; **intensive course** *n* Intensivkurs *m*

intent [ɪn'tent] *adj*: **to be ~ on doing sth** fest entschlossen sein, etw zu tun; **intention** [ɪn'tenʃən] *n* Absicht *f*; **intentional**, **intentionally** *adj*, *adv* absichtlich

interact [ɪntər'ækt] *vi* aufeinander einwirken; **interaction** *n* Interaktion *f*, Wechselwirkung *f*; **interactive** *adj* interaktiv

interchange ['ɪntətʃeɪndʒ] *n* (*of motorways*) Autobahnkreuz *nt*; **interchangeable** [ɪntə'tʃeɪndʒəbl] *adj* austauschbar

intercity [ɪntə'sɪtɪ] *n* Intercityzug *m*, IC *m*

intercom ['ɪntəkɒm] *n* (Gegen)sprechanlage *f*

intercourse ['ɪntəkɔːs] *n* (*sexual*) Geschlechtsverkehr *m*

interest ['ɪntrest] *n* Interesse *nt*; (*Fin: on money*) Zinsen *pl*; (*Comm: share*) Anteil *m*; **to be of ~** von Interesse sein (*to* für) ▷ *vt* interessieren; **interested** *adj* interessiert (*in* an +*dat*); **to be ~ed in** sich interessieren für; **are you ~ in coming?** hast du Lust, mitzukommen?; **interest-free** *adj* zinsfrei; **interesting** *adj* interessant; **interest rate** *n* Zinssatz *m*

interface ['ɪntəfeɪs] *n* (*Inform*) Schnittstelle *f*

interfere [ɪntə'fɪə°] *vi* (*meddle*) sich einmischen (*with*, in in +*akk*); **interference** *n* Einmischung *f*; (*TV, Radio*) Störung *f*

interior [ɪn'tɪərɪə°] *adj* Innen- ▷ *n* Innere(s) *nt*; (*of car*) Innenraum *m*; (*of house*) Innenausstattung *f*

intermediate [ɪntə'miːdɪət] *adj* Zwischen-; **~ stage** Zwischenstadium *nt*

intermission [ɪntə'mɪʃən] *n* Pause *f*

intern [ɪn'tɜːn] *n* Assistent(in) *m(f)*

internal [ɪn'tɜːnl] *adj* innere(r, s); (*flight*) Inlands-; **~ revenue** (*US*) Finanzamt *nt*; **internally** *adv* innen; (*in body*) innerlich

international [ɪntə'næʃnəl] *adj* international; **~ match** Länderspiel *nt*; **~ flight** Auslandsflug *m* ▷ *n* (*Sport: player*) Nationalspieler(in) *m(f)*

Internet ['ɪntənet] *n* (*Inform*) Internet *nt*; **Internet access** *n* Internetzugang *m*; **Internet auction** *n* Internetauktion *f*; **Internet banking** *n* Onlinebanking *nt*; **Internet café** *n* Internetcafé *nt*; **Internet connection** *n* Internetanschluss *m*; **Internet provider** *n* Internetprovider *m*

interpret [ɪn'tɜːprɪt] *vi*, *vt*

(*translate*) dolmetschen; (*explain*) interpretieren; **interpretation** [ɪntɜːprɪˈteɪʃən] *n* Interpretation *f*; **interpreter** [ɪnˈtɜːprɪtə*] *n* Dolmetscher(in) *m(f)*

interrogate [ɪnˈterəgeɪt] *vt* verhören; **interrogation** *n* Verhör *nt*

interrupt [ɪntəˈrʌpt] *vt* unterbrechen; **interruption** [ɪntəˈrʌpʃən] *n* Unterbrechung *f*

intersection [ɪntəˈsekʃən] *n* (*of roads*) Kreuzung *f*

interstate [ɪntəˈsteɪt] *n* (*US*) zwischenstaatlich; **~ highway** ≈ Bundesautobahn *f*

interval [ˈɪntəvəl] *n* (*space, time*) Abstand *m*; (*theatre etc*) Pause *f*

intervene [ɪntəˈviːn] *vi* eingreifen (*in* in); **intervention** [ɪntəˈvenʃən] *n* Eingreifen *nt*; (*Pol*) Intervention *f*

interview [ˈɪntəvjuː] *n* Interview *nt*; (*for job*) Vorstellungsgespräch *nt* ▷ *vt* interviewen; (*job applicant*) ein Vorstellungsgespräch führen mit; **interviewer** *n* Interviewer(in) *m(f)*

intestine [ɪnˈtestɪn] *n* Darm *m*; **~s** *pl* Eingeweide *pl*

intimate [ˈɪntɪmət] *adj* (*friends*) vertraut, eng; (*atmosphere*) gemütlich; (*sexually*) intim

intimidate [ɪnˈtɪmɪdeɪt] *vt* einschüchtern; **intimidation** *n* Einschüchterung *f*

into [ˈɪntʊ] *prep* in +*akk*; (*crash*) gegen; **to change ~ sth** (*turn ~*) zu etw werden; (*put on*) sich *dat* etw anziehen; **to translate ~ French** ins Französische übersetzen; **to be ~ sth** (*fam*) auf etw *akk* stehen

intolerable [ɪnˈtɒlərəbl] *adj* unerträglich

intolerant [ɪnˈtɒlərənt] *adj* intolerant

intoxicated [ɪnˈtɒksɪkeɪtɪd] *adj* betrunken; (*fig*) berauscht

intricate [ˈɪntrɪkət] *adj* kompliziert

intrigue [ɪnˈtriːg] *vt* faszinieren; **intriguing** *adj* faszinierend, fesselnd

introduce [ɪntrəˈdjuːs] *vt* (*person*) vorstellen (*to sb* jdm); (*sth new*) einführen (*to* in +*akk*); **introduction** [ɪntrəˈdʌkʃən] *n* Einführung *f* (*to* in +*akk*); (*to book*) Einleitung *f* (*to* zu); (*to person*) Vorstellung *f*

introvert [ˈɪntrəʊvɜːt] *n* Introvertierte(r) *mf*

intuition [ɪntjuːˈɪʃn] *n* Intuition *f*

invade [ɪnˈveɪd] *vt* einfallen in +*akk*

invalid [ˈɪnvəlɪd] *n* Kranke(r) *mf*; (*disabled*) Invalide *m* ▷ *adj* [ɪnˈvælɪd] (*not valid*) ungültig

invaluable [ɪnˈvæljʊəbl] *adj* äußerst wertvoll, unschätzbar

invariably [ɪnˈvɛərɪəblɪ] *adv* ständig; (*every time*) jedes Mal, ohne Ausnahme

invasion [ɪnˈveɪʒən] *n* Invasion *f* (*of* in +*akk*), Einfall *m* (*of* in +*akk*)

invent [ɪnˈvent] *vt* erfinden; **invention** [ɪnˈvenʃən] *n* Erfindung *f*; **inventor** *n* Erfinder(in) *m(f)*

inverted commas [ɪnˈvɜːtɪd ˈkɒməz] *npl* Anführungszeichen *pl*

invest [ɪnˈvest] *vt, vi* investieren (*in* in +*akk*)

investigate [ɪnˈvestɪgeɪt] *vt* untersuchen; **investigation** [ɪnvestɪˈgeɪʃən] *n* Untersuchung *f* (*into* +*gen*)

investment [ɪnˈvestmənt] *n* Investition *f*; **it's a good ~** es ist eine gute Anlage; (*it'll be useful*) es macht sich bezahlt

invigorating [ɪn'vɪgəreɪtɪŋ] *adj* erfrischend, belebend; *(tonic)* stärkend

invisible [ɪn'vɪzəbl] *adj* unsichtbar

invitation [ɪnvɪ'teɪʃən] *n* Einladung *f*; **invite** [ɪn'vaɪt] *vt* einladen

invoice ['ɪnvɔɪs] *n (bill)* Rechnung *f*

involuntary [ɪn'vɒləntərɪ] *adj* unbeabsichtigt

involve [ɪn'vɒlv] *vt* verwickeln *(in sth* in etw *akk); (entail)* zur Folge haben; **to be ~d in sth** *(participate in)* an etw *dat* beteiligt sein; **I'm not ~d** *(affected)* ich bin nicht betroffen

inward ['ɪnwəd] *adj* innere(r, s); **inwardly** *adv* innerlich; **inwards** *adv* nach innen

iodine ['aɪədiːn] *n* Jod *nt*

IOU [aɪəʊ'juː] *abbr* = **I owe you** Schuldschein *m*

IQ *abbr* = **intelligence quotient** IQ *m*

Iran [ɪ'rɑːn] *n* der Iran

Iraq [ɪ'rɑːk] *n* der Irak

Ireland ['aɪələnd] *n* Irland *nt*

iris ['aɪrɪs] *n (flower)* Schwertlilie *f; (of eye)* Iris *f*

Irish ['aɪrɪʃ] *adj* irisch; **~ coffee** Irish Coffee *m*; **~ Sea** die Irische See ▷ *n (language)* Irisch *nt*; **the ~** *pl* die Iren *pl*; **Irishman** *(pl* **-men)** *n* Ire *m*; **Irishwoman** *(pl* **-women)** *n* Irin *f*

iron ['aɪən] *n* Eisen *nt; (for ironing)* Bügeleisen *nt* ▷ *adj* eisern ▷ *vt* bügeln

ironic(al) [aɪ'rɒnɪk(əl)] *adj* ironisch

ironing board *n* Bügelbrett *nt*

irony ['aɪrənɪ] *n* Ironie *f*

irrational [ɪ'ræʃənl] *adj* irrational

irregular [ɪ'regjʊlə*] *adj* unregelmäßig; *(shape)* ungleichmäßig

irrelevant [ɪ'reləvənt] *adj* belanglos, irrelevant

irreplaceable [ɪrɪ'pleɪsəbl] *adj* unersetzlich

irresistible [ɪrɪ'zɪstəbl] *adj* unwiderstehlich

irrespective of [ɪrɪ'spektɪv ɒv] *prep* ungeachtet +*gen*

irresponsible [ɪrɪ'spɒnsəbl] *adj* verantwortungslos

irretrievable [ɪrɪ'triːvəbl] *adv* unwiederbringlich; *(loss)* unersetzlich

irritable ['ɪrɪtəbl] *adj* reizbar; **irritate** ['ɪrɪteɪt] *vt (annoy)* ärgern; *(deliberately)* reizen; **irritation** [ɪrɪ'teɪʃən] *n (anger)* Ärger *m; (Med)* Reizung *f*

IRS *abbr* = **Internal Revenue Service** *(US)* Finanzamt *nt*

is [ɪz] *present of* **be** ist

Islam ['ɪzlɑːm] *n* Islam *m*; **Islamic** [ɪz'læmɪk] *adj* islamisch

island ['aɪlənd] *n* Insel *f*; **Isle** [aɪl] *n (in names)* **the ~ of Man** die Insel Man; **the ~ of Wight** die Insel Wight; **the British ~s** die Britischen Inseln

isn't ['ɪznt] *contr of* **is not**

isolate ['aɪsəleɪt] *vt* isolieren; **isolated** *adj (remote)* abgelegen; *(cut off)* abgeschnitten *(from* von); **an ~ case** ein Einzelfall; **isolation** [aɪsə'leɪʃən] *n* Isolierung *f*

Israel ['ɪzreɪl] *n* Israel *nt*; **Israeli** [ɪz'reɪlɪ] *adj* israelisch ▷ *n* Israeli *m o f*

issue ['ɪʃuː] *n (matter)* Frage *f; (problem)* Problem *nt; (subject)* Thema *nt; (of newspaper etc)* Ausgabe *f*; **that's not the ~** darum geht es nicht ▷ *vt (give out)* ausgeben; *(document)* ausstellen; *(orders)* erteilen; *(book)* herausgeben

it [ɪt] *pron* **1** (*specific: subject*)
er/sie/es; (*direct object*) ihn/sie/es;
(*indirect object*) ihm/ihr/ihm;
about/from/in/of it
darüber/davon/darin/davon
2 (*impers*) es; **it's raining** es regnet;
it's Friday tomorrow morgen ist
Freitag; **who is it? — it's me** wer ist
da? — ich (bin's)

IT *abbr* = **information technology**
IT *f*

Italian [ɪ'tæljən] *adj* italienisch
▷ *n* Italiener(in) *m(f)*; (*language*)
Italienisch *nt*

italic [ɪ'tælɪk] *adj* kursiv ▷ *npl*: **in
~s** kursiv

Italy ['ɪtəlɪ] *n* Italien *nt*

itch [ɪtʃ] *n* Juckreiz *m*; **I have an
~** mich juckt es ▷ *vi* jucken; **he is
~ing to ...** es juckt ihn, zu ...; **itchy**
adj juckend

it'd ['ɪtd] *contr of* **it would; it had**

item ['aɪtəm] *n* (*article*)
Gegenstand *m*; (*in catalogue*)
Artikel *m*; (*on list, in accounts*)
Posten *m*; (*on agenda*) Punkt *m*; (*in
show programme*) Nummer *f*; (*in
news*) Bericht *m*; (*TV, radio*)
Meldung *f*

itinerary [aɪ'tɪnərərɪ] *n* Reiseroute *f*

it'll ['ɪtl] *contr of* **it will; it shall**

its [ɪts] *pron* sein; (*feminine form*)
ihr

it's [ɪts] *contr of* **it is; it has**

itself [ɪt'self] *pron* (*reflexive*) sich;
(*emphatic*) **the house ~** das Haus
selbst o an sich; **by ~** allein; **the
door closes (by) ~** die Tür schließt
sich von selbst

I've [aɪv] *contr of* **I have**

ivory ['aɪvərɪ] *n* Elfenbein *nt*

ivy ['aɪvɪ] *n* Efeu *m*

jab [dʒæb] *vt* (*needle, knife*)
stechen (*into* in +*akk*) ▷ *n* (*fam*)
Spritze *f*

jack [dʒæk] *n* (*Auto*) Wagenheber
m; (*Cards*) Bube *m*; **jack in** *vt* (*fam*)
aufgeben, hinschmeißen; **jack up**
vt (*car etc*) aufbocken

jacket ['dʒækɪt] *n* Jacke *f*; (*of
man's suit*) Jackett *nt*; (*of book*)
Schutzumschlag *m*; **jacket potato**
(*pl* **-es**) *n* (in der Schale)
gebackene Kartoffel

jack-knife ['dʒæknaɪf] (*pl
jack-knives*) *n* Klappmesser *nt*
▷ *vi* (*truck*) sich quer stellen

jackpot ['dʒækpɒt] *n* Jackpot *m*

jacuzzi® [dʒə'kuːzɪ] *n* (*bath*)
Whirlpool® *m*

jail [dʒeɪl] *n* Gefängnis *nt* ▷ *vt*
einsperren

jam [dʒæm] *n* Konfitüre *f*,
Marmelade *f*; (*traffic ~*) Stau *m* ▷ *vt*
(*street*) verstopfen; (*machine*)

blockieren; **to be ~med** (*stuck*) klemmen; **to ~ on the brakes** eine Vollbremsung machen

Jamaica [dʒə'meɪkə] *n* Jamaika *nt*

jam-packed *adj* proppenvoll

janitor ['dʒænɪtə°] *n* (*US*) Hausmeister(in) *m(f)*

Jan *abbr* = **January** Jan

January ['dʒænjʊərɪ] *n* Januar *m*

Japan [dʒə'pæn] *n* Japan *nt*; **Japanese** [dʒæpə'ni:z] *adj* japanisch ▷ *n* (*person*) Japaner(in) *m(f)*; (*language*) Japanisch *nt*

jar [dʒɑ:°] *n* Glas *nt*

jaundice ['dʒɔ:ndɪs] *n* Gelbsucht *f*

javelin ['dʒævlɪn] *n* Speer *m*; (*Sport*) Speerwerfen *nt*

jaw [dʒɔ:] *n* Kiefer *m*

jazz [dʒæz] *n* Jazz *m*

jealous ['dʒeləs] *adj* eifersüchtig (*of* auf +*akk*); **don't make me ~** mach mich nicht neidisch; **jealousy** *n* Eifersucht *f*

jeans [dʒi:nz] *npl* Jeans *pl*

jeep® [dʒi:p] *n* Jeep® *m*

jelly ['dʒelɪ] *n* Gelee *nt*; (*on meat*) Gallert *m* ▷ *n*; (*dessert*) Götterspeise *f*; (*US: jam*) Marmelade *f*; **jelly baby** *n* (*sweet*) Gummibärchen *nt*; **jellyfish** *n* Qualle *f*

jeopardize ['dʒepədaɪz] *vt* gefährden

jerk [dʒɜ:k] *n* Ruck *m*; (*fam: idiot*) Trottel *m* ▷ *vt* ruckartig bewegen ▷ *vi* (*rope*) rucken; (*muscles*) zucken

Jerusalem [dʒə'ru:sələm] *n* Jerusalem *nt*

jet [dʒet] *n* (*of water etc*) Strahl *m*; (*nozzle*) Düse *f*; (*aircraft*) Düsenflugzeug *nt*; **jet foil** *n* Tragflächenboot *nt*; **jetlag** *n* Jetlag *m* (*Müdigkeit nach langem Flug*)

Jew [dʒu:] *n* Jude *m*, Jüdin *f*

jewel ['dʒu:əl] *n* Edelstein *m*; (*esp fig*) Juwel *nt*; **jeweller, jeweler** (*US*) *n* Juwelier(in) *m(f)*; **jewellery, jewelry** (*US*) *n* Schmuck *m*

Jewish ['dʒu:ɪʃ] *adj* jüdisch; **she's ~** sie ist Jüdin

jigsaw (puzzle) ['dʒɪgsɔ:(pʌzl)] *n* Puzzle *nt*

jilt [dʒɪlt] *vt* den Laufpass geben +*dat*

jingle ['dʒɪŋgl] *n* (*advert*) Jingle *m*; (*verse*) Reim *m*

jitters ['dʒɪtəz] *npl* (*fam*) **to have the ~** Bammel haben; **jittery** *adj* (*fam*) ganz nervös

job [dʒɒb] *n* (*piece of work*) Arbeit *f*; (*task*) Aufgabe *f*; (*occupation*) Stellung *f*, Job *m*; **what's your ~?** was machen Sie beruflich?; **it's a good ~ you did that** gut, dass du das gemacht hast; **jobcentre** *n* Arbeitsvermittlungsstelle *f*, Arbeitsamt *nt*; **job-hunting** *n*: **to go ~** auf Arbeitssuche gehen; **jobless** *adj* arbeitslos; **job seeker** *n* Arbeitssuchende(r) *mf*; **jobseeker's allowance** *n* Arbeitslosengeld *nt*; **job-sharing** *n* Arbeitsplatzteilung *f*

jockey ['dʒɒkɪ] *n* Jockey *m*

jog [dʒɒg] *vt* (*person*) anstoßen ▷ *vi* (*run*) joggen; **jogging** *n* Jogging *nt*; **to go ~** joggen gehen

john [dʒɒn] *n* (*US fam*) Klo *nt*

join [dʒɔɪn] *vt* (*put together*) verbinden (*to* mit); (*club etc*) beitreten +*dat*; **to ~ sb** sich jdm anschließen; (*sit with*) sich zu jdm setzen ▷ *vi* (*unite*) sich vereinigen; (*rivers*) zusammenfließen ▷ *n* Verbindungsstelle *f*; (*seam*) Naht *f*; **join in** *vi*, *vt* mitmachen (*sth* bei etw)

joint [dʒɔɪnt] *n* (*of bones*) Gelenk *nt*; (*in pipe etc*) Verbindungsstelle *f*; (*of meat*) Braten *m*; (*of marijuana*)

Joint m ▷ adj gemeinsam; **joint account** n Gemeinschaftskonto nt; **jointly** adv gemeinsam

joke [dʒəʊk] n Witz m; (prank) Streich m; **for a ~** zum Spaß; **it's no ~** das ist nicht zum Lachen ▷ vi Witze machen; **you must be joking** das ist ja wohl nicht dein Ernst!

jolly ['dʒɒlɪ] adj lustig, vergnügt

Jordan ['dʒɔːdən] n (country) Jordanien nt; (river) Jordan m

jot down [dʒɒt daʊn] vt sich notieren; **jotter** n Notizbuch nt

journal ['dʒɜːnl] n (diary) Tagebuch nt; (magazine) Zeitschrift f; **journalism** n Journalismus m; **journalist** n Journalist(in) m(f)

journey ['dʒɜːnɪ] n Reise f; (esp on stage, by car, train) Fahrt f

joy [dʒɔɪ] n Freude f (at über +akk); **joystick** n (Inform) Joystick m; (Aviat) Steuerknüppel m

judge [dʒʌdʒ] n Richter(in) m(f); (Sport) Punktrichter(in) m(f) ▷ vt beurteilen (by nach); **as far as I can ~** meinem Urteil nach ▷ vi urteilen (by nach); **judg(e)ment** n (Jur) Urteil nt; (opinion) Ansicht f; **an error of ~** Fehleinschätzung f

judo ['dʒuːdəʊ] n Judo nt

jug [dʒʌg] n Krug m

juggle ['dʒʌgl] vi (lit, fig) jonglieren (with mit)

juice [dʒuːs] n Saft m; **juicy** adj saftig; (story, scandal) pikant

July [dʒuːˈlaɪ] n Juli m; see also **September**

jumble ['dʒʌmbl] n Durcheinander nt ▷ vt: **to ~ (up)** durcheinanderwerfen; (facts) durcheinanderbringen; **jumble sale** n (for charity) Flohmarkt m; Wohltätigkeitsbasar m

jumbo ['dʒʌmbəʊ] adj (sausage etc) Riesen-; **jumbo jet** n Jumbojet m

jump [dʒʌmp] vi springen; (nervously) zusammenzucken; **to ~ to conclusions** voreilige Schlüsse ziehen; **to ~ from one thing to another** dauernd das Thema wechseln ▷ vt (a. fig: omit) überspringen; **to ~ the lights** bei Rot über die Kreuzung fahren; **to ~ the queue** sich vordrängen ▷ n Sprung m; (for horses) Hindernis nt; **jumper** n Pullover m; (US: dress) Trägerkleid nt; (person, horse) Springer(in) m(f); **jumper cable** n (US), **jump lead** n (Brit Auto) Starthilfekabel nt

junction ['dʒʌŋkʃən] n (of roads) Kreuzung f; (Rail) Knotenpunkt m

June [dʒuːn] n Juni m; see also **September**

jungle ['dʒʌŋgl] n Dschungel m

junior ['dʒuːnɪə*] adj (younger) jünger; (for lower position) untergeordnet (to sb jdm) ▷ n: **she's two years my ~** sie ist zwei Jahre jünger als ich; **junior high (school)** n (US) ≈ Mittelschule f; **junior school** n (Brit) Grundschule f

junk [dʒʌŋk] n (trash) Plunder m; **junk food** n Nahrungsmittel pl mit geringem Nährwert, Junkfood nt; **junkie** n (fam) Junkie m, Fixer(in) m(f); (fig: fan) Freak m; **junk mail** n Reklame f; (Inform) Junkmail f; **junk shop** n Trödelladen m

jury ['dʒʊərɪ] n Geschworene pl; (in competition) Jury f

just [dʒʌst] adj gerecht ▷ adv (recently) gerade; (exactly) genau; **~ as expected** genau wie erwartet; **~ as nice** genauso nett; (barely) **~ in time** gerade noch rechtzeitig; (immediately) **~ before/after ...** gleich vor/nach ...; (small distance) **~ round the corner** gleich um die Ecke; (a little)

~ over an hour etwas mehr als eine
Stunde; (only) **~ the two of us** nur
wir beide; **~ a moment** Moment
mal; (absolutely, simply) **it was
~ fantastic** es war einfach klasse;
~ about so etwa; (more or less)
mehr oder weniger; **~ about
ready** fast fertig

justice ['dʒʌstɪs] n Gerechtigkeit
f; **justifiable** [dʒʌstɪ'faɪəbl] adj
berechtigt; **justifiably** adv zu
Recht; **justify** ['dʒʌstɪfaɪ] vt
rechtfertigen

jut [dʒʌt] vi: **to ~ (out)**
herausragen

juvenile ['dʒuːvənaɪl] n adj
Jugend-, jugendlich ▷ n
Jugendliche(r) mf

k abbr = **thousand**; **15k** 15 000
K abbr = **kilobyte** KB
kangaroo [kæŋgə'ruː] n Känguru
nt
karaoke [kærɪ'əʊkɪ] n Karaoke nt
karate [kə'rɑːtɪ] n Karate nt
kart [kɑːt] n Gokart m
kayak ['kaɪæk] n Kajak m o nt;
kayaking ['kaɪækɪŋ] n Kajakfahren nt
Kazakhstan [kæzæk'stɑːn] n
Kasachstan nt
kebab [kə'bæb] n (shish ~)
Schaschlik nt o m; (doner ~) Kebab
m
keel [kiːl] n (Naut) Kiel m; **keel
over** vi (boat) kentern; (person)
umkippen
keen [kiːn] adj begeistert (on
von); (hardworking) eifrig; (mind,
wind) scharf; (interest, feeling) stark;
to be ~ on sb von jdm angetan
sein; **she's ~ on riding** sie reitet

gern; **to be ~ to do sth** darauf
erpicht sein, etw zu tun
keep [ki:p] (**kept, kept**) vt
(retain) behalten; (secret) für sich
behalten; (observe) einhalten;
(promise) halten; (run: shop, diary,
accounts) führen; (animals) halten;
(support, family etc) unterhalten,
versorgen; (store) aufbewahren; **to
~ sb waiting** jdn warten lassen; **to
~ sb from doing sth** jdn davon
abhalten, etw zu tun; **to ~ sth
clean/secret** etw sauber/geheim
halten; **"~ clear"** „(bitte) frei
halten"; **~ this to yourself**
behalten Sie das für sich ▷ vi
(food) sich halten; (remain, with adj)
bleiben; **~ quiet** sei ruhig!; **~ left**
links fahren; **to ~ doing sth**
(repeatedly) etw immer wieder tun;
~ at it mach weiter so!; **it ~s
happening** es passiert immer
wieder ▷ n (livelihood) Unterhalt
m; **keep back** vi zurückbleiben
▷ vt zurückhalten; (information)
verschweigen; (from sb jdm); **keep
off** vt (person, animal) fernhalten;
"~ off the grass" „Betreten des
Rasens verboten"; **keep on** vi
weitermachen; (walking)
weitergehen; (in car) weiterfahren;
to ~ doing sth (persistently) etw
immer wieder tun ▷ vt (coat etc)
anbehalten; **keep out** vt nicht
hereinlassen ▷ vi draußen
bleiben; **~** (on sign) Eintritt
verboten; **keep to** vt (road, path)
bleiben auf +dat; (plan etc) sich
halten an +akk; **to ~ the point** bei
der Sache bleiben; **keep up** vi
Schritt halten (with mit) ▷ vt
(maintain) aufrechterhalten;
(speed) halten; **to ~ appearances**
den Schein wahren; **keep it up!**
(fam) weiter so!
keeper n (museum etc)
Aufseher(in) m(f); (goal~) Torwart

m; (zoo ~) Tierpfleger(in) m(f);
keep-fit n Fitnesstraining nt;
~ exercises Gymnastik f
kennel ['kenl] n Hundehütte f;
kennels n Hundepension f
Kenya ['kenjə] n Kenia nt
kept [kept] pt, pp of **keep**
kerb ['kɜ:b] n Randstein m
kerosene ['kerəsi:n] n (US)
Petroleum m
ketchup ['ketʃʌp] n Ketchup nt o
m
kettle ['ketl] n Kessel m
key [ki:] n Schlüssel m; (of piano,
computer) Taste f; (Mus) Tonart f;
(for map etc) Zeichenerklärung f
▷ vt: **to ~ (in)** (Inform) eingeben
▷ adj entscheidend; **keyboard** n
(piano, computer) Tastatur f;
keyhole n Schlüsselloch nt;
keypad n (Inform)
Nummernblock m; **keyring** n
Schlüsselring m
kick [kɪk] n Tritt m; (Sport) Stoß
m; **I get a ~ out of it** (fam) es turnt
mich an ▷ vt, vi treten; **kick out**
vt (fam) rausschmeißen (of aus);
kick-off n (Sport) Anstoß m
kid [kɪd] n (child) Kind nt ▷ vt
(tease) auf den Arm nehmen ▷ vi
Witze machen; **you're ~ding** das
ist doch nicht dein Ernst!; **no
~ding** aber echt!
kidnap ['kɪdnæp] vt entführen;
kidnapper n Entführer(in) m(f);
kidnapping n Entführung f
kidney ['kɪdnɪ] n Niere f; **kidney
machine** n künstliche Niere
kill [kɪl] vt töten; (esp
intentionally) umbringen; (weeds)
vernichten; **killer** n Mörder(in)
m(f)
kilo ['ki:ləʊ] (pl **-s**) n Kilo nt;
kilobyte n Kilobyte nt;
kilogramme n Kilogramm nt;
kilometer (US), **kilometre** n
Kilometer m; **~s per hour**

Stundenkilometer *pl*; **kilowatt** *n* Kilowatt *nt*

kilt [kɪlt] *n* Schottenrock *m*

kind [kaɪnd] *adj* nett, freundlich (*to* zu) ▷ *n* Art *f*; (*of coffee, cheese etc*) Sorte *f*; **what ~ of ...?** was für ein(e) ...?; **this ~ of ...** so ein(e) ...; **~ of** (+ *adj*) irgendwie

kindergarten ['kɪndəgɑːtn] *n* Kindergarten *m*

kindly ['kaɪndlɪ] *adj* nett, freundlich ▷ *adv* liebenswürdigerweise; **kindness** ['kaɪndnəs] *n* Freundlichkeit *f*

king [kɪŋ] *n* König *m*; **kingdom** *n* Königreich *nt*; **kingfisher** *n* Eisvogel *m*; **king-size** *adj* im Großformat; (*bed*) extra groß

kipper ['kɪpə°] *n* Räucherhering *m*

kiss [kɪs] *n* Kuss *m*; **~ of life** Mund-zu-Mund-Beatmung *f* ▷ *vt* küssen

kit [kɪt] *n* (*equipment*) Ausrüstung *f*; (*fam*) Sachen *pl*; (*sports ~*) Sportsachen *pl*; (*belongings, clothes*) Sachen *pl*; (*for building sth*) Bausatz *m*

kitchen ['kɪtʃɪn] *n* Küche *f*; **kitchen foil** *n* Alufolie *f*; **kitchen scales** *n* Küchenwaage *f*; **kitchen unit** *n* Küchenschrank *m*; **kitchenware** *n* Küchengeschirr *nt*

kite [kaɪt] *n* Drachen *m*

kitten ['kɪtn] *n* Kätzchen *nt*

kiwi ['kiːwiː] *n* (*fruit*) Kiwi *f*

km *abbr* = **kilometres** km

knack [næk] *n* Dreh *m*, Trick *m*; **to get/have got the ~** den Dreh herauskriegen/heraushaben; **knackered** ['nækəd] *adj* (*Brit fam*) fix und fertig, kaputt

knee [niː] *n* Knie *nt*; **kneecap** *n* Kniescheibe *f*; **knee-jerk** *adj* (*reaction*) reflexartig; **kneel** [niːl] (**knelt** *o* **kneeled, knelt** *o* **kneeled**)

vi knien; (*action, ~ down*) sich hinknien

knelt [nelt] *pt, pp of* **kneel**

knew [njuː] *pt of* **know**

knickers ['nɪkəz] *npl* (*Brit fam*) Schlüpfer *m*

knife [naɪf] (*pl* **knives**) *n* Messer *nt*

knight [naɪt] *n* Ritter *m*; (*in chess*) Pferd *nt*, Springer *m*

knit [nɪt] *vt, vi* stricken; **knitting** *n* (*piece of work*) Strickarbeit *f*; (*activity*) Stricken *nt*; **knitting needle** *n* Stricknadel *f*; **knitwear** *n* Strickwaren *pl*

knob [nɒb] *n* (*on door*) Knauf *m*; (*on radio etc*) Knopf *m*

knock [nɒk] *vt* (*with hammer etc*) schlagen; (*accidentally*) stoßen; **to ~ one's head** sich *dat* den Kopf anschlagen ▷ *vi* klopfen (*on, at* an +*akk*) ▷ *n* (*blow*) Schlag *m*; (*on door*) Klopfen *nt*; **there was a ~ (at the door)** es hat geklopft; **knock down** *vt* (*object*) umstoßen; (*person*) niederschlagen; (*with car*) anfahren; (*building*) abreißen; **knock out** *vt* (*stun*) bewusstlos schlagen; (*boxer*) k.o. schlagen; **knock over** *vt* umstoßen; (*with car*) anfahren; **knocker** *n* Türklopfer *m*; **knockout** *n* Knockout *m*, K.o. *m*

knot [nɒt] *n* Knoten *m*

know [nəʊ] (**knew, known**) *vt, vi* wissen; (*be acquainted with: people, places*) kennen; (*recognize*) erkennen; (*language*) können; **I'll let you ~** ich sage dir Bescheid; **I ~ some French** ich kann etwas Französisch; **to get to ~ sb** jdn kennenlernen; **to be ~n as** bekannt sein als; **know about** *vt* Bescheid wissen über +*akk*; (*subject*) sich auskennen in +*dat*; (*cars, horses etc*) sich auskennen mit; **know of** *vt* kennen; **not that**

I ~ nicht dass ich wüsste;
know-all n (fam) Klugscheißer m;
know-how n Kenntnis f,
Know-how nt; **knowing** adj
wissend; (look, smile) vielsagend;
knowledge ['nɒlɪdʒ] n Wissen
nt; (of a subject) Kenntnisse pl; **to
(the best of) my ~** meines
Wissens
known [nəʊn] pp of **know**
knuckle ['nʌkl] n (Finger)knöchel m; (Gastr) Hachse f;
knuckle down vi sich an die
Arbeit machen
Koran [kɒ'rɑːn] n Koran m
Korea [kə'rɪə] n Korea nt
Kosovo ['kɒsɒvəʊ] n der Kosovo
kph abbr = **kilometres per hour**
km/h
Kremlin ['kremlɪn] n: **the ~** der
Kreml
Kurd [kɛːd] n Kurde m, Kurdin f;
Kurdish adj kurdisch
Kuwait [kʊ'weɪt] n Kuwait nt

L abbr (Brit Auto) = **learner**
LA abbr = **Los Angeles**
lab [læb] n (fam) Labor nt
label ['leɪbl] n Etikett nt; (tied)
Anhänger m; (adhesive) Aufkleber
m; (record ~) Label nt ▷ vt
etikettieren; (pej) abstempeln
laboratory [lə'bɒrətərɪ] n Labor
nt

laborious [lə'bɔːrɪəs] adj
mühsam; **labor** (US), **labour**
['leɪbə°] n Arbeit f; (Med) Wehen
pl; **to be in ~** Wehen haben ▷ adj

(*Pol*) Labour-; **~ Party** Labour Party f; **labor union** n (*US*) Gewerkschaft f; **labourer** n Arbeiter(in) m(f)

lace [leɪs] n (*fabric*) Spitze f; (*of shoe*) Schnürsenkel m ▷ vt: **to ~ (up)** zuschnüren; **lace-up** n Schnürschuh m

lack [læk] vt, vi: **to be ~ing** fehlen; **sb ~s o is ~ing in sth** es fehlt jdm an etw dat; **we ~ the time** uns fehlt die Zeit ▷ n Mangel m (*of* an +dat)

lacquer ['lækə*] n Lack m; (*Brit: hair ~*) Haarspray nt

lad [læd] n Junge m

ladder ['lædə*] n Leiter f; (*in tight*) Laufmasche f

laddish ['lædɪʃ] adj (*Brit*) machohaft

laden ['leɪdn] adj beladen (*with* mit)

ladies ['leɪdɪz], **ladies' room** n Damentoilette f

lad mag n Männerzeitschrift f

lady ['leɪdɪ] n Dame f; (*as title*) Lady f; **ladybird, ladybug** (*US*) n Marienkäfer m; **Ladyshave®** n Epiliergerät nt

lag [læg] vi: **to ~ (behind)** zurückliegen ▷ vt (*pipes*) isolieren

lager ['lɑːgə*] n helles Bier; **~ lout** betrunkener Rowdy

lagging ['lægɪn] n Isolierung f

laid [leɪd] pt, pp of **lay**; **laid-back** adj (*fam*) cool, gelassen

lain [leɪn] pp of **lie**

lake [leɪk] n See m; **the Lake District** Seengebiet im Nordwesten Englands

lamb [læm] n Lamm nt; (*meat*) Lammfleisch nt; **lamb chop** n Lammkotelett nt

lame [leɪm] adj lahm; (*excuse*) faul; (*argument*) schwach

lament [lə'ment] n Klage f ▷ vt beklagen

laminated ['læmɪneɪtɪd] adj beschichtet

lamp [læmp] n Lampe f; (*in street*) Laterne f; (*in car*) Licht nt, Scheinwerfer m; **lamppost** n Laternenpfahl m; **lampshade** n Lampenschirm m

land [lænd] n Land nt ▷ vi (*from ship*) an Land gehen; (*Aviat*) landen ▷ vt (*passengers*) absetzen; (*goods*) abladen; (*plane*) landen **landing** n Landung f; (*on stairs*) Treppenabsatz m; **landing stage** n Landesteg m; **landing strip** n Landebahn f

landlady n Hauswirtin f, Vermieterin f; **landlord** n (*of house*) Hauswirt m, Vermieter m; (*of pub*) Gastwirt m; **landmark** n Wahrzeichen nt; (*event*) Meilenstein m; **landowner** n Grundbesitzer(in) m(f); **landscape** n Landschaft f; (*format*) Querformat nt; **landslide** n (*Geo*) Erdrutsch m

lane [leɪn] n (*in country*) enge Landstraße, Weg m; (*in town*) Gasse f; (*of motorway*) Spur f; (*Sport*) Bahn f; **to get in ~** (*in car*) sich einordnen

language ['læŋgwɪdʒ] n Sprache f; (*style*) Ausdrucksweise f

lantern ['læntən] n Laterne f

lap [læp] n Schoß m; (*in race*) Runde f ▷ vt (*in race*) überholen

lapse [læps] n (*mistake*) Irrtum m; (*moral*) Fehltritt m ▷ vi ablaufen

laptop ['læptɒp] n Laptop m

large [lɑːdʒ] adj groß; **by and ~** im Großen und Ganzen; **largely** adv zum größten Teil; **large-scale** adj groß angelegt, Groß-

lark [lɑːk] n (*bird*) Lerche f

laryngitis [lærɪn'dʒaɪtɪs] n Kehlkopfentzündung f; **larynx** ['lærɪŋks] n Kehlkopf m

laser ['leɪzə*] n Laser m; **laser printer** n Laserdrucker m

lash [læʃ] vt peitschen; **lash out** vi (with fists) um sich schlagen; (spend money) sich in Unkosten stürzen (on mit)

lass [læs] n Mädchen nt

last [lɑːst] adj letzte(r, s); **the ~ but one** der/die/das vorletzte; **~ night** gestern Abend; **~ but not least** nicht zuletzt ▷ adv zuletzt; (last time) das letzte Mal; **at ~** endlich ▷ n (person) Letzte(r) mf; (thing) Letzte(s) nt; **he was the ~ to leave** er ging als Letzter ▷ vi (continue) dauern; (remain in good condition) durchhalten; (remain good) sich halten; (money) ausreichen; **lasting** adj dauerhaft; (impression) nachhaltig; **lastly** adv schließlich; **last-minute** adj in letzter Minute; **last name** n Nachname m

late [leɪt] adj spät; (after proper time) zu spät; (train etc) verspätet; (dead) verstorben; **to be ~** zu spät kommen; (train etc) Verspätung haben ▷ adv spät; (after proper time) zu spät; **late availibility flight** n Last-Minute-Flug m; **lately** adv in letzter Zeit; **late opening** n verlängerte Öffnungszeiten pl; **later** ['leɪtə°] adj, adv später; **see you ~** bis später; **latest** ['leɪtɪst] adj späteste(r, s); (most recent) neueste(r, s) ▷ n: **the ~** (news) das Neueste; **at the ~** spätestens

Latin ['lætɪn] n Latein nt ▷ adj lateinisch; **Latin America** n Lateinamerika nt; **Latin-American** adj lateinamerikanisch ▷ n Lateinamerikaner(in) m(f)

latter ['lætə°] adj (second of two) letztere(r, s); (last: part, years) letzte(r, s), später

Latvia ['lætvɪə] n Lettland nt;

Latvian ['lætvɪən] ▷ adj lettisch; ▷ n (person) Lette m; Lettin f; (language) Lettisch nt

laugh [lɑːf] n Lachen nt; **for a ~** aus Spaß ▷ vi lachen (at, about über +akk); **to ~ at sb** sich über jdn lustig machen; **it's no ~ing matter** es ist nicht zum Lachen; **laughter** ['lɑːftə°] n Gelächter nt

launch [lɔːntʃ] n (launching, of ship) Stapellauf m; (of rocket) Abschuss m; (of product) Markteinführung f; (with hype) Lancierung f; (event) Eröffnungsfeier f ▷ vt (ship) vom Stapel lassen; (rocket) abschießen; (product) einführen; (with hype) lancieren; (project) in Gang setzen

launder ['lɔːndə°] vt waschen und bügeln; (fig: money) waschen; **laundrette** [lɔːn'dret] n (Brit), **laundromat** ['lɔːndrəmæt] n (US) Waschsalon m; **laundry** ['lɔːndrɪ] n (place) Wäscherei f; (clothes) Wäsche f

lavatory ['lævətrɪ] n Toilette f

lavender ['lævɪndə°] n Lavendel m

lavish ['lævɪʃ] adj verschwenderisch; (furnishings etc) üppig; (gift) großzügig

law [lɔː] n Gesetz nt; (system) Recht nt; (for study) Jura; (of sport) Regel f; **against the ~** gesetzwidrig; **law-abiding** adj gesetzestreu; **law court** n Gerichtshof m; **lawful** adj rechtmäßig

lawn [lɔːn] n Rasen m; **lawnmower** n Rasenmäher m

lawsuit ['lɔːsuːt] n Prozess m; **lawyer** ['lɔːjə°] n Rechtsanwalt m, Rechtsanwältin f

laxative ['læksətɪv] n Abführmittel nt

lay [leɪ] pt of **lie** ▷ vt (**laid**, **laid**) legen; (table) decken; (vulg)

poppen, bumsen; (*egg*) legen ▷ *adj*
Laien-; **lay down** *vt* hinlegen; **lay
off** *vt* (*workers*) (vorübergehend)
entlassen; (*stop attacking*) in Ruhe
lassen; **lay on** *vt* (*provide*)
anbieten; (*organize*) veranstalten,
bereitstellen; **layabout** *n*
Faulenzer(in) *m(f)*; **lay-by** *n*
Parkbucht *f*; (*bigger*) Parkplatz *m*
layer ['leɪə°] *n* Schicht *f*
layman ['leɪmən] *n* Laie *m*
layout ['leɪaʊt] *n* Gestaltung *f*;
(*of book etc*) Lay-out *nt*
laze [leɪz] *vi* faulenzen; **laziness**
['leɪzɪnɪs] *n* Faulheit *f*; **lazy**
['leɪzi] *adj* faul; (*day, time*)
gemütlich
lb *abbr* = **pound** Pfd.
lead [led] *n* Blei *nt* ▷ *vt, vi* [li:d]
(**led, led**) führen; (*group etc*) leiten;
to ~ the way vorangehen; **this is
~ing us nowhere** das bringt uns
nicht weiter ▷ [li:d] *n* (*race*)
Führung *f*; (*distance, time ahead*)
Vorsprung *m* (*over* vor +*dat*); (*of
police*) Spur *f*; (*Theat*) Hauptrolle *f*;
(*dog's*) Leine *f*; (*Elec: flex*) Leitung *f*;
lead astray *vt* irreführen; **lead
away** *vt* wegführen; **lead back** *vi*
zurückführen; **lead on** *vt*
anführen; **lead to** *vt* (*street*)
hinführen nach; (*result in*) führen
zu; **lead up to** *vt* (*drive*) führen zu
leaded ['ledɪd] *adj* (*petrol*)
verbleit
leader ['li:də°] *n* Führer(in) *m(f)*;
(*of party*) Vorsitzende(r) *mf*; (*of
project, expedition*) Leiter(in) *m(f)*;
(*Sport: in race*) der/die Erste; (*in
league*) Tabellenführer *m*;
leadership ['li:dəʃɪp] *n* Führung
f
lead-free ['led'fri:] *adj* (*petrol*)
bleifrei
leading ['li:dɪŋ] *adj* führend,
wichtig
leaf [li:f] (*pl* **leaves**) *n* Blatt *nt*;

leaflet ['li:flɪt] *n* Prospekt *m*;
(*pamphlet*) Flugblatt *nt*; (*with
instructions*) Merkblatt *nt*
league [li:g] *n* Bund *m*; (*Sport*)
Liga *f*
leak [li:k] *n* (*gap*) undichte Stelle;
(*escape*) Leck *nt*; **to take a ~** (*fam*)
pinkeln gehen ▷ *vi* (*pipe etc*)
undicht sein; (*liquid etc*) auslaufen;
leaky *adj* undicht
lean [li:n] *adj* (*meat*) mager; (*face*)
schmal; (*person*) drahtig ▷ *vi*
(**leant** *o* **leaned, leant** *o* **leaned**)
(*not vertical*) sich neigen; (*rest*) **to
~ against sth** sich an etw *akk*
lehnen; (*support oneself*) **to ~ on
sth** sich auf etw *akk* stützen ▷ *vt*
lehnen (*on, against* an +*akk*); **lean
back** *vi* sich zurücklehnen; **lean
forward** *vi* sich vorbeugen; **lean
over** *vi* sich hinüberbeugen; **lean
towards** *vt* tendieren zu
leant [lent] *pt, pp of* **lean**
leap [li:p] *n* Sprung *m* ▷ *vi* (**leapt**
o **leaped, leapt** *o* **leaped**)
springen; **leapt** [lept] *pt, pp of*
leap; leap year *n* Schaltjahr *nt*
learn [lɜ:n] (**learnt** *o* **learned,
learnt** *o* **learned**) *vt, vi* lernen;
(*find out*) erfahren; **to ~ (how) to
swim** schwimmen lernen;
learned ['lɜ:nɪd] *adj* gelehrt;
learner *n* Anfänger(in) *m(f)*; (*Brit:
driver*) Fahrschüler(in) *m(f)*
learnt [lɜ:nt] *pt, pp of* **learn**
lease [li:s] *n* (*of land, premises etc*)
Pacht *f*; (*contract*) Pachtvertrag *m*;
(*of house, car etc*) Miete *f*; (*contract*)
Mietvertrag *m* ▷ *vt* pachten;
(*house, car etc*) mieten; **lease out**
vt vermieten; **leasing** ['li:sɪŋ] *n*
Leasing *nt*
least [li:st] *adj* wenigste(r, s);
(*slightest*) geringste(r, s) ▷ *adv* am
wenigsten; **~ expensive**
billigste(r, s) ▷ *n*: **the ~** das
Mindeste; **not in the ~** nicht im

geringsten; **at ~** wenigstens; (*with number*) mindestens

leather ['leðə*] n Leder nt ▷ adj ledern, Leder-

leave [liːv] n (*time off*) Urlaub m; **on ~** auf Urlaub; **to take one's ~** Abschied nehmen (*of* von) ▷ vt (**left, left**) (*place, person*) verlassen; (*not remove, not change*) lassen; (*~ behind: message, scar etc*) hinterlassen; (*forget*) hinter sich lassen; (*after death*) hinterlassen (*to sb* jdm); (*entrust*) überlassen (*to sb* jdm); **to be left** (*remain*) übrig bleiben; **~ me alone** lass mich in Ruhe!; **don't ~ it to the last minute** warte nicht bis zur letzten Minute ▷ vi (*weg*)gehen, (*weg*)fahren; (*on journey*) abreisen; (*bus, train*) abfahren (*for* nach); **leave behind** vt zurücklassen; (*scar etc*) hinterlassen; (*forget*) hinter sich lassen; **leave out** vt auslassen; (*person*) ausschließen (*of* von)

leaves [liːvz] pl of **leaf**

leaving do [liːvɪŋ duː] n Abschiedsfeier f

Lebanon ['lebənən] n: **the ~** der Libanon

lecture ['lektʃə*] n Vortrag m; (*at university*) Vorlesung f; **to give a ~** einen Vortrag/eine Vorlesung halten; **lecturer** n Dozent(in) m(f); **lecture theatre** n Hörsaal m

led [led] pt, pp of **lead**

LED abbr = **light-emitting diode** Leuchtdiode f

ledge [ledʒ] n Leiste f; (*window ~*) Sims m o nt

leek [liːk] n Lauch m

left [left] pt, pp of **leave** ▷ adj linke(r, s) ▷ adv (*position*) links; (*movement*) nach links ▷ n (*side*) linke Seite; **the Left** (*Pol*) die Linke; **on/to the ~** links (*of* von); **move/fall to the ~** nach links

rücken/fallen; **left-hand** adj linke(r, s); **~ bend** Linkskurve f; **~ drive** Linkssteuerung f; **left-handed** adj linkshändig; **left-hand side** n linke Seite

left-luggage locker n Gepäckschließfach nt; **left-luggage office** n Gepäckaufbewahrung f

leftovers npl Reste pl

left wing n linker Flügel; **left-wing** adj (*Pol*) linksgerichtet

leg [leg] n Bein nt; (*of meat*) Keule f

legacy ['legəsɪ] n Erbe nt, Erbschaft f

legal ['liːgəl] adj Rechts-, rechtlich; (*allowed*) legal; (*limit, age*) gesetzlich; **~ aid** Rechtshilfe f; **legalize** vt legalisieren; **legally** adv legal

legend ['ledʒənd] n Legende f

legible, legibly ['ledʒəbl, -blɪ] adj, adv leserlich

legislation [ledʒɪs'leɪʃn] n Gesetze pl

legitimate [lɪ'dʒɪtɪmət] adj rechtmäßig, legitim

legroom ['legrʊm] n Beinfreiheit f

leisure ['leʒə*] n (*time*) Freizeit f ▷ adj Freizeit-; **~ centre** Freizeitzentrum nt; **leisurely** ['leʒəlɪ] adj gemächlich

lemon ['lemən] n Zitrone f; **lemonade** [lemə'neɪd] n Limonade f; **lemon curd** n Brotaufstrich aus Zitronen, Butter, Eiern und Zucker; **lemon juice** n Zitronensaft m; **lemon sole** n Seezunge f

lend [lend] (**lent, lent**) vt leihen; **to ~ sb sth** jdm etw leihen; **to (sb) ~ a hand** (jdm) behilflich sein; **lending library** n Leihbücherei f

length [leŋθ] n Länge f; **4 metres in ~** 4 Meter lang; **what**

~ is it? wie lange ist es?; **for any ~ of time** für längere Zeit; **at ~** (lengthily) ausführlich; **lengthen** ['leŋθən] vt verlängern; **lengthy** adj sehr lange; (dragging) langwierig

lenient ['liːnɪənt] adj nachsichtig

lens [lenz] n Linse f; (Foto) Objektiv nt

lent [lent] pt, pp of **lend**

Lent [lent] n Fastenzeit f

lentil ['lentl] n (Bot) Linse f

Leo ['liːəʊ] (pl -s) n (Astr) Löwe m

leopard ['lepəd] n Leopard m

lesbian ['lezbɪən] adj lesbisch ▷ n Lesbe f

less [les] adj, adv, n weniger; **~ and ~** immer weniger; (~ often) immer seltener; **lessen** ['lesn] vi abnehmen, nachlassen ▷ vt verringern; (pain) lindern; **lesser** ['lesə*] adj geringer; (amount) kleiner

lesson ['lesn] n (at school) Stunde f; (unit of study) Lektion f; (fig) Lehre f; (Rel) Lesung f; **~s start at 9** der Unterricht beginnt um 9

let [let] (**let, let**) vt lassen; (lease) vermieten; **to ~ sb have sth** jdm etw geben; **~'s go** gehen wir; **to ~ go (of sth)** (etw) loslassen; **let down** vt herunterlassen; (fail to help) im Stich lassen; (disappoint) enttäuschen; **let in** vt hereinlassen; **let off** vt (bomb) hochgehen lassen; (person) laufen lassen; **let out** vt hinauslassen; (secret) verraten; (scream etc) ausstoßen; **let up** vi nachlassen; (stop) aufhören

lethal ['liːθəl] adj tödlich

let's contr = **let us**

letter ['letə*] n (of alphabet) Buchstabe m; (message) Brief m; (official ~) Schreiben nt; **letter bomb** n Briefbombe f; **letterbox** n Briefkasten m

lettuce ['letɪs] n Kopfsalat m

leukaemia, leukemia (US) [luːˈkiːmɪə] n Leukämie f

level ['levl] adj (horizontal) waagerecht; (ground) eben; (two things, two runners) auf selber Höhe; **to be ~ with sb/sth** mit jdm/etw auf gleicher Höhe sein; **~ on points** punktgleich ▷ adv (run etc) auf gleicher Höhe, gleich auf; **to draw ~** (in race) gleichziehen (with mit); (in game) ausgleichen ▷ n (altitude) Höhe f; (standard) Niveau nt; (amount, degree) Grad m; **to be on a ~ with** auf gleicher Höhe sein mit ▷ vt (ground) einebnen; **level crossing** n (Brit) (schienengleicher) Bahnübergang m; **level-headed** adj vernünftig

lever ['liːvə*, (US) 'levə*] n Hebel m; (fig) Druckmittel nt; **lever up** vt hochstemmen

liability [laɪəˈbɪlɪtɪ] n Haftung f; (burden) Belastung f; (obligation) Verpflichtung f; **liable** ['laɪəbl] adj: **to be ~ for sth** (responsible) für etw haften; **~ for tax** steuerpflichtig

liar ['laɪə*] n Lügner(in) m(f)

Lib Dem [lɪb'dem] abbr = **Liberal Democrat**

liberal ['lɪbərəl] adj (generous) großzügig; (broad-minded) liberal; **Liberal Democrat** n (Brit Pol) Liberaldemokrat(in) m(f) ▷ adj liberaldemokratisch

liberate ['lɪbəreɪt] vt befreien; **liberation** [lɪbə'reɪʃn] n Befreiung f

Liberia [laɪ'bɪərɪə] n Liberia nt

liberty ['lɪbətɪ] n Freiheit f

Libra ['liːbrə] n (Astr) Waage f

library ['laɪbrərɪ] n Bibliothek f; (lending ~) Bücherei f

Libya ['lɪbɪə] n Libyen nt
lice [laɪs] pl of **louse**
licence ['laɪsəns] n (permit)
Genehmigung f; (Comm) Lizenz f;
(driving ~) Führerschein m; **license**
['laɪsəns] n (US) see **licence** ▷ vt
genehmigen; **licensed** adj
(restaurant etc) mit
Schankerlaubnis; **license plate** n
(US Auto) Nummernschild nt;
licensing hours npl
Ausschankzeiten pl
lick [lɪk] vt lecken ▷ n Lecken
nt
licorice ['lɪkərɪs] n Lakritze f
lid [lɪd] n Deckel m; (eye~) Lid nt
lie [laɪ] n Lüge f; ~ **detector**
Lügendetektor m ▷ vi lügen; **to**
~ **to sb** jdn belügen ▷ vi (**lay, lain**)
(rest, be situated) liegen; (~ down)
sich legen; (snow) liegen bleiben;
to be lying third an dritter Stelle
liegen; **lie about** vi herumliegen;
lie down vi sich hinlegen
Liechtenstein ['lɪktənstaɪn] n
Liechtenstein nt
lie in [laɪ'ɪn] n: **to have a**
~ ausschlafen
life [laɪf] (pl **lives**) n Leben nt; **to**
get ~ lebenslänglich bekommen;
there isn't much ~ **here** hier ist
nicht viel los; **how many lives**
were lost? wie viele sind ums
Leben gekommen?; **life assurance**
n Lebensversicherung f; **lifebelt** n
Rettungsring m; **lifeboat** n
Rettungsboot n; **lifeguard** n
Bademeister(in) m(f),
Rettungsschwimmer(in) m(f); **life**
insurance n Lebensversicherung
f; **life jacket** n Schwimmweste f;
lifeless adj (dead) leblos; **lifelong**
adj lebenslang; **life preserver** n
(US) Rettungsring m; **life-saving**
adj lebensrettend; **life-size(d)** adj
in Lebensgröße; **life span** n
Lebensspanne f; **life style** n

Lebensstil m; **lifetime** n
Lebenszeit f
lift [lɪft] vt (hoch)heben; (ban)
aufheben ▷ n (Brit: elevator)
Aufzug m, Lift m; **to give sb a** ~ jdn
im Auto mitnehmen; **lift up** vt
hochheben; **lift-off** n Start m
ligament ['lɪgəmənt] n Band nt
light [laɪt] (**lit** o **lighted, lit** o
lighted) vt beleuchten; (fire,
cigarette) anzünden ▷ n Licht nt;
(lamp) Lampe f; ~**s** pl (Auto)
Beleuchtung f; (traffic ~s) Ampel f;
in the ~ **of** angesichts +gen ▷ adj
(bright) hell; (not heavy, easy) leicht;
(punishment) milde; (taxes) niedrig;
~ **blue/green** hellblau/hellgrün;
light up vt beleuchten; (fire,
illuminate) beleuchten
▷ vi (a. eyes) aufleuchten
light bulb n Glühbirne f
lighten ['laɪtn] vi hell werden
▷ vt (give light to) erhellen; (make
less heavy) leichter machen; (fig)
erleichtern
lighter ['laɪtə°] n (cigarette ~)
Feuerzeug nt
light-hearted adj unbeschwert;
lighthouse n Leuchtturm m;
lighting n Beleuchtung f; **lightly**
adv leicht; **light meter** n (Foto)
Belichtungsmesser m
lightning ['laɪtnɪŋ] n Blitz m
lightweight adj leicht
like [laɪk] vt mögen, gernhaben;
he ~s swimming er schwimmt
gern; **would you** ~ ...? hättest
du/hätten Sie gern ...?; **I'd** ~ **to go**
home ich möchte nach Hause
(gehen); **I don't** ~ **the film** der
Film gefällt mir nicht ▷ prep wie;
what's it/he ~? wie ist es/er?; **he**
looks ~ **you** er sieht dir/Ihnen
ähnlich; ~ **that/this** so; **likeable**
['laɪkəbl] adj sympathisch
likelihood ['laɪklɪhʊd] n Wahrscheinlichkeit f; **likely** ['laɪklɪ]
adj wahrscheinlich; **the bus is**

~ to be late der Bus wird wahrscheinlich Verspätung haben; **he's not** (**at all**) **~ to come** (höchst)wahrscheinlich kommt er nicht

like-minded [laɪk'maɪndɪd] *adj* gleich gesinnt

likewise ['laɪkwaɪz] *adv* ebenfalls; **to do ~** das Gleiche tun

liking ['laɪkɪŋ] *n* (*for person*) Zuneigung *f*; (*for type, things*) Vorliebe *f* (*for* für)

lilac ['laɪlək] *n* Flieder *m* ▷ *adj* fliederfarben

lily ['lɪlɪ] *n* Lilie *f*; **~ of the valley** Maiglöckchen *nt*

limb [lɪm] *n* Glied *nt*

limbo ['lɪmbəʊ] *n*: **in ~** (*plans*) auf Eis gelegt

lime [laɪm] *n* (*tree*) Linde *f*; (*fruit*) Limone *f*; (*substance*) Kalk *m*; **lime juice** *n* Limonensaft *m*; **limelight** *n* (*fig*) Rampenlicht *nt*

limerick ['lɪmərɪk] *n* Limerick *m* (*fünfzeiliges komisches Gedicht*)

limestone ['laɪmstəʊn] *n* Kalkstein *m*

limit ['lɪmɪt] *n* Grenze *f*; (*for pollution etc*) Grenzwert *m*; **there's a ~ to that** dem sind Grenzen gesetzt; **to be over the ~** (*speed*) das Tempolimit überschreiten; (*alcohol consumption*) fahruntüchtig sein; **that's the ~** jetzt reicht's!, das ist die Höhe! ▷ *vt* beschränken (*to* auf +*akk*); (*freedom, spending*) einschränken; **limitation** [lɪmɪ'teɪʃən] *n* Beschränkung *f*; (*of freedom, spending*) Einschränkung *f*; **limited** *adj* begrenzt; **~ liability company** Gesellschaft *f* mit beschränkter Haftung, GmbH *f*; **public ~ company** Aktiengesellschaft *f*

limousine ['lɪməziːn] *n* Limousine *f*

limp [lɪmp] *vi* hinken ▷ *adj* schlaff

line [laɪn] *n* Linie *f*; (*written*) Zeile *f*; (*rope*) Leine *f*; (*on face*) Falte *f*; (*row*) Reihe *f*; (*US: queue*) Schlange *f*; (*Rail*) Bahnlinie *f*; (*between A and B*) Strecke *f*; (*Tel*) Leitung *f*; (*range of items*) Kollektion *f*; **hold the ~** bleiben Sie am Apparat!; **to stand in ~** Schlange stehen; **in ~ with** in Übereinstimmung mit; **something along those ~s** etwas in dieser Art; **drop me a ~** schreib mir ein paar Zeilen; **~s** (*Theat*) Text *m* ▷ *vt* (*clothes*) füttern; (*streets*) säumen; **lined** *adj* (*paper*) liniert; (*face*) faltig; **line up** *vi* sich aufstellen; (*US: form queue*) sich anstellen

linen ['lɪnɪn] *n* Leinen *nt*; (*sheets etc*) Wäsche *f*

liner ['laɪnə*] *n* Überseedampfer *m*, Passagierschiff *nt*

linger ['lɪŋgə*] *vi* verweilen; (*smell*) nicht weggehen

lingerie ['lænʒəriː] *n* Damenunterwäsche *f*

lining ['laɪnɪŋ] *n* (*of clothes*) Futter *nt*; (*brake ~*) Bremsbelag *m*

link [lɪŋk] *n* (*connection*) Verbindung *f*; (*of chain*) Glied *nt*; (*relationship*) Beziehung *f* (*with* zu); (*between events*) Zusammenhang *m*; (*Internet*) Link *m* ▷ *vt* verbinden

lion ['laɪən] *n* Löwe *m*; **lioness** *n* Löwin *f*

lip [lɪp] *n* Lippe *f*; **lipstick** *n* Lippenstift *m*

liqueur [lɪ'kjʊə*] *n* Likör *m*

liquid ['lɪkwɪd] *n* Flüssigkeit *f* ▷ *adj* flüssig

liquidate ['lɪkwɪdeɪt] *vt* liquidieren

liquidizer ['lɪkwɪdaɪzə*] *n* Mixer *m*

liquor ['lɪkə*] *n* Spirituosen *pl*

liquorice ['lɪkərɪs] n Lakritze f
Lisbon ['lɪzbən] n Lissabon nt
lisp [lɪsp] vt, vi lispeln
list [lɪst] n Liste f ▷ vi (ship)
Schlagseite haben ▷ vt auflisten,
aufzählen; **~ed building** unter
Denkmalschutz stehendes
Gebäude
listen ['lɪsn] vi zuhören, horchen
(for sth auf etw akk); **listen to** vt
(person) zuhören +dat; (radio)
hören; (advice) hören auf; **listener**
n Zuhörer(in) m(f); (to radio)
Hörer(in) m(f)
lit [lɪt] pt, pp of **light**
liter ['liːtə*] n (US) Liter m
literacy ['lɪtərəsɪ] n Fähigkeit f
zu lesen und zu schreiben; **literal**
['lɪtərəl] adj (translation, meaning)
wörtlich; (actual) buchstäblich;
literally adv (translate, take sth)
wörtlich; (really) buchstäblich,
wirklich; **literary** ['lɪtərərɪ] adj
literarisch; (critic, journal etc)
Literatur-; (language) gehoben;
literature ['lɪtrətʃə*] n Literatur
f; (brochures etc)
Informationsmaterial nt
Lithuania [lɪθjuː'eɪnjə] n Litauen
nt; **Lithuanian** [lɪθjuː'eɪnjən]
▷ adj litauisch; ▷ n (person)
Litauer(in) m(f); (language)
Litauisch nt
litre ['liːtə*] n Liter m
litter ['lɪtə*] n Abfälle pl; (of
animals) Wurf m ▷ vt: **to be ~ed
with** übersät sein mit; **litter bin** n
Abfalleimer m
little ['lɪtl] adj (**smaller,
smallest**) klein; (in quantity)
wenig; **a ~ while ago** vor kurzer
Zeit ▷ adv, n (**fewer, fewest**)
wenig; **a ~** ein bisschen, ein
wenig; **~ as possible** so wenig
wie möglich; **for as ~ as £5** ab nur
5 Pfund; **I see very ~ of them** ich
sehe sie sehr selten; **~ by ~** nach

und nach; **little finger** n kleiner
Finger
live [laɪv] adj lebendig; (Elec)
geladen, unter Strom; (TV, Radio:
event) live; **~ broadcast**
Direktübertragung f ▷ [lɪv] vi
leben; (not die) überleben; (dwell)
wohnen; **you ~ and learn** man
lernt nie aus ▷ vt (life) führen; **to
~ a life of luxury** im Luxus leben;
live on vi weiterleben ▷ vt: **to
~ sth** von etw leben; (feed) sich von
etw ernähren; **to earn enough to
~** genug verdienen, um davon zu
leben; **live together** vi
zusammenleben; **live up to** vt
(reputation) gerecht werden +dat;
(expectations) entsprechen +dat;
live with vt (parents etc) wohnen
bei; (partner) zusammenleben mit;
(difficulty) **you'll just have to ~ it**
du musst dich/Sie müssen sich
eben damit abfinden
liveliness ['laɪvlɪnɪs] n Lebhaf-
tigkeit f; **lively** ['laɪvlɪ] adj
lebhaft
liver ['lɪvə*] n Leber f
lives [laɪvz] pl of **life**
livestock ['laɪvstɒk] n Vieh nt
living ['lɪvɪŋ] n Lebensunterhalt
m; **what do you do for a ~?** was
machen Sie beruflich? ▷ adj
lebend; **living room** n
Wohnzimmer n
lizard ['lɪzəd] n Eidechse f
llama ['lɑːmə] n (Zool) Lama nt
load [ləʊd] n Last f; (cargo)
Ladung f; (Tech, fig) Belastung f; **~s
of** (fam) massenhaft; **it was a ~ of
rubbish** (fam) es war
grottenschlecht ▷ vt (vehicle)
beladen; (Inform) laden; (film)
einlegen
loaf [ləʊf] (pl **loaves**) n: **a ~ of
bread** ein (Laib) Brot (m)nt
loan [ləʊn] n (item leant)
Leihgabe f; (Fin) Darlehen nt; **on**

~ geliehen ▷ vt leihen (to sb
jdm)
loathe [ləʊð] vt verabscheuen
loaves [ləʊvz] pl of **loaf**
lobby ['lɒbɪ] n Vorhalle f; (Pol)
Lobby f
lobster ['lɒbstə°] n Hummer m
local ['ləʊkəl] adj (traffic, time etc)
Orts-; (radio, news, paper) Lokal-;
(government, authority) Kommunal-;
(anaesthetic) örtlich; ~ **call** (Tel)
Ortsgespräch nt; ~ **elections**
Kommunalwahlen pl; ~ **time**
Ortszeit f; ~ **train** Nahverkehrszug
m; **the ~ shops** die Geschäfte am
Ort ▷ n (pub) Stammlokal nt; **the
~s** pl die Ortsansässigen pl; **locally**
adv örtlich, am Ort
locate [ləʊ'keɪt] vt (find)
ausfindig machen; (position)
legen; (establish) errichten; **to be
~d** sich befinden (in, at in +dat);
location [ləʊ'keɪʃən] n (position)
Lage f; (Cine) Drehort m
loch [lɒx] n (Scot) See m
lock [lɒk] n Schloss nt; (Naut)
Schleuse f; (of hair) Locke f ▷ vt
(door etc) abschließen ▷ vi (door
etc) sich abschließen lassen;
(wheels) blockieren; **lock in** vt
einschließen, einsperren; **lock out**
vt aussperren; **lock up** vt (house)
abschließen; (person) einsperren
locker ['lɒkə°] n Schließfach nt;
locker room n (US)
Umkleideraum m
locksmith ['lɒksmɪθ] n Schlos-
ser(in) m(f)
locust ['ləʊkəst] n Heuschrecke f
lodge [lɒdʒ] n (small house)
Pförtnerhaus nt; (porter's ~)
Pförtnerloge f ▷ vi in Untermiete
wohnen (with bei); (get stuck)
stecken bleiben; **lodger** n
Untermieter(in) m(f); **lodging** n
Unterkunft f
loft [lɒft] n Dachboden m

log [lɒg] n Klotz m; (Naut) Log nt;
to keep a ~ of sth über etw Buch
führen; **log in** vi (Inform) sich
einloggen; **log off** vi (Inform) sich
ausloggen; **log on** vi (Inform) sich
einloggen; **log out** vi (Inform) sich
ausloggen
logic ['lɒdʒɪk] n Logik f; **logical**
adj logisch
logo ['lɒgəʊ] (pl **-s**) n Logo nt
loin [lɔɪn] n Lende f
loiter ['lɔɪtə°] vi sich herumtreiben
lollipop ['lɒlɪpɒp] n Lutscher m;
~ **man/lady** (Brit) Schülerlotse m,
Schülerlotsin f
lolly ['lɒlɪ] n Lutscher m
London ['lʌndən] n London nt;
Londoner n Londoner(in) m(f)
loneliness ['ləʊnlɪnɪs] n Einsamkeit f; **lonely** ['ləʊnlɪ], (esp
US) **lonesome** ['ləʊnsəm] adj
einsam
long [lɒŋ] adj lang; (distance)
weit; **it's a ~ way** es ist weit (to
nach); **for a ~ time** lange; **how ~ is
the film?** wie lange dauert der
Film?; **in the ~ run** auf die Dauer
▷ adv lange; **not for ~** nicht lange;
~ **ago** vor langer Zeit; **before**
~ bald; **all day ~** den ganzen Tag;
no ~er nicht mehr; **as ~ as** solange
▷ vi sich sehnen (for nach); (be
waiting) sehnsüchtig warten (for
auf); **long-distance call** n
Ferngespräch nt; **long drink** n
Longdrink m; **long-haul flight** n
Langstreckenflug m; **longing** n
Sehnsucht f (for nach); **longingly**
adv sehnsüchtig; **longitude**
['lɒŋgɪtjuːd] n Länge f; **long jump**
n Weitsprung m; **long-life milk** n
H-Milch f; **long-range** adj
Langstrecken-, Fern-; ~ **missile**
Langstreckenrakete f;
long-sighted adj weitsichtig;
long-standing adj alt,
langjährig; **long-term** adj

langfristig; (car park, effect etc) Langzeit-; **~ unemployment** Langzeitarbeitslosigkeit f; **long wave** n Langwelle f

loo [luː] n (Brit fam) Klo nt

look [lʊk] n Blick m; (appearance) **~(s)** pl Aussehen nt; **I'll have a ~** ich schau mal nach; **to have a ~ at sth** sich dat ansehen; **can I have a ~?** darf ich mal sehen? ▷ vi schauen, gucken; (with prep) sehen; (search) nachsehen; (appear) aussehen; (**I'm) just ~ing** ich schaue nur; **it ~s like rain** es sieht nach Regen aus ▷ vt: **~ what you've done** sieh dir mal an, was du da angestellt hast; (appear) **he ~s his age** man sieht ihm sein Alter an; **to ~ one's best** sehr vorteilhaft aussehen; **look after** vt (care for) sorgen für; (keep an eye on) aufpassen auf +akk; **look at** vt ansehen, anschauen; **look back** vi sich umsehen; (fig) zurückblicken; **look down on** vt (fig) herabsehen auf +akk; **look for** vt suchen; **look forward to** vt sich freuen auf +akk; **look into** vt (investigate) untersuchen; **look out** vi hinaussehen (of the window zum Fenster); (watch out) Ausschau halten (for nach); (be careful) aufpassen, Acht geben (for auf +akk); **~!** Vorsicht!; **look up** vi aufsehen ▷ vt (word etc) nachschlagen; **look up to** vt aufsehen zu

loony ['luːnɪ] adj (fam) bekloppt

loop [luːp] n Schleife f

loose [luːs] adj locker; (knot, button) lose; **loosen** vt lockern; (knot) lösen

loot [luːt] n Beute f

lop-sided ['lɒpˈsaɪdɪd] adj schief

lord [lɔːd] n (ruler) Herr m; (Brit: title) Lord m; **the Lord** (God) Gott der Herr; **the (House of) Lords** (Brit) das Oberhaus

lorry ['lɒrɪ] n (Brit) Lastwagen m

lose [luːz] (lost, lost) vt verlieren; (chance) verpassen; **to ~ weight** abnehmen; **to ~ one's life** umkommen ▷ vi verlieren; (clock, watch) nachgehen; **loser** n Verlierer(in) m(f); **loss** [lɒs] n Verlust m; **lost** [lɒst] pt, pp of **lose**; **we're ~** wir haben uns verlaufen ▷ adj verloren; **lost-and-found** (US), **lost property (office)** n Fundbüro nt

lot [lɒt] n (fam: batch) Menge f, Haufen m, Stoß m; **this is the first ~** das ist die erste Ladung; **a ~** viel(e); **a ~ of money** viel Geld; **~s of people** viele Leute; **the (whole) ~** alles; (people) alle

lotion ['ləʊʃən] n Lotion f

lottery ['lɒtərɪ] n Lotterie f

loud [laʊd] adj laut; (colour) schreiend; **loudspeaker** n Lautsprecher m; (of stereo) Box f

lounge [laʊndʒ] n Wohnzimmer nt; (in hotel) Aufenthaltsraum m; (at airport) Warteraum m ▷ vi sich herumlümmeln

louse [laʊs] (pl lice) n Laus f; **lousy** ['laʊzɪ] adj (fam) lausig

lout [laʊt] n Rüpel m

lovable ['lʌvəbl] adj liebenswert

love [lʌv] n Liebe f (of zu); (person, address) Liebling m, Schatz m; (Sport) null; **to be in ~** verliebt sein (with sb in jdn); **to fall in ~** sich verlieben (with sb in jdn); **to make ~** (sexually) sich lieben; **to make ~ to** (o with) **sb** mit jdm schlafen; (in letter) **he sends his ~** er lässt grüßen; **give her my ~** grüße sie von mir; **~, Tom** liebe Grüße, Tom ▷ vt (person) lieben; (activity) sehr gerne mögen; **to ~ to do sth** etw für sein Leben gerne tun; **I'd ~ a cup of tea** ich würde liebend gern eine Tasse Tee; **love affair** n (Liebes)verhältnis nt; **love letter** n

Liebesbrief *m*; **love life** *n*
Liebesleben *nt*; **lovely** ['lʌvlɪ] *adj*
schön, wunderschön; (*charming*)
reizend; **we had a ~ time** es war
sehr schön; **lover** ['lʌvə] *n* Lieb-
haber(in) *m(f)*; **loving** *adj* liebevoll

low [ləʊ] *adj* niedrig; (*rank*)
niedere(r, s); (*level, note, neckline*)
tief; (*intelligence, density*) gering;
(*quality, standard*) schlecht; (*not
loud*) leise; (*depressed*)
niedergeschlagen; **we're ~ on
petrol** wir haben kaum noch
Benzin ▷ *n* (*Meteo*) Tief *nt*;
low-calorie *adj* kalorienarm;
lowcut *adj* (*dress*) tief
ausgeschnitten; **low-emission**
adj schadstoffarm; **lower** ['ləʊə*]
adj niedriger; (*storey, class etc*)
untere(r, s) ▷ *vt* herunterlassen;
(*eyes, price*) senken; (*pressure*)
verringern; **low-fat** *adj* fettarm;
low tide [ləʊ'taɪd] *n* Ebbe *f*
loyal ['lɔɪəl] *adj* treu; **loyalty** *n*
Treue *f*
lozenge ['lɒzɪndʒ] *n* Pastille *f*

- **L-PLATES**

Als **L-Plates** werden in
Großbritannien die weißen
Schilder mit einem roten „L"
bezeichnet, die vorn und hinten
an jedem von einem
Fahrschüler gesteuerten
Fahrzeug befestigt werden
müssen. Fahrschüler müssen
einen vorläufigen Führerschein
beantragen und dürfen damit
unter der Aufsicht eines
erfahrenen Autofahrers auf
allen Straßen außer
Autobahnen fahren.

Ltd *abbr* = **limited** ≈ GmbH *f*
lubricant ['luːbrɪkənt] *n*
Schmiermittel *nt*, Gleitmittel *nt*
luck [lʌk] *n* Glück *nt*; **bad ~** Pech

nt; **luckily** *adv* glücklicherweise,
zum Glück; **lucky** *adj* (*number, day
etc*) Glücks-; **to be ~** Glück haben
ludicrous ['luːdɪkrəs] *adj*
grotesk
luggage ['lʌgɪdʒ] *n* Gepäck *nt*;
luggage compartment *n*
Gepäckraum *m*; **luggage rack** *n*
Gepäcknetz *nt*
lukewarm ['luːkwɔːm] *adj*
lauwarm
lullaby ['lʌləbaɪ] *n* Schlaflied *nt*
lumbago [lʌm'beɪgəʊ] *n* Hexenschuss *m*
luminous ['luːmɪnəs] *adj*
leuchtend
lump [lʌmp] *n* Klumpen *m*; (*Med*)
Schwellung *f*; (*in breast*) Knoten *m*;
(*of sugar*) Stück *nt*; **lump sum** *n*
Pauschalsumme *f*; **lumpy** *adj*
klumpig
lunacy ['luːnəsɪ] *n* Wahnsinn *m*;
lunatic ['luːnətɪk] *adj* wahnsinnig ▷ *n* Wahnsinnige(r) *mf*
lunch, luncheon [lʌntʃ, -ən] *n*
Mittagessen *nt*; **to have ~** zu
Mittag essen; **lunch break, lunch
hour** *n* Mittagspause *f*;
lunchtime *n* Mittagszeit *f*
lung [lʌŋ] *n* Lunge *f*
lurch [lɜːtʃ] *n*: **to leave sb in the
~** jdn im Stich lassen
lurid ['ljʊərɪd] *adj* (*colour*) grell;
(*details*) widerlich
lurk [lɜːk] *vi* lauern
lust [lʌst] *n* (sinnliche) Begierde
(*for* nach)
Luxembourg ['lʌksəmbɜːg] *n*
Luxemburg *nt*; **Luxembourger**
[lʌksəm'bɜːgə*] *n* Luxemburger(in)
m(f)
luxurious [lʌg'ʒʊərɪəs] *adj* luxuriös, Luxus-; **luxury** ['lʌkʃərɪ] *n*
(*a.* luxuries *pl*) Luxus *m*; **~ goods**
Luxusgüter *pl*
lynx [lɪŋks] *n* Luchs *m*
lyrics ['lɪrɪks] *npl* Liedtext *m*

m *abbr* = **metre** m

M *abbr* (*street*) = **Motorway** A; (*size*)
= **medium** M

MA *abbr* = **Master of Arts**
Magister Artium *m*

ma [mɑ:] *n* (*fam*) Mutti *f*

mac [mæk] *n* (*Brit fam*)
Regenmantel *m*

macaroon [mækə'ru:n] *n*
Makrone *f*

Macedonia [mæsɪdəʊnɪə] *n*
Mazedonien *nt*

machine [mə'ʃi:n] *n* Maschine *f*;
machine gun *n*
Maschinengewehr *nt*; **machinery**
[mə'ʃi:nərɪ] *n* Maschinen *pl*; (*fig*)
Apparat *m*; **machine washable**
adj waschmaschinenfest

mackerel ['mækrəl] *n* Makrele *f*

macro ['mækrəʊ] (*pl* **-s**) *n*
(*Inform*) Makro *nt*

mad [mæd] *adj* wahnsinnig,
verrückt; (*dog*) tollwütig; (*angry*)
wütend, sauer (*at* auf +*akk*); (*fam*)
~ about (*fond of*) verrückt nach; **to
work like ~** wie verrückt arbeiten;
are you ~? spinnst du/spinnen
Sie?

madam ['mædəm] *n* gnädige
Frau

mad cow disease
[mæd'kaʊdɪ'zi:z] *n* Rinder-
wahnsinn *m*; **maddening** *adj*
zum Verrücktwerden

made [meɪd] *pt, pp of* **make**

made-to-measure
['meɪdtə'meʒə*] *adj* nach Maß;
~ suit Maßanzug *m*

madly ['mædlɪ] *adv* wie verrückt;
(*with adj*) wahnsinnig; **madman**
['mædmən] (*pl* **-men**) *n*
Verrückte(r) *m*; **madwoman**
['mædwʊmən] (*pl* **-women**) *n*
Verrückte *f*; **madness** ['mædnɪs]
n Wahnsinn *m*

magazine ['mægəzi:n] *n*
Zeitschrift *f*

maggot ['mægət] *n* Made *f*

magic ['mædʒɪk] *n* Magie *f*;
(*activity*) Zauberei *f*; (*fig: effect*)
Zauber *m*; **as if by ~** wie durch
Zauberei ▷ *adj* Zauber-; (*powers*)
magisch; **magician** [mə'dʒɪʃən]
n Zauberer *m*, Zaub(r)erin *f*

magnet ['mægnɪt] *n* Magnet *m*;
magnetic [mæg'netɪk] *adj*
magnetisch; **magnetism**
['mægnɪtɪzəm] *n* (*fig*)
Anziehungskraft *f*

magnificent, **magnificently**
[mæg'nɪfɪsənt, -lɪ] *adj, adv*
herrlich, großartig

magnify ['mægnɪfaɪ] *vt* vergrößern; **magnifying glass** *n*
Vergrößerungsglas *nt*, Lupe *f*

magpie ['mægpaɪ] *n* Elster *f*

maid [meɪd] *n* Dienstmädchen
nt; **maiden name** *n*
Mädchenname *m*; **maiden
voyage** *n* Jungfernfahrt *f*

mail [meɪl] n Post f; (e-mail) Mail f ▷ vt (post) aufgeben; (send) mit der Post schicken (to an +akk); **mailbox** n (US) Briefkasten m; (Inform) Mailbox f; **mailing list** n Adressenliste f; **mailman** n (pl **-men**) (US) Briefträger m; **mail order** n Bestellung f per Post; **mail order firm** n Versandhaus nt; **mailshot** n Mailing nt

main [meɪn] adj Haupt-; **~ course** Hauptgericht nt; **the ~ thing** die Hauptsache f ▷ n (pipe) Hauptleitung f; **mainframe** n Großrechner m; **mainland** n Festland nt; **mainly** adv hauptsächlich; **main road** n Hauptverkehrsstraße f; **main street** n (US) Hauptstraße f

maintain [meɪnˈteɪn] vt (keep up) aufrechterhalten; (machine, roads) instand halten; (service) warten; (claim) behaupten; **maintenance** [ˈmeɪntənəns] n Instandhaltung f; (Tech) Wartung f

maize [meɪz] n Mais m

majestic [məˈdʒestɪk] adj majestätisch; **majesty** [ˈmædʒɪstɪ] n Majestät f; **Your/His/Her Majesty** Eure/Seine/Ihre Majestät

major [ˈmeɪdʒə*] adj (bigger) größer; (important) bedeutend; **~ part** Großteil m; (role) wichtige Rolle; **~ road** Hauptverkehrsstraße f; (Mus) **A ~** A-Dur nt ▷ vi (US) **to ~ in sth** etw als Hauptfach studieren

Majorca [məˈjɔːkə] n Mallorca nt

majority [məˈdʒɒrɪtɪ] n Mehrheit f; **to be in the ~** in der Mehrzahl sein

make [meɪk] n Marke f ▷ vt (**made, made**) machen; (manufacture) herstellen; (clothes) anfertigen; (dress) nähen; (soup) zubereiten; (bread, cake) backen; (tea, coffee) kochen; (speech) halten; (earn) verdienen; (decision) treffen; **it's made of gold** es ist aus Gold; **to ~ sb do sth** jdn dazu bringen, etw zu tun; (force) jdn zwingen, etw zu tun; **she made us wait** sie ließ uns warten; **what ~s you think that?** wie kommen Sie darauf?; **it ~s the room look smaller** es lässt den Raum kleiner wirken; **to ~ (it to) the airport** (reach) den Flughafen erreichen; (in time) es zum Flughafen schaffen; **he never really made it** er hat es nie zu etwas gebracht; **she didn't ~ it through the night** sie hat die Nacht nicht überlebt; (calculate) **I ~ it £5/a quarter to six** nach meiner Rechnung kommt es auf 5 Pfund/nach meiner Uhr ist es dreiviertel sechs; **he's just made for this job** er ist für diese Arbeit wie geschaffen; **make for** vt zusteuern auf +akk; **make of** vt (think of) halten von; **I couldn't ~ anything of it** ich wurde daraus nicht schlau; **make off** vi sich davonmachen (with mit); **make out** vi zurechtkommen ▷ vt (cheque) ausstellen; (list) aufstellen; (understand) verstehen; (discern) ausmachen; **to ~ (that) ...** es so hinstellen, als ob ...; **make up** vt (team etc) bilden; (face) schminken; (invent: story etc) erfinden; **to ~ one's mind** sich entscheiden; **to make (it) up with sb** sich mit jdm aussöhnen ▷ vi sich versöhnen; **make up for** vt ausgleichen; (time) aufholen

make-believe adj Fantasie-; **makeover** n gründliche Veränderung, Verschönerung f; **maker** n (Comm) Hersteller(in) m(f); **makeshift** adj behelfsmäßig; **make-up** n

Make-up *nt*, Schminke *f*; **making** ['meɪkɪŋ] *n* Herstellung *f*

maladjusted [mælə'dʒʌstɪd] *adj* verhaltensgestört

malaria [mə'lɛərɪə] *n* Malaria *f*

Malaysia [mə'leɪʒɪə] *n* Malaysia *nt*

male [meɪl] *n* Mann *m*; (*animal*) Männchen *nt* ▷ *adj* männlich; **~ chauvinist** Chauvi *m*, Macho *m*; **~ nurse** Krankenpfleger *m*

malfunction [mæl'fʌnkʃən] *vi* nicht richtig funktionieren ▷ *n* Defekt *m*

malice ['mælɪs] *n* Bosheit *f*; **malicious** [mə'lɪʃəs] *adj* boshaft; (*behaviour, action*) böswillig; (*damage*) mutwillig

malignant [mə'lɪgnənt] *adj* bösartig

mall [mɔːl] *n* (*US*) Einkaufszentrum *nt*

malnutrition [mælnjʊ'trɪʃən] *n* Unterernährung *f*

malt [mɔːlt] *n* Malz *nt*

Malta ['mɔːltə] *n* Malta *nt*; **Maltese** [mɔːl'tiːz] *adj* maltesisch ▷ *n* (*person*) Malteser(in) *m(f)*; (*language*) Maltesisch *nt*

maltreat [mæl'triːt] *vt* schlecht behandeln; (*violently*) misshandeln

mammal ['mæməl] *n* Säugetier *nt*

mammoth ['mæməθ] *adj* Mammut-, Riesen-

man [mæn] (*pl* **men**) *n* (*male*) Mann *m*; (*human race*) der Mensch, die Menschen *pl*; (*in chess*) Figur *f* ▷ *vt* besetzen

manage ['mænɪdʒ] *vi* zurechtkommen; **can you ~?** schaffst du es?; **to ~ without sth** ohne etw auskommen, auf etw verzichten können ▷ *vt* (*control*) leiten; (*musician, sportsman*) managen; (*cope with*) fertig werden mit; (*task,* *portion, climb etc*) schaffen; **to ~ to do sth** es schaffen, etw zu tun;

manageable *adj* (*object*) handlich; (*task*) zu bewältigen;

management *n* Leitung *f*; (*directors*) Direktion *f*; (*subject*) Management *nt*, Betriebswirtschaft *f*;

management consultant *n* Unternehmensberater(in) *m(f)*;

manager *n* Geschäftsführer(in) *m(f)*; (*departmental ~*) Abteilungsleiter(in) *m(f)*; (*of branch, bank*) Filialleiter(in) *m(f)*; (*of musician, sportsman*) Manager(in) *m(f)*; **managing director** *n* Geschäftsführer(in) *m(f)*

mane [meɪn] *n* Mähne *f*

maneuver (*US*) *see* **manoeuvre**

mango ['mæŋgəʊ] (*pl* **-es**) *n* Mango *f*

man-hour *n* Arbeitsstunde *f*

manhunt *n* Fahndung *f*

mania ['meɪnɪə] *n* Manie *f*; **maniac** ['meɪnɪæk] *n* Wahnsinnige(r) *mf*; (*fan*) Fanatiker(in) *m(f)*

manicure ['mænɪkjʊə*] *n* Maniküre *f*

manipulate [mə'nɪpjʊleɪt] *vt* manipulieren

mankind [mæn'kaɪnd] *n* Menschheit *f*

manly ['mænlɪ] *adj* männlich

man-made ['mænmeɪd] *adj* (*product*) künstlich

manner ['mænə*] *n* Art *f*; **in this ~** auf diese Art und Weise; **~s** *pl* Manieren *pl*

manoeuvre [mə'nuːvə*] *n* Manöver *nt* ▷ *vt, vi* manövrieren

manor ['mænə*] *n*: **~ (house)** Herrenhaus *nt*

manpower ['mænpaʊə*] *n* Arbeitskräfte *pl*

mansion ['mænʃən] *n* Villa *f*; (*of old family*) Herrenhaus *nt*

manslaughter ['mænslɔːtə*] n Totschlag m

mantelpiece ['mæntlpiːs] n Kaminsims m

manual ['mænjʊəl] adj manuell, Hand- ▷ n Handbuch nt

manufacture [mænjʊ'fæktʃə*] vt herstellen ▷ n Herstellung f; **manufacturer** n Hersteller m

manure [mə'njʊə*] n Dung m; (esp artificial) Dünger m

many ['menɪ] (**more, most**) adj, pron viele; **~ times** oft; **not ~ people** nicht viele Leute; **too ~ problems** zu viele Probleme

map [mæp] n Landkarte f; (of town) Stadtplan m

maple ['meɪpl] n Ahorn m

marathon ['mærəθən] n Marathon m

marble ['mɑːbl] n Marmor m; (for playing) Murmel f

march [mɑːtʃ] vi marschieren ▷ n Marsch m; (protest) Demonstration f

March [mɑːtʃ] n März m; see also **September**

mare [meə] n Stute f

margarine [mɑːdʒə'riːn] n Margarine f

margin ['mɑːdʒɪn] n Rand m; (extra amount) Spielraum m; (Comm) Gewinnspanne f; **marginal** adj (difference etc) geringfügig

marijuana [mærjuː'ɑːnə] n Marihuana nt

marine [mə'riːn] adj Meeres-

marital ['mærɪtl] adj ehelich; **~ status** Familienstand m

maritime ['mærɪtaɪm] adj See-

marjoram ['mɑːdʒərəm] n Majoran m

mark [mɑːk] n (spot) Fleck m; (at school) Note f; (sign) Zeichen nt ▷ vt (make ~) Flecken machen auf +akk; (indicate) markieren; (schoolwork) benoten, korrigieren, Flecken machen auf +akk;

markedly ['mɑːkɪdlɪ] adv merklich; (with comp adj) wesentlich;

marker n (in book) Lesezeichen nt; (pen) Marker m

market ['mɑːkɪt] n Markt m; (stock ~) Börse f ▷ vt (Comm: new product) auf den Markt bringen; (goods) vertreiben; **marketing** n Marketing nt; **market leader** n Marktführer m; **market place** n Marktplatz m; **market research** n Marktforschung f

marmalade ['mɑːməleɪd] n Orangenmarmelade f

maroon [mə'ruːn] adj rötlich braun

marquee [mɑː'kiː] n großes Zelt

marriage ['mærɪdʒ] n Ehe f; (wedding) Heirat f (to mit); **married** ['mærɪd] adj (person) verheiratet

marrow ['mærəʊ] n (bone ~) Knochenmark nt; (vegetable) Kürbis m

marry ['mærɪ] vt heiraten; (join) trauen; (take as husband, wife) heiraten ▷ vi: **to ~ / to get married** heiraten

marsh [mɑːʃ] n Marsch f, Sumpf m

marshal ['mɑːʃəl] n (at rally etc) Ordner m; (US: police) Bezirkspolizeichef m

martial arts ['mɑːʃəl'ɑːts] npl Kampfsportarten pl

martyr ['mɑːtə*] n Märtyrer(in) m(f)

marvel ['mɑːvəl] n Wunder nt ▷ vi staunen (at über +akk); **marvellous, marvelous** (US) adj wunderbar

marzipan [mɑːzɪ'pæn] n Marzipan nt o m

mascara [mæ'skɑːrə] n Wimperntusche f

mascot ['mæskɒt] *n* Maskottchen *nt*

masculine ['mæskjʊlɪn] *adj*
männlich

mashed [mæʃt] *adj* ~ **potatoes**
pl Kartoffelbrei *m*, Kartoffelpüree
nt

mask [mɑ:sk] *n* (*a. Inform*) Maske
f ▷ *vt* (*feelings*) verbergen

masochist ['mæsəʊkɪst] *n*
Masochist(in) *m(f)*

mason ['meɪsn] *n* (*stone~*)
Steinmetz(in) *m(f)*; **masonry** *n*
Mauerwerk *nt*

mass [mæs] *n* Masse *f*; (*of people*)
Menge *f*; (*Rel*) Messe *f*; **~es of**
massenhaft

massacre ['mæsəkə*] *n* Blutbad
nt

massage ['mæsɑ:ʒ] *n* Massage *f*
▷ *vt* massieren

massive ['mæsɪv] *adj* (*powerful*)
gewaltig; (*very large*) riesig

mass media ['mæs'mi:dɪə] *npl*
Massenmedien *pl*; **mass-produce**
vt in Massenproduktion
herstellen; **mass production** *n*
Massenproduktion *f*

master ['mɑ:stə*] *n* Herr *m*; (*of
dog*) Besitzer *m*, Herrchen *nt*;
(*teacher*) Lehrer *m*; (*artist*) Meister
m ▷ *vt* meistern; (*language etc*)
beherrschen; **masterly** *adj*
meisterhaft; **masterpiece** *n*
Meisterwerk *nt*

masturbate ['mæstəbeɪt] *vi*
masturbieren

mat [mæt] *n* Matte *f*; (*for table*)
Untersetzer *m*

match [mætʃ] *n* Streichholz
nt; (*Sport*) Wettkampf *m*; (*ball
games*) Spiel *nt*; (*tennis*) Match
nt ▷ *vt* (*be like, suit*) passen zu;
(*equal*) gleichkommen +*dat*
▷ *vi* zusammenpassen; **matchbox**
n Streichholzschachtel *f*;
matching *adj* (*one item*)

passend; (*two items*)
zusammenpassend

mate [meɪt] *n* (*companion*)
Kumpel *m*; (*of animal*) Weibchen
nt/Männchen *nt* ▷ *vi* sich paaren

material [mə'tɪərɪəl] *n* Material
nt; (*for book etc, cloth*) Stoff *m*;
materialistic [mətɪərɪə'lɪstɪk]
adj materialistisch; **materialize**
[mə'tɪərɪəlaɪz] *vi* zustande
kommen; (*hope*) wahr werden

maternal [mə'tɜ:nl] *adj*
mütterlich; **maternity**
[mə'tɜ:nɪtɪ] *adj*: ~ **dress**
Umstandskleid *nt*; ~ **leave**
Elternzeit *f* (der Mutter); ~ **ward**
Entbindungsstation *f*

math [mæθ] *n* (*US fam*) Mathe *f*;
mathematical [mæθə'mætɪkəl]
adj mathematisch; **mathematics**
[mæθə'mætɪks] *nsing* Mathematik
f; **maths** [mæθs] *nsing* (*Brit fam*)
Mathe *f*

matinée ['mætɪneɪ] *n* Nachmit-
tagsvorstellung *f*

matter ['mætə*] *n* (*substance*)
Materie *f*; (*affair*) Sache *f*; **a
personal** ~ eine persönliche
Angelegenheit; **a** ~ **of taste** eine
Frage des Geschmacks; **no
~ how/what** egal wie/was;
what's the ~? was ist los?; **as a
** ~ **of fact** eigentlich; **a** ~ **of time**
eine Frage der Zeit ▷ *vi* darauf
ankommen, wichtig sein; **it
doesn't** ~ es macht nichts;
matter-of-fact *adj* sachlich,
nüchtern

mattress ['mætrəs] *n* Matratze *f*

mature [mə'tjʊə*] *adj* reif ▷ *vi*
reif werden; **maturity**
[mə'tjʊərɪtɪ] *n* Reife *f*

maximum ['mæksɪməm] *adj*
Höchst-, höchste(r, s); ~ **speed**
Höchstgeschwindigkeit *f* ▷ *n*
Maximum *nt*

may [meɪ] (**might**) *vb aux* (*be*

possible) können; (*have permission*) dürfen; **it ~ rain** es könnte regnen; **~ I smoke?** darf ich rauchen?; **it ~ not happen** es passiert vielleicht gar nicht; **we ~ as well go** wir können ruhig gehen

May [meɪ] *n* Mai *m*; *see also* **September**

maybe ['meɪbiː] *adv* vielleicht

May Day ['meɪdeɪ] *n* der erste Mai

mayo ['meɪəʊ] (*US fam*), **mayonnaise** [meɪə'neɪz] *n* Mayo *f*, Mayonnaise *f*, Majonäse *f*

mayor [mɛə*] *n* Bürgermeister *m*

maze [meɪz] *n* Irrgarten *m*; (*fig*) Wirrwarr *nt*

MB *abbr* = **megabyte** MB *nt*

O KEYWORD

me [miː] *pron* **1** (*direct*) mich; **it's me** ich bin's
2 (*indirect*) mir; **give them to me** gib sie mir
3 (*after prep*) (*+akk*) mich; (*+dat*) mir; **with/without me** mit mir/ohne mich

meadow ['medəʊ] *n* Wiese *f*

meal [miːl] *n* Essen *nt*, Mahlzeit *f*; **to go out for a ~** essen gehen; **meal pack** *n* (*US*) tiefgekühltes Fertiggericht; **meal time** *n* Essenszeit *f*

mean [miːn] (**meant, meant**) *vt* (*signify*) bedeuten; (*have in mind*) meinen; (*intend*) vorhaben; **I ~ it** ich meine das ernst; **what do you ~ (by that)?** was willst du damit sagen?; **to ~ to do sth** etw tun wollen; **it was ~t for you** es war für dich bestimmt (*o gedacht*); **it was ~t to be a joke** es sollte ein Witz sein ▷ *vi*: **he ~s well** er

meint es gut ▷ *adj* (*stingy*) geizig; (*spiteful*) gemein (*to zu*); **meaning** ['miːnɪŋ] *n* Bedeutung *f*; (*of life, poem*) Sinn *m*; **meaningful** *adj* sinnvoll; **meaningless** *adj* (*text*) ohne Sinn

means [miːnz] (*pl* **means**) *n* Mittel *nt*; (*pl: funds*) Mittel *pl*; **by ~ of** durch, mittels; **by all ~** selbstverständlich; **by no ~** keineswegs; **~ of transport** Beförderungsmittel

meant [ment] *pt, pp of* **mean**

meantime ['miːn'taɪm] *adv*: **in the ~** inzwischen; **meanwhile** ['miːn'waɪl] *adv* inzwischen

measles ['miːzlz] *nsing* Masern *pl*; **German ~** Röteln *pl*

measure ['meʒə*] *vt, vi* messen ▷ *n* (*unit, device for measuring*) Maß *nt*; (*step*) Maßnahme *f*; **to take ~s** Maßnahmen ergreifen; **measurement** *n* (*amount measured*) Maß *nt*

meat [miːt] *n* Fleisch *nt*; **meatball** *n* Fleischbällchen *nt*

mechanic [mɪ'kænɪk] *n* Mechaniker(in) *m(f)*; **mechanical** *adj* mechanisch; **mechanics** *nsing* Mechanik *f*; **mechanism** ['mekənɪzəm] *n* Mechanismus *m*

medal ['medl] *n* Medaille *f*; (*decoration*) Orden *m*; **medalist** (*US*), **medallist** ['medəlɪst] *n* Medaillengewinner(in) *m(f)*

media ['miːdɪə] *npl* Medien *pl*

median strip ['miːdɪən strɪp] *n* (*US*) Mittelstreifen *m*

mediate ['miːdɪeɪt] *vi* vermitteln

medical ['medɪkəl] *adj* medizinisch; (*treatment etc*) ärztlich; **~ student** Medizinstudent(in) *m(f)* ▷ *n* Untersuchung *f*; **Medicare** ['medɪkɛə*] *n* (*US*) Krankenkasse *f* für ältere Leute; **medication**

[medɪˈkeɪʃən] n Medikamente pl;
to be on ~ Medikamente nehmen;
medicinal [meˈdɪsɪnl] adj Heil-;
~ herbs Heilkräuter pl; **medicine**
[ˈmedsɪn] n Arznei f; (science)
Medizin f

medieval [medɪˈiːvəl] adj
mittelalterlich

mediocre [miːdɪˈəʊkə*] adj
mittelmäßig

meditate [ˈmedɪteɪt] vi meditieren; (fig) nachdenken (on über
+akk)

Mediterranean
[medɪtəˈreɪnɪən] n (sea)
Mittelmeer nt; (region)
Mittelmeerraum m

medium [ˈmiːdɪəm] adj (quality,
size) mittlere(r, s); (steak)
halbdurch; **~ (dry)** (wine)
halbtrocken; **~ sized** mittelgroß;
~ wave Mittelwelle f ▷ n (pl
media) Medium nt; (means) Mittel
nt

meet [miːt] (**met, met**) vt
treffen; (by arrangement) sich
treffen mit; (difficulties) stoßen auf
+akk; (get to know) kennenlernen;
(requirement, demand) gerecht
werden +dat; (deadline) einhalten;
pleased to ~ you sehr angenehm!;
to ~ sb at the station jdn vom
Bahnhof abholen ▷ vi sich
treffen; (become acquainted) sich
kennenlernen; **we've met**
(before) wir kennen uns schon;
meet up vt sich treffen (with
mit); **meet with** vt (group)
zusammenkommen mit;
(difficulties, resistance etc) stoßen
auf +akk; **meeting** n Treffen nt;
(business ~) Besprechung f; (of
committee) Sitzung f; (assembly)
Versammlung f; **meeting place**,
meeting point n Treffpunkt m

megabyte [ˈmegəbaɪt] n
Megabyte nt

melody [ˈmelədɪ] n Melodie f
melon [ˈmelən] n Melone f
melt [melt], vt, vi schmelzen
member [ˈmembə*] n Mitglied
nt; (of tribe, species) Angehörige(r)
mf; **Member of Parliament**
Parlamentsabgeordnete(r) mf;
membership n Mitgliedschaft f;
membership card n
Mitgliedskarte f

memento [məˈmentəʊ] (pl **-es**)
n Andenken nt (of an +akk)

memo [ˈmeməʊ] (pl **-s**) n
Mitteilung f, Memo nt; **memo pad**
n Notizblock m

memorable [ˈmemərəbl] adj
unvergesslich; **memorial**
[mɪˈmɔːrɪəl] n Denkmal nt (to
für); **memorize** [ˈmeməraɪz] vt
sich einprägen, auswendig lernen;
memory [ˈmemərɪ] n Gedächtnis nt; (Inform: of computer)
Speicher m; (sth recalled)
Erinnerung f; **in ~ of** zur
Erinnerung an +akk

men [men] pl of **man**

menace [ˈmenɪs] n Bedrohung f;
(danger) Gefahr f

mend [mend] vt reparieren;
(clothes) flicken ▷ n: **to be on the**
~ auf dem Wege der Besserung
sein

meningitis [menɪnˈdʒaɪtɪs] n
Hirnhautentzündung f

menopause [ˈmenəʊpɔːz] n
Wechseljahre pl

mental [ˈmentl] adj geistig;
mentality [menˈtælɪtɪ] n Mentalität f; **mentally** [ˈmentlɪ] adv
geistig; **~ handicapped** geistig
behindert; **~ ill** geisteskrank

mention [ˈmenʃən] n Erwäh-
nung f ▷ vt erwähnen (to sb jdm
gegenüber); **don't ~ it** bitte sehr,
gern geschehen

menu [ˈmenjuː] n Speisekarte f;
(Inform) Menü nt

merchandise ['mɜːtʃəndaɪz] n Handelsware f; **merchant** ['mɜːtʃənt] adj Handels-

merciful ['mɜːsɪfʊl] adj gnädig; **mercifully** adv glücklicherweise

mercury ['mɜːkjʊrɪ] n Quecksilber nt

mercy ['mɜːsɪ] n Gnade f

mere [mɪə°] adj bloß; **merely** ['mɪəlɪ] adv bloß, lediglich

merge [mɜːdʒ] vi verschmelzen; (Auto) sich einfädeln; (Comm) fusionieren; **merger** n (Comm) Fusion f

meringue [məˈræŋ] n Baiser nt

merit ['merɪt] n Verdienst nt; (advantage) Vorzug m

merry ['merɪ] adj fröhlich; (fam: tipsy) angeheitert; **Merry Christmas** Fröhliche Weihnachten!; **merry-go-round** n Karussell nt

mess [mes] n Unordnung f; (muddle) Durcheinander nt; (dirty) Schweinerei f; (trouble) Schwierigkeiten pl; **in a ~** (muddled) durcheinander; (untidy) unordentlich; (fig: person) in der Klemme; **to make a ~ of sth** etw verpfuschen; **to look a ~** unmöglich aussehen; **mess about** vi (tinker with) herummurksen (with an +dat); (play the fool) herumalbern; (do nothing in particular) herumgammeln; **mess up** vt verpfuschen; (make untidy) in Unordnung bringen; (dirty) schmutzig machen

message ['mesɪdʒ] n Mitteilung f, Nachricht f; (meaning) Botschaft f; **can I give him a ~?** kann ich ihm etwas ausrichten?; **please leave a ~** (on answerphones) bitte hinterlassen Sie eine Nachricht; **I get the ~** ich hab's verstanden

messenger ['mesɪndʒə°] n Bote m

messy ['mesɪ] adj (untidy) unordentlich; (situation etc) verfahren

met [met] pt, pp of **meet**

metal ['metl] n Metall nt; **metallic** [mɪˈtælɪk] adj metallisch

meteorology [miːtɪəˈrɒlədʒɪ] n Meteorologie f

meter ['miːtə°] n Zähler m; (parking meter) Parkuhr f; (US) see **metre**

method ['meθəd] n Methode f; **methodical** [mɪˈθɒdɪkəl] adj methodisch

meticulous [mɪˈtɪkjʊləs] adj (peinlich) genau

metre ['miːtə°] n Meter m o nt; **metric** ['metrɪk] adj metrisch; **~ system** Dezimalsystem nt

Mexico ['meksɪkəʊ] n Mexiko nt

mice [maɪs] pl of **mouse**

mickey ['mɪkɪ] n: **to take the ~ (out of sb)** (fam) (jdn) auf den Arm nehmen

microchip ['maɪkrəʊtʃɪp] n (Inform) Mikrochip m; **microphone** n Mikrofon nt; **microscope** n Mikroskop nt; **microwave (oven)** n Mikrowelle(nherd) f(m)

mid [mɪd] adj: **in ~ January** Mitte Januar; **he's in his ~ forties** er ist Mitte vierzig

midday ['mɪddeɪ] n Mittag m; **at ~** mittags

middle ['mɪdl] n Mitte f; (waist) Taille f; **in the ~ of** mitten in +dat; **to be in the ~ of doing sth** gerade dabei sein, etw zu tun ▷ adj mittlere(r, s), Mittel-; **the ~ one** der/die/das Mittlere; **middle-aged** adj mittleren Alters; **Middle Ages** npl: **the ~** das Mittelalter; **middle-class** adj mittelständisch; (bourgeois) bürgerlich; **middle classes** npl: **the ~** der Mittelstand; **Middle East** n: **the ~** der Nahe Osten; **middle name** n zweiter Vorname

Midlands ['mɪdləndz] npl: **the ~** Mittelengland nt

midnight ['mɪdnaɪt] n Mitternacht f

midst [mɪdst] n: **in the ~ of** mitten in +dat

midsummer ['mɪdsʌmə°] n Hochsommer m; **Midsummer's Day** Sommersonnenwende f

midway [mɪd'weɪ] adv auf halbem Wege; **~ through the film** nach der Hälfte des Films; **midweek** [mɪd'wiːk] adj, adv in der Mitte der Woche

midwife ['mɪdwaɪf] (pl **-wives**) n Hebamme f

midwinter [mɪd'wɪntə°] n tiefster Winter

might [maɪt] pt of **may**; (possibility) könnte; (permission) dürfte; (would) würde; **they ~ still come** sie könnten noch kommen; **he ~ have let me know** er hätte mir doch Bescheid sagen können; **I thought she ~ change her mind** ich dachte schon, sie würde sich anders entscheiden ▷ n Macht f, Kraft f

mighty ['maɪtɪ] adj gewaltig; (powerful) mächtig

migraine ['miːɡreɪn] n Migräne f

migrant ['maɪɡrənt] n (bird) Zugvogel m; **~ worker** Gastarbeiter(in) m(f); Migrant(in) m(f); **migrate** [maɪ'ɡreɪt] vi abwandern; (birds) nach Süden ziehen

mike [maɪk] n (fam) Mikro nt

Milan [mɪ'læn] n Mailand nt

mild [maɪld] adj mild; (person) sanft; **mildly** adv: **to put it**

~ gelinde gesagt; mildness n Milde f

mile [maɪl] n Meile f (= 1,609 km); **for ~s (and ~s)** ≈ kilometerweit; **~s per hour** Meilen pro Stunde; **~s better than** hundertmal besser als; **mileage** n Meilen pl, Meilenzahl f; **mileometer** [maɪ'lɒmɪtə°] n ≈ Kilometerzähler m; **milestone** n (a. fig) Meilenstein m

militant ['mɪlɪtənt] adj militant; **military** ['mɪlɪtərɪ] adj Militär-, militärisch

milk [mɪlk] n Milch f ▷ vt melken; **milk chocolate** n Vollmilchschokolade f; **milkman** (pl **-men**) n Milchmann m; **milk shake** n Milchshake m, Milchmixgetränk nt

mill [mɪl] n Mühle f; (factory) Fabrik f

millennium [mɪ'lenɪəm] n Jahrtausend nt

milligramme ['mɪlɪɡræm] n Milligramm nt; **milliliter** (US), **millilitre** n Milliliter m; **millimeter** (US), **millimetre** n Millimeter m

million ['mɪljən] n Million f; **five ~** fünf Millionen; **~s of people** Millionen von Menschen; **millionaire** [mɪljə'nɛə°] n Millionär(in) m(f)

mime [maɪm] n Pantomime f ▷ vt, vi mimen; **mimic** ['mɪmɪk] n Imitator(in) m(f) ▷ vt, vi nachahmen; **mimicry** ['mɪmɪkrɪ] n Nachahmung f

mince [mɪns] vt (zer)hacken ▷ n (meat) Hackfleisch nt; **mincemeat** n süße Gebäckfüllung aus Rosinen, Äpfeln, Zucker, Gewürzen und Talg; **mince pie** n mit 'mincemeat' gefülltes süßes Weihnachtsgebäck

mind [maɪnd] n (intellect)

Verstand *m*; (*also person*) Geist *m*; **out of sight, out of ~** aus den Augen, aus dem Sinn; **he is out of his ~** er ist nicht bei Verstand; **to keep sth in ~** etw im Auge behalten; **do you have sth in ~?** denken Sie an etwas Besonderes?; **I've a lot on my ~** mich beschäftigt so vieles im Moment; **to change one's ~** es sich *dat* anders überlegen ▷ *vt* (*look after*) aufpassen auf +*akk*; (*object to*) etwas haben gegen; **~ you, ...** allerdings ...; **I wouldn't ~ ...** ich hätte nichts gegen ...; **"~ the step"** „Vorsicht Stufe!" ▷ *vi* etwas dagegen haben; **do you ~ if I ...** macht es Ihnen etwas aus, wenn ich ...; **I don't ~** es ist mir egal, meinetwegen; **never ~** macht nichts

mine [maɪn] *pron* meine(r, s); **this is ~** das gehört mir; **a friend of ~** ein Freund von mir ▷ *n* (*coalmine*) Bergwerk *nt*; (*Mil*) Mine *f*; **miner** *n* Bergarbeiter(in) *m(f)*

mineral ['mɪnərəl] *n* Mineral *nt*; **mineral water** *n* Mineralwasser *nt*

mingle ['mɪŋɡl] *vi* sich mischen (*with* unter +*akk*)

miniature ['mɪnɪtʃə*] *adj* Miniatur-

minibar ['mɪnɪbɑː] *n* Minibar *f*; **minibus** *n* Kleinbus *m*; **minicab** *n* Kleintaxi *nt*

minimal ['mɪnɪml] *adj* minimal; **minimize** ['mɪnɪmaɪz] *vt* auf ein Minimum reduzieren; **minimum** ['mɪnɪməm] *n* Minimum *nt* ▷ *adj* Mindest-

mining ['maɪnɪŋ] *n* Bergbau *m*

miniskirt *n* Minirock *m*

minister ['mɪnɪstə*] *n* (*Pol*) Minister(in) *m(f)*; (*Rel*) Pastor(in) *m(f)*, Pfarrer(in) *m(f)*; **ministry** ['mɪnɪstrɪ] *n* (*Pol*) Ministerium *nt*

minor ['maɪnə*] *adj* kleiner; (*insignificant*) unbedeutend; (*operation, offence*) harmlos; **~ road** Nebenstraße *f*; (*Mus*) **A ~** a-Moll *nt* ▷ *n* (*Brit: under 18*) Minderjährige(r) *mf*; **minority** [maɪˈnɒrɪtɪ] *n* Minderheit *f*

mint [mɪnt] *n* Minze *f*; (*sweet*) Pfefferminz(bonbon) *nt*; **mint sauce** *n* Minzsoße *f*

minus ['maɪnəs] *prep* minus; (*without*) ohne

minute [maɪˈnjuːt] *adj* winzig; **in ~ detail** genauestens ▷ ['mɪnɪt] *n* Minute *f*; **just a ~** Moment mal!; **any ~** jeden Augenblick; **~s** *pl* (*of meeting*) Protokoll *nt*

miracle ['mɪrəkl] *n* Wunder *nt*; **miraculous** [mɪˈrækjʊləs] *adj* unglaublich

mirage ['mɪrɑːʒ] *n* Fata Morgana *f*, Luftspiegelung *f*

mirror ['mɪrə*] *n* Spiegel *m*

misbehave [mɪsbɪˈheɪv] *vi* sich schlecht benehmen

miscalculation ['mɪskælkjʊˈleɪʃən] *n* Fehlkalkulation *f*; (*misjudgement*) Fehleinschätzung *f*

miscarriage ['mɪsˈkærɪdʒ] *n* (*Med*) Fehlgeburt *f*

miscellaneous [mɪsɪˈleɪnɪəs] *adj* verschieden

mischief ['mɪstʃɪf] *n* Unfug *m*; **mischievous** ['mɪstʃɪvəs] *adj* (*person*) durchtrieben; (*glance*) verschmitzt

misconception [mɪskənˈsepʃən] *n* falsche Vorstellung

misconduct [mɪsˈkɒndʌkt] *n* Vergehen *nt*

miser ['maɪzə*] *n* Geizhals *m*

miserable ['mɪzərəbl] *adj* (*person*) todunglücklich; (*conditions, life*) elend; (*pay, weather*) miserabel

miserly ['maɪzəlɪ] *adj* geizig

misery ['mɪzərɪ] n Elend nt;
(suffering) Qualen pl

misfit ['mɪsfɪt] n Außensei-
ter(in) m(f)

misfortune [mɪs'fɔːtʃən] n Pech
nt

misguided [mɪs'gaɪdɪd] adj irrig;
(optimism) unangebracht

misinform [mɪsɪn'fɔːm] vt falsch
informieren

misinterpret [mɪsɪn'tɜːprɪt] vt
falsch auslegen

misjudge [mɪs'dʒʌdʒ] vt falsch
beurteilen

mislay [mɪs'leɪ] irr vt verlegen

mislead [mɪs'liːd] irr vt
irreführen; **misleading** adj
irreführend

misprint ['mɪsprɪnt] n Druck-
fehler m

mispronounce [mɪsprə'naʊns]-
vt falsch aussprechen

miss [mɪs] vt (fail to hit, catch)
verfehlen; (not notice, hear) nicht
mitbekommen; (be too late for)
verpassen; (chance) versäumen;
(regret the absence of) vermissen; **I
~ you** du fehlst mir ▷ vi nicht
treffen; (shooting) daneben-
schießen; (ball, shot etc) daneben-
gehen; **miss out** vt auslassen
▷ vi: **to ~ on sth** etw verpassen

Miss [mɪs] n (unmarried woman)
Fräulein nt

missile ['mɪsaɪl] n Geschoss nt;
(rocket) Rakete f

missing ['mɪsɪŋ] adj (person)
vermisst; (thing) fehlend; **to be/go
~** vermisst werden, fehlen

mission ['mɪʃən] n (Pol, Mil, Rel)
Auftrag m, Mission f; **missionary**
['mɪʃənrɪ] n Missionar(in) m(f)

mist [mɪst] n (feiner) Nebel m;
(haze) Dunst m; **mist over, mist up**
vi sich beschlagen

mistake [mɪs'teɪk] n Fehler m;
by ~ aus Versehen ▷ irr vt

(**mistook, mistaken**)
(misunderstand) falsch verstehen;
(mix up) verwechseln (for mit);
there's no mistaking ... ... ist
unverkennbar; (meaning) ...
ist unmissverständlich;
mistaken adj (idea, identity)
falsch; **to be ~** sich irren,
falschliegen

mistletoe ['mɪsltəʊ] n Mistel f

mistreat [mɪs'triːt] vt schlecht
behandeln

mistress ['mɪstrɪs] n (lover)
Geliebte f

mistrust [mɪs'trʌst] n Misstrauen nt (of gegen) ▷ vt
misstrauen +dat

misty ['mɪstɪ] adj neblig; (hazy)
dunstig

misunderstand
[mɪsʌndə'stænd] irr vt, vi falsch
verstehen; **misunderstanding** n
Missverständnis nt; (disagreement)
Differenz f

mitten ['mɪtn] n Fausthandschuh m

mix [mɪks] n (mixture) Mischung f
▷ vt mischen; (blend) vermischen
(with mit); (drinks, music) mixen; **to
~ business with pleasure** das
Angenehme mit dem Nützlichen
verbinden ▷ vi (liquids) sich
vermischen lassen; **mix up** vt
(mix) zusammenmischen; (confuse)
verwechseln (with mit); **mixed** adj
gemischt; **a ~ bunch** eine bunt
gemischte Truppe; **~ grill** Mixed
Grill m; **~ vegetables**
Mischgemüse nt; **mixer** n (for
food) Mixer m; **mixture** ['mɪkstʃə*]
n Mischung f; (Med) Saft m;
mix-up n Durcheinander nt,
Missverständnis nt

ml abbr = **millilitre** ml

mm abbr = **millimetre** mm

moan [məʊn] n Stöhnen nt;
(complaint) Gejammer nt ▷ vi

stöhnen; (*complain*) jammern, meckern (*about* über +*akk*)

mobile ['məʊbaɪl] *adj* beweglich; (*on wheels*) fahrbar ▷ *n* (*phone*) Handy *nt*; **mobile phone** *n* Mobiltelefon *nt*, Handy *nt*

mobility [məʊ'bɪlɪtɪ] *n* Beweglichkeit *f*

mock [mɒk] *vt* verspotten ▷ *adj* Schein-; **mockery** *n* Spott *m*

mod cons ['mɒd'kɒnz] *abbr* = **modern conveniences** (moderner) Komfort

mode [məʊd] *n* Art *f*; (*Inform*) Modus *m*

model ['mɒdl] *n* Modell *nt*; (*example*) Vorbild *nt*; (*fashion ~*) Model *nt* ▷ *adj* (*miniature*) Modell-; (*perfect*) Muster- ▷ *vt* (*make*) formen ▷ *vi*: **she ~s for Versace** sie arbeitet als Model bei Versace

modem ['məʊdem] *n* Modem *nt*

moderate ['mɒdərət] *adj* mäßig; (*views, politics*) gemäßigt; (*income, success*) mittelmäßig ▷ *n* (*Pol*) Gemäßigte(r) *mf* ▷ ['mɒdəreɪt] *vt* mäßigen; **moderation** [mɒdə'reɪʃən] *n* Mäßigung *f*; **in ~** mit Maßen

modern ['mɒdən] *adj* modern; **~ history** neuere Geschichte; **~ Greek** Neugriechisch *nt*; **modernize** ['mɒdənaɪz] *vt* modernisieren

modest ['mɒdɪst] *adj* bescheiden; **modesty** *n* Bescheidenheit *f*

modification [mɒdɪfɪ'keɪʃən] *n* Abänderung *f*; **modify** ['mɒdɪfaɪ] *vt* abändern

moist [mɔɪst] *adj* feucht; **moisten** ['mɔɪsn] *vt* befeuchten; **moisture** ['mɔɪstʃə*] *n* Feuchtigkeit *f*; **moisturizer** *n* Feuchtigkeitscreme *f*

molar ['məʊlə*] *n* Backenzahn *m*

mold (*US*) *see* **mould**

mole [məʊl] *n* (*spot*) Leberfleck *m*; (*animal*) Maulwurf *m*

molecule ['mɒlɪkjuːl] *n* Molekül *nt*

molest [məʊ'lest] *vt* belästigen

molt (*US*) *see* **moult**

molten ['məʊltən] *adj* geschmolzen

mom [mɒm] *n* (*US*) Mutti *f*

moment ['məʊmənt] *n* Moment *m*, Augenblick *m*; **just a ~** Moment mal!; **at** (*o* **for**) **the ~** im Augenblick; **in a ~** gleich

momentous [məʊ'mentəs] *adj* bedeutsam

Monaco ['mɒnəkəʊ] *n* Monaco *nt*

monarchy ['mɒnəkɪ] *n* Monarchie *f*

monastery ['mɒnəstrɪ] *n* (*for monks*) Kloster *nt*

Monday ['mʌndeɪ] *n* Montag *m*; *see also* **Tuesday**

monetary ['mʌnɪtərɪ] *adj* (*reform, policy, union*) Währungs-; **~ unit** Geldeinheit *f*

money ['mʌnɪ] *n* Geld *nt*; **to get one's ~'s worth** auf seine Kosten kommen; **money order** *n* Postanweisung *f*

mongrel ['mʌŋgrəl] *n* Promenadenmischung *f*

monitor ['mɒnɪtə*] *n* (*screen*) Monitor *m* ▷ *vt* (*progress etc*) überwachen; (*broadcasts*) abhören

monk [mʌŋk] *n* Mönch *m*

monkey ['mʌŋkɪ] *n* Affe *m*; **~ business** Unfug *m*

monopolize [mə'nɒpəlaɪz] *vt* monopolisieren; (*fig: person, thing*) in Beschlag nehmen; **monopoly** [mə'nɒpəlɪ] *n* Monopol *nt*

monotonous [mə'nɒtənəs] *adj* eintönig, monoton

monsoon [mɒn'suːn] *n* Monsun *m*

monster ['mɒnstə*] *n* (*animal,*

thing) Monstrum *nt* ▷ *adj* Riesen-;
monstrosity [mɒnˈstrɒsɪtɪ] *n*
Monstrosität *f*; (*thing*) Ungetüm
nt
Montenegro [mɒntɪˈniːgrəʊ] *n*
Montenegro *nt*
month [mʌnθ] *n* Monat *m*;
monthly *adj* monatlich; (*ticket*,
salary) Monats- ▷ *adv* monatlich
▷ *n* (*magazine*) Monatsschrift *f*
monty [ˈmɒntɪ] *n*: **to go the full
~** (*fam: strip*) alle Hüllen fallen
lassen; (*go the whole hog*) aufs
Ganze gehen
monument [ˈmɒnjʊmənt] *n*
Denkmal *nt* (*to* für); **monumental**
[mɒnjʊˈmentl] *adj* (*huge*)
gewaltig
mood [muːd] *n* (*of person*)
Laune *f*; (*a. general*) Stimmung *f*;
**to be in a good/bad
~** gute/schlechte Laune haben;
to be in the ~ for sth zu etw
aufgelegt sein; **I'm not in the
~** ich fühle mich nicht danach;
moody *adj* launisch
moon [muːn] *n* Mond *m*; **to be
over the ~** (*fam*) überglücklich
sein; **moonlight** *n* Mondlicht *nt*
▷ *vi* schwarzarbeiten; **moonlit**
adj (*night, landscape*) mondhell
moor [mɔː*] *n* Moor *nt* ▷ *vt, vi*
festmachen; **moorings** *npl*
Liegeplatz *m*; **moorland** *n*
Moorland *nt*, Heideland *nt*
moose [muːs] (*pl* -) *n* Elch *m*
mop [mɒp] *n* Mopp *m*; **mop up**
vt aufwischen
mope [məʊp] *vi* Trübsal blasen
moped [ˈməʊped] *n* (*Brit*) Moped
nt
moral [ˈmɒrəl] *adj* moralisch;
(*values*) sittlich ▷ *n* Moral *f*; **~s** *pl*
Moral *f*; **morale** [mɒˈrɑːl] *n*
Stimmung *f*, Moral *f*; **morality**
[məˈrælɪtɪ] *n* Moral *f*, Ethik *f*
morbid [ˈmɔːbɪd] *adj* krankhaft

○ **KEYWORD**

more [mɔː*] *adj* (*greater in number
etc*) mehr; (*additional*) noch mehr;
do you want (some) more tea?
möchtest du/möchten Sie noch
etwas Tee?; **I have no** *o* **I don't
have any more money** ich habe
kein Geld mehr
▷ *pron* (*greater amount*) mehr;
(*further o additional amount*) noch
mehr; **is there any more?** gibt
es noch mehr?; (*left over*) ist noch
etwas da?; **there's no more** es ist
nichts mehr da
▷ *adv* mehr; **more
dangerous/easily** *etc* **(than)**
gefährlicher/einfacher *etc* (als);
more and more immer mehr;
more and more excited immer
aufgeregter; **more or less** mehr
oder weniger; **more than ever**
mehr denn je; **more beautiful
than ever** schöner denn je

moreish *adj* (*food*) **these
crisps are really ~** ich kann mit
diesen Chips einfach nicht
aufhören; **moreover** *adv*
außerdem
morgue [mɔːg] *n* Leichen-
schaushaus *nt*
morning [ˈmɔːnɪŋ] *n* Morgen *m*;
in the ~ am Morgen, morgens;
(*tomorrow*) morgen früh; **this
~** heute morgen ▷ *adj* Morgen-;
(*early*) Früh-; (*walk etc*)
morgendlich; **morning after pill**
n die Pille danach; **morning
sickness** *n* Schwangerschafts-
übelkeit *f*
Morocco [məˈrɒkəʊ] *n* Marokko
nt
moron [ˈmɔːrɒn] *n* Idiot(in) *m(f)*
morphine [ˈmɔːfiːn] *n* Morphium *nt*

morsel ['mɔːsl] *n* Bissen *m*

mortal ['mɔːtl] *adj* sterblich; (*wound*) tödlich ▷ *n* Sterbliche(r) *mf*; **mortality** [mɔː'tælɪtɪ] *n* (*death rate*) Sterblichkeitsziffer *f*; **mortally** *adv* tödlich

mortgage ['mɔːgɪdʒ] *n* Hypothek *f* ▷ *vt* mit einer Hypothek belasten

mortified ['mɔːtɪfaɪd] *adj*: **I was ~** es war mir schrecklich peinlich

mortuary ['mɔːtjʊərɪ] *n* Leichenhalle *f*

mosaic [məʊ'zeɪɪk] *n* Mosaik *nt*

Moscow ['mɒskəʊ] *n* Moskau *nt*

Moslem ['mɒzlem] *adj*, *n see* **Muslim**

mosque [mɒsk] *n* Moschee *f*

mosquito [mɒ'skiːtəʊ] (*pl* **-es**) *n* (Stech)mücke *f*; (*tropical*) Moskito *m*; **~ net** Moskitonetz *nt*

moss [mɒs] *n* Moos *nt*

most [məʊst] *adj* meiste *pl*, die meisten; **in ~ cases** in den meisten Fällen ▷ *adv* (*with verbs*) am meisten; (*with adj*) ...ste; (*with adv*) am ...sten; (*very*) äußerst, höchst; **he ate (the) ~** er hat am meisten gegessen; **the ~ beautiful/interesting** der/die/das schönste/interessanteste; **~ interesting** hochinteressant! ▷ *n* das meiste, der größte Teil; (*people*) die meisten; **~ of the money/players** das meiste Geld/die meisten Spieler; **for the ~ part** zum größten Teil; **five at the ~** höchstens fünf; **to make the ~ of sth** etw voll ausnützen; **mostly** *adv* (*most of the time*) meistens; (*mainly*) hauptsächlich; (*for the most part*) größtenteils

MOT *abbr* = **Ministry of Transport**; **~ (test)** ≈ TÜV *m*

motel [məʊ'tel] *n* Motel *nt*

moth [mɒθ] *n* Nachtfalter *m*; (*wool-eating*) Motte *f*; **mothball** *n* Mottenkugel *f*

mother ['mʌðə*] *n* Mutter *f* ▷ *vt* bemuttern; **mother-in-law** (*pl* **mothers-in-law**) *n* Schwiegermutter *f*; **mother-to-be** (*pl* **mothers-to-be**) *n* werdende Mutter

motif [məʊ'tiːf] *n* Motiv *nt*

motion ['məʊʃən] *n* Bewegung *f*; (*in meeting*) Antrag *m*; **motionless** *adj* bewegungslos

motivate ['məʊtɪveɪt] *vt* motivieren; **motive** ['məʊtɪv] *n* Motiv *nt*

motor ['məʊtə*] *n* Motor *m*; (*fam: car*) Auto *nt* ▷ *adj* Motor-; **Motorail train®** *n* (*Brit*) Autoreisezug *m*; **motorbike** *n* Motorrad *nt*; **motorboat** *n* Motorboot *m*; **motorcycle** *n* Motorrad *nt*; **motor industry** *n* Automobilindustrie *f*; **motoring** ['məʊtərɪŋ] *n* Autofahren *nt*; **~ organization** Automobilklub *m*; **motorist** ['məʊtərɪst] *n* Autofahrer(in) *m(f)*; **motor oil** *n* Motorenöl *nt*; **motor racing** *n* Autorennsport *m*; **motor scooter** *n* Motorroller *m*; **motor show** *n* Automobilausstellung *f*; **motor vehicle** *n* Kraftfahrzeug *nt*; **motorway** *n* (*Brit*) Autobahn *f*

motto ['mɒtəʊ] (*pl* **-es**) *n* Motto *nt*

mould [məʊld] *n* Form *f*; (*mildew*) Schimmel *m* ▷ *vt* (*a. fig*) formen; **mouldy** ['məʊldɪ] *adj* schimmelig

moult [məʊlt] *vi* sich mausern, haaren

mount [maʊnt] *vt* (*horse*) steigen auf +*akk*; (*exhibition etc*) organisieren; (*painting*) mit einem Passepartout versehen ▷ *vi*: **to ~ (up)** (an)steigen ▷ *n* Passepartout *nt*

mountain ['maʊntɪn] n Berg m;
mountain bike n Mountainbike
nt; **mountaineer** [maʊntɪ'nɪə*]
n Bergsteiger(in) m(f);
mountaineering [maʊntɪ'nɪərɪŋ]
n Bergsteigen nt; **mountainous**
adj bergig; **mountainside** n
Berghang m

mourn [mɔːn] vt betrauern ▷ vi
trauern (for um); **mourner** n
Trauernde(r) mf; **mournful** adj
trauervoll; **mourning** n Trauer f;
to be in ~ trauern (for um)

mouse [maʊs] (pl **mice**) n (a.
Inform) Maus f; **mouse mat**,
mouse pad (US) n Mauspad nt;
mouse trap n Mausefalle f

mousse [muːs] n (Gastr) Creme f;
(styling ~) Schaumfestiger m

moustache [mə'stæʃ] n
Schnurrbart m

mouth [maʊθ] n Mund m; (of
animal) Maul nt; (of cave) Eingang
m; (of bottle etc) Öffnung f; (of river)
Mündung f; **to keep one's ~ shut**
(fam) den Mund halten; **mouthful**
n (of drink) Schluck m; (of food)
Bissen m; **mouth organ** n
Mundharmonika f; **mouthwash** n
Mundwasser nt; **mouthwatering**
adj appetitlich, lecker

move [muːv] n (movement)
Bewegung f; (in game) Zug m; (step)
Schritt m; (moving house) Umzug m;
to make a ~ (in game) ziehen;
(leave) sich auf den Weg machen;
to get a ~ on (**with sth**) sich (mit
etw) beeilen ▷ vt bewegen;
(object) rücken; (car) wegfahren;
(transport: goods) befördern;
(people) transportieren; (in job)
versetzen; (emotionally) bewegen,
rühren; **I can't ~ it** (stuck, too heavy)
ich bringe es nicht von der Stelle;
to ~ (house) umziehen ▷ vi sich
bewegen; (change place) gehen;
(vehicle, ship) fahren; (move house,

town etc) umziehen; (in game)
ziehen; **move about** vi sich
bewegen; (travel) unterwegs sein;
move away vi weggehen; (move
town) wegziehen; **move in** vi (to
house) einziehen; **move off** vi
losfahren; **move on** vi
weitergehen; (vehicle)
weiterfahren; **move out** vi
ausziehen; **move up** vi (in queue
etc) aufrücken; **movement** n
Bewegung f

movie ['muːvɪ] n Film m; **the ~s**
(the cinema) das Kino; **movie
theatre** n (US) Kino nt

moving ['muːvɪŋ] adj (emotionally) ergreifend, berührend

mow [məʊ] (**mowed, mown** o
mowed) vt mähen; **mower** n
(lawn~) Rasenmäher m

mown [məʊn] pp of **mow**

Mozambique [məʊzæm'biːk] n
Mosambik nt

MP abbr = **Member of Parliament**
Parlamentsabgeordnete(r) mf

mph abbr = **miles per hour** Meilen
pro Stunde

MPV abbr = **multi-purpose
vehicle** Mehrzweckfahrzeug nt

MP3 player [empiː'θriː 'pleɪə*]
n MP3-Player m

Mr [mɪstə*] n (written form of
address) Herr

Mrs ['mɪsɪz] n (written form of
address) Frau

Ms [məz] n (written form of address
for any woman, married or unmarried)
Frau

MS n abbr = **multiple sclerosis** MS
f

Mt abbr = **Mount** Berg m

much [mʌtʃ] (**more, most**) adj
viel; **we haven't got ~ time** wir
haben nicht viel Zeit; **how
~ money?** wie viel Geld? ▷ adv
viel; (with verb) sehr; **~ better** viel
besser; **I like it very ~** es gefällt

mir sehr gut; **I don't like it ~** ich
mag es nicht besonders; **thank
you very ~** danke sehr; **I thought
as ~** das habe ich mir gedacht;
~ as I like him so sehr ich ihn mag;
we don't see them ~ wir sehen
sie nicht sehr oft; **~ the same** fast
gleich ▷ n viel; **as ~ as you want**
so viel du willst; **he's not ~ of a
cook** er ist kein großer Koch

muck [mʌk] n (fam) Dreck m;
muck about vi (fam)
herumalbern; **muck up** vt (fam)
dreckig machen; (spoil)
vermasseln; **mucky** adj dreckig

mucus ['mju:kəs] n Schleim m

mud [mʌd] n Schlamm m

muddle ['mʌdl] n Durcheinander nt; **to be in a ~** ganz
durcheinander sein ▷ vt: **to
~ (up)** durcheinanderbringen;
muddled adj konfus

muddy ['mʌdɪ] adj schlammig;
(shoes) schmutzig; **mudguard**
['mʌdgɑ:d] n Schutzblech nt

muesli ['mu:zlɪ] n Müsli nt

muffin ['mʌfɪn] n Muffin m;
(Brit) weiches, flaches Milchbrötchen
aus Hefeteig, das meist getoastet und
mit Butter gegessen wird

muffle ['mʌfl] vt (sound)
dämpfen; **muffler** n (US)
Schalldämpfer m

mug [mʌg] n (cup) Becher m;
(fam: fool) Trottel m ▷ vt (attack
and rob) überfallen; **mugging** n
Raubüberfall m

muggy ['mʌgɪ] adj (weather)
schwül

mule [mju:l] n Maulesel m

mull over [mʌl 'əʊvə*] vt
nachdenken über +akk

mulled [mʌld] adj: **~ wine**
Glühwein m

multicolored (US),
multicoloured ['mʌltɪ'kʌləd]
adj bunt; **multicultural** adj

multikulturell; **multi-grade** adj:
~ oil Mehrbereichsöl nt;
multilingual adj mehrsprachig;
multinational n (company) Multi
m

multiple ['mʌltɪpl] n Viel-
fache(s) nt ▷ adj mehrfach;
(several) mehrere; **multiple-choice
(method)** n Multiple-
-Choice-Verfahren nt; **multiple
sclerosis** ['mʌltɪplskle'rəʊsɪs] n
Multiple Sklerose f

multiplex ['mʌltɪpleks] adj, n:
~ (cinema) Multiplexkino nt

multiplication [mʌltɪplɪ'keɪʃən]
n Multiplikation f; **multiply**
['mʌltɪplaɪ] vt multiplizieren (by
mit) ▷ vi sich vermehren

multi-purpose ['mʌltɪ'pɜ:pəs]-
adj Mehrzweck-; **multistorey (car
park)** n Parkhaus nt;
multitasking n (Inform)
Multitasking nt

mum [mʌm] n (fam: mother)
Mutti f, Mami f

mumble ['mʌmbl] vt, vi
murmeln

mummy ['mʌmɪ] n (dead body)
Mumie f; (fam: mother) Mutti f,
Mami f

mumps [mʌmps] nsing Mumps
m

munch [mʌntʃ] vt, vi mampfen

Munich ['mju:nɪk] n München
nt

municipal [mju:'nɪsɪpəl] adj
städtisch

mural ['mjʊərəl] n Wand-
gemälde nt

murder ['mɜ:də*] n Mord m; **the
traffic was ~** der Verkehr war die
Hölle ▷ vt ermorden; **murderer** n
Mörder(in) m(f)

murky ['mɜ:kɪ] adj düster;
(water) trüb

murmur ['mɜ:mə*] vt, vi
murmeln

muscle ['mʌsl] n Muskel m;
muscular ['mʌskjulə*] adj (strong)
muskulös; (cramp, pain etc) Muskel-
museum [mjuː'zɪəm] n Museum
nt
mushroom ['mʌʃruːm] n (ess-
barer) Pilz; (button ~) Champignon
m ▷ vi (fig) emporschießen
mushy ['mʌʃɪ] adj breiig; ~ **peas**
Erbsenmus nt
music ['mjuːzɪk] n Musik f;
(printed) Noten pl; **musical** adj
(sound) melodisch; (person)
musikalisch; ~ **instrument**
Musikinstrument nt ▷ n (show)
Musical nt; **musically** adv
musikalisch; **musician**
[mjuː'zɪʃən] n Musiker(in) m(f)
Muslim ['muzlɪm] adj
moslemisch ▷ n Moslem m,
Muslime f
mussel ['mʌsl] n Miesmuschel f
must [mʌst] (**had to, had to**) vb
aux (need to) müssen; (in negation)
dürfen; **I ~n't forget that** ich darf
das nicht vergessen; (certainty) **he
~ be there by now** er ist
inzwischen bestimmt schon da;
(assumption) **I ~ have lost it** ich
habe es wohl verloren; ~ **you?**
muss das sein? ▷ n Muss nt
mustache ['mʌstæʃ] n (US)
Schnurrbart m
mustard ['mʌstəd] n Senf m; **to
cut the ~** es bringen
mustn't ['mʌsnt] contr of **must
not**
mute [mjuːt] adj stumm
mutter ['mʌtə*] vt, vi murmeln
mutton ['mʌtn] n Ham-
melfleisch nt
mutual ['mjuːtjʊəl] adj gegenseitig; **by ~ consent** in
gegenseitigem Einvernehmen
my [maɪ] adj mein; **I've hurt
~ leg** ich habe mir das Bein
verletzt

Myanmar ['maɪænmaː] n
Myanmar nt
myself [maɪ'self] pron (reflexive)
mich akk, mir dat; **I've hurt ~** ich
habe mich verletzt; **I've bought
~ a flat** ich habe mir eine
Wohnung gekauft; **I need it for
~** ich brauche es für mich (selbst);
(emphatic) **I did it ~** ich habe es
selbst gemacht; (all) **by ~** allein
mysterious [mɪ'stɪərɪəs] adj
geheimnisvoll, mysteriös;
(inexplicable) rätselhaft; **mystery**
['mɪstərɪ] n Geheimnis nt; (puzzle)
Rätsel nt; **it's a ~ to me** es ist mir
schleierhaft; **mystify** ['mɪstɪfaɪ]
vt verblüffen
myth [mɪθ] n Mythos m; (fig:
untrue story) Märchen nt; **mythical**
adj mythisch; (fig: untrue)
erfunden; **mythology**
[mɪ'θɒlədʒɪ] n Mythologie f

n

abbr = **north** N

nag [næg] *vt, vi* herumnörgeln (*sb* an jdm); **nagging** *n* Nörgelei *f*

nail [neɪl] *n* Nagel *m* ▷ *vt* nageln (*to* an); **nail down** *vt* festnageln; **nailbrush** *n* Nagelbürste *f*; **nail clippers** *npl* Nagelknipser *m*; **nailfile** *n* Nagelfeile *f*; **nail polish** *n* Nagellack *m*; **nail polish remover** *n* Nagellackentferner *m*; **nail scissors** *npl* Nagelschere *f*; **nail varnish** *n* Nagellack *m*

naive [naɪˈiːv] *adj* naiv

naked [ˈneɪkɪd] *adj* nackt

name [neɪm] *n* Name *m*; **his ~ is ...** er heißt ...; **what's your ~?** wie heißen Sie?; (*reputation*) **to have a good/bad ~** einen guten/schlechten Ruf haben ▷ *vt* nennen (*after* nach); (*sth new*) benennen; (*nominate*) ernennen (*as* als/zu); **a boy ~d ...** ein Junge

namens ...; **namely** *adv* nämlich; **name plate** *n* Namensschild *nt*

nan bread [ˈnɑːnˈbred] *n* (*warm serviertes*) *indisches Fladenbrot*

nanny [ˈnænɪ] *n* Kindermädchen *nt*

nap [næp] *n*: **to have/take a ~** ein Nickerchen machen

napkin [ˈnæpkɪn] *n* (*at table*) Serviette *f*

Naples [ˈneɪplz] *n* Neapel *nt*

nappy [ˈnæpɪ] *n* (Brit) Windel *f*

narcotic [nɑːˈkɒtɪk] *n* Rauschgift *nt*

narrate [nəˈreɪt] *vt* erzählen; **narration** [nəˈreɪʃən] , **narrative** [ˈnærətɪv] *n* Erzählung *f*; **narrator** [nəˈreɪtə*] *n* Erzähler(in) *m(f)*

narrow [ˈnærəʊ] *adj* eng, schmal; (*victory, majority*) knapp; **to have a ~ escape** mit knapper Not davonkommen ▷ *vi* sich verengen; **narrow down** *vt* einschränken (*to sth* auf etw *akk*); **narrow-minded** *adj* engstirnig

nasty [ˈnɑːstɪ] *adj* ekelhaft; (*person*) fies; (*remark*) gehässig; (*accident, wound etc*) schlimm

nation [ˈneɪʃən] *n* Nation *f*; **national** [ˈnæʃənl] *adj* national; **~ anthem** Nationalhymne *f*; **National Health Service** (Brit) staatlicher Gesundheitsdienst; **~ insurance** (Brit) Sozialversicherung *f*; **~ park** Nationalpark *m*; **~ service** Wehrdienst *m*; **~ socialism** (Hist) Nationalsozialismus *m* ▷ *n* Staatsbürger(in) *m(f)*

● **NATIONAL TRUST**
●
● Der **National Trust** ist ein 1895
● gegründeter Natur- und
● Denkmalschutzverband in
● Großbritannien, der Gebäude
● und Gelände von besonderem

- historischen oder ästhetischen
- Interesse erhält und der
- Öffentlichkeit zugänglich
- macht.

nationality [næʃ'nælɪtɪ] *n*
Staatsangehörigkeit *f*,
Nationalität *f*; **nationalize**
['næʃnəlaɪz] *vt* verstaatlichen;
nationwide *adj, adv* landesweit
native ['neɪtɪv] *adj* einheimisch;
(*inborn*) angeboren, natürlich;
Native American Indianer(in)
m(f); **~ country** Heimatland *nt*; **a**
~ German ein gebürtiger
Deutscher, eine gebürtige
Deutsche; **~ language**
Muttersprache *f*; **~ speaker**
Muttersprachler(in) *m(f)* ▷ *n*
Einheimische(r) *mf*; (*in colonial
context*) Eingeborene(r) *mf*
nativity play [nə'tɪvətɪpleɪ] *n*
Krippenspiel *nt*
NATO ['neɪtəʊ] *acr* = **North**
Atlantic Treaty Organization
Nato *f*
natural ['nætʃrəl] *adj* natürlich;
(*law, science, forces etc*) Natur-;
(*inborn*) angeboren; **~ gas** Erdgas
nt; **~ resources** Bodenschätze *pl*;
naturally *adv* natürlich; (*by
nature*) von Natur aus; **it comes**
~ to her es fällt ihr leicht
nature ['neɪtʃə°] *n* Natur *f*;
(*type*) Art *f*; **it is not in my ~** es
entspricht nicht meiner Art;
by ~ von Natur aus; **nature
reserve** *n* Naturschutzgebiet *nt*
naughty ['nɔːtɪ] *adj* (*child*)
ungezogen; (*cheeky*) frech
nausea ['nɔːsɪə] *n* Übelkeit *f*
nautical ['nɔːtɪkəl] *adj* nautisch;
~ mile Seemeile *f*
nave [neɪv] *n* Hauptschiff *nt*
navel ['neɪvl] *n* Nabel *m*
navigate ['nævɪgeɪt] *vi* navi-
gieren; (*in car*) lotsen, dirigieren;

navigation [nævɪ'geɪʃən] *n*
Navigation *f*; (*in car*) Lotsen *nt*
navy ['neɪvɪ] *n* Marine *f*; **~ blue**
Marineblau *nt*
Nazi ['nɑːtsɪ] *n* Nazi *m*
NB *abbr* = **nota bene** NB
NE *abbr* = **northeast** NO
near [nɪə°] *adj* nahe; **in the**
~ future in nächster Zukunft; **that**
was a ~ miss (*o thing*) das war
knapp; (*with price*) **... or ~est offer**
Verhandlungsbasis ... ▷ *adv* in der
Nähe; **so ~** so nahe; **come ~er**
näher kommen; (*event*) näher
rücken ▷ *prep*: **~ (to)** (*space*) nahe
an +*dat*; (*vicinity*) in der Nähe +*gen*;
~ the sea nahe am Meer; **~ the
station** in der Nähe des Bahnhofs,
in Bahnhofsnähe; **nearby** *adj*
nahe gelegen ▷ *adv* in der Nähe;
nearly *adv* fast; **nearside** *n*
(*Auto*) Beifahrerseite *f*;
near-sighted *adj* kurzsichtig
neat [niːt] *adj* ordentlich; (*work,
writing*) sauber; (*undiluted*) pur
necessarily [nesə'serəlɪ] *adv*
notwendigerweise; **not ~** nicht
unbedingt; **necessary** ['nesəsərɪ]
adj notwendig, nötig; **it's ~ to ...**
man muss ...; **it's not ~ for him to
come** er braucht nicht
mitzukommen; **necessity**
[nɪ'sesɪtɪ] *n* Notwendigkeit *f*; **the
bare necessities** das absolut
Notwendigste; **there is no ~ to ...**
man braucht nicht (zu) ..., man
muss nicht ...
neck [nek] *n* Hals *m*; (*size*)
Halsweite *f*; **back of the ~** Nacken
m; **necklace** ['neklɪs] *n*
Halskette *f*; **necktie** *n* (*US*)
Krawatte *f*
nectarine ['nektərɪn] *n* Nektarine *f*
née [neɪ] *adj* geborene
need [niːd] *n* (*requirement*)
Bedürfnis *nt* (*for* für); (*necessity*)

Notwendigkeit f; (poverty) Not f; **to be in ~ of sth** etw brauchen; **if ~(s) be** wenn nötig; **there is no ~ to ...** man braucht nicht (zu) ..., man muss nicht ... ▷ vt brauchen; **I ~ to speak to you** ich muss mit dir reden; **you ~n't go** du brauchst nicht (zu) gehen, du musst nicht gehen

needle ['niːdl] n Nadel f

needless, needlessly ['niːdlɪs, -lɪ] adj, adv unnötig; **~ to say** selbstverständlich

needy ['niːdɪ] adj bedürftig

negative ['negətɪv] n (Ling) Verneinung f; (Foto) Negativ nt ▷ adj negativ; (answer) verneinend

neglect [nɪ'glekt] n Vernachlässigung f ▷ vt vernachlässigen; **to ~ to do sth** es versäumen, etw zu tun; **negligence** ['neglɪdʒəns] n Nachlässigkeit f; **negligent** adj nachlässig

negligible ['neglɪdʒəbl] adj unbedeutend; (amount) geringfügig

negotiate [nɪ'gəʊʃɪeɪt] vi verhandeln; **negotiation** [nɪgəʊʃɪ'eɪʃən] n Verhandlung f

neigh [neɪ] vi (horse) wiehern

neighbor (US), **neighbour** ['neɪbə*] n Nachbar(in) m(f); **neighbo(u)rhood** n Nachbarschaft f; **neighbo(u)ring** adj benachbart

neither ['naɪðə*] adj, pron keine(r, s) von beiden; **~ of you/us** keiner von euch/uns beiden ▷ adv: **~ ... nor ...** weder ... noch ... ▷ conj: **I'm not going - ~ am I** ich gehe nicht - ich auch nicht

neon ['niːɒn] n Neon nt; **~ sign** (advertisement) Leuchtreklame f

nephew ['nefjuː] n Neffe m

nerd [nɜːv] n (fam) Schwachkopf m; **he's a real computer ~** er ist ein totaler Computerfreak

nerve [nɜːv] n Nerv m; **he gets on my ~s** er geht mir auf die Nerven; (courage) **to keep/lose one's ~** die Nerven behalten/verlieren; (cheek) **to have the ~ to do sth** die Frechheit besitzen, etw zu tun; **nerve-racking** adj nervenaufreibend; **nervous** ['nɜːvəs] adj (apprehensive) ängstlich; (on edge) nervös; **nervous breakdown** n Nervenzusammenbruch m

nest [nest] n Nest nt ▷ vi nisten

net [net] n Netz nt; **the Net** (Internet) das Internet; **on the ~** im Netz ▷ adj (price, weight) Netto-; **~ profit** Reingewinn m; **netball** n Netzball m

Netherlands ['neðələndz] npl: **the ~** die Niederlande pl

nettle ['netl] n Nessel f

network ['netwɜːk] n Netz nt; (TV, Radio) Sendenetz nt; (Inform) Netzwerk nt; **networking** n Networking n (das Knüpfen und Pflegen von Kontakten, die dem beruflichen Fortkommen dienen)

neurosis [njʊə'rəʊsɪs] n Neurose f; **neurotic** [njʊə'rɒtɪk] adj neurotisch

neuter ['njuːtə*] adj (Bio) geschlechtslos; (Ling) sächlich

neutral ['njuːtrəl] adj neutral ▷ n (gear in car) Leerlauf m

never ['nevə*] adv nie(mals); **~ before** noch nie; **~ mind** macht nichts!; **never-ending** adj endlos; **nevertheless** [nevəðə'les] adv trotzdem

new [njuː] adj neu; **this is all ~ to me** das ist für mich noch ungewohnt; **newcomer** n Neuankömmling m; (in job, subject) Neuling m

New England [njuː'ɪŋglənd] n Neuengland nt

Newfoundland ['nju:fəndlənd] *n* Neufundland *nt*

newly ['nju:lɪ] *adv* neu; **~ made** (*cake*) frisch gebacken; **newly-weds** *npl* Frischvermählte *pl*; **new moon** *n* Neumond *m*

news [nju:z] *nsing* (*item of ~*) Nachricht *f*; (*Radio, TV*) Nachrichten *pl*; **good ~** ein erfreuliche Nachricht; **what's the ~?** was gibt's Neues?; **have you heard the ~?** hast du das Neueste gehört?; **that's ~ to me** das ist mir neu; **newsagent, news dealer** (*US*) *n* Zeitungshändler(in) *m(f)*; **news bulletin** *n* Nachrichtensendung *f*; **news flash** *n* Kurzmeldung *f*; **newsgroup** *n* (*Inform*) Diskussionsforum *nt*, Newsgroup *f*; **newsletter** *n* Mitteilungsblatt *nt*; **newspaper** ['nju:speɪpə*] *n* Zeitung *f*

New Year ['nju:'jɪə*] *n* das neue Jahr; **Happy ~** (ein) frohes Neues Jahr!; (*toast*) Prosit Neujahr!; **~'s Day** Neujahr *nt*, Neujahrstag *m*; **~'s Eve** Silvesterabend *m*; **~'s resolution** *guter Vorsatz fürs neue Jahr*

New York [nju:'jɔ:k] *n* New York *nt*

New Zealand [nju:'zi:lənd] *n* Neuseeland *nt* ▷ *adj* neuseeländisch; **New Zealander** *n* Neuseeländer(in) *m(f)*

next [nekst] *adj* nächste(r, s); **the week after ~** übernächste Woche; **~ time I see him** wenn ich ihn das nächste Mal sehe; **you're ~** du bist jetzt dran ▷ *adv* als Nächstes; (*then*) dann, darauf; **~ to** neben +*dat*; **~ to last** vorletzte(r, s); **~ to impossible** nahezu unmöglich; **the ~ best thing** das Nächstbeste; **~ door** nebenan

NHS *abbr* = **National Health Service**

Niagara Falls [naɪ'ægrə'fɔ:lz] *npl* Niagarafälle *pl*

nibble ['nɪbl] *vt* knabbern an +*dat*; **nibbles** *npl* Knabberzeug *nt*

Nicaragua [nɪkə'rægjʊə] *n* Nicaragua *nt*

nice [naɪs] *adj* nett, sympathisch; (*taste, food, drink*) gut; (*weather*) schön; **~ and ...** schön ...; **be ~ to him** sei nett zu ihm; **have a ~ day** (*US*) schönen Tag noch!; **nicely** *adv* nett; (*well*) gut; **that'll do ~** das genügt vollauf

nick [nɪk] *vt* (*fam: steal*) klauen; (*capture*) schnappen

nickel ['nɪkl] *n* (*Chem*) Nickel *nt*; (*US: coin*) Nickel *m*

nickname ['nɪkneɪm] *n* Spitzname *m*

nicotine ['nɪkəti:n] *n* Nikotin *nt*; **nicotine patch** *n* Nikotinpflaster *nt*

niece [ni:s] *n* Nichte *f*

Nigeria [naɪ'dʒɪərɪə] *n* Nigeria *nt*

night [naɪt] *n* Nacht *f*; (*before bed*) Abend *m*; **good ~** gute Nacht!; **at** (*o by*) **~** nachts; **to have an early ~** früh schlafen gehen; **nightcap** *n* Schlummertrunk *m*; **nightclub** *n* Nachtklub *m*; **nightdress** *n* Nachthemd *nt*; **nightie** ['naɪtɪ] *n* (*fam*) Nachthemd *nt*

nightingale ['naɪtɪŋgeɪl] *n* Nachtigall *f*

night life ['naɪtlaɪf] *n* Nachtleben *nt*; **nightly** *adv* (*every evening*) jeden Abend; (*every night*) jede Nacht; **nightmare** ['naɪtmεə*] *n* Albtraum *m*; **nighttime** *n* Nacht *f*; **at ~** nachts

nil [nɪl] *n* (*Sport*) null

Nile [naɪl] *n* Nil *m*

nine [naɪn] *num* neun; **~ times out of ten** so gut wie immer ▷ *n* (*a. bus etc*) Neun *f*; *see also* **eight**; **nineteen** [naɪn'ti:n] *num*

neunzehn ▷ n (a. bus etc)
Neunzehn f; see also **eight**;
nineteenth adj neunzehnte(r, s);
see also **eighth**; **ninetieth**
['naɪntɪəθ] adj neunzigste(r, s);
see also **eighth**; **ninety** ['naɪntɪ]
num neunzig ▷ n Neunzig f; see
also **eight**; **ninth** [naɪnθ] adj
neunte(r, s) ▷ n (fraction) Neuntel
nt; see also **eighth**

nipple ['nɪpl] n Brustwarze f
nitrogen ['naɪtrədʒən] n Stick-
stoff m

KEYWORD

no [nəʊ] (pl **noes**) adv (opposite of
yes) nein; **to answer no** (to
question) mit Nein antworten; (to
request) Nein o nein sagen; **no
thank you** nein, danke
▷ adj (not any) kein(e); **I have no
money/time** ich habe kein
Geld/keine Zeit; **"no smoking"**
„Rauchen verboten"
▷ n Nein nt; (no vote) Neinstimme f

nobility [nəʊ'bɪlɪtɪ] n Adel m;
noble ['nəʊbl] adj (rank) adlig;
(quality) edel ▷ n Adlige(r)
mf
nobody ['nəʊbədɪ] pron niemand; (emphatic) keiner; **~ knows**
keiner weiß es; **~ else** sonst
niemand, kein anderer ▷ n
Niemand m
no-claims bonus
[nəʊ'kleɪmzbəʊnəs] n Schadenfreiheitsrabatt m
nod [nɒd] vi, vt nicken; **nod off** vi
einnicken
noise [nɔɪz] n (loud) Lärm m;
(sound) Geräusch nt; **noisy** adj
laut; (crowd) lärmend
nominate ['nɒmɪneɪt] vt (in
election) aufstellen; (appoint)
ernennen

nominative ['nɒmɪnətɪv] n
(Ling) Nominativ m
nominee [nɒmɪ'niː] n Kandi-
dat(in) m(f)
non- [nɒn] pref Nicht-; (with adj)
nicht-, un-; **non-alcoholic** adj
alkoholfrei
none [nʌn] pron keine(r, s); **~ of
them** keiner von ihnen; **~ of it is
any use** nichts davon ist
brauchbar; **there are ~ left** es sind
keine mehr da; (with comparative)
to be ~ the wiser auch nicht
schlauer sein; **I was ~ the worse
for it** es hat mir nichts geschadet
nonentity [nɒ'nentɪtɪ] n Null
f
nonetheless [nʌnðə'les] adv
nichtsdestoweniger, dennoch
non-event n Reinfall m;
non-existent adj nicht
vorhanden; **non-fiction** n
Sachbücher pl; **non-iron** adj
bügelfrei; **non-polluting** adj
schadstofffrei; **non-resident** n:
"open to ~s" „auch für
Nichthotelgäste"; **non-returnable**
adj: **~ bottle** Einwegflasche f
nonsense ['nɒnsəns] n Unsinn
m; **don't talk ~** red keinen Unsinn
non-smoker [nɒn'sməʊkə°] n
Nichtraucher(in) m(f);
non-smoking adj Nichtraucher-;
~ area Nichtraucherbereich m;
nonstop adj (train) durchgehend;
(flight) Nonstop- ▷ adv (talk)
ununterbrochen; (travel) ohne
Unterbrechung; (fly) ohne
Zwischenlandung; **non-violent**
adj gewaltfrei
noodles ['nuːdlz] npl Nudeln pl
noon [nuːn] n Mittag m; **at ~** um
12 Uhr mittags
no one ['nəʊwʌn] pron
niemand; (emphatic) keiner; **~ else**
sonst niemand, kein anderer
nor [nɔː] conj: **neither ... ~ ...**

weder ... noch ...; **I don't smoke,
~ does he** ich rauche nicht, er
auch nicht
norm [nɔːm] n Norm f
normal ['nɔːməl] adj normal; **to
get back to ~** sich wieder
normalisieren; **normally** adv
(usually) normalerweise
north [nɔːθ] n Norden m; **to the
~ of** nördlich von ▷ adv (go, face)
nach Norden ▷ adj Nord-; **~ wind**
Nordwind m; **North America** n
Nordamerika nt; **northbound** adj
(in) Richtung Norden; **northeast**
n Nordosten m; **to the ~ of**
nordöstlich von ▷ adv (go, face)
nach Nordosten ▷ adj Nordost-;
northern ['nɔːðən] adj nördlich;
~ France Nordfrankreich nt;
Northern Ireland n Nordirland
nt; **North Pole** n Nordpol m;
North Sea n Nordsee f;
northwards adv nach Norden;
northwest n Nordwesten m; **to
the ~ of** nordwestlich von ▷ adv
(go, face) nach Nordwesten ▷ adj
Nordwest-
Norway ['nɔːweɪ] n Norwegen
nt; **Norwegian** [nɔːˈwiːdʒən] adj
norwegisch ▷ n (person)
Norweger(in) m(f); (language)
Norwegisch nt
nos. abbr = **numbers** Nr.
nose [nəʊz] n Nase f; **nose
around** vi herumschnüffeln;
nosebleed n Nasenbluten nt;
nose-dive n Sturzflug m; **to take
a ~** abstürzen
nosey ['nəʊzɪ] see **nosy**
nostalgia [nɒˈstældʒɪə] n Nos-
talgie f (for nach); **nostalgic** adj
nostalgisch
nostril ['nɒstrɪl] n Nasenloch nt
nosy ['nəʊzɪ] adj neugierig
not [nɒt] adv nicht; **~ a** kein;
~ one of them kein einziger von
ihnen; **he is ~ an expert** er ist kein

Experte; **I told him ~ to** (**do it**) ich
sagte ihm, er solle es nicht tun;
~ at all überhaupt nicht,
keineswegs; (don't mention it) gern
geschehen; **~ yet** noch nicht
notable ['nəʊtəbl] adj bemerkenswert; **note** [nəʊt] n (written)
Notiz f; (short letter) paar Zeilen pl;
(on scrap of paper) Zettel m;
(comment in book etc) Anmerkung f;
(bank~) Schein m; (Mus: sign) Note
f; (sound) Ton m; **to make a ~ of
sth** sich dat etw notieren; **~s** (of
lecture etc) Aufzeichnungen pl; **to
take ~s** sich dat Notizen machen
(of über +akk) ▷ vt (notice)
bemerken (that dass); (write down)
notieren; **notebook** n Notizbuch
nt; (Inform) Notebook nt; **notepad**
n Notizblock m; **notepaper** n
Briefpapier nt
nothing ['nʌθɪŋ] n nichts; **~
but ...** lauter ...; **for ~** umsonst; **he
thinks ~ of it** er macht sich nichts
daraus
notice ['nəʊtɪs] n (announcement)
Bekanntmachung f; (on ~ board)
Anschlag m; (attention) Beachtung
f; (advance warning) Ankündigung
f; (to leave job, flat etc) Kündigung f;
at short ~ kurzfristig; **until
further ~** bis auf weiteres; **to give
sb ~** jdm kündigen; **to hand in
one's ~** kündigen; **to take (no)
~ of (sth)** etw (nicht) beachten;
take no ~ kümmere dich nicht
darum! ▷ vt bemerken;
noticeable adj erkennbar;
(visible) sichtbar; **to be ~** auffallen;
notice board n Anschlagtafel f
notification [nəʊtɪfɪˈkeɪʃən] n
Benachrichtigung f (of von); **notify**
['nəʊtɪfaɪ] vt benachrichtigen (of
von)
notion ['nəʊʃən] n Idee f
notorious [nəʊˈtɔːrɪəs] adj
berüchtigt

nought [nɔːt] n Null f
noun [naʊn] n Substantiv nt
nourish ['nʌrɪʃ] vt nähren;
 nourishing adj nahrhaft;
 nourishment n Nahrung f
novel ['nɒvəl] n Roman m ▷ adj
 neuartig; **novelist** n
 Schriftsteller(in) m(f); **novelty** n
 Neuheit f
November [nəʊ'vembə*] n
 November m; see also **September**
novice ['nɒvɪs] n Neuling m
now [naʊ] adv (at the moment)
 jetzt; (introductory phrase) also;
 right ~ jetzt gleich; **just ~** gerade;
 by ~ inzwischen; **from ~ on** ab
 jetzt; **~ and again** (o **then**) ab und
 zu; **nowadays** adv heutzutage
nowhere ['nəʊweə*] adv nirgends; **we're getting ~** wir
 kommen nicht weiter; **~ near**
 noch lange nicht
nozzle ['nɒzl] n Düse f
nuclear ['njuːklɪə*] adj (energy
 etc) Kern-; **~ power station**
 Kernkraftwerk nt; **nuclear waste**
 n Atommüll m
nude [njuːd] adj nackt ▷ n (person) Nackte(r) mf; (painting etc) Akt
 m
nudge [nʌdʒ] vt stupsen; **nudist**
 ['njuːdɪst] n Nudist(in) m(f),
 FKK-Anhänger(in) m(f); **nudist
 beach** n FKK-Strand m
nuisance ['njuːsns] n Ärgernis
 nt; (person) Plage f; **what a ~** wie
 ärgerlich!
nuke [njuːk] (US fam) n (bomb)
 Atombombe f ▷ vt eine
 Atombombe werfen auf +akk
numb [nʌm] adj taub, gefühllos
 ▷ vt betäuben
number ['nʌmbə*] n Nummer f;
 (Math) Zahl f; (quantity) (An)zahl f;
 in small/large ~s in
 kleinen/großen Mengen; **a ~ of
 times** mehrmals ▷ vt (give a

number to) nummerieren; (count)
 zählen (among zu); **his days are
 ~ed** seine Tage sind gezählt;
 number plate n (Brit Auto)
 Nummernschild nt
numeral ['njuːmərəl] n Ziffer f;
 numerical [njuː'merɪkəl] adj
 numerisch; (superiority)
 zahlenmäßig; **numerous**
 ['njuːmərəs] adj zahlreich
nun [nʌn] n Nonne f
Nuremberg ['njʊərəmbɜːg] n
 Nürnberg m
nurse [nɜːs] n Krankenschwester
 f; (male ~) Krankenpfleger m ▷ vt
 (patient) pflegen; (baby) stillen;
 nursery n Kinderzimmer nt; (for
 plants) Gärtnerei f; (tree)
 Baumschule f; **nursery rhyme** n
 Kinderreim m; **nursery school** n
 Kindergarten m; **~ teacher**
 Kindergärtner(in) m(f),
 Erzieher(in) m(f); **nursing** n
 (profession) Krankenpflege f;
 ~ home Privatklinik f
nut [nʌt] n Nuss f; (Tech: for bolt)
 Mutter f; **nutcase** n (fam)
 Spinner(in) m(f); **nutcracker** n,
 nutcrackers npl Nussknacker m
nutmeg ['nʌtmeg] n Muskat m,
 Muskatnuss f
nutrient ['njuːtrɪənt] n Nährstoff
 m
nutrition [njuː'trɪʃən] n Ernährung f; **nutritious** [njuː'trɪʃəs]
 adj nahrhaft
nuts [nʌts] (fam) adj verrückt; **to
 be ~ about sth** nach etw verrückt
 sein ▷ npl (testicles) Eier pl
nutshell ['nʌtʃel] n Nussschale f;
 in a ~ kurz gesagt
nutter ['nʌtə*] n (fam)
 Spinner(in) m(f); **nutty** ['nʌtɪ]
 adj (fam) verrückt
NW abbr = **northwest** NW
nylon® ['naɪlɒn] n Nylon® nt
 ▷ adj Nylon-

O [əʊ] *n* (*Tel*) Null *f*

oak [əʊk] *n* Eiche *f* ▷ *adj* Eichen-

OAP *abbr* = **old-age pensioner** Rentner(in) *m(f)*

oar [ɔː*] *n* Ruder *nt*

oasis [əʊ'eɪsɪs] (*pl* **oases**) *n* Oase *f*

oatcake ['əʊtkeɪk] *n* Haferkeks *m*

oath [əʊθ] *n* (*statement*) Eid *m*

oats [əʊts] *npl* Hafer *m*; (*Gastr*) Haferflocken *pl*

obedience [ə'biːdɪəns] *n* Gehorsam *m*; **obedient** *adj* gehorsam; **obey** [ə'beɪ] *vt, vi* gehorchen +*dat*

object ['ɒbdʒekt] *n* Gegenstand *m*; (*abstract*) Objekt *nt*; (*purpose*) Ziel *nt* ▷ [ə'bdʒekt] *vi* dagegen sein; (*raise objection*) Einwände erheben (*to* gegen); (*morally*) Anstoß nehmen (*to* an +*dat*); **do you ~ to my smoking?** haben Sie etwas dagegen, wenn ich rauche?; **objection** [əb'dʒekʃən] *n* Einwand *m*

objective [əb'dʒektɪv] *n* Ziel *nt* ▷ *adj* objektiv; **objectivity** [ɒbdʒek'tɪvɪtɪ] *n* Objektivität *f*

obligation [ɒblɪ'geɪʃən] *n* (*duty*) Pflicht *f*; (*commitment*) Verpflichtung *f*; **no ~** unverbindlich; **obligatory** [ə'blɪɡətərɪ] *adj* obligatorisch; **oblige** [ə'blaɪdʒ] *vt*: **to ~ sb to do sth** jdn (dazu) zwingen, etw zu tun; **he felt ~d to accept the offer** er fühlte sich verpflichtet, das Angebot anzunehmen

oblique [ə'bliːk] *adj* schräg; (*angle*) schief

oboe ['əʊbəʊ] *n* Oboe *f*

obscene [əb'siːn] *adj* obszön

obscure [əb'skjʊə*] *adj* unklar; (*unknown*) unbekannt

observant [əb'zɜːvənt] *adj* aufmerksam; **observation** [ɒbzə'veɪʃən] *n* (*watching*) Beobachtung *f*; (*remark*) Bemerkung *f*; **observe** [əb'zɜːv] *vt* (*notice*) bemerken; (*watch*) beobachten; (*customs*) einhalten

obsessed [əb'sest] *adj* besessen (*with an idea etc* von einem Gedanken etc); **obsession** [əb'seʃən] *n* Manie *f*

obsolete ['ɒbsəliːt] *adj* veraltet

obstacle ['ɒbstəkl] *n* Hindernis *nt* (*to* für); **to be an ~ to sth** einer Sache im Weg stehen

obstinate ['ɒbstɪnət] *adj* hartnäckig

obstruct [əb'strʌkt] *vt* versperren; (*pipe*) verstopfen; (*hinder*) behindern, aufhalten; **obstruction** [əb'strʌkʃən] *n* Blockierung *f*; (*of pipe*) Verstopfung *f*; (*obstacle*) Hindernis *nt*

obtain [əb'teɪn] *vt* erhalten; **obtainable** *adj* erhältlich

obvious [ˈɒbvɪəs] *adj* offensichtlich; **it was ~ to me that ...** es war mir klar, dass ...; **obviously** *adj* offensichtlich

occasion [əˈkeɪʒən] *n* Gelegenheit *f*; (*special event*) (großes) Ereignis *nt*; **on the ~ of** anlässlich +*gen*; **special ~** besonderer Anlass; **occasional, occasionally** *adj, adv* gelegentlich

occupant [ˈɒkjʊpənt] *n* (*of house*) Bewohner(in) *m(f)*; (*of vehicle*) Insasse *m*, Insassin *f*; **occupation** [ɒkjʊˈpeɪʃən] *n* Beruf *m*; (*pastime*) Beschäftigung *f*; (*of country etc*) Besetzung *f*; **occupied** *adj* (*country, seat, toilet*) besetzt; (*person*) beschäftigt; **to keep sb/oneself ~** jdn/sich beschäftigen; **occupy** [ˈɒkjʊpaɪ] *vt* (*country*) besetzen; (*time*) beanspruchen; (*mind, person*) beschäftigen

occur [əˈkɜː*] *vi* vorkommen; **~ to sb** jdm einfallen; **occurrence** [əˈkʌrəns] *n* (*event*) Ereignis *nt*; (*presence*) Vorkommen *nt*

ocean [ˈəʊʃən] *n* Ozean *m*; (*US: sea*) das Meer *nt*

o'clock [əˈklɒk] *adv*: **5 ~** 5 Uhr; **at 10 ~** um 10 Uhr

octagon [ˈɒktəgən] *n* Achteck *nt*

October [ɒkˈtəʊbə*] *n* Oktober *m*; *see also* **September**

octopus [ˈɒktəpəs] *n* Tintenfisch *m*

odd [ɒd] *adj* (*strange*) sonderbar; (*not even*) ungerade; (*one missing*) einzeln; **to be the ~ one out** nicht dazugehören; **~ jobs** Gelegenheitsarbeiten *pl*; **odds** *npl* Chancen *pl*; **against all ~** entgegen allen Erwartungen; **~ and ends** (*fam*) Kleinkram *pl*

odometer [əʊˈdɒmətə*] *n* (*US Auto*) Meilenzähler *m*

odor (*US*), **odour** [ˈəʊdə*] *n* Geruch *m*

KEYWORD

of [ɒv, əv] *prep* **1** von +*dat* ≈ use of gen; **the history of Germany** die Geschichte Deutschlands; **a friend of ours** ein Freund von uns; **a boy of 10** ein 10-jähriger Junge; **that was kind of you** das war sehr freundlich von Ihnen **2** (*expressing quantity, amount, dates etc*) **a kilo of flour** ein Kilo Mehl; **how much of this do you need?** wie viel brauchen Sie (davon)?; **there were 3 of them** (*people*) sie waren zu dritt; (*objects*) es gab 3 (davon); **a cup of tea/vase of flowers** eine Tasse Tee/Vase mit Blumen; **the 5th of July** der 5. Juli **3** (*from, out of*) aus; **a bridge made of wood** eine Holzbrücke, eine Brücke aus Holz

off [ɒf] *adv* (*away*) weg, fort; (*free*) frei; (*switch*) ausgeschaltet; (*milk*) sauer; **a mile ~** eine Meile entfernt; **I'll be ~ now** ich gehe jetzt; **to have the day/Monday ~** heute/Montag freihaben; **the lights are ~** die Lichter sind aus; **the concert is ~** das Konzert fällt aus; **I got 10 % ~** ich habe 10 % Nachlass bekommen ▷ *prep* (*away from*) von; **to jump/fall ~ the roof** vom Dach springen/fallen; **to get ~ the bus** aus dem Bus aussteigen; **he's ~ work/school** er hat frei/schulfrei; **to take £20 ~ the price** den Preis um 20 Pfund herabsetzen

offence [əˈfens] *n* (*crime*) Straftat *f*; (*minor*) Vergehen *nt*; (*to feelings*) Kränkung *f*; **to cause/take ~** Anstoß

erregen/nehmen; **offend** [ə'fend]
vt kränken; (*eye, ear*) beleidigen;
offender *n* Straffällige(r) *mf*;
offense (*US*) *see* **offence**;
offensive [ə'fensɪv] *adj* anstößig;
(*insulting*) beleidigend; (*smell*) übel,
abstoßend ▷ *n* (*Mil*) Offensive *f*

offer ['ɒfə*] *n* Angebot *nt*; **on
~** (*Comm*) im Angebot ▷ *vt*
anbieten (*to sb* jdm); (*money, a
chance etc*) bieten

offhand [ɒf'hænd] *adj* lässig
▷ *adv* (*say*) auf Anhieb

office ['ɒfɪs] *n* Büro *nt*; (*position*)
Amt *nt*; **doctor's ~** (*US*) Arztpraxis
f; **office block** *n* Bürogebäude *nt*;
office hours *npl* Dienstzeit *f*;
(*notice*) Geschäftszeiten *pl*; **officer**
['ɒfɪsə*] *n* (*Mil*) Offizier(in) *m(f)*;
(*official*) Polizeibeamte(r) *m*,
Polizeibeamtin *f*; **office worker**
['ɒfɪswɜːkə*] *n* Büroangestellte(r)
mf; **official** [ə'fɪʃəl] *adj* offiziell;
(*report etc*) amtlich; **~ language**
Amtssprache *f* ▷ *n* Beamte(r) *m*,
Beamtin *f*, Repräsentant(in)
m(f)

off-licence ['ɒflaɪsəns] *n* (*Brit*)
Wein- und Spirituosenhandlung *f*;
off-line *adj* (*Inform*) offline;
off-peak *adj* außerhalb der
Stoßzeiten; (*rate, ticket*) verbilligt;
off-putting *adj* abstoßend,
entmutigend, irritierend;
off-season *adj* außerhalb der
Saison

offshore ['ɒfʃɔː*] *adj* küstennah,
Küsten-; (*oil rig*) im Meer; **offside**
['ɒf'saɪd] *n* (*Auto*) Fahrerseite *f*;
(*Sport*) Abseits *nt*

often ['ɒfən] *adv* oft; **every so
~** von Zeit zu Zeit

oil [ɔɪl] *n* Öl *nt* ▷ *vt* ölen; **oil level**
n Ölstand *m*; **oil painting** *n*
Ölgemälde *nt*; **oil-rig** *n*
(Öl)bohrinsel *f*; **oil slick** *n*
Ölteppich *m*; **oil tanker** *n*

Öltanker *m*; (*truck*) Tankwagen *m*;
oily *adj* ölig; (*skin, hair*) fettig

ointment ['ɔɪntmənt] *n* Salbe *f*

OK, **okay** [əʊ'keɪ] *adj* (*fam*) okay,
in Ordnung; **that's ~ by** (*o* **with**)
me das ist mir recht

old [əʊld] *adj* alt; **old age** *n* Alter
nt; **~ pension** Rente *f*; **~ pensioner**
Rentner(in) *m(f)*; **old-fashioned**
adj altmodisch; **old people's
home** *n* Altersheim *nt*

olive ['ɒlɪv] *n* Olive *f*; **olive oil** *n*
Olivenöl *nt*

Olympic [əʊ'lɪmpɪk] *adj* olym-
pisch; **the ~ Games, the ~s** *pl* die
Olympischen Spiele *pl*, die
Olympiade

omelette ['ɒmlət] *n* Omelett *nt*

omission [əʊ'mɪʃən] *n* Auslas-
sung *f*; **omit** [əʊ'mɪt] *vt*
auslassen

O   **KEYWORD**

on [ɒn] *prep* **1** (*indicating position*)
auf +*dat*; (*with vb of motion*) auf
+*akk*; (*on vertical surface, part of
body*) an +*dat*; **it's on the table**
es ist auf dem Tisch; **she put the
book on the table** sie legte das
Buch auf den Tisch; **on the left**
links

2 (*indicating means, method,
condition etc*) **on foot** (*go, be*) zu
Fuß; **on the train/plane** (*go*) mit
dem Zug/Flugzeug; (*be*) im
Zug/Flugzeug; **on the
telephone/television** am
Telefon/im Fernsehen; **to be on
drugs** Drogen nehmen; **to be on
holiday/business** im Urlaub/auf
Geschäftsreise sein

3 (*referring to time*) **on Friday** (am)
Freitag; **on Fridays** freitags; **on
June 20th** am 20. Juni; **a week on
Friday** Freitag in einer Woche; **on
arrival he ...** als er ankam, ... er ...

4 (*about, concerning*) über +*akk*
▷ *adv* **1** (*referring to dress*) an; **she put her boots/hat on** sie zog ihre Stiefel an/setzte ihren Hut auf
2 (*further, continuously*) weiter; **to walk on** weitergehen
▷ *adj* **1** (*functioning, in operation: machine, TV, light*) an; (*tap*) aufgedreht; (*brakes*) angezogen; **is the meeting still on?** findet die Versammlung noch statt?; **there's a good film on** es läuft ein guter Film
2 that's not on! (*inf*) (*of behaviour*) das ist nicht drin!

once [wʌns] *adv* (*one time, in the past*) einmal; **at ~** sofort; (*at the same time*) gleichzeitig; **~ more** noch einmal; **for ~** ausnahmsweise (einmal); **~ in a while** ab und zu mal ▷ *conj* wenn ... einmal; **~ you've got used to it** sobald Sie sich daran gewöhnt haben

oncoming [ˈɒnkʌmɪŋ] *adj* entgegenkommend; **~ traffic** Gegenverkehr *m*

 KEYWORD

one [wʌn] *num* eins; (*with noun, referring back to noun*) ein/eine/ein; **it is one (o'clock)** es ist eins, es ist ein Uhr; **one hundred and fifty** einhundertfünfzig
▷ *adj* **1** (*sole*) einzige(r, s); **the one book which** das einzige Buch, welches
2 (*same*) derselbe/dieselbe/dasselbe; **they came in the one car** sie kamen alle in dem einen Auto
3 (*indef*) **one day I discovered ...** eines Tages bemerkte ich ...
▷ *pron* **1** eine(r, s); **do you have a red one?** haben Sie einen

roten/eine rote/ein rotes?; **this one** diese(r, s); **that one** der/die/das; **which one?** welche(r, s)?; **one by one** einzeln
2 one another einander; **do you two ever see one another?** seht ihr beide euch manchmal?
3 (*impers*) man; **one never knows** man kann nie wissen; **to cut one's finger** sich in den Finger schneiden

one-off *adj* einmalig ▷ *n*: **a ~** etwas Einmaliges; **one-parent family** *n* Einelternfamilie *f*; **one-piece** *adj* einteilig; **oneself** *pron* (*reflexive*) sich; **one-way** *adj*: **~ street** Einbahnstraße *f*; **~ ticket** (*US*) einfache Fahrkarte

onion [ˈʌnjən] *n* Zwiebel *f*

on-line [ˈɒnlaɪn] *adj* (*Inform*) online; **~ banking** Homebanking *nt*

only [ˈəʊnlɪ] *adv* nur; (*with time*) erst; **~ yesterday** erst gestern; **he's ~ four** er ist erst vier; **~ just arrived** gerade erst angekommen
▷ *adj* einzige(r, s); **~ child** Einzelkind *nt*

o.n.o. *abbr* = **or nearest offer** VB

onside [ɒnˈsaɪd] *adv* (*Sport*) nicht im Abseits

onto [ˈɒntʊ] *prep* auf +*akk*; (*vertical surface*) an +*akk*; **to be ~ sb** jdm auf die Schliche gekommen sein

onwards [ˈɒnwədz] *adv* voran, vorwärts; **from today ~** von heute an, ab heute

open [ˈəʊpən] *adj* offen; **in the ~ air** im Freien; **~ to the public** für die Öffentlichkeit zugänglich; **the shop is ~ all day** das Geschäft hat den ganzen Tag offen ▷ *vt* öffnen, aufmachen; (*meeting, account, new building*) eröffnen; (*road*) dem Verkehr übergeben ▷ *vi* (*door, window etc*) aufgehen, sich öffnen; (*shop, bank*) öffnen, aufmachen; (*begin*) anfangen (*with* mit); **open-air** *adj* Freiluft-; **open day** *n* Tag *m* der offenen Tür; **opening** *n* Öffnung *f*; (*beginning*) Anfang *m*; (*official, of exhibition etc*) Eröffnung *f*; (*opportunity*) Möglichkeit *f*; **~ hours** (*o* **times**) Öffnungszeiten *pl*; **openly** *adv* offen; **open-minded** *adj* aufgeschlossen; **open-plan** *adj*: **~ office** Großraumbüro *nt*

opera ['ɒpərə] *n* Oper *f*; **opera glasses** *npl* Opernglas *nt*; **opera house** *n* Oper *f*, Opernhaus *nt*; **opera singer** *n* Opernsänger(in) *m(f)*

operate ['ɒpəreɪt] *vt* (*machine*) bedienen; (*brakes, lights*) betätigen ▷ *vi* (*machine*) laufen; (*bus etc*) verkehren (*between* zwischen); **to ~** (**on sb**) (*Med*) (jdn) operieren; **operating theatre** *n* Operationssaal *m*; **operation** [ɒpə'reɪʃən] *n* (*of machine*) Bedienung *f*; (*functioning*) Funktionieren *nt*; (*Med*) Operation *f* (*on* an +*dat*); (*undertaking*) Unternehmen *nt*; **in ~** (*machine*) in Betrieb; **to have an ~** operiert werden (*for* wegen); **operator** ['ɒpəreɪtə*] *n*: **to phone the ~** die Vermittlung anrufen

opinion [ə'pɪnjən] *n* Meinung *f* (*on* zu); **in my ~** meiner Meinung nach

opponent [ə'pəʊnənt] *n* Gegner(in) *m(f)*

opportunity [ɒpə'tjuːnɪtɪ] *n* Gelegenheit *f*

oppose [ə'pəʊz] *vt* sich widersetzen +*dat*; (*idea*) ablehnen; **opposed** *adj*: **to be ~ to sth** gegen etw sein; **as ~ to** im

Gegensatz zu; **opposing** *adj* (*team*) gegnerisch; (*points of view*) entgegengesetzt

opposite ['ɒpəzɪt] *adj* (*house*) gegenüberliegend; (*direction*) entgegengesetzt; **the ~ sex** das andere Geschlecht ▷ *adv* gegenüber ▷ *prep* gegenüber +*dat*; **~ me** mir gegenüber ▷ *n* Gegenteil *nt*

opposition [ɒpə'zɪʃən] *n* Widerstand *m* (*to* gegen); (*Pol*) Opposition *f*

oppress [ə'pres] *vt* unterdrücken; **oppressive** *adj* (*heat*) drückend

opt [ɒpt] *vi*: **to ~ for sth** sich für etw entscheiden; **to ~ to do sth** sich entscheiden, etw zu tun

optician [ɒp'tɪʃən] *n* Optiker(in) *m(f)*

optimist ['ɒptɪmɪst] *n* Optimist(in) *m(f)*; **optimistic** [ɒptɪ'mɪstɪk] *adj* optimistisch

option ['ɒpʃən] *n* Möglichkeit *f*; (*Comm*) Option *f*; **to have no ~** keine Wahl haben; **optional** *adj* freiwillig; **~ extras** (*Auto*) Extras *pl*

or [ɔː*] *conj* oder; (*otherwise*) sonst; (*after neg*) noch; **hurry up, ~** (*else*) **we'll be late** beeil dich, sonst kommen wir zu spät

oral ['ɔːrəl] *adj* mündlich; **~ sex** Oralverkehr *m* ▷ *n* (*exam*) Mündliche(s) *nt*; **oral surgeon** *n* Kieferchirurg(in) *m(f)*

orange ['ɒrɪndʒ] *n* Orange *f* ▷ *adj* orangefarben; **orange juice** *n* Orangensaft *m*

orbit ['ɔːbɪt] *n* Umlaufbahn *f*; **to be out of ~** (*fam*) nicht zu erreichen sein ▷ *vt* umkreisen

orchard ['ɔːtʃəd] *n* Obstgarten *m*

orchestra ['ɔːkɪstrə] *n* Orchester *nt*; (*US Theat*) Parkett *nt*

orchid ['ɔːkɪd] *n* Orchidee *f*

ordeal [ɔːˈdiːl] *n* Tortur *f*;
(*emotional*) Qual *f*
order [ˈɔːdə*] *n* (*sequence*)
Reihenfolge *f*; (*good arrangement*)
Ordnung *f*; (*command*) Befehl *m*;
(*Jur*) Anordnung *f*; (*condition*)
Zustand *m*; (*Comm*) Bestellung *f*;
out of ~ (*not functioning*) außer
Betrieb; (*unsuitable*) nicht
angebracht; **in ~** (*items*) richtig
geordnet; (*all right*) in Ordnung; **in
~ to do sth** um etw zu tun ▷ *vt*
(*arrange*) ordnen; (*command*)
befehlen; **to ~ sb to do sth** jdm
befehlen, etw zu tun; (*food,
product*) bestellen; **order form** *n*
Bestellschein *m*
ordinary [ˈɔːdnrɪ] *adj* gewöhnlich, normal; (*average*)
durchschnittlich
ore [ɔː*] *n* Erz *nt*
organ [ˈɔːgən] *n* (*Mus*) Orgel *f*;
(*Anat*) Organ *nt*
organic [ɔːˈgænɪk] *adj* organisch;
(*farming, vegetables*) Bio-, Öko-;
~ farmer Biobauer *m*, Biobäuerin
f; **~ food** Biokost *f*
organization [ɔːgənaɪˈzeɪʃən] *n*
Organisation *f*; (*arrangement*)
Ordnung *f*; **organize** [ˈɔːgənaɪz]
vt organisieren; **organizer** *n*
(elektronisches) Notizbuch
orgasm [ˈɔːgæzəm] *n* Orgasmus
m
orgy [ˈɔːdʒɪ] *n* Orgie *f*
oriental [ɔːrɪˈentəl] *adj*
orientalisch
orientation [ˈɔːrɪenteɪʃən] *n*
Orientierung *f*
origin [ˈɒrɪdʒɪn] *n* Ursprung
m; (*of person*) Herkunft *f*;
original [əˈrɪdʒɪnl] *adj* (*first*)
ursprünglich; (*painting*) original;
(*idea*) originell ▷ *n* Original *nt*;
originality [ərɪdʒɪˈnælɪtɪ] *n*
Originalität *f*; **originally** *adv*
ursprünglich

Orkneys [ˈɔːknɪz] *npl*, **Orkney
Islands** *npl* Orkneyinseln *pl*
ornament [ˈɔːnəmənt] *n*
Schmuckgegenstand *m*;
ornamental [ɔːnəˈmentl] *adj*
dekorativ
orphan [ˈɔːfən] *n* Waise *f*,
Waisenkind *nt*; **orphanage**
[ˈɔːfənɪdʒ] *n* Waisenhaus *nt*
orthodox [ˈɔːθədɒks] *adj*
orthodox
orthopaedic, **orthopedic** (*US*)
[ɔːθəʊˈpiːdɪk] *adj* orthopädisch
ostentatious [ɒstenˈteɪʃəs] *adj*
protzig
ostrich [ˈɒstrɪtʃ] *n* (*Zool*) Strauß
m
other [ˈʌðə*] *adj*, *pron* andere(r,
s); **any ~ questions?** sonst noch
Fragen?; **the ~ day** neulich; **every
~ day** jeden zweiten Tag; **any
person ~ than him** alle außer ihm;
**someone/something or
~** irgendjemand/irgendetwas;
otherwise *adv* sonst; (*differently*)
anders
OTT *adj abbr* = **over the top**
übertrieben
otter [ˈɒtə*] *n* Otter *m*
ought [ɔːt] *vb aux* (*obligation*)
sollte; (*probability*) dürfte; (*stronger*)
müsste; **you ~ to do that** du
solltest/Sie sollten das tun; **he
~ to win** er müsste gewinnen;
that ~ to do das müsste reichen
ounce [aʊns] *n* Unze *f* (28,35 g)
our [aʊə*] *adj* unser; **ours** *pron*
unsere(r, s); **this is ~** das gehört
uns; **a friend of ~** ein Freund von
uns; **ourselves** *pron* (*reflexive*)
uns; **we enjoyed ~** wir haben uns
amüsiert; **we've got the house
to ~** wir haben das Haus für uns;
(*emphatic*) **we did it ~** wir haben
es selbst gemacht; (**all**) **by
~** allein
out [aʊt] *adv* hinaus/heraus; (*not*

indoors) draußen; (not at home)
nicht zu Hause; (not alight) aus;
(unconscious) bewusstlos;
(published) herausgekommen;
(results) bekannt gegeben; **have
you been ~ yet?** warst du/waren
Sie schon draußen?; **I was ~ when
they called** ich war nicht da, als
sie vorbeikamen; **to be ~ and
about** unterwegs sein; **the sun is
~** die Sonne scheint; **the fire is
~** das Feuer ist ausgegangen;
(wrong) **the calculation is (way)
~** die Kalkulation stimmt (ganz
und gar) nicht; **they're ~ to get
him** sie sind hinter ihm her ▷ vt
(fam) outen

outback ['aʊtbæk] n (in Australia)
the ~ das Hinterland

outboard ['aʊtbɔːd] adj: **~ motor**
Außenbordmotor m

outbreak ['aʊtbreɪk] n Ausbruch m

outburst ['aʊtbɜːst] n Ausbruch m

outcome ['aʊtkʌm] n Ergebnis
nt

outcry ['aʊtkraɪ] n (public protest)
Protestwelle f (against gegen)

outdo [aʊt'duː] irr vt übertreffen

outdoor ['aʊtdɔː*] adj Außen-;
(Sport) im Freien; **~ swimming
pool** Freibad nt; **outdoors**
[aʊt'dɔːz] adv draußen, im Freien

outer ['aʊtə*] adj äußere(r, s);
outer space n Weltraum m

outfit ['aʊtfɪt] n Ausrüstung f;
(clothes) Kleidung f

outgoing ['aʊtgəʊɪŋ] adj
kontaktfreudig

outgrow [aʊt'grəʊ] irr vt
(clothes) herauswachsen aus

outing ['aʊtɪŋ] n Ausflug m

outlet ['aʊtlet] n Auslass m,
Abfluss m; (US) Steckdose f; (shop)
Verkaufsstelle f

outline ['aʊtlaɪn] n Umriss m;
(summary) Abriss m

outlive [aʊt'lɪv] vt überleben

outlook ['aʊtlʊk] n Aussicht(en)
f(pl); (prospects) Aussichten pl;
(attitude) Einstellung f
(on zu)

outnumber [aʊt'nʌmbə*] vt
zahlenmäßig überlegen sein +dat;
~ed zahlenmäßig unterlegen

out of ['aʊtɒv] prep (motion,
motive, origin) aus; (position, away
from) außerhalb +gen;
~ danger/sight/breath außer
Gefahr/Sicht/Atem; **made ~ wood**
aus Holz gemacht; **we are ~ bread**
wir haben kein Brot mehr;
out-of-date adj veraltet;
out-of-the-way adj abgelegen

outpatient ['aʊtpeɪʃənt] n
ambulanter Patient, ambulante
Patientin

output ['aʊtpʊt] n Produktion f;
(of engine) Leistung f; (Inform)
Ausgabe f

outrage ['aʊtreɪdʒ] n (great
anger) Empörung f (at über);
(wicked deed) Schandtat f; (crime)
Verbrechen nt; (indecency) Skandal
m; **outrageous** [aʊt'reɪdʒəs] adj
unerhört; (clothes, behaviour etc)
unmöglich, schrill

outright ['aʊtraɪt] adv (killed)
sofort ▷ adj total; (denial) völlig;
(winner) unbestritten

outside [aʊt'saɪd] n Außenseite
f; **on the ~** außen ▷ adj äuße-
re(r, s), Außen-; (chance) sehr
gering ▷ adv außen; **to go ~** nach
draußen gehen ▷ prep außerhalb
+gen; **outsider** n Außenseiter(in)
m(f)

outskirts ['aʊtskɜːts] npl (of
town) Stadtrand m

outstanding [aʊt'stændɪŋ] adj
hervorragend; (debts etc)
ausstehend

outward ['aʊtwəd] adj äuß-
ere(r, s); **~ journey** Hinfahrt f;

outwardly *adv* nach außen hin;
outwards *adv* nach außen
oval ['əʊvəl] *adj* oval
ovary ['əʊvərɪ] *n* Eierstock *m*
ovation [əʊ'veɪʃən] *n* Ovation *f*,
Applaus *m*
oven ['ʌvn] *n* Backofen *m*; **oven
glove** *n* Topfhandschuh *m*;
ovenproof *adj* feuerfest;
oven-ready *adj* bratfertig
over ['əʊvə*] *prep* (*position*) über
+*dat*; (*motion*) über +*akk*; **they
spent a long time ~ it** sie haben
lange dazu gebraucht; **from all
~ England** aus ganz England;
~ £20 mehr als 20 Pfund; **~ the
phone/radio** am Telefon/im
Radio; **to talk ~ a glass of wine**
sich bei einem Glas Wein
unterhalten; **~ and above this**
darüber hinaus; **~ the summer**
während des Sommers ▷ *adv*
(*across*) hinüber/herüber; (*finished*)
vorbei; (*match, play etc*) zu Ende;
(*left*) übrig; (*more*) mehr;
~ there/in America da
drüben/drüben in Amerika; **~ to
you** du bist/Sie sind dran; **it's (all)
~ between us** es ist aus zwischen
uns; **~ and ~ again** immer wieder;
to start (all) ~ again noch einmal
von vorn anfangen; **children of 8
and ~** Kinder ab 8 Jahren
over- ['əʊvə*] *pref* über-
overall ['əʊvərɔːl] *n* (*Brit*) Kittel
m ▷ *adj* (*situation*) allgemein;
(*length*) Gesamt-; **~ majority**
absolute Mehrheit ▷ *adv*
insgesamt; **overalls** *npl* Overall
m
overboard ['əʊvəbɔːd] *adv* über
Bord
overbooked [əʊvə'bʊkt] *adj*
überbucht; **overbooking** *n*
Überbuchung *f*
overcharge [əʊvə'tʃɑːdʒ] *vt* zu
viel verlangen von

overcoat ['əʊvəkəʊt] *n* Wintermantel *m*
overcome [əʊvə'kʌm] *irr vt*
überwinden; **~ by sleep/emotion**
von Schlaf/Rührung übermannt;
we shall ~ wir werden siegen
overcooked [əʊvə'kʊkt] *adj*
verkocht; (*meat*) zu lange gebraten
overcrowded [əʊvə'kraʊdɪd]
adj überfüllt
overdo [əʊvə'duː] *irr vt* übertreiben; **overdone** *adj*
übertrieben; (*food*) zu lange
gekocht; (*meat*) zu lange gebraten
overdose ['əʊvədəʊs] *n* Über-
dosis *f*
overdraft ['əʊvədrɑːft] *n* Kon-
toüberziehung *f*; **overdrawn**
[əʊvə'drɔːn] *adj* überzogen
overdue [əʊvə'djuː] *adj*
überfällig
overestimate [əʊvər'estɪmeɪt]
vt überschätzen
overexpose [əʊvərɪks'pəʊz] *vt* (*Foto*)
überbelichten
overflow [əʊvə'fləʊ] *vi*
überlaufen
overhead ['əʊvəhed] *adj* (*Aviat*)
~ locker Gepäckfach *nt*;
~ projector Overheadprojektor *m*;
~ railway Hochbahn *f*
▷ [əʊvə'hed] *adv* oben;
overhead, (*Brit*) **overheads** *n*
(*Comm*) allgemeine
Geschäftskosten *pl*
overhear [əʊvə'hɪə*] *irr vt* zufällig
mit anhören
overheat [əʊvə'hiːt] *vi* (*engine*)
heiß laufen
overjoyed [əʊvə'dʒɔɪd] *adj*
überglücklich (*at* über)
overland ['əʊvəlænd] *adj* Über-
land- ▷ [əʊvə'lænd] *adv* (*travel*)
über Land
overlap [əʊvə'læp] *vi* (*dates etc*)
sich überschneiden; (*objects*) sich
teilweise decken

overload [əʊvə'ləʊd] *vt* überladen

overlook [əʊvə'lʊk] *vt* (*view from above*) überblicken; (*not notice*) übersehen; (*pardon*) hinwegsehen über +*akk*

overnight [əʊvə'naɪt] *adj* (*journey, train*) Nacht-; **~ bag** Reisetasche *f*; **~ stay** Übernachtung *f* ▷ *adv* über Nacht

overpass ['əʊvəpɑːs] *n* Überführung *f*

overpay [əʊvə'peɪ] *vt* überbezahlen

overrule [əʊvə'ruːl] *vt* verwerfen; (*decision*) aufheben

overseas [əʊvə'siːz] *adj* Übersee-; ausländisch; (*fam*) Auslands- ▷ *adv* (*go*) nach Übersee; (*live, work*) in Übersee

oversee [əʊvə'siː] *irr vt* beaufsichtigen

overshadow [əʊvə'ʃædəʊ] *vt* überschatten

overshoot [əʊvə'ʃuːt] *irr vt* (*runway*) hinausschießen über +*akk*; (*turning*) vorbeifahren +*dat*

oversight ['əʊvəsaɪt] *n* Versehen *nt*

oversimplify [əʊvə'sɪmplɪfaɪ] *vt* zu sehr vereinfachen

oversleep [əʊvə'sliːp] *irr vi* verschlafen

overtake [əʊvə'teɪk] *irr vt, vi* überholen

overtime ['əʊvətaɪm] *n* Überstunden *pl*

overturn [əʊvə'tɜːn] *vt, vi* umkippen

overweight [əʊvə'weɪt] *adj*: **to be ~** Übergewicht haben

overwhelm [əʊvə'welm] *vt* überwältigen; **overwhelming** *adj* überwältigend

overwork [əʊvə'wɜːk] *n* Überarbeitung *f* ▷ *vi* sich überarbeiten; **overworked** *adj* überarbeitet

owe [əʊ] *vt* schulden; **to ~ sth to sb** (*money*) jdm etw schulden; (*favour etc*) jdm etw verdanken; **how much do I ~ you?** was bin ich dir/Ihnen schuldig?; **owing to** *prep* wegen +*gen*

owl [aʊl] *n* Eule *f*

own [əʊn] *vt* besitzen ▷ *adj* eigen; **on one's ~** allein; **he has a flat of his ~** er hat eine eigene Wohung; **own up** *vi*: **to ~ to sth** etw zugeben; **owner** *n* Besitzer(in) *m(f)*; (*of business*) Inhaber(in) *m(f)*; **ownership** *n* Besitz *m*; **under new ~** unter neuer Leitung

ox [ɒks] (*pl* **oxen**) *n* Ochse *m*; **oxtail** ['ɒksteɪl] *n* Ochsenschwanz *m*; **~ soup** Ochsenschwanzsuppe *f*; **oxygen** ['ɒksɪdʒən] *n* Sauerstoff *m*

oyster ['ɔɪstə*] *n* Auster *f*

oz *abbr* = **ounces** Unzen *pl*

Oz ['ɒz] *n* (*fam*) Australien *nt*

ozone ['əʊzəʊn] *n* Ozon *nt*; **~ layer** Ozonschicht *f*

p *abbr* = **page** S.; *abbr* = **penny, pence**

p.a. *abbr* = **per annum**

pace [peɪs] *n* (*speed*) Tempo *nt*; (*step*) Schritt *m*; **pacemaker** *n* (*Med*) Schrittmacher *m*

Pacific [pə'sɪfɪk] *n*: **the ~ (Ocean)** der Pazifik; **Pacific Standard Time** *n* pazifische Zeit

pacifier ['pæsɪfaɪə] *n* (*US: for baby*) Schnuller *m*

pack [pæk] *n* (*of cards*) Spiel *nt*; (*esp US: of cigarettes*) Schachtel *f*; (*gang*) Bande *f*; (*US: backpack*) Rucksack *m* ▷ *vt* (*case*) packen; (*clothes*) einpacken ▷ *vi* (*for holiday*) packen; **pack in** *vt* (*Brit fam: job*) hinschmeißen; **package** ['pækɪdʒ] *n* (*a. Inform, fig*) Paket *nt*; **package deal** *n* Pauschalangebot *nt*; **package holiday, package tour** *n* Pauschalreise *f*; **packaging** *n*

(*material*) Verpackung *f*; **packed lunch** *n* (*Brit*) Lunchpaket *nt*; **packet** *n* Päckchen *nt*; (*of cigarettes*) Schachtel *f*

pad [pæd] *n* (*of paper*) Schreibblock *m*; (*padding*) Polster *nt*; **padded envelope** *n* wattierter Umschlag; **padding** *n* (*material*) Polsterung *f*

paddle ['pædl] *n* (*for boat*) Paddel *nt* ▷ *vi* (*in boat*) paddeln; **paddling pool** *n* (*Brit*) Planschbecken *nt*

padlock ['pædlɒk] *n* Vorhänge-schloss *nt*

page [peɪdʒ] *n* (*of book etc*) Seite *f*

pager ['peɪdʒə*] *n* Piepser *m*

paid [peɪd] *pt, pp of* **pay** ▷ *adj* bezahlt

pain [peɪn] *n* Schmerz *m*; **to be in ~** Schmerzen haben; **she's a (real) ~** sie nervt; **painful** *adj* (*physically*) schmerzhaft; (*embarrassing*) peinlich; **painkiller** *n* schmerzstillendes Mittel

painstaking *adj* sorgfältig

paint [peɪnt] *n* Farbe *f* ▷ *vt* anstreichen; (*picture*) malen; **paintbrush** *n* Pinsel *m*; **painter** *n* Maler(in) *m(f)*; **painting** *n* (*picture*) Bild *nt*, Gemälde *nt*

pair [pɛə*] *n* Paar *nt*; **a ~ of shoes** ein Paar Schuhe; **a ~ of scissors** eine Schere; **a ~ of trousers** eine Hose

pajamas [pə'dʒɑːməz] *npl* (*US*) Schlafanzug *m*

Pakistan [pɑːkɪ'stɑːn] *n* Paki-stan *nt*

pal [pæl] *n* (*fam*) Kumpel *m*

palace ['pæləs] *n* Palast *m*

pale [peɪl] *adj* (*face*) blass, bleich; (*colour*) hell

palm [pɑːm] *n* (*of hand*) Handfläche *f*; **~ (tree)** Palme *f*; **palmtop (computer)** *n* Palmtop(com-puter) *m*

pamper ['pæmpə*] vt
verhätscheln
pan [pæn] n (saucepan) Topf m;
(frying pan) Pfanne f; **pancake**
['pænkeɪk] n Pfannkuchen m;
Pancake Day n (Brit)
Fastnachtsdienstag m
pandemic [pæn'demɪk] n Pandemie f
panel ['pænl] n (of wood) Tafel f;
(in discussion) Diskussionsteil-
nehmer pl; (in jury) Jurymitglieder
pl
panic ['pænɪk] n Panik f ▷ vi in
Panik geraten; **panicky** ['pænɪkɪ]
adj panisch
pansy ['pænzɪ] n (flower)
Stiefmütterchen nt
panties ['pæntɪz] npl (Damen)-
slip m
pantomime ['pæntəmaɪm] n
(Brit) um die Weihnachtszeit
aufgeführte Märchenkomödie
pants [pænts] npl Unterhose f;
(esp US: trousers) Hose f
pantyhose ['pæntɪhəʊz] npl
(US) Strumpfhose f; **panty-liner** n
Slipeinlage f
paper ['peɪpə*] n Papier nt;
(newspaper) Zeitung f; (exam)
Klausur f; (for reading at conference)
Referat nt; **~s** pl (identity papers)
Papiere pl; **~ bag** Papiertüte f;
~ cup Pappbecher m ▷ vt (wall)
tapezieren; **paperback** n
Taschenbuch nt; **paper clip** n
Büroklammer f; **paper feed** n (of
printer) Papiereinzug m; **paper
round** n: **to do a ~** Zeitungen
austragen; **paperwork** n
Schreibarbeit f
parachute ['pærəʃuːt] n Fallschirm m ▷ vi abspringen
paracetamol [pærə'siːtəmɒl] n
(tablet) Paracetamoltablette
f
parade [pə'reɪd] n (procession)

Umzug m; (Mil) Parade f ▷ vi
vorbeimarschieren
paradise ['pærədaɪs] n Paradies
nt
paragliding ['pærəglaɪdɪŋ] n
Gleitschirmfliegen nt
paragraph ['pærəgrɑːf] n Absatz
m
parallel ['pærəlel] adj parallel
▷ n (Math, fig) Parallele f
paralyze ['pærəlaɪz] vt lähmen;
(fig) lahmlegen
paranoid ['pærənɔɪd] adj
paranoid
paraphrase ['pærəfreɪz] vt
umschreiben; (sth spoken) anders
ausdrücken
parasailing ['pærəseɪlɪŋ] n
Parasailing nt
parasol ['pærəsɒl] n Sonnenschirm m
parcel ['pɑːsl] n Paket nt
pardon ['pɑːdn] n (Jur)
Begnadigung f; **~ me/I beg your
~** verzeih/verzeihen Sie bitte;
(objection) aber ich bitte dich/Sie; **I
beg your ~?/~ me?** wie bitte?
parent ['peərənt] n Elternteil m;
~s pl Eltern pl; **~s-in-law** pl
Schwiegereltern pl; **parental**
[pə'rentl] adj elterlich, Eltern-
parish ['pærɪʃ] n Gemeinde f
park [pɑːk] n Park m ▷ vt, vi
parken; **parking** n Parken nt; **"no
~"** „Parken verboten"; **parking
brake** n (US) Handbremse f;
parking disc n Parkscheibe f;
parking fine n Geldbuße f für
falsches Parken; **parking lights**
npl (US) Standlicht nt; **parking lot**
n (US) Parkplatz m; **parking meter**
n Parkuhr f; **parking place** n,
parking space n Parkplatz m;
parking ticket n Strafzettel m
parliament ['pɑːləmənt] n Parlament nt
parrot ['pærət] n Papagei m

parsley ['pɑːslɪ] n Petersilie f
parsnip ['pɑːsnɪp] n Pastinake f
(längliches, weißes Wurzelgemüse)
part [pɑːt] n Teil m; (of machine)
Teil nt; (Theat) Rolle f; (US: in hair)
Scheitel m; **to take ~** teilnehmen
(in an +dat); **for the most ~** zum
größten Teil ▷ adj Teil- ▷ vt
(separate) trennen; (hair) scheiteln
▷ vi (people) sich trennen
partial ['pɑːʃəl] adj (incomplete)
teilweise, Teil-
participant [pɑːˈtɪsɪpənt] n
Teilnehmer(in) m(f); **participate**
[pɑːˈtɪsɪpeɪt] vi teilnehmen (in an
+dat)
particular [pəˈtɪkjʊlə°] adj
(specific) bestimmt; (exact) genau;
(fussy) eigen; **in ~** insbesondere
▷ n **~s** pl (details) Einzelheiten pl;
(about person) Personalien pl;
particularly adv besonders
parting ['pɑːtɪŋ] n (farewell) Abschied m; (Brit: in hair) Scheitel m
partly ['pɑːtlɪ] adv teilweise
partner ['pɑːtnə°] n Partner(in)
m(f); **partnership** n
Partnerschaft f
partridge ['pɑːtrɪdʒ] n Rebhuhn
nt
part-time ['pɑːt'taɪm] adj
Teilzeit- ▷ adv: **to work ~** Teilzeit
arbeiten
party ['pɑːtɪ] n (celebration) Party
f; (Pol, Jur) Partei f; (group) Gruppe f
▷ vi feiern
pass [pɑːs] vt (on foot)
vorbeigehen an +dat; (in car etc)
vorbeifahren an +dat; (time)
verbringen; (exam) bestehen; (law)
verabschieden; **to ~ sth to sb, to
~ sb sth** jdm etw reichen; **to ~ the
ball to sb** jdm den Ball zuspielen
▷ vi (on foot) vorbeigehen; (in car
etc) vorbeifahren; (years) vergehen;
(in exam) bestehen ▷ n (document)
Ausweis m; (Sport) Pass m; **pass**

away vi (die) verscheiden; **pass
by** vi (on foot) vorbeigehen; (in car
etc) vorbeifahren ▷ vt (on foot)
vorbeigehen an +dat; (in car etc)
vorbeifahren an +dat; **pass on** vt
weitergeben (to an +akk); (disease)
übertragen (to auf +akk); **pass out**
vi (faint) ohnmächtig werden;
pass round vt herumreichen
passage ['pæsɪdʒ] n (corridor)
Gang m; (in book, music) Passage f;
passageway n Durchgang m
passenger ['pæsɪndʒə°] n Pas-
sagier(in) m(f); (on bus) Fahrgast
m; (on train) Reisende(r) mf; (in car)
Mitfahrer(in) m(f)
passer-by ['pɑːsə'baɪ] (pl
passers-by) n Passant(in) m(f)
passion ['pæʃən] n Leidenschaft
f; **passionate** ['pæʃənɪt] adj
leidenschaftlich; **passion fruit** n
Passionsfrucht
passive ['pæsɪv] adj passiv;
~ smoking Passivrauchen nt ▷ n:
~ (voice) (Ling) Passiv nt
passport ['pɑːspɔːt] n (Reise)-
pass m; **passport control** n
Passkontrolle f
password ['pɑːswɜːd] n (Inform)
Passwort nt
past [pɑːst] n Vergangenheit f
▷ adv (by) vorbei; **it's five ~** es ist
fünf nach ▷ adj (years) vergangen;
(president etc) ehemalig; **in the
~ two months** in den letzten zwei
Monaten ▷ prep (telling time)
nach; **half ~ 10** halb 11; **to go ~ sth**
an etw dat vorbeigehen/-fahren
pasta ['pæstə] n Nudeln pl
paste [peɪst] vt (stick) kleben;
(Inform) einfügen ▷ n (glue)
Kleister m
pastime ['pɑːstaɪm] n Zeitvertreib m
pastry ['peɪstrɪ] n Teig m; (cake)
Stückchen
pasty ['pæstɪ] n (Brit) Pastete f

patch [pætʃ] n (area) Fleck m; (for mending) Flicken ▷ vt flicken; **patchy** adj (uneven) ungleichmäßig
pâté ['pæteɪ] n Pastete f
paternal [pə'tɜ:nl] adj väterlich; **~ grandmother** Großmutter f väterlicherseits; **paternity leave** [pə'tɜ:nɪtɪli:v] n Elternzeit f (des Vaters)
path [pɑ:θ] n (a. Inform) Pfad m; (a. fig) Weg m
pathetic [pə'θetɪk] adj (bad) kläglich, erbärmlich; **it's ~** es ist zum Heulen
patience ['peɪʃəns] n Geduld f; (Brit Cards) Patience f; **patient** adj geduldig ▷ n Patient(in) m(f)
patio ['pætɪəʊ] n Terrasse f
patriotic [pætrɪ'ɒtɪk] adj patriotisch
patrol car [pə'trəʊlkɑ:ʳ] n Streifenwagen m; **patrolman** (pl **-men**) n (US) Streifenpolizist m
patron ['peɪtrən] n (sponsor) Förderer m, Förderin f; (in shop) Kunde m, Kundin f
patronize ['pætrənaɪz] vt (treat condescendingly) von oben herab behandeln; **patronizing** adj (attitude) herablassend
pattern ['pætən] n Muster nt
pause [pɔ:z] n Pause f ▷ vi (speaker) innehalten
pavement n (Brit) Bürgersteig m; (US) Pflaster nt
pay [peɪ] (**paid, paid**) vt bezahlen; **he paid (me) £20 for it** er hat (mir) 20 Pfund dafür gezahlt; **to ~ attention** Acht geben (to auf +akk); **to ~ sb a visit** jdn besuchen ▷ vi zahlen; (be profitable) sich bezahlt machen; **to ~ for sth** etw bezahlen ▷ n Bezahlung f, Lohn m; **pay back** vt (money) zurückzahlen; **pay in** vt (into account) einzahlen; **payable**

adj zahlbar; (due) fällig; **payday** n Zahltag m; **payee** [peɪ'i:] n Zahlungsempfänger(in) m(f); **payment** n Bezahlung f; (money) Zahlung f; **pay-per-view** adj Pay-per-View-; **pay phone** n Münzfernsprecher m; **pay TV** n Pay-TV nt
PC abbr = **personal computer** PC m; abbr = **politically correct** politisch korrekt
PDA abbr = **personal digital assistant** PDA m
PE abbr = **physical education** (school) Sport m
pea [pi:] n Erbse f
peace [pi:s] n Frieden m; **peaceful** adj friedlich
peach [pi:tʃ] n Pfirsich m
peacock ['pi:kɒk] n Pfau m
peak [pi:k] n (of mountain) Gipfel m; (fig) Höhepunkt m; **peak period** n Stoßzeit f; (season) Hochsaison
peanut ['pi:nʌt] n Erdnuss f; **peanut butter** n Erdnussbutter f
pear [peəʳ] n Birne f
pearl [pɜ:l] n Perle f
pebble ['pebl] n Kiesel m
pecan [pɪ'kæn] n Pekannuss
peck [pek] vt, vi picken; **peckish** adj (Brit fam) ein bisschen hungrig
peculiar [pɪ'kju:lɪəʳ] adj (odd) seltsam; **~ to** charakteristisch für; **peculiarity** [pɪkjʊlɪ'ærɪtɪ] n (singular quality) Besonderheit f; (strangeness) Eigenartigkeit f
pedal ['pedl] n Pedal nt
pedestrian [pɪ'destrɪən] n Fußgänger(in) m(f); **pedestrian crossing** n Fußgängerüberweg m
pee [pi:] vi (fam) pinkeln
peel [pi:l] n Schale f ▷ vt schälen ▷ vi (paint etc) abblättern; (skin etc) sich schälen
peer [pɪəʳ] n Gleichaltrige(r) mf ▷ vi starren

peg [peg] n (for coat etc) Haken m; (for tent) Hering m; (**clothes**) ~ (Wäsche)klammer f

pelvis ['pɛlvɪs] n Becken nt

pen [pɛn] n (ball-point) Kuli m, Kugelschreiber; (fountain ~) Füller m

penalize ['piːnəlaɪz] vt (punish) bestrafen; **penalty** ['pɛnltɪ] n (punishment) Strafe f; (in football) Elfmeter m

pence [pɛns] pl of **penny**

pencil ['pɛnsl] n Bleistift m; **pencil sharpener** n (Bleistift)spitzer m

penetrate ['pɛnɪtreɪt] vt durchdringen; (enter into) eindringen in +akk

penfriend ['pɛnfrɛnd] n Brieffreund(in) m(f)

penguin ['pɛŋgwɪn] n Pinguin m

penicillin [pɛnɪ'sɪlɪn] n Penizillin nt

peninsula [pɪ'nɪnsjʊlə] n Halbinsel f

penis ['piːnɪs] n Penis m

penknife ['pɛnnaɪf] (pl **penknives**) n Taschenmesser nt

penny ['pɛnɪ] (pl **pence** o **pennies**) n (Brit) Penny m; (US) Centstück nt

pension ['pɛnʃən] n Rente f; (for civil servants, executives etc) Pension f; **pensioner** n Rentner(in) m(f); **pension plan**, **pension scheme** n Rentenversicherung f

penultimate [pɪ'nʌltɪmət] adj vorletzte(r, s)

people ['piːpl] npl (persons) Leute pl; (von Staat) Volk nt; (inhabitants) Bevölkerung f; **people carrier** n Minivan m

pepper ['pɛpə*] n Pfeffer m; (vegetable) Paprika m; **peppermint** n (sweet) Pfefferminz nt

per [pɜː*] prep pro; ~ **annum** pro Jahr; ~ **cent** Prozent nt

percentage [pə'sɛntɪdʒ] n Prozentsatz m

perceptible [pə'sɛptəbl] adj wahrnehmbar

percolator ['pɜːkəleɪtə*] n Kaffeemaschine f

percussion [pɜː'kʌʃən] n (Mus) Schlagzeug nt

perfect ['pɜːfɪkt] adj perfekt; (utter) völlig ▷ [pə'fɛkt] vt vervollkommnen; **perfectly** adv perfekt; (utterly) völlig

perform [pə'fɔːm] vt (task) ausführen; (play) aufführen; (Med: operation) durchführen ▷ vi (Theat) auftreten; **performance** n (show) Vorstellung f; (efficiency) Leistung f

perfume ['pɜːfjuːm] n Duft m; (substance) Parfüm nt

perhaps [pə'hæps] adv vielleicht

period ['pɪərɪəd] n (length of time) Zeit f; (in history) Zeitalter nt; (school) Stunde f; (Med) Periode f; (US: full stop) Punkt m; **for a ~ of three years** für einen Zeitraum von drei Jahren; **periodical** [pɪərɪ'ɒdɪkəl] n Zeitschrift f

peripheral [pə'rɪfərəl] n (Inform) Peripheriegerät nt

perjury ['pɜːdʒərɪ] n Meineid m

perm [pɜːm] n Dauerwelle f

permanent, permanently ['pɜːmənənt, -lɪ] adj, adv ständig

permission [pə'mɪʃən] n Erlaubnis f; **permit** ['pɜːmɪt] n Genehmigung f ▷ [pə'mɪt] vt erlauben, zulassen; **to ~ sb to do sth** jdm erlauben, etw zu tun

persecute ['pɜːsɪkjuːt] vt verfolgen

perseverance [pɜːsɪ'vɪərəns] n Ausdauer f

persist [pə'sɪst] vi (in belief etc) bleiben (in bei); (rain, smell) andauern; **persistent** adj beharrlich

person ['pɜ:sn] n Mensch m; (*in official context*) Person f; **in ~** persönlich; **personal** adj persönlich; (*private*) privat; **personality** [pɜ:sə'nælɪtɪ] n Persönlichkeit f; **personal organizer** n Organizer m; **personal stereo** (*pl* **-s**) n Walkman® m; **personnel** [pɜ:sə'nel] n Personal nt

perspective [pə'spektɪv] n Perspektive f

persuade [pə'sweɪd] vt überreden; (*convince*) überzeugen; **persuasive** [pə'sweɪsɪv] adj überzeugend

perverse [pə'vɜ:s] adj eigensinnig; abwegig; **pervert** ['pɜ:vɜ:t] n Perverse(r) mf ▷ [pə'vɜ:t] vt (*morally*) verderben; **perverted** [pə'vɜ:tɪd] adj pervers

pessimist ['pesɪmɪst] n Pessimist(in) m(f); **pessimistic** [pesɪ'mɪstɪk] adj pessimistisch

pest [pest] n (*insect*) Schädling m; (*fig: person*) Nervensäge f; (*thing*) Plage f; **pester** ['pestə*] vt plagen; **pesticide** ['pestɪsaɪd] n Schädlingsbekämpfungsmittel nt

pet [pet] n (*animal*) Haustier nt; (*person*) Liebling m

petal ['petl] n Blütenblatt nt

petition [pə'tɪʃən] n Petition f

petrol ['petrəl] n (*Brit*) Benzin nt; **petrol pump** n (*at garage*) Zapfsäule f; **petrol station** n Tankstelle f; **petrol tank** n Benzintank m

pharmacy ['fɑ:məsɪ] n (*shop*) Apotheke f; (*science*) Pharmazie f

phase [feɪz] n Phase f

PhD abbr = **Doctor of Philosophy** Dr. phil; (*dissertation*) Doktorarbeit f; **to do one's ~** promovieren

pheasant ['feznt] n Fasan m

phenomenon [fɪ'nɒmɪnən] (*pl* **phenomena**) n Phänomen nt

Philippines ['fɪlɪpi:nz] npl Philippinen pl

philosophical [fɪlə'sɒfɪkəl] adj philosophisch; (*fig*) gelassen; **philosophy** [fɪ'lɒsəfɪ] n Philosophie f

phone [fəʊn] n Telefon nt ▷ vt, vi anrufen; **phone book** n Telefonbuch nt; **phone bill** n Telefonrechnung f; **phone booth**, **phone box** (*Brit*) n Telefonzelle f; **phonecall** n Telefonanruf m; **phonecard** n Telefonkarte f; **phone-in** n Rundfunkprogramm, bei dem Hörer anrufen können; **phone number** n Telefonnummer f

photo ['fəʊtəʊ] (*pl* **-s**) n Foto nt; **photo booth** n Fotoautomat m; **photocopier** ['fəʊtəʊ'kɒpɪə*] n Kopiergerät nt; **photocopy** ['fəʊtəʊkɒpɪ] n Fotokopie f ▷ vt fotokopieren; **photograph** ['fəʊtəgrɑ:f] n Fotografie f, Aufnahme f ▷ vt fotografieren; **photographer** [fə'tɒgrəfə*] n Fotograf(in) m(f); **photography** [fə'tɒgrəfɪ] n Fotografie f

phrase [freɪz] n (*expression*) Redewendung f, Ausdruck m; **phrase book** n Sprachführer m

physical ['fɪzɪkəl] adj (*bodily*) körperlich, physisch ▷ n ärztliche Untersuchung f; **physically** adv (*bodily*) körperlich, physisch; **~ handicapped** körperbehindert

physics ['fɪzɪks] nsing Physik f

physiotherapy [fɪzɪə'θerəpɪ] n Physiotherapie f

physique [fɪ'zi:k] n Körperbau m

piano ['pjɑ:nəʊ] (*pl* **-s**) n Klavier nt

pick [pɪk] vt (*flowers, fruit*) pflücken; (*choose*) auswählen; (*team*) aufstellen; **pick out** vt auswählen; **pick up** vt (*lift up*) aufheben; (*collect*) abholen; (*learn*) lernen

pickle ['pɪkl] n (food) (Mixed) Pickles pl ▷ vt einlegen

pickpocket ['pɪkpɒkɪt] n Taschendieb(in) m(f)

picnic ['pɪknɪk] n Picknick nt

picture ['pɪktʃə*] n Bild nt; **to go to the ~s** (Brit) ins Kino gehen ▷ vt (visualize) sich vorstellen; **picture book** n Bilderbuch nt; **picturesque** [pɪktʃə'resk] adj malerisch

pie [paɪ] n (meat) Pastete f; (fruit) Kuchen m

piece [piːs] n Stück nt; (part) Teil nt; (in chess) Figur f; (in draughts) Stein m; **a ~ of cake** ein Stück Kuchen; **to fall to ~s** auseinanderfallen

pier [pɪə*] n Pier m

pierce [pɪəs] vt durchstechen, durchbohren; (cold, sound) durchdringen; **pierced** adj (part of body) gepierct; **piercing** adj durchdringend

pig [pɪg] n Schwein nt

pigeon ['pɪdʒən] n Taube f; **pigeonhole** n (compartment) Ablegefach nt

piggy ['pɪgɪ] adj (fam) verfressen; **pigheaded** ['pɪg'hedɪd] adj dickköpfig; **piglet** ['pɪglət] n Ferkel nt; **pigsty** ['pɪgstaɪ] n Schweinestall m; **pigtail** ['pɪgteɪl] n Zopf m

pile [paɪl] n (heap) Haufen m; (one on top of another) Stapel m; **pile up** vi (accumulate) sich anhäufen

piles [paɪlz] npl Hämorr(ho)iden pl

pile-up ['paɪlʌp] n (Auto) Massenkarambolage f

pilgrim ['pɪlgrɪm] n Pilger(in) m(f)

pill [pɪl] n Tablette f; **the ~** die (Antibaby)pille; **to be on the ~** die Pille nehmen

pillar ['pɪlə*] n Pfeiler m

pillow ['pɪləʊ] n (Kopf)kissen nt; **pillowcase** n (Kopf)kissenbezug m

pilot ['paɪlət] n (Aviat) Pilot(in) m(f)

pimple ['pɪmpl] n Pickel m

pin [pɪn] n (for fixing) Nadel f; (in sewing) Stecknadel f; (Tech) Stift m; **I've got ~s and needles in my leg** mein Bein ist mir eingeschlafen ▷ vt (fix with ~) heften (to an +akk)

PIN [pɪn] acr = **personal identification number ~ (number)** PIN f, Geheimzahl f

pinch [pɪntʃ] n (of salt) Prise f ▷ vt zwicken; (fam: steal) klauen ▷ vi (shoe) drücken

pine [paɪn] n Kiefer f

pineapple ['paɪnæpl] n Ananas f

pink [pɪŋk] adj rosa

pinstripe(d) ['pɪnstraɪp(t)] adj Nadelstreifen-

pint [paɪnt] n Pint nt (Brit: 0,57 l, US: 0,473l); (Brit: glass of beer) Bier nt

pious ['paɪəs] adj fromm

pip [pɪp] n (of fruit) Kern m

pipe [paɪp] n (for smoking) Pfeife f; (for water, gas) Rohrleitung f

pirate ['paɪərɪt] n Pirat(in) m(f); **pirated copy** n Raubkopie f

Pisces ['paɪsiːz] nsing (Astr) Fische pl; **she's a ~** sie ist Fisch

piss [pɪs] vi (vulg) pissen ▷ n (vulg) Pisse f; **to take the ~ out of sb** jdn verarschen; **piss off** vi (vulg) sich verpissen; **~!** verpiss dich!; **pissed** adj (Brit fam: drunk) sturzbesoffen; (US fam: annoyed) stocksauer

pistachio [pɪ'stɑːʃɪəʊ] (pl **-s**) n Pistazie f

piste [piːst] n (Ski) Piste f

pistol ['pɪstl] n Pistole f

pit [pɪt] n (hole) Grube f; (coalmine) Zeche f; **the ~s** (motor racing) die Box; **to be the ~s** (fam) grottenschlecht sein

pitch [pɪtʃ] n (Sport) Spielfeld nt; (Mus: of instrument) Tonlage f; (of voice) Stimmlage f ▷ vt (tent)

aufschlagen; (*throw*) werfen;
pitch-black *adj* pechschwarz
pitcher ['pɪtʃə*] *n* (*US: jug*) Krug *m*
pitiful ['pɪtɪfʊl] *adj* (*contemptible*) jämmerlich
pitta bread ['pɪtə] *n* Pittabrot *nt*
pity ['pɪtɪ] *n* Mitleid *nt*; **what a ~** wie schade; **it's a ~** es ist schade ▷ *vt* Mitleid haben mit
pizza ['pi:tsə] *n* Pizza *f*
place [pleɪs] *n* *m* (*spot, in text*) Stelle *f*; (*town etc*) Ort; (*house*) Haus *nt*; (*position, seat, on course*) Platz *m*; **~ of birth** Geburtsort *m*; **at my ~** bei mir; **in third ~** auf dem dritten Platz; **to three decimal ~s** bis auf drei Stellen nach dem Komma; **out of ~** nicht an der richtigen Stelle; (*fig: remark*) unangebracht; **in ~ of** anstelle von; **in the first ~** (*firstly*) erstens; (*immediately*) gleich; (*in any case*) überhaupt ▷ *vt* (*put*) stellen, setzen; (*lay flat*) legen; (*advertisement*) setzen (*in* in +*akk*); (*Comm: order*) aufgeben; **place mat** *n* Set *nt*
plague [pleɪg] *n* Pest *f*
plaice [pleɪs] *n* Scholle *f*
plain [pleɪn] *adj* (*clear*) klar, deutlich; (*simple*) einfach; (*not beautiful*) unattraktiv; (*yoghurt*) Natur-; (*Brit: chocolate*) (Zart)bitter- ▷ *n* Ebene *f*; **plainly** *adv* (*frankly*) offen; (*simply*) einfach; (*obviously*) eindeutig
plait [plæt] *n* Zopf *m* ▷ *vt* flechten
plan [plæn] *n* Plan *m*; (*for essay etc*) Konzept *nt* ▷ *vt* planen; **to ~ to do sth, to ~ on doing sth** vorhaben, etw zu tun ▷ *vi* planen
plane [pleɪn] *n* (*aircraft*) Flugzeug *nt*; (*tool*) Hobel *m*
planet ['plænɪt] *n* Planet *m*
plank [plæŋk] *n* Brett *nt*
plant [plɑ:nt] *n* Pflanze *f*; (*equipment*) Maschinen *pl*; (*factory*) Werk *nt* ▷ *vt* (*tree etc*) pflanzen;

plantation [plæn'teɪʃən] *n* Plantage *f*
plaque [plæk] *n* Gedenktafel *f*; (*on teeth*) Zahnbelag *m*
plaster ['plɑ:stə*] *n* (*Brit Med: sticking ~*) Pflaster *nt*; (*on wall*) Verputz *m*; **to have one's arm in ~** den Arm in Gips haben
plastered ['plɑ:stəd] *adj* (*fam*) besoffen; **to get (absolutely) ~** sich besaufen
plastic ['plæstɪk] *n* Kunststoff *m*; **to pay with ~** mit Kreditkarte bezahlen ▷ *adj* Plastik-; **plastic bag** *n* Plastiktüte *f*; **plastic surgery** *n* plastische Chirurgie *f*
plate [pleɪt] *n* (*for food*) Teller *m*; (*flat sheet*) Platte *f*; (*plaque*) Schild *nt*
platform ['plætfɔ:m] *n* (*Rail*) Bahnsteig *m*; (*at meeting*) Podium *nt*
platinum ['plætɪnəm] *n* Platin *nt*
play [pleɪ] *n* Spiel *nt*; (*Theat*) (Theater)stück *nt* ▷ *vt* spielen; (*another player or team*) spielen gegen; **to ~ the piano** Klavier spielen; **to ~ a part in** (*fig*) eine Rolle spielen ▷ *vi* spielen; **play at** *vt*: **what are you ~ing at?** was soll das?; **play back** *vt* abspielen; **play down** *vt* herunterspielen
playacting *n* Schauspielerei *f*; **playback** *n* Wiedergabe *f*; **player** *n* Spieler(in) *m(f)*; **playful** *adj* (*person*) verspielt; (*remark*) scherzhaft; **playground** *n* Spielplatz *m*; (*in school*) Schulhof *m*; **playgroup** *n* Spielgruppe *f*; **playing card** *n* Spielkarte *f*; **playing field** *n* Sportplatz *m*; **playmate** *n* Spielkamerad(in) *m(f)*; **playwright** *n* Dramatiker(in) *m(f)*
plc *abbr* = **public limited company** AG *f*

plea [pliː] *n* Bitte *f* (for um)

plead [pliːd] *vi* dringend bitten (*with sb* jdn); (*Jur*) **to ~ guilty** sich schuldig bekennen

pleasant, **pleasantly** ['pleznt, -lɪ] *adj, adv* angenehm

please [pliːz] *adv* bitte; **more tea? - yes, ~** noch Tee? - ja, bitte ▷ *vt* (*be agreeable to*) gefallen *+dat*; **~ yourself** wie du willst/Sie wollen; **pleased** *adj* zufrieden; (*glad*) erfreut; **~ to meet you** freut mich, angenehm; **pleasing** *adj* erfreulich; **pleasure** ['pleʒəʳ] *n* Vergnügen *nt*, Freude *f*; **it's a ~** gern geschehen

pledge [pledʒ] *n* (*promise*) Versprechen *nt* ▷ *vt* (*promise*) versprechen

plenty ['plentɪ] *n*: **~ of** eine Menge, viel(e); **to be ~** genug sein, reichen; **I've got ~** ich habe mehr als genug ▷ *adv* (*US fam*) ganz schön

pliable ['plaɪəbl] *adj* biegsam

pliers ['plaɪəz] *npl* (Kombi)zange *f*

plimsoll ['plɪmsəl] *n* (*Brit*) Turnschuh *m*

plonk [plɒŋk] *n* (*Brit fam: wine*) billiger Wein ▷ *vt*: **to ~ sth** (**down**) etw hinknallen

plot [plɒt] *n* (*of story*) Handlung *f*; (*conspiracy*) Komplott *nt*; (*of land*) Stück *nt* Land, Grundstück *nt* ▷ *vi* ein Komplott schmieden

plough, **plow** (*US*) [plaʊ] *n* Pflug *m* ▷ *vt, vi* (*Agr*) pflügen; **ploughman's lunch** *n* (*Brit*) in einer Kneipe serviertes Gericht aus Käse, Brot, Mixed Pickles etc

pluck [plʌk] *vt* (*eyebrows, guitar*) zupfen; (*chicken*) rupfen; **pluck up** *vt*: **to ~** (**one's**) **courage** Mut aufbringen

plug [plʌg] *n* (*for sink, bath*) Stöpsel *m*; (*Elec*) Stecker *m*; (*Auto*)

(Zünd)kerze *f*; (*fam: publicity*) Schleichwerbung *f* ▷ *vt* (*fam: advertise*) Reklame machen für; **plug in** *vt* anschließen

plum [plʌm] *n* Pflaume *f* ▷ *adj* (*fam: job etc*) Super-

plumber ['plʌməʳ] *n* Klempner(in) *m(f)*; **plumbing** ['plʌmɪŋ] *n* (*fittings*) Leitungen *pl*; (*craft*) Installieren *nt*

plump [plʌmp] *adj* rundlich

plunge [plʌndʒ] *vt* (*knife*) stoßen; (*into water*) tauchen ▷ *vi* stürzen; (*into water*) tauchen

plural ['plʊərəl] *n* Plural *m*

plus [plʌs] *prep* plus; (*as well as*) und ▷ *adj* Plus-; **20 ~** mehr als 20 ▷ *n* (*fig*) Plus *nt*

plywood ['plaɪwʊd] *n* Sperrholz *nt*

pm *abbr* = **post meridiem**; **at 3 ~** um 3 Uhr nachmittags; **at 8 ~** um 8 Uhr abends

pneumonia [njuːˈməʊnɪə] *n* Lungenentzündung *f*

poached [pəʊtʃt] *adj* (*egg*) pochiert, verloren

PO Box *abbr* = **post office box** Postfach *nt*

pocket ['pɒkɪt] *n* Tasche *f* ▷ *vt* (*put in ~*) einstecken; **pocketbook** *n* (*US: wallet*) Brieftasche *f*; **pocket calculator** *n* Taschenrechner *m*; **pocket money** *n* Taschengeld *nt*

poem ['pəʊəm] *n* Gedicht *nt*; **poet** ['pəʊɪt] *n* Dichter(in) *m(f)*; **poetic** [pəʊˈetɪk] *adj* poetisch; **poetry** ['pəʊɪtrɪ] *n* (*art*) Dichtung *f*; (*poems*) Gedichte *pl*

point [pɔɪnt] *n* Punkt *m*; (*spot*) Stelle *f*; (*sharp tip*) Spitze *f*; (*moment*) Zeitpunkt *m*; (*purpose*) Zweck *m*; (*idea*) Argument *nt*; (*decimal*) Dezimalstelle *f*; **~s** *pl* (*Rail*) Weiche *f*; **~ of view** Standpunkt *m*; **three ~ two** drei Komma zwei; **at some ~** irgendwann (mal); **to get**

to the ~ zur Sache kommen;
there's no ~ es hat keinen Sinn; **I
was on the ~ of leaving** ich wollte
gerade gehen ▷ vt (gun etc)
richten (at, at +akk); **to ~ one's
finger at** mit dem Finger zeigen
auf +akk ▷ vi (with finger etc)
zeigen (at, to auf +akk); **point out**
vt (indicate) aufzeigen; (mention)
hinweisen auf +akk; **pointed** adj
spitz; (question) gezielt; **pointer** n
(on dial) Zeiger m; (tip) Hinweis m;
pointless adj sinnlos

poison ['pɔɪzn] n Gift nt ▷ vt
vergiften; **poisonous** adj giftig

poke [pəʊk] vt (with stick, finger)
stoßen, stupsen; (put) stecken

Poland ['pəʊlənd] n Polen nt

polar ['pəʊlə°] adj Polar-, polar;
~ bear Eisbär m

pole [pəʊl] n Stange f; (Geo, Elec)
Pol m

Pole [pəʊl] n Pole m, Polin f

pole vault n Stabhochsprung m

police [pə'liːs] n Polizei f; **police
car** n Polizeiwagen m; **policeman**
(pl **-men**) n Polizist m; **police
station** n (Polizei)wache f;
policewoman (pl **-women**) n
Polizistin f

policy ['pɒlɪsɪ] n (plan) Politik f;
(principle) Grundsatz m; (insurance
~) (Versicherungs)police f

polio ['pəʊlɪəʊ] n Kinderlähmung f

polish ['pɒlɪʃ] n (for furniture)
Politur f; (for floor) Wachs nt; (for
shoes) Creme f; (shine) Glanz m;
(fig) Schliff m ▷ vt polieren;
(shoes) putzen; (fig) den letzten
Schliff geben +dat

Polish ['pəʊlɪʃ] adj polnisch ▷ n
Polnisch nt

polite [pə'laɪt] adj höflich;
politeness n Höflichkeit f

political, politically [pə'lɪtɪkəl, -ɪ]
adj, adv politisch; **~ly correct**
politisch korrekt; **politician**
[pɒlɪ'tɪʃən] n Politiker(in) m(f);
politics ['pɒlɪtɪks] nsing o pl
Politik f

poll [pəʊl] n (election) Wahl f;
(opinion ~) Umfrage f

pollen ['pɒlən] n Pollen m,
Blütenstaub m; **pollen count** n
Pollenflug m

polling station ['pəʊlɪŋsteɪʃən]
n Wahllokal nt

pollute [pə'luːt] vt verschmutzen; **pollution** [pə'luːʃən] n
Verschmutzung f

pompous ['pɒmpəs] adj aufge-
blasen; (language) geschwollen

pond [pɒnd] n Teich m

pony ['pəʊnɪ] n Pony nt;
ponytail n Pferdeschwanz m

poodle ['puːdl] n Pudel m

pool [puːl] n (swimming ~)
Schwimmbad nt; (private)
Swimmingpool m; (of spilt liquid,
blood) Lache f; (game) Poolbillard
nt ▷ vt (money etc)
zusammenlegen

poor [pɔː°] adj arm; (not good)
schlecht ▷ npl **the ~** die Armen
pl; **poorly** adv (badly) schlecht
▷ adj (Brit) krank

pop [pɒp] n (music) Pop m; (noise)
Knall m ▷ vt (put) stecken;
(balloon) platzen lassen ▷ vi
(balloon) platzen; (cork) knallen; **to
~ in** (person) vorbeischauen; **pop
concert** n Popkonzert nt;
popcorn n Popcorn nt

Pope [pəʊp] n Papst m

pop group ['pɒpgruːp] n
Popgruppe f; **pop music** n
Popmusik f

poppy ['pɒpɪ] n Mohn m

Popsicle® ['pɒpsɪkl] n (US) Eis
nt am Stiel

pop star ['pɒpstɑː°] n Popstar m

popular ['pɒpjʊlə°] adj (well-
-liked) beliebt (with bei);
(widespread) weit verbreitet

population [pɒpjʊ'leɪʃən] n Bevölkerung f; (of town) Einwohner pl

porcelain ['pɔːslɪn] n Porzellan nt

porch [pɔːtʃ] n Vorbau m; (US: verandah) Veranda f

porcupine ['pɔːkjʊpaɪn] n Stachelschwein nt

pork [pɔːk] n Schweinefleisch nt; **pork chop** n Schweinekotelett; **pork pie** n Schweinefleischpastete f

porn [pɔːn] n Porno m; **pornographic** [pɔːnə'græfɪk] adj pornografisch; **pornography** [pɔː'nɒgrəfɪ] n Pornografie f

porridge ['pɒrɪdʒ] n Haferbrei m

port [pɔːt] n (harbour) Hafen m; (town) Hafenstadt f; (Naut: left side) Backbord nt; (wine) Portwein m; (Inform) Anschluss m

portable ['pɔːtəbl] adj tragbar; (radio) Koffer-

portal ['pɔːtl] n (Inform) Portal nt

porter ['pɔːtə*] n Pförtner(in) m(f); (for luggage) Gepäckträger m

porthole ['pɔːthəʊl] n Bullauge nt

portion ['pɔːʃən] n Teil m; (of food) Portion f

portrait ['pɔːtrɪt] n Porträt nt

portray [pɔː'treɪ] vt darstellen

Portugal ['pɔːtʃʊgl] n Portugal nt; **Portuguese** [pɔːtʃʊ'giːz] adj portugiesisch ▷ n Portugiese m, Portugiesin f; (language) Portugiesisch nt

pose [pəʊz] n Haltung f ▷ vi posieren ▷ vt (threat, problem) darstellen

posh [pɒʃ] adj (fam) piekfein

position [pə'zɪʃən] n Stellung f; (place) Position f, Lage f; (job) Stelle f; (opinion) Standpunkt m; **to be in a ~ to do sth** in der Lage sein, etw zu tun; **in third ~** auf dem dritten Platz ▷ vt aufstellen; (Inform: cursor) positionieren

positive ['pɒzɪtɪv] adj positiv; (convinced) sicher

possess [pə'zes] vt besitzen; **possession** [pə'zeʃən] n ~(s pl) Besitz m; **possessive** adj (person) besitzergreifend

possibility [pɒsə'bɪlɪtɪ] n Möglichkeit f; **possible** ['pɒsəbl] adj möglich; **if ~** wenn möglich; **as big/soon as ~** so groß/bald wie möglich; **possibly** adv (perhaps) vielleicht; **I've done all I ~ can** ich habe mein Möglichstes getan

post [pəʊst] n (mail) Post f; (pole) Pfosten m; (job) Stelle f ▷ vt (letters) aufgeben; **to keep sb ~ed** jdn auf dem Laufenden halten; **postage** ['pəʊstɪdʒ] n Porto nt; **~ and packing** Porto und Verpackung; **postal** adj Post-; (Brit) **~ order** Postanweisung f; **postbox** n Briefkasten m; **postcard** n Postkarte f; **postcode** n (Brit) Postleitzahl f

poster ['pəʊstə*] n Plakat nt, Poster nt

postgraduate [pəʊst'grædjuːt] n jmd, der seine Studien nach dem ersten akademischen Grad weiterführt

postman ['pəʊstmən] (pl **-men**) n Briefträger m; **postmark** n Poststempel m

postmortem [pəʊst'mɔːtəm] n Autopsie f

post office ['pəʊstɒfɪs] n Post® f

postpone [pə'spəʊn] vt verschieben (till auf +akk)

posture ['pɒstʃə*] n Haltung f

pot [pɒt] n Topf m; (tea~, coffee ~) Kanne f; (fam: marijuana) Pot nt ▷ vt (plant) eintopfen

potato [pə'teɪtəʊ] (pl **-es**) n Kartoffel f; **potato chips** (US) npl Kartoffelchips pl; **potato peeler** n Kartoffelschäler m

potent ['pəutənt] *adj* stark
potential [pəu'tenʃəl] *adj*
potenziell ▷ *n* Potenzial *nt*;
potentially *adv* potenziell
pothole ['pɒthəʊl] *n* Höhle *f*; (*in road*) Schlagloch *nt*
potter about ['pɒtərəbaʊt] *vi* herumhantieren
pottery ['pɒtəri] *n* (*objects*) Töpferwaren *pl*
potty ['pɒti] *adj* (*Brit fam*) verrückt ▷ *n* Töpfchen *nt*
poultry ['pəʊltri] *n* Geflügel *nt*
pounce [paʊns] *vi*: **to ~ on** sich stürzen auf +*akk*
pound [paʊnd] *n* (*money*) Pfund *nt*; (*weight*) Pfund *nt* (0,454 *kg*); **a ~ of cherries** ein Pfund Kirschen; **ten-~ note** Zehnpfundschein *m*
pour [pɔːʳ] *vt* (*liquid*) gießen; (*rice, sugar etc*) schütten; **to ~ sb sth** (*drink*) jdm etw eingießen; **pouring** *adj* (*rain*) strömend
poverty ['pɒvəti] *n* Armut *f*
powder ['paʊdəʳ] *n* Pulver *nt*; (*cosmetic*) Puder *m*; **powdered milk** *n* Milchpulver *nt*; **powder room** *n* Damentoilette *f*
power ['paʊəʳ] *n* Macht *f*; (*ability*) Fähigkeit *f*; (*strength*) Stärke *f*; (*Elec*) Strom *m*; **to be in ~** an der Macht sein ▷ *vt* betreiben, antreiben;
power-assisted steering *n* Servolenkung *f*; **power cut** *n* Stromausfall *m*; **powerful** *adj* (*politician etc*) mächtig; (*engine, government*) stark; (*argument*) durchschlagend; **powerless** *adj* machtlos; **power station** *n* Kraftwerk *nt*
p&p *abbr* = **postage and packing**
PR *abbr* = **public relations** ▷ *abbr* = **proportional representation**
practical, practically ['præktikəl,

-i] *adj, adv* praktisch; **practice** ['præktis] *n* (*training*) Übung *f*; (*custom*) Gewohnheit *f*; (*doctor's, lawyer's*) Praxis *f*; **in ~** (*in reality*) in der Praxis; **out of ~** außer Übung; **to put sth into ~** etw in die Praxis umsetzen ▷ *vt, vi* (*US*) see
practise; **practise** ['præktis] *vt* (*instrument, movement*) üben; (*profession*) ausüben ▷ *vi* üben; (*doctor, lawyer*) praktizieren
Prague [prɑːg] *n* Prag *nt*
praise [preiz] *n* Lob *nt* ▷ *vt* loben
pram [præm] *n* (*Brit*) Kinderwagen *m*
prawn [prɔːn] *n* Garnele *f*, Krabbe *f*; **prawn crackers** *npl* Krabbenchips *pl*
pray [prei] *vi* beten; **to ~ for sth** (*fig*) stark auf etw akk hoffen;
prayer ['preəʳ] *n* Gebet *nt*
pre- [priː] *pref* vor-, prä-
preach [priːtʃ] *vi* predigen
prearrange [priːə'reindʒ] *vt* im Voraus vereinbaren
precaution [pri'kɔːʃən] *n* Vorsichtsmaßnahme *f*
precede [pri'siːd] *vt* vorausgehen +*dat*; **preceding** *adj* vorhergehend
precinct ['priːsiŋkt] *n* (*Brit: pedestrian ~*) Fußgängerzone *f*; (*Brit: shopping ~*) Einkaufsviertel *nt*; (*US: district*) Bezirk *m*
precious ['preʃəs] *adj* kostbar; **~ stone** Edelstein *m*
précis ['preisiː] *n* Zusammenfassung *f*
precise, precisely [pri'sais, -li] *adj, adv* genau
precondition [priːkən'diʃən] *n* Vorbedingung *f*
predecessor ['priːdisesəʳ] *n* Vorgänger(in) *m(f)*
predicament [pri'dikəmənt] *n* missliche Lage

predict [prɪˈdɪkt] vt voraussagen; **predictable** adj vorhersehbar; (person) berechenbar

predominant [prɪˈdɒmɪnənt] adj vorherrschend; **predominantly** adv überwiegend

preface [ˈprefɪs] n Vorwort nt

prefer [prɪˈfɜː*] vt vorziehen (to dat), lieber mögen (to als); **to ~ to do sth** etw lieber tun; **preferably** [ˈprefrəblɪ] adv vorzugsweise, am liebsten; **preference** [ˈprefərəns] n (liking) Vorliebe f; **preferential** [prefəˈrenʃəl] adj: **to get ~ treatment** bevorzugt behandelt werden

prefix [ˈpriːfɪks] n (US Tel) Vorwahl f

pregnancy [ˈpregnənsɪ] n Schwangerschaft f; **pregnant** [ˈpregnənt] adj schwanger; **two months ~** im zweiten Monat schwanger

prejudice [ˈpredʒʊdɪs] n Vorurteil nt; **prejudiced** adj (person) voreingenommen

preliminary [prɪˈlɪmɪnərɪ] adj (measures) vorbereitend; (results) vorläufig; (remarks) einleitend

premature [ˈpremətʃʊə*] adj vorzeitig; (hasty) voreilig

premiere [ˈpremɪeə*] n Premiere f

premises [ˈpremɪsɪz] npl (offices) Räumlichkeiten pl; (of factory, school) Gelände nt

premium-rate [ˈpriːmɪəmreɪt] adj (Tel) zum Höchsttarif

preoccupied [priːˈɒkjʊpaɪd] adj: **to be ~ with sth** mit etw sehr beschäftigt sein

prepaid [priːˈpeɪd] adj vorausbezahlt; (envelope) frankiert

preparation [prepəˈreɪʃən] n Vorbereitung f; **prepare** [prɪˈpeə*] vt vorbereiten (for auf +akk); (food)

zubereiten; **to be ~d to do sth** bereit sein, etw zu tun ▷ vi sich vorbereiten (for auf +akk)

prerequisite [priːˈrekwɪzɪt] n Voraussetzung f

prescribe [prɪˈskraɪb] vt vorschreiben; (Med) verschreiben; **prescription** [prɪˈskrɪpʃən] n Rezept nt

presence [ˈprezns] n Gegenwart f; **present** [ˈprezmt] adj (in attendance) anwesend (at bei); (current) gegenwärtig; **~ tense** Gegenwart f, Präsens nt ▷ n Gegenwart f; (gift) Geschenk nt; **at ~** zurzeit ▷ [prɪˈzent] vt (TV, Radio) präsentieren; (problem) darstellen; (report etc) vorlegen; **to ~ sb with sth** jdm etw überreichen; **present-day** adj heutig; **presently** adv bald; (at present) zurzeit

preservative [prɪˈzɜːvətɪv] n Konservierungsmittel nt; **preserve** [prɪˈzɜːv] vt erhalten; (food) einmachen, konservieren

president [ˈprezɪdənt] n Präsident(in) m(f); **presidential** [prezɪˈdenʃəl] adj Präsidenten-; (election) Präsidentschafts-

press [pres] n (newspapers, machine) Presse f ▷ vt (push) drücken; **to ~ a button** auf einen Knopf drücken ▷ vi (push) drücken; **pressing** adj dringend; **press-stud** n Druckknopf m; **press-up** n (Brit) Liegestütz m; **pressure** [ˈpreʃə*] n Druck m; **to be under ~** unter Druck stehen; **to put ~ on sb** jdn unter Druck setzen; **pressure cooker** n Schnellkochtopf m; **pressurize** [ˈpreʃəraɪz] vt (person) unter Druck setzen

presumably [prɪˈzjuːməblɪ] adv vermutlich; **presume** [prɪˈzjuːm] vt, vi annehmen

presumptuous [prɪ'zʌmptʃʊəs] *adj* anmaßend

presuppose [pri:sə'pəʊz] *vt* voraussetzen

pretend [prɪ'tend] *vt*: **to ~ that** so tun als ob; **to ~ to do sth** vorgeben, etw zu tun ▷ *vi*: **she's ~ing** sie tut nur so

pretentious [prɪ'tenʃəs] *adj* anmaßend; (*person*) wichtigtuerisch

pretty ['prɪtɪ] *adj* hübsch ▷ *adv* ziemlich

prevent [prɪ'vent] *vt* verhindern; **to ~ sb from doing sth** jdn daran hindern, etw zu tun

preview ['pri:vju:] *n* (*Cine*) Voraufführung *f*; (*trailer*) Vorschau *f*

previous, **previously** ['pri:vɪəs, -lɪ] *adj*, *adv* früher

prey [preɪ] *n* Beute *f*

price [praɪs] *n* Preis *m* ▷ *vt*: **it's ~d at £10** es ist mit 10 Pfund ausgezeichnet; **priceless** *adj* unbezahlbar; **price list** *n* Preisliste *f*; **price tag** *n* Preisschild *nt*

prick [prɪk] *n* Stich *m*; (*vulg: penis*) Schwanz *m*; (*vulg: person*) Arsch *m* ▷ *vt* stechen in +*akk*; **to ~ one's finger** sich *dat* in den Finger stechen; **prickly** ['prɪklɪ] *adj* stachelig

pride [praɪd] *n* Stolz *m*; (*arrogance*) Hochmut *m* ▷ *vt*: **to ~ oneself on sth** auf etw *akk* stolz sein

priest [pri:st] *n* Priester *m*

primarily ['praɪmərɪlɪ] *adv* vorwiegend; **primary** ['praɪmərɪ] *adj* Haupt-; **~ education** Grundschulausbildung *f*; **~ school** Grundschule *f*

prime [praɪm] *adj* Haupt-; (*excellent*) erstklassig ▷ *n*: **in one's ~** in den besten Jahren; **prime minister** *n* Premierminister(in) *m(f)*; **prime time** *n* (*TV*) Hauptsendezeit *f*

primitive ['prɪmɪtɪv] *adj* primitiv

primrose ['prɪmrəʊz] *n* Schlüsselblume *f*

prince [prɪns] *n* Prinz *m*; (*ruler*) Fürst *m*; (*princess* [prɪn'ses] *n* Prinzessin *f*; Fürstin *f*

principal ['prɪnsɪpəl] *adj* Haupt-, wichtigste(r, s) ▷ *n* (*school*) Rektor(in) *m(f)*

principle ['prɪnsəpl] *n* Prinzip *nt*; **in ~** im Prinzip; **on ~** aus Prinzip

print [prɪnt] *n* (*picture*) Druck *m*; (*Foto*) Abzug *m*; (*made by feet, fingers*) Abdruck *m*; **out of ~** vergriffen ▷ *vt* drucken; (*photo*) abziehen; (*write in block letters*) in Druckschrift schreiben; **print out** *vt* (*Inform*) ausdrucken; **printed matter** *n* Drucksache *f*; **printer** *n* Drucker *m*; **printout** *n* (*Inform*) Ausdruck *m*

prior ['praɪə*] *adj* früher; **a ~ engagement** eine vorher getroffene Verabredung; **~ to sth** vor etw *dat*; **~ to going abroad, she had ...** bevor sie ins Ausland ging, hatte sie ...

priority [praɪ'ɒrɪtɪ] *n* (*thing having precedence*) Priorität *f*

prison ['prɪzn] *n* Gefängnis *nt*; **prisoner** *n* Gefangene(r) *mf*; **~ of war** Kriegsgefangene(r) *mf*

privacy ['prɪvəsɪ] *n* Privatleben *nt*; **private** ['praɪvɪt] *adj* privat; (*confidential*) vertraulich ▷ *n* einfacher Soldat; **in ~** privat; **privately** *adv* privat; (*confidentially*) vertraulich; **privatize** ['praɪvətaɪz] *vt* privatisieren

privilege ['prɪvɪlɪdʒ] *n* Privileg *nt*; **privileged** *adj* privilegiert

prize [praɪz] *n* Preis *m*; **prize money** *n* Preisgeld *nt*; **prizewinner** *n* Gewinner(in) *m(f)*; **prizewinning** *adj* preisgekrönt

pro [prəʊ] (pl **-s**) n (professional) Profi m; **the ~s and cons** pl das Für und Wider

pro- [prəʊ] pref pro-

probability [prɒbə'bɪlətɪ] n Wahrscheinlichkeit f; **probable**, **probably** ['prɒbəbl, -blɪ] adj, adv wahrscheinlich

probation [prə'beɪʃən] n Probezeit f; (Jur) Bewährung f

probe [prəʊb] n (investigation) Untersuchung f ▷ vt untersuchen

problem ['prɒbləm] n Problem nt; **no ~** kein Problem!

procedure [prə'si:dʒə*] n Verfahren nt

proceed [prə'si:d] vi (continue) fortfahren; (set about sth) vorgehen ▷ vt: **to ~ to do sth** anfangen, etw zu tun; **proceedings** npl (Jur) Verfahren nt; **proceeds** ['prəʊsi:ds] npl Erlös m

process ['prəʊses] n Prozess m, Vorgang m; (method) Verfahren nt ▷ vt (application etc) bearbeiten; (food, data) verarbeiten; (film) entwickeln

procession [prə'seʃən] n Umzug m

processor ['prəʊsesə*] n (Inform) Prozessor m; (Gastr) Küchenmaschine f

produce ['prɒdju:s] n (Agr) Produkte pl, Erzeugnisse pl ▷ [prə'dju:s] vt (manufacture) herstellen, produzieren; (on farm) erzeugen; (film, play, record) produzieren; (cause) hervorrufen; (evidence, results) liefern; **producer** n (manufacturer) Hersteller(in) m(f); (of film, play, record) Produzent(in) m(f); **product** ['prɒdʌkt] n Produkt nt, Erzeugnis nt; **production** [prə'dʌkʃən] n Produktion f; (Theat) Inszenierung f; **productive** [prə'dʌktɪv] adj produktiv; (land) ertragreich

prof [prɒf] n (fam) Prof m

profession [prə'feʃən] n Beruf m; **professional** [prə'feʃənl] n Profi m ▷ adj beruflich; (expert) fachlich; (sportsman, actor etc) Berufs-

professor [prə'fesə*] n Professor(in) m(f); (US: lecturer) Dozent(in) m(f)

proficient [prə'fɪʃənt] adj kompetent (in in +dat)

profile ['prəʊfaɪl] n Profil nt; **to keep a low ~** sich rarmachen

profit ['prɒfɪt] n Gewinn m ▷ vi profitieren (by, from von); **profitable** adj rentabel

profound [prə'faʊnd] adj tief; (idea, thinker) tiefgründig; (knowledge) profund

program ['prəʊgræm] n (Inform) Programm nt; (US) see **programme** ▷ vt (Inform) programmieren; (US) see **programme**

programme ['prəʊgræm] n Programm nt; (TV, Radio) Sendung f ▷ vt programmieren; **programmer** n Programmierer(in) m(f); **programming** n (Inform) Programmieren nt; **~ language** Programmiersprache f

progress ['prəʊgres] n Fortschritt m; **to make ~** Fortschritte machen ▷ [prə'gres] vi (work, illness etc) fortschreiten; (improve) Fortschritte machen; **progressive** [prə'gresɪv] adj (person, policy) fortschrittlich; **progressively** [prə'gresɪvlɪ] adv zunehmend

prohibit [prə'hɪbɪt] vt verbieten

project ['prɒdʒekt] n Projekt nt

projector [prə'dʒektə*] n Projektor m

prolong [prə'lɒŋ] vt verlängern

prom [prɒm] n (at seaside) Promenade f; (Brit: concert) Konzert nt (bei dem ein Großteil des Publikums im Parkett Stehplätze hat); (US:

dance) Ball für die Schüler und Studenten von Highschools oder Colleges

prominent ['prɒmɪnənt] _adj_ (_politician, actor etc_) prominent; (_easily seen_) auffallend

promiscuous [prə'mɪskjʊəs] _adj_ promisk

promise ['prɒmɪs] _n_ Versprechen _nt_ ▷ _vt_ versprechen; **to ~ sb sth** jdm etw versprechen; **to ~ to do sth** versprechen, etw zu tun ▷ _vi_ versprechen; **promising** _adj_ vielversprechend

promote [prə'məʊt] _vt_ (_in rank_) befördern; (_help on_) fördern; (_Comm_) werben für; **promotion** [prə'məʊʃən] _n_ (_in rank_) Beförderung _f_; (_Comm_) Werbung _f_ (_of für_)

prompt [prɒmpt] _adj_ prompt; (_punctual_) pünktlich ▷ _adv_: **at two o'clock ~** Punkt zwei Uhr ▷ _vt_ (_Theat: actor_) soufflieren +_dat_

prone [prəʊn] _adj_: **to be ~ to sth** zu etw neigen

pronounce [prə'naʊns] _vt_ (_word_) aussprechen; **pronounced** _adj_ ausgeprägt; **pronunciation** [prənʌnsɪ'eɪʃən] _n_ Aussprache _f_

proof [pru:f] _n_ Beweis _m_; (_of alcohol_) Alkoholgehalt _m_

prop [prɒp] _n_ Stütze _f_; (_Theat_) Requisit _nt_ ▷ _vt_: **to ~ sth against sth** etw gegen etw lehnen; **prop up** _vt_ stützen; (_fig_) unterstützen

proper ['prɒpə*] _adj_ richtig; (_morally correct_) anständig

property ['prɒpətɪ] _n_ (_possession_) Eigentum _nt_; (_house_) Haus _nt_; (_land_) Grundbesitz _m_; (_characteristic_) Eigenschaft _f_

proportion [prə'pɔ:ʃən] _n_ Verhältnis _nt_; (_share_) Teil _m_; **~s** _pl_ (_size_) Proportionen _pl_; **in ~ to** im Verhältnis zu; **proportional** _adj_

proportional; **~ representation** Verhältniswahlrecht _nt_

proposal [prə'pəʊzl] _n_ Vorschlag _m_; **~ (of marriage)** (Heirats)antrag _m_; **propose** [prə'pəʊz] _vt_ vorschlagen ▷ _vi_ (_offer marriage_) einen Heiratsantrag machen (_to sb_ jdm)

proprietor [prə'praɪətə*] _n_ Besitzer(in) _m(f)_; (_of pub, hotel_) Inhaber(in) _m(f)_

prose [prəʊz] _n_ Prosa _f_

prosecute ['prɒsɪkju:t] _vt_ verfolgen (_for wegen_)

prospect ['prɒspekt] _n_ Aussicht _f_

prosperity [prɒ'sperɪtɪ] _n_ Wohlstand _m_; **prosperous** _adj_ wohlhabend; (_business_) gut gehend

prostitute ['prɒstɪtju:t] _n_ Prostituierte(r) _mf_

protect [prə'tekt] _vt_ schützen (_from, against_ vor +_dat_, gegen); **protection** [prə'tekʃən] _n_ Schutz _m_ (_from, against_ vor +_dat_, gegen); **protective** _adj_ beschützend; (_clothing etc_) Schutz-

protein ['prəʊti:n] _n_ Protein _nt_

protest ['prəʊtest] _n_ Protest _m_; (_demonstration_) Protestkundgebung _f_ ▷ [prə'test] _vi_ protestieren (_against_ gegen); (_demonstrate_) demonstrieren

Protestant ['prɒtəstənt] _adj_ protestantisch ▷ _n_ Protestant(in) _m(f)_

proud, proudly [praʊd, -lɪ] _adj, adv_ stolz (_of_ auf +_akk_)

prove [pru:v] _vt_ beweisen; (_turn out to be_) sich erweisen als

proverb ['prɒvɜ:b] _n_ Sprichwort _nt_

provide [prə'vaɪd] _vt_ zur Verfügung stellen; (_drinks, music etc_) sorgen für; (_person_) versorgen (_with_ mit); **provide for** _vt_ (_family_ *etc*) sorgen für; **provided** *conj*: **~ (that)** vorausgesetzt, dass; **provider** *n* (*Inform*) Provider *m*

provision [prəˈvɪʒən] *n* (*condition*) Bestimmung *f*; **~s** *pl* (*food*) Proviant *m*

provisional, provisionally [prəˈvɪʒənl, -ɪ] *adj, adv* provisorisch

provoke [prəˈvəʊk] *vt* provozieren; (*cause*) hervorrufen

proximity [prɒkˈsɪmɪtɪ] *n* Nähe *f*

prudent [ˈpruːdənt] *adj* klug; (*person*) umsichtig

prudish [ˈpruːdɪʃ] *adj* prüde

prune [pruːn] *n* Backpflaume *f* ▷ *vt* (*tree etc*) zurechtstutzen

PS *abbr* = **postscript** PS *nt*

psalm [sɑːm] *n* Psalm *m*

pseudo [ˈsjuːdəʊ] *adj* pseudo-, Pseudo-; **pseudonym** [ˈsjuːdənɪm] *n* Pseudonym *nt*

PST *abbr* = **Pacific Standard Time**

psychiatric [saɪkɪˈætrɪk] *adj* psychiatrisch; (*illness*) psychisch; **psychiatrist** [saɪˈkaɪətrɪst] *n* Psychiater(in) *m(f)*; **psychiatry** [saɪˈkaɪətrɪ] *n* Psychiatrie *f*; **psychic** [ˈsaɪkɪk] *adj* übersinnlich; **I'm not ~** ich kann keine Gedanken lesen; **psychoanalysis** [saɪkəʊəˈnæləsɪs] *n* Psychoanalyse *f*; **psychoanalyst** [saɪkəʊˈænəlɪst] *n* Psychoanalytiker(in) *m(f)*; **psychological** [saɪkəˈlɒdʒɪkəl] *adj* psychologisch; **psychology** [saɪˈkɒlədʒɪ] *n* Psychologie *f*; **psychopath** [ˈsaɪkəʊpæθ] *n* Psychopath(in) *m(f)*

pt *abbr* = **pint**

pto *abbr* = **please turn over** b.w.

pub [pʌb] *n* (*Brit*) Kneipe *f*

- **PUB**
-
- Ein **pub** ist ein Gasthaus mit
- einer Lizenz zum Ausschank von
- alkoholischen Getränken. Ein
- „Pub" besteht meist aus
- verschiedenen gemütlichen
- (**lounge, snug**) oder
- einfacheren (**public bar**)
- Räumen, in denen oft auch
- Spiele wie Darts, Domino und
- Poolbillard zur Verfügung
- stehen. In „Pubs" werden vor
- allem mittags auch Mahlzeiten
- angeboten (**pub lunch**). Die
- Sperrstunde wurde 2005
- aufgehoben. Dennoch sind
- „Pubs" oft nur von 11 bis 23 Uhr
- geöffnet. Nachmittags bleiben
- sie häufig geschlossen.

puberty [ˈpjuːbətɪ] *n* Pubertät *f*

public [ˈpʌblɪk] *n*: **the** (**general**) **~** die (breite) Öffentlichkeit; **in ~** in der Öffentlichkeit ▷ *adj* öffentlich; (*relating to the State*) Staats-; **~ convenience** (*Brit*) öffentliche Toilette; **~ holiday** gesetzlicher Feiertag; **~ opinion** die öffentliche Meinung; **~ relations** *pl* Öffentlichkeitsarbeit *f*, Public Relations *pl*; **~ school** (*Brit*) Privatschule *f*; **publication** [pʌblɪˈkeɪʃən] *n* Veröffentlichung *f*; **publicity** [pʌbˈlɪsɪtɪ] *n* Publicity *f*; (*advertisements*) Werbung *f*; **publish** [ˈpʌblɪʃ] *vt* veröffentlichen; **publisher** *n* Verleger(in) *m(f)*; (*company*) Verlag *m*; **publishing** *n* Verlagswesen *nt*

pub lunch [ˈpʌbˈlʌntʃ] *n* (*oft einfacheres*) *Mittagessen in einer Kneipe*

pudding [ˈpʊdɪŋ] *n* (*course*) Nachtisch *m*

puddle [ˈpʌdl] *n* Pfütze *f*

puff [pʌf] *vi* (*pant*) schnaufen

puffin [ˈpʌfɪn] *n* Papageientaucher *m*

puff paste (US), **puff pastry** ['pʌf'peɪstrɪ] n Blätterteig m
pull [pʊl] n Ziehen nt; **to give sth a ~** an etw dat ziehen ▷ vt (cart, tooth) ziehen; (rope, handle) ziehen an +dat; (fam: date) abschleppen; **to ~ a muscle** sich dat einen Muskel zerren; **to ~ sb's leg** jdn auf den Arm nehmen ▷ vi ziehen; **pull apart** vt (separate) auseinanderziehen; **pull down** vt (blind) herunterziehen; (house) abreißen; **pull in** vi hineinfahren; (stop) anhalten; **pull off** vt (deal etc) zuwege bringen; (clothes) ausziehen; **pull on** vt (clothes) anziehen; **pull out** vi (car from lane) ausscheren; (train) abfahren; (withdraw) aussteigen (of aus) ▷ vt herausziehen; (tooth) ziehen; (troops) abziehen; **pull round, pull through** vi durchkommen; **pull up** vt (raise) hochziehen; (chair) heranziehen ▷ vi anhalten
pullover ['pʊləʊvə*] n Pullover m
pulp [pʌlp] n Brei m; (of fruit) Fruchtfleisch nt
pulpit ['pʊlpɪt] n Kanzel f
pulse [pʌls] n Puls m
pump [pʌmp] n Pumpe f; (in petrol station) Zapfsäule f; **pump up** vt (tyre etc) aufpumpen
pumpkin ['pʌmpkɪn] n Kürbis m
pun [pʌn] n Wortspiel nt
punch [pʌntʃ] n (blow) (Faust)schlag m; (tool) Locher m; (hot drink) Punsch m; (cold drink) Bowle f ▷ vt (strike) schlagen; (ticket, paper) lochen
punctual, punctually ['pʌŋktjʊəl, -ɪ] adj, adv pünktlich
punctuation [pʌŋktjʊ'eɪʃən] n Interpunktion f; **punctuation mark** n Satzeichen nt
puncture ['pʌŋktʃə*] n (flat tyre) Reifenpanne f

punish ['pʌnɪʃ] vt bestrafen; **punishment** n Strafe f; (action) Bestrafung f
pupil ['pjuːpl] n (school) Schüler(in) m(f)
puppet ['pʌpɪt] n Marionette f
puppy ['pʌpɪ] n junger Hund
purchase ['pɜːtʃɪs] n Kauf m ▷ vt kaufen
pure [pjʊə*] adj rein; (clean) sauber; (utter) pur; **purely** ['pjuːəlɪ] adv rein; **purify** ['pjʊərɪfaɪ] vt reinigen; **purity** ['pjʊərɪtɪ] n Reinheit f
purple ['pɜːpl] adj violett
purpose ['pɜːpəs] n Zweck m; (of person) Absicht f; **on ~** absichtlich
purr [pɜː*] vi (cat) schnurren
purse [pɜːs] n Geldbeutel m; (US: handbag) Handtasche f
pursue [pə'sjuː] vt (person, car) verfolgen; (hobby, studies) nachgehen +dat; **pursuit** [pə'sjuːt] n (chase) Verfolgung f; (occupation) Beschäftigung f; (hobby) Hobby nt
pus [pʌs] n Eiter m
push [pʊʃ] n Stoß m ▷ vt (person) stoßen; (car, chair etc) schieben; (button) drücken; (drugs) dealen ▷ vi (in crowd) drängeln; **push in** vi (in queue) sich vordrängeln; **push off** vi (fam: leave) abhauen; **push on** vi (with job) weitermachen; **push up** vt (prices) hochtreiben; **pushchair** n (Brit) Sport(kinder)wagen m; **pusher** n (of drugs) Dealer(in) m(f); **push-up** n (US) Liegestütz m; **pushy** adj (fam) aufdringlich, penetrant
put [pʊt] (put, put) vt tun; (upright) stellen; (flat) legen; (express) ausdrücken; (write) schreiben; **he ~ his hand in his pocket** er steckte die Hand in die Tasche; **he ~ his hand on her shoulder** er legte ihr die Hand auf

die Schulter; **to ~ money into one's account** Geld auf sein Konto einzahlen; **put aside** vt (money) zurücklegen; **put away** vt (tidy away) wegräumen; **put back** vt zurücklegen; (clock) zurückstellen; **put down** vt (in writing) aufschreiben; (Brit: animal) einschläfern; (rebellion) niederschlagen; **to put the phone down** (den Hörer) auflegen; **to put one's name down for sth** sich für etw eintragen; **put forward** vt (idea) vorbringen; (name) vorschlagen; (clock) vorstellen; **put in** vt (install) einbauen; (submit) einreichen; **put off** vt (switch off) ausschalten; (postpone) verschieben; **to put sb off doing sth** jdn davon abbringen, etw zu tun; **put on** vt (switch on) anmachen; (clothes) anziehen; (hat, glasses) aufsetzen; (make-up, CD) auflegen; (play) aufführen; **to put the kettle on** Wasser aufsetzen; **to put weight on** zunehmen; **put out** vt (hand, foot) ausstrecken; (light, cigarette) ausmachen; **put up** vt (hand) hochheben; (picture) aufhängen; (tent) aufstellen; (building) errichten; (price) erhöhen; (person) unterbringen; **to ~ with** sich abfinden mit; **I won't ~ with it** das lasse ich mir nicht gefallen

putt [pʌt] vt, vi (Sport) putten

puzzle ['pʌzl] n Rätsel nt; (toy) Geduldsspiel nt; (**jigsaw**) ~ Puzzle nt ▷ vt vor ein Rätsel stellen; **it ~s me** es ist mir ein Rätsel; **puzzling** adj rätselhaft

pyjamas [pɪ'dʒɑːməz] npl Schlafanzug m

pylon ['paɪlən] n Mast m

pyramid ['pɪrəmɪd] n Pyramide f

quack [kwæk] vi quaken

quaint [kweɪnt] adj (idea, tradition) kurios; (picturesque) malerisch

qualification [kwɒlɪfɪ'keɪʃən] n (for job) Qualifikation f; (from school, university) Abschluss m; **qualified** ['kwɒlɪfaɪd] adj (for job) qualifiziert; **qualify** vt (limit) einschränken; **to be qualified to do sth** berechtigt sein, etw zu tun ▷ vi (finish training) seine Ausbildung abschließen; (contest etc) sich qualifizieren

quality ['kwɒlɪtɪ] n Qualität f; (characteristic) Eigenschaft f

quantity ['kwɒntɪtɪ] n Menge f, Quantität f

quarantine ['kwɒrəntiːn] n Quarantäne f

quarrel ['kwɒrəl] n Streit m ▷ vi sich streiten

quarter ['kwɔːtə*] n Viertel nt;

(of year) Vierteljahr nt; (US: coin) Vierteldollar m; **a ~ of an hour** eine Viertelstunde; **~ to/past** (Brit) (o **~ of/after** (US)) **three** Viertel vor/nach drei ▷ vt vierteln; **quarter final** n Viertelfinale nt; **quarters** npl (Mil) Quartier nt

quartet [kwɔː'tet] n Quartett nt

quay [kiː] n Kai m

queasy ['kwiːzɪ] adj: **I feel ~** mir ist übel

queen [kwiːn] n Königin f; (in cards, chess) Dame f

queer [kwɪə*] adj (strange) seltsam, sonderbar; (pej: homosexual) schwul ▷ n (pej) Schwule(r) m

quench [kwentʃ] vt (thirst) löschen

query ['kwɪərɪ] n Frage f ▷ vt infrage stellen; (bill) reklamieren

question ['kwestʃən] n Frage f; **that's out of the ~** das kommt nicht infrage ▷ vt (person) befragen; (suspect) verhören; (express doubt about) bezweifeln; **questionable** adj zweifelhaft; (improper) fragwürdig; **question mark** n Fragezeichen nt; **questionnaire** [kwestʃə'nɛə*] n Fragebogen m

queue [kjuː] n (Brit) Schlange f; **to jump the ~** sich vordrängeln ▷ vi: **to ~ (up)** Schlange stehen

quibble ['kwɪbl] vi kleinlich sein; (argue) streiten

quiche [kiːʃ] n Quiche

quick [kwɪk] adj schnell; (short) kurz; **be ~** mach schnell!; **quickly** adv schnell

quid [kwɪd] (pl **quid**) n (Brit fam) Pfund nt; **20 ~** 20 Pfund

quiet ['kwaɪət] adj (not noisy) leise; (peaceful, calm) still, ruhig; **be ~** sei still!; **to keep ~ about sth** über etw akk nichts sagen ▷ n

Stille f, Ruhe f; **quiet down** (US), **quieten down** ['kwaɪətən'daʊn] vi sich beruhigen ▷ vt beruhigen; **quietly** adv leise; (calmly) ruhig

quilt [kwɪlt] n (Stepp)decke f

quit [kwɪt] (**quit** o **quitted, quit** o **quitted**) vt (leave) verlassen; (job) aufgeben; **to ~ doing sth** aufhören, etw zu tun ▷ vi aufhören; (resign) kündigen

quite [kwaɪt] adv (fairly) ziemlich; (completely) ganz, völlig; **I don't ~ understand** ich verstehe das nicht ganz; **~ a few** ziemlich viele; **~ so** richtig!

quits [kwɪts] adj: **to be ~ with sb** mit jdm quitt sein

quiver ['kwɪvə*] vi zittern

quiz [kwɪz] n (competition) Quiz nt

quota ['kwəʊtə] n Anteil m; (Comm, Pol) Quote f

quotation [kwəʊ'teɪʃən] n Zitat nt; (price) Kostenvoranschlag m; **quotation marks** npl Anführungszeichen pl; **quote** [kwəʊt] vt (text, author) zitieren; (price) nennen ▷ n Zitat nt; (price) Kostenvoranschlag m; **in ~s** in Anführungszeichen

r

rabbi ['ræbaɪ] n Rabbiner m
rabbit ['ræbɪt] n Kaninchen nt
rabies ['reɪbiːz] nsing Tollwut f
raccoon [rə'kuːn] n Waschbär m
race [reɪs] n (competition) Rennen
nt; (people) Rasse f ▷ vt um die
Wette laufen/fahren ▷ vi (rush)
rennen; **racecourse** n Rennbahn
f; **racehorse** n Rennpferd nt;
racetrack n Rennbahn f
racial ['reɪʃəl] adj Rassen-;
~ discrimination
Rassendiskriminierung f
racing ['reɪsɪŋ] n: (**horse**)
~ Pferderennen nt; (**motor**)
~ Autorennen nt; **racing car** n
Rennwagen m
racism ['reɪsɪzəm] n Rassismus
m; **racist** n Rassist(in) m(f) ▷ adj
rassistisch
rack [ræk] n Ständer m, Gestell nt
▷ vt: **to ~ one's brains** sich dat
den Kopf zerbrechen

racket ['rækɪt] n (Sport) Schläger
m; (noise) Krach m
radar ['reɪdɑː*] n Radar nt o m;
radar trap n Radarfalle f
radiation [reɪdɪ'eɪʃən] n (radioactive) Strahlung f
radiator ['reɪdɪeɪtə*] n Heizkörper m; (Auto) Kühler m
radical ['rædɪkəl] adj radikal
radio ['reɪdɪəʊ] (pl **-s**) n
Rundfunk m, Radio nt
radioactivity [reɪdɪəʊæk'tɪvɪtɪ]
n Radioaktivität f
radio alarm ['reɪdɪəʊə'lɑːm] n
Radiowecker m; **radio station** n
Rundfunkstation f
radiotherapy [reɪdɪəʊ'θerəpɪ]
n Strahlenbehandlung f
radish ['rædɪʃ] n Radieschen nt
radius ['reɪdɪəs] n Radius m;
within a five-mile ~ im Umkreis
von fünf Meilen (of um)
raffle ['ræfl] n Tombola f; **raffle
ticket** n Los nt
raft [rɑːft] n Floß nt
rag [ræg] n Lumpen m; (for
cleaning) Lappen m
rage [reɪdʒ] n Wut f; **to be all the
~** der letzte Schrei sein ▷ vi toben;
(disease) wüten
raid [reɪd] n Überfall m (on auf
+akk); (by police) Razzia f (on gegen)
▷ vt (bank etc) überfallen; (by
police) eine Razzia machen in +dat
rail [reɪl] n (on stairs, balcony etc)
Geländer nt; (of ship) Reling f; (Rail)
Schiene f; **railcard** n (Brit) ≈
Bahncard® f; **railing** n Geländer
nt; **~s** pl (fence) Zaun m; **railroad** n
(US) Eisenbahn f; **railroad station**
n (US) Bahnhof m; **railway** n (Brit)
Eisenbahn f; **railway line** n
Bahnlinie f; (track) Gleis m; **railway
station** n Bahnhof m
rain [reɪn] n Regen m ▷ vi
regnen; **it's ~ing** es regnet;
rainbow n Regenbogen m;

raincoat n Regenmantel m;
rainfall n Niederschlag m;
rainforest n Regenwald m; **rainy**
adj regnerisch
raise [reɪz] n (US: of wages/salary)
Gehalts-/Lohnerhöhung f ▷ vt
(lift) hochheben; (increase)
erhöhen; (family) großziehen;
(livestock) züchten; (money)
aufbringen; (objection) erheben; **to**
~ one's voice laut werden
raisin ['reɪzən] n Rosine f
rally ['rælɪ] n (Pol) Kundgebung f;
(Auto) Rallye f; (Tennis) Ballwechsel
m
RAM [ræm] acr = **random access**
memory RAM m
ramble ['ræmbl] n Wanderung f
▷ vi (walk) wandern; (talk)
schwafeln
ramp [ræmp] n Rampe f
ran [ræn] pt of **run**
ranch [rɑːntʃ] n Ranch f
rancid ['rænsɪd] adj ranzig
random ['rændəm] adj
willkürlich ▷ n: **at ~** (choose)
willkürlich; (fire) ziellos
rang [ræŋ] pt of **ring**
range [reɪndʒ] n (selection)
Auswahl f (of an +dat); (Comm)
Sortiment nt (of an +dat); (of
missile, telescope) Reichweite f; (of
mountains) Kette f; **in this price**
~ in dieser Preisklasse ▷ vi: **to**
~ from ... to ... gehen von ... bis ...;
(temperature, sizes, prices) liegen
zwischen ... und ...
rank [ræŋk] n (Mil) Rang m; (social
position) Stand m ▷ vt einstufen
ransom ['rænsəm] n Lösegeld nt
rap [ræp] n (Mus) Rap m
rape [reɪp] n Vergewaltigung f
▷ vt vergewaltigen
rapid, **rapidly** ['ræpɪd, -lɪ] adj, adv
schnell
rapist ['reɪpɪst] n Vergewaltiger
m

rare [rɛə*] adj selten, rar;
(especially good) vortrefflich; (steak)
blutig; **rarely** adv selten; **rarity**
['rɛərɪtɪ] n Seltenheit f
rash [ræʃ] adj unbesonnen ▷ n
(Med) (Haut)ausschlag m
rasher ['ræʃə*] n: **~ (of bacon)**
(Speck)scheibe f
raspberry ['rɑːzbərɪ] n Himbeere f
rat [ræt] n Ratte f; (pej: person)
Schwein nt
rate [reɪt] n (proportion, frequency)
Rate f; (speed) Tempo nt; **~ (of**
exchange) (Wechsel)kurs m; **~ of**
inflation Inflationsrate f; **~ of**
interest Zinssatz m; **at any ~** auf
jeden Fall ▷ vt (evaluate)
einschätzen (as als)
rather ['rɑːðə*] adv (in preference)
lieber; (fairly) ziemlich; **I'd ~ stay**
here ich würde lieber hierbleiben;
I'd ~ not lieber nicht; **or ~** (more
accurately) vielmehr
ratio ['reɪʃɪəʊ] (pl **-s**) n Verhältnis
nt
rational ['ræʃənl] adj rational;
rationalize ['ræʃnəlaɪz] vt
rationalisieren
rattle ['rætl] n (toy) Rassel f ▷ vt
(keys, coins) klimpern mit; (person)
durcheinanderbringen ▷ vi (window) klappern; (bottles) klirren;
rattle off vt herunterrasseln;
rattlesnake n Klapperschlange
f
rave [reɪv] vi (talk wildly)
fantasieren; (rage) toben; (enthuse)
schwärmen (about von) ▷ n (Brit:
event) Raveparty f
raven ['reɪvn] n Rabe m
raving ['reɪvɪŋ] adv: **~ mad** total
verrückt
ravishing ['rævɪʃɪŋ] adj
hinreißend
raw [rɔː] adj (food) roh; (skin)
wund; (climate) rau

ray [reɪ] n (of light) Strahl m; **~ of hope** Hoffnungsschimmer m

razor ['reɪzə*] n Rasierapparat m; **razor blade** n Rasierklinge f

Rd n abbr = **road** Str.

re [riː] prep (Comm) betreffs +gen

RE abbr = **religious education**

reach [riːtʃ] n: **within/out of (sb's) ~** in/außer (jds) Reichweite; **within easy ~ of the shops** nicht weit von den Geschäften ▷ vt (arrive at, contact) erreichen; (come down/up as far as) reichen bis zu; (contact) **can you ~ it?** kommst du/kommen Sie dran?; **reach for** vt greifen nach; **reach out** vi die Hand ausstrecken; **to ~ for** greifen nach

react [riːˈækt] vi reagieren (to auf +akk); **reaction** [riːˈækʃən] n Reaktion f (to auf +akk); **reactor** [rɪˈæktə*] n Reaktor m

read [riːd] (**read, read**) vt lesen; (meter) ablesen; **to ~ sth to sb** jdm etw vorlesen ▷ vi lesen; **to ~ to sb** jdm vorlesen; **it ~s well** es liest sich gut; **it ~s as follows** es lautet folgendermaßen; **read out** vt vorlesen; **read through** vt durchlesen; **read up on** vt nachlesen über +akk; **readable** adj (book) lesenswert; (handwriting) lesbar; **reader** n Leser(in) m(f); **readership** n Leserschaft f

readily ['redɪlɪ] adv (willingly) bereitwillig; **~ available** leicht erhältlich

reading ['riːdɪŋ] n (action) Lesen nt; (from meter) Zählerstand m; **reading glasses** npl Lesebrille f; **reading lamp** n Leselampe f; **reading list** n Leseliste f; **reading matter** n Lektüre f

readjust [riːəˈdʒʌst] vt (mechanism etc) neu einstellen ▷ vi sich wieder anpassen (to an +akk)

ready ['redɪ] adj fertig, bereit; **to**
be **~ to do sth** (willing) bereit sein, etw zu tun; **are you ~ to go?** bist du so weit?; **to get sth ~** etw fertig machen; **to get (oneself) ~** sich fertig machen; **ready cash** n Bargeld nt; **ready-made** adj (product) Fertig-; (clothes) Konfektions-; **~ meal** Fertiggericht nt

real [rɪəl] adj wirklich; (actual) eigentlich; (genuine) echt; (idiot etc) richtig ▷ adv (fam, esp US) echt; **for ~** diesmal ist es ernst; **this time it's for ~** diesmal ist es ernst; **get ~** sei realistisch!; **real ale** n Ale nt; **real estate** n Immobilien pl

realistic, realistically [rɪəˈlɪstɪk, -əlɪ] adj, adv realistisch; **reality** [riːˈælɪtɪ] n Wirklichkeit f; **in ~** in Wirklichkeit; **reality TV** n Reality-TV nt; **realization** [rɪəlaɪˈzeɪʃən] n (awareness) Erkenntnis f; **realize** ['rɪəlaɪz] vt (understand) begreifen; (plan, idea) realisieren; **I ~d (that) ...** mir wurde klar, dass ...

really ['rɪəlɪ] adv wirklich

real time [rɪəlˈtaɪm] n (Inform) **in ~** in Echtzeit

realtor ['rɪəltɔ*] n (US) Grundstücksmakler(in) m(f)

reappear [riːəˈpɪə*] vi wieder erscheinen

rear [rɪə*] adj hintere(r, s), Hinter- ▷ n (of building, vehicle) hinterer Teil; **at the ~ of** hinter +dat; (inside) hinten in +dat; **rear light** n (Auto) Rücklicht nt

rearm [riːˈɑːm] vi wieder aufrüsten

rearrange [riːəˈreɪndʒ] vt (furniture, system) umstellen; (meeting) verlegen (for auf +akk)

rear-view mirror ['rɪəvjuːˈmɪrə*] n Rückspiegel m; **rear window** n (Auto) Heckscheibe f

reason ['riːzn] n (cause) Grund m
(for für); (ability to think) Verstand
m; (common sense) Vernunft f; **for
some ~** aus irgendeinem Grund
▷ vi: **to ~ with sb** mit jdm
vernünftig reden; **reasonable** adj
(person, price) vernünftig; (offer)
akzeptabel; (chance) reell; (food,
weather) ganz gut; **reasonably** adv
vernünftig; (fairly) ziemlich

reassure [riːə'ʃʊə*] vt beruhigen; **she ~d me that ...** sie
versicherte mir, dass ...

rebel ['rebl] n Rebell(in) m(f)
▷ [rɪ'bel] vi rebellieren; **rebellion**
[rɪ'beliən] n Aufstand m

reboot [riː'buːt] vt, vi (Inform)
rebooten

rebound [rɪ'baʊnd] vi (ball etc)
zurückprallen

rebuild [riː'bɪld] irr vt wieder
aufbauen

recall [rɪ'kɔːl] vt (remember) sich
erinnern an +akk; (call back)
zurückrufen

recap ['riːkæp] vt, vi
rekapitulieren

receipt [rɪ'siːt] n (document)
Quittung f; (receiving) Empfang m;
~s pl (money) Einnahmen pl

receive [rɪ'siːv] vt (news etc)
erhalten, bekommen; (visitor)
empfangen; **receiver** n (Tel)
Hörer m; (Radio) Empfänger m

recent ['riːsnt] adj (event) vor
Kurzem stattgefunden; (photo)
neueste(r,s); (invention) neu; **in
~ years** in den letzten Jahren;
recently adv vor Kurzem; (in the
last few days or weeks) in letzter Zeit

reception [rɪ'sepʃən] n Empfang
m; **receptionist** n (in hotel)
Empfangschef m, Empfangsdame
f; (woman in firm) Empfangsdame f;
(Med) Sprechstundenhilfe f

recess [rɪ'ses] n (in wall) Nische
f; (US: in school) Pause f

recession [rɪ'seʃən] n Rezession
f

recharge [riː'tʃɑːdʒ] vt (battery)
aufladen; **rechargeable**
[riː'tʃɑːdʒəbl] adj wiederaufladbar

recipe ['resɪpɪ] n Rezept nt (for
für)

recipient [rɪ'sɪpɪənt] n
Empfänger(in) m(f)

reciprocal [rɪ'sɪprəkəl] adj
gegenseitig

recite [rɪ'saɪt] vt vortragen;
(details) aufzählen

reckless ['rekləs] adj leichtsinnig; (driving) gefährlich

reckon ['rekən] vt (calculate)
schätzen; (think) glauben ▷ vi: **to
~ with/on** rechnen mit

reclaim [rɪ'kleɪm] vt (baggage)
abholen; (expenses, tax)
zurückverlangen

recline [rɪ'klaɪn] vi (person) sich
zurücklehnen; **reclining seat** n
Liegesitz m

recognition [rekəg'nɪʃən] n
(acknowledgement) Anerkennung f;
in ~ of in Anerkennung +gen;
recognize ['rekəgnaɪz] vt
erkennen; (approve officially)
anerkennen

recommend [rekə'mend] vt
empfehlen; **recommendation**
[rekəmen'deɪʃən] n Empfehlung f

reconfirm [riːkən'fɜːm] vt (flight
etc) rückbestätigen

reconsider [riːkən'sɪdə*] vt noch
einmal überdenken ▷ vi es sich
dat noch einmal überlegen

reconstruct [riːkən'strʌkt] vt
wieder aufbauen; (crime)
rekonstruieren

record ['rekɔːd] n (Mus)
(Schall)platte f; (best performance)
Rekord m; **~s** pl (files) Akten pl; **to
keep a ~ of** Buch führen über +akk
▷ adj (time etc) Rekord- ▷ [rɪ'kɔːd]
vt (write down) aufzeichnen; (on

tape etc) aufnehmen; **~ed message**
Ansage *f*; **recorded delivery** *n*
(*Brit*) **by ~** per Einschreiben
recorder [rɪ'kɔːdə*] *n* (*Mus*)
Blockflöte *f*; (**cassette**)
~ (Kassetten)rekorder *m*;
recording [rɪ'kɔːdɪŋ] *n* (*on tape
etc*) Aufnahme *f*; **record player**
['rekɔːdpleɪə*] *n* Plattenspieler *m*
recover [rɪ'kʌvə*] *vt* (*money, item*)
zurückbekommen; (*appetite,
strength*) wiedergewinnen ▷ *vi*
sich erholen
recreation [rekrɪ'eɪʃən] *n*
Erholung *f*; **recreational** *adj*
Freizeit-; **~ vehicle** (*US*)
Wohnmobil *nt*
recruit [rɪ'kruːt] *n* (*Mil*)
Rekrut(in) *m(f)*; (*in firm,
organization*) neues Mitglied ▷ *vt*
(*Mil*) rekrutieren; (*members*)
anwerben; (*staff*) einstellen;
recruitment agency *n*
Personalagentur *f*
rectangle ['rektæŋgl] *n*
Rechteck *nt*; **rectangular**
[rek'tæŋgʊlə*] *adj* rechteckig
rectify ['rektɪfaɪ] *vt* berichtigen
recuperate [rɪ'kuːpəreɪt] *vi* sich
erholen
recyclable [riː'saɪkləbl] *adj*
recyclebar, wiederverwertbar;
recycle [riː'saɪkl] *vt* recyceln,
wiederverwerten; **~d paper**
Recyclingpapier *nt*; **recycling** *n*
Recycling *nt*, Wiederverwertung *f*
red [red] *adj* rot ▷ *n*: **in the ~** in
den roten Zahlen; **Red Cross** *n*
Rotes Kreuz; **red cabbage** *n*
Rotkohl *m*; **redcurrant** *n* (rote)
Johannisbeere
redeem [rɪ'diːm] *vt* (*Comm*)
einlösen
red-handed [red'hændɪd] *adj*:
to catch sb ~ jdn auf frischer Tat
ertappen; **redhead** *n*
Rothaarige(r) *mf*

redial [riː'daɪəl] *vt, vi* nochmals
wählen
redirect [riːdaɪ'rekt] *vt* (*traffic*)
umleiten; (*forward*) nachsenden
red light [red'laɪt] *n* (*traffic
signal*) rotes Licht; **to go through
the ~** bei Rot über die Ampel
fahren; **red meat** *n*
Rind-, Lamm-, Rehfleisch
redo [riː'duː] *irr vt* nochmals
machen
reduce [rɪ'djuːs] *vt* reduzieren
(*to* auf +*akk*, *by* um); **reduction**
[rɪ'dʌkʃən] *n* Reduzierung *f*; (*in
price*) Ermäßigung *f*
redundant [rɪ'dʌndənt] *adj*
überflüssig; **to be made
~** entlassen werden
red wine [red'waɪn] *n* Rotwein
m
reef [riːf] *n* Riff *nt*
reel [riːl] *n* Spule *f*; (*on fishing rod*)
Rolle *f*; **reel off** *vt* herunterrasseln
ref [ref] *n* (*fam: referee*) Schiri *m*
refectory [rɪ'fektərɪ] *n* (*at
college*) Mensa *f*
refer [rɪ'fɜː*] *vt*: **to ~ sb to sb/sth**
jdn an jdn/etw verweisen; **to
~ sth to sb** (*query, problem*) etw an
jdn weiterleiten ▷ *vi*: **to ~ to**
(*mention, allude to*) sich beziehen
auf +*akk*; (*book*) nachschlagen in
+*dat*
referee [refə'riː] *n* Schiedsrich-
ter(in) *m(f)*; (*in boxing*) Ringrichter
m; (*Brit: for job*) Referenz *f*
reference ['refrəns] *n* (*allusion*)
Anspielung *f* (*to* auf +*akk*); (*for job*)
Referenz *f*; (*in book*) Verweis *m*;
~ (**number**) (*in document*)
Aktenzeichen *nt*; **with ~ to** mit
Bezug auf +*akk*; **reference book** *n*
Nachschlagewerk *nt*
referendum [refə'rendəm] (*pl
referenda*) *n* Referendum *nt*
refill ['riːfɪl] *vt* [riː'fɪl] nachfüllen
▷ *n* (*for ballpoint pen*) Ersatzmine *f*

refine [rɪ'faɪn] *vt* (*purify*)
raffinieren; (*improve*) verfeinern;
refined *adj* (*genteel*) fein
reflect [rɪ'flekt] *vt* reflektieren;
(*fig*) widerspiegeln ▷ *vi*
nachdenken (*on* über +*akk*);
reflection [rɪ'flekʃən] *n* (*image*)
Spiegelbild *nt*; (*thought*)
Überlegung *f*; **on ~** nach reiflicher
Überlegung
reflex ['riːfleks] *n* Reflex *m*
reform [rɪ'fɔːm] *n* Reform *f* ▷ *vt*
reformieren; (*person*) bessern
refrain [rɪ'freɪn] *vi*: **to ~ from
doing sth** es unterlassen, etw zu
tun
refresh [rɪ'freʃ] *vt* erfrischen;
refresher course *n*
Auffrischungskurs *m*; **refreshing**
adj erfrischend; **refreshments** *npl*
Erfrischungen *pl*
refrigerator [rɪ'frɪdʒəreɪtə°] *n*
Kühlschrank *m*
refuel [riː'fjʊəl] *vt, vi* auftanken
refugee [refjʊ'dʒiː] *n* Flüchtling
m
refund ['riːfʌnd] *n* (*of money*)
Rückerstattung *f*; **to get a ~ (on
sth**) sein Geld (für etw)
zurückbekommen ▷ [rɪ'fʌnd] *vt*
zurückerstatten
refusal [rɪ'fjuːzəl] *n* (*to do sth*)
Weigerung *f*; **refuse** ['refjuːs] *n*
Müll *m*, Abfall *m* ▷ [rɪ'fjuːz] *vt*
ablehnen; **to ~ sb sth** jdm etw
verweigern; **to ~ to do sth** sich
weigern, etw zu tun ▷ *vi* sich
weigern
regain [rɪ'geɪn] *vt* wiedergewinnen, wiedererlangen; **to
~ consciousness** wieder zu
Bewusstsein kommen
regard [rɪ'gɑːd] *n*: **with ~ to** in
Bezug auf +*akk*; **in this ~** in dieser
Hinsicht; **~s** (*at end of letter*) mit
freundlichen Grüßen; **give my ~s
to ...** viele Grüße an ... +*akk* ▷ *vt*:

to ~ sb/sth as sth jdn/etw als etw
betrachten; **as ~s ...** was ...
betrifft; **regarding** *prep* bezüglich
+*gen*; **regardless** *adj*: **~ of** ohne
Rücksicht auf +*akk* ▷ *adv*
trotzdem; **to carry on ~** einfach
weitermachen
regime [reɪ'ʒiːm] *n* (*Pol*) Regime
nt
region ['riːdʒən] *n* (*of country*)
Region *f*, Gebiet *nt*; **in the ~ of**
(*about*) ungefähr; **regional** *adj*
regional
register ['redʒɪstə°] *n* Register
nt; (*school*) Namensliste *f* ▷ *vt*
(*with an authority*) registrieren
lassen; anmelden ▷ *vi* (*at hotel, for course*)
sich anmelden; (*at university*) sich
einschreiben; **registered** *adj*
eingetragen; (*letter*)
eingeschrieben; **by ~ post** per
Einschreiben; **registration**
[redʒɪ'streɪʃən] *n* (*for course*)
Anmeldung *f*; (*at university*)
Einschreibung *f*; (*Auto: number*)
(polizeiliches) Kennzeichen;
registration form *n*
Anmeldeformular *nt*; **registration
number** *n* (*Auto*) (polizeiliches)
Kennzeichen; **registry office**
['redʒɪstrɪɒfɪs] *n* Standesamt *nt*
regret [rɪ'gret] *n* Bedauern *nt*
▷ *vt* bedauern; **regrettable** *adj*
bedauerlich
regular ['regjʊlə°] *adj* regelmäßig; (*size*) normal ▷ *n* (*client*)
Stammkunde *m*, Stammkundin *f*;
(*in bar*) Stammgast *m*; (*petrol*)
Normalbenzin *nt*; **regularly** *adv*
regelmäßig
regulate ['regjʊleɪt] *vt*
regulieren; (*using rules*) regeln;
regulation [regjʊ'leɪʃən] *n* (*rule*)
Vorschrift *f*
rehabilitation [riːəbɪlɪ'teɪʃən]
n Rehabilitation *f*

rehearsal [rɪˈhɜːsəl] n Probe f;
rehearse vt, vi proben
reign [reɪn] n Herrschaft f ▷ vi
herrschen (over über +akk)
reimburse [riːɪmˈbɜːs] vt (person) entschädigen; (expenses)
zurückerstatten
reindeer [ˈreɪndɪə°] n Rentier nt
reinforce [riːɪnˈfɔːs] vt
verstärken
reinstate [riːɪnˈsteɪt] vt
(employee) wieder einstellen;
(passage in text) wieder aufnehmen
reject [ˈriːdʒekt] n (Comm)
Ausschussartikel m ▷ [rɪˈdʒekt]
vt ablehnen; **rejection**
[rɪˈdʒekʃən] n Ablehnung f
relapse [rɪˈlæps] n Rückfall m
relate [rɪˈleɪt] vt (story) erzählen;
(connect) in Verbindung bringen (to
mit) ▷ vi: **to ~ to** (refer) sich
beziehen auf +akk; **related** adj
verwandt (to mit); **relation**
[rɪˈleɪʃən] n (relative) Verwandte(r)
mf; (connection) Beziehung f; **~s** pl
(dealings) Beziehungen pl;
relationship n (connection)
Beziehung f; (between people)
Verhältnis nt
relative [ˈrelətɪv] n Verwandte(r)
mf ▷ adj relativ; **relatively** adv
relativ, verhältnismäßig
relax [rɪˈlæks] vi sich
entspannen; **~!** reg dich nicht auf!
▷ vt (grip, conditions) lockern;
relaxation [riːlækˈseɪʃən] n (rest)
Entspannung f; **relaxed** adj
entspannt; **relaxing** adj
entspannend
release [rɪˈliːs] n (from prison)
Entlassung f; **new/recent ~** (film,
CD) Neuerscheinung f ▷ vt
(animal, hostage) freilassen;
(prisoner) entlassen; (handbrake)
lösen; (news) veröffentlichen;
(film, CD) herausbringen
relent [rɪˈlent] vi nachgeben;

relentless, **relentlessly** adj, adv
(merciless) erbarmungslos;
(neverending) unaufhörlich
relevance [ˈreləvəns] n
Relevanz f (to für); **relevant** adj
relevant (to für)
reliable, **reliably** [rɪˈlaɪəbl, -blɪ]
adj, adv zuverlässig; **reliant**
[rɪˈlaɪənt] adj: **~ on** abhängig von
relic [ˈrelɪk] n (from past) Relikt nt
relief [rɪˈliːf] n (from anxiety, pain)
Erleichterung f; (assistance) Hilfe f;
relieve [rɪˈliːv] vt (pain) lindern;
(boredom) überwinden; (take over
from) ablösen; **I'm ~d** ich bin
erleichtert
religion [rɪˈlɪdʒən] n Religion f;
religious [rɪˈlɪdʒəs] adj religiös
relish [ˈrelɪʃ] n (for food) würzige
Soße ▷ vt (enjoy) genießen; **I
don't ~ the thought of it** der
Gedanke behagt mir gar nicht
reluctant [rɪˈlʌktənt] adj
widerwillig; **to be ~ to do sth** etw
nur ungern tun; **reluctantly** adv
widerwillig
rely on [rɪˈlaɪ ɒn] vt sich
verlassen auf +akk; (depend on) I
abhängig sein von
remain [rɪˈmeɪn] vi bleiben; (be
left over) übrig bleiben; **remainder**
n (a. Math) Rest m; **remaining** adj
übrig; **remains** npl Überreste pl
remark [rɪˈmɑːk] n Bemerkung f
▷ vt: **to ~ that** bemerken, dass
▷ vi: **to ~ on sth** über etw akk eine
Bemerkung machen; **remarkable**,
remarkably adj, adv
bemerkenswert
remarry [riːˈmærɪ] vi wieder
heiraten
remedy [ˈremədɪ] n Mittel nt (for
gegen) ▷ vt abhelfen +dat
remember [rɪˈmembə°] vt sich
erinnern an +akk; **to ~ to do sth**
daran denken, etw zu tun; **I
~ seeing her** ich erinnere mich

daran, sie gesehen zu haben; **I must ~ that** das muss ich mir merken ▷ vi sich erinnern

Remembrance Day
[rɪˈmembrənsˈdeɪ] n (Brit) ≈ Volkstrauertag m

● **REMEMBRANCE DAY**
●
● **Remembrance Sunday/Day** ist
● der britische Gedenktag für die
● Gefallenen der beiden
● Weltkriege und anderer Kriege.
● Er fällt auf einen Sonntag vor
● oder nach dem 11. November
● (am 11.11.1918 endete der Erste
● Weltkrieg) und wird mit einer
● Schweigeminute,
● Kranzniederlegungen an
● Kriegerdenkmälern und dem
● Tragen von Anstecknadeln in
● Form einer Mohnblume
● begangen.

remind [rɪˈmaɪnd] vt: **to ~ sb of/about sb/sth** jdn an jdn/etw erinnern; **to ~ sb to do sth** jdn daran erinnern, etw zu tun; **that ~s me** dabei fällt mir ein ...; **reminder** n (to pay) Mahnung f

reminisce [remɪˈnɪs] vi in Erinnerungen schwelgen (about an +akk); **reminiscent** [remɪˈnɪsənt] adj: **to be ~ of** erinnern an +akk

remittance n Überweisung f (to an +akk)

remnant [ˈremnənt] n Rest m

remote [rɪˈməʊt] adj (place) abgelegen; (slight) gering ▷ n (TV) Fernbedienung f; **remote control** n Fernsteuerung f; (device) Fernbedienung f

removal [rɪˈmuːvəl] n Entfernung f; (Brit: move from house) Umzug m; **removal firm** n (Brit) Spedition f; **remove** [rɪˈmuːv] vt entfernen; (lid) abnehmen;

(clothes) ausziehen; (doubt, suspicion) zerstreuen

rename [riːˈneɪm] vt umbenennen

renew [rɪˈnjuː] vt erneuern; (licence, passport, library book) verlängern lassen

renounce [rɪˈnaʊns] vt verzichten auf +akk; (faith, opinion) abschwören +dat

renovate [ˈrenəveɪt] vt renovieren

renowned [rɪˈnaʊnd] adj berühmt (for für)

rent [rent] n Miete f; **for ~** (US) zu vermieten ▷ vt (as hirer, tenant) mieten; (as owner) vermieten; **~ed car** Mietwagen m; **rent out** vt vermieten; **rental** n Miete f; (for car, TV etc) Leihgebühr f ▷ adj Miet-

reorganize [riːˈɔːgənaɪz] vt umorganisieren

rep [rep] n (Comm) Vertreter(in) m(f)

repair [rɪˈpeə*] n Reparatur f ▷ vt reparieren; (damage) wiedergutmachen; **repair kit** n Flickzeug nt

repay [riːˈpeɪ] irr vt (money) zurückzahlen; **to ~ sb for sth** (fig) sich bei jdm für etw revanchieren

repeat [rɪˈpiːt] n (Radio, TV) Wiederholung f ▷ vt wiederholen; **repetition** [repəˈtɪʃən] n Wiederholung f; **repetitive** [rɪˈpetɪtɪv] adj sich wiederholend

rephrase [riːˈfreɪz] vt anders formulieren

replace [rɪˈpleɪs] vt ersetzen (with durch); (put back) zurückstellen, zurücklegen; **replacement** n (thing, person) Ersatz m; (temporarily in job) Vertretung f; **replacement part** n Ersatzteil nt

replay [ˈriːpleɪ] n: (**action**)

~ Wiederholung f ▷ [riːˈpleɪ] vt (game) wiederholen

replica [ˈreplɪkə] n Kopie f

reply [rɪˈplaɪ] n Antwort f ▷ vi antworten; **to ~ to sb/sth** jdm/auf etw akk antworten ▷ vt: **to ~ that** antworten, dass

report [rɪˈpɔːt] n Bericht m; (school) Zeugnis nt ▷ vt (tell) berichten; (give information against) melden; (to police) anzeigen ▷ vi (present oneself) sich melden; **to ~ sick** sich krankmelden; **report card** n (US: school) Zeugnis nt; **reporter** n Reporter(in) m(f)

represent [reprɪˈzent] vt darstellen; (speak for) vertreten; **representation** [reprɪzenˈteɪʃən] n (picture etc) Darstellung f; **representative** [reprɪˈzentətɪv] n Vertreter(in) m(f); (US Pol) Abgeordnete(r) mf ▷ adj repräsentativ (of für)

reprimand [ˈreprɪmɑːnd] n Tadel m ▷ vt tadeln

reprint [ˈriːprɪnt] n Nachdruck m

reproduce [riːprəˈdjuːs] vt (copy) reproduzieren ▷ vi (Bio) sich fortpflanzen; **reproduction** [riːprəˈdʌkʃən] n (copy) Reproduktion f; (Bio) Fortpflanzung f

reptile [ˈreptaɪl] n Reptil nt

republic [rɪˈpʌblɪk] n Republik f; **republican** adj republikanisch ▷ n Republikaner(in) m(f)

repulsive [rɪˈpʌlsɪv] adj abstoßend

reputable [ˈrepjʊtəbl] adj seriös

reputation [repjʊˈteɪʃən] n Ruf m; **he has a ~ for being difficult** er hat den Ruf, schwierig zu sein

request [rɪˈkwest] n Bitte f (for um); **on ~** auf Wunsch ▷ vt bitten um; **to ~ sb to do sth** jdn bitten, etw zu tun

require [rɪˈkwaɪə*] vt (need)

brauchen; (desire) verlangen; **what qualifications are ~d?** welche Qualifikationen sind erforderlich?; **required** adj erforderlich; **requirement** n (condition) Anforderung f; (need) Bedingung f

rerun [ˈriːrʌn] n Wiederholung f

rescue [ˈreskjuː] n Rettung f; **to come to sb's ~** jdm zu Hilfe kommen ▷ vt retten; **rescue party** n Rettungsmannschaft f

research [rɪˈsɜːtʃ] n Forschung f ▷ vi forschen (into über +akk) ▷ vt erforschen; **researcher** n Forscher(in) m(f)

resemblance [rɪˈzembləns] n Ähnlichkeit f (to mit); **resemble** [rɪˈzembl] vt ähneln +dat

resent [rɪˈzent] vt übel nehmen

reservation [rezəˈveɪʃən] n (booking) Reservierung f; (doubt) Vorbehalt m; **I have a ~** (in hotel, restaurant) ich habe reserviert; **reserve** [rɪˈzɜːv] n (store) Vorrat m (of an +dat); (manner) Zurückhaltung f; (Sport) Reservespieler(in) m(f); (game ~) Naturschutzgebiet nt ▷ vt (book in advance) reservieren; **reserved** adj reserviert

reservoir [ˈrezəvwɑː*] n (for water) Reservoir nt

reside [rɪˈzaɪd] vi wohnen; **residence** [ˈrezɪdəns] n Wohnsitz m; (living) Aufenthalt m; **~ permit** Aufenthaltsgenehmigung f; **~ hall** Studentenwohnheim nt; **resident** [ˈrezɪdənt] n (in house) Bewohner(in) m(f); (in town, area) Einwohner(in) m(f)

resign [rɪˈzaɪn] vt (post) zurücktreten von; (job) kündigen ▷ vi (from post) zurücktreten; (from job) kündigen; **resignation** [rezɪgˈneɪʃən] n (from post)

Rücktritt m; (from job) Kündigung f; **resigned** adj resigniert; **he is ~ to it** er hat sich damit abgefunden

resist [rɪ'zɪst] vt widerstehen +dat; **resistance** n Widerstand m (to gegen)

resit [riː'sɪt] (Brit) irr vt wiederholen ▷ ['riːsɪt] n Wiederholungsprüfung f

resolution [rezə'luːʃən] n (intention) Vorsatz m; (decision) Beschluss m

resolve [rɪ'zɒlv] vt (problem) lösen

resort [rɪ'zɔːt] n (holiday ~) Urlaubsort m; (health ~) Kurort m; **as a last ~** als letzter Ausweg ▷ vi: **to ~ to** greifen zu; (violence) anwenden

resources [rɪ'sɔːsɪz] npl (money) (Geld)mittel pl; (mineral ~) Bodenschätze pl

respect [rɪ'spekt] n Respekt m (for vor +dat); (consideration) Rücksicht f (for auf +akk); **with ~ to** in Bezug auf +akk; **in this ~** in dieser Hinsicht; **with all due ~** bei allem Respekt ▷ vt respektieren; **respectable** [rɪ'spektəbl] adj (person, family) angesehen; (district) anständig; (achievement, result) beachtlich; **respected** [rɪ'spektɪd] adj angesehen

respective [rɪ'spektɪv] adj jeweilig; **respectively** adv: **5 % and 10 % ~** 5 % beziehungsweise 10 %

respiratory [rɪ'spɪrətərɪ] adj: **~ problems** (o **trouble**) Atembeschwerden pl

respond [rɪ'spɒnd] vi antworten (to auf +akk); (react) reagieren (to auf +akk); (to treatment) ansprechen (to auf +akk); **response** [rɪ'spɒns] n Antwort f; (reaction) Reaktion f; **in ~ to** als Antwort auf +akk

responsibility [rɪspɒnsə'bɪlɪtɪ] n Verantwortung f; **that's her ~** dafür ist sie verantwortlich; **responsible** [rɪ'spɒnsəbl] adj verantwortlich (for für); (trustworthy) verantwortungsbewusst; (job) verantwortungsvoll

rest [rest] n (relaxation) Ruhe f; (break) Pause f; (remainder) Rest m; **to have** (o **take**) **a ~** sich ausruhen; (break) Pause machen; **the ~ of the wine/the people** der Rest des Weins/der Leute ▷ vi (relax) sich ausruhen; (lean) lehnen (on, against an +dat, gegen)

restaurant ['restərɒnt] n Restaurant nt; **restaurant car** n (Brit) Speisewagen m

restful ['restfʊl] adj (holiday etc) erholsam, ruhig; **restless** ['restləs] adj unruhig

restore [rɪ'stɔː°] vt (painting, building) restaurieren; (order) wiederherstellen; (give back) zurückgeben

restrain [rɪ'streɪn] vt (person, feelings) zurückhalten; **to ~ oneself** sich beherrschen

restrict [rɪ'strɪkt] vt beschränken (to auf +akk); **restricted** adj beschränkt; **restriction** [rɪ'strɪkʃən] n Einschränkung f (on +gen)

rest room ['restruːm] n (US) Toilette f

result [rɪ'zʌlt] n Ergebnis nt; (consequence) Folge f; **as a ~ of** infolge +gen ▷ vi: **to ~ in** führen zu; **to ~ from** sich ergeben aus

resume [rɪ'zjuːm] vt (work, negotiations) wieder aufnehmen; (journey) fortsetzen

résumé ['rezjʊmeɪ] n Zusammenfassung f; (US: curriculum vitae) Lebenslauf m

resuscitate [rɪ'sʌsɪteɪt] *vt* wiederbeleben

retail ['riːteɪl] *adv* im Einzelhandel; **retailer** *n* Einzelhändler(in) *m(f)*

retain [rɪ'teɪn] *vt* behalten; (*heat*) halten

rethink [riː'θɪŋk] *irr vt* noch einmal überdenken

retire [rɪ'taɪə*] *vi* (*from work*) in den Ruhestand treten; (*withdraw*) sich zurückziehen; **retired** *adj* (*person*) pensioniert; **retirement** *n* (*time of life*) Ruhestand *m*; **retirement age** *n* Rentenalter *nt*

retrace [rɪ'treɪs] *vt* zurückverfolgen

retrain [riː'treɪn] *vi* sich umschulen lassen

retreat [rɪ'triːt] *n* (*Mil*) Rückzug *m* (*from aus*); (*refuge*) Zufluchtsort *m* ⊳ *vi* (*Mil*) sich zurückziehen; (*step back*) zurückweichen

retrieve [rɪ'triːv] *vt* (*recover*) wiederbekommen; (*rescue*) retten; (*data*) abrufen

retrospect ['retrəʊspekt] *n*: **in ~** rückblickend; **retrospective** [retrəʊ'spektɪv] *adj* rückblickend; (*pay rise*) rückwirkend

return [rɪ'tɜːn] *n* (*going back*) Rückkehr *f*; (*giving back*) Rückgabe *f*; (*profit*) Gewinn *m*; (*Brit*: ~ *ticket*) Rückfahrkarte *f*; (*plane ticket*) Rückflugticket *nt*; (*Tennis*), Return *m*; **in ~** als Gegenleistung (*for* für); **many happy ~s** (**of the day**) herzlichen Glückwunsch zum Geburtstag! ⊳ *vi* (*person*) zurückkehren; (*doubts, symptoms*) wieder auftreten; **to ~ to school/work** wieder in die Schule/die Arbeit gehen ⊳ *vt* (*give back*) zurückgeben; **I ~ed his call** ich habe ihn zurückgerufen; **returnable** *adj* (*bottle*) Pfand-;

return flight *n* (*Brit*) Rückflug *m*; (*both ways*) Hin- und Rückflug *m*; **return key** *n* (*Inform*) Eingabetaste *f*; **return ticket** *n* (*Brit*) Rückfahrkarte *f*; (*for plane*) Rückflugticket *nt*

reunification [riːjuːnɪfɪ'keɪʃən] *n* Wiedervereinigung *f*

reunion [riː'juːnjən] *n* (*party*) Treffen *nt*; **reunite** [riːjuː'naɪt] *vt* wieder vereinigen

reusable [riː'juːzəbl] *adj* wiederverwendbar

reveal [rɪ'viːl] *vt* (*make known*) enthüllen; (*secret*) verraten; (*show*) zeigen; **revealing** *adj* aufschlussreich; (*dress*) freizügig

revenge [rɪ'vendʒ] *n* Rache *f*; (*in game*) Revanche *f*; **to take ~ on sb** (**for sth**) sich an jdm (für etw) rächen

revenue ['revənjuː] *n* Einnahmen *pl*

reverse [rɪ'vɜːs] *n* (*back*) Rückseite *f*; (*opposite*) Gegenteil *nt*; (*Auto*) ~ (**gear**) Rückwärtsgang *m* ⊳ *adj*: **in ~ order** in umgekehrter Reihenfolge ⊳ *vt* (*order*) umkehren; (*decision*) umstoßen; (*car*) zurücksetzen; **to ~ the charges** (*Brit*) ein R-Gespräch führen ⊳ *vi* (*Auto*) rückwärtsfahren

review [rɪ'vjuː] *n* (*of book, film etc*) Rezension *f*; Kritik *f*; **to be under ~** überprüft werden ⊳ *vt* (*book, film etc*) rezensieren; (*re-examine*) überprüfen

revise [rɪ'vaɪz] *vt* revidieren; (*text*) überarbeiten; (*Brit: in school*) wiederholen ⊳ *vi* (*Brit, in school*) (für eine Prüfung) lernen; **revision** [rɪ'vɪʒən] *n* (*of text*) Überarbeitung *f*; (*Brit, in school*) Wiederholung *f*

revitalize [riː'vaɪtəlaɪz] *vt* neu beleben

revive [rɪ'vaɪv] vt (person)
wiederbeleben; (tradition, interest)
wieder aufleben lassen ▷ vi
(regain consciousness) wieder zu
sich kommen

revolt [rɪ'vəʊlt] n Aufstand m;
revolting adj widerlich

revolution [revə'luːʃən] n (Pol,
fig) Revolution f; (turn)
Umdrehung f; **revolutionary** adj
revolutionär ▷ n Revolutionär(in)
m(f)

revolve [rɪ'vɒlv] vi sich drehen
(around um); **revolver** n Revolver
m; **revolving door** n Drehtür
f

reward [rɪ'wɔːd] n Belohnung f
▷ vt belohnen; **rewarding** adj
lohnend

rewind [riː'waɪnd] irr vt (tape)
zurückspulen

rewrite [riː'raɪt] irr vt (write
again; recast) umschreiben

rheumatism ['ruːmətɪzəm] n
Rheuma nt

Rhine [raɪn] n Rhein m

rhinoceros [raɪ'nɒsərəs] n
Nashorn nt

Rhodes [rəʊdz] n Rhodos nt

rhubarb ['ruːbɑːb] n Rhabarber
m

rhyme [raɪm] n Reim m ▷ vi
sich reimen (with auf +akk)

rhythm ['rɪðəm] n Rhythmus m

rib [rɪb] n Rippe f

ribbon ['rɪbən] n Band nt

rice [raɪs] n Reis m; **rice pudding**
n Milchreis m

rich [rɪtʃ] adj reich; (food) schwer
▷ npl: **the ~** die Reichen pl

rickety ['rɪkɪtɪ] adj wackelig

rid [rɪd] (**rid, rid**) vt: **to get ~ of**
sb/sth jdn/etw loswerden

ridden ['rɪdn] pp of **ride**

riddle ['rɪdl] n Rätsel nt

ride [raɪd] (**rode, ridden**) vt
(horse) reiten; (bicycle) fahren ▷ vi

(on horse) reiten; (on bike) fahren
▷ n (in vehicle, on bike) Fahrt f; (on
horse) (Aus)ritt m; **to go for a ~** (in
car, on bike) spazieren fahren; (on
horse) reiten gehen; **to take sb for**
a ~ (fam) jdn verarschen; **rider** n
(on horse) Reiter(in) m(f); (on bike)
Fahrer(in) m(f)

ridiculous [rɪ'dɪkjʊləs] adj
lächerlich; **don't be ~** red keinen
Unsinn!

riding ['raɪdɪŋ] n Reiten nt; **to go**
~ reiten gehen ▷ adj Reit-

rifle ['raɪfl] n Gewehr nt

rig [rɪg] n: **oil ~** Bohrinsel f ▷ vt
(election etc) manipulieren

right [raɪt] adj (correct, just)
richtig; (opposite of left) rechte(r, s);
(clothes, job etc) passend; **to be**
~ (person) recht haben; (clock)
richtig gehen; **that's ~** das
stimmt! ▷ n Recht nt (to auf +akk);
(side) rechte Seite; **the Right** (Pol)
die Rechte; **to take a ~** (Auto)
rechts abbiegen; **on the ~** rechts
(of von); **to the ~** nach rechts; (on
the ~) rechts (of von) ▷ adv
(towards the ~) nach rechts;
(directly) direkt; (exactly) genau; **to**
turn ~ (Auto) rechts abbiegen;
~ away sofort; **~ now** im
Moment; (immediately) sofort;
right angle n rechter Winkel;
right-hand drive n
Rechtssteuerung f ▷ adj
rechtsgesteuert; **right-handed**
adj: **he is ~** er ist Rechtshänder;
right-hand side n rechte Seite;
on the ~ auf der rechten Seite;
rightly adv zu Recht; **right of**
way n: **to have ~** (Auto) Vorfahrt
haben; **right wing** n (Pol, Sport)
rechter Flügel; **right-wing** adj
Rechts-; **~ extremist**
Rechtsradikale(r) mf

rigid ['rɪdʒɪd] adj (stiff) starr;
(strict) streng

rigorous, **rigorously** ['rɪgərəs, -lɪ] *adj, adv* streng

rim [rɪm] *n* (*of cup etc*) Rand *m*; (*of wheel*) Felge *f*

rind [raɪnd] *n* (*of cheese*) Rinde *f*; (*of bacon*) Schwarte *f*; (*of fruit*) Schale *f*

ring [rɪŋ] (**rang, rung**) *vt, vi* (*bell*) läuten; (*Tel*) anrufen ▷ *n* (*on finger, in boxing*) Ring *m*; (*circle*) Kreis *m*; (*at circus*) Manege *f*; **to give sb a ~** (*Tel*) jdn anrufen; **ring back** *vt, vi* zurückrufen; **ring up** *vt, vi* anrufen

ring binder *n* Ringbuch *nt*

ringleader *n* Anführer(in) *m(f)*

ring road *n* (*Brit*) Umgehungsstraße *f*

ringtone *n* Klingelton *m*

rink [rɪŋk] *n* (*ice ~*) Eisbahn *f*; (*for roller-skating*) Rollschuhbahn *f*

rinse [rɪns] *vt* spülen

riot ['raɪət] *n* Aufruhr *m*

rip [rɪp] *n* Riss *m* ▷ *vt* zerreißen; **to ~ sth open** etw aufreißen ▷ *vi* reißen; **rip off** *vt* (*fam: person*) übers Ohr hauen; **rip up** *vt* zerreißen

ripe [raɪp] *adj* (*fruit*) reif; **ripen** *vi* reifen

rip-off ['rɪpɒf] *n*: **that's a ~** (*fam: too expensive*) das ist Wucher

rise [raɪz] (**rose, risen**) *vi* (*from sitting, lying*) aufstehen; (*sun*) aufgehen; (*prices, temperature*) steigen; (*ground*) ansteigen; (*in revolt*) sich erheben ▷ *n* (*increase*) Anstieg *m* (*in +gen*); (*pay ~*) Gehaltserhöhung *f*; (*to power, fame*) Aufstieg *m* (*to zu*); (*slope*) Steigung *f*; **risen** ['rɪzn] *pp of* **rise**

risk [rɪsk] *n* Risiko *nt* ▷ *vt* riskieren; **to ~ doing sth** es riskieren, etw zu tun; **risky** *adj* riskant

risotto [rɪ'zɒtəʊ] (*pl* **-s**) *n* Risotto *nt*

ritual ['rɪtjʊəl] *n* Ritual *nt* ▷ *adj* rituell

rival ['raɪvəl] *n* Rivale *m*, Rivalin *f* (*for um*); (*Comm*) Konkurrent(in) *m(f)*; **rivalry** *n* Rivalität *f*; (*Comm, Sport*) Konkurrenz *f*

river ['rɪvə*] *n* Fluss *m*; **the River Thames** (*Brit*), **the Thames River** (*US*) die Themse; **riverside** *n* Flussufer *nt* ▷ *adj* am Flussufer

road [rəʊd] *n* Straße *f*; (*fig*) Weg *m*; **on the ~** (*travelling*) unterwegs, mit dem Auto/Bus *etc* fahren; **roadblock** *n* Straßensperre *f*; **roadmap** *n* Straßenkarte *f*; **road rage** *n* aggressives Verhalten im Straßenverkehr; **roadside** *n*: **at** (*o* **by**) **the ~** am Straßenrand; **roadsign** *n* Verkehrsschild *nt*; **road tax** *n* Kraftfahrzeugssteuer *f*; **roadworks** *npl* Bauarbeiten *pl*; **roadworthy** *adj* fahrtüchtig

roar [rɔː*] *n* (*of person, lion*) Brüllen *nt*; (*von Verkehr*) Donnern *nt* ▷ *vi* (*person, lion*) brüllen (*with vor* *+dat*)

roast [rəʊst] *n* Braten *m* ▷ *adj*: **~ beef** Rinderbraten *m*; **~ chicken** Brathähnchen *nt*; **~ pork** Schweinebraten *m*; **~ potatoes** *pl* im Backofen gebratene Kartoffeln ▷ *vt* (*meat*) braten

rob [rɒb] *vt* bestehlen; (*bank, shop*) ausrauben; **robber** *n* Räuber(in) *m(f)*; **robbery** *n* Raub *m*

robe [rəʊb] *n* (*US: dressing gown*) Morgenrock *m*; (*of judge, priest etc*) Robe *f*, Talar *m*

robin ['rɒbɪn] *n* Rotkehlchen *nt*

robot ['rəʊbɒt] *n* Roboter *m*

robust [rəʊ'bʌst] *adj* robust; (*defence*) stark

rock [rɒk] *n* (*substance*) Stein *m*; (*boulder*) Felsbrocken *m*; (*Mus*) Rock *m*; **stick of ~** (*Brit*) Zuckerstange *f*; **on the ~s** (*drink*) mit Eis; (*marriage*) gescheitert ▷ *vt, vi* (*swing*) schaukeln; (*dance*) rocken; **rock climbing** *n* Klettern *nt*; **to go ~** klettern gehen

rocket ['rɒkɪt] *n* Rakete *f*; (*in salad*) Rucola *m*

rocking chair ['rɒkɪŋtʃɛəᵊ] *n* Schaukelstuhl *m*

rocky ['rɒkɪ] *adj* (*landscape*) felsig; (*path*) steinig

rod [rɒd] *n* (*bar*) Stange *f*; (*fishing* ~) Rute *f*

rode [rəʊd] *pt of* **ride**

rogue [rəʊg] *n* Schurke *m*, Gauner *m*

role [rəʊl] *n* Rolle *f*; **role model** *n* Vorbild *nt*

roll [rəʊl] *n* (*of film, paper etc*) Rolle *f*; (*bread* ~) Brötchen *nt* ▷ *vt* (*move by ~ing*) rollen; (*cigarette*) drehen ▷ *vi* (*move by ~ing*) rollen; (*ship*) schlingern; (*camera*) laufen; **roll out** *vt* (*pastry*) ausrollen; **roll over** *vi* (*person*) sich umdrehen; **roll up** *vi* (*fam: arrive*) antanzen ▷ *vt* (*carpet*) aufrollen; **to roll one's sleeves up** die Ärmel hochkrempeln

roller *n* (*hair* ~) (Locken)wickler *m*; **Rollerblades®** *npl* Inlineskates *pl*; **rollerblading** *n* Inlineskaten *nt*; **roller coaster** *n* Achterbahn *f*; **roller skates** *npl* Rollschuhe *pl*; **roller-skating** *n* Rollschuhlaufen *nt*; **rolling pin** *n* Nudelholz *nt*; **roll-on (deodorant)** *n* Deoroller *m*

ROM [rɒm] *acr* = **read only memory** ROM *m*

Roman ['rəʊmən] *adj* römisch ▷ *n* Römer(in) *m(f)*; **Roman Catholic** *adj* römisch-katholisch ▷ *n* Katholik(in) *m(f)*

romance [rəʊ'mæns] *n* Romantik *f*; (*love affair*) Romanze *f*

Romania [rəʊ'meɪnɪə] *n* Rumänien *nt*; **Romanian** *adj* rumänisch ▷ *n* Rumäne *m*, Rumänin *f*; (*language*) Rumänisch *nt*

romantic [rəʊ'mæntɪk] *adj* romantisch

roof [ruːf] *n* Dach *nt*; **roof rack** *n* Dachgepäckträger *m*

rook [rʊk] *n* (*in chess*) Turm *m*

room [ruːm] *n* Zimmer *nt*, Raum *m*; (*large, for gatherings etc*) Saal *m*; (*space*) Platz *m*; (*fig*) Spielraum *m*; **to make ~ for** Platz machen für; **roommate** *n* Zimmergenosse *m*, Zimmergenossin *f*; Mitbewohner(in) *m(f)*; **room service** *n* Zimmerservice *m*; **roomy** *adj* geräumig; (*garment*) weit

root [ruːt] *n* Wurzel *f*; **root out** *vt* (*eradicate*) ausrotten; **root vegetable** *n* Wurzelgemüse *nt*

rope [rəʊp] *n* Seil *nt*; **to know the ~s** (*fam*) sich auskennen

rose [rəʊz] *pt of* **rise** ▷ *n* Rose *f*

rosé ['rəʊzeɪ] *n* Rosé(wein) *m*

rot [rɒt] *vi* verfaulen

rota ['rəʊtə] *n* (*Brit*) Dienstplan *m*

rotate [rəʊ'teɪt] *vt* (*turn*) rotieren lassen ▷ *vi* rotieren; **rotation** [rəʊ'teɪʃən] *n* (*turning*) Rotation *f*; **in ~** abwechselnd

rotten ['rɒtn] *adj* (*decayed*) faul; (*mean*) gemein; (*unpleasant*) scheußlich; (*ill*) elend

rough [rʌf] *adj* (*not smooth*) rau; (*path*) uneben; (*coarse, violent*) grob; (*crossing*) stürmisch; (*without comforts*) hart; (*unfinished, makeshift*) grob; (*approximate*) ungefähr; **~ draft** Rohentwurf *m*; **I have a ~ idea** ich habe eine ungefähre Vorstellung ▷ *adv*: **to sleep ~** im Freien schlafen ▷ *vt*: **to ~ it** primitiv leben ▷ *n*: **to write sth in ~** etw ins Unreine schreiben; **roughly** *adv* grob; (*approximately*) ungefähr

round [raʊnd] *adj* rund ▷ *adv*: **all ~** (*on all sides*) rundherum; **the long way ~** der längere Weg; **I'll be ~ at 8** ich werde um acht Uhr da sein; **the other way ~** umgekehrt ▷ *prep* (*surrounding*) um (... herum); **~** (**about**) (*approximately*) ungefähr; **~ the corner** um die Ecke; **to go ~ the world** um die Welt reisen; **she lives ~ here** sie wohnt hier in der Gegend ▷ *n* Runde *f*; (*of bread, toast*) Scheibe *f*; **it's my ~** (*of drinks*) die Runde geht auf mich ▷ *vt* (*corner*) biegen um; **round off** *vt* abrunden; **round up** *vt* (*number, price*) aufrunden

roundabout *n* (*Brit Auto*) Kreisverkehr *m*; (*Brit: merry-go-round*) Karussell *nt* ▷ *adj* umständlich; **round-the-clock** *adj* rund um die Uhr; **round trip** *n* Rundreise *f*; **round-trip ticket** *n* (*US*) Rückfahrkarte *f*; (*for plane*) Rückflugticket *nt*

rouse [raʊz] *vt* (*from sleep*) wecken

route [ruːt] *n* Route *f*; (*bus, plane etc service*) Linie *f*; (*fig*) Weg *m*

routine [ruːˈtiːn] *n* Routine *f* ▷ *adj* Routine-

row [rəʊ] *n* (*line*) Reihe *f*; **three times in a ~** dreimal hintereinander ▷ *vt, vi* (*boat*) rudern ▷ [raʊ] *n* (*noise*) Krach *m*; (*dispute*) Streit *m*

rowboat [ˈrəʊbəʊt] *n* (*US*) Ruderboot *nt*

row house [ˈrəʊhaʊs] *n* (*US*) Reihenhaus *nt*

rowing [ˈrəʊɪŋ] *n* Rudern *nt*; **rowing boat** *n* (*Brit*) Ruderboot *nt*; **rowing machine** *n* Rudergerät *nt*

royal [ˈrɔɪəl] *adj* königlich; **royalty** *n* (*family*) Mitglieder *pl* der königlichen Familie; **royalties** *pl* (*from book, music*) Tantiemen *pl*

RSPCA *abbr* = **Royal Society for the Prevention of Cruelty to Animals** *britischer Tierschutzverein*

RSPCC *abbr* = **Royal Society for the Prevention of Cruelty to Children** *britischer Kinderschutzverein*

RSVP *abbr* = **répondez s'il vous plaît** u. A. w. g.

rub [rʌb] *vt* reiben; **rub in** *vt* einmassieren; **rub out** *vt* (*with eraser*) ausradieren

rubber [ˈrʌbəʳ] *n* Gummi *m*; (*Brit: eraser*) Radiergummi *m*; (*US fam: contraceptive*) Gummi *m*; **rubber band** *n* Gummiband *nt*; **rubber stamp** *n* Stempel *m*

rubbish [ˈrʌbɪʃ] *n* Abfall *m*; (*nonsense*) Quatsch *m*; (*poor-quality thing*) Mist *m*; **don't talk ~** red keinen Unsinn!; **rubbish bin** *n* Mülleimer *m*; **rubbish dump** *n* Müllabladeplatz *m*

rubble [ˈrʌbl] *n* Schutt *m*

ruby [ˈruːbɪ] *n* (*stone*) Rubin *m*

rucksack [ˈrʌksæk] *n* Rucksack *m*

rude [ruːd] *adj* (*impolite*) unhöflich; (*indecent*) unanständig

rug [rʌg] *n* Teppich *m*; (*next to bed*) Bettvorleger *m*; (*for knees*) Wolldecke *f*

rugby [ˈrʌgbɪ] *n* Rugby *nt*

rugged [ˈrʌgɪd] *adj* (*coastline*) zerklüftet; (*features*) markant

ruin [ˈruːɪn] *n* Ruine *f*; (*financial, social*) Ruin *m* ▷ *vt* ruinieren

rule [ruːl] *n* Regel *f*; (*governing*) Herrschaft *f*; **as a ~** in der Regel ▷ *vt, vi* (*govern*) regieren; (*decide*) entscheiden; **ruler** *n* Lineal *nt*; (*person*) Herrscher(in) *m(f)*

rum [rʌm] *n* Rum *m*

rumble [ˈrʌmbl] *vi* (*stomach*) knurren; (*train, truck*) rumpeln

rummage [ˈrʌmɪdʒ] *vi*: **~** (**around**) herumstöbern

rumor (US), **rumour** ['ruːmə*] n
Gerücht nt

run [rʌn] (**ran, run**) vt (race,
distance) laufen; (machine, engine,
computer program, water) laufen
lassen; (manage) leiten, führen;
(car) unterhalten; **I ran her home**
ich habe sie nach Hause gefahren
▷ vi laufen; (move quickly) rennen;
(bus, train) fahren; (path etc)
verlaufen; (machine, engine,
computer program) laufen; (flow)
fließen; (colours, make-up)
verlaufen; **it ~s in the family** es liegt in
der Familie ▷ n (on foot) Lauf m;
(in car) Spazierfahrt f; (series) Reihe
f; (sudden demand) Ansturm m (on
auf +akk); (in tights) Laufmasche f;
(in cricket, baseball) Lauf m; **to go
for a ~** laufen gehen; (in car) eine
Spazierfahrt machen; **in the long
~** auf die Dauer; **on the ~** auf der
Flucht (from vor +dat); **run about**
vi herumlaufen; **run away** vi
weglaufen; **run down** vt (with car)
umfahren; (criticize)
heruntermachen; **to be ~** (tired)
abgespannt sein; **run into** vt
(meet) zufällig treffen; (problem)
stoßen auf +akk; **run off** vi
weglaufen; **run out** vi (person)
hinausrennen; (liquid) auslaufen;
(lease, time) ablaufen; (money,
supplies) ausgehen; **he ran ~ of
money** ihm ging das Geld aus; **run
over** vt (with car) überfahren; **run
up** vt (debt, bill) machen

rung [rʌŋ] pp of **ring**

runner ['rʌnə*] n (athlete)
Läufer(in) m(f); **to do a ~** (fam)
wegrennen; **runner bean** n (Brit)
Stangenbohne f

running ['rʌnɪŋ] n (Sport) Laufen
nt; (management) Leitung f,
Führung f ▷ adj (water) fließend;
~ costs Betriebskosten pl; (for car)
Unterhaltskosten pl; **3 days** = 3
Tage hintereinander

runny ['rʌnɪ] adj (food) flüssig;
(nose) laufend

runway ['rʌnweɪ] n Start- und
Landebahn f

rural ['rʊərəl] adj ländlich

rush [rʌʃ] n Eile f; (for tickets etc)
Ansturm m (for auf +akk); **to be in a
~** es eilig haben; **there's no ~** es
eilt nicht ▷ vt (do too quickly)
hastig machen; (meal) hastig
essen; **to ~ sb to hospital** jdn auf
dem schnellsten Weg ins
Krankenhaus bringen; **don't ~ me**
dräng mich nicht ▷ vi (hurry)
eilen; **don't ~** lass dir Zeit; **rush
hour** n Hauptverkehrszeit f

rusk [rʌsk] n Zwieback m

Russia ['rʌʃə] n Russland nt;
Russian adj russisch ▷ n Russe
m, Russin f; (language) Russisch nt

rust [rʌst] n Rost m ▷ vi rosten;
rustproof ['rʌstpruːf] adj rostfrei; **rusty** ['rʌstɪ] adj rostig

ruthless ['ruːθləs] adj rücksichtslos; (treatment, criticism)
schonungslos

rye [raɪ] n Roggen m; **rye bread**
n Roggenbrot nt

S

S *abbr* = **south** S

sabotage ['sæbətɑːʒ] *vt* sabotieren

sachet ['sæʃeɪ] *n* Päckchen *nt*

sack [sæk] *n* (*bag*) Sack *m*; **to get the ~** (*fam*) rausgeschmissen werden ▷ *vt* (*fam*) rausschmeißen

sacred ['seɪkrɪd] *adj* heilig

sacrifice ['sækrɪfaɪs] *n* Opfer *nt* ▷ *vt* opfern

sad [sæd] *adj* traurig

saddle ['sædl] *n* Sattel *m*

sadistic [sə'dɪstɪk] *adj* sadistisch

sadly ['sædlɪ] *adv* (*unfortunately*) leider

safari [sə'fɑːrɪ] *n* Safari

safe [seɪf] *adj* (*free from danger*) sicher; (*out of danger*) in Sicherheit; (*careful*) vorsichtig; **have a ~ journey** gute Fahrt! ▷ *n* Safe *m*; **safeguard** *n* Schutz *m* ▷ *vt* schützen (*against* vor +*dat*); **safely** *adv* sicher; (*arrive*) wohlbehalten;

(*drive*) vorsichtig; **safety** *n* Sicherheit *f*; **safety belt** *n* Sicherheitsgurt *m*; **safety pin** *n* Sicherheitsnadel *f*

Sagittarius [sædʒɪ'tɛərɪəs] *n* (*Astr*) Schütze *m*

Sahara [sə'hɑːrə] *n*: **the ~** (**Desert**) die (Wüste) Sahara

said [sed] *pt, pp of* **say**

sail [seɪl] *n* Segel *nt*; **to set ~** losfahren (*for* nach) ▷ *vi* (*in yacht*) segeln; (*on ship*) mit dem Schiff fahren; (*ship*) auslaufen (*for* nach) ▷ *vt* (*yacht*) segeln mit; (*ship*) steuern; **sailboat** *n* (*US*) Segelboot *nt*; **sailing** *n*: **to go ~** segeln gehen; **sailing boat** *n* (*Brit*) Segelboot *nt*; **sailor** *n* Seemann *m*; (*in navy*) Matrose *m*

saint [seɪnt] *n* Heilige(r) *mf*

sake [seɪk] *n*: **for the ~ of** um +*gen* ... willen; **for your ~** deinetwegen, dir zuliebe

salad ['sæləd] *n* Salat *m*; **salad cream** *n* (*Brit*) majonäseartige Salatsoße; **salad dressing** *n* Salatsoße *f*

salary ['sælərɪ] *n* Gehalt *nt*

sale [seɪl] *n* Verkauf *m*; (*at reduced prices*) Ausverkauf *m*; **the ~s** *pl* (*in summer, winter*) der Schlussverkauf; **for ~** zu verkaufen; **sales clerk** *n* (*US*) Verkäufer(in) *m(f)*; **salesman** (*pl* **-men**) *n* Verkäufer *m*; (*rep*) Vertreter *m*; **sales rep** *n* Vertreter(in) *m(f)*; **sales tax** *n* (*US*) Verkaufssteuer *f*; **saleswoman** (*pl* **-women**) *n* Verkäuferin *f*; (*rep*) Vertreterin *f*

salmon ['sæmən] *n* Lachs *m*

saloon [sə'luːn] *n* (*ship's lounge*) Salon *m*; (*US: bar*) Kneipe *f*

salt [sɔːlt] *n* Salz *nt* ▷ *vt* (*flavour*) salzen; (*roads*) mit Salz streuen; **salt cellar**, **salt shaker** (*US*) *n* Salzstreuer *m*; **salty** *adj* salzig

salvage ['sælvɪdʒ] *vt* bergen (*from* aus); (*fig*) retten
same [seɪm] *adj*: **the ~** (*similar*) der/die/das gleiche, die gleichen *pl*; (*identical*) der-/die-/dasselbe, dieselben *pl*; **they live in the ~ house** sie wohnen im selben Haus ▷ *pron*: **the ~** (*similar*) der/die/das Gleiche, die Gleichen *pl*; (*identical*) der-/die-/dasselbe, dieselben *pl*; **all the ~** trotzdem; **the ~ to you** gleichfalls; **it's all the ~ to me** es ist mir egal ▷ *adv*: **the ~** gleich; **they look the ~** sie sehen gleich aus
sample ['sɑːmpl] *n* Probe *f*; (*of fabric*) Muster *nt* ▷ *vt* probieren
sanctions ['sæŋkʃənz] *npl* (*Pol*) Sanktionen *pl*
sanctuary ['sæŋktjʊərɪ] *n* (*refuge*) Zuflucht *f*; (*for animals*) Schutzgebiet *nt*
sand [sænd] *n* Sand *m*
sandal ['sændl] *n* Sandale *f*
sandpaper *n* Sandpapier *nt* ▷ *vt* schmirgeln
sandwich ['sænwɪdʒ] *n* Sandwich *nt*
sandy ['sændɪ] *adj* (*full of sand*) sandig; **~ beach** Sandstrand *m*
sane [seɪn] *adj* geistig gesund, normal; (*sensible*) vernünftig
sang [sæŋ] *pt of* **sing**
sanitary ['sænɪtərɪ] *adj* hygienisch; **sanitary napkin** (*US*), **sanitary towel** *n* Damenbinde *f*
sank [sæŋk] *pt of* **sink**
Santa (Claus) ['sæntə('klɔːz)] *n* der Weihnachtsmann
sarcastic [sɑː'kæstɪk] *adj* sarkastisch
sardine [sɑː'diːn] *n* Sardine *f*
Sardinia [sɑː'dɪnɪə] *n* Sardinien *nt*
sari [sɑːrɪ] *n* Sari *m* (*von indischen Frauen getragenes Gewand*)
sat [sæt] *pt, pp of* **sit**

Sat *abbr* = **Saturday** Sa.
satellite ['sætəlaɪt] *n* Satellit *m*; **satellite dish** *n* Satellitenschüssel *f*; **satellite TV** *n* Satellitenfernsehen *nt*
satin ['sætɪn] *n* Satin *m*
satisfaction [sætɪs'fækʃən] *n* (*contentment*) Zufriedenheit *f*; **is that to your ~?** bist du/sind Sie damit zufrieden?; **satisfactory** [sætɪs'fæktərɪ] *adj* zufriedenstellend; **satisfied** ['sætɪsfaɪd] *adj* zufrieden (*with* mit); **satisfy** ['sætɪsfaɪ] *vt* zufriedenstellen; (*convince*) überzeugen; (*conditions*) erfüllen; (*need, demand*) befriedigen; **satisfying** *adj* befriedigend
Saturday ['sætədeɪ] *n* Samstag *m*, Sonnabend *m*; *see also* **Tuesday**
sauce [sɔːs] *n* Soße *f*; **saucepan** *n* Kochtopf *m*; **saucer** *n* Untertasse *f*
saucy ['sɔːsɪ] *adj* frech
Saudi Arabia ['saʊdɪə'reɪbɪə] *n* Saudi-Arabien *nt*
sauna ['sɔːnə] *n* Sauna *f*
sausage ['sɒsɪdʒ] *n* Wurst *f*; **sausage roll** *n* mit Wurst gefülltes Blätterteigröllchen
savage ['sævɪdʒ] *adj* (*person, attack*) brutal; (*animal*) wild
save [seɪv] *vt* (*rescue*) retten (*from* vor +dat); (*money, time, electricity etc*) sparen; (*strength*) schonen; (*Inform*) speichern; **to ~ sb's life** jdm das Leben retten ▷ *vi* sparen ▷ *n* (*in football*) Parade *f*; **save up** *vi* sparen (*for* auf +akk); **saving** *n* (*of money*) Sparen *nt*; **~s** *pl* Ersparnisse *pl*; **~s account** Sparkonto *nt*
savory (*US*), **savoury** ['seɪvərɪ] *adj* (*not sweet*) pikant
saw [sɔː] (**sawed, sawn**) *vt, vi* sägen ▷ *n* (*tool*) Säge *f* ▷ *pt of* **see**; **sawdust** *n* Sägemehl *nt*

saxophone ['sæksəfəʊn] *n*
Saxophon *nt*

say [seɪ] (**said, said**) *vt* sagen (*to sb* jdm); (*prayer*) sprechen; **what does the letter ~?** was steht im Brief?; **the rules ~ that ...** in den Regeln heißt es, dass ...; **he's said to be rich** er soll reich sein ▷ *n*: **to have a ~ in sth** bei etw ein Mitspracherecht haben ▷ *adv* zum Beispiel; **saying** *n* Sprichwort *nt*

scab [skæb] *n* (*on cut*) Schorf *m*

scaffolding ['skæfəʊldɪŋ] *n* (Bau)gerüst *nt*

scale [skeɪl] *n* (*of map etc*) Maßstab *m*; (*on thermometer etc*) Skala *f*; (*of pay*) Tarifsystem *nt*; (*Mus*) Tonleiter *f*; (*of fish, snake*) Schuppe *f*; **to ~** maßstabsgerecht; **on a large/small ~** in großem/kleinem Umfang; **scales** *npl* (*for weighing*) Waage *f*

scalp [skælp] *n* Kopfhaut *f*

scan [skæn] *vt* (*examine*) genau prüfen; (*read quickly*) überfliegen; (*Inform*) scannen ▷ *n* (*Med*) Ultraschall *m*; **scan in** *vt* (*Inform*) einscannen

scandal ['skændl] *n* Skandal *m*; **scandalous** *adj* skandalös

Scandinavia [skændɪ'neɪvɪə] *n* Skandinavien *nt*; **Scandinavian** *adj* skandinavisch ▷ *n* Skandinavier(in) *m(f)*

scanner ['skænə*] *n* Scanner *m*

scapegoat ['skeɪpgəʊt] *n* Sündenbock *m*

scar [skɑː*] *n* Narbe *f*

scarce ['skeəs] *adj* selten; (*in short supply*) knapp; **scarcely** *adv* kaum

scare ['skeə*] *n* (*general alarm*) Panik *f* ▷ *vt* erschrecken; **to be ~d** Angst haben (*of* vor +*dat*)

scarf [skɑːf] (*pl* -**scarves**) *n* Schal *m*; (*on head*) Kopftuch *nt*

scarlet ['skɑːlət] *adj* scharlachrot; **scarlet fever** *n* Scharlach *m*

scary ['skeərɪ] *adj* (*film, story*) gruselig

scatter ['skætə*] *vt* verstreuen; (*seed, gravel*) streuen; (*disperse*) auseinandertreiben

scene [siːn] *n* (*location*) Ort *m*; (*division of play*) (*Theat*) Szene *f*; (*view*) Anblick *m*; **to make a ~** eine Szene machen; **scenery** ['siːnərɪ] *n* (*landscape*) Landschaft *f*; (*Theat*) Kulissen *pl*; **scenic** ['siːnɪk] *adj* (*landscape*) malerisch; **~ route** landschaftlich schöne Strecke

scent [sent] *n* (*perfume*) Parfüm *nt*; (*smell*) Duft *m*

sceptical ['skeptɪkəl] *adj* (*Brit*) skeptisch

schedule ['ʃedjuːl, 'skedʒʊəl] *n* (*plan*) Programm *nt*; (*of work*) Zeitplan *m*; (*list*) Liste *f*; (*US: of trains, buses, air traffic*) Fahr-, Flugplan *m*; **on ~** planmäßig; **to be behind ~ with sth** mit etw in Verzug sein ▷ *vt*: **the meeting is ~d for next Monday** die Besprechung ist für nächsten Montag angesetzt; **scheduled** *adj* (*departure, arrival*) planmäßig; **~ flight** Linienflug *m*

scheme [skiːm] *n* (*plan*) Plan *m*; (*project*) Projekt *nt*; (*dishonest*) Intrige *f* ▷ *vi* intrigieren

schizophrenic [skɪtsə'frenɪk] *adj* schizophren

scholar ['skɒlə*] *n* Gelehrte(r) *mf*; **scholarship** *n* (*grant*) Stipendium *nt*

school [skuːl] *n* Schule *f*; (*university department*) Fachbereich *m*; (*US: university*) Universität *f*; **school bag** *n* Schultasche *f*; **schoolbook** *n* Schulbuch *nt*; **schoolboy** *n* Schüler *m*; **school bus** *n* Schulbus *m*; **schoolgirl** *n*

Schülerin f; **schoolteacher** n Lehrer(in) m(f); **schoolwork** n Schularbeiten pl

sciatica [saɪˈætɪkə] n Ischias m

science [ˈsaɪəns] n Wissenschaft f; (natural ~) Naturwissenschaft f; **science fiction** n Sciencefiction f; **scientific** [saɪənˈtɪfɪk] adj wissenschaftlich; **scientist** [ˈsaɪəntɪst] n Wissenschaftler(in) m(f); (in natural sciences) Naturwissenschaftler(in) m(f)

scissors [ˈsɪzəz] npl Schere f

scone [skɒn] n kleines süßes Hefebrötchen mit oder ohne Rosinen, das mit Butter oder Dickrahm und Marmelade gegessen wird

scoop [sku:p] n (exclusive story) Exklusivbericht m; **a ~ of ice-cream** eine Kugel Eis ▷ vt: **to ~ (up)** schaufeln

scooter [ˈsku:tə*] n (Motor)-roller m; (toy) (Tret)roller m

scope [skəʊp] n Umfang m; (opportunity) Möglichkeit f

score [skɔ:*] n (Sport) Spielstand m; (final result) Spielergebnis nt; (in quiz etc) Punktestand m; (Mus) Partitur f; **to keep (the) ~** mitzählen ▷ vt (goal) schießen; (points) punkten ▷ vi (keep ~) mitzählen; **scoreboard** n Anzeigetafel f

scorn [skɔ:n] n Verachtung f; **scornful** adj verächtlich

Scorpio [ˈskɔ:pɪəʊ] (pl **-s**) n (Astr) Skorpion m

scorpion [ˈskɔ:pɪən] n Skorpion m

Scot [skɒt] n Schotte m, Schottin f; **Scotch** [skɒtʃ] n (whisky) schottischer Whisky, Scotch m

Scotch tape® n (US) Tesafilm® m

Scotland [ˈskɒtlənd] n Schottland nt; **Scotsman** (pl **-men**) n Schotte m; **Scotswoman** (pl **-women**) n Schottin f; **Scottish** adj schottisch

scout [skaʊt] n (boy ~) Pfadfinder m

scowl [skaʊl] vi finster blicken

scrambled eggs npl Rührei nt

scrap [skræp] n (bit) Stückchen nt, Fetzen m; (metal) Schrott m ▷ vt (car) verschrotten; (plan) verwerfen; **scrapbook** n Sammelalbum nt

scrape [skreɪp] n (scratch) Kratzer m ▷ vt (car) schrammen; (wall) streifen; **to ~ one's knee** sich das Knie schürfen; **scrape through** vi (exam) mit knapper Not bestehen

scrap heap [ˈskræphi:p] n Schrotthaufen m; **scrap metal** n Schrott m; **scrap paper** n Schmierpapier nt

scratch [skrætʃ] n (mark) Kratzer m; **to start from ~** von vorne anfangen ▷ vt kratzen; (car) zerkratzen; **to ~ one's arm** sich am Arm kratzen ▷ vi kratzen; (~ oneself) sich kratzen

scream [skri:m] n Schrei m ▷ vi schreien (with vor +dat); **to ~ at sb** jdn anschreien

screen [skri:n] n (TV, Inform) Bildschirm m; (Cine) Leinwand f ▷ vt (protect) abschirmen; (hide) verdecken; (film) zeigen; (applicants, luggage) überprüfen; **screenplay** n Drehbuch nt; **screensaver** n (Inform) Bildschirmschoner m

screw [skru:] n Schraube f ▷ vt (vulg: have sex with) ficken; **to ~ sth to sth** etw an etw akk schrauben; **to ~ off/on** (lid) ab-/aufschrauben; **screw up** vt (paper) zusammenknüllen; (make a mess of) vermasseln; **screwdriver** n Schraubenzieher m; **screw top** n Schraubverschluss m

scribble ['skrɪbl] *vt, vi* kritzeln
script [skrɪpt] *n* (*of play*) Text *m*; (*of film*) Drehbuch *nt*; (*style of writing*) Schrift *f*
scroll down ['skrəʊl'daʊn] *vi* (*Inform*) runterscrollen; **scroll up** *vi* (*Inform*) raufscrollen; **scroll bar** *n* (*Inform*) Scrollbar *f*
scrub [skrʌb] *vt* schrubben; **scrubbing brush, scrub brush** (*US*) *n* Scheuerbürste *f*
scruffy ['skrʌfɪ] *adj* vergammelt
scrupulous, scrupulously ['skruːpjʊləs, -lɪ] *adj, adv* gewissenhaft; (*painstaking*) peinlich genau
scuba-diving ['skuːbədaɪvɪŋ] *n* Sporttauchen *nt*
sculptor ['skʌlptə*] *n* Bildhauer(in) *m(f)*; **sculpture** ['skʌlptʃə*] *n* (*Art*) Bildhauerei *f*; (*statue*) Skulptur *f*
sea [siː] *n* Meer *nt*, See *f*; **seafood** *n* Meeresfrüchte *pl*; **sea front** *n* Strandpromenade *f*; **seagull** *n* Möwe *f*
seal [siːl] *n* (*animal*) Robbe *f*; (*stamp, impression*) Siegel *nt*; (*Tech*) Verschluss *m*; (*ring etc*) Dichtung *f* ▷ *vt* versiegeln; (*envelope*) zukleben
seam [siːm] *n* Naht *f*
search [sɜːtʃ] *n* Suche *f* (*for* nach); **to do a ~ for** (*Inform*) suchen nach; **in ~ of** auf der Suche nach ▷ *vi* suchen (*for* nach) ▷ *vt* durchsuchen; **search engine** *n* (*Inform*) Suchmaschine *f*
seashell ['siːʃel] *n* Muschel *f*; **seashore** *n* Strand *m*; **seasick** *adj* seekrank; **seaside** *n*: **at the ~** am Meer; **to go to the ~** ans Meer fahren; **seaside resort** *n* Seebad *nt*
season ['siːzn] *n* Jahreszeit *f*; (*Comm*) Saison *f*; **high/low**

~ Hoch-/Nebensaison *f* ▷ *vt* (*flavour*) würzen
seasoning *n* Gewürz *nt*
season ticket *n* (*Rail*) Zeitkarte *f*; (*Theat*) Abonnement *nt*; (*Sport*) Dauerkarte *f*
seat [siːt] *n* (*place*) Platz *m*; (*chair*) Sitz *m*; **take a ~** setzen Sie sich ▷ *vt*: **the hall ~s 300** der Saal hat 300 Sitzplätze; **please be ~ed** bitte setzen Sie sich; **to remain ~ed** sitzen bleiben; **seat belt** *n* Sicherheitsgurt *m*
sea view ['siːvjuː] *n* Seeblick *m*; **seaweed** *n* Seetang *m*
secluded [sɪ'kluːdɪd] *adj* abgelegen
second ['sekənd] *adj* zweite(r, s); **the ~ of June** der zweite Juni ▷ *adv* (*in ~ position*) an zweiter Stelle; (*secondly*) zweitens; **he came ~** er ist Zweiter geworden ▷ *n* (*of time*) Sekunde *f*; (*moment*) Augenblick *m*; **~ (gear)** der zweite Gang; (**~ helping**) zweite Portion; **just a ~** (einen) Augenblick!; **secondary** *adj* (*less important*) zweitrangig; **~ education** höhere Schulbildung *f*; **~ school** weiterführende Schule; **second-class** *adj* (*ticket*) zweiter Klasse; **~ stamp** *Briefmarke für nicht bevorzugt beförderte Sendungen* ▷ *adv* (*travel*) zweiter Klasse; **second-hand** *adj, adv* gebraucht; (*information*) aus zweiter Hand; **secondly** *adv* zweitens; **second-rate** *adj* (*pej*) zweitklassig
secret ['siːkrət] *n* Geheimnis *nt* ▷ *adj* geheim; (*admirer*) heimlich
secretary ['sekrətrɪ] *n* Sekretär(in) *m(f)*; (*minister*) Minister(in) *m(f)*; **Secretary of State** *n* (*US*) Außenminister(in) *m(f)*; **secretary's office** *n* Sekretariat *nt*

secretive ['siːkrətɪv] *adj* (*person*) geheimnistuerisch; **secretly** ['siːkrətlɪ] *adv* heimlich

sect [sekt] *n* Sekte *f*

section ['sekʃən] *n* (*part*) Teil *m*; (*of document*) Abschnitt *m*; (*department*) Abteilung *f*

secure [sɪˈkjʊəʳ] *adj* (*safe*) sicher (*from* vor +*dat*); (*firmly fixed*) fest ▷ *vt* (*make firm*) befestigen; (*window, door*) fest verschließen; **securely** *adv* fest; (*safely*) sicher; **security** [sɪˈkjʊərɪtɪ] *n* Sicherheit *f*

sedative ['sedətɪv] *n* Beruhigungsmittel *nt*

seduce [sɪˈdjuːs] *vt* verführen; **seductive** [sɪˈdʌktɪv] *adj* verführerisch; (*offer*) verlockend

see [siː] (**saw, seen**) *vt* sehen; (*understand*) verstehen; (*check*) nachsehen; (*accompany*) bringen; (*visit*) besuchen; (*talk to*) sprechen; **to ~ the doctor** zum Arzt gehen; **to ~ sb home** jdn nach Hause begleiten; **I saw him swimming** ich habe ihn schwimmen sehen; **~ you** tschüs!; **~ you on Friday** bis Freitag! ▷ *vi* sehen; (*understand*) verstehen; (*check*) nachsehen; (**you**) **~** siehst du!; **we'll ~** mal sehen; **see about** *vt* (*attend to*) sich kümmern um; **see off** *vt* (*say goodbye to*) verabschieden; **see out** *vt* (*show out*) zur Tür bringen; **see through** *vt*: **to see sth through** etw zu Ende bringen; **to ~ sb/sth** jdn/etw durchschauen; **see to** *vt* sich kümmern um; **~ it that ...** sieh zu, dass ...

seed [siːd] *n* (*of plant*) Samen *m*; (*in fruit*) Kern *m*; **seedless** *adj* kernlos

seedy ['siːdɪ] *adj* zwielichtig

seek [siːk] (**sought, sought**) *vt* suchen; (*fame*) streben nach; **to ~ sb's advice** jdn um Rat fragen

seem [siːm] *vi* scheinen; **he ~s (to be) honest** er scheint ehrlich zu sein; **it ~s to me that ...** es scheint mir, dass ...

seen [siːn] *pp* of **see**

seesaw ['siːsɔː] *n* Wippe *f*

see-through *adj* durchsichtig

segment ['segmənt] *n* Teil *m*

seize [siːz] *vt* packen; (*confiscate*) beschlagnahmen; (*opportunity, power*) ergreifen

seldom ['seldəm] *adv* selten

select [sɪˈlekt] *adj* (*exclusive*) exklusiv ▷ *vt* auswählen; **selection** [sɪˈlekʃən] *n* Auswahl *f* (*of* an +*dat*); **selective** *adj* (*choosy*) wählerisch

self [self] (*pl* **selves**) *n* Selbst *nt*, Ich *nt*; **he's his old ~ again** er ist wieder ganz der Alte; **self-adhesive** *adj* selbstklebend; **self-assured** *adj* selbstsicher; **self-catering** *adj* für Selbstversorger; **self-centred** *adj* egozentrisch; **self-confidence** *n* Selbstbewusstsein *nt*; **self-confident** *adj* selbstbewusst; **self-conscious** *adj* befangen, verklemmt; **self-contained** *adj* (*flat*) separat; **self-control** *n* Selbstbeherrschung *f*; **self-defence** *n* Selbstverteidigung *f*; **self-employed** *adj* selbstständig; **self-evident** *adj* offensichtlich

selfish, selfishly ['selfɪʃ, -lɪ] *adj, adv* egoistisch, selbstsüchtig; **selfless, selflessly** *adj, adv* selbstlos

self-pity [self'pɪtɪ] *n* Selbstmitleid *nt*; **self-portrait** *n* Selbstporträt *nt*; **self-respect** *n* Selbstachtung *f*; **self-service** *n* Selbstbedienung *f* ▷ *adj* Selbstbedienungs-

sell [sel] (**sold, sold**) *vt* verkaufen; **to ~ sb sth, to ~ sth to**

sb jdm etw verkaufen; **do you ~ postcards?** haben Sie Postkarten? ▷ vi (product) sich verkaufen; **sell out** vt: **to be sold ~** ausverkauft sein; **sell-by date** n Haltbarkeitsdatum nt

Sellotape® ['seləteɪp] n (Brit) Tesafilm® m

semester [sɪ'mestə*] n Semester nt

semi ['semɪ] n (Brit: house) Doppelhaushälfte f; **semicircle** n Halbkreis m; **semicolon** n Semikolon nt; **semidetached (house)** n (Brit) Doppelhaushälfte f; **semifinal** n Halbfinale nt

seminar ['semɪnɑ:*] n Seminar nt

semiskimmed milk ['semɪskɪmd'mɪlk] n Halbfettmilch f

senate ['senət] n Senat m; **senator** n Senator(in) m(f)

send [send] (**sent, sent**) vt schicken; **to ~ sb sth, to ~ sth to sb** jdm etw schicken; **~ her my best wishes** grüße sie von mir; **send away** vt wegschicken ▷ vi: **to ~ for** anfordern; **send back** vt zurückschicken; **send for** vt (person) holen lassen; (by post) anfordern; **send off** vt (by post) abschicken; **send out** vt (invitations etc) verschicken ▷ vi: **to ~ for sth** etw holen lassen

sender ['sendə*] n Absender(in) m(f)

senior ['si:nɪə*] adj (older) älter; (high-ranking) höher; (pupils) älter; **he is ~ to me** er ist mir übergeordnet ▷ n: **he's eight years my ~** er ist acht Jahre älter als ich; **senior citizen** n Senior(in) m(f)

sensation [sen'seɪʃən] n Gefühl nt; (excitement, person, thing)

Sensation f; **sensational** adj sensationell

sense [sens] n (faculty, meaning) Sinn m; (feeling) Gefühl nt; (understanding) Verstand m; **~ of smell/taste** Geruchs-/Geschmackssinn m; **to have a ~ of humour** Humor haben; **to make ~** (sentence etc) einen Sinn ergeben; (be sensible) Sinn machen; **in a ~** gewissermaßen ▷ vt spüren; **senseless** adj (stupid) sinnlos

sensible, sensibly ['sensəbl, -blɪ] adj, adv vernünftig

sensitive ['sensɪtɪv] adj empfindlich (to gegen); (easily hurt) sensibel; (subject) heikel

sensual ['sensjʊəl] adj sinnlich

sensuous ['sensjʊəs] adj sinnlich

sent [sent] pt, pp of **send**

sentence ['sentəns] n (Ling) Satz m; (Jur) Strafe f ▷ vt verurteilen (to zu)

sentiment ['sentɪmənt] n (sentimentality) Sentimentalität f; (opinion) Ansicht f; **sentimental** [sentɪ'mentl] adj sentimental

separate ['seprət] adj getrennt, separat; (individual) einzeln ▷ ['sepəreɪt] vt trennen (from von); **they are ~d** (couple) sie leben getrennt ▷ vi sich trennen; **separately** adv getrennt; (singly) einzeln

September [sep'tembə*] n September m; **in ~** im September; **on the 2nd of ~** am 2. September; **at the beginning/in the middle/at the end of ~** Anfang/Mitte/Ende September; **last/next ~** letzten/nächsten September

septic ['septɪk] adj vereitert

sequel ['si:kwəl] n (to film, book) Fortsetzung f (to von)

sequence ['si:kwəns] n (order) Reihenfolge f

Serbia ['sɜ:bjə] n Serbien nt

sergeant ['sɑ:dʒənt] n Polizeimeister(in) m(f); (Mil) Feldwebel(in) m(f)

serial ['sɪərɪəl] n (TV) Serie f; (in newspaper etc) Fortsetzungsroman m ▷ adj (Inform) seriell; **~ number** Seriennummer f

series ['sɪərɪz] nsing Reihe f; (TV, Radio) Serie f

serious ['sɪərɪəs] adj ernst; (injury, illness, mistake) schwer; (discussion) ernsthaft; **are you ~?** ist das dein Ernst?; **seriously** adv ernsthaft; (hurt) schwer; **~?** im Ernst?; **to take sb ~** jdn ernst nehmen

sermon ['sɜ:mən] n (Rel) Predigt f

servant ['sɜ:vənt] n Diener(in) m(f); **serve** [sɜ:v] vt (customer) bedienen; (food) servieren; (one's country etc) dienen +dat; (sentence) verbüßen; **I'm being ~d** ich werde schon bedient; **it ~s him right** es geschieht ihm recht ▷ vi dienen (as als), aufschlagen ▷ n Aufschlag m

server n (Inform) Server m

service ['sɜ:vɪs] n (in shop, hotel) Bedienung f; (activity, amenity) Dienstleistung f; (set of dishes) Service nt; (Auto) Inspektion f; (Tech) Wartung f; (Rel) Gottesdienst m, Aufschlag m; **train/bus ~** Zug-/Busverbindung f; **"~ not included"** „Bedienung nicht inbegriffen" ▷ vt (Auto, Tech) warten; **service area** n (on motorway) Raststätte f (mit Tankstelle); **service charge** n Bedienung f; **service provider** n (Inform) Provider m; **service station** n Tankstelle f

session ['seʃən] n (of court, assembly) Sitzung f

set [set] (**set, set**) vt (place) stellen; (lay flat) legen; (arrange) anordnen; (table) decken; (trap, record) aufstellen; (time, price) festsetzen; (watch, alarm) stellen (for auf +akk); **to ~ sb a task** jdm eine Aufgabe stellen; **to ~ free** freilassen; **to ~ a good example** ein gutes Beispiel geben; **the novel is ~ in London** der Roman spielt in London ▷ vi (sun) untergehen; (become hard) fest werden; (bone) zusammenwachsen ▷ n (collection of things) Satz m; (of cutlery, furniture) Garnitur f; (group of people) Kreis m; (Radio, TV) Apparat m, Satz m; (Theat) Bühnenbild nt; (Cine) (Film)kulisse f ▷ adj (agreed, prescribed) festgelegt; (ready) bereit; **~ meal** Menü nt; **set aside** vt (money) beiseitelegen; (time) einplanen; **set off** vi aufbrechen (for nach) ▷ vt (alarm) auslösen; (enhance) hervorheben; **set out** vi aufbrechen (for nach) ▷ vt (chairs, chesspieces etc) aufstellen; (state) darlegen; **to ~ to do sth** (intend) beabsichtigen, etw zu tun; **set up** vt (firm, organization) gründen; (stall, tent, camera) aufbauen; (meeting) vereinbaren ▷ vi: **to ~ as a doctor** sich als Arzt niederlassen

setback n Rückschlag m

settee [se'ti:] n Sofa nt, Couch f

setting ['setɪŋ] n (of novel, film) Schauplatz m; (surroundings) Umgebung f

settle ['setl] vt (bill, debt) begleichen; (dispute) beilegen; (question) klären; (stomach) beruhigen ▷ vi: **to ~ (down)** (feel at home) sich einleben; (calm down) sich beruhigen; **settle in** vi (in place) sich einleben; (in job) sich eingewöhnen; **settle up** vi (be)zahlen; **to ~ with sb** mit jdm abrechnen; **settlement** n (of bill, debt) Begleichung f; (colony) Siedlung f; **to reach a ~** sich einigen

setup ['setʌp] n (organization) Organisation f; (situation) Situation f

seven ['sevn] num sieben ▷ n Sieben f; see also **eight**; **seventeen** ['sevn'tiːn] num siebzehn ▷ n Siebzehn f; see also **eight**; **seventeenth** adj siebzehnte(r, s); see also **eighth**; **seventh** ['sevnθ] adj siebte(r, s) ▷ n (fraction) Siebtel nt; see also **eighth**; **seventieth** ['sevntɪɪθ] adj siebzigste(r, s); see also **eighth**; **seventy** ['sevntɪ] num siebzig; **~-one** einundsiebzig ▷ n Siebzig f; **to be in one's seventies** in den Siebzigern sein; see also **eight**

several ['sevrəl] adj, pron mehrere

severe [sɪ'vɪə*] adj (strict) streng; (serious) schwer; (pain) stark; (winter) hart; **severely** adv (harshly) hart; (seriously) schwer

sew [səʊ] (**sewed, sewn**) vt, vi nähen

sewage ['suːɪdʒ] n Abwasser nt; **sewer** ['sʊə*] n Abwasserkanal m

sewing ['səʊɪŋ] n Nähen nt; **sewing machine** n Nähmaschine f

sewn [səʊn] pp of **sew**

sex [seks] n Sex m; (gender) Geschlecht nt; **to have ~** Sex haben (with mit); **sexism** ['seksɪzəm] n Sexismus m; **sexist** ['seksɪst] adj sexistisch ▷ n Sexist(in) m(f); **sex life** n Sex(ual)leben nt

sexual ['seksjʊəl] adj sexuell; **~ discrimination/harassment** sexuelle Diskriminierung/ Belästigung; **~ intercourse** Geschlechtsverkehr m; **sexuality** [seksjʊ'ælɪtɪ] n Sexualität f; **sexually** adv sexuell

sexy ['seksɪ] adj sexy, geil

Seychelles ['seɪʃelz] npl Seychellen pl

shabby ['ʃæbɪ] adj schäbig

shack [ʃæk] n Hütte f

shade [ʃeɪd] n (shadow) Schatten m; (for lamp) (Lampen)schirm m; (colour) Farbton m; **~s** (US: sunglasses) Sonnenbrille f ▷ vt (from sun) abschirmen; (in drawing) schattieren

shadow ['ʃædəʊ] n Schatten m

shady ['ʃeɪdɪ] adj schattig; (fig) zwielichtig

shake [ʃeɪk] (**shook, shaken**) vt schütteln; (shock) erschüttern; **to ~ hands with sb** jdm die Hand geben; **to ~ one's head** den Kopf schütteln ▷ vi (tremble) zittern; (building, ground) schwanken; **shake off** vt abschütteln; **shaken** ['ʃeɪkn] pp of **shake**; **shaky** ['ʃeɪkɪ] adj (trembling) zittrig; (table, chair, position) wackelig; (weak) unsicher

shall [ʃæl] (**should**) vb aux werden; (in questions) sollen; **I ~ do my best** ich werde mein Bestes tun; **~ I come too?** soll ich mitkommen?; **where ~ we go?** wo gehen wir hin?

shallow ['ʃæləʊ] adj (a. fig) seicht; (person) oberflächlich

shame [ʃeɪm] n (feeling of ~) Scham f; (disgrace) Schande f; **what a ~!** wie schade!; **~ on you!** schäm dich/schämen Sie sich!; **it's a ~ that ...** schade, dass ...

shampoo [ʃæm'puː] n Shampoo nt; **to have a ~ and set** sich die Haare waschen und legen lassen ▷ vt (hair) waschen; (carpet) schamponieren

shandy ['ʃændɪ] n Radler m, Alsterwasser nt

shan't [ʃɑːnt] contr of **shall not**

shape [ʃeɪp] n Form f; (unidentified figure) Gestalt f; **in the ~ of** in Form +gen; **to be in good ~** (healthwise) in guter Verfassung sein; **to take ~** (plan, idea) Gestalt annehmen ▷ vt (clay, person) formen; **-shaped** [ʃeɪpt] suf -förmig; **shapeless** adj formlos

share [ʃɛə°] n Anteil +dat (in, of an m); (Fin) Aktie f ▷ vt, vi teilen; **shareholder** n Aktionär(in) m(f)

shark [ʃɑːk] n (Zool) Haifisch m

sharp [ʃɑːp] adj scharf; (pin) spitz; (person) scharfsinnig; (pain) heftig; (increase, fall) abrupt; **C/F ~** (Mus) Cis/Dis nt ▷ adv: **at 2 o'clock ~** Punkt 2 Uhr; **sharpen** vt (knife) schärfen; (pencil) spitzen; **sharpener** n (pencil ~) Spitzer m

shatter [ʃætə°] vt zerschmettern; (fig) zerstören ▷ vi zerspringen; **shattered** adj (exhausted) kaputt

shave [ʃeɪv] (**shaved, shaved** o **shaven**) vt rasieren ▷ vi sich rasieren ▷ n Rasur f; **that was a close ~** (fig) das war knapp; **shave off** vt: **to shave one's beard off** sich den Bart abrasieren; **shaven** [ʃeɪvn] pp of **shave** ▷ adj (head) kahl geschoren; **shaver** n (Elec) Rasierapparat m; **shaving brush** n Rasierpinsel m; **shaving foam** n Rasierschaum m; **shaving tackle** n Rasierzeug nt

shawl [ʃɔːl] n Tuch nt

she [ʃiː] pron sie

shed [ʃed] (**shed, shed**) n Schuppen m ▷ vt (tears, blood) vergießen; (hair, leaves) verlieren

she'd [ʃiːd] contr of **she had; she would**

sheep [ʃiːp] (pl -) n Schaf nt; **sheepdog** n Schäferhund m; **sheepskin** n Schaffell nt

sheer [ʃɪə°] adj (madness) rein; (steep) steil; **by ~ chance** rein zufällig

sheet [ʃiːt] n (on bed) Betttuch nt; (of paper) Blatt nt; (of metal) Platte f; (of glass) Scheibe f; **a ~ of paper** ein Blatt Papier

shelf [ʃelf] (pl **shelves**) n Bücherbord nt, Regal nt; **shelves** pl (item of furniture) Regal nt

she'll [ʃiːl] contr of **she will; she shall**

shell [ʃel] n (of egg, nut) Schale f; (sea~) Muschel f ▷ vt (peas, nuts) schälen; **shellfish** n (as food) Meeresfrüchte pl

shelter [ʃeltə°] n (protection) Schutz m; (accommodation) Unterkunft f; (bus ~) Wartehäuschen nt ▷ vt schützen (from vor +dat) ▷ vi sich unterstellen; **sheltered** adj (spot) geschützt; (life) behütet

shelve [ʃelv] vt (fig) aufschieben; **shelves** pl of **shelf**

shepherd [ʃepəd] n Schäfer m; **shepherd's pie** n Hackfleischauflauf mit Decke aus Kartoffelpüree

sherry [ʃerɪ] n Sherry m

she's [ʃiːz] contr of **she is; she has**

shield [ʃiːld] n Schild m; (fig) Schutz m ▷ vt schützen (from vor +dat)

shift [ʃɪft] n (change) Veränderung f; (period at work, workers) Schicht f; (on keyboard) Umschalttaste f ▷ vt (furniture etc) verrücken; (stain) entfernen; **to ~ gear(s)** (US Auto) schalten ▷ vi (move) sich bewegen; (move up) rutschen; **shift key** n Umschalttaste f

shin [ʃɪn] n Schienbein nt

shine [ʃaɪn] (**shone, shone**) vi (be shiny) glänzen; (sun) scheinen; (lamp) leuchten ▷ vt (polish) polieren ▷ n Glanz m

shingles [ˈʃɪŋglz] nsing (Med) Gürtelrose f

shiny [ˈʃaɪnɪ] adj glänzend

ship [ʃɪp] n Schiff nt ▷ vt (send) versenden; (by ship) verschiffen; **shipment** n (goods) Sendung f; (sent by ship) Ladung f; **shipwreck** n Schiffbruch m; **shipyard** n Werft f

shirt [ʃɜːt] n Hemd nt

shit [ʃɪt] n (vulg) Scheiße f; (person) Arschloch nt; ~! Scheiße!; **shitty** [ˈʃɪtɪ] adj (fam) beschissen

shiver [ˈʃɪvə°] vi zittern (with vor +dat)

shock [ʃɒk] n (mental, emotional) Schock m; **to be in** ~ unter Schock stehen; **to get a** ~ (Elec) einen Schlag bekommen ▷ vt schockieren; **shock absorber** n Stoßdämpfer m; **shocked** adj schockiert (by über +akk); **shocking** adj schockierend; (awful) furchtbar

shoe [ʃuː] n Schuh m; **shoehorn** n Schuhlöffel m; **shoelace** n Schnürsenkel m; **shoe polish** n Schuhcreme f

shone [ʃɒn] pt, pp of **shine**

shook [ʃʊk] pt of **shake**

shoot [ʃuːt] (**shot, shot**) vt (wound) anschießen; (kill) erschießen; (Cine) drehen; (fam: heroin) drücken ▷ vi (with gun, move quickly) schießen; **to** ~ **at sb** auf jdn schießen ▷ n (of plant) Trieb m; **shooting** n (exchange of gunfire) Schießerei f; (killing) Erschießung f

shop [ʃɒp] n Geschäft nt, Laden m ▷ vi einkaufen; **shop assistant** n Verkäufer(in) m(f); **shopkeeper** n Geschäftsinhaber(in) m(f); **shoplifting** n Ladendiebstahl m; **shopper** n Käufer(in) m(f); **shopping** n (activity) Einkaufen nt; (goods) Einkäufe pl; **to do the**

~ einkaufen; **to go** ~ einkaufen gehen; **shopping bag** n Einkaufstasche f; **shopping cart** n (US) Einkaufswagen m; **shopping center** (US), **shopping centre** n Einkaufszentrum nt; **shopping list** n Einkaufszettel m; **shopping trolley** n (Brit) Einkaufswagen m; **shop window** n Schaufenster nt

shore [ʃɔː°] n Ufer nt; **on** ~ an Land

short [ʃɔːt] adj kurz; (person) klein; **to be** ~ **of money** knapp bei Kasse sein; **to be** ~ **of time** wenig Zeit haben; ~ **of breath** kurzatmig; **to cut** ~ (holiday) abbrechen; **we are two** ~ wir haben zwei zu wenig; **it's** ~ **for ...** das ist die Kurzform von ... ▷ n (drink, Elec) Kurze(r) m; **shortage** n Knappheit f (of an +dat); **shortbread** n Buttergebäck nt; **short circuit** n Kurzschluss m; **shortcoming** n Unzulänglichkeit f; (of person) Fehler m; **shortcut** n (quicker route) Abkürzung f; (Inform) Shortcut m; **shorten** vt kürzen; (in time) verkürzen; **shorthand** n Stenografie f; **shortlist** n: **to be on the** ~ in der engeren Wahl sein; **short-lived** adj kurzlebig; **shortly** adv bald; **shorts** npl Shorts pl; **short-sighted** adj (a. fig) kurzsichtig; **short-sleeved** adj kurzärmelig; **short-stay car park** n Kurzzeitparkplatz m; **short story** n Kurzgeschichte f; **short-term** adj kurzfristig; **short wave** n Kurzwelle f

shot [ʃɒt] pt, pp of **shoot** ▷ n (from gun, in football) Schuss m; (Foto, Cine) Aufnahme f; (injection) Spritze f; (of alcohol) Schuss m

should [ʃʊd] pt of **shall** ▷ vb aux: **I** ~ **go now** ich sollte jetzt gehen; **what** ~ **I do?** was soll ich tun?; **you** ~**n't have said that** das hättest du/hätten Sie nicht sagen sollen; **that ~ be enough** das müsste reichen

shoulder ['ʃəʊldə*] n Schulter f

shouldn't ['ʃʊdnt] contr of **should not**

should've ['ʃʊdəv] contr of **should have**

shout [ʃaʊt] n Schrei m; (call) Ruf m ▷ vt rufen; (order) brüllen ▷ vi schreien; **to ~ at** anschreien; **to ~ for help** um Hilfe rufen

shove [ʃʌv] vt (person) schubsen; (car, table etc) schieben ▷ vi (in crowd) drängeln

shovel ['ʃʌvl] n Schaufel f ▷ vt schaufeln

show [ʃəʊ] (showed, shown) vt zeigen; **to ~ sb sth, to ~ sth to sb** jdm etw zeigen; **to ~ sb in** jdn hereinführen; **to ~ sb out** jdn zur Tür bringen ▷ n (Cine, Theat) Vorstellung f; (TV) Show f; (exhibition) Ausstellung f; **show off** vi (pej) angeben; **show round** vt herumführen; **to show sb round the house/the town** jdm das Haus/die Stadt zeigen; **show up** vi (arrive) auftauchen

shower ['ʃaʊə*] n Dusche f; (rain) Schauer m; **to have** (o **take**) **a ~** duschen ▷ vi (wash) duschen

showing ['ʃəʊɪŋ] n (Cine) Vorstellung f

shown [ʃəʊn] pp of **show**

showroom ['ʃəʊruːm] n Ausstellungsraum m

shrank [ʃræŋk] pt of **shrink**

shred [ʃred] n (of paper, fabric) Fetzen m ▷ vt (in shredder) (im Reißwolf) zerkleinern; **shredder** n (for paper) Reißwolf m

shrimp [ʃrɪmp] n Garnele f

shrink [ʃrɪŋk] (shrank, shrunk) vi schrumpfen; (clothes) eingehen

shrivel ['ʃrɪvl] vi: **to ~ (up)**

schrumpfen; (skin) runzlig werden; (plant) welken

Shrove Tuesday ['ʃrəʊv'tjuːzdeɪ] n Fastnachtsdienstag m

shrub [ʃrʌb] n Busch m, Strauch m

shrug [ʃrʌg] vt, vi: **to ~ (one's shoulders)** die Achseln zucken

shrunk [ʃrʌŋk] pp of **shrink**

shudder ['ʃʌdə*] vi schaudern; (ground, building) beben

shuffle ['ʃʌfl] vt, vi mischen

shut [ʃʌt] (shut, shut) vt zumachen, schließen; **~ your face!** (fam) halt den Mund! ▷ vi schließen ▷ adj geschlossen; **we're ~** wir haben geschlossen; **shut down** vt schließen; (computer) ausschalten ▷ vi schließen; (computer) sich ausschalten; **shut in** vt einschließen; **shut out** vt (lock out) aussperren; **to shut oneself out** sich aussperren; **shut up** vt (lock up) abschließen; (silence) zum Schweigen bringen ▷ vi (keep quiet) den Mund halten; **~!** halt den Mund!; **shutter** n (on window) (Fenster)laden m; **shutter release** n Auslöser m; **shutter speed** n Belichtungszeit f

shuttle bus ['ʃʌtlbʌs] n Shuttlebus m

shuttlecock ['ʃʌtlkɒk] n Federball m

shuttle service ['ʃʌtlsɜːvɪs] n Pendelverkehr m

shy [ʃaɪ] adj schüchtern; (animal) scheu

Siberia [saɪ'bɪərɪə] n Sibirien nt

Sicily ['sɪsɪlɪ] n Sizilien nt

sick [sɪk] adj krank; (joke) makaber; **to be ~** (Brit: vomit) sich übergeben; **to be off ~** wegen Krankheit fehlen; **I feel ~** mir ist schlecht; **to be ~ of sb/sth** jdn/etw satthaben; **it makes me**

~ *(fig)* es ekelt mich an; **sickbag** *n* Spucktüte *f*; **sick leave** *n*: **to be on** ~ krankgeschrieben sein; **sickness** *n* Krankheit *f*; *(Brit: nausea)* Übelkeit *f*; **sickness benefit** *n* *(Brit)* Krankengeld *nt*

side [saɪd] *n* Seite *f*; *(of road)* Rand *m*; *(of mountain)* Hang *m*; *(Sport)* Mannschaft *f*; **by my** ~ neben mir; ~ **by** ~ nebeneinander ▷ *adj (door, entrance)* Seiten-; **sideboard** *n* Anrichte *f*; **sideburns** *npl* Koteletten *pl*; **side dish** *n* Beilage *f*; **side effect** *n* Nebenwirkung *f*; **sidelight** *n* *(Brit Auto)* Parklicht *nt*; **side order** *n* Beilage *f*; **side road** *n* Nebenstraße *f*; **side street** *n* Seitenstraße *f*; **sidewalk** *n* *(US)* Bürgersteig *m*; **sideways** *adv* seitwärts

sieve [sɪv] *n* Sieb *nt*

sift [sɪft] *vt (flour etc)* sieben

sigh [saɪ] *vi* seufzen

sight [saɪt] *n (power of seeing)* Sehvermögen *nt*; *(view, thing seen)* Anblick *m*; ~**s** *pl (of city etc)* Sehenswürdigkeiten *pl*; **to have bad** ~ schlecht sehen; **to lose** ~ **of** aus den Augen verlieren; **out of** ~ außer Sicht; **sightseeing** *n*: **to go** ~ Sehenswürdigkeiten besichtigen; ~ **tour** Rundfahrt *f*

sign [saɪn] *n* Zeichen *nt*; *(notice, road* ~*)* Schild *nt* ▷ *vt* unterschreiben ▷ *vi* unterschreiben; **to** ~ **for sth** den Empfang einer Sache *gen* bestätigen; **to** ~ **in/out** sich ein-/austragen; **sign on** *vi (Brit: register as unemployed)* sich arbeitslos melden; **sign up** *vi (for course)* sich einschreiben; *(Mil)* sich verpflichten

signal ['sɪgnl] *n* Signal *nt* ▷ *vi (car driver)* blinken

signature ['sɪgnətʃə°] *n* Unterschrift *f*

significant [sɪg'nɪfɪkənt] *adj (important)* bedeutend, wichtig; *(meaning sth)* bedeutsam; **significantly** *adv (considerably)* bedeutend

sign language ['saɪnlæŋgwɪdʒ] *n* Zeichensprache *f*; **signpost** *n* Wegweiser *m*

silence ['saɪləns] *n* Stille *f*; *(of person)* Schweigen *nt*; ~! Ruhe! ▷ *vt* zum Schweigen bringen; **silent** *adj* still; *(taciturn)* schweigsam; **she remained** ~ sie schwieg

silk [sɪlk] *n* Seide *f* ▷ *adj* Seiden-

silly ['sɪlɪ] *adj* dumm, albern; **don't do anything** ~ mach keine Dummheiten; **the** ~ **season** das Sommerloch

silver ['sɪlvə°] *n* Silber *nt*; *(coins)* Silbermünzen *pl* ▷ *adj* Silber-, silbern; **silver-plated** *adj* versilbert; **silver wedding** *n* silberne Hochzeit

similar ['sɪmɪlə°] *adj* ähnlich *(to dat)*; **similarity** [sɪmɪ'lærɪtɪ] *n* Ähnlichkeit *f (to* mit*)*; **similarly** *adv (equally)* ebenso

simple ['sɪmpl] *adj* einfach; *(unsophisticated)* schlicht; **simplify** ['sɪmplɪfaɪ] *vt* vereinfachen; **simply** *adv* einfach; *(merely)* bloß; *(dress)* schlicht

simulate ['sɪmjʊleɪt] *vt* simulieren

simultaneous, simultaneously [sɪməl'teɪnɪəs, -lɪ] *adj, adv* gleichzeitig

sin [sɪn] *n* Sünde *f* ▷ *vi* sündigen

since [sɪns] *adv* seitdem; *(in the meantime)* inzwischen ▷ *prep* seit +*dat*; **ever** ~ **1995** schon seit 1995 ▷ *conj (time)* seit, seitdem; *(because)* da, weil; **ever** ~ **I've known her** seit ich sie kenne; **it's ages** ~ **I've seen him** ich habe ihn seit Langem nicht mehr gesehen

sincere [sɪn'sɪə*] *adj* aufrichtig;
sincerely *adv* aufrichtig;
Yours ~ mit freundlichen
Grüßen
sing [sɪŋ] (**sang, sung**) *vt, vi*
singen
Singapore [sɪŋgə'pɔ:*] *n* Singapur *nt*
singer [ˈsɪŋə*] *n* Sänger(in) *m(f)*
single [ˈsɪŋgl] *adj* (*one only*)
einzig; (*not double*) einfach; (*bed,
room*) Einzel-; (*unmarried*) ledig;
(*Brit: ticket*) einfach ▷ *n* (*Brit:
ticket*) einfache Fahrkarte; (*Mus*)
Single *f*; **a ~ to London, please**
(*Brit Rail*) einfach nach London,
bitte; **single out** *vt* (*choose*)
auswählen; **single-handed,
single-handedly** *adv* im
Alleingang; **single parent** *n*
Alleinerziehende(r) *mf*; **single
supplement** *n* (*for hotel room*)
Einzelzimmerzuschlag *m*
singular [ˈsɪŋgjʊlə*] *n* Singular
m
sinister [ˈsɪnɪstə*] *adj*
unheimlich
sink [sɪŋk] (**sank, sunk**) *vt* (*ship*)
versenken ▷ *vi* sinken ▷ *n*
Spülbecken *nt*; (*in bathroom*)
Waschbecken *nt*
sip [sɪp] *vt* nippen an +*dat*
sir [sɜ:*] *n*: **yes, ~** ja(, mein Herr);
can I help you, ~? kann ich Ihnen
helfen?; **Sir James** (*title*) Sir James
sister [ˈsɪstə*] *n* Schwester *f*;
(*Brit: nurse*) Oberschwester *f*;
sister-in-law (*pl* **sisters-in-law**) *n*
Schwägerin *f*
sit [sɪt] (**sat, sat**) *vi* (*be sitting*)
sitzen; (*~ down*) sich setzen;
(*committee, court*) tagen ▷ *vt* (*Brit:
exam*) machen; **sit down** *vi* sich
hinsetzen; **sit up** *vi* (*from lying
position*) sich aufsetzen
sitcom [ˈsɪtkɒm] *n* Situ-
ationskomödie *f*

site [saɪt] *n* Platz *m*; (*building ~*)
Baustelle *f*; (*web~*) Site *f*
sitting [ˈsɪtɪŋ] *n* (*meeting, for
portrait*) Sitzung *f*; **sitting room** *n*
Wohnzimmer *nt*
situated [ˈsɪtjʊeɪtɪd] *adj*: **to be
~** liegen
situation [sɪtjʊ'eɪʃən] *n* (*circumstances*) Situation *f*, Lage *f*; (*job*)
Stelle *f*; **"~s vacant/wanted"** (*Brit*)
„Stellenangebote/Stellengesuche"
six [sɪks] *num* sechs ▷ *n* Sechs *f*;
see also **eight**; **sixpack** *n* (*of beer
etc*) Sechserpack *nt*; **sixteen**
[ˈsɪks'ti:n] *num* sechzehn ▷ *n*
Sechzehn *f*; *see also* **eight**;
sixteenth *adj* sechzehnte(r, s); *see
also* **eighth**; **sixth** [sɪksθ] *adj*
sechste(r, s); **~ form** (*Brit*) ≈
Oberstufe *f* ▷ *n* (*fraction*) Sechstel
nt; *see also* **eighth**; **sixtieth**
[ˈsɪkstɪɪθ] *adj* sechzigste(r, s); *see
also* **eighth**; **sixty** [ˈsɪkstɪ] *num*
sechzig; **~-one** einundsechzig ▷ *n*
Sechzig *f*; **to be in one's sixties** in
den Sechzigern sein; *see also* **eight**
size [saɪz] *n* Größe *f*; **what ~ are
you?** welche Größe hast du/haben
Sie?; **a ~ too big** eine Nummer zu
groß
sizzle [ˈsɪzl] *vi* (*Gastr*) brutzeln
skate [skeɪt] *n* Schlittschuh *m*;
(*roller ~*) Rollschuh *m* ▷ *vi*
Schlittschuh laufen; (*roller-~*)
Rollschuh laufen; **skateboard** *n*
Skateboard *nt*; **skating** *n* Eislauf
m; (*roller-~*) Rollschuhlauf *m*;
skating rink *n* Eisbahn *f*; (*for
roller-skating*) Rollschuhbahn *f*
skeleton [ˈskelɪtn] *n* (*a. fig*)
Skelett *nt*
skeptical *n* (*US*) *see* **sceptical**
sketch [sketʃ] *n* Skizze *f*; (*Theat*)
Sketch *m* ▷ *vt* skizzieren;
sketchbook *n* Skizzenbuch *nt*
ski [ski:] *n* Ski *m* ▷ *vi* Ski laufen;
ski boot *n* Skistiefel *m*

skid [skɪd] *vi* (*Auto*) schleudern
skier ['skiːə*] *n* Skiläufer(in) *m(f)*;
skiing *n* Skilaufen *nt*; **to go ~** Ski
laufen gehen; **~ holiday** Skiurlaub
m; **skiing instructor** *n*
Skilehrer(in) *m(f)*
skilful, skilfully ['skɪlfʊl, -fəlɪ]
adj, adv geschickt
ski-lift ['skiːlɪft] *n* Skilift *m*
skill [skɪl] *n* Geschick *nt*; (*acquired
technique*) Fertigkeit *f*; **skilled** *adj*
geschickt (*at, in* in +*dat*); (*worker*)
Fach-; (*work*) fachmännisch
skim [skɪm] *vt*: **to ~ (off)** (*fat etc*)
abschöpfen; **to ~ (through)** (*read*)
überfliegen; **skimmed milk** *n*
Magermilch *f*
skin [skɪn] *n* Haut *f*; (*fur*) Fell *nt*;
(*peel*) Schale *f*; **skin diving** *n*
Sporttauchen *nt*; **skinny** *adj* dünn
skip [skɪp] *vi* hüpfen; (*with rope*)
seilspringen ▷ *vt* (*miss out*)
überspringen; (*meal*) ausfallen
lassen; (*school, lesson*) schwänzen
ski pants ['skiːpænts] *npl*
Skihose *f*; **ski pass** *n* Skipass *m*;
ski pole *n* Skistock *m*; **ski resort**
n Skiort *m*
skirt [skɜːt] *n* Rock *m*
ski run ['skiːrʌn] *n* (Ski)abfahrt
f; **ski stick** *n* Skistock *m*; **ski tow**
n Schlepplift *m*
skittle ['skɪtl] *n* Kegel *m*; **~s**
(*game*) Kegeln *nt*
skive [skaɪv] *vi*: **to ~ (off)** (*Brit*)
(*from school*) schwänzen; (*from
work*) blaumachen
skull [skʌl] *n* Schädel *m*
sky [skaɪ] *n* Himmel *m*;
skydiving *n* Fallschirmspringen
nt; **skylight** *n* Dachfenster *nt*;
skyscraper *n* Wolkenkratzer *m*
slam [slæm] *vt* (*door*) zuschlagen;
slam on *vt*: **to slam the brakes
on** voll auf die Bremse treten
slander ['slɑːndə*] *n* Verleumdung *f* ▷ *vt* verleumden

slang [slæŋ] *n* Slang *m*
slap [slæp] *n* Klaps *m*; (*across face*)
Ohrfeige *f* ▷ *vt* schlagen; **to ~ sb's
face** jdn ohrfeigen
slash [slæʃ] *n* (*punctuation mark*)
Schrägstrich *m* ▷ *vt* (*face, tyre*)
aufschlitzen; (*prices*) stark
herabsetzen
slate [sleɪt] *n* (*rock*) Schiefer *m*;
(*roof ~*) Schieferplatte *f*
slaughter ['slɔːtə*] *vt* (*animals*)
schlachten; (*people*) abschlachten
Slav [slɑːv] *adj* slawisch ▷ *n*
Slawe *m*, Slawin *f*
slave [sleɪv] *n* Sklave *m*, Sklavin *f*;
slave away *vi* schuften;
slave-driver *n* (*fam*)
Sklaventreiber(in) *m(f)*; **slavery**
['sleɪvərɪ] *n* Sklaverei *f*
sleaze [sliːz] *n* (*corruption*)
Korruption *f*; **sleazy** *adj* (*bar,
district*) zwielichtig
sledge ['sledʒ] *n* Schlitten *m*
sleep [sliːp] (**slept, slept**) *vi*
schlafen; **to ~ with sb** mit jdm
schlafen ▷ *n* Schlaf *m*; **to put to
~** (*animal*) einschläfern; **sleep in** *vi*
(*lie in*) ausschlafen; **sleeper** *n*
(*Rail: train*) Schlafwagenzug *m*;
(*carriage*) Schlafwagen *m*; **sleeping
bag** *n* Schlafsack *m*; **sleeping car**
n Schlafwagen *m*; **sleeping pill** *n*
Schlaftablette *f*; **sleepless** *adj*
schlaflos; **sleepy** *adj* schläfrig;
(*place*) verschlafen
sleet [sliːt] *n* Schneeregen *m*
sleeve [sliːv] *n* Ärmel *m*;
sleeveless *adj* ärmellos
sleigh [sleɪ] *n* (Pferde)schlitten
m
slender ['slendə*] *adj* schlank;
(*fig*) gering
slept [slept] *pt, pp of* **sleep**
slice [slaɪs] *n* Scheibe *f*; (*of cake,
tart, pizza*) Stück *nt* ▷ *vt*: **to ~ (up)**
in Scheiben schneiden; **sliced
bread** *n* geschnittenes Brot

slid [slɪd] *pt, pp of* **slide**

slide [slaɪd] (**slid, slid**) *vt* gleiten lassen; (*push*) schieben ▷ *vi* gleiten; (*slip*) rutschen ▷ *n* (*Foto*) Dia *nt*; (*in playground*) Rutschbahn *f*; (*Brit: for hair*) Spange *f*

slight [slaɪt] *adj* leicht; (*problem, difference*) klein; **not in the ~est** nicht im Geringsten; **slightly** *adv* etwas; (*injured*) leicht

slim [slɪm] *adj* (*person*) schlank; (*book*) dünn; (*chance, hope*) gering ▷ *vi* abnehmen

slime [slaɪm] *n* Schleim *m*; **slimy** *adj* schleimig

sling [slɪŋ] (**slung, slung**) *vt* werfen ▷ *n* (*for arm*) Schlinge *f*

slip [slɪp] *n* (*mistake*) Flüchtigkeitsfehler *m*; **~ of paper** Zettel *m* ▷ *vt* (*put*) stecken; **to ~ on/off** (*garment*) an-/ausziehen; **it ~ped my mind** ich habe es vergessen ▷ *vi* (*lose balance*) (aus)rutschen; **slip away** *vi* (*leave*) sich wegstehlen; **slipper** *n* Hausschuh *m*; **slippery** *adj* (*path, road*) glatt; (*soap, fish*) glitschig; **slip-road** *n* (*Brit: onto motorway*) Auffahrt *f*; (*off motorway*) Ausfahrt *f*

slit [slɪt] (**slit, slit**) *vt* aufschlitzen ▷ *n* Schlitz *m*

slope [sləʊp] *n* Neigung *f*; (*side of hill*) Hang *m* ▷ *vi* (*be sloping*) schräg sein; **sloping** *adj* (*floor, roof*) schräg

sloppy ['slɒpɪ] *adj* (*careless*) schlampig; (*sentimental*) rührselig

slot [slɒt] *n* (*opening*) Schlitz *m*; (*Inform*) Steckplatz *m*; **we have a ~ free at 2** (*free time*) um 2 ist noch ein Termin frei; **slot machine** *n* Automat *m*; (*for gambling*) Spielautomat *m*

Slovak ['sləʊvæk] *adj* slowakisch ▷ *n* (*person*) Slowake *m*, Slowakin *f*; (*language*) Slowakisch *nt*; **Slovakia** [sləʊ'vækɪə] *n* Slowakei *f*

Slovene ['sləʊviːn], **Slovenian** [sləʊ'viːnɪən] *adj* slowenisch ▷ *n* (*person*) Slowene *m*, Slowenin *f*; (*language*) Slowenisch *nt*; **Slovenia** [sləʊ'viːnɪə] *n* Slowenien *nt*

slow [sləʊ] *adj* langsam; (*business*) flau; **to be ~** (*clock*) nachgehen; (*stupid*) begriffsstutzig sein; **slow down** *vi* langsamer werden; (*when driving/walking*) langsamer fahren/gehen; **slowly** *adv* langsam; **slow motion** *n*: **in ~** in Zeitlupe

slug [slʌg] *n* (*Zool*) Nacktschnecke *f*

slum [slʌm] *n* Slum *m*

slump [slʌmp] *n* Rückgang *m* (*in an +dat*) ▷ *vi* (*onto chair etc*) sich fallen lassen; (*prices*) stürzen

slung [slʌŋ] *pt, pp of* **sling**

slur [slɜː*] *n* (*insult*) Verleumdung *f*; **slurred** [slɜːd] *adj* undeutlich

slush [slʌʃ] *n* (*snow*) Schneematsch *m*; **slushy** *adj* matschig; (*fig*) schmalzig

slut [slʌt] *n* (*pej*) Schlampe *f*

smack [smæk] *n* Klaps *m* ▷ *vt*: **to ~ sb** jdm einen Klaps geben ▷ *vi*: **to ~ of** riechen nach

small [smɔːl] *adj* klein; **small ads** *npl* (*Brit*) Kleinanzeigen *pl*; **small change** *n* Kleingeld *nt*; **small letters** *npl*: **in ~** in Kleinbuchstaben; **smallpox** *n* Pocken *pl*; **small print** *n*: **the ~** das Kleingedruckte; **small-scale** *adj* (*map*) in kleinem Maßstab; **small talk** *n* Konversation *f*, Smalltalk *m*

smart [smɑːt] *adj* (*elegant*) schick; (*clever*) clever; **smartarse**, **smartass** (*US*) *n* (*fam*) Klugscheißer (*in*) *m(f)*; **smart card** *n* Chipkarte *f*; **smartly** *adv* (*dressed*) schick

smash [smæʃ] *n* (*car crash*) Zusammenstoß *m*, Schmetterball

$m \triangleright vt$ (*break*) zerschlagen; (*fig: record*) brechen, deutlich übertreffen $\triangleright vi$ (*break*) zerbrechen; **to ~ into** (*car*) krachen gegen

smear [smɪə*] n (*mark*) Fleck m; (*Med*) Abstrich m; (*fig*) Verleumdung $f \triangleright vt$ (*spread*) schmieren; (*make dirty*) beschmieren; (*fig*) verleumden

smell [smel] (**smelt** o **smelled, smelt** o **smelled**) vt riechen $\triangleright vi$ riechen (*of* nach); (*unpleasantly*) stinken $\triangleright n$ Geruch m; (*unpleasant*) Gestank m; **smelly** *adj* übel riechend; **smelt** [smelt] *pt*, *pp of* **smell**

smile [smaɪl] n Lächeln $nt \triangleright vi$ lächeln; **to ~ at sb** jdn anlächeln

smock [smɒk] n Kittel m

smog [smɒg] n Smog m

smoke [sməʊk] n Rauch $m \triangleright vt$ rauchen; (*food*) räuchern $\triangleright vi$ rauchen; **smoke alarm** n Rauchmelder m; **smoked** *adj* (*food*) geräuchert; **smoke-free** *adj* (*zone, building*) rauchfrei; **smoker** n Raucher(in) $m(f)$; **smoking** n Rauchen nt; **"no ~"** „Rauchen verboten"

smooth [smuːð] *adj* glatt; (*flight, crossing*) ruhig; (*movement*) geschmeidig; (*without problems*) reibungslos; (*pej: person*) aalglatt $\triangleright vt$ (*hair, dress*) glatt streichen; (*surface*) glätten; **smoothly** *adv* reibungslos; **to run ~** (*engine*) ruhig laufen

smudge [smʌdʒ] vt (*writing, lipstick*) verschmieren

smug [smʌg] *adj* selbstgefällig

smuggle ['smʌgl] vt schmuggeln; **to ~ in/out** herein-/herausschmuggeln

smutty ['smʌtɪ] *adj* (*obscene*) schmutzig

snack [snæk] n Imbiss m; **to have**

a ~ eine Kleinigkeit essen; **snack bar** n Imbissstube f

snail [sneɪl] n Schnecke f; **snail mail** n (*fam*) Schneckenpost f

snake [sneɪk] n Schlange f

snap [snæp] n (*photo*) Schnappschuss $m \triangleright adj$ (*decision*) spontan $\triangleright vt$ (*break*) zerbrechen; (*rope*) zerreißen $\triangleright vi$ (*break*) brechen; (*rope*) reißen; (*bite*) schnappen (*at* nach); **snap off** vt (*break*) abbrechen; **snap fastener** n (*US*) Druckknopf m; **snapshot** n Schnappschuss m

snatch [snætʃ] vt (*grab*) schnappen

sneak [sniːk] vi (*move*) schleichen; **sneakers** *npl* (*US*) Turnschuhe *pl*

sneeze [sniːz] vi niesen

sniff [snɪf] vi schniefen; (*smell*) schnüffeln (*at* an +*dat*) $\triangleright vt$ schnuppern an +*dat*; (*glue*) schnüffeln

snob [snɒb] n Snob m; **snobbish** *adj* versnobt

snog [snɒg] vi, vt knutschen

snooker ['snuːkə*] n Snooker nt

snoop [snuːp] vi: **to ~ (around)** (herum)schnüffeln

snooze [snuːz] n, vi: **to (have a) ~** ein Nickerchen machen

snore [snɔː*] vi schnarchen

snorkel ['snɔːkl] n Schnorchel m; **snorkelling** n Schnorcheln nt; **to go ~** schnorcheln gehen

snout [snaʊt] n Schnauze f

snow [snəʊ] n Schnee $m \triangleright vi$ schneien; **snowball** n Schneeball m; **snowboard** n Snowboard nt; **snowboarding** n Snowboarding nt; **snowdrift** n Schneewehe f; **snowdrop** n Schneeglöckchen nt; **snowflake** n Schneeflocke f; **snowman** (*pl* **-men**) n Schneemann m; **snowplough**,

snowplow (*US*) *n* Schneepflug *m*;
snowstorm *n* Schneesturm *m*;
snowy *adj* (*region*) schneereich;
(*landscape*) verschneit
snug [snʌg] *adj* (*person, place*)
gemütlich
snuggle up ['snʌgl'ʌp] *vi*: **to
~ to sb** sich an jdn ankuscheln

○ **KEYWORD**

so [səʊ] *adv* 1 (*thus*) so; (*likewise*)
auch; **so saying he walked away**
indem er das sagte, ging er; **if so**
wenn ja; **I didn't do it — you did
so!** ich hab das nicht gemacht —
hast du wohl!; **so do I, so am I** *etc*
ich auch; **so it is!** tatsächlich!; **I
hope/think so** hoffentlich/ich
glaube schon; **so far** bis jetzt
2 (*in comparisons etc: to such a
degree*) so; **so quickly/big (that)**
so schnell/groß, dass; **I'm so glad
to see you** ich freue mich so,
dich/Sie zu sehen
3 **so many** so viele; **so much work**
so viel Arbeit; **I love you so much**
ich liebe dich so sehr
4 (*phrases*) **10 or so** etwa 10; **so
long!** (*inf*) (*goodbye*) tschüss!
▷ *conj* 1 (*expressing purpose*) **so as to**
um ... zu; **so (that)** damit
2 (*expressing result*) also; **so I was
right after all** ich hatte also doch
recht; **so you see ...** wie du
siehst/Sie sehen ...

soak [səʊk] *vt* durchnässen;
(*leave in liquid*) einweichen; **I'm ~ed**
ich bin klatschnass; **soaking** *adj*:
~ (**wet**) klatschnass
soap [səʊp] *n* Seife *f*; **soap
(opera)** *n* Seifenoper *f*; **soap
powder** *n* Waschpulver *nt*
sob [sɒb] *vi* schluchzen
sober ['səʊbə°] *adj* nüchtern;
sober up *vi* nüchtern werden

so-called ['səʊ'kɔːld] *adj*
sogenannt
soccer ['sɒkə°] *n* Fußball *m*
sociable ['səʊʃəbl] *adj* gesellig
social ['səʊʃəl] *adj* sozial;
(*sociable*) gesellig; **socialist** *adj*
sozialistisch ▷ *n* Sozialist(in)
m(f); **socialize** *vi* unter die Leute
gehen; **social security** *n* (*Brit*)
Sozialhilfe *f*; (*US*)
Sozialversicherung *f*
society [sə'saɪətɪ] *n* Gesellschaft
f; (*club*) Verein *m*
sock [sɒk] *n* Socke *f*
socket ['sɒkɪt] *n* (*Elec*) Steckdose
f
soda ['səʊdə] *n* (~ *water*) Soda *f*;
(*US: pop*) Limo *f*; **soda water** *n*
Sodawasser *nt*
sofa ['səʊfə] *n* Sofa *nt*; **sofa bed**
n Schlafcouch *f*
soft [sɒft] *adj* weich; (*quiet*) leise;
(*lighting*) gedämpft; (*kind*)
gutmütig; (*weak*) nachgiebig;
~ **drink** alkoholfreies Getränk;
softly *adv* sanft; (*quietly*) leise;
software *n* (*Inform*) Software *f*
soil [sɔɪl] *n* Erde *f*; (*ground*) Boden
m
solar ['səʊlə°] *adj* Sonnen-, Solar-
solarium [sə'lɛərɪəm] *n*
Solarium *nt*
sold [səʊld] *pt, pp of* **sell**
soldier ['səʊldʒə°] *n* Soldat(in)
m(f)
sole [səʊl] *n* Sohle *f*; (*fish*)
Seezunge *f* ▷ *vt* besohlen ▷ *adj*
einzig; (*owner, responsibility*)
alleinig; **solely** *adv* nur
solemn ['sɒləm] *adj* feierlich;
(*person*) ernst
solicitor [sə'lɪsɪtə°] *n* (*Brit*)
Rechtsanwalt *m*, Rechtsanwältin *f*
solid ['sɒlɪd] *adj* (*hard*) fest; (*gold,
oak etc*) massiv; (~*ly built*) solide;
(*meal*) kräftig; **three hours** ~ drei
volle Stunden

solitary ['sɒlɪtərɪ] *adj* einsam; (*single*) einzeln; **solitude** ['sɒlɪtjuːd] *n* Einsamkeit *f*
solo ['səʊləʊ] *n* (Mus) Solo *nt*
soluble ['sɒljʊbl] *adj* löslich; **solution** [sə'luːʃən] *n* Lösung *f* (*to +gen*); **solve** [sɒlv] *vt* lösen
somber (US), **sombre** ['sɒmbə*] *adj* düster

⭕ **KEYWORD**

some [sʌm] *adj* 1 (*a certain amount o number of*) einige; (*a few*) ein paar; (*with singular nouns*) etwas; **some tea/biscuits** etwas Tee/ein paar Kekse; **I've got some money, but not much** ich habe ein bisschen Geld, aber nicht viel
2 (*certain: in contrasts*) manche(r, s); **some people say that ...** manche Leute sagen, dass ...
3 (*unspecified*) irgendein(e); **some woman was asking for you** da hat eine Frau nach dir/Ihnen gefragt; **some day** eines Tages; **some day next week** irgendwann nächste Woche
▷ *pron* 1 (*a certain number*) einige; **have you got some?** hast du/haben Sie welche?
2 (*a certain amount*) etwas; **I've read some of the book** ich habe das Buch teilweise gelesen
▷ *adv*: **some 10 people** etwa 10 Leute

somebody *pron* jemand; **~ (or other)** irgendjemand; **~ else** jemand anders; **someday** *adv* irgendwann; **somehow** *adv* irgendwie; **someone** *pron see* **somebody**; **someplace** *adv* (US) *see* **somewhere**; **something** ['sʌmθɪŋ] *pron* etwas; **~ (or other)** irgendetwas; **~ else** etwas anderes; **~ nice** etwas Nettes;

would you like ~ to drink? möchtest du/möchten Sie etwas trinken? ▷ *adv*: **~ like 20** ungefähr 20; **sometime** *adv* irgendwann; **sometimes** *adv* manchmal; **somewhat** *adv* ein wenig; **somewhere** *adv* irgendwo; (*to a place*) irgendwohin; **~ else** irgendwo anders; (*to another place*) irgendwo anders hin
son [sʌn] *n* Sohn *m*
song [sɒŋ] *n* Lied *nt*; Song *m*
son-in-law ['sʌnɪnlɔː] (*pl* **sons-in-law**) *n* Schwiegersohn *m*
soon [suːn] *adv* bald; (*early*) früh; **too ~** zu früh; **as ~ as I ...** sobald ich ...; **as ~ as possible** so bald wie möglich; **sooner** *adv* (*time*) früher; (*for preference*) lieber
soot [sʊt] *n* Ruß *m*
soothe [suːð] *vt* beruhigen; (*pain*) lindern
sophisticated [sə'fɪstɪkeɪtɪd] *adj* (*person*) kultiviert; (*machine*) hoch entwickelt; (*plan*) ausgeklügelt
sophomore ['sɒfəmɔː*] *n* (US) College-Student(in) *m(f)* im zweiten Jahr
soppy ['sɒpɪ] *adj* (*fam*) rührselig
soprano [sə'prɑːnəʊ] *n* Sopran *m*
sore [sɔː*] *adj*: **to be ~** wehtun; **to have a ~ throat** Halsschmerzen haben ▷ *n* wunde Stelle
sorrow ['sɒrəʊ] *n* Kummer *m*
sorry ['sɒrɪ] *adj* (*sight, figure*) traurig; (**I'm**) ~ (*excusing*) Entschuldigung!; **I'm ~** (*regretful*) es tut mir leid; **~?** wie bitte?; **I feel ~ for him** er tut mir leid
sort [sɔːt] *n* 1 Art *f*; **what ~ of film is it?** was für ein Film ist das?; **a ~ of** eine Art *+gen*; **all ~s of things** alles Mögliche ▷ *adv*: **~ of** (*fam*) irgendwie ▷ *vt* sortieren; **everything's ~ed** (*dealt with*) alles

ist geregelt; **sort out** vt (*classify etc*) sortieren; (*problems*) lösen

sought [sɔːt] *pt, pp of* **seek**

soul [səʊl] *n* Seele *f*; (*music*) Soul *m*

sound [saʊnd] *adj* (*healthy*) gesund; (*safe*) sicher; (*sensible*) vernünftig; (*theory*) stichhaltig; (*thrashing*) tüchtig ▷ *n* (*noise*) Geräusch *nt*; (*Mus*) Klang *m*; (*TV*) Ton *m* ▷ *vt*: **to ~ the alarm** Alarm schlagen; **to ~ one's horn** hupen ▷ *vi* (*seem*) klingen (*like* wie); **soundcard** *n* (*Inform*) Soundkarte *f*; **sound effects** *npl* Klangeffekte *pl*; **soundproof** *adj* schalldicht; **soundtrack** *n* (*of film*) Filmmusik *f*, Soundtrack *m*

soup [suːp] *n* Suppe *f*

sour ['saʊə°] *adj* sauer; (*fig*) mürrisch

source [sɔːs] *n* Quelle *f*; (*fig*) Ursprung *m*

sour cream [saʊə'kriːm] *n* saure Sahne

south [saʊθ] *n* Süden *m*; **to the ~ of** südlich von ▷ *adv* (*go, face*) nach Süden ▷ *adj* Süd-; **South Africa** *n* Südafrika *nt*; **South African** *adj* südafrikanisch ▷ *n* Südafrikaner(in) *m(f)*; **South America** *n* Südamerika *nt*; **South American** *adj* südamerikanisch ▷ *n* Südamerikaner(in) *m(f)*; **southbound** *adj* (in) Richtung Süden; **southern** ['sʌðən] *adj* Süd-, südlich; **~ Europe** Südeuropa *nt*; **southwards** ['saʊθwədz] *adv* nach Süden

souvenir [suːvə'nɪə°] *n* Andenken *nt* (*of an* +*akk*)

sow [səʊ] (**sowed, sown** *o* **sowed**) *vt* (*a. fig*) säen; (*field*) besäen ▷ [saʊ] *n* (*pig*) Sau *f*

soya bean ['sɔɪə'biːn] *n* Sojabohne *f*

soy sauce ['sɔɪ'sɔːs] *n* Sojasoße *f*

spa [spɑː] *n* (*place*) Kurort *m*

space [speɪs] *n* (*room*) Platz *m*, Raum *m*; (*outer ~*) Weltraum *m*; (*gap*) Zwischenraum *m*; (*for parking*) Lücke *f*; **space bar** *n* Leertaste *f*; **spacecraft** (*pl -*) *n* Raumschiff *nt*; **space ship** *n* Raumschiff *nt*; **space shuttle** *n* Raumfähre *f*

spacing ['speɪsɪŋ] *n* (*in text*) Zeilenabstand *m*; **double ~** zweizeiliger Abstand

spacious ['speɪʃəs] *adj* geräumig

spade [speɪd] *n* Spaten *m*; **~s** Pik *nt*

spaghetti [spə'getɪ] *nsing* Spaghetti *pl*

Spain [speɪn] *n* Spanien *nt*

spam [spæm] *n* (*Inform*) Spam *m*

Spaniard ['spænɪəd] *n* Spanier(in) *m(f)*; **Spanish** ['spænɪʃ] *adj* spanisch ▷ *n* (*language*) Spanisch *nt*

spanner ['spænə°] *n* (*Brit*) Schraubenschlüssel *m*

spare [speə°] *adj* (*as replacement*) Ersatz-; **~ part** Ersatzteil *nt*; **~ room** Gästezimmer *nt*; **~ time** Freizeit *f*; **~ tyre** Ersatzreifen *m* ▷ *n* (*~ part*) Ersatzteil *nt* ▷ *vt* (*lives, feelings*) verschonen; **can you ~ (me) a moment?** hättest du/hätten Sie einen Moment Zeit?

spark [spɑːk] *n* Funke *m*; **sparkle** ['spɑːkl] *vi* funkeln; **sparkling wine** *n* Schaumwein *m*, Sekt *m*; **spark plug** ['spɑːkplʌg] *n* Zündkerze *f*

sparrow ['spærəʊ] *n* Spatz *m*

sparse [spɑːs] *adj* spärlich; **sparsely** *adv*: **~ populated** dünn besiedelt

spasm ['spæzəm] *n* Krampf *m*

spat [spæt] *pt, pp of* **spit**

speak [spiːk] (**spoke, spoken**) *vt* sprechen; **can you ~ French?** sprechen Sie Französisch?; **to**

~ one's mind seine Meinung sagen ▷ vi sprechen (to mit, zu); (make speech) reden; **~ing** (Tel) am Apparat; **so to ~** sozusagen; **~ for yourself** das meinst auch nur du!; **speak up** vi (louder) lauter sprechen; **speaker** n Sprecher(in) m(f); (public ~) Redner(in) m(f); (loud~) Lautsprecher m, Box f

special ['speʃəl] adj besondere(r, s), speziell ▷ n (on menu) Tagesgericht nt; (TV, Radio) Sondersendung f; **special delivery** n Eilzustellung f; **special effects** npl Spezialeffekte pl; **specialist** n Spezialist(in) m(f); (Tech) Fachmann m, Fachfrau f; (Med) Facharzt m, Fachärztin f; **speciality** [speʃɪ'ælɪtɪ] n Spezialität f; **specialize** vi sich spezialisieren (in auf +akk); **specially** adv besonders; (specifically) extra; **special offer** n Sonderangebot nt; **specialty** n (US) see **speciality**

species ['spi:ʃi:z] nsing Art f

specific [spə'sɪfɪk] adj spezifisch; (precise) genau; **specify** ['spesɪfaɪ] vt genau angeben

specimen ['spesɪmən] n (sample) Probe f; (example) Exemplar nt

specs [speks] npl (fam) Brille f

spectacle ['spektəkl] n Schauspiel nt

spectacles npl Brille f

spectacular [spek'tækjʊlə°] adj spektakulär

spectator [spek'teɪtə°] n Zuschauer(in) m(f)

sped [sped] pt, pp of **speed**

speech [spi:tʃ] n (address) Rede f; (faculty) Sprache f; **to make a ~** eine Rede halten; **speechless** adj sprachlos (with vor +dat)

speed [spi:d] (**sped** o **speeded**, **sped** o **speeded**) vi rasen; (exceed ~ limit) zu schnell fahren ▷ n Geschwindigkeit f; (of film) Lichtempfindlichkeit f; **speed up** vt beschleunigen ▷ vi schneller werden/fahren; (drive faster) schneller fahren; **speedboat** n Rennboot nt; **speed bump** n Bodenschwelle f; **speed camera** n Blitzgerät nt; **speed limit** n Geschwindigkeitsbegrenzung f; **speedometer** [spɪ'dɒmɪtə°] n Tachometer m; **speed trap** n Radarfalle f; **speedy** adj schnell

spell [spel] (**spelt** o **spelled**, **spelt** o **spelled**) vt buchstabieren; **how do you ~ ...?** wie schreibt man ...? ▷ n (period) Weile f; (enchantment) Zauber m; **a cold/hot ~** (weather) ein Kälteeinbruch/eine Hitzewelle; **spellchecker** n (Inform) Rechtschreibprüfung f; **spelling** n Rechtschreibung f; (of a word) Schreibweise f; **~ mistake** Schreibfehler m

spelt [spelt] pt, pp of **spell**

spend [spend] (**spent, spent**) vt (money) ausgeben (on für); (time) verbringen; **spending money** n Taschengeld nt

spent [spent] pt, pp of **spend**

sperm [spɜ:m] n Sperma nt

sphere [sfɪə°] n (globe) Kugel f; (fig) Sphäre f

spice [spaɪs] n Gewürz nt; (fig) Würze f ▷ vt würzen; **spicy** ['spaɪsɪ] adj würzig; (fig) pikant

spider ['spaɪdə°] n Spinne f

spike [spaɪk] n (on railing etc) Spitze f; (on shoe, tyre) Spike m

spill [spɪl] (**spilt** o **spilled**, **spilt** o **spilled**) vt verschütten

spin [spɪn] (**spun, spun**) vi (turn) sich drehen; (washing) schleudern; **my head is ~ning** mir dreht sich alles ▷ vt (turn) drehen; (coin) hochwerfen ▷ n (turn) Drehung f

spinach ['spɪnɪtʃ] n Spinat m

spin doctor n Spindoktor m
(Verantwortlicher für die
schönrednerische Öffentlichkeitsarbeit
besonders von Politikern)

spin-drier ['spɪndraɪə°] n
Wäscheschleuder f; **spin-dry** vt
schleudern

spine [spaɪn] n Rückgrat nt; (of
animal, plant) Stachel m; (of book)
Rücken m

spiral ['spaɪrəl] n Spirale f ▷ adj
spiralförmig; **spiral staircase** n
Wendeltreppe f

spire ['spaɪə°] n Turmspitze f

spirit ['spɪrɪt] n (essence, soul)
Geist m; (humour, mood) Stimmung
f; (courage) Mut m; (verve) Elan m;
~s pl (drinks) Spirituosen pl

spiritual ['spɪrɪtjʊəl] adj geistig;
(Rel) geistlich

spit [spɪt] (**spat, spat**) vi
spucken ▷ n (for roasting)
(Brat)spieß m; (saliva) Spucke f;
spit out vt ausspucken

spite [spaɪt] n Boshaftigkeit f; **in
~ of** trotz +gen; **spiteful** adj
boshaft

spitting image ['spɪtɪŋ'ɪmɪdʒ]
n: **he's the ~ of you** er ist
dir/Ihnen wie aus dem Gesicht
geschnitten

splash [splæʃ] vt (person, object)
bespritzen ▷ vi (liquid) spritzen;
(play in water) planschen

splendid ['splendɪd] adj herrlich

splinter ['splɪntə°] n Splitter
m

split [splɪt] (**split, split**) vt (stone,
wood) spalten; (share) teilen ▷ vi
(stone, wood) sich spalten; (seam)
platzen ▷ n (in stone, wood) Spalt
m; (in clothing) Riss m; (fig)
Spaltung f; **split up** vi (couple) sich
trennen ▷ vt (divide up) aufteilen;
split ends npl (Haar)spliss m;
splitting adj (headache) rasend

spoil [spɔɪl] (**spoiled** o **spoilt,**

spoiled o **spoilt**) vt verderben;
(child) verwöhnen ▷ vi (food)
verderben

spoilt [spɔɪlt] pt, pp of **spoil**

spoke [spəʊk] pt of **speak** ▷ n
Speiche f

spoken ['spəʊkən] pp of **speak**

spokesperson ['spəʊkspɜːsən]
(pl **-people**) n Sprecher(in) m(f)

sponge [spʌndʒ] n (for washing)
Schwamm m; **sponge bag** n
Kulturbeutel m; **sponge cake** n
Biskuitkuchen m

sponsor ['spɒnsə°] n (of event,
programme) Sponsor(in) m(f) ▷ vt
unterstützen; (event, programme)
sponsern

spontaneous, spontaneously
[spɒn'teɪnɪəs, -lɪ] adj, adv
spontan

spool [spuːl] n Spule f

spoon [spuːn] n Löffel m

sport [spɔːt] n Sport m; **sports
car** n Sportwagen m; **sports
centre** n Sportzentrum nt;
sports club n Sportverein m;
sportsman (pl **-men**) n Sportler
m; **sportswear** n Sportkleidung f;
sportswoman (pl **-women**) n
Sportlerin f; **sporty** adj sportlich

spot [spɒt] n (dot) Punkt m; (of
paint, blood etc) Fleck m; (place)
Stelle f; (pimple) Pickel m; **on the
~** vor Ort; (at once) auf der Stelle
▷ vt (notice) entdecken; (difference)
erkennen; **spotless** adj (clean)
blitzsauber; **spotlight** n (lamp)
Scheinwerfer m; **spotty** adj
(pimply) pickelig

spouse [spaʊs] n Gatte m,
Gattin f

spout [spaʊt] n Schnabel m

sprain [spreɪn] n Verstauchung
f ▷ vt: **to ~ one's ankle** sich den
Knöchel verstauchen

sprang [spræŋ] pt of **spring**

spray [spreɪ] n (liquid in can)

Spray nt o m; (~ (can)) Spraydose f
▷ vt (plant, insects) besprühen;
(car) spritzen

spread [spred] (**spread, spread**)
vt (open out) ausbreiten; (news,
disease) verbreiten; (butter, jam)
streichen; (bread, surface)
bestreichen ▷ vi (news, disease,
fire) sich verbreiten ▷ n (of disease,
religion etc) Verbreitung f; (for bread)
Aufstrich m; **spreadsheet** n
(Inform) Tabellenkalkulation f

spring [sprɪŋ] (**sprang, sprung**)
vi (leap) springen ▷ n (season)
Frühling m; (coil) Feder f; (water)
Quelle f; **springboard** n
Sprungbrett nt; **spring onion** n
(Brit) Frühlingszwiebel f; **spring
roll** n (Brit) Frühlingsrolle f;
springy adj (mattress) federnd

sprinkle ['sprɪŋkl] vt streuen;
(liquid) (be)träufeln; **to ~ sth with
sth** etw mit etw bestreuen; (with
liquid) etw mit etw besprengen;
sprinkler n (for lawn)
Rasensprenger m; (for fire)
Sprinkler m

sprint [sprɪnt] vi rennen; (Sport)
sprinten

sprout [spraʊt] n (of plant) Trieb
m; (from seed) Keim m; (**Brussels**)
~s pl Rosenkohl m ▷ vi sprießen

sprung [sprʌŋ] pp of **spring**

spun [spʌn] pt, pp of **spin**

spy [spaɪ] n Spion(in) m(f) ▷ vi
spionieren; **to ~ on sb** jdm
nachspionieren ▷ vt erspähen

squad [skwɒd] n (Sport) Kader m;
(police ~) Kommando nt

square [skwɛə*] n (shape)
Quadrat nt; (open space) Platz m;
(on chessboard etc) Feld nt ▷ adj (in
shape) quadratisch; **2 ~ metres** 2
Quadratmeter; **2 metres ~** 2 Meter
im Quadrat ▷ vt: **3 ~d** 3 hoch 2;
square root n Quadratwurzel f

squash [skwɒʃ] n (drink)

Fruchtsaftgetränk nt; (Sport)
Squash nt; (US: vegetable) Kürbis m
▷ vt zerquetschen

squat [skwɒt] vi (be crouching)
hocken; **to ~ (down)** sich
(hin)hocken

squeak [skwiːk] vi (door, shoes
etc) quietschen; (animal) quieken

squeal [skwiːl] vi (person)
kreischen (with vor +dat)

squeeze [skwiːz] vt drücken;
(orange) auspressen ▷ vi: **to ~ into
the car** sich in den Wagen
hineinzwängen; **squeeze up** vi
(on bench etc) zusammenrücken

squid [skwɪd] n Tintenfisch m

squint [skwɪnt] vi schielen; (in
bright light) blinzeln

squirrel ['skwɪrəl] n Eichhörnchen nt

squirt [skwɜːt] vt, vi (liquid)
spritzen

Sri Lanka [sriːˈlæŋkə] n Sri
Lanka nt

st abbr = **stone** Gewichtseinheit (6,35
kg)

St abbr = **saint** St.; abbr = **street** Str.

stab [stæb] vt (person) einstechen
auf +akk; (to death) erstechen;
stabbing adj (pain) stechend

stabilize ['steɪbəlaɪz] vt
stabilisieren ▷ vi sich
stabilisieren

stable ['steɪbl] n Stall m ▷ adj
stabil

stack [stæk] n (pile) Stapel m
▷ vt: **to ~ (up)** (auf)stapeln

stadium ['steɪdɪəm] n Stadion
nt

staff [stɑːf] n (personnel) Personal
nt, Lehrkräfte pl

stag [stæg] n Hirsch m

stag night n (Brit)
Junggesellenabschied m

stage [steɪdʒ] n (Theat) Bühne f;
(of project, life etc) Stadium nt; (of
journey) Etappe f; **at this ~** zu

diesem Zeitpunkt ▷ vt (Theat) aufführen, inszenieren; (demonstration) veranstalten

stagger ['stægə°] vi wanken ▷ vt (amaze) verblüffen; **staggering** adj (amazing) umwerfend; (amount, price) schwindelerregend

stagnate [stæg'neɪt] vi (fig) stagnieren

stain [steɪn] n Fleck m; **stained-glass window** n Buntglasfenster nt; **stainless steel** n rostfreier Stahl; **stain remover** n Fleck(en)entferner m

stair [stɛə°] n (Treppen)stufe f; **~s** pl Treppe f; **staircase** n Treppe f

stake [steɪk] n (post) Pfahl m; (in betting) Einsatz m; (Fin) Anteil m (in an +dat); **to be at ~** auf dem Spiel stehen

stale [steɪl] adj (bread) alt; (beer) schal

stalk [stɔːk] n Stiel m ▷ vt (wild animal) sich anpirschen an +akk; (person) nachstellen +dat

stall [stɔːl] n (in market) (Verkaufs)stand m; (in stable) Box f; **~s** pl (Theat) Parkett nt ▷ vt (engine) abwürgen ▷ vi (driver) den Motor abwürgen; (car) stehen bleiben; (delay) Zeit schinden

stamina ['stæmɪnə] n Durchhaltevermögen nt

stammer ['stæmə°] vi, vt stottern

stamp [stæmp] n (postage ~) Briefmarke f; (for document) Stempel m ▷ vt (passport etc) stempeln; (mail) frankieren; **stamped addressed envelope** n frankierter Rückumschlag

stand [stænd] (**stood, stood**) vi stehen; (as candidate) kandidieren ▷ vt (place) stellen; (endure) aushalten; **I can't ~ her** ich kann sie nicht ausstehen ▷ n (stall)

Stand m; (seats in stadium) Tribüne f; (for coats, bicycles) Ständer m; (for small objects) Gestell nt; **stand around** vi herumstehen; **stand by** vi (be ready) sich bereithalten; (be inactive) danebenstehen ▷ vt (fig: person) halten zu; (decision, promise) stehen zu; **stand for** vt (represent) stehen für; (tolerate) hinnehmen; **stand in for** vt einspringen für; **stand out** vi (be noticeable) auffallen; **stand up** vi (get up) aufstehen ▷ vt (girlfriend, boyfriend) versetzen; **stand up for** vt sich einsetzen für; **stand up to** vt: **to ~ sb** jdm die Stirn bieten

standard ['stændəd] n (norm) Norm f; **~ of living** Lebensstandard m ▷ adj Standard-

standardize ['stændədaɪz] vt vereinheitlichen

stand-by ['stændbaɪ] n (thing in reserve) Reserve f; **on ~** in Bereitschaft ▷ adj (flight, ticket) Stand-by-; **standing order** n (at bank) Dauerauftrag m; **standpoint** ['stændpɔɪnt] n Standpunkt m; **standstill** ['stændstɪl] n Stillstand m; **to come to a ~** stehen bleiben; (fig) zum Erliegen kommen

stank [stæŋk] pt of **stink**

staple ['steɪpl] n (for paper) Heftklammer f ▷ vt heften (to an +akk); **stapler** n Hefter m

star [stɑː°] n Stern m; (person) Star m ▷ vt: **the film ~s Hugh Grant** der Film zeigt Hugh Grant in der Hauptrolle ▷ vi die Hauptrolle spielen

starch [stɑːtʃ] n Stärke f

stare [stɛə°] vi starren; **to ~ at** anstarren

starfish ['stɑːfɪʃ] n Seestern m

star sign ['stɑːsaɪn] n Sternzeichen nt

start [stɑːt] n (beginning) Anfang m, Beginn m; (Sport) Start m; (lead) Vorsprung m; **from the ~** von Anfang an ▷ vt anfangen; (car, engine) starten; (business, family) gründen; **to ~ to do sth, to ~ doing sth** anfangen, etw zu tun ▷ vi (begin) anfangen; (car) anspringen; (on journey) aufbrechen; (Sport) starten; (jump) zusammenfahren; **~ing from Monday** ab Montag; **start off** vt (discussion, process etc) anfangen, beginnen ▷ vi (begin) anfangen, beginnen; (on journey) aufbrechen; **start over** vi (US) wieder anfangen; **start up** vi (in business) anfangen ▷ vt (car, engine) starten; (business) gründen; **starter** n (Brit: first course) Vorspeise f; (Auto) Anlasser m; **starting point** n (a. fig) Ausgangspunkt m

startle ['stɑːtl] vt erschrecken; **startling** adj überraschend

starve [stɑːv] vi hungern; (to death) verhungern; **I'm starving** ich habe einen Riesenhunger

state [steɪt] n (condition) Zustand m; (Pol) Staat m; **the (United) States** die (Vereinigten) Staaten ▷ adj Staats-; (control, education) staatlich ▷ vt erklären; (facts, name etc) angeben; **stated** adj (fixed) festgesetzt

statement ['steɪtmənt] n (official declaration) Erklärung f; (to police) Aussage f; (from bank) Kontoauszug m

state-of-the-art [steɪtəvðiːˈɑːt] adj hochmodern, auf dem neuesten Stand der Technik

static ['stætɪk] adj (unchanging) konstant

station ['steɪʃən] n (for trains, buses) Bahnhof m; (underground ~) Station f; (police ~, fire ~) Wache f; (TV, Radio) Sender m ▷ vt (Mil) stationieren

stationer's ['steɪʃənəz] n: **~ (shop)** Schreibwarengeschäft nt; **stationery** n Schreibwaren pl

station wagon ['steɪʃənwægən] n (US) Kombiwagen m

statistics [stəˈtɪstɪks] nsing (science) Statistik f; (figures) Statistiken pl

statue ['stætjuː] n Statue f

status ['steɪtəs] n Status m; (prestige) Ansehen nt; **status bar** n (Inform) Statuszeile f

stay [steɪ] n Aufenthalt m ▷ vi bleiben; (with friends, in hotel) wohnen (with bei); **to ~ the night** übernachten; **stay away** vi wegbleiben; **to ~ from sb** sich von jdm fernhalten; **stay behind** vi zurückbleiben; (at work) länger bleiben; **stay in** vi (at home) zu Hause bleiben; **stay out** vi (not come home) wegbleiben; **stay up** vi (at night) aufbleiben

steady ['stedɪ] adj (speed) gleichmäßig; (progress, increase) stetig; (job, income, girlfriend) fest; (worker) zuverlässig; (hand) ruhig; **they've been going ~ for two years** sie sind seit zwei Jahren fest zusammen ▷ vt (nerves) beruhigen; **to ~ oneself** Halt finden

steak [steɪk] n Steak nt; (of fish) Filet nt

steal [stiːl] (stole, stolen) vt stehlen; **to ~ sth from sb** jdm etw stehlen

steam [stiːm] n Dampf m ▷ vt (Gastr) dämpfen; **steam up** vi (window) beschlagen; **steamer** n (Gastr) Dampfkochtopf m; (ship) Dampfer m; **steam iron** n Dampfbügeleisen nt

steel [stiːl] n Stahl m ▷ adj Stahl-

steep [stiːp] *adj* steil
steeple ['stiːpl] *n* Kirchturm *m*
steer [stɪə°] *vt, vi* steuern; (*car, bike etc*) lenken; **steering** *n* (*Auto*) Lenkung *f*; **steering wheel** *n* Steuer *nt*, Lenkrad *nt*
stem [stem] *n* (*of plant, glass*) Stiel *m*
step [step] *n* Schritt *m*; (*stair*) Stufe *f*; (*measure*) Maßnahme *f*; **~ by ~** Schritt für Schritt ▷ *vi* treten; **~ this way, please** hier entlang, bitte; **step down** *vi* (*resign*) zurücktreten
stepbrother *n* Stiefbruder *m*; **stepchild** (*pl* **-children**) *n* Stiefkind *nt*; **stepfather** *n* Stiefvater *m*
stepladder *n* Trittleiter *f*
stepmother *n* Stiefmutter *f*; **stepsister** *n* Stiefschwester *f*
stereo ['sterɪəʊ] (*pl* **-s**) *n*: **~ (system)** Stereoanlage *f*
sterile ['steraɪl] *adj* steril; **sterilize** ['sterɪlaɪz] *vt* sterilisieren
sterling ['stɜːlɪŋ] *n* (*Fin*) das Pfund Sterling
stew [stjuː] *n* Eintopf *m*
steward ['stjuːəd] *n* (*on plane, ship*) Steward *m*; **stewardess** *n* Stewardess *f*
stick [stɪk] (**stuck, stuck**) *vt* (*with glue etc*) kleben; (*pin etc*) stecken; (*fam: put*) tun ▷ *vi* (*get jammed*) klemmen; (*hold fast*) haften ▷ *n* Stock *m*; (*hockey ~*) Schläger *m*; (*of chalk*) Stück *nt*; (*of celery, rhubarb*) Stange *f*; **stick out** *vt*: **to stick one's tongue out (at sb)** (jdm) die Zunge herausstrecken ▷ *vi* (*protrude*) vorstehen; (*ears*) abstehen; (*be noticeable*) auffallen; **stick to** *vt* (*rules, plan etc*) sich halten an +*akk*; **sticker** ['stɪkə°] *n* Aufkleber *m*; **sticky** ['stɪkɪ] *adj* klebrig;

(*weather*) schwül; **~ label** Aufkleber *m*; **~ tape** Klebeband *nt*
stiff [stɪf] *adj* steif
stifle ['staɪfl] *vt* (*yawn etc, opposition*) unterdrücken; **stifling** *adj* drückend
still [stɪl] *adj* still; (*drink*) ohne Kohlensäure ▷ *adv* (*yet, even now*) (immer) noch; (*all the same*) immerhin; **he ~ doesn't believe me** er glaubt mir immer noch nicht; **keep ~** halt still!; **bigger/better ~** noch größer/besser
still life (*pl* **still lives**) *n* Stillleben *nt*
stimulate ['stɪmjʊleɪt] *vt* anregen, stimulieren; **stimulating** *adj* anregend
sting [stɪŋ] (**stung, stung**) *vt* (*wound with ~*) stechen ▷ *vi* (*eyes, ointment etc*) brennen ▷ *n* (*insect wound*) Stich *m*
stingy ['stɪndʒɪ] *adj* (*fam*) geizig
stink [stɪŋk] (**stank, stunk**) *vi* stinken (*of* nach) ▷ *n* Gestank *m*
stir [stɜː°] *vt* (*mix*) (um)rühren; **stir up** *vt* (*mob*) aufhetzen; (*memories*) wachrufen; **to ~ trouble** Unruhe stiften; **stir-fry** *vt* (*unter Rühren*) kurz anbraten
stitch [stɪtʃ] *n* (*in sewing*) Stich *m*; (*in knitting*) Masche *f*; **to have a ~** (*pain*) Seitenstechen haben; **he had to have ~es** er musste genäht werden; **she had her ~es out** ihr wurden die Fäden gezogen; **to be in ~es** (*fam*) sich kaputtlachen ▷ *vt* nähen; **stitch up** *vt* (*hole, wound*) nähen
stock [stɒk] *n* (*supply*) Vorrat *m* (*of an* +*dat*); (*of shop*) Bestand *m*; (*for soup etc*) Brühe *f*; **~s and shares** *pl* Aktien und Wertpapiere *pl*; **to be in/out of ~** vorrätig/nicht vorrätig sein; **to**

take ~ Inventur machen; (*fig*) Bilanz ziehen ▷ *vt* (*keep in shop*) führen; **stock up** *vi* sich eindecken (*on, with* mit)

stockbroker *n* Börsenmakler(in) *m(f)*

stock cube *n* Brühwurfel *m*

stock exchange *n* Börse *f*

stocking ['stɒkɪŋ] *n* Strumpf *m*

stock market ['stɒkmɑːkɪt] *n* Börse *f*

stole [stəʊl] *pt of* **steal**; **stolen** ['stəʊlən] *pp of* **steal**

stomach ['stʌmək] *n* Magen *m*; (*belly*) Bauch *m*; **on an empty ~** auf leeren Magen; **stomach-ache** *n* Magenschmerzen *pl*; **stomach upset** *n* Magenverstimmung *f*

stone [stəʊn] *n* Stein *m*; (*seed*) Kern *m*, Stein *m*; (*weight*) *britische Gewichtseinheit (6,35 kg)* ▷ *adj* Stein-, aus Stein; **stony** *adj* (*ground*) steinig

stood [stʊd] *pt, pp of* **stand**

stool [stuːl] *n* Hocker *m*

stop [stɒp] *n* Halt *m*; (*for bus, tram, train*) Haltestelle *f*; **to come to a ~** anhalten ▷ *vt* (*vehicle, passer-by*) anhalten; (*put an end to*) ein Ende machen +*dat*; (*cease*) aufhören mit; (*prevent from happening*) verhindern; (*bleeding*) stillen; (*engine, machine*) abstellen; (*payments*) einstellen; (*cheque*) sperren; **to ~ doing sth** aufhören, etw zu tun; **to ~ sb (from) doing sth** jdn daran hindern, etw zu tun; **~ it** hör auf (damit)! ▷ *vi* (*vehicle*) anhalten; (*during journey*) Halt machen; (*pedestrian, clock, heart*) stehen bleiben; (*rain, noise*) aufhören; (*stay*) bleiben; **stop by** *vi* vorbeischauen; **stop over** *vi* Halt machen; (*overnight*) übernachten; **stopgap** *n* Provisorium *nt*, Zwischenlösung *f*; **stopover** *n* (*on journey*)

Zwischenstation *f*; **stopper** *n* Stöpsel *m*; **stop sign** *n* Stoppschild *nt*; **stopwatch** *n* Stoppuhr *f*

storage ['stɔːrɪdʒ] *n* Lagerung *f*; **store** [stɔː°] *n* (*supply*) Vorrat *m* (*of* an +*dat*); (*place for storage*) Lager *nt*; (*large shop*) Kaufhaus *nt*; (*US: shop*) Geschäft *nt* ▷ *vt* lagern; (*Inform*) speichern; **storecard** *n* Kundenkreditkarte *f*; **storeroom** *n* Lagerraum *m*

storey ['stɔːrɪ] *n* (*Brit*) Stock *m*, Stockwerk *nt*

storm [stɔːm] *n* Sturm *m*; (*thunder~*) Gewitter *nt* ▷ *vt, vi* (*with movement*) stürmen; **stormy** *adj* stürmisch

story ['stɔːrɪ] *n* Geschichte *f*; (*plot*) Handlung *f*; (*US: of building*) Stock *m*, Stockwerk *nt*

stout [staʊt] *adj* (*fat*) korpulent

stove [stəʊv] *n* Herd *m*; (*for heating*) Ofen *m*

stow [stəʊ] *vt* verstauen; **stowaway** *n* blinder Passagier

straight [streɪt] *adj* (*not curved*) gerade; (*hair*) glatt; (*honest*) ehrlich; (*with* zu); (*fam: heterosexual*) hetero ▷ *adv* (*directly*) direkt; (*immediately*) sofort; (*drink*) pur; (*think*) klar; **~ ahead** geradeaus; **to go ~ on** geradeaus weitergehen/ weiterfahren; **straightaway** *adv* sofort; **straightforward** *adj* einfach; (*person*) aufrichtig, unkompliziert

strain [streɪn] *n* Belastung *f* ▷ *vt* (*eyes*) überanstrengen; (*rope, relationship*) belasten; (*vegetables*) abgießen; **to ~ a muscle** sich einen Muskel zerren; **strained** *adj* (*laugh, smile*) gezwungen; (*relations*) gespannt; **~ muscle** Muskelzerrung *f*; **strainer** *n* Sieb *nt*

strand [strænd] *n* (*of wool*) Faden

m; (of hair) Strähne f ▷ _vt:_ **to be (left) ~ed** (_person_) festsitzen

strange [streɪndʒ] _adj_ seltsam; (_unfamiliar_) fremd; **strangely** _adv_ seltsam; **~ enough** seltsamerweise; **stranger** _n_ Fremde(r) _mf;_ **I'm a ~ here** ich bin hier fremd

strangle ['stræŋgl] _vt_ (_kill_) erdrosseln

strap [stræp] _n_ Riemen _m;_ (_on dress etc_) Träger _m;_ (_on watch_) Band _nt_ ▷ _vt_ (_fasten_) festschnallen (_to_ an +_dat_); **strapless** _adj_ trägerlos

strategy ['strætɪdʒɪ] _n_ Strategie f

straw [strɔ:] _n_ Stroh _nt;_ (_drinking ~_) Strohhalm _m_

strawberry _n_ Erdbeere f

stray [streɪ] _n_ streunendes Tier ▷ _adj_ (_cat, dog_) streunend ▷ _vi_ streunen

streak ['stri:k] _n_ (_of colour, dirt_) Streifen _m;_ (_in hair_) Strähne f; (_in character_) Zug _m_

stream [stri:m] _n_ (_flow of liquid_) Strom _m;_ (_brook_) Bach _m_ ▷ _vi_ strömen; **streamer** _n_ (_of paper_) Luftschlange f

street [stri:t] _n_ Straße f; **streetcar** _n_ (_US_) Straßenbahn f; **street lamp, street light** _n_ Straßenlaterne f; **street map** _n_ Stadtplan _m_

strength [streŋθ] _n_ Kraft f, Stärke f; **strengthen** _vt_ verstärken; (_fig_) stärken

strenuous ['strenjʊəs] _adj_ anstrengend

stress [stres] _n_ Stress _m;_ (_on word_) Betonung f; **to be under ~** im Stress sein ▷ _vt_ betonen; (_put under ~_) stressen; **stressed** _adj:_ **~ (out)** gestresst

stretch [stretʃ] _n_ (_of land_) Stück _nt;_ (_of road_) Strecke f ▷ _vt_ (_material, shoes_) dehnen; (_rope, canvas_) spannen; (_person in job etc_) fordern; **to ~ one's legs** (_walk_) sich die Beine vertreten ▷ _vi_ (_person_) sich strecken; (_area_) sich erstrecken (_to_ bis zu); **stretch out** _vt:_ **to stretch one's hand/legs out** die Hand/die Beine ausstrecken, ausstrecken ▷ _vi_ (_reach_) sich strecken; (_lie down_) sich ausstrecken; **stretcher** _n_ Tragbahre f

strict, strictly [strɪkt, -lɪ] _adj, adv_ (_severe(ly)_) streng; (_exact(ly)_) genau; **~ speaking** genauer gesagt

strike [straɪk] (_struck, struck_) _vt_ (_match_) anzünden; (_hit_) schlagen; (_find_) finden; **it struck me as strange** es kam mir seltsam vor ▷ _vi_ (_stop work_) streiken; (_attack_) zuschlagen; (_clock_) schlagen ▷ _n_ (_by workers_) Streik _m;_ **to be on ~** streiken; **strike up** _vt_ (_conversation_) anfangen; (_friendship_) schließen; **striking** _adj_ auffallend

string [strɪŋ] _n_ (_for tying_) Schnur f; (_Mus, Tennis_) Saite f; **the ~s** _pl_ (_section of orchestra_) die Streicher _pl_

strip [strɪp] _n_ Streifen _m;_ (_Brit: of footballer etc_) Trikot _nt_ ▷ _vi_ (_undress_) sich ausziehen, strippen

stripe [straɪp] _n_ Streifen _m;_ **striped** _adj_ gestreift

stripper ['strɪpə*] _n_ Stripper(in) _m(f);_ (_paint ~_) Farbentferner _m_

strip-search ['strɪpsɜ:tʃ] _n_ Leibesvisitation f (_bei der man sich ausziehen muss_)

striptease ['strɪpti:z] _n_ Strip-tease _m_

stroke [strəʊk] _n_ (_Med, Tennis etc_) Schlag _m;_ (_of pen, brush_) Strich _m_ ▷ _vt_ streicheln

stroll [strəʊl] _n_ Spaziergang _m_ ▷ _vi_ spazieren; **stroller** _n_ (_US: for baby_) Buggy _m_

strong [strɒŋ] _adj_ stark; (_healthy_)

robust; (*wall, table*) stabil; (*shoes*) fest; (*influence, chance*) groß; **strongly** *adv* stark; (*believe*) fest; (*constructed*) stabil

struck [strʌk] *pt, pp of* **strike**

structural, structurally [ˈstrʌktʃərəl, -lɪ] *adj* strukturell; **structure** [ˈstrʌktʃə°] *n* Struktur *f*; (*building, bridge*) Konstruktion *f*, Bau *m*

struggle [ˈstrʌgl] *n* Kampf *m* (*for* um) ▷ *vi* (*fight*) kämpfen (*for* um); (*do sth with difficulty*) sich abmühen; **to ~ to do sth** sich abmühen, etw zu tun

stub [stʌb] *n* (*of cigarette*) Kippe *f*; (*of ticket, cheque*) Abschnitt *m* ▷ *vt*: **to ~ one's toe** sich *dat* den Zeh stoßen (*on* an +*dat*)

stubble [ˈstʌbl] *n* Stoppelbart *m*; (*field*) Stoppeln *pl*

stubborn [ˈstʌbən] *adj* (*person*) stur

stuck [stʌk] *pt, pp of* **stick** ▷ *adj*: **to be ~** (*jammed*) klemmen; (*at a loss*) nicht mehr weiterwissen; **to get ~** (*car in snow etc*) stecken bleiben

student [ˈstjuːdənt] *n* Student(in) *m(f)*, Schüler(in) *m(f)*

studio [ˈstjuːdɪəʊ] (*pl* **-s**) *n* Studio *nt*

studious [ˈstjuːdɪəs] *adj* fleißig

study [ˈstʌdɪ] *n* (*investigation*) Untersuchung *f*; (*room*) Arbeitszimmer *nt* ▷ *vt, vi* studieren

stuff [stʌf] *n* Zeug *nt*, Sachen *pl* ▷ *vt* (*push*) stopfen; (*Gastr*) füllen; **to ~ oneself** (*fam*) sich vollstopfen; **stuffing** *n* (*Gastr*) Füllung *f*

stuffy [ˈstʌfɪ] *adj* (*room*) stickig; (*person*) spießig

stumble [ˈstʌmbl] *vi* stolpern; (*when speaking*) stocken

stun [stʌn] *vt* (*shock*) fassungslos

machen; **I was ~ned** ich war fassungslos (*o* völlig überrascht)

stung [stʌŋ] *pt, pp of* **sting**

stunk [stʌŋk] *pp of* **stink**

stunning [ˈstʌnɪŋ] *adj* (*marvellous*) fantastisch; (*beautiful*) atemberaubend; (*very surprising, shocking*) überwältigend; unfassbar

stunt [stʌnt] *n* (*Cine*) Stunt *m*

stupid [ˈstjuːpɪd] *adj* dumm; **stupidity** [stjuːˈpɪdɪtɪ] *n* Dummheit *f*

sturdy [ˈstɜːdɪ] *adj* robust; (*building, car*) stabil

stutter [ˈstʌtə°] *vi, vt* stottern

stye [staɪ] *n* (*Med*) Gerstenkorn *nt*

style [staɪl] *n* Stil *m* ▷ *vt* (*hair*) stylen; **styling mousse** *n* Schaumfestiger *m*; **stylish** [ˈstaɪlɪʃ] *adj* elegant, schick

subconscious [sʌbˈkɒnʃəs] *adj* unterbewusst ▷ *n*: **the ~** das Unterbewusstsein

subdivide [sʌbdɪˈvaɪd] *vt* unterteilen

subject [ˈsʌbdʒɪkt] *n* (*topic*) Thema *nt*; (*in school*) Fach *nt*; (*citizen*) Staatsangehörige(r) *mf*; (*of kingdom*) Untertan(in) *m(f)*; (*Ling*) Subjekt *nt*; **to change the ~** das Thema wechseln ▷ *adj* [səbˈdʒekt] **to be ~ to** (*dependent on*) abhängen von; (*under control of*) unterworfen sein +*dat*

subjective [səbˈdʒektɪv] *adj* subjektiv

sublet [sʌbˈlet] *irr vt* untervermieten (*to* an +*akk*)

submarine [sʌbməˈriːn] *n* U-Boot *nt*

submerge [səbˈmɜːdʒ] *vt* (*put in water*) eintauchen ▷ *vi* tauchen

submit [səbˈmɪt] *vt* (*application, claim*) einreichen ▷ *vi* (*surrender*) sich ergeben

subordinate [səˈbɔːdɪnət] *adj*

untergeordnet (*to +dat*) ▷ *n* Untergebene(r) *mf*

subscribe [səb'skraɪb] *vi*: **to ~ to** (*magazine etc*) abonnieren; **subscription** [səb'skrɪpʃən] *n* (*to magazine etc*) Abonnement *nt*; (*to club etc*) (Mitglieds)beitrag *m*

subsequent ['sʌbsɪkwənt] *adj* nach(folgend); **subsequently** *adv* später, anschließend

subside [səb'saɪd] *vi* (*floods*) zurückgehen; (*storm*) sich legen; (*building*) sich senken

substance ['sʌbstəns] *n* Substanz *f*

substantial [səb'stænʃəl] *adj* beträchtlich; (*improvement*) wesentlich; (*meal*) reichhaltig; (*furniture*) solide

substitute ['sʌbstɪtjuːt] *n* Ersatz *m*; (*Sport*) Ersatzspieler(in) *m(f)* ▷ *vt*: **to ~ A for B** B durch A ersetzen

subtitle ['sʌbtaɪtl] *n* Untertitel *m*

subtle ['sʌtl] *adj* (*difference, taste*) fein; (*plan*) raffiniert

subtotal ['sʌbtəʊtl] *n* Zwischensumme *f*

subtract [səb'trækt] *vt* abziehen (*from* von)

suburb ['sʌbɜːb] *n* Vorort *m*; **in the ~s** am Stadtrand; **suburban** [sə'bɜːbən] *adj* vorstädtisch, Vorstadt-

subway ['sʌbweɪ] *n* (*Brit*) Unterführung *f*; (*US Rail*) U-Bahn *f*

succeed [sək'siːd] *vi* erfolgreich sein; **he ~ed** (**in doing it**) es gelang ihm(, es zu tun) ▷ *vt* nachfolgen +*dat*; **succeeding** *adj* nachfolgend; **success** [sək'ses] *n* Erfolg *m*; **successful, successfully** *adj, adv* erfolgreich

successive [sək'sesɪv] *adj* aufeinanderfolgend; **successor** *n* Nachfolger(in) *m(f)*

succulent ['sʌkjʊlənt] *adj* saftig

succumb [sə'kʌm] *vi* erliegen (*to +dat*)

such [sʌtʃ] *adj* solche(r, s); **~ a book** so ein Buch, ein solches Buch; **it was ~ a success that ...** es war solch ein Erfolg, dass ...; **~ as** wie ▷ *adv* so; **~ a hot day** so ein heißer Tag ▷ *pron*: **as ~** als solche(r, s)

suck [sʌk] *vt* (*toffee etc*) lutschen; (*liquid*) saugen; **it ~s** (*fam*) das ist beschissen

Sudan [su'dɑːn] *n*: (**the**) **~** der Sudan

sudden ['sʌdn] *adj* plötzlich; **all of a ~** ganz plötzlich; **suddenly** *adv* plötzlich

sue [suː] *vt* verklagen

suede [sweɪd] *n* Wildleder *nt*

suffer ['sʌfə*] *vt* erleiden ▷ *vi* leiden; **to ~ from** (*Med*) leiden an +*dat*

sufficient, sufficiently [sə'fɪʃənt, -lɪ] *adj, adv* ausreichend

suffocate ['sʌfəkeɪt] *vt, vi* ersticken

sugar ['ʃʊgə*] *n* Zucker *m* ▷ *vt* zuckern; **sugar bowl** *n* Zuckerdose *f*; **sugary** *adj* (*sweet*) süß

suggest [sə'dʒest] *vt* vorschlagen; (*imply*) andeuten; **I ~ saying nothing** ich schlage vor, nichts zu sagen; **suggestion** [sə'dʒestʃən] *n* (*proposal*) Vorschlag *m*; **suggestive** *adj* vielsagend; (*sexually*) anzüglich

suicide ['suɪsaɪd] *n* (*act*) Selbstmord *m*; **suicide bomber** *n* Selbstmordattentäter(in) *m(f)*; **suicide bombing** *n* Selbstmordattentat *nt*

suit [suːt] *n* (*man's clothes*) Anzug *m*; (*lady's clothes*) Kostüm *nt*; (*Cards*) Farbe *f* ▷ *vt* (*be convenient for*) passen +dat; (clothes, colour) stehen +dat; (climate, food) bekommen +dat; **suitable** adj geeignet (for für); **suitcase** n Koffer m

suite [swiːt] n (of rooms) Suite f; (sofa and chairs) Sitzgarnitur f

sulk [sʌlk] vi schmollen; **sulky** adj eingeschnappt

sultana [sʌl'tɑːnə] n (raisin) Sultanine f

sum [sʌm] n Summe f; (money a.) Betrag m; (calculation) Rechenaufgabe f; **sum up** vt, vi (summarize) zusammenfassen

summarize ['sʌməraiz] vt, vi zusammenfassen; **summary** n Zusammenfassung f

summer ['sʌmə*] n Sommer m; **summer camp** n (US) Ferienlager nt; **summer holidays** n Sommerferien pl; **summertime** n: **in (the)** ~ im Sommer

summit ['sʌmit] n (a. Pol) Gipfel m

summon ['sʌmən] vt (doctor, fire brigade etc) rufen; (to one's office) zitieren; **summon up** vt (courage, strength) zusammennehmen

summons ['sʌmənz] nsing (Jur) Vorladung f

sumptuous ['sʌmptjʊəs] adj luxuriös; (meal) üppig

sun [sʌn] n Sonne f ▷ vt: **to ~ oneself** sich sonnen

Sun abbr = **Sunday** So.

sunbathe vi sich sonnen; **sunbathing** n Sonnenbaden nt; **sunbed** n Sonnenbank f; **sunblock** n Sunblocker m; **sunburn** n Sonnenbrand m; **sunburnt** adj: **to be/get ~** einen Sonnenbrand haben/bekommen

sundae ['sʌndei] n Eisbecher m

Sunday ['sʌndi] n Sonntag m; see also **Tuesday**

sung [sʌŋ] pp of **sing**

sunglasses ['sʌnglɑːsiz] npl

Sonnenbrille f; **sunhat** n Sonnenhut m

sunk [sʌŋk] pp of **sink**

sunlamp ['sʌnlæmp] n Höhensonne f; **sunlight** n Sonnenlicht nt; **sunny** ['sʌni] adj sonnig; **sun protection factor** n Lichtschutzfaktor m; **sunrise** n Sonnenaufgang m; **sunroof** n (Auto) Schiebedach nt; **sunscreen** n Sonnenschutzmittel nt; **sunset** n Sonnenuntergang m; **sunshade** n Sonnenschirm m; **sunshine** n Sonnenschein m; **sunstroke** n Sonnenstich m; **suntan** n (Sonnen)bräune f; **to get/have a ~** braun werden/sein; **~ lotion** (o **oil**) Sonnenöl nt

super ['suːpə*] adj (fam) toll

superb, superbly [suː'pɜːb, -li] adj, adv ausgezeichnet

superficial, superficially [suːpə'fiʃəl, -i] adj, adv oberflächlich

superfluous [sʊ'pɜːfluəs] adj überflüssig

superglue ['suːpəgluː] n Sekundenkleber m

superior [sʊ'piəriə*] adj (better) besser (to als); (higher in rank) höhergestellt (to als), höher ▷ n (in rank) Vorgesetzte(r) mf

supermarket ['suːpəmɑːkit] n Supermarkt m

supersede [suːpə'siːd] vt ablösen

supersonic [suːpə'sɒnik] adj Überschall-

superstition [suːpə'stiʃən] n Aberglaube m; **superstitious** [suːpə'stiʃəs] adj abergläubisch

superstore ['suːpəstɔː*] n Verbrauchermarkt m

supervise ['suːpəvaiz] vt beaufsichtigen; **supervisor** ['suːpəvaizə] n Aufsicht f; (at university) Doktorvater m

supper ['sʌpə°] n Abendessen nt; (late-night snack) Imbiss
supplement ['sʌplɪmənt] n (extra payment) Zuschlag m; (of newspaper) Beilage f ▷ vt ergänzen; **supplementary** [sʌplɪ'mentərɪ] adj zusätzlich
supplier [sə'plaɪə°] n Lieferant(in) m(f); **supply** [sə'plaɪ] vt (deliver) liefern; (drinks, music etc) sorgen für; **to ~ sb with sth** (provide) jdn mit etw versorgen ▷ n (stock) Vorrat m (of an +dat)
support [sə'pɔːt] n Unterstützung f; (Tech) Stütze f ▷ vt (hold up) tragen, stützen; (provide for) ernähren, unterhalten; (speak in favour of) unterstützen; **he ~s Manchester United** er ist Manchester-United-Fan
suppose [sə'pəʊz] vt (assume) annehmen; **I ~ so** ich denke schon; **I ~ not** wahrscheinlich nicht; **you're not ~d to smoke here** du darfst/Sie dürfen hier nicht rauchen; **supposedly** [sə'pəʊzɪdlɪ] adv angeblich; **supposing** conj angenommen
suppress [sə'pres] vt unterdrücken
surcharge ['sɜːtʃɑːdʒ] n Zuschlag m
sure [ʃʊə°] adj sicher; **I'm (not) ~** ich bin mir (nicht) sicher; **make ~ you lock up** vergiss/vergessen Sie nicht abzuschließen ▷ adv: **~!** klar!; **~ enough** tatsächlich; **surely** adv: **~ you don't mean it?** das ist nicht dein/Ihr Ernst, oder?
surf [sɜːf] n Brandung f ▷ vi (Sport) surfen ▷ vt: **to ~ the net** im Internet surfen
surface ['sɜːfɪs] n Oberfläche f ▷ vi auftauchen; **surface mail** n: **by ~** auf dem Land-/Seeweg
surfboard ['sɜːfbɔːd] n Surfbrett nt; **surfer** n Surfer(in) m(f);

surfing n Surfen nt; **to go ~** surfen gehen
surgeon ['sɜːdʒən] n Chirurg(in) m(f); **surgery** ['sɜːdʒərɪ] n (operation) Operation f; (room) Praxis f, Sprechzimmer nt; (consulting time) Sprechstunde f; **to have ~** operiert werden
surname ['sɜːneɪm] n Nachname m
surpass [sɜː'pɑːs] vt übertreffen
surplus ['sɜːpləs] n Überschuss m (of an +dat)
surprise [sə'praɪz] n Überraschung f ▷ vt überraschen; **surprising** adj überraschend; **surprisingly** adv überraschenderweise, erstaunlicherweise
surrender [sə'rendə°] vi sich ergeben (to +dat) ▷ vt (weapon, passport) abgeben
surround [sə'raʊnd] vt umgeben; (stand all round) umringen; **surrounding** adj (countryside) umliegend ▷ n **~s** pl Umgebung f
survey ['sɜːveɪ] n (opinion poll) Umfrage f; (of literature etc) Überblick m (of über +akk); (of land) Vermessung f ▷ [sɜː'veɪ] vt (look out over) überblicken; (land) vermessen
survive [sə'vaɪv] vt, vi überleben
susceptible [sə'septəbl] adj empfänglich (to für); (Med) anfällig (to für)
sushi ['suːʃɪ] n Sushi nt
suspect ['sʌspekt] n Verdächtige(r) mf ▷ adj verdächtig ▷ [sə'spekt] vt verdächtigen (of +gen); (think likely) vermuten
suspend [sə'spend] vt (from work) suspendieren; (payment) vorübergehend einstellen; (player) sperren; (hang up) aufhängen; **suspender** n (Brit) Strumpfhalter

m; **~s** pl (US: for trousers) Hosenträger pl

suspense [sə'spens] n Spannung f

suspicious [sə'spɪʃəs] adj misstrauisch (of sb/sth jdm/etw gegenüber); (causing suspicion) verdächtig

swallow ['swɒləʊ] n (bird) Schwalbe f ▷ vt, vi schlucken

swam [swæm] pt of **swim**

swamp [swɒmp] n Sumpf m

swan [swɒn] n Schwan m

swap [swɒp] vt, vi tauschen; **to ~ sth for sth** etw gegen etw eintauschen

sway [sweɪ] vi schwanken

swear [sweə°] (**swore, sworn**) vi (promise) schwören; (curse) fluchen; **to ~ at sb** jdn beschimpfen; **swear by** vt (have faith in) schwören auf +akk; **swearword** n Fluch m

sweat [swet] n Schweiß m ▷ vi schwitzen; **sweatband** n Schweißband nt; **sweater** n Pullover m; **sweatshirt** n Sweatshirt nt; **sweaty** adj verschwitzt

swede [swiːd] n Steckrübe f

Swede [swiːd] n Schwede m, Schwedin f; **Sweden** n Schweden nt; **Swedish** adj schwedisch ▷ n (language) Schwedisch nt

sweep [swiːp] (**swept, swept**) vt, vi (with brush) kehren, fegen; **sweep up** vt (dirt etc) zusammenkehren, zusammenfegen

sweet [swiːt] n (Brit: candy) Bonbon nt; (dessert) Nachtisch m ▷ adj süß; (kind) lieb; **sweet-and-sour** adj süßsauer; **sweetcorn** n Mais m; **sweeten** vt (tea etc) süßen; **sweetener** n (substance) Süßstoff m; **sweet potato** n Süßkartoffel f

swell [swel] (**swelled, swollen** o **swelled**) vi: **to ~ (up)** (an)schwellen ▷ adj (US fam) toll; **swelling** n (Med) Schwellung f

sweltering ['sweltərɪŋ] adj (heat) drückend

swept [swept] pt, pp of **sweep**

swift, **swiftly** [swɪft] adj, adv schnell

swig [swɪg] n (fam) Schluck m

swim [swɪm] (**swam, swum**) vi schwimmen ▷ n: **to go for a ~** schwimmen gehen; **swimmer** n Schwimmer(in) m(f); **swimming** n Schwimmen nt; **to go ~** schwimmen gehen; **swimming cap** n (Brit) Badekappe f; **swimming costume** n (Brit) Badeanzug m; **swimming pool** n Schwimmbad nt; (private, in hotel) Swimmingpool m; **swimming trunks** npl (Brit) Badehose f; **swimsuit** n Badeanzug m

swindle ['swɪndl] vt betrügen (out of um)

swine [swaɪn] n (person) Schwein nt

swing [swɪŋ] (**swung, swung**) vt, vi (object) schwingen ▷ n (for child) Schaukel f

swipe [swaɪp] vt (credit card etc) durchziehen; (fam: steal) klauen; **swipe card** n Magnetkarte f

Swiss [swɪs] adj schweizerisch ▷ n Schweizer(in) m(f)

switch [swɪtʃ] n (Elec) Schalter m ▷ vi (change) wechseln (to zu); **switch off** vt abschalten, ausschalten; **switch on** vt anschalten, einschalten; **switchboard** n (Tel) Vermittlung f

Switzerland ['swɪtsələnd] n die Schweiz

swivel ['swɪvl] vi sich drehen ▷ vt drehen; **swivel chair** n Drehstuhl m

swollen ['swəʊlən] pp of **swell**

▷ *adj* (*Med*) geschwollen; (*stomach*) aufgebläht

swop [swɒp] *see* **swap**

sword [sɔːd] *n* Schwert *nt*

swore [swɔːʳ] *pt of* **swear**

sworn [swɔːn] *pp of* **swear**

swot [swɒt] *vi* (*Brit fam*) büffeln (*for* für)

swum [swʌm] *pp of* **swim**

swung [swʌŋ] *pt, pp of* **swing**

syllable ['sɪləbl] *n* Silbe *f*

syllabus ['sɪləbəs] *n* Lehrplan *m*

symbol ['sɪmbəl] *n* Symbol *nt*; **symbolic** [sɪm'bɒlɪk] *adj* symbolisch; **symbolize** *vt* symbolisieren

symmetrical [sɪ'metrɪkəl] *adj* symmetrisch

sympathetic [sɪmpə'θetɪk] *adj* mitfühlend; (*understanding*) verständnisvoll; **sympathize** ['sɪmpəθaɪz] *vi* mitfühlen (*with sb* mit jdm); **sympathy** ['sɪmpəθɪ] *n* Mitleid *nt*; (*after death*) Beileid *nt*; (*understanding*) Verständnis *nt*

symphony ['sɪmfənɪ] *n* Sinfonie *f*

symptom ['sɪmptəm] *n* (*a. fig*) Symptom *nt*

synagogue ['sɪnəgɒg] *n* Synagoge *f*

synonym ['sɪnənɪm] *n* Synonym *nt*; **synonymous** [sɪ'nɒnɪməs] *adj* synonym (*with* mit)

synthetic [sɪn'θetɪk] *adj* (*material*) synthetisch

syphilis ['sɪfɪlɪs] *n* Syphilis *f*

Syria ['sɪrɪə] *n* Syrien *nt*

syringe [sɪ'rɪndʒ] *n* Spritze *f*

system ['sɪstəm] *n* System *nt*; **systematic** [sɪstə'mætɪk] *adj* systematisch; **system disk** *n* (*Inform*) Systemdiskette *f*; **system(s) software** *n* (*Inform*) Systemsoftware *f*

tab [tæb] *n* (*for hanging up coat etc*) Aufhänger *m*; (*Inform*) Tabulator *m*; **to pick up the ~** (*fam*) die Rechnung übernehmen

table ['teɪbl] *n* Tisch *m*; (*list*) Tabelle *f*; **~ of contents** Inhaltsverzeichnis *nt*; **tablecloth** *n* Tischdecke *f*; **tablelamp** *n* Tischlampe *f*; **tablemat** *n* Set *nt*; **tablespoon** *n* Servierlöffel *m*; (*in recipes*) Esslöffel *m*

tablet ['tæblət] *n* (*Med*) Tablette *f*

table tennis ['teɪbltenɪs] *n* Tischtennis *nt*; **table wine** *n* Tafelwein *m*

tabloid ['tæblɔɪd] *n* Boulevardzeitung *f*

taboo [tə'buː] *n* Tabu *nt* ▷ *adj* tabu

tacit, tacitly ['tæsɪt, -lɪ] *adj, adv* stillschweigend

tack [tæk] *n* (*small nail*) Stift *m*; (*US: thumb~*) Reißzwecke *f*

tackle ['tækl] n (Sport) Angriff m; (equipment) Ausrüstung f ▷ vt (deal with) in Angriff nehmen; (Sport) angreifen; (verbally) zur Rede stellen (about wegen)

tacky ['tækɪ] adj trashig, heruntergekommen

tact [tækt] n Takt m; **tactful**, **tactfully** adj, adv taktvoll; **tactic(s)** ['tæktɪk(s)] n(pl) Taktik f; **tactless**, **tactlessly** ['tæktləs, -lɪ] adj, adv taktlos

tag [tæg] n (label) Schild nt; (with maker's name) Etikett nt

Tahiti [taːˈhiːtɪ] n Tahiti nt

tail [teɪl] n Schwanz m; **heads or ~s?** Kopf oder Zahl?; **tailback** n (Brit) Rückstau m; **taillight** n (Auto) Rücklicht nt

tailor ['teɪlə°] n Schneider(in) m(f)

tailpipe ['teɪlpaɪp] n (US Auto) Auspuffrohr nt

tainted ['teɪntɪd] adj (US: food) verdorben

Taiwan [taɪˈwæn] n Taiwan nt

take [teɪk] (**took, taken**) vt nehmen; (~ along with one) mitnehmen; (~ to a place) bringen; (subtract) abziehen (from von); (capture: person) fassen; (gain, obtain) bekommen; (Fin, Comm) einnehmen; (train, taxi) nehmen, fahren mit; (trip, walk, holiday, exam, course, photo) machen; (bath) nehmen; (phone call) entgegennehmen; (decision, precautions) treffen; (risk) eingehen; (advice, job) annehmen; (consume) zu sich nehmen; (tablets) nehmen; (heat, pain) ertragen; (react to) aufnehmen; (have room for) Platz haben für; **I'll ~ it** (item in shop) ich nehme es; **how long does it ~?** wie lange dauert es?; **it ~s 4 hours** man braucht 4 Stunden; **do you ~ sugar?** nimmst

du/nehmen Sie Zucker?; **I ~ it that ...** ich nehme an, dass ...; **to ~ part in** teilnehmen an; **to ~ place** stattfinden; **take after** vt nachschlagen +dat; **take along** vt mitnehmen; **take apart** vt auseinandernehmen; **take away** vt (remove) wegnehmen (from sb jdm); (subtract) abziehen (from von); **take back** vt (return) zurückbringen; (retract) zurücknehmen; (remind) zurückversetzen (to in +akk); **take down** vt (picture, curtains) abnehmen; (write down) aufschreiben; **take in** vt (understand) begreifen; (give accommodation to) aufnehmen; (deceive) hereinlegen; (include) einschließen; (show, film etc) mitnehmen; **take off** vi (plane) starten ▷ vt (clothing) ausziehen; (hat, lid) abnehmen; (deduct) abziehen; (Brit: imitate) nachmachen; **to take a day off** sich einen Tag freinehmen; **take on** vt (undertake) übernehmen; (employ) einstellen; (Sport) antreten gegen; **take out** vt (wallet etc) herausnehmen; (person, dog) ausführen; (insurance) abschließen; (money from bank) abheben; (book from library) ausleihen; **take over** vt übernehmen ▷ vi: **he took over (from me)** er hat mich abgelöst; **take to** vt: **I've taken to her/it** ich mag sie/es; **to ~ doing sth** (begin) anfangen, etw zu tun; **take up** vt (carpet) hochnehmen; (space) einnehmen; (time) in Anspruch nehmen; (hobby) anfangen mit; (new job) antreten; (offer) annehmen

takeaway n (Brit: meal) Essen nt zum Mitnehmen

taken ['teɪkn] pp of **take** ▷ adj

(seat) besetzt; **to be ~ with** angetan sein von

takeoff ['teɪkɒf] n (Aviat) Start m; (imitation) Nachahmung f; **takeout** (US) see **takeaway**; **takeover** n (Comm) Übernahme f

takings ['teɪkɪŋz] npl Einnahmen pl

tale [teɪl] n Geschichte f

talent ['tælənt] n Talent nt; **talented** adj begabt

talk [tɔːk] n (conversation) Gespräch nt; (rumour) Gerede nt; (to audience) Vortrag m ▷ vi sprechen, reden; (have conversation) sich unterhalten; **to ~ to** (o **with**) **sb** (about sth) mit jdm (über etw akk) sprechen ▷ vt (language) sprechen; (nonsense) reden; (politics, business) reden über +akk; **to ~ sb into doing/out of doing sth** jdn überreden/jdm ausreden, etw zu tun; **talk over** vt besprechen

talkative adj gesprächig; **talk show** n Talkshow f

tall [tɔːl] adj groß; (building, tree) hoch; **he is 6ft ~** er ist 1,80m groß

tame [teɪm] adj zahm; (joke, story) fade ▷ vt (animal) zähmen

tampon ['tæmpɒn] n Tampon m

tan [tæn] n (on skin) (Sonnen)bräune f; **to get/have a ~** braun werden/sein ▷ vi braun werden

tangerine [tændʒə'riːn] n Mandarine f

tango ['tæŋɡəʊ] n Tango m

tank [tæŋk] n Tank m; (for fish) Aquarium nt; (Mil) Panzer m

tanker ['tæŋkə*] n (ship) Tanker m; (vehicle) Tankwagen m

tanned [tænd] adj (by sun) braun

tantalizing ['tæntəlaɪzɪŋ] adj verlockend

Tanzania [tænzə'nɪə] n Tansania nt

tap [tæp] n (for water) Hahn m ▷ vt, vi (strike) klopfen; **to ~ sb on the shoulder** jdm auf die Schulter klopfen; **tap-dance** vi steppen

tape [teɪp] n (adhesive ~) Klebeband nt; (for tape recorder) Tonband nt; (cassette) Kassette f; (video) Video nt ▷ vt (record) aufnehmen; **tape up** vt (parcel) zukleben; **tape measure** n Maßband nt; **tape recorder** n Tonbandgerät nt

tapestry ['tæpɪstrɪ] n Wandteppich m

tap water ['tæpwɔːtə*] n Leitungswasser nt

target ['tɑːɡɪt] n Ziel nt; (board) Zielscheibe f; **target group** n Zielgruppe f

tariff ['tærɪf] n (price list) Preisliste f; (tax) Zoll m

tarmac ['tɑːmæk] n (Aviat) Rollfeld nt

tart [tɑːt] n (fruit ~) (Obst)kuchen m; (small) (Obst)törtchen nt; (fam, pej: prostitute) Nutte f; (fam: promiscuous person) Schlampe f

tartan ['tɑːtən] n Schottenkaro nt; (material) Schottenstoff m

tartar(e) sauce ['tɑːtə'sɔːs] n Remouladensoße f

task [tɑːsk] n Aufgabe f; (duty) Pflicht f; **taskbar** n (Inform) Taskbar f

Tasmania [tæz'meɪnɪə] n Tasmanien nt

taste [teɪst] n Geschmack m; (sense of ~) Geschmackssinn m; (small quantity) Kostprobe f; **it has a strange ~** es schmeckt komisch ▷ vt schmecken; (try) probieren ▷ vi (food) schmecken (of nach); **to ~ good/strange** gut/komisch schmecken; **tasteful, tastefully** adj, adv geschmackvoll; **tasteless, tastelessly** adj, adv geschmacklos; **tasty** adj lecker

tattered ['tætəd] adj (clothes) zerlumpt; (fam: person) angespannt; **I'm absolutely ~** ich bin mit den Nerven am Ende

tattoo [tə'tu:] n (on skin) Tätowierung f

taught [tɔːt] pt, pp of **teach**

Taurus ['tɔːrəs] n (Astr) Stier m

tax [tæks] n Steuer f (on auf +akk) ▷ vt besteuern; **taxable** adj steuerpflichtig; **taxation** [tæk'seɪʃən] n Besteuerung f; **tax bracket** n Steuerklasse f; **tax disc** n (Brit Auto) Steuermarke f; **tax-free** adj steuerfrei

taxi ['tæksɪ] n Taxi nt ▷ vi (plane) rollen; **taxi driver** n Taxifahrer(in) m(f); **taxi rank** (Brit), **taxi stand** n Taxistand m

tax return ['tæksrɪ'tɜːn] n Steuererklärung f

tea [ti:] n Tee m; (afternoon ~) ≈ Kaffee und Kuchen; (meal) frühes Abendessen; **teabag** n Teebeutel m; **tea break** n Tee(pause f

teach [ti:tʃ] (**taught, taught**) vt (person, subject) unterrichten; **to ~ sb (how) to dance** jdm das Tanzen beibringen ▷ vi unterrichten; **teacher** n Lehrer(in) m(f); **teaching** n (activity) Unterrichten nt; (profession) Lehrberuf m

teacup ['ti:kʌp] n Teetasse f

team [ti:m] n (Sport) Mannschaft f, Team nt; **teamwork** n Teamarbeit f

teapot ['ti:pɒt] n Teekanne f

tear [tɪə°] n (in eye) Träne f

tear [tɛə°] (**tore, torn**) vt zerreißen; **to ~ a muscle** sich einen Muskel zerren ▷ n (in material etc) Riss m; **tear down** vt (building) abreißen; **tear up** vt (paper) zerreißen

tearoom ['ti:rʊm] n Teestube f,

Café, in dem in erster Linie Tee serviert wird

tease [ti:z] vt (person) necken (about wegen)

tea set ['ti:set] n Teeservice nt; **teashop** n Teestube f; **teaspoon** n Teelöffel m; **tea towel** n Geschirrtuch nt

technical ['teknɪkəl] adj technisch; (knowledge, term, dictionary) Fach-; **technically** adv technisch; **technique** [tek'ni:k] n Technik f

techno ['teknəʊ] n Techno f

technological [teknə'lɒdʒɪkəl] adj technologisch; **technology** [tek'nɒlədʒɪ] n Technologie f, Technik f

tedious ['ti:dɪəs] adj langweilig

teen(age) ['ti:n(eɪdʒ)] adj (fashions etc) Teenager-; **teenager** n Teenager m; **teens** [ti:nz] npl: **in one's ~** im Teenageralter

teeth [ti:θ] pl of **tooth**

teetotal ['ti:'təʊtl] adj abstinent

telegraph pole ['telɪgrɑ:fpəʊl] n (Brit) Telegrafenmast m

telephone ['telɪfəʊn] n Telefon nt ▷ vi telefonieren ▷ vt anrufen; **telephone banking** n Telefonbanking nt; **telephone book** n Telefonbuch nt; **telephone booth, telephone box** (Brit) n Telefonzelle f; **telephone call** n Telefonanruf m; **telephone directory** n Telefonbuch nt; **telephone number** n Telefonnummer f

telephoto lens ['telɪfəʊtəʊ'lenz] n Teleobjektiv nt

telescope ['telɪskəʊp] n Teleskop nt

televise ['telɪvaɪz] vt im Fernsehen übertragen; **television** ['telɪvɪʒən] n Fernsehen nt; **television programme** n Fernsehsendung f; **television (set)** n Fernseher m

teleworking ['telɪwɜːkɪŋ] *n*
Telearbeit *f*

tell [tel] (**told, told**) *vt* (*say,
inform*) sagen (*sb sth* jdm etw);
(*story*) erzählen; (*truth*) sagen;
(*difference*) erkennen; (*reveal secret*)
verraten; **to ~ sb about sth** jdm
von etw erzählen; **to ~ sth from
sth** etw von etw unterscheiden
▷ *vi* (*be sure*) wissen; **tell apart** *vt*
unterscheiden; **tell off** *vt*
schimpfen

telling *adj* aufschlussreich

telly ['telɪ] *n* (*Brit fam*) Glotze *f*; **on
(the)** ~ in der Glotze

temp [temp] *n* Aushilfskraft *f*
▷ *vi* als Aushilfskraft arbeiten

temper ['tempə°] *n* (*anger*) Wut *f*;
(*mood*) Laune *f*; **to lose one's ~** die
Beherrschung verlieren; **to have a
bad ~** jähzornig sein;
temperamental
[tempərə'mentl] *adj* (*moody*)
launisch

temperature ['temprɪtʃə°] *n*
Temperatur *f*; (*Med: high* ~) Fieber
nt; **to have a ~** Fieber haben

temple ['templ] *n* Tempel *m*;
(*Anat*) Schläfe *f*

temporarily ['tempərərɪlɪ] *adv*
vorübergehend; **temporary**
['tempərərɪ] *adj* vorübergehend;
(*road, building*) provisorisch

tempt [tempt] *vt* in Versuchung
führen; **I'm ~ed to accept** ich bin
versucht anzunehmen;
temptation [temp'teɪʃən] *n*
Versuchung *f*; **tempting** *adj*
verlockend

ten [ten] *num* zehn ▷ *n* Zehn *f*;
see also **eight**

tenant ['tenənt] *n* Mieter(in)
m(f); (*of land*) Pächter(in) *m(f)*

tend [tend] *vi*: **to ~ to do sth**
(*person*) dazu neigen, etw zu tun;
to ~ towards neigen zu;
tendency ['tendənsɪ] *n* Tendenz

f; **to have a ~ to do sth** (*person*)
dazu neigen, etw zu tun

tender ['tendə°] *adj* (*loving*)
zärtlich; (*sore*) empfindlich; (*meat*)
zart

tendon ['tendən] *n* Sehne *f*

Tenerife [tenə'riːf] *n* Teneriffa *nt*

tenner ['tenə°] *n* (*Brit fam: note*)
Zehnpfundschein *m*; (*amount*) zehn
Pfund

tennis ['tenɪs] *n* Tennis *nt*;
tennis ball *n* Tennisball *m*; **tennis
court** *n* Tennisplatz *m*; **tennis
racket** *n* Tennisschläger *m*

tenor [tenə°] *n* Tenor *m*

tenpin bowling, tenpins (*US*)
['tenpɪn'bəʊlɪŋ, 'tenpɪnz] *n*
Bowling *nt*

tense [tens] *adj* angespannt;
(*stretched tight*) gespannt; **tension**
['tenʃən] *n* Spannung *f*; (*strain*)
Anspannung *f*

tent [tent] *n* Zelt *nt*

tenth [tenθ] *adj* zehnte(r, s) ▷ *n*
(*fraction*) Zehntel *nt*; *see also* **eighth**

tent peg ['tentpeg] *n* Hering *m*;
tent pole *n* Zeltstange *f*

term [tɜːm] *n* (*in school, at
university*) Trimester *nt*; (*expression*)
Ausdruck *m*; **~s** *pl* (*conditions*)
Bedingungen *pl*; **to be on good ~s
with sb** mit jdm gut auskommen;
to come to ~s with sth sich mit
etw abfinden; **in the long/short
~** langfristig/kurzfristig; **in ~s
of ...** was ... betrifft

terminal ['tɜːmɪnl] *n* (*bus ~ etc*)
Endstation *f*; (*Aviat*) Terminal *m*;
(*Inform*) Terminal *nt*; (*Elec*) Pol *m*
▷ *adj* (*Med*) unheilbar; **terminally**
adv (*ill*) unheilbar

terminate ['tɜːmɪneɪt] *vt* (*contract*) lösen; (*pregnancy*) abbrechen
▷ *vi* (*train, bus*) enden

terminology [tɜːmɪ'nɒlədʒɪ] *n*
Terminologie *f*

terrace ['terəs] *n* (*of houses*)

Häuserreihe f; (in garden etc)
Terrasse f; **terraced** adj (garden)
terrassenförmig angelegt;
terraced house n (Brit)
Reihenhaus nt
terrible ['terəbl] adj schrecklich
terrific [tə'rɪfɪk] adj (very good)
fantastisch
terrify ['terɪfaɪ] vt erschrecken;
to be terrified schreckliche Angst
haben (of vor +dat)
territory ['terɪtərɪ] n Gebiet nt
terror ['terə°] n Schrecken m;
(Pol) Terror m; **terrorism** n
Terrorismus m; **terrorist** n
Terrorist(in) m(f)
test [test] n Test m, Klassenarbeit
f; (driving ~) Prüfung f; **to put to
the ~** auf die Probe stellen ▷ vt
testen, prüfen; (patience, courage
etc) auf die Probe stellen
Testament ['testəmənt] n: **the
Old/New ~** das Alte/Neue
Testament
test-drive ['testdraɪv] vt Probe
fahren
testicle ['testɪkl] n Hoden m
testify ['testɪfaɪ] vi (Jur)
aussagen
test tube ['testtjuːb] n
Reagenzglas nt
tetanus ['tetənəs] n Tetanus m
text [tekst] n Text m; (of
document) Wortlaut m; (sent by
mobile phone) SMS f ▷ vt (message)
simsen, SMSen; **to ~ sb** jdm
simsen, jdm eine SMS schicken;
I'll ~ it to you ich schicke es dir per
SMS
textbook n Lehrbuch nt
texting ['tekstɪŋ] n SMS-
Messaging nt; **text message** n
SMS f; **text messaging** n
SMS-Messaging nt
texture ['tekstʃə°] n
Beschaffenheit f
Thailand ['taɪlənd] n Thailand nt

Thames [temz] n Themse f
than [ðæn] prep, conj als;
bigger/faster ~ me
größer/schneller als ich; **I'd rather
walk ~ drive** ich gehe lieber zu
Fuß als mit dem Auto
thank [θæŋk] vt danken +dat;
~ you danke; **~ you very much**
vielen Dank; **thankful** adj
dankbar; **thankfully** adv (luckily)
zum Glück; **thankless** adj
undankbar; **thanks** npl Dank m;
~ danke!; ~ to dank +gen

- THANKSGIVING DAY

- **Thanksgiving (Day)** ist ein
- Feiertag in den USA, der auf den
- vierten Donnerstag im
- November fällt. Er soll daran
- erinnern, wie die Pilgerväter die
- gute Ernte im Jahre 1621
- feierten. In Kanada gibt es einen
- ähnlichen Erntedanktag (der
- aber nichts mit den Pilgervätern
- zu tun hat) am zweiten Montag
- im Oktober.

O **KEYWORD**

that [ðæt, ðət] adj (demonstrative)
(pl those) der/die/das, jene(r, s);
that one das da
▷ pron **1** (demonstrative) (pl those)
das; **who's/what's that?** wer ist
da/was ist das?; **is that you?** bist
du/sind Sie das?; **that's what he
said** genau das hat er gesagt;
what happened after that? was
passierte danach?; **that is** das
heißt
2 (relative) (subj) der/die/das, die;
(direct obj) den/die/das, die;
(indirect obj) dem/der/dem, denen;
all (that) I have alles, was ich
habe
3 (relative) (of time); **the day (that)**

an dem Tag, als; **the winter (that) he came** in dem Winter, in dem er kam
▷ *conj* dass; **he thought that I was ill** er dachte, dass ich krank sei, er dachte, ich sei krank
▷ *adv* (*demonstrative*) so; **I can't work that much** ich kann nicht so viel arbeiten

that's [ðæts] *contr of* **that is; that has**

thaw [θɔː] *vi* tauen; (*frozen food*) auftauen ▷ *vt* auftauen lassen

⬤ **KEYWORD**

the [ðə, ðiː] *def art* **1** der/die/das; **to play the piano/violin** Klavier/Geige spielen; **I'm going to the butcher's/the cinema** ich gehe zum Fleischer/ins Kino; **Elizabeth the First** Elisabeth die Erste
2 (+*adj to form noun*) das, die; **the rich and the poor** die Reichen und die Armen
3 (*in comparisons*) **the more he works the more he earns** je mehr er arbeitet, desto mehr verdient er

theater (*US*), **theatre** ['θɪətə*] *n* Theater *nt*; (*for lectures etc*) Saal *m*
theft [θeft] *n* Diebstahl *m*
their [ðɛə*] *adj* ihr; (*unidentified person*) sein; **they cleaned ~ teeth** sie putzten sich die Zähne; **someone has left ~ umbrella here** jemand hat seinen Schirm hier vergessen; **theirs** *pron* ihre(r, s); (*unidentified person*) seine(r, s); **it's ~** es gehört ihnen; **a friend of ~** ein Freund von ihnen; **someone has left ~ here** jemand hat seins hier liegen lassen
them [ðem, ðəm] *pron* (*direct object*) sie; (*indirect object*) ihnen;

(*unidentified person*) ihn/ihm, sie/ihr; **do you know ~?** kennst du/kennen Sie sie?; **can you help ~?** kannst du/können Sie ihnen helfen?; **it's ~** sie sind's; **if anyone has a problem you should help ~** wenn jemand ein Problem hat, solltest du/sollten Sie ihm helfen
theme [θiːm] *n* Thema *nt*; (*Mus*) Motiv *nt*; **~ park** Themenpark *m*; **~ song** Titelmusik *f*
themselves [ðəm'selvz] *pron* sich; **they hurt ~** sie haben sich verletzt; **they ~ were not there** sie selbst waren nicht da; **they did it ~** sie haben es selbst gemacht; **they are not dangerous in ~** an sich sind sie nicht gefährlich; (**all**) **by ~** allein
then [ðen] *adv* (*at that time*) damals; (*next*) dann; (*therefore*) also; (*furthermore*) ferner; **from ~ on** von da an; **by ~** bis dahin
▷ *adj* damalig
theoretical, theoretically [θɪə'retɪkəl, -ɪ] *adj, adv* theoretisch
theory ['θɪərɪ] *n* Theorie *f*; **in ~** theoretisch
therapy ['θerəpɪ] *n* Therapie *f*

⬤ **KEYWORD**

there [ðɛə*] *adv* **1 there is/there are** es *o* da ist/sind; (*there exists/exist also*) es gibt; **there are 3 of them** (*people, things*) es gibt 3 davon; **there has been an accident** da war ein Unfall
2 (*place*) da, dort; (*direction*) dahin, dorthin; **put it in/on there** leg es dahinein/dorthinauf
3 there, there (*esp to child*) na, na

thereabouts *adv* (*approximately*) so ungefähr; **therefore** *adv* daher, deshalb

thermometer [θəˈmɒmɪtə°] n
Thermometer nt

Thermos® [ˈθɜːməs] n: ~ **(flask)**
Thermosflasche® f

these [ðiːz] pron, adj diese; **I
don't like ~ apples** ich mag diese
Äpfel nicht; **~ are not my books**
das sind nicht meine Bücher

thesis [ˈθiːsɪs] (pl theses) n (for
PhD) Doktorarbeit f

they [ðeɪ] pron pl sie; (people in
general) man; (unidentified person)
er/sie; **~ are rich** sie sind reich;
~ say that ... man sagt, dass ...; **if
anyone looks at this, ~ will see
that ...** wenn sich jemand dies
ansieht, wird er erkennen, dass ...

they'd [ðeɪd] contr of **they had;
they would**

they'll [ðeɪl] contr of **they will;
they shall**

they've [ðeɪv] contr of **they have**

thick [θɪk] adj dick; (fog) dicht;
(liquid) dickflüssig; (fam: stupid)
dumm; **thicken** vi (fog) dichter
werden ▷ vt
(sauce) eindicken
(sauce) dick werden ▷ vt

thief [θiːf] (pl thieves) n
Dieb(in) m(f)

thigh [θaɪ] n Oberschenkel m

thimble [ˈθɪmbl] n Fingerhut m

thin [θɪn] adj dünn

thing [θɪŋ] n Ding nt; (affair)
Sache f; **my ~s** pl meine Sachen pl;
how are ~s? wie geht's?; **I can't
see a ~** ich kann nichts sehen; **he
knows a ~ or two about cars** er
kennt sich mit Autos aus

think [θɪŋk] (thought, thought)
vt, vi denken; (believe) meinen; **I
~ so** ich denke schon; **I don't ~ so**
ich glaube nicht; **think about** vt
denken an +akk; (reflect on)
nachdenken über +akk; (have
opinion of) halten von; **think of** vt
denken an +akk; (devise) sich
ausdenken; (have opinion of) halten

von; (remember) sich erinnern an
+akk; **think over** vt überdenken;
think up vt sich ausdenken

third [θɜːd] adj dritte(r, s); **the
Third World** die Dritte Welt ▷ n
(fraction) Drittel nt; **in ~ (gear)** im
dritten Gang; see also **eighth**;
thirdly adv drittens; **third-party
insurance** n Haftpflichtversicherung f

thirst [θɜːst] n Durst m (for nach);
thirsty adj: **to be ~** Durst haben

thirteen [ˈθɜːˈtiːn] num dreizehn
▷ n Dreizehn f; see also **eight**;
thirteenth adj dreizehnte(r, s);
see also **eighth**; **thirtieth** [ˈθɜːtɪɪθ]
adj dreißigste(r, s); see also **eighth**;
thirty [ˈθɜːtɪ] num dreißig;
~-one einunddreißig ▷ n Dreißig
f; **to be in one's thirties** in den
Dreißigern sein; see also **eight**

○ **KEYWORD**

this [ðɪs] adj (demonstrative) (pl
these) diese(r, s); **this evening**
heute Abend; **this one** diese(r, s)
(da)
▷ pron (demonstrative) (pl these)
dies, das; **who/what is this?**
wer/was ist das?; **this is where I
live** hier wohne ich; **this is what
he said** das hat er gesagt; **this is
Mr Brown** dies ist Mr Brown; (on
telephone) hier ist Mr Brown
▷ adv (demonstrative) **this
high/long** etc so groß/lang etc

thistle [ˈθɪsl] n Distel f

thong [θɒŋ] n String m

thorn [θɔːn] n Dorn m, Stachel m

thorough [ˈθʌrə] adj gründlich;
thoroughly adv gründlich; (agree
etc) völlig

those [ðəʊz] pron die da, jene;
~ who diejenigen, die ▷ adj die,
jene

though [ðəʊ] *conj* obwohl; **as ~** als ob ▷ *adv* aber

thought [θɔːt] *pt, pp of* **think** ▷ *n* Gedanke *m*; *(thinking)* Überlegung *f*; **thoughtful** *adj (kind)* rücksichtsvoll; *(attentive)* aufmerksam; *(in Gedanken versunken)* nachdenklich; **thoughtless** *adj (unkind)* rücksichtslos, gedankenlos

thousand ['θaʊzənd] *num:* **(one) ~, a ~** tausend; **five ~** fünftausend; **~s of** Tausende von

thrash [θræʃ] *vt (hit)* verprügeln; *(defeat)* vernichtend schlagen

thread [θred] *n* Faden *m* ▷ *vt (needle)* einfädeln; *(beads)* auffädeln

threat [θret] *n* Drohung *f*; *(danger)* Bedrohung *f (to* für); **threaten** *vt* bedrohen; **threatening** *adj* bedrohlich

three [θriː] *num* drei ▷ *n* Drei *f*; *see also* **eight**; **three-dimensional** *adj* dreidimensional; **three-piece suit** *n* Anzug *m* mit Weste; **three-quarters** *npl* drei Viertel *pl*

threshold ['θreʃhəʊld] *n* Schwelle *f*

threw [θruː] *pt of* **throw**

thrifty ['θrɪftɪ] *adj* sparsam

thrilled [θrɪld] *adj:* **to be ~ (with sth)** sich (über etw *akk*) riesig freuen; **thriller** *n* Thriller *m*; **thrilling** *adj* aufregend

thrive [θraɪv] *vi* gedeihen *(on* bei); *(fig, business)* florieren

throat [θrəʊt] *n* Hals *m*, Kehle *f*

throbbing ['θrɒbɪŋ] *adj (pain, headache)* pochend

thrombosis [θrɒm'bəʊsɪs] *n* Thrombose *f*; **deep vein ~** tiefe Venenthrombose *f*

throne [θrəʊn] *n* Thron *m*

through [θruː] *prep* durch; *(time)* während +*gen*; *(because of)* aus, durch; *(US: up to and including)* bis;

arranged ~ him durch ihn arrangiert ▷ *adv* durch; **to put sb ~** *(Tel)* jdn verbinden *(to* mit) ▷ *adj (ticket, train)* durchgehend; **~ flight** Direktflug *m*; **to be ~ with sb/sth** mit jdm/etw fertig sein;

throughout [θru'aʊt] *prep (place)* überall in +*dat*; *(time)* während +*gen*; **~ the night** die ganze Nacht hindurch ▷ *adv* überall; *(time)* die ganze Zeit

throw [θrəʊ] **(threw, thrown)** *vt* werfen; *(rider)* abwerfen; *(party)* geben; **to ~ sth to sb, to ~ sb sth** jdm etw zuwerfen; **I was ~n by his question** seine Frage hat mich aus dem Konzept gebracht ▷ *n* Wurf *m*; **throw away** *vt* wegwerfen; **throw in** *vt (include)* dazugeben; **throw out** *vt (unwanted object)* wegwerfen; *(person)* hinauswerfen *(of* aus); **throw up** *vt, vi (fam: vomit)* sich übergeben; **throw-in** *n* Einwurf *m*

thrown [θrəʊn] *pp of* **throw**

thru *(US) see* **through**

thrush [θrʌʃ] *n* Drossel *f*

thrust [θrʌst] **(thrust, thrust)** *vt, vi (push)* stoßen

thruway ['θruːweɪ] *n (US)* Schnellstraße *f*

thumb [θʌm] *n* Daumen *m* ▷ *vt:* **to ~ a lift** per Anhalter fahren; **thumbtack** *n (US)* Reißzwecke *f*

thunder ['θʌndə°] *n* Donner *m* ▷ *vi* donnern; **thunderstorm** *n* Gewitter *nt*

Thur(s) *abbr* = **Thursday** Do.

Thursday ['θɜːzdɪ] *n* Donnerstag *m*; *see also* **Tuesday**

thus [ðʌs] *adv (in this way)* so; *(therefore)* somit, also

thyme [taɪm] *n* Thymian *m*

Tibet [tɪ'bet] *n* Tibet *nt*

tick [tɪk] *n (Brit: mark)* Häkchen *nt* ▷ *vt (name)* abhaken; *(box, answer)* ankreuzen ▷ *vi (clock)* ticken

ticket ['tɪkɪt] n (for train, bus)
(Fahr)karte f; (plane ~) Flugschein
m, Ticket nt; (for theatre, match,
museum etc) (Eintritts)karte f; (price
~) (Preis)schild nt; (raffle ~) Los nt;
(for car park) Parkschein m; (for
traffic offence) Strafzettel m; **ticket
collector, ticket inspector** (Brit)
n Fahrkartenkontrolleur(in) m(f);
ticket machine n (for public
transport) Fahrscheinautomat m;
(in car park) Parkscheinautomat m;
ticket office n (Rail)
Fahrkartenschalter m; (Theat)
Kasse f
tickle ['tɪkl] vt kitzeln; **ticklish**
['tɪklɪʃ] adj kitzlig
tide [taɪd] n Gezeiten pl; **the ~ is
in/out** es ist Flut/Ebbe
tidy ['taɪdɪ] adj ordentlich ▷ vt
aufräumen; **tidy up** vt, vi
aufräumen
tie [taɪ] n (neck~) Krawatte f;
(Sport) Unentschieden nt; (bond)
Bindung f ▷ vt (attach, do up)
binden (to an +akk); (~ together)
zusammenbinden; (knot) machen
▷ vi (Sport) unentschieden spielen;
tie down vt festbinden (to an
+dat); (fig) binden; **tie up** vt (dog)
anbinden; (parcel) verschnüren;
(shoelace) binden; (boat)
festmachen; **I'm tied up** (fig) ich
bin beschäftigt
tiger ['taɪgə°] n Tiger m
tight [taɪt] adj (clothes) eng;
(knot) fest; (screw, lid) fest sitzend;
(control, security measures) streng;
(timewise) knapp; (schedule) eng
▷ adv (shut) fest; (pull) stramm;
hold ~ festhalten!; **sleep ~** schlaf
gut!; **tighten** vt (knot, rope, screw)
anziehen; (belt) enger machen;
(restrictions, control) verschärfen;
tights npl (Brit) Strumpfhose
f
tile [taɪl] n (on roof) Dachziegel m;

(on wall, floor) Fliese f; **tiled** adj
(roof) Ziegel-; (floor, wall) gefliest
till [tɪl] n Kasse f ▷ prep, conj see
until
tilt [tɪlt] vt kippen; (head) neigen
▷ vi sich neigen
time [taɪm] n Zeit f; (occasion)
Mal nt; (Mus) Takt m; **local
~** Ortszeit; **what ~ is it?, what's
the ~?** wie spät ist es?, wie viel Uhr
ist es?; **to take one's ~ (over sth)**
sich (bei etw) Zeit lassen; **to have
a good ~** Spaß haben; **in two
weeks' ~** in zwei Wochen; **at ~s**
manchmal; **at the same
~** gleichzeitig; **all the ~** die ganze
Zeit; **by the ~ he ...** bis er ...; (in
past) als er ...; **for the ~ being**
vorläufig; **in ~** (not late)
rechtzeitig; **on ~** pünktlich; **the
first ~** das erste Mal; **this
~** diesmal; **five ~s** fünfmal; **five ~s
six** fünf mal sechs; **four ~s a year**
viermal im Jahr; **three at a ~** drei
auf einmal ▷ vt (with stopwatch)
stoppen; **you ~d that well** das
hast du/haben Sie gut getimt;
time difference n
Zeitunterschied m; **time limit** n
Frist f; **timer** n Timer m; (switch)
Schaltuhr f; **time-saving** adj
zeitsparend; **time switch** n
Schaltuhr f; **timetable** n (for
public transport) Fahrplan m;
(school) Stundenplan m; **time zone**
n Zeitzone f
timid ['tɪmɪd] adj ängstlich
timing ['taɪmɪŋ] n (coordination)
Timing nt, zeitliche Abstimmung
tin [tɪn] n (metal) Blech nt; (Brit:
can) Dose f; **tinfoil** n Alufolie f;
tinned [tɪnd] adj (Brit) aus der
Dose; **tin opener** n (Brit)
Dosenöffner m
tinsel ['tɪnsəl] n ≈ Lametta nt
tint [tɪnt] n (Farb)ton m; (in hair)
Tönung f; **tinted** adj getönt

tiny ['taɪnɪ] *adj* winzig
tip [tɪp] *n* (*money*) Trinkgeld *nt*; (*hint*) Tipp *m*; (*end*) Spitze *f*; (*of cigarette*) Filter *m*; (*Brit: rubbish ~*) Müllkippe *f* ⊳ *vt* (*waiter*) Trinkgeld geben +*dat*; **tip over** *vt*, *vi* (*overturn*) umkippen
tipsy ['tɪpsɪ] *adj* beschwipst
tiptoe ['tɪptəʊ] *n*: **on ~** auf Zehenspitzen
tire ['taɪə°] *n* (*US*) *see* **tyre** ⊳ *vt* müde machen ⊳ *vi* müde werden; **tired** *adj* müde; **to be ~ of sb/sth** jdn/etw satthaben; **to be ~ of doing sth** es satthaben, etw zu tun; **tireless, tirelessly** *adv* unermüdlich; **tiresome** *adj* lästig; **tiring** *adj* ermüdend
Tirol [tɪ'rəʊl] *see* **Tyrol**
tissue ['tɪʃuː] *n* (*Anat*) Gewebe *nt*; (*paper handkerchief*) Tempotaschentuch® *nt*, Papier(taschen)tuch *nt*; **tissue paper** *n* Seidenpapier *nt*
tit [tɪt] *n* (*bird*) Meise *f*; (*fam: breast*) Titte *f*
title ['taɪtl] *n* Titel *m*
titter ['tɪtə] *vi* kichern

◯ KEYWORD

to [tuː, tə] *prep* **1** (*direction*) zu, nach; **I go to France/school** ich gehe nach Frankreich/zur Schule; **to the left** nach links
2 (*as far as*) bis
3 (*with expressions of time*) vor; **a quarter to 5** Viertel vor 5
4 (*for, of*) für; **secretary to the director** Sekretärin des Direktors
5 (*expressing indirect object*) **to give sth to sb** jdm etw geben; **to talk to sb** mit jdm sprechen; **I sold it to a friend** ich habe es einem Freund verkauft
6 (*in relation to*) zu; **30 miles to the gallon** 30 Meilen pro Gallone

7 (*purpose, result*) zu; **to my surprise** zu meiner Überraschung
⊳ *with vb* **1** (*infin*) **to go/eat** gehen/essen; **to want to do sth** etw tun wollen; **to try/start to do sth** versuchen/anfangen, etw zu tun; **he has a lot to lose** er hat viel zu verlieren
2 (*with vb omitted*) **I don't want to** ich will (es) nicht
3 (*purpose, result*) um; **I did it to help you** ich tat es, um dir/Ihnen zu helfen
4 (*after adj etc*) **ready to use** gebrauchsfertig; **too old/young to ...** zu alt/jung, um ... zu ...
⊳ *adv*: **push/pull the door to** die Tür zuschieben/zuziehen

toad [təʊd] *n* Kröte *f*; **toadstool** *n* Giftpilz *m*
toast [təʊst] *n* (*bread, drink*) Toast *m*; **a piece** (*o slice*) **of ~** eine Scheibe Toast; **to propose a ~ to sb** einen Toast auf jdn ausbringen ⊳ *vt* (*bread*) toasten; (*person*) trinken auf +*akk*; **toaster** *n* Toaster *m*
tobacco [tə'bækəʊ] (*pl* -**es**) *n* Tabak *m*; **tobacconist's** [tə'bækənɪsts] *n*: **~** (**shop**) Tabakladen *m*
toboggan [tə'bɒgən] *n* Schlitten *m*
today [tə'deɪ] *adv* heute; **a week ~** heute in einer Woche; **~'s newspaper** die Zeitung von heute
toddler ['tɒdlə°] *n* Kleinkind *nt*
toe [təʊ] *n* Zehe *f*, Zeh *m*; **toenail** *n* Zehennagel *m*
toffee ['tɒfɪ] *n* (*sweet*) Karamellbonbon *nt*; **toffee apple** *n* kandierter Apfel; **toffee-nosed** *adj* hochnäsig
tofu ['təʊfuː] *n* Tofu *m*
together [tə'geðə°] *adv*

zusammen; **I tied them ~** ich habe sie zusammengebunden

toilet ['tɔɪlət] n Toilette f; **to go to the ~** auf die Toilette gehen; **toilet bag** n Kulturbeutel m; **toilet paper** n Toilettenpapier nt; **toiletries** ['tɔɪlətrɪz] npl Toilettenartikel pl; **toilet roll** n Rolle f Toilettenpapier

token ['təʊkən] n Marke f; (in casino) Spielmarke f; (voucher, gift ~) Gutschein m; (sign) Zeichen nt

Tokyo ['təʊkɪəʊ] n Tokio nt

told [təʊld] pt, pp of **tell**

tolerant ['tɒlərənt] adj tolerant (of gegenüber); **tolerate** ['tɒləreɪt] vt tolerieren; (noise, pain, heat) ertragen

toll [təʊl] n (charge) Gebühr f; **the death ~** die Zahl der Toten; **toll-free** adj, adv (US Tel) gebührenfrei; **toll road** n gebührenpflichtige Straße

tomato [tə'mɑːtəʊ] (pl **-es**) n Tomate f; **tomato juice** n Tomatensaft m; **tomato ketchup** n Tomatenketchup m o nt; **tomato sauce** n Tomatensoße f; (Brit: ketchup) Tomatenketchup m o nt

tomb [tuːm] n Grabmal nt; **tombstone** n Grabstein m

tomorrow [tə'mɒrəʊ] adv morgen; **~ morning** morgen früh; **~ evening** morgen Abend; **the day after ~** übermorgen; **a week (from) ~/~ week** morgen in einer Woche

ton [tʌn] n (Brit) Tonne f (1016 kg); (US) Tonne f (907 kg); **~s of books** (fam) eine Menge Bücher

tone [təʊn] n Ton m; **tone down** vt mäßigen; **toner** ['təʊnə°] n (for printer) Toner m; **toner cartridge** n Tonerpatrone f

tongs [tɒŋz] npl Zange f; (curling ~) Lockenstab m

tongue [tʌŋ] n Zunge f

tonic ['tɒnɪk] n (Med) Stärkungsmittel nt; **~ (water)** Tonic nt; **gin and ~** Gin m Tonic

tonight [tə'naɪt] adv heute Abend; (during night) heute Nacht

tonsils ['tɒnslz] n Mandeln pl; **tonsillitis** [tɒnsɪ'laɪtɪs] n Mandelentzündung f

too [tuː] adv zu; (also) auch; **~ fast** zu schnell; **~ much/many** zu viel/viele; **me ~** ich auch; **she liked it ~** ihr gefiel es auch

took [tʊk] pt of **take**

tool [tuːl] n Werkzeug nt; **toolbar** n (Inform) Symbolleiste f; **toolbox** n Werkzeugkasten m

tooth [tuːθ] (pl **teeth**) n Zahn m; **toothache** n Zahnschmerzen pl; **toothbrush** n Zahnbürste f; **toothpaste** n Zahnpasta f; **toothpick** n Zahnstocher m

top [tɒp] n (of tower, class, company etc) Spitze f; (of mountain) Gipfel m; (of tree) Krone f; (of street) oberes Ende; (of tube, pen) Kappe f; (of box) Deckel m; (of bikini) Oberteil nt; (sleeveless) Top nt; **at the ~ of the page** oben auf der Seite; **at the ~ of the league** an der Spitze der Liga; **on ~** oben; **on ~ of** auf +dat; (in addition to) zusätzlich zu; **in ~ (gear)** im höchsten Gang; **over the ~** übertrieben ▷ adj (floor, shelf) oberste(r, s); (price, note) höchste(r, s); (best) Spitzen-; (pupil, school) beste(r, s) ▷ vt (exceed) übersteigen; (be better than) übertreffen; (league) an erster Stelle liegen in +dat; **~ped with cream** mit Sahne obendrauf; **top up** vt auffüllen; **can I top you up?** darf ich dir nachschenken?

topic ['tɒpɪk] n Thema nt; **topical** adj aktuell

topless ['tɒpləs] adj, adv oben ohne

topping ['tɒpɪŋ] n (on top of pizza, ice-cream etc) Belag m, Garnierung f

top-secret ['tɒp'siːkrət] adj streng geheim

torch [tɔːtʃ] n (Brit) Taschenlampe f

tore [tɔː*] pt of **tear**

torment ['tɔːment] vt quälen

torn [tɔːn] pp of **tear**

tornado [tɔː'neɪdəʊ] (pl **-es**) n Tornado m

torrential [tə'renʃəl] adj (rain) sintflutartig

tortoise ['tɔːtəs] n Schildkröte f

torture ['tɔːtʃə*] n Folter f; (fig) Qual f ▷ vt foltern

Tory ['tɔːrɪ] (Brit) n Tory m, Konservative(r) mf ▷ adj Tory-

toss [tɒs] vt (throw) werfen; (salad) anmachen; **to ~ a coin** eine Münze werfen ▷ n: **I don't give a ~** (fam) es ist mir scheißegal

total ['təʊtl] n (of figures, money) Gesamtsumme f; **a ~ of 30** insgesamt 30; **in ~** insgesamt ▷ adj total; (sum etc) Gesamt- ▷ vt (amount to) sich belaufen auf +akk; **totally** adv total

touch [tʌtʃ] n (act of ~ing) Berührung f; (sense of ~) Tastsinn m; (trace) Spur f; **to be/keep in ~ with sb** mit jdm in Verbindung stehen/bleiben; **to get in ~ with sb** sich mit jdm in Verbindung setzen; **to lose ~ with sb** den Kontakt zu jdm verlieren ▷ vt (feel) berühren; (emotionally) bewegen; **touch on** vt (topic) berühren; **touchdown** n (Aviat) Landung f; (Sport) Touchdown m; **touching** adj (moving) rührend; **touch screen** n Touchscreen m, Berührungsbildschirm m; **touchy** adj empfindlich, zickig

tough [tʌf] adj hart; (meat) zäh; (material) robust; (meat) zäh

tour ['tʊə*] n Tour f (of durch); (of town, building) Rundgang m (of durch); (of pop group etc) Tournee f ▷ vt eine Tour/einen Rundgang/eine Tournee machen durch ▷ vi (on holiday) umherreisen; **tour guide** n Reiseleiter(in) m(f)

tourism ['tʊərɪzəm] n Tourismus m, Fremdenverkehr m; **tourist** n Tourist(in) m(f); **tourist class** n Touristenklasse f; **tourist guide** n (book) Reiseführer m; (person) Fremdenführer(in) m(f); **tourist office** n Fremdenverkehrsamt nt

tournament ['tʊənəmənt] n Turnier nt

tour operator ['tʊərɒpəreɪtə*] n Reiseveranstalter m

tow [təʊ] vt abschleppen; (caravan, trailer) ziehen; **tow away** vt abschleppen

towards [tə'wɔːdz] prep: **~ me** mir entgegen, auf mich zu; **we walked ~ the station** wir gingen in Richtung Bahnhof; **my feelings ~ him** meine Gefühle ihm gegenüber; **she was kind ~ me** sie war nett zu mir

towel ['taʊəl] n Handtuch nt

tower ['taʊə*] n Turm m; **tower block** n (Brit) Hochhaus nt

town [taʊn] n Stadt f; **town center** (US), **town centre** n Stadtmitte f, Stadtzentrum nt; **town hall** n Rathaus nt

towrope ['təʊrəʊp] n Abschleppseil nt; **tow truck** n (US) Abschleppwagen m

toxic ['tɒksɪk] adj giftig, Gift-

toy [tɔɪ] n Spielzeug nt; **toy with** vt spielen mit; **toyshop** n Spielwarengeschäft nt

trace [treɪs] n Spur f; **without**

~ spurlos ▷ vt (find) ausfindig machen; **tracing paper** n Pauspapier nt

track [træk] n (mark) Spur f; (path) Weg m; (Rail) Gleis nt; (on CD, record) Stück nt; **to keep/lose ~ of sb/sth** jdn/etw im Auge behalten/aus den Augen verlieren; **track down** vt ausfindig machen; **trackball** n (Inform) Trackball m; **tracksuit** n Trainingsanzug m

tractor ['træktə*] n Traktor m

trade [treɪd] n (commerce) Handel m; (business) Geschäft nt; (skilled job) Handwerk nt ▷ vi handeln (in mit) ▷ vt (exchange) tauschen (for gegen); **trademark** n Warenzeichen nt; **tradesman** (pl **-men**) n (shopkeeper) Geschäftsmann m; (workman) Handwerker m; **trade(s) union** n (Brit) Gewerkschaft f

tradition [trə'dɪʃən] n Tradition f; **traditional, traditionally** adj, adv traditionell

traffic ['træfɪk] n Verkehr m; (pej: trading) Handel m (in mit); **traffic circle** n (US) Kreisverkehr m; **traffic island** n Verkehrsinsel f; **traffic jam** n Stau m; **traffic lights** npl Verkehrsampel f; **traffic warden** n (Brit) ≈ Politesse f

tragedy ['trædʒədɪ] n Tragödie f; **tragic** ['trædʒɪk] adj tragisch

trail [treɪl] n Spur f; (path) Weg m ▷ vt (follow) verfolgen; (drag) schleppen; (drag behind) hinter sich herziehen; (Sport) zurückliegen hinter +dat ▷ vi (hang loosely) schleifen; (Sport) weit zurückliegen; **trailer** n Anhänger m; (US: caravan) Wohnwagen m; (Cine) Trailer m

train [treɪn] n (Rail) Zug m ▷ vt (teach) ausbilden; (Sport) trainieren ▷ vi (Sport) trainieren; **to ~ as** (o **to be**) **a teacher** eine Ausbildung als Lehrer machen; **trained** adj (person, voice) ausgebildet; **trainee** n Auszubildende(r) mf; (academic, practical) Praktikant(in) m(f); **traineeship** n Praktikum nt; **trainer** n (Sport) Trainer(in) m(f); **~s** (Brit: shoes) Turnschuhe pl; **training** n Ausbildung f; (Sport) Training nt; **train station** n Bahnhof m

tram [træm] n (Brit) Straßenbahn f

tramp [træmp] n Landstreicher(in) m(f) ▷ vi trotten

tranquillizer ['træŋkwɪlaɪzə*] n Beruhigungsmittel nt

transaction n (piece of business) Geschäft nt

transatlantic ['trænzət'læntɪk] adj transatlantisch; **~ flight** Transatlantikflug m

transfer ['trænsfə*] n (of money) Überweisung f; (US: ticket) Umsteigekarte f ▷ [træns'fз:*] vt (money) überweisen (to sb an jdn); (patient) verlegen; (employee) versetzen; (Sport) transferieren ▷ vi (on journey) umsteigen; **transferable** [træns'fз:rəbl] adj übertragbar

transform [træns'fɔ:m] vt umwandeln; **transformation** [trænsfə'meɪʃən] n Umwandlung f

transfusion [træns'fju:ʒən] n Transfusion f

transistor [træn'zɪstə*] n Transistor m; **~ (radio)** Transistorradio nt

transition [træn'zɪʃən] n Übergang m (from ... to von ... zu)

transit lounge ['trænzɪtlaʊndʒ] n Transitraum m; **transit passenger** n Transitreisende(r) mf

translate [trænz'leɪt] vt, vi
übersetzen; **translation**
[trænz'leɪʃən] n Übersetzung f;
translator [trænz'leɪtə*] n
Übersetzer(in) m(f)
transmission [trænz'mɪʃən] n
(Auto) Getriebe nt
transparent [træns'pærənt] adj
durchsichtig; (fig) offenkundig
transplant [træns'plɑ:nt] (Med)
vt transplantieren ▷ ['trænsplɑ:nt]
n (operation) Transplantation f
transport ['trænspɔ:t] n (of
goods, people) Beförderung f; **public
~** öffentliche Verkehrsmittel pl
▷ [træns'pɔ:t] vt befördern,
transportieren; **transportation**
[trænspɔ:'teɪʃən] n see **transport**
trap [træp] n Falle f ▷ vt: **to be
~ped** (in snow, job etc) festsitzen
trash [træʃ] n (book, film etc)
Schund m; (US: refuse) Abfall m;
trash can n (US) Abfalleimer m;
trashy adj niveaulos; (novel)
Schund-
traumatic [trɔ:'mætɪk] adj
traumatisch
travel ['trævl] n Reisen nt ▷ vi
(journey) reisen ▷ vt (distance)
zurücklegen; (country) bereisen;
travel agency, **travel agent** n
(company) Reisebüro nt; **traveler**
(US) see **traveller**; **traveler's
check** (US) see **traveller's cheque**;
travel insurance n
Reiseversicherung f; **traveller** n
Reisende(r) mf; **traveller's cheque**
n (Brit) Reisescheck m; **travelsick**
n reisekrank
tray [treɪ] n Tablett nt; (for mail
etc) Ablage f; (of printer, photocopier)
Fach nt
tread [tred] n (on tyre) Profil nt;
tread on [tred] (**trod, trodden**)
vt treten auf +akk
treasure ['treʒə*] n Schatz m
▷ vt schätzen

treat [tri:t] n besondere Freude;
it's my ~ das geht auf meine
Kosten ▷ vt behandeln; **to ~ sb
(to sth)** jdn (zu etw) einladen; **to
~ oneself to sth** sich etw leisten;
treatment ['tri:tmənt] n
Behandlung f
treaty ['tri:tɪ] n Vertrag m
tree [tri:] n Baum m
tremble ['trembl] vi zittern
tremendous [trə'mendəs] adj
gewaltig; (fam: very good) toll
trench [trentʃ] n Graben m
trend [trend] n Tendenz f;
(fashion) Mode f, Trend m; **trendy**
adj trendy
trespass ['trespəs] vi: **"no ~ing"**
„Betreten verboten"
trial ['traɪəl] n (Jur) Prozess m;
(test) Versuch m; **by ~ and error**
durch Ausprobieren; **trial period**
n (for employee) Probezeit f
triangle ['traɪæŋgl] n Dreieck nt;
(Mus) Triangel m; **triangular**
[traɪ'æŋgjʊlə*] adj dreieckig
tribe [traɪb] n Stamm m
trick [trɪk] n Trick m; (mischief)
Streich m ▷ vt hereinlegen
tricky ['trɪkɪ] adj (difficult)
schwierig, heikel; (situation)
verzwickt
trifle ['traɪfl] n Kleinigkeit f; (Brit
Gastr) Trifle nt (Nachspeise aus
Biskuit, Wackelpudding, Obst,
Vanillesoße und Sahne)
trigger ['trɪgə*] n (of gun) Abzug
m ▷ vt: **to ~ (off)** auslösen
trim [trɪm] vt (hair, beard)
nachschneiden; (nails) schneiden;
(hedge) stutzen ▷ n: **just a ~,
please** nur etwas nachschneiden,
bitte; **trimmings** npl (decorations)
Verzierungen pl; (extras) Zubehör
nt; (Gastr) Beilagen pl
trip [trɪp] n Reise f; (outing)
Ausflug m ▷ vi stolpern (over über
+akk)

triple [ˈtrɪpl] *adj* dreifach ▷ *adv*:
~ **the price** dreimal so teuer ▷ *vi*
sich verdreifachen; **triplet**
[ˈtrɪplɪt] *n* Drilling *m*
tripod [ˈtraɪpɒd] *n* (*Foto*) Stativ
nt
trite [traɪt] *adj* banal
triumph [ˈtraɪʌmf] *n* Triumph *m*
trivial [ˈtrɪvɪəl] *adj* trivial
trod [trɒd] *pt of* **tread**
trodden *pp of* **tread**
trolley [ˈtrɒlɪ] *n* (*Brit: in shop*)
Einkaufswagen *m*; (*for luggage*)
Kofferkuli *m*; (*serving* ~) Teewagen
m
trombone [trɒmˈbəʊn] *n*
Posaune *f*
troops [truːps] *npl* (*Mil*) Truppen
pl
trophy [ˈtrəʊfɪ] *n* Trophäe *f*
tropical [ˈtrɒpɪkl] *adj* tropisch
trouble [ˈtrʌbl] *n* (*problems*)
Schwierigkeiten *pl*; (*worry*) Sorgen
pl; (*effort*) Mühe *f*; (*unrest*) Unruhen
pl; (*Med*) Beschwerden *pl*; **to be in**
~ in Schwierigkeiten sein; **to get**
into ~ (*with authority*) Ärger
bekommen; **to make**
~ Schwierigkeiten machen ▷ *vt*
(*worry*) beunruhigen; (*disturb*)
stören; **my back's troubling me**
mein Rücken macht mir zu
schaffen; **sorry to** ~ **you** ich muss
dich/Sie leider kurz stören;
troubled *adj* (*worried*)
beunruhigt; **trouble-free** *adj*
problemlos; **troublemaker** *n*
Unruhestifter(in) *m(f)*;
troublesome *adj* lästig
trousers [ˈtraʊzəz] *npl* Hose *f*;
trouser suit *n* (*Brit*) Hosenanzug
m
trout [traʊt] *n* Forelle *f*
truck [trʌk] *n* Lastwagen *m*; (*Brit*
Rail) Güterwagen *m*; **trucker** *n*
(*US: driver*) Lastwagenfahrer(in)
m(f)

true [truː] *adj* (*factually correct*)
wahr; (*genuine*) echt; **to come**
~ wahr werden
truly [ˈtruːlɪ] *adv* wirklich; **Yours**
~ (*in letter*) mit freundlichen
Grüßen
trumpet [ˈtrʌmpɪt] *n* Trompete
f
trunk [trʌŋk] *n* (*of tree*) Stamm
m; (*Anat*) Rumpf *m*; (*of elephant*)
Rüssel *m*; (*piece of luggage*)
Überseekoffer *m*; (*US Auto*)
Kofferraum *m*; **trunks** *npl*:
(**swimming**) ~ Badehose *f*
trust [trʌst] *n* (*confidence*)
Vertrauen *nt* (*in zu*) ▷ *vt* vertrauen
+*dat*; **trusting** *adj* vertrauensvoll;
trustworthy *adj*
vertrauenswürdig
truth [truːθ] *n* Wahrheit *f*;
truthful *adj* ehrlich; (*statement*)
wahrheitsgemäß
try [traɪ] *n* Versuch *m* ▷ *vt*
(*attempt*) versuchen; (~ *out*)
ausprobieren; (*sample*) probieren;
(*Jur: person*) vor Gericht stellen;
(*courage, patience*) auf die Probe
stellen ▷ *vi* versuchen; (*make*
effort) sich bemühen; ~ **and come**
versuch zu kommen; **try on** *vt*
(*clothes*) anprobieren; **try out** *vt*
ausprobieren
T-shirt [ˈtiːʃɜːt] *n* T-Shirt *nt*
tub [tʌb] *n* (*for ice-cream,*
margarine) Becher *m*
tube [tjuːb] *n* (*pipe*) Rohr *nt*; (*of*
rubber, plastic) Schlauch *m*; (*for*
toothpaste, glue etc) Tube *f*; **the**
Tube (*in London*) die U-Bahn
tube station [ˈtjuːbsteɪʃən] *n*
U-Bahn-Station *f*
tuck [tʌk] *vt* (*put*) stecken; **tuck**
in *vt* (*shirt*) in die Hose stecken;
(*blanket*) feststecken; (*person*)
zudecken ▷ *vi* (*eat*) zulangen
Tue(s) *abbr* = **Tuesday** Di.
Tuesday [ˈtjuːzdɪ] *n* Dienstag *m*;

on ~ (am) Dienstag; **on ~s** dienstags; **this/last/next ~** diesen/letzten/nächsten Dienstag; **(on) ~ morning/ afternoon/evening** (am) Dienstagmorgen/-nachmittag/ -abend; **every ~** jeden Dienstag; **a week on ~/~ week** Dienstag in einer Woche

tug [tʌg] vt ziehen; **she ~ged his sleeve** sie zog an seinem Ärmel ▷ vi ziehen (at an +dat)

tuition [tjuˈɪʃən] n Unterricht m; (US: fees) Studiengebühren pl; **~ fees** pl Studiengebühren pl

tulip [ˈtjuːlɪp] n Tulpe f

tumble [ˈtʌmbl] vi (person, prices) fallen; **tumble dryer** n Wäschetrockner m; **tumbler** n (glass) (Becher)glas nt

tummy [ˈtʌmɪ] n (fam) Bauch m; **tummyache** n (fam) Bauchweh nt

tumor (US), **tumour** [ˈtjuːmə*] n Tumor m

tuna [ˈtjuːnə] n Thunfisch m

tune [tjuːn] n Melodie f; **to be in/out of ~** (instrument) gestimmt/verstimmt sein; (singer) richtig/falsch singen ▷ vt (instrument) stimmen; (radio) einstellen (to auf +akk); **tuner** n (in stereo system) Tuner m

Tunisia [tjuːˈnɪzɪə] n Tunesien nt

tunnel [ˈtʌnl] n Tunnel m; (under road, railway) Unterführung f

turban [ˈtɜːbən] n Turban m

turbulence [ˈtɜːbjʊləns] n (Aviat) Turbulenzen pl; **turbulent** adj stürmisch

Turk [tɜːk] n Türke m, Türkin f

turkey [ˈtɜːkɪ] n Truthahn m

Turkey [ˈtɜːkɪ] n die Türkei; **Turkish** adj türkisch ▷ n (language) Türkisch nt

turmoil [ˈtɜːmɔɪl] n Aufruhr m

turn [tɜːn] n (rotation) Drehung f; (performance) Nummer f; **to make a left ~** nach links abbiegen; **at the ~ of the century** um die Jahrhundertwende; **it's your ~** du bist/Sie sind dran; **in ~, by ~s** abwechselnd; **to take ~s** sich abwechseln ▷ vt (wheel, key, screw) drehen; (to face other way) umdrehen; (corner) biegen um; (page) umblättern; (transform) verwandeln (into in +akk) ▷ vi (rotate) sich drehen; (to face other way) sich umdrehen; (change direction: driver, car) abbiegen; (become) werden; (weather) umschlagen; **to ~ into sth** (become) sich in etw akk verwandeln; **to ~ cold/green** kalt/grün werden; **to ~ left/right** links/rechts abbiegen; **turn away** vt (person) abweisen; **turn back** vt (person) zurückweisen ▷ vi (go back) umkehren; **turn down** vt (refuse) ablehnen; (radio, TV) leiser stellen; (heating) kleiner stellen; **turn off** vi abbiegen ▷ vt (switch off) ausschalten; (tap) zudrehen; (engine, electricity) abstellen; **turn on** vt (switch on) einschalten; (tap) aufdrehen; (engine, electricity) anstellen; (fam: person) anmachen, antörnen; **turn out** vt (light) ausmachen; (pockets) leeren ▷ vi (develop) sich entwickeln; **as it turned out** wie sich herausstellte; **turn over** vt (page) umblättern ▷ vi (person) umdrehen; (car) sich überschlagen; (TV) umschalten (to auf +akk); **turn round** vt (to face other way) umdrehen ▷ vi (person) sich umdrehen; (go back) umkehren; **turn to** vt sich zuwenden +dat; **turn up** vi (person, lost object) auftauchen ▷ vt (radio, TV) lauter stellen; (heating) höher stellen; **turning** n (in road) Abzweigung f; **turning point** n Wendepunkt m

turnip ['tɜːnɪp] n Rübe f

turnover ['tɜːnəʊvə*] n (Fin) Umsatz m

turnpike ['tɜːnpaɪk] n (US) gebührenpflichtige Autobahn

turntable ['tɜːnteɪbl] n (on record player) Plattenteller m

turn-up ['tɜːnʌp] n (Brit: on trousers) Aufschlag m

turquoise ['tɜːkwɔɪz] adj türkis

turtle ['tɜːtl] n (Brit) Wasserschildkröte f; (US) Schildkröte f

tutor ['tjuːtə*] n (private) Privatlehrer(in) m(f); (Brit: at university) Tutor(in) m(f)

tux [tʌks] , **tuxedo** [tʌkˈsiːdəʊ] (pl **-s**) n (US) Smoking m

TV ['tiːˈviː] n Fernsehen nt; (~ set) Fernseher m; **to watch ~** fernsehen; **on ~** im Fernsehen ▷ adj Fernseh-; **~ programme** Fernsehsendung f

tweed [twiːd] n Tweed m

tweezers ['twiːzəz] npl Pinzette f

twelfth [twelfθ] adj zwölfte(r, s); see also **eighth**; **twelve** [twelv] num zwölf ▷ n Zwölf f; see also **eight**

twentieth ['twentɪɪθ] adj zwanzigste(r, s); see also **eighth**; **twenty** ['twentɪ] num zwanzig; **~-one** einundzwanzig ▷ n Zwanzig f; **to be in one's twenties** in den Zwanzigern sein; see also **eight**

twice [twaɪs] adv zweimal; **~ as much/many** doppelt so viel/viele

twig [twɪg] n Zweig m

twilight ['twaɪlaɪt] n (in evening) Dämmerung f

twin [twɪn] n Zwilling m ▷ adj (brother etc) Zwillings-; **~ beds** zwei Einzelbetten ▷ vt: **York is ~ned with Münster** York ist eine Partnerstadt von Münster

twinge [twɪndʒ] n (pain) stechender Schmerz

twinkle ['twɪŋkl] vi funkeln

twin room ['twɪnˈruːm] n Zweibettzimmer nt; **twin town** n Partnerstadt f

twist [twɪst] vt (turn) drehen, winden; (distort) verdrehen; **I've ~ed my ankle** ich bin mit dem Fuß umgeknickt

two [tuː] num zwei; **to break sth in ~** etw in zwei Teile brechen ▷ n Zwei f; **the ~ of them** die beiden; see also **eight; two-dimensional** adj zweidimensional; (fig) oberflächlich; **two-faced** adj falsch, heuchlerisch; **two-piece** adj zweiteilig; **two-way** adj: **~ traffic** Gegenverkehr

type [taɪp] n (sort) Art f; (typeface) Schrift(art) f; **what ~ of car is it?** was für ein Auto ist das?; **he's not my ~** er ist nicht mein Typ; **typeface** n Schrift(art) f; **typewriter** n Schreibmaschine f

typhoid ['taɪfɔɪd] n Typhus m

typhoon [taɪˈfuːn] n Taifun m

typical ['tɪpɪkəl] adj typisch (of für)

typing error ['taɪpɪŋerə*] n Tippfehler m

tyre [taɪə*] n (Brit) Reifen m; **tyre pressure** n Reifendruck m

Tyrol [tɪˈrəʊl] n: **the ~** Tirol nt

U

UFO ['juːfəʊ] *acr* = **unidentified flying object** Ufo *nt*

Uganda [juːˈɡændə] *n* Uganda *nt*

ugly ['ʌglɪ] *adj* hässlich

UHT *adj abbr* = **ultra-heat treated** ~ **milk** H-Milch *f*

UK *abbr* = **United Kingdom**

Ukraine [juːˈkreɪn] *n*: **the** ~ die Ukraine

ulcer ['ʌlsə°] *n* Geschwür *nt*

ulterior [ʌlˈtɪərɪə°] *adj*: ~ **motive** Hintergedanke *m*

ultimate ['ʌltɪmət] *adj* (*final*) letzte(r, s); (*authority*) höchste(r, s); **ultimately** *adv* letzten Endes; (*eventually*) schließlich; **ultimatum** [ʌltɪˈmeɪtəm] *n* Ultimatum *nt*

ultra- ['ʌltrə] *pref* ultra-

ultrasound ['ʌltrəsaʊnd] *n* (*Med*) Ultraschall *m*

umbrella [ʌmˈbrelə] *n* Schirm *m*

umpire ['ʌmpaɪə°] *n* Schiedsrichter(in) *m(f)*

umpteen ['ʌmptiːn] *num* (*fam*) zig; ~ **times** zigmal

un- [ʌn] *pref* un-

UN *nsing abbr* = **United Nations** VN, Vereinte Nationen *pl*

unable [ʌnˈeɪbl] *adj*: **to be** ~ **to do sth** etw nicht tun können

unacceptable [ʌnəkˈseptəbl] *adj* unannehmbar

unaccountably [ʌnəˈkaʊntəblɪ] *adv* unerklärlicherweise

unaccustomed [ʌnəˈkʌstəmd] *adj*: **to be** ~ **to sth** etw nicht gewohnt sein

unanimous, **unanimously** [juːˈnænɪməs, -lɪ] *adj, adv* einmütig

unattached [ʌnəˈtætʃt] *adj* (*without partner*) ungebunden

unattended [ʌnəˈtendɪd] *adj* (*luggage, car*) unbeaufsichtigt

unauthorized [ʌnˈɔːθəraɪzd] *adj* unbefugt

unavailable [ʌnəˈveɪləbl] *adj* nicht erhältlich; (*person*) nicht erreichbar

unavoidable [ʌnəˈvɔɪdəbl] *adj* unvermeidlich

unaware [ʌnəˈwɛə°] *adj*: **to be** ~ **of sth** sich einer Sache *dat* nicht bewusst sein; **I was** ~ **that ...** ich wusste nicht, dass ...

unbalanced [ʌnˈbælənst] *adj* unausgewogen; (*mentally*) gestört

unbearable [ʌnˈbɛərəbl] *adj* unerträglich

unbeatable [ʌnˈbiːtəbl] *adj* unschlagbar

unbelievable [ʌnbɪˈliːvəbl] *adj* unglaublich

unblock [ʌnˈblɒk] *vt* (*pipe*) frei machen

unbutton [ʌnˈbʌtn] *vt* aufknöpfen

uncertain [ʌn'sɜːtən] *adj*
unsicher
uncle [ʌŋkl] *n* Onkel *m*
uncomfortable [ʌn'kʌmfətəbl]
adj unbequem
unconditional [ʌnkən'dɪʃənl]
adj bedingungslos
unconscious [ʌn'kɒnʃəs] *adj*
(*Med*) bewusstlos; **to be ~ of sth**
sich einer Sache *dat* nicht bewusst
sein; **unconsciously** *adv*
unbewusst
uncork [ʌn'kɔːk] *vt* entkorken
uncover [ʌn'kʌvə*] *vt*
aufdecken
undecided [ʌndɪ'saɪdɪd] *adj*
unschlüssig
undeniable [ʌndɪ'naɪəbl] *adj*
unbestreitbar
under [ʌndə*] *prep* (*beneath*)
unter +*dat*; (*with motion*) unter
+*akk*; **children ~ eight** Kinder
unter acht; **~ an hour** weniger als
eine Stunde ▷ *adv* (*beneath*)
unten; (*with motion*) darunter;
children aged eight and ~ Kinder
bis zu acht Jahren; **under-age** *adj*
minderjährig
undercarriage [ʌndəkærɪdʒ] *n*
Fahrgestell *nt*
underdog [ʌndədɒg] *n* (*outsider*)
Außenseiter(in) *m(f)*
underdone [ʌndə'dʌn] *adj*
(*Gastr*) nicht gar, durch;
(*deliberately*) nicht durchgebraten
underestimate [ʌndər-
'estɪmeɪt] *vt* unterschätzen
underexposed [ʌndərɪks'pəʊzd]
adj (*Foto*) unterbelichtet
undergo [ʌndə'gəʊ] *irr vt*
(*experience*) durchmachen;
(*operation*, *test*) sich unterziehen
+*dat*
undergraduate [ʌndə'grædjʊət]
n Student(in) *m(f)*
underground [ʌndəgraʊnd] *adj*
unterirdisch ▷ *n* (*Brit Rail*) U-Bahn

f; **underground station** *n*
U-Bahn-Station *f*
underlie [ʌndə'laɪ] *irr vt*
zugrunde liegen +*dat*
underline [ʌndə'laɪn] *vt*
unterstreichen
underlying [ʌndə'laɪɪŋ] *adj*
zugrunde liegend
underneath [ʌndə'niːθ] *prep*
unter; (*with motion*) unter +*akk*
▷ *adv* darunter
underpants [ʌndəpænts] *npl*
Unterhose *f*; **undershirt**
[ʌndəʃɜːt] *n* (*US*) Unterhemd *nt*;
undershorts [ʌndəʃɔːts] *npl* (*US*)
Unterhose *f*
understand [ʌndə'stænd] *irr vt*,
vi verstehen; **I ~ that ...** (*been told*)
ich habe gehört, dass ...;
(*sympathize*) ich habe Verständnis
dafür, dass ...; **to make oneself
understood** sich verständlich
machen; **understandable** *adj*
verständlich; **understanding** *adj*
verständnisvoll
undertake [ʌndə'teɪk] *irr vt*
(*task*) übernehmen; **to ~ to do sth**
sich verpflichten, etw zu tun;
undertaker *n* Leichenbestat-
ter(in) *m(f)*; **~'s** (*firm*)
Bestattungsinstitut *nt*
underwater [ʌndə'wɔːtə*] *adv*
unter Wasser ▷ *adj* Unterwasser-
underwear [ʌndəwɛə*] *n*
Unterwäsche *f*
undesirable [ʌndɪ'zaɪərəbl] *adj*
unerwünscht
undo [ʌn'duː] *irr vt* (*unfasten*)
aufmachen; (*work*)
zunichtemachen; (*Inform*)
rückgängig machen
undoubtedly [ʌn'daʊtɪdlɪ] *adv*
zweifellos
undress [ʌn'dres] *vt* ausziehen;
to get ~ed sich ausziehen ▷ *vi*
sich ausziehen
undue [ʌn'djuː] *adj* übermäßig

unduly [ʌn'djuːlɪ] *adv* übermäßig

unearth [ʌn'ɜːθ] *vt* (*dig up*) ausgraben; (*find*) aufstöbern

unease [ʌn'iːz] *n* Unbehagen *nt*; **uneasy** (*person*) unbehaglich; **I'm ~ about it** mir ist nicht wohl dabei

unemployed [ʌnɪm'plɔɪd] *adj* arbeitslos ▷ ▷ *npl*: **the ~** die Arbeitslosen *pl*; **unemployment** [ʌnɪm'plɔɪmənt] *n* Arbeitslosigkeit *f*; **unemployment benefit** *n* Arbeitslosengeld *nt*

unequal [ʌn'iːkwəl] *adj* ungleich

uneven [ʌn'iːvən] *adj* (*surface, road*) uneben; (*contest*) ungleich

unexpected [ʌnɪk'spektɪd] *adj* unerwartet

unfair [ʌn'feə°] *adj* unfair

unfamiliar [ʌnfə'mɪljə°] *adj*: **to be ~ with sb/sth** jdn/etw nicht kennen

unfasten [ʌn'fɑːsn] *vt* aufmachen

unfit [ʌn'fɪt] *adj* ungeeignet (*for* für); (*in bad health*) nicht fit

unforeseen [ʌnfɔː'siːn] *adj* unvorhergesehen

unforgettable [ʌnfə'getəbl] *adj* unvergesslich

unforgivable [ʌnfə'gɪvəbl] *adj* unverzeihlich

unfortunate [ʌn'fɔːtʃnət] *adj* (*unlucky*) unglücklich; **it is ~ that ...** es ist bedauerlich, dass ...; **unfortunately** *adv* leider

unfounded [ʌn'faʊndɪd] *adj* unbegründet

unhappy [ʌn'hæpɪ] *adj* (*sad*) unglücklich, unzufrieden; **to be ~ with sth** mit etw unzufrieden sein

unhealthy [ʌn'helθɪ] *adj* ungesund

unheard-of [ʌn'hɜːdɒv] *adj*

(*unknown*) gänzlich unbekannt; (*outrageous*) unerhört

unhelpful [ʌn'helpfʊl] *adj* nicht hilfreich

unhitch [ʌn'hɪtʃ] *vt* (*caravan, trailer*) abkoppeln

unhurt [ʌn'hɜːt] *adj* unverletzt

uniform ['juːnɪfɔːm] *n* Uniform *f* ▷ *adj* einheitlich

unify ['juːnɪfaɪ] *vt* vereinigen

unimportant [ʌnɪm'pɔːtənt]- *adj* unwichtig

uninhabited [ʌnɪn'hæbɪtɪd] *adj* unbewohnt

uninstall [ʌnɪn'stɔːl] *vt* (*Inform*) deinstallieren

unintentional [ʌnɪn'tenʃənl] *adj* unabsichtlich

union ['juːnjən] *n* (*uniting*) Vereinigung *f*; (*alliance*) Union *f*; **Union Jack** *n* Union Jack *m* (*britische Nationalflagge*)

unique [juː'niːk] *adj* einzigartig

unit ['juːnɪt] *n* Einheit *f*; (*of system, machine*) Teil *nt*; (*in school*) Lektion *f*

unite [juː'naɪt] *vt* vereinigen; **the United Kingdom** das Vereinigte Königreich; **the United Nations** *pl* die Vereinten Nationen *pl*; **the United States (of America)** *pl* die Vereinigten Staaten (von Amerika) *pl* ▷ *vi* sich vereinigen

universe ['juːnɪvɜːs] *n* Universum *nt*

university [juːnɪ'vɜːsɪtɪ] *n* Universität *f*

unkind [ʌn'kaɪnd] *adj* unfreundlich (*to* zu)

unknown [ʌn'nəʊn] *adj* unbekannt (*to +dat*)

unleaded [ʌn'ledɪd] *adj* bleifrei

unless [ən'les] *conj* es sei denn, wenn ... nicht; **don't do it ~ I tell you to** mach das nicht, es sei denn, ich sage es dir; **~ I'm**

mistaken ... wenn ich mich nicht irre ...

unlicensed [ʌn'laɪsənst] *adj* (*to sell alcohol*) ohne Lizenz

unlike [ʌn'laɪk] *prep* (*in contrast to*) im Gegensatz zu; **it's ~ her to be late** es sieht ihr gar nicht ähnlich, zu spät zu kommen; **unlikely** [ʌn'laɪklɪ] *adj* unwahrscheinlich

unload [ʌn'ləʊd] *vt* ausladen

unlock [ʌn'lɒk] *vt* aufschließen

unlucky [ʌn'lʌkɪ] *adj* unglücklich; **to be ~** Pech haben

unmistakable [ʌnmɪ'steɪkəbl] *adj* unverkennbar

unnecessary [ʌn'nesəsərɪ] *adj* unnötig

unobtainable [ʌnəb'teɪnəbl] *adj* nicht erhältlich

unoccupied [ʌn'ɒkjʊpaɪd] *adj* (*seat*) frei; (*building, room*) leer stehend

unpack [ʌn'pæk] *vt, vi* auspacken

unpleasant [ʌn'pleznt] *adj* unangenehm

unplug [ʌn'plʌg] *vt*: **to ~ sth** den Stecker von etw herausziehen

unprecedented [ʌn'presɪdəntɪd] *adj* beispiellos

unpredictable [ʌnprɪ'dɪktəbl] *adj* (*person, weather*) unberechenbar

unreasonable [ʌn'riːznəbl] *adj* unvernünftig; (*demand*) übertrieben

unreliable [ʌnrɪ'laɪəbl] *adj* unzuverlässig

unsafe [ʌn'seɪf] *adj* nicht sicher; (*dangerous*) gefährlich

unscrew [ʌn'skruː] *vt* abschrauben

unsightly [ʌn'saɪtlɪ] *adj* unansehnlich

unskilled [ʌn'skɪld] *adj* (*worker*) ungelernt

unsuccessful [ʌnsək'sesfʊl] *adj* erfolglos

unsuitable [ʌn'suːtəbl] *adj* ungeeignet (*for* für)

until [ən'tɪl] *prep* bis; **not ~** erst; **from Monday ~ Friday** von Montag bis Freitag; **he didn't come home ~ midnight** er kam erst um Mitternacht nach Hause; **~ then** bis dahin ▷ *conj* bis; **she won't come ~ you invite her** sie kommt erst, wenn du sie einlädst/wenn Sie sie einladen

unusual, unusually [ʌn'juːʒʊəl, -ɪ] *adj, adv* ungewöhnlich

unwanted [ʌn'wɒntɪd] *adj* unerwünscht, ungewollt

unwell [ʌn'wel] *adj* krank; **to feel ~** sich nicht wohlfühlen

unwilling [ʌn'wɪlɪŋ] *adj*: **to be ~ to do sth** nicht bereit sein, etw zu tun

unwind [ʌn'waɪnd] *irr vt* abwickeln ▷ *vi* (*relax*) sich entspannen

unwrap [ʌn'ræp] *vt* auspacken

unzip [ʌn'zɪp] *vt* den Reißverschluss aufmachen an +*dat*; (*Inform*) entzippen

O **KEYWORD**

up [ʌp] *prep*: **to be up sth** oben auf etw *dat* sein; **to go up sth** (auf) etw *akk* hinaufgehen; **go up that road** gehen Sie die Straße hinauf
▷ *adv* **1** (*upwards, higher*) oben; **put it up a bit higher** stell es etwas weiter nach oben; **up there** da oben, dort oben; **up above** hoch oben

2 to be up (*out of bed*) auf sein; (*prices, level*) gestiegen sein; (*building, tent*) stehen

3 up to (*as far as*) bis; **up to now** bis jetzt

4 to be up to (*depending on*): **it's up to you** das hängt von dir ab; (*equal to*): **he's not up to it** (*job, task etc*) er ist dem nicht gewachsen; (*inf: be doing*) (*showing disapproval, suspicion*) **what is he up to?** was führt er im Schilde?; **it's not up to me to decide** die Entscheidung liegt nicht bei mir; **his work is not up to the required standard** seine Arbeit entspricht nicht dem geforderten Niveau
▷ *n*: **ups and downs** (*in life, career*) Höhen und Tiefen *pl*

upbringing ['ʌpbrɪŋɪŋ] *n* Erziehung *f*

update [ʌp'deɪt] *n* (*list etc*) Aktualisierung *f*; (*software*) Update *nt* ▷ *vt* (*list etc, person*) auf den neuesten Stand bringen, aktualisieren

upgrade [ʌp'greɪd] *vt* (*computer*) aufrüsten; **we were ~d** das Hotel hat uns ein besseres Zimmer gegeben

upheaval [ʌp'hiːvəl] *n* Aufruhr *m*; (*Pol*) Umbruch *m*

uphill [ʌp'hɪl] *adv* bergauf

upon [ə'pɒn] *prep see* **on**

upper ['ʌpə*] *adj* obere(r, s); (*arm, deck*) Ober-

upright ['ʌpraɪt] *adj, adv* aufrecht

uprising ['ʌpraɪzɪŋ] *n* Aufstand *m*

uproar ['ʌprɔː*] *n* Aufruhr *m*

upset [ʌp'set] *irr vt* (*overturn*) umkippen; (*disturb*) aufregen; (*sadden*) bestürzen; (*offend*) kränken; (*plans*) durcheinanderbringen ▷ *adj* (*disturbed*) aufgeregt; (*sad*) bestürzt; (*offended*) gekränkt; **~ stomach** ['ʌpset] Magenverstimmung *f*

upside down [ʌpsaɪd'daʊn]

adv verkehrt herum; (*fig*) drunter und drüber; **to turn sth ~** (*box etc*) etw umdrehen/durchwühlen

upstairs [ʌp'steəz] *adv* oben; (*go, take*) nach oben

up-to-date ['ʌptə'deɪt] *adj* modern; (*fashion, information*) aktuell; **to keep sb ~** jdn auf dem Laufenden halten

upwards ['ʌpwədz] *adv* nach oben

urban ['ɜːbən] *adj* städtisch, Stadt-

urge [ɜːdʒ] *n* Drang *m* ▷ *vt*: **to ~ sb to do sth** jdn drängen, etw zu tun; **urgent, urgently** ['ɜːdʒənt, -lɪ] *adj, adv* dringend

urine ['jʊərɪn] *n* Urin *m*

us [ʌs] *pron* uns; **do they know ~?** kennen sie uns?; **can he help ~?** kann er uns helfen?; **it's ~** wir sind's; **both of ~** wir beide

US, USA *nsing abbr* = **United States (of America)** USA *pl*

use [juːs] *n* (*using*) Gebrauch *m*; (*for specific purpose*) Benutzung *f*; **to make ~ of** Gebrauch machen von; **in/out of ~** in/außer Gebrauch; **it's no ~** (*doing that*) es hat keinen Zweck(, das zu tun); **it's (of) no ~ to me** das kann ich nicht brauchen ▷ [juːz] *vt* benutzen, gebrauchen; (*for specific purpose*) verwenden; (*method*) anwenden; **use up** *vt* aufbrauchen

used [juːzd] *adj* (*secondhand*) gebraucht ▷ *vb aux*: **to be ~d to sb/sth** an jdn/etw gewöhnt sein; **to get ~d to sb/sth** sich an jdn/etw gewöhnen; **she ~d to live here** sie hat früher mal hier gewohnt; **useful** *adj* nützlich; **useless** *adj* nutzlos; (*unusable*) unbrauchbar; (*pointless*) zwecklos; **user** ['juːzə*] *n* Benutzer(in) *m(f)*;

user-friendly *adj*
benutzerfreundlich
usual ['juːʒʊəl] *adj* üblich,
gewöhnlich; **as ~** wie üblich;
usually *adv* normalerweise
utensil [juːˈtensl] *n* Gerät *nt*
uterus ['juːtərəs] *n* Gebärmutter
f
utilize ['juːtɪlaɪz] *vt* verwenden
utmost ['ʌtməʊst] *adj* äußerst;
to do one's ~ sein Möglichstes
tun
utter ['ʌtə*] *adj* völlig ▷ *vt* von
sich geben; **utterly** *adv* völlig
U-turn ['juːtɜːn] *n* (*Auto*) Wende
f; **to do a ~** wenden; (*fig*) eine
Kehrtwendung machen

vacancy ['veɪkənsɪ] *n* (*job*)
offene Stelle; (*room*) freies Zimmer;
vacant ['veɪkənt] *adj* (*room,
toilet*) frei; (*post*) offen; (*building*)
leer stehend; **vacate** [vəˈkeɪt] *vt*
(*room, building*) räumen; (*seat*) frei
machen
vacation [vəˈkeɪʃən] *n* (*US*)
Ferien *pl*, Urlaub *m*; (*at university*)
(Semester)ferien *pl*; **to go on ~** in
Urlaub fahren; **~ course**
Ferienkurs *m*
vaccinate ['væksɪneɪt] *vt*
impfen; **vaccination**
[væksɪˈneɪʃən] *n* Impfung *f*; **~ card**
Impfpass *m*
vacuum ['vækjʊm] *n* Vakuum *nt*
▷ *vt, vi* (staub)saugen; **vacuum
(cleaner)** *n* Staubsauger *m*
vagina [vəˈdʒaɪnə] *n* Scheide *f*
vague [veɪɡ] *adj* (*imprecise*) vage;
(*resemblance*) entfernt; **vaguely**
adv in etwa, irgendwie

vain [veɪn] *adj* (*attempt*) vergeblich; (*conceited*) eitel; **in ~** vergeblich, umsonst; **vainly** *adv* (*in vain*) vergeblich

valentine (card) ['væləntaɪn(kɑːd)] *n* Valentinskarte *f*; **Valentine's Day** *n* Valentinstag *m*

valid ['vælɪd] *adj* (*ticket, passport etc*) gültig; (*argument*) stichhaltig; (*claim*) berechtigt

valley ['vælɪ] *n* Tal *nt*

valuable ['væljʊəbl] *adj* wertvoll; (*time*) kostbar; **valuables** *npl* Wertsachen *pl*

value ['væljuː] *n* Wert *m* ▷ *vt* (*appreciate*) schätzen; **value added tax** *n* Mehrwertsteuer *f*

valve [vælv] *n* Ventil *nt*

van [væn] *n* (*Auto*) Lieferwagen *m*

vanilla [vəˈnɪlə] *n* Vanille *f*

vanish [ˈvænɪʃ] *vi* verschwinden

vanity [ˈvænɪtɪ] *n* Eitelkeit *f*; **vanity case** *n* Schminkkoffer *m*

vapor (*US*), **vapour** [ˈveɪpə°] *n* (*mist*) Dunst *m*; (*steam*) Dampf *m*

variable [ˈvɛərɪəbl] *adj* (*weather, mood*) unbeständig; (*quality*) unterschiedlich; (*speed, height*) regulierbar; **varied** [ˈvɛərɪd] *adj* (*interests, selection*) vielseitig; (*career*) bewegt; (*work, diet*) abwechslungsreich; **variety** [vəˈraɪətɪ] *n* (*diversity*) Abwechslung *f*; (*assortment*) Vielfalt *f* (*of an +dat*); (*type*) Art *f*; **various** [ˈvɛərɪəs] *adj* verschieden

varnish [ˈvɑːnɪʃ] *n* Lack *m* ▷ *vt* lackieren

vary [ˈvɛərɪ] *vt* (*alter*) verändern ▷ *vi* (*be different*) unterschiedlich sein; (*fluctuate*) sich verändern; (*prices*) schwanken

vase [vɑːz, ?? veɪz] (*US*) *n* Vase *f*

vast [vɑːst] *adj* riesig; (*area*) weit

VAT [væt] *abbr* = **value added tax** Mehrwertsteuer *f*, MwSt.

Vatican [ˈvætɪkən] *n*: **the ~** der Vatikan

VCR [viːsiːˈɑː°] *abbr* = **video cassette recorder** Videorekorder *m*

VD [viːˈdiː] *abbr* = **venereal disease** Geschlechtskrankheit *f*

VDU [viːdiːˈjuː] *abbr* = **visual display unit**

veal [viːl] *n* Kalbfleisch *nt*

vegan [ˈviːgən] *n* Veganer(in) *m(f)*

vegetable [ˈvedʒtəbl] *n* Gemüse *nt*

vegetarian [vedʒɪˈtɛərɪən] *n* Vegetarier(in) *m(f)* ▷ *adj* vegetarisch

veggie [ˈvedʒɪ] *n* (*fam*) Vegetarier(in) *m(f)*; Gemüse *nt* ▷ *adj* vegetarisch; **veggieburger** *n* Veggieburger *m*, Gemüseburger *m*

vehicle [ˈviːɪkl] *n* Fahrzeug *nt*

veil [veɪl] *n* Schleier *m*

vein [veɪn] *n* Ader *f*

Velcro® [ˈvelkrəʊ] *n* Klettband *nt*

velvet [ˈvelvɪt] *n* Samt *m*

vending machine [ˈvendɪŋməʃiːn] *n* Automat *m*

venetian blind [vɪˈniːʃənˈblaɪnd] *n* Jalousie *f*

Venezuela [veneˈzweɪlə] *n* Venezuela *nt*

Venice [ˈvenɪs] *n* Venedig *nt*

venison [ˈvenɪsn] *n* Rehfleisch *nt*

vent [vent] *n* Öffnung *f*

ventilate [ˈventɪleɪt] *vt* lüften; **ventilation** [ventɪˈleɪʃən] *n* Belüftung *f*; **ventilator** [ˈventɪleɪtə°] *n* (*in room*) Ventilator *m*; **to be on a ~** (*Med*) künstlich beatmet werden

venture [ˈventʃə°] *n* (*project*)

Unternehmung f; (Comm)
Unternehmen nt ▷ vi (go) (sich)
wagen
venue ['venju:] n (for concert etc)
Veranstaltungsort m; (Sport)
Austragungsort m
verb [vɜ:b] n Verb nt; **verbal** adj
(agreement) mündlich; (skills)
sprachlich; **verbally** adv
mündlich
verdict ['vɜ:dɪkt] n Urteil nt
verge [vɜ:dʒ] n (of road)
(Straßen)rand m; **to be on the ~ of
doing sth** im Begriff sein, etw zu
tun ▷ vi: **to ~ on** grenzen an +akk
verification [verɪfɪ'keɪʃən] n
(confirmation) Bestätigung f;
(check) Überprüfung f; **verify**
['verɪfaɪ] vt (confirm) bestätigen;
(check) überprüfen
vermin ['vɜ:mɪn] npl Schädlinge
pl; (insects) Ungeziefer nt
verruca [ve'ru:kə] n Warze f
versatile ['vɜ:sətaɪl] adj
vielseitig
verse [vɜ:s] n (poetry) Poesie f;
(stanza) Strophe f
version ['vɜ:ʃən] n Version f
versus ['vɜ:səs] prep gegen
vertical ['vɜ:tɪkəl] adj senkrecht,
vertikal
very ['verɪ] adv sehr; **~ much** sehr
▷ adj: **the ~ book I need** genau
das Buch, das ich brauche; **at that
~ moment** gerade in dem
Augenblick; **at the ~ top** ganz
oben; **the ~ best** der/die/das
Allerbeste
vest [vest] n (Brit) Unterhemd nt;
(US: waistcoat) Weste f
vet [vet] n Tierarzt m, Tierärztin f
veto ['vi:təʊ] n (pl **-es**) Veto nt
▷ vt sein Veto einlegen gegen
VHF abbr = **very high frequency**
UKW
via ['vaɪə] prep über +akk
viable ['vaɪəbl] adj (plan)

realisierbar; (company) rentabel
vibrate [vaɪ'breɪt] vi vibrieren;
vibration [vaɪ'breɪʃən] n Vibration f
vicar ['vɪkə*] n Pfarrer(in) m(f)
vice [vaɪs] n (evil) Laster nt; (Tech)
Schraubstock m ▷ pref Vize-;
~-chairman stellvertretender
Vorsitzender; **~-president**
Vizepräsident(in) m(f)
vice versa ['vaɪs'vɜ:sə] adv
umgekehrt
vicinity [vɪ'sɪnɪtɪ] n: **in the ~** in
der Nähe (of +gen)
vicious ['vɪʃəs] adj (violent)
brutal; (malicious) gemein; **vicious
circle** n Teufelskreis m
victim ['vɪktɪm] n Opfer nt
Victorian [vɪk'tɔ:rɪən] adj
viktorianisch
victory ['vɪktərɪ] n Sieg m
video ['vɪdɪəʊ] (pl **-s**) adj Video-
▷ n Video nt; (recorder)
Videorekorder m ▷ vt (auf Video)
aufnehmen; **video camera** n
Videokamera f; **video cassette** n
Videokassette f; **video clip** n
Videoclip m; **video game** n
Videospiel nt; **video recorder** n
Videorekorder m; **video shop** n
Videothek f; **videotape** n
Videoband nt ▷ vt (auf Video)
aufnehmen
Vienna [vɪ'enə] n Wien nt
Vietnam [vjet'næm] n Vietnam
nt
view [vju:] n (sight) Blick m (of auf
+akk); (vista) Aussicht f; (opinion)
Ansicht f, Meinung f; **in ~ of**
angesichts +gen ▷ vt (situation,
event) betrachten; (house)
besichtigen; **viewer** n (for slides)
Diabetrachter m; (TV)
Zuschauer(in) m(f); **viewpoint** n
(fig) Standpunkt m
vigilant ['vɪdʒɪlənt] adj
wachsam

vile [vaɪl] *adj* abscheulich;
(*weather, food*) scheußlich
village [ˈvɪlɪdʒ] *n* Dorf *nt*;
villager *n* Dorfbewohner(in) *m(f)*
villain [ˈvɪlən] *n* Schurke *m*; (*in
film, story*) Bösewicht *m*
vine [vaɪn] *n* (Wein)rebe *f*
vinegar [ˈvɪnɪgəˈ] *n* Essig *m*
vineyard [ˈvɪnjəd] *n* Weinberg
m
vintage [ˈvɪntɪdʒ] *n* (*of wine*)
Jahrgang *m*; **vintage wine** *n* edler
Wein
vinyl [ˈvaɪnɪl] *n* Vinyl *nt*
viola [vɪˈəʊlə] *n* Bratsche *f*
violate [ˈvaɪəleɪt] *vt* (*treaty*)
brechen; (*rights, rule*) verletzen
violence [ˈvaɪələns] *n* (*brutality*)
Gewalt *f*; (*of person*)
Gewalttätigkeit *f*; **violent** *adj*
(*brutal*) brutal; (*death*) gewaltsam
violet [ˈvaɪələt] *n* Veilchen *nt*
violin [vaɪəˈlɪn] *n* Geige *f*, Violine
f
VIP *abbr* = **very important person**
VIP *mf*
virgin [ˈvɜːdʒɪn] *n* Jungfrau *f*
Virgo [ˈvɜːgəʊ] *n* (*Astr*) Jungfrau *f*
virile [ˈvɪraɪl] *adj* (*man*) männlich
virtual [ˈvɜːtjʊəl] *adj* (*Inform*)
virtuell; **virtually** *adv* praktisch;
virtual reality *n* virtuelle
Realität
virtue [ˈvɜːtjuː] *n* Tugend *f*; **by
~ of** aufgrund +*gen*; **virtuous**
[ˈvɜːtjʊəs] *adj* tugendhaft
virus [ˈvaɪrəs] *n* (*Med, Inform*)
Virus *m*
visa [ˈviːzə] *n* Visum *nt*
visibility [vɪzɪˈbɪlɪtɪ] *n* (*Meteo*)
Sichtweite *f*; **good/poor
~** gute/schlechte Sicht; **visible**
[ˈvɪzəbl] *adj* sichtbar; (*evident*)
sichtlich; **visibly** *adv* sichtlich
vision [ˈvɪʒən] *n* (*power of sight*)
Sehvermögen *nt*; (*foresight*)
Weitblick *m*; (*dream, image*) Vision *f*

visit [ˈvɪzɪt] *n* Besuch *m*; (*stay*)
Aufenthalt *m* ▷ *vt* besuchen;
visiting hours *npl* Besuchszeiten
pl; **visitor** *n* Besucher(in) *m(f)*; **~s'
book** Gästebuch *nt*; **visitor centre**
n Informationszentrum *nt*
visor [ˈvaɪzəˈ] *n* (*on helmet*) Visier
nt; (*Auto*) Blende *f*
visual [ˈvɪzjʊəl] *adj* Seh-; (*image,
joke*) visuell; **~ aid** *n*
Anschauungsmaterial *nt*;
~ display unit Monitor *m*;
visualize *vt* sich vorstelle;
visually *adv* visuell; **~ impaired**
sehbehindert
vital [ˈvaɪtl] *adj* (*essential*)
unerlässlich, wesentlich;
(*argument, moment*) entscheidend;
vitality [vaɪˈtælɪtɪ] *n* Vitalität *f*;
vitally *adv* äußerst
vitamin [ˈvɪtəmɪn] *n* Vitamin *nt*
vivacious [vɪˈveɪʃəs] *adj* lebhaft
vivid [ˈvɪvɪd] *adj* (*description*)
anschaulich; (*memory*) lebhaft;
(*colour*) leuchtend
V-neck [ˈviːnek] *n* V-Ausschnitt
m
vocabulary [vəʊˈkæbjʊlərɪ] *n*
Wortschatz *m*, Vokabular *nt*
vocal [ˈvəʊkəl] *adj* (*of the voice*)
Stimm-; (*group*) Gesangs-; (*protest,
person*) lautstark
vocation [vəʊˈkeɪʃən] *n* Berufung *f*; **vocational** *adj* Berufs-
vodka [ˈvɒdkə] *n* Wodka *m*
voice [vɔɪs] *n* Stimme *f* ▷ *vt*
äußern; **voice mail** *n* Voicemail *f*
void [vɔɪd] *n* Leere *f* ▷ *adj* (*Jur*)
ungültig; **~ of** (ganz) ohne
volcano [vɒlˈkeɪnəʊ] *n* (*pl* -**es**) *n*
Vulkan *m*
volley [ˈvɒlɪ] *n* (*Tennis*) Volley *m*;
volleyball *n* Volleyball *m*
volt [vəʊlt] *n* Volt *nt*; **voltage** *n*
Spannung *f*
volume [ˈvɒljuːm] *n* (*of sound*)
Lautstärke *f*; (*space occupied by sth*)

Volumen nt; (size, amount) Umfang m; (book) Band m; **volume control** n Lautstärkeregler m

voluntary, **voluntarily** ['vɒləntərɪ, -lɪ] adj, adv freiwillig; (unpaid) ehrenamtlich; **volunteer** [vɒlən'tɪə°] n Freiwillige(r) mf ▷ vi sich freiwillig melden ▷ vt: **to ~ to do sth** sich anbieten, etw zu tun

voluptuous [və'lʌptjʊəs] adj sinnlich

vomit ['vɒmɪt] vi sich übergeben

vote [vəʊt] n Stimme f; (ballot) Wahl f; (result) Abstimmungsergebnis nt; (right to vote) Wahlrecht nt ▷ vt (elect) wählen; **they ~d him chairman** sie wählten ihn zum Vorsitzenden ▷ vi wählen; **to ~ for/against sth** für/gegen etw stimmen; **voter** n Wähler(in) m(f)

voucher ['vaʊtʃə°] n Gutschein m

vow [vaʊ] n Gelöbnis nt ▷ vt: **~ to do sth** geloben, etw zu tun

vowel ['vaʊəl] n Vokal m

voyage ['vɔɪɪdʒ] n Reise f

vulgar ['vʌlgə°] adj vulgär, ordinär

vulnerable ['vʌlnərəbl] adj verwundbar; (sensitive) verletzlich

vulture ['vʌltʃə°] n Geier m

W abbr = **west** W

wade [weɪd] vi (in water) waten

wafer ['weɪfə°] n Waffel f; (Rel) Hostie f; **wafer-thin** adj hauchdünn

waffle ['wɒfl] n Waffel f; (Brit fam: empty talk) Geschwafel nt ▷ vi (Brit fam) schwafeln

wag [wæg] vt (tail) wedeln mit

wage [weɪdʒ] n Lohn m

waggon (Brit), **wagon** ['wægən] n (horse-drawn) Fuhrwerk nt; (Brit Rail) Waggon m; (US Auto) Wagen m

waist [weɪst] n Taille f; **waistcoat** n (Brit) Weste f; **waistline** n Taille f

wait [weɪt] n Wartezeit f ▷ vi warten (for auf +akk); **to ~ and see** abwarten; **~ a minute** Moment mal!; **wait up** vi aufbleiben

waiter n Kellner m; **~!** Herr Ober!

waiting n: **"no ~"** „Halteverbot";

waiting list n Warteliste f;
waiting room n (Med)
Wartezimmer nt; (Rail) Wartesaal
m
waitress n Kellnerin f
wake [weɪk] (**woke** o **waked,
woken** o **waked**) vt wecken ▷ vi
aufwachen; **wake up** vt
aufwecken ▷ vi aufwachen;
wake-up call n (Tel) Weckruf m
Wales ['weɪlz] n Wales nt
walk [wɔːk] n Spaziergang m;
(ramble) Wanderung f; (route) Weg
m; **to go for a ~** spazieren gehen;
it's only a five-minute ~ es sind
nur fünf Minuten zu Fuß ▷ vi
gehen; (stroll) spazieren gehen;
(ramble) wandern ▷ vt (dog)
ausführen; **walking** n: **to go
~** wandern; **walking shoes** npl
Wanderschuhe pl; **walking stick** n
Spazierstock m
Walkman® (pl -s) n Walkman®
m
wall [wɔːl] n (inside) Wand f;
(outside) Mauer f
wallet ['wɒlɪt] n Brieftasche
f
wallpaper ['wɔːlpeɪpə*] n
Tapete f, (Inform)
Bildschirmhintergrund m ▷ vt
tapezieren
walnut ['wɔːlnʌt] n (nut)
Walnuss f
waltz [wɔːlts] n Walzer m
wander ['wɒndə*] vi (person)
herumwandern
want [wɒnt] n (lack) Mangel m
(of an +dat); (need) Bedürfnis nt; **for
~ of** aus Mangel an +dat ▷ vt
(desire) wollen; (need) brauchen; **I
~ to stay here** ich will hier
bleiben; **he doesn't ~ to** er will
nicht
WAP phone ['wæpfəʊn] n
WAP-Handy nt
war [wɔː*] n Krieg m

ward [wɔːd] n (in hospital)
Station f; (child) Mündel nt
warden ['wɔːdən] n Aufseher(in)
m(f); (in youth hostel) Herbergsvater
m, Herbergsmutter f
wardrobe ['wɔːdrəʊb] n
Kleiderschrank m
warehouse ['wɛəhaʊs] n
Lagerhaus nt
warfare ['wɔːfɛə*] n Krieg m;
(techniques) Kriegsführung f
warm [wɔːm] adj warm;
(welcome) herzlich; **I'm ~** mir ist
warm ▷ vt wärmen; (food)
aufwärmen; **warm over** vt (US:
food) aufwärmen; **warm up** vt
(food) aufwärmen; (room)
erwärmen ▷ vi (food, room) warm
werden; (Sport) sich aufwärmen;
warmly adv warm; (welcome)
herzlich; **warmth** n Wärme f; (of
welcome) Herzlichkeit f
warn [wɔːn] vt warnen (of,
against vor +dat); **to ~ sb not to do
sth** jdn davor warnen, etw zu tun;
warning n Warnung f; **warning
light** h Warnlicht nt; **warning
triangle** n (Auto) Warndreieck nt
warranty ['wɒrəntɪ] n Garantie
f
wart [wɔːt] n Warze f
wary ['wɛərɪ] adj vorsichtig;
(suspicious) misstrauisch
was [wɒz, wəz] pt of **be**
wash [wɒʃ] n: **to have a ~** sich
waschen; **it's in the ~** es ist in der
Wäsche ▷ vt waschen; (plates,
glasses etc) abwaschen; **to ~ one's
hands** sich dat die Hände
waschen; **to ~ the dishes** (das
Geschirr) abwaschen ▷ vi (clean
oneself) sich waschen; **wash off** vt
abwaschen; **wash up** vi (Brit:
wash dishes) abwaschen; (US: clean
oneself) sich waschen; **washable**
adj waschbar; **washbag** n (US)
Kulturbeutel m; **washbasin** n

Waschbecken nt; **washcloth** n (US) Waschlappen m; **washer** n (Tech) Dichtungsring m; (washing machine) Waschmaschine f; **washing** n (laundry) Wäsche f; **washing machine** n Waschmaschine f; **washing powder** n Waschpulver nt; **washing-up** n (Brit) Abwasch m; **to do the ~** abwaschen; **washing-up liquid** n (Brit) Spülmittel nt; **washroom** n (US) Toilette f

wasn't ['wɒznt] contr of was not
wasp [wɒsp] n Wespe f
waste [weɪst] n (materials) Abfall m; (wasting) Verschwendung f; **it's a ~ of time** das ist Zeitverschwendung ▷ adj (superfluous) überschüssig ▷ vt verschwenden (on an +akk); (opportunity) vertun; **waste bin** n Abfalleimer m; **wastepaper basket** n Papierkorb m
watch [wɒtʃ] n (timepiece) (Armband)uhr f ▷ vt (observe) beobachten; (guard) aufpassen auf +akk; (film, play, programme) sich dat ansehen; **to ~ TV** fernsehen ▷ vi zusehen; (guard) Wache halten; **to ~ for sb/sth** nach jdm/etw Ausschau halten; **~ out** pass auf! **watchdog** n Wachhund m; (fig) Aufsichtsbehörde f; **watchful** adj wachsam
water ['wɔːtə°] n Wasser nt ▷ vt (plant) gießen ▷ vi (eye) tränen; **my mouth is ~ing** mir läuft das Wasser im Mund zusammen; **water down** vt verdünnen; **watercolor** (US), **watercolour** n (painting) Aquarell nt; (paint) Wasserfarbe f; **watercress** n (Brunnen)kresse f; **waterfall** n Wasserfall m; **watering can** n Gießkanne f; **water level** n

Wasserstand m; **watermelon** n Wassermelone f; **waterproof** adj wasserdicht; **water-skiing** n Wasserskilaufen nt; **water sports** npl Wassersport m; **watertight** adj wasserdicht; **water wings** npl Schwimmflügel pl; **watery** adj wässerig
wave [weɪv] n Welle f ▷ vt (move to and fro) schwenken; (hand, flag) winken mit ▷ vi (person) winken; (flag) wehen; **wavelength** n Wellenlänge f; **to be on the same ~** (fig) die gleiche Wellenlänge haben; **wavy** ['weɪvɪ] adj wellig
wax [wæks] n Wachs nt; (in ear) Ohrenschmalz m
way [weɪ] n Weg m; (direction) Richtung f; (manner) Art f; **can you tell me the ~ to ... ?** wie komme ich (am besten) zu ... ?; **we went the wrong ~** wir sind in die falsche Richtung gefahren/gegangen; **to lose one's ~** sich verirren; **to make ~ for sb/sth** jdm/etw Platz machen; **to get one's own ~** seinen Willen durchsetzen; **"give ~"** (Auto) „Vorfahrt achten"; **the other ~ round** andersherum; **one ~ or another** irgendwie; **in a ~** in gewisser Weise; **in the ~** im Weg; **by the ~** übrigens; **"~ in"** „Eingang"; **"~ out"** „Ausgang"; **no ~** (fam) kommt nicht infrage!
we [wiː] pron wir
weak [wiːk] adj schwach; **weaken** vt schwächen ▷ vi schwächer werden
wealth [welθ] n Reichtum m; **wealthy** adj reich
weapon ['wepən] n Waffe f
wear [weə°] (wore, worn) vt (have on) tragen; **what shall I ~?** was soll ich anziehen? ▷ vi (become worn) sich abnutzen ▷ n: **~ (and tear)** Abnutzung f; **wear**

off vi (diminish) nachlassen; **wear out** vt abnutzen; (person) erschöpfen ▷ vi sich abnutzen

weather ['weðə*] n Wetter nt; **I'm feeling under the ~** ich fühle mich nicht ganz wohl; **weather forecast** n Wettervorhersage f

weave [wi:v] (**wove** o **weaved, woven** o **weaved**) vt (cloth) weben; (basket etc) flechten

web [web] n (a. fig) Netz nt; **the Web** das Web, das Internet; **webcam** ['webkæm] n Webcam f; **web page** n Webseite f; **website** n Website f

we'd [wi:d] contr of **we had; we would**

Wed abbr = **Wednesday** Mi.

wedding ['wedɪŋ] n Hochzeit f; **wedding anniversary** n Hochzeitstag m; **wedding dress** n Hochzeitskleid nt; **wedding ring** n Ehering m

wedding shower n (US) Party für die zukünftige Braut

wedge [wedʒ] n (under door etc) Keil m; (of cheese etc) Stück nt, Ecke f

Wednesday ['wenzdeɪ] n Mittwoch m; see also **Tuesday**

wee [wi:] adj klein ▷ vi (fam) Pipi machen

weed [wi:d] n Unkraut nt ▷ vt jäten

week [wi:k] n Woche f; **twice a ~** zweimal in der Woche; **a ~ on Friday/Friday ~** Freitag in einer Woche; **a ~ last Friday** letzten Freitag vor einer Woche; **in two ~s' time, in two ~s** in zwei Wochen; **for ~s** wochenlang; **weekday** n Wochentag m; **weekend** n Wochenende nt; **weekend break** n Wochenendurlaub m; **weekly** adj, adv wöchentlich; (magazine) Wochen-

weep [wi:p] (**wept, wept**) vi weinen

weigh [weɪ] vt, vi wiegen; **it ~s 20 kilos** es wiegt 20 Kilo; **weigh up** vt abwägen; (person) einschätzen; **weight** [weɪt] n Gewicht nt; **to lose/put on ~** abnehmen/zunehmen; **weightlifting** n Gewichtheben nt; **weight training** n Krafttraining nt; **weighty** adj (important) schwerwiegend

weird [wɪəd] adj seltsam; **weirdo** ['wɪədəʊ] n Spinner(in) m(f)

welcome ['welkəm] n Empfang m ▷ adj willkommen; (news) angenehm; **~ to London** willkommen in London! ▷ vt begrüßen; **welcoming** adj freundlich

welfare ['welfɛə*] n Wohl nt; (US: social security) Sozialhilfe f; **welfare state** n Wohlfahrtsstaat m

well [wel] n Brunnen m ▷ adj (in good health) gesund; **are you ~?** geht es dir/Ihnen gut?; **to feel ~** sich wohlfühlen; **get ~ soon** gute Besserung! ▷ interj nun; **~, I don't know** nun, ich weiß nicht ▷ adv gut; **~ done** gut gemacht!; **it may ~ be** das kann wohl sein; **as ~** (in addition) auch; **~ over 60** weit über 60

we'll [wi:l] contr of **we will; we shall**

well-behaved [welbɪ'heɪvd] adj brav; **well-being** n Wohl nt; **well-built** adj (person) gut gebaut; **well-done** adj (steak) durchgebraten; **well-earned** adj wohlverdient

wellingtons ['welɪŋtənz] npl Gummistiefel pl

well-known [wel'nəʊn] adj bekannt; **well-off** adj (wealthy)

wohlhabend; **well-paid** adj gut
bezahlt

Welsh [welʃ] adj walisisch ▷ n
(language) Walisisch nt; **the ~** pl die
Waliser pl; **Welshman** (pl **-men**) n
Waliser m; **Welshwoman** (pl
-women) n Waliserin f

went [went] pt of **go**

wept [wept] pt, pp of **weep**

were [wɜː] pt of **be**

we're [wɪə*] contr of **we are**

weren't [wɜːnt] contr of **were not**

west [west] n Westen m; **the
West** (Pol) der Westen ▷ adv (go,
face) nach Westen ▷ adj West-;
westbound adj (in) Richtung
Westen; **western** adj
West-, westlich; **Western Europe**
Westeuropa nt ▷ n (Cine) Western
m; **West Germany** n: (**the
former**) **~** (das ehemalige)
Westdeutschland,
Westdeutschland n; **westwards**
['westwədz] adv nach Westen

wet [wet] (**wet, wet**) vt: **to
~ oneself** in die Hose machen
▷ adj nass, feucht; **"~ paint"**
„frisch gestrichen"; **wet suit** n
Taucheranzug m

we've [wiːv] contr of **we have**

whale [weɪl] n Wal m

wharf [wɔːf] (pl **-s** o **wharves**) n
Kai m

KEYWORD

what [wɒt] adj **1** (in questions)
welche(r, s) was für ein(e);
what size is it? welche Größe ist
das?
2 (in exclamations) was für ein(e);
what a mess! was für ein
Durcheinander!
▷ pron (interrogative/relative) was;
what are you doing? was machst
du/machen Sie gerade?; **what are
you talking about?** wovon redest

du/reden Sie?; **what's your
name?** wie heißt du/heißen Sie?;
what is it called? wie heißt das?;
what about …? wie wär's mit …?;
I saw what you did ich habe
gesehen, was du gemacht
hast/Sie gemacht haben
▷ excl (disbelieving) wie, was;
what, no coffee! wie, kein
Kaffee?; **I've crashed the car —
what!** ich hatte einen
Autounfall — was!

whatever pron: **I'll do ~ you
want** ich tue alles, was du
willst/Sie wollen; **~ he says** egal,
was er sagt

what's [wɒts] contr of **what is;
what has**

wheat [wiːt] n Weizen m

wheel [wiːl] n Rad nt; (steering
wheel) Lenkrad nt ▷ vt (bicycle,
trolley) schieben; **wheelbarrow** n
Schubkarren m; **wheelchair** n
Rollstuhl m; **wheel clamp** n
Parkkralle f

KEYWORD

when [wen] adv wann
▷ conj **1** (at, during, after the time
that) wenn; (in past) als; **she was
reading when I came in** sie las,
als ich hereinkam; **be careful
when you cross the road** sei
vorsichtig, wenn du über die
Straße gehst/seien Sie vorsichtig,
wenn Sie über die Straße gehen
2 (on, at which) als; **on the day
when I met him** an dem Tag, an
dem ich ihn traf
3 (whereas) wo … doch

whenever adv (every time) immer
wenn; **come ~ you like** komm,
wann immer du willst/kommen
Sie, wann immer sie wollen

᠆here [wɛə*] adv wo; **~ are you
going?** wohin gehst du/gehen
Sie?; **~ are you from?** woher
kommst du/kommen Sie? ▷ conj
wo; **that's ~ I used to live** da habe
ich früher gewohnt; **whereabouts**
[wɛərə'baʊts] adv wo ▷ npl
['wɛərəbaʊts] Aufenthaltsort
m; **whereas** [wɛər'æz] conj
während, wohingegen; **whereby**
adv wodurch; **wherever**
[wɛər'evə*] conj wo immer;
~ that may be wo immer das sein
mag; **~ I go** überall, wohin ich
gehe

whether ['wɛðə*] conj ob

○ **KEYWORD**

which [wɪtʃ] adj **1** (interrogative)
(direct, indirect) welche(r, s); **which
one?** welche(r, s)?
2 in which case in diesem Fall; **by
which time** zu dieser Zeit
▷ pron **1** (interrogative) welche(r, s);
(of people also) wer
2 (relative) der/die/das; (referring to
people) was; **the apple which you
ate/which is on the table** der
Apfel, den du gegessen hast/der
auf dem Tisch liegt; **he said he
saw her, which is true** er sagte, er
habe sie gesehen, was auch
stimmt

whichever adj, pron welche(r, s)
auch immer

while [waɪl] n: **a ~** eine Weile; **for
a ~** eine Zeit lang; **a short ~ ago**
vor Kurzem ▷ conj während;
(although) obwohl

whine [waɪn] vi (person)
jammern

whip [wɪp] n Peitsche f ▷ vt
(beat) peitschen; **~ped cream**
Schlagsahne f

whirl [wɜːl] vt, vi herumwirbeln;

whirlpool n (in river, sea) Strudel
m; (pool) Whirlpool m

whisk [wɪsk] n Schneebesen m
▷ vt (cream etc) schlagen

whisker ['wɪskə*] n (of animal)
Schnurrhaar nt; **~s** pl (of man)
Backenbart m

whisk(e)y ['wɪski] n Whisky m

whisper ['wɪspə*] vi, vt flüstern;
to ~ sth to sb jdm etw zuflüstern

whistle ['wɪsl] n Pfiff m;
(instrument) Pfeife f ▷ vt, vi pfeifen

white [waɪt] n (of egg) Eiweiß nt;
(of eye) Weiße nt ▷ adj weiß; (with
fear) blass; (coffee) mit
Milch/Sahne; **White House** n:
the ~ das Weiße Haus; **white lie** n
Notlüge f; **white meat** n helles
Fleisch; **white sauce** n weiße
Soße; **white water rafting** n
Rafting nt; **white wine** n
Weißwein m

Whitsun ['wɪtsn] n Pfingsten
nt

○ **KEYWORD**

who [huː] pron **1** (interrogative)
wer; (akk) wen; (dat) wem; **who is
it?, who's there?** wer ist da?
2 (relative) der/die/das; **the
woman/man who spoke to me**
die Frau/der Mann, die/der mit
mir sprach

whoever [huː'evə*] pron wer
auch immer; **~ you choose** wen
auch immer du wählst/Sie wählen

whole [həʊl] adj ganz ▷ n Gan-
ze(s) nt; **the ~ of my family** meine
ganze Familie; **on the ~** im Großen
und Ganzen; **wholefood** n (Brit)
Vollwertkost f; **~ store** Bioladen m;
wholeheartedly adv voll und
ganz; **wholemeal** adj (Brit)
Vollkorn-; **wholesale** adv (buy,
sell) im Großhandel; **wholesome**

adj gesund; **whole wheat** adj
Vollkorn-; **wholly** ['həʊlɪ] adv
völlig

○ **KEYWORD**

whom [hu:m] pron **1**
(interrogative) (akk) wen; (dat) wem;
whom did you see? wen hast
du/haben Sie gesehen?; **to whom
did you give it?** wem hast
du/haben Sie es gegeben?
2 (relative) (akk) den/die/das; (dat)
dem/der/dem; **the man whom
I saw/to whom I spoke** der
Mann, den ich sah/mit dem ich
sprach

whooping cough ['hu:pɪŋkɒf]
n Keuchhusten m
whose [hu:z] adj (in questions)
wessen; (in relative clauses)
dessen/deren/dessen, deren pl;
~ bike is that? wessen Fahrrad ist
das? ▷ pron (in questions) wessen;
~ is this? wem gehört das?

○ **KEYWORD**

why [waɪ] adv warum, weshalb
▷ conj warum, weshalb; **that's
not why I'm here** ich bin nicht
deswegen hier; **that's the reason
why** deshalb
▷ excl (expressing surprise, shock) na
so was; (explaining) also dann;
why, it's you! na so was, du
bist/Sie sind es!

wicked ['wɪkɪd] adj böse; (fam:
great) geil
wide [waɪd] adj breit; (skirt,
trousers) weit; (selection) groß
▷ adv weit; **wide-angle lens** n
Weitwinkelobjektiv nt;
wide-awake adj hellwach;
widely adv weit; **~ known**

allgemein bekannt; **widen** vt
verbreitern; (fig) erweitern;
wide-open adj weit offen;
widescreen TV n
Breitbildfernseher m; **widespread**
adj weit verbreitet
widow ['wɪdəʊ] n Witwe f;
widowed adj verwitwet;
widower n Witwer m
width [wɪdθ] n Breite f
wife [waɪf] (pl **wives**) n
(Ehe)frau f
wig [wɪg] n Perücke f
wiggle ['wɪgl] vt wackeln mit
wild [waɪld] adj wild; (violent)
heftig; (plan, idea) verrückt ▷ n: **in
the ~** in freier Wildbahn; **wildlife**
n Tier- und Pflanzenwelt f; **wildly**
adv wild; (exaggerated) maßlos

○ **KEYWORD**

will [wɪl] vb aux **1** (forms future
tense) werden; **I will finish it
tomorrow** ich mache es morgen
zu Ende
2 (in conjectures, predictions) **he will**
o **he'll be there by now** er dürfte
jetzt da sein; **that will be the
postman** das wird der Postbote
sein
3 (in commands, requests, offers) **will
you be quiet!** sei/seien Sie
endlich still!; **will you help me?**
hilfst du/helfen Sie mir?; **will you
have a cup of tea?** trinkst
du/trinken Sie eine Tasse Tee?; **I
won't put up with it!** das lasse ich
mir nicht gefallen!
▷ vt wollen
▷ n Wille m; (jur) Testament
nt

willing adj bereitwillig; **to be ~ to
do sth** bereit sein, etw zu tun;
willingly adv gern(e)
willow ['wɪləʊ] n Weide f

willpower ['wɪlpaʊə*] n Willenskraft f
wimp [wɪmp] n Weichei nt
win [wɪn] **(won, won)** vt, vi gewinnen ▷ n Sieg m; **win over**, **win round** vt für sich gewinnen
wind [waɪnd] **(wound, wound)** vt (rope, bandage) wickeln; **wind down** vt (car window) herunterkurbeln; **wind up** vt (clock) aufziehen; (car window) hochkurbeln; (meeting, speech) abschließen; (person) aufziehen, ärgern
wind [wɪnd] n Wind m; (Med) Blähungen pl
wind instrument ['wɪndɪnstrʊmənt] n Blasinstrument nt; **windmill** n Windmühle f
window ['wɪndəʊ] n Fenster nt; (counter) Schalter m; **~ of opportunity** Chance f, Gelegenheit f; **window box** n Blumenkasten m; **windowpane** n Fensterscheibe f; **window-shopping** n: **to go ~** einen Schaufensterbummel machen; **windowsill** n Fensterbrett nt
windpipe ['wɪndpaɪp] n Luftröhre f; **windscreen** n (Brit) Windschutzscheibe f; **windscreen wiper** n (Brit) Scheibenwischer m; **windshield** n (US) Windschutzscheibe f; **windshield wiper** n (US) Scheibenwischer m; **windsurfer** n Windsurfer(in) m(f); (board) Surfbrett nt; **windsurfing** n Windsurfen nt
windy ['wɪndɪ] adj windig
wine [waɪn] n Wein m; **wine bar** n Weinlokal nt; **wineglass** n Weinglas nt; **wine list** n Weinkarte f; **wine tasting** n (event) Weinprobe f

wing [wɪŋ] n Flügel m; (Brit Auto) Kotflügel m; **~s** pl (Theat) Kulissen pl
wink [wɪŋk] vi zwinkern; **to ~ at sb** jdm zuzwinkern
winner ['wɪnə*] n Gewinner(in) m(f); (Sport) Sieger(in) m(f); **winning** adj (team, horse etc) siegreich; **~ number** Gewinnzahl f ▷ n **~s** pl Gewinn m
winter ['wɪntə*] n Winter m; **winter sports** npl Wintersport m; **wint(e)ry** ['wɪntrɪ] adj winterlich
wipe [waɪp] vt abwischen; **to ~ one's nose** sich dat die Nase putzen; **to ~ one's feet** (on mat) sich dat die Schuhe abtreten; **wipe off** vt abwischen; **wipe out** vt (destroy) vernichten; (data, debt) löschen; (epidemic etc) ausrotten
wire ['waɪə*] n Draht m; (Elec) Leitung f; (US: telegram) Telegramm nt ▷ vt (plug in) anschließen; (US Tel) telegrafieren (sb sth jdm etw); **wireless** ['waɪələs] adj drahtlos
wisdom ['wɪzdəm] n Weisheit f; **wisdom tooth** n Weisheitszahn m
wise, **wisely** [waɪz, -lɪ] adj, adv weise
wish [wɪʃ] n Wunsch m (for nach); **with best ~es** (in letter) herzliche Grüße ▷ vt wünschen, wollen; **to ~ sb good luck/Merry Christmas** jdm viel Glück/frohe Weihnachten wünschen; **I ~ I'd never seen him** ich wünschte, ich hätte ihn nie gesehen
witch [wɪtʃ] n Hexe f

⭕ **KEYWORD**

with [wɪð] prep **1** (accompanying, in the company of) mit; **we stayed with friends** wir übernachteten bei Freunden; **I'll be with you in a minute** einen Augenblick, ich bin sofort da; **I'm not with you** (I don't understand) das verstehe ich nicht; **to be with it** (inf) (up-to-date) auf dem Laufenden sein; (alert) (voll) da sein inf

2 (descriptive, indicating manner etc) mit; **the man with the grey hat** der Mann mit dem grauen Hut; **red with anger** rot vor Wut

withdraw [wɪð'drɔ:] irr vt zurückziehen; (money) abheben; (comment) zurücknehmen ▷ vi sich zurückziehen

wither ['wɪðə*] vi (plant) verwelken

withhold [wɪð'həʊld] irr vt vorenthalten (from sb jdm)

within [wɪð'ɪn] prep innerhalb +gen; **~ walking distance** zu Fuß erreichbar

without [wɪð'aʊt] prep ohne; **~ asking** ohne zu fragen

withstand [wɪð'stænd] irr vt standhalten +dat

witness ['wɪtnəs] n Zeuge m, Zeugin f ▷ vt Zeuge sein; **witness box, witness stand** (US) n Zeugenstand m

witty ['wɪtɪ] adj geistreich

wives ['waɪvz] pl of **wife**

WMD abbr = **weapon of mass destruction** Massenvernichtungswaffe

wobble ['wɒbl] vi wackeln; **wobbly** adj wackelig

wok [wɒk] n Wok m

woke [wəʊk] pt of **wake**

woken ['wəʊkn] pp of **wake**

wolf [wʊlf] n (pl **wolves**) n Wolf m

woman ['wʊmən] n (pl **women**) Frau f

womb [wu:m] n Gebärmutter f

women ['wɪmɪn] pl of **woman**

won [wʌn] pt, pp of **win**

wonder ['wʌndə*] n (marvel) Wunder nt; (surprise) Staunen nt ▷ vt, vi (speculate) sich fragen; **I ~ what/if ...** ich frage mich, was/ob ...; **wonderful** adj, adv wunderbar

won't [wəʊnt] contr of **will not**

wood [wʊd] n Holz nt; **~s** Wald m; **wooden** adj Holz-; (fig) hölzern; **woodpecker** n Specht m; **woodwork** n (wooden parts) Holzteile pl; (in school) Werken nt

wool [wʊl] n Wolle f; **woollen, woolen** (US) adj Woll-

word [wɜ:d] n Wort nt; (promise) Ehrenwort nt; **~s** pl (of song) Text m; **to have a ~ with sb** mit jdm sprechen; **in other ~s** mit anderen Worten ▷ vt formulieren; **wording** n Wortlaut m, Formulierung f; **word processing** n Textverarbeitung f; **word processor** n (program) Textverarbeitungsprogramm nt

wore [wɔ:*] pt of **wear**

work [wɜ:k] n Arbeit f; (of art, literature) Werk nt; **~ of art** Kunstwerk nt; **he's at ~** er ist in/auf der Arbeit; **out of ~** arbeitslos ▷ vi arbeiten (at, on an +dat); (machine, plan) funktionieren; (medicine) wirken; (succeed) klappen ▷ vt (machine) bedienen; **work out** vi (plan) klappen; (sum) aufgehen; (person) trainieren ▷ vt (price, speed etc) ausrechnen; (plan) ausarbeiten; **work up** vt: **to get worked up** sich aufregen; **workaholic** [wɜ:kə'hɒlɪk] n Arbeitstier nt; **worker** n Arbeiter(in) m(f); **working class** n Arbeiterklasse f; **workman** (pl **-men**) n Handwerker m; **workout** n (Sport) Fitnesstraining nt, Konditionstraining nt; **work permit** n Arbeitserlaubnis f;

workplace n Arbeitsplatz m;
workshop n Werkstatt f;
(meeting) Workshop m; **work
station** n (Inform) Workstation
f

world [wɜːld] n Welt f; **world
championship** n Weltmeisterschaft f; **World War** n: ~ I/II, the
First/Second ~ der Erste/Zweite
Weltkrieg; **world-wide** adj, adv
weltweit; **World Wide Web** n
World Wide Web nt

worm [wɜːm] n Wurm m

worn [wɔːn] pp of **wear** ▷ adj
(clothes) abgetragen; (tyre)
abgefahren; **worn-out** adj
abgenutzt; (person) erschöpft

worried ['wʌrɪd] adj besorgt; **be
~ about** sich dat Sorgen machen
um; **worry** ['wʌrɪ] n Sorge f ▷ vt
Sorgen machen +dat ▷ vi sich
Sorgen machen (about um); **don't
~!** keine Sorge!; **worrying** adj
beunruhigend

worse [wɜːs] adj comparative of
bad; schlechter; (pain, mistake etc)
schlimmer ▷ adv comparative of
badly; schlechter; **worsen** vt
verschlechtern ▷ vi sich
verschlechtern

worship ['wɜːʃɪp] vt anbeten,
anhimmeln

worst [wɜːst] adj superlative of
bad; schlechteste(r, s); (pain,
mistake etc) schlimmste(r, s) ▷ adv
superlative of **badly**; am
schlechtesten ▷ n: **the ~ is over**
das Schlimmste ist vorbei; **at (the)
~** schlimmstenfalls

worth [wɜːθ] n Wert m; **£10 ~ of
food** Essen für 10 Pfund ▷ adj: **it is
~ £50** es ist 50 Pfund wert;
~ seeing sehenswert; **it's ~ it**
(rewarding) es lohnt sich;
worthless adj wertlos;
worthwhile adj lohnend,
lohnenswert; **worthy** ['wɜːðɪ]

adj (deserving respect) würdig; **to
be ~ of sth** etw verdienen

○ **KEYWORD**

would [wʊd] vb aux 1 (conditional
tense) **if you asked him he would
do it** wenn du ihn fragtest/Sie ihn
fragten, würde er es tun; **if you
had asked him he would have
done it** wenn du ihn gefragt
hättest/Sie ihn gefragt hätten,
hätte er es getan
2 (in offers, invitations, requests)
would you like a biscuit?
möchtest du/möchten Sie einen
Keks?; **would you ask him to
come in?** würdest du/würden Sie
ihn bitte hereinbitten?
3 (in indirect speech) **I said I would
do it** ich sagte, ich würde es tun
4 (emphatic) **it WOULD have to
snow today!** es musste ja
ausgerechnet heute schneien!
5 (insistence) **she wouldn't behave**
sie wollte sich partout nicht
anständig benehmen
6 (conjecture) **it would have been
midnight** es mag ungefähr
Mitternacht gewesen sein; **it
would seem so** es sieht wohl so
aus
7 (indicating habit) **he would go
there on Mondays** er ging jeden
Montag dorthin

wouldn't ['wʊdnt] contr of
would not
would've ['wʊdəv] contr of
would have
wound [wuːnd] n Wunde f ▷ vt
verwunden; (fig) verletzen
▷ [waʊnd] pt, pp of **wind**
wove [wəʊv] pt of **weave**
woven ['wəʊvn] pp of **weave**
wrap [ræp] vt (parcel, present)
einwickeln; **to ~ sth round sth**

etw um etw wickeln; **wrap up** vt
(parcel, present) einwickeln ▷ vi
(dress warmly) sich warm anziehen;
wrapper n (of sweet) Papier nt;
wrapping paper n Packpapier nt;
(giftwrap) Geschenkpapier nt
wreath [riːθ] n Kranz m
wreck [rek] n (ship, plane, car)
Wrack nt; **a nervous ~** ein
Nervenbündel m ▷ vt (car) zu
Schrott fahren; (fig) zerstören;
wreckage ['rekɪdʒ] n Trümmer pl
wrench [rentʃ] n (tool)
Schraubenschlüssel m
wrestling ['reslɪŋ] n Ringen nt
wring out ['rɪŋ'aʊt] (**wrung,
wrung**) vt auswringen
wrinkle ['rɪŋkl] n Falte f
wrist [rɪst] n Handgelenk nt;
wristwatch n Armbanduhr f
write [raɪt] (**wrote, written**) vt
schreiben; (cheque) ausstellen ▷ vi
schreiben; **to ~ to sb** jdm
schreiben; **write down** vt
aufschreiben; **write off** vt (debt,
person) abschreiben; (car) zu
Schrott fahren ▷ vi: **to ~ off for
sth** etw anfordern; **write out** vt
(name etc) ausschreiben; (cheque)
ausstellen; **write-protected** adj
(Inform) schreibgeschützt; **writer**
n Verfasser(in) m(f); (author)
Schriftsteller(in) m(f); **writing** n
Schrift f; (profession) Schreiben nt;
in ~ schriftlich; **writing paper** n
Schreibpapier nt
written ['rɪtən] pp of **write**
wrong [rɒŋ] adj (incorrect) falsch;
(morally) unrecht; **you're ~** du
hast/Sie haben unrecht; **what's
~ with your leg?** was ist mit
deinem/Ihrem Bein los?; **you've
got the ~ number** du bist/Sie sind
falsch verbunden; **I dialled the
~ number** ich habe mich
verwählt; **don't get me
~** versteh/verstehen Sie mich

nicht falsch; **to go ~** (plan)
schiefgehen; **wrongly** adv falsch;
(unjustly) zu Unrecht
wrote [rəʊt] pt of **write**
WWW abbr = **World Wide Web**
WWW

xenophobia [zenə'fəubɪə] *n*
Ausländerfeindlichkeit *f*
XL *abbr* = **extra large** XL, übergroß
Xmas ['krɪsməs] *n* Weihnachten
nt
X-ray ['eksreɪ] *n* (*picture*)
Röntgenaufnahme *f* ▷ *vt* röntgen
xylophone ['zaɪləfəun] *n* Xylo

yacht [jɒt] *n* Jacht *f*; **yachting** *n*
Segeln *nt*; **to go ~** segeln gehen
yam [jæm] *n* (*US*) Süßkartoffel
f
yard [jɑːd] *n* Hof *m*; (*US: garden*)
Garten *m*; (*measure*) Yard *nt* (0,91 m)
yawn [jɔːn] *vi* gähnen
yd *abbr* = **yard(s)**
year ['jɪə*] *n* Jahr *nt*; **this/last/
next ~** dieses/letztes/nächstes
Jahr; **he is 28 ~s old** er ist 28 Jahre
alt; **~s ago** vor Jahren; **a
five-year-old** ein(e)
Fünfjährige(r); **yearly** *adj, adv*
jährlich
yearn [jɜːn] *vi* sich sehnen (*for*
nach +*dat*); **to ~ to do sth** sich
danach sehnen, etw zu tun
yeast [jiːst] *n* Hefe *f*
yell [jel] *vi, vt* schreien; **to ~ at sb**
jdn anschreien
yellow ['jeləu] *adj* gelb; **~ card**

(*Sport*) gelbe Karte; **~ fever** Gelbfieber *nt*; **~ line** (*Brit*) ≈ Halteverbot *nt*; **double ~ line** (*Brit*) ≈ absolutes Halteverbot; **the Yellow Pages®** *pl* die Gelben Seiten *pl*

yes [jes] *adv* ja; (*answering negative question*) doch; **to say ~ to sth** ja zu etw sagen ▷ *n* Ja *nt*

yesterday ['jestədeɪ] *adv* gestern; **~ morning/evening** gestern Morgen/Abend; **the day before ~** vorgestern; **~'s newspaper** die Zeitung von gestern

yet [jet] *adv* (*still*) noch; (*up to now*) bis jetzt; (*in a question: already*) schon; **he hasn't arrived ~** er ist noch nicht gekommen; **have you finished ~?** bist du/sind Sie schon fertig?; **~ again** schon wieder; **as ~** bis jetzt ▷ *conj* doch

yield [jiːld] *n* Ertrag *m* ▷ *vt* (*result, crop*) hervorbringen; (*profit, interest*) bringen ▷ *vi* nachgeben (*to* +*dat*); (*Mil*) sich ergeben (*to* +*dat*); **"~"** (*US Auto*) „Vorfahrt beachten"

yoga ['jəʊgə] *n* Yoga *nt*

yog(h)urt ['jɒgət] *n* Jog(h)urt *m*

yolk [jəʊk] *n* Eigelb *nt*

Yorkshire pudding ['jɔːkʃəˈpʊdɪŋ] *n* gebackener Eierteig, der meist zum Roastbeef gegessen wird

 KEYWORD

you [juː] *pron* **1** (*subj, in comparisons*) (*familiar form*) (*sg*) du; (*pl*) ihr; (*in letters*) Du, Ihr; (*polite form*) Sie; **you Germans** ihr Deutschen; **she's younger than you** sie ist jünger als du/ihr/Sie **2** (*direct object, after prep* +*akk*) (*familiar form*) (*sg*) dich; (*pl*) euch; (*in letters*) Dich, Euch; (*polite form*)

Sie; **I know you** ich kenne dich/euch/Sie **3** (*indirect object, after prep* +*dat*) (*familiar form*) (*sg*) dir; (*pl*) euch; (*in letters*) Dir, Euch; (*polite form*) Ihnen; **I gave it to you** ich gab es dir/euch/Ihnen **4** (*impers*) (*one*) (*subj*) man; (*direct object*) einen; (*indirect object*) einem; **fresh air does you good** frische Luft tut (einem) gut

you'd [juːd] *contr of* **you had; you would**; **~ better leave** du solltest/Sie sollten gehen

you'll [juːl] *contr of* **you will; you shall**

young [jʌŋ] *adj* jung ▷ *n* **the ~** *pl* (*~ people*) die jungen Leute *pl*; (*animals*) die Jungen *pl*; **youngster** ['jʌŋstə°] *n* Jugendliche(r) *mf*

your ['jɔː°] *adj sing* dein; *polite form* Ihr; *pl* euer; *polite form* Ihr; **have you hurt ~ leg?** hast du dir/haben Sie sich das Bein verletzt?

you're ['jʊə°] *contr of* **you are**

yours ['jɔːz] *pron sing* deine(r, s); *polite form* Ihre(r, s); *pl* eure(r, s); *polite form* Ihre(r, s); **is this ~?** gehört das dir/Ihnen?; **a friend of ~** ein Freund von dir/Ihnen

yourself [jɔːˈself] *pron sing* dich; *polite form* sich; **have you hurt ~?** hast du dich/haben Sie sich verletzt?; **did you do it ~?** hast du/haben Sie es selbst gemacht?; **(all) by ~** allein; **yourselves** *pron pl* euch; *polite form* sich; **have you hurt ~?** habt ihr euch/haben Sie sich verletzt?; **did you do it ~?** habt ihr/haben Sie es selbst gemacht?; **(all) by ~** allein

youth [juːθ] *n* (*period*) Jugend *f*; (*young man*) junger Mann *m*; (*young people*) Jugend *f*; **youth group** *n*

Jugendgruppe f: **youth hostel** n Jugendherberge f

you've [juːv] contr of **you have**

yucky ['jʌkɪ] adj (fam) eklig

yummy ['jʌmɪ] adj (fam) lecker

yuppie, **yuppy** ['jʌpɪ] n Yuppie m

zap [zæp] vt (Inform) löschen; (in computer game) abknallen ▷ vi (TV) zappen; **zapper** n (TV) Fernbedienung f; **zapping** n (TV) ständiges Umschalten, Zapping nt

zebra ['zebrə, ?? 'ziːbrə] (US) n Zebra nt; **zebra crossing** n (Brit) Zebrastreifen m

zero [zɪərəʊ] (pl **-es**) n Null f; **10 degrees below ~** 10 Grad unter null

zest [zest] n (enthusiasm) Begeisterung f

zigzag ['zɪgzæg] n Zickzack m ▷ vi (person, vehicle) im Zickzack gehen/fahren; (path) im Zickzack verlaufen

zinc [zɪŋk] n Zink nt

zip [zɪp] n (Brit) Reißverschluss m ▷ vt: **to ~ (up)** den Reißverschluss zumachen; (Inform) zippen; **zip code** n (US) Postleitzahl f; **Zip disk®** n (Inform) ZIP-Diskette® f;

Zip drive® n (Inform)
ZIP-Laufwerk® nt; **Zip file®** n
(Inform) ZIP-Datei® f; **zipper** n
(US) Reißverschluss m

zit [zɪt] n (fam) Pickel m

zodiac [ˈzəʊdɪæk] n Tierkreis m;
sign of the ~ Tierkreiszeichen
nt

zone [zəʊn] n Zone f; (area)
Gebiet nt; (in town) Bezirk m

zoo [zuː] n Zoo m

zoom [zuːm] vi (move fast)
brausen, sausen ▷ n: **~ (lens)**
Zoomobjektiv nt; **zoom in** vi
(Foto) heranzoomen (on an +akk)

zucchini [zuːˈkiːnɪ] (pl -(**s**)) n
(US) Zucchini f